THE MODERN LIBRARY
OF THE WORLD'S BEST BOOKS

THE COMEDIES OF

SHAKESPEARE

The
Comedies
of
Shakespeare

THE MODERN LIBRARY

NEW YORK

FIRST *Modern Library* EDITION, 1943

Random House IS THE PUBLISHER OF

THE MODERN LIBRARY

BENNETT A. CERF · DONALD S. KLOPFER · ROBERT K. HAAS

Manufactured in the United States of America

Printed by Parkway Printing Company   Bound by H. Wolff

CONTENTS

CONTENTS

THE TEMPEST

THE TEMPEST

ACT ONE

SCENE ONE

On a Ship at Sea. A tempestuous noise of thunder and lightning heard.

Enter a Shipmaster and a Boatswain severally

MASTER. Boatswain!

BOATSWAIN. Here, master: what cheer?

MASTER. Good, speak to the mariners: fall to 't yarely, or we
 run ourselves aground: bestir, bestir.   *Exit*
                    Enter Mariners

BOATSWAIN. Heigh, my hearts! Cheerly, cheerly, my hearts!
 Yare, yare! Take in the topsail. Tend to the master's
 whistle! Blow, till thou burst thy wind, if room enough!
         Enter Alonso, Sebastian,
       Antonio, Ferdinand, Gonzalo, and others

ALONSO. Good boatswain, have care. Where 's the master?
 Play the men.

BOATSWAIN. I pray now, keep below.

ANTONIO. Where is the master, bos'n?

BOATSWAIN. Do you not hear him? You mar our labour: keep
 your cabins: you do assist the storm.

GONZALO. Nay, good, be patient.

BOATSWAIN. When the sea is. Hence! What cares these roar-
 ers for the name of king? To cabin! silence! trouble us not.

GONZALO. Good, yet remember whom thou hast aboard.

BOATSWAIN. None that I more love than myself. You are a
 counsellor: if you can command these elements to silence, and work the peace of the present, we will not
 hand a rope more; use your authority: if you cannot,
 give thanks you have lived so long, and make yourself

ready in your cabin for the mischance of the hour, if it
so hap.—Cheerly, good hearts!—Out of our way, I say.

Exit

GONZALO. I have great comfort from this fellow: methinks
he hath no drowning mark upon him; his complexion is
perfect gallows. Stand fast, good Fate, to his hanging!
Make the rope of his destiny our cable, for our own doth
little advantage! If he be not born to be hanged, our
case is miserable.   *Exeunt*

Re-enter Boatswain

BOATSWAIN. Down with the topmast! Yare! Lower, lower!
Bring her to try with main-course. (*A cry within*) A
plague upon this howling! They are louder than the
weather, or our office.—

Re-enter Sebastian, Antonio, and Gonzalo

Yet again! What do you here? Shall we give o'er, and
drown? Have you a mind to sink?

SEBASTIAN. A pox o' your throat, you bawling, blasphe-
mous, incharitable dog!

BOATSWAIN. Work you, then.

ANTONIO. Hang, cur, hang! you whoreson, insolent noise-
maker, we are less afraid to be drowned than thou art.

GONZALO. I 'll warrant him for drowning; though the ship
were no stronger than a nutshell, and as leaky as an unstanched wench.

BOATSWAIN. Lay her a-hold, a-hold! Set her two courses!
Off to sea again! Lay her off!

Enter Mariners, wet

MARINERS. All lost! To prayers, to prayers! All lost!

Exeunt

BOATSWAIN. What, must our mouths be cold?

GONZALO. The king and prince at prayers! Let us assist
them,
For our case is as theirs.

SEBASTIAN.   I am out of patience.

ANTONIO. We are merely cheated of our lives by drunkards.—
This wide-chapp'd rascal,—would thou might'st lie
drowning,
The washing of ten tides!

GONZALO.   He 'll be hang'd yet,
Though every drop of water swear against it,

And gape at wid'st to glut him.
(*A confused noise within*)   'Mercy on us!'—
'We split, we split!'—'Farewell, my wife and children!'—
'Farewell, brother!'—'We split, we split, we split!'—

ANTONIO. Let 's all sink wi' the king.   *Exit*

SEBASTIAN. Let 's take leave of him.   *Exit*

GONZALO. Now would I give a thousand furlongs of sea for
an acre of barren ground; long heath, brown furze, any
thing. The wills above be done! But I would fain die a
dry death.   *Exit*

SCENE TWO

The Island: before the Cell of Prospero.

Enter Prospero and Miranda

MIRANDA. If by your art, my dearest father, you have
Put the wild waters in this roar, allay them.
The sky, it seems, would pour down stinking pitch,
But that the sea, mounting to th' welkin's cheek,
Dashes the fire out. O! I have suffer'd
With those that I saw suffer: a brave vessel,
Who had, no doubt, some noble creatures in her,
Dash'd all to pieces. O! the cry did knock
Against my very heart. Poor souls, they perish'd.
Had I been any god of power, I would
Have sunk the sea within the earth, or e'er
It should the good ship so have swallow'd and
The fraughting souls within her.

PROSPERO.   Be collected:
No more amazement. Tell your piteous heart
There 's no harm done.

MIRANDA.   O, woe the day!

PROSPERO.   No harm.
I have done nothing but in care of thee,—
Of thee, my dear one! thee, my daughter!—who
Art ignorant of what thou art, nought knowing
Of whence I am: nor that I am more better
Than Prospero, master of a full poor cell,
And thy no greater father.

MIRANDA. More to know
Did never meddle with my thoughts.

PROSPERO. 'Tis time
I should inform thee further. Lend thy hand,
And pluck my magic garment from me.—So:

Lays down his mantle

Lie there, my art.—Wipe thou thine eyes; have comfort.
The direful spectacle of the wrack, which touch'd
The very virtue of compassion in thee,
I have with such provision in mine art
So safely order'd, that there is no soul—
No, not so much perdition as an hair,
Betid to any creature in the vessel
Which thou heard'st cry, which thou saw'st sink. Sit down;
For thou must now know further.

MIRANDA. You have often
Begun to tell me what I am, but stopp'd,
And left me to a bootless inquisition,
Concluding, 'Stay; not yet.'

PROSPERO. The hour 's now come,
The very minute bids thee ope thine ear;
Obey and be attentive. Canst thou remember
A time before we came unto this cell?
I do not think thou canst, for then thou wast not
Out three years old.

MIRANDA. Certainly, sir, I can.

PROSPERO. By what? by any other house or person?
Of anything the image tell me, that
Hath kept with thy remembrance.

MIRANDA. 'Tis far off;
And rather like a dream than an assurance
That my remembrance warrants. Had I not
Four or five women once that tended me?

PROSPERO. Thou hadst, and more, Miranda. But how is it
That this lives in thy mind? What seest thou else
In the dark backward and abysm of time?
If thou remember'st aught ere thou cam'st here,
How thou cam'st here, thou may'st.

MIRANDA. But that I do not.

PROSPERO. Twelve year since, Miranda, twelve year since,
Thy father was the Duke of Milan and

A prince of power.

MIRANDA. Sir, are not you my father?

PROSPERO. Thy mother was a piece of virtue, and
She said thou wast my daughter; and thy father
Was Duke of Milan, and his only heir
A princess,—no worse issued.

MIRANDA. O, the heavens!
What foul play had we that we came from thence?
Or blessed was 't we did?

PROSPERO. Both, both, my girl:
By foul play, as thou say'st, were we heav'd thence;
But blessedly holp hither.

MIRANDA. O! my heart bleeds
To think o' the teen that I have turn'd you to,
Which is from my remembrance. Please you, further.

PROSPERO. My brother and thy uncle, call'd Antonio,—
I pray thee, mark me,—that a brother should
Be so perfidious!—he whom next thyself,
Of all the world I lov'd, and to him put
The manage of my state; as at that time
Through all the signiories it was the first,
And Prospero the prime duke; being so reputed
In dignity, and for the liberal arts,
Without a parallel: those being all my study,
The government I cast upon my brother,
And to my state grew stranger, being transported
And rapt in secret studies. Thy false uncle—
Dost thou attend me?

MIRANDA. Sir, most heedfully.

PROSPERO. Being once perfected how to grant suits,
How to deny them, who t' advance, and who
To trash for over-topping; new created
The creatures that were mine, I say, or chang'd 'em,
Or else new form'd 'em: having both the key
Of officer and office, set all hearts i' the state
To what tune pleas'd his ear; that now he was
The ivy which had hid my princely trunk,
And suck'd my verdure out on't.—Thou attend'st not.

MIRANDA. O, good sir! I do.

PROSPERO. I pray thee, mark me.
I, thus neglecting worldly ends, all dedicated
To closeness and the bettering of my mind

With that, which, but by being so retir'd,
O'erpriz'd all popular rate, in my false brother
Awak'd an evil nature; and my trust,
Like a good parent, did beget of him
A falsehood in its contrary as great
As my trust was; which had, indeed no limit,
A confidence sans bound. He being thus lorded,
Not only with what my revenue yielded,
But what my power might else exact,—like one,
Who having, into truth, by telling of it,
Made such a sinner of his memory,
To credit his own lie,—he did believe
He was indeed the duke; out o' the substitution,
And executing th' outward face of royalty,
With all prerogative:—Hence his ambition growing,—
Dost thou hear?

MIRANDA.   Your tale, sir, would cure deafness.

PROSPERO. To have no screen between this part he play'd
And him he play'd it for, he needs will be
Absolute Milan. Me, poor man,—my library
Was dukedom large enough: of temporal royalties
He thinks me now incapable; confederates,—
So dry he was for sway,—wi' the king of Naples
To give him annual tribute, do him homage;
Subject his coronet to his crown, and bend
The dukedom, yet unbow'd,—alas, poor Milan!—
To most ignoble stooping.

MIRANDA.   O the heavens!

PROSPERO. Mark his condition and the event; then tell me
If this might be a brother.

MIRANDA.   I should sin
To think but nobly of my grandmother:
Good wombs have borne bad sons.

PROSPERO.   Now the condition.
This King of Naples, being an enemy
To me inveterate, hearkens my brother's suit;
Which was, that he, in lieu o' the premises
Of homage and I know not how much tribute,
Should presently extirpate me and mine
Out of the dukedom, and confer fair Milan,
With all the honours on my brother: whereon,
A treacherous army levied, one midnight

Fated to the purpose did Antonio open
The gates of Milan; and, i' the dead of darkness,
The ministers for the purpose hurried thence
Me and thy crying self.

MIRANDA.   Alack, for pity!
I, not rememb'ring how I cried out then,
Will cry it o'er again: it is a hint,
That wrings mine eyes to 't.

PROSPERO.   Hear a little further,
And then I 'll bring thee to the present business
Which now 's upon us; without the which this story
Were most impertinent.

MIRANDA.   Wherefore did they not
That hour destroy us?

PROSPERO.   Well demanded, wench:
My tale provokes that question. Dear, they durst not,
So dear the love my people bore me, nor set
A mark so bloody on the business; but
With colours fairer painted their foul ends.
In few, they hurried us aboard a bark,
Bore us some leagues to sea; where they prepar'd
A rotten carcass of a boat, not rigg'd,
Nor tackle, sail, nor mast; the very rats
Instinctively have quit it: there they hoist us,
To cry to the sea that roar'd to us; to sigh
To the winds whose pity, sighing back again,
Did us but loving wrong.

MIRANDA.   Alack! what trouble
Was I then to you!

PROSPERO.   O, a cherubin
Thou wast, that did preserve me! Thou didst smile,
Infused with a fortitude from heaven,
When I have deck'd the sea with drops full salt,
Under my burden groan'd; which rais'd in me
An undergoing stomach, to bear up
Against what should ensue.

MIRANDA.   How came we ashore?

PROSPERO. By Providence divine.
Some food we had and some fresh water that
A noble Neapolitan, Gonzalo,
Out of his charity,—who being then appointed
Master of this design,—did give us; with

Rich garments, linens, stuffs, and necessaries,
Which since have steaded much; so, of his gentleness,
Knowing I lov'd my books, he furnish'd me,
From mine own library with volumes that
I prize above my dukedom.

MIRANDA.   Would I might
But ever see that man!

PROSPERO.   Now I arise:—*Resumes his mantle*
Sit still, and hear the last of our sea-sorrow.
Here in this island we arriv'd; and here
Have I, thy schoolmaster, made thee more profit
Than other princes can, that have more time
For vainer hours and tutors not so careful.

MIRANDA. Heavens thank you for 't! And now, I pray you,
     sir,—
For still 'tis beating in my mind,—your reason
For raising this sea-storm?

PROSPERO.   Know thus far forth.
By accident most strange, bountiful Fortune,
Now my dear lady, hath mine enemies
Brought to this shore; and by my prescience
I find my zenith doth depend upon
A most auspicious star, whose influence
If now I court not but omit, my fortunes
Will ever after droop. Here cease more questions;
Thou art inclin'd to sleep; 'tis a good dulness,
And give it way;—I know thou canst not choose.—

                                        Miranda sleeps
Come away, servant, come! I 'm ready now.
Approach, my Ariel; come!

                              Enter Ariel

ARIEL. All hail, great master! Grave sir, hail! I come
To answer thy best pleasure; be 't to fly,
To swim, to dive into the fire, to ride
On the curl'd clouds: to thy strong bidding task
Ariel and all his quality.

PROSPERO.   Hast thou, spirit,
Perform'd to point the tempest that I bade thee?

ARIEL. To every article.
I boarded the king's ship; now on the beak,
Now in the waist, the deck, in every cabin,
I flam'd amazement: sometime I 'd divide

And burn in many places; on the topmast,
The yards, and boresprit, would I flame distinctly,
Then meet, and join: Jove's lightnings, the precursors
O' the dreadful thunder-claps, more momentary
And sight-outrunning were not: the fire and cracks
Of sulphurous roaring the most mighty Neptune
Seem to besiege and make his bold waves tremble,
Yea, his dread trident shake.

PROSPERO.   My brave spirit!
Who was so firm, so constant, that this coil
Would not infect his reason?

ARIEL.   Not a soul
But felt a fever of the mad and play'd
Some tricks of desperation. All but mariners,
Plunged in the foaming brine and quit the vessel,
Then all a-fire with me: the king's son, Ferdinand,
With hair up-staring,—then like reeds, not hair,—
Was the first man that leap'd; cried, 'Hell is empty,
And all the devils are here.'

PROSPERO.   Why, that 's my spirit!
But was not this nigh shore?

ARIEL.   Close by, my master.

PROSPERO. But are they, Ariel, safe?

ARIEL.   ·   Not a hair perish'd;
On their sustaining garments not a blemish,
But fresher than before: and, as thou bad'st me,
In troops I have dispers'd them 'bout the isle.
The king's son have I landed by himself;
Whom I left cooling of the air with sighs
In an odd angle of the isle and sitting,
His arms in this sad knot.

PROSPERO.   Of the king's ship
The mariners, say how thou hast dispos'd,
And all the rest o' the fleet.

ARIEL.   Safely in harbour
Is the king's ship; in the deep nook, where once
Thou call'dst me up at midnight to fetch dew
From the still-vex'd Bermoothes; there she 's hid:
The mariners all under hatches stow'd;
Who, with a charm join'd to their suffer'd labour,
I have left asleep: and for the rest o' the fleet
Which I dispers'd, they all have met again,

And are upon the Mediterranean flote,
Bound sadly home for Naples,
Supposing that they saw the king's ship wrack'd,
And his great person perish.

PROSPERO.   Ariel, thy charge
Exactly is perform'd; but there 's more work.
What is the time o' th' day?

ARIEL.   Past the mid season.

PROSPERO. At least two glasses. The time 'twixt six and
    now
Must by us both be spent most preciously.

ARIEL. Is there more toil? Since thou dost give me pains,
Let me remember thee what thou hast promis'd,
Which is not yet perform'd me.

PROSPERO.   How now! moody?
What is 't thou canst demand?

ARIEL.   My liberty.

PROSPERO. Before the time be out! no more!

ARIEL.   I prithee
Remember, I have done thee worthy service;
Told thee no lies, made no mistakings, serv'd
Without or grudge or grumblings: thou didst promise
To bate me a full year.

PROSPERO.   Dost thou forget
From what a torment I did free thee?

ARIEL.   No.

PROSPERO. Thou dost; and think'st it much to tread the
    ooze
Of the salt deep,
To run upon the sharp wind of the north,
To do me business in the veins o' th' earth
When it is bak'd with frost.

ARIEL.   I do not, sir.

PROSPERO. Thou liest, malignant thing! Hast thou forgot
The foul witch Sycorax, who with age and envy
Was grown into a hoop? Hast thou forgot her?

ARIEL. No, sir.

PROSPERO.   Thou hast. Where was she born? Speak; tell
    me.

ARIEL. Sir, in Argier.

PROSPERO.   O! was she so? I must,
Once in a month, recount what thou hast been,

Which thou forget'st. This damn'd witch, Sycorax,
For mischiefs manifold and sorceries terrible
To enter human hearing, from Argier,
Thou know'st, was banish'd: for one thing she did
They would not take her life. Is not this true?

ARIEL. Ay, sir.

PROSPERO. This blue-ey'd hag was hither brought with
    child
  And here was left by the sailors. Thou, my slave,
  As thou report'st thyself, wast then her servant:
  And, for thou wast a spirit too delicate
  To act her earthly and abhorr'd commands,
  Refusing her grand hests, she did confine thee,
  By help of her more potent ministers,
  And in her most unmitigable rage,
  Into a cloven pine; within which rift
  Imprison'd, thou didst painfully remain
  A dozen years; within which space she died
  And left thee there, where thou didst vent thy groans
  As fast as mill-wheels strike. Then was this island,—
  Save for the son that she did litter here,
  A freckled whelp hag-born,—not honour'd with
  A human shape.

ARIEL.   Yes; Caliban her son.

PROSPERO. Dull thing, I say so; he that Caliban,
  Whom now I keep in service. Thou best know'st
  What torment I did find thee in; thy groans
  Did make wolves howl and penetrate the breasts
  Of ever-angry bears; it was a torment
  To lay upon the damn'd, which Sycorax
  Could not again undo; it was mine art,
  When I arriv'd and heard thee, that made gape
  The pine, and let thee out.

ARIEL.   I thank thee, master.

PROSPERO. If thou more murmur'st, I will rend an oak
  And peg thee in his knotty entrails till
  Thou hast howl'd away twelve winters.

ARIEL.   Pardon, master;
  I will be correspondent to command,
  And do my spiriting gently.

PROSPERO.   Do so; and after two days
  I will discharge thee.

ARIEL. That 's my noble master!
What shall I do? say what? what shall I do?

PROSPERO. Go make thyself like a nymph of the sea: be
  subject
To no sight but thine and mine; invisible
To every eyeball else. Go, take this shape,
And hither come in 't: go, hence with diligence!

Exit Ariel

Awake, dear heart, awake! thou hast slept well;
Awake!

MIRANDA. (*Waking*) The strangeness of your story put
Heaviness in me.

PROSPERO. Shake it off. Come on;
We 'll visit Caliban my slave, who never
Yields us kind answer.

MIRANDA. 'Tis a villain, sir,
I do not love to look on.

PROSPERO. But, as 'tis,
We cannot miss him: he does make our fire,
Fetch in our wood; and serves in offices
That profit us.—What ho! slave! Caliban!
Thou earth, thou! speak.

CALIBAN. (*Within*) There 's wood enough within.

PROSPERO. Come forth, I say; there 's other business for thee:
Come, thou tortoise! When?

Re-enter Ariel, like a water-nymph

Fine apparition! My quaint Ariel,
Hark in thine ear.

ARIEL. My lord, it shall be done. *Exit*

PROSPERO. Thou poisonous slave, got by the devil himself
Upon thy wicked dam, come forth!

Enter Caliban

CALIBAN. As wicked dew as e'er my mother brush'd
With raven's feather from unwholesome fen
Drop on you both! A south-west blow on ye,
And blister you all o'er!

PROSPERO. For this, be sure, to-night thou shalt have cramps,
Side-stitches that shall pen thy breath up; urchins
Shall forth at vast of night, that they may work
All exercise on thee: thou shalt be pinch'd
As thick as honeycomb, each pinch more stinging
Than bees that made them.

CALIBAN.   I must eat my dinner.
This island 's mine, by Sycorax my mother,
Which thou tak'st from me. When thou camest first,
Thou strok'dst me, and mad'st much of me; wouldst give
    me
Water with berries in 't; and teach me how
To name the bigger light, and how the less,
That burn by day and night: and then I lov'd thee
And show'd thee all the qualities o' th' isle,
The fresh springs, brine-pits, barren place, and fertile.
Cursed be I that did so!—All the charms
Of Sycorax, toads, beetles, bats, light on you!
For I am all the subjects that you have,
Which first was mine own king; and here you sty me
In this hard rock, whiles you do keep from me
The rest o' th' island.
PROSPERO.   Thou most lying slave,
Whom stripes may move, not kindness! I have us'd thee,
Filth as thou art, with human care; and lodg'd thee
In mine own cell, till thou didst seek to violate
The honour of my child.
CALIBAN. Oh ho! Oh ho!—would it had been done!
Thou didst prevent me; I had peopled else
This isle with Calibans.
PROSPERO.   Abhorred slave,
Which any print of goodness will not take,
Being capable of all ill! I pitied thee,
Took pains to make thee speak, taught thee each hour
One thing or other: when thou didst not, savage,
Know thine own meaning, but wouldst gabble like
A thing most brutish, I endow'd thy purposes
With words that made them known: but thy vile race,
Though thou didst learn, had that in 't which good na-
    tures
Could not abide to be with; therefore wast thou
Deservedly confin'd into this rock,
Who hadst deserv'd more than a prison.
CALIBAN. You taught me language; and my profit on 't
Is, I know how to curse: the red plague rid you,
For learning me your language!
PROSPERO.   Hag-seed, hence!
Fetch us in fuel; and be quick, thou 'rt best,

To answer other business. Shrug'st thou, malice?
If thou neglect'st, or dost unwillingly
What I command, I 'll rack thee with old cramps,
Fill all thy bones with aches; make thee roar,
That beasts shall tremble at thy din.

CALIBAN.   No, pray thee!—
   (*Aside*) I must obey: his art is of such power,
It would control my dam's god, Setebos,
And make a vassal of him.

PROSPERO.   So, slave; hence! *Exit Caliban*
                           Re-enter Ariel, invisible,
              playing and singing; Ferdinand following

ARIEL'S SONG

Come unto these yellow sands,
   And then take hands:
Curtsied when you have, and kiss'd,—
   The wild waves whist,—
Foot it featly here and there;
And, sweet sprites, the burden bear.
            Hark, hark!
                     Burden: Bow, wow, *dispersedly*
            The watch-dogs bark:
                     Burden: Bow, wow, *dispersedly*
            Hark, hark! I hear
The strain of strutting Chanticleer
                     Cry: Cock-a-diddle-dow.

FERDINAND. Where should this music be? I' th' air, or th'
   earth?
It sounds no more;—and sure, it waits upon
Some god o' th' island. Sitting on a bank,
Weeping again the king my father's wrack,
This music crept by me upon the waters,
Allaying both their fury, and my passion,
With its sweet air: thence I have follow'd it,—
Or it hath drawn me rather,—but 'tis gone.
No, it begins again.

ARIEL'S SONG

Full fathom five thy father lies;
   Of his bones are coral made:
Those are pearls that were his eyes:
   Nothing of him that doth fade,

But doth suffer a sea-change
Into something rich and strange.
Sea-nymphs hourly ring his knell:
　　　　　　　　　Burden: ding-dong
　Hark! now I hear them,—ding-dong, bell.

FERDINAND. The ditty does remember my drown'd father.
This is no mortal business, nor no sound
That the earth owes:—I hear it now above me.

PROSPERO. The fringed curtains of thine eye advance,
And say what thou seest yond.

MIRANDA. 　　　　　　　　　What is 't? a spirit?
Lord, how it looks about! Believe me, sir,
It carries a brave form:—but 'tis a spirit.

PROSPERO. No, wench; it eats and sleeps, and hath such
　　senses
As we have, such; this gallant which thou see'st,
Was in the wrack; and, but he 's something stain'd
With grief,—that beauty's canker,—thou might'st call him
A goodly person: he hath lost his fellows
And strays about to find 'em.

MIRANDA. 　　　　　　　I might call him
A thing divine; for nothing natural
I ever saw so noble.

PROSPERO. 　　　　　(*Aside*) It goes on, I see,
As my soul prompts it.—Spirit, fine spirit! I 'll free thee
Within two days for this.

FERDINAND. 　　　　Most sure, the goddess
On whom these airs attend!—Vouchsafe, my prayer
May know if you remain upon this island;
And that you will some good instruction give
How I may bear me here: my prime request,
Which I do last pronounce, is,—O you wonder!—
If you be maid or no?

MIRANDA. 　　　　　No wonder, sir;
But certainly a maid.

FERDINAND. 　　　　My language! heavens!—
I am the best of them that speak this speech,
Were I but where 'tis spoken.

PROSPERO. 　　　　　How! the best?
What wert thou, if the King of Naples heard thee?

FERDINAND. A single thing, as I am now, that wonders
To hear thee speak of Naples. He does hear me;

And, that he does, I weep: myself am Naples,
Who with mine eyes,—ne'er since at ebb,—beheld
The king, my father wrack'd.

MIRANDA.   Alack, for mercy!

FERDINAND. Yes, faith, and all his lords; the Duke of Milan
And his brave son being twain.

PROSPERO.   (*Aside*) The Duke of Milan
And his more braver daughter could control thee,
If now 'twere fit to do 't.—At the first sight (*Aside*)
They have changed eyes:—delicate Ariel,
I 'll set thee free for this!—(*To Ferdinand*) A word, good
    sir;
I fear you have done yourself some wrong: a word.

MIRANDA. (*Aside*) Why speaks my father so ungently?
    This
Is the third man that e'er I saw; the first
That e'er I sigh'd for: pity move my father
To be inclin'd my way!

FERDINAND.   (*Aside*) O! if a virgin,
And your affection not gone forth, I 'll make you
The Queen of Naples.

PROSPERO.   Soft, sir: one word more—
    (*Aside*) They are both in either's powers: but this swift
        business
I must uneasy make, lest too light winning
Make the prize light.—(*To Ferdinand*) One word more:
    I charge thee
That thou attend me. Thou dost here usurp
The name thou ow'st not; and hast put thyself
Upon this island as a spy, to win it
From me, the lord on 't.

FERDINAND.   No, as I am a man.

MIRANDA. There 's nothing ill can dwell in such a temple
If the ill spirit have so fair a house,
Good things will strive to dwell with 't.

PROSPERO.   (*To Ferdinand*) Follow me.—
    (*To Miranda*) Speak not you for him; he 's a traitor.—
        (*To Ferdinand*) Come;
I 'll manacle thy neck and feet together:
Sea-water shalt thou drink; thy food shall be
The fresh-brook mussels, wither'd roots and husks

Wherein the acorn cradled. Follow.

FERDINAND.   No;
I will resist such entertainment till
Mine enemy has more power.
                    He draws, and is charmed from moving

MIRANDA.   O dear father!
Make not too rash a trial of him, for
He 's gentle, and not fearful.

PROSPERO.   What! I say,
My foot my tutor?—Put thy sword up, traitor;
Who mak'st a show, but dar'st not strike, thy conscience
Is so possess'd with guilt: come from thy ward,
For I can here disarm thee with this stick
And make thy weapon drop.

MIRANDA.   Beseech you, father!

PROSPERO. Hence! Hang not on my garments.

MIRANDA.   Sir, have pity:
I 'll be his surety.

PROSPERO.   Silence! One word more
Shall make me chide thee, if not hate thee. What!
An advocate for an imposter? Hush!
Thou think'st there is no more such shapes as he,
Having seen but him and Caliban. Foolish wench!
To the most of men this is a Caliban
And they to him are angels.

MIRANDA.   My affections
Are then most humble; I have no ambition
To see a goodlier man.

PROSPERO. (*To Ferdinand*) Come on; obey:
Thy nerves are in their infancy again,
And have no vigour in them.

FERDINAND.   So they are:
My spirits, as in a dream, are all bound up.
My father's loss, the weakness which I feel,
The wrack of all my friends, or this man's threats,
To whom I am subdued, are but light to me,
Might I but through my prison once a day
Behold this maid: all corners else o' th' earth
Let liberty make use of; space enough
Have I in such a prison.

PROSPERO. (*Aside*) It works.—(*To Ferdinand*) Come on.—

Thou hast done well, fine Ariel!—(*To Ferdinand*) Follow me.—

(*To Ariel*) Hark, what thou else shalt do me.

MIRANDA.   Be of comfort;
My father 's of a better nature, sir,
Than he appears by speech: this is unwonted,
Which now came from him.

PROSPERO.   Thou shalt be as free
As mountain winds; but then exactly do
All points of my command.

ARIEL.   To the syllable.

PROSPERO. (*To Ferdinand*) Come, follow.—Speak not for
him.   *Exeunt*

ACT TWO

SCENE ONE

Another Part of the Island.

Enter Alonso, Sebastian, Antonio, Gonzalo, Adrian,
Francisco, and others

GONZALO. Beseech you, sir, be merry: you have cause,
So have we all, of joy; for our escape
Is much beyond our loss. Our hint of woe
Is common: every day some sailor's wife,
The masters of some merchant and the merchant,
Have just our theme of woe; but for the miracle,
I mean our preservation, few in millions
Can speak like us: then wisely, good sir, weigh
Our sorrow with our comfort.

ALONSO.   Prithee, peace.

SEBASTIAN. He receives comfort like cold porridge.

ANTONIO. The visitor will not give him o'er so.

SEBASTIAN. Look, he 's winding up the watch of his wit; by
and by it will strike.

GONZALO. Sir,—

SEBASTIAN. One: tell.

GONZALO. When every grief is entertain'd that 's offer'd,
Comes to the entertainer—

SEBASTIAN. A dollar.

GONZALO. Dolour comes to him, indeed: you have spoken
truer than you purposed.

SEBASTIAN. You have taken it wiselier than I meant you
should.

GONZALO. Therefore, my lord,—

ANTONIO. Fie, what a spendthrift is he of his tongue!

ALONSO. I prithee, spare.

GONZALO. Well, I have done: but yet—

SEBASTIAN. He will be talking.

ANTONIO. Which, of he or Adrian, for a good wager, firs
begins to crow?

SEBASTIAN. The old cock.

ANTONIO. The cockerel.

SEBASTIAN. Done. The wager?

ANTONIO. A laughter.

SEBASTIAN. A match!

ADRIAN. Though this island seem to be desert,—

SEBASTIAN. Ha, ha, ha! So you 're paid.

ADRIAN. Uninhabitable, and almost inaccessible,—

SEBASTIAN. Yet—

ADRIAN. Yet—

ANTONIO. He could not miss it.

ADRIAN. It must needs be of subtle, tender, and delicat
temperance.

ANTONIO. Temperance was a delicate wench.

SEBASTIAN. Ay, and a subtle; as he most learnedly deliv
ered.

ADRIAN. The air breathes upon us here most sweetly.

SEBASTIAN. As if it had lungs, and rotten ones.

ANTONIO. Or as 'twere perfumed by a fen.

GONZALO. Here is everything advantageous to life.

ANTONIO. True; save means to live.

SEBASTIAN. Of that there 's none, or little.

GONZALO. How lush and lusty the grass looks! how green

ANTONIO. The ground indeed is tawny.

SEBASTIAN. With an eye of green in 't.

ANTONIO. He misses not much.

SEBASTIAN. No; he doth but mistake the truth totally.

GONZALO. But the rarity of it is,—which is indeed almos
beyond credit,—

SEBASTIAN. As many vouch'd rarities are.

GONZALO. That our garments, being, as they were, drenche
in the sea, hold notwithstanding their freshness an
glosses; being rather new-dyed than stain'd with sal
water.

ANTONIO. If but one of his pockets could speak, would i
not say he lies?

SEBASTIAN. Ay, or very falsely pocket up his report.

GONZALO. Methinks, our garments are now as fresh a
when we put them on first in Afric, at the marriage of the
king's fair daughter Claribel to the King of Tunis.

SEBASTIAN. 'Twas a sweet marriage, and we prosper well
in our return.

ADRIAN. Tunis was never graced before with such a paragon to their queen.

GONZALO. Not since widow Dido's time.

ANTONIO. Widow! a pox o' that! How came that widow in?
Widow Dido!

SEBASTIAN. What if he had said, widower Æneas too?
Good Lord, how you take it!

ADRIAN. Widow Dido, said you? You make me study of
that: she was of Carthage, not of Tunis.

GONZALO. This Tunis, sir, was Carthage.

ADRIAN. Carthage?

GONZALO. I assure you, Carthage.

ANTONIO. His word is more than the miraculous harp.

SEBASTIAN. He hath rais'd the wall, and houses too.

ANTONIO. What impossible matter will he make easy next?

SEBASTIAN. I think he will carry this island home in his
pocket, and give it his son for an apple.

ANTONIO. And, sowing the kernels of it in the sea, bring
forth more islands.

ALONSO. Ay?

ANTONIO. Why, in good time.

GONZALO. (To Alonso) Sir, we were talking that our garments seem now as fresh as when we were at Tunis at
the marriage of your daughter, who is now queen.

ANTONIO. And the rarest that e'er came there.

SEBASTIAN. Bate, I beseech you, widow Dido.

ANTONIO. O! widow Dido; ay, widow Dido.

GONZALO. Is not, sir, my doublet as fresh as the first day I
wore it? I mean, in a sort.

ANTONIO. That sort was well fish'd for.

GONZALO. When I wore it at your daughter's marriage?

ALONSO. You cram these words into mine ears, against
The stomach of my sense. Would I had never
Married my daughter there! for, coming thence,
My son is lost; and, in my rate, she too,
Who is so far from Italy remov'd,
I ne'er again shall see her. O thou, mine heir
Of Naples and of Milan! what strange fish
Hath made his meal on thee?

FRANCISCO.   Sir, he may live:

I saw him beat the surges under him,
And ride upon their backs: he trod the water,
Whose enmity he flung aside, and breasted
The surge most swoln that met him: his bold head
'Bove the contentious waves he kept, and oar'd
Himself with his good arms in lusty stroke
To the shore, that o'er his wave-worn basis bow'd,
As stooping to relieve him. I not doubt
He came alive to land.

ALONSO.   No, no; he 's gone.

SEBASTIÀN. Sir, you may thank yourself for this great loss
That would not bless our Europe with your daughter,
But rather lose her to an African;
Where she at least is banish'd from your eye,
Who hath cause to wet the grief on 't.

ALONSO.   Prithee, peace.

SEBASTIAN. You were kneel'd to and importun'd otherwis
By all of us; and the fair soul herself
Weigh'd between loathness and obedience, at
Which end o' the beam should bow. We have lost you
  son,
I fear, for ever: Milan and Naples have
More widows in them of this business' making,
Than we bring men to comfort them; the fault 's
Your own.

ALONSO. So is the dearest of the loss.

GONZALO. My lord Sebastian,
The truth you speak doth lack some gentleness
And time to speak it in; you rub the sore,
When you should bring the plaster.

SEBASTIAN.   Very well.

ANTONIO. And most chirurgeonly.

GONZALO. It is foul weather in us all, good sir,
When you are cloudy.

SEBASTIAN.   Foul weather?

ANTONIO.   Very foul.

GONZALO. Had I plantation of this isle, my lord,—

ANTONIO. He 'd sow 't with nettle-seed.

SEBASTIAN.   Or docks, or mallows

GONZALO. And were the king on 't, what would I do?

SEBASTIAN. 'Scape being drunk for want of wine.

GONZALO. I' the commonwealth I would by contraries

Execute all things; for no kind of traffic
Would I admit; no name of magistrate;
Letters should not be known; riches, poverty,
And use of service, none; contract, succession,
Bourn, bound of land, tilth, vineyard, none;
No use of metal, corn, or wine, or oil;
No occupation; all men idle, all;
And women too, but innocent and pure;
No sovereignty,—

EBASTIAN.   Yet he would be king on 't.

NTONIO. The latter end of his commonwealth forgets the
beginning.

ONZALO. All things in common nature should produce
Without sweat or endeavour: treason, felony,
Sword, pike, knife, gun, or need of any engine,
Would I not have; but nature should bring forth,
Of its own kind, all foison, all abundance,
To feed my innocent people.

EBASTIAN. No marrying 'mong his subjects?

NTONIO. None, man; all idle; whores and knaves.

ONZALO. I would with such perfection govern, sir,
To excel the golden age.

EBASTIAN.   Save his Majesty!

NTONIO. Long live Gonzalo!

ONZALO.   And,—do you mark me, sir?

LONSO. Prithee, no more: thou dost talk nothing to me.

ONZALO. I do well believe your Highness; and did it to
minister occasion to these gentlemen, who are of such
sensible and nimble lungs that they always use to laugh
at nothing.

NTONIO. 'Twas you we laugh'd at.

ONZALO. Who in this kind of merry fooling am nothing to
you; so you may continue and laugh at nothing still.

NTONIO. What a blow was there given!

EBASTIAN. An it had not fallen flat-long.

ONZALO. You are gentlemen of brave mettle: you would
lift the moon out of her sphere, if she would continue in
it five weeks without changing.

Enter Ariel, invisible, playing solemn music

EBASTIAN. We would so, and then go a-bat-fowling.

NTONIO. Nay, good my lord, be not angry.

ONZALO. No, I warrant you; I will not adventure my dis-

cretion so weakly. Will you laugh me asleep, for I am
very heavy?

ANTONIO. Go sleep, and hear us.

All sleep but Alonso, Sebastian, and Antonio.

ALONSO. What! all so soon asleep! I wish mine eyes
Would, with themselves, shut up my thoughts: I find
They are inclin'd to do so.

SEBASTIAN.   Please you, sir,
Do not omit the heavy offer of it:
It seldom visits sorrow; when it doth
It is a comforter.

ANTONIO.   We two, my lord,
Will guard your person while you take your rest,
And watch your safety.

ALONSO.   Thank you. Wondrous heavy.

Alonso sleeps. Exit Ariel

SEBASTIAN. What a strange drowsiness possesses them!

ANTONIO. It is the quality o' the climate.

SEBASTIAN.   Why
Doth it not then our eyelids sink? I find not
Myself dispos'd to sleep.

ANTONIO.   Nor I: my spirits are nimble.
They fell together all, as by consent;
They dropp'd, as by a thunder-stroke. What might,
Worthy Sebastian? O! what might?—No more:—
And yet methinks I see it in thy face,
What thou should'st be. The occasion speaks thee; and
My strong imagination sees a crown
Dropping upon thy head.

SEBASTIAN.   What! art thou waking?

ANTONIO. Do you not hear me speak?

SEBASTIAN.   I do; and surely,
It is a sleepy language, and thou speak'st
Out of thy sleep. What is it thou didst say?
This is a strange repose, to be asleep
With eyes wide open; standing, speaking, moving,
And yet so fast asleep.

ANTONIO.   Noble Sebastian,
Thou let'st thy fortune sleep—die rather; wink'st
Whiles thou art waking.

SEBASTIAN.   Thou dost snore distinctly:
There 's meaning in thy snores.

ANTONIO. I am more serious than my custom: you
　　Must be so too, if heed me; which to do
　　Trebles thee o'er.
SEBASTIAN.　　　　　Well; I am standing water.
ANTONIO. I 'll teach you how to flow.
SEBASTIAN.　　　　　　　Do so: to ebb,
　　Hereditary sloth instructs me.
ANTONIO.　　　　　　O!
　　If you but knew how you the purpose cherish
　　Whiles thus you mock it! how, in stripping it,
　　You more invest it! Ebbing men, indeed,
　　Most often do so near the bottom run
　　By their own fear or sloth.
SEBASTIAN.　　　　　　Prithee, say on:
　　The setting of thine eye and cheek proclaim
　　A matter from thee, and a birth indeed
　　Which throes thee much to yield.
ANTONIO.　　　　　　Thus, sir:
　　Although this lord of weak remembrance, this
　　Who shall be of as little memory
　　When he is earth'd, hath here almost persuaded,—
　　For he 's a spirit of persuasion, only
　　Professes to persuade,—the king, his son 's alive,
　　'Tis as impossible that he 's undrown'd
　　As he that sleeps here swims.
SEBASTIAN.　　　　　　I have no hope
　　That he 's undrown'd.
ANTONIO.　　　O! out of that 'no hope,'
　　What great hope have you! no hope that way is
　　Another way so high a hope that even
　　Ambition cannot pierce a wink beyond,
　　But doubts discovery there. Will you grant with me
　　That Ferdinand is drown'd?
SEBASTIAN.　　　　　He 's gone.
ANTONIO.　　　　　Then tell me
　　Who 's the next heir of Naples?
SEBASTIAN.　　　　　Claribel.
ANTONIO. She that is Queen of Tunis; she that dwells
　　Ten leagues beyond man's life; she that from Naples
　　Can have no note, unless the sun were post—
　　The man i' th' moon 's too slow—till new-born chins
　　Be rough and razorable: she that, from whom?

We all were sea-swallow'd, though some cast again,
And by that destiny to perform an act
Whereof what 's past is prologue, what to come
In yours and my discharge.

SEBASTIAN.   What stuff is this!—How say you?
'Tis true my brother's daughter 's Queen of Tunis;
So is she heir of Naples; 'twixt which regions
There is some space.

ANTONIO.   A space whose every cubit
Seems to cry out, 'How shall that Claribel
Measure us back to Naples?—Keep in Tunis,
And let Sebastian wake!'—Say, this were death
That now hath seiz'd them; why, they were no worse
Than now they are. There be that can rule Naples
As well as he that sleeps; lords that can prate
As amply and unnecessarily
As this Gonzalo: I myself could make
A chough of as deep chat. O, that you bore
The mind that I do! what a sleep were this
For your advancement! Do you understand me?

SEBASTIAN. Methinks I do.

ANTONIO.   And how does your content
Tender your own good fortune?

SEBASTIAN.   I remember
You did supplant your brother Prospero.

ANTONIO.   True:
And look how well my garments sit upon me;
Much feater than before; my brother's servants
Were then my fellows; now they are my men.

SEBASTIAN. But, for your conscience,—

ANTONIO. Ay, sir; where lies that? If it were a kibe,
'Twould put me to my slipper: but I feel not
This deity in my bosom: twenty consciences,
That stand 'twixt me and Milan, candied be they,
And melt ere they molest! Here lies your brother,
No better than the earth he lies upon,
If he were that which now he 's like, that 's dead;
Whom I, with this obedient steel,—three inches of it,—
Can lay to bed for ever; whiles you, doing thus,
To the perpetual wink for aye might put
This ancient morsel, this Sir Prudence, who
Should not upbraid our course. For all the rest,

They 'll take suggestion as a cat laps milk;
They 'll tell the clock to any business that
We say befits the hour.

SEBASTIAN. Thy case, dear friend,
Shall be my precedent: as thou got'st Milan,
I 'll come by Naples. Draw thy sword: one stroke
Shall free thee from the tribute which thou pay'st,
And I the king shall love thee.

ANTONIO. Draw together;
And when I rear my hand, do you the like,
To fall it on Gonzalo.

SEBASTIAN. O! but one word. *They converse apart*
Music. Re-enter Ariel, invisible.

ARIEL. My master through his art foresees the danger
That you, his friend, are in; and sends me forth—
For else his project dies—to keep thee living.

Sings in Gonzalo's ear

While you here do snoring lie,
Open-ey'd Conspiracy
His time doth take.
If of life you keep a care,
Shake off slumber, and beware:
Awake! awake!

ANTONIO. Then let us both be sudden.

GONZALO. Now, good angels
Preserve the king! *They wake*

ALONSO. Why, how now! ho, awake! Why are you drawn?
Wherefore this ghastly looking?

GONZALO. What 's the matter?

SEBASTIAN. Whiles we stood here securing your repose,
Even now, we heard a hollow burst of bellowing
Like bulls, or rather lions; did 't not wake you?
It struck mine ear most terribly.

ALONSO. I heard nothing.

ANTONIO. O! 'twas a din to fright a monster's ear,
To make an earthquake: sure it was the roar
Of a whole herd of lions.

ALONSO. Heard you this, Gonzalo?

GONZALO. Upon mine honour, sir, I heard a humming,
And that a strange one too, which did awake me.
I shak'd you, sir, and cried; as mine eyes open'd,
I saw their weapons drawn:—there was a noise,

That 's verily. 'Tis best we stand upon our guard,
Or that we quit this place: let 's draw our weapons.

ALONSO. Lead off this ground, and let 's make further search
For my poor son.

GONZALO.   Heavens keep him from these beasts!
For he is, sure, i' the island.

ALONSO.   Lead away.

Exit with the others

ARIEL. Prospero my lord shall know what I have done:
So, king, go safely on to seek thy son.   *Exit*

SCENE TWO

Another Part of the Island.

*Enter Caliban, with
a burden of wood. A noise of thunder heard*

CALIBAN. All the infections that the sun sucks up
From bogs, fens, flats, on Prosper fall, and make him
By inch-meal a disease! His spirits hear me,
And yet I needs must curse. But they 'll nor pinch,
Fright me with urchin-shows, pitch me i' the mire,
Nor lead me, like a firebrand, in the dark
Out of my way, unless he bid 'em; but
For every trifle are they set upon me:
Sometime like apes, that mow and chatter at me
And after bite me; then like hedge-hogs, which
Lie tumbling in my bare-foot way and mount
Their pricks at my foot-fall; sometime am I
All wound with adders, who with cloven tongues
Do hiss me into madness.—

Enter Trinculo

                    Lo now! lo!
Here comes a spirit of his, and to torment me
For bringing wood in slowly: I 'll fall flat;
Perchance he will not mind me.

TRINCULO. Here 's neither bush nor shrub to bear off any
weather at all, and another storm brewing; I hear it sing
i' the wind; yond same black cloud, yond huge one, looks

like a foul bombard that would shed his liquor. If it
should thunder as it did before, I know not where to hide
my head: yond same cloud cannot choose but fall by
pailfuls.—What have we here? a man or a fish? Dead or
alive? A fish: he smells like a fish; a very ancient and
fish-like smell; a kind of not of the newest Poor-John. A
strange fish! Were I in England now,—as once I was,—
and had but this fish painted, not a holiday fool there but
would give a piece of silver: there would this monster
make a man; any strange beast there makes a man.
When they will not give a doit to relieve a lame beggar,
they will lay out ten to see a dead Indian. Legg'd like a
man! and his fins like arms! Warm, o' my troth! I do now
let loose my opinion, hold it no longer; this is no fish, but
an islander, that hath lately suffered by a thunderbolt.
(*Thunder*) Alas, the storm is come again: my best way
is to creep under his gaberdine; there is no other shelter
hereabout: misery acquaints a man with strange bedfel-
lows. I will here shroud till the dregs of the storm be
past.

Enter Stephano, singing; a bottle in his hand

STEPHANO. I shall no more to sea, to sea,
            Here shall I die a-shore:—
This is a very scurvy tune to sing at a man's funeral:
Well, here 's my comfort.   *Drinks*
        The master, the swabber, the boatswain and I,
            The gunner and his mate,
    Lov'd Mall, Meg, and Marian and Margery,
            But none of us car'd for Kate;
        For she had a tongue with a tang,
            Would cry to a sailor, 'Go hang!'
    She lov'd not the savour of tar nor of pitch,
    Yet a tailor might scratch her where-e'er she did itch:
            Then to sea, boys, and let her go hang.
This is a scurvy tune too: but here 's my comfort.
                                               Drinks

CALIBAN. Do not torment me: O!

STEPHANO. What 's the matter? Have we devils here? Do
you put tricks upon us with savages and men of Ind? Ha!
I have not 'scaped drowning, to be afeard now of your
four legs; for it hath been said, 'As proper a man as ever
went on four legs cannot make him give ground': and it

shall be said so again while Stephano breathes at 's nostrils.

CALIBAN. The spirit torments me: O!

STEPHANO. This is some monster of the isle with four legs, who hath got, as I take it, an ague. Where the devil should he learn our language? I will give him some relief, if it be but for that: if I can recover him and keep him tame and get to Naples with him, he 's a present for any emperor that ever trod on neat's-leather.

CALIBAN. Do not torment me, prithee; I 'll bring my wood home faster.

STEPHANO. He 's in his fit now and does not talk after the wisest. He shall taste of my bottle: if he have never drunk wine afore it will go near to remove his fit. If I can recover him, and keep him tame, I will not take too much for him: he shall pay for him that hath him, and that soundly.

CALIBAN. Thou dost me yet but little hurt; thou wilt anon, I know it by thy trembling: now Prosper works upon thee.

STEPHANO. Come on your ways: open your mouth; here is that which will give language to you, cat. Open your mouth: this will shake your shaking, I can tell you, and that soundly (*Gives Caliban drink*): you cannot tell who 's your friend: open your chaps again.

TRINCULO. I should know that voice: it should be—but he is drowned; and these are devils. O! defend me.

STEPHANO. Four legs and two voices; a most delicate monster! His forward voice now is to speak well of his friend; his backward voice is to utter foul speeches, and to detract. If all the wine in my bottle will recover him, I will help his ague. Come. Amen! I will pour some in thy other mouth.

TRINCULO. Stephano!

STEPHANO. Doth thy other mouth call me? Mercy! mercy! This is a devil, and no monster: I will leave him; I have no long spoon.

TRINCULO. Stephano!—if thou beest Stephano, touch me, and speak to me; for I am Trinculo:—be not afeard—thy good friend Trinculo.

STEPHANO. If thou beest Trinculo, come forth. I 'll pull thee by the lesser legs: if any be Trinculo's legs, these are

they. Thou art very Trinculo indeed! How cam'st thou to
be the siege of this moon-calf? Can he vent Trinculos?

TRINCULO. I took him to be killed with a thunder-stroke.
But art thou not drowned, Stephano? I hope now thou
art not drowned. Is the storm overblown? I hid me under
the dead moon-calf's gaberdine for fear of the storm. And
art thou living, Stephano? O Stephano! two Neapolitans
'scaped!

STEPHANO. Prithee, do not turn me about: my stomach is
not constant.

CALIBAN. (*Aside*) These be fine things an if they be not
sprites.
That 's a brave god and bears celestial liquor:
I will kneel to him.

STEPHANO. How didst thou 'scape? How cam'st thou
hither? Swear by this bottle, how thou cam'st hither. I
escaped upon a butt of sack, which the sailors heaved
overboard, by this bottle! which I made of the bark of a
tree with mine own hands, since I was cast ashore.

CALIBAN. I 'll swear upon that bottle, to be thy true subject;
for the liquor is not earthly.

STEPHANO. Here: swear then, how thou escapedst.

TRINCULO. Swam ashore, man, like a duck: I can swim like
a duck, I 'll be sworn.

STEPHANO. Here, kiss the book (*Gives Trinculo drink*).
Though thou canst swim like a duck, thou art made like a
goose.

TRINCULO. O Stephano! hast any more of this?

STEPHANO. The whole butt, man: my cellar is in a rock by
the seaside, where my wine is hid. How now, moon-calf!
how does thine ague?

CALIBAN. Hast thou not dropped from heaven?

STEPHANO. Out o' the moon, I do assure thee: I was the
man in the moon, when time was.

CALIBAN. I have seen thee in her, and I do adore thee; my
mistress showed me thee, and thy dog, and thy bush.

STEPHANO. Come, swear to that; kiss the book; I will furnish it anon with new contents; swear.

TRINCULO. By this good light, this is a very shallow monster.—I afeard of him!—a very weak monster.—the man i'
the moon! a most poor credulous monster!—Well drawn,
monster, in good sooth.

CALIBAN. I 'll show thee every fertile inch o' the island;
    And I will kiss thy foot. I prithee, be my god.

TRINCULO. By this light, a most perfidious and drunken
    monster: when his god 's asleep, he 'll rob his bottle.

CALIBAN. I 'll kiss thy foot: I 'll swear myself thy subject.

STEPHANO. Come on then; down, and swear.

TRINCULO. I shall laugh myself to death at this puppy-
    headed monster. A most scurvy monster! I could find in
    my heart to beat him,—

STEPHANO. Come, kiss.

TRINCULO. But that the poor monster 's in drink: an abom-
    inable monster!

CALIBAN. I 'll shew thee the best springs; I 'll pluck thee
    berries;
    I 'll fish for thee, and get thee wood enough.
    A plague upon the tyrant that I serve!
    I 'll bear him no more sticks, but follow thee,
    Thou wondrous man.

TRINCULO. A most ridiculous monster, to make a wonder of
    a poor drunkard!

CALIBAN. I prithee, let me bring thee where crabs grow;
    And I with my long nails will dig thee pig-nuts;
    Show thee a jay's nest and instruct thee how
    To snare the nimble marmozet; I 'll bring thee
    To clust'ring filberts, and sometimes I 'll get thee
    Young scamels from the rock. Wilt thou go with me?

STEPHANO. I prithee now, lead the way, without any more
    talking.—Trinculo, the king and all our company else be-
    ing drowned, we will inherit here.—Here; bear my bottle.
    —Fellow Trinculo, we 'll fill him by and by again.

CALIBAN. Farewell, master; farewell, farewell!

                           Sings drunkenly

TRINCULO. A howling monster, a drunken monster.

CALIBAN.   No more dams I 'll make for fish;
              Nor fetch in firing
                At requiring,
           Nor scrape trenchering, nor wash dish;
             'Ban, 'Ban, Ca—Caliban,
             Has a new master—Get a new man.

    Freedom, high-day! high-day, freedom! freedom! high-
    day, freedom!

STEPHANO. O brave monster! lead the way.   *Exeunt*

ACT THREE

SCENE ONE

Before Prospero's Cell.

Enter Ferdinand, bearing a log

FERDINAND. There be some sports are painful, and their la-
bour
Delight in them sets off: some kinds of baseness
Are nobly undergone, and most poor matters
Point to rich ends. This my mean task
Would be as heavy to me as odious; but
The mistress which I serve quickens what 's dead
And makes my labours pleasures: O! she is
Ten times more gentle than her father 's crabbed,
And he 's compos'd of harshness. I must remove
Some thousands of these logs and pile them up,
Upon a sore injunction: my sweet mistress
Weeps when she sees me work, and says such baseness
Had never like executor. I forget:
But these sweet thoughts do even refresh my labours,
Most busiest when I do it.

Enter Miranda; and Prospero behind

MIRANDA.   Alas! now pray you,
Work not so hard: I would the lightning had
Burnt up those logs that you are enjoin'd to pile!
Pray, set it down and rest you: when this burns,
'Twill weep for having wearied you. My father
Is hard at study; pray now, rest yourself:
He 's safe for these three hours.

FERDINAND.   O most dear mistress,
The sun will set, before I shall discharge
What I must strive to do.

MIRANDA.   If you 'll sit down,
I 'll bear your logs the while. Pray, give me that;

I 'll carry it to the pile.

FERDINAND.   No, precious creature:
I had rather crack my sinews, break my back,
Than you should such dishonour undergo,
While I sit lazy by.

MIRANDA.   It would become me
As well as it does you: and I should do it
With much more ease; for my good will is to it,
And yours it is against.

PROSPERO. (*Aside*) Poor worm! thou art infected:
This visitation shows it.

MIRANDA.   You look wearily.

FERDINAND. No, noble mistress; 'tis fresh morning with me
When you are by at night. I do beseech you—
Chiefly that I might set it in my prayers—
What is your name?

MIRANDA.   Miranda.—O my father!
I have broke your hest to say so.

FERDINAND.   Admir'd Miranda!
Indeed, the top of admiration; worth
What 's dearest to the world! Full many a lady
I have ey'd with best regard, and many a time
The harmony of their tongues hath into bondage
Brought my too diligent ear: for several virtues
Have I lik'd several women; never any
With so full soul but some defect in her
Did quarrel with the noblest grace she ow'd,
And put it to the foil: but you, O you!
So perfect and so peerless, are created
Of every creature's best.

MIRANDA.   I do not know
One of my sex; no woman's face remember,
Save, from my glass, mine own; nor have I seen
More that I may call men than you, good friend,
And my dear father: how features are abroad,
I am skill-less of; but, by my modesty,—
The jewel in my dower,—I would not wish
Any companion in the world but you;
Nor can imagination form a shape,
Besides yourself, to like of. But I prattle
Something too wildly and my father's precepts
I therein do forget.

FERDINAND.   I am in my condition
   A prince, Miranda; I do think, a king;—
   I would not so!—and would no more endure
   This wooden slavery than to suffer
   The flesh-fly blow my mouth.—Hear my soul speak:—
   The very instant that I saw you did
   My heart fly to your service; there resides,
   To make me slave to it; and for your sake
   Am I this patient log-man.

MIRANDA.   Do you love me?

FERDINAND. O heaven! O earth! bear witness to this sound,
   And crown what I profess with kind event
   If I speak true: if hollowly, invert
   What best is boded me to mischief! I,
   Beyond all limit of what else i' the world,
   Do love, prize, honour you.

MIRANDA.   I am a fool
   To weep at what I am glad of.

PROSPERO.   (Aside) Fair encounter
   Of two most rare affections! Heavens rain grace
   On that which breeds between them!

FERDINAND.   Wherefore weep you?

MIRANDA. At mine unworthiness, that dare not offer
   What I desire to give; and much less take
   What I shall die to want. But this is trifling;
   And all the more it seeks to hide itself
   The bigger bulk it shows. Hence, bashful cunning!
   And prompt me, plain and holy innocence!
   I am your wife, if you will marry me;
   If not, I 'll die your maid: to be your fellow
   You may deny me; but I 'll be your servant
   Whether you will or no.

FERDINAND.   My mistress, dearest;
   And I thus humble ever.

MIRANDA.   My husband then?

FERDINAND. Ay, with a heart as willing
   As bondage e'er of freedom: here 's my hand.

MIRANDA. And mine, with my heart in 't: and now farewell
   Till half an hour hence.

FERDINAND.   A thousand thousand!
              Exeunt Ferdinand and Miranda severally

PROSPERO. So glad of this as they, I cannot be,

Who are surpris'd withal; but my rejoicing
At nothing can be more. I 'll to my book;
For yet, ere supper time, must I perform
Much business appertaining.   *Exit*

SCENE TWO

Another Part of the Island.

Enter Caliban, with a bottle, Stephano, and Trinculo

STEPHANO. Tell not me:—when the butt is out, we will
drink water; not a drop before: therefore bear up, and
board 'em.—Servant-monster, drink to me.

TRINCULO. Servant-monster! the folly of this island! They
say there 's but five upon this isle: we are three of them;
if th' other two be brained like us, the state totters.

STEPHANO. Drink, servant-monster, when I bid thee: thy
eyes are almost set in thy head.

TRINCULO. Where should they be set else? He were a brave
monster indeed, if they were set in his tail.

STEPHANO. My man-monster hath drowned his tongue in
sack: for my part, the sea cannot drown me; I swam, ere
I could recover the shore, five-and-thirty leagues, off and
on, by this light. Thou shalt be my lieutenant, monster,
or my standard.

TRINCULO. Your lieutenant, if you list; he 's no standard.

STEPHANO. We 'll not run, Monsieur monster.

TRINCULO. Nor go neither: but you 'll lie, like dogs; and yet
say nothing neither.

STEPHANO. Moon-calf, speak once in thy life, if thou beest
a good moon-calf.

CALIBAN. How does thy honour? Let me lick thy shoe. I 'll
not serve him; he is not valiant.

TRINCULO. Thou liest, most ignorant monster: I am in case
to justle a constable. Why, thou deboshed fish thou, was
there ever a man a coward that hath drunk so much sack
as I to-day? Wilt thou tell a monstrous lie, being but half
a fish and half a monster?

CALIBAN. Lo, how he mocks me! wilt thou let him, my
lord?

TRINCULO. 'Lord' quoth he!—that a monster should be such
   a natural!

CALIBAN. Lo, lo, again! Bite him to death, I prithee.

STEPHANO. Trinculo, keep a good tongue in your head: if
   you prove a mutineer, the next tree! The poor monster 's
   my subject, and he shall not suffer indignity.

CALIBAN. I thank my noble lord. Wilt thou be pleas'd
   To hearken once again the suit I made thee?

STEPHANO. Marry, will I; kneel, and repeat it: I will stand,
   and so shall Trinculo.

                Enter Ariel, invisible

CALIBAN. As I told thee before, I am subject to a tyrant, a
   sorcerer, that by his cunning hath cheated me of the
   island.

ARIEL. Thou liest.

CALIBAN. Thou liest, thou jesting monkey thou;
   I would my valiant master would destroy thee;
   I do not lie.

STEPHANO. Trinculo, if you trouble him any more in his
   tale, by this hand, I will supplant some of your teeth.

TRINCULO. Why, I said nothing.

STEPHANO. Mum then and no more.—(*To Caliban*) Proceed.

CALIBAN. I say, by sorcery he got this isle;
   From me he got it: if thy greatness will,
   Revenge it on him,—for, I know, thou dar 'st;
   But this thing dare not,—

STEPHANO. That 's most certain.

CALIBAN. Thou shalt be lord of it and I 'll serve thee.

STEPHANO. How now shall this be compassed? Canst thou
   bring me to the party?

CALIBAN. Yea, yea, my lord: I 'll yield him thee asleep,
   Where thou may'st knock a nail into his head.

ARIEL. Thou liest; thou canst not.

CALIBAN. What a pied ninny's this! Thou scurvy patch!—
   I do beseech thy greatness, give him blows,
   And take his bottle from him: when that 's gone
   He shall drink nought but brine; for I 'll not show him
   Where the quick freshes are.

STEPHANO. Trinculo, run into no further danger: interrupt
   the monster one word further, and, by this hand, I 'll turn
   my mercy out o' doors and make a stock-fish of thee.

TRINCULO. Why, what did I? I did nothing. I 'll go further
off.

STEPHANO. Didst thou not say he lied?

ARIEL. Thou liest.

STEPHANO. Do I so? Take thou that. (*Strikes Trinculo*) As
you like this, give me the lie another time.

TRINCULO. I did not give thee the lie:—Out o' your wits
and hearing too?—A pox o' your bottle! this can sack and
drinking do.—A murrain on your monster, and the devil
take your fingers!

CALIBAN. Ha, ha, ha!

STEPHANO. Now, forward with your tale.—Prithee stand
further off.

CALIBAN. Beat him enough: after a little time
I 'll beat him too.

STEPHANO.   Stand further.—Come, proceed.

CALIBAN. Why, as I told thee, 'tis a custom with him
I' the afternoon to sleep: there thou may'st brain him,
Having first seiz'd his books; or with a log
Batter his skull, or paunch him with a stake,
Or cut his wezand with thy knife. Remember
First to possess his books; for without them
He 's but a sot, as I am, nor hath not
One spirit to command: they all do hate him
As rootedly as I. Burn but his books;
He has brave utensils,—for so he calls them,—
Which, when he has a house, he 'll deck withal:
And that most deeply to consider is
The beauty of his daughter; he himself
Calls her a nonpareil: I never saw a woman,
But only Sycorax my dam and she;
But she as far surpasseth Sycorax
As great'st does least.

STEPHANO.   Is it so brave a lass?

CALIBAN. Ay, lord; she will become thy bed, I warrant,
And bring thee forth brave brood.

STEPHANO. Monster, I will kill this man; his daughter and
I will be king and queen,—save our graces! and Trinculo
and thyself shall be viceroys. Dost thou like the plot,
Trinculo?

TRINCULO. Excellent.

STEPHANO. Give me thy hand: I am sorry I beat thee; but,

while thou livest, keep a good tongue in thy head.

CALIBAN. Within this half hour will he be asleep;
Wilt thou destroy him then?

STEPHANO.   Ay, on mine honour.

ARIEL. This will I tell my master.

CALIBAN. Thou mak'st me merry: I am full of pleasure.
Let us be jocund: will you troll the catch
You taught me but while-ere?

STEPHANO. At thy request, monster, I will do reason, any
reason: Come on, Trinculo, let us sing.   *Sings*
     Flout 'em, and scout 'em; and scout 'em, and flout 'em;
     Thought is free.

CALIBAN. That 's not the tune.

     Ariel plays the tune on a Tabor and Pipe

STEPHANO. What is this same?

TRINCULO. This is the tune of our catch, played by the picture of Nobody.

STEPHANO. If thou beest a man, show thyself in thy likeness: if thou beest a devil, take 't as thou list.

TRINCULO. O, forgive me my sins!

STEPHANO. He that dies pays all debts: I defy thee.—Mercy
upon us!

CALIBAN. Art thou afeard?

STEPHANO. No, monster, not I.

CALIBAN. Be not afeard: the isle is full of noises,
Sounds and sweet airs, that give delight, and hurt not.
Sometimes a thousand twangling instruments
Will hum about mine ears; and sometime voices,
That, if I then had wak'd after long sleep,
Will make me sleep again: and then, in dreaming,
The clouds methought would open and show riches
Ready to drop upon me; that, when I wak'd
I cried to dream again.

STEPHANO. This will prove a brave kingdom to me, where I
shall have my music for nothing.

CALIBAN. When Prospero is destroyed.

STEPHANO. That shall be by and by: I remember the story.

TRINCULO. The sound is going away: let 's follow it, and
after do our work.

STEPHANO. Lead, monster; we 'll follow.—I would I could
see this taborer! he lays it on. Wilt come?

TRINCULO. I 'll follow, Stephano.   *Exeunt*

SCENE THREE

Another Part of the Island.

Enter Alonso, Sebastian, Antonio, Gonzalo, Adrian,
Francisco, and others

GONZALO. By'r lakin, I can go no further, sir;
  My old bones ache: here 's a maze trod indeed,
  Through forth-rights, and meanders! by your patience,
  I needs must rest me.

ALONSO.   Old lord, I cannot blame thee,
  Who am myself attach'd with weariness,
  To the dulling of my spirits: sit down, and rest.
  Even here I will put off my hope, and keep it
  No longer for my flatterer: he is drown'd
  Whom thus we stray to find; and the sea mocks
  Our frustrate search on land. Well, let him go.

ANTONIO. *(Aside to Sebastian)* I am right glad that he 's so
  out of hope.
  Do not, for one repulse, forego the purpose
  That you resolv'd to effect.

SEBASTIAN. *(Aside to Antonio)* The next advantage
  Will we take throughly.

ANTONIO. *(Aside to Sebastian)* Let it be to-night;
  For, now they are oppress'd with travel, they
  Will not, nor cannot, use such vigilance
  As when they are fresh.

SEBASTIAN. *(Aside to Antonio)* I say to-night: no more.
      Solemn and strange music; and Prospero
above, invisible. Enter below several strange Shapes, bring-
ing in a banquet: they dance about it with gentle actions of
salutation; and, inviting the King, &c., to eat, they depart.

ALONSO. What harmony is this? My good friends, hark!

GONZALO. Marvellous sweet music!

ALONSO. Give us kind keepers, heavens! What were these?

SEBASTIAN. A living drollery. Now I will believe
  That there are unicorns; that in Arabia
  There is one tree, the phœnix' throne; one phœnix

At this hour reigning there.

ANTONIO.   I 'll believe both;
And what does else want credit, come to me,
And I 'll be sworn 'tis true: travellers ne'er did lie,
Though fools at home condemn them.

GONZALO.   If in Naples
I should report this now, would they believe me?
If I should say I saw such islanders,—
For, certes, these are people of the island,—
Who, though they are of monstrous shape, yet, note,
Their manners are more gentle-kind than of
Our human generation you shall find
Many, nay, almost any.

PROSPERO.   (*Aside*) Honest lord,
Thou hast said well; for some of you there present
Are worse than devils.

ALONSO.   I cannot too much muse,
Such shapes, such gesture, and such sound, expressing,—
Although they want the use of tongue,—a kind
Of excellent dumb discourse.

PROSPERO.   (*Aside*) Praise in departing.

FRANCISCO. They vanish'd strangely.

SEBASTIAN.   No matter, since
They have left their viands behind; for we have stom-
    achs.—
Will 't please you to taste of what is here?

ALONSO.   Not I.

GONZALO. Faith, sir, you need not fear. When we were boys,
Who would believe that there were mountaineers
Dew-lapp'd like bulls, whose throats had hanging at them
Wallets of flesh? or that there were such men
Whose heads stood in their breasts? which now we find
Each putter-out of five for one will bring us
Good warrant of.

ALONSO.   I will stand to and feed,
Although my last; no matter, since I feel
The best is past.—Brother, my lord the duke,
Stand to and do as we.

                        Thunder and lightning.
*Enter Ariel like a harpy; claps his wings upon the table;
    and, with a quaint device, the banquet vanishes.*

ARIEL. You are three men of sin, whom Destiny—

That hath to instrument this lower world
And what is in 't,—the never-surfeited sea
Hath caused to belch up you; and on this island
Where man doth not inhabit; you 'mongst men
Being most unfit to live. I have made you mad;

Seeing Alonso, Sebastian, &c., draw their sword

And even with such-like valour men hang and drown
Their proper selves. You fools! I and my fellows
Are ministers of fate: the elements
Of whom your swords are temper'd, may as well
Wound the loud winds, or with bemock'd-at stabs
Kill the still-closing waters, as diminish
One dowle that 's in my plume; my fellow-ministers
Are like invulnerable. If you could hurt,
Your swords are now too massy for your strengths,
And will not be uplifted. But, remember,—
For that 's my business to you,—that you three
From Milan did supplant good Prospero;
Expos'd unto the sea, which hath requit it,
Him and his innocent child: for which foul deed
The powers, delaying, not forgetting, have
Incens'd the seas and shores, yea, all the creatures,
Against your peace. Thee of thy son, Alonso,
They have bereft; and do pronounce, by me,
Lingering perdition,—worse than any death
Can be at once,—shall step by step attend
You and your ways; whose wraths to guard you from—
Which here in this most desolate isle, else falls
Upon your heads,—is nothing but heart-sorrow
And a clear life ensuing.

He vanishes in thunder:
then, to soft music, enter the Shapes again, and dance with
mocks and mows, and carry out the table

PROSPERO. (*Aside*) Bravely the figure of this harpy hast thou
Perform'd, my Ariel; a grace it had, devouring:
Of my instruction hast thou nothing bated
In what thou hadst to say: so, with good life
And observation strange, my meaner ministers
Their several kinds have done. My high charms work,
And these mine enemies are all knit up
In their distractions: they now are in my power;
And in these fits I leave them, while I visit

Young Ferdinand,—whom they suppose is drown'd,—
And his and mine lov'd darling.   *Exit above*

ɢONZALO. I' the name of something holy, sir, why stand you
In this strange stare?

ᴀLONSO.   O, it is monstrous! monstrous!
Methought the billows spoke and told me of it;
The winds did sing it to me; and the thunder,
That deep and dreadful organ-pipe, pronounc'd
The name of Prosper: it did bass my trespass.
Therefore my son i' th' ooze is bedded; and
I 'll seek him deeper than e'er plummet sounded,
And with him there lie mudded.   *Exit*

ꜱEBASTIAN.   But one fiend at a time,
I 'll fight their legions o'er.

ᴀNTONIO.   I 'll be thy second.
                         Exeunt Sebastian and Antonio

ɢONZALO. All three of them are desperate; their great guilt,
Like poison given to work a great time after,
Now 'gins to bite the spirits.—I do beseech you
That are of suppler joints, follow them swiftly
And hinder them from what this ecstasy
May now provoke them to.

ᴀDRIAN.   Follow, I pray you. *Exeunt*

ACT FOUR

SCENE ONE

Before Prospero's Cell.

Enter Prospero, Ferdinand, and Miranda

PROSPERO. If I have too austerely punish'd you,
　　Your compensation makes amends; for I
　　Have given you here a third of mine own life,
　　Or that for which I live; whom once again
　　I tender to thy hand: all thy vexations
　　Were but my trials of thy love, and thou
　　Hast strangely stood the test: here, afore Heaven,
　　I ratify this my rich gift. O Ferdinand!
　　Do not smile at me that I boast her off,
　　For thou shalt find she will outstrip all praise,
　　And make it halt behind her.
FERDINAND.　　　　　　　　　　I do believe it
　　Against an oracle.
PROSPERO. Then, as my gift and thine own acquisition
　　Worthily purchas'd, take my daughter: but
　　If thou dost break her virgin knot before
　　All sanctimonious ceremonies may
　　With full and holy rite be minister'd,
　　No sweet aspersion shall the heavens let fall
　　To make this contract grow; but barren hate,
　　Sour-ey'd disdain and discord shall bestrew
　　The union of your beds with weeds so loathly
　　That you shall hate it both: therefore take heed,
　　As Hymen's lamps shall light you.
FERDINAND.　　　　　　　　　　As I hope
　　For quiet days, fair issue and long life,
　　With such love as 'tis now, the murkiest den,
　　The most opportune place, the strong'st suggestion
　　Our worser genius can, shall never melt

Mine honour into lust, to take away
The edge of that day's celebration
When I shall think, or Phœbus' steeds are founder'd,
Or Night kept chain'd below.

ROSPERO. Fairly spoke:
Sit then, and talk with her, she is thine own.
What, Ariel! my industrious servant Ariel!

Enter Ariel

RIEL. What would my potent master? Here I am.

ROSPERO. Thou and thy meaner fellows your last service
Did worthily perform; and I must use you
In such another trick. Go bring the rabble,
O'er whom I give thee power, here to this place:
Incite them to quick motion; for I must
Bestow upon the eyes of this young couple
Some vanity of mine art: it is my promise,
And they expect it from me.

RIEL. Presently?

ROSPERO. Ay, with a twink.

RIEL. Before you can say, 'Come,' and 'Go,'
And breathe twice; and cry, 'so, so,'
Each one, tripping on his toe,
Will be here with mop and mow.
Do you love me, master? no?

ROSPERO. Dearly, my delicate Ariel. Do not approach
Till thou dost hear me call.

RIEL. Well, I can conceive. *Exit*

ROSPERO. Look thou be true; do not give dalliance
Too much the rein: the strongest oaths are straw
To the fire i' the blood: be more abstemious,
Or else good night your vow!

FERDINAND. I warrant yôu, sir;
The white-cold virgin snow upon my heart
Abates the ardour of my liver.

ROSPERO. Well.—
Now come, my Ariel! bring a corollary,
Rather than want a spirit: appear, and pertly.
No tongue! all eyes! be silent. *Soft music*

A Masque. Enter Iris.

IS. Ceres, most bounteous lady, thy rich leas
Of wheat, rye, barley, vetches, oats, and peas;

Thy turfy mountains, where live nibbling sheep,
And flat meads thatch'd with stover, them to keep;
Thy banks with pioned and twilled brims,
Which spongy April at thy hest betrims,
To make cold nymphs chaste crowns; and thy broom
    groves,
Whose shadow the dismissed bachelor loves,
Being lass-lorn; thy pole-clipt vineyard;
And thy sea-marge, sterile and rocky-hard,
Where thou thyself dost air: the queen o' the sky,
Whose watery arch and messenger am I,
Bids thee leave these; and with her sovereign grace,
Here on this grass-plot, in this very place,
To come and sport; her peacocks fly amain:
Approach, rich Ceres, her to entertain.

Enter Ceres

CERES. Hail, many-colour'd messenger, that ne'er
Dost disobey the wife of Jupiter;
Who with thy saffron wings upon my flowers
Diffusest honey-drops, refreshing showers:
And with each end of thy blue bow dost crown
My bosky acres, and my unshrubb'd down,
Rich scarf to my proud earth; why hath thy queen
Summon'd me hither, to this short-grass'd green?
IRIS. A contract of true love to celebrate,
And some donation freely to estate
On the bless'd lovers.
CERES.   Tell me, heavenly bow,
If Venus or her son, as thou dost know,
Do now attend the queen? since they did plot
The means that dusky Dis my daughter got,
Her and her blind boy's scandal'd company
I have forsworn.
IRIS.   Of her society
Be not afraid; I met her deity
Cutting the clouds towards Paphos and her son
Dove-drawn with her. Here thought they to have done
Some wanton charm upon this man and maid,
Whose vows are, that no bed-rite shall be paid
Till Hymen's torch be lighted; but in vain:
Mars's hot minion is return'd again:

Her waspish-headed son has broke his arrows,
Swears he will shoot no more, but play with sparrows,
And be a boy right out.

CERES.   Highest queen of state,
Great Juno comes; I know her by her gait.

Enter Juno

JUNO. How does my bounteous sister? Go with me
To bless this twain, that they may prosperous be,
And honour'd in their issue.

SONG

JUNO.   Honour, riches, marriage-blessing,
               Long continuance, and increasing,
               Hourly joys be still upon you!
               Juno sings her blessings on you.

CERES.   Earth's increase, foison plenty,
               Barns and garners never empty:
               Vines, with clust'ring bunches growing;
               Plants with goodly burden bowing;
               Spring come to you at the farthest
               In the very end of harvest!
               Scarcity and want shall shun you;
               Ceres' blessing so is on you.

FERDINAND. This is a most majestic vision, and
Harmonious charmingly: May I be bold
To think these spirits?

PROSPERO.   Spirits, which by mine art
I have from their confines call'd to enact
My present fancies.

FERDINAND.   Let me live here ever:
So rare a wonder'd father and a wise,
Makes this place Paradise.

Juno and Ceres whisper, and send Iris on employment

PROSPERO.   Sweet, now, silence!
Juno and Ceres whisper seriously,
There 's something else to do: hush, and be mute,
Or else our spell is marr'd.

IRIS. You nymphs, call'd Naiades, of the windring brooks,
With your sedg'd crowns, and ever-harmless looks,
Leave your crisp channels, and on this green land
Answer your summons: Juno does command.
Come, temperate nymphs, and help to celebrate
A contract of true love: be not too late.

Enter certain Nymphs

You sun-burn'd sicklemen, of August weary,
Come hither from the furrow, and be merry:
Make holiday: your rye-straw hats put on,
And these fresh nymphs encounter every one
In country footing.

Enter certain Reapers, properly habited:
they join with the Nymphs in a graceful dance; towar
the end whereof Prospero starts suddenly, and speaks; af
which, to a strange, hollow, and confused
noise, they heavily vanish

PROSPERO. (*Aside*) I had forgot that foul conspiracy
Of the beast Caliban, and his confederates
Against my life: the minute of their plot
Is almost come.—(*To the Spirits*) Well done! avoid; no
more!

FERDINAND. This is strange: your father 's in some passi
That works him strongly.

MIRANDA.   Never till this day
Saw I him touch'd with anger so distemper'd.

PROSPERO. You do look, my son, in a mov'd sort,
As if you were dismay'd: be cheerful, sir:
Our revels now are ended. These our actors,
As I foretold you, were all spirits and
Are melted into air, into thin air:
And, like the baseless fabric of this vision,
The cloud-capp'd towers, the gorgeous palaces,
The solemn temples, the great globe itself,
Yea, all which it inherit, shall dissolve
And, like this insubstantial pageant faded,
Leave not a rack behind. We are such stuff
As dreams are made on, and our little life
Is rounded with a sleep.—Sir, I am vex'd:
Bear with my weakness; my old brain is troubled.
Be not disturb'd with my infirmity.
If you be pleas'd, retire into my cell
And there repose: a turn or two I 'll walk,
To still my beating mind.

FERDINAND, MIRANDA. We wish your peace.   *Exe*

PROSPERO. Come with a thought!—(*To them*) I thank th
Ariel, come!

Enter Ariel

EL. Thy thoughts I cleave to. What's thy pleasure?

OSPERO. Spirit,
We must prepare to meet with Caliban.

EL. Ay, my commander; when I presented Ceres,
I thought to have told thee of it; but I fear'd
Lest I might anger thee.

OSPERO. Say again, where didst thou leave these varlets?

EL. I told you, sir, they were red-hot with drinking;
So full of valour that they smote the air
For breathing in their faces; beat the ground
For kissing of their feet; yet always bending
Towards their project. Then I beat my tabor;
At which, like unback'd colts, they prick'd their ears,
Advanc'd their eyelids, lifted up their noses
As they smelt music: so I charm'd their ears
That, calf-like, they my lowing follow'd through
Tooth'd briers, sharp furzes, pricking goss and thorns,
Which enter'd their frail shins: at last I left them
I' the filthy-mantled pool beyond your cell,
There dancing up to the chins, that the foul lake
O'erstunk their feet.

OSPERO.　　　　This was well done, my bird.
Thy shape invisible retain thou still:
The trumpery in my house, go bring it hither,
For stale to catch these thieves.

EL.　　　　　　I go, I go.　　　*Exit*

OSPERO. A devil, a born devil, on whose nature
Nurture can never stick; on whom my pains,
Humanely taken, are all lost, quite lost;
And as with age his body uglier grows,
So his mind cankers. I will plague them all,
Even to roaring.

Re-enter Ariel, loaden with glistering apparel, &c.
　　　　　Come, hang them on this line.
　　Prospero and Ariel remain invisible.
　Enter Caliban, Stephano, and Trinculo, all wet.

LIBAN. Pray you, tread softly, that the blind mole may
　not
Hear a foot fall: we now are near his cell.

EPHANO. Monster, your fairy, which you say is a harmless fairy, has done little better than played the Jack with
us.

TRINCULO. Monster, I do smell all horse-piss; at which
nose is in great indignation.

STEPHANO. So is mine.—Do you hear, monster? If I shou
take a displeasure against you, look you,—

TRINCULO. Thou wert but a lost monster.

CALIBAN. Good my lord, give me thy favour still:
Be patient, for the prize I 'll bring thee to
Shall hoodwink this mischance: therefore speak softly;
All 's hush'd as midnight yet.

TRINCULO. Ay, but to lose our bottles in the pool,—

STEPHANO. There is not only disgrace and dishonour
that, monster, but an infinite loss.

TRINCULO. That 's more to me than my wetting: yet this
your harmless fairy, monster.

STEPHANO. I will fetch off my bottle, though I be o'er e
for my labour.

CALIBAN. Prithee, my king, be quiet. Seest thou here,
This is the mouth o' the cell: no noise, and enter.
Do that good mischief, which may make this island
Thine own for ever, and I, thy Caliban,
For aye thy foot-licker.

STEPHANO. Give me thy hand: I do begin to have bloo
thoughts.

TRINCULO. O king Stephano! O peer! O worthy Stepha
look, what a wardrobe here is for thee!

CALIBAN. Let it alone, thou fool; it is but trash.

TRINCULO. O, ho, monster! we know what belongs to a fr
pery.—O king Stephano!

STEPHANO. Put off that gown, Trinculo; by this hand, I
have that gown.

TRINCULO. Thy Grace shall have it.

CALIBAN. The dropsy drown this fool! what do you mear
To dote thus on such luggage? Let 's along,
And do the murder first: if he awake,
From toe to crown he 'll fill our skin with pinches;
Make us strange stuff.

STEPHANO. Be you quiet, monster.—Mistress line, is not t
my jerkin? Now is the jerkin under the line: now, jerk
you are like to lose your hair and prove a bald jerkin

TRINCULO. Do, do: we steal by line and level, an 't
your Grace.

STEPHANO. I thank thee for that jest; here 's a garment

't: wit shall not go unrewarded while I am king of this
country: 'Steal by line and level,' is an excellent pass of
pate; there 's another garment for 't.

INCULO. Monster, come, put some lime upon your fingers, and away with the rest.

LIBAN. I will have none on 't: we shall lose our time,
And all be turn'd to barnacles, or to apes
With foreheads villanous low.

EPHANO. Monster, lay-to your fingers: help to bear this
away where my hogshead of wine is, or I 'll turn you out
of my kingdom. Go to; carry this.

INCULO. And this.

EPHANO. Ay, and this.

A noise of hunters heard.

*Enter divers Spirits, in shape of hounds, and hunt them
about; Prospero and Ariel setting them on.*

OSPERO. Hey, Mountain, hey!

IEL. Silver! there it goes, Silver!

OSPERO. Fury, Fury! there, Tyrant, there! hark, hark!

Caliban, Stephano, and Trinculo are driven out

Go, charge my goblins that they grind their joints
With dry convulsions; shorten up their sinews
With aged cramps, and more pinch-spotted make them
Than pard, or cat o' mountain.

IEL.   Hark! they roar.

OSPERO. Let them be hunted soundly. At this hour
Lie at my mercy all mine enemies:
Shortly shall all my labours end, and thou
Shalt have the air at freedom; for a little,
Follow, and do me service.   *Exeunt*

ACT FIVE

SCENE ONE

Before the Cell of Prospero.

Enter Prospero in his magic robes; and Ariel

PROSPERO. Now does my project gather to a head:
My charms crack not; my spirits obey, and time
Goes upright with his carriage. How 's the day?
ARIEL. On the sixth hour; at which time, my lord,
You said our work should cease.
PROSPERO.   I did say so
When first I rais'd the tempest. Say, my spirit,
How fares the king and 's followers?
ARIEL.   Confin'd together
In the same fashion as you gave in charge;
Just as you left them: all prisoners, sir,
In the line-grove which weather-fends your cell;
They cannot budge till your release. The king,
His brother, and yours, abide all three distracted,
And the remainder mourning over them,
Brimful of sorrow and dismay; but chiefly
Him, that you term'd, sir, 'The good old lord Gonzalo'
His tears run down his beard, like winter's drops
From eaves of reeds; your charm so strongly works the
That if you now beheld them, your affections
Would become tender.
PROSPERO.   Dost thou think so, spirit?
ARIEL. Mine would, sir, were I human.
PROSPERO.   And mine shall.
Hast thou, which art but air, a touch, a feeling
Of their afflictions, and shall not myself,
One of their kind, that relish all as sharply,
Passion as they, be kindlier mov'd than thou art?
Though with their high wrongs I am struck to the qu

Where we, in all her trim, freshly beheld
Our royal, good, and gallant ship; our master
Capering to eye her: on a trice, so please you,
Even in a dream, were we divided from them,
And were brought moping hither.

ARIEL. (*Aside to Prospero*) Was 't well done?

PROSPERO. (*Aside to Ariel*) Bravely, my diligence! Thou
  shalt be free.

ALONSO. This is as strange a maze as e'er men trod;
  And there is in this business more than nature
  Was ever conduct of: some oracle
  Must rectify our knowledge.

PROSPERO.   Sir, my liege,
  Do not infest your mind with beating on
  The strangeness of this business: at pick'd leisure
  Which shall be shortly, single I 'll resolve you,—
  Which to you shall seem probable,—of every
  These happen'd accidents; till when, be cheerful,
  And think of each thing well.—(*Aside to Ariel*) Come
    hither, spirit;
  Set Caliban and his companions free;
  Untie the spell. (*Exit Ariel*) How fares my gracious sir?
  There are yet missing of your company
  Some few odd lads that you remember not.

Re-enter Ariel, driving in
Caliban, Stephano, and Trinculo, in their stolen apparel

STEPHANO. Every man shift for all the rest, and let no man
  take care for himself, for all is but fortune.—Coragio!
  bully-monster, Coragio!

TRINCULO. If these be true spies which I wear in my head,
  here 's a goodly sight.

CALIBAN. O Setebos! these be brave spirits, indeed.
  How fine my master is! I am afraid
  He will chastise me.

SEBASTIAN.   Ha, ha!
  What things are these, my lord Antonio?
  Will money buy them?

ANTONIO.   Very like; one of them
  Is a plain fish, and, no doubt, marketable.

PROSPERO. Mark but the badges of these men, my lords,
  Then say, if they be true.—This mis-shapen knave,—
  His mother was a witch; and one so strong

That could control the moon, make flows and ebbs,
And deal in her command without her power.
These three have robb'd me; and this demi-devil,—
For he 's a bastard one,—had plotted with them
To take my life: two of these fellows you
Must know and own; this thing of darkness I
Acknowledge mine.

CALIBAN.   I shall be pinch'd to death.

ALONSO. Is not this Stephano, my drunken butler?

SEBASTIAN. He is drunk now: where had he wine?

ALONSO. And Trinculo is reeling-ripe: where should they
Find this grand liquor that hath gilded them?
How cam'st thou in this pickle?

TRINCULO. I have been in such a pickle since I saw you last
that, I fear me, will never out of my bones: I shall not
fear fly-blowing.

SEBASTIAN. Why, how now, Stephano!

STEPHANO. O! touch me not: I am not Stephano, but a
cramp.

PROSPERO. You 'd be king of the isle, sirrah?

STEPHANO. I should have been a sore one then.

ALONSO. This is a strange thing as e'er I look'd on.

Pointing to Caliban

PROSPERO. He is as disproportion'd in his manners
As in his shape.—Go, sirrah, to my cell;
Take with you your companions: as you look
To have my pardon, trim it handsomely.

CALIBAN. Ay, that I will; and I 'll be wise hereafter,
And seek for grace. What a thrice-double ass
Was I, to take this drunkard for a god,
And worship this dull fool!

PROSPERO.   Go to; away!

ALONSO. Hence, and bestow your luggage where you found
it.

SEBASTIAN. Or stole it, rather.

Exeunt Caliban, Stephano, and Trinculo

PROSPERO. Sir, I invite your Highness and your train
To my poor cell, where you shall take your rest
For this one night; which—part of it—I 'll waste
With such discourse as, I not doubt, shall make it
Go quick away; the story of my life
And the particular accidents gone by

Since I came to this isle: and in the morn
I 'll bring you to your ship, and so to Naples,
Where I have hope to see the nuptial
Of these our dear-beloved solemniz'd;
And thence retire me to my Milan, where
Every third thought shall be my grave.

ALONSO.   I long
To hear the story of your life, which must
Take the ear strangely.

PROSPERO.   I 'll deliver all;
And promise you calm seas, auspicious gales
And sail so expeditious that shall catch
Your royal fleet far off.—(*Aside to Ariel*) My Ariel, chick,
That is thy charge: then to the elements
Be free, and fare thou well!—Please you, draw near.

                                        Exeunt

EPILOGUE

Spoken by Prospero

Now my charms are all o'erthrown,
And what strength I have 's mine own;
Which is most faint: now, 'tis true,
I must be here confin'd by you,
Or sent to Naples. Let me not,
Since I have my dukedom got
And pardon'd the deceiver, dwell
In this bare island by your spell;
But release me from my bands
With the help of your good hands.
Gentle breath of yours my sails
Must fill, or else my project fails,
Which was to please. Now I want
Spirits to enforce, art to enchant;
And my ending is despair,
Unless I be reliev'd by prayer,
Which pierces so that it assaults
Mercy itself and frees all faults.
As you from crimes would pardon'd be,
Let your indulgence set me free.

THE TWO GENTLEMEN OF VERONA

THE TWO GENTLEMEN
OF VERONA

CAST OF CHARACTERS

Duke of Milan, Father to Silvia

Valentine
Proteus } the Two Gentlemen

Antonio, Father to Proteus
Thurio, a foolish rival to Valentine
Eglamour, Agent for Silvia, in her escape
Speed, a clownish Servant to Valentine
Launce, the like to Proteus
Panthino, Servant to Antonio

Host, where Julia lodges in Milan
Outlaws with Valentine

Julia, beloved of Proteus
Silvia, beloved of Valentine
Lucetta, waiting-woman to Julia

Servants, Musicians

SCENE

Verona; Milan; and the frontiers of Mantua

THE TWO GENTLEMEN
OF VERONA

ACT ONE

SCENE ONE

Verona. An open place.

Enter Valentine and Proteus

VALENTINE. Cease to persuade, my loving Proteus:
Home-keeping youth have ever homely wits.
Were 't not affection chains thy tender days
To the sweet glances of thy honour'd love,
I rather would entreat thy company
To see the wonders of the world abroad
Than, living dully sluggardiz'd at home,
Wear out thy youth with shapeless idleness.
But since thou lov'st, love still, and thrive therein,
Even as I would when I to love begin.

PROTEUS. Wilt thou be gone? Sweet Valentine, adieu!
Think on thy Proteus, when thou haply seest
Some rare noteworthy object in thy travel:
Wish me partaker in thy happiness
When thou dost meet good hap; and in thy danger,
If ever danger do environ thee,
Commend thy grievance to my holy prayers,
For I will be thy beadsman, Valentine.

VALENTINE. And on a love-book pray for my success?

PROTEUS. Upon some book I love I 'll pray for thee.

VALENTINE. That 's on some shallow story of deep love,
How young Leander cross'd the Hellespont.

PROTEUS. That 's a deep story of a deeper love;
For he was more than over shoes in love.

VALENTINE. 'Tis true; for you are over boots in love,
 And yet you never swum the Hellespont.
PROTEUS. Over the boots? Nay, give me not the boots.
VALENTINE. No, I will not, for it boots thee not.
PROTEUS.   What?
VALENTINE. To be in love, where scorn is bought with
  groans;
 Coy looks with heart-sore sighs; one fading moment's mirth
 With twenty watchful, weary, tedious nights:
 If haply won, perhaps a hapless gain;
 If lost, why then a grievous labour won:
 However, but a folly bought with wit,
 Or else a wit by folly vanquished.
PROTEUS. So, by your circumstance, you call me fool.
VALENTINE. So, by your circumstance, I fear you 'll prove.
PROTEUS. 'Tis love you cavil at: I am not Love.
VALENTINE. Love is your master, for he masters you;
 And he that is so yoked by a fool,
 Methinks, should not be chronicled for wise.
PROTEUS. Yet writers say, as in the sweetest bud
 The eating canker dwells, so eating love
 Inhabits in the finest wits of all.
VALENTINE. And writers say, as the most forward bud
 Is eaten by the canker ere it blow,
 Even so by love the young and tender wit
 Is turned to folly; blasting in the bud,
 Losing his verdure even in the prime,
 And all the fair effects of future hopes.
 But wherefore waste I time to counsel thee
 That art a votary to fond desire?
 Once more adieu! my father at the road
 Expects my coming, there to see me shipp'd.
PROTEUS. And thither will I bring thee, Valentine.
VALENTINE. Sweet Proteus, no; now let us take our leave.
 To Milan let me hear from thee by letters
 Of thy success in love, and what news else
 Betideth here in absence of thy friend;
 And I likewise will visit thee with mine.
PROTEUS. All happiness bechance to thee in Milan!
VALENTINE. As much to you at home! and so, farewell. *Exit*
PROTEUS. He after honour hunts, I after love:
 He leaves his friends to dignify them more;

I leave myself, my friends and all, for love.
Thou, Julia, thou hast metamorphos'd me;—
Made me neglect my studies, lose my time,
War with good counsel, set the world at nought;
Made wit with musing weak, heart sick with thought.

Enter Speed

SPEED. Sir Proteus, save you! Saw you my master?

PROTEUS. But now he parted hence, to embark for Milan.

SPEED. Twenty to one, then, he is shipp'd already,
And I have play'd the sheep, in losing him.

PROTEUS. Indeed, a sheep doth very often stray,
An if the shepherd be a while away.

SPEED. You conclude that my master is a shepherd, then,
and I a sheep?

PROTEUS. I do.

SPEED. Why then my horns are his horns, whether I wake
or sleep.

PROTEUS. A silly answer, and fitting well a sheep.

SPEED. This proves me still a sheep.

PROTEUS. True, and thy master a shepherd.

SPEED. Nay, that I can deny by a circumstance.

PROTEUS. It shall go hard but I 'll prove it by another.

SPEED. The shepherd seeks the sheep, and not the sheep
the shepherd; but I seek my master, and my master seeks
not me: therefore I am no sheep.

PROTEUS. The sheep for fodder follow the shepherd, the
shepherd for food follows not the sheep; thou for wages
followest thy master, thy master for wages follows not
thee: therefore thou art a sheep.

SPEED. Such another proof will make me cry 'baa.'

PROTEUS. But, dost thou hear? gavest thou my letter to
Julia?

SPEED. Ay, sir: I, a lost mutton, gave your letter to her, a
laced mutton; and she, a laced mutton, gave me, a lost
mutton, nothing for my labour.

PROTEUS. Here 's too small a pasture for such store of muttons.

SPEED. If the ground be overcharged, you were best stick
her.

PROTEUS. Nay, in that you are astray; 'twere best pound you.

SPEED. Nay, sir, less than a pound shall serve me for carrying your letter.

PROTEUS. You mistake: I mean the pound,—a pinfold.

SPEED. From a pound to a pin? fold it over and over,
'Tis threefold too little for carrying a letter to your lover.

PROTEUS. But what said she? (*Speed nods*) Did she nod?

SPEED. Ay.

PROTEUS. Nod, ay? why, that 's noddy.

SPEED. You mistook, sir: I say she did nod; and you ask me
if she did nod; and I say, Ay.

PROTEUS. And that set together is—noddy.

SPEED. Now you have taken the pains to set it together,
take it for your pains.

PROTEUS. No, no; you shall have it for bearing the letter.

SPEED. Well, I perceive I must be fain to bear with you.

PROTEUS. Why, sir, how do you bear with me?

SPEED. Marry, sir, the letter very orderly; having nothing
but the word 'noddy' for my pains.

PROTEUS. Beshrew me, but you have a quick wit.

SPEED. And yet it cannot overtake your slow purse.

PROTEUS. Come, come; open the matter in brief: what said
she?

SPEED. Open your purse, that the money and the matter
may be both at once delivered.

PROTEUS. Well, sir, here is for your pains (*Giving him money*)
What said she?

SPEED. Truly, sir, I think you'll hardly win her.

PROTEUS. Why? couldst thou perceive so much from her?

SPEED. Sir, I could perceive nothing at all from her; no, not
so much as a ducat for delivering your letter. And being
so hard to me that brought your mind, I fear she 'll prove
as hard to you in telling your mind. Give her no token
but stones, for she 's as hard as steel.

PROTEUS. What! said she nothing?

SPEED. No, not so much as 'Take this for thy pains.' To testify your bounty, I thank you, you have testerned me; in
requital whereof, henceforth carry your letters yourself.
And so, sir, I 'll commend you to my master.

PROTEUS. Go, go, be gone, to save your ship from wrack;
Which cannot perish, having thee aboard,
Being destin'd to a drier death on shore.—   *Exit Speed*
I must go send some better messenger:
I fear my Julia would not deign my lines,
Receiving them from such a worthless post.   *Exit*

SCENE TWO

Verona. The Garden of Julia's House.

Enter Julia and Lucetta

JULIA. But say, Lucetta, now we are alone,
  Wouldst thou then counsel me to fall in love?
LUCETTA. Ay, madam, so you stumble not unheedfully.
JULIA. Of all the fair resort of gentlemen
  That every day with parle encounter me,
  In thy opinion which is worthiest love?
LUCETTA. Please you repeat their names, I'll show my mind
  According to my shallow simple skill.
JULIA. What think'st thou of the fair Sir Eglamour?
LUCETTA. As of a knight well-spoken, neat and fine;
  But, were I you, he never should be mine.
JULIA. What think'st thou of the rich Mercatio?
LUCETTA. Well of his wealth; but of himself, so so.
JULIA. What think'st thou of the gentle Proteus?
LUCETTA. Lord, Lord! to see what folly reigns in us!
JULIA. How now! what means this passion at his name?
LUCETTA. Pardon, dear madam; 'tis a passing shame
  That I, unworthy body as I am,
  Should censure thus on lovely gentlemen.
JULIA. Why not on Proteus, as of all the rest?
LUCETTA. Then thus,—of many good I think him best.
JULIA. Your reason?
LUCETTA. I have no other but a woman's reason:
  I think him so because I think him so.
JULIA. And wouldst thou have me cast my love on him?
LUCETTA. Ay, if you thought your love not cast away.
JULIA. Why, he, of all the rest hath never moved me.
LUCETTA. Yet he of all the rest, I think, best loves ye.
JULIA. His little speaking shows his love but small.
LUCETTA. Fire that's closest kept burns most of all.
JULIA. They do not love that do not show their love.
LUCETTA. O! they love least that let men know their love.
JULIA. I would I knew his mind.
LUCETTA.   Peruse this paper, madam.
                                      Gives a letter

JULIA. 'To Julia.'—Say from whom?

LUCETTA.   That the contents will show.

JULIA. Say, say, who gave it thee?

LUCETTA. Sir Valentine's page, and sent, I think, from Pro-
    teus.

   He would have given it you, but I, being in the way,
   Did in your name receive it; pardon the fault, I pray.

JULIA. Now, by my modesty, a goodly broker!

   Dare you presume to harbour wanton lines?

   To whisper and conspire against my youth?

   Now, trust me, 'tis an office of great worth

   And you an officer fit for the place.

   There, take the paper: see it be return'd;

   Or else return no more into my sight.

LUCETTA. To plead for love deserves more fee than hate.

JULIA. Will ye be gone?

LUCETTA.   That you may ruminate.   *Exit*

JULIA. And yet I would I had o'erlook'd the letter.

   It were a shame to call her back again

   And pray her to a fault for which I chid her.

   What fool is she, that knows I am a maid,

   And would not force the letter to my view!

   Since maids, in modesty, say 'No' to that

   Which they would have the profferer construe 'Ay.'

   Fie, fie! how wayward is this foolish love

   That, like a testy babe, will scratch the nurse

   And presently all humbled kiss the rod!

   How churlishly I chid Lucetta hence,

   When willingly I would have had her here:

   How angerly I taught my brow to frown,

   When inward joy enforc'd my heart to smile.

   My penance is, to call Lucetta back

   And ask remission for my folly past.

   What ho! Lucetta!

Re-enter Lucetta

LUCETTA.   What would your ladyship?

JULIA. Is it near dinner-time?

LUCETTA.   I would it were;

   That you might kill your stomach on your meat

   And not upon your maid.

JULIA. What is 't that you took up so gingerly?

LUCETTA. Nothing.

JULIA. Why didst thou stoop, then?

LUCETTA.   To take a paper up
  That I let fall.

JULIA.   And is that paper nothing?

LUCETTA. Nothing concerning me.

JULIA. Then let it lie for those that it concerns.

LUCETTA. Madam, it will not lie where it concerns,
  Unless it have a false interpreter.

JULIA. Some love of yours hath writ to you in rime.

LUCETTA. That I might sing it, madam, to a tune:
  Give me a note: your ladyship can set.

JULIA. As little by such toys as may be possible;
  Best sing it to the tune of 'Light o' Love.'

LUCETTA. It is too heavy for so light a tune.

JULIA. Heavy! belike it hath some burden, then?

LUCETTA. Ay; and melodious were it, would you sing it.

JULIA. And why not you?

LUCETTA.   I cannot reach so high.

JULIA. Let 's see your song. (*Taking the letter*) How now,
  minion!

LUCETTA. Keep tune there still, so you will sing it out:
  And yet methinks, I do not like this tune.

JULIA. You do not?

LUCETTA.   No, madam; it is too sharp.

JULIA. You, minion, are too saucy.

LUCETTA. Nay, now you are too flat
  And mar the concord with too harsh a descant:
  There wanteth but a mean to fill your song.

JULIA. The mean is drown'd with your unruly bass.

LUCETTA. Indeed, I bid the base for Proteus.

JULIA. This babble shall not henceforth trouble me.
  Here is a coil with protestation!—*Tears the letter*
  Go, get you gone, and let the papers lie:
  You would be fingering them, to anger me.

LUCETTA. She makes it strange; but she would be best
  pleas'd
  To be so anger'd with another letter.   *Exit*

JULIA. Nay, would I were so anger'd with the same!
  O hateful hands, to tear such loving words!
  Injurious wasps, to feed on such sweet honey
  And kill the bees that yield it with your stings!
  I 'll kiss each several paper for amends.

Look, here is writ 'kind Julia': unkind Julia!
As in revenge of thy ingratitude,
I throw thy name against the bruising stones,
Trampling contemptuously on thy disdain.
And here is writ 'love-wounded Proteus':
Poor wounded name! my bosom, as a bed
Shall lodge thee till thy wound be thoroughly heal'd;
And thus I search it with a sovereign kiss.
But twice or thrice was 'Proteus' written down:
Be calm, good wind, blow not a word away
Till I have found each letter in the letter
Except mine own name; that some whirlwind bear
Unto a ragged, fearful-hanging rock,
And throw it thence into the raging sea!
Lo! here in one line is his name twice writ,
'Poor forlorn Proteus, passionate Proteus,
To the sweet Julia':—that I 'll tear away;
And yet I will not, sith so prettily
He couples it to his complaining names:
Thus will I fold them one upon another:
Now kiss, embrace, contend, do what you will.

Re-enter Lucetta

LUCETTA. Madam,
Dinner is ready, and your father stays.
JULIA. Well, let us go.
LUCETTA. What! shall these papers lie like tell-tales here?
JULIA. If you respect them, best to take them up.
LUCETTA. Nay, I was taken up for laying them down;
Yet here they shall not lie, for catching cold.
JULIA. I see you have a month's mind to them.
LUCETTA. Ay, madam, you may say what sights you see;
I see things too, although you judge I wink.
JULIA. Come, come; will 't please you go?   *Exeunt*

SCENE THREE

Verona. A Room in Antonio's House.

Enter Antonio and Panthino

ANTONIO. Tell me, Panthino, what sad talk was that
  Wherewith my brother held you in the cloister?
PANTHINO. 'Twas of his nephew Proteus, your son.
ANTONIO. Why, what of him?
PANTHINO.   He wonder'd that your lordship
  Would suffer him to spend his youth at home,
  While other men, of slender reputation,
  Put forth their sons to seek preferment out:
  Some to the wars, to try their fortune there;
  Some to discover islands far away;
  Some to the studious universities.
  For any or for all these exercises
  He said that Proteus your son was meet,
  And did request me to importune you
  To let him spend his time no more at home,
  Which would be great impeachment to his age,
  In having known no travel in his youth.
ANTONIO. Nor need'st thou much importune me to that
  Whereon this month I have been hammering.
  I have consider'd well his loss of time,
  And how he cannot be a perfect man,
  Not being tried and tutor'd in the world:
  Experience is by industry achiev'd
  And perfected by the swift course of time.
  Then tell me, whither were I best to send him?
PANTHINO. I think your lordship is not ignorant
  How his companion, youthful Valentine,
  Attends the emperor in his royal court.
ANTONIO. I know it well.
PANTHINO. 'Twere good, I think, your lordship sent him
    thither:
  There shall he practise tilts and tournaments,
  Hear sweet discourse, converse with noblemen,
  And be in eye of every exercise
  Worthy his youth and nobleness of birth.

ANTONIO. I like thy counsel; well hast thou advis'd:
    And that thou mayst perceive how well I like it
    The execution of it shall make known.
    Even with the speediest expedition
    I will dispatch him to the emperor's court.

PANTHINO. To-morrow, may it please you, Don Alphonso
    With other gentlemen of good esteem,
    Are journeying to salute the emperor
    And to commend their service to his will.

ANTONIO. Good company; with them shall Proteus go:
    And in good time:—now will we break with him.

Enter Proteus

PROTEUS. Sweet love! sweet lines! sweet life!
    Here is her hand, the agent of her heart;
    Here is her oath for love, her honour's pawn.
    O! that our fathers would applaud our loves,
    To seal our happiness with their consents!
    O heavenly Julia!

ANTONIO. How now! what letter are you reading there?

PROTEUS. May 't please your lordship, 'tis a word or two
    Of commendations sent from Valentine,
    Deliver'd by a friend that came from him.

ANTONIO. Lend me the letter; let me see what news.

PROTEUS. There is no news, my lord; but that he writes
    How happily he lives, how well belov'd
    And daily graced by the emperor;
    Wishing me with him, partner of his fortune.

ANTONIO. And how stand you affected to his wish?

PROTEUS. As one relying on your lordship's will
    And not depending on his friendly wish.

ANTONIO. My will is something sorted with his wish.
    Muse not that I thus suddenly proceed;
    For what I will, I will, and there an end.
    I am resolv'd that thou shalt spend some time
    With Valentinus in the emperor's court:
    What maintenance he from his friends receives,
    Like exhibition thou shalt have from me.
    To-morrow be in readiness to go:
    Excuse it not, for I am peremptory.

PROTEUS. My lord, I cannot be so soon provided:
    Please you, deliberate a day or two.

ANTONIO. Look, what thou want'st shall be sent after thee:

No more of stay; to-morrow thou must go.
Come on, Panthino: you shall be employ'd
To hasten on his expedition.

Exeunt Antonio and Panthino

PROTEUS. Thus have I shunn'd the fire for fear of burning,
And drench'd me in the sea, where I am drown'd.
I fear'd to show my father Julia's letter,
Lest he should take exceptions to my love;
And with the vantage of mine own excuse
Hath he excepted most against my love,
O! how this spring of love resembleth
    The uncertain glory of an April day,
Which now shows all the beauty of the sun,
    And by and by a cloud takes all away!

Re-enter Panthino

PANTHINO. Sir Proteus, your father calls for you:
He is in haste; therefore, I pray you, go.
PROTEUS. Why, this it is: my heart accords thereto,
And yet a thousand times it answers, 'no.'   *Exeunt*

ACT TWO

SCENE ONE

Milan. A Room in the Duke's Palace.

Enter Valentine and Speed

SPEED. Sir, your glove.   *Offering a glove*
VALENTINE.   Not mine; my gloves are on.
SPEED. Why, then this may be yours, for this is but one.
VALENTINE. Ha! let me see: ay, give it me, it 's mine;
Sweet ornament that decks a thing divine!
Ah Silvia! Silvia!
SPEED. (*Calling*) Madam Silvia! Madam Silvia!
VALENTINE. How now, sirrah?
SPEED. She is not within hearing, sir.
VALENTINE. Why, sir, who bade you call her?
SPEED. Your worship, sir; or else I mistook.
VALENTINE. Well, you 'll still be too forward.
SPEED. And yet I was last chidden for being too slow.
VALENTINE. Go to, sir. Tell me, do you know Madam Silvia?
SPEED. She that your worship loves?
VALENTINE. Why, how know you that I am in love?
SPEED. Marry, by these special marks: first, you have
learned, like Sir Proteus, to wreathe your arms, like a
malecontent; to relish a love-song, like a robin-redbreast;
to walk alone, like one that had the pestilence; to sigh,
like a schoolboy that had lost his A B C; to weep, like a
young wench that had buried her grandam; to fast, like
one that takes diet; to watch, like one that fears robbing;
to speak puling, like a beggar at Hallowmas. You were
wont, when you laughed, to crow like a cock; when you
walked, to walk like one of the lions; when you fasted, it
was presently after dinner; when you looked sadly, it was
for want of money: and now you are metamorphosed

with a mistress, that, when I look on you, I can hardly think you my master.

VALENTINE. Are all these things perceived in me?

SPEED. They are all perceived without ye.

VALENTINE. Without me? they cannot.

SPEED. Without you? nay, that 's certain; for, without you were so simple, none else would: but you are so without these follies, that these follies are within you and shine through you like the water in an urinal, that not an eye that sees you but is a physician to comment on your malady.

VALENTINE. But tell me, dost thou know my lady Silvia?

SPEED. She that you gaze on so as she sits at supper?

VALENTINE. Hast thou observed that? even she, I mean.

SPEED. Why, sir, I know her not.

VALENTINE. Dost thou know her by my gazing on her, and yet knowest her not?

SPEED. Is she not hard-favoured, sir?

VALENTINE. Not so fair, boy, as well-favoured.

SPEED. Sir, I know that well enough.

VALENTINE. What dost thou know?

SPEED. That she is not so fair, as, of you, well-favoured.

VALENTINE. I mean that her beauty is exquisite, but her favour infinite.

SPEED. That 's because the one is painted and the other out of all count.

VALENTINE. How painted? and how out of count?

SPEED. Marry, sir, so painted to make her fair, that no man counts of her beauty.

VALENTINE. How esteemest thou me? I account of her beauty.

SPEED. You never saw her since she was deformed.

VALENTINE. How long hath she been deformed?

SPEED. Ever since you loved her.

VALENTINE. I have loved her ever since I saw her, and still I see her beautiful.

SPEED. If you love her you cannot see her.

VALENTINE. Why?

SPEED. Because Love is blind. O! that you had mine eyes; or your own eyes had the lights they were wont to have when you chid at Sir Proteus for going ungartered!

VALENTINE. What should I see then?

SPEED. Your own present folly and her passing deformity: for he, being in love, could not see to garter his hose; and you, being in love, cannot see to put on your hose.

VALENTINE. Belike, boy, then, you are in love; for last morning you could not see to wipe my shoes.

SPEED. True, sir; I was in love with my bed. I thank you, you swinged me for my love, which makes me the bolder to chide you for yours.

VALENTINE. In conclusion, I stand affected to her.

SPEED. I would you were set, so your affection would cease.

VALENTINE. Last night she enjoined me to write some lines to one she loves.

SPEED. And have you.

VALENTINE. I have.

SPEED. Are they not lamely writ?

VALENTINE. No, boy, but as well as I can do them. Peace! here she comes.

Enter Silvia

SPEED. (*Aside*) O excellent motion! O exceeding puppet! now will he interpret to her.

VALENTINE. Madam and mistress, a thousand good-morrows.

SPEED. (*Aside*) O! give ye good even: here 's a million of manners.

SILVIA. Sir Valentine and servant, to you two thousand.

SPEED. (*Aside*) He should give her interest, and she gives it him.

VALENTINE. As you enjoin'd me, I have writ your letter
Unto the secret nameless friend of yours;
Which I was much unwilling to proceed in
But for my duty to your ladyship.   *Gives a letter*

SILVIA. I thank you, gentle servant. 'Tis very clerkly done.

VALENTINE. Now, trust me, madam, it came hardly off;
For, being ignorant to whom it goes
I writ at random, very doubtfully.

SILVIA. Perchance you think too much of so much pains?

VALENTINE. No, madam; so it stead you, I will write,
Please you command, a thousand times as much.
And yet—

SILVIA. A pretty period! Well, I guess the sequel;
And yet I will not name it; and yet I care not;
And yet take this again; and yet I thank you,

Meaning henceforth to trouble you no more.

SPEED. (*Aside*) And yet you will; and yet another yet.

VALENTINE. What means your ladyship? do you not like it?

SILVIA. Yes, yes: the lines are very quaintly writ,
But since unwillingly, take them again:
Nay, take them. *Gives back the letter*

VALENTINE. Madam, they are for you.

SILVIA. Ay, ay; you writ them, sir, at my request,
But I will none of them; they are for you.
I would have had them writ more movingly.

VALENTINE. Please you, I 'll write your ladyship another.

SILVIA. And when it 's writ, for my sake read it over:
And if it please you, so; if not, why, so.

VALENTINE. If it please me, madam, what then?

SILVIA. Why, if it please you, take it for your labour:
And so, good-morrow, servant. *Exit*

SPEED. (*Aside*) O jest unseen, inscrutable, invisible
As a nose on a man's face, or a weathercock on a steeple!
My master sues to her, and she hath taught her suitor,
He being her pupil, to become her tutor.
O excellent device! was there ever heard a better,
That my master, being scribe, to himself should write the
letter?

VALENTINE. How now, sir! what are you reasoning with
yourself?

SPEED. Nay, I was riming; 'tis you that have the reason.

VALENTINE. To do what?

SPEED. To be a spokesman from Madam Silvia.

VALENTINE. To whom?

SPEED. To yourself. Why, she wooes you by a figure.

VALENTINE. What figure?

SPEED. By a letter, I should say.

VALENTINE. Why, she hath not writ to me?

SPEED. What need she, when she hath made you write to
yourself? Why, do you not perceive the jest?

VALENTINE. No, believe me.

SPEED. No believing you, indeed, sir. But did you perceive
her earnest?

VALENTINE. She gave me none, except an angry word.

SPEED. Why, she hath given you a letter.

VALENTINE. That 's the letter I writ to her friend.

SPEED. And that letter hath she delivered, and there an end.

VALENTINE. I would it were no worse.

SPEED. I 'll warrant you, 'tis as well:

'For often have you writ to her, and she, in modesty,
    Or else for want of idle time, could not again reply;
    Or fearing else some messenger that might her mind dis-
        cover,
    Herself hath taught her love himself to write unto her
        lover.'

All this I speak in print, for in print I found it.
Why muse you, sir? 'tis dinner-time.

VALENTINE. I have dined.

SPEED. Ay, but hearken, sir: though the chameleon Love
can feed on the air, I am one that am nourished by my
victuals and would fain have meat. O! be not like your
mistress: be moved, be moved.   *Exeunt*

SCENE TWO

Verona. A Room in Julia's House.

Enter Proteus and Julia

PROTEUS. Have patience, gentle Julia.

JULIA. I must, where is no remedy.

PROTEUS. When possibly I can, I will return.

JULIA. If you turn not, you will return the sooner.
    Keep this remembrance for thy Julia's sake.

                                        Gives him a ring

PROTEUS. Why, then, we 'll make exchange: here, take you
    this.   *Gives her another*

JULIA. And seal the bargain with a holy kiss.

PROTEUS. Here is my hand for my true constancy;
    And when that hour o'erslips me in the day
    Wherein I sigh not, Julia, for thy sake,
    The next ensuing hour some foul mischance
    Torment me for my love's forgetfulness!
    My father stays my coming; answer not.
    The tide is now: nay, not thy tide of tears;
    That tide will stay me longer than I should.
    Julia, farewell.   *Exit Julia*
                What! gone without a word?

Ay, so true love should do: it cannot speak;
For truth hath better deeds than words to grace it.
                    Enter Panthino
PANTHINO. Sir Proteus, you are stay'd for.
PROTEUS.   Go; I come, I come.
Alas! this parting strikes poor lovers dumb.   *Exeunt*

        SCENE THREE

        Verona. A Street.

        Enter Launce, leading a dog

LAUNCE. Nay, 'twill be this hour ere I have done weeping:
all the kind of the Launces have this very fault. I have
received my proportion, like the prodigious son, and am
going with Sir Proteus to the imperial's court. I think
Crab my dog be the sourest-natured dog that lives: my
mother weeping, my father wailing, my sister crying, our
maid howling, our cat wringing her hands, and all our
house in a great perplexity, yet did not this cruel-hearted
cur shed one tear. He is a stone, a very pebble stone, and
has no more pity in him than a dog; a Jew would have
wept to have seen our parting: why, my grandam, having no eyes, look you, wept herself blind at my parting.
Nay, I 'll show you the manner of it. This shoe is my
father; no, this left shoe is my father: no, no, this left
shoe is my mother; nay, that cannot be so neither:—yes,
it is so; it is so; it hath the worser sole. This shoe, with
the hole in, is my mother, and this is my father. A vengeance on 't! there 'tis: now, sir, this staff is my sister;
for, look you, she is as white as a lily and as small as a
wand: this hat is Nan, our maid: I am the dog; no, the
dog is himself, and I am the dog,—O! the dog is me, and
I am myself: ay, so, so. Now come I to my father;
'Father, your blessing'; now should not the shoe speak a
word for weeping: now should I kiss my father; well, he
weeps on. Now come I to my mother;—O, that she could
speak now like a wood woman! Well, I kiss her; why,
there 'tis; here 's my mother's breath up and down. Now
come I to my sister; mark the moan she makes: Now the

dog all this while sheds not a tear nor speaks a word; but
see how I lay the dust with my tears.

Enter Panthino

PANTHINO. Launce, away, away, aboard! thy master is
shipped, and thou art to post after with oars. What 's
the matter? why weepest thou, man? Away, ass! you 'll
lose the tide if you tarry any longer.

LAUNCE. It is no matter if the tied were lost; for it is the unkindest tied that ever any man tied.

PANTHINO. What 's the unkindest tide?

LAUNCE. Why, he that 's tied here, Crab, my dog.

PANTHINO. Tut, man, I mean thou 'lt lose the flood; and, in
losing the flood, lose thy voyage, and, in losing thy voyage, lose thy master; and, in losing thy master, lose thy
service; and, in losing thy service—Why dost thou stop
my mouth?

LAUNCE. For fear thou shouldst lose thy tongue.

PANTHINO. Where should I lose my tongue?

LAUNCE. In thy tale.

PANTHINO. In thy tail!

LAUNCE. Lose the tide, and the voyage, and the master,
and the service, and the tied! Why, man, if the river
were dry, I am able to fill it with my tears; if the wind
were down, I could drive the boat with my sighs.

PANTHINO. Come, come away, man; I was sent to call thee.

LAUNCE. Sir, call me what thou darest.

PANTHINO. Wilt thou go?

LAUNCE. Well, I will go.   *Exeunt*

SCENE FOUR

Milan. A Room in the Duke's Palace.

Enter Valentine, Silvia, Thurio, and Speed

SILVIA. Servant!

VALENTINE. Mistress?

SPEED. Master, Sir Thurio frowns on you.

VALENTINE. Ay, boy, it 's for love.

SPEED. Not of you.

VALENTINE. Of my mistress, then.

SPEED. 'Twere good you knock'd him.

SILVIA. Servant, you are sad.

VALENTINE. Indeed, madam, I seem so.

THURIO. Seem you that you are not?

VALENTINE. Haply I do.

THURIO. So do counterfeits.

VALENTINE. So do you.

THURIO. What seem I that I am not?

VALENTINE. Wise.

THURIO. What instance of the contrary?

VALENTINE. Your folly.

THURIO. And how quote you my folly?

VALENTINE. I quote it in your jerkin.

THURIO. My jerkin is a doublet.

VALENTINE. Well, then, I 'll double your folly.

THURIO. How?

SILVIA. What, angry, Sir Thurio! do you change colour?

VALENTINE. Give him leave, madam; he is a kind of chameleon.

THURIO. That hath more mind to feed on your blood than live in your air.

VALENTINE. You have said, sir.

THURIO. Ay, sir, and done too, for this time.

VALENTINE. I know it well, sir: you always end ere you begin.

SILVIA. A fine volley of words, gentlemen, and quickly shot off.

VALENTINE. 'Tis indeed, madam; we thank the giver.

SILVIA. Who is that, servant?

VALENTINE. Yourself, sweet lady; for you gave the fire. Sir Thurio borrows his wit from your ladyship's looks, and spends what he borrows kindly in your company.

THURIO. Sir, if you spend word for word with me, I shall make your wit bankrupt.

VALENTINE. I know it well, sir: you have an exchequer of words, and, I think, no other treasure to give your followers; for it appears by their bare liveries that they live by your bare words.

SILVIA. No more, gentlemen, no more. Here comes my father.

Enter Duke

DUKE. Now, daughter Silvia, you are hard beset.
Sir Valentine, your father 's in good health:

What say you to a letter from your friends
Of much good news?

VALENTINE.   My lord, I will be thankful
To any happy messenger from thence.

DUKE. Know ye Don Antonio, your countryman?

VALENTINE. Ay, my good lord; I know the gentleman
To be of worth and worthy estimation,
And not without desert so well reputed.

DUKE. Hath he not a son?

VALENTINE. Ay, my good lord; a son that well deserves
The honour and regard of such a father.

DUKE. You know him well?

VALENTINE. I know him as myself; for from our infancy
We have convers'd and spent our hours together:
And though myself have been an idle truant,
Omitting the sweet benefit of time
To clothe mine age with angel-like perfection,
Yet hath Sir Proteus,—for that 's his name,—
Made use and fair advantage of his days:
His years but young, but his experience old;
His head unmellow'd, but his judgment ripe;
And, in a word,—for far behind his worth
Come all the praises that I now bestow,—
He is complete in feature and in mind
With all good grace to grace a gentleman.

DUKE. Beshrew me, sir, but if he make this good,
He is as worthy for an empress' love
As meet to be an emperor's counsellor.
Well, sir, this gentleman is come to me
With commendation from great potentates;
And here he means to spend his time a while:
I think, 'tis no unwelcome news to you.

VALENTINE. Should I have wish'd a thing, it had been he.

DUKE. Welcome him then according to his worth.
Silvia, I speak to you; and you, Sir Thurio:—
For Valentine, I need not cite him to it.
I 'll send him hither to you presently.   *Exit*

VALENTINE. This is the gentleman I told your ladyship
Had come along with me, but that his mistress
Did hold his eyes lock'd in her crystal looks.

SILVIA. Belike that now she hath enfranchis'd them
Upon some other pawn for fealty.

VALENTINE. Nay, sure, I think she holds them prisoners
 still.

SILVIA. Nay, then he should be blind; and, being blind,
 How could he see his way to seek out you?

VALENTINE. Why, lady, Love hath twenty pairs of eyes.

THURIO. They say that Love hath not an eye at all.

VALENTINE. To see such lovers, Thurio, as yourself:
 Upon a homely object Love can wink.

SILVIA. Have done, have done. Here comes the gentleman.

Enter Proteus

VALENTINE. Welcome, dear Proteus! Mistress, I beseech
 you,
 Confirm his welcome with some special favour.

SILVIA. His worth is warrant for his welcome hither,
 If this be he you oft have wish'd to hear from.

VALENTINE. Mistress, it is: sweet lady, entertain him
 To be my fellow-servant to your ladyship.

SILVIA. Too low a mistress for so high a servant.

PROTEUS. Not so, sweet lady; but too mean a servant
 To have a look of such a worthy mistress.

VALENTINE. Leave off discourse of disability:
 Sweet lady, entertain him for your servant.

PROTEUS. My duty will I boast of, nothing else.

SILVIA. And duty never yet did want his meed.
 Servant, you are welcome to a worthless mistress.

PROTEUS. I'll die on him that says so but yourself.

SILVIA. That you are welcome?

PROTEUS.   That you are worthless.

Enter a Servant

SERVANT. Madam, my lord your father would speak with
 you.

SILVIA. I wait upon his pleasure. (*Exit Servant*) Come, Sir
 Thurio,
 Go with me. Once more, new servant, welcome:
 I'll leave you to confer of home-affairs;
 When you have done, we look to hear from you.

PROTEUS. We'll both attend upon your ladyship.

Exeunt Silvia, Thurio, and Speed

VALENTINE. Now, tell me, how do all from whence you
 came?

PROTEUS. Your friends are well and have them much commended.

VALENTINE. And how do yours?

PROTEUS.   I left them all in health.

VALENTINE. How does your lady and how thrives your
  love?

PROTEUS. My tales of love were wont to weary you;
  I know you joy not in a love-discourse.

VALENTINE. Ay, Proteus, but that life is alter'd now:
  I have done penance for contemning love;
  Whose high imperious thoughts have punish'd me
  With bitter fasts, with penitential groans,
  With nightly tears and daily heart-sore sighs;
  For, in revenge of my contempt of love,
  Love hath chas'd sleep from my enthralled eyes,
  And made them watchers of mine own heart's sorrow.
  O, gentle Proteus! Love 's a mighty lord,
  And hath so humbled me as I confess,
  There is no woe to his correction,
  Nor to his service no such joy on earth.
  Now no discourse, except it be of love;
  Now can I break my fast, dine, sup and sleep,
  Upon the very naked name of love.

PROTEUS. Enough; I read your fortune in your eye.
  Was this the idol that you worship so?

VALENTINE. Even she; and is she not a heavenly saint?

PROTEUS. No; but she is an earthly paragon.

VALENTINE. Call her divine.

PROTEUS.   I will not flatter her.

VALENTINE. O! flatter me, for love delights in praises.

PROTEUS. When I was sick you gave me bitter pills,
  And I must minister the like to you.

VALENTINE. Then speak the truth by her; if not divine,
  Yet let her be a principality,
  Sovereign to all the creatures on the earth.

PROTEUS. Except my mistress.

VALENTINE.   Sweet, except not any,
  Except thou wilt except against my love.

PROTEUS. Have I not reason to prefer mine own?

VALENTINE. And I will help thee to prefer her too:
  She shall be dignified with this high honour,—
  To bear my lady's train, lest the base earth
  Should from her vesture chance to steal a kiss,
  And, of so great a favour growing proud,

Disdain to root the summer-swelling flower,
And make rough winter everlastingly.

PROTEUS. Why, Valentine, what braggardism is this?

VALENTINE. Pardon me, Proteus: all I can is nothing
To her whose worth makes other worthies nothing.
She is alone.

PROTEUS. Then, let her alone.

VALENTINE. Not for the world: why, man, she is mine own,
And I as rich in having such a jewel
As twenty seas, if all their sand were pearl,
The water nectar, and the rocks pure gold.
Forgive me that I do not dream on thee,
Because thou see'st me dote upon my love.
My foolish rival, that her father likes
Only for his possessions are so huge,
Is gone with her along, and I must after,
For love, thou know'st, is full of jealousy.

PROTEUS. But she loves you?

VALENTINE. Ay, and we are betroth'd: nay, more, our mar-
riage-hour,
With all the cunning manner of our flight,
Determin'd of: how I must climb her window,
The ladder made of cords, and all the means
Plotted and 'greed on for my happiness.
Good Proteus, go with me to my chamber,
In these affairs to aid me with thy counsel.

PROTEUS. Go on before; I shall inquire you forth:
I must unto the road, to disembark
Some necessaries that I needs must use,
And then I 'll presently attend you.

VALENTINE. Will you make haste?

PROTEUS. I will.   *Exit Valentine*
Even as one heat another heat expels,
Or as one nail by strength drives out another,
So the remembrance of my former love
Is by a newer object quite forgotten.
Is it mine eye, or Valentinus' praise,
Her true perfection, or my false transgression,
That makes me reasonless to reason thus?
She 's fair; and so is Julia that I love,—
That I did love, for now my love is thaw'd,
Which, like a waxen image 'gainst a fire,

Bears no impression of the thing it was.
Methinks my zeal to Valentine is cold,
And that I love him not as I was wont:
O! but I love his lady too-too much;
And that's the reason I love him so little.
How shall I dote on her with more advice,
That thus without advice begin to love her?
'Tis but her picture I have yet beheld,
And that hath dazzled my reason's light;
But when I look on her perfections,
There is no reason but I shall be blind.
If I can check my erring love, I will;
If not, to compass her I'll use my skill.   *Exit*

SCENE FIVE

Milan. A Street.

Enter Speed and Launce

SPEED. Launce! by mine honesty, welcome to Milan!

LAUNCE. Forswear not thyself, sweet youth, for I am not welcome. I reckon this always that a man is never undone till he be hanged; nor never welcome to a place till some certain shot be paid and the hostess say, 'Welcome!'

SPEED. Come on, you madcap, I'll to the alehouse with you presently; where, for one shot of five pence, thou shalt have five thousand welcomes. But, sirrah, how did thy master part with Madam Julia?

LAUNCE. Marry, after they closed in earnest, they parted very fairly in jest.

SPEED. But shall she marry him?

LAUNCE. No.

SPEED. How then? Shall he marry her?

LAUNCE. No, neither.

SPEED. What, are they broken?

LAUNCE. No, they are both as whole as a fish.

SPEED. Why then, how stands the matter with them?

LAUNCE. Marry, thus; when it stands well with him, it stands well with her.

SPEED. What an ass art thou! I understand thee not.

LAUNCE. What a block art thou, that thou canst not! My staff understands me.

SPEED. What thou sayest?

LAUNCE. Ay, and what I do too: look thee, I 'll but lean, and my staff understands me.

SPEED. It stands under thee, indeed.

LAUNCE. Why, stand-under and under-stand is all one.

SPEED. But tell me true, will 't be a match?

LAUNCE. Ask my dog: if he say ay, it will; if he say no, it will; if he shake his tail and say nothing, it will.

SPEED. The conclusion is, then, that it will.

LAUNCE. Thou shalt never get such a secret from me but by a parable.

SPEED. 'Tis well that I get it so. But, Launce, how sayest thou, that my master is become a notable lover?

LAUNCE. I never knew him otherwise.

SPEED. Than how?

LAUNCE. A notable lubber, as thou reportest him to be.

SPEED. Why, thou whoreson ass, thou mistakest me.

LAUNCE. Why, fool, I meant not thee; I meant thy master.

SPEED. I tell thee, my master is become a hot lover.

LAUNCE. Why, I tell thee, I care not though he burn himself in love. If thou wilt go with me to the alehouse so; if not, thou art a Hebrew, a Jew, and not worth the name of a Christian.

SPEED. Why?

LAUNCE. Because thou hast not so much charity in thee as to go to the ale with a Christian. Wilt thou go?

SPEED. At thy service.   *Exeunt*

SCENE SIX

Milan. A Room in the Duke's Palace.

Enter Proteus

PROTEUS. To leave my Julia, shall I be forsworn;
To love fair Silvia, shall I be forsworn;
To wrong my friend, I shall be much forsworn;
And even that power which gave me first my oath
Provokes me to this threefold perjury:
Love bade me swear, and Love bids me forswear.

O sweet-suggesting Love! if thou hast sinn'd,
Teach me, thy tempted subject, to excuse it.
At first I did adore a twinkling star,
But now I worship a celestial sun.
Unheedful vows may heedfully be broken;
And he wants wit that wants resolved will
To learn his wit to exchange the bad for better.
Fie, fie, unreverend tongue! to call her bad,
Whose sovereignty so oft thou hast preferr'd
With twenty thousand soul-confirming oaths.
I cannot leave to love, and yet I do;
But there I leave to love where I should love.
Julia I lose and Valentine I lose:
If I keep them, I needs must lose myself;
If I lose them, thus find I by their loss,
For Valentine, myself; for Julia, Silvia.
I to myself am dearer than a friend,
For love is still most precious in itself;
And Silvia—witness heaven that made her fair!—
Shows Julia but a swarthy Ethiope.
I will forget that Julia is alive,
Remembering that my love to her is dead;
And Valentine I 'll hold an enemy,
Aiming at Silvia as a sweeter friend.
I cannot now prove constant to myself
Without some treachery us'd to Valentine:
This night he meaneth with a corded ladder
To climb celestial Silvia's chamber-window,
Myself in counsel, his competitor.
Now presently, I 'll give her father notice
Of their disguising and pretended flight;
Who, all enrag'd, will banish Valentine;
For Thurio, he intends, shall wed his daughter;
But, Valentine being gone, I 'll quickly cross,
By some sly trick blunt Thurio's dull proceeding.
Love, lend me wings to make my purpose swift,
As thou hast lent me wit to plot this drift!   *Exit*

SCENE SEVEN

Verona. A Room in Julia's House.

Enter Julia and Lucetta

JULIA. Counsel, Lucetta; gentle girl, assist me:
   And e'en in kind love I do conjure thee,
   Who art the table wherein all my thoughts
   Are visibly character'd and engrav'd,
   To lesson me and tell me some good mean
   How, with my honour, I may undertake
   A journey to my loving Proteus.
LUCETTA. Alas! the way is wearisome and long.
JULIA. A true-devoted pilgrim is not weary
   To measure kingdoms with his feeble steps;
   Much less shall she that hath Love's wings to fly,
   And when the flight is made to one so dear,
   Of such divine perfection, as Sir Proteus.
LUCETTA. Better forbear till Proteus make return.
JULIA. O! know'st thou not his looks are my soul's food?
   Pity the dearth that I have pined in,
   By longing for that food so long a time.
   Didst thou but know the inly touch of love,
   Thou wouldst as soon go kindle fire with snow
   As seek to quench the fire of love with words.
LUCETTA. I do not seek to quench your love's hot fire,
   But qualify the fire's extreme rage,
   Lest it should burn above the bounds of reason.
JULIA. The more thou damm'st it up, the more it burns.
   The current that with gentle murmur glides,
   Thou know'st, being stopp'd, impatiently doth rage;
   But when his fair course is not hindered,
   He makes sweet music with th' enamell'd stones,
   Giving a gentle kiss to every sedge
   He overtaketh in his pilgrimage;
   And so by many winding nooks he strays
   With willing sport, to the wild ocean.
   Then let me go and hinder not my course:
   I'll be as patient as a gentle stream
   And make a pastime of each weary step,

Till the last step have brought me to my love;
And there I 'll rest, as after much turmoil
A blessed soul doth in Elysium.

LUCETTA. But in what habit will you go along?

JULIA. Not like a woman; for I would prevent
The loose encounters of lascivious men.
Gentle Lucetta, fit me with such weeds
As may beseem some well-reputed page.

LUCETTA. Why, then, your ladyship must cut your hair.

JULIA. No, girl; I 'll knit it up in silken strings
With twenty odd-conceited true-love knots:
To be fantastic may become a youth
Of greater time than I shall show to be.

LUCETTA. What fashion, madam, shall I make your
breeches?

JULIA. That fits as well as 'Tell me, good my lord,
What compass will you wear your farthingale?'
Why, even what fashion thou best lik'st, Lucetta.

LUCETTA. You must needs have them with a cod-piece,
madam.

JULIA. Out, out, Lucetta! that will be ill-favour'd.

LUCETTA. A round hose, madam, now 's not worth a pin,
Unless you have a cod-piece to stick pins on.

JULIA. Lucetta, as thou lov'st me, let me have
What thou think'st meet and is most mannerly.
But tell me, wench, how will the world repute me
For undertaking so unstaid a journey?
I fear me, it will make me scandaliz'd.

LUCETTA. If you think so, then stay at home and go not.

JULIA. Nay, that I will not.

LUCETTA. Then never dream on infamy, but go.
If Proteus like your journey when you come,
No matter who 's displeas'd when you are gone.
I fear me, he will scarce be pleas'd withal.

JULIA. That is the least, Lucetta, of my fear:
A thousand oaths, an ocean of his tears,
And instances of infinite of love
Warrant me welcome to my Proteus.

LUCETTA. All these are servants to deceitful men.

JULIA. Base men, that use them to so base effect;
But truer stars did govern Proteus' birth:
His words are bonds, his oaths are oracles,

His love sincere, his thoughts immaculate,
His tears pure messengers sent from his heart,
His heart as far from fraud as heaven from earth.
LUCETTA. Pray heaven he prove so when you come to him!
JULIA. Now, as thou lov'st me, do him not that wrong
  To bear a hard opinion of his truth:
  Only deserve my love by loving him,
  And presently go with me to my chamber,
  To take a note of what I stand in need of
  To furnish me upon my longing journey.
  All that is mine I leave at thy dispose,
  My goods, my lands, my reputation;
  Only, in lieu thereof, dispatch me hence.
  Come, answer not, but to it presently!
  I am impatient of my tarriance.   *Exeunt*

ACT THREE

SCENE ONE

Milan. An anteroom in the Duke's Palace.

Enter Duke, Thurio, and Proteus

DUKE. Sir Thurio, give us leave, I pray, awhile;
　　We have some secrets to confer about.　　　*Exit Thurio*
　　Now tell me, Proteus, what 's your will with me?
PROTEUS. My gracious lord, that which I would discover
　　The law of friendship bids me to conceal;
　　But when I call to mind your gracious favours
　　Done to me, undeserving as I am,
　　My duty pricks me on to utter that
　　Which else no worldly good should draw from me.
　　Know, worthy prince, Sir Valentine, my friend,
　　This night intends to steal away your daughter:
　　Myself am one made privy to the plot.
　　I know you have determin'd to bestow her
　　On Thurio, whom your gentle daughter hates;
　　And should she thus be stol'n away from you
　　It would be much vexation to your age.
　　Thus, for my duty's sake, I rather chose
　　To cross my friend in his intended drift,
　　Than, by concealing it, heap on your head
　　A pack of sorrows which would press you down,
　　Being unprevented, to your timeless grave.
DUKE. Proteus, I thank thee for thine honest care,
　　Which to requite, command me while I live.
　　This love of theirs myself have often seen,
　　Haply, when they have judg'd me fast asleep,
　　And oftentimes have purpos'd to forbid
　　Sir Valentine her company and my court;
　　But fearing lest my jealous aim might err
　　And so unworthily disgrace the man,—

A rashness that I ever yet have shunn'd,—
I gave him gentle looks, thereby to find
That which thyself hast now disclos'd to me.
And, that thou mayst perceive my fear of this,
Knowing that tender youth is soon suggested,
I nightly lodge her in an upper tower,
The key whereof myself have ever kept;
And thence she cannot be convey'd away.

PROTEUS. Know, noble lord, they have devis'd a mean
How he her chamber-window will ascend
And with a corded ladder fetch her down;
For which the youthful lover now is gone
And this way comes he with it presently;
Where, if it please you, you may intercept him.
But, good my lord, do it so cunningly
That my discovery be not aimed at;
For love of you, not hate unto my friend,
Hath made me publisher of this pretence.

DUKE. Upon mine honour, he shall never know
That I had any light from thee of this.

PROTEUS. Adieu, my lord: Sir Valentine is coming. *Exit*

Enter Valentine

DUKE. Sir Valentine, whither away so fast?

VALENTINE. Please it your Grace, there is a messenger
That stays to bear my letters to my friends,
And I am going to deliver them.

DUKE. Be they of much import?

VALENTINE. The tenour of them doth but signify
My health and happy being at your court.

DUKE. Nay then, no matter: stay with me awhile;
I am to break with thee of some affairs
That touch me near, wherein thou must be secret.
'Tis not unknown to thee that I have sought
To match my friend Sir Thurio to my daughter.

VALENTINE. I know it well, my lord; and sure, the match
Were rich and honourable; besides, the gentleman
Is full of virtue, bounty, worth, and qualities
Beseeming such a wife as your fair daughter.
Cannot your Grace win her to fancy him?

DUKE. No, trust me: she is peevish, sullen, froward,
Proud, disobedient, stubborn, lacking duty;
Neither regarding that she is my child,

Nor fearing me as if I were her father:
And, may I say to thee, this pride of hers,
Upon advice, hath drawn my love from her;
And, where I thought the remnant of mine age
Should have been cherish'd by her child-like duty,
I now am full resolv'd to take a wife
And turn her out to who will take her in:
Then let her beauty be her wedding-dower;
For me and my possessions she esteems not.

VALENTINE. What would your Grace have me to do in this?

DUKE. There is a lady of Verona here,
    Whom I affect; but she is nice and coy
    And nought esteems my aged eloquence:
    Now therefore, would I have thee to my tutor,
    For long agone I have forgot to court;
    Besides, the fashion of the time is chang'd,
    How and which way I may bestow myself
    To be regarded in her sun-bright eye.

VALENTINE. Win her with gifts, if she respect not words:
    Dumb jewels often in their silent kind
    More than quick words do move a woman's mind.

DUKE. But she did scorn a present that I sent her.

VALENTINE. A woman sometime scorns what best contents
        her.
    Send her another; never give her o'er,
    For scorn at first makes after-love the more.
    If she do frown, 'tis not in hate of you,
    But rather to beget more love in you;
    If she do chide, 'tis not to have you gone;
    For why the fools are mad if left alone.
    Take no repulse, whatever she doth say;
    For, 'get you gone,' she doth not mean, 'away!'
    Flatter and praise, commend, extol their graces;
    Though ne'er so black, say they have angels' faces.
    That man that hath a tongue, I say, is no man,
    If with his tongue he cannot win a woman.

DUKE. But she I mean is promis'd by her friends
    Unto a youthful gentleman of worth,
    And kept severely from resort of men,
    That no man hath access by day to her.

VALENTINE. Why then, I would resort to her by night.

DUKE. Ay, but the doors be lock'd and keys kept safe,

That no man hath recourse to her by night.

VALENTINE. What lets but one may enter at her window?

DUKE. Her chamber is aloft, far from the ground,
And built so shelving that one cannot climb it
Without apparent hazard of his life.

VALENTINE. Why then, a ladder quaintly made of cords,
To cast up, with a pair of anchoring hooks,
Would serve to scale another Hero's tower,
So bold Leander would adventure it.

DUKE. Now, as thou art a gentleman of blood,
Advise me where I may have such a ladder.

VALENTINE. When would you use it? pray, sir, tell me that.

DUKE. This very night; for Love is like a child,
That longs for every thing that he can come by.

VALENTINE. By seven o'clock I 'll get you such a ladder.

DUKE. But hark thee; I will go to her alone:
How shall I best convey the ladder thither?

VALENTINE. It will be light, my lord, that you may bear it
Under a cloak that is of any length.

DUKE. A cloak as long as thine will serve the turn?

VALENTINE. Ay, my good lord.

DUKE.   Then let me see thy cloak:
I 'll get me one of such another length.

VALENTINE. Why, any cloak will serve the turn, my lord.

DUKE. How shall I fashion me to wear a cloak?
I pray thee, let me feel thy cloak upon me.

                              Pulls open Valentine's cloak
What letter is this same? What 's here?—'To Silvia!'
And here an engine fit for my proceeding!
I 'll be so bold to break the seal for once.   *Reads*
'My thoughts do harbour with my Silvia nightly;
  And slaves they are to me that send them flying:
O! could their master come and go as lightly,
  Himself would lodge where senseless they are lying!
My herald thoughts in thy pure bosom rest them;
  While I, their king, that thither them importune,
Do curse the grace that with such grace hath bless'd
    them,
  Because myself do want my servants' fortune:
I curse myself, for they are sent by me,
That they should harbour where their lord would be.'
What 's here?

'Silvia, this night I will enfranchise thee.'
'Tis so; and here's the ladder for the purpose.
Why, Phæthon,—for thou art Merops' son,—
Wilt thou aspire to guide the heavenly car
And with thy daring folly burn the world?
Wilt thou reach stars, because they shine on thee?
Go, base intruder! overweening slave!
Bestow thy fawning smiles on equal mates,
And think my patience, more than thy desert,
Is privilege for thy departure hence.
Thank me for this more than for all the favours
Which all too much I have bestow'd on thee.
But if thou linger in my territories
Longer than swiftest expedition
Will give thee time to leave our royal court,
By heaven! my wrath shall far exceed the love
I ever bore my daughter or thyself.
Be gone! I will not hear thy vain excuse;
But, as thou lov'st thy life, make speed from hence.   *Exit*

VALENTINE.   And why not death rather than living torment?
To die is to be banish'd from myself;
And Silvia is myself: banish'd from her
Is self from self,—a deadly banishment!
What light is light, if Silvia be not seen?
What joy is joy, if Silvia be not by?
Unless it be to think that she is by
And feed upon the shadow of perfection.
Except I be by Silvia in the night,
There is no music in the nightingale;
Unless I look on Silvia in the day,
There is no day for me to look upon.
She is my essence; and I leave to be,
If I be not by her fair influence
Foster'd, illumin'd, cherish'd, kept alive.
I fly not death, to fly his deadly doom:
Tarry I here, I but attend on death;
But, fly I hence, I fly away from life.

Enter Proteus and Launce

PROTEUS.   Run, boy; run, run, and seek him out.
LAUNCE.   Soho! soho!
PROTEUS.   What seest thou?

LAUNCE. Him we go to find: there 's not a hair on 's head
but 'tis a Valentine.

PROTEUS. Valentine?

VALENTINE. No.

PROTEUS. Who then? his spirit?

VALENTINE. Neither.

PROTEUS. What then?

VALENTINE. Nothing.

LAUNCE. Can nothing speak? Master, shall I strike?

PROTEUS. Who would'st thou strike?

LAUNCE. Nothing.

PROTEUS. Villain, forbear.

LAUNCE. Why, sir, I 'll strike nothing: I pray you,—

PROTEUS. Sirrah, I say, forbear.—Friend Valentine, a word.

VALENTINE. My ears are stopp'd and cannot hear good news,
So much of bad already hath possess'd them.

PROTEUS. Then in dumb silence will I bury mine,
For they are harsh, untuneable and bad.

VALENTINE. Is Silvia dead?

PROTEUS. No, Valentine.

VALENTINE. No Valentine, indeed, for sacred Silvia!
Hath she forsworn me?

PROTEUS. No, Valentine.

VALENTINE. No Valentine, if Silvia have forsworn me!
What is your news?

LAUNCE. Sir, there is a proclamation that you are vanished.

PROTEUS. That thou art banished, O, that 's the news,
From hence, from Silvia, and from me thy friend.

VALENTINE. O, I have fed upon this woe already,
And now excess of it will make me surfeit.
Doth Silvia know that I am banished?

PROTEUS. Ay, ay; and she hath offer'd to the doom—
Which, unrevers'd, stands in effectual force—
A sea of melting pearl, which some call tears:
Those at her father's churlish feet she tender'd;
With them, upon her knees, her humble self;
Wringing her hands, whose whiteness so became them
As if but now they waxed pale for woe:
But neither bended knees, pure hands held up,
Sad sighs, deep groans, nor silver-shedding tears,
Could penetrate her uncompassionate sire;

But Valentine, if he be ta'en, must die.
Besides, her intercession chaf'd him so,
When she for thy repeal was suppliant,
That to close prison he commanded her,
With many bitter threats of biding there.

VALENTINE. No more; unless the next word that thou
speak'st
Have some malignant power upon my life:
If so, I pray thee, breathe it in mine ear,
As ending anthem of my endless dolour.

PROTEUS. Cease to lament for that thou canst not help,
And study help for that which thou lament'st.
Time is the nurse and breeder of all good.
Here if thou stay, thou canst not see thy love;
Besides, thy staying will abridge thy life.
Hope is a lover's staff; walk hence with that
And manage it against despairing thoughts.
Thy letters may be here, though thou art hence;
Which, being writ to me, shall be deliver'd
Even in the milk-white bosom of thy love.
The time now serves not to expostulate:
Come, I'll convey thee through the city-gate,
And, ere I part with thee, confer at large
Of all that may concern thy love-affairs.
As thou lov'st Silvia, though not for thyself,
Regard thy danger, and along with me!

VALENTINE. I pray thee, Launce, and if thou seest my boy,
Bid him make haste and meet me at the North-gate.

PROTEUS. Go, sirrah, find him out. Come, Valentine.

VALENTINE. O my dear Silvia! hapless Valentine!

Exeunt Valentine and Proteus

LAUNCE. I am but a fool, look you; and yet I have the wit
to think my master is a kind of a knave: but that's all
one, if he be but one knave. He lives not now that knows
me to be in love: yet I am in love; but a team of horse
shall not pluck that from me, nor who 'tis I love; and yet
'tis a woman; but what woman, I will not tell myself;
and yet 'tis a milkmaid; yet 'tis not a maid, for she hath
had gossips; yet 'tis a maid, for she is her master's maid,
and serves for wages. She hath more qualities than a
water-spaniel,—which is much in a bare Christian. (*Pulling out a paper*) Here is the catelog of her condition.

'Imprimis, She can fetch and carry.' Why, a horse can do no more: nay, a horse cannot fetch, but only carry; therefore, is she better than a jade. 'Item, She can milk'; look you, a sweet virtue in a maid with clean hands.

Enter Speed

SPEED. How now, Signior Launce! what news with your mastership?

LAUNCE. With my master's ship? why, it is at sea.

SPEED. Well, your old vice still; mistake the word. What news, then, in your paper?

LAUNCE. The blackest news that ever thou heardest.

SPEED. Why, man, how black?

LAUNCE. Why, as black as ink.

SPEED. Let me read them.

LAUNCE. Fie on thee, jolthead! thou canst not read.

SPEED. Thou liest; I can.

LAUNCE. I will try thee. Tell me this: who begot thee?

SPEED. Marry, the son of my grandfather.

LAUNCE. O, illiterate loiterer! it was the son of thy grandmother. This proves that thou canst not read.

SPEED. Come, fool, come: try me in thy paper.

LAUNCE. There; and Saint Nicholas be thy speed!

SPEED. (*Reads*) 'Imprimis. She can milk.'

LAUNCE. Ay, that she can.

SPEED. 'Item. She brews good ale.'

LAUNCE. And thereof comes the proverb, 'Blessing of your heart, you brew good ale.'

SPEED. 'Item. She can sew.'

LAUNCE. That 's as much as to say, Can she so?

SPEED. 'Item. She can knit.'

LAUNCE. What need a man care for a stock with a wench, when she can knit him a stock?

SPEED. 'Item. She can wash and scour.'

LAUNCE. A special virtue; for then she need not be washed and scoured.

SPEED. 'Item. She can spin.'

LAUNCE. Then may I set the world on wheels, when she can spin for her living.

SPEED. 'Item. She hath many nameless virtues.'

LAUNCE. That 's as much as to say, bastard virtues; that, indeed, know not their fathers, and therefore have no names.

SPEED. 'Here follow her vices.'

LAUNCE. Close at the heels of her virtues.

SPEED. 'Item. She is not to be kissed fasting, in respect of her breath.'

LAUNCE. Well, that fault may be mended with a breakfast. Read on.

SPEED. 'Item. She hath a sweet mouth.'

LAUNCE. That makes amends for her sour breath.

SPEED. 'Item. She doth talk in her sleep.'

LAUNCE. It 's no matter for that, so she sleep not in her talk.

SPEED. 'Item. She is slow in words.'

LAUNCE. O villain, that set this down among her vices! To be slow in words is a woman's only virtue: I pray thee, out with 't, and place it for her chief virtue.

SPEED. 'Item. She is proud.'

LAUNCE. Out with that too: it was Eve's legacy, and cannot be ta'en from her.

SPEED. 'Item. She hath no teeth.'

LAUNCE. I care not for that neither, because I love crusts.

SPEED. 'Item. She is curst.'

LAUNCE. Well; the best is, she hath no teeth to bite.

SPEED. 'Item. She will often praise her liquor.'

LAUNCE. If her liquor be good, she shall: if she will not, I will; for good things should be praised.

SPEED. 'Item. She is too liberal.'

LAUNCE. Of her tongue she cannot, for that 's writ down she is slow of: of her purse she shall not, for that I 'll keep shut: now, of another thing she may, and that cannot I help. Well, proceed.

SPEED. 'Item. She hath more hair than wit, and more faults than hairs, and more wealth than faults.'

LAUNCE. Stop there; I 'll have her: she was mine, and not mine, twice or thrice in that last article. Rehearse that once more.

SPEED. 'Item. She hath more hair than wit.'—

LAUNCE. More hair than wit it may be; I 'll prove it: the cover of the salt hides the salt, and therefore it is more than the salt; the hair, that covers the wit is more than the wit, for the greater hides the less. What 's next?

SPEED. 'And more faults than hairs.'—

LAUNCE. That 's monstrous! O, that that were out!

SPEED. 'And more wealth than faults.'

LAUNCE. Why, that word makes the faults gracious. Well,
  I 'll have her; and if it be a match, as nothing is impossible,—

SPEED. What then?

LAUNCE. Why, then will I tell thee,—that thy master stays
  for thee at the North-gate.

SPEED. For me?

LAUNCE. For thee! ay; who art thou? he hath stayed for a
  better man than thee.

SPEED. And must I go to him?

LAUNCE. Thou must run to him, for thou hast stayed so
  long that going will scarce serve the turn.

SPEED. Why didst not tell me sooner? pox of your love-
  letters!   *Exit*

LAUNCE. Now will he be swing'd for reading my letter. An
  unmannerly slave, that will thrust himself into secrets.
  I 'll after, to rejoice in the boy's correction.   *Exit*

SCENE TWO

Milan. A Room in the Duke's Palace.

Enter Duke and Thurio

DUKE. Sir Thurio, fear not but that she will love you,
  Now Valentine is banish'd from her sight.

THURIO. Since his exile she hath despis'd me most,
  Forsworn my company and rail'd at me,
  That I am desperate of obtaining her.

DUKE. This weak impress of love is as a figure
  Trenched in ice, which with an hour's heat
  Dissolves to water and doth lose his form.
  A little time will melt her frozen thoughts,
  And worthless Valentine shall be forgot.

Enter Proteus

  How now, Sir Proteus! Is your countryman
  According to our proclamation gone?

PROTEUS. Gone, my good lord.

DUKE. My daughter takes his going grievously.

PROTEUS. A little time, my lord, will kill that grief.

DUKE. So I believe; but Thurio thinks not so.

Proteus, the good conceit I hold of thee,—
For thou hast shown some sign of good desert,—
Makes me the better to confer with thee.

PROTEUS. Longer than I prove loyal to your Grace
Let me not live to look upon your Grace.

DUKE. Thou know'st how willingly I would effect
The match between Sir Thurio and my daughter.

PROTEUS. I do, my lord.

DUKE. And also, I think, thou art not ignorant
How she opposes her against my will.

PROTEUS. She did, my lord, when Valentine was here.

DUKE. Ay, and perversely she persevers so.
What might we do to make the girl forget
The love of Valentine, and love Sir Thurio?

PROTEUS. The best way is to slander Valentine
With falsehood, cowardice, and poor descent,
Three things that women highly hold in hate.

DUKE. Ay, but she 'll think that it is spoke in hate.

PROTEUS. Ay, if his enemy deliver it:
Therefore it must with circumstance be spoken
By one whom she esteemeth as his friend.

DUKE. Then you must undertake to slander him.

PROTEUS. And that, my lord, I shall be loath to do:
'Tis an ill office for a gentleman,
Especially against his very friend.

DUKE. Where your good word cannot advantage him,
Your slander never can endamage him:
Therefore the office is indifferent,
Being entreated to it by your friend.

PROTEUS. You have prevail'd, my lord. If I can do it,
By aught that I can speak in his dispraise,
She shall not long continue love to him.
But say this weed her love from Valentine,
It follows not that she will love Sir Thurio.

THURIO. Therefore, as you unwind her love from him,
Lest it should ravel and be good to none,
You must provide to bottom it on me;
Which must be done by praising me as much
As you in worth dispraise Sir Valentine.

DUKE. And, Proteus, we dare trust you in this kind,
Because we know, on Valentine's report,
You are already Love's firm votary

And cannot soon revolt and change your mind.
Upon this warrant shall you have access
Where you with Silvia may confer at large;
For she is lumpish, heavy, melancholy,
And, for your friend's sake, will be glad of you;
Where you may temper her, by your persuasion,
To hate young Valentine and love my friend.

PROTEUS. As much as I can do I will effect.
But you, Sir Thurio, are not sharp enough;
You must lay lime to tangle her desires
By wailful sonnets, whose composed rimes
Should be full-fraught with serviceable vows.

DUKE. Ay,
Much is the force of heaven-bred poesy.

PROTEUS. Say that upon the altar of her beauty
You sacrifice your tears, your sighs, your heart.
Write till your ink be dry, and with your tears
Moist it again, and frame some feeling line
That may discover such integrity:
For Orpheus' lute was strung with poets' sinews,
Whose golden touch could soften steel and stones,
Make tigers tame and huge leviathans
Forsake unsounded deeps to dance on sands.
After your dire-lamenting elegies,
Visit by night your lady's chamber-window
With some sweet consort: to their instruments
Tune a deploring dump; the night's dead silence
Will well become such sweet-complaining grievance.
This, or else nothing, will inherit her.

DUKE. This discipline shows thou hast been in love.

THURIO. And thy advice this night I 'll put in practice.
Therefore, sweet Proteus, my direction-giver,
Let us into the city presently
To sort some gentlemen well skill'd in music.
I have a sonnet that will serve the turn
To give the onset to thy good advice.

DUKE. About it, gentlemen!

PROTEUS. We 'll wait upon your Grace till after-supper,
And afterward determine our proceedings.

DUKE. Even now about it! I will pardon you.   *Exeunt*

ACT FOUR

SCENE ONE

A Forest between Milan and Verona.

Enter certain Outlaws

FIRST OUTLAW. Fellows, stand fast; I see a passenger.

SECOND OUTLAW. If there be ten, shrink not, but down with
    'em.

Enter Valentine and Speed

THIRD OUTLAW. Stand, sir, and throw us that you have
    about ye;

If not, we 'll make you sit and rifle you.

SPEED. Sir, we are undone: these are the villains

That all the travellers do fear so much.

VALENTINE. My friends,—

FIRST OUTLAW. That 's not so, sir; we are your enemies.

SECOND OUTLAW. Peace! we 'll hear him.

THIRD OUTLAW. Ay, by my beard, will we, for he is a
    proper man.

VALENTINE. Then know, that I have little wealth to lose.

A man I am cross'd with adversity:

My riches are these poor habiliments,

Of which if you should here disfurnish me,

You take the sum and substance that I have.

SECOND OUTLAW. Whither travel you?

VALENTINE. To Verona.

FIRST OUTLAW. Whence came you?

VALENTINE. From Milan.

THIRD OUTLAW. Have you long sojourn'd there?

VALENTINE. Some sixteen months; and longer might have
    stay'd

If crooked fortune had not thwarted me.

SECOND OUTLAW. What! were you banish'd thence?

VALENTINE. I was.

SECOND OUTLAW. For what offence?

VALENTINE. For that which now torments me to rehearse.
I kill'd a man, whose death I much repent;
But yet I slew him manfully, in fight,
Without false vantage or base treachery.

FIRST OUTLAW. Why, ne'er repent it, if it were done so.
But were you banish'd for so small a fault?

VALENTINE. I was, and held me glad of such a doom.

SECOND OUTLAW. Have you the tongues?

VALENTINE. My youthful travel therein made me happy,
Or else I often had been miserable.

THIRD OUTLAW. By the bare scalp of Robin Hood's fat friar,
This fellow were a king for our wild faction!

FIRST OUTLAW. We 'll have him: Sirs, a word.

SPEED. Master, be one of them;
It is an honourable kind of thievery.

VALENTINE. Peace, villain!

SECOND OUTLAW. Tell us this: have you anything to take to?

VALENTINE. Nothing, but my fortune.

THIRD OUTLAW. Know then, that some of us are gentlemen,
Such as the fury of ungovern'd youth
Thrust from the company of awful men:
Myself was from Verona banished
For practising to steal away a lady,
An heir, and near allied unto the duke.

SECOND OUTLAW. And I from Mantua, for a gentleman,
Who, in my mood, I stabb'd unto the heart.

FIRST OUTLAW. And I for such like petty crimes as these.
But to the purpose; for we cite our faults,
That they may hold excus'd our lawless lives;
And, partly, seeing you are beautified
With goodly shape, and by your own report
A linguist, and a man of such perfection
As we do in our quality much want—

SECOND OUTLAW. Indeed, because you are a banish'd man,
Therefore, above the rest, we parley to you.
Are you content to be our general?
To make a virtue of necessity
And live, as we do, in this wilderness?

THIRD OUTLAW. What say'st thou? wilt thou be of our consort?
Say 'ay,' and be the captain of us all:

We 'll do thee homage and be rul'd by thee,
Love thee as our commander and our king.

FIRST OUTLAW. But if thou scorn our courtesy, thou diest.

SECOND OUTLAW. Thou shalt not live to brag what we have
offer'd.

VALENTINE. I take your offer and will live with you,
Provided that you do no outrages
On silly women, or poor passengers.

THIRD OUTLAW. No; we detest such vile, base practices.
Come, go with us; we 'll bring thee to our crews,
And show thee all the treasure we have got,
Which, with ourselves, all rest at thy dispose.   *Exeunt*

SCENE TWO

Milan. The Court of the Duke's Palace.

Enter Proteus

PROTEUS. Already have I been false to Valentine,
And now I must be as unjust to Thurio.
Under the colour of commending him,
I have access my own love to prefer:
But Silvia is too fair, too true, too holy,
To be corrupted with my worthless gifts.
When I protest true loyalty to her,
She twits me with my falsehood to my friend;
When to her beauty I commend my vows,
She bids me think how I have been forsworn
In breaking faith with Julia whom I lov'd:
And notwithstanding all her sudden quips,
The least whereof would quell a lover's hope,
Yet, spaniel-like, the more she spurns my love,
The more it grows, and fawneth on her still.
But here comes Thurio: now must we to her window,
And give some evening music to her ear.

Enter Thurio, and Musicians

THURIO. How now, Sir Proteus! are you crept before us?

PROTEUS. Ay, gentle Thurio; for you know that love
Will creep in service where it cannot go.

THURIO. Ay; but I hope, sir, that you love not here.

PROTEUS. Sir, but I do; or else I would be hence.

THURIO. Who? Silvia?

PROTEUS. Ay, Silvia, for your sake.

THURIO. I thank you for your own. Now, gentlemen,
Let 's tune, and to it lustily a while.

Enter Host and Julia behind. Julia in boy's clothes

HOST. Now, my young guest, methinks you 're allycholly: I
pray you, why is it?

JULIA. Marry, mine host, because I cannot be merry.

HOST. Come, we 'll have you merry. I 'll bring you where
you shall hear music and see the gentleman that you
asked for.

JULIA. But shall I hear him speak?

HOST. Ay, that you shall.

JULIA. That will be music.   *Music plays*

HOST. Hark! hark!

JULIA. Is he among these?

HOST. Ay; but peace! let 's hear 'em.

SONG

Who is Silvia? what is she?
    That all our swains commend her?
Holy, fair, and wise is she;
    The heaven such grace did lend her,
That she might admired be.

Is she kind as she is fair?
    For beauty lives with kindness:
Love doth to her eyes repair,
    To help him of his blindness;
And, being help'd, inhabits there.

Then to Silvia let us sing,
    That Silvia is excelling;
She excels each mortal thing
    Upon the dull earth dwelling;
To her let us garlands bring.

HOST. How now! Are you sadder than you were before?
How do you, man? the music likes you not.

JULIA. You mistake; the musician likes me not.

HOST. Why, my pretty youth?

JULIA. He plays false, father.

HOST. How? out of tune on the strings?

JULIA. Not so; but yet so false that he grieves my very
heart-strings.

HOST. You have a quick ear.

JULIA. Ay; I would I were deaf; it makes me have a slow
heart.

HOST. I perceive you delight not in music.

JULIA. Not a whit,—when it jars so.

HOST. Hark! what fine change is in the music!

JULIA. Ay, that change is the spite.

HOST. You would have them always play but one thing?

JULIA. I would always have one play but one thing.
But, host, doth this Sir Proteus that we talk on
Often resort unto this gentlewoman?

HOST. I will tell you what Launce, his man, told me: he
lov'd her out of all nick.

JULIA. Where is Launce?

HOST. Gone to seek his dog; which, to-morrow, by his master's command, he must carry for a present to his lady.

JULIA. Peace! stand aside: the company parts.

PROTEUS. Sir Thurio, fear not you: I will so plead
That you shall say my cunning drift excels.

THURIO. Where meet we?

PROTEUS. At Saint Gregory's well.

THURIO. Farewell.   *Exeunt Thurio and Musicians*
                    Enter Silvia, above, at her window

PROTEUS. Madam, good even to your ladyship.

SILVIA. I thank you for your music, gentlemen.
Who is that that spake?

PROTEUS. One, lady, if you knew his pure heart's truth,
You would quickly learn to know him by his voice.

SILVIA. Sir Proteus, as I take it.

PROTEUS. Sir Proteus, gentle lady, and your servant.

SILVIA. What is your will?

PROTEUS.   That I may compass yours.

SILVIA. You have your wish; my will is even this:
That presently you hie you home to bed.
Thou subtle, perjur'd, false, disloyal man!
Think'st thou I am so shallow, so conceitless,
To be seduced by thy flattery,
That hast deceiv'd so many with thy vows?

Return, return, and make thy love amends.
For me, by this pale queen of night I swear,
I am so far from granting thy request
That I despise thee for thy wrongful suit,
And by and by intend to chide myself
Even for this time I spend in talking to thee.

PROTEUS. I grant, sweet love, that I did love a lady:
But she is dead.

JULIA. (*Aside*) 'Twere false, if I should speak it;
For I am sure she is not buried.

SILVIA. Say that she be; yet Valentine thy friend
Survives; to whom, thyself art witness,
I am betroth'd: and art thou not asham'd
To wrong him with thy importunacy?

PROTEUS. I likewise hear that Valentine is dead.

SILVIA. And so suppose am I; for in his grave,
Assure thyself my love is buried.

PROTEUS. Sweet lady, let me rake it from the earth.

SILVIA. Go to thy lady's grave and call hers thence;
Or, at the least, in hers sepulchre thine.

JULIA. (*Aside*) He heard not that.

PROTEUS. Madam, if your heart be so obdurate,
Vouchsafe me yet your picture for my love,
The picture that is hanging in your chamber:
To that I'll speak, to that I'll sigh and weep;
For since the substance of your perfect self
Is else devoted, I am but a shadow,
And to your shadow will I make true love.

JULIA. (*Aside*) If 'twere a substance, you would, sure, deceive it,
And make it but a shadow, as I am.

SILVIA. I am very loath to be your idol, sir;
But, since your falsehood shall become you well
To worship shadows and adore false shapes,
Send to me in the morning and I'll send it.
And so, good rest.

PROTEUS.   As wretches have o'er night
That wait for execution in the morn.

Exeunt Proteus, and Silvia, above

JULIA. Host, will you go?

HOST. By my halidom, I was fast asleep.

JULIA. Pray you, where lies Sir Proteus?

HOST. Marry, at my house. Trust me, I think
　　'tis almost day.

JULIA. Not so; but it hath been the longest night
　　That e'er I watch'd and the most heaviest.　　*Exeunt*

SCENE THREE

The Same.

Enter Eglamour

EGLAMOUR. This is the hour that Madam Silvia
　　Entreated me to call, and know her mind:
　　There 's some great matter she 'd employ me in.
　　Madam, Madam!

　　　　　　　Enter Silvia above, at her window

SILVIA.　　　　　　Who calls?

EGLAMOUR.　　　　　　　Your servant, and your friend;
　　One that attends your ladyship's command.

SILVIA. Sir Eglamour, a thousand times good-morrow.

EGLAMOUR. As many, worthy lady, to yourself.
　　According to your ladyship's impose,
　　I am thus early come to know what service
　　It is your pleasure to command me in.

SILVIA. O Eglamour, thou art a gentleman—
　　Think not I flatter, for I swear I do not—
　　Valiant, wise, remorseful, well-accomplish'd.
　　Thou art not ignorant what dear good will
　　I bear unto the banish'd Valentine,
　　Nor how my father would enforce me marry
　　Vain Thurio, whom my very soul abhors.
　　Thyself hast lov'd; and I have heard thee say
　　No grief did ever come so near thy heart
　　As when thy lady and thy true love died,
　　Upon whose grave thou vow'dst pure chastity.
　　Sir Eglamour, I would to Valentine,
　　To Mantua, where, I hear, he makes abode;
　　And, for the ways are dangerous to pass,
　　I do desire thy worthy company,
　　Upon whose faith and honour I repose.
　　Urge not my father's anger, Eglamour,
　　But think upon my grief, a lady's grief,
　　And on the justice of my flying hence,

To keep me from a most unholy match,
Which heaven and fortune still rewards with plagues.
I do desire thee, even from a heart
As full of sorrows as the sea of sands,
To bear me company and go with me:
If not, to hide what I have said to thee,
That I may venture to depart alone.

EGLAMOUR. Madam, I pity much your grievances;
Which since I know they virtuously are plac'd,
I give consent to go along with you.
Recking as little what betideth me
As much I wish all good befortune you.
When will you go?

SILVIA.   This evening coming.

EGLAMOUR. Where shall I meet you?

SILVIA.   At Friar Patrick's cell,
Where I intend holy confession.

EGLAMOUR. I will not fail your ladyship.
  Good-morrow, gentle lady.

SILVIA. Good-morrow, kind Sir Eglamour.   *Exeunt*

SCENE FOUR

The Same.

Enter Launce with his dog

LAUNCE. When a man's servant shall play the cur with him,
look you, it goes hard; one that I brought up of a puppy;
one that I saved from drowning, when three or four of
his blind brothers and sisters went to it. I have taught
him, even as one would say precisely, 'Thus would I
teach a dog.' I was sent to deliver him as a present to
Mistress Silvia from my master, and I came no sooner
into the dining-chamber but he steps me to her trencher
and steals her capon's leg. O! 'tis a foul thing when a cur
cannot keep himself in all companies. I would have, as
one should say, one that takes upon him to be a dog indeed, to be, as it were, a dog at all things. If I had not
had more wit than he, to take a fault upon me that he
did, I think verily he had been hanged for 't: sure as I
live, he had suffered for 't: you shall judge. He thrusts

me himself into the company of three or four gentleman-like dogs under the duke's table: he had not been there—bless the mark—a pissing-while, but all the chamber smelt him. 'Out with the dog!' says one; 'What cur is that?' says another; 'Whip him out,' says the third; 'Hang him up,' says the duke. I, having been acquainted with the smell before, knew it was Crab, and goes me to the fellow that whips the dogs: 'Friend,' quoth I, 'you mean to whip the dog?' 'Ay, marry, do I,' quoth he. 'You do him the more wrong,' quoth I; ''twas I did the thing you wot of.' He makes me no more ado, but whips me out of the chamber. How many masters would do this for his servant? Nay, I 'll be sworn, I have sat in the stocks for puddings he hath stolen, otherwise he had been exe-cuted; I have stood on the pillory for geese he hath killed, otherwise he had suffered for 't; thou thinkest not of this now. Nay, I remember the trick you served me when I took my leave of Madam Silvia: did not I bid thee still mark me and do as I do? When didst thou see me heave up my leg and make water against a gentle-woman's farthingale? Didst thou ever see me do such a trick?

Enter Proteus, and Julia in boy's clothes

PROTEUS. Sebastian is thy name? I like thee well
And will employ thee in some service presently.

JULIA. In what you please: I will do what I can.

PROTEUS. I hope thou wilt. (*To Launce*) How now, you
    whoreson peasant!
Where have you been these two days loitering?

LAUNCE. Marry, sir, I carried Mistress Silvia the dog you
    bade me.

PROTEUS. And what says she to my little jewel?

LAUNCE. Marry, she says, your dog was a cur, and tells you,
    currish thanks is good enough for such a present.

PROTEUS. But she received my dog?

LAUNCE. No, indeed, did she not: here have I brought him
    back again.

PROTEUS. What! didst thou offer her this from me?

LAUNCE. Ay, sir: the other squirrel was stolen from me by
    the hangman boys in the market-place; and then I of-fered her mine own, who is a dog as big as ten of yours,
    and therefore the gift the greater.

PROTEUS. Go, get thee hence, and find my dog again,
    Or ne'er return again into my sight.
    Away, I say! Stay'st thou to vex me here?
    A slave that still an end turns me to shame.   *Exit Launce*
    Sebastian, I have entertained thee
    Partly, that I have need of such a youth,
    That can with some discretion do my business,
    For 't is no trusting to yond foolish lout;
    But chiefly for thy face and thy behaviour,
    Which, if my augury deceive me not,
    Witness good bringing up, fortune, and truth:
    Therefore, know thou, for this I entertain thee.
    Go presently, and take this ring with thee.
    Deliver it to Madam Silvia:
    She lov'd me well deliver'd it to me.
JULIA. It seems, you lov'd not her, to leave her token.
    She 's dead, belike?
PROTEUS.   Not so: I think, she lives.
JULIA. Alas!
PROTEUS. Why dost thou cry 'alas'?
JULIA.   I cannot choose
    But pity her.
PROTEUS. Wherefore should'st thou pity her?
JULIA. Because methinks that she lov'd you as well
    As you do love your lady Silvia.
    She dreams on him that has forgot her love;
    You dote on her, that cares not for your love.
    'Tis pity, love should be so contrary;
    And thinking on it makes me cry, 'alas!'
PROTEUS. Well, well, give her that ring and therewithal
    This letter: that 's her chamber. Tell my lady
    I claim the promise for her heavenly picture.
    Your message done, hie home unto my chamber,
    Where thou shalt find me sad and solitary.   *Exit*
JULIA. How many women would do such a message?
    Alas, poor Proteus! thou hast entertain'd
    A fox to be the shepherd of thy lambs.
    Alas, poor fool! why do I pity him
    That with his very heart despiseth me?
    Because he loves her, he despiseth me;
    Because I love him, I must pity him.
    This ring I gave him when he parted from me,

To bind him to remember my good will;
And now am I—unhappy messenger—
To plead for that which I would not obtain,
To carry that which I would have refus'd,
To praise his faith which I would have disprais'd.
I am my master's true-confirmed love,
But cannot be true servant to my master,
Unless I prove false traitor to myself.
Yet will I woo for him; but yet so coldly
As heaven it knows, I would not have him speed.

Enter Silvia, attended

Gentlewoman, good day! I pray you, be my mean
To bring me where to speak with Madam Silvia.

SILVIA. What would you with her, if that I be she?

JULIA. If you be she, I do entreat your patience
To hear me speak the message I am sent on.

SILVIA. From whom?

JULIA. From my master, Sir Proteus, madam.

SILVIA. O! he sends you for a picture?

JULIA. Ay, madam.

SILVIA. Ursula, bring my picture there. *A picture brought*
Go, give your master this: tell him from me,
One Julia, that his changing thoughts forget,
Would better fit his chamber than this shadow.

JULIA. Madam, please you peruse this letter.—*Gives a letter*
Pardon me, madam, I have unadvis'd
Delivered you a paper that I should not:
This is the letter to your ladyship.   *Gives another letter*

SILVIA. I pray thee, let me look on that again.

JULIA. It may not be: good madam, pardon me.

SILVIA. There, hold.
I will not look upon your master's lines:
I know, they are stuff'd with protestations
And full of new-found oaths, which he will break
As easily as I do tear his paper.   *Tears the second letter*

JULIA. Madam, he sends your ladyship this ring.

SILVIA. The more shame for him that he sends it me;
For, I have heard him say a thousand times,
His Julia gave it him at his departure.
Though his false finger have profan'd the ring,
Mine shall not do his Julia so much wrong.

JULIA. She thanks you.

SILVIA. What say'st thou?

JULIA. I thank you, madam, that you tender her.
  Poor gentlewoman! my master wrongs her much.

SILVIA. Dost thou know her?

JULIA. Almost as well as I do know myself:
  To think upon her woes, I do protest
  That I have wept a hundred several times.

SILVIA. Belike she thinks that Proteus hath forsook her.

JULIA. I think she doth, and that 's her cause of sorrow.

SILVIA. Is she not passing fair?

JULIA. She hath been fairer, madam, than she is.
  When she did think my master lov'd her well,
  She, in my judgment, was as fair as you;
  But since she did neglect her looking-glass
  And threw her sun-expelling mask away,
  The air hath starv'd the roses in her cheeks
  And pinch'd the lily-tincture of her face,
  That now she is become as black as I.

SILVIA. How tall was she?

JULIA. About my stature; for, at Pentecost,
  When all our pageants of delight were play'd,
  Our youth got me to play the woman's part,
  And I was trimm'd in Madam Julia's gown,
  Which served me as fit, by all men's judgments,
  As if the garment had been made for me:
  Therefore I know she is about my height.
  And at that time I made her weep agood;
  For I did play a lamentable part.
  Madam, 'twas Ariadne passioning
  For Theseus' perjury and unjust flight;
  Which I so lively acted with my tears
  That my poor mistress, mov'd therewithal
  Wept bitterly, and would I might be dead
  If I in thought felt not her very sorrow!

SILVIA. She is beholding to thee, gentle youth.—
  Alas, poor lady, desolate and left!
  I weep myself to think upon thy words.
  Here, youth, there is my purse: I give thee this
  For thy sweet mistress' sake, because thou lov'st her.
  Farewell.

JULIA. And she shall thank you for 't, if e'er you know
      her.—   *Exit Silvia, with Attendants*

A virtuous gentlewoman, mild and beautiful.
I hope my master's suit will be but cold,
Since she respects my mistress' love so much.
Alas, how love can trifle with itself!
Here is her picture: let me see; I think,
If I had such a tire, this face of mine
Were full as lovely as is this of hers;
And yet the painter flatter'd her a little,
Unless I flatter with myself too much.
Her hair is auburn, mine is perfect yellow:
If that be all the difference in his love
I 'll get me such a colour'd periwig.
Her eyes are grey as glass, and so are mine:
Ay, but her forehead 's low, and mine 's as high.
What should it be that he respects in her
But I can make respective in myself,
If this fond Love were not a blinded god?
Come, shadow, come, and take this shadow up,
For 'tis thy rival. O thou senseless form!
Thou shalt be worshipp'd, kiss'd, lov'd, and ador'd,
And, were there sense in his idolatry,
My substance should be statue in thy stead.
I 'll use thee kindly for thy mistress' sake,
That us'd me so; or else, by Jove I vow,
I should have scratch'd out your unseeing eyes,
To make my master out of love with thee.   *Exit*

ACT FIVE

SCENE ONE

Milan. An Abbey.

Enter Eglamour

EGLAMOUR. The sun begins to gild the western sky,
And now it is about the very hour
That Silvia at Friar Patrick's cell should meet me.
She will not fail; for lovers break not hours,
Unless it be to come before their time,
So much they spur their expedition.
See, where she comes.

Enter Silvia
                    Lady, a happy evening!

SILVIA. Amen, amen! go on, good Eglamour,
Out at the postern by the abbey-wall.
I fear I am attended by some spies.

EGLAMOUR. Fear not: the forest is not three leagues off;
If we recover that, we 're sure enough.   *Exeunt*

SCENE TWO

Milan. A Room in the Duke's Palace.

Enter Thurio, Proteus, and Julia

THURIO. Sir Proteus, what says Silvia to my suit?

PROTEUS. O, sir, I find her milder than she was;
And yet she takes exceptions at your person.

THURIO. What! that my leg is too long?

PROTEUS. No, that it is too little.

THURIO. I 'll wear a boot to make it somewhat rounder.

JULIA. *(Aside)* But love will not be spurr'd to what it
loathes.

THURIO. What says she to my face?

PROTEUS. She says it is a fair one.

THURIO. Nay then, the wanton lies; my face is black.

PROTEUS. But pearls are fair, and the old saying is,
    'Black men are pearls in beauteous ladies' eyes.'

JULIA. (*Aside*) 'Tis true, such pearls as put out ladies'
    eyes;
    For I had rather wink than look on them.

THURIO. How likes she my discourse?

PROTEUS. Ill, when you talk of war.

THURIO. But well, when I discourse of love and peace?

JULIA. (*Aside*) But better, indeed, when you hold your
    peace.

THURIO. What says she to my valour?

PROTEUS. O, sir, she makes no doubt of that.

JULIA. (*Aside*) She needs not, when she knows it coward-
    ice.

THURIO. What says she to my birth?

PROTEUS. That you are well deriv'd.

JULIA. (*Aside*) True; from a gentleman to a fool.

THURIO. Considers she my possessions?

PROTEUS. O, ay; and pities them.

THURIO. Wherefore?

JULIA. (*Aside*) That such an ass should owe them.

PROTEUS. That they are out by lease.

JULIA. Here comes the duke.

Enter Duke

DUKE. How now, Sir Proteus! how now, Thurio!
    Which of you saw Sir Eglamour of late?

THURIO. Not I.

PROTEUS.   Nor I.

DUKE.   Saw you my daughter?

PROTEUS.   Neither.

DUKE. Why then,
    She 's fled unto that peasant Valentine,
    And Eglamour is in her company.
    'Tis true; for Friar Laurence met them both,
    As he in penance wander'd through the forest;
    Him he knew well, and guess'd that it was she,
    But, being mask'd, he was not sure of it;
    Besides, she did intend confession
    At Patrick's cell this even, and there she was not.

These likelihoods confirm her flight from hence.
Therefore, I pray you, stand not to discourse,
But mount you presently and meet with me
Upon the rising of the mountain-foot,
That leads towards Mantua, whither they are fled.
Dispatch, sweet gentlemen, and follow me.   *Exit*

THURIO. Why, this it is to be a peevish girl,
That flies her fortune when it follows her.
I 'll after, more to be reveng'd on Eglamour
Than for the love of reckless Silvia.   *Exit*

PROTEUS. And I will follow, more for Silvia's love
Than hate of Eglamour that goes with her.   *Exit*

JULIA. And I will follow, more to cross that love
Than hate for Silvia that is gone for love.   *Exit*

SCENE THREE

Frontiers of Mantua. The Forest.

Enter Outlaws with Silvia

FIRST OUTLAW. Come, come,
Be patient; we must bring you to our captain.

SILVIA. A thousand more mischances than this one
Have learn'd me how to brook this patiently.

SECOND OUTLAW. Come, bring her away.

FIRST OUTLAW. Where is the gentleman that was with her?

THIRD OUTLAW. Being nimble-footed, he hath outrun us;
But Moyses and Valerius follow him.
Go thou with her to the west end of the wood;
There is our captain. We 'll follow him that 's fled:
The thicket is beset; he cannot 'scape.
            Exeunt all except the First Outlaw and Silvia

FIRST OUTLAW. Come, I must bring you to our captain's
cave.
Fear not; he bears an honourable mind,
And will not use a woman lawlessly.

SILVIA. O Valentine! this I endure for thee.   *Exeunt*

SCENE FOUR

Another Part of the Forest.

Enter Valentine

VALENTINE. How use doth breed a habit in a man!
This shadowy desart, unfrequented woods,
I better brook than flourishing peopled towns.
Here can I sit alone, unseen of any,
And to the nightingale's complaining notes
Tune my distresses and record my woes.
O thou that dost inhabit in my breast,
Leave not the mansion so long tenantless,
Lest, growing ruinous, the building fall
And leave no memory of what it was!
Repair me with thy presence, Silvia!
Thou gentle nymph, cherish thy forlorn swain!

Noise within

What halloing and what stir is this to-day?
These are my mates, that make their wills their law,
Have some unhappy passenger in chase.
They love me well; yet I have much to do
To keep them from uncivil outrages.
Withdraw thee, Valentine: who 's this comes here?

Steps aside

Enter Proteus, Silvia, and Julia

PROTEUS. Madam, this service I have done for you—
Though you respect not aught your servant doth—
To hazard life and rescue you from him
That would have forc'd your honour and your love.
Vouchsafe me, for my meed, but one fair look;
A smaller boon than this I cannot beg,
And less than this, I am sure, you cannot give.

VALENTINE. (*Aside*) How like a dream is this I see and hear!
Love, lend me patience to forbear awhile.

SILVIA. O, miserable, unhappy that I am!

PROTEUS. Unhappy were you, madam, ere I came;
But by my coming I have made you happy.

SILVIA. By thy approach thou mak'st me most unhappy.

JULIA. (*Aside*) And me, when he approacheth to your
  presence.
SILVIA. Had I been seized by a hungry lion,
  I would have been a breakfast to the beast,
  Rather than have false Proteus rescue me.
  O! heaven be judge how I love Valentine,
  Whose life 's as tender to me as my soul,
  And full as much—for more there cannot be—
  I do detest false perjur'd Proteus.
  Therefore be gone, solicit me no more.
PROTEUS. What dangerous action, stood it next to death,
  Would I not undergo for one calm look!
  O, 'tis the curse in love, and still approv'd,
  When women cannot love where they 're belov'd!
SILVIA. When Proteus cannot love where he 's belov'd.
  Read over Julia's heart, thy first best love,
  For whose dear sake thou didst then rend thy faith
  Into a thousand oaths; and all those oaths
  Descended into perjury to love me.
  Thou hast no faith left now, unless thou 'dst two,
  And that 's far worse than none: better have none
  Than plural faith which is too much by one.
  Thou counterfeit to thy true friend!
PROTEUS.   In love
  Who respects friend?
SILVIA.   All men but Proteus.
PROTEUS. Nay, if the gentle spirit of moving words
  Can no way change you to a milder form,
  I 'll woo you like a soldier, at arms' end,
  And love you 'gainst the nature of love,—force ye.
SILVIA. O heaven!
PROTEUS.   I 'll force thee yield to my desire.
VALENTINE. (*Coming forward*) Ruffian, let go that rude
  uncivil touch;
  Thou friend of an ill fashion!
PROTEUS.   Valentine!
VALENTINE. Thou common friend, that 's without faith or
  love—
  For such is a friend now—treacherous man!
  Thou hast beguil'd my hopes: nought but mine eye
  Could have persuaded me. Now I dare not say
  I have one friend alive: thou wouldst disprove me.

Who should be trusted now, when one's right hand
Is perjur'd to the bosom? Proteus,
I am sorry I must never trust thee more,
But count the world a stranger for thy sake.
The private wound is deep'st. O time most curst!
'Mongst all foes that a friend should be the worst!

PROTEUS. My shame and guilt confound me.
Forgive me, Valentine. If hearty sorrow
Be a sufficient ransom for offence,
I tender 't here: I do as truly suffer
As e'er I did commit.

VALENTINE.   Then, I am paid;
And once again I do receive thee honest.
Who by repentance is not satisfied
Is nor of heaven, nor earth; for these are pleas'd.
By penitence the Eternal's wrath 's appeas'd:
And, that my love may appear plain and free,
All that was mine in Silvia I give thee.

JULIA. O me unhappy!   *Swoons*

PROTEUS. Look to the boy.

VALENTINE. Why, boy! why, wag! how now! what 's the
    matter?
Look up; speak.

JULIA. O good sir, my master charg'd me
To deliver a ring to Madam Silvia,
Which out of my neglect was never done.

PROTEUS. Where is that ring, boy?

JULIA.   Here 'tis: this is it.   *Gives a ring*

PROTEUS. How! let me see.
Why this is the ring I gave to Julia.

JULIA. O, cry you mercy, sir; I have mistook:
This is the ring you sent to Silvia.   *Shows another ring*

PROTEUS. But how cam'st thou by this ring?
At my depart I gave this unto Julia.

JULIA. And Julia herself did give it me;
And Julia herself hath brought it hither.

PROTEUS. How! Julia!

JULIA. Behold her that gave aim to all thy oaths,
And entertain'd them deeply in her heart:
How oft hast thou with perjury cleft the root!
O Proteus! let this habit make thee blush.
Be thou asham'd that I have took upon me

Such an immodest raiment; if shame live
In a disguise of love.
It is the lesser blot, modesty finds,
Women to change their shapes than men their minds.

PROTEUS. Than men their minds! 'tis true. O heaven! were
    man
But constant, he were perfect: that one error
Fills him with faults; makes him run through all the sins:
Inconstancy falls off ere it begins.
What is in Silvia's face, but I may spy
More fresh in Julia's with a constant eye?

VALENTINE. Come, come, a hand from either.
Let me be blest to make this happy close:
'Twere pity two such friends should be long foes.

PROTEUS. Bear witness, heaven, I have my wish, for ever.

JULIA. And I mine.

Enter Outlaws with Duke and Thurio

OUTLAW. A prize! a prize! a prize!

VALENTINE. Forbear, forbear, I say; it is my lord the duke.
Your Grace is welcome to a man disgrac'd,
Banished Valentine.

DUKE.   Sir Valentine!

THURIO. Yonder is Silvia; and Silvia 's mine.

VALENTINE. Thurio, give back, or else embrace thy death;
Come not within the measure of my wrath;
Do not name Silvia thine; if once again,
Verona shall not hold thee. Here she stands;
Take but possession of her with a touch;
I dare thee but to breathe upon my love.

THURIO. Sir Valentine, I care not for her, I.
I hold him but a fool that will endanger
His body for a girl that loves him not:
I claim her not, and therefore she is thine.

DUKE. The more degenerate and base art thou,
To make such means for her as thou hast done,
And leave her on such slight conditions.
Now, by the honour of my ancestry,
I do applaud thy spirit, Valentine,
And think thee worthy of an empress' love.
Know then, I here forget all former griefs,
Cancel all grudge, repeal thee home again,
Plead a new state in thy unrivall'd merit,

To which I thus subscribe: Sir Valentine,
Thou art a gentleman and well deriv'd;
Take thou thy Silvia, for thou hast deserv'd her.

VALENTINE. I thank your Grace; the gift hath made me happy.
I now beseech you, for your daughter's sake,
To grant one boon that I shall ask of you.

DUKE. I grant it, for thine own, whate'er it be.

VALENTINE. These banish'd men, that I have kept withal,
Are men endu'd with worthy qualities:
Forgive them what they have committed here,
And let them be recall'd from their exile.
They are reformed, civil, full of good,
And fit for great employment, worthy lord.

DUKE. Thou hast prevail'd; I pardon them, and thee:
Dispose of them as thou know'st their deserts.
Come, let us go: we will include all jars
With triumphs, mirth, and rare solemnity.

VALENTINE. And as we walk along, I dare be bold
With our discourse to make your Grace to smile.
What think you of this page, my lord?

DUKE. I think the boy hath grace in him: he blushes.

VALENTINE. I warrant you, my lord, more grace than boy.

DUKE. What mean you by that saying?

VALENTINE. Please you, I 'll tell you as we pass along,
That you will wonder what hath fortuned.
Come, Proteus; 'tis your penance, but to hear
The story of your loves discovered:
That done, our day of marriage shall be yours;
One feast, one house, one mutual happiness.   *Exeunt*

THE MERRY WIVES OF WINDSOR

SCENE

Windsor; and the Neighbourhood

THE MERRY WIVES OF WINDSOR

ACT ONE

SCENE ONE

Windsor. Before Page's House.

Enter Justice Shallow, Slender, and Sir Hugh Evans

SHALLOW. Sir Hugh, persuade me not; I will make a Star-chamber matter of it; if he were twenty Sir John Falstaffs he shall not abuse Robert Shallow, esquire.

SLENDER. In the county of Gloster, justice of peace, and 'coram.'

SHALLOW. Ay, cousin Slender, and 'cust-alorum.'

SLENDER. Ay, and 'rato-lorum' too; and a gentleman born, Master Parson; who writes himself 'armigero' in any bill, warrant, quittance, or obligation,—'armigero.'

SHALLOW. Ay, that I do; and have done any time these three hundred years.

SLENDER. All his successors gone before him hath done 't; and all his ancestors that come after him may: they may give the dozen white luces in their coat.

SHALLOW. It is an old coat.

EVANS. The dozen white louses do become an old coat well; it agrees well, passant; it is a familiar beast to man, and signifies love.

SHALLOW. The luce is the fresh fish; the salt fish is an old coat.

SLENDER. I may quarter, coz?

SHALLOW. You may, by marrying.

EVANS. It is marring indeed, if he quarter it.

SHALLOW. Not a whit.

EVANS. Yes, py 'r lady; if he has a quarter of your coat, there is but three skirts for yourself, in my simple conjectures:

but that is all one. If Sir John Falstaff have committed disparagements unto you, I am of the Church, and will be glad to do my benevolence to make atonements and compromises between you.

SHALLOW. The Council shall hear it; it is a riot.

EVANS. It is not meet the Council hear a riot; there is no fear of Got in a riot. The Council, look you, shall desire to hear the fear of Got, and not to hear a riot; take your vizaments in that.

SHALLOW. Ha! o' my life, if I were young again, the sword should end it.

EVANS. It is petter that friends is the sword, and end it; and there is also another device in my prain, which, peradventure, prings goot discretions with it. There is Anne Page, which is daughter to Master Thomas Page, which is pretty virginity.

SLENDER. Mistress Anne Page? She has brown hair, and speaks small like a woman.

EVANS. It is that fery person for all the orld, as just as you will desire; and seven hundred pounds of moneys, and gold and silver, is her grandsire, upon his death's-bed,— Got deliver to a joyful resurrections!—give, when she is able to overtake seventeen years old. It were a goot motion if we leave our pribbles and prabbles, and desire a marriage between Master Abraham and Mistress Anne Page.

SHALLOW. Did her grandsire leave her seven hundred pound?

EVANS. Ay, and her father is make her a petter penny.

SHALLOW. I know the young gentlewoman; she has good gifts.

EVANS. Seven hundred pounds and possibilities is goot gifts.

SHALLOW. Well, let us see honest Master Page. Is Falstaff there?

EVANS. Shall I tell you a lie? I do despise a liar as I do despise one that is false; or as I despise one that is not true. The knight, Sir John, is there; and, I beseech you, be ruled by your well-willers. I will peat the door for Master Page. (Knocks) What, hoa! Got pless your house here!

PAGE. (Within) Who's there?

EVANS. Here is Got's plessing, and your friend, and Justice Shallow; and here young Master Slender, that peradventures shall tell you another tale, if matters grow to your likings.

Enter Page

PAGE. I am glad to see your worships well. I thank you for my venison, Master Shallow.

SHALLOW. Master Page, I am glad to see you: much good do it your good heart! I wished your venison better; it was ill killed. How doth good Mistress Page?—And I thank you always with my heart, la! with my heart.

PAGE. Sir, I thank you.

SHALLOW. Sir, I thank you; by yea and no, I do.

PAGE. I am glad to see you, good Master Slender.

SLENDER. How does your fallow greyhound, sir? I heard say he was outrun on Cotsall.

PAGE. It could not be judged, sir.

SLENDER. You 'll not confess, you 'll not confess.

SHALLOW. That he will not: 'tis your fault, 'tis your fault. 'Tis a good dog.

PAGE. A cur, sir.

SHALLOW. Sir, he 's a good dog, and a fair dog; can there be more said? he is good and fair. Is Sir John Falstaff here?

PAGE. Sir, he is within; and I would I could do a good office between you.

EVANS. It is spoke as a Christians ought to speak.

SHALLOW. He hath wronged me, Master Page.

PAGE. Sir, he doth in some sort confess it.

SHALLOW. If it be confessed, it is not redressed: is not that so, Master Page? He hath wronged me; indeed, he hath; —at a word, he hath,—believe me: Robert Shallow, esquire, saith, he is wronged.

PAGE. Here comes Sir John.

Enter Sir John Falstaff, Bardolph, Nym, and Pistol

FALSTAFF. Now, Master Shallow, you 'll complain of me to the king?

SHALLOW. Knight, you have beaten my men, killed my deer, and broke open my lodge.

FALSTAFF. But not kissed your keeper's daughter?

SHALLOW. Tut, a pin! This shall be answered.

FALSTAFF. I will answer it straight: I have done all this. That is now answered.

SHALLOW. The Council shall know this.

FALSTAFF. 'Twere better for you if it were known in counsel: you 'll be laughed at.

EVANS. Pauca verba, Sir John; goot worts.

FALSTAFF. Good worts! Good cabbage. Slender, I broke your head: what matter have you against me?

SLENDER. Marry, sir, I have matter in my head against you; and against your cony-catching rascals, Bardolph, Nym, and Pistol. They carried me to the tavern, and made me drunk, and afterwards picked my pocket.

BARDOLPH. You Banbury cheese!

SLENDER. Ay, it is no matter.

PISTOL. How now, Mephistophilus!

SLENDER. Ay, it is no matter.

NYM. Slice, I say! pauca, pauca; slice! that 's my humour.

SLENDER. Where 's Simple, my man? can you tell, cousin?

EVANS. Peace, I pray you. Now let us understand: there is three umpires in this matter, as I understand; that is— Master Page, fidelicet, Master Page; and there is myself, fidelicet, myself; and the three party is, lastly and finally, mine host of the Garter.

PAGE. We three, to hear it and end it between them.

EVANS. Fery goot: I will make a prief of it in my note-book; and we will afterwards ork upon the cause with as great discreetly as we can.

FALSTAFF. Pistol!

PISTOL. He hears with ears.

EVANS. The tevil and his tam! what phrase is this, 'He hears with ear'? Why, it is affectations.

FALSTAFF. Pistol, did you pick Master Slender's purse?

SLENDER. Ay, by these gloves, did he,—or I would I might never come in mine own great chamber again else,—of seven groats in mill-sixpences, and two Edward shovel-boards, that cost me two shilling and two pence a-piece of Yead Miller, by these gloves.

FALSTAFF. Is this true, Pistol?

EVANS. No; it is false, if it is a pick-purse.

PISTOL. Ha, thou mountain foreigner!—Sir John and master mine,

I combat challenge of this latten bilbo.
Word of denial in thy labras here!
Word of denial: froth and scum, thou liest.

SLENDER. By these gloves, then, 'twas he.

NYM. Be avised, sir, and pass good humours. I will say, 'marry trap,' with you, if you run the nuthook's humour on me: that is the very note of it.

SLENDER. By this hat, then, he in the red face had it; for though I cannot remember what I did when you made me drunk, yet I am not altogether an ass.

FALSTAFF. What say you, Scarlet and John?

BARDOLPH. Why, sir, for my part, I say, the gentleman had drunk himself out of his five sentences.

EVANS. It is his 'five senses'; fie, what the ignorance is!

BARDOLPH. And being fap, sir, was, as they say, cashier'd; and so conclusions pass'd the careires.

SLENDER. Ay, you spake in Latin then too; but 'tis no matter. I 'll ne'er be drunk whilst I live again, but in honest, civil, godly company, for this trick: if I be drunk, I 'll be drunk with those that have the fear of God, and not with drunken knaves.

EVANS. So Got udge me, that is a virtuous mind.

FALSTAFF. You hear all these matters denied, gentlemen; you hear it.

Enter Anne Page,
with wine; Mistress Ford and Mistress Page

PAGE. Nay, daughter, carry the wine in; we 'll drink within.
Exit Anne Page

SLENDER. O heaven! this is Mistress Anne Page.

PAGE. How now, Mistress Ford!

FALSTAFF. Mistress Ford, by my troth, you are very well met: by your leave, good mistress.   *Kissing her*

PAGE. Wife, bid these gentlemen welcome. Come, we have a hot venison pasty to dinner: come, gentlemen, I hope we shall drink down all unkindness.

Exeunt all but Shallow, Slender, and Evans

SLENDER. I had rather than forty shillings I had my Book of Songs and Sonnets here.

Enter Simple

How now, Simple! Where have you been? I must wait on myself, must I? You have not the Book of Riddles about you, have you?

SIMPLE. Book of Riddles! Why, did you not lend it to Alice Shortcake upon All-Hallowmas last, a fortnight afore Michaelmas?

SHALLOW. Come, coz; come, coz; we stay for you. A word

with you, coz; marry, this, coz: there is, as 'twere a
tender, a kind of tender, made afar off by Sir Hugh here:
do you understand me?

SLENDER. Ay, sir, you shall find me reasonable: if it be so, I
shall do that that is reason.

SHALLOW. Nay, but understand me.

SLENDER. So I do, sir.

EVANS. Give ear to his motions, Master Slender: I will description the matter to you, if you pe capacity of it.

SLENDER. Nay, I will do as my cousin Shallow says. I pray
you pardon me; he 's a justice of peace in his country,
simple though I stand here.

EVANS. But that is not the question; the question is concerning your marriage.

SHALLOW. Ay, there 's the point, sir.

EVANS. Marry, is it, the very point of it; to Mistress Anne
Page.

SLENDER. Why, if it be so, I will marry her upon any reasonable demands.

EVANS. But can you affection the 'oman? Let us command
to know that of your mouth or of your lips; for divers
philosophers hold that the lips is parcel of the mouth:
therefore, precisely, can you carry your good will to the
maid?

SHALLOW. Cousin Abraham Slender, can you love her?

SLENDER. I hope, sir, I will do as it shall become one that
would do reason.

EVANS. Nay, Got's lords and his ladies! you must speak possitable, if you can carry her your desires towards her.

SHALLOW. That you must. Will you, upon good dowry,
marry her?

SLENDER. I will do a greater thing than that, upon your request, cousin, in any reason.

SHALLOW. Nay, conceive me, conceive me, sweet coz: what
I do, is to pleasure you, coz. Can you love the maid?

SLENDER. I will marry her, sir, at your request; but if there
be no great love in the beginning, yet heaven may de-
crease it upon better acquaintance, when we are married
and have more occasion to know one another; I hope,
upon familiarity will grow more contempt: but if you
say, 'Marry her,' I will marry her; that I am freely dissolved, and dissolutely.

EVANS. It is a fery discretion answer; save, the faul is in the ort 'dissolutely': the ort is, according to our meaning, 'resolutely.' His meaning is goot.

SHALLOW. Ay, I think my cousin meant well.

SLENDER. Ay, or else I would I might be hanged, la!

SHALLOW. Here comes fair Mistress Anne.

Re-enter Anne Page

Would I were young for your sake, Mistress Anne.

ANNE. The dinner is on the table; my father desires your worships' company.

SHALLOW. I will wait on him, fair Mistress Anne.

EVANS. Od's plessed will! I will not be absence at the grace.

Exeunt Shallow and Evans

ANNE. Will 't please your worship to come in, sir?

SLENDER. No, I thank you, forsooth, heartily; I am very well.

ANNE. The dinner attends you, sir.

SLENDER. I am not a-hungry, I thank you forsooth. Go, sirrah, for all you are my man, go wait upon my cousin Shallow. (*Exit Simple*) A justice of peace sometime may be beholding to his friend for a man. I keep but three men and a boy yet, till my mother be dead; but what though? Yet I live like a poor gentleman born.

ANNE. I may not go in without your worship: they will not sit till you come.

SLENDER. I' faith, I 'll eat nothing; I thank you as much as though I did.

ANNE. I pray you, sir, walk in.

SLENDER. I had rather walk here, I thank you. I bruised my shin th' other day with playing at sword and dagger with a master of fence; three veneys for a dish of stewed prunes;—and, by my troth, I cannot abide the smell of hot meat since. Why do your dogs bark so? Be there bears i' the town?

ANNE. I think there are, sir; I heard them talked of.

SLENDER. I love the sport well; but I shall as soon quarrel at it as any man in England. You are afraid if you see the bear loose, are you not?

ANNE. Ay, indeed, sir.

SLENDER. That 's meat and drink to me, now: I have seen Sackerson loose twenty times, and have taken him by the chain; but, I warrant you, the women have so cried and

shrieked at it, that it passed: but women, indeed, cannot
abide 'em; they are very ill-favoured rough things.

Re-enter Page

PAGE. Come, gentle Master Slender, come; we stay for you.

SLENDER. I 'll eat nothing, I thank you, sir.

PAGE. By cock and pie, you shall not choose, sir! come,
come.

SLENDER. Nay, pray you, lead the way.

PAGE. Come on, sir.

SLENDER. Mistress Anne, yourself shall go first.

ANNE. Not I, sir; pray you, keep on.

SLENDER. Truly, I will not go first: truly, la! I will not do
you that wrong.

ANNE. I pray you, sir.

SLENDER. I 'll rather be unmannerly than troublesome. You
do yourself wrong, indeed, la! *Exeunt*

SCENE TWO

The Same.

Enter Sir Hugh Evans and Simple

EVANS. Go your ways, and ask of Doctor Caius' house,
which is the way: and there dwells one Mistress Quickly,
which is in the manner of his nurse, or his try nurse, or
his cook, or his laundry, his washer, and his wringer.

SIMPLE. Well, sir.

EVANS. Nay, it is better yet. Give her this letter; for it is a
'oman that altogether 's acquaintance with Mistress Anne
Page: and the letter is, to desire and require her to solicit
your master's desires to Mistress Anne Page. I pray you,
be gone: I will make an end of my dinner; there 's pip-
pins and seese to come. *Exeunt*

SCENE THREE

A Room in the Garter Inn.

Enter Falstaff, Host, Bardolph, Nym, Pistol, and Robin

FALSTAFF. Mine host of the Garter!

HOST. What says my bully-rook? Speak scholarly and wisely.

FALSTAFF. Truly, mine host, I must turn away some of my followers.

HOST. Discard, bully Hercules; cashier: let them wag; trot, trot.

FALSTAFF. I sit at ten pounds a week.

HOST. Thou 'rt an emperor, Cæsar, Keisar, and Pheezar. I will entertain Bardolph; he shall draw, he shall tap: said I well, bully Hector?

FALSTAFF. Do so, good mine host.

HOST. I have spoke; let him follow. (*To Bardolph*) Let me see thee froth and lime: I am at a word; follow.

FALSTAFF. Bardolph, follow him. A tapster is a good trade: an old cloak makes a new jerkin; a withered serving-man, a fresh tapster. Go; adieu.

BARDOLPH. It is a life that I have desired. I will thrive.

PISTOL. O base Hungarian wight! wilt thou the spigot wield?   *Exit Bardolph*

NYM. He was gotten in drink; is not the humour conceited?

FALSTAFF. I am glad I am so acquit of this tinderbox; his thefts were too open; his filching was like an unskilful singer; he kept not time.

NYM. The good humour is to steal at a minim's rest.

PISTOL. 'Convey,' the wise it call. 'Steal!' foh! a fico for the phrase!

FALSTAFF. Well, sirs, I am almost out at heels.

PISTOL. Why, then, let kibes ensue.

FALSTAFF. There is no remedy; I must cony-catch, I must shift.

PISTOL. Young ravens must have food.

FALSTAFF. Which of you know Ford of this town?

PISTOL. I ken the wight: he is of substance good.

FALSTAFF. My honest lads, I will tell you what I am about.

PISTOL. Two yards, and more.

FALSTAFF. No quips now, Pistol! Indeed, I am in the waist two yards about; but I am now about no waste; I am about thrift. Briefly, I do mean to make love to Ford's wife: I spy entertainment in her; she discourses, she carves, she gives the leer of invitation: I can construe the action of her familiar style; and the hardest voice of her behaviour, to be Englished rightly, is, 'I am Sir John Falstaff's.'

PISTOL. He hath studied her well, and translated her well, out of honesty into English.

NYM. The anchor is deep: will that humour pàss?

FALSTAFF. Now, the report goes she has all the rule of her husband's purse; he hath a legion of angels.

PISTOL. As many devils entertain, and 'To her, boy,' say I.

NYM. The humour rises; it is good: humour me the angels.

FALSTAFF. I have writ me here a letter to her; and here another to Page's wife, who even now gave me good eyes too, examined my parts with most judicious œilliades: sometimes the beam of her view gilded my foot, sometimes my portly belly.

PISTOL. Then did the sun on dunghill shine.

NYM. I thank thee for that humour.

FALSTAFF. O! she did so course o'er my exteriors with such a greedy intention, that the appetite of her eye did seem to scorch me up like a burning-glass. Here 's another letter to her: she bears the purse too; she is a region in Guiana, all gold and bounty. I will be 'cheator to them both, and they shall be exchequers to me: they shall be my East and West Indies, and I will trade to them both. (*To Pistol*) Go bear thou this letter to Mistress Page; (*To Nym*) and thou this to Mistress Ford. We will thrive, lads, we will thrive.

PISTOL. Shall I Sir Pandarus of Troy become,

And by my side wear steel? Then, Lucifer take all!

NYM. I will run no base humour: here, take the humour-letter. I will keep the haviour of reputation.

FALSTAFF. (*To Robin*) Hold, sirrah, bear you these letters tightly:

Sail like my pinnace to these golden shores.

Rogues, hence! avaunt! vanish like hailstones, go;

Trudge, plod away o' the hoof; seek shelter, pack!

Falstaff will learn the humour of this age,
French thrift, you rogues: myself and skirted page.
                                    Exeunt Falstaff and Robin

PISTOL. Let vultures gripe thy guts! for gourd and fullam
     holds,
And high and low beguile the rich and poor.
Tester I 'll have in pouch when thou shalt lack,
Base Phrygian Turk!

NYM. I have operations in my head, which be humours of
     revenge.

PISTOL. Wilt thou revenge?

NYM. By welkin and her star!

PISTOL. With wit or steel?

NYM. With both the humours, I:
I will discuss the humour of this love to Page.

PISTOL.   And I to Ford shall eke unfold
               How Falstaff, varlet vile,
               His dove will prove, his gold will hold,
               And his soft couch defile.

NYM. My humour shall not cool: I will incense Page to deal
     with poison; I will possess him with yellowness, for the
     revolt of mine is dangerous: that is my true humour.

PISTOL. Thou art the Mars of malcontents: I second thee;
     troop on.   *Exeunt*

SCENE FOUR

A Room in Doctor Caius's House.

Enter Mistress Quickly and Simple

QUICKLY. What, John Rugby!—
                         Enter Rugby
I pray thee, go to the casement, and see if you can see
my master, Master Doctor Caius, coming: if he do, i'
faith, and find anybody in the house, here will be an old
abusing of God's patience and the king's English.

RUGBY. I 'll go watch.

QUICKLY. Go; and we 'll have a posset for 't soon at night, in
faith, at the latter end of a sea-coal fire. (*Exit Rugby*)
An honest, willing, kind fellow, as ever servant shall
come in house withal; and, I warrant you, no tell-tale,

nor no breed-bate: his worst fault is, that he is given to
prayer; he is something peevish that way, but nobody
but has his fault; but let that pass. Peter Simple you say
your name is?

SIMPLE. Ay, for fault of a better.

QUICKLY. And Master Slender 's your master?

SIMPLE. Ay, forsooth.

QUICKLY. Does he not wear a great round beard like a
glover's paring-knife?

SIMPLE. No, forsooth: he hath but a little whey-face, with a
little yellow beard—a cane-coloured beard.

QUICKLY. A softly-sprighted man, is he not?

SIMPLE. Ay, forsooth; but he is as tall a man of his hands as
any is between this and his head: he hath fought with a
warrener.

QUICKLY. How say you?—O! I should remember him: does
he not hold up his head, as it were, and strut in his gait?

SIMPLE. Yes, indeed, does he.

QUICKLY. Well, heaven send Anne Page no worse fortune!
Tell Master Parson Evans I will do what I can for your
master: Anne is a good girl, and I wish—

Re-enter Rugby

RUGBY. Out, alas! here comes my master.

QUICKLY. We shall all be shent. Run in here, good young
man; go into this closet. (*Shuts Simple in the closet*) He
will not stay long. What, John Rugby! John, what, John,
I say! Go, John, go inquire for my master; I doubt he be
not well, that he comes not home.   *Exit Rugby*

(*Sings*) 'And down, down, adown-a,' &c.

Enter Doctor Caius

CAIUS. Vat is you sing? I do not like dese toys. Pray you, go
and vetch me in my closet une boitine verde; a box, a
green-a box: do intend vat I speak? a green-a box.

QUICKLY. Ay, forsooth; I 'll fetch it you. (*Aside*) I am glad
he went not in himself: if he had found the young man,
he would have been horn-mad.

CAIUS. Fe, fe, fe, fe! ma foi, il fait fort chaud. Je m'en vais à
la cour,—la grande affaire.

QUICKLY. Is it this, sir?

CAIUS. Oui; mettez le au mon pocket; dépêchez, quickly.—
Vere is dat knave Rugby?

QUICKLY. What, John Rugby! John!

Re-enter Rugby

RUGBY. Here, sir.

CAIUS. You are John Rugby, and you are Jack Rugby:
come, take-a your rapier, and come after my heel to de
court.

RUGBY. 'Tis ready, sir, here in the porch.

CAIUS. By my trot, I tarry too long.—Od's me! Qu'ay j'ou-
blié? dere is some simples in my closet, dat I vill not for
de varld I shall leave behind.

QUICKLY. (*Aside*) Ay me! he 'll find the young man there,
and be mad.

CAIUS. O diable! diable! vat is in my closet?—Villain! larron!
(*Pulling Simple out*) Rugby, my rapier!

QUICKLY. Good master, be content.

CAIUS. Verefore shall I be content-a?

QUICKLY. The young man is an honest man.

CAIUS. Vat shall de honest man do in my closet? Dere is no
honest man dat shall come in my closet.

QUICKLY. I beseech you, be not so phlegmatic. Hear the
truth of it: he came of an errand to me from Parson
Hugh.

CAIUS. Vell.

SIMPLE. Ay, forsooth, to desire her to—

QUICKLY. Peace, I pray you.

CAIUS. Peace-a your tongue!—Speak-a your tale.

SIMPLE. To desire this honest gentlewoman, your maid, to
speak a good word to Mistress Anne Page for my master
in the way of marriage.

QUICKLY. This is all, indeed, la! but I 'll ne'er put my finger
in the fire, and need not.

CAIUS. Sir Hugh send-a you?—Rugby, baillez me some
paper: tarry you a little-a while.   *Writes*

QUICKLY. I am glad he is so quiet: if he had been throughly
moved, you should have heard him so loud, and so melancholy. But, notwithstanding, man, I 'll do your master
what good I can; and the very yea and the no is, the
French doctor, my master,—I may call him my master,
look you, for I keep his house; and I wash, wring, brew,
bake, scour, dress meat and drink, make the beds, and do
all myself,—

SIMPLE. 'Tis a great charge to come under one body's hand.

QUICKLY. Are you avis'd o' that? you shall find it a great

charge: and to be up early and down late; but notwithstanding,—to tell you in your ear,—I would have no
words of it,—my master himself is in love with Mistress
Anne Page: but notwithstanding that, I know Anne's
mind, that's neither here nor there.

CAIUS. You jack'nape, give-a dis letter to Sir Hugh; by gar,
it is a shallenge: I vill cut his troat in de Park; and I vill
teach a scurvy jack-a-nape priest to meddle or make. You
may be gone; it is not good you tarry here: by gar, I vill
cut all his two stones; by gar, he shall not have a stone to
trow at his dog.   *Exit Simple*

QUICKLY. Alas! he speaks but for his friend.

CAIUS. It is no matter-a for dat:—do not you tell-a me dat I
shall have Anne Page for myself? By gar, I vill kill de
Jack priest; and I have appointed mine host of de Jar-
tiere to measure our weapon. By gar, I vill myself have
Anne Page.

QUICKLY. Sir, the maid loves you, and all shall be well. We
must give folks leave to prate: what, the good-jer!

CAIUS. Rugby, come to the court vit me. By gar, if I have
not Anne Page, I shall turn your head out of my door.
Follow my heels, Rugby.   *Exeunt Caius and Rugby*

QUICKLY. You shall have An fool's-head of your own. No, I
know Anne's mind for that: never a woman in Windsor
knows more of Anne's mind than I do; nor can do more
than I do with her, I thank heaven.

FENTON. (*Within*) Who's within there? ho!

QUICKLY. Who's there, I trow? Come near the house, I
pray you.

Enter Fenton

FENTON. How now, good woman! how dost thou?

QUICKLY. The better, that it pleases your good worship to
ask.

FENTON. What news? How does pretty Mistress Anne?

QUICKLY. In truth, sir, and she is pretty, and honest, and
gentle; and one that is your friend, I can tell you that by
the way; I praise heaven for it.

FENTON. Shall I do any good, thinkest thou? Shall I not lose
my suit?

QUICKLY. Troth, sir, all is in his hands above; but notwithstanding, Master Fenton, I'll be sworn on a book, she
loves you. Have not your worship a wart above your eye?

FENTON. Yes, marry have I; what of that?

QUICKLY. Well, thereby hangs a tale. Good faith, it is such another Nan; but, I detest, an honest maid as ever broke bread: we had an hour's talk of that wart. I shall never laugh but in that maid's company;—but, indeed, she is given too much to allicholy and musing. But for you—well, go to.

FENTON. Well, I shall see her to-day. Hold, there's money for thee; let me have thy voice in my behalf: if thou seest her before me, commend me.

QUICKLY. Will I? i' faith, that we will: and I will tell your worship more of the wart the next time we have confidence; and of other wooers.

FENTON. Well, farewell; I am in great haste now.

QUICKLY. Farewell to your worship.—(*Exit Fenton*) Truly, an honest gentleman: but Anne loves him not; for I know Anne's mind as well as another does. Out upon 't! what have I forgot?   *Exit*

ACT TWO

SCENE ONE

Before Page's House.

Enter Mistress Page, with a Letter

MRS. PAGE. What! have I 'scaped love-letters in the holiday-time of my beauty, and am I now a subject for them? Let me see. (*Reads*)

'Ask me no reason why I love you; for though Love use Reason for his physician, he admits him not for his counsellor. You are not young, no more am I; go to then, there 's sympathy; you are merry, so am I; ha! ha! then, there 's more sympathy; you love sack, and so do I; would you desire better sympathy? Let it suffice thee, Mistress Page, at the least, if the love of a soldier can suffice, that I love thee. I will not say, pity me,—'tis not a soldier-like phrase; but I say, love me. By me,

Thine own true knight,
By day or night,
Or any kind of light,
With all his might
For thee to fight,
'John Falstaff.'

What a Herod of Jewry is this! O wicked, wicked world! one that is well-nigh worn to pieces with age, to show himself a young gallant. What an unweighed behaviour hath this Flemish drunkard picked, (with the devil's name!) out of my conversation, that he dares in this manner assay me? Why, he hath not been thrice in my company! What should I say to him? I was then frugal of my mirth:—heaven forgive me! Why, I 'll exhibit a bill in the parliament for the putting down of men. How shall I be revenged on him? for revenged I will be, as sure as his guts are made of puddings.

Enter Mistress Ford

MRS. FORD. Mistress Page, trust me, I was going to your house.

MRS. PAGE. And, trust me, I was coming to you. You look very ill.

MRS. FORD. Nay, I 'll ne'er believe that: I have to show to the contrary.

MRS. PAGE. Faith, but you do, in my mind.

MRS. FORD. Well, I do then: yet, I say I could show you to the contrary. O, Mistress Page! give me some counsel.

MRS. PAGE. What 's the matter, woman?

MRS. FORD. O woman, if it were not for one trifling respect, I could come to such honour!

MRS. PAGE. Hang the trifle, woman; take the honour. What is it?—dispense with trifles;—what is it?

MRS. FORD. If I would but go to hell for an eternal moment or so, I could be knighted.

MRS. PAGE. What? thou liest. Sir Alice Ford! These knights will hack; and so thou shouldst not alter the article of thy gentry.

MRS. FORD. We burn daylight: here, read, read; perceive how I might be knighted. I shall think the worse of fat men as long as I have an eye to make difference of men's liking: and yet he would not swear; praised women's modesty; and gave such orderly and well-behaved reproof to all uncomeliness, that I would have sworn his disposition would have gone to the truth of his words; but they do no more adhere and keep place together than the Hundredth Psalm to the tune of 'Green Sleeves.' What tempest, I trow, threw this whale, with so many tuns of oil in his belly, ashore at Windsor? How shall I be revenged on him? I think, the best way were to entertain him with hope, till the wicked fire of lust have melted him in his own grease. Did you ever hear the like?

MRS. PAGE. Letter for letter, but that the name of Page and Ford differs! To thy great comfort in this mystery of ill opinions, here 's the twin brother of thy letter: but let thine inherit first; for, I protest, mine never shall. I warrant, he hath a thousand of these letters, writ with blank space for different names, sure more, and these are of the second edition. He will print them, out of doubt; for he cares not what he puts into the press, when he would put

us two: I had rather be a giantess, and lie under Mount
Pelion. Well, I will find you twenty lascivious turtles ere
one chaste man.

MRS. FORD. Why, this is the very same; the very hand, the
very words. What doth he think of us?

MRS. PAGE. Nay, I know not: it makes me almost ready to
wrangle with mine own honesty. I 'll entertain myself like
one that I am not acquainted withal; for, sure, unless he
know some strain in me, that I know not myself, he
would never have boarded me in this fury.

MRS. FORD. Boarding call you it? I 'll be sure to keep him
above deck.

MRS. PAGE. So will I: if he come under my hatches, I 'll
never to sea again. Let 's be revenged on him: let 's appoint him a meeting; give him a show of comfort in his
suit, and lead him on with a fine-baited delay, till he hath
pawned his horses to mine host of the Garter.

MRS. FORD. Nay, I will consent to act any villany against
him, that may not sully the chariness of our honesty. O,
that my husband saw this letter! it would give eternal
food to his jealousy.

MRS. PAGE. Why, look, where he comes; and my good man
too: he 's as far from jealousy, as I am from giving him
cause; and that, I hope, is an unmeasurable distance.

MRS. FORD. You are the happier woman.

MRS. PAGE. Let 's consult together against this greasy
knight. Come hither.   *They retire*

Enter Ford, Pistol, Page, and Nym

FORD. Well, I hope it be not so.

PISTOL. Hope is a curtal dog in some affairs:
Sir John affects thy wife.

FORD. Why, sir, my wife is not young.

PISTOL. He wooes both high and low, both rich and poor,
Both young and old, one with another, Ford.
He loves the galimaufry: Ford, perpend.

FORD. Love my wife!

PISTOL. With liver burning hot: prevent, or go thou,
Like Sir Actæon he, with Ringwood at thy heels.—
O! odious is the name!

FORD. What name, sir?

PISTOL. The horn, I say. Farewell:
Take heed; have open eye, for thieves do foot by night:

Take heed, ere summer comes or cuckoo-birds do sing.
Away, sir Corporal Nym!
Believe it, Page; he speaks sense.   *Exit*

FORD. (*Aside*) I will be patient: I will find out this.

NYM. (*To Page*) And this is true; I like not the humour of
lying. He hath wronged me in some humours: I should
have borne the humoured letter to her, but I have a
sword and it shall bite upon my necessity. He loves your
wife; there 's the short and the long. My name is Corporal Nym; I speak, and I avouch 'tis true: my name is
Nym, and Falstaff loves your wife. Adieu. I love not the
humour of bread and cheese; and there 's the humour of
it. Adieu.   *Exit*

PAGE. (*Aside*) 'The humour of it,' quoth 'a! here 's a fellow
frights humour out of his wits.

FORD. I will seek out Falstaff.

PAGE. I never heard such a drawling, affecting rogue.

FORD. If I do find it: well.

PAGE. I will not believe such a Cataian, though the priest o'
the town commended him for a true man.

FORD. 'Twas a good sensible fellow: well.

PAGE. How now, Meg!

MRS. PAGE. Whither go you, George?—Hark you.

MRS. FORD. How now, sweet Frank! why art thou melancholy?

FORD. I melancholy! I am not melancholy. Get you home,
go.

MRS. FORD. Faith, thou hast some crotchets in thy head
now. Will you go, Mistress Page?

MRS. PAGE. Have with you, you 'll come to dinner, George?
(*Aside to Mrs. Ford*) Look, who comes yonder: she shall
be our messenger to this paltry knight.

MRS. FORD. Trust me, I thought on her: she 'll fit it.

Enter Mistress Quickly

MRS. PAGE. You are come to see my daughter Anne?

QUICKLY. Ay, forsooth; and, I pray, how does good Mistress
Anne?

MRS. PAGE. Go in with us, and see: we 'd have an hour's
talk with you.   *Exeunt Mistress
                    Page, Mistress Ford, and Mistress Quickly*

PAGE. How now, Master Ford!

FORD. You heard what this knave told me, did you not?

PAGE. Yes; and you heard what the other told me?

FORD. Do you think there is truth in them?

PAGE. Hang 'em, slaves! I do not think the knight would offer it: but these that accuse him in his intent towards our
wives, are a yoke of his discarded men; very rogues, now
they be out of service.

FORD. Were they his men?

PAGE. Marry, were they.

FORD. I like it never the better for that. Does he lie at the
Garter?

PAGE. Ay, marry, does he. If he should intend this voyage
towards my wife, I would turn her loose to him; and
what he gets more of her than sharp words, let it lie on
my head.

FORD. I do not misdoubt my wife, but I would be loth to
turn them together. A man may be too confident: I
would have nothing 'lie on my head': I cannot be thus
satisfied.

PAGE. Look, where my ranting host of the Garter comes.
There is either liquor in his pate or money in his purse
when he looks so merrily.—

Enter Host and Shallow

How now, mine host!

HOST. How now, bully-rook! thou 'rt a gentleman. Cavaliero-
justice, I say!

SHALLOW. I follow, mine host, I follow. Good even and
twenty, good Master Page! Master Page, will you go with
us? we have sport in hand.

HOST. Tell him, cavaliero-justice; tell him, bully-rook.

SHALLOW. Sir, there is a fray to be fought between Sir
Hugh the Welsh priest and Caius the French doctor.

FORD. Good mine host o' the Garter, a word with you.

HOST. What sayest thou, my bully-rook?   *They go aside*

SHALLOW. (*To Page*) Will you go with us to behold it? My
merry host hath had the measuring of their weapons,
and, I think, hath appointed them contrary places; for,
believe me, I hear the parson is no jester. Hark, I will tell
you what our sport shall be.   *They go aside*

HOST. Hast thou no suit against my knight, my guest-cava-
lier?

FORD. None, I protest: but I 'll give you a pottle of burnt

sack to give me recourse to him and tell him my name is
Brook, only for a jest.

HOST. My hand, bully: thou shalt have egress and regress;
said I well? and thy name shall be Brook. It is a merry
knight. Will you go, mynheers?

SHALLOW. Have with you, mine host.

PAGE. I have heard, the Frenchman hath good skill in his
rapier.

SHALLOW. Tut, sir! I could have told you more. In these
times you stand on distance, your passes, stoccadoes, and
I know not what: 'tis the heart, Master Page; 'tis here, 'tis
here. I have seen the time with my long sword I would
have made you four tall fellows skip like rats.

HOST. Here, boys, here, here! shall we wag?

PAGE. Have with you. I had rather hear them scold than
fight. *Exeunt Host, Shallow, and Page*

FORD. Though Page be a secure fool, and stands so firmly
on his wife's frailty, yet I cannot put off my opinion so
easily. She was in his company at Page's house, and what
they made there, I know not. Well, I will look further
into 't; and I have a disguise to sound Falstaff. If I find
her honest, I lose not my labour; if she be otherwise, 'tis
labour well bestowed. *Exit*

SCENE TWO

A Room in the Garter Inn.

Enter Falstaff and Pistol

FALSTAFF. I will not lend thee a penny.

PISTOL. Why, then the world 's mine oyster,
Which I with sword will open.
I will retort the sum in equipage.

FALSTAFF. Not a penny. I have been content, sir, you
should lay my countenance to pawn: I have grated upon
my good friends for three reprieves for you and your
coach-fellow Nym; or else you had looked through the
grate, like a geminy of baboons. I am damned in hell for
swearing to gentlemen my friends, you were good soldiers and tall fellows; and when Mistress Bridget lost the

handle of her fan, I took 't upon mine honour thou hadst
it not.

PISTOL. Didst thou not share? Hadst thou not fifteen pence?

FALSTAFF. Reason, you rogue, reason: thinkest thou, I 'll endanger my soul gratis? At a word, hang no more about
me; I am no gibbet for you: go: a short knife and a
throng!—to your manor of Pichthatch! go. You 'll not bear
a letter for me, you rogue!—you stand upon your honour!
—Why, thou unconfinable baseness, it is as much as I can
do to keep the terms of mine honour precise. I, I, I, myself sometimes, leaving the fear of God on the left hand
and hiding mine honour in my necessity, am fain to shuffle, to hedge and to lurch; and yet you, rogue, will ensconce your rags, your cat-a-mountain looks, your red-
lattice phrases, and your bold-beating oaths, under the
shelter of your honour! You will not do it, you!

PISTOL. I do relent: what wouldst thou more of man?

Enter Robin

ROBIN. Sir, here 's a woman would speak with you.

FALSTAFF. Let her approach.

Enter Mistress Quickly

QUICKLY. Give your worship good-morrow.

FALSTAFF. Good-morrow, good wife.

QUICKLY. Not so, an 't please your worship.

FALSTAFF. Good maid, then.

QUICKLY. I 'll be sworn
As my mother was, the first hour I was born.

FALSTAFF. I do believe the swearer. What with me?

QUICKLY. Shall I vouchsafe your worship a word or two?

FALSTAFF. Two thousand, fair woman; and I 'll vouchsafe
thee the hearing.

QUICKLY. There is one Mistress Ford, sir,—I pray, come a
little nearer this ways:—I myself dwell with Master Doctor Caius.

FALSTAFF. Well, on: Mistress Ford, you say,—

QUICKLY. Your worship says very true:—I pray your worship, come a little nearer this ways.

FALSTAFF. I warrant thee, nobody hears; mine own people,
mine own people.

QUICKLY. Are they so? God bless them, and make them his
servants!

FALSTAFF. Well: Mistress Ford; what of her?

QUICKLY. Why, sir, she 's a good creature. Lord, Lord! your worship 's a wanton! Well, heaven forgive you, and all of us, I pray!

FALSTAFF. Mistress Ford; come, Mistress Ford,—

QUICKLY. Marry, this is the short and the long of it. You have brought her into such a canaries as 'tis wonderful: the best courtier of them all, when the court lay at Windsor, could never have brought her to such a canary; yet there has been knights, and lords, and gentlemen, with their coaches, I warrant you, coach after coach, letter after letter, gift after gift; smelling so sweetly—all musk, and so rushling, I warrant you, in silk and gold; and in such alligant terms; and in such wine and sugar of the best and the fairest, that would have won any woman's heart; and, I warrant you, they could never get an eye-wink of her. I had myself twenty angels given me this morning; but I defy all angels, in any such sort, as they say, but in the way of honesty: and, I warrant you, they could never get her so much as sip on a cup with the proudest of them all; and yet there has been earls, nay, which is more, pensioners; but, I warrant you, all is one with her.

FALSTAFF. But what says she to me? Be brief, my good she-Mercury.

QUICKLY. Marry, she hath received your letter; for the which she thanks you a thousand times; and she gives you to notify that her husband will be absence from his house between ten and eleven.

FALSTAFF. Ten and eleven?

QUICKLY. Ay, forsooth; and then you may come and see the picture, she says, that you wot of: Master Ford, her husband, will be from home. Alas! the sweet woman leads an ill life with him; he 's a very jealousy man; she leads a very frampold life with him, good heart.

FALSTAFF. Ten and eleven. Woman, commend me to her; I will not fail her.

QUICKLY. Why, you say well. But I have another messenger to your worship: Mistress Page hath her hearty commendations to you too: and let me tell you in your ear, she 's as fartuous a civil modest wife, and one, I tell you, that will not miss you morning nor evening prayer, as any is in Windsor, whoe'er be the other: and she bade me tell

your worship that her husband is seldom from home;
but, she hopes there will come a time. I never knew a
woman so dote upon a man: surely, I think you have
charms, la; yes, in truth.

FALSTAFF. Not I, I assure thee: setting the attraction of my
good parts aside, I have no other charms.

QUICKLY. Blessing on your heart for 't!

FALSTAFF. But, I pray thee, tell me this: has Ford's wife
and Page's wife acquainted each other how they love
me?

QUICKLY. That were a jest indeed! They have not so little
grace, I hope: that were a trick, indeed! But Mistress
Page would desire you to send her your little page, of all
loves: her husband has a marvellous infection to the little
page; and, truly, Master Page is an honest man. Never a
wife in Windsor leads a better life than she does: do
what she will, say what she will, take all, pay all, go to
bed when she list, rise when she list, all is as she will:
and, truly she deserves it; for if there be a kind woman in
Windsor, she is one. You must send her your page; no
remedy.

FALSTAFF. Why, I will.

QUICKLY. Nay, but do so, then; and, look you, he may come
and go between you both; and in any case have a nay-
word, that you may know one another's mind, and the
boy never need to understand any thing; for 'tis not good
that children should know any wickedness: old folks, you
know, have discretion, as they say, and know the world

FALSTAFF. Fare thee well: commend me to them both
There 's my purse; I am yet thy debtor.—Boy, go along
with this woman.—(*Exeunt Mistress Quickly and Robin*)
This news distracts me.

PISTOL. This punk is one of Cupid's carriers.
Clap on more sails; pursue; up with your fights;
Give fire! She is my prize, or ocean whelm them all! *Exi*

FALSTAFF. Sayest thou so, old Jack? Go thy ways; I 'll make
more of thy old body than I have done. Will they ye
look after thee? Wilt thou, after the expense of so much
money, be now a gainer? Good body, I thank thee. Le
them say 'tis grossly done; so it be fairly done, no matter

Enter Bardolph, with a cup of Sack

BARDOLPH. Sir John, there 's one Master Brook below would

fain speak with you, and be acquainted with you; and
hath sent your worship a morning's draught of sack.

FALSTAFF. Brook is his name?

BARDOLPH. Ay, sir.

FALSTAFF. Call him in. (*Exit Bardolph*) Such Brooks are
welcome to me, that o'erflow such liquor. Ah, ha! Mistress Ford and Mistress Page, have I encompassed you?
Go to; via!

Re-enter Bardolph, with Ford disguised

FORD. Bless you, sir!

FALSTAFF. And you, sir; would you speak with me?

FORD. I make bold to press with so little preparation upon
you.

FALSTAFF. You 're welcome. What 's your will?—Give us
leave, drawer. *Exit Bardolph*

FORD. Sir, I am a gentleman that have spent much: my
name is Brook.

FALSTAFF. Good Master Brook, I desire more acquaintance
of you.

FORD. Good Sir John, I sue for yours: not to charge you; for
I must let you understand I think myself in better plight
for a lender than you are: the which hath something em-
boldened me to this unseasoned intrusion; for, they say,
if money go before, all ways do lie open.

FALSTAFF. Money is a good soldier, sir, and will on.

FORD. Troth, and I have a bag of money here troubles me:
if you will help to bear it, Sir John, take all, or half, for
easing me of the carriage.

FALSTAFF. Sir, I know not how I may deserve to be your
porter.

FORD. I will tell you, sir, if you will give me the hearing.

FALSTAFF. Speak, good Master Brook; I shall be glad to be
your servant.

FORD. Sir, I hear you are a scholar,—I will be brief with
you, and you have been a man long known to me, though
I had never so good means, as desire, to make myself acquainted with you. I shall discover a thing to you, wherein I must very much lay open mine own imperfection;
but, good Sir John, as you have one eye upon my follies,
as you hear them unfolded, turn another into the register
of your own, that I may pass with a reproof the easier,

sith you yourself know how easy it is to be such an offender.

FALSTAFF. Very well, sir; proceed.

FORD. There is a gentlewoman in this town, her husband's
name is Ford.

FALSTAFF. Well, sir.

FORD. I have long loved her, and, I protest to you, bestowed much on her; followed her with a doting observance; engrossed opportunities to meet her; fee'd every
slight occasion that could but niggardly give me sight of
her; not only bought many presents to give her, but have
given largely to many to know what she would have
given. Briefly, I have pursued her as love hath pursued
me; which hath been on the wing of all occasions. But
whatsoever I have merited, either in my mind or in my
means, meed, I am sure, I have received none; unless experience be a jewel that I have purchased at an infinite
rate; and that hath taught me to say this,

Love like a shadow flies when substance love pursues;
Pursuing that that flies, and flying what pursues.

FALSTAFF. Have you received no promise of satisfaction at
her hands?

FORD. Never.

FALSTAFF. Have you importuned her to such a purpose?

FORD. Never.

FALSTAFF. Of what quality was your love, then?

FORD. Like a fair house built upon another man's ground;
so that I have lost my edifice by mistaking the place
where I erected it.

FALSTAFF. To what purpose have you unfolded this to me?

FORD. When I have told you that, I have told you all. Some
say, that though she appear honest to me, yet in other
places she enlargeth her mirth so far that there is shrewd
construction made of her. Now, Sir John, here is the
heart of my purpose: you are a gentleman of excellent
breeding, admirable discourse, of great admittance, authentic in your place and person, generally allowed for
your many war-like, court-like, and learned preparations.

FALSTAFF. O, sir!

FORD. Believe it, for you know it. There is money; spend it,
spend it; spend more; spend all I have; only give me so

much of your time in exchange of it, as to lay an amiable siege to the honesty of this Ford's wife: use your art of wooing, win her to consent to you; if any man may, you may as soon as any.

FALSTAFF. Would it apply well to the vehemency of your affection, that I should win what you would enjoy? Methinks you prescribe to yourself very preposterously.

FORD. O, understand my drift. She dwells so securely on the excellency of her honour, that the folly of my soul dares not present itself: she is too bright to be looked against. Now, could I come to her with any detection in my hand, my desires had instance and argument to commend themselves: I could drive her then from the ward of her purity, her reputation, her marriage-vow, and a thousand other her defences, which now are too-too strongly embattled against me. What say you to 't, Sir John?

FALSTAFF. Master Brook, I will first make bold with your money; next, give me your hand; and last, as I am a gentleman, you shall, if you will, enjoy Ford's wife.

FORD. O good sir!

FALSTAFF. I say you shall.

FORD. Want no money, Sir John; you shall want none.

FALSTAFF. Want no Mistress Ford, Master Brook; you shall want none. I shall be with her, I may tell you, by her own appointment; even as you came in to me, her assistant or go-between parted from me: I say I shall be with her between ten and eleven; for at that time the jealous rascally knave her husband will be forth. Come you to me at night; you shall know how I speed.

FORD. I am blest in your acquaintance. Do you know Ford, sir?

FALSTAFF. Hang him, poor cuckoldly knave! I know him not. Yet I wrong him, to call him poor: they say the jealous wittolly knave hath masses of money; for the which his wife seems to me well-favoured. I will use her as the key of the cuckoldly rogue's coffer; and there 's my harvest-home.

FORD. I would you knew Ford, sir, that you might avoid him, if you saw him.

FALSTAFF. Hang him, mechanical salt-butter rogue! I will stare him out of his wits; I will awe him with my cudgel:

it shall hang like a meteor o'er the cuckold's horns. Master Brook, thou shalt know I will predominate over the peasant, and thou shalt lie with his wife. Come to me soon at night. Ford 's a knave, and I will aggravate his style; thou, Master Brook, shalt know him for knave and cuckold. Come to me soon at night.   *Exit*

FORD. What a damned Epicurean rascal is this! My heart is ready to crack with impatience. Who says this is improvident jealousy? My wife hath sent to him, the hour is fixed, the match is made. Would any man have thought this? See the hell of having a false woman! My bed shall be abused, my coffers ransacked, my reputation gnawn at; and I shall not only receive this villanous wrong, but stand under the adoption of abominable terms, and by him that does me this wrong. Terms! names! Amaimon sounds well; Lucifer, well; Barbason, well; yet they are devils' additions, the names of fiends: but Cuckold! Wittol!—Cuckold! the devil himself hath not such a name. Page is an ass, a secure ass: he will trust his wife; he will not be jealous. I will rather trust a Fleming with my butter, Parson Hugh the Welshman with my cheese, an Irishman with my aqua-vitæ bottle, or a thief to walk my ambling gelding, than my wife with herself: then she plots, then she ruminates, then she devises; and what they think in their hearts they may effect, they will break their hearts but they will effect. God be praised for my jealousy! Eleven o'clock the hour: I will prevent this, detect my wife, be revenged on Falstaff, and laugh at Page. I will about it; better three hours too soon than a minute too late. Fie, fie, fie! cuckold! cuckold! cuckold!   *Exit*

SCENE THREE

A Field near Windsor.

Enter Caius and Rugby

CAIUS. Jack Rugby!

RUGBY. Sir?

CAIUS. Vat is de clock, Jack?

RUGBY. 'Tis past the hour, sir, that Sir Hugh promised to meet.

CAIUS. By gar, he has save his soul, dat he is no come: he has pray his Pible vell, dat he is no come. By gar, Jack Rugby, he is dead already, if he be come.

RUGBY. He is wise, sir; he knew your worship would kill him, if he came.

CAIUS. By gar, de herring is no dead so as I vill kill him. Take your rapier, Jack; I vill tell you how I vill kill him.

RUGBY. Alas, sir! I cannot fence.

CAIUS. Villany, take your rapier.

RUGBY. Forbear; here 's company.

Enter Host, Shallow, Slender, and Page

HOST. Bless thee, bully doctor!

SHALLOW. Save you, Master Doctor Caius!

PAGE. Now, good Master doctor!

SLENDER. Give you good-morrow, sir.

CAIUS. Vat be all you, one, two, tree, four, come for?

HOST. To see thee fight, to see thee foin, to see thee traverse; to see thee here, to see thee there; to see thee pass thy punto, thy stock, thy reverse, thy distance, thy montant. Is he dead, my Ethiopian? is he dead, my Francisco? ha, bully! What says my Æsculapius? my Galen? my heart of elder? ha! is he dead, bully stale? is he dead?

CAIUS. By gar, he is de coward Jack priest of de vorld; he is not show his face.

HOST. Thou art a Castilian King Urinal! Hector of Greece, my boy!

CAIUS. I pray you, bear vitness that me have stay six or seven, two, tree hours for him, and he is no come.

SHALLOW. He is the wiser man, Master doctor: he is a curer of souls, and you a curer of bodies; if you should fight, you go against the hair of your professions. Is it not true, Master Page?

PAGE. Master Shallow, you have yourself been a great fighter, though now a man of peace.

SHALLOW. Bodykins, Master Page, though I now be old and of the peace, if I see a sword out, my finger itches to make one. Though we are justices and doctors and churchmen, Master Page, we have some salt of our youth in us; we are the sons of women, Master Page.

PAGE. 'Tis true, Master Shallow.

SHALLOW. It will be found so, Master Page. Master Doctor Caius, I am come to fetch you home. I am sworn of the

peace: you have showed yourself a wise physician, and
Sir Hugh hath shown himself a wise and patient churchman. You must go with me, Master doctor.

HOST. Pardon, guest-justice.—A word, Monsieur Mockwater.

CAIUS. Mock-vater! vat is dat?

HOST. Mock-water, in our English tongue, is valour, bully.

CAIUS. By gar, den, I have as mush mock-vater as de Englishman.—Scurvy jack-dog priest! by gar, me vill cut his
ears.

HOST. He will clapper-claw thee tightly, bully.

CAIUS. Clapper-de-claw! vat is dat?

HOST. That is, he will make thee amends.

CAIUS. By gar, me do look, he shall clapper-de-claw me;
for, by gar, me vill have it.

HOST. And I will provoke him to 't, or let him wag.

CAIUS. Me tank you for dat.

HOST. And moreover, bully,—But first, Master guest, and
Master Page, and eke Cavaliero Slender, go you through
the town to Frogmore.   *Aside to them*

PAGE. Sir Hugh is there, is he?

HOST. He is there: see what humour he is in; and I will
bring the doctor about by the fields. Will it do well?

SHALLOW. We will do it.

PAGE, SHALLOW, AND SLENDER. Adieu, good Master doctor.
                    Exeunt Page, Shallow, and Slender

CAIUS. By gar, me vill kill de priest; for he speak for a jack-
an-ape to Anne Page.

HOST. Let him die. Sheathe thy impatience; throw cold
water on thy choler: go about the fields with me through
Frogmore: I will bring thee where Mistress Anne Page is,
at a farmhouse a-feasting; and thou shalt woo her. Cried
I aim? said I well?

CAIUS. By gar, me tank you for dat: by gar, I love you; and
I shall procure-a you de good guest, de earl, de knight,
de lords, de gentlemen, my patients.

HOST. For the which I will be thy adversary toward Anne
Page: said I well?

CAIUS. By gar, 'tis good; vell said.

HOST. Let us wag, then.

CAIUS. Come at my heels, Jack Rugby.   *Exeunt*

ACT THREE

SCENE ONE

A Field near Frogmore.

Enter Sir Hugh Evans and Simple

EVANS. I pray you now, good Master Slender's serving-man, and friend Simple by your name, which way have you looked for Master Caius, that calls himself doctor of physic?

SIMPLE. Marry, sir, the pittie-ward, the park-ward, every way; old Windsor way, and every way but the town way.

EVANS. I most fehemently desire you you will also look that way.

SIMPLE. I will, sir. *Exit*

EVANS. Pless my soul! how full of chollors I am, and trempling of mind! I shall be glad if he have deceived me. How melancholies I am! I will knog his urinals about his knave's costard when I have goot opportunities for the 'ork: pless my soul! *Sings*

> To shallow rivers, to whose falls
> Melodious birds sing madrigals;
> There will we make our peds of roses,
> And a thousand fragrant posies.
> To shallow—

Mercy on me! I have a great dispositions to cry. *Sings*

> Melodious birds sing madrigals,—
> When as I sat in Pabylon,—
> And a thousand vagram posies.
> To shallow,—

Re-enter Simple

SIMPLE. Yonder he is coming, this way, Sir Hugh.

EVANS. He's welcome. *Sings*

> To shallow rivers, to whose falls—

Heaven prosper the right!—what weapons is he?

SIMPLE. No weapons, sir. There comes my master, Master
Shallow, and another gentleman, from Frogmore, over
the stile, this way.

EVANS. Pray you, give me my gown; or else keep it in your
arms.   *Reads in a book*

Enter Page, Shallow, and Slender

SHALLOW. How now, Master Parson! Good-morrow, good
Sir Hugh. Keep a gamester from the dice, and a good
student from his book, and it is wonderful.

SLENDER. (*Aside*) Ah, sweet Anne Page!

PAGE. Save you, good Sir Hugh!

EVANS. Pless you from His mercy sake, all of you!

SHALLOW. What, the sword and the word! do you study
them both, Master Parson?

PAGE. And youthful still in your doublet and hose! this raw
rheumatic day?

EVANS. There is reasons and causes for it.

PAGE. We are come to you to do a good office, Master Parson.

EVANS. Fery well: what is it?

PAGE. Yonder is a most reverend gentleman, who, belike
having received wrong by some person, is at most odds
with his own gravity and patience that ever you saw.

SHALLOW. I have lived fourscore years and upward; I never
heard a man of his place, gravity, and learning, so wide
of his own respect.

EVANS. What is he?

PAGE. I think you know him; Master Doctor Caius, the renowned French physician.

EVANS. Got's will, and his passion of my heart! I had as lief
you would tell me of a mess of porridge.

PAGE. Why?

EVANS. He has no more knowledge in Hibbocrates and Galen,—and he is a knave besides; a cowardly knave as you
would desires to be acquainted withal.

PAGE. I warrant you, he 's the man should fight with him.

SLENDER. (*Aside*) O, sweet Anne Page!

SHALLOW. It appears so, by his weapons. Keep them asunder: here comes Doctor Caius.

Enter Host, Caius, and Rugby

PAGE. Nay, good Master parson, keep in your weapon.

SHALLOW. So do you, good Master doctor.

HOST. Disarm them, and let them question: let them keep their limbs whole and hack our English.

CAIUS. I pray you, let-a me speak a word vit your ear: verefore vill you not meet-a me?

EVANS. (*Aside to Caius*) Pray you, use your patience: in good time.

CAIUS. By gar, you are de coward, de Jack dog, John ape.

EVANS. (*Aside to Caius*) Pray you, let us not be laughingstogs to other men's humours; I desire you in friendship, and I will one way or other make you amends: (*Aloud*) I will knog your urinals about your knave's cogscomb for missing your meetings and appointments.

CAIUS. Diable!—Jack Rugby,—mine host de Jarretierre— have I not stay for him to kill him? have I not, at de place I did appoint?

EVANS. As I am a Christians soul, now, look you, this is the place appointed: I 'll be judgment by mine host of the Garter.

HOST. Peace, I say, Gallia and Guallia; French and Welsh, soul-curer and body-curer!

CAIUS. Ay, dat is very good; excellent.

HOST. Peace, I say! hear mine host of the Garter. Am I politic? am I subtle? am I a Machiavel? Shall I lose my doctor? no; he gives me the potions and the motions. Shall I lose my parson, my priest, my Sir Hugh? no; he gives me the proverbs and the no-verbs. Give me thy hand, terrestrial; so;—give me thy hand, celestial; so. Boys of art, I have deceived you both; I have directed you to wrong places: your hearts are mighty, your skins are whole, and let burnt sack be the issue. Come, lay their swords to pawn. Follow me, lads of peace; follow, follow, follow.

SHALLOW. Trust me, a mad host!—Follow, gentlemen, follow.

SLENDER. (*Aside*) O, sweet Anne Page!

Exeunt Shallow, Slender, Page, and Host

CAIUS. Ha! do I perceive dat? have you make-a de sot of us, ha, ha?

EVANS. This is well; he has made us his vlouting-stog. I desire you that we may be friends and let us knog our prains together to be revenge on this same scall, scurvy, cogging companion, the host of the Garter.

CAIUS. By gar, vit all my heart. He promise to bring me vere is Anne Page: by gar, he deceive me too.

EVANS. Well, I will smite his noddles. Pray you, follow.

Exeunt

SCENE TWO

A Street in Windsor.

Enter Mistress Page and Robin

MRS. PAGE. Nay, keep your way, little gallant: you were wont to be a follower, but now you are a leader. Whether had you rather lead mine eyes, or eye your master's heels?

ROBIN. I had rather, forsooth, go before you like a man than follow him like a dwarf.

MRS. PAGE. O! you are a flattering boy: now I see you 'll be a courtier.

Enter Ford

FORD. Well met, Mistress Page. Whither go you?

MRS. PAGE. Truly, sir, to see your wife. Is she at home?

FORD. Ay; and as idle as she may hang together, for want of company. I think, if your husbands were dead, you two would marry.

MRS. PAGE. Be sure of that,—two other husbands.

FORD. Where had you this pretty weathercock?

MRS. PAGE. I cannot tell what the dickens his name is my husband had him of. What do you call your knight's name, sirrah?

ROBIN. Sir John Falstaff.

FORD. Sir John Falstaff!

MRS. PAGE. He, he; I can never hit on 's name. There is such a league between my good man and he! Is your wife at home indeed?

FORD. Indeed she is.

MRS. PAGE. By your leave, sir: I am sick till I see her.

Exeunt Mistress Page and Robin

FORD. Has Page any brains? Hath he any eyes? Hath he any thinking? Sure, they sleep; he hath no use of them. Why, this boy will carry a letter twenty mile, as easy as a cannon will shoot point-blank twelve score. He pieces out his wife's inclination; he gives her folly motion and advantage: and now she 's going to my wife, and Falstaff's boy with her. A man may hear this shower sing in the wind: and Falstaff's boy with her! Good plots! they are laid; and our revolted wives share damnation together. Well; I will take him, then torture my wife, pluck the borrowed veil of modesty from the so seeming Mistress Page, divulge Page himself for a secure and wilful Actæon; and to these violent proceedings all my neighbours shall cry aim. (*Clock strikes*) The clock gives me my cue, and my assurance bids me search; there I shall find Falstaff. I shall be rather praised for this than mocked; for it is as positive as the earth is firm, that Falstaff is there: I will go.

Enter Page, Shallow,
Slender, Host, Sir Hugh Evans, Caius, and Rugby

PAGE, SHALLOW, &C. Well met, Master Ford.

FORD. Trust me, a good knot. I have good cheer at home; and I pray you all go with me.

SHALLOW. I must excuse myself, Master Ford.

SLENDER. And so must I, sir: we have appointed to dine with Mistress Anne, and I would not break with her for more money than I 'll speak of.

SHALLOW. We have lingered about a match between Anne Page and my cousin Slender, and this day we shall have our answer.

SLENDER. I hope I have your good will, father Page.

PAGE. You have, Master Slender; I stand wholly for you: but my wife, Master doctor, is for you altogether.

CAIUS. Ay, by gar; and de maid is love-a me: my nursh-a Quickly tell me so mush.

HOST. What say you to young Master Fenton? He capers, he dances, he has eyes of youth, he writes verses, he speaks holiday, he smells April and May: he will carry 't, he will carry 't; 'tis in his buttons; he will carry 't.

PAGE. Not by my consent, I promise you. The gentleman is of no having: he kept company with the wild prince and Pointz; he is of too high a region; he knows too much. No, he shall not knit a knot in his fortunes with the finger of my substance: if he take her, let him take her simply; the wealth I have waits on my consent, and my consent goes not that way.

FORD. I beseech you heartily, some of you go home with
me to dinner: besides your cheer, you shall have sport; I
will show you a monster. Master doctor, you shall go; so
shall you, Master Page; and you, Sir Hugh.

SHALLOW. Well, fare you well: we shall have the freer wooing at Master Page's.   *Exeunt Shallow and Slender*

CAIUS. Go home, John Rugby; I come anon.   *Exit Rugby*

HOST. Farewell, my hearts: I will to my honest knight Falstaff, and drink canary with him.   *Exit Host*

FORD. (*Aside*) I think I shall drink in pipe-wine first with
him; I 'll make him dance. Will you go, gentles?

ALL. Have with you to see this monster.   *Exeunt*

SCENE THREE

A Room in Ford's House.

Enter Mistress Ford and Mistress Page

MRS. FORD. What, John! what, Robert!

MRS. PAGE. Quickly, quickly:—Is the buck-basket—

MRS. FORD. I warrant. What, Robin, I say!
                    Enter Servants with a Basket

MRS. PAGE. Come, come, come.

MRS. FORD. Here, set it down.

MRS. PAGE. Give your men the charge; we must be brief.

MRS. FORD. Marry, as I told you before, John, and Robert,
be ready here hard by in the brew-house; and when I
suddenly call you, come forth, and without any pause or
staggering, take this basket on your shoulders: that done,
trudge with it in all haste, and carry it among the whit-
sters in Datchet-mead, and there empty it in the muddy
ditch, close by the Thames side.

MRS. PAGE. You will do it?

MRS. FORD. I have told them over and over; they lack no direction. Be gone, and come when you are called.

                              Exeunt Servants

MRS. PAGE. Here comes little Robin.

                    Enter Robin

MRS. FORD. How now, my eyas-musket! what news with
you?

ROBIN. My master, Sir John, is come in at your back-door, Mistress Ford, and requests your company.

MRS. PAGE. You little Jack-a-Lent, have you been true to us?

ROBIN. Ay, I'll be sworn. My master knows not of your being here, and hath threatened to put me into everlasting liberty if I tell you of it; for he swears he'll turn me away.

MRS. PAGE. Thou'rt a good boy; this secrecy of thine shall be a tailor to thee and shall make thee a new doublet and hose. I'll go hide me.

MRS. FORD. Do so. Go tell thy master I am alone. (*Exit Robin*) Mistress Page, remember you your cue.

MRS. PAGE. I warrant thee; if I do not act it, hiss me. *Exit*

MRS. FORD. Go to, then: we'll use this unwholesome humidity, this gross watery pumpion; we'll teach him to know turtles from jays.

Enter Falstaff

FALSTAFF. 'Have I caught my heavenly jewel?' Why, now let me die, for I have lived long enough: this is the period of my ambition: O this blessed hour!

MRS. FORD. O, sweet Sir John!

FALSTAFF. Mistress Ford, I cannot cog, I cannot prate, Mistress Ford. Now shall I sin in my wish: I would thy husband were dead. I'll speak it before the best lord, I would make thee my lady.

MRS. FORD. I your lady, Sir John! Alas, I should be a pitiful lady.

FALSTAFF. Let the court of France show me such another. I see how thine eye would emulate the diamond: thou hast the right arched beauty of the brow that becomes the ship-tire, the tire-valiant, or any tire of Venetian admittance.

MRS. FORD. A plain kerchief, Sir John: my brows become nothing else; nor that well neither.

FALSTAFF. By the Lord, thou art a traitor to say so: thou wouldst make an absolute courtier; and the firm fixture of thy foot would give an excellent motion to thy gait in a semi-circled farthingale. I see what thou wert, if Fortune thy foe were not, Nature thy friend. Come, thou canst not hide it.

MRS. FORD. Believe me, there's no such thing in me.

FALSTAFF. What made me love thee? let that persuade thee

there 's something extraordinary in thee. Come, I cannot
cog and say thou art this and that, like a many of these
lisping hawthorn-buds, that come like women in men's
apparel, and smell like Bucklersbury in simple-time; I
cannot; but I love thee; none but thee; and thou deservest it.

MRS. FORD. Do not betray me, sir. I fear you love Mistress
Page.

FALSTAFF. Thou mightst as well say, I love to walk by the
Counter-gate, which is as hateful to me as the reek of a
lime-kiln.

MRS. FORD. Well, heaven knows how I love you; and you
shall one day find it.

FALSTAFF. Keep in that mind; I 'll deserve it.

MRS. FORD. Nay, I must tell you, so you do, or else I could
not be in that mind.

ROBIN. (*Within*) Mistress Ford! Mistress Ford! here 's Mistress Page at the door, sweating and blowing and looking
wildly, and would needs speak with you presently.

FALSTAFF. She shall not see me: I will ensconce me behind
the arras.

MRS. FORD. Pray you, do so: she 's a very tattling woman
                                    Falstaff hides himself
        Re-enter Mistress Page and Robin
What 's the matter? how now!

MRS. PAGE. O Mistress Ford! what have you done? You 're
shamed, you are overthrown, you 're undone for ever!

MRS. FORD. What 's the matter, good Mistress Page?

MRS. PAGE. O well-a-day, Mistress Ford! having an honest
man to your husband, to give him such cause of suspicion!

MRS. FORD. What cause of suspicion?

MRS. PAGE. What cause of suspicion! Out upon you! how
am I mistook in you!

MRS. FORD. Why, alas, what 's the matter?

MRS. PAGE. Your husband's coming hither, woman, with all
the officers of Windsor, to search for a gentleman that he
says is here now in the house by your consent, to take an
ill advantage of his absence: you are undone.

MRS. FORD. (*Aside*) Speak louder.—'Tis not so, I hope.

MRS. PAGE. Pray heaven it be not so, that you have such a
man here! but 'tis most certain your husband 's coming

with half Windsor at his heels, to search for such a one. I come before to tell you. If you know yourself clear, why, I am glad of it; but if you have a friend here, convey, convey him out. Be not amazed; call all your senses to you: defend your reputation, or bid farewell to your good life for ever.

MRS. FORD. What shall I do?—There is a gentleman, my dear friend; and I fear not mine own shame so much as his peril: I had rather than a thousand pound he were out of the house.

MRS. PAGE. For shame! never stand 'you had rather' and 'you had rather': your husband 's here at hand; bethink you of some conveyance: in the house you cannot hide him. O, how have you deceived me! Look, here is a basket: if he be of any reasonable stature, he may creep in here; and throw foul linen upon him, as if it were going to bucking: or—it is whiting-time—send him by your two men to Datchet-mead.

MRS. FORD. He 's too big to go in there. What shall I do?

FALSTAFF. (*Coming forward*) Let me see 't, let me see 't, O, let me see 't! I 'll in, I 'll in. Follow your friend's counsel. I 'll in.

MRS. PAGE. What, Sir John Falstaff! Are these your letters, knight?

FALSTAFF. I love thee, and none but thee; help me away: let me creep in here. I 'll never—
He gets into the basket; they cover him with foul linen

MRS. PAGE. Help to cover your master, boy. Call your men, Mistress Ford. You dissembling knight!

MRS. FORD. What, John! Robert! John!   *Exit Robin*
Re-enter Servants
Go, take up these clothes here quickly; where 's the cowl-staff? look, how you drumble! carry them to the laundress in Datchet-mead; quickly, come.

Enter Ford, Page, Caius, and Sir Hugh Evans

FORD. Pray you, come near: if I suspect without cause, why then make sport at me; then let me be your jest; I deserve it. How now! what goes here? whither bear you this?

SERVANTS. To the laundress, forsooth.

MRS. FORD. Why, what have you to do whither they bear it? You were best meddle with buck-washing.

FORD. Buck! I would I could wash myself of the buck!
Buck, buck, buck! Ay, buck; I warrant you, buck; and of
the season too, it shall appear. (*Exeunt Servants with the
basket*) Gentlemen, I have dreamed to-night; I 'll tell
you my dream. Here, here, here be my keys: ascend my
chambers; search, seek, find out: I 'll warrant we 'll un-
kennel the fox. Let me stop this way first. (*Locking the
door*) So, now uncape.

PAGE. Good Master Ford, be contented: you wrong yourself too much.

FORD. True, Master Page. Up, gentlemen; you shall see
sport anon: follow me, gentlemen.   *Exit*

EVANS. This is fery fantastical humours and jealousies.

CAIUS. By gar, 'tis no de fashion of France; it is not jealous
in France.

PAGE. Nay, follow him, gentlemen; see the issue of his
search.   *Exeunt Page, Caius, and Evans*

MRS. PAGE. Is there not a double excellency in this?

MRS. FORD. I know not which pleases me better; that my
husband is deceived, or Sir John.

MRS. PAGE. What a taking was he in when your husband
asked who was in the basket!

MRS. FORD. I am half afraid he will have need of washing;
so throwing him into the water will do him a benefit.

MRS. PAGE. Hang him, dishonest rascal! I would all of the
same strain were in the same distress.

MRS. FORD. I think my husband hath some special suspicion
of Falstaff's being here; for I never saw him so gross in
his jealousy till now.

MRS. PAGE. I will lay a plot to try that; and we will yet
have more tricks with Falstaff: his dissolute disease will
scarce obey this medicine.

MRS. FORD. Shall we send that foolish carrion Mistress
Quickly to him, and excuse his throwing into the water;
and give him another hope, to betray him to another punishment?

MRS. PAGE. We will do it: let him be sent for to-morrow,
eight o'clock, to have amends.

Re-enter Ford, Page, Caius, and Sir Hugh Evans

FORD. I cannot find him: may be the knave bragged of that
he could not compass.

MRS. PAGE. (*Aside to Mrs. Ford*) Heard you that?

MRS. FORD. (*Aside to Mrs. Page*) Ay, ay, peace.—You use me well, Master Ford, do you?

FORD. Ay, I do so.

MRS. FORD. Heaven make you better than your thoughts!

FORD. Amen!

MRS. PAGE. You do yourself mighty wrong, Master Ford.

FORD. Ay, ay; I must bear it.

EVANS. If there pe any pody in the house, and in the chambers, and in the coffers, and in the presses, heaven forgive my sins at the day of judgment!

CAIUS. By gar, nor I too, dere is no bodies.

PAGE. Fie, fie, Master Ford: are you not ashamed? What spirit, what devil suggests this imagination? I would not ha' your distemper in this kind for the wealth of Windsor Castle.

FORD. 'Tis my fault, Master Page: I suffer for it.

EVANS. You suffer for a pad conscience: your wife is as honest a 'omans as I will desires among five thousand, and five hundred too.

CAIUS. By gar, I see 'tis an honest woman.

FORD. Well; I promised you a dinner. Come, come, walk in the Park: I pray you, pardon me; I will hereafter make known to you why I have done this. Come, wife; come, Mistress Page. I pray you, pardon me; pray heartily, pardon me.

PAGE. Let 's go in, gentlemen; but, trust me, we 'll mock him. I do invite you to-morrow morning to my house to breakfast; after, we 'll a-birding together: I have a fine hawk for the bush. Shall it be so?

FORD. Any thing.

EVANS. If there is one, I shall make two in the company.

CAIUS. If dere be one or two, I shall make-a de turd.

FORD. Pray you go, Master Page.

EVANS. I pray you now, remembrance to-morrow on the lousy knave, mine host.

CAIUS. Dat is good; by gar, vit all my heart.

EVANS. A lousy knave! to have his gibes and his mockeries!

Exeunt

SCENE FOUR

A Room in Page's House.

Enter Fenton, Anne Page, and Mistress Quickly.
Mistress Quickly stands apart.

FENTON. I see I cannot get thy father's love;
  Therefore no more turn me to him, sweet Nan.

ANNE. Alas! how then?

FENTON.   Why, thou must be thyself.
  He doth object, I am too great of birth,
  And that my state being gall'd with my expense,
  I seek to heal it only by his wealth.
  Besides these, other bars he lays before me,
  My riots past, my wild societies;
  And tells me 'tis a thing impossible
  I should love thee but as a property.

ANNE. May be he tells you true.

FENTON. No, heaven so speed me in my time to come!
  Albeit I will confess thy father's wealth
  Was the first motive that I woo'd thee, Anne:
  Yet, wooing thee, I found thee of more value
  Than stamps in gold or sums in sealed bags;
  And 'tis the very riches of thyself
  That now I aim at.

ANNE.   Gentle Master Fenton,
  Yet seek my father's love; still seek it, sir:
  If opportunity and humblest suit
  Cannot attain it, why, then,—hark you hither.

They converse apart
Enter Shallow and Slender

SHALLOW. Break their talk, Mistress Quickly: my kinsman
  shall speak for himself.

SLENDER. I 'll make a shaft or a bolt on 't. 'Slid, 'tis but ven-
  turing.

SHALLOW. Be not dismayed.

SLENDER. No, she shall not dismay me: I care not for that,
  but that I am afeard.

QUICKLY. Hark ye; Master Slender would speak a word
  with you.

ANNE. I come to him. (*Aside*) This is my father's choice.
O, what a world of vile ill-favour'd faults
Looks handsome in three hundred pounds a year!

QUICKLY. And how does good Master Fenton? Pray you, a
word with you.

SHALLOW. She 's coming; to her, coz. O boy, thou hadst a
father!

SLENDER. I had a father, Mistress Anne; my uncle can tell
you good jests of him. Pray you, uncle, tell Mistress Anne
the jest, how my father stole two geese out of a pen, good
uncle.

SHALLOW. Mistress Anne, my cousin loves you.

SLENDER. Ay, that I do; as well as I love any woman in
Glostershire.

SHALLOW. He will maintain you like a gentlewoman.

SLENDER. Ay, that I will, come cut and long-tail, under the
degree of a squire.

SHALLOW. He will make you a hundred and fifty pounds
jointure.

ANNE. Good Master Shallow, let him woo for himself.

SHALLOW. Marry, I thank you for it; I thank you for that
good comfort. She calls you, coz: I 'll leave you.

ANNE. Now, Master Slender.

SLENDER. Now, good Mistress Anne.—

ANNE. What is your will?

SLENDER. My will? od 's heartlings! that 's a pretty jest, indeed! I ne'er made my will yet, I thank heaven; I am not
such a sickly creature, I give heaven praise.

ANNE. I mean, Master Slender, what would you with me?.

SLENDER. Truly, for mine own part, I would little or nothing with you. Your father and my uncle have made motions: if it be my luck, so; if not, happy man be his dole!
They can tell you how things go better than I can: you
may ask your father; here he comes.

Enter Page and Mistress Page

PAGE. Now, Master Slender: love him, daughter Anne.
Why, how now! what does Master Fenton here?
You wrong me, sir, thus still to haunt my house:
I told you, sir, my daughter is dispos'd of.

FENTON. Nay, Master Page, be not impatient.

MRS. PAGE. Good Master Fenton, come not to my child.

PAGE. She is no match for you.

FENTON. Sir, will you hear me?

PAGE.   No, good Master Fenton.
Come, Master Shallow; come, son Slender, in.
Knowing my mind, you wrong me, Master Fenton.

Exeunt Page, Shallow, and Slender

QUICKLY. Speak to Mistress Page.

FENTON. Good Mistress Page, for that I love your daughter
In such a righteous fashion as I do,
Perforce, against all checks, rebukes and manners,
I must advance the colours of my love
And not retire: let me have your good will.

ANNE. Good mother, do not marry me to yond fool.

MRS. PAGE. I mean it not; I seek you a better husband.

QUICKLY. That 's my master, Master doctor.

ANNE. Alas! I had rather be set quick i' the earth,
And bowl'd to death with turnips.

MRS. PAGE. Come, trouble not yourself. Good Master Fenton,
I will not be your friend, nor enemy:
My daughter will I question how she loves you,
And as I find her, so am I affected.
'Till then, farewell, sir: she must needs go in;
Her father will be angry.

FENTON. Farewell, gentle mistress. Farewell, Nan.

Exeunt Mistress Page and Anne

QUICKLY. This is my doing, now: 'Nay,' said I, 'will you cast
away your child on a fool, and a physician? Look on
Master Fenton.' This is my doing.

FENTON. I thank thee: and I pray thee, once to-night
Give my sweet Nan this ring. There 's for thy pains.

QUICKLY. Now heaven send thee good fortune! (*Exit Fenton*) A kind heart he hath: a woman would run through
fire and water for such a kind heart. But yet I would my
master had Mistress Anne; or I would Master Slender
had her; or, in sooth, I would Master Fenton had her. I
will do what I can for them all three, for so I have promised, and I 'll be as good as my word; but speciously for
Master Fenton. Well, I must of another errand to Sir
John Falstaff from my two mistresses: what a beast am I
to slack it!

SCENE FIVE

A Room in the Garter Inn.

Enter Falstaff and Bardolph

FALSTAFF. Bardolph, I say,—

BARDOLPH. Here, sir.

FALSTAFF. Go fetch me a quart of sack; put a toast in 't. (*Exit Bardolph*) Have I lived to be carried in a basket, and to be thrown in the Thames like a barrow of butcher's offal? Well, if I be served such another trick, I 'll have my brains ta'en out, and buttered, and give them to a dog for a new year's gift. The rogues slighted me into the river with as little remorse as they would have drowned a blind bitch's puppies, fifteen i' the litter; and you may know by my size that I have a kind of alacrity in sinking: if the bottom were as deep as hell, I should down. I had been drowned but that the shore was shelvy and shallow; a death that I abhor, for the water swells a man, and what a thing should I have been when I had been swelled! I should have been a mountain of mummy.

Re-enter Bardolph, with the sack

BARDOLPH. Here 's Mistress Quickly, sir, to speak with you.

FALSTAFF. Come, let me pour in some sack to the Thames water, for my belly 's as cold as if I had swallowed snowballs for pills to cool the reins. Call her in.

BARDOLPH. Come in, woman.

Enter Mistress Quickly

QUICKLY. By your leave. I cry you mercy: give your worship good-morrow.

FALSTAFF. Take away these chalices. Go brew me a pottle of sack finely.

BARDOLPH. With eggs, sir?

FALSTAFF. Simple of itself; I 'll no pullet-sperm in my brewage. (*Exit Bardolph*)—How now!

QUICKLY. Marry, sir, I come to your worship from Mistress Ford.

FALSTAFF. Mistress Ford! I have had ford enough; I was thrown into the ford; I have my belly full of ford.

QUICKLY. Alas the day! good heart, that was not her fault:

She does so take on with her men; they mistook their erection.

FALSTAFF. So did I mine, to build upon a foolish woman's promise.

QUICKLY. Well, she laments, sir, for it, that it would yearn your heart to see it. Her husband goes this morning a-birding: she desires you once more to come to her between eight and nine. I must carry her word quickly: she 'll make you amends, I warrant you.

FALSTAFF. Well, I will visit her: tell her so; and bid her think what a man is: let her consider his frailty, and then judge of my merit.

QUICKLY. I will tell her.

FALSTAFF. Do so. Between nine and ten, sayest thou?

QUICKLY. Eight and nine, sir.

FALSTAFF. Well, be gone: I will not miss her.

QUICKLY. Peace be with you, sir.   *Exit*

FALSTAFF. I marvel I hear not of Master Brook; he sent me word to stay within. I like his money well. O! here he comes.

Enter Ford, disguised

FORD. Bless you, sir!

FALSTAFF. Now, Master Brook, you come to know what hath passed between me and Ford's wife?

FORD. That, indeed, Sir John, is my business.

FALSTAFF. Master Brook, I will not lie to you: I was at her house the hour she appointed me.

FORD. And how sped you, sir?

FALSTAFF. Very ill-favouredly, Master Brook.

FORD. How so, sir? did she change her determination?

FALSTAFF. No, Master Brook; but the peaking cornuto her husband, Master Brook, dwelling in a continual 'larum of jealousy, comes me in the instant of our encounter, after we had embraced, kissed, protested, and, as it were, spoke the prologue of our comedy; and at his heels a rabble of his companions, thither provoked and instigated by his distemper, and, forsooth, to search his house for his wife's love.

FORD. What! while you were there?

FALSTAFF. While I was there.

FORD. And did he search for you, and could not find you?

FALSTAFF. You shall hear. As good luck would have it,

comes in one Mistress Page; gives intelligence of Ford's
approach; and in her invention, and Ford's wife's distraction, they conveyed me into a buck-basket.

FORD. A buck-basket!

FALSTAFF. By the Lord, a buck-basket! rammed me in with
foul shirts and smocks, socks, foul stockings, greasy nap-
kins; that, Master Brook, there was the rankest compound of villanous smell that ever offended nostril.

FORD. And how long lay you there?

FALSTAFF. Nay, you shall hear, Master Brook, what I have
suffered to bring this woman to evil for your good. Being
thus crammed in the basket, a couple of Ford's knaves,
his hinds, were called forth by their mistress to carry me
in the name of foul clothes to Datchet-lane: they took me
on their shoulders; met the jealous knave their master in
the door, who asked them once or twice what they had in
their basket. I quaked for fear lest the lunatic knave
would have searched it; but Fate, ordaining he should be
a cuckold, held his hand. Well; on went he for a search,
and away went I for foul clothes. But mark the sequel,
Master Brook: I suffered the pangs of three several
deaths: first, an intolerable fright, to be detected with a
jealous rotten bell-wether; next, to be compassed, like a
good bilbo, in the circumference of a peck, hilt to point,
heel to head; and then, to be stopped in, like a strong
distillation, with stinking clothes that fretted in their own
grease: think of that, a man of my kidney, think of that,
that am as subject to heat as butter; a man of continual
dissolution and thaw: it was a miracle to 'scape suffoca-
tion. And in the height of this bath, when I was more
than half stewed in grease, like a Dutch dish, to be
thrown into the Thames, and cooled, glowing hot, in that
surge, like a horse-shoe; think of that, hissing hot, think
of that, Master Brook!

FORD. In good sadness, sir, I am sorry that for my sake you
have suffered all this. My suit then is desperate; you 'll
undertake her no more?

FALSTAFF. Master Brook, I will be thrown into Etna, as I
have been into Thames, ere I will leave her thus. Her
husband is this morning gone a-birding: I have received
from her another embassy of meeting; 'twixt eight and
nine is the hour, Master Brook.

FORD. 'Tis past eight already, sir.

FALSTAFF. Is it? I will then address me to my appointment.
Come to me at your convenient leisure, and you shall
know how I speed, and the conclusion shall be crowned
with your enjoying her: adieu. You shall have her, Master Brook; Master Brook, you shall cuckold Ford.   *Exit*

FORD. Hum! ha! is this a vision? it this a dream? do I sleep?
Master Ford, awake! awake, Master Ford! there 's a hole
made in your best coat, Master Ford. This 'tis to be married: this 'tis to have linen and buck-baskets! Well, I will
proclaim myself what I am: I will now take the lecher;
he is at my house; he cannot 'scape me; 'tis impossible he
should; he cannot creep into a half-penny purse, nor into
a pepper-box; but, lest the devil that guides him should
aid him, I will search impossible places. Though what I
am I cannot avoid, yet to be what I would not, shall not
make me tame: if I have horns to make me mad, let the
proverb go with me; I 'll be horn-mad.   *Exit*

ACT FOUR

SCENE ONE

Windsor. The Street.

Enter Mistress Page, Mistress Quickly, and William

MRS. PAGE. Is he at Master Ford's already, thinkest thou?

QUICKLY. Sure he is by this, or will be presently; but truly, he is very courageous mad about his throwing into the water. Mistress Ford desires you to come suddenly.

MRS. PAGE. I 'll be with her by and by: I 'll but bring my young man here to school. Look, where his master comes; 'tis a playing-day, I see.

Enter Sir Hugh Evans

How now, Sir Hugh! no school to-day?

EVANS. No; Master Slender is get the boys leave to play.

QUICKLY. Blessing of his heart!

MRS. PAGE. Sir Hugh, my husband says my son profits nothing in the world at his book: I pray you, ask him some questions in his accidence.

EVANS. Come hither, William; hold up your head; come.

MRS. PAGE. Come on, sirrah; hold up your head; answer your master, be not afraid.

EVANS. William, how many numbers is in nouns?

WILLIAM. Two.

QUICKLY. Truly, I thought there had been one number more, because they say 'Od's nouns.'

EVANS. Peace your tattlings! What is 'fair,' William?

WILLIAM. Pulcher.

QUICKLY. Polecats! there are fairer things than polecats, sure.

EVANS. You are a very simplicity 'oman: I pray you peace. What is 'lapis,' William?

WILLIAM. A stone.

EVANS. And what is 'a stone,' William?

WILLIAM. A pebble.

EVANS. No, it is 'lapis': I pray you remember in your prain.

WILLIAM. Lapis.

EVANS. That is a good William. What is he, William, that does lend articles?

WILLIAM. Articles are borrowed of the pronoun, and be thus declined, Singulariter, nominativo, hic, hæc, hoc.

EVANS. Nominativo, hig, hag, hog; pray you, mark: genitivo, hujus. Well, what is your accusative case?

WILLIAM. Accusativo, hinc.

EVANS. I pray you, have your remembrance, child; accusativo, hung, hang, hog.

QUICKLY. Hang hog is Latin for bacon, I warrant you.

EVANS. Leave your prabbles, 'oman. What is the focative case, William?

WILLIAM. O vocativo, O.

EVANS. Remember, William; focative is caret.

QUICKLY. And that 's a good root.

EVANS. 'Oman, forbear.

MRS. PAGE. Peace!

EVANS. What is your genitive case plural, William?

WILLIAM. Genitive case?

EVANS. Ay.

WILLIAM. Genitive, horum, harum, horum.

QUICKLY. Vengeance of Jenny's case! fie on her! Never name her, child, if she be a whore.

EVANS. For shame, 'oman!

QUICKLY. You do ill to teach the child such words. He teaches him to hick and to hack, which they 'll do fast enough of themselves, and to call 'horum': fie upon you!

EVANS. 'Oman, art thou lunatics? hast thou no understandings for thy cases and the numbers and the genders? Thou art as foolish Christian creatures as I would desires.

MRS. PAGE. Prithee, hold thy peace.

EVANS. Show me now, William, some declensions of your pronouns.

WILLIAM. Forsooth, I have forgot.

EVANS. It is qui, quæ, quod; if you forget your 'quis,' your 'quæs,' and your 'quods,' you must be preeches. Go your ways and play; go.

MRS. PAGE. He is a better scholar than I thought he was.

EVANS. He is a good sprag memory. Farewell, Mistress
  Page.

MRS. PAGE. Adieu, good Sir Hugh.   *Exit Sir Hugh*
  Get you home, boy. Come, we stay too long.   *Exeunt*

SCENE TWO

A Room in Ford's House.

Enter Falstaff and Mistress Ford

FALSTAFF. Mistress Ford, your sorrow hath eaten up my
  sufferance. I see you are obsequious in your love, and I
  profess requital to a hair's breadth; not only, Mistress
  Ford, in the simple office of love, but in all the accoutre-
  ment, complement and ceremony of it. But are you sure
  of your husband now?

MRS. FORD. He 's a-birding, sweet Sir John.

MRS. PAGE. (*Within*) What ho! gossip Ford! what ho!

MRS. FORD. Step into the chamber, Sir John.   *Exit Falstaff*
                    Enter Mistress Page

MRS. PAGE. How now, sweet heart! who 's at home besides
  yourself?

MRS. FORD. Why, none but mine own people.

MRS. PAGE. Indeed!

MRS. FORD. No, certainly.—(*Aside to her*) Speak louder.

MRS. PAGE. Truly, I am so glad you have nobody here.

MRS. FORD. Why?

MRS. PAGE. Why, woman, your husband is in his old lunes
  again: he so takes on yonder with my husband; so rails
  against all married mankind; so curses all Eve's daughters, of what complexion soever; and so buffets himself
  on the forehead, crying, 'Peer out, peer out!' that any
  madness I ever yet beheld seemed but tameness, civility
  and patience, to this his distemper he is in now. I am
  glad the fat knight is not here.

MRS. FORD. Why, does he talk of him?

MRS. PAGE. Of none but him; and swears he was carried
  out, the last time he searched for him, in a basket: protests to my husband he is now here, and hath drawn him

and the rest of their company from their sport, to make
another experiment of his suspicion. But I am glad the
knight is not here; now he shall see his own foolery.

MRS. FORD. How near is he, Mistress Page?

MRS. PAGE. Hard by; at street end; he will be here anon.

MRS. FORD. I am undone! the knight is here.

MRS. PAGE. Why then you are utterly shamed, and he 's but
a dead man. What a woman are you! Away with him,
away with him! better shame than murder.

MRS. FORD. Which way should he go? How should I bestow
him? Shall I put him into the basket again?

Re-enter Falstaff

FALSTAFF. No, I 'll come no more i' the basket. May I not go
out ere he come?

MRS. PAGE. Alas! three of Master Ford's brothers watch the
door with pistols, that none shall issue out; otherwise you
might slip away ere he came. But what make you here?

FALSTAFF. What shall I do? I 'll creep up into the chimney.

MRS. FORD. There they always use to discharge their bird-
ing-pieces.

MRS. PAGE. Creep into the kiln-hole.

FALSTAFF. Where is it?

MRS. FORD. He will seek there, on my word. Neither press,
coffer, chest, trunk, well, vault, but he hath an abstract
for the remembrance of such places, and goes to them by
his note: there is no hiding you in the house.

FALSTAFF. I 'll go out, then.

MRS. PAGE. If you go out in your own semblance, you die,
Sir John. Unless you go out disguised,—

MRS. FORD. How might we disguise him?

MRS. PAGE. Alas the day! I know not. There is no woman's
gown big enough for him; otherwise, he might put on a
hat, a muffler, and a kerchief, and so escape.

FALSTAFF. Good hearts, devise something: any extremity
rather than a mischief.

MRS. FORD. My maid's aunt, the fat woman of Brainford,
has a gown above.

MRS. PAGE. On my word, it will serve him; she 's as big as
he is: and there 's her thrummed hat and her muffler too.
Run up, Sir John.

MRS. FORD. Go, go, sweet Sir John: Mistress Page and I
will look some linen for your head.

MRS. PAGE. Quick, quick! we 'll come dress you, straight; put on the gown the while.   *Exit Falstaff*

MRS. FORD. I would my husband would meet him in this shape: he cannot abide the old woman of Brainford; he swears she 's a witch; forbade her my house, and hath threatened to beat her.

MRS. PAGE. Heaven guide him to thy husband's cudgel, and the devil guide his cudgel afterwards!

MRS. FORD. But is my husband coming?

MRS. PAGE. Ay, in good sadness, is he; and talks of the basket too, howsoever he hath had intelligence.

MRS. FORD. We 'll try that; for I 'll appoint my men to carry the basket again, to meet him at the door with it, as they did last time.

MRS. PAGE. Nay, but he 'll be here presently: let 's go dress him like the witch of Brainford.

MRS. FORD. I 'll first direct my men what they shall do with the basket. Go up; I 'll bring linen for him straight.   *Exit*

MRS. PAGE. Hang him, dishonest varlet! we cannot misuse him enough.

We 'll leave a proof, by that which we will do,
Wives may be merry, and yet honest too:
We do not act that often jest and laugh;
'Tis old, but true, 'Still swine eats all the draff.'   *Exit*
    Re-enter Mistress Ford, with two Servants

MRS. FORD. Go, sirs, take the basket again on your shoulders: your master is hard at door; if he bid you set it down, obey him. Quickly; dispatch.   *Exit*

FIRST SERVANT. Come, come, take it up.

SECOND SERVANT. Pray heaven, it be not full of knight again.

FIRST SERVANT. I hope not; I had as lief bear so much lead.
    Enter Ford, Page, Shallow, Caius, and Sir Hugh Evans

FORD. Ay, but if it prove true, Master Page, have you any way then to unfool me again? Set down the basket, villains. Somebody call my wife. Youth in a basket! O you panderly rascals! there 's a knot, a ging, a pack, a conspiracy against me: now shall the devil be shamed. What, wife, I say! Come, come forth! Behold what honest clothes you send forth to bleaching!

PAGE. Why, this passes! Master Ford, you are not to go loose any longer; you must be pinioned.

EVANS. Why, this is lunatics! this is mad as a mad dog!

SHALLOW. Indeed, Master Ford, this is not well, indeed.

FORD. So say I too, sir.—

Re-enter Mistress Ford

Come hither, Mistress Ford, the honest woman, the modest wife, the virtuous creature, that hath the jealous fool to her husband! I suspect without cause, mistress, do I?

MRS. FORD. Heaven be my witness, you do, if you suspect me in any dishonesty.

FORD. Well said, brazen-face! hold it out. Come forth, sir-rah!   *Pulls the clothes out of the basket*

PAGE. This passes!

MRS. FORD. Are you not ashamed? let the clothes alone.

FORD. I shall find you anon.

EVANS. 'Tis unreasonable. Will you take up your wife's clothes? Come away.

FORD. Empty the basket, I say!

MRS. FORD. Why, man, why?

FORD. Master Page, as I am an honest man, there was one conveyed out of my house yesterday in this basket: why may not he be there again? In my house I am sure he is; my intelligence is true; my jealousy is reasonable. Pluck me out all the linen.

MRS. FORD. If you find a man there he shall die a flea's death.

PAGE. Here 's no man.

SHALLOW. By my fidelity, this is not well, Master Ford; this wrongs you.

EVANS. Master Ford, you must pray, and not follow the imaginations of your own heart: this is jealousies.

FORD. Well, he 's not here I seek for.

PAGE. No, nor nowhere else but in your brain.

Servants carry away the basket

FORD. Help to search my house this one time: if I find not what I seek, show no colour for my extremity; let me for ever be your table-sport; let them say of me, 'As jealous as Ford, that searched a hollow walnut for his wife's leman.' Satisfy me once more; once more search with me.

MRS. FORD. What ho, Mistress Page! come you and the old woman down; my husband will come into the chamber.

FORD. Old woman! What old woman 's that?

MRS. FORD. Why, it is my maid's aunt of Brainford.

FORD. A witch, a quean, an old cozening quean! Have I not
forbid her my house? She comes of errands, does she?
We are simple men; we do not know what 's brought to
pass under the profession of fortune-telling. She works
by charms, by spells, by the figure, and such daubery as
this is, beyond our element: we know nothing. Come
down, you witch, you hag, you; come down, I say!

MRS. FORD. Nay, good, sweet husband! good gentlemen, let
him not strike the old woman.

Enter Falstaff in women's clothes, led by Mistress Page

MRS. PAGE. Come, Mother Prat; come, give me your hand.

FORD. I 'll 'prat' her.—(*Beats him*) Out of my door, you
witch, you rag, you baggage, you polecat, you ronyon!
out, out! I 'll conjure you, I 'll fortune-tell you.

Exit Falstaff

MRS. PAGE. Are you not ashamed? I think you have killed
the poor woman.

MRS. FORD. Nay, he will do it. 'Tis a goodly credit for you.

FORD. Hang her, witch!

EVANS. By yea and no, I think the 'oman is a witch indeed:
I like not when a 'oman has a great peard; I spy a great
peard under her muffler.

FORD. Will you follow, gentlemen? I beseech you, follow:
see but the issue of my jealousy. If I cry out thus upon no
trail, never trust me when I open again.

PAGE. Let 's obey his humour a little further. Come, gentlemen.   *Exeunt Ford, Page, Shallow, Caius, and Evans*

MRS. PAGE. Trust me, he beat him most pitifully.

MRS. FORD. Nay, by the mass, that he did not; he beat him
most unpitifully methought.

MRS. PAGE. I 'll have the cudgel hallowed and hung o'er the
altar: it hath done meritorious service.

MRS. FORD. What think you? May we, with the warrant of
womanhood and the witness of a good conscience, pursue him with any further revenge?

MRS. PAGE. The spirit of wantonness is, sure, scared out of
him: if the devil have him not in fee-simple, with fine
and recovery, he will never, I think, in the way of waste,
attempt us again.

MRS. FORD. Shall we tell our husbands how we have served
him?

MRS. PAGE. Yes, by all means; if it be but to scrape the fig-

ures out of your husband's brains. If they can
find in their hearts the poor unvirtuous fat knight shall
be any further afflicted, we two will still be the ministers.

MRS. FORD. I 'll warrant they 'll have him publicly shamed,
and methinks there would be no period to the jest,
should he not be publicly shamed.

MRS. PAGE. Come, to the forge with it then; shape it: I
would not have things cool.   *Exeunt*

SCENE THREE

A Room in the Garter Inn.

Enter Host and Bardolph

BARDOLPH. Sir, the Germans desire to have three of your
horses: the duke himself will be to-morrow at court, and
they are going to meet him.

HOST. What duke should that be comes so secretly? I hear
not of him in the court. Let me speak with the gentlemen; they speak English?

BARDOLPH. Ay, sir; I 'll call them to you.

HOST. They shall have my horses, but I 'll make them pay;
I 'll sauce them: they have had my house a week at command; I have turned away my other guests: they must
come off; I 'll sauce them. Come.   *Exeunt*

SCENE FOUR

A Room in Ford's House.

*Enter Page, Ford, Mistress Page, Mistress Ford,
and Sir Hugh Evans*

EVANS. 'Tis one of the pest discretions of a 'oman as ever I
did look upon.

PAGE. And did he send you both these letters at an instant?

MRS. PAGE. Within a quarter of an hour.

FORD. Pardon me, wife. Henceforth do what thou wilt;
I rather will suspect the sun with cold
Than thee with wantonness: now doth thy honour stand,
In him that was of late an heretic,
As firm as faith.

PAGE.   'Tis well, 'tis well; no more.
  Be not as extreme in submission
  As an offence;
  But let our plot go forward: let our wives
  Yet once again, to make us public sport,
  Appoint a meeting with this old fat fellow,
  Where we may take him and disgrace him for it.

FORD. There is no better way than that they spoke of.

PAGE. How? to send him word they 'll meet him in the park
  at midnight? Fie, fie! he 'll never come.

EVANS. You say he has been thrown into the rivers, and has
  been grievously peaten as an old 'oman: methinks there
  should be terrors in him that he should not come; methinks his flesh is punished, he shall have no desires.

PAGE. So think I too.

MRS. FORD. Devise but how you 'll use him when he comes,
  And let us two devise to bring him thither.

MRS. PAGE. There is an old tale goes that Herne the hunter,
  Sometime a keeper here in Windsor forest,
  Doth all the winter-time, at still midnight,
  Walk round about an oak, with great ragg'd horns;
  And there he blasts the tree, and takes the cattle,
  And makes milch-kine yield blood, and shakes a chain
  In a most hideous and dreadful manner:
  You have heard of such a spirit, and well you know
  The superstitious idle-headed eld
  Receiv'd and did deliver to our age
  This tale of Herne the hunter for a truth.

PAGE. Why, yet there want not many that do fear
  In deep of night to walk by this Herne's oak.
  But what of this?

MRS. FORD.   Marry, this is our device;
  That Falstaff at that oak shall meet with us,
  Disguis'd like Herne with huge horns on his head.

PAGE. Well, let it not be doubted but he 'll come,
  And in this shape when you have brought him thither,
  What shall be done with him? what is your plot?

MRS. PAGE. That likewise have we thought upon, and thus:
  Nan Page my daughter, and my little son,
  And three or four more of their growth, we 'll dress
  Like urchins, ouphs and fairies, green and white,
  With rounds of waxen tapers on their heads,

And rattles in their hands. Upon a sudden,
As Falstaff, she, and I, are newly met,
Let them from forth a sawpit rush at once
With some diffused song: upon their sight,
We two in great amazedness will fly:
Then let them all encircle him about,
And, fairy-like, to pinch the unclean knight;
And ask him why, that hour of fairy revel,
In their so sacred paths he dares to tread
In shape profane.

MRS. FORD.   And till he tell the truth,
Let the supposed fairies pinch him sound
And burn him with their tapers.

MRS. PAGE.   The truth being known,
We 'll all present ourselves, dis-horn the spirit,
And mock him home to Windsor.

FORD.   The children must
Be practis'd well to this, or they 'll ne'er do 't.

EVANS. I will teach the children their behaviours; and I will
be like a jack-an-apes also, to burn the knight with my
taber.

FORD. That will be excellent. I 'll go buy them vizards.

MRS. PAGE. My Nan shall be the queen of all the fairies,
Finely attired in a robe of white.

PAGE. That silk will I go buy:—(*Aside*) and in that time
Shall Master Slender steal my Nan away,
And marry her at Eton. Go, send to Falstaff straight.

FORD. Nay, I 'll to him again in name of Brook;
He 'll tell me all his purpose. Sure, he 'll come.

MRS. PAGE. Fear not you that. Go, get us properties,
And tricking for our fairies.

EVANS. Let us about it: it is admirable pleasures and fery
honest knaveries.   *Exeunt Page, Ford, and Evans*

MRS. PAGE. Go, Mistress Ford,   *Exit Mistress Ford*
Send Quickly to Sir John, to know his mind.
I 'll to the doctor: he hath my good will,
And none but he, to marry with Nan Page.
That Slender, though well landed, is an idiot;
And him my husband best of all affects:
The doctor is well money'd, and his friends
Potent at court: he, none but he, shall have her,
Though twenty thousand worthier come to crave her.

                                              Exit

SCENE FIVE

A Room in the Garter Inn.

Enter Host and Simple

HOST. What wouldst thou have, boor? what, thickskin? speak, breathe, discuss; brief, short, quick, snap.

SIMPLE. Marry, sir, I come to speak with Sir John Falstaff from Master Slender.

HOST. There 's his chamber, his house, his castle, his standing-bed and truckle-bed: 'tis painted about with the story of the Prodigal, fresh and new. Go knock and call: he 'll speak like an Anthropophaginian unto thee: knock, I say.

SIMPLE. There 's an old woman, a fat woman, gone up into his chamber: I 'll be so bold as stay, sir, till she come down; I come to speak with her, indeed.

HOST. Ha! a fat woman! the knight may be robbed: I 'll call. Bully knight! Bully Sir John! speak from thy lungs military: art thou there? it is thine host, thine Ephesian, calls.

FALSTAFF. (*Above*) How now, mine host!

HOST. Here 's a Bohemian-Tartar tarries the coming down of thy fat woman. Let her descend, bully; let her descend; my chambers are honourable: fie! privacy? fie!

Enter Falstaff

FALSTAFF. There was, mine host, an old fat woman even now with me, but she 's gone.

SIMPLE. Pray you, sir, was 't not the wise woman of Brainford?

FALSTAFF. Ay, marry, was it, muscle-shell: what would you with her?

SIMPLE. My master, sir, Master Slender, sent to her, seeing her go thorough the streets, to know, sir, whether one Nym, sir, that beguiled him of a chain, had the chain or no.

FALSTAFF. I spake with the old woman about it.

SIMPLE. And what says she, I pray, sir?

FALSTAFF. Marry, she says that the very same man that beguiled Master Slender of his chain cozened him of it.

SIMPLE. I would I could have spoken with the woman herself: I had other things to have spoken with her too, from him.

FALSTAFF. What are they? let us know.

HOST. Ay, come; quick.

SIMPLE. I may not conceal them, sir.

HOST. Conceal them, or thou diest.

SIMPLE. Why, sir, they were nothing but about Mistress
Anne Page; to know if it were my master's fortune to
have her or no.

FALSTAFF. 'Tis, 'tis his fortune.

SIMPLE. What, sir?

FALSTAFF. To have her, or no. Go; say the woman told me
so.

SIMPLE. May I be bold to say so, sir?

FALSTAFF. Ay, Sir Tike; who more bold?

SIMPLE. I thank your worship: I shall make my master glad
with these tidings.   *Exit*

HOST. Thou art clerkly, thou art clerkly, Sir John. Was
there a wise woman with thee?

FALSTAFF. Ay, that there was, mine host; one that hath
taught me more wit than ever I learned before in my life:
and I paid nothing for it neither, but was paid for my
learning.

Enter Bardolph

BARDOLPH. Out, alas, sir! cozenage, mere cozenage!

HOST. Where be my horses? speak well of them, varletto.

BARDOLPH. Run away, with the cozeners; for so soon as I
came beyond Eton, they threw me off, from behind one
of them, in a slough of mire; and set spurs and away, like
three German devils, three Doctor Faustuses.

HOST. They are gone but to meet the duke, villain. Do not
say they be fled; Germans are honest men.

Enter Sir Hugh Evans

EVANS. Where is mine host?

HOST. What is the matter, sir?

EVANS. Have a care of your entertainments: there is a
friend of mine come to town, tells me, there is three
cozen-germans that has cozened all the hosts of Readins,
of Maidenhead, of Colebrook, of horses and money. I tell
you for good will, look you: you are wise and full of
gibes and vlouting-stogs, and 'tis not convenient you
should be cozened. Fare you well.   *Exit*

Enter Doctor Caius

CAIUS. Vere is mine host de Jarteer?

HOST. Here, Master doctor, in perplexity and doubtful di-
lemma.

CAIUS. I cannot tell vat is dat; but it is tell-a me dat you
make grand preparation for a duke de Jamany: by my
trot, dere is no duke dat de court is know to come. I tell
you for good vill: adieu.   *Exit*

HOST. Hue and cry, villain! go. Assist me, knight; I am undone. Fly, run, hue and cry, villain! I am undone!
                            Exeunt Host and Bardolph

FALSTAFF. I would all the world might be cozened, for I
have been cozened and beaten too. If it should come to
the ear of the court how I have been transformed, and
how my transformation hath been washed and cudgelled, they would melt me out of my fat drop by drop,
and liquor fishermen's boots with me: I warrant they
would whip me with their fine wits till I were as crest-
fallen as a dried pear. I never prospered since I forswore
myself at primero. Well, if my wind were but long
enough to say my prayers, I would repent.

                    Enter Mistress Quickly

Now, whence come you?

QUICKLY. From the two parties, forsooth.

FALSTAFF. The devil take one party and his dam the other!
and so they shall be both bestowed. I have suffered more
for their sakes, more than the villanous inconstancy of
man's disposition is able to bear.

QUICKLY. And have not they suffered? Yes, I warrant; speciously one of them: Mistress Ford, good heart, is beaten
black and blue, that you cannot see a white spot about
her.

FALSTAFF. What tellest thou me of black and blue? I was
beaten myself into all the colours of the rainbow; and I
was like to be apprehended for the witch of Brainford:
but that my admirable dexterity of wit, my counterfeiting
the action of an old woman, delivered me, the knave constable had set me i' the stocks, i' the common stocks, for
a witch.

QUICKLY. Sir, let me speak with you in your chamber; you
shall hear how things go, and, I warrant, to your content.
Here is a letter will say somewhat. Good hearts! what
ado here is to bring you together! Sure, one of you does
not serve heaven well, that you are so crossed.
                                                   Exeunt

FALSTAFF. Come up into my chamber.

SCENE SIX

Another Room in the Garter Inn.

Enter Fenton and Host

HOST. Master Fenton, talk not to me: my mind is heavy; I
will give over all.

FENTON. Yet hear me speak. Assist me in my purpose,
And, as I am a gentleman, I 'll give thee
A hundred pound in gold more than your loss.

HOST. I will hear you, Master Fenton; and I will, at the
least, keep your counsel.

FENTON. From time to time I have acquainted you
With the dear love I bear to fair Anne Page;
Who, mutually hath answer'd my affection,
So far forth as herself might be her chooser,
Even to my wish. I have a letter from her
Of such contents as you will wonder at;
The mirth whereof so larded with my matter,
That neither singly can be manifested,
Without the show of both; wherein fat Falstaff
Hath a great scare: the image of the jest
I 'll show you here at large. (*Pointing to the Letter*) Hark,
  good mine host:
To-night at Herne's oak, just 'twixt twelve and one,
Must my sweet Nan present the Fairy Queen;
The purpose why, is here: in which disguise,
While other jests are something rank on foot,
Her father hath commanded her to slip
Away with Slender, and with him at Eton
Immediately to marry: she hath consented:
Now, sir,
Her mother, even strong against that match
And firm for Doctor Caius, hath appointed
That he shall likewise shuffle her away,
While other sports are tasking of their minds;
And at the deanery, where a priest attends,
Straight marry her: to this her mother's plot
She, seemingly obedient, likewise hath
Made promise to the doctor. Now, thus it rests:

Her father means she shall be all in white,
And in that habit, when Slender sees his time
To take her by the hand and bid her go,
She shall go with him: her mother hath intended,
The better to denote her to the doctor,—
For they must all be mask'd and vizarded—
That quaint in green she shall be loose enrob'd,
With ribands pendent, flaring 'bout her head;
And when the doctor spies his vantage ripe,
To pinch her by the hand: and on that token
The maid hath given consent to go with him.

HOST. Which means she to deceive, father or mother?

FENTON. Both, my good host, to go along with me:
And here it rests, that you 'll procure the vicar
To stay for me at church 'twixt twelve and one,
And, in the lawful name of marrying,
To give our hearts united ceremony.

HOST. Well, husband your device; I 'll to the vicar.
Bring you the maid, you shall not lack a priest.

FENTON. So shall I evermore be bound to thee;
Besides, I 'll make a present recompense.

ACT FIVE

SCENE ONE

A Room in the Garter Inn.

Enter Falstaff and Mistress Quickly

FALSTAFF. Prithee, no more prattling; go: I 'll hold. This is
the third time; I hope good luck lies in odd numbers.
Away! go. They say there is divinity in odd numbers,
either in nativity, chance or death. Away!

QUICKLY. I 'll provide you a chain, and I 'll do what I can to
get you a pair of horns.

FALSTAFF. Away, I say; time wears: hold up your head,
and mince.   *Exit Mistress Quickly*

Enter Ford, disguised

How now, Master Brook! Master Brook, the matter will
be known to-night, or never. Be you in the Park about
midnight, at Herne's oak, and you shall see wonders.

FORD. Went you not to her yesterday, sir, as you told me
you had appointed?

FALSTAFF. I went to her, Master Brook, as you see, like a
poor old man; but I came from her, Master Brook, like a
poor old woman. That same knave Ford, her husband,
hath the finest mad devil of jealousy in him, Master
Brook, that ever governed frenzy. I will tell you: he beat
me grievously, in the shape of a woman; for in the shape
of a man, Master Brook, I fear not Goliath with a weaver's beam, because I know also life is a shuttle. I am in
haste: go along with me; I 'll tell you all, Master Brook.
Since I plucked geese, played truant, and whipped top, I
knew not what it was to be beaten till lately. Follow me:
I 'll tell you strange things of this knave Ford, on whom
to-night I will be revenged, and I will deliver his wife
into your hand. Follow. Strange things in hand, Master
Brook! Follow.   *Exeunt*

SCENE TWO

Windsor Park.

Enter Page, Shallow, and Slender

PAGE. Come, come; we 'll couch i' the castle-ditch till we
see the light of our fairies. Remember, son Slender, my
daughter.

SLENDER. Ay, forsooth; I have spoke with her and we have
a nay-word how to know one another. I come to her in
white, and cry, 'mum'; she cries, 'budget'; and by that
we know one another.

SHALLOW. That 's good too: but what needs either your
'mum', or her 'budget'? the white will decipher her well
enough. It hath struck ten o'clock.

PAGE. The night is dark; light and spirits will become it
well. Heaven prosper our sport! No man means evil but
the devil, and we shall know him by his horns. Let 's
away; follow me.   *Exeunt*

SCENE THREE

The Street in Windsor.

Enter Mistress Page, Mistress Ford, and Dr. Caius

MRS. PAGE. Master Doctor, my daughter is in green: when
you see your time, take her by the hand, away with her
to the deanery, and dispatch it quickly. Go before into
the Park: we two must go together.

CAIUS. I know vat I have to do. Adieu.

MRS. PAGE. Fare you well, sir. (*Exit Caius*) My husband
will not rejoice so much at the abuse of Falstaff, as he
will chafe at the doctor's marrying my daughter: but 'tis
no matter; better a little chiding than a great deal of
heart break.

MRS. FORD. Where is Nan now and her troop of fairies, and
the Welsh devil, Hugh?

MRS. PAGE. They are all couched in a pit hard by Herne's
oak, with obscured lights; which, at the very instant of

Falstaff's and our meeting, they will at once display to the night.

MRS. FORD. That cannot choose but amaze him.

MRS. PAGE. If he be not amazed, he will be mocked; if he be amazed, he will every way be mocked.

MRS. FORD. We 'll betray him finely.

MRS. PAGE. Against such lewdsters and their lechery,
Those that betray them do no treachery.

MRS. FORD. The hour draws on: to the oak, to the oak!

Exeunt

SCENE FOUR

Windsor Park.

Enter Sir Hugh Evans, disguised, and others as Fairies

EVANS. Trib, trib, fairies: come; and remember your parts. Be pold, I pray you; follow me into the pit, and when I give the watch-ords, do as I pid you. Come, come; trib, trib.

Exeunt

SCENE FIVE

Another part of the Park.

Enter Falstaff disguised as Herne, with a buck's head on

FALSTAFF. The Windsor bell hath struck twelve; the minute draws on. Now, the hot-blooded gods assist me! Remember, Jove, thou wast a bull for thy Europa; love set on thy horns. O powerful love! that, in some respects, makes a beast a man; in some other, a man a beast. You were also, Jupiter, a swan for the love of Leda; O omnipotent love! how near the god drew to the complexion of a goose! A fault done first in the form of a beast; O Jove, a beastly fault! and then another fault in the semblance of a fowl: think on 't, Jove; a foul fault! When gods have hot backs, what shall poor men do? For me, I am here a Windsor stag; and the fattest, I think, i' the forest: send me a cool rut-time, Jove, or who can blame me to piss my tallow? Who comes here? my doe?

Enter Mistress Ford and Mistress Page

MRS. FORD. Sir John! art thou there, my deer? my male deer?

FALSTAFF. My doe with the black scut! Let the sky rain potatoes; let it thunder to the tune of 'Green Sleeves'; hail kissing-comfits and snow eringoes; let there come a tempest of provocation, I will shelter me here.

Embracing her

MRS. FORD. Mistress Page is come with me, sweetheart.

FALSTAFF. Divide me like a brib'd buck, each a haunch: I will keep my sides to myself, my shoulders for the fellow of this walk, and my horns I bequeath your husbands. Am I a woodman, ha? Speak I like Herne the hunter? Why, now is Cupid a child of conscience; he makes restitution. As I am a true spirit, welcome!   *Noise within*

MRS. PAGE. Alas! what noise?

MRS. FORD. Heaven forgive our sins!

FALSTAFF. What should this be?

MRS. FORD. ⎫
MRS. PAGE. ⎬ Away, away!   *They run off*

FALSTAFF. I think the devil will not have me damned, lest the oil that is in me should set hell on fire; he would never else cross me thus.

Enter Sir Hugh Evans, like a Satyr; Pistol as Hobgoblin; Anne Page, as the Fairy Queen, attended by her Brother and Others, as Fairies, with waxen tapers on their heads

ANNE. Fairies, black, grey, green, and white,
  You moonshine revellers, and shades of night,
  You orphan heirs of fixed destiny,
  Attend your office and your quality.
  Crier Hobgoblin, make the fairy oyes.

PISTOL. Elves, list your names: silence, you airy toys!
  Cricket, to Windsor chimneys shalt thou leap:
  Where fires thou find'st unrak'd and hearths unswept,
  There pinch the maids as blue as bilberry:
  Our radiant queen hates sluts and sluttery.

FALSTAFF. They are fairies; he that speaks to them shall die:
  I 'll wink and couch: no man their works must eye.

Lies down upon his face

EVANS. Where 's Bede? Go you, and where you find a maid
  That, ere she sleep, has thrice her prayers said,

Rein up the organs of her fantasy,
Sleep she as sound as careless infancy;
But those that sleep and think not on their sins,
Pinch them, arms, legs, backs, shoulders, sides, and shins.

ANNE. About, about!
Search Windsor castle, elves, within and out:
Strew good luck, ouphs, on every sacred room,
That it may stand till the perpetual doom,
In state as wholesome as in state 'tis fit,
Worthy the owner, and the owner it.
The several chairs of order look you scour
With juice of balm and every precious flower:
Each fair instalment, coat, and several crest,
With loyal blazon, ever more be blest!
And nightly, meadow-fairies, look you sing,
Like to the Garter's compass, in a ring:
The expressure that it bears, green let it be,
More fertile-fresh than all the field to see;
And, 'Honi soit qui mal y pense' write
In emerald tufts, flowers purple, blue, and white;
Like sapphire, pearl, and rich embroidery,
Buckled below fair knighthood's bending knee:
Fairies use flowers for their charactery.
Away! disperse! But, till 'tis one o'clock,
Our dance of custom round about the oak
Of Herne the hunter, let us not forget.

EVANS. Pray you, lock hand in hand; yourselves in order
    set;
And twenty glow-worms shall our lanthorns be,
To guide our measure round about the tree.
But, stay; I smell a man of middle-earth.

FALSTAFF. Heavens defend me from that Welsh fairy, lest
he transform me to a piece of cheese!

PISTOL. Vile worm, thou wast o'erlook'd even in thy birth.

ANNE. With trial-fire touch me his finger-end:
If he be chaste, the flame will back descend
And turn him to no pain; but if he start,
It is the flesh of a corrupted heart.

PISTOL. A trial! come.

EVANS.   Come, will this wood take fire?
                    They burn him with their tapers

FALSTAFF. Oh, oh, oh!

ANNE. Corrupt, corrupt, and tainted in desire!
   About him, fairies, sing a scornful rime;
   And, as you trip, still pinch him to your time.

SONG

   Fie on sinful fantasy!
   Fie on lust and luxury!
   Lust is but a bloody fire,
   Kindled with unchaste desire,
   Fed in heart, whose flames aspire,
   As thoughts do blow them higher and higher.
   Pinch him, fairies, mutually;
   Pinch him for his villany;
   Pinch him, and burn him, and turn him about,
   Till candles and star-light and moonshine be out.

   During this song, the Fairies pinch
   Falstaff. Doctor Caius comes one way, and
   steals away a Fairy in green; Slender another way,
and takes off a Fairy in white; and Fenton comes, and steals
away Anne Page. A noise of hunting is heard within. The
Fairies run away. Falstaff pulls off his buck's head, and rises

   Enter Page, Ford, Mistress
   Page and Mistress Ford. They lay hold on Falstaff

PAGE. Nay, do not fly: I think we have watch'd you now:
   Will none but Herne the hunter serve your turn?

MRS. PAGE. I pray you, come, hold up the jest no higher.
   Now, good Sir John, how like you Windsor wives?
   See you these, husband? do not these fair yokes
   Become the forest better than the town?

FORD. Now sir, who 's a cuckold now? Master Brook, Falstaff 's a knave, a cuckoldly knave; here are his horns,
   Master Brook: and, Master Brook, he hath enjoyed nothing of Ford's but his buck-basket, his cudgel, and twenty
   pounds of money, which must be paid too, Master Brook;
   his horses are arrested for it, Master Brook.

MRS. FORD. Sir John, we have had ill luck; we could never
   meet. I will never take you for my love again, but I will
   always count you my deer.

FALSTAFF. I do begin to perceive that I am made an ass.

FORD. Ay, and an ox too; both the proofs are extant.

FALSTAFF. And these are not fairies? I was three or four

times in the thought they were not fairies; and yet the
guiltiness of my mind, the sudden surprise of my powers,
drove the grossness of the foppery into a received belief,
in despite of the teeth of all rime and reason, that they
were fairies. See now how wit may be made a Jack-a-
Lent, when 'tis upon ill employment!

EVANS. Sir John Falstaff, serve Got, and leave your desires,
and fairies will not pinse you.

FORD. Well said, fairy Hugh.

EVANS. And leave you your jealousies too, I pray you.

FORD. I will never mistrust my wife again, till thou art able
to woo her in good English.

FALSTAFF. Have I laid my brain in the sun and dried it,
that it wants matter to prevent so gross o'er-reaching as
this? Am I ridden with a Welsh goat too? Shall I have a
coxcomb of frize? 'Tis time I were choked with a piece of
toasted cheese.

EVANS. Seese is not goot to give putter: your pelly is all
putter.

FALSTAFF. 'Seese' and 'putter'! Have I lived to stand at the
taunt of one that makes fritters of English? This is
enough to be the decay of lust and late-walking through
the realm.

MRS. PAGE. Why, Sir John, do you think, though we would
have thrust virtue out of our hearts by the head and
shoulders, and have given ourselves without scruple to
hell, that ever the devil could have made you our delight?

FORD. What, a hodge-pudding? a bag of flax?

MRS. PAGE. A puffed man?

PAGE. Old, cold, withered, and of intolerable entrails?

FORD. And one that is as slanderous as Satan?

PAGE. And as poor as Job?

FORD. And as wicked as his wife?

EVANS. And given to fornications, and to taverns, and sack
and wine and metheglins, and to drinkings and swearings
and starings, pribbles and prabbles?

FALSTAFF. Well, I am your theme: you have the start of
me; I am dejected; I am not able to answer the Welsh
flannel. Ignorance itself is a plummet o'er me: use me as
you will.

FORD. Marry, sir, we 'll bring you to Windsor, to one Master

Brook, that you have cozened of money, to whom you
should have been a pander: over and above that you
have suffered, I think, to repay that money will be a biting affliction.

MRS. FORD. Nay, husband, let that go to make amends;
Forgive that sum, and so we 'll all be friends.

FORD. Well, here 's my hand: all is forgiven at last.

PAGE. Yet be cheerful, knight: thou shalt eat a posset to-
night at my house; where I will desire thee to laugh at
my wife, that now laughs at thee. Tell her, Master Slender hath married her daughter.

MRS. PAGE. (*Aside*) Doctors doubt that: if Anne Page be
my daughter, she is, by this, Doctor Caius' wife.

Enter Slender

SLENDER. Whoa, ho! ho! father Page!

PAGE. Son, how now! how now, son! have you dispatched?

SLENDER. Dispatched! I 'll make the best in Glostershire
know on 't; would I were hanged, la, else!

PAGE. Of what, son?

SLENDER. I came yonder at Eton to marry Mistress Anne
Page, and she 's a great lubberly boy: if it had not been
i' the church, I would have swinged him, or he should
have swinged me. If I did not think it had been Anne
Page, would I might never stir! and 'tis a postmaster's
boy.

PAGE. Upon my life, then, you took the wrong.

SLENDER. What need you tell me that? I think so, when I
took a boy for a girl. If I had been married to him, for all
he was in woman's apparel, I would not have had him.

PAGE. Why, this is your own folly. Did not I tell you how
you should know my daughter by her garments?

SLENDER. I went to her in white, and cried, 'mum,' and she
cried 'budget,' as Anne and I had appointed; and yet it
was not Anne, but a postmaster's boy.

EVANS. Jeshu! Master Slender, cannot you see put marry
poys?

PAGE. O I am vexed at heart: what shall I do?

MRS. PAGE. Good George, be not angry: I knew of your
purpose; turned my daughter into green; and, indeed,
she is now with the doctor at the deanery, and there married.

Enter Doctor Caius

CAIUS. Vere is Mistress Page? By gar, I am cozened: I ha'
married un garçon, a boy; un paysan, by gar, a boy; it is
not Anne Page: by gar, I am cozened.

MRS. PAGE. Why, did you not take her in green?

CAIUS. Ay, by gar, and 'tis a boy: by gar, I'll raise all Windsor.

FORD. This is strange. Who hath got the right Anne?

PAGE. My heart misgives me: here comes Master Fenton.

Enter Fenton and Anne Page

How now, Master Fenton!

ANNE. Pardon, good father! good my mother, pardon!

PAGE. Now, mistress, how chance you went not with Master Slender?

MRS. PAGE. Why went you not with Master Doctor, maid?

FENTON. You do amaze her: hear the truth of it.
You would have married her most shamefully,
Where there was no proportion held in love.
The truth is, she and I, long since contracted,
Are now so sure that nothing can dissolve us.
The offence is holy that she hath committed,
And this deceit loses the name of craft,
Of disobedience, or unduteous title,
Since therein she doth evitate and shun
A thousand irreligious cursed hours,
Which forced marriage would have brought upon her.

FORD. Stand not amaz'd: here is no remedy:
In love the heavens themselves do guide the state:
Money buys lands, and wives are sold by fate.

FALSTAFF. I am glad, though you have ta'en a special stand
to strike at me, that your arrow hath glanced.

PAGE. Well, what remedy?—Fenton, heaven give thee joy!
What cannot be eschew'd must be embrac'd.

FALSTAFF. When night-dogs run all sorts of deer are chas'd.

MRS. PAGE. Well, I will muse no further. Master Fenton,
Heaven give you many, many merry days!
Good husband, let us every one go home,
And laugh this sport o'er by a country fire;
Sir John and all.

FORD.   Let it be so. Sir John,
To Master Brook you yet shall hold your word;
For he to-night shall lie with Mistress Ford.   *Exeunt*

MEASURE FOR MEASURE

CAST OF CHARACTERS

VINCENTIO, *the Duke*
ANGELO, *Lord Deputy in the Duke's absence*
ESCALUS, *an Ancient Lord, joined with Angelo*
    in the deputation
CLAUDIO, *a young Gentleman*
LUCIO, *a Fantastic*
Two other like Gentlemen
VARRIUS, *a Gentleman attending on the Duke*
Provost

THOMAS ⎱ *two Friars*
PETER ⎰

A Justice
ELBOW, *a simple Constable*
FROTH, *a foolish Gentleman*
POMPEY, *Tapster to Mistress Overdone*
ABHORSON, *an Executioner*
BARNARDINE, *a dissolute Prisoner*

ISABELLA, *sister to Claudio*
MARIANA, *betrothed to Angelo*
JULIET, *beloved of Claudio*
FRANCISCA, *a Nun*
MISTRESS OVERDONE, *a Bawd*

Lords, Officers, Citizens, Boy, and Attendants

SCENE
Vienna

MEASURE FOR MEASURE

ACT ONE

SCENE ONE

An Apartment in the Duke's Palace.

Enter Duke, Escalus, Lords, and Attendants

DUKE. Escalus.

ESCALUS. My lord?

DUKE. Of government the properties to unfold,
    Would seem in me to affect speech and discourse,
    Since I am put to know that your own science
    Exceeds, in that, the lists of all advice
    My strength can give you: then no more remains,
    But that, to your sufficiency, as your worth is able,
    And let them work. The nature of our people
    Our city's institutions, and the terms
    For common justice, you're as pregnant in,
    As art and practice hath enriched any
    That we remember. There is our commission,   *Giving it*
    From which we would not have you warp. Call hither,
    I say, bid come before us Angelo.   *Exit an Attendant*
    What figure of us think you he will bear?
    For you must know, we have with special soul
    Elected him our absence to supply,
    Lent him our terror, drest him with our love,
    And given his deputation all the organs
    Of our own power: what think you of it?

ESCALUS. If any in Vienna be of worth
    To undergo such ample grace and honour,
    It is Lord Angelo.

DUKE.   Look where he comes.
               Enter Angelo

ANGELO. Always obedient to your Grace's will
  I come to know your pleasure.

DUKE.   Angelo,
  There is a kind of character in thy life,
  That, to th' observer doth thy history
  Fully unfold. Thy self and thy belongings
  Are not thine own so proper, as to waste
  Thyself upon thy virtues, they on thee.
  Heaven doth with us as we with torches do,
  Not light them for themselves; for if our virtues
  Did not go forth of us, 'twere all alike
  As if we had them not. Spirits are not finely touch'd
  But to fine issues, nor Nature never lends
  The smallest scruple of her excellence,
  But, like a thrifty goddess, she determines
  Herself the glory of a creditor,
  Both thanks and use. But I do bend my speech
  To one that can my part in him advertise;
  Hold, therefore, Angelo: *Tendering his commission*
  In our remove be thou at full ourself;
  Mortality and mercy in Vienna
  Live in thy tongue and heart. Old Escalus,
  Though first in question, is thy secondary.
  Take thy commission.   *Giving it*

ANGELO.   Now, good my lord,
  Let there be some more test made of my metal,
  Before so noble and so great a figure
  Be stamp'd upon it.

DUKE.   No more evasion:
  We have with a leaven'd and prepared choice
  Proceeded to you; therefore take your honours.
  Our haste from hence is of so quick condition
  That it prefers itself, and leaves unquestion'd
  Matters of needful value. We shall write to you,
  As time and our concernings shall importune,
  How it goes with us: and do look to know
  What doth befall you here. So, fare you well:
  To the hopeful execution do I leave you
  Of your commissions.

ANGELO.   Yet, give leave, my lord,
  That we may bring you something on the way.

DUKE. My haste may not admit it;

Nor need you, on mine honour, have to do
With any scruple: your scope is as mine own,
So to enforce or qualify the laws
As to your soul seems good. Give me your hand;
I 'll privily away: I love the people,
But do not like to stage me to their eyes.
Though it do well, I do not relish well
Their loud applause and Aves vehement,
Nor do I think the man of safe discretion
That does affect it. Once more, fare you well.

ANGELO. The heavens give safety to your purposes!

ESCALUS. Lead forth and bring you back in happiness!

DUKE. I thank you. Fare you well.   *Exit*

ESCALUS. I shall desire you, sir, to give me leave
To have free speech with you; and it concerns me
To look into the bottom of my place:
A power I have, but of what strength and nature
I am not yet instructed.

ANGELO. 'Tis so with me. Let us withdraw together,
And we may soon our satisfaction have
Touching that point.

ESCALUS.   I 'll wait upon your honour. *Exeunt*

SCENE TWO

A Street.

Enter Lucio and two Gentlemen

LUCIO. If the duke with the other dukes comes not to composition with the King of Hungary, why then, all the
dukes fall upon the king.

FIRST GENTLEMAN. Heaven grant us its peace, but not the
King of Hungary's!

SECOND GENTLEMAN. Amen.

LUCIO. Thou concludest like the sanctimonious pirate, that
went to sea with the Ten Commandments, but scraped
one out of the table.

SECOND GENTLEMAN. 'Thou shalt not steal'?

LUCIO. Ay, that he razed.

FIRST GENTLEMAN. Why, 'twas a commandment to command the captain and all the rest from their functions:

they put forth to steal. There 's not a soldier of us all, that, in the thanksgiving before meat, doth relish the petition well that prays for peace.

SECOND GENTLEMAN. I never heard any soldier dislike it.

LUCIO. I believe thee, for I think thou never wast where grace was said.

SECOND GENTLEMAN. No? a dozen times at least.

FIRST GENTLEMAN. What, in metre?

LUCIO. In any proportion or in any language.

FIRST GENTLEMAN. I think, or in any religion.

LUCIO. Ay; why not? Grace is grace, despite of all controversy: as, for example, thou thyself art a wicked villain, despite of all grace.

FIRST GENTLEMAN. Well, there went but a pair of shears between us.

LUCIO. I grant; as there may between the lists and the velvet: thou art the list.

FIRST GENTLEMAN. And thou the velvet: thou art good velvet; thou art a three-piled piece, I warrant thee. I had as lief be a list of an English kersey as be piled, as thou art piled, for a French velvet. Do I speak feelingly now?

LUCIO. I think thou dost; and, indeed, with most painful feeling of thy speech: I will, out of thine own confession, learn to begin thy health; but, whilst I live, forget to drink after thee.

FIRST GENTLEMAN. I think I have done myself wrong, have I not?

SECOND GENTLEMAN. Yes, that thou hast, whether thou art tainted or free.

LUCIO. Behold, behold, where Madam Mitigation comes! I have purchased as many diseases under her roof as come to—

SECOND GENTLEMAN. To what, I pray?

LUCIO. Judge.

SECOND GENTLEMAN. To three thousand dolours a year.

FIRST GENTLEMAN. Ay, and more.

LUCIO. A French crown more.

FIRST GENTLEMAN. Thou art always figuring diseases in me; but thou art full of error: I am sound.

LUCIO. Nay, not as one would say, healthy; but so sound as things that are hollow: thy bones are hollow; impiety has made a feast of thee.

Enter Mistress Overdone

FIRST GENTLEMAN. How now! which of your hips has the most profound sciatica?

MRS. OVERDONE. Well, well; there 's one yonder arrested and carried to prison was worth five thousand of you all.

SECOND GENTLEMAN. Who 's that, I pray thee?

MRS. OVERDONE. Marry, sir, that 's Claudio, Signior Claudio.

FIRST GENTLEMAN. Claudio to prison! 'Tis not so.

MRS. OVERDONE. Nay, but I know 'tis so. I saw him arrested; saw him carried away; and, which is more, within these three days his head to be chopped off.

LUCIO. But, after all this fooling, I would not have it so. Art thou sure of this?

MRS. OVERDONE. I am too sure of it; and it is for getting Madam Julietta with child.

LUCIO. Believe me, this may be: he promised to meet me two hours since, and he was ever precise in promise-keeping.

SECOND GENTLEMAN. Besides, you know, it draws something near to the speech we had to such a purpose.

FIRST GENTLEMAN. But most of all, agreeing with the proclamation.

LUCIO. Away! let 's go learn the truth of it.

Exeunt Lucio and Gentlemen

MRS. OVERDONE. Thus, what with the war, what with the sweat, what with the gallows and what with poverty, I am custom-shrunk.

Enter Pompey

How now! what 's the news with you?

POMPEY. Yonder man is carried to prison.

MRS. OVERDONE. Well: what has he done?

POMPEY. A woman.

MRS. OVERDONE. But what 's his offence?

POMPEY. Groping for trouts in a peculiar river.

MRS. OVERDONE. What, is there a maid with child by him?

POMPEY. No; but there 's a woman with maid by him. You have not heard of the proclamation, have you?

MRS. OVERDONE. What proclamation, man?

POMPEY. All houses of resort in the suburbs of Vienna must be plucked down.

MRS. OVERDONE. And what shall become of those in the city?

POMPEY. They shall stand for seed: they had gone down too, but that a wise burgher put in for them.

MRS. OVERDONE. But shall all our houses of resort in the suburbs be pulled down?

POMPEY. To the ground, mistress.

MRS. OVERDONE. Why, here 's a change indeed in the commonwealth! What shall become of me?

POMPEY. Come; fear not you: good counsellors lack no clients: though you change your place, you need not change your trade; I 'll be your tapster still. Courage! there will be pity taken on you; you that have worn your eyes almost out in the service, you will be considered.

MRS. OVERDONE. What 's to do here, Thomas tapster? Let 's withdraw.

POMPEY. Here comes Signior Claudio, led by the provost to prison; and there 's Madam Juliet.   *Exeunt*

> *Enter Provost, Claudio, Juliet, and Officers*

CLAUDIO. Fellow, why dost thou show me thus to the world?
Bear me to prison where I am committed.

PROVOST. I do it not in evil disposition,
But from Lord Angelo by special charge.

CLAUDIO. Thus can the demi-god Authority
Make us pay down for our offence by weight.
The words of heaven; on whom it will, it will;
On whom it will not, so: yet still 'tis just.

> *Re-enter Lucio and two Gentlemen*

LUCIO. Why, how now, Claudio! whence comes this restraint?

CLAUDIO. From too much liberty, my Lucio, liberty:
As surfeit is the father of much fast,
So every scope by the immoderate use
Turns to restraint. Our natures do pursue—
Like rats that ravin down their proper bane,—
A thirsty evil, and when we drink we die.

LUCIO. If I could speak so wisely under an arrest, I would send for certain of my creditors. And yet, to say the truth, I had as lief have the foppery of freedom as the morality of imprisonment. What 's thy offence, Claudio?

CLAUDIO. What but to speak of would offend again.

LUCIO. What, is 't murder?

CLAUDIO. No.

LUCIO. Lechery?

CLAUDIO. Call it so.

PROVOST. Away, sir! you must go.

CLAUDIO. One word, good friend. Lucio, a word with you.

Takes him aside

LUCIO. A hundred, if they 'll do you any good.
Is lechery so looked after?

CLAUDIO. Thus stands it with me: upon a true contract
I got possession of Julietta's bed:
You know the lady; she is fast my wife,
Save that we do the denunciation lack
Of outward order: this we came not to,
Only for propagation of a dower
Remaining in the coffer of her friends,
From whom we thought it meet to hide our love
Till time had made them for us. But it chances
The stealth of our most mutual entertainment
With character too gross is writ on Juliet.

LUCIO. With child, perhaps?

CLAUDIO.   Unhappily, even so.
And the new deputy now for the duke,—
Whether it be the fault and glimpse of newness,
Or whether that the body public be
A horse whereon the governor doth ride,
Who, newly in the seat, that it may know
He can command, lets it straight feel the spur;
Whether the tyranny be in his place,
Or in his eminence that fills it up,
I stagger in:—but this new governor
Awakes me all the enrolled penalties
Which have, like unscour'd armour, hung by the wall
So long that nineteen zodiacs have gone round,
And none of them been worn; and, for a name,
Now puts the drowsy and neglected act
Freshly on me: 'tis surely for a name.

LUCIO. I warrant it is: and thy head stands so tickle on thy
shoulders that a milkmaid, if she be in love, may sigh it
off. Send after the duke and appeal to him.

CLAUDIO. I have done so, but he 's not to be found.
I prithee, Lucio, do me this kind service.
This day my sister should the cloister enter,

And there receive her approbation:
Acquaint her with the danger of my state;
Implore her, in my voice, that she make friends
To the strict deputy; bid herself assay him:
I have great hope in that; for in her youth
There is a prone and speechless dialect,
Such as move men; beside, she hath prosperous art
When she will play with reason and discourse,
And well she can persuade.

LUCIO. I pray she may: as well for the encouragement of
the like, which else would stand under grievous imposition, as for the enjoying of thy life, who I would be sorry
should be thus foolishly lost at a game of tick-tack. I 'll to
her.

CLAUDIO. I thank you, good friend Lucio.

LUCIO. Within two hours.

CLAUDIO.   Come, officer, away!   *Exeunt*

SCENE THREE

A Monastery.

Enter Duke and Friar Thomas

DUKE. No, holy father; throw away that thought:
Believe not that the dribbling dart of love
Can pierce a complete bosom. Why I desire thee
To give me secret harbour, hath a purpose
More grave and wrinkled than the aims and ends
Of burning youth.

FRIAR THOMAS.   May your Grace speak of it?

DUKE. My holy sir, none better knows than you
How I have ever lov'd the life remov'd,
And held in idle price to haunt assemblies
Where youth, and cost, and witless bravery keeps.
I have deliver'd to Lord Angelo—
A man of stricture and firm abstinence—
My absolute power and place here in Vienna,
And he supposes me travell'd to Poland;
For so I have strew'd it in the common ear,
And so it is receiv'd. Now, pious sir,
You will demand of me why I do this?

FRIAR THOMAS. Gladly, my lord.

DUKE. We have strict statutes and most biting laws,—
    The needful bits and curbs to headstrong steeds,—
    Which for this fourteen years we have let sleep;
    Even like an o'ergrown lion in a cave,
    That goes not out to prey. Now, as fond fathers,
    Having bound up the threat'ning twigs of birch,
    Only to stick it in their children's sight
    For terror, not to use, in time the rod
    Becomes more mock'd than fear'd; so our decrees,
    Dead to infliction, to themselves are dead,
    And liberty plucks justice by the nose;
    The baby beats the nurse, and quite athwart
    Goes all decorum.

FRIAR THOMAS.   It rested in your Grace
    T' unloose this tied-up justice when you pleas'd;
    And it in you more dreadful would have seem'd
    Than in Lord Angelo.

DUKE.   I do fear, too dreadful:
    Sith 'twas my fault to give the people scope,
    'Twould be my tyranny to strike and gall them
    For what I bid them do: for we bid this be done,
    When evil deeds have their permissive pass
    And not the punishment. Therefore, indeed, my father,
    I have on Angelo impos'd the office,
    Who may, in the ambush of my name, strike home,
    And yet my nature never in the sight
    To do it slander. And to behold his sway,
    I will, as 'twere a brother of your order,
    Visit both prince and people: therefore, I prithee,
    Supply me with the habit, and instruct me
    How I may formally in person bear me
    Like a true friar. Moe reasons for this action
    At our more leisure shall I render you;
    Only, this one: Lord Angelo is precise;
    Stands at a guard with envy; scarce confesses
    That his blood flows, or that his appetite
    Is more to bread than stone: hence shall we see,
    If power change purpose, what our seemers be.   *Exeunt*

SCENE FOUR

A Nunnery.

Enter Isabella and Francisca

ISABELLA. And have you nuns no further privileges?

FRANCISCA. Are not these large enough?

ISABELLA. Yes, truly; I speak not as desiring more,
But rather wishing a more strict restraint
Upon the sisterhood, the votarists of Saint Clare.

LUCIO. (*Within*) Ho! Peace be in this place!

ISABELLA.   Who's that which calls?

FRANCISCA. It is a man's voice. Gentle Isabella,
Turn you the key, and know his business of him:
You may, I may not; you are yet unsworn.
When you have vow'd, you must not speak with men
But in the presence of the prioress:
Then, if you speak, you must not show your face,
Or, if you show your face, you must not speak.
He calls again; I pray you, answer him.   *Exit*

ISABELLA. Peace and prosperity! Who is't that calls?

Enter Lucio

LUCIO. Hail, virgin, if you be, as those cheek-roses
Proclaim you are no less! Can you so stead me
As bring me to the sight of Isabella,
A novice of this place, and the fair sister
To her unhappy brother Claudio?

ISABELLA. Why 'her unhappy brother'? let me ask;
The rather for I now must make you know
I am that Isabella and his sister.

LUCIO. Gentle and fair, your brother kindly greets you:
Not to be weary with you, he's in prison.

ISABELLA. Woe me! for what?

LUCIO. For that which, if myself might be his judge,
He should receive his punishment in thanks:
He hath got his friend with child.

ISABELLA. Sir, make me not your story.

LUCIO.   It is true.
I would not, though 'tis my familiar sin
With maids to seem the lapwing and to jest,

Tongue far from heart, play with all virgins so:
I hold you as a thing ensky'd and sainted;
By your renouncement an immortal spirit,
And to be talk'd with in sincerity,
As with a saint.

ISABELLA. You do blaspheme the good in mocking me.
LUCIO. Do not believe it. Fewness and truth, 'tis thus:
Your brother and his lover have embrac'd:
As those that feed grow full, as blossoming time
That from the seedness the bare fallow brings
To teeming foison, even so her plenteous womb
Expresseth his full tilth and husbandry.

ISABELLA. Some one with child by him? My cousin Juliet?
LUCIO. Is she your cousin?
ISABELLA. Adoptedly; as school-maids change their names
By vain, though apt affection.
LUCIO.   She it is.
ISABELLA. O! let him marry her.
LUCIO.   This is the point.
The duke is very strangely gone from hence;
Bore many gentlemen, myself being one,
In hand and hope of action; but we do learn
By those that know the very nerves of state,
His givings out were of an infinite distance
From his true-meant design. Upon his place,
And with full line of his authority,
Governs Lord Angelo; a man whose blood
Is very snow-broth; one who never feels
The wanton stings and motions of the sense,
But doth rebate and blunt his natural edge
With profits of the mind, study and fast.
He,—to give fear to use and liberty,
Which have for long run by the hideous law,
As mice by lions, hath pick'd out an act,
Under whose heavy sense your brother's life
Falls into forfeit: he arrests him on it,
And follows close the rigour of the statute,
To make him an example. All hope is gone,
Unless you have the grace by your fair prayer
To soften Angelo; and that 's my pith of business
Twixt you and your poor brother.

ISABELLA. Doth he so seek his life?

LUCIO.   He 's censur'd him
    Already; and, as I hear, the provost hath
    A warrant for his execution.

ISABELLA. Alas! what poor ability 's in me
    To do him good?

LUCIO.   Assay the power you have.

ISABELLA. My power? alas! I doubt—

LUCIO.   Our doubts are traitors,
    And make us lose the good we oft might win,
    By fearing to attempt. Go to Lord Angelo,
    And let him learn to know, when maidens sue,
    Men give like gods; but when they weep and kneel,
    All their petitions are as freely theirs
    As they themselves would owe them.

ISABELLA. I 'll see what I can do.

LUCIO.   But speedily.

ISABELLA. I will about it straight;
    No longer staying but to give the Mother
    Notice of my affair. I humbly thank you:
    Commend me to my brother; soon at night
    I 'll send him certain word of my success.

LUCIO. I take my leave of you.

ISABELLA.   Good sir, adieu.   *Exeunt*

ACT TWO

SCENE ONE

A Hall in Angelo's House.

*Enter Angelo, Escalus, a Justice, Provost, Officers,
and other Attendants*

ANGELO. We must not make a scarecrow of the law,
Setting it up to fear the birds of prey,
And let it keep one shape, till custom make it
Their perch and not their terror.

ESCALUS.   Ay, but yet
Let us be keen and rather cut a little,
Than fall, and bruise to death. Alas! this gentleman,
Whom I would save, had a most noble father.
Let but your honour know,—
Whom I believe to be most strait in virtue,—
That, in the working of your own affections,
Had time coher'd with place or place with wishing,
Or that the resolute acting of your blood
Could have attain'd the effect of your own purpose,
Whether you had not, some time in your life,
Err'd in this point which now you censure him,
And pull'd the law upon you.

ANGELO. 'Tis one thing to be tempted, Escalus,
Another thing to fall. I not deny,
The jury, passing on the prisoner's life,
May in the sworn twelve have a thief or two
Guiltier than him they try; what 's open made to justice,
That justice seizes: what know the laws
That thieves do pass on thieves? 'Tis very pregnant,
The jewel that we find, we stoop and take it
Because we see it; but what we do not see
We tread upon, and never think of it.
You may not so extenuate his offence

For I have had such faults; but rather tell me,
When I, that censure him, do so offend,
Let mine own judgment pattern out my death,
And nothing come in partial. Sir, he must die.

ESCALUS. Be it as your wisdom will.

ANGELO.   Where is the provost?

PROVOST. Here, if it like your honour.

ANGELO.   See that Claudio
Be executed by nine to-morrow morning:
Bring him his confessor, let him be prepar'd;
For that's the utmost of his pilgrimage.   *Exit Provost*

ESCALUS. Well, heaven forgive him, and forgive us all!
Some rise by sin, and some by virtue fall:
Some run from brakes of ice, and answer none,
And some condemnèd for a fault alone.

Enter Elbow and Officers, with Froth and Pompey

ELBOW. Come, bring them away: if these be good people in
a common-weal that do nothing but use their abuses in
common houses, I know no law: bring them away.

ANGELO. How now, sir! What's your name, and what's the
matter?

ELBOW. If it please your honour, I am the poor duke's constable, and my name is Elbow: I do lean upon justice, sir;
and do bring in here before your good honour two notorious benefactors.

ANGELO. Benefactors! Well; what benefactors are they? are
they not malefactors?

ELBOW. If it please your honour, I know not well what they
are; but precise villains they are, that I am sure of, and
void of all profanation in the world that good Christians
ought to have.

ESCALUS. This comes off well: here's a wise officer.

ANGELO. Go to: what quality are they of? Elbow is your
name? Why dost thou not speak, Elbow?

POMPEY. He cannot, sir: he's out at elbow.

ANGELO. What are you, sir?

ELBOW. He, sir! a tapster, sir; parcel-bawd; one that serves
a bad woman, whose house, sir, was, as they say, plucked
down in the suburbs; and now she professes a hot-house,
which, I think, is a very ill house too.

ESCALUS. How know you that?

ELBOW. My wife, sir, whom I detest before heaven and your honour,—

ESCALUS. How! thy wife?

ELBOW. Ay, sir; whom, I thank heaven, is an honest woman,—

ESCALUS. Dost thou detest her therefore?

ELBOW. I say, sir, I will detest myself also, as well as she, that this house, if it be not a bawd's house, it is pity of her life, for it is a naughty house.

ESCALUS. How dost thou know that, constable?

ELBOW. Marry, sir, by my wife; who, if she had been a woman cardinally given, might have been accused in fornication, adultery, and all uncleanliness there.

ESCALUS. By the woman's means?

ELBOW. Ay, sir, by Mistress Overdone's means; but as she spit in his face, so she defied him.

POMPEY. Sir, if it please your honour, this is not so.

ELBOW. Prove it before these varlets here, thou honourable man, prove it.

ESCALUS. (*To Angelo*) Do you hear how he misplaces?

POMPEY. Sir, she came in, great with child, and longing,— saving your honour's reverence,—for stewed prunes. Sir, we had but two in the house, which at that very distant time stood, as it were, in a fruit-dish, a dish of some three-pence; your honours have seen such dishes; they are not China dishes, but very good dishes.

ESCALUS. Go to, go to: no matter for the dish, sir.

POMPEY. No, indeed, sir, not of a pin; you are therein in the right: but to the point. As I say, this Mistress Elbow, being, as I say, with child, and being great-bellied, and longing, as I said, for prunes, and having but two in the dish, as I said, Master Froth here, this very man, having eaten the rest, as I said, and, as I say, paying for them very honestly; for, as you know, Master Froth, I could not give you three-pence again.

FROTH. No, indeed.

POMPEY. Very well: you being then, if you be remembered, cracking the stones of the foresaid prunes,—

FROTH. Ay, so I did, indeed.

POMPEY. Why, very well: I telling you then, if you be remembered, that such a one and such a one were past cure of the thing you wot of, unless they kept very good diet, as I told you,—

FROTH. All this is true.

POMPEY. Why, very well then.—

ESCALUS. Come, you are a tedious fool: to the purpose. What was done to Elbow's wife, that he hath cause to complain of? Come me to what was done to her.

POMPEY. Sir, your honour cannot come to that yet.

ESCALUS. No, sir, nor I mean it not.

POMPEY. Sir, but you shall come to it, by your honour's leave. And, I beseech you, look into Master Froth here, sir; a man of fourscore pound a year, whose father died at Hallowmas. Was 't not at Hallowmas, Master Froth?

FROTH. All-hallownd eve.

POMPEY. Why, very well: I hope here be truths. He, sir, sitting, as I say, in a lower chair, sir; 'twas in the Bunch of Grapes, where indeed, you have a delight to sit, have you not?

FROTH. I have so, because it is an open room and good for winter.

POMPEY. Why, very well then: I hope here be truths.

ANGELO. This will last out a night in Russia,
When nights are longest there: I 'll take my leave,
And leave you to the hearing of the cause,
Hoping you 'll find good cause to whip them all.

ESCALUS. I think no less. Good-morrow to your lordship.

Exit Angelo

Now, sir, come on: what was done to Elbow's wife, once more?

POMPEY. Once, sir? there was nothing done to her once.

ELBOW. I beseech you, sir, ask him what this man did to my wife.

POMPEY. I beseech your honour, ask me.

ESCALUS. Well, sir, what did this gentleman to her?

POMPEY. I beseech you, sir, look in this gentleman's face. Good Master Froth, look upon his honour; 'tis for a good purpose. Doth your honour mark his face?

ESCALUS. Ay, sir, very well.

POMPEY. Nay, I beseech you, mark it well.

ESCALUS. Well, I do so.

POMPEY. Doth your honour see any harm in his face?

ESCALUS. Why, no.

POMPEY. I 'll be supposed upon a book, his face is the worst
thing about him. Good, then; if his face be the worst
thing about him, how could Master Froth do the constable's wife any harm? I would know that of your honour.

ESCALUS. He 's in the right. Constable, what say you to it?

ELBOW. First, an' it like you, the house is a respected
house; next, this is a respected fellow, and his mistress is
a respected woman.

POMPEY. By this hand, sir, his wife is a more respected person than any of us all.

ELBOW. Varlet, thou liest: thou liest, wicked varlet. The
time is yet to come that she was ever respected with
man, woman, or child.

POMPEY. Sir, she was respected with him before he married
with her.

ESCALUS. Which is the wiser here? Justice, or Iniquity? Is
this true?

ELBOW. O thou caitiff! O thou varlet! O thou wicked Hannibal! I respected with her before I was married to her?
If ever I was respected with her, or she with me, let not
your worship think me the poor duke's officer. Prove this,
thou wicked Hannibal, or I 'll have mine action of battery
on thee.

ESCALUS. If he took you a box o' th' ear, you might have
your action of slander too.

ELBOW. Marry, I thank your good worship for it. What is 't
your worship's pleasure I shall do with this wicked caitiff?

ESCALUS. Truly, officer, because he hath some offences in
him that thou wouldst discover if thou couldst, let him
continue in his courses till thou knowest what they are.

ELBOW. Marry, I thank your worship for it. Thou seest,
thou wicked varlet, now, what 's come upon thee: thou
art to continue now, thou varlet, thou art to continue.

ESCALUS. Where were you born, friend?

FROTH. Here in Vienna, sir.

ESCALUS. Are you of fourscore pounds a year?

FROTH. Yes, an 't please you, sir.

ESCALUS. So. (*To Pompey*) What trade are you of, sir?

POMPEY. A tapster; a poor widow's tapster.

ESCALUS. Your mistress' name?

POMPEY. Mistress Overdone.

ESCALUS. Hath she had any more than one husband?

POMPEY. Nine, sir; Overdone by the last.

ESCALUS. Nine!—Come hither to me, Master Froth. Master
Froth, I would not have you acquainted with tapsters;
they will draw you, Master Froth, and you will hang
them. Get you gone, and let me hear no more of you.

FROTH. I thank your worship. For mine own part, I never
come into any room in a taphouse, but I am drawn in.

ESCALUS. Well: no more of it, Master Froth: farewell. (*Exit
Froth*)—Come you hither to me, Master tapster. What 's
your name, Master tapster?

POMPEY. Pompey.

ESCALUS. What else?

POMPEY. Bum, sir.

ESCALUS. Troth, and your bum is the greatest thing about
you, so that, in the beastliest sense, you are Pompey the
Great. Pompey, you are partly a bawd, Pompey, howsoever you colour it in being a tapster, are you not? Come,
tell me true; it shall be the better for you.

POMPEY. Truly, sir, I am a poor fellow that would live.

ESCALUS. How would you live, Pompey? by being a bawd?
What do you think of the trade, Pompey? is it a lawful
trade?

POMPEY. If the law would allow it, sir.

ESCALUS. But the law will not allow it, Pompey; nor it shall
not be allowed in Vienna.

POMPEY. Does your worship mean to geld and splay all the
youth of the city?

ESCALUS. No, Pompey.

POMPEY. Truly, sir, in my humble opinion, they will to 't
then. If your worship will take order for the drabs and
the knaves, you need not to fear the bawds.

ESCALUS. There are pretty orders beginning, I can tell you:
it is but heading and hanging.

POMPEY. If you head and hang all that offend that way but
for ten year together, you 'll be glad to give out a commission for more heads. If this law hold in Vienna ten
year, I 'll rent the fairest house in it after threepence a
bay. If you live to see this come to pass, say, Pompey
told you so.

ESCALUS. Thank you, good Pompey; and, in requital of
your prophecy, hark you: I advise you, let me not find

you before me again upon any complaint whatsoever; no,
not for dwelling where you do; if I do, Pompey, I shall
beat you to your tent, and prove a shrewd Cæsar to you.
In plain dealing, Pompey, I shall have you whipt. So, for
this time, Pompey, fare you well.

POMPEY. I thank your worship for your good counsel;—
(*Aside*) but I shall follow it as the flesh and fortune shall
better determine.
Whip me! No, no; let carman whip his jade;
The valiant heart 's not whipt out of his trade.   *Exit*

ESCALUS. Come hither to me, Master Elbow; come hither,
Master constable. How long have you been in this place
of constable?

ELBOW. Seven year and a half, sir.

ESCALUS. I thought, by your readiness in the office, you had
continued in it some time. You say, seven years together?

ELBOW. And a half, sir.

ESCALUS. Alas! it hath been great pains to you! They do you
wrong to put you so oft upon 't. Are there not men in
your ward sufficient to serve it?

ELBOW. Faith, sir, few of any wit in such matters. As they
are chosen, they are glad to choose me for them: I do it
for some piece of money, and go through with all.

ESCALUS. Look you bring me in the names of some six or
seven, the most sufficient of your parish.

ELBOW. To your worship's house, sir?

ESCALUS. To my house. Fare you well.   *Exit Elbow*
What 's o'clock, think you?

JUSTICE. Eleven, sir.

ESCALUS. I pray you home to dinner with me.

JUSTICE. I humbly thank you.

ESCALUS. It grieves me for the death of Claudio;
But there is no remedy.

JUSTICE. Lord Angelo is severe.

ESCALUS.   It is but needful:
Mercy is not itself, that oft looks so;
Pardon is still the nurse of second woe.
But yet, poor Claudio! There 's no remedy.
Come, sir.   *Exeunt*

SCENE TWO

Another Room in the Same.

Enter Provost and a Servant

SERVANT. He 's hearing of a cause: he will come straight:
I 'll tell him of you.

PROVOST.   Pray you, do. (*Exit Servant*) I 'll know
His pleasure; may be he will relent. Alas!
He hath but as offended in a dream:
All sects, all ages smack of this vice, and he
To die for it!

Enter Angelo

ANGELO.   Now, what 's the matter, provost?

PROVOST. Is it your will Claudio shall die to-morrow?

ANGELO. Did I not tell thee, yea? hadst thou not order?
Why dost thou ask again?

PROVOST.   Lest I might be too rash.
Under your good correction, I have seen,
When, after execution, Judgment hath
Repented o'er his doom.

ANGELO.   Go to; let that be mine:
Do you your office, or give up your place,
And you shall well be spar'd.

PROVOST.   I crave your honour's pardon.
What shall be done, sir, with the groaning Juliet?
She 's very near her hour.

ANGELO.   Dispose of her
To some more fitter place; and that with speed.

Re-enter Servant

SERVANT. Here is the sister of the man condemn'd
Desires access to you.

ANGELO.   Hath he a sister?

PROVOST. Ay, my good lord; a very virtuous maid,
And to be shortly of a sisterhood,
If not already.

ANGELO.   Well, let her be admitted.   *Exit Servant*
See you the fornicatress be remov'd:
Let her have needful, but not lavish, means;
There shall be order for 't.

Enter Isabella and Lucio

PROVOST.   God save your honour!
                                  Offering to retire
ANGELO. Stay a little while.—(*To Isabella*) You 're welcome.
     What 's your will?
ISABELLA. I am a woful suitor to your honour,
     Please but your honour hear me.
ANGELO.   Well; what 's your suit?
ISABELLA. There is a vice that most I do abhor,
     And most desire should meet the blow of justice,
     For which I would not plead, but that I must;
     For which I must not plead, but that I am
     At war 'twixt will and will not.
ANGELO.   Well; the matter?
ISABELLA. I have a brother is condemn'd to die:
     I do beseech you, let it be his fault,
     And not my brother.
PROVOST.   (*Aside*) Heaven give thee moving graces!
ANGELO. Condemn the fault, and not the actor of it?
     Why, every fault 's condemn'd ere it be done.
     Mine were the very cipher of a function,
     To fine the faults whose fine stands in record,
     And let go by the actor.
ISABELLA.   O just, but severe law!
     I had a brother, then.—Heaven keep your honour!
                                            Retiring
LUCIO. (*Aside to Isabella*) Give 't not o'er so: to him again,
     entreat him;
     Kneel down before him, hang upon his gown;
     You are too cold; if you should need a pin,
     You could not with more tame a tongue desire it.
     To him, I say!
ISABELLA. Must he needs die?
ANGELO.   Maiden, no remedy.
ISABELLA. Yes; I do think that you might pardon him,
     And neither heaven nor man grieve at the mercy.
ANGELO. I will not do 't.
ISABELLA.   But can you, if you would?
ANGELO. Look, what I will not, that I cannot do.
ISABELLA. But might you do 't, and do the world no wrong,
     If so your heart were touch'd with that remorse
     As mine is to him?

ANGELO.   He 's sentenc'd: 'tis too late.

LUCIO. (*Aside to Isabella*) You are too cold.

ISABELLA. Too late? Why, no; I, that do speak a word,
    May call it back again. Well, believe this,
    No ceremony that to great ones 'longs,
    Not the king's crown, nor the deputed sword,
    The marshal's truncheon, nor the judge's robe,
    Become them with one half so good a grace
    As mercy does.
    If he had been as you, and you as he,
    You would have slipt like him; but he, like you,
    Would not have been so stern.

ANGELO.   Pray you, be gone.

ISABELLA. I would to heaven I had your potency,
    And you were Isabel! Should it then be thus?
    No; I would tell what 'twere to be a judge,
    And what a prisoner.

LUCIO. (*Aside to Isabella*) Ay, touch him; there 's the vein.

ANGELO. Your brother is a forfeit of the law
    And you but waste your words.

ISABELLA.   Alas! alas!
    Why, all the souls that were were forfeit once;
    And He that might the vantage best have took,
    Found out the remedy. How would you be,
    If He, which is the top of judgment, should
    But judge you as you are? O! think on that,
    And mercy then will breathe within your lips,
    Like man new made.

ANGELO.   Be you content, fair maid;
    It is the law, not I, condemn your brother:
    Were he my kinsman, brother, or my son,
    It should be thus with him: he must die to-morrow.

ISABELLA. To-morrow! O! that 's sudden! Spare him, spare
    him!
    He 's not prepar'd for death. Even for our kitchens
    We kill the fowl of season: shall we serve heaven
    With less respect than we do minister
    To our gross selves? Good, good my lord, bethink you:
    Who is it that hath died for this offence?
    There 's many have committed it.

LUCIO.   (*Aside to Isabella*) Ay, well said.

ANGELO. The law hath not been dead, though it hath slept:

Those many had not dar'd to do that evil,
If that the first that did th' edict infringe
Had answer'd for his deed: now 'tis awake,
Takes note of what is done, and, like a prophet,
Looks in a glass, that shows what future evils,
Either new, or by remissness new-conceiv'd,
And so in progress to be hatch'd and born,
Are now to have no successive degrees,
But, ere they live, to end.

ISABELLA.   Yet show some pity.

ANGELO. I show it most of all when I show justice;
For then I pity those I do not know,
Which a dismiss'd offence would after gall,
And do him right, that, answering one foul wrong,
Lives not to act another. Be satisfied:
Your brother dies to-morrow: be content.

ISABELLA. So you must be the first that gives this sentence,
And he that suffers. O! it is excellent
To have a giant's strength, but it is tyrannous
To use it like a giant.

LUCIO. (*Aside to Isabella*) That 's well said.

ISABELLA. Could great men thunder
As Jove himself does, Jove would ne'er be quiet,
For every pelting, petty officer
Would use his heaven for thunder; nothing but thunder,
Merciful heaven!
Thou rather with thy sharp and sulphurous bolt
Split'st the unwedgeable and gnarled oak
Than the soft myrtle; but man, proud man,
Drest in a little brief authority,
Most ignorant of what he 's most assur'd,
His glassy essence, like an angry ape,
Plays such fantastic tricks before high heaven
As make the angels weep; who, with our spleens,
Would all themselves laugh mortal.

LUCIO. (*Aside to Isabella*) O, to him, to him, wench! He
    will relent:
He 's coming: I perceive 't.

PROVOST.   (*Aside*) Pray heaven she win him!

ISABELLA. We cannot weigh our brother with ourself:
Great men may jest with saints; 'tis wit in them,
But, in the less foul profanation.

LUCIO. (*Aside to Isabella*) Thou 'rt in the right, girl: more o' that.

ISABELLA. That in the captain 's but a choleric word,
Which in the soldier is flat blasphemy.

LUCIO. (*Aside to Isabella*) Art advis'd o' that? more on 't.

ANGELO. Why do you put these sayings upon me?

ISABELLA. Because authority, though it err like others,
Hath yet a kind of medicine in itself,
That skins the vice o' the top. Go to your bosom;
Knock there, and ask your heart what it doth know
That 's like my brother's fault: if it confess
A natural guiltiness such as is his,
Let it not sound a thought upon your tongue
Against my brother's life.

ANGELO.   She speaks, and 'tis
Such sense that my sense breeds with it. Fare you well.

ISABELLA. Gentle my lord, turn back.

ANGELO. I will bethink me. Come again to-morrow.

ISABELLA. Hark how I 'll bribe you. Good my lord, turn back.

ANGELO. How! bribe me?

ISABELLA. Ay, with such gifts that heaven shall share with you.

LUCIO. (*Aside to Isabella*) You had marr'd all else.

ISABELLA. Not with fond sicles of the tested gold,
Or stones whose rates are either rich or poor
As fancy values them; but with true prayers
That shall be up at heaven and enter there
Ere sun-rise: prayers from preserved souls,
From fasting maids whose minds are dedicate
To nothing temporal.

ANGELO.   Well; come to me to-morrow.

LUCIO. (*Aside to Isabella*) Go to; 'tis well: away!

ISABELLA. Heaven keep your honour safe!

ANGELO.   (*Aside*) Amen:
For I am that way going to temptation,
Where prayers cross.

ISABELLA.   At what hour to-morrow
Shall I attend your lordship?

ANGELO.   At any time 'fore noon.

ISABELLA. Save your honour!

                                Exeunt Isabella, Lucio, and Provost

ANGELO.   From thee; even from thy virtue!
  What 's this? what 's this? Is this her fault or mine?
  The tempter or the tempted, who sins most?
  Ha!
  Not she; nor doth she tempt: but it is I,
  That, lying by the violet in the sun,
  Do as the carrion does, not as the flower,
  Corrupt with virtuous season. Can it be
  That modesty may more betray our sense
  Than woman's lightness? Having waste ground enough,
  Shall we desire to raze the sanctuary,
  And pitch our evils there? O, fie, fie, fie!
  What dost thou, or what art thou, Angelo?
  Dost thou desire her foully for those things
  That make her good? O, let her brother live!
  Thieves for their robbery have authority
  When judges steal themselves. What! do I love her,
  That I desire to hear her speak again,
  And feast upon her eyes? What is 't I dream on?
  O cunning enemy, that, to catch a saint,
  With saints dost bait thy hook! Most dangerous
  Is that temptation that doth goad us on
  To sin in loving virtue: never could the strumpet,
  With all her double vigour, art and nature,
  Once stir my temper; but this virtuous maid
  Subdues me quite. Ever till now,
  When men were fond, I smil'd and wonder'd how.   *Exit*

SCENE THREE

A Room in a Prison.

Enter Duke, disguised as a Friar, and Provost

DUKE. Hail to you, provost! So I think you are.
PROVOST. I am the provost. What 's your will, good friar?
DUKE. Bound by my charity and my bless'd order,
  I come to visit the afflicted spirits
  Here in the prison: do me the common right
  To let me see them and to make me know
  The nature of their crimes, that I may minister
  To them accordingly.

PROVOST. I would do more than that, if more were needful.
  Look, here comes one: a gentlewoman of mine,
  Who, falling in the flaws of her own youth,
  Hath blister'd her report. She is with child,
  And he that got it, sentenc'd; a young man
  More fit to do another such offence,
  Than die for this.

Enter Juliet

DUKE. When must he die?
PROVOST.   As I do think, to-morrow.
  (*To Juliet*) I have provided for you: stay a while,
  And you shall be conducted.
DUKE. Repent you, fair one, of the sin you carry?
JULIET. I do, and bear the shame most patiently.
DUKE. I 'll teach you how you shall arraign your conscience,
  And try your penitence, if it be sound,
  Or hollowly put on.
JULIET.   I 'll gladly learn.
DUKE. Love you the man that wrong'd you?
JULIET. Yes, as I love the woman that wrong'd him.
DUKE. So then it seems your most offenceful act
  Was mutually committed?
JULIET.   Mutually.
DUKE. Then was your sin of heavier kind than his.
JULIET. I do confess it, and repent it, father.
DUKE. 'Tis meet so, daughter: but lest you do repent,
  As that the sin hath brought you to this shame,
  Which sorrow is always toward ourselves, not heaven,
  Showing we would not spare heaven as we love it,
  But as we stand in fear,—
JULIET. I do repent me, as it is an evil,
  And take the shame with joy.
DUKE.   There rest.
  Your partner, as I hear, must die to-morrow,
  And I am going with instruction to him.
  God's grace go with you! Benedicite!   *Exit*
JULIET. Must die to-morrow! O injurious love,
  That respites me a life, whose very comfort
  Is still a dying horror!
PROVOST.   'Tis pity of him.   *Exeunt*

SCENE FOUR

A Room in Angelo's House.

Enter Angelo

ANGELO. When I would pray and think, I think and pray
To several subjects: heaven hath my empty words,
Whilst my invention, hearing not my tongue,
Anchors on Isabel: heaven in my mouth,
As if I did but only chew his name,
And in my heart the strong and swelling evil
Of my conception. The state, whereon I studied,
Is like a good thing, being often read,
Grown fear'd and tedious; yea, my gravity,
Wherein, let no man hear me, I take pride,
Could I with boot change for an idle plume,
Which the air beats for vain. O place! O form!
How often dost thou with thy case, thy habit,
Wrench awe from fools, and tie the wiser souls
To thy false seeming! Blood, thou art blood:
Let 's write good angel on the devil's horn,
'Tis not the devil's crest.

Enter a Servant

How now! who 's there?

SERVANT.　　　　　　　　One Isabel, a sister,
Desires access to you.

ANGELO.　　　　　　Teach her the way.　*Exit Servant*
O heavens!
Why does my blood thus muster to my heart,
Making both it unable for itself,
And dispossessing all my other parts
Of necessary fitness?
So play the foolish throngs with one that swounds;
Come all to help him, and so stop the air
By which he should revive: and even so
The general, subject to a well-wish'd king,
Quit their own part, and in obsequious fondness
Crowd to his presence, where their untaught love
Must needs appear offence.

Enter Isabella

How now, fair maid!

ISABELLA. I am come to know your pleasure.

ANGELO. That you might know it, would much better please
  me,
  Than to demand what 'tis. Your brother cannot live.

ISABELLA. Even so. Heaven keep your honour!

ANGELO. Yet may he live awhile; and, it may be,
  As long as you or I: yet he must die.

ISABELLA. Under your sentence?

ANGELO. Yea.

ISABELLA. When, I beseech you? that in his reprieve,
  Longer or shorter, he may be so fitted
  That his soul sicken not.

ANGELO. Ha! fie, these filthy vices! It were as good
  To pardon him that hath from nature stolen
  A man already made, as to remit
  Their saucy sweetness that do coin heaven's image
  In stamps that are forbid: 'tis all as easy
  Falsely to take away a life true made,
  As to put metal in restrained means
  To make a false one.

ISABELLA. 'Tis set down so in heaven, but not in earth.

ANGELO. Say you so? Then I shall pose you quickly.
  Which had you rather, that the most just law
  Now took your brother's life; or, to redeem him,
  Give up your body to such sweet uncleanness
  As she that he hath stain'd?

ISABELLA.   Sir, believe this,
  I had rather give my body than my soul.

ANGELO. I talk not of your soul. Our compell'd sins
  Stand more for number than for accompt.

ISABELLA.   How say you?

ANGELO. Nay, I 'll not warrant that; for I can speak
  Against the thing I say. Answer to this:
  I, now the voice of the recorded law,
  Pronounce a sentence on your brother's life:
  Might there not be a charity in sin
  To save this brother's life?

ISABELLA.   Please you to do 't,
  I 'll take it as a peril to my soul;
  It is no sin at all, but charity.

ANGELO. Pleas'd you to do 't, at peril of your soul,

Were equal poise of sin and charity.

ISABELLA. That I do beg his life, if it be sin,
Heaven let me bear it! you granting of my suit,
If that be sin, I 'll make it my morn prayer
To have it added to the faults of mine,
And nothing of your answer.

ANGELO.   Nay, but hear me.
Your sense pursues not mine: either you are ignorant,
Or seem so craftily; and that 's not good.

ISABELLA. Let me be ignorant, and in nothing good,
But graciously to know I am no better.

ANGELO. Thus wisdom wishes to appear most bright
When it doth tax itself; as these black masks
Proclaim an enshield beauty ten times louder
Than beauty could, display'd. But mark me;
To be received plain, I 'll speak more gross:
Your brother is to die.

ISABELLA. So.

ANGELO. And his offence is so, as it appears,
Accountant to the law upon that pain.

ISABELLA. True.

ANGELO. Admit no other way to save his life,—
As I subscribe not that, nor any other,
But in the loss of question,—that you, his sister,
Finding yourself desir'd of such a person,
Whose credit with the judge, or own great place,
Could fetch your brother from the manacles
Of the all-building law; and that there were
No earthly mean to save him, but that either
You must lay down the treasures of your body
To this suppos'd, or else to let him suffer;
What would you do?

ISABELLA. As much for my poor brother as myself:
That is, were I under the terms of death,
Th' impression of keen whips I 'd wear as rubies,
And strip myself to death, as to a bed
That, longing, have been sick for, ere I 'd yield
My body up to shame.

ANGELO.   Then must your brother die.

ISABELLA. And 'twere the cheaper way:
Better it were a brother died at once,
Than that a sister, by redeeming him,

Should die for ever.

ANGELO. Were not you then as cruel as the sentence
That you have slander'd so?

ISABELLA. Ignomy in ransom and free pardon
Are of two houses: lawful mercy
Is nothing kin to foul redemption.

ANGELO. You seem'd of late to make the law a tyrant;
And rather prov'd the sliding of your brother
A merriment than a vice.

ISABELLA. O, pardon me, my lord! it oft falls out,
To have what we would have, we speak not what we
mean.
I something do excuse the thing I hate,
For his advantage that I dearly love.

ANGELO. We are all frail.

ISABELLA.   Else let my brother die,
If not a feodary, but only he
Owe and succeed thy weakness.

ANGELO. Nay, women are frail too.

ISABELLA. Ay, as the glasses where they view themselves,
Which are as easy broke as they make forms.
Women! Help heaven! men their creation mar
In profiting by them. Nay, call us ten times frail,
For we are soft as our complexions are,
And credulous to false prints.

ANGELO.   I think it well:
And from this testimony of your own sex,—
Since I suppose we are made to be no stronger
Than faults may shake our frames,—let me be bold;
I do arrest your words. Be that you are,
That is, a woman; if you be more, you 're none;
If you be one, as you are well express'd
By all external warrants, show it now,
By putting on the destin'd livery.

ISABELLA. I have no tongue but one: gentle my lord,
Let me entreat you speak the former language.

ANGELO. Plainly conceive, I love you.

ISABELLA. My brother did love Juliet; and you tell me
That he shall die for 't.

ANGELO. He shall not, Isabel, if you give me love.

ISABELLA. I know your virtue hath a licence in 't,
Which seems a little fouler than it is,

To pluck on others.

ANGELO.   Believe me, on mine honour,
My words express my purpose.

ISABELLA. Ha! little honour to be much believ'd,
And most pernicious purpose! Seeming, seeming!
I will proclaim thee, Angelo; look for 't:
Sign me a present pardon for my brother,
Or with an outstretch'd throat I 'll tell the world aloud
What man thou art.

ANGELO.   Who will believe thee, Isabel?
My unsoil'd name, the austereness of my life,
My vouch against you, and my place i' the state,
Will so your accusation overweigh,
That you shall stifle in your own report
And smell of calumny. I have begun;
And now I give my sensual race the rein:
Fit thy consent to my sharp appetite;
Lay by all nicety and prolixious blushes,
That banish what they sue for; redeem thy brother
By yielding up thy body to my will,
Or else he must not only die the death,
But thy unkindness shall his death draw out
To lingering sufferance. Answer me to-morrow,
Or, by the affection that now guides me most,
I 'll prove a tyrant to him. As for you,
Say what you can, my false o'erweighs your true.   *Exit*

ISABELLA. To whom should I complain? Did I tell this,
Who would believe me? O perilous mouths!
That bear in them one and the self-same tongue,
Either of condemnation or approof,
Bidding the law make curt'sy to their will;
Hooking both right and wrong to th' appetite,
To follow as it draws. I 'll to my brother:
Though he hath fallen by prompture of the blood,
Yet hath he in him such a mind of honour,
That, had he twenty heads to tender down
On twenty bloody blocks, he 'd yield them up,
Before his sister should her body stoop
To such abhorr'd pollution.
Then, Isabel, live chaste, and, brother, die:
More than our brother is our chastity.
I 'll tell him yet of Angelo's request,
And fit his mind to death, for his soul's rest.   *Exit*

ACT THREE

SCENE ONE

A Room in the Prison.

Enter Duke, as a friar, Claudio, and Provost

DUKE. So then you hope of pardon from Lord Angelo?

CLAUDIO. The miserable have no other medicine
  But only hope:
  I have hope to live, and am prepar'd to die.

DUKE. Be absolute for death; either death or life
  Shall thereby be the sweeter. Reason thus with life:
  If I do lose thee, I do lose a thing
  That none but fools would keep: a breath thou art,
  Servile to all the skyey influences,
  That dost this habitation, where thou keep'st,
  Hourly afflict. Merely, thou art death's fool;
  For him thou labour'st by thy flight to shun,
  And yet run'st toward him still. Thou art not noble;
  For all th' accommodations that thou bear'st
  Are nurs'd by baseness. Thou art by no means valiant;
  For thou dost fear the soft and tender fork
  Of a poor worm. Thy best of rest is sleep,
  And that thou oft provok'st; yet grossly fear'st
  Thy death, which is no more. Thou art not thyself;
  For thou exist'st on many a thousand grains
  That issue out of dust. Happy thou art not;
  For what thou hast not, still thou striv'st to get,
  And what thou hast, forget'st. Thou art not certain;
  For thy complexion shifts to strange effects,
  After the moon. If thou art rich, thou'rt poor;
  For, like an ass whose back with ingots bows,
  Thou bear'st thy heavy riches but a journey,
  And death unloads thee. Friend hast thou none;
  For thine own bowels, which do call thee sire,

The mere effusion of thy proper loins,
Do curse the gout, serpigo, and the rheum,
For ending thee no sooner. Thou hast nor youth nor age;
But, as it were, an after-dinner's sleep,
Dreaming on both; for all thy blessed youth
Becomes as aged, and doth beg the alms
Of palsied eld; and when thou art old and rich,
Thou hast neither heat, affection, limb, nor beauty,
To make thy riches pleasant. What 's yet in this
That bears the name of life? Yet in this life
Lie hid moe thousand deaths: yet death we fear,
That makes these odds all even.

CLAUDIO.   I humbly thank you.
To sue to live, I find I seek to die,
And, seeking death, find life: let it come on.

ISABELLA. (*Within*) What ho! Peace here; grace and good
    company!

PROVOST. Who 's there? come in: the wish deserves a wel-
    come.

DUKE. Dear sir, ere long I 'll visit you again.

CLAUDIO. Most holy sir, I thank you.

                Enter Isabella

ISABELLA. My business is a word or two with Claudio.

PROVOST. And very welcome. Look, signior; here 's your
    sister.

DUKE. Provost, a word with you.

PROVOST. As many as you please.

DUKE. Bring me to hear them speak, where I may be con-
    ceal'd.   *Exeunt Duke and Provost*

CLAUDIO. Now, sister, what 's the comfort?

ISABELLA. Why, as all comforts are; most good, most good
    indeed.
    Lord Angelo, having affairs to heaven,
    Intends you for his swift ambassador,
    Where you shall be an everlasting leiger:
    Therefore, your best appointment make with speed;
    To-morrow you set on.

CLAUDIO.   Is there no remedy?

ISABELLA. None, but such remedy, as to save a head
    To cleave a heart in twain.

CLAUDIO.   But is there any?

ISABELLA. Yes, brother, you may live:

There is a devilish mercy in the judge,
If you 'll implore it, that will free your life,
But fetter you till death.

CLAUDIO.   Perpetual durance?

ISABELLA. Ay, just; perpetual durance, a restraint,
Though all the world's vastidity you had,
To a determin'd scope.

CLAUDIO.   But in what nature?

ISABELLA. In such a one as, you consenting to 't,
Would bark your honour from that trunk you bear,
And leave you naked.

CLAUDIO.   Let me know the point.

ISABELLA. O, I do fear thee, Claudio; and I quake,
Lest thou a feverous life shouldst entertain,
And six or seven winters more respect
Than a perpetual honour. Dar'st thou die?
The sense of death is most in apprehension,
And the poor beetle, that we tread upon,
In corporal sufferance finds a pang as great
As when a giant dies.

CLAUDIO.   Why give you me this shame?
Think you I can a resolution fetch
From flowery tenderness? If I must die,
I will encounter darkness as a bride,
And hug it in mine arms.

ISABELLA. There spake my brother: there my father's grave
Did utter forth a voice. Yes, thou must die:
Thou art too noble to conserve a life
In base appliances. This outward-sainted deputy,
Whose settled visage and deliberate word
Nips youth i' the head, and follies doth enmew
As falcon doth the fowl, is yet a devil;
His filth within being cast, he would appear
A pond as deep as hell.

CLAUDIO.   The prenzie Angelo?

ISABELLA. O, 'tis the cunning livery of hell,
The damned'st body to invest and cover
In prenzie guards! Dost thou think, Claudio?
If I would yield him my virginity,
Thou mightst be freed.

CLAUDIO.   O heavens! it cannot be.

ISABELLA. Yes, he would give 't thee, from this rank offence,
  So to offend him still. This night 's the time
  That I should do what I abhor to name,
  Or else thou diest to-morrow.

CLAUDIO.   Thou shalt not do 't.

ISABELLA. O! were it but my life,
  I 'd throw it down for your deliverance
  As frankly as a pin.

CLAUDIO.   Thanks, dear Isabel.

ISABELLA. Be ready, Claudio, for your death to-morrow.

CLAUDIO. Yes. Has he affections in him,
  That thus can make him bite the law by the nose,
  When he would force it? Sure, it is no sin;
  Or of the deadly seven it is the least.

ISABELLA. Which is the least?

CLAUDIO. If it were damnable, he being so wise,
  Why would he for the momentary trick
  Be perdurably fin'd? O Isabel!

ISABELLA. What says my brother?

CLAUDIO.   Death is a fearful thing.

ISABELLA. And shamed life a hateful.

CLAUDIO. Ay, but to die, and go we know not where;
  To lie in cold obstruction and to rot;
  This sensible warm motion to become
  A kneaded clod; and the delighted spirit
  To bathe in fiery floods, or to reside
  In thrilling region of thick-ribbed ice;
  To be imprison'd in the viewless winds
  And blown with restless violence round about
  The pendant world; or to be worse than worst
  Of those that lawless and incertain thoughts
  Imagine howling: 'tis too horrible!
  The weariest and most loathed worldly life
  That age, ache, penury and imprisonment
  Can lay on nature is a paradise
  To what we fear of death.

ISABELLA. Alas! alas!

CLAUDIO.   Sweet sister, let me live:
  What sin you do to save a brother's life,
  Nature dispenses with the deed so far
  That it becomes a virtue.

ISABELLA.   O you beast!
O faithless coward! O dishonest wretch!
Wilt thou be made a man out of my vice?
Is 't not a kind of incest, to take life
From thine own sister's shame? What should I think?
Heaven shield my mother play'd my father fair;
For such a warped slip of wilderness
Ne'er issu'd from his blood. Take my defiance;
Die, perish! Might but my bending down
Reprieve thee from thy fate, it should proceed.
I 'll pray a thousand prayers for thy death,
No word to save thee.

CLAUDIO. Nay, hear me, Isabel.

ISABELLA.   O, fie, fie, fie!
Thy sin 's not accidental, but a trade.
Mercy to thee would prove itself a bawd:
'Tis best that thou diest quickly.   *Going*

CLAUDIO.   O hear me, Isabella.

Re-enter Duke

DUKE. Vouchsafe a word, young sister, but one word.

ISABELLA. What is your will?

DUKE. Might you dispense with your leisure, I would by
and by have some speech with you: the satisfaction I
would require is likewise your own benefit.

ISABELLA. I have no superfluous leisure: my stay must be
stolen out of other affairs; but I will attend you a while.

DUKE. (*Aside to Claudio*) Son, I have overheard what hath
past between you and your sister. Angelo had never the
purpose to corrupt her; only he hath made an assay of
her virtue to practise his judgment with the disposition
of natures. She, having the truth of honour in her, hath
made him that gracious denial which he is most glad to
receive: I am confessor to Angelo, and I know this to be
true; therefore prepare yourself to death. Do not satisfy
your resolution with hopes that are fallible: to-morrow
you must die; go to your knees and make ready.

CLAUDIO. Let me ask my sister pardon. I am so out of love
with life that I will sue to be rid of it.

DUKE. Hold you there: farewell.   *Exit Claudio*

Re-enter Provost

Provost, a word with you.

PROVOST. What 's your will, father?

DUKE. That now you are come, you will be gone. Leave me awhile with the maid: my mind promises with my habit no loss shall touch her by my company.

PROVOST. In good time.   *Exit*

DUKE. The hand that hath made you fair hath made you good: the goodness that is cheap in beauty makes beauty brief in goodness; but grace, being the soul of your complexion, shall keep the body of it ever fair. The assault that Angelo hath made to you, fortune hath conveyed to my understanding; and, but that frailty hath examples for his falling, I should wonder at Angelo. How would you do to content this substitute, and to save your brother?

ISABELLA. I am now going to resolve him; I had rather my brother die by the law than my son should be unlawfully born. But O, how much is the good duke deceived in Angelo! If ever he return and I can speak to him, I will open my lips in vain, or discover his government.

DUKE. That shall not be much amiss: yet, as the matter now stands, he will avoid your accusation; 'he made trial of you only.' Therefore, fasten your ear on my advisings: to the love I have in doing good a remedy presents itself. I do make myself believe that you may most uprighteously do a poor wronged lady a merited benefit, redeem your brother from the angry law, do no stain to your own gracious person, and much please the absent duke, if peradventure he shall ever return to have hearing of this business.

ISABELLA. Let me hear you speak further. I have spirit to do anything that appears not foul in the truth of my spirit.

DUKE. Virtue is bold, and goodness never fearful. Have you not heard speak of Mariana, the sister of Frederick, the great soldier who miscarried at sea?

ISABELLA. I have heard of the lady, and good words went with her name.

DUKE. She should this Angelo have married; was affianced to her by oath, and the nuptial appointed: between which time of the contract, and limit of the solemnity, her brother Frederick was wracked at sea, having in that perished vessel the dowry of his sister. But mark how heavily this befell to the poor gentlewoman: there she lost a noble and renowned brother, in his love toward her ever most kind and natural; with him the portion and sinew of her fortune, her marriage-dowry; with both, her combinate husband, this well-seeming Angelo.

ISABELLA. Can this be so? Did Angelo so leave her?

DUKE. Left her in her tears, and dried not one of them with his comfort; swallowed his vows whole, pretending in her discoveries of dishonour: in few, bestowed her on her own lamentation, which she yet wears for his sake; and he, a marble to her tears, is washed with them, but relents not.

ISABELLA. What a merit were it in death to take this poor maid from the world! What corruption in this life, that it will let this man live! But how out of this can she avail?

DUKE. It is a rupture that you may easily heal; and the cure of it not only saves your brother, but keeps you from dishonour in doing it.

ISABELLA. Show me how, good father.

DUKE. This forenamed maid hath yet in her the continuance of her first affection: his unjust unkindness, that in all reason should have quenched her love, hath, like an impediment in the current, made it more violent and unruly. Go you to Angelo: answer his requiring with a plausible obedience: agree with his demands to the point; only refer yourself to this advantage, first, that your stay with him may not be long, that the time may have all shadow and silence in it, and the place answer to convenience. This being granted in course, and now follows all, we shall advise this wronged maid to stead up your appointment, go in your place; if the encounter acknowledge itself hereafter, it may compel him to her recompense; and here by this is your brother saved, your honour untainted, the poor Mariana advantaged, and the corrupt deputy scaled. The maid will I frame and make fit for his attempt. If you think well to carry this, as you may, the doubleness of the benefit defends the deceit from reproof. What think you of it?

ISABELLA. The image of it gives me content already, and I trust it will grow to a most prosperous perfection.

DUKE. It lies much in your holding up. Haste you speedily to Angelo: if for this night he entreat you to his bed, give him promise of satisfaction. I will presently to St. Luke's;

there, at the moated grange, resides this dejected Mariana: at that place call upon me, and dispatch with Angelo, that it may be quickly.

ISABELLA. I thank you for this comfort. Fare you well, good
father.   *Exeunt*

SCENE TWO

The Street before the Prison.

Enter Duke, as a friar; to him Elbow, Pompey, and Officers

ELBOW. Nay, if there be no remedy for it, but that you will
needs buy and sell men and women like beasts, we shall
have all the world drink brown and white bastard.

DUKE. O heavens! what stuff is here?

POMPEY. 'Twas never merry world, since, of two usuries,
the merriest was put down, and the worser allowed by
order of law a furred gown to keep him warm; and
furred with fox and lamb skins too, to signify that craft,
being richer than innocency, stands for the facing.

ELBOW. Come your way, sir. Bless you, good father friar.

DUKE. And you, good brother father. What offence hath
this man made you, sir?

ELBOW. Marry, sir, he hath offended the law: and, sir, we
take him to be a thief too, sir; for we have found upon
him, sir, a strange picklock, which we have sent to the
deputy.

DUKE. Fie, sirrah: a bawd, a wicked bawd!
The evil that thou causest to be done,
That is thy means to live. Do thou but think
What 'tis to cram a maw or clothe a back
From such a filthy vice: say to thyself,
From their abominable and beastly touches
I drink, I eat, array myself, and live.
Canst thou believe thy living is a life,
So stinkingly depending? Go mend, go mend.

POMPEY. Indeed, it does stink in some sort, sir; but yet, sir,
I would prove—

DUKE. Nay, if the devil have given thee proofs for sin,
Thou wilt prove his. Take him to prison, officer;
Correction and instruction must both work

Ere this rude beast will profit.

ELBOW. He must before the deputy, sir; he has given him
warning. The deputy cannot abide a whoremaster: if he
be a whoremonger, and comes before him, he were as
good go a mile on his errand.

DUKE. That we were all, as some would seem to be,
From our faults, as faults from seeming, free!

ELBOW. His neck will come to your waist,—a cord, sir.

POMPEY. I spy comfort: I cry, bail. Here 's a gentleman
and a friend of mine.

Enter Lucio

LUCIO. How now, noble Pompey! What, at the wheels of
Cæsar? Art thou led in triumph? What, is there none of
Pygmalion's images, newly made woman, to be had now,
for putting the hand in the pocket and extracting it
clutched? What reply? ha? What say'st thou to this tune,
matter and method? Is 't not drowned i' the last rain, ha?
What sayest thou, Trot? Is the world as it was, man?
Which is the way? Is it sad, and few words, or how? The
trick of it?

DUKE. Still thus, and thus, still worse!

LUCIO. How doth my dear morsel, thy mistress? Procures
she still, ha?

POMPEY. Troth, sir, she hath eaten up all her beef, and she
is herself in the tub.

LUCIO. Why, 'tis good; it is the right of it; it must be so:
ever your fresh whore and your powdered bawd: an unshunned consequence; it must be so. Art going to prison,
Pompey?

POMPEY. Yes, faith, sir.

LUCIO. Why, 'tis not amiss, Pompey. Farewell. Go, say I
sent thee thither. For debt, Pompey? or how?

ELBOW. For being a bawd, for being a bawd.

LUCIO. Well, then, imprison him. If imprisonment be the
due of a bawd, why, 'tis his right: bawd is he, doubtless,
and of antiquity too; bawd-born. Farewell, good Pompey. Commend me to the prison, Pompey. You will turn
good husband now, Pompey; you will keep the house.

POMPEY. I hope, sir, your good worship will be my bail.

LUCIO. No, indeed will I not, Pompey; it is not the wear. I
will pray, Pompey, to increase your bondage: if you take

it not patiently, why, your mettle is the more. Adieu,
trusty Pompey. Bless you, friar.

DUKE. And you.

LUCIO. Does Bridget paint still, Pompey, ha?

ELBOW. Come your ways, sir; come.

POMPEY. You will not bail me then, sir?

LUCIO. Then, Pompey, nor now. What news abroad, friar?
What news?

ELBOW. Come your ways, sir; come.

LUCIO. Go to kennel, Pompey; go.

Exeunt Elbow, Pompey and Officers

What news, friar, of the duke.

DUKE. I know none. Can you tell me of any?

LUCIO. Some say he is with the Emperor of Russia; other
some, he is in Rome: but where is he, think you?

DUKE. I know not where; but wheresoever, I wish him well.

LUCIO. It was a mad fantastical trick of him to steal from
the state, and usurp the beggary he was never born to.
Lord Angelo dukes it well in his absence; he puts transgression to 't.

DUKE. He does well in 't.

LUCIO. A little more lenity to lechery would do no harm in
him: something too crabbed that way, friar.

DUKE. It is too general a vice, and severity must cure it.

LUCIO. Yes, in good sooth, the vice is of a great kindred; it
is well allied; but it is impossible to extirp it quite, friar,
till eating and drinking be put down. They say this Angelo was not made by man and woman after this downright way of creation: is it true, think you?

DUKE. How should he be made, then?

LUCIO. Some report a sea-maid spawn'd him; some that he
was begot between two stock-fishes. But it is certain that
when he makes water his urine is congealed ice; that I
know to be true; and he is a motion generative; that 's
infallible.

DUKE. You are pleasant, sir, and speak apace.

LUCIO. Why, what a ruthless thing is this in him, for the rebellion of a cod-piece to take away the life of a man!
Would the duke that is absent have done this? Ere he
would have hanged a man for the getting a hundred bastards, he would have paid for the nursing a thousand: he

had some feeling of the sport; he knew the service, and that instructed him to mercy.

DUKE. I never heard the absent duke much detected for women; he was not inclined that way.

LUCIO. O, sir, you are deceived.

DUKE. 'Tis not possible.

LUCIO. Who? not the duke? yes, your beggar of fifty, and his use was to put a ducat in her clack-dish; the duke had crotchets in him. He would be drunk too; that let me inform you.

DUKE. You do him wrong, surely.

LUCIO. Sir, I was an inward of his. A shy fellow was the duke; and, I believe I know the cause of his withdrawing.

DUKE. What, I prithee, might be the cause?

LUCIO. No, pardon; 'tis a secret must be locked within the teeth and the lips; but this I can let you understand, the greater file of the subject held the duke to be wise.

DUKE. Wise! why, no question but he was.

LUCIO. A very superficial, ignorant, unweighing fellow.

DUKE. Either this is envy in you, folly, or mistaking; the very stream of his life and the business he hath helmed must, upon a warranted need, give him a better proclamation. Let him be but testimonied in his own bringings forth, and he shall appear to the envious a scholar, a statesman and a soldier. Therefore you speak unskilfully; or, if your knowledge be more, it is much darkened in your malice.

LUCIO. Sir, I know him, and I love him.

DUKE. Love talks with better knowledge, and knowledge with dearer love.

LUCIO. Come, sir, I know what I know.

DUKE. I can hardly believe that, since you know not what you speak. But, if ever the duke return,—as our prayers are he may,—let me desire you to make your answer before him: if it be honest you have spoke, you have courage to maintain it. I am bound to call upon you; and, I pray you, your name?

LUCIO. Sir, my name is Lucio, well known to the duke.

DUKE. He shall know you better, sir, if I may live to report you.

LUCIO. I fear you not,

DUKE. O! you hope the duke will return no more, or you
  imagine me too unhurtful an opposite. But indeed I can
  do you little harm; you 'll forswear this again.

LUCIO. I 'll be hanged first: thou art deceived in me, friar.
  But no more of this. Canst thou tell if Claudio die to-
  morrow or no?

DUKE. Why should he die, sir?

LUCIO. Why? for filling a bottle with a tundish. I would the
  duke we talk of were returned again; this ungenitured
  agent will unpeople the province with continency; sparrows must not build in his house-eaves, because they are
  lecherous. The duke yet would have dark deeds darkly
  answered; he would never bring them to light: would he
  were returned! Marry, this Claudio is condemned for untrussing. Farewell, good friar; I prithee, pray for me. The
  duke, I say to thee again, would eat mutton on Fridays.
  He 's not past it yet, and I say to thee, he would mouth
  with a beggar, though she smelt brown bread and garlic:
  say that I said so. Farewell.   *Exit*

DUKE. No might nor greatness in mortality
  Can censure 'scape: back-wounding calumny
  The whitest virtue strikes. What king so strong
  Can tie the gall up in the slanderous tongue?
  But who comes here?
            Enter Escalus,
  Provost, and Officers with Mistress Overdone

ESCALUS. Go; away with her to prison!

MRS. OVERDONE. Good my lord, be good to me; your honour is accounted a merciful man; good my lord.

ESCALUS. Double and treble admonition, and still forfeit in
  the same kind? This would make mercy swear, and play
  the tyrant.

PROVOST. A bawd of eleven years' continuance, may it
  please your honour.

MRS. OVERDONE. My lord, this is one Lucio's information
  against me. Mistress Kate Keepdown was with child by
  him in the duke's time; he promised her marriage; his
  child is a year and a quarter old, come Philip and Jacob:
  I have kept it myself, and see how he goes about to
  abuse me!

ESCALUS. That fellow is a fellow of much licence: let him
  be called before us. Away with her to prison! Go to; no

more words. (*Exeunt Officers with Mistress Overdone*)
Provost, my brother Angelo will not be altered; Claudio
must die to-morrow. Let him be furnished with divines,
and have all charitable preparation: if my brother
wrought by my pity, it should not be so with him.

PROVOST. So please you, this friar hath been with him, and
advised him for the entertainment of death.

ESCALUS. Good even, good father.

DUKE. Bliss and goodness on you!

ESCALUS. Of whence are you?

DUKE. Not of this country, though my chance is now
To use it for my time: I am a brother
Of gracious order, late come from the See,
In special business from his Holiness.

ESCALUS. What news abroad i' the world?

DUKE. None, but there is so great a fever on goodness, that
the dissolution of it must cure it: novelty is only in request; and it is as dangerous to be aged in any kind of
course, as it is virtuous to be constant in any undertaking: there is scarce truth enough alive to make societies
secure, but security enough to make fellowships ac-
cursed. Much upon this riddle runs the wisdom of the
world. This news is old enough, yet it is every day's
news. I pray you, sir, of what disposition was the duke?

ESCALUS. One that, above all other strifes, contended especially to know himself.

DUKE. What pleasure was he given to?

ESCALUS. Rather rejoicing to see another merry, than merry
at anything which professed to make him rejoice: a gentleman of all temperance. But leave we him to his events,
with a prayer they may prove prosperous; and let me desire to know how you find Claudio prepared. I am made
to understand, that you have lent him visitation.

DUKE. He professes to have received no sinister measure
from his judge, but most willingly humbles himself to the
determination of justice; yet had he framed to himself, by
the instruction of his frailty, many deceiving promises of
life, which I, by my good leisure have discredited to him,
and now is he resolved to die.

ESCALUS. You have paid the heavens your function, and the
prisoner the very debt of your calling. I have laboured
for the poor gentleman to the extremest shore of my

modesty; but my brother justice have I found so severe, that he hath forced me to tell him he is indeed Justice.

DUKE. If his own life answer the straitness of his proceeding, it shall become him well; wherein if he chance to fail, he hath sentenced himself.

ESCALUS. I am going to visit the prisoner. Fare you well.

DUKE. Peace be with you! *Exeunt Escalus and Provost*

    He, who the sword of heaven will bear
    Should be as holy as severe;
    Pattern in himself to know,
    Grace to stand, and virtue go;
    More nor less to others paying
    Than by self offences weighing.
    Shame to him whose cruel striking
    Kills for faults of his own liking!
    Twice treble shame on Angelo,
    To weed my vice and let his grow!
    O, what may man within him hide,
    Though angel on the outward side!
    How many likeness made in crimes,
    Making practice on the times,
    To draw with idle spiders' strings
    Most pond'rous and substantial things!
    Craft against vice I must apply:
    With Angelo to-night shall lie
    His old betrothed but despis'd:
    So disguise shall, by the disguis'd,
    Pay with falsehood false exacting,
    And perform an old contracting. *Exit*

ACT FOUR

SCENE ONE

The moated Grange at St. Luke's.

Enter Mariana and a Boy: Boy sings

> Take, O take those lips away,
>> That so sweetly were forsworn;
> And those eyes, the break of day,
>> Lights that do mislead the morn:
> But my kisses bring again, bring again,
>> Seals of love, but seal'd in vain, seal'd in vain.

MARIANA. Break off thy song, and haste thee quick away:
Here comes a man of comfort, whose advice
Hath often still'd my brawling discontent.   *Exit Boy*

Enter Duke, disguised as before

I cry you mercy, sir; and well could wish
You had not found me here so musical:
Let me excuse me, and believe me so,
My mirth it much displeas'd, but pleas'd my woe.

DUKE. 'Tis good; though music oft hath such a charm
To make bad good, and good provoke to harm.
I pray you tell me, hath anybody inquired for me here
to-day? Much upon this time have I promised here to
meet.

MARIANA. You have not been inquired after: I have sat
here all day.

DUKE. I do constantly believe you. The time is come even
now. I shall crave your forbearance a little; may be I will
call upon you anon, for some advantage to yourself.

MARIANA. I am always bound to you.   *Exit*

Enter Isabella

DUKE. Very well met, and well come.
What is the news from this good deputy?

ISABELLA. He hath a garden circummur'd with brick,

Whose western side is with a vineyard back'd;
And to that vineyard is a planched gate,
That makes his opening with this bigger key;
This other doth command a little door
Which from the vineyard to the garden leads;
There have I made my promise
Upon the heavy middle of the night
To call upon him.

DUKE. But shall you on your knowledge find this way?

ISABELLA. I have ta'en a due and wary note upon't:
With whispering and most guilty diligence,
In action all of precept, he did show me
The way twice o'er.

DUKE.   Are there no other tokens
Between you 'greed concerning her observance?

ISABELLA. No, none, but only a repair i' the dark;
And that I have possess'd him my most stay
Can be but brief; for I have made him know
I have a servant comes with me along,
That stays upon me, whose persuasion is
I come about my brother.

DUKE.   'Tis well borne up.
I have not yet made known to Mariana
A word of this. What ho! within! come forth.

Re-enter Mariana

I pray you, be acquainted with this maid:
She comes to do you good.

ISABELLA.   I do desire the like.

DUKE. Do you persuade yourself that I respect you?

MARIANA. Good friar, I know you do, and oft have found it.

DUKE. Take then this your companion by the hand,
Who hath a story ready for your ear.
I shall attend your leisure: but make haste;
The vaporous night approaches.

MARIANA.   Will 't please you walk aside?

                    Exeunt Mariana and Isabella

DUKE. O place and greatness! millions of false eyes
Are stuck upon thee: volumes of report
Run with these false and most contrarious quests
Upon thy doings: thousand escapes of wit
Make thee the father of their idle dream,
And rack thee in their fancies!

Re-enter Mariana and Isabella

　　　　　　　　　　　Welcome! How agreed?

ISABELLA. She 'll take the enterprise upon her, father,
　　If you advise it.

DUKE. 　　　　　　It is not my consent,
　　But my entreaty too.

ISABELLA. 　　　　　　Little have you to say
　　When you depart from him, but, soft and low,
　　'Remember now my brother.'

MARIANA. 　　　　　　　　Fear me not.

DUKE. Nor, gentle daughter, fear you not at all.
　　He is your husband on a pre-contract:
　　To bring you thus together, 'tis no sin,
　　Sith that the justice of your title to him
　　Doth flourish the deceit. Come, let us go:
　　Our corn 's to reap, for yet our tithe 's to sow.　　*Exeunt*

SCENE TWO

A Room in the Prison.

Enter Provost and Pompey

PROVOST. Come hither, sirrah. Can you cut off a man's
　　head?

POMPEY. If the man be a bachelor, sir, I can; but if he be a
　　married man, he is his wife's head, and I can never cut
　　off a woman's head.

PROVOST. Come, sir, leave me your snatches, and yield me
　　a direct answer. To-morrow morning are to die Claudio
　　and Barnardine. Here is in our prison a common execu-
　　tioner, who in his office lacks a helper: if you will take it
　　on you to assist him, it shall redeem you from your gyves;
　　if not, you shall have your full time of imprisonment, and
　　your deliverance with an unpitied whipping, for you
　　have been a notorious bawd.

POMPEY. Sir, I have been an unlawful bawd time out of
　　mind; but yet I will be content to be a lawful hangman.
　　I would be glad to receive some instruction from my fel-
　　low partner.

PROVOST. What ho, Abhorson! Where 's Abhorson, there?

Enter Abhorson

ABHORSON. Do you call, sir?

PROVOST. Sirrah, here 's a fellow will help you to-morrow in your execution. If you think it meet, compound with him by the year, and let him abide here with you; if not, use him for the present, and dismiss him. He cannot plead his estimation with you; he hath been a bawd.

ABHORSON. A bawd, sir? Fie upon him! he will discredit our mystery.

PROVOST. Go to, sir; you weigh equally; a feather will turn the scale.   *Exit*

POMPEY. Pray, sir, by your good favour—for surely, sir, a good favour you have, but that you have a hanging look, —do you call, sir, your occupation a mystery?

ABHORSON. Ay, sir; a mystery.

POMPEY. Painting, sir, I have heard say, is a mystery; and your whores, sir, being members of my occupation, using painting, do prove my occupation a mystery: but what mystery there should be in hanging, if I should be hanged, I cannot imagine.

ABHORSON. Sir, it is a mystery.

POMPEY. Proof?

ABHORSON. Every true man's apparel fits your thief.

POMPEY. If it be too little for your thief, your true man thinks it big enough; if it be too big for your thief, your thief thinks it little enough: so, every true man's apparel fits your thief.

Re-enter Provost

PROVOST. Are you agreed?

POMPEY. Sir, I will serve him; for I do find that your hang-man is a more penitent trade than your bawd, he doth often ask forgiveness.

PROVOST. You, sirrah, provide your block and your axe to-morrow four o'clock.

ABHORSON. Come on, bawd; I will instruct thee in my trade; follow.

POMPEY. I do desire to learn, sir; and, I hope, if you have occasion to use me for your own turn, you shall find me yare; for, truly, sir, for your kindness I owe you a good turn.

PROVOST. Call hither Barnardine and Claudio:

Exeunt Pompey and Abhorson

The one has my pity; not a jot the other,
Being a murderer, though he were my brother.

Enter Claudio

Look, here 's the warrant, Claudio, for thy death:
'Tis now dead midnight, and by eight to-morrow
Thou must be made immortal. Where 's Barnardine?

CLAUDIO. As fast lock'd up in sleep as guiltless labour
When it lies starkly in the traveller's bones;
He will not wake.

PROVOST.   Who can do good on him?
Well, go; prepare yourself. (*Knocking within*) But hark,
    what noise?—
Heaven give your spirits comfort!—(*Exit Claudio*) By and
    by.
I hope it is some pardon or reprieve
For the most gentle Claudio.

Enter Duke, disguised as before
                              Welcome, father.

DUKE. The best and wholesom'st spirits of the night
Envelop you, good provost! Who call'd here of late?

PROVOST. None since the curfew rung.

DUKE. Not Isabel?

PROVOST.   No.

DUKE.   They will, then, ere 't be long.

PROVOST. What comfort is for Claudio?

DUKE. There 's some in hope.

PROVOST.   It is a bitter deputy.

DUKE. Not so, not so: his life is parallel'd
Even with the stroke and line of his great justice:
He doth with holy abstinence subdue
That in himself which he spurs on his power
To qualify in others: were he meal'd with that
Which he corrects, then were he tyrannous;
But this being so, he 's just.—(*Knocking within*) Now
    are they come.   *Exit Provost*
This is a gentle provost: seldom when
The steeled gaoler is the friend of men.   *Knocking*
How now! What noise? That spirit 's possess'd with haste
That wounds the unsisting postern with these strokes.

Re-enter Provost

PROVOST. There he must stay until the officer
Arise to let him in; he is call'd up.

DUKE. Have you no countermand for Claudio yet,
But he must die to-morrow?

PROVOST. None, sir, none.

DUKE. As near the dawning, provost, as it is,
You shall hear more ere morning.

PROVOST. Happily
You something know; yet, I believe there comes
No countermand: no such example have we.
Besides, upon the very siege of justice,
Lord Angelo hath to the public ear
Profess'd the contrary.

Enter a Messenger

This is his lordship's man.

DUKE. And here comes Claudio's pardon.

MESSENGER. (*Giving a paper*) My lord hath sent you this
note; and by me this further charge, that you swerve not
from the smallest article of it, neither in time, matter, or
other circumstance. Good-morrow; for, as I take it, it is
almost day.

PROVOST. I shall obey him. *Exit Messenger*

DUKE. (*Aside*) This is his pardon, purchased by such sin
For which the pardoner himself is in;
Hence hath offence his quick celerity,
When it is borne in high authority.
When vice makes mercy, mercy 's so extended,
That for the fault's love is the offender friended.
Now, sir, what news?

PROVOST. I told you: Lord Angelo, belike thinking me re-
miss in mine office, awakens me with this unwonted putting on; methinks strangely, for he hath not used it before.

DUKE. Pray you, let 's hear.

PROVOST. (*Reads*) 'Whatsoever you may hear to the contrary, let Claudio be executed by four of the clock; and,
in the afternoon, Barnardine. For my better satisfaction,
let me have Claudio's head sent me by five. Let this be
duly performed; with a thought that more depends on it
than we must yet deliver. Thus fail not to do your office,
as you will answer it at your peril.' What say you to this,
sir?

DUKE. What is that Barnardine who is to be executed this
afternoon?

PROVOST. A Bohemian born, but here nursed up and bred;
one that is a prisoner nine years old.

DUKE. How came it that the absent duke had not either delivered him to his liberty or executed him? I have heard
it was ever his manner to do so.

PROVOST. His friends still wrought reprieves for him; and,
indeed, his fact, till now in the government of Lord Angelo, came not to an undoubtful proof.

DUKE. It is now apparent?

PROVOST. Most manifest, and not denied by himself.

DUKE. Hath he borne himself penitently in prison? How
seems he to be touched?

PROVOST. A man that apprehends death no more dreadfully
but as a drunken sleep; careless, reckless, and fearless of
what 's past, present, or to come; insensible of mortality,
and desperately mortal.

DUKE. He wants advice.

PROVOST. He will hear none. He hath evermore had the liberty of the prison: give him leave to escape hence, he
would not: drunk many times a day, if not many days
entirely drunk. We have very oft awaked him, as if to
carry him to execution, and showed him a seeming warrant for it: it hath not moved him at all.

DUKE. More of him anon. There is written in your brow,
provost, honesty and constancy: if I read it not truly, my
ancient skill beguiles me; but, in the boldness of my cunning I will lay myself in hazard. Claudio, whom here
you have warrant to execute, is no greater forfeit to the
law than Angelo who hath sentenced him. To make you
understand this in a manifested effect, I crave but four
days' respite, for the which you are to do me both a present and a dangerous courtesy.

PROVOST. Pray, sir, in what?

DUKE. In the delaying death.

PROVOST. Alack! how may I do it, having the hour limited,
and an express command, under penalty, to deliver his
head in the view of Angelo? I may make my case as
Claudio's to cross this in the smallest.

DUKE. By the vow of mine order I warrant you, if my instructions may be your guide. Let this Barnardine be this
morning executed, and his head borne to Angelo.

PROVOST. Angelo hath seen them both, and will discover the favour.

DUKE. O! death 's a great disguiser, and you may add to it. Shave the head, and tie the beard; and say it was the desire of the penitent to be so bared before his death: you know the course is common. If anything fall to you upon this, more than thanks and good fortune, by the saint whom I profess, I will plead against it with my life.

PROVOST. Pardon me, good father; it is against my oath.

DUKE. Were you sworn to the duke or to the deputy?

PROVOST. To him, and to his substitutes.

DUKE. You will think you have made no offence, if the duke avouch the justice of your dealing?

PROVOST. But what likelihood is in that?

DUKE. Not a resemblance, but a certainty. Yet since I see you fearful, that neither my coat, integrity, nor persuasion can with ease attempt you, I will go further than I meant, to pluck all fears out of you. Look you, sir; here is the hand and seal of the duke: you know the character, I doubt not, and the signet is not strange to you.

PROVOST. I know them both.

DUKE. The contents of this is the return of the duke: you shall anon over-read it at your pleasure, where you shall find within these two days, he will be here. This is a thing that Angelo knows not, for he this very day receives letters of strange tenour; perchance of the duke's death; perchance, his entering into some monastery; but, by chance, nothing of what is writ. Look, the unfolding star calls up the shepherd. Put not yourself into amazement how these things should be: all difficulties are but easy when they are known. Call your executioner, and off with Barnardine's head: I will give him a present shrift and advise him for a better place. Yet you are amaz'd, but this shall absolutely resolve you. Come away; it is almost clear dawn.   *Exeunt*

SCENE THREE

Another Room in the Same.

Enter Pompey

POMPEY. I am as well acquainted here as I was in our house of profession: one would think it were Mistress Overdone's own house, for here be many of her old customers. First, here's young Master Rash; he's in for a commodity of brown paper and old ginger, nine-score and seventeen pounds, of which he made five marks, ready money: marry, then ginger was not much in request, for the old women were all dead. Then is there here one Master Caper, at the suit of Master Three-pile the mercer, for some four suits of peach-colour'd satin, which now peaches him a beggar. Then have we young Dizy, and young Master Deep-vow, and Master Copperspur, and Master Starve-lackey the rapier and dagger man, and young Drop-heir that kill'd lusty Pudding, and Master Forthlight, the tilter, and brave Master Shoe-tie the great traveller, and wild Half-can that stabbed Pots, and, I think, forty more; all great doers in our trade, and are now 'for the Lord's sake.'

Enter Abhorson

ABHORSON. Sirrah, bring Barnardine hither.

POMPEY. Master Barnardine! you must rise and be hanged, Master Barnardine.

ABHORSON. What ho! Barnardine!

BARNARDINE. (*Within*) A pox o' your throats! Who makes that noise there? What are you?

POMPEY. Your friends, sir; the hangman. You must be so good, sir, to rise and be put to death.

BARNARDINE. (*Within*) Away! you rogue, away! I am sleepy.

ABHORSON. Tell him he must awake, and that quickly too.

POMPEY. Pray, Master Barnardine, awake till you are executed, and sleep afterwards.

ABHORSON. Go in to him, and fetch him out.

POMPEY. He is coming, sir, he is coming; I hear his straw rustle.

ABHORSON. Is the axe upon the block, sirrah?

POMPEY. Very ready, sir.

Enter Barnardine

BARNARDINE. How now, Abhorson! what 's the news with you?

ABHORSON. Truly, sir, I would desire you to clap into your prayers; for, look you, the warrant 's come.

BARNARDINE. You rogue, I have been drinking all night; I am not fitted for 't.

POMPEY. O, the better, sir; for he that drinks all night, and is hang'd betimes in the morning, may sleep the sounder all the next day.

ABHORSON. Look you, sir; here comes your ghostly father: do we jest now, think you?

Enter Duke, disguised as before

DUKE. Sir, induced by my charity, and hearing how hastily you are to depart, I am come to advise you, comfort you, and pray with you.

BARNARDINE. Friar, not I: I have been drinking hard all night, and I will have more time to prepare me, or they shall beat out my brains with billets. I will not consent to die this day, that 's certain.

DUKE. O, sir, you must; and therefore, I beseech you look forward on the journey you shall go.

BARNARDINE. I swear I will not die to-day for any man's persuasion.

DUKE. But hear you.

BARNARDINE. Not a word: if you have anything to say to me, come to my ward; for thence will not I to-day.   *Exit*

Enter Provost

DUKE. Unfit to live or die. O, gravel heart!
After him fellows: bring him to the block.

Exeunt Abhorson and Pompey

PROVOST. Now, sir, how do you find the prisoner?

DUKE. A creature unprepar'd, unmeet for death;
And, to transport him in the mind he is
Were damnable.

PROVOST.   Here in the prison, father,
There died this morning of a cruel fever
One Ragozine, a most notorious pirate,
A man of Claudio's years; his beard and head
Just of his colour. What if we do omit
This reprobate till he were well inclin'd,

And satisfy the deputy with the visage
Of Ragozine, more like to Claudio?

DUKE. O, 'tis an accident that heaven provides!
Dispatch it presently: the hour draws on
Prefix'd by Angelo. See this be done,
And sent according to command, whiles I
Persuade this rude wretch willingly to die.

PROVOST. This shall be done, good father, presently.
But Barnardine must die this afternoon:
And how shall we continue Claudio,
To save me from the danger that might come
If he were known alive?

DUKE.   Let this be done:
Put them in secret holds, both Barnardine and Claudio:
Ere twice the sun hath made his journal greeting
To the under generation, you shall find
Your safety manifested.

PROVOST. I am your free dependant.

DUKE. Quick, dispatch,
And send the head to Angelo.   *Exit Provost*
Now will I write letters to Angelo,—
The provost, he shall bear them,—whose contents
Shall witness to him I am near at home,
And that, by great injunctions, I am bound
To enter publicly: him I 'll desire
To meet me at the consecrated fount
A league below the city; and from thence,
By cold gradation and well-balanc'd form,
We shall proceed with Angelo.

Re-enter Provost

PROVOST. Here is the head; I 'll carry it myself.

DUKE. Convenient is it. Make a swift return,
For I would commune with you of such things
That want no ear but yours.

PROVOST.   I 'll make all speed.   *Exit*

ISABELLA. (*Within*) Peace, ho, be here!

DUKE. The tongue of Isabel. She 's come to know
If yet her brother's pardon be come hither;
But I will keep her ignorant of her good,
To make her heavenly comforts of despair,
When it is least expected.

Enter Isabella

ISABELLA.   Ho! by your leave.

DUKE. Good-morning to you, fair and gracious daughter.

ISABELLA. The better, given me by so holy a man.
  Hath yet the deputy sent my brother's pardon?

DUKE. He hath releas'd him, Isabel, from the world:
  His head is off and sent to Angelo.

ISABELLA. Nay, but it is not so.

DUKE. It is no other: show your wisdom, daughter,
  In your close patience.

ISABELLA. O! I will to him and pluck out his eyes!

DUKE. You shall not be admitted to his sight.

ISABELLA. Unhappy Claudio! Wretched Isabel!
  Injurious world! Most damned Angelo!

DUKE. This nor hurts him nor profits you a jot;
  Forbear it therefore; give your cause to heaven.
  Mark what I say, which you shall find
  By every syllable a faithful verity.
  The duke comes home to-morrow; nay, dry your eyes:
  One of our convent, and his confessor,
  Gives me this instance: already he hath carried
  Notice to Escalus and Angelo,
  Who do prepare to meet him at the gates,
  There to give up their power. If you can, pace your wis-
    dom
  In that good path that I would wish it go,
  And you shall have your bosom on this wretch,
  Grace of the duke, revenges to your heart,
  And general honour.

ISABELLA.   I am directed by you.

DUKE. This letter then to Friar Peter give;
  'Tis that he sent me of the duke's return:
  Say, by this token, I desire his company
  At Mariana's house to-night. Her cause and yours,
  I'll perfect him withal, and he shall bring you
  Before the duke; and to the head of Angelo
  Accuse him home, and home. For my poor self,
  I am combined by a sacred vow
  And shall be absent. Wend you with this letter.
  Command these fretting waters from your eyes
  With a light heart: trust not my holy order,
  If I pervert your course. Who's here?

Enter Lucio

LUCIO. Good even. Friar, where is the provost?

DUKE. Not within, sir.

LUCIO. O pretty Isabella, I am pale at mine heart to see
thine eyes so red: thou must be patient. I am fain to dine
and sup with water and bran; I dare not for my head fill
my belly; one fruitful meal would set me to 't. But they
say the duke will be here to-morrow. By my troth, Isabel,
I loved thy brother: if the old fantastical duke of dark
corners had been at home, he had lived.   *Exit Isabella*

DUKE. Sir, the duke is marvellous little beholding to your
reports; but the best is, he lives not in them.

LUCIO. Friar, thou knowest not the duke so well as I do:
he 's a better woodman than thou takest him for.

DUKE. Well, you 'll answer this one day. Fare ye well.

LUCIO. Nay, tarry; I 'll go along with thee: I can tell thee
pretty tales of the duke.

DUKE. You have told me too many of him already, sir, if
they be true; if not true, none were enough.

LUCIO. I was once before him for getting a wench with
child.

DUKE. Did you such a thing?

LUCIO. Yes, marry, did I; but I was fain to forswear it: they
would else have married me to the rotten medlar.

DUKE. Sir, your company is fairer than honest. Rest you
well.

LUCIO. By my troth, I 'll go with thee to the lane's end. If
bawdy talk offend you, we 'll have very little of it. Nay,
friar, I am a kind of burr; I shall stick.   *Exeunt*

SCENE FOUR

A Room in Angelo's House.

Enter Angelo and Escalus

ESCALUS. Every letter he hath writ hath disvouched other.

ANGELO. In most uneven and distracted manner. His actions show much like to madness: pray heaven his wisdom be not tainted! And why meet him at the gates, and
redeliver our authorities there?

ESCALUS. I guess not.

ANGELO. And why should we proclaim it in an hour before
  his entering, that if any crave redress of injustice, they
  should exhibit their petitions in the street?
ESCALUS. He shows his reason for that: to have a dispatch
  of complaints, and to deliver us from devices hereafter,
  which shall then have no power to stand against us.
ANGELO. Well, I beseech you, let it be proclaim'd:
  Betimes i' the morn I 'll call you at your house;
  Give notice to such men of sort and suit
  As are to meet him.
ESCALUS. I shall, sir: fare you well.
ANGELO. Good-night.—   *Exit Escalus*
  This deed unshapes me quite, makes me unpregnant
  And dull to all proceedings. A deflower'd maid,
  And by an eminent body that enforc'd
  The law against it! But that her tender shame
  Will not proclaim against her maiden loss,
  How might she tongue me! Yet reason dares her no:
  For my authority bears so credent bulk,
  That no particular scandal once can touch:
  But it confounds the breather. He should have liv'd,
  Save that his riotous youth, with dangerous sense,
  Might in the times to come have ta'en revenge,
  By so receiving a dishonour'd life
  With ransom of such shame. Would yet he had liv'd!
  Alack! when once our grace we have forgot,
  Nothing goes right: we would, and we would not.   *Exit*

                    SCENE FIVE

              Fields without the Town.

        Enter Duke, in his own habit, and Friar Peter

DUKE. These letters at fit time deliver me.   *Giving letters*
  The provost knows our purpose and our plot.
  The matter being afoot, keep your instruction,
  And hold you ever to our special drift,
  Though sometimes you do blench from this to that,
  As cause doth minister. Go call at Flavius' house,
  And tell him where I stay: give the like notice
  To Valentinus, Rowland, and to Crassus,

And bid them bring the trumpets to the gate;
But send me Flavius first.

FRIAR PETER.   It shall be speeded well.   *Exit*

Enter Varrius

DUKE. I thank thee, Varrius; thou hast made good haste.
Come, we will walk. There 's other of our friends
Will greet us here anon, my gentle Varrius.   *Exeunt*

SCENE SIX

Street near the City Gate.

Enter Isabella and Mariana

ISABELLA. To speak so indirectly I am loath:
I would say the truth; but to accuse him so,
That is your part: yet I 'm advis'd to do it;
He says, to veil full purpose.

MARIANA.   Be rul'd by him.

ISABELLA. Besides, he tells me that if peradventure
He speak against me on the adverse side,
I should not think it strange; for 'tis a physic
That 's bitter to sweet end.

MARIANA. I would, Friar Peter—

ISABELLA.   O, peace! the friar is come.

Enter Friar Peter

FRIAR PETER. Come; I have found you out a stand most fit,
Where you may have such vantage on the duke,
He shall not pass you. Twice have the trumpets sounded:
The generous and gravest citizens
Have hent the gates, and very near upon
The duke is ent'ring: therefore hence, away!   *Exeunt*

ACT FIVE

SCENE ONE

A public Place near the City Gate.

*Mariana, veiled, Isabella, and Friar Peter, at their stand.
Enter Duke, Varrius, Lords, Angelo, Escalus, Lucio,
Provost, Officers, and Citizens at several doors*

DUKE. My very worthy cousin, fairly met!
  Our old and faithful friend, we are glad to see you.

ANGELO. }
ESCALUS. } Happy return be to your royal Grace!

DUKE. Many and hearty thankings to you both.
  We have made inquiry of you; and we hear
  Such goodness of your justice, that our soul
  Cannot but yield you forth to public thanks,
  Forerunning more requital.

ANGELO.   You make my bonds still greater.

DUKE. O! your desert speaks loud; and I should wrong it,
  To lock it in the wards of covert bosom,
  When it deserves, with characters of brass,
  A forted residence 'gainst the tooth of time
  And razure of oblivion. Give me your hand,
  And let the subject see, to make them know
  That outward courtesies would fain proclaim
  Favours that keep within. Come, Escalus,
  You must walk by us on our other hand;
  And good supporters are you.

     Friar Peter and Isabella come forward

FRIAR PETER. Now is your time: speak loud and kneel before him.

ISABELLA. Justice, O royal duke! Vail your regard
  Upon a wrong'd—I'd fain have said, a maid!
  O worthy prince! dishonour not your eye
  By throwing it on any other object

Till you have heard me in my true complaint
And given me justice, justice, justice, justice!

DUKE. Relate your wrongs: in what? by whom? be brief;
Here is Lord Angelo shall give you justice:
Reveal yourself to him.

ISABELLA.   O worthy duke!
You bid me seek redemption of the devil.
Hear me yourself; for that which I must speak
Must either punish me, not being believ'd,
Or wring redress from you. Hear me, O, hear me, hear!

ANGELO. My lord, her wits, I fear me, are not firm:
She hath been a suitor to me for her brother
Cut off by course of justice,—

ISABELLA.   By course of justice!

ANGELO. And she will speak most bitterly and strange.

ISABELLA. Most strange, but yet most truly, will I speak.
That Angelo 's forsworn, is it not strange?
That Angelo 's a murderer, is 't not strange?
That Angelo is an adulterous thief,
A hypocrite, a virgin-violator;
Is it not strange, and strange?

DUKE.   Nay, it is ten times strange.

ISABELLA. It is not truer he is Angelo
Than this is all as true as it is strange;
Nay, it is ten times true; for truth is truth
To the end of reckoning.

DUKE.   Away with her! poor soul,
She speaks this in the infirmity of sense.

ISABELLA. O prince, I conjure thee, as thou believ'st
There is another comfort than this world,
That thou neglect me not, with that opinion
That I am touch'd with madness. Make not impossible
That which but seems unlike. 'Tis not impossible
But one, the wicked'st caitiff on the ground,
May seem as shy, as grave, as just, as absolute
As Angelo; even so may Angelo,
In all his dressings, characts, titles, forms,
Be an arch-villain. Believe it, royal prince:
If he be less, he 's nothing; but he 's more,
Had I more name for badness.

DUKE.   By mine honesty,
If she be mad,—as I believe no other,—

Her madness hath the oddest frame of sense,
Such a dependency of thing on thing,
As e'er I heard in madness.

ISABELLA.   O gracious duke!
Harp not on that; nor do not banish reason
For inequality; but let your reason serve
To make the truth appear where it seems hid,
And hide the false seems true.

DUKE.   Many that are not mad
Have, sure, more lack of reason. What would you say?

ISABELLA. I am sister of one Claudio,
Condemn'd upon the act of fornication
To lose his head; condemn'd by Angelo.
I, in probation of a sisterhood,
Was sent to by my brother; one Lucio
As then the messenger,—

LUCIO.   That's I, an't like your Grace:
I came to her from Claudio, and desir'd her
To try her gracious fortune with Lord Angelo
For her poor brother's pardon.

ISABELLA.   That's he indeed.

DUKE. You were not bid to speak.

LUCIO.   No, my good lord,
Nor wish'd to hold my peace.

DUKE.   I wish you now, then;
Pray you, take note of it; and when you have
A business for yourself, pray heaven you then
Be perfect.

LUCIO. I warrant your honour.

DUKE. The warrant's for yourself: take heed to it.

ISABELLA. This gentleman told somewhat of my tale,—

LUCIO. Right.

DUKE. It may be right; but you are in the wrong
To speak before your time. Proceed.

ISABELLA.   I went
To this pernicious caitiff deputy.

DUKE. That's somewhat madly spoken.

ISABELLA.   Pardon it;
The phrase is to the matter.

DUKE. Mended again: the matter; proceed.

ISABELLA. In brief, to set the needless process by,
How I persuaded, how I pray'd, and kneel'd,

How he refell'd me, and how I replied,—
For this was of much length,—the vile conclusion
I now begin with grief and shame to utter.
He would not, but by gift of my chaste body
To his concupiscible intemperate lust,
Release my brother; and, after much debatement,
My sisterly remorse confutes mine honour,
And I did yield to him. But the next morn betimes,
His purpose surfeiting, he sends a warrant
For my poor brother's head.

DUKE.   This is most likely!

ISABELLA. O, that it were as like as it is true!

DUKE. By heaven, fond wretch! thou know'st not what thou
          speak'st,
Or else thou art suborn'd against his honour
In hateful practice. First, his integrity
Stands without blemish; next, it imports no reason
That with such vehemency he should pursue
Faults proper to himself: if he had so offended,
He would have weigh'd thy brother by himself,
And not have cut him off. Some one hath set you on:
Confess the truth, and say by whose advice
Thou cam'st here to complain.

ISABELLA.   And is this all?
Then, O you blessed ministers above,
Keep me in patience; and, with ripen'd time
Unfold the evil which is here wrapt up
In countenance! Heaven shield your Grace from woe,
As I, thus wrong'd, hence unbelieved go!

DUKE. I know you 'd fain be gone. An officer!
To prison with her! Shall we thus permit
A blasting and a scandalous breath to fall
On him so near us? This needs must be a practice.
Who knew of your intent and coming hither?

ISABELLA. One that I would were here, Friar Lodowick.

DUKE. A ghostly father, belike. Who knows that Lodowick?

LUCIO. My lord, I know him; 'tis a meddling friar;
I do not like the man: had he been lay, my lord,
For certain words he spake against your Grace
In your retirement, I had swing'd him soundly.

DUKE. Words against me! This' a good friar, belike!
And to set on this wretched woman here

Against our substitute! Let this friar be found.

LUCIO. But yesternight, my lord, she and that friar,
    I saw them at the prison: a saucy friar,
    A very scurvy fellow.

FRIAR PETER.   Bless'd be your royal Grace!
    I have stood by, my lord, and I have heard
    Your royal ear abus'd. First, hath this woman
    Most wrongfully accus'd your substitute,
    Who is as free from touch or soil with her,
    As she from one ungot.

DUKE.   We did believe no less.
    Know you that Friar Lodowick that she speaks of?

FRIAR PETER. I know him for a man divine and holy;
    Not scurvy, nor a temporary meddler,
    As he's reported by this gentleman;
    And, on my trust, a man that never yet
    Did, as he vouches, misreport your Grace.

LUCIO. My lord, most villanously; believe it.

FRIAR PETER. Well; he in time may come to clear himself,
    But at this instant he is sick, my lord,
    Of a strange fever. Upon his mere request,
    Being come to knowledge that there was complaint
    Intended 'gainst Lord Angelo, came I hither,
    To speak, as from his mouth, what he doth know
    Is true and false; and what he with his oath
    And all probation will make up full clear,
    Whensoever he's convented. First, for this woman,
    To justify this worthy nobleman,
    So vulgarly and personally accus'd,
    Her shall you hear disproved to her eyes,
    Till she herself confess it.

DUKE.   Good friar, let's hear it.
                 Isabella is carried off
           guarded; and Mariana comes forward
    Do you not smile at this, Lord Angelo?—
    O heaven, the vanity of wretched fools!
    Give us some seats. Come, cousin Angelo;
    In this I'll be impartial; be you judge
    Of your own cause. Is this the witness, friar?
    First, let her show her face, and after speak.

MARIANA. Pardon, my lord; I will not show my face
    Until my husband bid me.

DUKE.   What, are you married?

MARIANA. No, my lord.

DUKE.   Are you a maid?

MARIANA.   No, my lord.

DUKE. A widow, then?

MARIANA.   Neither, my lord.

DUKE.   Why, you
Are nothing, then: neither maid, widow, nor wife?

LUCIO. My lord, she may be a punk; for many of them are
neither maid, widow, nor wife.

DUKE. Silence that fellow: I would he had some cause
To prattle for himself.

LUCIO. Well, my lord.

MARIANA. My lord, I do confess I ne'er was married;
And I confess besides I am no maid:
I have known my husband yet my husband knows not
That ever he knew me.

LUCIO. He was drunk then, my lord: it can be no better.

DUKE. For the benefit of silence, would thou wert so too!

LUCIO. Well, my lord.

DUKE. This is no witness for Lord Angelo.

MARIANA. Now I come to 't, my lord:
She that accuses him of fornication,
In self-same manner doth accuse my husband;
And charges him, my lord, with such a time,
When, I 'll depose, I had him in mine arms,
With all th' effect of love.

ANGELO. Charges she moe than me?

MARIANA.   Not that I know.

DUKE. No? you say your husband.

MARIANA. Why, just, my lord, and that is Angelo,
Who thinks he knows that he ne'er knew my body
But knows he thinks that he knows Isabel's.

ANGELO. This is a strange abuse. Let 's see thy face.

MARIANA. My husband bids me; now I will unmask.
This is that face, thou cruel Angelo,   *Unveiling*
Which once thou swor'st was worth the looking on:
This is the hand which, with a vow'd contract,
Was fast belock'd in thine: this is the body
That took away the match from Isabel,
And did supply thee at thy garden-house
In her imagin'd person.

DUKE.   Know you this woman?

LUCIO. Carnally, she says.

DUKE.   Sirrah, no more!

LUCIO. Enough, my lord.

ANGELO. My lord, I must confess I know this woman;
    And five years since there was some speech of marriage
    Betwixt myself and her, which was broke off,
    Partly for that her promised proportions
    Came short of composition; but, in chief
    For that her reputation was disvalu'd
    In levity: since what time of five years
    I never spake with her, saw her, nor heard from her,
    Upon my faith and honour.

MARIANA.   Noble prince,
    As there comes light from heaven and words from breath,
    As there is sense in truth and truth in virtue,
    I am affianc'd this man's wife as strongly
    As words could make up vows: and, my good lord,
    But Tuesday night last gone in 's garden-house
    He knew me as a wife. As this is true,
    Let me in safety raise me from my knees
    Or else for ever be confixed here,
    A marble monument.

ANGELO.   I did but smile till now:
    Now, good my lord, give me the scope of justice;
    My patience here is touch'd. I do perceive
    These poor informal women are no more
    But instruments of some more mightier member
    That sets them on. Let me have way, my lord,
    To find this practice out.

DUKE.   Ay, with my heart;
    And punish them unto your height of pleasure.
    Thou foolish friar, and thou pernicious woman,
    Compact with her that 's gone, think'st thou thy oaths,
    Though they would swear down each particular saint,
    Were testimonies against his worth and credit
    That 's seal'd in approbation? You, Lord Escalus,
    Sit with my cousin; lend him your kind pains
    To find out this abuse, whence 'tis deriv'd.
    There is another friar that set them on;
    Let him be sent for.

FRIAR PETER. Would he were here, my lord; for he indeed
    Hath set the women on to this complaint:
    Your provost knows the place where he abides
    And he may fetch him.

DUKE.   Go do it instantly.   *Exit Provost*
    And you, my noble and well-warranted cousin,
    Whom it concerns to hear this matter forth,
    Do with your injuries as seems you best,
    In any chastisement: I for awhile will leave you;
    But stir not you, till you have well determin'd
    Upon these slanderers.

ESCALUS. My lord, we 'll do it throughly.—   *Exit Duke*
    Signior Lucio, did not you say you knew that Friar Lodo-
    wick to be a dishonest person?

LUCIO. Cucullus non facit monachum: honest in nothing,
    but in his clothes; and one that hath spoke most villanous
    speeches of the duke.

ESCALUS. We shall entreat you to abide here till he come
    and enforce them against him. We shall find this friar a
    notable fellow.

LUCIO. As any in Vienna, on my word.

ESCALUS. Call that same Isabel here once again: I would
    speak with her. (*Exit an Attendant*) Pray you, my lord,
    give me leave to question; you shall see how I 'll handle
    her.

LUCIO. Not better than he, by her own report.

ESCALUS. Say you?

LUCIO. Marry, sir, I think, if you handled her privately, she
    would sooner confess: perchance, publicly, she 'll be
    ashamed.

ESCALUS. I will go darkly to work with her.

LUCIO. That 's the way: for women are light at midnight.

           Re-enter Officers with Isabella

ESCALUS. (*To Isabella*) Come on, mistress: here 's a gentle-
    woman denies all that you have said.

LUCIO. My lord, here comes the rascal I spoke of; here with
    the provost.

ESCALUS. In very good time: speak not you to him, till we
    call upon you.

    Enter Duke, disguised as a friar, and Provost

LUCIO. Mum.

ESCALUS. Come, sir. Did you set these women on to slander
   Lord Angelo? They have confessed you did.

DUKE. 'Tis false.

ESCALUS. How! know you where you are?

DUKE. Respect to your great place! and let the devil
   Be sometime honour'd for his burning throne.
   Where is the duke? 'Tis he should hear me speak.

ESCALUS. The duke 's in us, and we will hear you speak:
   Look you speak justly.

DUKE. Boldly, at least. But, O, poor souls!
   Come you to seek the lamb here of the fox?
   Good-night to your redress! Is the duke gone?
   Then is your cause gone too. The duke 's unjust,
   Thus to retort your manifest appeal,
   And put your trial in the villain's mouth
   Which here you come to accuse.

LUCIO. This is the rascal: this is he I spoke of.

ESCALUS. Why, thou unreverend and unhallow'd friar!
   Is 't not enough thou hast suborn'd these women
   To accuse this worthy man, but, in foul mouth,
   And in the witness of his proper ear,
   To call him villain?
   And then to glance from him to the duke himself,
   To tax him with injustice? Take him hence;
   To the rack with him! We 'll touse you joint by joint,
   But we will know his purpose. What! 'unjust'?

DUKE. Be not so hot; the duke
   Dare no more stretch this finger of mine than he
   Dare rack his own: his subject am I not,
   Nor here provincial. My business in this state
   Made me a looker-on here in Vienna,
   Where I have seen corruption boil and bubble
   Till it o'er-run the stew: laws for all faults,
   But faults so countenanc'd, that the strong statutes
   Stand like the forfeits in a barber's shop,
   As much in mock as mark.

ESCALUS. Slander to the state! Away with him to prison!

ANGELO. What can you vouch against him, Signior Lucio?
   Is this the man that you did tell us of?

LUCIO. 'Tis he, my lord. Come hither, goodman bald-pate:
   do you know me?

DUKE. I remember you, sir, by the sound of your voice: I
met you at the prison, in the absence of the duke.

LUCIO. O! did you so? And do you remember what you said
of the duke?

DUKE. Most notedly, sir.

LUCIO. Do you so, sir? And was the duke a flesh-monger, a
fool, and a coward, as you then reported him to be?

DUKE. You must, sir, change persons with me, ere you make
that my report: you, indeed, spoke so of him; and much
more, much worse.

LUCIO. O thou damnable fellow! Did not I pluck thee by
the nose for thy speeches?

DUKE. I protest I love the duke as I love myself.

ANGELO. Hark how the villain would close now, after his
treasonable abuses!

ESCALUS. Such a fellow is not to be talk'd withal.
Away with him to prison! Where is the provost?
Away with him to prison! Lay bolts enough on him, let
him speak no more. Away with those giglots too, and
with the other confederate companion!

                         The Provost lays hands on the Duke

DUKE. Stay, sir; stay awhile.

ANGELO. What! resists he? Help him, Lucio.

LUCIO. Come, sir; come, sir; come, sir; foh! sir. Why, you
bald-pated, lying rascal, you must be hooded, must you?
show your knave's visage, with a pox to you! show your
sheep-biting face, and be hanged an hour! Will 't not off?

               Pulls off the friar's hood, and discovers the Duke

DUKE. Thou art the first knave that e'er made a duke.
First, provost, let me bail these gentle three.
(*To Lucio*) Sneak not away, sir; for the friar and you
Must have a word anon. Lay hold on him.

LUCIO. This may prove worse than hanging.

DUKE. (*To Escalus*) What you have spoke I pardon; sit you
down:
We 'll borrow place of him. (*To Angelo*) Sir, by your
leave.
Hast thou or word, or wit, or impudence,
That yet can do thee office? If thou hast,
Rely upon it till my tale be heard,
And hold no longer out.

ANGELO.   O my dread lord!

I should be guiltier than my guiltiness,
To think I can be undiscernible
When I perceive your Grace, like power divine,
Hath look'd upon my passes. Then, good prince,
No longer session hold upon my shame,
But let my trial be mine own confession:
Immediate sentence then and sequent death
Is all the grace I beg.

DUKE.   Come hither, Mariana.
Say, wast thou e'er contracted to this woman?

ANGELO. I was, my lord.

DUKE. Go take her hence, and marry her instantly.
Do you the office, friar; which consummate,
Return him here again. Go with him, provost.

　　　Exeunt Angelo, Mariana, Friar Peter, and Provost

ESCALUS. My lord, I am more amaz'd at his dishonour
Than at the strangeness of it.

DUKE.   Come hither, Isabel.
Your friar is now your prince: as I was then
Advertising and holy to your business,
Not changing heart with habit, I am still
Attorney'd at your service.

ISABELLA.   O, give me pardon,
That I, your vassal, have employ'd and pain'd
Your unknown sovereignty!

DUKE.   You are pardon'd, Isabel:
And now, dear maid, be you as free to us.
Your brother's death, I know, sits at your heart;
And you may marvel why I obscur'd myself,
Labouring to save his life, and would not rather
Make rash remonstrance of my hidden power
Than let him so be lost. O most kind maid!
It was the swift celerity of his death,
Which I did think with slower foot came on,
That brain'd my purpose: but, peace be with him!
That life is better life, past fearing death,
Than that which lives to fear: make it your comfort,
So happy is your brother.

ISABELLA.   I do, my lord.

　　Re-enter Angelo, Mariana, Friar Peter, and Provost

DUKE. For this new-married man approaching here,
Whose salt imagination yet hath wrong'd

Your well-defended honour, you must pardon
For Mariana's sake. But as he adjudg'd your brother,—
Being criminal, in double violation
Of sacred chastity, and of promise-breach,
Thereon dependent, for your brother's life,—
The very mercy of the law cries out
Most audible, even from his proper tongue,
'An Angelo for Claudio, death for death!'
Haste still pays haste, and leisure answers leisure,
Like doth quit like, and Measure still for Measure.
Then, Angelo, thy fault 's thus manifested,
Which, though thou wouldst deny, denies thee vantage.
We do condemn thee to the very block
Where Claudio stoop'd to death, and with like haste.
Away with him!

MARIANA.   O, my most gracious lord!
I hope you will not mock me with a husband.

DUKE. It is your husband mock'd you with a husband.
Consenting to the safeguard of your honour,
I thought your marriage fit; else imputation,
For that he knew you, might reproach your life
And choke your good to come. For his possessions,
Although by confiscation they are ours,
We do instate and widow you withal,
To buy you a better husband.

MARIANA.   O my dear lord!
I crave no other, nor no better man.

DUKE. Never crave him; we are definitive.

MARIANA. (Kneeling) Gentle my liege—

DUKE.   You do but lose your labour.
Away with him to death! (To Lucio) Now, sir, to you.

MARIANA. O my good lord! Sweet Isabel, take my part:
Lend me your knees, and, all my life to come,
I 'll lend you all my life to do you service.

DUKE. Against all sense you do importune her:
Should she kneel down in mercy of this fact,
Her brother's ghost his paved bed would break,
And take her hence in horror.

MARIANA.   Isabel,
Sweet Isabel, do yet but kneel by me:
Hold up your hands, say nothing, I 'll speak all.
They say best men are moulded out of faults,

And, for the most, become much more the better
For being a little bad: so may my husband.
O, Isabel! will you not lend a knee?

DUKE. He dies for Claudio's death.

ISABELLA.   (*Kneeling*) Most bounteous sir,
Look, if it please you, on this man condemn'd,
As if my brother liv'd. I partly think
A due sincerity govern'd his deeds,
Till he did look on me: since it is so,
Let him not die. My brother had but justice,
In that he did the thing for which he died:
For Angelo,
His act did not o'ertake his bad intent;
And must be buried but as an intent
That perish'd by the way. Thoughts are no subjects;
Intents but merely thoughts.

MARIANA.   Merely, my lord.

DUKE. Your suit 's unprofitable: stand up, I say.
I have bethought me of another fault.
Provost, how came it Claudio was beheaded
At an unusual hour?

PROVOST.   It was commanded so.

DUKE. Had you a special warrant for the deed?

PROVOST. No, my good lord; it was by private message.

DUKE. For which I do discharge you of your office:
Give up your keys.

PROVOST.   Pardon me, noble lord:
I thought it was a fault, but knew it not,
Yet did repent me, after more advice;
For testimony whereof, one in the prison,
That should by private order else have died
I have reserv'd alive.

DUKE.   What 's he?

PROVOST.   His name is Barnardine.

DUKE. I would thou hadst done so by Claudio.
Go, fetch him hither: let me look upon him. *Exit Provost*

ESCALUS. I am sorry, one so learned and so wise
As you, Lord Angelo, have still appear'd,
Should slip so grossly, both in the heat of blood,
And lack of temper'd judgment afterward.

ANGELO. I am sorry that such sorrow I procure;
And so deep sticks it in my penitent heart

That I crave death more willingly than mercy:
'Tis my deserving, and I do entreat it.

Re-enter Provost,
with Barnardine, Claudio muffled, and Juliet

DUKE. Which is that Barnardine?

PROVOST.   This, my lord.

DUKE. There was a friar told me of this man.
Sirrah, thou art said to have a stubborn soul,
That apprehends no further than this world,
And squar'st thy life according. Thou 'rt condemn'd:
But, for those earthly faults, I quit them all,
And pray thee take this mercy to provide
For better times to come. Friar, advise him:
I leave him to your hand.—What muffled fellow 's that?

PROVOST. This is another prisoner that I sav'd,
That should have died when Claudio lost his head,
As like almost to Claudio as himself.   *Unmuffles Claudio*

DUKE. (*To Isabella*) If he be like your brother, for his sake
Is he pardon'd; and, for your lovely sake
Give me your hand, and say you will be mine,
He is my brother too. But fitter time for that.
By this, Lord Angelo perceives he 's safe:
Methinks I see a quickening in his eye.
Well, Angelo, your evil quits you well:
Look that you love your wife; her worth worth yours.—
I find an apt remission in myself,
And yet here 's one in place I cannot pardon.—
(*To Lucio*) You, sirrah, that knew me for a fool, a cow-
ard;
One all of luxury, an ass, a madman:
Wherein have I so deserv'd of you,
That you extol me thus?

LUCIO. 'Faith, my lord, I spoke it but according to the trick.
If you will hang me for it, you may; but I had rather it
would please you I might be whipped.

DUKE. Whipp'd first, sir, and hang'd after.
Proclaim it, provost, round about the city,
If any woman 's wrong'd by this lewd fellow,—
As I have heard him swear himself there 's one
Whom he begot with child, let her appear,
And he shall marry her: the nuptial finish'd,
Let him be whipp'd and hang'd.

LUCIO. I beseech your Highness, do not marry me to a
　　whore. Your Highness said even now, I made you a duke:
　　good my lord, do not recompense me in making me a
　　cuckold.
DUKE. Upon mine honour, thou shalt marry her.
　　Thy slanders I forgive; and therewithal
　　Remit thy other forfeits. Take him to prison,
　　And see our pleasure herein executed.
LUCIO. Marrying a punk, my lord, is pressing to death,
　　whipping, and hanging.
DUKE. Slandering a prince deserves it.
　　She, Claudio, that you wrong'd, look you restore.
　　Joy to you, Mariana! love her, Angelo:
　　I have confess'd her and I know her virtue.
　　Thanks, good friend Escalus, for thy much goodness:
　　There 's more behind that is more gratulate.
　　Thanks, provost, for thy care and secrecy;
　　We shall employ thee in a worthier place.
　　Forgive him, Angelo, that brought you home
　　The head of Ragozine for Claudio's:
　　The offence pardons itself. Dear Isabel,
　　I have a motion much imports your good;
　　Whereto if you 'll a willing ear incline,
　　What 's mine is yours, and what is yours is mine.
　　So, bring us to our palace; where we 'll show
　　What 's yet behind, that 's meet you all should know.
　　　　　　　　　　　　　　　　　　　　　Exeunt

THE COMEDY OF
ERRORS

SCENE

Ephesus

THE COMEDY OF ERRORS

ACT ONE

SCENE ONE

A Hall in the Duke's Palace.

Enter Duke, Ægeon, Gaoler, Officers, and other Attendants

ÆGEON. Proceed, Solinus, to procure my fall,
    And by the doom of death end woes and all.
DUKE. Merchant of Syracusa, plead no more.
    I am not partial to infringe our laws:
    The enmity and discord which of late
    Sprung from the rancorous outrage of your duke
    To merchants, our well-dealing countrymen,
    Who, wanting guilders to redeem their lives,
    Have seal'd his rigorous statutes with their bloods,
    Excludes all pity from our threat'ning looks.
    For, since the mortal and intestine jars
    'Twixt thy seditious countrymen and us,
    It hath in solemn synods been decreed,
    Both by the Syracusians and ourselves,
    T' admit no traffic to our adverse towns:
    Nay, more, if any, born at Ephesus
    Be seen at Syracusian marts and fairs;
    Again, if any Syracusian born
    Come to the bay of Ephesus, he dies,
    His goods confiscate to the duke's dispose;
    Unless a thousand marks be levied,
    To quit the penalty and to ransom him.
    Thy substance, valu'd at the highest rate,
    Cannot amount unto a hundred marks;
    Therefore, by law thou art condemn'd to die.
ÆGEON. Yet this my comfort: when your words are done,

My woes end likewise with the evening sun.
DUKE. Well, Syracusian; say, in brief the cause
Why thou departedst from thy native home,
And for what cause thou cam'st to Ephesus.
ÆGEON. A heavier task could not have been impos'd
Than I to speak my griefs unspeakable;
Yet, that the world may witness that my end
Was wrought by nature, not by vile offence,
I 'll utter what my sorrow gives me leave.
In Syracusa was I born, and wed
Unto a woman, happy but for me,
And by me too, had not our hap been bad.
With her I liv'd in joy: our wealth increas'd
By prosperous voyages I often made
To Epidamnum; till my factor's death,
And the great care of goods at random left,
Drew me from kind embracements of my spouse:
From whom my absence was not six months old,
Before herself,—almost at fainting under
The pleasing punishment that women bear,—
Had made provision for her following me,
And soon and safe arrived where I was.
There had she not been long but she became
A joyful mother of two goodly sons;
And, which was strange, the one so like the other,
As could not be distinguish'd but by names.
That very hour, and in the self-same inn,
A meaner woman was delivered
Of such a burden, male twins, both alike.
Those,—for their parents were exceeding poor,—
I bought, and brought up to attend my sons.
My wife, not meanly proud of two such boys,
Made daily motions for our home return:
Unwilling I agreed; alas! too soon
We came aboard.
A league from Epidamnum had we sail'd,
Before the always-wind-obeying deep
Gave any tragic instance of our harm:
But longer did we not retain much hope;
For what obscured light the heavens did grant
Did but convey unto our fearful minds
A doubtful warrant of immediate death;

Which, though myself would gladly have embrac'd,
Yet the incessant weepings of my wife,
Weeping before for what she saw must come,
And piteous plainings of the pretty babes,
That mourn'd for fashion, ignorant what to fear,
Forc'd me to seek delays for them and me.
And this it was, for other means was none:
The sailors sought for safety by our boat,
And left the ship, then sinking-ripe, to us:
My wife, more careful for the latter-born,
Had fasten'd him unto a small spare mast,
Such as seafaring men provide for storms;
To him one of the other twins was bound,
Whilst I had been like heedful of the other.
The children thus dispos'd, my wife and I,
Fixing our eyes on whom our care was fix'd,
Fasten'd ourselves at either end the mast;
And floating straight, obedient to the stream,
Were carried towards Corinth, as we thought.
At length the sun, gazing upon the earth,
Dispers'd those vapours that offended us;
And, by the benefit of his wished light
The seas wax'd calm, and we discovered
Two ships from far making amain to us;
Of Corinth that, of Epidaurus this:
But ere they came,—O! let me say no more;
Gather the sequel by that went before.

DUKE. Nay, forward, old man; do not break off so;
    For we may pity, though not pardon thee.

ÆGEON. O! had the gods done so, I had not now
    Worthily term'd them merciless to us!
    For, ere the ships could meet by twice five leagues,
    We were encounter'd by a mighty rock;
    Which, being violently borne upon,
    Our helpful ship was splitted in the midst;
    So that, in this unjust divorce of us
    Fortune had left to both of us alike
    What to delight in, what to sorrow for.
    Her part, poor soul! seeming as burdened
    With lesser weight, but not with lesser woe,
    Was carried with more speed before the wind,
    And in our sight they three were taken up

By fishermen of Corinth, as we thought.
At length, another ship had seized on us,
And, knowing whom it was their hap to save,
Gave healthful welcome to their ship-wrack'd guests;
And would have reft the fishers of their prey,
Had not their bark been very slow of sail;
And therefore homeward did they bend their course.
Thus have you heard me sever'd from my bliss,
That by misfortune was my life prolong'd,
To tell sad stories of my own mishaps.

DUKE. And, for the sake of them thou sorrowest for,
Do me the favour to dilate at full
What hath befall'n of them and thee till now.

ÆGEON. My youngest boy, and yet my eldest care,
At eighteen years became inquisitive
After his brother; and importun'd me
That his attendant—for his case was like,
Reft of his brother, but retain'd his name—
Might bear him company in the quest of him;
Whom whilst I labour'd of a love to see,
I hazarded the loss of whom I lov'd.
Five summers have I spent in furthest Greece,
Roaming clean through the bounds of Asia,
And, coasting homeward, came to Ephesus,
Hopeless to find, yet loath to leave unsought
Or that or any place that harbours men.
But here must end the story of my life;
And happy were I in my timely death,
Could all my travels warrant me they live.

DUKE. Hapless Ægeon, whom the fates have mark'd
To bear the extremity of dire mishap!
Now, trust me, were it not against our laws,
Against my crown, my oath, my dignity,
Which princes, would they, may not disannul,
My soul should sue as advocate for thee.
But though thou art adjudged to the death
And passed sentence may not be recall'd
But to our honour's great disparagement,
Yet will I favour thee in what I can:
Therefore, merchant, I 'll limit thee this day
To seek thy life by beneficial help.
Try all the friends thou hast in Ephesus;

Beg thou, or borrow, to make up the sum,
And live; if no, then thou art doom'd to die.
Gaoler, take him to thy custody

GAOLER. I will, my lord.

ÆGEON. Hopeless and helpless doth Ægeon wend,
But to procrastinate his lifeless end.   *Exeunt*

SCENE TWO

The Mart.

*Enter Antipholus of Syracuse, Dromio of Syracuse,
and a Merchant*

MERCHANT. Therefore, give out you are of Epidamnum,
Lest that your goods too soon be confiscate.
This very day, a Syracusian merchant
Is apprehended for arrival here;
And, not being able to buy out his life,
According to the statute of the town,
Dies ere the weary sun set in the west.
There is your money that I had to keep.

ANTIPHOLUS OF SYRACUSE. Go bear it to the Centaur, where
we host,
And stay there, Dromio, till I come to thee.
Within this hour it will be dinner-time:
Till that, I 'll view the manners of the town,
Peruse the traders, gaze upon the buildings,
And then return and sleep within mine inn,
For with long travel I am stiff and weary.
Get thee away.

DROMIO OF SYRACUSE. Many a man would take you at your
word,
And go indeed, having so good a mean.   *Exit*

ANTIPHOLUS OF SYRACUSE. A trusty villain, sir, that very oft,
When I am dull with care and melancholy,
Lightens my humour with his merry jests.
What, will you walk with me about the town,
And then go to my inn and dine with me?

MERCHANT. I am invited, sir, to certain merchants,
Of whom I hope to make much benefit;
I crave your pardon. Soon at five o'clock,

Please you, I 'll meet with you upon the mart,
And afterward consort you till bed-time:
My present business calls me from you now.

ANTIPHOLUS OF SYRACUSE. Farewell till then: I will go lose myself,
And wander up and down to view the city.

MERCHANT. Sir, I commend you to your own content.   *Exit*

ANTIPHOLUS OF SYRACUSE. He that commends me to mine own content,
Commends me to the thing I cannot get.
I to the world am like a drop of water
That in the ocean seeks another drop;
Who, falling there to find his fellow forth,
Unseen, inquisitive, confounds himself:
So I, to find a mother and a brother,
In quest of them, unhappy, lose myself.

Enter Dromio of Ephesus

Here comes the almanack of my true date.
What now? How chance thou art return'd so soon?

DROMIO OF EPHESUS. Return'd so soon! rather approach'd too late:
The capon burns, the pig falls from the spit,
The clock hath strucken twelve upon the bell;
My mistress made it one upon my cheek:
She is so hot because the meat is cold;
The meat is cold because you come not home;
You come not home because you have no stomach;
You have no stomach, having broke your fast;
But we, that know what 'tis to fast and pray,
Are penitent for your default to-day.

ANTIPHOLUS OF SYRACUSE. Stop in your wind, sir: tell me this, I pray:
Where have you left the money that I gave you?

DROMIO OF EPHESUS. O!—sixpence, that I had o' Wednesday last
To pay the saddler for my mistress' crupper;
The saddler had it, sir; I kept it not.

ANTIPHOLUS OF SYRACUSE. I am not in a sportive humour now.
Tell me, and dally not, where is the money?
We being strangers here, how dar'st thou trust
So great a charge from thine own custody?

DROMIO OF EPHESUS. I pray you, jest, sir, as you sit at
    dinner.
  I from my mistress come to you in post;
  If I return, I shall be post indeed,
  For she will score your fault upon my pate.
  Methinks your maw, like mine, should be your clock
  And strike you home without a messenger.
ANTIPHOLUS OF SYRACUSE. Come, Dromio, come; these jests
    are out of season;
  Reserve them till a merrier hour than this.
  Where is the gold I gave in charge to thee?
DROMIO OF EPHESUS. To me, sir? why, you gave no gold to
    me.
ANTIPHOLUS OF SYRACUSE. Come on, sir knave, have done
    your foolishness,
  And tell me how thou hast dispos'd thy charge.
DROMIO OF EPHESUS. My charge was but to fetch you from
    the mart
  Home to your house, the Phœnix, sir, to dinner:
  My mistress and her sister stays for you.
ANTIPHOLUS OF SYRACUSE. Now, as I am a Christian,
    answer me,
  In what safe place you have bestow'd my money:
  Or I shall break that merry sconce of yours
  That stands on tricks when I am undispos'd.
  Where is the thousand marks thou hadst of me?
DROMIO OF EPHESUS. I have some marks of yours upon my
    pate,
  Some of my mistress' marks upon my shoulders,
  But not a thousand marks between you both.
  If I should pay your worship those again,
  Perchance you will not bear them patiently.
ANTIPHOLUS OF SYRACUSE. Thy mistress' marks! what mis-
    tress, slave, hast thou?
DROMIO OF EPHESUS. Your worship's wife, my mistress at
    the Phœnix;
  She that doth fast till you come home to dinner,
  And prays that you will hie you home to dinner.
ANTIPHOLUS OF SYRACUSE. What! wilt thou flout me thus
    unto my face,
  Being forbid? There, take you that, sir knave. *Strikes him*

DROMIO OF EPHESUS. What mean you, sir? for God's sake,
    hold your hands!

    Nay, an you will not, sir, I 'll take my heels.   *Exit*

ANTIPHOLUS OF SYRACUSE. Upon my life, by some device or
    other

    The villain is o'er-raught of all my money.

    They say this town is full of cozenage;

    As, nimble jugglers that deceive the eye,

    Dark-working sorcerers that change the mind,

    Soul-killing witches that deform the body,

    Disguised cheaters, prating mountebanks,

    And many such-like liberties of sin:

    If it prove so, I will be gone the sooner.

    I 'll to the Centaur, to go seek this slave:

    I greatly fear my money is not safe.   *Exit*

ACT TWO

SCENE ONE

The House of Antipholus of Ephesus.

Enter Adriana and Luciana

ADRIANA. Neither my husband, nor the slave return'd,
That in such haste I sent to seek his master!
Sure, Luciana, it is two o'clock.

LUCIANA. Perhaps some merchant hath invited him,
And from the mart he 's somewhere gone to dinner.
Good sister, let us dine and never fret:
A man is master of his liberty:
Time is their master, and, when they see time,
They 'll go or come: if so, be patient, sister.

ADRIANA. Why should their liberty than ours be more?

LUCIANA. Because their business still lies out o' door.

ADRIANA. Look, when I serve him so, he takes it ill.

LUCIANA. O! know he is the bridle of your will.

ADRIANA. There 's none but asses will be bridled so.

LUCIANA. Why, headstrong liberty is lash'd with woe.
There 's nothing situate under heaven's eye
But hath his bound, in earth, in sea, in sky:
The beasts, the fishes, and the winged fowls,
Are their males' subjects and at their controls.
Men, more divine, the masters of all these,
Lords of the wide world, and wild wat'ry seas,
Indu'd with intellectual sense and souls,
Of more pre-eminence than fish and fowls,
Are masters to their females and their lords:
Then, let your will attend on their accords.

ADRIANA. This servitude makes you to keep unwed.

LUCIANA. Not this, but troubles of the marriage-bed.

ADRIANA. But, were you wedded, you would bear some
sway.

LUCIANA. Ere I learn love, I 'll practise to obey.

ADRIANA. How if your husband start some other where?

LUCIANA. Till he come home again, I would forbear.

ADRIANA. Patience unmov'd! no marvel though she pause;
 They can be meek that have no other cause.
 A wretched soul, bruis'd with adversity,
 We bid be quiet when we hear it cry;
 But were we burden'd with like weight of pain,
 As much, or more, we should ourselves complain:
 So thou, that hast no unkind mate to grieve thee,
 With urging helpless patience wouldst relieve me:
 But if thou live to see like right bereft,
 This fool-begged patience in thee will be left.

LUCIANA. Well, I will marry one day, but to try.
 Here comes your man: now is your husband nigh.

Enter Dromio of Ephesus

ADRIANA. Say, is your tardy master now at hand?

DROMIO OF EPHESUS. Nay, he 's at two hands with me, and
 that my two ears can witness.

ADRIANA. Say, didst thou speak with him? Know'st thou his
 mind?

DROMIO OF EPHESUS. Ay, ay, he told his mind upon mine
 ear.
 Beshrew his hand, I scarce could understand it.

LUCIANA. Spake he so doubtfully, thou couldst not feel his
 meaning?

DROMIO OF EPHESUS. Nay, he struck so plainly, I could too
 well feel his blows; and withal so doubtfully, that I could
 scarce understand them.

ADRIANA. But say, I prithee, is he coming home?
 It seems he hath great care to please his wife.

DROMIO OF EPHESUS. Why, mistress, sure my master is
 horn-mad.

ADRIANA. Horn-mad, thou villain!

DROMIO OF EPHESUS. I mean not cuckold-mad; but, sure, he
 is stark mad.
 When I desir'd him to come home to dinner,
 He ask'd me for a thousand marks in gold:
 ' 'Tis dinner time,' quoth I; 'my gold!' quoth he:
 'Your meat doth burn,' quoth I; 'my gold!' quoth he:
 'Will you come home?' quoth I: 'my gold!' quoth he:
 'Where is the thousand marks I gave thee, villain?'

'The pig,' quoth I, 'is burn'd;' 'my gold!' quoth he:
'My mistress, sir,' quoth I: 'hang up thy mistress!
I know not thy mistress: out on thy mistress!'

LUCIANA. Quoth who?

DROMIO OF EPHESUS. Quoth my master:
'I know,' quoth he, 'no house, no wife, no mistress.'
So that my errand, due unto my tongue,
I thank him, I bear home upon my shoulders;
For, in conclusion, he did beat me there.

ADRIANA. Go back again, thou slave, and fetch him home.

DROMIO OF EPHESUS. Go back again, and be new beaten
    home?
For God's sake, send some other messenger.

ADRIANA. Back, slave, or I will break thy pate across.

DROMIO OF EPHESUS. And he will bless that cross with other
    beating:
Between you, I shall have a holy head.

ADRIANA. Hence, prating peasant! fetch thy master home.

DROMIO OF EPHESUS. Am I so round with you as you with
    me,
That like a football you do spurn me thus?
You spurn me hence, and he will spurn me hither:
If I last in this service, you must case me in leather. *Exit*

LUCIANA. Fie, how impatience low'reth in your face!

ADRIANA. His company must do his minions grace,
Whilst I at home starve for a merry look.
Hath homely age the alluring beauty took
From my poor cheek? then, he hath wasted it:
Are my discourses dull? barren my wit?
If voluble and sharp discourse be marr'd,
Unkindness blunts it more than marble hard:
Do their gay vestments his affections bait?
That 's not my fault; he 's master of my state:
What ruins are in me that can be found
By him not ruin'd? then is he the ground
Of my defeatures. My decayed fair
A sunny look of his would soon repair;
But, too unruly deer, he breaks the pale
And feeds from home: poor I am but his stale.

LUCIANA. Self-harming jealousy! fie! beat it hence.

ADRIANA. Unfeeling fools can with such wrongs dispense.
I know his eye doth homage otherwhere,

Or else what lets it but he would be here?
Sister, you know he promis'd me a chain:
Would that alone, alone he would detain,
So he would keep fair quarter with his bed!
I see, the jewel best enamelled
Will lose his beauty; and though gold bides still
That others touch, yet often touching will
Wear gold; and no man that hath a name,
By falsehood and corruption doth it shame.
Since that my beauty cannot please his eye,
I 'll weep what 's left away, and weeping die.

LUCIANA. How many fond fools serve mad jealousy!

Exeunt

SCENE TWO

A public Place.

Enter Antipholus of Syracuse

ANTIPHOLUS OF SYRACUSE. The gold I gave to Dromio is
laid up
Safe at the Centaur; and the heedful slave
Is wander'd forth, in care to seek me out.
By computation, and mine host's report,
I could not speak with Dromio since at first
I sent him from the mart. See, here he comes.

Enter Dromio of Syracuse

How now, sir! is your merry humour alter'd?
As you love strokes, so jest with me again.
You know no Centaur? You receiv'd no gold?
Your mistress sent to have me home to dinner?
My house was at the Phœnix? Wast thou mad,
That thus so madly thou didst answer me?

DROMIO OF SYRACUSE. What answer, sir? when spake I such
a word?

ANTIPHOLUS OF SYRACUSE. Even now, even here, not half-
an-hour since.

DROMIO OF SYRACUSE. I did not see you since you sent me
hence,
Home to the Centaur, with the gold you gave me.

ANTIPHOLUS OF SYRACUSE. Villain, thou didst deny the gold's receipt,

And told'st me of a mistress and a dinner;

For which, I hope, thou felt'st I was displeas'd.

DROMIO OF SYRACUSE. I am glad to see you in this merry vein:

What means this jest? I pray you, master, tell me.

ANTIPHOLUS OF SYRACUSE. Yea, dost thou jeer, and flout me in the teeth?

Think'st thou I jest? Hold, take thou that, and that.

Beating him

DROMIO OF SYRACUSE. Hold, sir, for God's sake! now your jest is earnest:

Upon what bargain do you give it me?

ANTIPHOLUS OF SYRACUSE. Because that I familiarly sometimes

Do use you for my fool, and chat with you,

Your sauciness will jest upon my love,

And make a common of my serious hours.

When the sun shines let foolish gnats make sport,

But creep in crannies when he hides his beams.

If you will jest with me, know my aspect,

And fashion your demeanour to my looks,

Or I will beat this method in your sconce.

DROMIO OF SYRACUSE. Sconce, call you it? so you would leave battering, I had rather have it a head: an you use these blows long, I must get a sconce for my head and insconce it too; or else I shall seek my wit in my shoulders. But, I pray, sir, why am I beaten?

ANTIPHOLUS OF SYRACUSE. Dost thou not know?

DROMIO OF SYRACUSE. Nothing, sir, but that I am beaten.

ANTIPHOLUS OF SYRACUSE. Shall I tell you why?

DROMIO OF SYRACUSE. Ay, sir, and wherefore; for they say every why hath a wherefore.

ANTIPHOLUS OF SYRACUSE. Why, first,—for flouting me; and then, wherefore,—

For urging it the second time to me.

DROMIO OF SYRACUSE. Was there ever any man thus beaten out of season,

When, in the why and the wherefore is neither rime nor reason?

Well, sir, I thank you.

ANTIPHOLUS OF SYRACUSE. Thank me, sir! for what?

DROMIO OF SYRACUSE. Marry, sir, for this something that you gave me for nothing.

ANTIPHOLUS OF SYRACUSE. I 'll make you amends next, to give you nothing for something. But say, sir, is it dinner-time?

DROMIO OF SYRACUSE. No, sir: I think the meat wants that I have.

ANTIPHOLUS OF SYRACUSE. In good time, sir; what 's that?

DROMIO OF SYRACUSE. Basting.

ANTIPHOLUS OF SYRACUSE. Well, sir, then 'twill be dry.

DROMIO OF SYRACUSE. If it be, sir, I pray you eat none of it.

ANTIPHOLUS OF SYRACUSE. Your reason?

DROMIO OF SYRACUSE. Lest it make you choleric, and purchase me another dry basting.

ANTIPHOLUS OF SYRACUSE. Well, sir, learn to jest in good time: there 's a time for all things.

DROMIO OF SYRACUSE. I durst have denied that, before you were so choleric.

ANTIPHOLUS OF SYRACUSE. By what rule, sir?

DROMIO OF SYRACUSE. Marry, sir, by a rule as plain as the plain bald pate of Father Time himself.

ANTIPHOLUS OF SYRACUSE. Let 's hear it.

DROMIO OF SYRACUSE. There 's no time for a man to recover his hair that grows bald by nature.

ANTIPHOLUS OF SYRACUSE. May he not do it by fine and recovery?

DROMIO OF SYRACUSE. Yes, to pay a fine for a periwig and recover the lost hair of another man.

ANTIPHOLUS OF SYRACUSE. Why is Time such a niggard of hair, being, as it is, so plentiful an excrement?

DROMIO OF SYRACUSE. Because it is a blessing that he bestows on beasts: and what he hath scanted men in hair, he hath given them in wit.

ANTIPHOLUS OF SYRACUSE. Why, but there 's many a man hath more hair than wit.

DROMIO OF SYRACUSE. Not a man of those but he hath the wit to lose his hair.

ANTIPHOLUS OF SYRACUSE. Why, thou didst conclude hairy men plain dealers without wit.

DROMIO OF SYRACUSE. The plainer dealer, the sooner lost: yet he loseth it in a kind of jollity.

ANTIPHOLUS OF SYRACUSE. For what reason?

DROMIO OF SYRACUSE. For two; and sound ones too.

ANTIPHOLUS OF SYRACUSE. Nay, not sound, I pray you.

DROMIO OF SYRACUSE. Sure ones then.

ANTIPHOLUS OF SYRACUSE. Nay, not sure, in a thing falsing.

DROMIO OF SYRACUSE. Certain ones then.

ANTIPHOLUS OF SYRACUSE. Name them.

DROMIO OF SYRACUSE. The one, to save the money that he
spends in tiring; the other, that at dinner they should not
drop in his porridge.

ANTIPHOLUS OF SYRACUSE. You would all this time have
proved there is no time for all things.

DROMIO OF SYRACUSE. Marry, and did, sir; namely, no time
to recover hair lost by nature.

ANTIPHOLUS OF SYRACUSE. But your reason was not substantial, why there is no time to recover.

DROMIO OF SYRACUSE. Thus I mend it: Time himself is
bald, and therefore to the world's end will have bald followers.

ANTIPHOLUS OF SYRACUSE. I knew 'twould be a bald conclusion. But soft! Who wafts us yonder?

Enter Adriana and Luciana

ADRIANA. Ay, ay, Antipholus, look strange, and frown:
Some other mistress hath thy sweet aspects,
I am not Adriana, nor thy wife.
The time was once when thou unurg'd wouldst vow
That never words were music to thine ear,
That never object pleasing in thine eye,
That never touch well welcome to thy hand,
That never meat sweet-savour'd in thy taste,
Unless I spake, or look'd, or touch'd, or carv'd to thee.
How comes it now, my husband, O! how comes it,
That thou art thus estranged from thyself?
Thyself I call it, being strange to me,
That, undividable, incorporate,
Am better than thy dear self's better part.
Ah! do not tear away thyself from me,
For know, my love, as easy mayst thou fall
A drop of water in the breaking gulf,
And take unmingled thence that drop again,
Without addition or diminishing,
As take from me thyself and not me too.

How dearly would it touch thee to the quick,
Shouldst thou but hear I were licentious,
And that this body, consecrate to thee,
By ruffian lust should be contaminate!
Wouldst thou not spit at me and spurn at me,
And hurl the name of husband in my face,
And tear the stain'd skin off my harlet-brow,
And from my false hand cut the wedding-ring
And break it with a deep-divorcing vow?
I know thou canst; and therefore, see thou do it.
I am possess'd with an adulterate blot;
My blood is mingled with the crime of lust:
For if we two be one and thou play false,
I do digest the poison of thy flesh,
Being strumpeted by thy contagion.
Keep then fair league and truce with thy true bed;
I live unstain'd, thou undishonoured.

ANTIPHOLUS OF SYRACUSE. Plead you to me, fair dame? I
    know you not:
In Ephesus I am but two hours old,
As strange unto your town as to your talk;
Who, every word by all my wit being scann'd,
Want wit in all one word to understand.

LUCIANA. Fie, brother: how the world is chang'd with you!
When were you wont to use my sister thus?
She sent for you by Dromio home to dinner.

ANTIPHOLUS OF SYRACUSE. By Dromio?

DROMIO OF SYRACUSE. By me?

ADRIANA. By thee; and this thou didst return from him,
That he did buffet thee, and in his blows,
Denied my house for his, me for his wife.

ANTIPHOLUS OF SYRACUSE. Did you converse, sir, with this
    gentlewoman?
What is the course and drift of your compact?

DROMIO OF SYRACUSE. I, sir? I never saw her till this time.

ANTIPHOLUS OF SYRACUSE. Villain, thou liest; for even her
    very words
Didst thou deliver to me on the mart.

DROMIO OF SYRACUSE. I never spake with her in all my life.

ANTIPHOLUS OF SYRACUSE. How can she thus then call us by
    our names,
Unless it be by inspiration?

ADRIANA. How ill agrees it with your gravity
　　To counterfeit thus grossly with your slave,
　　Abetting him to thwart me in my mood!
　　Be it my wrong you are from me exempt,
　　But wrong not that wrong with a more contempt.
　　Come, I will fasten on this sleeve of thine;
　　Thou art an elm, my husband, I a vine,
　　Whose weakness, married to thy stronger state,
　　Makes me with thy strength to communicate:
　　If aught possess thee from me, it is dross,
　　Usurping ivy, brier, or idle moss;
　　Who, all for want of pruning, with intrusion
　　Infect thy sap and live on thy confusion.

ANTIPHOLUS OF SYRACUSE. To me she speaks; she moves me
　　　　for her theme!
　　What! was I married to her in my dream?
　　Or sleep I now and think I hear all this?
　　What error drives our eyes and ears amiss?
　　Until I know this sure uncertainty,
　　I 'll entertain the offer'd fallacy.

LUCIANA. Dromio, go bid the servants spread for dinner.

DROMIO OF SYRACUSE. O, for my beads! I cross me for a
　　　　sinner.
　　This is the fairy land: O! spite of spites,
　　We talk with goblins, owls, and elvish sprites:
　　If we obey them not, this will ensue,
　　They 'll suck our breath, or pinch us black and blue.

LUCIANA. Why prat'st thou to thyself and answer'st not?
　　Dromio, thou drone, thou snail, thou slug, thou sot!

DROMIO OF SYRACUSE. I am transformed, master, am not I?

ANTIPHOLUS OF SYRACUSE. I think thou art, in mind, and so
　　　　am I.

DROMIO OF SYRACUSE. Nay, master, both in mind and in my
　　　　shape.

ANTIPHOLUS OF SYRACUSE. Thou hast thine own form.

DROMIO OF SYRACUSE.　　　　　　　　No, I am an ape.

LUCIANA. If thou art chang'd to aught, 'tis to an ass.

DROMIO OF SYRACUSE. 'Tis true; she rides me and I long for
　　　　grass.
　　'Tis so, I am an ass; else it could never be
　　But I should know her as well as she knows me.

ADRIANA. Come, come; no longer will I be a fool,

To put the finger in the eye and weep,
Whilst man and master laugh my woes to scorn.
Come, sir, to dinner. Dromio, keep the gate.
Husband, I 'll dine above with you to-day,
And shrive you of a thousand idle pranks.
Sirrah, if any ask you for your master,
Say he dines forth, and let no creature enter.
Come, sister. Dromio, play the porter well.

ANTIPHOLUS OF SYRACUSE. (*Aside*) Am I in earth, in heaven,
 or in hell?
Sleeping or waking? mad or well-advis'd?
Known unto these, and to myself disguis'd!
I 'll say as they say, and persever so,
And in this mist at all adventures go.

DROMIO OF SYRACUSE. Master, shall I be porter at the gate?

ADRIANA. Ay; and let none enter, lest I break your pate.

LUCIANA. Come, come, Antipholus; we dine too late.

           Exeunt

ACT THREE

SCENE ONE

Before the House of Antipholus of Ephesus.

*Enter Antipholus of Ephesus, Dromio of Ephesus,
Angelo, and Balthazar*

ANTIPHOLUS OF EPHESUS. Good Signior Angelo, you must
    excuse us all;
  My wife is shrewish when I keep not hours;
  Say that I linger'd with you at your shop
  To see the making of her carkanet,
  And that to-morrow you will bring it home.
  But here 's a villain, that would face me down
  He met me on the mart, and that I beat him,
  And charg'd him with a thousand marks in gold,
  And that I did deny my wife and house.
  Thou drunkard, thou, what didst thou mean by this?
DROMIO OF EPHESUS. Say what you will, sir, but I know
    what I know;
  That you beat me at the mart, I have your hand to show:
  If the skin were parchment and the blows you gave were
    ink,
  Your own handwriting would tell you what I think.
ANTIPHOLUS OF EPHESUS. I think thou art an ass.
DROMIO OF EPHESUS.   Marry, so it doth appear
  By the wrongs I suffer and the blows I bear.
  I should kick, being kick'd; and, being at that pass,
  You would keep from my heels and beware of an ass.
ANTIPHOLUS OF EPHESUS. You are sad, Signior Balthazar:
    pray God, our cheer
  May answer my good will and your good welcome here.
BALTHAZAR. I hold your dainties cheap, sir, and your wel-
  come dear.

ANTIPHOLUS OF EPHESUS. O, Signior Balthazar, either at flesh or fish,
A table-full of welcome makes scarce one dainty dish.

BALTHAZAR. Good meat, sir, is common; that every churl affords.

ANTIPHOLUS OF EPHESUS. And welcome more common, for that 's nothing but words.

BALTHAZAR. Small cheer and great welcome makes a merry feast.

ANTIPHOLUS OF EPHESUS. Ay, to a niggardly host and more sparing guest:
But though my cates be mean, take them in good part;
Better cheer may you have, but not with better heart.
But soft! my door is lock'd. Go bid them let us in.

DROMIO OF EPHESUS. Maud, Bridget, Marian, Cicely, Gillian, Ginn!

DROMIO OF SYRACUSE. (Within) Mome, malt-horse, capon, coxcomb, idiot, patch!
Either get thee from the door or sit down at the hatch.
Dost thou conjure for wenches, that thou call'st for such store,
When one is one too many? Go, get thee from the door.

DROMIO OF EPHESUS. What patch is made our porter?—My master stays in the street.

DROMIO OF SYRACUSE. (Within) Let him walk from whence he came, lest he catch cold on 's feet.

ANTIPHOLUS OF EPHESUS. Who talks within there? ho! open the door.

DROMIO OF SYRACUSE. (Within) Right, sir; I 'll tell you when, an you 'll tell me wherefore.

ANTIPHOLUS OF EPHESUS. Wherefore? for my dinner: I have not din'd to-day.

DROMIO OF SYRACUSE. Nor to-day here you must not; come again when you may.

ANTIPHOLUS OF EPHESUS. What art thou that keep'st me out from the house I owe?

DROMIO OF SYRACUSE. (Within) The porter for this time, sir, and my name is Dromio.

DROMIO OF EPHESUS. O villain! thou hast stolen both mine office and my name:
The one ne'er got me credit, the other mickle blame.
If thou hadst been Dromio to-day in my place,

Thou wouldst have chang'd thy face for a name, or thy
    name for an ass.

LUCE. (*Within*) What a coil is there, Dromio! who are those
    at the gate?

DROMIO OF EPHESUS. Let my master in, Luce.

LUCE. (*Within*)   Faith, no; he comes too late;
    And so tell your master.

DROMIO OF EPHESUS.   O Lord! I must laugh.
Have at you with a proverb: Shall I set in my staff?

LUCE. (*Within*) Have at you with another: that 's—when?
    can you tell?

DROMIO OF SYRACUSE. (*Within*) If thy name be call'd Luce,
    —Luce, thou hast answer'd him well.

ANTIPHOLUS OF EPHESUS. Do you hear, you minion? you 'll
    let us in, I trow?

LUCE. (*Within*) I thought to have ask'd you.

DROMIO OF SYRACUSE. (*Within*)   And you said, no.

DROMIO OF EPHESUS. So come, help: well struck! there was
    blow for blow.

ANTIPHOLUS OF EPHESUS. Thou baggage, let me in.

LUCE. (*Within*) Can you tell for whose sake?

DROMIO OF EPHESUS. Master, knock the door hard.

LUCE. (*Within*) Let him knock till it ache.

ANTIPHOLUS OF EPHESUS. You 'll cry for this, minion, if I beat
    the door down.

LUCE. (*Within*) What needs all that, and a pair of stocks
    in the town?

ADRIANA. (*Within*) Who is that at the door that keeps all
    this noise?

DROMIO OF SYRACUSE. (*Within*) By my troth your town is
    troubled with unruly boys.

ANTIPHOLUS OF EPHESUS. Are you there, wife? you might
    have come before.

ADRIANA. (*Within*) Your wife, sir knave! go, get you from
    the door.

DROMIO OF EPHESUS. If you went in pain, master, this
    'knave' would go sore.

ANGELO. Here is neither cheer, sir, nor welcome: we would
    fain have either.

BALTHAZAR. In debating which was best, we shall part
    with neither.

DROMIO OF EPHESUS. They stand at the door, master: bid
　them welcome hither.

ANTIPHOLUS OF EPHESUS. There is something in the wind,
　that we cannot get in.

DROMIO OF EPHESUS. You would say so, master, if your gar-
　ments were thin.

　Your cake here is warm within; you stand here in the
　cold:

　It would make a man mad as a buck to be so bought and
　sold.

ANTIPHOLUS OF EPHESUS. Go fetch me something: I 'll break
　ope the gate.

DROMIO OF SYRACUSE. (*Within*) Break any breaking here,
　and I 'll break your knave's pate.

DROMIO OF EPHESUS. A man may break a word with you,
　sir, and words are but wind:

　Ay, and break it in your face, so he break it not behind.

DROMIO OF SYRACUSE. (*Within*) It seems thou wantest break-
　ing: out upon thee, hind!

DROMIO OF EPHESUS. Here 's too much 'out upon thee!' I
　pray thee, let me in.

DROMIO OF SYRACUSE. (*Within*) Ay, when fowls have no
　feathers, and fish have no fin.

ANTIPHOLUS OF EPHESUS. Well, I 'll break in. Go borrow me
　a crow.

DROMIO OF EPHESUS. A crow without feather? Master,
　mean you so?

　For a fish without a fin, there 's a fowl without a feather:

　If a crow help us in, sirrah, we 'll pluck a crow together.

ANTIPHOLUS OF EPHESUS. Go get thee gone: fetch me an
　iron crow.

BALTHAZAR. Have patience, sir; O! let it not be so;

　Herein you war against your reputation,

　And draw within the compass of suspect

　The unviolated honour of your wife.

　Once this,—your long experience of her wisdom,

　Her sober virtue, years, and modesty,

　Plead on her part some cause to you unknown;

　And doubt not, sir, but she will well excuse

　Why at this time the doors are made against you.

　Be rul'd by me: depart in patience,

　And let us to the Tiger all to dinner;

And about evening come yourself alone,
To know the reason of this strange restraint.
If by strong hand you offer to break in
Now in the stirring passage of the day,
A vulgar comment will be made of it,
And that supposed by the common rout
Against your yet ungalled estimation,
That may with foul intrusion enter in
And dwell upon your grave when you are dead;
For slander lives upon succession,
For ever housed where it gets possession.

ANTIPHOLUS OF EPHESUS. You have prevail'd: I will depart
    in quiet,
And, in despite of mirth, mean to be merry.
I know a wench of excellent discourse,
Pretty and witty, wild and yet, too, gentle:
There will we dine: this woman that I mean,
My wife,—but, I protest, without desert,—
Hath oftentimes upbraided me withal:
To her will we to dinner. (*To Angelo*) Get you home,
And fetch the chain; by this I know 'tis made:
Bring it, I pray you, to the Porpentine;
For there 's the house: that chain will I bestow,
Be it for nothing but to spite my wife,
Upon mine hostess there. Good sir, make haste.
Since mine own doors refuse to entertain me,
I 'll knock elsewhere, to see if they 'll disdain me.

ANGELO. I 'll meet you at that place some hour hence.

ANTIPHOLUS OF EPHESUS. Do so. This jest shall cost me
    some expense.   *Exeunt*

SCENE TWO

The Same.

Enter Luciana and Antipholus of Syracuse

LUCIANA. And may it be that you have quite forgot
    A husband's office? Shall, Antipholus,
Even in the spring of love, thy love-springs rot?
    Shall love, in building, grow so ruinous?
If you did wed my sister for her wealth,

Then, for her wealth's sake use her with more kind-
      ness:
Or, if you like elsewhere, do it by stealth;
      Muffle your false love with some show of blindness;
Let not my sister read it in your eye;
      Be not thy tongue thy own shame's orator;
Look sweet, speak fair, become disloyalty;
      Apparel vice like virtue's harbinger;
Bear a fair presence, though your heart be tainted;
      Teach sin the carriage of a holy saint;
Be secret-false: what need she be acquainted?
      What simple thief brags of his own attaint?
'Tis double wrong to truant with your bed,
      And let her read it in thy looks at board:
Shame hath a bastard fame, well managed;
      Ill deeds are doubled with an evil word.
Alas! poor women, make us but believe,
      Being compact of credit, that you love us;
Though others have the arm, show us the sleeve;
      We in your motion turn, and you may move us.
Then, gentle brother, get you in again;
      Comfort my sister, cheer her, call her wife:
'Tis holy sport to be a little vain,
      When the sweet breath of flattery conquers strife.

ANTIPHOLUS OF SYRACUSE. Sweet mistress,—what your name
            is else, I know not,
      Nor by what wonder you do hit of mine,—
Less in your knowledge and your grace you show not
      Than our earth's wonder; more than earth divine.
Teach me, dear creature, how to think and speak:
      Lay open to my earthy-gross conceit,
Smother'd in errors, feeble, shallow, weak,
      The folded meaning of your words' deceit.
Against my soul's pure truth why labour you
      To make it wander in an unknown field?
Are you a god? would you create me new?
      Transform me then, and to your power I 'll yield.
But if that I am I, then well I know
      Your weeping sister is no wife of mine,
Nor to her bed no homage do I owe:
      Far more, far more, to you do I decline.
O! train me not, sweet mermaid, with thy note,

> To drown me in thy sister flood of tears:
> Sing, siren, for thyself, and I will dote:
> > Spread o'er the silver waves thy golden hairs,
> And as a bed I 'll take them and there lie;
> > And, in that glorious supposition think
> He gains by death that hath such means to die:
> > Let Love, being light, be drowned if she sink!

LUCIANA. What! are you mad, that you do reason so?

ANTIPHOLUS OF SYRACUSE. Not mad, but mated; how, I do not know.

LUCIANA. It is a fault that springeth from your eye.

ANTIPHOLUS OF SYRACUSE. For gazing on your beams, fair sun, being by.

LUCIANA. Gaze where you should, and that will clear your sight.

ANTIPHOLUS OF SYRACUSE. As good to wink, sweet love, as look on night.

LUCIANA. Why call you me love? call my sister so.

ANTIPHOLUS OF SYRACUSE. Thy sister's sister.

LUCIANA.   That 's my sister.

ANTIPHOLUS OF SYRACUSE.   No;
> It is thyself, mine own self's better part;
> Mine eye's clear eye, my dear heart's dearer heart;
> My food, my fortune, and my sweet hope's aim,
> My sole earth's heaven, and my heaven's claim.

LUCIANA. All this my sister is, or else should be.

ANTIPHOLUS OF SYRACUSE. Call thyself sister, sweet, for I aim thee.
> Thee will I love and with thee lead my life:
> Thou hast no husband yet nor I no wife.
> Give me thy hand.

LUCIANA.   O! soft, sir; hold you still:
> I 'll fetch my sister, to get her good will.   *Exit*

Enter Dromio of Syracuse, hastily

ANTIPHOLUS OF SYRACUSE. Why, how now, Dromio! Where run'st thou so fast?

DROMIO OF SYRACUSE. Do you know me, sir? am I Dromio? am I your man? am I myself?

ANTIPHOLUS OF SYRACUSE. Thou art Dromio, thou art my man, thou art thyself.

DROMIO OF SYRACUSE. I am an ass, I am a woman's man and besides myself.

ANTIPHOLUS OF SYRACUSE. What woman's man? and how besides thyself?

DROMIO OF SYRACUSE. Marry, sir, besides myself, I am due to a woman; one that claims me, one that haunts me, one that will have me.

ANTIPHOLUS OF SYRACUSE. What claim lays she to thee?

DROMIO OF SYRACUSE. Marry, sir, such claim as you would lay to your horse; and she would have me as a beast: not that, I being a beast, she would have me; but that she, being a very beastly creature, lays claim to me.

ANTIPHOLUS OF SYRACUSE. What is she?

DROMIO OF SYRACUSE. A very reverent body; aye, such a one as a man may not speak of, without he say, 'Sir-reverence.' I have but lean luck in the match, and yet is she a wondrous fat marriage.

ANTIPHOLUS OF SYRACUSE. How dost thou mean a fat marriage?

DROMIO OF SYRACUSE. Marry, sir, she's the kitchen-wench, and all grease; and I know not what use to put her to but to make a lamp of her and run from her by her own light. I warrant her rags and the tallow in them will burn a Poland winter; if she lives till doomsday, she'll burn a week longer than the whole world.

ANTIPHOLUS OF SYRACUSE. What complexion is she of?

DROMIO OF SYRACUSE. Swart, like my shoe, but her face nothing like so clean kept: for why she sweats; a man may go over shoes in the grime of it.

ANTIPHOLUS OF SYRACUSE. That's a fault that water will mend.

DROMIO OF SYRACUSE. No, sir, 'tis in grain; Noah's flood could not do it.

ANTIPHOLUS OF SYRACUSE. What's her name?

DROMIO OF SYRACUSE. Nell, sir; but her name and three quarters,—that is, an ell and three quarters,—will not measure her from hip to hip.

ANTIPHOLUS OF SYRACUSE. Then she bears some breadth?

DROMIO OF SYRACUSE. No longer from head to foot than from hip to hip: she is spherical, like a globe; I could find out countries in her.

ANTIPHOLUS OF SYRACUSE. In what part of her body stands Ireland?

DROMIO OF SYRACUSE. Marry, sir, in her buttocks: I found it out by the bogs.

ANTIPHOLUS OF SYRACUSE. Where Scotland?

DROMIO OF SYRACUSE. I found it by the barrenness; hard in the palm of the hand.

ANTIPHOLUS OF SYRACUSE. Where France?

DROMIO OF SYRACUSE. In her forehead; armed and reverted, making war against her heir.

ANTIPHOLUS OF SYRACUSE. Where England?

DROMIO OF SYRACUSE. I looked for the chalky cliffs, but I could find no whiteness in them: but I guess it stood in her chin, by the salt rheum that ran between France and it.

ANTIPHOLUS OF SYRACUSE. Where Spain?

DROMIO OF SYRACUSE. Faith, I saw not; but I felt it hot in her breath.

ANTIPHOLUS OF SYRACUSE. Where America, the Indies?

DROMIO OF SYRACUSE. O, sir! upon her nose, all o'er embellished with rubies, carbuncles, sapphires, declining their rich aspect to the hot breath of Spain, who sent whole armadoes of caracks to be ballast at her nose.

ANTIPHOLUS OF SYRACUSE. Where stood Belgia, the Netherlands?

DROMIO OF SYRACUSE. O, sir! I did not look so low. To conclude, this drudge, or diviner, laid claim to me; call'd me Dromio; swore I was assured to her; told me what privy marks I had about me, as the mark of my shoulder, the mole in my neck, the great wart on my left arm, that I, amazed, ran from her as a witch.

And, I think, if my breast had not been made of faith and my heart of steel,

She had transform'd me to a curtal dog and made me turn i' the wheel.

ANTIPHOLUS OF SYRACUSE. Go hie thee presently post to the road:

An if the wind blow any way from shore,

I will not harbour in this town to-night:

If any bark put forth, come to the mart,

Where I will walk till thou return to me.

If every one knows us and we know none,

'Tis time, I think, to trudge, pack, and be gone.

DROMIO OF SYRACUSE. As from a bear a man would run for life,

  So fly I from her that would be my wife.   *Exit*

ANTIPHOLUS OF SYRACUSE. There 's none but witches do inhabit here,

  And therefore 'tis high time that I were hence.

  She that doth call me husband, even my soul

  Doth for a wife abhor; but her fair sister,

  Possess'd with such a gentle sovereign grace,

  Of such enchanting presence and discourse,

  Hath almost made me traitor to myself:

  But, lest myself be guilty to self-wrong,

  I 'll stop mine ears against the mermaid's song.

            Enter Angelo, with the chain

ANGELO. Master Antipholus!

ANTIPHOLUS OF SYRACUSE. Ay, that 's my name.

ANGELO. I know it well, sir: lo, here is the chain.

  I thought to have ta'en you at the Porpentine;

  The chain unfinish'd made me stay thus long.

ANTIPHOLUS OF SYRACUSE. What is your will that I shall do with this?

ANGELO. What please yourself, sir: I have made it for you.

ANTIPHOLUS OF SYRACUSE. Made it for me, sir! I bespoke it not.

ANGELO. Not once, nor twice, but twenty times you have.

  Go home with it, and please your wife withal;

  And soon at supper-time I 'll visit you,

  And then receive my money for the chain.

ANTIPHOLUS OF SYRACUSE. I pray you, sir, receive the money now,

  For fear you ne'er see chain nor money more.

ANGELO. You are a merry man, sir: fare you well.

            Exit, leaving the chain

ANTIPHOLUS OF SYRACUSE. What I should think of this, I cannot tell:

  But this I think, there 's no man is so vain

  That would refuse so fair and offer'd chain.

  I see, a man here needs not live by shifts,

  When in the streets he meets such golden gifts.

  I 'll to the mart, and there for Dromio stay:

  If any ship put out, then straight away.   *Exit*

ACT FOUR

SCENE ONE

A Public Place.

Enter Second Merchant, Angelo, and an Officer

MERCHANT. You know since Pentecost the sum is due,
    And since I have not much importun'd you;
    Nor now I had not, but that I am bound
    To Persia, and want guilders for my voyage:
    Therefore make present satisfaction,
    Or I 'll attach you by this officer.
ANGELO. Even just the sum that I do owe to you
    Is growing to me by Antipholus;
    And in the instant that I met with you
    He had of me a chain: at five o'clock
    I shall receive the money for the same.
    Pleaseth you walk with me down to his house,
    I will discharge my bond, and thank you too.
            Enter Antipholus of
Ephesus and Dromio of Ephesus from the Courtezan's
OFFICER. That labour may you save: see where he comes.
ANTIPHOLUS OF EPHESUS. While I go to the goldsmith's
        house, go thou
    And buy a rope's end, that I will bestow
    Among my wife and her confederates,
    For locking me out of my doors by day.
    But soft! I see the goldsmith. Get thee gone;
    Buy thou a rope, and bring it home to me.
DROMIO OF EPHESUS. I buy a thousand pound a year: I buy
        a rope!   *Exit*
ANTIPHOLUS OF EPHESUS. A man is well holp up that trusts
        to you:
    I promised your presence and the chain;
    But neither chain nor goldsmith came to me.

Belike you thought our love would last too long,
If it were chain'd together, and therefore came not.

ANGELO. Saving your merry humour, here's the note
How much your chain weighs to the utmost carat.
The fineness of the gold, and chargeful fashion,
Which doth amount to three odd ducats more
Than I stand debted to this gentleman:
I pray you see him presently discharg'd,
For he is bound to sea and stays but for it.

ANTIPHOLUS OF EPHESUS. I am not furnish'd with the present money;
Besides, I have some business in the town.
Good signior, take the stranger to my house,
And with you take the chain, and bid my wife
Disburse the sum on the receipt thereof:
Perchance I will be there as soon as you.

ANGELO. Then, you will bring the chain to her yourself?

ANTIPHOLUS OF EPHESUS. No; bear it with you, lest I come not time enough.

ANGELO. Well, sir, I will. Have you the chain about you?

ANTIPHOLUS OF EPHESUS. An if I have not, sir, I hope you have,
Or else you may return without your money.

ANGELO. Nay, come, I pray you, sir, give me the chain:
Both wind and tide stays for this gentleman,
And I, to blame, have held him here too long.

ANTIPHOLUS OF EPHESUS. Good Lord! you use this dalliance to excuse
Your breach of promise to the Porpentine.
I should have chid you for not bringing it,
But, like a shrew, you first begin to brawl.

MERCHANT. The hour steals on; I pray you, sir, dispatch.

ANGELO. You hear how he importunes me: the chain!

ANTIPHOLUS OF EPHESUS. Why, give it to my wife and fetch your money.

ANGELO. Come, come; you know I gave it you even now.
Either send the chain or send by me some token.

ANTIPHOLUS OF EPHESUS. Fie! now you run this humour out of breath.
Come, where's the chain? I pray you, let me see it.

MERCHANT. My business cannot brook this dalliance.
Good sir, say whe'r you'll answer me or no:

If not, I 'll leave him to the officer.

ANTIPHOLUS OF EPHESUS. I answer you! what should I answer you?

ANGELO. The money that you owe me for the chain.

ANTIPHOLUS OF EPHESUS. I owe you none till I receive the chain.

ANGELO. You know I gave it you half an hour since.

ANTIPHOLUS OF EPHESUS. You gave me none: you wrong me much to say so.

ANGELO. You wrong me more, sir, in denying it:
Consider how it stands upon my credit.

MERCHANT. Well, officer, arrest him at my suit.

OFFICER. I do;
And charge you in the duke's name to obey me.

ANGELO. This touches me in reputation.
Either consent to pay this sum for me,
Or I attach you by this officer.

ANTIPHOLUS OF EPHESUS. Consent to pay thee that I never had!
Arrest me, foolish fellow, if thou dar'st.

ANGELO. Here is thy fee: arrest him, officer.
I would not spare my brother in this case,
If he should scorn me so apparently.

OFFICER. I do arrest you, sir: you hear the suit.

ANTIPHOLUS OF EPHESUS. I do obey thee till I give thee bail.
But, sirrah, you shall buy this sport as dear
As all the metal in your shop will answer.

ANGELO. Sir, sir, I shall have law in Ephesus,
To your notorious shame, I doubt it not.

Enter Dromio of Syracuse

DROMIO OF SYRACUSE. Master, there is a bark of Epidamnum
That stays but till her owner comes aboard,
And then she bears away. Our fraughtage, sir,
I have convey'd aboard, and I have bought
The oil, the balsamum, and aqua-vitæ.
The ship is in her trim; the merry wind
Blows fair from land; they stay for nought at all
But for their owner, master, and yourself.

ANTIPHOLUS OF EPHESUS. How now! a madman! Why, thou peevish sheep,
What ship of Epidamnum stays for me?

DROMIO OF SYRACUSE. A ship you sent me to,
    to hire waftage.

ANTIPHOLUS OF EPHESUS. Thou drunken slave, I sent thee
    for a rope;
And told thee to what purpose, and what end.

DROMIO OF SYRACUSE. You sent me for a rope's end as soon:
You sent me to the bay, sir, for a bark.

ANTIPHOLUS OF EPHESUS. I will debate this matter at more
    leisure,
And teach your ears to list me with more heed.
To Adriana, villain, hie thee straight;
Give her this key, and tell her, in the desk
That 's cover'd o'er with Turkish tapestry,
There is a purse of ducats: let her send it.
Tell her I am arrested in the street,
And that shall bail me. Hie thee, slave, be gone!
On, officer, to prison till it come.

Exeunt Merchant, Angelo,
Officer, and Antipholus of Ephesus

DROMIO OF SYRACUSE. To Adriana! That is where we din'd,
Where Dowsabel did claim me for her husband:
She is too big, I hope, for me to compass.
Thither I must, although against my will,
For servants must their masters' minds fulfil.   *Exit*

SCENE TWO

A Room in the House of Antipholus of Ephesus.

Enter Adriana and Luciana

ADRIANA. Ah! Luciana, did he tempt thee so?
    Mightst thou perceive austerely in his eye
That he did plead in earnest? yea or no?
    Look'd he or red or pale? or sad or merrily?
What observation mad'st thou in this case
Of his heart's meteors tilting in his face?

LUCIANA. First he denied you had in him no right.

ADRIANA. He meant he did me none; the more my spite.

LUCIANA. Then swore he that he was a stranger here.

ADRIANA. And true he swore, though yet forsworn he were.

LUCIANA. Then pleaded I for you.

ADRIANA.   And what said he?

LUCIANA. That love I begg'd for you he begg'd of me.

ADRIANA. With what persuasion did he tempt thy love?

LUCIANA. With words that in an honest suit might move.
First, he did praise my beauty, then my speech.

ADRIANA. Didst speak him fair?

LUCIANA.   Have patience, I beseech.

ADRIANA. I cannot, nor I will not hold me still:
My tongue, though not my heart, shall have his will.
He is deformed, crooked, old and sere,
Ill-fac'd, worse bodied, shapeless everywhere;
Vicious, ungentle, foolish, blunt, unkind,
Stigmatical in making, worse in mind.

LUCIANA. Who would be jealous then, of such a one?
No evil lost is wail'd when it is gone.

ADRIANA. Ah! but I think him better than I say,
And yet would herein others' eyes were worse.
Far from her nest the lapwing cries away:
My heart prays for him, though my tongue do curse.

Enter Dromio of Syracuse

DROMIO OF SYRACUSE. Here, go: the desk! the purse! sweet,
now, make haste.

LUCIANA. How hast thou lost thy breath?

DROMIO OF SYRACUSE.   By running fast.

ADRIANA. Where is thy master, Dromio? is he well?

DROMIO OF SYRACUSE. No, he 's in Tartar limbo, worse than
hell.
A devil in an everlasting garment hath him,
One whose hard heart is button'd up with steel;
A fiend, a fairy, pitiless and rough;
A wolf, nay, worse, a fellow all in buff;
A back-friend, a shoulder-clapper, one that counter-
mands
The passages of alleys, creeks and narrow lands;
A hound that runs counter and yet draws dryfoot well;
One that, before the judgment, carries poor souls to hell.

ADRIANA. Why, man, what is the matter?

DROMIO OF SYRACUSE. I do not know the matter: he is
'rested on the case.

ADRIANA. What, is he arrested? tell me at whose suit.

DROMIO OF SYRACUSE. I know not at whose suit he is arrested well;

But he 's in a suit of buff which 'rested him, that can I
    tell.

Will you send him, mistress, redemption, the money in
    his desk?

ADRIANA. Go fetch it, sister.—(*Exit Luciana*) This I won-
    der at:

That he, unknown to me, should be in debt:

Tell me, was he arrested on a band?

DROMIO OF SYRACUSE. Not on a band, but on a stronger
    thing;

A chain, a chain. Do you not hear it ring?

ADRIANA. What, the chain?

DROMIO OF SYRACUSE. No, no, the bell: 'tis time that I were
    gone:

It was two ere I left him, and now the clock strikes one.

ADRIANA. The hours come back! that did I never hear.

DROMIO OF SYRACUSE. O yes; if any hour meet a sergeant, a'
    turns back for very fear.

ADRIANA. As if Time were in debt! how fondly dost thou
    reason!

DROMIO OF SYRACUSE. Time is a very bankrupt, and owes
    more than he 's worth to season.

Nay, he 's a thief too: have you not heard men say,

That Time comes stealing on by night and day?

If Time be in debt and theft, and a sergeant in the way,

Hath he not reason to turn back an hour in a day?

          Re-enter Luciana

ADRIANA. Go, Dromio: there 's the money, bear it straight,

And bring thy master home immediately.

Come, sister; I am press'd down with conceit;

Conceit, my comfort and my injury.   *Exeunt*

SCENE THREE

A Public Place.

Enter Antipholus of Syracuse

ANTIPHOLUS OF SYRACUSE. There 's not a man I meet but
    doth salute me,

As if I were their well acquainted friend;

And every one doth call me by my name.

Some tender money to me; some invite me;
Some other give me thanks for kindnesses;
Some offer me commodities to buy:
Even now a tailor call'd me in his shop
And show'd me silks that he had bought for me,
And therewithal, took measure of my body.
Sure these are but imaginary wiles,
And Lapland sorcerers inhabit here.

Enter Dromio of Syracuse

DROMIO OF SYRACUSE. Master, here 's the gold you sent me for.
What! have you got the picture of old Adam new apparelled?

ANTIPHOLUS OF SYRACUSE. What gold is this? What Adam dost thou mean?

DROMIO OF SYRACUSE. Not that Adam that kept the Paradise, but that Adam that keeps the prison: he that goes in the calf's skin that was killed for the Prodigal: he that came behind you, sir, like an evil angel, and bid you forsake your liberty.

ANTIPHOLUS OF SYRACUSE. I understand thee not.

DROMIO OF SYRACUSE. No? why, 'tis a plain case: he that went, like a base-viol, in a case of leather; the man, sir, that, when gentlemen are tired, gives them a fob, and 'rests them; he, sir, that takes pity on decayed men and gives them suits of durance; he that sets up his rest to do more exploits with his mace than a morris-pike.

ANTIPHOLUS OF SYRACUSE. What, thou meanest an officer?

DROMIO OF SYRACUSE. Ay, sir, the sergeant of the band; he that brings any man to answer it that breaks his band; one that thinks a man always going to bed, and says, 'God give you good rest!'

ANTIPHOLUS OF SYRACUSE. Well, sir, there rest in your foolery. Is there any ship puts forth to-night? may we be gone?

DROMIO OF SYRACUSE. Why, sir, I brought you word an hour since that the bark Expedition put forth to-night; and then were you hindered by the sergeant to tarry for the hoy Delay. Here are the angels that you sent for to deliver you.

ANTIPHOLUS OF SYRACUSE. The fellow is distract, and so am I;

And here we wander in illusions:
Some blessed power deliver us from hence!

Enter a Courtezan

COURTEZAN. Well met, well met, Master Antipholus.
I see, sir, you have found the goldsmith now:
Is that the chain you promis'd me to-day?

ANTIPHOLUS OF SYRACUSE. Satan, avoid! I charge thee
tempt me not!

DROMIO OF SYRACUSE. Master, is this Mistress Satan?

ANTIPHOLUS OF SYRACUSE. It is the devil.

DROMIO OF SYRACUSE. Nay, she is worse, she is the devil's
dam, and here she comes in the habit of a light wench:
and thereof comes that the wenches say, 'God damn me';
that's as much as to say, 'God make me a light wench.' It
is written, they appear to men like angels of light: light is
an effect of fire, and fire will burn; ergo, light wenches
will burn. Come not near her.

COURTEZAN. Your man and you are marvellous merry, sir.
Will you go with me? we 'll mend our dinner here.

DROMIO OF SYRACUSE. Master, if you do, expect spoonmeat,
so bespeak a long spoon.

ANTIPHOLUS OF SYRACUSE. Why, Dromio?

DROMIO OF SYRACUSE. Marry, he must have a long spoon
that must eat with the devil.

ANTIPHOLUS OF SYRACUSE. Avoid thee, fiend! what tell'st
thou me of supping?
Thou art, as you are all, a sorceress:
I conjure thee to leave me and be gone.

COURTEZAN. Give me the ring of mine you had at dinner,
Or, for my diamond, the chain you promis'd,
And I 'll be gone, sir, and not trouble you.

DROMIO OF SYRACUSE. Some devils ask but the parings of
one's nail,
A rush, a hair, a drop of blood, a pin,
A nut, a cherry-stone;
But she, more covetous, would have a chain.
Master, be wise: an if you give it her,
The devil will shake her chain and fright us with it.

COURTEZAN. I pray you, sir, my ring, or else the chain:
I hope you do not mean to cheat me so.

ANTIPHOLUS OF SYRACUSE. Avaunt, thou witch! Come, Dromio, let us go.

DROMIO OF SYRACUSE. 'Fly pride,' says the peacock: mistress, that you know.

> *Exeunt Antipholus of*
> *Syracuse, and Dromio of Syracuse*

COURTEZAN. Now, out of doubt, Antipholus is mad,
Else would he never so demean himself.
A ring he hath of mine worth forty ducats,
And for the same he promis'd me a chain:
Both one and other he denies me now.
The reason that I gather he is mad,
Besides this present instance of his rage,
Is a mad tale he told to-day at dinner,
Of his own doors being shut against his entrance.
Belike his wife, acquainted with his fits,
On purpose shut the doors against his way.
My way is now to hie home to his house,
And tell his wife, that, being lunatic,
He rush'd into my house, and took perforce
My ring away. This course I fittest choose,
For forty ducats is too much to lose.   *Exit*

SCENE FOUR

A Street.

Enter Antipholus of Ephesus and the Officer

ANTIPHOLUS OF EPHESUS. Fear me not, man; I will not
break away:
I 'll give thee, ere I leave thee, so much money,
To warrant thee, as I am 'rested for.
My wife is in a wayward mood to-day,
And will not lightly trust the messenger.
That I should be attach'd in Ephesus,
I tell you, 'twill sound harshly in her ears.

Enter Dromio of Ephesus with a rope's end

Here comes my man: I think he brings the money.
How now, sir! have you that I sent you for?

DROMIO OF EPHESUS. Here 's that, I warrant you, will pay
them all.

ANTIPHOLUS OF EPHESUS. But where 's the money?

DROMIO OF EPHESUS. Why, sir, I gave the money for the
    rope.

ANTIPHOLUS OF EPHESUS. Five hundred ducats, villain, for
    a rope?

DROMIO OF EPHESUS. I 'll serve you, sir, five hundred at the
    rate.

ANTIPHOLUS OF EPHESUS. To what end did I bid thee hie
    thee home?

DROMIO OF EPHESUS. To a rope's end, sir; and to that end
    am I return'd.

ANTIPHOLUS OF EPHESUS. And to that end, sir, I will wel-
    come you.   *Beats him*

OFFICER. Good sir, be patient.

DROMIO OF EPHESUS. Nay, 'tis for me to be patient; I am in
    adversity.

OFFICER. Good now, hold thy tongue.

DROMIO OF EPHESUS. Nay, rather persuade him to hold his
    hands.

ANTIPHOLUS OF EPHESUS. Thou whoreson, senseless villain!

DROMIO OF EPHESUS. I would I were senseless, sir, that I
    might not feel your blows.

ANTIPHOLUS OF EPHESUS. Thou art sensible in nothing but
    blows, and so is an ass.

DROMIO OF EPHESUS. I am an ass indeed: you may prove it
    by my long ears. I have served him from the hour of my
    nativity to this instant, and have nothing at his hands for
    my service but blows. When I am cold, he heats me with
    beating; when I am warm, he cools me with beating; I
    am waked with it when I sleep; raised with it when I sit;
    driven out of doors with it when I go from home; wel-
    comed home with it when I return; nay, I bear it on my
    shoulders, as a beggar wont her brat; and, I think, when
    he hath lamed me, I shall beg with it from door to door.

ANTIPHOLUS OF EPHESUS. Come, go along; my wife is com-
    ing yonder.

    Enter Adriana, Luciana, the Courtezan, and Pinch

DROMIO OF EPHESUS. Mistress, respice finem, respect your
    end; or rather, to prophesy like the parrot, 'Beware the
    rope's end.'

ANTIPHOLUS OF EPHESUS. Wilt thou still talk?   *Beats him*

COURTEZAN. How say you now? is not your husband mad?

ADRIANA. His incivility confirms no less.

Good Doctor Pinch, you are a conjurer;
Establish him in his true sense again,
And I will please you what you will demand.

LUCIANA. Alas! how fiery and how sharp he looks.

COURTEZAN. Mark how he trembles in his ecstasy!

PINCH. Give me your hand and let me feel your pulse.

ANTIPHOLUS OF EPHESUS. There is my hand, and let it feel
 your ear.   *Strikes him*

PINCH. I charge thee, Satan, hous'd within this man,
To yield possession to my holy prayers,
And to thy state of darkness hie thee straight:
I conjure thee by all the saints in heaven.

ANTIPHOLUS OF EPHESUS. Peace, doting wizard, peace! I am
 not mad.

ADRIANA. O! that thou wert not, poor distressed soul!

ANTIPHOLUS OF EPHESUS. You minion, you, are these your
 customers?
Did this companion with the saffron face
Revel and feast it at my house to-day,
Whilst upon me the guilty doors were shut
And I denied to enter in my house?

ADRIANA. O husband, God doth know you din'd at home;
Where would you had remain'd until this time,
Free from these slanders and this open shame!

ANTIPHOLUS OF EPHESUS. Din'd at home! Thou villain, what
 say'st thou?

DROMIO OF EPHESUS. Sir, sooth to say, you did not dine at
 home.

ANTIPHOLUS OF EPHESUS. Were not my doors lock'd up and
 I shut out?

DROMIO OF EPHESUS. Perdy, your doors were lock'd and you
 shut out.

ANTIPHOLUS OF EPHESUS. And did not she herself revile me
 there?

DROMIO OF EPHESUS. Sans fable, she herself revil'd you
 there.

ANTIPHOLUS OF EPHESUS. Did not her kitchen-maid rail,
 taunt, and scorn me?

DROMIO OF EPHESUS. Certes, she did; the kitchen-vestal
 scorn'd you.

ANTIPHOLUS OF EPHESUS. And did not I in rage depart from
 thence?

DROMIO OF EPHESUS. In verity you did: my bones bear witness,
    That since have felt the vigour of his rage.

ADRIANA. Is 't good to soothe him in these contraries?

PINCH. It is no shame: the fellow finds his vein,
    And, yielding to him humours well his frenzy.

ANTIPHOLUS OF EPHESUS. Thou hast suborn'd the goldsmith
    to arrest me.

ADRIANA. Alas! I sent you money to redeem you,
    By Dromio here, who came in haste for it.

DROMIO OF EPHESUS. Money by me! heart and good will
    you might;
    But surely, master, not a rag of money.

ANTIPHOLUS OF EPHESUS. Went'st not thou to her for a
    purse of ducats?

ADRIANA. He came to me, and I deliver'd it.

LUCIANA. And I am witness with her that she did.

DROMIO OF EPHESUS. God and the rope-maker bear me witness
    That I was sent for nothing but a rope!

PINCH. Mistress, both man and master is possess'd:
    I know it by their pale and deadly looks.
    They must be bound and laid in some dark room.

ANTIPHOLUS OF EPHESUS. Say, wherefore didst thou lock me
    forth to-day?
    And why dost thou deny the bag of gold?

ADRIANA. I did not, gentle husband, lock thee forth.

DROMIO OF EPHESUS. And, gentle master, I receiv'd no gold;
    But I confess, sir, that we were lock'd out.

ADRIANA. Dissembling villain! thou speak'st false in both.

ANTIPHOLUS OF EPHESUS. Dissembling harlot! thou art false
    in all;
    And art confederate with a damned pack
    To make a loathsome abject scorn of me;
    But with these nails I 'll pluck out those false eyes
    That would behold in me this shameful sport.

ADRIANA. O! bind him, bind him, let him not come near me.

PINCH. More company! the fiend is strong within him.

LUCIANA. Ay me! poor man, how pale and wan he looks!

    Enter three or four and bind Antipholus of Ephesus

ANTIPHOLUS OF EPHESUS. What, will you murder me? Thou
    gaoler, thou,

I am thy prisoner: wilt thou suffer them
To make a rescue?
OFFICER.   Masters, let him go:
He is my prisoner, and you shall not have him.
PINCH. Go bind this man, for he is frantic too.
                    They bind Dromio of Ephesus
ADRIANA. What wilt thou do, thou peevish officer?
Hast thou delight to see a wretched man
Do outrage and displeasure to himself?
OFFICER. He is my prisoner: if I let him go,
The debt he owes will be requir'd of me.
ADRIANA. I will discharge thee ere I go from thee:
Bear me forthwith unto his creditor,
And, knowing how the debt grows, I will pay it.
Good Master doctor, see him safe convey'd
Home to my house. O most unhappy day!
ANTIPHOLUS OF EPHESUS. O most unhappy strumpet!
DROMIO OF EPHESUS. Master, I am here enter'd in bond for
you.
ANTIPHOLUS OF EPHESUS. Out on thee, villain! wherefore
dost thou mad me?
DROMIO OF EPHESUS. Will you be bound for nothing? be
mad, good master; cry, 'the devil!'
LUCIANA. God help, poor souls! how idly do they talk.
ADRIANA. Go bear him hence. Sister, go you with me.—
                    Exeunt Pinch and Assistants
        with Antipholus of Ephesus and Dromio of Ephesus
Say now, whose suit is he arrested at?
OFFICER. One Angelo, a goldsmith; do you know him?
ADRIANA. I know the man. What is the sum he owes?
OFFICER. Two hundred ducats.
ADRIANA.   Say, how grows it due?
OFFICER. Due for a chain your husband had of him.
ADRIANA. He did bespeak a chain for me, but had it not.
COURTEZAN. When as your husband all in rage, to-day
Came to my house, and took away my ring,—
The ring I saw upon his finger now,—
Straight after did I meet him with a chain.
ADRIANA. It may be so, but I did never see it.
Come, gaoler, bring me where the goldsmith is:
I long to know the truth hereof at large.

Enter Antipholus of
Syracuse and Dromio of Syracuse, with rapiers drawn

LUCIANA. God, for thy mercy! they are loose again.

ADRIANA. And come with naked swords. Let 's call more
help
To have them bound again.

OFFICER.   Away! they 'll kill us.
                    Exeunt Adriana, Luciana, and Officer

ANTIPHOLUS OF SYRACUSE. I see, these witches are afraid of
swords.

DROMIO OF SYRACUSE. She that would be your wife now ran
from you.

ANTIPHOLUS OF SYRACUSE. Come to the Centaur; fetch our
stuff from thence:
I long that we were safe and sound aboard.

DROMIO OF SYRACUSE. Faith, stay here this night, they will
surely do us no harm; you saw they speak us fair, give us
gold: methinks they are such a gentle nation, that, but
for the mountain of mad flesh that claims marriage of me,
I could find in my heart to stay here still, and turn witch.

ANTIPHOLUS OF SYRACUSE. I will not stay to-night for all the
town;
Therefore away, to get our stuff aboard.   *Exeunt*

ACT FIVE

SCENE ONE

A Street before an Abbey.

Enter Merchant and Angelo

ANGELO. I am sorry, sir, that I have hinder'd you;
　　But, I protest, he had the chain of me,
　　Though most dishonestly he doth deny it.

MERCHANT. How is the man esteem'd here in the city?

ANGELO. Of very reverend reputation, sir,
　　Of credit infinite, highly belov'd,
　　Second to none that lives here in the city:
　　His word might bear my wealth at any time.

MERCHANT. Speak softly: yonder, as I think, he walks.

Enter Antipholus of Syracuse and Dromio of Syracuse

ANGELO. 'Tis so; and that self chain about his neck
　　Which he forswore most monstrously to have.
　　Good sir, draw near to me, I 'll speak to him.
　　Signior Antipholus, I wonder much
　　That you would put me to this shame and trouble;
　　And not without some scandal to yourself,
　　With circumstance and oaths so to deny
　　This chain which now you wear so openly:
　　Beside the charge, the shame, imprisonment,
　　You have done wrong to this my honest friend,
　　Who, but for staying on our controversy,
　　Had hoisted sail and put to sea to-day.
　　This chain you had of me; can you deny it?

ANTIPHOLUS OF SYRACUSE. I think I had: I never did deny
　　it.

MERCHANT. Yes, that you did, sir, and forswore it too.

ANTIPHOLUS OF SYRACUSE. Who heard me to deny it or for-
　　swear it?

MERCHANT. These ears of mine, thou know'st, did hear
    thee.
    Fie on thee, wretch! 'tis pity that thou liv'st
    To walk where any honest men resort.
ANTIPHOLUS OF SYRACUSE. Thou art a villain to impeach me
    thus:
    I 'll prove mine honour and mine honesty
    Against thee presently, if thou dar'st stand.
MERCHANT. I dare, and do defy thee for a villain.

They draw

Enter Adriana, Luciana, Courtezan, and Others

ADRIANA. Hold! hurt him not, for God's sake! he is mad.
    Some get within him, take his sword away.
    Bind Dromio too, and bear them to my house.
DROMIO OF SYRACUSE. Run, master, run; for God's sake,
    take a house!
    This is some priory: in, or we are spoil'd.

Exeunt Antipholus of
Syracuse and Dromio of Syracuse to the Abbey
Enter the Abbess

ABBESS. Be quiet, people. Wherefore throng you hither?
ADRIANA. To fetch my poor distracted husband hence.
    Let us come in, that we may bind him fast,
    And bear him home for his recovery.
ANGELO. I knew he was not in his perfect wits.
MERCHANT. I am sorry now that I did draw on him.
ABBESS. How long hath this possession held the man?
ADRIANA. This week he hath been heavy, sour, sad,
    And much different from the man he was;
    But, till this afternoon his passion
    Ne'er brake into extremity of rage.
ABBESS. Hath he not lost much wealth by wrack of sea?
    Buried some dear friend? Hath not else his eye
    Stray'd his affection in unlawful love?
    A sin prevailing much in youthful men,
    Who give their eyes the liberty of gazing.
    Which of these sorrows is he subject to?
ADRIANA. To none of these, except it be the last;
    Namely, some love that drew him oft from home.
ABBESS. You should for that have reprehended him.
ADRIANA. Why, so I did.
ABBESS.   Ay, but not rough enough.

ADRIANA. As roughly as my modesty would let me.

ABBESS. Haply, in private.

ADRIANA.   And in assemblies too.

ABBESS. Ay, but not enough.

ADRIANA. It was the copy of our conference:
    In bed, he slept not for my urging it;
    At board, he fed not for my urging it;
    Alone, it was the subject of my theme;
    In company I often glanced it:
    Still did I tell him it was vile and bad.

ABBESS. And thereof came it that the man was mad:
    The venom clamours of a jealous woman
    Poison more deadly than a mad dog's tooth.
    It seems, his sleeps were hinder'd by thy railing,
    And thereof comes it that his head is light.
    Thou say'st his meat was sauc'd with thy upbraidings:
    Unquiet meals make ill digestions;
    Thereof the raging fire of fever bred:
    And what's a fever but a fit of madness?
    Thou say'st his sports were hinder'd by thy brawls:
    Sweet recreation barr'd, what doth ensue
    But moody moping, and dull melancholy,
    Kinsman to grim and comfortless despair,
    And at her heels a huge infectious troop
    Of pale distemperatures and foes to life?
    In food, in sport, and life-preserving rest
    To be disturb'd, would mad or man or beast:
    The consequence is then, thy jealous fits
    Have scar'd thy husband from the use of wits.

LUCIANA. She never reprehended him but mildly
    When he demean'd himself rough, rude, and wildly.
    Why bear you these rebukes and answer not?

ADRIANA. She did betray me to my own reproof.
    Good people, enter, and lay hold on him.

ABBESS. No; not a creature enters in my house.

ADRIANA. Then, let your servants bring my husband forth.

ABBESS. Neither: he took this place for sanctuary,
    And it shall privilege him from your hands
    Till I have brought him to his wits again,
    Or lose my labour in assaying it.

ADRIANA. I will attend my husband, be his nurse,
    Diet his sickness, for it is my office,

And will have no attorney but myself;
And therefore let me have him home with me.

ABBESS. Be patient; for I will not let him stir
Till I have us'd the approved means I have,
With wholesome syrups, drugs, and holy prayers,
To make of him a formal man again.
It is a branch and parcel of mine oath,
A charitable duty of my order;
Therefore depart and leave him here with me.

ADRIANA. I will not hence and leave my husband here;
And ill it doth beseem your holiness
To separate the husband and the wife.

ABBESS. Be quiet, and depart. Thou shalt not have him.

Exit

LUCIANA. Complain unto the duke of this indignity.

ADRIANA. Come, go: I will fall prostrate at his feet,
And never rise until my tears and prayers
Have won his Grace to come in person hither,
And take perforce my husband from the abbess.

SECOND MERCHANT. By this, I think, the dial points at five:
Anon, I 'm sure, the duke himself in person
Comes this way to the melancholy vale,
The place of death and sorry execution,
Behind the ditches of the abbey here.

ANGELO. Upon what cause?

SECOND MERCHANT. To see a reverend Syracusian merchant,
Who put unluckily into this bay
Against the laws and statutes of this town,
Beheaded publicly for his offence.

ANGELO. See where they come: we will behold his death.

LUCIANA. Kneel to the duke before he pass the abbey.

*Enter Duke attended; Ægeon
bare-headed; with the Headsman and other Officers*

DUKE. Yet once again proclaim it publicly,
If any friend will pay the sum for him,
He shall not die; so much we tender him.

ADRIANA. Justice, most sacred duke, against the abbess!

DUKE. She is a virtuous and a reverend lady:
It cannot be that she hath done thee wrong.

ADRIANA. May it please your Grace, Antipholus, my husband,

Whom I made lord of me and all I had,
At your important letters, this ill day
A most outrageous fit of madness took him,
That desperately he hurried through the street,—
With him his bondman, all as mad as he,—
Doing displeasure to the citizens
By rushing in their houses, bearing thence
Rings, jewels, anything his rage did like.
Once did I get him bound and sent him home,
Whilst to take order for the wrongs I went
That here and there his fury had committed.
Anon, I wot not by what strong escape,
He broke from those that had the guard of him,
And with his mad attendant and himself,
Each one with ireful passion, with drawn swords,
Met us again, and, madly bent on us
Chas'd us away, till, raising of more aid
We came again to bind them. Then they fled
Into this abbey, whither we pursu'd them;
And here the abbess shuts the gates on us,
And will not suffer us to fetch him out,
Nor send him forth that we may bear him hence.
Therefore, most gracious duke, with thy command
Let him be brought forth, and borne hence for help.

DUKE. Long since thy husband serv'd me in my wars,
And I to thee engag'd a prince's word,
When thou didst make him master of thy bed,
To do him all the grace and good I could.
Go, some of you, knock at the abbey gate
And bid the Lady Abbess come to me.
I will determine this before I stir.

Enter a Servant

SERVANT. O mistress, mistress! shift and save yourself!
My master and his man are both broke loose,
Beaten the maids a-row and bound the doctor,
Whose beard they have sing'd off with brands of fire;
And ever as it blaz'd they threw on him
Great pails of puddled mire to quench the hair.
My master preaches patience to him, and the while
His man with scissors nicks him like a fool;
And sure, unless you send some present help,
Between them they will kill the conjurer.

ADRIANA. Peace, fool! thy master and his man are here,
And that is false thou dost report to us.

SERVANT. Mistress, upon my life, I tell you true;
I have not breath'd almost, since I did see it.
He cries for you and vows, if he can take you,
To scotch your face, and to disfigure you.   *Cry within*
Hark, hark! I hear him, mistress: fly, be gone!

DUKE. Come, stand by me; fear nothing. Guard with hal-
berds!

ADRIANA. Ay me, it is my husband! Witness you,
That he is borne about invisible:
Even now we hous'd him in the abbey here,
And now he 's here, past thought of human reason.

Enter Antipholus of Ephesus and Dromio of Ephesus

ANTIPHOLUS OF EPHESUS. Justice, most gracious duke! O!
grant me justice,
Even for the service that long since I did thee,
When I bestrid thee in the wars and took
Deep scars to save thy life; even for the blood
That then I lost for thee, now grant me justice.

ÆGEON. Unless the fear of death doth make me dote,
I see my son Antipholus and Dromio!

ANTIPHOLUS OF EPHESUS. Justice, sweet prince, against that
woman there!
She whom thou gav'st to me to be my wife,
That hath abused and dishonour'd me,
Even in the strength and height of injury!
Beyond imagination is the wrong
That she this day hath shameless thrown on me.

DUKE. Discover how, and thou shalt find me just.

ANTIPHOLUS OF EPHESUS. This day, great duke, she shut the
doors upon me,
While she with harlots feasted in my house.

DUKE. A grievous fault! Say, woman, didst thou so?

ADRIANA. No, my good lord: myself, he, and my sister
To-day did dine together. So befall my soul
As this is false he burdens me withal!

LUCIANA. Ne'er may I look on day, nor sleep on night,
But she tells to your Highness simple truth!

ANGELO. O perjur'd woman! They are both forsworn:
In this the madman justly chargeth them!

ANTIPHOLUS OF EPHESUS. My liege, I am advised what I say:

Neither disturb'd with the effect of wine,
Nor heady-rash, provok'd with raging ire,
Albeit my wrongs might make one wiser mad.
This woman lock'd me out this day from dinner:
That goldsmith there, were he not pack'd with her,
Could witness it, for he was with me then;
Who parted with me to go fetch a chain,
Promising to bring it to the Porpentine,
Where Balthazar and I did dine together.
Our dinner done, and he not coming thither,
I went to seek him: in the street I met him,
And in his company that gentleman.
There did this perjur'd goldsmith swear me down
That I this day of him receiv'd the chain,
Which, God he knows, I saw not; for the which
He did arrest me with an officer.
I did obey, and sent my peasant home
For certain ducats: he with none return'd.
Then fairly I bespoke the officer
To go in person with me to my house.
By the way we met
My wife, her sister, and a rabble more
Of vile confederates: along with them
They brought one Pinch, a hungry lean-fac'd villain,
A mere anatomy, a mountebank,
A threadbare juggler, and a fortune-teller,
A needy, hollow-ey'd, sharp-looking wretch,
A living-dead man. This pernicious slave,
Forsooth, took on him as a conjurer,
And, gazing in mine eyes, feeling my pulse,
And with no face, as 'twere, out-facing me,
Cries out, I was possess'd. Then, altogether
They fell upon me, bound me, bore me thence,
And in a dark and dankish vault at home
There left me and my man, both bound together;
Till, gnawing with my teeth my bonds in sunder,
I gain'd my freedom, and immediately
Ran hither to your Grace; whom I beseech
To give me ample satisfaction
For these deep shames and great indignities.

ANGELO. My lord, in truth, thus far I witness with him,
That he din'd not at home, but was lock'd out.

DUKE. But had he such a chain of thee, or no?

ANGELO. He had, my lord; and when he ran in here,
These people saw the chain about his neck.

SECOND MERCHANT. Besides, I will be sworn these ears of
mine
Heard you confess you had the chain of him
After you first forswore it on the mart;
And thereupon I drew my sword on you;
And then you fled into this abbey here,
From whence, I think, you are come by miracle.

ANTIPHOLUS OF EPHESUS. I never came within these abbey
walls;
Nor ever didst thou draw thy sword on me;
I never saw the chain, so help me heaven!
And this is false you burden me withal.

DUKE. Why, what an intricate impeach is this!
I think you all have drunk of Circe's cup.
If here you hous'd him, here he would have been;
If he were mad, he would not plead so coldly;
You say he din'd at home; the goldsmith here
Denies that saying. Sirrah, what say you?

DROMIO OF EPHESUS. Sir, he din'd with her there, at the
Porpentine.

COURTEZAN. He did, and from my finger snatch'd that ring.

ANTIPHOLUS OF EPHESUS. 'Tis true, my liege; this ring I had
of her.

DUKE. Saw'st thou him enter at the abbey here?

COURTEZAN. As sure, my liege, as I do see your Grace.

DUKE. Why, this is strange. Go call the abbess hither.

Exit an Attendant

I think you are all mated or stark mad.

ÆGEON. Most mighty duke, vouchsafe me speak a word:
Haply I see a friend will save my life,
And pay the sum that may deliver me.

DUKE. Speak freely, Syracusian, what thou wilt.

ÆGEON. Is not your name, sir, called Antipholus?
And is not that your bondman Dromio?

DROMIO OF EPHESUS. Within this hour I was his bondman,
sir;
But he, I thank him, gnaw'd in two my cords:
Now am I Dromio and his man, unbound.

ÆGEON. I am sure you both of you remember me.

DROMIO OF EPHESUS. Ourselves we do remember, sir, by
    you;
    For lately we were bound, as you are now.
    You are not Pinch's patient, are you, sir?

ÆGEON. Why look you strange on me? you know me well.

ANTIPHOLUS OF EPHESUS. I never saw you in my life till
    now.

ÆGEON. O! grief hath chang'd me since you saw me last,
    And careful hours, with Time's deformed hand,
    Have written strange defeatures in my face:
    But tell me yet, dost thou not know my voice?

ANTIPHOLUS OF EPHESUS. Neither.

ÆGEON. Dromio, nor thou?

DROMIO OF EPHESUS. No, trust me, sir, not I.

ÆGEON. I am sure thou dost.

DROMIO OF EPHESUS. Ay, sir; but I am sure I do not; and
    whatsoever a man denies, you are now bound to believe
    him.

ÆGEON. Not know my voice! O, time's extremity,
    Hast thou so crack'd and splitted my poor tongue
    In seven short years, that here my only son
    Knows not my feeble key of untun'd cares?
    Though now this grained face of mine be hid
    In sap-consuming winter's drizzled snow,
    And all the conduits of my blood froze up,
    Yet hath my night of life some memory,
    My wasting lamps some fading glimmer left,
    My dull deaf ears a little use to hear:
    All these old witnesses, I cannot err,
    Tell me thou art my son Antipholus.

ANTIPHOLUS OF EPHESUS. I never saw my father in my life.

ÆGEON. But seven years since, in Syracusa, boy,
    Thou know'st we parted: but perhaps, my son,
    Thou sham'st to acknowledge me in misery.

ANTIPHOLUS OF EPHESUS. The duke and all that know me in
    the city
    Can witness with me that it is not so:
    I ne'er saw Syracusa in my life.

DUKE. I tell thee, Syracusian, twenty years
    Have I been patron to Antipholus,
    During which time he ne'er saw Syracusa.
    I see thy age and dangers make thee dote.

Re-enter Abbess, with
Antipholus of Syracuse and Dromio of Syracuse

ABBESS. Most mighty duke, behold a man much wrong'd.

All gather to see him

ADRIANA. I see two husbands, or mine eyes deceive me!

DUKE. One of these men is Genius to the other;
    And so of these: which is the natural man,
    And which the spirit? Who deciphers them?

DROMIO OF SYRACUSE. I, sir, am Dromio: command him
    away.

DROMIO OF EPHESUS. I, sir, am Dromio: pray let me stay.

ANTIPHOLUS OF SYRACUSE. Ægeon art thou not? or else his
    ghost?

DROMIO OF SYRACUSE. O! my old master; who hath bound
    him here?

ABBESS. Whoever bound him, I will loose his bonds,
    And gain a husband by his liberty.
    Speak, old Ægeon, if thou be'st the man
    That hadst a wife once call'd Æmilia,
    That bore thee at a burden two fair sons.
    O! if thou be'st the same Ægeon, speak,
    And speak unto the same Æmilia!

ÆGEON. If I dream not, thou art Æmilia:
    If thou art she, tell me where is that son
    That floated with thee on the fatal raft?

ABBESS. By men of Epidamnum, he and I,
    And the twin Dromio, all were taken up:
    But by and by rude fishermen of Corinth
    By force took Dromio and my son from them,
    And me they left with those of Epidamnum.
    What then became of them, I cannot tell;
    I to this fortune that you see me in.

DUKE. Why, here begins his morning story right:
    These two Antipholus', these two so like,
    And these two Dromios, one in semblance,
    Besides her urging of her wrack at sea;
    These are the parents to these children,
    Which accidentally are met together.
    Antipholus, thou cam'st from Corinth first?

ANTIPHOLUS OF SYRACUSE. No, sir, not I; I came from Syra-
    cuse.

DUKE. Stay, stand apart; I know not which is which.

ANTIPHOLUS OF EPHESUS. I came from Corinth, my most
    gracious lord,—

DROMIO OF EPHESUS. And I with him.

ANTIPHOLUS OF EPHESUS. Brought to this town by that most
    famous warrior,

Duke Menaphon, your most renowned uncle.

ADRIANA. Which of you two did dine with me to-day?

ANTIPHOLUS OF SYRACUSE. I, gentle mistress.

ADRIANA. And are not you my husband?

ANTIPHOLUS OF EPHESUS. No; I say nay to that.

ANTIPHOLUS OF SYRACUSE. And so do I; yet did she call me
    so;

And this fair gentlewoman, her sister here,
Did call me brother. (*To Luciana*) What I told you then,
I hope I shall have leisure to make good,
If this be not a dream I see and hear.

ANGELO. That is the chain, sir, which you had of me.

ANTIPHOLUS OF SYRACUSE. I think it be, sir; I deny it not.

ANTIPHOLUS OF EPHESUS. And you, sir, for this chain ar-
    rested me.

ANGELO. I think I did, sir; I deny it not.

ADRIANA. I sent you money, sir, to be your bail,
By Dromio; but I think he brought it not.

DROMIO OF EPHESUS. No, none by me.

ANTIPHOLUS OF SYRACUSE. This purse of ducats I receiv'd
    from you,

And Dromio, my man, did bring them me.
I see we still did meet each other's man,
And I was ta'en for him, and he for me,
And thereupon these errors are arose.

ANTIPHOLUS OF EPHESUS. These ducats pawn I for my
    father here.

DUKE. It shall not need: thy father hath his life.

COURTEZAN. Sir, I must have that diamond from you.

ANTIPHOLUS OF EPHESUS. There, take it; and much thanks
    for my good cheer.

ABBESS. Renowned duke, vouchsafe to take the pains
To go with us into the abbey here,
And hear at large discoursed all our fortunes;
And all that are assembled in this place,
That by this sympathized one day's error
Have suffer'd wrong, go keep us company,

And we shall make full satisfaction.
Thirty-three years have I but gone in travail
Of you, my sons; and, till this present hour
My heavy burdens ne'er delivered.
The duke, my husband, and my children both,
And you the calendars of their nativity,
Go to a gossip's feast, and joy with me:
After so long grief such festivity!

DUKE. With all my heart I 'll gossip at this feast.

         Exeunt Duke, Abbess,
Ægeon, Courtezan, Merchant, Angelo, and Attendants

DROMIO OF SYRACUSE. Master, shall I fetch your stuff from
   shipboard?

ANTIPHOLUS OF EPHESUS. Dromio, what stuff of mine hast
   thou embark'd?

DROMIO OF SYRACUSE. Your goods that lay at host, sir, in the
   Centaur.

ANTIPHOLUS OF SYRACUSE. He speaks to me. I am your master, Dromio:

Come, go with us; we 'll look to that anon:
Embrace thy brother there; rejoice with him.

         Exeunt Antipholus of Syracuse
and Antipholus of Ephesus, Adriana and Luciana

DROMIO OF SYRACUSE. There is a fat friend at your master's
   house,

That kitchen'd me for you to-day at dinner:
She now shall be my sister, not my wife.

DROMIO OF EPHESUS. Methinks you are my glass, and not
   my brother:

I see by you I am a sweet-fac'd youth.
Will you walk in to see their gossiping?

DROMIO OF SYRACUSE. Not I, sir; you are my elder.

DROMIO OF EPHESUS. That 's a question: how shall we try
   it?

DROMIO OF SYRACUSE. We 'll draw cuts for the senior: till
   then lead thou first.

DROMIO OF EPHESUS. Nay, then, thus:

We came into the world like brother and brother;
And now let 's go hand in hand, not one before another.

         Exeunt

MUCH ADO ABOUT NOTHING

CAST OF CHARACTERS

DON PEDRO, *Prince of Arragon*
DON JOHN, *his bastard Brother*
CLAUDIO, *a young Lord of Florence*
BENEDICK, *a young Lord of Padua*
LEONATO, *Governor of Messina*
ANTONIO, *his Brother*
BALTHAZAR, *Servant to Don Pedro*

BORACHIO
CONRADE } *followers of Don John*

DOGBERRY, *a Constable*
VERGES, *a Headborough*
FRIAR FRANCIS
A Sexton
A Boy

HERO, *Daughter to Leonato*
BEATRICE, *Niece to Leonato*
MARGARET } *Waiting-gentlewomen*
URSULA } *attending on Hero*

Messengers, Watch, Attendants, &c.

SCENE

Messina

MUCH ADO ABOUT NOTHING

ACT ONE

SCENE ONE

Before Leonato's House.

Enter Leonato, Hero, Beatrice and others,
with a Messenger

LEONATO. I learn in this letter that Don Pedro of Arragon comes this night to Messina.

MESSENGER. He is very near by this. He was not three leagues off when I left him.

LEONATO. How many gentlemen have you lost in this action?

MESSENGER. But few of any sort, and none of name.

LEONATO. A victory is twice itself when the achiever brings home full numbers. I find here that Don Pedro hath bestowed much honour on a young Florentine called Claudio.

MESSENGER. Much deserved on his part and equally remembered by Don Pedro. He hath borne himself beyond the promise of his age, doing in the figure of a lamb the feats of a lion: he hath indeed better bettered expectation than you must expect of me to tell you how.

LEONATO. He hath an uncle here in Messina will be very much glad of it.

MESSENGER. I have already delivered him letters, and there appears much joy in him; even so much that joy could not show itself modest enough without a badge of bitterness.

LEONATO. Did he break out into tears?

MESSENGER. In great measure.

LEONATO. A kind overflow of kindness. There are no faces

truer than those that are so washed: how much better is
it to weep at joy than to joy at weeping!

BEATRICE. I pray you is Signior Mountanto returned from
the wars or no?

MESSENGER. I know none of that name, lady: there was
none such in the army of any sort.

LEONATO. What is he that you ask for, niece?

HERO. My cousin means Signior Benedick of Padua.

MESSENGER. O! he is returned, and as pleasant as ever he
was.

BEATRICE. He set up his bills here in Messina and challenged Cupid at the flight; and my uncle's fool, reading
the challenge, subscribed for Cupid, and challenged him
at the bird-bolt. I pray you, how many hath he killed and
eaten in these wars? But how many hath he killed? for,
indeed, I promised to eat all of his killing.

LEONATO. Faith, niece, you tax Signior Benedick too much;
but he 'll be meet with you, I doubt it not.

MESSENGER. He hath done good service, lady, in these wars.

BEATRICE. You had musty victual, and he hath holp to eat
it: he is a very valiant trencher-man; he hath an excellent
stomach.

MESSENGER. And a good soldier too, lady.

BEATRICE. And a good soldier to a lady; but what is he to a
lord?

MESSENGER. A lord to a lord, a man to a man; stuffed with
all honourable virtues.

BEATRICE. It is so, indeed; he is no less than a stuffed man;
but for the stuffing,—well, we are all mortal.

LEONATO. You must not, sir, mistake my niece. There is a
kind of merry war betwixt Signior Benedick and her:
they never meet but there 's a skirmish of wit between
them.

BEATRICE. Alas! he gets nothing by that. In our last conflict
four of his five wits went halting off, and now is the
whole man governed with one! so that if he have wit
enough to keep himself warm, let him bear it for a difference between himself and his horse; for it is all the
wealth that he hath left to be known a reasonable creature. Who is his companion now? He hath every month a
new sworn brother.

MESSENGER. Is 't possible?

BEATRICE. Very easily possible: he wears his faith but as the fashion of his hat; it ever changes with the next block.

MESSENGER. I see, lady, the gentleman is not in your books.

BEATRICE. No; an he were, I would burn my study. But, I pray you, who is his companion? Is there no young squarer now that will make a voyage with him to the devil?

MESSENGER. He is most in the company of the right noble Claudio.

BEATRICE. O Lord! he will hang upon him like a disease: he is sooner caught than the pestilence, and the taker runs presently mad. God help the noble Claudio! if he have caught the Benedick, it will cost him a thousand pound ere a' be cured.

MESSENGER. I will hold friends with you, lady.

BEATRICE. Do, good friend.

LEONATO. You will never run mad, niece.

BEATRICE. No, not till a hot January.

MESSENGER. Don Pedro is approached.

Enter Don Pedro, Don John,
Claudio, Benedick, Balthazar, and Others

DON PEDRO. Good Signior Leonato, you are come to meet your trouble: the fashion of the world is to avoid cost, and you encounter it.

LEONATO. Never came trouble to my house in the likeness of your Grace, for trouble being gone, comfort should remain; but when you depart from me, sorrow abides and happiness takes his leave.

DON PEDRO. You embrace your charge too willingly. I think this is your daughter.

LEONATO. Her mother hath many times told me so.

BENEDICK. Were you in doubt, sir, that you asked her?

LEONATO. Signior Benedick, no; for then you were a child.

DON PEDRO. You have it full, Benedick: we may guess by this what you are, being a man. Truly, the lady fathers herself. Be happy, lady, for you are like an honourable father.

BENEDICK. If Signior Leonato be her father, she would not have his head on her shoulders for all Messina, as like him as she is.

BEATRICE. I wonder that you will still be talking, Signior Benedick: nobody marks you.

BENEDICK. What! my dear Lady Disdain, are you yet living?

BEATRICE. Is it possible Disdain should die while she hath such meet food to feed it as Signior Benedick? Courtesy itself must convert to disdain, if you come in her presence.

BENEDICK. Then is courtesy a turncoat. But it is certain I am loved of all ladies, only you excepted; and I would I could find in my heart that I had not a hard heart; for, truly, I love none.

BEATRICE. A dear happiness to women: they would else have been troubled with a pernicious suitor. I thank God and my cold blood, I am of your humour for that: I had rather hear my dog bark at a crow than a man swear he loves me.

BENEDICK. God keep your ladyship still in that mind; so some gentleman or other shall 'scape a predestinate scratched face.

BEATRICE. Scratching could not make it worse, an 'twere such a face as yours were.

BENEDICK. Well, you are a rare parrot-teacher.

BEATRICE. A bird of my tongue is better than a beast of yours.

BENEDICK. I would my horse had the speed of your tongue, and so good a continuer. But keep your way, i' God's name; I have done.

BEATRICE. You always end with a jade's trick: I know you of old.

DON PEDRO. This is the sum of all, Leonato: Signior Claudio, and Signior Benedick, my dear friend Leonato hath invited you all. I tell him we shall stay here at the least a month, and he heartily prays some occasion may detain us longer: I dare swear he is no hypocrite, but prays from his heart.

LEONATO. If you swear, my lord, you shall not be forsworn. (*To Don John*) Let me bid you welcome, my lord: being reconciled to the prince your brother, I owe you all duty.

DON JOHN. I thank you: I am not of many words, but I thank you.

LEONATO. Please it your Grace lead on?

DON PEDRO. Your hand, Leonato; we will go together.

Exeunt all but Benedick and Claudio

CLAUDIO. Benedick, didst thou note the daughter of Signior Leonato?

BENEDICK. I noted her not; but I looked on her.

CLAUDIO. Is she not a modest young lady?

BENEDICK. Do you question me, as an honest man should do, for my simple true judgment; or would you have me speak after my custom, as being a professed tyrant to their sex?

CLAUDIO. No; I pray thee speak in sober judgment.

BENEDICK. Why, i' faith, methinks she 's too low for a high praise, too brown for a fair praise, and too little for a great praise: only this commendation I can afford her, that were she other than she is, she were unhandsome, and being no other but as she is, I do not like her.

CLAUDIO. Thou thinkest I am in sport: I pray thee tell me truly how thou likest her.

BENEDICK. Would you buy her, that you inquire after her?

CLAUDIO. Can the world buy such a jewel?

BENEDICK. Yea, and a case to put it into. But speak you this with a sad brow, or do you play the flouting Jack, to tell us Cupid is a good hare-finder, and Vulcan a rare carpenter? Come, in what key shall a man take you, to go in the song?

CLAUDIO. In mine eye she is the sweetest lady that ever I looked on.

BENEDICK. I can see yet without spectacles and I see no such matter: there 's her cousin an she were not possessed with a fury, exceeds her as much in beauty as the first of May doth the last of December. But I hope you have no intent to turn husband, have you?

CLAUDIO. I would scarce trust myself, though I had sworn to the contrary, if Hero would be my wife.

BENEDICK. Is 't come to this, i' faith? Hath not the world one man but he will wear his cap with suspicion? Shall I never see a bachelor of threescore again? Go to, i' faith; an thou wilt needs thrust thy neck into a yoke, wear the print of it, and sigh away Sundays. Look! Don Pedro is returned to seek you.

Re-enter Don Pedro

DON PEDRO. What secret hath held you here, that you followed not to Leonato's?

BENEDICK. I would your Grace would constrain me to tell.

DON PEDRO. I charge thee on thy allegiance.

BENEDICK. You hear, Count Claudio: I can be secret as a dumb man; I would have you think so; but on my allegiance, mark you this, on my allegiance: he is in love. With who? Now that is your Grace's part. Mark how short his answer is: with Hero, Leonato's short daughter.

CLAUDIO. If this were so, so were it uttered.

BENEDICK. Like the old tale, my lord: 'it is not so, nor 'twas not so; but, indeed, God forbid it should be so.'

CLAUDIO. If my passion change not shortly, God forbid it should be otherwise.

DON PEDRO. Amen, if you love her; for the lady is very well worthy.

CLAUDIO. You speak this to fetch me in, my lord.

DON PEDRO. By my troth, I speak my thought.

CLAUDIO. And in faith, my lord, I spoke mine.

BENEDICK. And by my two faiths and troths, my lord, I spoke mine.

CLAUDIO. That I love her, I feel.

DON PEDRO. That she is worthy, I know.

BENEDICK. That I neither feel how she should be loved nor know how she should be worthy, is the opinion that fire cannot melt out of me: I will die in it at the stake.

DON PEDRO. Thou wast ever an obstinate heretic in the despite of beauty.

CLAUDIO. And never could maintain his part but in the force of his will.

BENEDICK. That a woman conceived me, I thank her; that she brought me up, I likewise give her most humble thanks: but that I will have a recheat winded in my forehead, or hang my bugle in an invisible baldrick, all women shall pardon me. Because I will not do them the wrong to mistrust any, I will do myself the right to trust none; and the fine is,—for the which I may go the finer,— I will live a bachelor.

DON PEDRO. I shall see thee, ere I die, look pale with love.

BENEDICK. With anger, with sickness, or with hunger, my lord; not with love: prove that ever I lose more blood with love than I will get again with drinking, pick out mine eyes with a ballad-maker's pen, and hang me up at the door of a brothel-house for the sign of blind Cupid.

DON PEDRO. Well, if ever thou dost fall from this faith, thou
wilt prove a notable argument.

BENEDICK. If I do, hang me in a bottle like a cat and shoot
at me; and he that hits me, let him be clapped on the
shoulder, and called Adam.

DON PEDRO. Well, as time shall try:

'In time the savage bull doth bear the yoke.'

BENEDICK. The savage bull may; but if ever the sensible
Benedick bear it, pluck off the bull's horns and set them
in my forehead; and let me be vilely painted, and in such
great letters as they write, 'Here is good horse to hire,' let
them signify under my sign 'Here you may see Benedick
the married man.'

CLAUDIO. If this should ever happen, thou wouldst be horn-
mad.

DON PEDRO. Nay, if Cupid have not spent all his quiver in
Venice, thou wilt quake for this shortly.

BENEDICK. I look for an earthquake too then.

DON PEDRO. Well, you will temporize with the hours. In the
meantime, good Signior Benedick, repair to Leonato's:
commend me to him and tell him I will not fail him at
supper; for indeed he hath made great preparation.

BENEDICK. I have almost matter enough in me for such an
embassage; and so I commit you—

CLAUDIO. To the tuition of God: from my house, if I had
it,—

DON PEDRO. The sixth of July: your loving friend, Benedick.

BENEDICK. Nay, mock not, mock not. The body of your discourse is sometime guarded with fragments, and the
guards are but slightly basted on neither: ere you flout
old ends any further, examine your conscience: and so I
leave you.   *Exit*

CLAUDIO. My liege, your Highness now may do me good.

DON PEDRO. My love is thine to teach: teach it but how,
And thou shalt see how apt it is to learn
Any hard lesson that may do thee good.

CLAUDIO. Hath Leonato any son, my lord?

DON PEDRO. No child but Hero; she 's his only heir.
Dost thou affect her, Claudio?

CLAUDIO.   O! my lord,
When you went onward on this ended action,
I looked upon her with a soldier's eye,

That lik'd, but had a rougher task in hand
Than to drive liking to the name of love;
But now I am return'd, and that war-thoughts
Have left their places vacant, in their rooms
Come thronging soft and delicate desires,
All prompting me how fair young Hero is,
Saying, I lik'd her ere I went to wars.

DON PEDRO. Thou wilt be like a lover presently,
And tire the hearer with a book of words.
If thou dost love fair Hero, cherish it,
And I will break with her, and with her father,
And thou shalt have her. Was 't not to this end
That thou began'st to twist so fine a story?

CLAUDIO. How sweetly do you minister to love,
That know love's grief by his complexion!
But lest my liking might too sudden seem,
I would have salv'd it with a longer treatise.

DON PEDRO. What need the bridge much broader than the
    flood?
The fairest grant is the necessity.
Look, what will serve is fit: 'tis once, thou lov'st,
And I will fit thee with the remedy.
I know we shall have revelling to-night:
I will assume thy part in some disguise,
And tell fair Hero I am Claudio;
And in her bosom I 'll unclasp my heart,
And take her hearing prisoner with the force
And strong encounter of my amorous tale:
Then, after to her father will I break;
And the conclusion is, she shall be thine.
In practice let us put it presently.   *Exeunt*

SCENE TWO

A Room in Leonato's House.

Enter Leonato and Antonio, meeting

LEONATO. How now, brother! Where is my cousin, your
son? Hath he provided this music?

ANTONIO. He is very busy about it. But, brother, I can tell
you strange news that you yet dreamt not of.

LEONATO. Are they good?

ANTONIO. As the event stamps them: but they have a good cover; they show well outward. The prince and Count Claudio, walking in a thick-pleached alley in my orchard, were thus much overheard by a man of mine: the prince discovered to Claudio that he loved my niece your daughter, and meant to acknowledge it this night in a dance; and, if he found her accordant, he meant to take the present time by the top and instantly break with you of it.

LEONATO. Hath the fellow any wit that told you this?

ANTONIO. A good sharp fellow: I will send for him; and question him yourself.

LEONATO. No, no; we will hold it as a dream till it appear itself: but I will acquaint my daughter withal, that she may be the better prepared for an answer, if peradventure this be true. Go you, and tell her of it. (*Several persons cross the stage*) Cousins, you know what you have to do. O! I cry you mercy, friend; go you with me, and I will use your skill. Good cousin, have a care this busy time.   *Exeunt*

SCENE THREE

Another Room in Leonato's House.

Enter Don John and Conrade

CONRADE. What the good-year, my lord! why are you thus out of measure sad?

DON JOHN. There is no measure in the occasion that breeds; therefore the sadness is without limit.

CONRADE. You should hear reason.

DON JOHN. And when I have heard it, what blessing brings it?

CONRADE. If not a present remedy, at least a patient sufferance.

DON JOHN. I wonder that thou, being,—as thou say'st thou art,—born under Saturn, goest about to apply a moral medicine to a mortifying mischief. I cannot hide what I am: I must be sad when I have cause, and smile at no man's jests; eat when I have stomach, and wait for no man's leisure; sleep when I am drowsy, and tend on no man's business; laugh when I am merry, and claw no man in his humour.

CONRADE. Yea; but you must not make the full show of this till you may do it without controlment. You have of late stood out against your brother, and he hath ta'en you newly into his grace; where it is impossible you should take true root but by the fair weather that you make yourself: it is needful that you frame the season for your own harvest.

DON JOHN. I had rather be a canker in a hedge than a rose in his grace; and it better fits my blood to be disdained of all than to fashion a carriage to rob love from any: in this, though I cannot be said to be a flattering honest man, it must not be denied but I am a plain-dealing villain. I am trusted with a muzzle and enfranchised with a clog; therefore I have decreed not to sing in my cage. If I had my mouth, I would bite; if I had my liberty, I would do my liking: in the meantime, let me be that I am, and seek not to alter me.

CONRADE. Can you make no use of your discontent?

DON JOHN. I make all use of it, for I use it only. Who comes here?

Enter Borachio

What news, Borachio?

BORACHIO. I came yonder from a great supper: the prince, your brother, is royally entertained by Leonato; and I can give you intelligence of an intended marriage.

DON JOHN. Will it serve for any model to build mischief on? What is he for a fool that betroths himself to unquietness?

BORACHIO. Marry, it is your brother's right hand.

DON JOHN. Who? the most exquisite Claudio?

BORACHIO. Even he.

DON JOHN. A proper squire! And who, and who? which way looks he?

BORACHIO. Marry, on Hero, the daughter and heir of Leonato.

DON JOHN. A very forward March-chick! How came you to this?

BORACHIO. Being entertained for a perfumer, as I was smoking a musty room, comes me the prince and Claudio,

hand in hand, in sad conference: I whipt me behind the
arras, and there heard it agreed upon that the prince
should woo Hero for himself, and having obtained her,
give her to Count Claudio.

DON JOHN. Come, come; let us thither: this may prove food
to my displeasure. That young start-up hath all the glory
of my overthrow: if I can cross him any way, I bless myself every way. You are both sure, and will assist me?

CONRADE. ⎱ To the death, my lord.
BORACHIO. ⎰

DON JOHN. Let us to the great supper: their cheer is the
greater that I am subdued. Would the cook were of my
mind! Shall we go to prove what's to be done?

BORACHIO. We'll wait upon your lordship.   *Exeunt*

ACT TWO

SCENE ONE

A Hall in Leonato's House.

Enter Leonato, Antonio, Hero, Beatrice, and Others

LEONATO. Was not Count John here at supper?

ANTONIO. I saw him not.

BEATRICE. How tartly that gentleman looks! I never can see
him but I am heart-burned an hour after.

HERO. He is of a very melancholy disposition.

BEATRICE. He were an excellent man that were made just
in the mid-way between him and Benedick: the one is
too like an image, and says nothing; and the other too
like my lady's eldest son, evermore tattling.

LEONATO. Then half Signior Benedick's tongue in Count
John's mouth, and half Count John's melancholy in Signior Benedick's face,—

BEATRICE. With a good leg and a good foot, uncle, and
money enough in his purse, such a man would win any
woman in the world, if a' could get her good will.

LEONATO. By my troth, niece, thou wilt never get thee a
husband, if thou be so shrewd of thy tongue.

ANTONIO. In faith, she 's too curst.

BEATRICE. Too curst is more than curst: I shall lessen God's
sending that way; for it is said, 'God sends a curst cow
short horns'; but to a cow too curst he sends none.

LEONATO. So, by being too curst, God will send you no
horns?

BEATRICE. Just, if he send me no husband; for the which
blessing I am at him upon my knees every morning and
evening. Lord! I could not endure a husband with a
beard on his face: I had rather lie in the woollen.

LEONATO. You may light on a husband that hath no beard.

BEATRICE. What should I do with him? dress him in my ap-

parel and make him my waiting-gentlewoman? He that
hath a beard is more than a youth, and he that hath no
beard is less than a man; and he that is more than a
youth is not for me; and he that is less than a man, I am
not for him: therefore I will even take sixpence in earnest
of the bear-ward, and lead his apes into hell.

LEONATO. Well then, go you into hell?

BEATRICE. No; but to the gate; and there will the devil
meet me, like an old cuckold, with horns on his head, and
say, 'Get you to heaven, Beatrice, get you to heaven;
here 's no place for you maids': so deliver I up my apes,
and away to Saint Peter for the heavens; he shows me
where the bachelors sit, and there live we as merry as the
day is long.

ANTONIO. (*To Hero*) Well, niece, I trust you will be ruled
by your father.

BEATRICE. Yes, faith; it is my cousin's duty to make curtsy,
and say, 'Father, as it please you':—but yet for all that,
cousin, let him be a handsome fellow, or else make another curtsy, and say, 'Father, as it please me.'

LEONATO. Well, niece, I hope to see you one day fitted with
a husband.

BEATRICE. Not till God make men of some other metal than
earth. Would it not grieve a woman to be over-mastered
with a piece of valiant dust? to make an account of her
life to a clod of wayward marl? No, uncle, I 'll none:
Adam's sons are my brethren; and truly, I hold it a sin to
match in my kindred.

LEONATO. Daughter, remember what I told you: if the
prince do solicit you in that kind, you know your answer.

BEATRICE. The fault will be in the music, cousin, if you be
not wooed in good time: if the prince be too important,
tell him there is measure in everything, and so dance out
the answer. For, hear me, Hero: wooing, wedding, and
repenting, is as a Scotch jig, a measure, and a cinque-
pace: the first suit is hot and hasty, like a Scotch jig, and
full as fantastical; the wedding, mannerly-modest, as a
measure, full of state and ancientry; and then comes Repentance, and, with his bad legs, falls into the cinque-
pace faster and faster, till he sink into his grave.

LEONATO. Cousin, you apprehend passing shrewdly.

BEATRICE. I have a good eye, uncle: I can see a church by
daylight.

LEONATO. The revellers are entering, brother: make good
room.

*Enter Don Pedro, Claudio, Benedick, Balthazar, Don John,
Borachio, Margaret, Ursula, and Others, masked*

DON PEDRO. Lady, will you walk about with your friend?

HERO. So you walk softly and look sweetly and say nothing,
I am yours for the walk; and especially when I walk
away.

DON PEDRO. With me in your company?

HERO. I may say so, when I please.

DON PEDRO. And when please you to say so?

HERO. When I like your favour; for God defend the lute
should be like the case!

DON PEDRO. My visor is Philemon's roof; within the house is
Jove.

HERO. Why, then, your visor should be thatch'd.

DON PEDRO. Speak low, if you speak love.   *Takes her aside*

BALTHAZAR. Well, I would you did like me.

MARGARET. So would not I, for your own sake; for I have
many ill qualities.

BALTHAZAR. Which is one?

MARGARET. I say my prayers aloud.

BALTHAZAR. I love you the better; the hearers may cry
Amen.

MARGARET. God match me with a good dancer!

BALTHAZAR. Amen.

MARGARET. And God keep him out of my sight when the
dance is done! Answer, clerk.

BALTHAZAR. No more words: the clerk is answered.

URSULA. I know you well enough: you are Signior Antonio.

ANTONIO. At a word, I am not.

URSULA. I know you by the waggling of your head.

ANTONIO. To tell you true, I counterfeit him.

URSULA. You could never do him so ill-well, unless you
were the very man. Here's his dry hand up and down:
you are he, you are he.

ANTONIO. At a word, I am not.

URSULA. Come, come; do you think I do not know you by
your excellent wit? Can virtue hide itself? Go to, mum,
you are he: graces will appear, and there's an end.

BEATRICE. Will you not tell me who told you so?

BENEDICK. No, you shall pardon me.

BEATRICE. Nor will you not tell me who you are?

BENEDICK. Not now.

BEATRICE. That I was disdainful, and that I had my good wit out of the 'Hundred Merry Tales.' Well, this was Signior Benedick that said so.

BENEDICK. What 's he?

BEATRICE. I am sure you know him well enough.

BENEDICK. Not I, believe me.

BEATRICE. Did he never make you laugh?

BENEDICK. I pray you, what is he?

BEATRICE. Why, he is the prince's jester: a very dull fool; only his gift is in devising impossible slanders: none but libertines delight in him; and the commendation is not in his wit, but in his villany; for he both pleases men and angers them, and then they laugh at him and beat him. I am sure he is in the fleet: I would he had boarded me!

BENEDICK. When I know the gentleman, I 'll tell him what you say.

BEATRICE. Do, do: he 'll but break a comparison or two on me; which, peradventure not marked or not laughed at, strikes him into melancholy; and then there 's a partridge wing saved, for the fool will eat no supper that night. (*Music within*) We must follow the leaders.

BENEDICK. In every good thing.

BEATRICE. Nay, if they lead to any ill, I will leave them at the next turning.

Dance. Then exeunt all
but Don John, Borachio, and Claudio

DON JOHN. Sure my brother is amorous on Hero, and hath withdrawn her father to break with him about it. The ladies follow her and but one visor remains.

BORACHIO. And that is Claudio: I know him by his bearing.

DON JOHN. Are not you Signior Benedick?

CLAUDIO. You know me well; I am he.

DON JOHN. Signior, you are very near my brother in his love: he is enamoured on Hero; I pray you, dissuade him from her; she is no equal for his birth: you may do the part of an honest man in it.

CLAUDIO. How know you he loves her?

DON JOHN. I heard him swear his affection.

BORACHIO. So did I too; and he swore he would marry her
  to-night.

DON JOHN. Come, let us to the banquet.

Exeunt Don John and Borachio

CLAUDIO. Thus answer I in name of Benedick,
  But hear these ill news with the ears of Claudio.
  'Tis certain so; the prince woos for himself.
  Friendship is constant in all other things
  Save in the office and affairs of love:
  Therefore all hearts in love use their own tongues;
  Let every eye negotiate for itself
  And trust no agent; for beauty is a witch
  Against whose charms faith melteth into blood.
  This is an accident of hourly proof,
  Which I mistrusted not. Farewell, therefore, Hero!

Re-enter Benedick

BENEDICK. Count Claudio?

CLAUDIO. Yea, the same.

BENEDICK. Come, will you go with me?

CLAUDIO. Whither?

BENEDICK. Even to the next willow, about your own business, count. What fashion will you wear the garland of?
  About your neck, like a usurer's chain? or under your
  arm, like a lieutenant's scarf? You must wear it one way,
  for the prince hath got your Hero.

CLAUDIO. I wish him joy of her.

BENEDICK. Why, that 's spoken like an honest drovier: so
  they sell bullocks. But did you think the prince would
  have served you thus?

CLAUDIO. I pray you, leave me.

BENEDICK. Ho! now you strike like the blind man: 'twas the
  boy that stole your meat, and you 'll beat the post.

CLAUDIO. If it will not be, I 'll leave you.   *Exit*

BENEDICK. Alas! poor hurt fowl. Now will he creep into
  sedges. But, that my lady Beatrice should know me, and
  not know me! The prince's fool! Ha! it may be I go under
  that title because I am merry. Yea, but so I am apt to do
  myself wrong; I am not so reputed: it is the base though
  bitter disposition of Beatrice that puts the world into her
  person, and so gives me out. Well, I 'll be revenged as I
  may.

Re-enter Don Pedro

DON PEDRO. Now, signior, where's the count? Did you see him?

BENEDICK. Troth, my lord, I have played the part of Lady Fame. I found him here as melancholy as a lodge in a warren. I told him, and I think I told him true, that your Grace had got the good will of this young lady; and I offered him my company to a willow tree, either to make him a garland, as being forsaken, or to bind him up a rod, as being worthy to be whipped.

DON PEDRO. To be whipped! What's his fault?

BENEDICK. The flat transgression of a school-boy, who, being overjoy'd with finding a bird's nest, shows it his companion, and he steals it.

DON PEDRO. Wilt thou make a trust a transgression? The transgression is in the stealer.

BENEDICK. Yet it had not been amiss the rod had been made, and the garland too; for the garland he might have worn himself, and the rod he might have bestowed on you, who, as I take it, have stolen his bird's nest.

DON PEDRO. I will but teach them to sing, and restore them to the owner.

BENEDICK. If their singing answer your saying, by my faith, you say honestly.

DON PEDRO. The Lady Beatrice hath a quarrel to you: the gentleman that danced with her told her she is much wronged by you.

BENEDICK. O! she misused me past the endurance of a block: an oak but with one green leaf on it, would have answered her: my very visor began to assume life and scold with her. She told me, not thinking I had been myself, that I was the prince's jester; that I was duller than a great thaw; huddling jest upon jest with such impossible conveyance upon me, that I stood like a man at a mark, with a whole army shooting at me. She speaks poniards, and every word stabs: if her breath were as terrible as her terminations, there were no living near her; she would infect to the north star. I would not marry her, though she were endowed with all that Adam had left him before he transgressed: she would have made Hercules have turned spit, yea, and have cleft his club to make the fire too. Come, talk not of her; you shall find her the infernal Ate in good apparel. I would to God some scholar would

conjure her, for certainly, while she is here, a man may
live as quiet in hell as in a sanctuary; and people sin
upon purpose because they would go thither; so, indeed,
all disquiet, horror and perturbation follow her.

Re-enter Claudio, Beatrice, Hero, and Leonato

DON PEDRO. Look! here she comes.

BENEDICK. Will your Grace command me any service to the
world's end? I will go on the slightest errand now to the
Antipodes that you can devise to send me on; I will fetch
you a toothpicker now from the furthest inch of Asia;
bring you the length of Prester John's foot; fetch you a
hair off the Great Cham's beard; do you any embassage
to the Pigmies, rather than hold three words' conference
with this harpy. You have no employment for me?

DON PEDRO. None, but to desire your good company.

BENEDICK. O God, sir, here 's a dish I love not: I cannot endure my Lady Tongue. *Exit*

DON PEDRO. Come, lady, come; you have lost the heart of
Signior Benedick.

BEATRICE. Indeed, my lord, he lent it me awhile; and I gave
him use for it, a double heart for a single one: marry,
once before he won it of me with false dice, therefore
your Grace may well say I have lost it.

DON PEDRO. You have put him down, lady, you have put
him down.

BEATRICE. So I would not he should do me, my lord, lest I
should prove the mother of fools. I have brought Count
Claudio, whom you sent me to seek.

DON PEDRO. Why, how now, count! wherefore are you sad?

CLAUDIO. Not sad, my lord.

DON PEDRO. How then? Sick?

CLAUDIO. Neither, my lord.

BEATRICE. The count is neither sad, nor sick, nor merry,
nor well; but civil count, civil as an orange, and something of that jealous complexion.

DON PEDRO. I' faith, lady, I think your blazon to be true;
though, I 'll be sworn, if he be so, his conceit is false.
Here, Claudio, I have wooed in thy name, and fair Hero
is won; I have broke with her father, and, his good will
obtained; name the day of marriage, and God give thee
joy!

LEONATO. Count, take of me my daughter, and with her my

fortunes: his Grace hath made the match, and all grace say Amen to it!

BEATRICE. Speak, count, 'tis your cue.

CLAUDIO. Silence is the perfectest herald of joy: I were but little happy, if I could say how much. Lady, as you are mine, I am yours: I give away myself for you and dote upon the exchange.

BEATRICE. Speak, cousin; or, if you cannot, stop his mouth with a kiss, and let not him speak neither.

DON PEDRO. In faith, lady, you have a merry heart.

BEATRICE. Yea, my lord; I thank it, poor fool, it keeps on the windy side of care. My cousin tells him in his ear that he is in her heart.

CLAUDIO. And so she doth, cousin.

BEATRICE. Good Lord, for alliance! Thus goes every one to the world but I, and I am sunburnt. I may sit in a corner and cry heigh-ho for a husband!

DON PEDRO. Lady Beatrice, I will get you one.

BEATRICE. I would rather have one of your father's getting. Hath your Grace ne'er a brother like you? Your father got excellent husbands, if a maid could come by them.

DON PEDRO. Will you have me, lady?

BEATRICE. No, my lord, unless I might have another for working days: your Grace is too costly to wear every day. But, I beseech your Grace, pardon me; I was born to speak all mirth and no matter.

DON PEDRO. Your silence most offends me, and to be merry best becomes you; for, out of question, you were born in a merry hour.

BEATRICE. No, sure, my lord, my mother cried; but then there was a star danced, and under that was I born. Cousins, God give you joy!

LEONATO. Niece, will you look to those things I told you of?

BEATRICE. I cry you mercy, uncle. By your Grace's pardon.

Exit

DON PEDRO. By my troth, a pleasant spirited lady.

LEONATO. There 's little of the melancholy element in her, my lord: she is never sad but when she sleeps; and not ever sad then, for I have heard my daughter say, she hath often dreamed of unhappiness and waked herself with laughing.

DON PEDRO. She cannot endure to hear tell of a husband.

LEONATO. O! by no means: she mocks all her wooers out of suit.

DON PEDRO. She were an excellent wife for Benedick.

LEONATO. O Lord! my lord, if they were but a week married, they would talk themselves mad.

DON PEDRO. Count Claudio, when mean you to go to church?

CLAUDIO. To-morrow, my lord. Time goes on crutches till love have all his rites.

LEONATO. Not till Monday, my dear son, which is hence a just seven-night; and a time too brief too, to have all things answer my mind.

DON PEDRO. Come, you shake the head at so long a breathing; but, I warrant thee, Claudio, the time shall not go dully by us. I will in the interim undertake one of Hercules' labours, which is, to bring Signior Benedick and the Lady Beatrice into a mountain of affection the one with the other. I would fain have it a match; and I doubt not but to fashion it, if you three will but minister such assistance as I shall give you direction.

LEONATO. My lord, I am for you, though it cost me ten nights' watchings.

CLAUDIO. And I, my lord.

DON PEDRO. And you too, gentle Hero?

HERO. I will do any modest office, my lord, to help my cousin to a good husband.

DON PEDRO. And Benedick is not the unhopefullest husband that I know. Thus far can I praise him; he is of a noble strain, of approved valour, and confirmed honesty. I will teach you how to humour your cousin, that she shall fall in love with Benedick; and I, with your two helps, will so practise on Benedick that, in despite of his quick wit and his queasy stomach, he shall fall in love with Beatrice. If we can do this, Cupid is no longer an archer: his glory shall be ours, for we are the only love-gods. Go in with me, and I will tell you my drift.   *Exeunt*

SCENE TWO

Another Room in Leonato's House.

Enter Don John and Borachio

DON JOHN. It is so; the Count Claudio shall marry the daughter of Leonato.

BORACHIO. Yea, my lord; but I can cross it.

DON JOHN. Any bar, any cross, any impediment will be medicinable to me: I am sick in displeasure to him, and whatsoever comes athwart his affection ranges evenly with mine. How canst thou cross this marriage?

BORACHIO. Not honestly, my lord; but so covertly that no dishonesty shall appear in me.

DON JOHN. Show me briefly how.

BORACHIO. I think I told your lordship, a year since, how much I am in the favour of Margaret, the waiting-gentle-woman to Hero.

DON JOHN. I remember.

BORACHIO. I can, at any unseasonable instant of the night, appoint her to look out at her lady's chamber-window.

DON JOHN. What life is in that, to be the death of this marriage?

BORACHIO. The poison of that lies in you to temper. Go you to the prince your brother; spare not to tell him, that he hath wronged his honour in marrying the renowned Claudio,—whose estimation do you mightily hold up,—to a con-taminated stale, such a one as Hero.

DON JOHN. What proof shall I make of that?

BORACHIO. Proof enough to misuse the prince, to vex Claudio, to undo Hero, and kill Leonato. Look you for any other issue?

DON JOHN. Only to despite them, I will endeavour any thing.

BORACHIO. Go, then; find me a meet hour to draw Don Pedro and the Count Claudio alone: tell them that you know that Hero loves me; intend a kind of zeal both to the prince and Claudio, as—in love of your brother's honour, who hath made this match, and his friend's reputation, who is thus like to be cozened with the semblance of a maid,—that you have discovered thus. They will scarcely believe this without trial: offer them instances, which shall bear no less likelihood than to see me at her chamber-window, hear me call Margaret Hero; hear Margaret term me Claudio; and bring them to see this the very night before the intended wedding: for in the meantime I will so fashion the matter that Hero shall be absent; and there shall appear such seeming truth of Hero's disloyalty, that jealousy shall be called assurance, and all the preparation overthrown.

DON JOHN. Grow this to what adverse issue it can, I will put it in practice. Be cunning in the working this, and thy fee is a thousand ducats.

BORACHIO. Be you constant in the accusation, and my cunning shall not shame me.

DON JOHN. I will presently go learn their day of marriage.

Exeunt

SCENE THREE

Leonato's Garden.

Enter Benedick

BENEDICK. Boy!

Enter a Boy

BOY. Signior?

BENEDICK. In my chamber-window lies a book; bring it hither to me in the orchard.

BOY. I am here already, sir.

BENEDICK. I know that; but I would have thee hence, and here again. (*Exit Boy*) I do much wonder that one man, seeing how much another man is a fool when he dedicates his behaviours to love, will, after he hath laughed at such shallow follies in others, become the argument of his own scorn by falling in love: and such a man is Claudio. I have known, when there was no music with him but the drum and the fife; and now had he rather hear the tabor and the pipe: I have known, when he would have walked ten mile afoot to see a good armour; and now will he lie ten nights awake, carving the fashion of a new doublet. He was wont to speak plain and to the purpose, like an hon-

est man and a soldier; and now is he turned orthogra-
pher; his words are a very fantastical banquet, just so
many strange dishes. May I be so converted, and see with
these eyes? I cannot tell; I think not: I will not be sworn
but love may transform me to an oyster; but I 'll take my
oath on it, till he have made an oyster of me, he shall
never make me such a fool. One woman is fair, yet I am
well; another is wise, yet I am well; another virtuous, yet
I am well; but till all graces be in one woman, one woman
shall not come in my grace. Rich she shall be, that 's certain; wise, or I 'll none; virtuous, or I 'll never cheapen her;
fair, or I 'll never look on her; mild, or come not near me;
noble, or not I for an angel; of good discourse, an excellent musician, and her hair shall be of what colour it
please God. Ha! the prince and Monsieur Love! I will
hide me in the arbour.   *Withdraws*

Enter Don Pedro, Leonato,
and Claudio, followed by Balthazar and Musicians

DON PEDRO. Come, shall we hear this music?

CLAUDIO. Yea, my good lord. How still the evening is,
As hush'd on purpose to grace harmony!

DON PEDRO. See you where Benedick hath hid himself?

CLAUDIO. O! very well, my lord: the music ended,
We 'll fit the kid-fox with a penny-worth.

DON PEDRO. Come, Balthazar, we 'll hear that song again.

BALTHAZAR. O! good my lord, tax not so bad a voice
To slander music any more than once.

DON PEDRO. It is the witness still of excellency,
To put a strange face on his own perfection.
I pray thee, sing, and let me woo no more.

BALTHAZAR. Because you talk of wooing, I will sing;
Since many a wooer doth commence his suit
To her he thinks not worthy; yet he wooes;
Yet will he swear he loves.

DON PEDRO.   Nay, pray thee, come;
Or if thou wilt hold longer argument,
Do it in notes.

BALTHAZAR.   Note this before my notes;
There 's not a note of mine that 's worth the noting.

DON PEDRO. Why these are very crotchets that he speaks;
Notes, notes, forsooth, and nothing!   *Music*

BENEDICK. Now, divine air! now is his soul ravished! Is it

not strange that sheeps' guts should hale souls out of men's bodies? Well, a horn for my money, when all 's done.

BALTHAZAR'S SONG

Sigh no more, ladies, sigh no more,
 Men were deceivers ever;
One foot in sea, and one on shore,
 To one thing constant never.
  Then sigh not so,
  But let them go,
 And be you blithe and bonny,
Converting all your sounds of woe
 Into Hey nonny, nonny.

Sing no more ditties, sing no mo
 Of dumps so dull and heavy;
The fraud of men was ever so,
 Since summer first was leavy.
  Then sigh not so,
  But let them go,
 And be you blithe and bonny,
Converting all your sounds of woe
 Into Hey nonny, nonny.

DON PEDRO. By my troth, a good song.

BALTHAZAR. And an ill singer, my lord.

DON PEDRO. Ha, no, no, faith; thou singest well enough for a shift.

BENEDICK. (*Aside*) An he had been a dog that should have howled thus, they would have hanged him; and I pray God his bad voice bode no mischief. I had as lief have heard the night-raven, come what plague could have come after it.

DON PEDRO. Yea, marry; dost thou hear, Balthazar? I pray thee, get us some excellent music, for to-morrow night we would have it at the Lady Hero's chamber-window.

BALTHAZAR. The best I can, my lord.

DON PEDRO. Do so: farewell. (*Exeunt Balthazar and Musicians*) Come hither, Leonato: what was it you told me of to-day, that your niece Beatrice was in love with Signior Benedick?

CLAUDIO. O! ay:—(*Aside to Don Pedro*) Stalk on, stalk on; the fowl sits. I did never think that lady would have loved any man.

LEONATO. No, nor I neither; but most wonderful that she should so dote on Signior Benedick, whom she hath in all outward behaviours seemed ever to abhor.

BENEDICK. (*Aside*) Is 't possible? Sits the wind in that corner?

LEONATO. By my troth, my lord, I cannot tell what to think of it but that she loves him with an enraged affection: it is past the infinite of thought.

DON PEDRO. May be she doth but counterfeit.

CLAUDIO. Faith, like enough.

LEONATO. O God! counterfeit! There was never counterfeit of passion came so near the life of passion as she discovers it.

DON PEDRO. Why, what effects of passion shows she?

CLAUDIO. (*Aside*) Bait the hook well: this fish will bite.

LEONATO. What effects, my lord? She will sit you; (*To Claudio*) You heard my daughter tell you how.

CLAUDIO. She did, indeed.

DON PEDRO. How, how, I pray you? You amaze me: I would have thought her spirit had been invincible against all assaults of affection.

LEONATO. I would have sworn it had, my lord; especially against Benedick.

BENEDICK. (*Aside*) I should think this a gull, but that the white-bearded fellow speaks it: knavery cannot, sure, hide itself in such reverence.

CLAUDIO. (*Aside*) He hath ta'en the infection: hold it up.

DON PEDRO. Hath she made her affection known to Benedick?

LEONATO. No; and swears she never will: that 's her torment.

CLAUDIO. 'Tis true, indeed; so your daughter says: 'Shall I,' says she, 'that have so oft encountered him with scorn, write to him that I love him?'

LEONATO. This says she now when she is beginning to write to him; for she 'll be up twenty times a night, and there will she sit in her smock till she have writ a sheet of paper: my daughter tells us all.

CLAUDIO. Now you talk of a sheet of paper, I remember a pretty jest your daughter told us of.

LEONATO. O! when she had writ it, and was reading it over, she found Benedick and Beatrice between the sheet?

CLAUDIO. That.

LEONATO. O! she tore the letter into a thousand halfpence; railed at herself, that she should be so immodest to write to one that she knew would flout her: 'I measure him,' says she, 'by my own spirit; for I should flout him, if he writ to me; yea, though I love him, I should.'

CLAUDIO. Then down upon her knees she falls, weeps, sobs, beats her heart, tears her hair, prays, curses; 'O sweet Benedick! God give me patience!'

LEONATO. She doth indeed; my daughter says so; and the ecstasy hath so much overborne her, that my daughter is sometimes afeard she will do a desperate outrage to herself. It is very true.

DON PEDRO. It were good that Benedick knew of it by some other, if she will not discover it.

CLAUDIO. To what end? He would but make a sport of it and torment the poor lady worse.

DON PEDRO. An he should, it were an alms to hang him. She 's an excellent sweet lady, and, out of all suspicion, she is virtuous.

CLAUDIO. And she is exceeding wise.

DON PEDRO. In everything but in loving Benedick.

LEONATO. O! my lord, wisdom and blood combating in so tender a body, we have ten proofs to one that blood hath the victory. I am sorry for her, as I have just cause, being her uncle and her guardian.

DON PEDRO. I would she had bestowed this dotage on me; I would have daffed all other respects and made her half myself. I pray you, tell Benedick of it, and hear what a' will say.

LEONATO. Were it good, think you?

CLAUDIO. Hero thinks surely she will die; for she says she will die if he love her not, and she will die ere she make her love known, and she will die if he woo her, rather than she will bate one breath of her accustomed crossness.

DON PEDRO. She doth well: if she should make tender of her love, 'tis very possible he 'll scorn it; for the man,—as you know all,—hath a contemptible spirit.

CLAUDIO. He is a very proper man.

DON PEDRO. He hath indeed a good outward happiness.

CLAUDIO. 'Fore God, and in my mind, very wise.

DON PEDRO. He doth indeed show some sparks that are like wit.

LEONATO. And I take him to be valiant.

DON PEDRO. As Hector, I assure you: and in the managing of quarrels you may say he is wise; for either he avoids them with great discretion, or undertakes them with a most Christian-like fear.

LEONATO. If he do fear God, a' must necessarily keep peace: if he break the peace, he ought to enter into a quarrel with fear and trembling.

DON PEDRO. And so will he do; for the man doth fear God, howsoever it seems not in him by some large jests he will make. Well, I am sorry for your niece. Shall we go seek Benedick, and tell him of her love?

CLAUDIO. Never tell him, my lord: let her wear it out with good counsel.

LEONATO. Nay, that 's impossible: she may wear her heart out first.

DON PEDRO. Well, we will hear further of it by your daughter: let it cool the while. I love Benedick well, and I could wish he would modestly examine himself, to see how much he is unworthy to have so good a lady.

LEONATO. My lord, will you walk? Dinner is ready.

CLAUDIO. (*Aside*) If he do not dote on her upon this, I will never trust my expectation.

DON PEDRO. (*Aside*) Let there be the same net spread for her; and that must your daughter and her gentlewoman carry. The sport will be, when they hold one an opinion of another's dotage, and no such matter: that 's the scene that I would see, which will be merely a dumb-show. Let us send her to call him in to dinner.

Exeunt Don Pedro, Claudio, and Leonato

BENEDICK. (*Advancing from the arbour*) This can be no trick: the conference was sadly borne. They have the truth of this from Hero. They seem to pity the lady: it seems, her affections have their full bent. Love me! why, it must be requited. I hear how I am censured: they say I will bear myself proudly, if I perceive the love come from her; they say too that she will rather die than give any sign of affection. I did never think to marry: I must not seem proud: happy are they that hear their detractions, and can put them to mending. They say the lady is fair:

'tis a truth, I can bear them witness; and virtuous: 'tis so,
I cannot reprove it; and wise, but for loving me: by my
troth, it is no addition to her wit, nor no great argument
of her folly, for I will be horribly in love with her. I may
chance have some odd quirks and remnants of wit broken
on me, because I have railed so long against marriage;
but doth not the appetite alter? A man loves the meat in
his youth that he cannot endure in his age. Shall quips
and sentences and these paper bullets of the brain awe a
man from the career of his humour? No; the world must
be peopled. When I said I would die a bachelor, I did not
think I should live till I were married. Here comes Beatrice. By this day! she 's a fair lady: I do spy some marks
of love in her.

Enter Beatrice

BEATRICE. Against my will I am sent to bid you come in to
dinner.

BENEDICK. Fair Beatrice, I thank you for your pains.

BEATRICE. I took no more pains for those thanks than you
take pains to thank me: if it had been painful, I would
not have come.

BENEDICK. You take pleasure then in the message?

BEATRICE. Yea, just so much as you may take upon a knife's
point, and choke a daw withal. You have no stomach, signior: fare you well.   *Exit*

BENEDICK. Ha! 'Against my will I am sent to bid you come
in to dinner,' there 's a double meaning in that. 'I took no
more pains for those thanks than you took pains to thank
me,' that 's as much as to say, Any pains that I take for you
is as easy as thanks. If I do not take pity of her, I am a villain; if I do not love her, I am a Jew. I will go get her picture.   *Exit*

ACT THREE

SCENE ONE

Leonato's Garden.

Enter Hero, Margaret, and Ursula

HERO. Good Margaret, run thee to the parlour;
　　There shalt thou find my cousin Beatrice
　　Proposing with the prince and Claudio:
　　Whisper her ear, and tell her, I and Ursula
　　Walk in the orchard, and our whole discourse
　　Is all of her; say that thou overheard'st us,
　　And bid her steal into the pleached bower,
　　Where honey-suckles, ripen'd by the sun,
　　Forbid the sun to enter; like favourites,
　　Made proud by princes, that advance their pride
　　Against that power that bred it. There will she hide her,
　　To listen our propose. This is thy office;
　　Bear thee well in it and leave us alone.
MARGARET. I 'll make her come, I warrant you, presently.

　　　　　　　　　　　　　　　　　　　　　Exit

HERO. Now, Ursula, when Beatrice doth come,
　　As we do trace this alley up and down,
　　Our talk must only be of Benedick:
　　When I do name him, let it be thy part
　　To praise him more than ever man did merit.
　　My talk to thee must be how Benedick
　　Is sick in love with Beatrice: of this matter
　　Is little Cupid's crafty arrow made,
　　That only wounds by hearsay.

　　　　　　　　Enter Beatrice, behind
　　　　　　　　　　　　　　Now begin;

　　For look where Beatrice, like a lapwing, runs
　　Close by the ground, to hear our conference.
URSULA. The pleasant'st angling is to see the fish

Cut with her golden oars the silver stream,
And greedily devour the treacherous bait:
So angle we for Beatrice; who even now
Is couched in the woodbine coverture.
Fear you not my part of the dialogue.

HERO. Then go we near her, that her ear lose nothing
Of the false sweet bait that we lay for it.

They advance to the bower

No, truly, Ursula, she is too disdainful;
I know her spirits are as coy and wild
As haggerds of the rock.

URSULA.   But are you sure
That Benedick loves Beatrice so entirely?

HERO. So says the prince, and my new-trothed lord.

URSULA. And did they bid you tell her of it, madam?

HERO. They did entreat me to acquaint her of it;
But I persuaded them, if they lov'd Benedick,
To wish him wrestle with affection,
And never to let Beatrice know of it.

URSULA. Why did you so? Doth not the gentleman
Deserve as full as fortunate a bed
As ever Beatrice shall couch upon?

HERO. O god of love! I know he doth deserve
As much as may be yielded to a man;
But nature never fram'd a woman's heart
Of prouder stuff than that of Beatrice;
Disdain and scorn ride sparkling in her eyes,
Misprising what they look on, and her wit
Values itself so highly, that to her
All matter else seems weak. She cannot love,
Nor take no shape nor project of affection,
She is so self-endear'd.

URSULA.   Sure, I think so;
And therefore certainly it were not good
She knew his love, lest she make sport at it.

HERO. Why, you speak truth. I never yet saw man,
How wise, how noble, young, how rarely featur'd,
But she would spell him backward: if fair-fac'd,
She would swear the gentleman should be her sister;
If black, why, Nature, drawing of an antick,
Made a foul blot; if tall, a lance ill-headed;
If low, an agate very vilely cut;

If speaking, why, a vane blown with all winds;
If silent, why, a block moved with none.
So turns she every man the wrong side out,
And never gives to truth and virtue that
Which simpleness and merit purchaseth.

URSULA. Sure, sure, such carping is not commendable.

HERO. No; not to be so odd and from all fashions
As Beatrice is, cannot be commendable.
But who dare tell her so? If I should speak,
She would mock me into air: O! she would laugh me
Out of myself, press me to death with wit.
Therefore let Benedick, like cover'd fire,
Consume away in sighs, waste inwardly:
It were a better death than die with mocks,
Which is as bad as die with tickling.

URSULA. Yet tell her of it: hear what she will say.

HERO. No; rather I will go to Benedick,
And counsel him to fight against his passion.
And, truly, I 'll devise some honest slanders
To stain my cousin with. One doth not know
How much an ill word may empoison liking.

URSULA. O! do not do your cousin such a wrong.
She cannot be so much without true judgment,—
Having so swift and excellent a wit
As she is priz'd to have,—as to refuse
So rare a gentleman as Signior Benedick.

HERO. He is the only man of Italy,
Always excepted my dear Claudio.

URSULA. I pray you, be not angry with me, madam,
Speaking my fancy: Signior Benedick,
For shape, for bearing, argument and valour,
Goes foremost in report through Italy.

HERO. Indeed, he hath an excellent good name.

URSULA. His excellence did earn it, ere he had it.
When are you married, madam?

HERO. Why, every day, to-morrow. Come, go in:
I 'll show thee some attires, and have thy counsel
Which is the best to furnish me to-morrow.

URSULA. She 's lim'd, I warrant you: we have caught her,
madam.

HERO. If it prove so, then loving goes by haps:
Some Cupid kills with arrows, some with traps.

Exeunt Hero and Ursula

BEATRICE. (*Advancing*) What fire is in mine ears? Can this
 be true?
 Stand I condemn'd for pride and scorn so much?
Contempt, farewell! and maiden pride, adieu!
 No glory lives behind the back of such.
And, Benedick, love on; I will requite thee,
 Taming my wild heart to thy loving hand:
If thou dost love, my kindness shall incite thee
 To bind our loves up in a holy band;
For others say thou dost deserve, and I
Believe it better than reportingly.   *Exit*

SCENE TWO

A Room in Leonato's House.

Enter Don Pedro, Claudio, Benedick, and Leonato

DON PEDRO. I do but stay till your marriage be consummate,
 and then go I toward Arragon.

CLAUDIO. I 'll bring you thither, my lord, if you 'll vouchsafe
 me.

DON PEDRO. Nay, that would be as great a soil in the new
 gloss of your marriage, as to show a child his new coat and
 forbid him to wear it. I will only be bold with Benedick
 for his company; for, from the crown of his head to the
 sole of his foot, he is all mirth; he hath twice or thrice cut
 Cupid's bow-string, and the little hangman dare not shoot
 at him. He hath a heart as sound as a bell, and his tongue
 is the clapper; for what his heart thinks his tongue speaks.

BENEDICK. Gallants, I am not as I have been.

LEONATO. So say I: methinks you are sadder.

CLAUDIO. I hope he be in love.

DON PEDRO. Hang him, truant! there 's no true drop of blood
 in him, to be truly touched with love. If he be sad, he
 wants money.

BENEDICK. I have the tooth-ache.

DON PEDRO. Draw it.

BENEDICK. Hang it.

CLAUDIO. You must hang it first, and draw it afterwards.

DON PEDRO. What! sigh for the tooth-ache?

LEONATO. Where is but a humour or a worm?

BENEDICK. Well, every one can master a grief but he that has it.

CLAUDIO. Yet say I, he is in love.

DON PEDRO. There is no appearance of fancy in him, unless it be a fancy that he hath to strange disguises; as, to be a Dutchman to-day, a Frenchman to-morrow, or in the shape of two countries at once, as a German from the waist downward, all slops, and a Spaniard from the hip upward, no doublet. Unless he have a fancy to this foolery, as it appears he hath, he is no fool for fancy, as you would have it appear he is.

CLAUDIO. If he be not in love with some woman, there is no believing old signs: a' brushes his hat a mornings; what should that bode?

DON PEDRO. Hath any man seen him at the barber's?

CLAUDIO. No, but the barber's man hath been seen with him; and the old ornament of his cheek hath already stuffed tennis-balls.

LEONATO. Indeed he looks younger than he did, by the loss of a beard.

DON PEDRO. Nay, a' rubs himself with civet: can you smell him out by that?

CLAUDIO. That's as much as to say the sweet youth's in love.

DON PEDRO. The greatest note of it is his melancholy.

CLAUDIO. And when was he wont to wash his face?

DON PEDRO. Yea, or to paint himself? for the which, I hear what they say of him.

CLAUDIO. Nay, but his jesting spirit; which is now crept into a lute-string, and new-governed by stops.

DON PEDRO. Indeed, that tells a heavy tale for him. Conclude, conclude he is in love.

CLAUDIO. Nay, but I know who loves him.

DON PEDRO. That would I know too: I warrant, one that knows him not.

CLAUDIO. Yes, and his ill conditions; and in despite of all, dies for him.

DON PEDRO. She shall be buried with her face upwards.

BENEDICK. Yet is this no charm for the tooth-ache. Old signior, walk aside with me: I have studied eight or nine wise words to speak to you, which these hobby-horses must not hear.   *Exeunt Benedick and Leonato*

DON PEDRO. For my life, to break with him about Beatrice.

CLAUDIO. 'Tis even so. Hero and Margaret have by this
played their parts with Beatrice, and then the two bears
will not bite one another when they meet.

Enter Don John

DON JOHN. My lord and brother, God save you!

DON PEDRO. Good den, brother.

DON JOHN. If your leisure served, I would speak with you.

DON PEDRO. In private?

DON JOHN. If it please you; yet Count Claudio may hear, for
what I would speak of concerns him.

DON PEDRO. What 's the matter?

DON JOHN. (*To Claudio*) Means your lordship to be married
to-morrow?

DON PEDRO. You know he does.

DON JOHN. I know not that, when he knows what I know.

CLAUDIO. If there be any impediment, I pray you discover it.

DON JOHN. You may think I love you not: let that appear
hereafter, and aim better at me by that I now will manifest. For my brother, I think he holds you well, and in
dearness of heart hath holp to effect your ensuing marriage; surely suit ill-spent, and labour ill bestowed!

DON PEDRO. Why, what 's the matter?

DON JOHN. I came hither to tell you; and circumstances
shortened,—for she hath been too long a talking of,—the
lady is disloyal.

CLAUDIO. Who, Hero?

DON JOHN. Even she: Leonato's Hero, your Hero, every
man's Hero.

CLAUDIO. Disloyal?

DON JOHN. The word 's too good to paint out her wickedness; I could say, she were worse: think you of a worse
title, and I will fit her to it. Wonder not till further warrant: go but with me to-night, you shall see her chamber-
window entered, even the night before her wedding-day:
if you love her then, to-morrow wed her; but it would better fit your honour to change your mind.

CLAUDIO. May this be so?

DON PEDRO. I will not think it.

DON JOHN. If you dare not trust that you see, confess not
that you know. If you will follow me, I will show you

enough; and when you have seen more and heard more, proceed accordingly.

CLAUDIO. If I see any thing to-night why I should not marry her to-morrow, in the congregation, where I should wed, there will I shame her.

DON PEDRO. And, as I wooed for thee to obtain her, I will join with·thee to disgrace her.

DON JOHN. I will disparage her no further till you are my witnesses: bear it coldly but till midnight, and let the issue show itself.

DON PEDRO. O day untowardly turned!

CLAUDIO. O mischief strangely thwarting!

DON JOHN. O plague right well prevented! So will you say when you have seen the sequel.   *Exeunt*

SCENE THREE

A Street.

Enter Dogberry and Verges, with the Watch

DOGBERRY. Are you good men and true?

VERGES. Yea, or else it were pity but they should suffer salvation, body and soul.

DOGBERRY. Nay, that were a punishment too good for them, if they should have any allegiance in them, being chosen for the prince's watch.

VERGES. Well, give them their charge, neighbour Dogberry.

DOGBERRY. First, who think you the most desartless man to be constable?

FIRST WATCH. Hugh Oatcake, sir, or George Seacoal; for they can write and read.

DOGBERRY. Come hither, neighbour Seacoal. God hath blessed you with a good name: to be a well-favoured man is the gift of fortune; but to write and read comes by nature.

SECOND WATCH. Both which, Master constable,—

DOGBERRY. You have: I knew it would be your answer. Well, for your favour, sir, why, give God thanks, and make no boast of it; and for your writing and reading, let that appear when there is no need of such vanity. You are thought here to be the most senseless and fit man for the constable of the watch; therefore bear you the lanthorn. This is your charge: you shall comprehend all vagrom men; you are to bid any man stand, in the prince's name.

WATCH. How, if a' will not stand?

DOGBERRY. Why, then, take no note of him, but let him go; and presently call the rest of the watch together, and thank God you are rid of a knave.

VERGES. If he will not stand when he is bidden, he is none of the prince's subjects.

DOGBERRY. True, and they are to meddle with none but the prince's subjects. You shall also make no noise in the streets: for, for the watch to babble and to talk is most tolerable and not to be endured.

SECOND WATCH. We will rather sleep than talk: we know what belongs to a watch.

DOGBERRY. Why, you speak like an ancient and most quiet watchman, for I cannot see how sleeping should offend; only have a care that your bills be not stolen. Well, you are to call at all the alehouses, and bid those that are drunk get them to bed.

WATCH. How if they will not?

DOGBERRY. Why then, let them alone till they are sober: if they make you not then the better answer, you may say they are not the men you took them for.

WATCH. Well, sir.

DOGBERRY. If you meet a thief, you may suspect him, by virtue of your office, to be no true man; and, for such kind of men, the less you meddle or make with them, why, the more is for your honesty.

SECOND WATCH. If we know him to be a thief, shall we not lay hands on him?

DOGBERRY. Truly, by your office, you may; but I think they that touch pitch will be defiled. The most peaceable way for you, if you do take a thief, is, to let him show himself what he is and steal out of your company.

VERGES. You have been always called a merciful man, partner.

DOGBERRY. Truly, I would not hang a dog by my will, much more a man who hath any honesty in him.

VERGES. If you hear a child cry in the night, you must call to the nurse and bid her still it.

SECOND WATCH. How if the nurse be asleep and will not hear us?

DOGBERRY. Why, then, depart in peace, and let the child wake her with crying; for the ewe that will not hear her lamb when it baes, will never answer a calf when he bleats.

VERGES. 'Tis very true.

DOGBERRY. This is the end of the charge. You constable, are to present the prince's own person: if you meet the prince in the night, you may stay him.

VERGES. Nay, by 'r lady, that I think, a' cannot.

DOGBERRY. Five shillings to one on 't, with any man that knows the statues, he may stay him: marry, not without the prince be willing; for, indeed, the watch ought to offend no man, and it is an offence to stay a man against his will.

VERGES. By 'r lady, I think it be so.

DOGBERRY. Ha, ah, ha! Well, masters, good-night: an there be any matter of weight chances, call up me: keep your fellows' counsels and your own, and good-night. Come, neighbour.

SECOND WATCH. Well, masters, we hear our charge: let us go sit here upon the church-bench till two, and then all go to bed.

DOGBERRY. One word more, honest neighbours. I pray you, watch about Signior Leonato's door; for the wedding being there to-morrow, there is a great coil to-night. Adieu; be vigitant, I beseech you.   *Exeunt Dogberry and Verges*
                    Enter Borachio and Conrade

BORACHIO. What, Conrade!

WATCH. (*Aside*) Peace! stir not.

BORACHIO. Conrade, I say!

CONRADE. Here, man, I am at thy elbow.

BORACHIO. Mass, and my elbow itched; I thought there would a scab follow.

CONRADE. I will owe thee an answer for that; and now forward with thy tale.

BORACHIO. Stand thee close then under this pent-house, for it drizzles rain, and I will, like a true drunkard, utter all to thee.

WATCH. (*Aside*) Some treason, masters; yet stand close.

BORACHIO. Therefore know, I have earned of Don John a thousand ducats.

CONRADE. Is it possible that any villany should be so dear?

BORACHIO. Thou shouldst rather ask if it were possible any villany should be so rich; for when rich villains have need of poor ones, poor ones may make what price they will.

CONRADE. I wonder at it.

BORACHIO. That shows thou art unconfirmed. Thou knowest that the fashion of a doublet, or a hat, or a cloak, is nothing to a man.

CONRADE. Yes, it is apparel.

BORACHIO. I mean, the fashion.

CONRADE. Yes, the fashion is the fashion.

BORACHIO. Tush! I may as well say the fool 's the fool. But seest thou not what a deformed thief this fashion is?

WATCH. (*Aside*) I know that Deformed; a' has been a vile thief this seven years; a' goes up and down like a gentleman: I remember his name.

BORACHIO. Didst thou not hear somebody?

CONRADE. No: 'twas the vane on the house.

BORACHIO. Seest thou not, I say, what a deformed thief this fashion is? how giddily he turns about all the hot bloods between fourteen and five-and-thirty? sometime fashioning them like Pharaoh's soldiers in the reechy painting; sometime like god Bel's priests in the old church-window; sometime like the shaven Hercules in the smirched worm-eaten tapestry, where his cod-piece seems as massy as his club?

CONRADE. All this I see, and I see that the fashion wears out more apparel than the man. But art not thou thyself giddy with the fashion too, that thou hast shifted out of thy tale into telling me of the fashion?

BORACHIO. Not so, neither; but know, that I have to-night wooed Margaret, the Lady Hero's gentlewoman, by the name of Hero: she leans me out at her mistress' chamber-window, bids me a thousand times good-night,—I tell this tale vilely:—I should first tell thee how the prince, Claudio, and my master, planted and placed and possessed by my master Don John, saw afar off in the orchard this amiable encounter.

CONRADE. And thought they Margaret was Hero?

BORACHIO. Two of them did, the prince and Claudio; but

the devil my master, knew she was Margaret; and partly by his oaths, which first possessed them, partly by the dark night, which did deceive them, but chiefly by my villany, which did confirm any slander that Don John had made, away went Claudio enraged; swore he would meet her, as he was appointed, next morning at the temple, and there, before the whole congregation, shame her with what he saw o'er night, and send her home again without a husband.

FIRST WATCH. We charge you in the prince's name, stand!

SECOND WATCH. Call up the right Master constable. We have here recovered the most dangerous piece of lechery that ever was known in the commonwealth.

FIRST WATCH. And one Deformed is one of them: I know him, a' wears a lock.

CONRADE. Masters, masters!

SECOND WATCH. You 'll be made bring Deformed forth, I warrant you.

CONRADE. Masters,—

FIRST WATCH. Never speak: we charge you let us obey you to go with us.

BORACHIO. We are like to prove a goodly commodity, being taken up of these men's bills.

CONRADE. A commodity in question, I warrant you. Come, we 'll obey you. *Exeunt*

SCENE FOUR

A Room in Leonato's House.

Enter Hero, Margaret, and Ursula

HERO. Good Ursula, wake my cousin Beatrice, and desire her to rise.

URSULA. I will, lady.

HERO. And bid her come hither.

URSULA. Well. *Exit*

MARGARET. Troth, I think your other rabato were better.

HERO. No, pray thee, good Meg, I 'll wear this.

MARGARET. By my troth 's not so good; and I warrant your cousin will say so.

HERO. My cousin 's a fool, and thou art another: I 'll wear none but this.

MARGARET. I like the new tire within excellently, if the hair were a thought browner; and your gown 's a most rare fashion, i' faith. I saw the·Duchess of Milan's gown that they praise so.

HERO. O! that exceeds, they say.

MARGARET. By my troth 's but a night-gown in respect of yours: cloth o' gold, and cuts, and laced with silver, set with pearls, down sleeves, side sleeves, and skirts round, underborne with a bluish tinsel; but for a fine, quaint, graceful, and excellent fashion, yours is worth ten on 't.

HERO. God give me joy to wear it! for my heart is exceeding heavy.

MARGARET. 'Twill be heavier soon by the weight of a man.

HERO. Fie upon thee! art not ashamed?

MARGARET. Of what, lady? of speaking honourably? is not marriage honourable in a beggar? Is not your lord honourable without marriage? I think you would have me say, 'saving your reverence, a husband': an bad thinking do not wrest true speaking, I 'll offend nobody. Is there any harm in 'the heavier for a husband'? None, I think, an it be the right husband and the right wife; otherwise 'tis light, and not heavy: ask my Lady Beatrice else; here she comes.

Enter Beatrice

HERO. Good-morrow, coz.

BEATRICE. Good-morrow, sweet Hero.

HERO. Why, how now! do you speak in the sick tune?

BEATRICE. I am out of all other tune, methinks.

MARGARET. Clap 's into 'Light o' love'; that goes without a burden: do you sing it, and I 'll dance it.

BEATRICE. Ye light o' love with your heels! Then, if your husband have stables enough, you 'll see he shall lack no barns.

MARGARET. O illegitimate construction! I scorn that with my heels.

BEATRICE. 'Tis almost five o'clock, cousin; 'tis time you were ready. By my troth, I am exceeding ill. Heigh-ho!

MARGARET. For a hawk, a horse, or a husband?

BEATRICE. For the letter that begins them all, H.

MARGARET. Well, an you be not turned Turk, there's no more sailing by the star.

BEATRICE. What means the fool, trow?

MARGARET. Nothing I; but God send every one their heart's desire!

HERO. These gloves the count sent me; they are an excellent perfume.

BEATRICE. I am stuffed, cousin, I cannot smell.

MARGARET. A maid, and stuffed! there's goodly catching of cold.

BEATRICE. O, God help me! God help me! how long have you professed apprehension?

MARGARET. Ever since you left it. Doth not my wit become me rarely!

BEATRICE. It is not seen enough, you should wear it in your cap. By my troth, I am sick.

MARGARET. Get you some of this distilled Carduus Benedictus, and lay it to your heart: it is the only thing for a qualm.

HERO. There thou prick'st her with a thistle.

BEATRICE. Benedictus! why Benedictus? You have some moral in this Benedictus.

MARGARET. Moral! no, by my troth, I have no moral meaning; I meant, plain holy-thistle. You may think, perchance, that I think you are in love: nay, by 'r lady, I am not such a fool to think what I list; nor I list not to think what I can; nor, indeed, I cannot think, if I would think my heart out of thinking, that you are in love, or that you will be in love, or that you can be in love. Yet Benedick was such another, and now is he become a man: he swore he would never marry; and yet now, in despite of his heart, he eats his meat without grudging: and how you may be converted, I know not; but methinks you look with your eyes as other women do.

BEATRICE. What pace is this that thy tongue keeps?

MARGARET. Not a false gallop.

Re-enter Ursula

URSULA. Madam, withdraw: the prince, the count, Signior Benedick, Don John, and all the gallants of the town, are come to fetch you to church.

HERO. Help to dress me, good coz, good Meg, good Ursula.

Exeunt

SCENE FIVE

Another Room in Leonato's House.

Enter Leonato with Dogberry and Verges

LEONATO. What would you with me, honest neighbour?

DOGBERRY. Marry, sir, I would have some confidence with you, that decerns you nearly.

LEONATO. Brief, I pray you; for you see it is a busy time with me.

DOGBERRY. Marry, this it is, sir.

VERGES. Yes, in truth it is, sir.

LEONATO. What is it, my good friends?

DOGBERRY. Goodman Verges, sir, speaks a little off the matter: an old man, sir, and his wits are not so blunt, as, God help, I would desire they were; but, in faith, honest as the skin between his brows.

VERGES. Yes, I thank God, I am as honest as any man living, that is an old man and no honester than I.

DOGBERRY. Comparisons are odorous: palabras, neighbour Verges.

LEONATO. Neighbours, you are tedious.

DOGBERRY. It pleases your worship to say so, but we are the poor duke's officers; but truly, for mine own part, if I were as tedious as a king, I could find in my heart to bestow it all of your worship.

LEONATO. All thy tediousness on me! ha?

DOGBERRY. Yea, an 't were a thousand pound more than 'tis; for I hear as good exclamation on your worship, as of any man in the city, and though I be but a poor man, I am glad to hear it.

VERGES. And so am I.

LEONATO. I would fain know what you have to say.

VERGES. Marry, sir, our watch to-night, excepting your worship's presence, ha' ta'en a couple of as arrant knaves as any in Messina.

DOGBERRY. A good old man, sir; he will be talking; as they say, 'when the age is in, the wit is out.' God help us! it is a world to see! Well said, i' faith, neighbour Verges: well, God 's a good man; an two men ride of a horse, one must

ride behind. An honest soul, i' faith, sir; by my troth he is,
as ever broke bread: but God is to be worshipped: all men
are not alike; alas! good neighbour.

LEONATO. Indeed, neighbour, he comes too short of you.

DOGBERRY. Gifts that God gives.

LEONATO. I must leave you.

DOGBERRY. One word, sir: our watch, sir, hath indeed com-
prehended two aspicious persons, and we would have
them this morning examined before your worship.

LEONATO. Take their examination yourself, and bring it me:
I am now in great haste, as may appear unto you.

DOGBERRY. It shall be suffigance.

LEONATO. Drink some wine ere you go: fare you well.

Enter a Messenger

MESSENGER. My lord, they stay for you to give your daughter to her husband.

LEONATO. I 'll wait upon them: I am ready.

Exeunt Leonato and Messenger

DOGBERRY. Go, good partner, go, get you to Francis Seacoal;
bid him bring his pen and inkhorn to the gaol: we are
now to examination these men.

VERGES. And we must do it wisely.

DOGBERRY. We will spare for no wit, I warrant you; here 's
that shall drive some of them to a *non-come*: only get the
learned writer to set down our excommunication, and
meet me at the gaol. *Exeunt*

ACT FOUR

SCENE ONE

The Inside of a Church.

*Enter Don Pedro, Don John, Leonato, Friar Francis,
Claudio, Benedick, Hero, Beatrice, &c.*

LEONATO. Come, Friar Francis, be brief: only to the plain
form of marriage, and you shall recount their particular
duties afterwards.

FRIAR. You come hither, my lord, to marry this lady?

CLAUDIO. No.

LEONATO. To be married to her, friar; you come to marry
her.

FRIAR. Lady, you come hither to be married to this count?

HERO. I do.

FRIAR. If either of you know any inward impediment, why
you should not be conjoined, I charge you, on your souls,
to utter it.

CLAUDIO. Know you any, Hero?

HERO. None, my lord.

FRIAR. Know you any, count?

LEONATO. I dare make his answer; none.

CLAUDIO. O! what men dare do! what men may do! what
men daily do, not knowing what they do!

BENEDICK. How now! Interjections? Why then, some be of
laughing, as ah! ha! he!

CLAUDIO. Stand thee by, friar. Father, by your leave:
Will you with free and unconstrained soul
Give me this maid, your daughter?

LEONATO. As freely, son, as God did give her me.

CLAUDIO. And what have I to give you back whose worth
May counterpoise this rich and precious gift?

DON PEDRO. Nothing, unless you render her again.

CLAUDIO. Sweet prince, you learn me noble thankfulness.

There, Leonato, take her back again:
Give not this rotten orange to your friend;
She 's but the sign and semblance of her honour.
Behold! how like a maid she blushes here.
O! what authority and show of truth
Can cunning sin cover itself withal.
Comes not that blood as modest evidence
To witness simple virtue? Would you not swear,
All you that see her, that she were a maid,
By these exterior shows? But she is none:
She knows the heat of a luxurious bed;
Her blush is guiltiness, not modesty.

LEONATO. What do you mean, my lord?

CLAUDIO.   Not to be married,
Not to knit my soul to an approved wanton.

LEONATO. Dear my lord, if you, in your own proof,
Have vanquish'd the resistance of her youth,
And made defeat of her virginity,—

CLAUDIO. I know what you would say: if I have known her,
You 'll say she did embrace me as a husband,
And so extenuate the 'forehand sin:
No, Leonato,
I never tempted her with word too large;
But, as a brother to his sister, show'd
Bashful sincerity and comely love.

HERO. And seem'd I ever otherwise to you?

CLAUDIO. Out on thee! Seeming! I will write against it:
You seem to me as Dian in her orb,
As chaste as is the bud ere it be blown;
But you are more intemperate in your blood
Than Venus, or those pamper'd animals
That rage in savage sensuality.

HERO. Is my lord well, that he doth speak so wide?

LEONATO. Sweet prince, why speak not you?

DON PEDRO.   What should I speak?
I stand dishonour'd, that have gone about
To link my dear friend to a common stale.

LEONATO. Are these things spoken, or do I but dream?

DON JOHN. Sir, they are spoken, and these things are true.

BENEDICK. This looks not like a nuptial.

HERO.   True! O God!

CLAUDIO. Leonato, stand I here?

Is this the prince? Is this the prince's brother?
Is this face Hero's? Are our eyes our own?

LEONATO. All this is so; but what of this, my lord?

CLAUDIO. Let me but move one question to your daughter;
And by that fatherly and kindly power
That you have in her, bid her answer truly.

LEONATO. I charge thee do so, as thou art my child.

HERO. O, God defend me! how am I beset!
What kind of catechizing call you this?

CLAUDIO. To make you answer truly to your name.

HERO. Is it not Hero? Who can blot that name
With any just reproach?

CLAUDIO.   Marry, that can Hero:
Hero itself can blot out Hero's virtue.
What man was he talk'd with you yesternight
Out at your window, betwixt twelve and one?
Now, if you are a maid, answer to this.

HERO. I talk'd with no man at that hour, my lord.

DON PEDRO. Why, then are you no maiden. Leonato,
I am sorry you must hear: upon mine honour,
Myself, my brother, and this grieved count,
Did see her, hear her, at that hour last night,
Talk with a ruffian at her chamber-window;
Who hath indeed, most like a liberal villain,
Confess'd the vile encounters they have had
A thousand times in secret.

DON JOHN. Fie, fie! they are not to be nam'd, my lord,
Not to be spoke of;
There is not chastity enough in language
Without offence to utter them. Thus, pretty lady,
I am sorry for thy much misgovernment.

CLAUDIO. O Hero! what a Hero hadst thou been,
If half thy outward graces had been plac'd
About thy thoughts and counsels of thy heart!
But fare thee well, most foul, most fair! Farewell,
Thou pure impiety, and impious purity!
For thee I 'll lock up all the gates of love,
And on my eyelids shall conjecture hang,
To turn all beauty into thoughts of harm,
And never shall it more be gracious.

LEONATO. Hath no man's dagger here a point for me?

Hero swoons

BEATRICE. Why, how now, cousin! wherefore sink you
    down?

DON JOHN. Come, let us go. These things, come thus to light,
    Smother her spirits up.

              Exeunt Don Pedro, Don John and Claudio

BENEDICK. How doth the lady?

BEATRICE.   Dead, I think! help, uncle!
    Hero! why, Hero! Uncle! Signior Benedick!
    Friar!

LEONATO. O Fate! take not away thy heavy hand:
    Death is the fairest cover for her shame
    That may be wish'd for.

BEATRICE.   How now, cousin Hero!

FRIAR. Have comfort, lady,

LEONATO. Dost thou look up?

FRIAR.   Yea; wherefore should she not?

LEONATO. Wherefore! Why, doth not every earthly thing
    Cry shame upon her? Could she here deny
    The story that is printed in her blood?
    Do not live, Hero; do not ope thine eyes;
    For, did I think thou wouldst not quickly die,
    Thought I thy spirits were stronger than thy shames,
    Myself would, on the rearward of reproaches,
    Strike at thy life. Griev'd I, I had but one?
    Chid I for that at frugal nature's frame?
    O! one too much by thee. Why had I one?
    Why ever wast thou lovely in mine eyes?
    Why had I not with charitable hand
    Took up a beggar's issue at my gates,
    Who smirched thus, and mir'd with infamy,
    I might have said, 'No part of it is mine;
    This shame derives itself from unknown loins'?
    But mine, and mine I lov'd, and mine I prais'd,
    And mine that I was proud on, mine so much
    That I myself was to myself not mine,
    Valuing of her; why, she—O! she is fallen
    Into a pit of ink, that the wide sea
    Hath drops too few to wash her clean again,
    And salt too little which may season give
    To her foul-tainted flesh.

BENEDICK.   Sir, sir, be patient.
    For my part, I am so attir'd in wonder,

I know not what to say.

BEATRICE. O! on my soul, my cousin is belied!

BENEDICK. Lady, were you her bedfellow last night?

BEATRICE. No, truly, not; although, until last night
  I have this twelvemonth been her bedfellow.

LEONATO. Confirm'd, confirm'd! O! that is stronger made,
  Which was before barr'd up with ribs of iron.
  Would the two princes lie? and Claudio lie,
  Who lov'd her so, that, speaking of her foulness,
  Wash'd it with tears? Hence from her! let her die.

FRIAR. Hear me a little;
  For I have only been silent so long,
  And given way unto this course of fortune,
  By noting of the lady: I have mark'd
  A thousand blushing apparitions
  To start into her face; a thousand innocent shames
  In angel whiteness bear away those blushes;
  And in her eye there hath appear'd a fire,
  To burn the errors that these princes hold
  Against her maiden truth. Call me a fool;
  Trust not my reading nor my observations,
  Which with experimental seal doth warrant
  The tenour of my book; trust not my age,
  My reverence, calling, nor divinity,
  If this sweet lady lie not guiltless here
  Under some biting error.

LEONATO.   Friar, it cannot be.
  Thou seest that all the grace that she hath left
  Is, that she will not add to her damnation
  A sin of perjury: she not denies it.
  Why seek'st thou then to cover with excuse
  That which appears in proper nakedness?

FRIAR. Lady, what man is he you are accus'd of?

HERO. They know that do accuse me, I know none;
  If I know more of any man alive
  Than that which maiden modesty doth warrant,
  Let all my sins lack mercy! O, my father!
  Prove you that any man with me convers'd
  At hours unmeet, or that I yesternight
  Maintain'd the change of words with any creature,
  Refuse me, hate me, torture me to death.

FRIAR. There is some strange misprision in the princes.

BENEDICK. Two of them have the very bent of honour;
　　And if their wisdoms be misled in this,
　　The practice of it lives in John the bastard,
　　Whose spirits toil in frame of villanies.
LEONATO. I know not. If they speak but truth of her,
　　These hands shall tear her; if they wrong her honour,
　　The proudest of them shall well hear of it.
　　Time hath not yet so dried this blood of mine,
　　Nor age so eat up my invention,
　　Nor fortune made such havoc of my means,
　　Nor my bad life reft me so much of friends,
　　But they shall find, awak'd in such a kind,
　　Both strength of limb and policy of mind,
　　Ability in means and choice of friends,
　　To quit me of them throughly.
FRIAR.　　　　　　　　　　　　　Pause awhile,
　　And let my counsel sway you in this case.
　　Your daughter here the princes left for dead;
　　Let her awhile be secretly kept in,
　　And publish it that she is dead indeed:
　　Maintain a mourning ostentation;
　　And on your family's old monument
　　Hang mournful epitaphs and do all rites
　　That appertain unto a burial.
LEONATO. What shall become of this? What will this do?
FRIAR. Marry, this well carried shall on her behalf
　　Change slander to remorse; that is some good
　　But not for that dream I on this strange course,
　　But on this travail look for greater birth.
　　She dying, as it must be so maintain'd,
　　Upon the instant that she was accus'd,
　　Shall be lamented, pitied and excus'd
　　Of every hearer; for it so falls out
　　That what we have we prize not to the worth
　　Whiles we enjoy it, but being lack'd and lost,
　　Why, then we rack the value, then we find
　　The virtue that possession would not show us
　　Whiles it was ours. So will it fare with Claudio:
　　When he shall hear she died upon his words,
　　The idea of her life shall sweetly creep
　　Into his study of imagination,
　　And every lovely organ of her life

Shall come apparell'd in more precious habit,
More moving-delicate, and full of life
Into the eye and prospect of his soul,
Than when she liv'd indeed: then shall he mourn,—
If ever love had interest in his liver,—
And wish he had not so accused her,
No, though he thought his accusation true.
Let this be so, and doubt not but success
Will fashion the event in better shape
Than I can lay it down in likelihood.
But if all aim but this be levell'd false,
The supposition of the lady's death
Will quench the wonder of her infamy:
And if it sort not well, you may conceal her,—
As best befits her wounded reputation,—
In some reclusive and religious life,
Out of all eyes, tongues, minds, and injuries.

BENEDICK. Signior Leonato, let the friar advise you:
And though you know my inwardness and love
Is very much unto the prince and Claudio,
Yet, by mine honour, I will deal in this
As secretly and justly as your soul
Should with your body.

LEONATO.   Being that I flow in grief,
The smallest twine may lead me.

FRIAR. 'Tis well consented: presently away;
For to strange sores strangely they strain the cure.
Come, lady, die to live: this wedding day
Perhaps is but prolong'd: have patience and endure.

                    Exeunt Friar, Hero, and Leonato

BENEDICK. Lady Beatrice, have you wept all this while?

BEATRICE. Yea, and I will weep a while longer.

BENEDICK. I will not desire that.

BEATRICE. You have no reason; I do it freely.

BENEDICK. Surely I do believe your fair cousin is wronged.

BEATRICE. Ah! how much might the man deserve of me that
would right her.

BENEDICK. Is there any way to show such friendship?

BEATRICE. A very even way, but no such friend.

BENEDICK. May a man do it?

BEATRICE. It is a man's office, but not yours.

BENEDICK. I do love nothing in the world so well as you: is not that strange?

BEATRICE. As strange as the thing I know not. It were as possible for me to say I loved nothing so well as you; but believe me not, and yet I lie not; I confess nothing, nor I deny nothing. I am sorry for my cousin.

BENEDICK. By my sword, Beatrice, thou lovest me.

BEATRICE. Do not swear by it, and eat it.

BENEDICK. I will swear by it that you love me; and I will make him eat it that says I love not you.

BEATRICE. Will you not eat your word?

BENEDICK. With no sauce that can be devised to it. I protest I love thee.

BEATRICE. Why then, God forgive me!

BENEDICK. What offence, sweet Beatrice?

BEATRICE. You have stayed me in a happy hour: I was about to protest I loved you.

BENEDICK. And do it with all thy heart.

BEATRICE. I love you with so much of my heart that none is left to protest.

BENEDICK. Come, bid me do anything for thee.

BEATRICE. Kill Claudio.

BENEDICK. Ha! not for the wide world.

BEATRICE. You kill me to deny it. Farewell.

BENEDICK. Tarry, sweet Beatrice.

BEATRICE. I am gone, though I am here: there is no love in you: nay, I pray you, let me go.

BENEDICK. Beatrice,—

BEATRICE. In faith, I will go.

BENEDICK. We 'll be friends first.

BEATRICE. You dare easier be friends with me than fight with mine enemy.

BENEDICK. Is Claudio thine enemy?

BEATRICE. Is he not approved in the height a villain, that hath slandered, scorned, dishonoured my kinswoman? O! that I were a man. What! bear her in hand until they come to take hands, and then, with public accusation, uncovered slander, unmitigated rancour,—O God, that I were a man! I would eat his heart in the market-place.

BENEDICK. Hear me, Beatrice,—

BEATRICE. Talk with a man out at a window! a proper saying!

BENEDICK. Nay, but Beatrice,—

BEATRICE. Sweet Hero! she is wronged, she is slandered, she is undone.

BENEDICK. Beat——

BEATRICE. Princes and counties! Surely, a princely testimony, a goodly Count Comfect; a sweet gallant, surely! O! that I were a man for his sake, or that I had any friend would be a man for my sake! But manhood is melted into curtsies, valour into compliment, and men are only turned into tongue, and trim ones too: he is now as valiant as Hercules, that only tells a lie and swears it. I cannot be a man with wishing, therefore I will die a woman with grieving.

BENEDICK. Tarry, good Beatrice. By this hand, I love thee.

BEATRICE. Use it for my love some other way than swearing by it.

BENEDICK. Think you in your soul the Count Claudio hath wronged Hero?

BEATRICE. Yea, as sure as I have a thought or a soul.

BENEDICK. Enough! I am engaged, I will challenge him. I will kiss your hand, and so leave you. By this hand, Claudio shall render me a dear account. As you hear of me, so think of me. Go, comfort your cousin: I must say she is dead; and so, farewell.   *Exeunt*

SCENE TWO

A Prison.

Enter Dogberry, Verges, and Sexton, in gowns; and the Watch, with Conrade and Borachio

DOGBERRY. Is our whole dissembly appeared?

VERGES. O! a stool and a cushion for the sexton.

SEXTON. Which be the malefactors?

DOGBERRY. Marry, that am I and my partner.

VERGES. Nay, that 's certain: we have the exhibition to examine.

SEXTON. But which are the offenders that are to be examined? Let them come before Master constable.

DOGBERRY. Yea, marry, let them come before me. What is your name, friend?

BORACHIO. Borachio.

DOGBERRY. Pray write down Borachio. Yours, sirrah?

CONRADE. I am a gentleman, sir, and my name is Conrade.

DOGBERRY. Write down Master Gentleman Conrade. Masters, do you serve God?

CONRADE. ⎱ Yea, sir, we hope.
BORACHIO. ⎰

DOGBERRY. Write down that they hope they serve God: and write God first; for God defend but God should go before such villains! Masters, it is proved already that you are little better than false knaves, and it will go near to be thought so shortly. How answer you for yourselves?

CONRADE. Marry, sir, we say we are none.

DOGBERRY. A marvellous witty fellow, I assure you; but I will go about with him. Come you hither, sirrah; a word in your ear: sir, I say to you, it is thought you are false knaves.

BORACHIO. Sir, I say to you we are none.

DOGBERRY. Well, stand aside. 'Fore God, they are both in a tale. Have you writ down, that they are none?

SEXTON. Master constable, you go not the way to examine: you must call forth the watch that are their accusers.

DOGBERRY. Yea, marry, that's the eftest way. Let the watch come forth. Masters, I charge you, in the prince's name, accuse these men.

FIRST WATCH. This man said, sir, that Don John, the prince's brother, was a villain.

DOGBERRY. Write down Prince John a villain. Why, that is flat perjury, to call a prince's brother villain.

BORACHIO. Master constable,—

DOGBERRY. Pray thee, fellow, peace: I do not like thy look, I promise thee.

SEXTON. What heard you him say else?

SECOND WATCH. Marry, that he had received a thousand ducats of Don John for accusing the Lady Hero wrongfully.

DOGBERRY. Flat burglary as ever was committed.

VERGES. Yea, by the mass, that it is.

SEXTON. What else, fellow?

FIRST WATCH. And that Count Claudio did mean, upon his words, to disgrace Hero before the whole assembly, and not marry her.

DOGBERRY. O villain! thou wilt be condemned into everlasting redemption for this.

SEXTON. What else?

SECOND WATCH. This is all.

SEXTON. And this is more, masters, than you can deny.
Prince John is this morning secretly stolen away: Hero
was in this manner accused, in this very manner refused,
and, upon the grief of this, suddenly died. Master Constable, let these men be bound, and brought to Leonato's:
I will go before and show him their examination.   *Exit*

DOGBERRY. Come, let them be opinioned.

VERGES. Let them be in the hands—

CONRADE. Off, coxcomb!

DOGBERRY. God's my life! where's the sexton? let him write
down the prince's officer coxcomb. Come, bind them.
Thou naughty varlet!

CONRADE. Away! you are an ass; you are an ass.

DOGBERRY. Dost thou not suspect my place? Dost thou not
suspect my years? O that he were here to write me down
an ass! but, masters, remember that I am an ass; though
it be not written down, yet forget not that I am an ass. No,
thou villain, thou art full of piety, as shall be proved upon
thee by good witness. I am a wise fellow; and, which is
more, an officer; and, which is more, a householder; and,
which is more, as pretty a piece of flesh as any in Messina;
and one that knows the law, go to; and a rich fellow
enough, go to; and a fellow that hath had losses; and one
that hath two gowns, and everything handsome about
him. Bring him away. O that I had been writ down an ass!
Exeunt

ACT FIVE

SCENE ONE

Before Leonato's House.

Enter Leonato and Antonio

ANTONIO. If you go on thus, you will kill yourself
    And 'tis not wisdom thus to second grief
    Against yourself.
LEONATO.   I pray thee, cease thy counsel,
    Which falls into mine ears as profitless
    As water in a sieve: give not me counsel;
    Nor let no comforter delight mine ear
    But such a one whose wrongs do suit with mine:
    Bring me a father that so lov'd his child,
    Whose joy of her is overwhelm'd like mine,
    And bid him speak of patience;
    Measure his woe the length and breadth of mine,
    And let it answer every strain for strain,
    As thus for thus and such a grief for such,
    In every lineament, branch, shape, and form:
    If such a one will smile, and stroke his beard;
    Bid sorrow wag, cry 'hem' when he should groan,
    Patch grief with proverbs; make misfortune drunk
    With candle-wasters; bring him yet to me,
    And I of him will gather patience.
    But there is no such man; for, brother, men
    Can counsel and speak comfort to that grief
    Which they themselves not feel; but, tasting it,
    Their counsel turns to passion, which before
    Would give preceptial medicine to rage,
    Fetter strong madness in a silken thread,
    Charm ache with air and agony with words.
    No, no; 'tis all men's office to speak patience
    To those that wring under the load of sorrow,

But no man's virtue nor sufficiency
To be so moral when he shall endure
The like himself. Therefore give me no counsel:
My griefs cry louder than advertisement.

ANTONIO. Therein do men from children nothing differ.

LEONATO. I pray thee, peace! I will be flesh and blood;
For there was never yet philosopher
That could endure the toothache patiently,
However they have writ the style of gods
And made a push at chance and sufferance.

ANTONIO. Yet bend not all the harm upon yourself;
Make those that do offend you suffer too.

LEONATO. There thou speak'st reason: nay, I will do so.
My soul doth tell me Hero is belied;
And that shall Claudio know; so shall the prince,
And all of them that thus dishonour her.

ANTONIO. Here come the prince and Claudio hastily.

Enter Don Pedro and Claudio

DON PEDRO. Good den, good den.

CLAUDIO.   Good-day to both of you.

LEONATO. Hear you, my lords,—

DON PEDRO.   We have some haste, Leonato.

LEONATO. Some haste, my lord! well, fare you well, my lord:
Are you so hasty now?—well, all is one.

DON PEDRO. Nay, do not quarrel with us, good old man.

ANTONIO. If he could right himself with quarrelling,
Some of us would lie low.

CLAUDIO.   Who wrongs him?

LEONATO. Marry, thou dost wrong me; thou dissembler,
thou.
Nay, never lay thy hand upon thy sword;
I fear thee not.

CLAUDIO.   Marry, beshrew my hand,
If it should give your age such cause of fear.
In faith, my hand meant nothing to my sword.

LEONATO. Tush, tush, man! never fleer and jest at me:
I speak not like a dotard nor a fool,
As, under privilege of age, to brag
What I have done being young, or what would do,
Were I not old. Know, Claudio, to thy head,
Thou hast so wrong'd mine innocent child and me
That I am forc'd to lay my reverence by,

And, with grey hairs and bruise of many days,
Do challenge thee to trial of a man.
I say thou hast belied mine innocent child:
Thy slander hath gone through and through her heart,
And she lies buried with her ancestors;
O! in a tomb where never scandal slept,
Save this of hers, fram'd by thy villany!

CLAUDIO. My villany?

LEONATO.　　　　　　　Thine, Claudio; thine, I say.

DON PEDRO. You say not right, old man.

LEONATO.　　　　　　　　　My lord, my lord,
I 'll prove it on his body, if he dare,
Despite his nice fence and his active practice,
His May of youth and bloom of lustihood.

CLAUDIO. Away! I will not have to do with you.

LEONATO. Canst thou so daff me? Thou hast kill'd my child;
If thou kill'st me, boy, thou shalt kill a man.

ANTONIO. He shall kill two of us, and men indeed:
But that 's no matter; let him kill one first:
Win me and wear me; let him answer me.
Come, follow me, boy; come, sir boy, come, follow me.
Sir boy, I 'll whip you from your foining fence;
Nay, as I am a gentleman, I will.

LEONATO. Brother,—

ANTONIO. Content yourself. God knows I lov'd my niece;
And she is dead, slander'd to death by villains,
That dare as well answer a man indeed
As I dare take a serpent by the tongue.
Boys, apes, braggarts, Jacks, milksops!

LEONATO.　　　　　　　　　Brother Antony,—

ANTONIO. Hold your content. What, man! I know them, yea,
And what they weigh, even to the utmost scruple,
Scambling, out-facing, fashion-monging boys,
That lie and cog and flout, deprave and slander,
Go antickly, show outward hideousness,
And speak off half a dozen dangerous words,
How they might hurt their enemies, if they durst;
And this is all!

LEONATO. But, brother Antony,—

ANTONIO.　　　　　　　Come, 'tis no matter:
Do not you meddle, let me deal in this.

DON PEDRO. Gentlemen both, we will not wake your pa-
tience.
My heart is sorry for your daughter's death;
But, on my honour, she was charg'd with nothing
But what was true and very full of proof.

LEONATO. My lord, my lord—

DON PEDRO.   I will not hear you.

LEONATO.   No?
Come, brother, away. I will be heard.—

ANTONIO. And shall, or some of us will smart for it.

Exeunt Leonato and Antonio
Enter Benedick

DON PEDRO. See, see; here comes the man we went to seek.

CLAUDIO. Now, signior, what news?

BENEDICK. Good-day, my lord.

DON PEDRO. Welcome, signior: you are almost come to part
almost a fray.

CLAUDIO. We had like to have had our two noses snapped
off with two old men without teeth.

DON PEDRO. Leonato and his brother. What thinkest thou?
Had we fought, I doubt we should have been too young
for them.

BENEDICK. In a false quarrel there is no true valour. I came
to seek you both.

CLAUDIO. We have been up and down to seek thee; for we
are high-proof melancholy, and would fain have it beaten
away. Wilt thou use thy wit?

BENEDICK. It is in my scabbard; shall I draw it?

DON PEDRO. Dost thou wear thy wit by thy side?

CLAUDIO. Never any did so, though very many have been
beside their wit. I will bid thee draw, as we do the minstrels; draw, to pleasure us.

DON PEDRO. As I am an honest man, he looks pale. Art thou
sick, or angry?

CLAUDIO. What, courage, man! What though care killed a
cat, thou hast mettle enough in thee to kill care.

BENEDICK. Sir, I shall meet your wit in the career, an you
charge it against me. I pray you choose another subject.

CLAUDIO. Nay then, give him another staff: this last was
broke cross.

DON PEDRO. By this light, he changes more and more: I
think he be angry indeed.

CLAUDIO. If he be, he knows how to turn his girdle.

BENEDICK. Shall I speak a word in your ear?

CLAUDIO. God bless me from a challenge!

BENEDICK. (*Aside to Claudio*) You are a villain, I jest not: I will make it good how you dare, with what you dare, and when you dare. Do me right, or I will protest your cowardice. You have killed a sweet lady, and her death shall fall heavy on you. Let me hear from you.

CLAUDIO. Well I will meet you, so I may have good cheer.

DON PEDRO. What, a feast, a feast?

CLAUDIO. I' faith, I thank him; he hath bid me to a calf's-head and a capon, the which if I do not carve most curiously, say my knife 's naught. Shall I not find a woodcock too?

BENEDICK. Sir, your wit ambles well; it goes easily.

DON PEDRO. I 'll tell thee how Beatrice praised thy wit the other day. I said, thou hadst a fine wit. 'True,' says she, 'a fine little one.' 'No,' said I, 'a great wit.' 'Right,' said she, 'a great gross one.' 'Nay,' said I, 'a good wit.' 'Just,' said she, 'it hurts nobody.' 'Nay,' said I, 'the gentleman is wise.' 'Certain,' said she, 'a wise gentleman.' 'Nay,' said I, 'he hath the tongues.' 'That I believe,' said she, 'for he swore a thing to me on Monday night, which he forswore on Tuesday morning: there 's a double tongue; there 's two tongues.' Thus did she, an hour together, trans-shape thy particular virtues; yet at last she concluded with a sigh, thou wast the properest man in Italy.

CLAUDIO. For the which she wept heartily and said she cared not.

DON PEDRO. Yea, that she did; but yet, for all that, an if she did not hate him deadly, she would love him dearly. The old man's daughter told us all.

CLAUDIO. All, all; and moreover, God saw him when he was hid in the garden.

DON PEDRO. But when shall we set the savage bull's horns on the sensible Benedick's head?

CLAUDIO. Yea, and text underneath, 'Here dwells Benedick the married man!'

BENEDICK. Fare you well, boy: you know my mind. I will leave you now to your gossip-like humour: you break jests as braggarts do their blades, which, God be thanked, hurt not. My lord, for your many courtesies I thank thee: I

must discontinue your company. Your brother the bastard
is fled from Messina: you have, among you, killed a sweet
and innocent lady. For my Lord Lack-beard there, he and
I shall meet; and till then, peace be with him.

DON PEDRO. He is in earnest.

CLAUDIO. In most profound earnest; and, I 'll warrant you,
for the love of Beatrice.

DON PEDRO. And hath challenged thee?

CLAUDIO. Most sincerely.

DON PEDRO. What a pretty thing man is when he goes in his
doublet and hose and leaves off his wit!

CLAUDIO. He is then a giant to an ape; but then is an ape a
doctor to such a man.

DON PEDRO. But, soft you; let me be: pluck up, my heart,
and be sad! Did he not say my brother was fled?

Enter Dogberry, Verges,
and the Watch, with Conrade and Borachio

DOGBERRY. Come, you sir: if justice cannot tame you, she
shall ne'er weigh more reasons in her balance. Nay, an
you be a cursing hypocrite once, you must be looked to.

DON PEDRO. How now! two of my brother's men bound!
Borachio, one!

CLAUDIO. Hearken after their offence, my lord.

DON PEDRO. Officers, what offence have these men done?

DOGBERRY. Marry, sir, they have committed false report;
moreover, they have spoken untruths; secondarily, they
are slanders; sixth and lastly, they have belied a lady;
thirdly, they have verified unjust things; and to conclude,
they are lying knaves.

DON PEDRO. First, I ask thee what they have done; thirdly, I
ask thee what 's their offence; sixth and lastly, why they
are committed; and, to conclude, what you lay to their
charge?

CLAUDIO. Rightly reasoned, and in his own division; and, by
my troth, there 's one meaning well suited.

DON PEDRO. Who have you offended, masters, that you are
thus bound to your answer? This learned constable is too
cunning to be understood. What 's your offence?

BORACHIO. Sweet prince, let me go no further to mine answer: do you hear me, and let this count kill me. I have
deceived even your very eyes: what your wisdoms could
not discover, these shallow fools have brought to light;

who, in the night overheard me confessing to this man
how Don John your brother incensed me to slander the
Lady Hero; how you were brought into the orchard and
saw me court Margaret in Hero's garments; how you disgraced her, when you should marry her. My villany they
have upon record; which I had rather seal with my death
than repeat over to my shame. The lady is dead upon
mine and my master's false accusation; and, briefly, I desire nothing but the reward of a villain.

DON PEDRO. Runs not this speech like iron through your
    blood?

CLAUDIO. I have drunk poison whiles he utter'd it.

DON PEDRO. But did my brother set thee on to this?

BORACHIO. Yea; and paid me richly for the practice of it.

DON PEDRO. He is compos'd and fram'd of treachery:
    And fled he is upon this villany.

CLAUDIO. Sweet Hero! now thy image doth appear
    In the rare semblance that I lov'd it first.

DOGBERRY. Come, bring away the plaintiffs: by this time
    our sexton hath reformed Signior Leonato of the matter.
    And masters, do not forget to specify, when time and
    place shall serve, that I am an ass.

VERGES. Here, here comes Master Signior Leonato, and the
    sexton too.

    Re-enter Leonato, Antonio, and the Sexton

LEONATO. Which is the villain? Let me see his eyes,
    That, when I note another man like him,
    I may avoid him. Which of these is he?

BORACHIO. If you would know your wronger, look on me.

LEONATO. Art thou the slave that with thy breath hast kill'd
    Mine innocent child?

BORACHIO.   Yea, even I alone.

LEONATO. No, not so, villain; thou beliest thyself:
    Here stand a pair of honourable men;
    A third is fled, that had a hand in it.
    I thank you, princes, for my daughter's death:
    Record it with your high and worthy deeds.
    'Twas bravely done, if you bethink you of it.

CLAUDIO. I know not how to pray your patience;
    Yet I must speak. Choose your revenge yourself;
    Impose me to what penance your invention
    Can lay upon my sin: yet sinn'd I not

But in mistaking.

DON PEDRO.   By my soul, nor I:
And yet, to satisfy this good old man,
I would bend under any heavy weight
That he 'll enjoin me to.

LEONATO. I cannot bid you bid my daughter live;
That were impossible: but, I pray you both,
Possess the people in Messina here
How innocent she died; and if your love
Can labour aught in sad invention,
Hang her an epitaph upon her tomb,
And sing it to her bones: sing it to-night.
To-morrow morning come you to my house,
And since you could not be my son-in-law,
Be yet my nephew. My brother hath a daughter,
Almost the copy of my child that 's dead,
And she alone is heir to both of us:
Give her the right you should have given her cousin,
And so dies my revenge.

CLAUDIO.   O noble sir,
Your over-kindness doth wring tears from me!
I do embrace your offer; and dispose
For henceforth of poor Claudio.

LEONATO. To-morrow then I will expect your coming;
To-night I take my leave. This naughty man
Shall face to face be brought to Margaret,
Who, I believe, was pack'd in all this wrong,
Hir'd to it by your brother.

BORACHIO.   No, by my soul she was not;
Nor knew not what she did when she spoke to me;
But always hath been just and virtuous
In anything that I do know by her.

DOGBERRY. Moreover, sir,—which, indeed, is not under
white and black,—this plaintiff here, the offender, did call
me ass: I beseech you, let it be remembered in his punishment. And also, the watch heard them talk of one Deformed: they say he wears a key in his ear and a lock
hanging by it, and borrows money in God's name, the
which he hath used so long and never paid, that now men
grow hard-hearted, and will lend nothing for God's sake.
Pray you, examine him upon that point.

LEONATO. I thank thee for thy care and honest pains.

DOGBERRY. Your worship speaks like a most thankful and reverend youth, and I praise God for you.

LEONATO. There 's for thy pains.

DOGBERRY. God save the foundation!

LEONATO. Go, I discharge thee of thy prisoner, and I thank thee.

DOGBERRY. I leave an arrant knave with your worship; which I beseech your worship to correct yourself, for the example of others. God keep your worship! I wish your worship well; God restore you to health! I humbly give you leave to depart, and if a merry meeting may be wished, God prohibit it! Come, neighbour.

Exeunt Dogberry and Verges

LEONATO. Until to-morrow morning, lords, farewell.

ANTONIO. Farewell, my lords: we look for you to-morrow.

DON PEDRO. We will not fail.

CLAUDIO. To-night I 'll mourn with Hero.

Exeunt Don Pedro and Claudio

LEONATO. (*To the Watch*) Bring you these fellows on. We 'll talk with Margaret,
How her acquaintance grew with this lewd fellow.

Exeunt

SCENE TWO

Leonato's Garden.

Enter Benedick and Margaret, meeting

BENEDICK. Pray thee, sweet Mistress Margaret, deserve well at my hands by helping me to the speech of Beatrice.

MARGARET. Will you then write me a sonnet in praise of my beauty?

BENEDICK. In so high a style, Margaret, that no man living shall come over it; for, in most comely truth, thou deservest it.

MARGARET. To have no man come over me! why, shall I always keep below stairs?

BENEDICK. Thy wit is as quick as the greyhound's mouth; it catches.

MARGARET. And yours as blunt as the fencer's foils, which hit, but hurt not.

BENEDICK. A most manly wit, Margaret; it will not hurt a woman: and so, I pray thee, call Beatrice. I give thee the bucklers.

MARGARET. Give us the swords, we have bucklers of our own.

BENEDICK. If you use them, Margaret, you must put in the pikes with a vice; and they are dangerous weapons for maids.

MARGARET. Well, I will call Beatrice to you, who I think hath legs.

BENEDICK. And therefore will come.   *Exit Margaret*

        The god of love,
        That sits above,
    And knows me, and knows me,
      How pitiful I deserve,—

I mean, in singing; but in loving, Leander the good swimmer, Troilus the first employer of pandars, and a whole book full of these quondam carpet-mongers, whose names yet run smoothly in the even road of a blank verse, why, they were never so truly turned over and over as my poor self, in love. Marry, I cannot show it in rime; I have tried: I can find out no rime to 'lady' but 'baby,' an innocent rime; for 'scorn,' 'horn,' a hard rime; for 'school,' 'fool,' a babbling rime; very ominous endings: no, I was not born under a riming planet, nor I cannot woo in festival terms.

Enter Beatrice

Sweet Beatrice, wouldst thou come when I called thee?

BEATRICE. Yea, signior; and depart when you bid me.

BENEDICK. O stay but till then!

BEATRICE. 'Then' is spoken; fare you well now: and yet, ere I go, let me go with that I came for; which is, with knowing what hath passed between you and Claudio.

BENEDICK. Only foul words; and thereupon I will kiss thee.

BEATRICE. Foul words is but foul wind, and foul wind is but foul breath, and foul breath is noisome; therefore I will depart unkissed.

BENEDICK. Thou hast frighted the word out of his right sense, so forcible is thy wit. But I must tell thee plainly, Claudio undergoes my challenge, and either I must shortly hear from him, or I will subscribe him a coward. And, I pray thee now, tell me, for which of my bad parts didst thou first fall in love with me?

BEATRICE. For them all together; which maintained so politic a state of evil that they will not admit any good part to intermingle with them. But for which of my good parts did you first suffer love for me?

BENEDICK. 'Suffer love,' a good epithet! I do suffer love indeed, for I love thee against my will.

BEATRICE. In spite of your heart, I think. Alas, poor heart! If you spite it for my sake, I will spite it for yours; for I will never love that which my friend hates.

BENEDICK. Thou and I are too wise to woo peaceably.

BEATRICE. It appears not in this confession: there 's not one wise man among twenty that will praise himself.

BENEDICK. An old, an old instance, Beatrice, that lived in the time of good neighbours. If a man do not erect in this age his own tomb ere he dies, he shall live no longer in monument than the bell rings and the widow weeps.

BEATRICE. And how long is that think you?

BENEDICK. Question: why, an hour in clamour and a quarter in rheum: therefore it is most expedient for the wise, —if Don Worm, his conscience, find no impediment to the contrary,—to be the trumpet of his own virtues, as I am to myself. So much for praising myself, who, I myself will bear witness, is praiseworthy. And now tell me, how doth your cousin?

BEATRICE. Very ill.

BENEDICK. And how do you?

BEATRICE. Very ill too.

BENEDICK. Serve God, love me, and mend. There will I leave you too, for here comes one in haste.

Enter Ursula

URSULA. Madam, you must come to your uncle. Yonder 's old coil at home: it is proved, my Lady Hero hath been falsely accused, the prince and Claudio mightily abused; and Don John is the author of all, who is fled and gone. Will you come presently?

BEATRICE. Will you go hear this news, signior?

BENEDICK. I will live in thy heart, die in thy lap, and be buried in thy eyes; and moreover I will go with thee to thy uncle's.   *Exeunt*

SCENE THREE

The Inside of a Church.

Enter Don Pedro, Claudio, and Attendants, with music and tapers

CLAUDIO. Is this the monument of Leonato?
A LORD. It is, my lord.
CLAUDIO. (*Reads from a scroll*)

> Done to death by slanderous tongues
>   Was the Hero that here lies:
> Death, in guerdon of her wrongs,
>   Gives her fame which never dies.
> So the life that died with shame
> Lives in death with glorious fame.

Hang thou there upon the tomb,
Praising her when I am dumb.

Now, music, sound, and sing your solemn hymn.

SONG

> Pardon, goddess of the night,
> Those that slew thy virgin knight;
> For the which, with songs of woe,
> Round about her tomb they go.
>   Midnight, assist our moan;
>   Help us to sigh and groan,
>   Heavily, heavily:
>   Graves, yawn and yield your dead,
>   Till death be uttered,
>   Heavily, heavily.

CLAUDIO. Now, unto thy bones good-night!
Yearly will I do this rite.
DON PEDRO. Good-morrow, masters: put your torches out.
The wolves have prey'd; and look, the gentle day,
Before the wheels of Phœbus, round about
Dapples the drowsy east with spots of grey.
Thanks to you all, and leave us: fare you well.
CLAUDIO. Good-morrow, masters: each his several way.

DON PEDRO. Come, let us hence, and put on other weeds;
    And then to Leonato's we will go.
CLAUDIO. And Hymen now with luckier issue speed 's,
    Than this for whom we render'd up this woe!   *Exeunt*

SCENE FOUR

A Room in Leonato's House.

Enter Leonato, Antonio, Benedick, Beatrice, Margaret,
Ursula, Friar Francis, and Hero

FRIAR. Did I not tell you she was innocent?
LEONATO. So are the prince and Claudio, who accus'd her
    Upon the error that you heard debated:
    But Margaret was in some fault for this,
    Although against her will, as it appears
    In the true course of all the question.
ANTONIO. Well, I am glad that all things sort so well.
BENEDICK. And so am I, being else by faith enforc'd
    To call young Claudio to a reckoning for it.
LEONATO. Well, daughter, and you gentlewomen all,
    Withdraw into a chamber by yourselves,
    And when I send for you, come hither mask'd:
    The prince and Claudio promis'd by this hour
    To visit me.   *Exeunt ladies*
              You know your office, brother;
    You must be father to your brother's daughter,
    And give her to young Claudio.
ANTONIO. Which I will do with confirm'd countenance.
BENEDICK. Friar, I must entreat your pains, I think.
FRIAR. To do what, signior?
BENEDICK. To bind me, or undo me; one of them.
    Signior Leonato, truth it is, good signior,
    Your niece regards me with an eye of favour.
LEONATO. That eye my daughter lent her: 'tis most true.
BENEDICK. And I do with an eye of love requite her.
LEONATO. The sight whereof I think, you had from me,
    From Claudio, and the prince. But what 's your will?
BENEDICK. Your answer, sir, is enigmatical:
    But, for my will, my will is your good will
    May stand with ours, this day to be conjoin'd

In the state of honourable marriage:

In which, good friar, I shall desire your help.

LEONATO. My heart is with your liking.

FRIAR.   And my help.

Here come the prince and Claudio.

Enter Don Pedro and Claudio, with Attendants

DON PEDRO. Good-morrow to this fair assembly.

LEONATO. Good-morrow, prince; good-morrow, Claudio:

We here attend you. Are you yet determin'd

To-day to marry with my brother's daughter?

CLAUDIO. I 'll hold my mind, were she an Ethiop.

LEONATO. Call her forth, brother: here 's the friar ready.

Exit Antonio

DON PEDRO. Good-morrow, Benedick. Why what 's the matter,

That you have such a February face,

So full of frost, of storm and cloudiness?

CLAUDIO. I think he thinks upon the savage bull.

Tush! fear not, man, we 'll tip thy horns with gold,

And all Europa shall rejoice at thee,

As once Europa did at lusty Jove,

When he would play the noble beast in love.

BENEDICK. Bull Jove, sir, had an amiable low:

And some such strange bull leap'd your father's cow,

And got a calf in that same noble feat,

Much like to you, for you have just his bleat.

CLAUDIO. For this I owe you: here come other reckonings.

Re-enter Antonio, with the ladies masked

Which is the lady I must seize upon?

ANTONIO. This same is she, and I do give you her.

CLAUDIO. Why, then she 's mine. Sweet, let me see your face.

LEONATO. No, that you shall not, till you take her hand

Before this friar, and swear to marry her.

CLAUDIO. Give me your hand: before this holy friar,

I am your husband, if you like of me.

HERO. And when I liv'd, I was your other wife: *Unmasking*

And when you lov'd, you were my other husband.

CLAUDIO. Another Hero!

HERO.   Nothing certainer:

One Hero died defil'd, but I do live,

And surely as I live, I am a maid.

DON PEDRO. The former Hero! Hero that is dead!

LEONATO. She died, my lord, but whiles her slander liv'd.

FRIAR. All this amazement can I qualify:
When after that the holy rites are ended,
I 'll tell you largely of fair Hero's death:
Meantime, let wonder seem familiar,
And to the chapel let us presently.

BENEDICK. Soft and fair, friar. Which is Beatrice?

BEATRICE. (*Unmasking*) I answer to that name. What is
your will?

BENEDICK. Do not you love me?

BEATRICE.   Why, no; no more than reason.

BENEDICK. Why, then, your uncle and the prince and Claudio
Have been deceived; for they swore you did.

BEATRICE. Do not you love me?

BENEDICK.   Troth, no; no more than reason.

BEATRICE. Why, then, my cousin, Margaret, and Ursula,
Are much deceiv'd; for they did swear you did.

BENEDICK. They swore that you were almost sick for me.

BEATRICE. They swore that you were well-nigh dead for
me.

BENEDICK. 'Tis no such matter. Then, you do not love me?

BEATRICE. No, truly, but in friendly recompense.

LEONATO. Come, cousin, I am sure you love the gentleman.

CLAUDIO. And I 'll be sworn upon 't that he loves her;
For here 's a paper written in his hand,
A halting sonnet of his own pure brain,
Fashion'd to Beatrice.

HERO.   And here 's another,
Writ in my cousin's hand, stolen from her pocket,
Containing her affection unto Benedick.

BENEDICK. A miracle! here 's our own hands against our
hearts. Come, I will have thee; but, by this light, I take
thee for pity.

BEATRICE. I would not deny you; but, by this good day, I
yield upon great persuasion, and partly to save your life,
for I was told you were in a consumption.

BENEDICK. Peace! I will stop your mouth.   *Kisses her*

DON PEDRO. How dost thou, Benedick, the married man?

BENEDICK. I 'll tell thee what, prince; a college of witcrack-
ers cannot flout me out of my humour. Dost thou think I

care for a satire or an epigram? No; if a man will be
beaten with brains, a' shall wear nothing handsome about
him. In brief, since I do purpose to marry, I will think
nothing to any purpose that the world can say against it;
and therefore never flout at me for what I have said
against it, for man is a giddy thing, and this is my conclusion. For thy part, Claudio, I did think to have beaten
thee; but, in that thou art like to be my kinsman, live un-
bruised, and love my cousin.

CLAUDIO. I had well hoped thou wouldst have denied Beatrice, that I might have cudgelled thee out of thy single
life, to make thee a double-dealer; which, out of question, thou wilt be, if my cousin do not look exceeding
narrowly to thee.

BENEDICK. Come, come, we are friends. Let 's have a dance
ere we are married, that we may lighten our own hearts
and our wives' heels.

LEONATO. We 'll have dancing afterward.

BENEDICK. First, of my word; therefore play, music! Prince,
thou art sad; get thee a wife, get thee a wife: there is no
staff more reverend than one tipped with horn.

Enter a Messenger

MESSENGER. My lord, your brother John is ta'en in flight,
And brought with armed men back to Messina.

BENEDICK. Think not on him till to-morrow: I 'll devise thee
brave punishments for him. Strike up, pipers!

Dance. Exeunt

LOVE'S LABOUR'S LOST

CAST OF CHARACTERS

FERDINAND, *King of Navarre*

BEROWNE
LONGAVILLE   } *Lords, attending on the King*
DUMAINE

BOYET   } *Lords, attending on the Princess of*
MARCADE } *France*

DON ADRIANO DE ARMADO, *a fantastical Spaniard*

SIR NATHANIEL, *a Curate*

HOLOFERNES, *a Schoolmaster*

DULL, *a Constable*

COSTARD, *a Clown*

MOTH, *Page to Armado*

A Forester

The PRINCESS of France

ROSALINE
MARIA   } *Ladies, attending on the Princess*
KATHARINE

JAQUENETTA, *a country Wench*

Officers and Others, Attendants on the King and
Princess

SCENE
Navarre

LOVE'S LABOUR'S LOST

ACT ONE

SCENE ONE

The King of Navarre's Park.

Enter the King, Berowne, Longaville, and Dumaine

KING. Let fame, that all hunt after in their lives,
Live register'd upon our brazen tombs,
And then grace us in the disgrace of death;
When, spite of cormorant devouring Time,
The endeavour of this present breath may buy
That honour which shall bate his scythe's keen edge,
And make us heirs of all eternity.
Therefore, brave conquerors,—for so you are,
That war against your own affections
And the huge army of the world's desires,—
Our late edict shall strongly stand in force:
Navarre shall be the wonder of the world;
Our court shall be a little academe,
Still and contemplative in living art.
You three, Berowne, Dumaine, and Longaville,
Have sworn for three years' term to live with me,
My fellow-scholars, and to keep those statutes
That are recorded in this schedule here:
Your oaths are pass'd; and now subscribe your names,
That his own hand may strike his honour down
That violates the smallest branch herein.
If you are arm'd to do, as sworn to do,
Subscribe to your deep oaths, and keep it too.
LONGAVILLE. I am resolv'd; 'tis but a three years' fast:
The mind shall banquet, though the body pine:
Fat paunches have lean pates, and dainty bits

Make rich the ribs, but bankrupt quite the wits.

DUMAINE. My loving lord, Dumaine is mortified:
The grosser manner of these world's delights
He throws upon the gross world's baser slaves:
To love, to wealth, to pomp, I pine and die;
With all these living in philosophy.

BEROWNE. I can but say their protestation over;
So much, dear liege, I have already sworn,
That is, to live and study here three years.
But there are other strict observances;
As, not to see a woman in that term,
Which I hope well is not enrolled there:
And one day in a week to touch no food,
And but one meal on every day beside;
The which I hope is not enrolled there:
And then, to sleep but three hours in the night,
And not be seen to wink of all the day,—
When I was wont to think no harm all night
And make a dark night too of half the day,—
Which I hope well is not enrolled there.
O! these are barren tasks, too hard to keep,
Not to see ladies, study, fast, not sleep.

KING. Your oath is pass'd to pass away from these.

BEROWNE. Let me say no, my liege, an if you please.
I only swore to study with your Grace,
And stay here in your court for three years' space.

LONGAVILLE. You swore to that, Berowne, and to the rest.

BEROWNE. By yea and nay, sir, then I swore in jest.
What is the end of study? Let me know.

KING. Why, that to know which else we should not know.

BEROWNE. Things hid and barr'd, you mean, from common
       sense?

KING. Ay, that is study's god-like recompense.

BEROWNE. Come on then; I will swear to study so,
To know the thing I am forbid to know;
As thus: to study where I well may dine,
    When I to feast expressly am forbid;
Or study where to meet some mistress fine,
    When mistresses from common sense are hid;
Or, having sworn too hard-a-keeping oath,
Study to break it, and not break my troth.
If study's gain be thus, and this be so,

Study knows that which yet it doth not know.
Swear me to this, and I will ne'er say no.

KING. These be the stops that hinder study quite,
And train our intellects to vain delight.

BEROWNE. Why, all delights are vain; but that most vain
Which, with pain purchas'd doth inherit pain:
As, painfully to pore upon a book,
    To seek the light of truth; while truth the while
Doth falsely blind the eyesight of his look:
    Light seeking light doth light of light beguile:
So, ere you find where light in darkness lies,
Your light grows dark by losing of your eyes.
Study me how to please the eye indeed,
    By fixing it upon a fairer eye,
Who dazzling so, that eye shall be his heed,
    And give him light that it was blinded by.
Study is like the heaven's glorious sun,
    That will not be deep-search'd with saucy looks;
Small have continual plodders ever won,
    Save base authority from others' books.
These earthly godfathers of heaven's lights
    That give a name to every fixed star,
Have no more profit of their shining nights
    Than those that walk and wot not what they are.
Too much to know is to know nought but fame;
And every godfather can give a name.

KING. How well he 's read, to reason against reading!

DUMAINE. Proceeded well, to stop all good proceeding!

LONGAVILLE. He weeds the corn, and still lets grow the
weeding.

BEROWNE. The spring is near, when green geese are
a-breeding.

DUMAINE. How follows that?

BEROWNE.   Fit in his place and time.

DUMAINE. In reason nothing.

BEROWNE.   Something then, in rime.

KING. Berowne is like an envious sneaping frost
    That bites the first-born infants of the spring.

BEROWNE. Well, say I am: why should proud summer boast
    Before the birds have any cause to sing?
Why should I joy in an abortive birth?
    At Christmas I no more desire a rose

Than wish a snow in May's new-fangled mirth;
    But like of each thing that in season grows.
So you, to study now it is too late,
    Climb o'er the house to unlock the little gate.

KING. Well, sit you out: go home, Berowne: adieu!

BEROWNE. No, my good lord; I have sworn to stay with
        you:
    And though I have for barbarism spoke more
        Than for that angel knowledge you can say,
    Yet confident I 'll keep to what I swore,
        And bide the penance of each three years' day.
    Give me the paper; let me read the same;
    And to the strict'st decrees I 'll write my name.

KING. How well this yielding rescues thee from shame!

BEROWNE. Item, 'That no woman shall come within a mile
    of my court.' Hath this been proclaimed?

LONGAVILLE. Four days ago.

BEROWNE. Let 's see the penalty. 'On pain of losing her
    tongue.' Who devised this penalty?

LONGAVILLE. Marry, that did I.

BEROWNE.   ` Sweet lord, and why?

LONGAVILLE. To fright them hence with that dread penalty.

BEROWNE. A dangerous law against gentility!
    Item. 'If any man be seen to talk with a woman within
    the term of three years, he shall endure such public shame
    as the rest of the court can possibly devise.'
    This article, my liege, yourself must break;
        For well you know here comes in embassy
    The French king's daughter with yourself to speak—
        A maid of grace and complete majesty—
    About surrender up of Aquitaine
        To her decrepit, sick, and bed-rid father:
    Therefore this article is made in vain,
        Or vainly comes th' admired princess hither.

KING. What say you, lords? why, this was quite forgot.

BEROWNE. So study evermore is overshot:
    While it doth study to have what it would,
    It doth forget to do the thing it should;
    And when it hath the thing it hunteth most,
    'Tis won as towns with fire; so won, so lost.

KING. We must of force dispense with this decree;
    She must lie here on mere necessity.

BEROWNE. Necessity will make us all forsworn
  Three thousand times within this three years' space;
For every man with his affects is born,
  Not by night master'd, but by special grace.
If I break faith this word shall speak for me,
I am forsworn 'on mere necessity.'
So to the laws at large I write my name: *Subscribes*
  And he that breaks them in the least degree
Stands in attainder of eternal shame:
  Suggestions are to others as to me;
But I believe, although I seem so loath,
I am the last that will last keep his oath.
But is there no quick recreation granted?
KING. Ay, that there is. Our court, you know, is haunted
  With a refined traveller of Spain;
A man in all the world's new fashion planted,
  That hath a mint of phrases in his brain;
One whom the music of his own vain tongue
  Doth ravish like enchanting harmony;
A man of complements, whom right and wrong
  Have chose as umpire of their mutiny:
This child of fancy, that Armado hight,
  For interim to our studies shall relate
In high-born words the worth of many a knight
  From tawny Spain lost in the world's debate.
How you delight, my lords, I know not, I;
But, I protest, I love to hear him lie,
And I will use him for my minstrelsy.
BEROWNE. Armado is a most illustrious wight,
  A man of fire-new words, fashion's own knight.
LONGAVILLE. Costard the swain and he shall be our sport;
  And, so to study, three years is but short.
      Enter Dull, with a letter, and Costard
DULL. Which is the duke's own person?
BEROWNE. This, fellow. What wouldst?
DULL. I myself reprehend his own person, for I am his
  Grace's tharborough: but I would see his own person in
  flesh and blood.
BEROWNE. This is he.
DULL. Signior Arm—Arm—commends you. There 's villany
  abroad: this letter will tell you more.
COSTARD. Sir, the contempts thereof are as touching me.

KING. A letter from the magnificent Armado.

BEROWNE. How long soever the matter, I hope in God for high words.

LONGAVILLE. A high hope for a low heaven: God grant us patience!

BEROWNE. To hear, or forbear laughing?

LONGAVILLE. To hear meekly, sir, and to laugh moderately; or to forbear both.

BEROWNE. Well, sir, be it as the style shall give us cause to climb in the merriness.

COSTARD. The matter is to me, sir, as concerning Jaquenetta. The manner of it is, I was taken with the manner.

BEROWNE. In what manner?

COSTARD. In manner and form following, sir; all those three: I was seen with her in the manor-house, sitting with her upon the form, and taken following her into the park; which, put together, is, in manner and form following. Now, sir, for the manner,—it is the manner of a man to speak to a woman, for the form,—in some form.

BEROWNE. For the following, sir?

COSTARD. As it shall follow in my correction; and God defend the right!

KING. Will you hear this letter with attention?

BEROWNE. As we would hear an oracle.

COSTARD. Such is the simplicity of man to hearken after the flesh.

KING. 'Great deputy, the welkin's vicegerent, and sole dominator of Navarre, my soul's earth's God, and body's fostering patron,'

COSTARD. Not a word of Costard yet.

KING. 'So it is,'—

COSTARD. It may be so; but if he say it is so, he is, in telling true, but so.—

KING. Peace!

COSTARD. Be to me and every man that dares not fight.

KING. No words!

COSTARD. Of other men's secrets, I beseech you.

KING. 'So it is, besieged with sable-coloured melancholy, I did commend the black-oppressing humour to the most wholesome physic of thy health-giving air; and, as I am a gentleman, betook myself to walk. The time when? About the sixth hour; when beasts most graze, birds best peck,

and men sit down to that nourishment which is called
supper: so much for the time when. Now for the ground
which; which, I mean, I walked upon; it is ycleped thy
park. Then for the place where; where, I mean, I did encounter that most obscene and preposterous event, that
draweth from my snow-white pen the ebon-coloured ink,
which here thou viewest, beholdest, surveyest, or seest.
But to the place where, it standeth north-north-east and
by east from the west corner of thy curious-knotted garden: there did I see that low-spirited swain, that base
minnow of thy mirth,'—

COSTARD. Me.

KING. 'that unlettered small-knowing soul,'—

COSTARD. Me.

KING. 'that shallow vessel,'—

COSTARD. Still me.

KING. 'which, as I remember, hight Costard,'—

COSTARD. O me.

KING. 'sorted and consorted, contrary to thy established proclaimed edict and continent canon, with—with,—O! with
but with this I passion to say wherewith,'—

COSTARD. With a wench.

KING. 'with a child of our grandmother Eve, a female; or,
for thy more sweet understanding, a woman. Him, I,—as
my ever-esteemed duty pricks me on,—have sent to thee,
to receive the meed of punishment, by thy sweet Grace's
officer, Antony Dull; a man of good repute, carriage,
bearing, and estimation.'

DULL. Me, an 't please you; I am Antony Dull.

KING. 'For Jaquenetta,—so is the weaker vessel called which
I apprehended with the aforesaid swain,—I keep her as a
vessel of thy law's fury; and shall, at the least of thy sweet
notice, bring her to trial. Thine, in all compliments of devoted and heart-burning heat of duty,

'Don Adriano de Armado.'

BEROWNE. This is not so well as I looked for, but the best
that ever I heard.

KING. Ay, the best for the worst. But, sirrah, what say you
to this?

COSTARD. Sir, I confess the wench.

KING. Did you hear the proclamation?

COSTARD. I do confess much of the hearing it, but little of
the marking of it.

KING. It was proclaimed a year's imprisonment to be taken with a wench.

COSTARD. I was taken with none, sir: I was taken with a damosel.

KING. Well, it was proclaimed 'damosel.'

COSTARD. This was no damosel neither, sir: she was a virgin.

KING. It is so varied too; for it was proclaimed 'virgin.'

COSTARD. If it were, I deny her virginity: I was taken with a maid.

KING. This maid will not serve your turn, sir.

COSTARD. This maid will serve my turn, sir.

KING. Sir, I will pronounce your sentence: you shall fast a week with bran and water.

COSTARD. I had rather pray a month with mutton and porridge.

KING. And Don Armado shall be your keeper.
My Lord Berowne, see him deliver'd o'er:
And go we, lords, to put in practice that
Which each to other hath so strongly sworn.

Exeunt King, Longaville, and Dumaine

BEROWNE. I 'll lay my head to any good man's hat,
These oaths and laws will prove an idle scorn.
Sirrah, come on.

COSTARD. I suffer for the truth, sir: for true it is I was taken with Jaquenetta, and Jaquenetta is a true girl; and therefore welcome the sour cup of prosperity! Affliction may one day smile again; and till then, sit thee down, sorrow!

Exeunt

SCENE TWO
The Same.

Enter Armado and Moth

ARMADO. Boy, what sign is it when a man of great spirit grows melancholy?

MOTH. A great sign, sir, that he will look sad.

ARMADO. Why, sadness is one and the self-same thing, dear imp.

MOTH. No, no; O Lord, sir, no.

ARMADO. How canst thou part sadness and melancholy, my

tender juvenal?

MOTH. By a familiar demonstration of the working, my tough senior.

ARMADO. Why tough senior? Why tough senior?

MOTH. Why tender juvenal? Why tender juvenal?

ARMADO. I spoke it, tender juvenal, as a congruent epitheton appertaining to thy young days, which we may nominate tender.

MOTH. And I, tough senior, as an appertinent title to your old time, which we may name tough.

ARMADO. Pretty, and apt.

MOTH. How mean you, sir? I pretty, and my saying apt? or I apt, and my saying pretty?

ARMADO. Thou pretty, because little.

MOTH. Little pretty, because little. Wherefore apt?

ARMADO. And therefore apt, because quick.

MOTH. Speak you this in my praise, master?

ARMADO. In thy condign praise.

MOTH. I will praise an eel with the same praise.

ARMADO. What! that an eel is ingenious?

MOTH. That an eel is quick.

ARMADO. I do say thou art quick in answers: thou heatest my blood.

MOTH. I am answered, sir.

ARMADO. I love not to be crossed.

MOTH. (Aside) He speaks the mere contrary: crosses love not him.

ARMADO. I have promised to study three years with the duke.

MOTH. You may do it in an hour, sir.

ARMADO. Impossible.

MOTH. How many is one thrice told?

ARMADO. I am ill at reckoning; it fitteth the spirit of a tapster.

MOTH. You are a gentleman and a gamester, sir.

ARMADO. I confess both: they are both the varnish of a complete man.

MOTH. Then, I am sure you know how much the gross sum of deuce-ace amounts to.

ARMADO. It doth amount to one more than two.

MOTH. Which the base vulgar do call three.

ARMADO. True.

MOTH. Why, sir, is this such a piece of study? Now, here 's three studied, ere you 'll thrice wink; and how easy it is to put 'years' to the word 'three,' and study three years in two words, the dancing horse will tell you.

ARMADO. A most fine figure!

MOTH. To prove you a cipher.

ARMADO. I will hereupon confess I am in love; and as it is base for a soldier to love, so am I in love with a base wench. If drawing my sword against the humour of affection would deliver me from the reprobate thought of it, I would take Desire prisoner, and ransom him to any French courtier for a new devised curtsy. I think scorn to sigh: methinks I should outswear Cupid. Comfort me, boy: what great men have been in love?

MOTH. Hercules, master.

ARMADO. Most sweet Hercules! More authority, dear boy, name more; and, sweet my child, let them be men of good repute and carriage.

MOTH. Samson, master: he was a man of good carriage, great carriage, for he carried the town-gates on his back like a porter; and he was in love.

ARMADO. O well-knit Samson! strong-jointed Samson! I do excel thee in my rapier as much as thou didst me in carrying gates. I am in love too. Who was Samson's love, my dear Moth?

MOTH. A woman, master.

ARMADO. Of what complexion?

MOTH. Of all the four, or the three, or the two, or one of the four.

ARMADO. Tell me precisely of what complexion.

MOTH. Of the sea-water green, sir.

ARMADO. Is that one of the four complexions?

MOTH. As I have read, sir; and the best of them too.

ARMADO. Green indeed is the colour of lovers; but to have a love of that colour, methinks Samson had small reason for it. He surely affected her for her wit.

MOTH. It was so, sir, for she had a green wit.

ARMADO. My love is most immaculate white and red.

MOTH. Most maculate thoughts, master, are masked under such colours.

ARMADO. Define, define, well-educated infant.

MOTH. My father's wit, and my mother's tongue, assist me!

ARMADO. Sweet invocation of a child; most pretty and pathetical!

MOTH. If she be made of white and red,
> Her faults will ne'er be known,
> For blushing cheeks by faults are bred,
> And fears by pale white shown:
> Then if she fear, or be to blame,
> By this you shall not know,
> For still her cheeks possess the same
> Which native she doth owe.

A dangerous rime, master, against the reason of white and red.

ARMADO. Is there not a ballad, boy, of the King and the Beggar?

MOTH. The world was very guilty of such a ballad some three ages since; but I think now 'tis not to be found; or, if it were, it would neither serve for the writing nor the tune.

ARMADO. I will have that subject newly writ o'er, that I may example my digression by some mighty precedent. Boy, I do love that country girl that I took in the park with the rational hind Costard: she deserves well.

MOTH. (*Aside*) To be whipped; and yet a better love than my master.

ARMADO. Sing, boy: my spirit grows heavy in love.

MOTH. And that's great marvel, loving a light wench.

ARMADO. I say, sing.

MOTH. Forbear till this company be past.

Enter Dull, Costard, and Jaquenetta

DULL. Sir, the duke's pleasure is, that you keep Costard safe: and you must let him take no delight nor no penance, but a' must fast three days a week. For this damsel, I must keep her at the park; she is allowed for the day-woman. Fare you well.

ARMADO. I do betray myself with blushing. Maid!

JAQUENETTA. Man?

ARMADO. I will visit thee at the lodge.

JAQUENETTA. That's hereby.

ARMADO. I know where it is situate.

JAQUENETTA. Lord, how wise you are!

ARMADO. I will tell thee wonders.

JAQUENETTA. With that face?

ARMADO. I love thee.

JAQUENETTA. So I heard you say.

ARMADO. And so farewell.

JAQUENETTA. Fair weather after you!

DULL. Come, Jaquenetta, away!

Exeunt Dull and Jaquenetta

ARMADO. Villain, thou shalt fast for thy offences ere thou be
pardoned.

COSTARD. Well, sir, I hope, when I do it, I shall do it on a
full stomach.

ARMADO. Thou shalt be heavily punished.

COSTARD. I am more bound to you than your fellows, for
they are but lightly rewarded.

ARMADO. Take away this villain: shut him up.

MOTH. Come, you transgressing slave: away!

COSTARD. Let me not be pent up, sir: I will fast, being loose.

MOTH. No, sir; that were fast and loose: thou shalt to prison.

COSTARD. Well, if ever I do see the merry days of desolation
that I have seen, some shall see—

MOTH. What shall some see?

COSTARD. Nay, nothing, Master Moth, but what they look
upon. It is not for prisoners to be too silent in their words;
and therefore I will say nothing: I thank God I have as
little patience as another man, and therefore I can be
quiet.   *Exeunt Moth and Costard*

ARMADO. I do affect the very ground, which is base, where
her shoe, which is baser, guided by her foot, which is
basest, doth tread. I shall be forsworn,—which is a great
argument of falsehood,—if I love. And how can that be
true love which is falsely attempted? Love is a familiar;
Love is a devil: there is no evil angel but Love. Yet was
Samson so tempted, and he had an excellent strength; yet
was Solomon so seduced, and he had a very good wit.
Cupid's butt-shaft is too hard for Hercules' club, and
therefore too much odds for a Spaniard's rapier. The first
and second clause will not serve my turn; the passado he
respects not, the duello he regards not: his disgrace is to
be called boy, but his glory is, to subdue men. Adieu, valour! rust, rapier! be still, drum! for your manager is in
love; yea, he loveth. Assist me some extemporal god of
rime, for I am sure I shall turn sonneter. Devise, wit;
write, pen; for I am for whole volumes in folio.   *Exit*

ACT TWO

SCENE ONE

*The King of Navarre's Park. A Pavilion and Tents
at a distance.*

*Enter the Princess of France, Rosaline, Maria, Katharine,
Boyet, Lords, and other Attendants*

BOYET. Now, madam, summon up your dearest spirits:
    Consider whom the king your father sends,
    To whom he sends, and what 's his embassy:
    Yourself, held precious in the world's esteem,
    To parley with the sole inheritor
    Of all perfections that a man may owe,
    Matchless Navarre; the plea of no less weight
    Than Aquitaine, a dowry for a queen.
    Be now as prodigal of all dear grace
    As Nature was in making graces dear
    When she did starve the general world beside,
    And prodigally gave them all to you.
PRINCESS. Good Lord Boyet, my beauty, though but mean,
    Needs not the painted flourish of your praise:
    Beauty is bought by judgment of the eye,
    Not utter'd by base sale of chapmen's tongues.
    I am less proud to hear you tell my worth
    Than you much willing to be counted wise
    In spending your wit in the praise of mine.
    But now to task the tasker: good Boyet,
    You are not ignorant, all-telling fame
    Doth noise abroad, Navarre hath made a vow,
    Till painful study shall out-wear three years,
    No woman may approach his silent court:
    Therefore to us seemth it a needful course,
    Before we enter his forbidden gates,
    To know his pleasure; and in that behalf,

Bold of your worthiness, we single you
As our best-moving fair solicitor.
Tell him, the daughter of the King of France,
On serious business, craving quick dispatch,
Importunes personal conference with his Grace.
Haste, signify so much; while we attend,
Like humble-visag'd suitors, his high will.

BOYET. Proud of employment, willingly I go.

PRINCESS. All pride is willing pride, and yours is so.

Exit Boyet

Who are the votaries, my loving lords,
That are vow-fellows with this virtuous duke?

FIRST LORD. Lord Longaville is one.

PRINCESS.   Know you the man?

MARIA. I know him, madam: at a marriage feast,
Between Lord Perigort and the beauteous heir
Of Jacques Falconbridge, solemnized
In Normandy, saw I this Longaville.
A man of sovereign parts he is esteem'd,
Well fitted in the arts, glorious in arms:
Nothing becomes him ill that he would well.
The only soil of his fair virtue's gloss,—
If virtue's gloss will stain with any soil,—
Is a sharp wit match'd with too blunt a will;
Whose edge hath power to cut, whose will still wills
It should none spare that come within his power.

PRINCESS. Some merry mocking lord, belike; is't so?

MARIA. They say so most that most his humours know.

PRINCESS. Such short-liv'd wits do wither as they grow.
Who are the rest?

KATHARINE. The young Dumaine, a well-accomplish'd youth,
Of all that virtue love for virtue lov'd:
Most power to do most harm, least knowing ill,
For he hath wit to make an ill shape good,
And shape to win grace though he had no wit.
I saw him at the Duke Alençon's once;
And much too little of that good I saw
Is my report to his great worthiness.

ROSALINE. Another of these students at that time
Was there with him, if I have heard a truth:
Berowne they call him; but a merrier man,
Within the limit of becoming mirth,

I never spent an hour's talk withal.
His eye begets occasion for his wit;
For every object that the one doth catch
The other turns to a mirth-moving jest,
Which his fair tongue, conceit's expositor,
Delivers in such apt and gracious words,
That aged ears play truant at his tales,
And younger hearings are quite ravished;
So sweet and voluble is his discourse.

PRINCESS. God bless my ladies! are they all in love,
That every one her own hath garnished
With such bedecking ornaments of praise?

FIRST LORD. Here comes Boyet.

Re-enter Boyet

PRINCESS.   Now, what admittance, lord?

BOYET. Navarre had notice of your fair approach;
And he and his competitors in oath
Were all address'd to meet you, gentle lady,
Before I came. Marry, thus much I have learnt;
He rather means to lodge you in the field,
Like one that comes here to besiege his court,
Than seek a dispensation for his oath,
To let you enter his unpeeled house.
Here comes Navarre.   *The Ladies mask*

Enter King, Longaville, Dumaine, Berowne, and Attendants

KING. Fair princess, welcome to the court of Navarre.

PRINCESS. 'Fair,' I give you back again; and 'welcome' I
have not yet: the roof of this court is too high to be yours,
and welcome to the wide fields too base to be mine.

KING. You shall be welcome, madam, to my court.

PRINCESS. I will be welcome, then: conduct me thither.

KING. Hear me, dear lady; I have sworn an oath.

PRINCESS. Our Lady help my lord! he 'll be forsworn.

KING. Not for the world, fair madam, by my will.

PRINCESS. Why, will shall break it; will, and nothing else.

KING. Your ladyship is ignorant what it is.

PRINCESS. Were my lord so, his ignorance were wise,
Where now his knowledge must prove ignorance.
I hear your Grace hath sworn out house-keeping:
'Tis deadly sin to keep that oath, my lord,
And sin to break it.
But pardon me, I am too sudden-bold:

To teach a teacher ill beseemeth me.
Vouchsafe to read the purpose of my coming,
And suddenly resolve me in my suit.   *Gives a paper*

KING. Madam, I will, if suddenly I may.

PRINCESS. You will the sooner that I were away,
For you 'll prove perjur'd if you make me stay.

BEROWNE. Did not I dance with you in Brabant once?

ROSALINE. Did not I dance with you in Brabant once?

BEROWNE. I know you did.

ROSALINE.   How needless was it then
To ask the question!

BEROWNE.   You must not be so quick.

ROSALINE. 'Tis 'long of you that spur me with such questions.

BEROWNE. Your wit 's too hot, it speeds too fast, 'twill tire.

ROSALINE. Not till it leave the rider in the mire.

BEROWNE. What time o' day?

ROSALINE. The hour that fools should ask.

BEROWNE. Now fair befall your mask!

ROSALINE. Fair fall the face it covers!

BEROWNE. And send you many lovers!

ROSALINE. Amen, so you be none.

BEROWNE. Nay, then I will be gone.

KING. Madam, your father here doth intimate
The payment of a hundred thousand crowns;
Being but the one half of an entire sum
Disbursed by my father in his wars.
But say that he, or we,—as neither have,—
Receiv'd that sum, yet there remains unpaid
A hundred thousand more; in surety of the which,
One part of Aquitaine is bound to us,
Although not valued to the money's worth.
If then the king your father will restore
But that one half which is unsatisfied,
We will give up our right in Aquitaine,
And hold fair friendship with his Majesty.
But that it seems, he little purposeth,
For here he doth demand to have repaid
A hundred thousand crowns; and not demands,
On payment of a hundred thousand crowns,
To have his title live in Aquitaine;
Which we much rather had depart withal,

And have the money by our father lent,
Than Aquitaine, so gelded as it is.
Dear princess, were not his requests so far
From reason's yielding, your fair self should make
A yielding 'gainst some reason in my breast,
And go well satisfied to France again.

PRINCESS. You do the king my father too much wrong
And wrong the reputation of your name,
In so unseeming to confess receipt
Of that which hath so faithfully been paid.

KING. I do protest I never heard of it;
And if you prove it, I 'll repay it back
Or yield up Aquitaine.

PRINCESS.   We arrest your word.
Boyet, you can produce acquittances
For such a sum from special officers
Of Charles his father.

KING.   Satisfy me so.

BOYET. So please your Grace, the packet is not come
Where that and other specialties are bound:
To-morrow you shall have a sight of them.

KING. It shall suffice me: at which interview
All liberal reason I will yield unto.
Meantime, receive such welcome at my hand
As honour, without breach of honour, may
Make tender of to thy true worthiness.
You may not come, fair princess, in my gates;
But here without you shall be so receiv'd,
As you shall deem yourself lodg'd in my heart,
Though so denied fair harbour in my house.
Your own good thoughts excuse me, and farewell:
To-morrow shall we visit you again.

PRINCESS. Sweet health and fair desires consort your Grace!

KING. Thy own wish wish I thee in every place!

                    Exeunt King and his Train

BEROWNE. Lady, I will commend you to mine own heart.

ROSALINE. Pray you, do my commendations; I would be glad
to see it.

BEROWNE. I would you heard it groan.

ROSALINE. Is the fool sick?

BEROWNE. Sick at the heart.

ROSALINE. Alack! let it blood.

BEROWNE. Would that do it good?

ROSALINE. My physic says, 'ay.'

BEROWNE. Will you prick 't with your eye?

ROSALINE. No point, with my knife.

BEROWNE. Now, God save thy life!

ROSALINE. And yours from long living!

BEROWNE. I cannot stay thanksgiving.   *Retiring*

DUMAINE. Sir, I pray you, a word: what lady is that same?

BOYET. The heir of Alençon, Katharine her name.

DUMAINE. A gallant lady. Monsieur, fare you well.   *Exit*

LONGAVILLE. I beseech you a word: what is she in the
     white?

BOYET. A woman sometimes, an you saw her in the light.

LONGAVILLE. Perchance light in the light. I desire her name.

BOYET. She hath but one for herself; to desire that, were a
     shame.

LONGAVILLE. Pray you, sir, whose daughter?

BOYET. Her mother's, I have heard.

LONGAVILLE. God's blessing on your beard!

BOYET. Good sir, be not offended.
     She is an heir of Falconbridge.

LONGAVILLE. Nay, my choler is ended.
     She is a most sweet lady.

BOYET. Not unlike, sir; that may be.   *Exit Longaville*

BEROWNE. What 's her name, in the cap?

BOYET. Rosaline, by good hap.

BEROWNE. Is she wedded or no?

BOYET. To her will, sir, or so.

BEROWNE. You are welcome, sir. Adieu.

BOYET. Farewell to me, sir, and welcome to you.

                              Exit Berowne.—Ladies unmask

MARIA. That last is Berowne, the merry madcap lord:
     Not a word with him but a jest.

BOYET.   And every jest but a word.

PRINCESS. It was well done of you to take him at his word.

BOYET. I was as willing to grapple, as he was to board.

MARIA. Two hot sheeps, marry!

BOYET.   And wherefore not ships?
     No sheep, sweet lamb, unless we feed on your lips.

MARIA. You sheep, and I pasture: shall that finish the jest?

BOYET. So you grant pasture for me.   *Offering to kiss her*

MARIA.   Not so, gentle beast.
     My lips are no common, though several they be.

BOYET. Belonging to whom?

MARIA.   To my fortunes and me.

PRINCESS. Good wits will be jangling; but, gentles, agree.
   This civil war of wits were much better us'd
   On Navarre and his book-men, for here 'tis abus'd.

BOYET. If my observation,—which very seldom lies,
   By the heart's still rhetoric disclosed with eye,
   Deceive me not now, Navarre is infected.

PRINCESS. With what?

BOYET. With that which we lovers entitle affected.

PRINCESS. Your reason.

BOYET. Why, all his behaviours did make their retire
   To the court of his eye, peeping thorough desire;
   His heart, like an agate, with your print impress'd,
   Proud with his form, in his eye pride express'd:
   His tongue, all impatient to speak and not see,
   Did stumble with haste in his eyesight to be;
   All senses to that sense did make their repair,
   To feel only looking on fairest of fair,
   Methought all his senses were lock'd in his eye,
   As jewels in crystal for some prince to buy;
   Who, tend'ring their own worth from where they were glass'd,
   Did point you to buy them, along as you pass'd.
   His face's own margent did quote such amazes,
   That all eyes saw his eyes enchanted with gazes,
   I 'll give you Aquitaine, and all that is his,
   An' you give him for my sake but one loving kiss.

PRINCESS. Come to our pavilion: Boyet is dispos'd.

BOYET. But to speak that in words which his eye hath disclos'd.
   I only have made a mouth of his eye,
   By adding a tongue which I know will not lie.

ROSALINE. Thou art an old love-monger, and speak'st skilfully.

MARIA. He is Cupid's grandfather and learns news of him.

ROSALINE. Then was Venus like her mother, for her father is but grim.

BOYET. Do you hear, my mad wenches?

MARIA.   No.

BOYET.   What, then, do you see?

ROSALINE. Ay, our way to be gone.

BOYET.   You are too hard for me.

                      Exeunt

ACT THREE

SCENE ONE

The King of Navarre's Park.

Enter Armado and Moth

ARMADO. Warble, child; make passionate my sense of hearing.

MOTH. (*Singing*) Concolinel,—

ARMADO. Sweet air! Go, tenderness of years; take this key, give enlargement to the swain, bring him festinately hither; I must employ him in a letter to my love.

MOTH. Master, will you win your love with a French brawl?

ARMADO. How meanest thou? brawling in French?

MOTH. No, my complete master; but to jig off a tune at the tongue's end, canary to it with your feet, humour it with turning up your eyelids, sigh a note and sing a note, sometime through the throat, as if you swallowed love by singing love, sometime through the nose, as if you snuffed up love by smelling love; with your hat penthouse-like o'er the shop of your eyes; with your arms crossed on your thin belly-doublet like a rabbit on a spit; or your hands in your pocket like a man after the old painting; and keep not too long in one tune, but a snip and away. These are complements, these are humours, these betray nice wenches, that would be betrayed without these; and make them men of note,—do you note me?—that most are affected to these.

ARMADO. How hast thou purchased this experience?

MOTH. By my penny of observation.

ARMADO. But O—but O,—

MOTH. 'The hobby-horse is forgot.'

ARMADO. Callest thou my love 'hobby-horse'?

MOTH. No, master; the hobby-horse is but a colt, and your love perhaps, a hackney. But have you forgot your love?

ARMADO. Almost I had.

MOTH. Negligent student! learn her by heart.

ARMADO. By heart, and in heart, boy.

MOTH. And out of heart, master: all those three I will prove.

ARMADO. What wilt thou prove?

MOTH. A man, if I live; and this, by, in, and without, upon the instant: by heart you love her, because your heart cannot come by her; in heart you love her, because your heart is in love with her; and out of heart you love her, being out of heart that you cannot enjoy her.

ARMADO. I am all these three.

MOTH. And three times as much more, and yet nothing at all.

ARMADO. Fetch hither the swain: he must carry me a letter.

MOTH. A message well sympathized; a horse to be ambassador for an ass.

ARMADO. Ha, ha! what sayest thou?

MOTH. Marry, sir, you must send the ass upon the horse, for he is very slow-gaited. But I go.

ARMADO. The way is but short: away!

MOTH. As swift as lead, sir.

ARMADO. Thy meaning, pretty ingenious?
Is not lead a metal heavy, dull, and slow?

MOTH. Minime, honest master; or rather, master, no.

ARMADO. I say, lead is slow.

MOTH.   You are too swift, sir, to say so:
Is that lead slow which is fir'd from a gun?

ARMADO. Sweet smoke of rhetoric!
He reputes me a cannon; and the bullet, that's he:
I shoot thee at the swain.

MOTH.   Thump then, and I flee.   *Exit*

ARMADO. A most acute juvenal; volable and free of grace!
By thy favour, sweet welkin, I must sigh in thy face:
Most rude melancholy, valour gives thee place.
My herald is return'd.

Re-enter Moth with Costard

MOTH. A wonder, master! here's a costard broken in a shin.

ARMADO. Some enigma, some riddle: come, thy l'envoy; begin.

COSTARD. No egma, no riddle, no l'envoy; no salve in the mail, sir. O! sir, plantain, a plain plantain: no l'envoy, no l'envoy: no salve, sir, but a plantain.

ARMADO. By virtue, thou enforcest laughter; thy silly

thought, my spleen; the heaving of my lungs provokes me
to ridiculous smiling: O! pardon me, my stars. Doth the
inconsiderate take salve for l'envoy, and the word l'envoy
for a salve?

MOTH. Do the wise think them other? Is not l'envoy a salve?

ARMADO. No, page: it is an epilogue or discourse, to make
plain
Some obscure precedence that hath tofore been sain.
I will example it:
          The fox, the ape, and the humble-bee
          Were still at odds, being but three.
There's the moral. Now the l'envoy.

MOTH. I will add the l'envoy. Say the moral again.

ARMADO. The fox, the ape, and the humble-bee
          Were still at odds, being but three.

MOTH.   Until the goose came out of door,
          And stay'd the odds by adding four.
Now will I begin your moral, and do you follow with my
l'envoy.
          The fox, the ape, and the humble-bee,
          Were still at odds, being but three.

ARMADO. Until the goose came out of door,
          Staying the odds by adding four.

MOTH. A good l'envoy, ending in the goose.
Would you desire more?

COSTARD. The boy hath sold him a bargain, a goose, that's
flat.
Sir, your pennyworth is good an your goose be fat.
To sell a bargain well is as cunning as fast and loose:
Let me see; a fat l'envoy; ay, that's a fat goose.

ARMADO. Come hither, come hither. How did this argument
begin?

MOTH. By saying that a costard was broken in a shin. Then
call'd you for the l'envoy.

COSTARD. True, and I for a plantain: thus came your argu-
ment in;
Then the boy's fat l'envoy, the goose that you bought;
And he ended the market.

ARMADO. But tell me; how was there a costard broken in a
shin?

MOTH. I will tell you sensibly.

COSTARD. Thou hast no feeling of it, Moth: I will speak that l'envoy:

> I, Costard, running out, that was safely within,
> Fell over the threshold and broke my shin.

ARMADO. We will talk no more of this matter.

COSTARD. Till there be more matter in the shin.

ARMADO. Sirrah Costard, I will enfranchise thee.

COSTARD. O! marry me to one Frances: I smell some l'envoy, some goose, in this.

ARMADO. By my sweet soul, I mean setting thee at liberty, enfreedoming thy person: thou wert immured, restrained, captivated, bound.

COSTARD. True, true, and now you will be my purgation and let me loose.

ARMADO. I give thee thy liberty, set thee from durance; and in lieu thereof, impose upon thee nothing but this:—(*Giving a letter*) Bear this significant to the country maid Jaquenetta. (*Giving money*) There is remuneration; for the best ward of mine honour is rewarding my dependents. Moth, follow.   *Exit*

MOTH. Like the sequel, I. Signior Costard, adieu.

COSTARD. My sweet ounce of man's flesh! my incony Jew!

Exit Moth

Now will I look to his remuneration. Remuneration! O! that's the Latin word for three farthings: three farthings, remuneration. 'What 's the price of this inkle?' 'One penny.' 'No, I 'll give you a remuneration': why, it carries it. Remuneration! why, it is a fairer name than French crown. I will never buy and sell out of this word.

Enter Berowne

BEROWNE. O! my good knave Costard, exceedingly well met.

COSTARD. Pray you, sir, how much carnation riband may a man buy for a remuneration?

BEROWNE. What is a remuneration?

COSTARD. Marry, sir, halfpenny farthing.

BEROWNE. Why then, three-farthing-worth of silk.

COSTARD. I thank your worship. God be wi' you!

BEROWNE. Stay, slave; I must employ thee:

> As thou wilt win my favour, good my knave,
> Do one thing for me that I shall entreat.

COSTARD. When would you have it done, sir?

BEROWNE. O, this afternoon.

COSTARD. Well, I will do it, sir! fare you well.

BEROWNE. O, thou knowest not what it is.

COSTARD. I shall know, sir, when I have done it.

BEROWNE. Why, villain, thou must know first.

COSTARD. I will come to your worship to-morrow morning.

BEROWNE. It must be done this afternoon. Hark, slave, it is
    but this:
    The princess comes to hunt here in the park,
    And in her train there is a gentle lady;
    When tongues speak sweetly, then they name her name,
    And Rosaline they call her: ask for her
    And to her white hand see thou do commend
    This seal'd-up counsel. (*Gives him a shilling*) There 's
    thy guerdon: go.

COSTARD. Gardon, O sweet gardon! better than remunera-
    tion; a 'leven-pence farthing better. Most sweet gardon;
    I will do it, sir, in print. Gardon! remuneration!   *Exit*

BEROWNE. And I,—
    Forsooth, in love! I, that have been love's whip;
    A very beadle to a humorous sigh;
    A critic, nay, a night-watch constable,
    A domineering pedant o'er the boy,
    Than whom no mortal so magnificent!
    This wimpled, whining, purblind, wayward boy,
    This senior-junior, giant-dwarf, Dan Cupid;
    Regent of love-rimes, lord of folded arms,
    The anointed sovereign of sighs and groans,
    Liege of all loiterers and malecontents,
    Dread prince of plackets, king of codpieces,
    Sole imperator and great general
    Of trotting 'paritors: O my little heart!
    And I to be a corporal of his field,
    And wear his colours like a tumbler's hoop!
    What I! I love! I sue! I seek a wife!
    A woman that is like a German clock,
    Still a-repairing, ever out of frame,
    And never going aright, being a watch,
    But being watch'd that it may still go right!
    Nay, to be perjur'd, which is worst of all;
    And, among three, to love the worst of all;

A wightly wanton with a velvet brow,
With two pitch balls stuck in her face for eyes;
Ay, and, by heaven, one that will do the deed
Though Argus were her eunuch and her guard:
And I to sigh for her! to watch for her!
To pray for her! Go to; it is a plague
That Cupid will impose for my neglect
Of his almighty dreadful little might.
Well, I will love, write, sigh, pray, sue, and groan:
Some men must love my lady, and some Joan.   *Exit*

ACT FOUR

SCENE ONE

The King of Navarre's Park.

Enter the Princess, Rosaline, Maria, Katharine,
Boyet, Lords, Attendants, and a Forester

PRINCESS. Was that the king, that spurr'd his horse so hard
  Against the steep uprising of the hill?
BOYET. I know not; but I think it was not he.
PRINCESS. Whoe'er a' was, a' show'd a mounting mind.
  Well, lords, to-day we shall have our dispatch;
  On Saturday we will return to France.
  Then, forester, my friend, where is the bush
  That we must stand and play the murderer in?
FORESTER. Hereby, upon the edge of yonder coppice;
  A stand where you may make the fairest shoot.
PRINCESS. I thank my beauty, I am fair that shoot,
  And thereupon thou speak'st the fairest shoot.
FORESTER. Pardon me, madam, for I meant not so.
PRINCESS. What, what? first praise me, and again say no?
  O short-liv'd pride! Not fair? alack for woe!
FORESTER. Yes, madam, fair.
PRINCESS.   Nay, never paint me now:
  Where fair is not, praise cannot mend the brow.
  Here, good my glass (*Gives money*):—Take this for tell-
    ing true:
  Fair payment for foul words is more than due.
FORESTER. Nothing but fair is that which you inherit.
PRINCESS. See, see! my beauty will be sav'd by merit.
  O heresy in fair, fit for these days!
  A giving hand, though foul, shall have fair praise.
  But come, the bow: now mercy goes to kill,
  And shooting well is then accounted ill.
  Thus will I save my credit in the shoot:
  Not wounding, pity would not let me do 't;

If wounding, then it was to show my skill,
That more for praise than purpose meant to kill.
And out of question so it is sometimes,
Glory grows guilty of detested crimes,
When, for fame's sake, for praise, an outward part,
We bend to that the working of the heart;
As I for praise alone now seek to spill
The poor deer's blood, that my heart means no ill.

BOYET. Do not curst wives hold that self-sovereignty
Only for praise' sake, when they strive to be
Lords o'er their lords?

PRINCESS. Only for praise; and praise we may afford
To any lady that subdues a lord.

Enter Costard

BOYET. Here comes a member of the commonwealth.

COSTARD. God dig-you-den all! Pray you, which is the head
lady?

PRINCESS. Thou shalt know her, fellow, by the rest that have
no heads.

COSTARD. Which is the greatest lady, the highest?

PRINCESS. The thickest, and the tallest.

COSTARD. The thickest, and the tallest! it is so; truth is truth.
An your waist, mistress, were as slender as my wit,
One o' these maids' girdles for your waist should be fit.
Are not you the chief woman? You are the thickest here.

PRINCESS. What's your will, sir? What's your will?

COSTARD. I have a letter from Monsieur Berowne to one
Lady Rosaline.

PRINCESS. O! thy letter, thy letter; he's a good friend of
mine.
Stand aside, good bearer. Boyet, you can carve;
Break up this capon.

BOYET.   I am bound to serve.
This letter is mistook; it importeth none here;
It is writ to Jaquenetta.

PRINCESS.   We will read it, I swear.
Break the neck of the wax, and every one give ear.

BOYET. 'By heaven, that thou art fair, is most infallible; true,
that thou art beauteous; truth itself, that thou art lovely.
More fairer than fair, beautiful than beauteous, truer than
truth itself, have commiseration on thy heroical vassal!
The magnanimous and most illustrate king Cophetua set

eye upon the pernicious and indubitate beggar Zenelophon, and he it was that might rightly say veni, vidi, vici; which to anatomize in the vulgar—O base and obscure vulgar!—videlicet, he came, saw, and overcame: he came, one; saw, two; overcame, three. Who came? the king: Why did he come? to see: Why did he see? to overcome: To whom came he? to the beggar: What saw he? the beggar. Whom overcame he? the beggar. The conclusion is victory: on whose side? the king's; the captive is enriched: on whose side? the beggar's. The catastrophe is a nuptial: on whose side? the king's, no, on both in one, or one in both. I am the king, for so stands the comparison; thou the beggar, for so witnesseth thy lowliness. Shall I command thy love? I may: Shall I enforce thy love? I could: Shall I entreat thy love? I will. What shalt thou exchange for rags? robes; for tittles? titles; for thyself? me. Thus, expecting thy reply, I profane my lips on thy foot, my eyes on thy picture, and my heart on thy every part.

> Thine, in the dearest design of Industry,
>
>   Don Adriano de Armado.

'Thus dost thou hear the Nemean lion roar
'Gainst thee, thou lamb, that standest as his prey:
Submissive fall his princely feet before,
        And he from forage will incline to play.
But if thou strive, poor soul, what art thou then?
Food for his rage, repasture for his den.'

PRINCESS. What plume of feathers is he that indited this letter?

What vane? what weathercock? did you ever hear better?

BOYET. I am much deceiv'd but I remember the style.

PRINCESS. Else your memory is bad, going o'er it erewhile.

BOYET. This Armado is a Spaniard, that keeps here in court;
A phantasime, a Monarcho, and one that makes sport
To the prince and his book-mates.

PRINCESS.   Thou, fellow, a word.
Who gave thee this letter?

COSTARD.   I told you; my lord.

PRINCESS. To whom shouldst thou give it?

COSTARD.   From my lord to my lady.

PRINCESS. From which lord, to which lady?

COSTARD. From my lord Berowne, a good master of mine,
To a lady of France, that he call'd Rosaline.

PRINCESS. Thou hast mistaken his letter. Come, lords, away.
Here, sweet, put up this: 'twill be thine another day.

Exeunt Princess and Train

BOYET. Who is the suitor? who is the suitor?

ROSALINE.   Shall I teach you to know?

BOYET. Ay, my continent of beauty.

ROSALINE.   Why, she that bears the bow.
Finely put off!

BOYET. My lady goes to kill horns; but, if thou marry,
Hang me by the neck if horns that year miscarry.
Finely put on!

ROSALINE. Well then, I am the shooter.

BOYET.   And who is your deer?

ROSALINE. If we choose by the horns, yourself: come not
near.
Finely put on, indeed!

MARIA. You still wrangle with her, Boyet, and she strikes at
the brow.

BOYET. But she herself is hit lower: have I hit her now?

ROSALINE. Shall I come upon thee with an old saying, that
was a man when King Pepin of France was a little boy, as
touching the hit it?

BOYET. So may I answer thee with one as old, that was a
woman when Queen Guinever of Britain was a little
wench, as touching the hit it.

ROSALINE. Thou canst not hit it, hit it, hit it,
Thou canst not hit it, my good man.

BOYET.   An I cannot, cannot, cannot,
An I cannot, another can.

Exeunt Rosaline and Katharine

COSTARD. By my troth, most pleasant: how both did fit it!

MARIA. A mark marvellous well shot, for they both did hit it!

BOYET. A mark! O! mark but that mark; a mark, says my
lady!
Let the mark have a prick in 't, to mete at, if it may be.

MARIA. Wide o' the bow hand! i' faith your hand is out.

COSTARD. Indeed a' must shoot nearer, or he 'll ne'er hit the
clout.

BOYET. An' if my hand be out, then belike your hand is in.

COSTARD. Then will she get the upshoot by cleaving the pin.

MARIA. Come, come, you talk greasily; your lips grow foul.

COSTARD. She's too hard for you at pricks, sir: challenge her
    to bowl.

BOYET. I fear too much rubbing. Good night, my good owl.

Exeunt Boyet and Maria

COSTARD. By my soul, a swain! a most simple clown!
    Lord, lord how the ladies and I have put him down!
    O' my troth, most sweet jests! most incony vulgar wit!
    When it comes so smoothly off, so obscenely, as it were, so
        fit,
    Armado, o' the one side, O! a most dainty man.
    To see him walk before a lady, and to bear her fan!
    To see him kiss his hand! and how most sweetly a' will
        swear!
    And his page o' t'other side, that handful of wit!
    Ah! heavens, it is a most pathetical nit.
    (*Shouting within*) Sola, sola!   *Exit running*

SCENE TWO

The Same.

Enter Holofernes, Sir Nathaniel, and Dull

NATHANIEL. Very reverend sport, truly: and done in the
    testimony of a good conscience.

HOLOFERNES. The deer was, as you know, sanguis, in blood;
    ripe as a pomewater, who now hangeth like a jewel in the
    ear of cælo, the sky, the welkin, the heaven; and anon
    falleth like a crab on the face of terra, the soil, the land,
    the earth.

NATHANIEL. Truly, Master Holofernes, the epithets are
    sweetly varied, like a scholar at the least: but, sir, I assure
    ye, it was a buck of the first head.

HOLOFERNES. Sir Nathaniel, haud credo.

DULL. 'Twas not a haud credo; 'twas a pricket.

HOLOFERNES. Most barbarous intimation! yet a kind of in-
    sinuation, as it were, in via, in way, of explication; facere,
    as it were, replication, or, rather, ostentare, to show, as it
    were, his inclination,—after his undressed, unpolished, un-
    educated, unpruned, untrained, or, rather, unlettered, or,
    ratherest, unconfirmed fashion,—to insert again my haud
    credo for a deer.

DULL. I said the deer was not a haud credo; 'twas a pricket.
HOLOFERNES. Twice sod simplicity, bis coctus!
 O! thou monster Ignorance, how deformed dost thou look!
NATHANIEL. Sir, he hath not fed of the dainties that are bred
  of a book;
 he hath not eat paper, as it were; he hath not drunk ink:
 his intellect is not replenished; he is only an animal, only
  sensible in the duller parts:
 And such barren plants are set before us, that we thankful
  should be,
 Which we of taste and feeling are, for those parts that do
  fructify in us more than he;
 For as it would ill become me to be vain, indiscreet, or a
  fool:
 So, were there a patch set on learning, to see him in a
  school:
 But, omne bene, say I; being of an old Father's mind,
 Many can brook the weather that love not the wind.
DULL. You two are book-men: can you tell by your wit,
 What was a month old at Cain's birth, that 's not five
  weeks old as yet?
HOLOFERNES. Dictynna, goodman Dull: Dictynna, goodman
  Dull.
DULL. What is Dictynna?
NATHANIEL. A title to Phœbe, to Luna, to the moon.
HOLOFERNES. The moon was a month old when Adam was
  no more;
 And raught not to five weeks when he came to five-score.
 The allusion holds in the exchange.
DULL. 'Tis true indeed: the collusion holds in the exchange.
HOLOFERNES. God comfort thy capacity! I say, the allusion
  holds in the exchange.
DULL. And I say the pollusion holds in the exchange, for the
  moon is never but a month old; and I say beside that 'twas
  a pricket that the princess killed.
HOLOFERNES. Sir Nathaniel, will you hear an extemporal
  epitaph on the death of the deer? and, to humour the ignorant, I have call'd the deer the princess killed, a pricket.
NATHANIEL. Perge, good Master Holofernes, perge; so it
  shall please you to abrogate scurrility.
HOLOFERNES. I will something affect the letter; for it argues
  facility.

> The preyful princess pierc'd and prick'd a pretty pleasing
> pricket;
>> Some say a sore; but not a sore, till now made sore with
>> shooting.
> The dogs did yell; put L to sore, then sorel jumps from
> thicket;
>> Or pricket, sore, or else sorel; the people fall a hooting.
> If sore be sore, then L to sore makes fifty sores one sorel!
> Of one sore I a hundred make, by adding but one more L.

NATHANIEL. A rare talent!

DULL. (*Aside*) If a talent be a claw, look how he claws him
with a talent.

HOLOFERNES. This is a gift that I have, simple, simple; a
foolish extravagant spirit, full of forms, figures, shapes,
objects, ideas, apprehensions, motions, revolutions: these
are begot in the ventricle of memory, nourished in the
womb of pia mater, and delivered upon the mellowing of
occasion. But the gift is good in those in whom it is acute,
and I am thankful for it.

NATHANIEL. Sir, I praise the Lord for you, and so may my
parishioners; for their sons are well tutored by you, and
their daughters profit very greatly under you: you are a
good member of the commonwealth.

HOLOFERNES. Mehercle! if their sons be ingenuous, they
shall want no instruction; if their daughters be capable, I
will put it to them. But, vir sapit qui pauca loquitur. A
soul feminine saluteth us.

Enter Jaquenetta and Costard

JAQUENETTA. God give you good-morrow, Master parson.

HOLOFERNES. Master parson, quasi pers-on. An if one should
be pierced, which is the one?

COSTARD. Marry, Master schoolmaster, he that is likest to a
hogshead.

HOLOFERNES. Piercing a hogshead! a good lustre or conceit
in a turf of earth; fire enough for a flint, pearl enough for a
swine: 'tis pretty; it is well.

JAQUENETTA. Good Master parson (*giving a letter to Nathaniel*), be so good as read me this letter: it was given me
by Costard, and sent me from Don Armado: I beseech
you, read it.

HOLOFERNES. 'Fauste, precor gelida quando pecus omne sub
umbra Ruminat,' and so forth. Ah! good old Mantuan. I

may speak of thee as the traveller doth of Venice:

> —Venetia, Venetia,
>> Chi non te vede, non te pretia.

Old Mantuan! old Mantuan! Who understandeth thee not, loves thee not. Ut, re, sol, la, mi, fa. Under pardon, sir, what are the contents? or, rather, as Horace says in his— What, my soul, verses?

NATHANIEL. Ay, sir, and very learned.

HOLOFERNES. Let me hear a staff, a stanze, a verse: lege, domine.

NATHANIEL. (*Reads*) 'If love make me forsworn, how shall I swear to love?
Ah! never faith could hold, if not to beauty vow'd;
Though to myself forsworn, to thee I 'll faithful prove;
Those thoughts to me were oaks, to thee like osiers bow'd.
Study his bias leaves and makes his book thine eyes,
Where all those pleasures live that art would comprehend:
If knowledge be the mark, to know thee shall suffice.
Well learned is that tongue that well can thee commend;
All ignorant that soul that sees thee without wonder;
Which is to me some praise that I thy parts admire.
Thy eye Jove's lightning bears, thy voice his dreadful thunder,
Which, not to anger bent, is music and sweet fire.
Celestial as thou art, O! pardon love this wrong,
That sings heaven's praise with such an earthly tongue!'

HOLOFERNES. You find not the apostrophas, and so miss the accent: let me supervise the canzonet. Here are only numbers ratified; but, for the elegancy, facility, and golden cadence of poesy, caret. Ovidious Naso was the man: and why, indeed, Naso, but for smelling out the odoriferous flowers of fancy, the jerks of invention? Imitari is nothing; so doth the hound his master, the ape his keeper, the 'tired horse his rider. But, damosella virgin, was this directed to you?

JAQUENETTA. Ay, sir; from one Monsieur Berowne, one of the strange queen's lords.

HOLOFERNES. I will overglance the superscript. To the snow-white hand of the most beauteous Lady Rosaline.'

I will look again on the intellect of the letter, for the nomination of the party writing to the person written unto: 'Your ladyship's, in all desired employment, Berowne.'— Sir Nathaniel, this Berowne is one of the votaries with the king; and here he hath framed a letter to a sequent of the stranger queen's, which, accidentally, or by the way of progression, hath miscarried. Trip and go, my sweet; deliver this paper into the royal hand of the king; it may concern much. Stay not thy compliment; I forgive thy duty: adieu.

JAQUENETTA. Good Costard, go with me. Sir, God save your life!

COSTARD. Have with thee, my girl.

Exeunt Costard and Jaquenetta

NATHANIEL. Sir, you have done this in the fear of God, very religiously; and, as a certain Father saith—

HOLOFERNES. Sir, tell not me of the Father; I do fear colourable colours. But to return to the verses: did they please you, Sir Nathaniel?

NATHANIEL. Marvellous well for the pen.

HOLOFERNES. I do dine to-day at the father's of a certain pupil of mine; where, if before repast it shall please you to gratify the table with a grace, I will, on my privilege I have with the parents of the foresaid child or pupil, undertake your ben venuto; where I will prove those verses to be very unlearned, neither savouring of poetry, wit, nor invention. I beseech your society.

NATHANIEL. And thank you too; for society—saith the text— is the happiness of life.

HOLOFERNES. And, certes, the text most infallibly concludes it.—(*To Dull*) Sir, I do invite you too: you shall not say me nay: pauca verba. Away! the gentles are at their game, and we will to our recreation.   *Exeunt*

SCENE THREE

The Same.

Enter Berowne, with a paper

BEROWNE. The king he is hunting the deer; I am coursing myself: they have pitched a toil; I am toiling in a pitch,—pitch that defiles: defile! a foul word! Well, sit thee down, sorrow! for so they say the fool said, and so say I, and I the fool: well proved, wit! By the Lord, this love is as mad as Ajax: it kills sheep: it kills me, I a sheep: well proved again o' my side! I will not love; if I do, hang me; i' faith, I will not. O! but her eye,—by this light, but for her eye, I would not love her; yes, for her two eyes. Well, I do nothing in the world but lie, and lie in my throat. By heaven, I do love, and it hath taught me to rime, and to be melancholy; and here is part of my rime, and here my melancholy. Well, she hath one o' my sonnets already: the clown bore it, the fool sent it, and the lady hath it: sweet clown, sweeter fool, sweetest lady! By the world, I would not care a pin if the other three were in. Here comes one with a paper: God give him grace to groan!   *Gets up into a tree*

Enter the King, with a paper

KING. Ah me!

BEROWNE. (*Aside*) Shot, by heaven! Proceed, sweet Cupid: thou hast thumped him with thy bird-bolt under the left pap. In faith, secrets!

KING. (*Reads*) 'So sweet a kiss the golden sun gives not
    To those fresh morning drops upon the rose,
As thy eye-beams, when their fresh rays have smote
    The night of dew that on my cheeks down flows;
Nor shines the silver moon one half so bright
    Through the transparent bosom of the deep,
As doth thy face through tears of mine give light;
    Thou shin'st in every tear that I do weep:
No drop but as a coach doth carry thee;
    So ridest thou triumphing in my woe.
Do but behold the tears that swell in me,
    And they thy glory through my grief will show:
But do not love thyself; then thou wilt keep

My tears for glasses, and still make me weep.
O queen of queens! how far thou dost excel,
No thought can think, nor tongue of mortal tell.'

How shall she know my griefs? I 'll drop the paper:
Sweet leaves, shade folly. Who is he comes here?

                                        Steps aside

What, Longaville! and reading! listen, ear.

                Enter Longaville, with a paper

BEROWNE. Now, in thy likeness, one more fool appear!
LONGAVILLE. Ay me! I am forsworn.
BEROWNE. Why, he comes in like a perjure, wearing papers.
KING. In love, I hope: sweet fellowship in shame!
BEROWNE. One drunkard loves another of the name.
LONGAVILLE. Am I the first that have been perjur'd so?
BEROWNE. I could put thee in comfort: not by two that I
    know:
  Thou mak'st the triumviry, the corner-cap of society,
  The shape of love's Tyburn, that hangs up simplicity.
LONGAVILLE. I fear these stubborn lines lack power to move.
  O sweet Maria, empress of my love!
  These numbers will I tear, and write in prose.
BEROWNE. O! rimes are guards on wanton Cupid's hose:
  Disfigure not his slop.
LONGAVILLE.   This same shall go. (*Reads*)
  'Did not the heavenly rhetoric of thine eye,
    'Gainst whom the world cannot hold argument,
  Persuade my heart to this false perjury?
    Vows for thee broke deserve not punishment.
  A woman I forswore; but I will prove,
    Thou being a goddess, I forswore not thee:
  My vow was earthly, thou a heavenly love;
    Thy grace, being gain'd, cures all disgrace in me.
  Vows are but breath, and breath a vapour is:
    Then thou, fair sun, which on my earth dost shine,
  Exhal'st this vapour-vow; in thee it is:
    If broken, then, it is no fault of mine:
  If by me broke, what fool is not so wise
  To lose an oath to win a paradise!'
BEROWNE. This is the liver-vein, which makes flesh a deity;
  A green goose a goddess; pure, pure idolatry.
  God amend us, God amend! we are much out o' the way.

LONGAVILLE. By whom shall I send this?—Company! stay.

Steps aside

BEROWNE. All hid, all hid; an old infant play.
Like a demi-god here sit I in the sky,
And wretched fools' secrets heedfully o'er-eye.
More sacks to the mill! O heavens! I have my wish.

Enter Dumaine, with a paper

Dumaine transform'd: four woodcocks in a dish!

DUMAINE. O most divine Kate!

BEROWNE. O most profane coxcomb!

DUMAINE. By heaven, the wonder of a mortal eye!

BEROWNE. By earth, she is but corporal; there you lie.

DUMAINE. Her amber hairs for foul have amber quoted.

BEROWNE. An amber-colour'd raven was well noted.

DUMAINE. As upright as the cedar.

BEROWNE.   Stoop, I say;
Her shoulder is with child.

DUMAINE.   As fair as day.

BEROWNE. Ay, as some days; but then no sun must shine.

DUMAINE. O! that I had my wish.

LONGAVILLE.   And I had mine!

KING. And I mine too, good Lord!

BEROWNE. Amen, so I had mine. Is not that a good word?

DUMAINE. I would forget her; but a fever she
Reigns in my blood, and will remember'd be.

BEROWNE. A fever in your blood! why, then incision
Would let her out in saucers: sweet misprision!

DUMAINE. Once more I 'll read the ode that I have writ.

BEROWNE. Once more I 'll mark how love can vary wit.

DUMAINE. (*Reads*) 'On a day, alack the day!
Love, whose month is ever May,
Spied a blossom passing fair
Playing in the wanton air:
Through the velvet leaves the wind,
All unseen, 'gan passage find;
That the lover, sick to death,
Wish'd himself the heaven's breath.
Air, quoth he, thy cheeks may blow
Air, would I might triumph so!
But alack! my hand is sworn
Ne'er to pluck thee from thy thorn:
Vow, alack! for youth unmeet,

     Youth so apt to pluck a sweet.
     Do not call it sin in me,
     That I am forsworn for thee;
     Thou for whom e'en Jove would swear
     Juno but an Ethiop were;
     And deny himself for Jove,
     Turning mortal for thy love.'
  This will I send, and something else more plain,
  That shall express my true love's fasting pain.
  O! would the King, Berowne, and Longaville
  Were lovers too. Ill, to example ill,
  Would from my forehead wipe a perjur'd note;
  For none offend where all alike do dote.

LONGAVILLE. (*Advancing*) Dumaine, thy love is far from charity,
  That in love's grief desir'st society:
  You may look pale, but I should blush, I know,
  To be o'erheard and taken napping so.

KING. (*Advancing*) Come, sir, you blush: as his your case is such;
  You chide at him, offending twice as much:
  You do not love Maria; Longaville
  Did never sonnet for her sake compile,
  Nor never lay his wreathed arms athwart
  His loving bosom to keep down his heart.
  I have been closely shrouded in this bush,
  And mark'd you both, and for you both did blush.
  I heard your guilty rimes, observ'd your fashion,
  Saw sighs reek from you, noted well your passion:
  Ay me! says one; O Jove! the other cries;
  One, her hairs were gold, crystal the other's eyes:
  (*To Longaville*) You would for paradise break faith and troth;
  (*To Dumaine*) And Jove, for your love, would infringe an oath.
  What will Berowne say, when that he shall hear
  A faith infringed, which such zeal did swear?
  How will he scorn! how will he spend his wit!
  How will he triumph, leap and laugh at it!
  For all the wealth that ever I did see,
  I would not have him know so much by me.

BEROWNE. Now step I forth to whip hypocrisy. *Descends*

Ah! good my liege, I pray thee, pardon me:
Good heart! what grace hast thou, thus to reprove
These worms for loving, that art most in love?
Your eyes do make no coaches; in your tears
There is no certain princess that appears:
You 'll not be perjur'd, 'tis a hateful thing:
Tush! none but minstrels like of sonneting.
But are you not asham'd? nay, are you not,
All three of you, to be thus much o'ershot?
You found his mote; the king your mote did see;
But I a beam do find in each of three.
O! what a scene of foolery have I seen,
Of sighs, of groans, of sorrow, and of teen;
O me! with what strict patience have I sat,
To see a king transformed to a gnat;
To see great Hercules whipping a gig,
And profound Solomon to tune a jig,
And Nestor play at push-pin with the boys,
And critic Timon laugh at idle toys!
Where lies thy grief? O! tell me, good Dumaine,
And, gentle Longaville, where lies thy pain?
And where my liege's? all about the breast:
A caudle, ho!

KING.   Too bitter is thy jest.
Are we betray'd thus to thy over-view?

BEROWNE. Not you to me, but I betray'd by you:
I, that am honest; I, that hold it sin
To break the vow I am engaged in;
I am betray'd, by keeping company
With men like men, men of inconstancy.
When shall you see me write a thing in rime?
Or groan for Joan? or spend a minute's time
In pruning me? When shall you hear that I
Will praise a hand, a foot, a face, an eye,
A gait, a state, a brow, a breast, a waist,
A leg, a limb?—

KING.   Soft! Whither away so fast?
A true man or a thief that gallops so?

BEROWNE. I post from love; good lover, let me go.
                Enter Jaquenetta and Costard

JAQUENETTA. God bless the king!

KING.   What present hast thou there?

COSTARD. Some certain treason.

KING.   What makes treason here?

COSTARD. Nay, it makes nothing, sir.

KING.   If it mar nothing neither,
The treason and you go in peace away together.

JAQUENETTA. I beseech your Grace, let this letter be read:
Our parson misdoubts it; 'twas treason, he said.

KING. Berowne, read it over—   *Giving the letter to him*
Where hadst thou it?

JAQUENETTA. Of Costard.

KING. Where hadst thou it?

COSTARD. Of Dun Adramadio, Dun Adramadio.

                          Berowne tears the letter

KING. How now! what is in you? why dost thou tear it?

BEROWNE. A toy, my liege, a toy: your Grace needs not fear
it.

LONGAVILLE. It did move him to passion, and therefore let 's
hear it.

DUMAINE. (*Picking up the pieces*) It is Berowne's writing,
and here is his name.

BEROWNE. (*To Costard*) Ah, you whoreson loggerhead, you
were born to do me shame.

Guilty, my lord, guilty; I confess, I confess.

KING. What?

BEROWNE. That you three fools lack'd me fool to make up
the mess;

He, he, and you, and you my liege, and I,

Are pick-purses in love, and we deserve to die.

O! dismiss this audience, and I shall tell you more.

DUMAINE. Now the number is even.

BEROWNE.   True, true; we are four.
Will these turtles be gone?

KING.   Hence, sirs; away!

COSTARD. Walk aside the true folk, and let the traitors stay.

                          Exeunt Costard and Jaquenetta

BEROWNE. Sweet lords, sweet lovers, O! let us embrace.
As true we are as flesh and blood can be:
The sea will ebb and flow, heaven show his face;
Young blood doth not obey an old decree:
We cannot cross the cause why we were born;
Therefore, of all hands must we be forsworn.

KING. What! did these rent lines show some love of thine?

BEROWNE. 'Did they,' quoth you? Who sees the heavenly
    Rosaline,
  That, like a rude and savage man of Inde,
    At the first opening of the gorgeous east,
  Bows not his vassal head, and, strucken blind,
    Kisses the base ground with obedient breast?
  What peremptory eagle-sighted eye
    Dares look upon the heaven of her brow,
  That is not blinded by her majesty?

KING. What zeal, what fury hath inspir'd thee now?
  My love, her mistress, is a gracious moon;
    She, an attending star, scarce seen a light.

BEROWNE. My eyes are then no eyes, nor I Berowne:
    O! but for my love, day would turn to night.
  Of all complexions the cull'd sovereignty
    Do meet, as at a fair, in her fair cheek;
  Where several worthies make one dignity,
    Where nothing wants that want itself doth seek.
  Lend me the flourish of all gentle tongues,—
    Fie, painted rhetoric! O! she needs it not:
  To things of sale a seller's praise belongs;
    She passes praise; then praise too short doth blot.
  A wither'd hermit, five-score winters worn,
    Might shake off fifty, looking in her eye:
  Beauty doth varnish age, as if new-born,
    And gives the crutch the cradle's infancy.
  O! 'tis the sun that maketh all things shine.

KING. By heaven, thy love is black as ebony.

BEROWNE. Is ebony like her? O wood divine!
  A wife of such wood were felicity.
  O! who can give an oath? where is a book?
    That I may swear beauty doth beauty lack,
  If that she learn not of her eye to look:
    No face is fair that is not full so black.

KING. O paradox! Black is the badge of hell,
  The hue of dungeons and the scowl of night;
  And beauty's crest becomes the heavens well.

BEROWNE. Devils soonest tempt, resembling spirit of light.
  O! if in black my lady's brows be deck'd,
    It mourns that painting and usurping hair
  Should ravish doters with a false aspect;

 And therefore is she born to make black fair.
Her favour turns the fashion of the days,
 For native blood is counted painting now;
And therefore red, that would avoid dispraise,
 Paints itself black, to imitate her brow.

DUMAINE. To look like her are chimney-sweepers black.

LONGAVILLE. And since her time are colliers counted bright.

KING. And Ethiops of their sweet complexion crack.

DUMAINE. Dark needs no candles now, for dark is light.

BEROWNE. Your mistresses dare never come in rain,
 For fear their colours should be wash'd away.

KING. 'Twere good yours did; for, sir, to tell you plain,
 I'll find a fairer face not wash'd to-day.

BEROWNE. I'll prove her fair, or talk till doomsday here.

KING. No devil will fright thee then so much as she.

DUMAINE. I never knew man hold vile stuff so dear.

LONGAVILLE. Look, here's thy love: (*Showing his shoe*) my
 foot and her face see.

BEROWNE. O! if the streets were paved with thine eyes,
 Her feet were much too dainty for such tread.

DUMAINE. O vile! then, as she goes, what upward lies
 The street should see as she walk'd over head.

KING. But what of this? Are we not all in love?

BEROWNE. Nothing so sure; and thereby all forsworn.

KING. Then leave this chat; and good Berowne, now prove
 Our loving lawful, and our faith not torn.

DUMAINE. Ay, marry, there; some flattery for this evil.

LONGAVILLE. O! some authority how to proceed;
 Some tricks, some quillets, how to cheat the devil.

DUMAINE. Some salve for perjury.

BEROWNE.   O, 'tis more than need.
 Have at you, then, affection's men-at-arms:
 Consider what you first did swear unto,
 To fast, to study, and to see no woman;
 Flat treason 'gainst the kingly state of youth.
 Say, can you fast? your stomachs are too young,
 And abstinence engenders maladies.
 And where that you have vow'd to study, lords,
 In that each of you hath forsworn his book,
 Can you still dream and pore and thereon look?
 For when would you, my lord, or you, or you,
 Have found the ground of study's excellence
 Without the beauty of a woman's face?

From women's eyes this doctrine I derive:
They are the ground, the books, the academes,
From whence doth spring the true Promethean fire.
Why, universal plodding poisons up
The nimble spirits in the arteries,
As motion and long-during action tires
The sinewy vigour of the traveller.
Now, for not looking on a woman's face,
You have in that forsworn the use of eyes,
And study too, the causer of your vow;
For where is any author in the world
Teaches such beauty as a woman's eye?
Learning is but an adjunct to ourself,
And where we are our learning likewise is:
Then when ourselves we see in ladies' eyes,
Do we not likewise see our learning there?
O! we have made a vow to study, lords,
And in that vow we have forsworn our books:
For when would you, my liege, or you, or you,
In leaden contemplation have found out
Such fiery numbers as the prompting eyes
Of beauty's tutors have enrich'd you with?
Other slow arts entirely keep the brain,
And therefore, finding barren practisers,
Scarce show a harvest of their heavy toil;
But love, first learned in a lady's eyes,
Lives not alone immured in the brain,
But, with the motion of all elements,
Courses as swift as thought in every power,
And gives to every power a double power,
Above their functions and their offices.
It adds a precious seeing to the eye;
A lover's eyes will gaze an eagle blind;
A lover's ear will hear the lowest sound,
When the suspicious head of theft is stopp'd:
Love's feeling is more soft and sensible
Than are the tender horns of cockled snails:
Love's tongue proves dainty Bacchus gross in taste.
For valour, is not Love a Hercules,
Still climbing trees in the Hesperides?
Subtle as Sphinx; as sweet and musical
As bright Apollo's lute, strung with his hair;
And when Love speaks, the voice of all the gods

Makes heaven drowsy with the harmony.
Never durst poet touch a pen to write
Until his ink were temper'd with Love's sighs;
O! then his lines would ravish savage ears,
And plant in tyrants mild humility.
From women's eyes this doctrine I derive:
They sparkle still the right Promethean fire;
They are the books, the arts, the academes,
That show, contain, and nourish all the world;
Else none at all in aught proves excellent.
Then fools you were these women to forswear,
Or, keeping what is sworn, you will prove fools.
For wisdom's sake, a word that all men love,
Or for love's sake, a word that loves all men,
Or for men's sake, the authors of these women;
Or women's sake, by whom we men are men,
Let us once lose our oaths to find ourselves,
Or else we lose ourselves to keep our oaths.
It is religion to be thus forsworn;
For charity itself fulfils the law;
And who can sever love from charity?

KING. Saint Cupid, then! and, soldiers, to the field!

BEROWNE. Advance your standards, and upon them, lords!
Pell-mell, down with them! but be first advis'd,
In conflict that you get the sun of them.

LONGAVILLE. Now to plain-dealing; lay these glozes by;
Shall we resolve to woo these girls of France?

KING. And win them too: therefore let us devise
Some entertainment for them in their tents.

BEROWNE. First, from the park let us conduct them thither;
Then homeward every man attach the hand
Of his fair mistress: in the afternoon
We will with some strange pastime solace them,
Such as the shortness of the time can shape;
For revels, dances, masks, and merry hours,
Forerun fair Love, strewing her way with flowers.

KING. Away, away! no time shall be omitted,
That will betime, and may by us be fitted.

BEROWNE. Allons! allons! Sow'd cockle reap'd no corn;
And justice always whirls in equal measure:
Light wenches may prove plagues to men forsworn;
If so, our copper buys no better treasure.   *Exeunt*

ACT FIVE

SCENE ONE

The King of Navarre's Park.

Enter Holofernes, Sir Nathaniel, and Dull

HOLOFERNES. Satis quod sufficit.

NATHANIEL. I praise God for you, sir: your reasons at dinner have been sharp and sententious; pleasant without scurrility, witty without affection, audacious without impudency, learned without opinion, and strange without heresy. I did converse this quondam day with a companion of the king's, who is intituled, nominated, or called, Don Adriano de Armado.

HOLOFERNES. Novi hominem tanquam te: his humour is lofty, his discourse peremptory, his tongue filed, his eye ambitious, his gait majestical, and his general behaviour vain, ridiculous, and thrasonical. He is too picked, too spruce, too affected, too odd, as it were, too peregrinate, as I may call it.

NATHANIEL. A most singular and choice epithet.

Draws out his table-book

HOLOFERNES. He draweth out the thread of his verbosity finer than the staple of his argument. I abhor such fanatical phantasimes, such insociable and point-devise companions; such rackers of orthography, as to speak dout, fine, when he should say, doubt; det, when he should pronounce, debt,—d, e, b, t, not d, e, t: he clepeth a calf, cauf; half, hauf; neighbour vocatur nebour, neigh abbreviated ne. This is abhominable, which he would call abominable,—it insinuateth me of insanie: anne intelligis, domine? To make frantic, lunatic.

NATHANIEL. Laus Deo bone intelligo.

HOLOFERNES. Bone? bone, for bene: Priscian a little scratched; 'twill serve.

Enter Armado, Moth, and Costard

NATHANIEL. Videsne quis venit?

HOLOFERNES. Video, et gaudeo.

ARMADO. (*To Moth*) Chirrah!

HOLOFERNES. Quare Chirrah, not sirrah?

ARMADO. Men of peace, well encountered.

HOLOFERNES. Most military sir, salutation.

MOTH. (*Aside to Costard*) They have been at a great feast of languages, and stolen the scraps.

COSTARD. O! they have lived long on the almsbasket of words. I marvel thy master hath not eaten thee for a word; for thou art not so long by the head as honorifica-bilitudinitatibus: thou art easier swallowed than a flap-dragon.

MOTH. Peace! the peal begins.

ARMADO. (*To Holofernes*) Monsieur, are you not lettered?

MOTH. Yes, yes; he teaches boys the hornbook. What is a, b, spelt backward, with the horn on his head?

HOLOFERNES. Ba, pueritia, with a horn added.

MOTH. Ba! most silly sheep with a horn. You hear his learning.

HOLOFERNES. Quis, quis, thou consonant?

MOTH. The third of the five vowels, if you repeat them; or the fifth, if I.

HOLOFERNES. I will repeat them,—a, e, i,—

MOTH. The sheep; the other two concludes it,—o, u.

ARMADO. Now, by the salt wave of the Mediterraneum, a sweet touch, a quick venew of wit! snip, snap, quick and home! it rejoiceth my intellect: true wit!

MOTH. Offered by a child to an old man; which is wit-old.

HOLOFERNES. What is the figure? what is the figure?

MOTH. Horns.

HOLOFERNES. Thou disputest like an infant; go, whip thy gig.

MOTH. Lend me your horn to make one, and I will whip about your infamy circum circa. A gig of a cuckold's horn.

COSTARD. An I had but one penny in the world, thou shouldst have it to buy gingerbread. Hold, there is the very remuneration I had of thy master, thou half-penny purse of wit, thou pigeon-egg of discretion. O! an the heavens were so pleased that thou wert but my bastard,

what a joyful father wouldst thou make me. Go to; thou
hast it ad dunghill, at the fingers' ends, as they say.

HOLOFERNES. O! I smell false Latin; dunghill for unguem.

ARMADO. Arts-man, præambula: we will be singled from
the barbarous. Do you not educate youth at the charge-
house on the top of the mountain?

HOLOFERNES. Or mons, the hill.

ARMADO. At your sweet pleasure, for the mountain.

HOLOFERNES. I do, sans question.

ARMADO. Sir, it is the king's most sweet pleasure and affection to congratulate the princess at her pavilion in the
posteriors of this day, which the rude multitude call the
afternoon.

HOLOFERNES. The posterior of the day, most generous sir, is
liable, congruent, and measurable for the afternoon: the
word is well culled, chose, sweet and apt, I do assure you,
sir; I do assure.

ARMADO. Sir, the king is a noble gentleman, and my familiar, I do assure ye, very good friend. For what is inward
between us, let it pass: I do beseech thee, remember thy
curtsy; I beseech thee, apparel thy head: and among
other importunate and most serious designs, and of great
import indeed, too, but let that pass: for I must tell thee,
it will please his Grace, by the world, sometime to lean
upon my poor shoulder, and with his royal finger, thus
dally with my excrement, with my mustachio: but, sweet
heart, let that pass. By the world, I recount no fable:
some certain special honours it pleaseth his greatness to
impart to Armado, a soldier, a man of travel, that hath
seen the world: but let that pass. The very all of all is,
but, sweet heart, I do implore secrecy, that the king
would have me present the princess, sweet chuck, with
some delightful ostentation, or show, or pageant, or antick, or firework. Now, understanding that the curate and
your sweet self are good at such eruptions and sudden
breaking out of mirth, as it were, I have acquainted you
withal, to the end to crave your assistance.

HOLOFERNES. Sir, you shall present before her the Nine
Worthies. Sir Nathaniel, as concerning some entertainment of time, some show in the posterior of this day, to
be rendered by our assistance, at the king's command,
and this most gallant, illustrate, and learned gentleman,

before the princess; I say, none so fit as to present the Nine Worthies.

NATHANIEL. Where will you find men worthy enough to present them?

HOLOFERNES. Joshua, yourself; myself, or this gallant gentleman, Judas Maccabæus; this swain, because of his great limb, or joint, shall pass Pompey the Great; the page, Hercules,—

ARMADO. Pardon, sir, error: he is not quantity enough for that Worthy's thumb: he is not so big as the end of his club.

HOLOFERNES. Shall I have audience? He shall present Hercules in minority: his enter and exit shall be strangling a snake; and I will have an apology for that purpose.

MOTH. An excellent device! so, if any of the audience hiss, you may cry, 'Well done, Hercules! now thou crushest the snake!' that is the way to make an offence gracious, though few have the grace to do it.

ARMADO. For the rest of the Worthies?—

HOLOFERNES. I will play three myself.

MOTH. Thrice-worthy gentleman!

ARMADO. Shall I tell you a thing?

HOLOFERNES. We attend.

ARMADO. We will have, if this fadge not, an antick. I beseech you, follow.

HOLOFERNES. Via, goodman Dull! thou hast spoken no word all this while.

DULL. Nor understood none neither, sir.

HOLOFERNES. Allons! we will employ thee.

DULL. I 'll make one in a dance, or so; or I will play the tabor to the Worthies, and let them dance the hay.

HOLOFERNES. Most dull, honest Dull, to our sport, away!

Exeunt

SCENE TWO

The Same. Before the Princess's Pavilion.

Enter the Princess, Katharine, Rosaline, and Maria

PRINCESS. Sweet hearts, we shall be rich ere we depart,
 If fairings come thus plentifully in:
 A lady wall'd about with diamonds!
 Look you what I have from the loving king.
ROSALINE. Madam, came nothing else along with that?
PRINCESS. Nothing but this! yes, as much love in rime
 As would be cramm'd up in a sheet of paper,
 Writ o' both sides the leaf, margent and all,
 That he was fain to seal on Cupid's name.
ROSALINE. That was the way to make his godhead wax;
 For he hath been five thousand years a boy.
KATHARINE. Ay, and a shrewd unhappy gallows too.
ROSALINE. You 'll ne'er be friends with him: a' kill'd your
 sister.
KATHARINE. He made her melancholy, sad, and heavy;
 And so she died: had she been light, like you,
 Of such a merry, nimble, stirring spirit,
 She might ha' been a grandam ere she died;
 And so may you, for a light heart lives long.
ROSALINE. What 's your dark meaning, mouse, of this light
 word?
KATHARINE. A light condition in a beauty dark.
ROSALINE. We need more light to find your meaning out.
KATHARINE. You 'll mar the light by taking it in snuff;
 Therefore, I 'll darkly end the argument.
ROSALINE. Look, what you do, you do it still i' the dark.
KATHARINE. So do not you, for you are a light wench.
ROSALINE. Indeed I weigh not you, and therefore light.
KATHARINE. You weigh me not. O! that 's you care not for
 me.
ROSALINE. Great reason; for, 'past cure is still past care.'
PRINCESS. Well bandied both; a set of wit well play'd.
 But Rosaline, you have a favour too:
 Who sent it? and what is it?
ROSALINE.   I would you knew:

An if my face were but as fair as yours,
My favour were as great; be witness this.
Nay, I have verses too, I thank Berowne:
The numbers true; and, were the numbering too,
I were the fairest goddess on the ground:
I am compared to twenty thousand fairs:
O! he hath drawn my picture in his letter.

PRINCESS. Anything like?

ROSALINE. Much in the letters, nothing in the praise.

PRINCESS. Beauteous as ink; a good conclusion.

KATHARINE. Fair as a text B in a copy-book.

ROSALINE. 'Ware pencils! how? Let me not die your debtor,
My red dominical, my golden letter:
O, that your face were not so full of O's!

KATHARINE. A pox of that jest! and beshrew all shrows!

PRINCESS. But what was sent to you from fair Dumaine?

KATHARINE. Madam, this glove.

PRINCESS.   Did he not send you twain?

KATHARINE. Yes, madam; and moreover,
Some thousand verses of a faithful lover:
A huge translation of hypocrisy,
Vilely compil'd, profound simplicity.

MARIA. This, and these pearls to me sent Longaville:
The letter is too long by half a mile.

PRINCESS. I think no less. Dost thou not wish in heart
The chain were longer and the letter short?

MARIA. Ay, or I would these hands might never part.

PRINCESS. We are wise girls to mock our lovers so.

ROSALINE. They are worse fools to purchase mocking so.
That same Berowne I 'll torture ere I go.
O that I knew he were but in by the week!
How I would make him fawn, and beg, and seek,
And wait the season, and observe the times,
And spend his prodigal wits in bootless rimes,
And shape his service wholly to my hests,
And make him proud to make me proud that jests!
So perttaunt-like would I o'ersway his state
That he should be my fool, and I his fate.

PRINCESS. None are so surely caught, when they are
    catch'd,
As wit turn'd fool: folly, in wisdom hatch'd,
Hath wisdom's warrant and the help of school

And wit's own grace to grace a learned fool.

ROSALINE. The blood of youth burns not with such excess
  As gravity's revolt to wantonness.

MARIA. Folly in fools bears not so strong a note
  As foolery in the wise, when wit doth dote;
  Since all the power thereof it doth apply
  To prove, by wit, worth in simplicity.

Enter Boyet

PRINCESS. Here comes Boyet, and mirth is in his face.

BOYET. O! I am stabb'd with laughter. Where 's her Grace?

PRINCESS. Thy news, Boyet?

BOYET.   Prepare, madam, prepare!—
  Arm, wenches, arm! encounters mounted are
  Against your peace: Love doth approach disguis'd,
  Armed in arguments; you 'll be surpris'd:
  Muster your wits; stand in your own defence
  Or hide your heads like cowards, and fly hence.

PRINCESS. Saint Denis to Saint Cupid! What are they
  That charge their breath against us? Say, scout, say.

BOYET. Under the cool shade of a sycamore
  I thought to close mine eyes some half an hour,
  When, lo! to interrupt my purpos'd rest,
  Toward that shade I might behold addrest
  The king and his companions: warily
  I stole into a neighbour thicket by,
  And overheard what you shall overhear;
  That, by and by, disguis'd they will be here.
  Their herald is a pretty knavish page,
  That well by heart hath conn'd his embassage:
  Action and accent did they teach him there;
  'Thus must thou speak, and thus thy body bear.'
  And ever and anon they made a doubt
  Presence majestical would put him out;
  'For,' quoth the king, 'an angel shalt thou see;
  Yet fear not thou, but speak audaciously.'
  The boy replied, 'An angel is not evil;
  I should have fear'd her had she been a devil.'
  With that all laugh'd and clapp'd him on the shoulder,
  Making the bold wag by their praises bolder.
  One rubb'd his elbow thus, and fleer'd, and swore
  A better speech was never spoke before;
  Another, with his finger and his thumb,

Cry'd 'Via! we will do 't, come what will come';
The third he caper'd and cried, 'All goes well';
The fourth turn'd on the toe, and down he fell.
With that, they all did tumble on the ground,
With such a zealous laughter, so profound,
That in this spleen ridiculous appears,
To check their folly, passion's solemn tears.

PRINCESS. But what, but what, come they to visit us?

BOYET. They do, they do; and are apparell'd thus,
Like Muscovites or Russians, as I guess.
Their purpose is to parle, to court and dance;
And every one his love-feat will advance
Unto his several mistress, which they 'll know
By favours several which they did bestow.

PRINCESS. And will they so? The gallants shall be task'd:
For, ladies, we will every one be mask'd,
And not a man of them shall have the grace,
Despite of suit, to see a lady's face.
Hold, Rosaline, this favour thou shalt wear,
And then the king will court thee for his dear:
Hold, take thou this, my sweet, and give me thine,
So shall Berowne take me for Rosaline,
And change you favours too; so shall your loves
Woo contrary, deceiv'd by these removes.

ROSALINE. Come on, then; wear the favours most in sight.

KATHARINE. But in this changing what is your intent?

PRINCESS. The effect of my intent is, to cross theirs:
They do it but in mocking merriment;
And mock for mock is only my intent.
Their several counsels they unbosom shall
To loves mistook and so be mock'd withal
Upon the next occasion that we meet,
With visages display'd, to talk and greet.

ROSALINE. But shall we dance, if they desire us to 't?

PRINCESS. No, to the death, we will not move a foot:
Nor to their penn'd speech render we no grace;
But while 'tis spoke each turn away her face.

BOYET. Why, that contempt will kill the speaker's heart,
And quite divorce his memory from his part.

PRINCESS. Therefore I do it; and I make no doubt,
The rest will ne'er come in, if he be out.
There 's no such sport as sport by sport o'erthrown,

To make theirs ours and ours none but our own:
So shall we stay, mocking intended game,
And they, well mock'd, depart away with shame.

Trumpets sound within

BOYET. The trumpet sounds: be mask'd; the maskers come.

The Ladies mask

Enter Blackamoors with music;
Moth; the King, Berowne, Longaville, and Dumaine
in Russian habits, and masked

MOTH. 'All hail, the richest beauties on the earth!'

BOYET. Beauties no richer than rich taffeta.

MOTH. 'A holy parcel of the fairest dames,

The Ladies turn their backs to him

That ever turn'd their—backs—to mortal views!'

BEROWNE. 'Their eyes,' villain, 'their eyes.'

MOTH. 'That ever turn'd their eyes to mortal views! Out'—

BOYET. True; 'out,' indeed.

MOTH. 'Out of your favours, heavenly spirits, vouchsafe
Not to behold'—

BEROWNE. 'Once to behold,' rogue.

MOTH. 'Once to behold with your sun-beamed eyes,
—with your sun-beamed eyes'—

BOYET. They will not answer to that epithet;
You were best call it 'daughter-beamed eyes.'

MOTH. They do not mark me, and that brings me out.

BEROWNE. Is this your perfectness? be gone, you rogue!

Exit Moth

ROSALINE. What would these strangers? Know their minds,
Boyet:
If they do speak our language, 'tis our will
That some plain man recount their purposes:
Know what they would.

BOYET. What would you with the princess?

BEROWNE. Nothing but peace and gentle visitation.

ROSALINE. What would they, say they?

BOYET. Nothing but peace and gentle visitation.

ROSALINE. Why, that they have; and bid them so be gone.

BOYET. She says, you have it, and you may be gone.

KING. Say to her, we have measur'd many miles,
To tread a measure with her on this grass.

BOYET. They say, that they have measur'd many a mile,
To tread a measure with you on this grass.

ROSALINE. It is not so. Ask them how many inches
   Is in one mile: if they have measur'd many,
   The measure then of one is easily told.
BOYET. If to come hither you have measur'd miles,
   And many miles, the princess bids you tell
   How many inches do fill up one mile.
BEROWNE. Tell her we measure them by weary steps.
BOYET. She hears herself.
ROSALINE.   How many weary steps,
   Of many weary miles you have o'ergone,
   Are number'd in the travel of one mile?
BEROWNE. We number nothing that we spend for you:
   Our duty is so rich, so infinite,
   That we may do it still without accompt.
   Vouchsafe to show the sunshine of your face,
   That we, like savages, may worship it.
ROSALINE. My face is but a moon, and clouded too.
KING. Blessed are clouds, to do as such clouds do!
   Vouchsafe, bright moon, and these thy stars, to shine,
   Those clouds remov'd, upon our watery eyne.
ROSALINE. O vain petitioner! beg a greater matter;
   Thou now request'st but moonshine in the water.
KING. Then, in our measure but vouchsafe one change.
   Thou bid'st me beg; this begging is not strange.
ROSALINE. Play, music, then! Nay, you must do it soon.
                               Music plays
   Not yet! no dance! thus change I like the moon.
KING. Will you not dance? How come you thus estrang'd?
ROSALINE. You took the moon at full, but now she 's chang'd.
KING. Yet still she is the moon, and I the man.
   The music plays; vouchsafe some motion to it.
ROSALINE. Our ears vouchsafe it.
KING.   But your legs should do it.
ROSALINE. Since you are strangers, and come here by chance,
   We 'll not be nice: take hands: we will not dance.
KING. Why take we hands then?
ROSALINE.   Only to part friends.
   Curtsy, sweet hearts; and so the measure ends.
KING. More measure of this measure: be not nice.
ROSALINE. We can afford no more at such a price.
KING. Prize you yourselves? what buys your company?

ROSALINE. Your absence only.
KING.   That can never be.
ROSALINE. Then cannot we be bought: and so, adieu;
  Twice to your visor, and half once to you!
KING. If you deny to dance, let 's hold more chat.
ROSALINE. In private, then.
KING.   I am best pleas'd with that.
                              They converse apart
BEROWNE. White-handed mistress, one sweet word with
  thee.
PRINCESS. Honey, and milk, and sugar; there are three.
BEROWNE. Nay then, two treys, an if you grow so nice,
  Metheglin, wort, and malmsey: well run, dice!
  There 's half a dozen sweets.
PRINCESS.   Seventh sweet, adieu:
  Since you can cog, I 'll play no more with you.
BEROWNE. One word in secret.
PRINCESS.   Let it not be sweet.
BEROWNE. Thou griev'st my gall.
PRINCESS.   Gall! bitter.
BEROWNE.   Therefore meet.
                              They converse apart
DUMAINE. Will you vouchsafe with me to change a word?
MARIA. Name it.
DUMAINE.   Fair lady,—
MARIA.   Say you so? Fair lord,
  Take that for your fair lady.
DUMAINE.   Please it you,
  As much in private, and I 'll bid adieu.
                              They converse apart
KATHARINE. What! was your visor made without a tongue?
LONGAVILLE. I know the reason, lady, why you ask.
KATHARINE. O! for your reason; quickly, sir; I long.
LONGAVILLE. You have a double tongue within your mask,
  And would afford my speechless visor half.
KATHARINE. 'Veal,' quoth the Dutchman. Is not 'veal' a calf?
LONGAVILLE. A calf, fair lady!
KATHARINE.   No, a fair lord calf.
LONGAVILLE. Let 's part the word.
KATHARINE.   No, I 'll not be your half:
  Take all, and wean it: it may prove an ox.

LONGAVILLE. Look, how you butt yourself in these sharp
     mocks.
     Will you give horns, chaste lady? do not so.
KATHARINE. Then die a calf, before your horns do grow.
LONGAVILLE. One word in private with you, ere I die.
KATHARINE. Bleat softly then; the butcher hears you cry.
                                        They converse apart
BOYET. The tongues of mocking wenches are as keen
     As is the razor's edge invisible,
   Cutting a smaller hair than may be seen,
     Above the sense of sense; so sensible
   Seemeth their conference; their conceits have wings
   Fleeter than arrows, bullets, wind, thought, swifter things.
ROSALINE. Not one word more, my maids: break off, break
     off.
BEROWNE. By heaven, all dry-beaten with pure scoff!
KING. Farewell, mad wenches: you have simple wits.
PRINCESS. Twenty adieus, my frozen Muscovits.
               Exeunt King, Lords, Music, and Attendants
     Are these the breed of wits so wonder'd at?
BOYET. Tapers they are, with your sweet breaths puff'd out.
ROSALINE. Well-liking wits they have; gross, gross; fat, fat.
PRINCESS. O poverty in wit, kingly-poor flout!
     Will they not, think you, hang themselves to-night?
     Or ever, but in visors, show their faces?
   This pert Berowne was out of countenance quite.
ROSALINE. O! they were all in lamentable cases.
   The king was weeping-ripe for a good word.
PRINCESS. Berowne did swear himself out of all suit.
MARIA. Dumaine was at my service, and his sword:
   'No point,' quoth I: my servant straight was mute.
KATHARINE. Lord Longaville said, I came o'er his heart;
     And trow you what he call'd me?
PRINCESS.   Qualm, perhaps.
KATHARINE. Yes, in good faith.
PRINCESS.   Go, sickness as thou art!
ROSALINE. Well, better wits have worn plain statute-caps.
   But will you hear? The king is my love sworn.
PRINCESS. And quick Berowne hath plighted faith to me.
KATHARINE. And Longaville was for my service born.
MARIA. Dumaine is mine, as sure as bark on tree.

BOYET. Madam, and pretty mistresses, give ear:
    Immediately they will again be here
    In their own shapes; for it can never be
    They will digest this harsh indignity.
PRINCESS. Will they return?
BOYET.   They will, they will, God knows;
    And leap for joy, though they are lame with blows:
    Therefore change favours; and, when they repair,
    Blow like sweet roses in this summer air.
PRINCESS. How blow? how blow? speak to be understood.
BOYET. Fair ladies mask'd, are roses in their bud:
    Dismask'd, their damask sweet commixture shown,
    Are angels vailing clouds, or roses blown.
PRINCESS. Avaunt perplexity! What shall we do
    If they return in their own shapes to woo?
ROSALINE. Good madam, if by me you 'll be advis'd,
    Let 's mock them still, as well known as disguis'd.
    Let us complain to them what fools were here,
    Disguis'd like Muscovites, in shapeless gear;
    And wonder what they were, and to what end
    Their shallow shows and prologue vilely penn'd,
    And their rough carriage so ridiculous,
    Should be presented at our tent to us.
BOYET. Ladies, withdraw: the gallants are at hand.
PRINCESS. Whip to our tents, as roes run over land.
            Exeunt Princess, Rosaline, Katharine, and Maria
                Enter the King, Berowne,
        Longaville, and Dumaine in their proper habits
KING. Fair sir, God save you! Where is the princess?
BOYET. Gone to her tent. Please it your Majesty,
    Command me any service to her thither?
KING. That she vouchsafe me audience for one word.
BOYET. I will; and so will she, I know, my lord.   *Exit*
BEROWNE. This fellow pecks up wit, as pigeons pease,
    And utters it again when God doth please:
    He is wit's pedlar, and retails his wares
    At wakes and wassails, meetings, markets, fairs;
    And we that sell by gross, the Lord doth know,
    Have not the grace to grace it with such show.
    This gallant pins the wenches on his sleeve;
    Had he been Adam, he had tempted Eve:
    He can carve too, and lisp: why, this is he

That kiss'd his hand away in courtesy;
This is the ape of form, monsieur the nice,
That, when he plays at tables, chides the dice
In honourable terms: nay, he can sing
A mean most meanly, and in ushering
Mend him who can: the ladies call him, sweet;
The stairs, as he treads on them, kiss his feet.
This is the flower that smiles on every one,
To show his teeth as white as whales-bone;
And consciences, that will not die in debt,
Pay him the due of honey tongu'd Boyet.

KING. A blister on his sweet tongue, with my heart,
That put Armado's page out of his part!

Re-enter the Princess, ushered
by Boyet; Rosaline, Maria, Katharine, and Attendants

BEROWNE. See where it comes! Behaviour, what wert thou,
Till this man show'd thee? and what art thou now?

KING. All hail, sweet madam, and fair time of day!

PRINCESS. 'Fair,' in 'all hail,' is foul, as I conceive.

KING. Construe my speeches better, if you may.

PRINCESS. Then wish me better: I will give you leave.

KING. We came to visit you, and purpose now
To lead you to our court: vouchsafe it then.

PRINCESS. This field shall hold me, and so hold your vow:
Nor God, nor I, delights in perjur'd men.

KING. Rebuke me not for that which you provoke:
The virtue of your eye must break my oath.

PRINCESS. Your nick-name virtue; vice you should have spoke;
For virtue's office never breaks men's troth.
Now, by my maiden honour, yet as pure
As the unsullied lily, I protest,
A world of torments though I should endure,
I would not yield to be your house's guest;
So much I hate a breaking cause to be
Of heavenly oaths, vow'd with integrity.

KING. O! you have liv'd in desolation here,
Unseen, unvisited, much to our shame.

PRINCESS. Not so, my lord; it is not so, I swear;
We have had pastime here and pleasant game.
A mess of Russians left us but of late.

KING. How, madam! Russians?

PRINCESS.   Ay, in truth, my lord;
  Trim gallants, full of courtship and of state.
ROSALINE. Madam, speak true. It is not so, my lord:
  My lady, to the manner of the days,
  In courtesy gives undeserving praise.
  We four, indeed, confronted were with four
  In Russian habit: here they stay'd an hour,
  And talk'd apace; and in that hour, my lord,
  They did not bless us with one happy word.
  I dare not call them fools; but this I think,
  When they are thirsty, fools would fain have drink.
BEROWNE. This jest is dry to me. Fair gentle sweet,
  Your wit makes wise things foolish: when we greet,
  With eyes best seeing, heaven's fiery eye,
  By light we lose light: your capacity
  Is of that nature that to your huge store
  Wise things seem foolish and rich things but poor.
ROSALINE. This proves you wise and rich, for in my eye—
BEROWNE. I am a fool, and full of poverty.
ROSALINE. But that you take what doth to you belong,
  It were a fault to snatch words from my tongue.
BEROWNE. O! I am yours, and all that I possess.
ROSALINE. All the fool mine?
BEROWNE.   I cannot give you less.
ROSALINE. Which of the visors was it that you wore?
BEROWNE. Where? when? what visor? why demand you
    this?
ROSALINE. There, then, that visor; that superfluous case
  That hid the worse, and show'd the better face.
KING. We are descried: they 'll mock us now downright.
DUMAINE. Let us confess, and turn it to a jest.
PRINCESS. Amaz'd, my lord? Why looks your Highness sad?
ROSALINE. Help! hold his brows! he 'll swound. Why look
    you pale?
  Sea-sick, I think, coming from Muscovy.
BEROWNE. Thus pour the stars down plagues for perjury.
    Can any face of brass hold longer out?—
  Here stand I, lady; dart thy skill at me;
    Bruise me with scorn, confound me with a flout;
  Thrust thy sharp wit quite through my ignorance;
    Cut me to pieces with thy keen conceit;
  And I will wish thee never more to dance,

Nor never more in Russian habit wait.
O! never will I trust to speeches penn'd,
    Nor to the motion of a school-boy's tongue,
Nor never come in visor to my friend,
    Nor woo in rime, like a blind harper's song,
Taffeta phrases, silken terms precise,
    Three-pil'd hyperboles, spruce affectation,
Figures pedantical; these summer flies
    Have blown me full of maggot ostentation:
I do forswear them; and I here protest,
    By this white glove,—how white the hand, God knows,—
Henceforth my wooing mind shall be express'd
    In russet yeas and honest kersey noes:
And, to begin, wench,—so God help me, la!—
My love to thee is sound, sans crack or flaw.

ROSALINE. Sans 'sans,' I pray you.

BEROWNE.   Yet I have a trick
Of the old rage: bear with me, I am sick;
I 'll leave it by degrees. Soft! let us see:
Write, 'Lord have mercy on us' on those three;
They are infected, in their hearts it lies;
They have the plague, and caught it of your eyes:
These lords are visited; you are not free,
For the Lord's tokens on you do I see.

PRINCESS. No, they are free that gave these tokens to us.

BEROWNE. Our states are forfeit: seek not to undo us.

ROSALINE. It is not so. For how can this be true,
That you stand forfeit, being those that sue?

BEROWNE. Peace! for I will not have to do with you.

ROSALINE. Nor shall not, if I do as I intend.

BEROWNE. Speak for yourselves: my wit is at an end.

KING. Teach us, sweet madam, for our rude transgression
Some fair excuse.

PRINCESS.   The fairest is confession.
Were you not here, but even now, disguis'd?

KING. Madam, I was.

PRINCESS.   And were you well advis'd?

KING. I was, fair madam.

PRINCESS.   When you then were here,
What did you whisper in your lady's ear?

KING. That more than all the world I did respect her.

PRINCESS. When she shall challenge this, you will reject her.
KING. Upon mine honour, no.
PRINCESS.   Peace! peace! forbear;
   Your oath once broke, you force not to forswear.
KING. Despise me, when I break this oath of mine.
PRINCESS. I will; and therefore keep it. Rosaline,
   What did the Russian whisper in your ear?
ROSALINE. Madam, he swore that he did hold me dear
   As precious eyesight, and did value me
   Above this world; adding thereto, moreover,
   That he would wed me, or else die my lover.
PRINCESS. God give thee joy of him! the noble lord
   Most honourably doth uphold his word.
KING. What mean you, madam? by my life, my troth,
   I never swore this lady such an oath.
ROSALINE. By heaven you did; and to confirm it plain,
   You gave me this: but take it, sir, again.
KING. My faith and this the princess I did give:
   I knew her by this jewel on her sleeve.
PRINCESS. Pardon me, sir, this jewel did she wear;
   And Lord Berowne, I thank him, is my dear.
   What, will you have me, or your pearl again?
BEROWNE. Neither of either; I remit both twain.
   I see the trick on 't: here was a consent,
   Knowing aforehand of our merriment,
   To dash it like a Christmas comedy.
   Some carry-tale, some please-man, some slight zany,
   Some mumble-news, some trencher-knight, some Dick,
   That smiles his cheek in years, and knows the trick
   To make my lady laugh when she 's dispos'd,
   Told our intents before; which once disclos'd,
   The ladies did change favours, and then we,
   Following the signs, woo'd but the sign of she.
   Now, to our perjury to add more terror,
   We are again forsworn, in will and error.
   Much upon this it is: (*To Boyet*) and might not you
   Forestall our sport, to make us thus untrue?
   Do not you know my lady's foot by the squire,
      And laugh upon the apple of her eye?
   And stand between her back, sir, and the fire,
      Holding a trencher, jesting merrily?
   You put our page out: go, you are allow'd;

Die when you will, a smock shall be your shroud.
You leer upon me, do you? There's an eye
Wounds like a leaden sword.

BOYET.   Full merrily
Hath this brave manage, this career, been run.

BEROWNE. Lo! he is tilting straight. Peace! I have done.

                    Enter Costard

Welcome, pure wit! thou partest a fair fray.

COSTARD. O Lord, sir, they would know
Whether the three Worthies shall come in or no.

BEROWNE. What, are there but three?

COSTARD.   No, sir; but it is vara fine,
For every one pursents three.

BEROWNE.   And three times thrice is nine.

COSTARD. Not so, sir; under correction, sir, I hope, it is not
so.
You cannot beg us, sir, I can assure you, sir; we know
what we know:
I hope, sir, three times thrice, sir,—

BEROWNE.   Is not nine.

COSTARD. Under correction, sir, we know whereuntil it doth
amount.

BEROWNE. By Jove, I always took three threes for nine.

COSTARD. O Lord, sir! it were pity you should get your living by reckoning, sir.

BEROWNE. How much is it?

COSTARD. O Lord, sir! the parties themselves, the actors, sir,
will show whereuntil it doth amount: for mine own part,
I am, as they say, but to parfect one man in one poor man,
Pompion the Great, sir.

BEROWNE. Art thou one of the Worthies?

COSTARD. It pleased them to think me worthy of Pompion
the Great: for mine own part, I know not the degree of
the Worthy, but I am to stand for him.

BEROWNE. Go, bid them prepare.

COSTARD. We will turn it finely off, sir; we will take some
care.   *Exit*

KING. Berowne, they will shame us; let them not approach.

BEROWNE. We are shame-proof, my lord; and 'tis some policy
To have one show worse than the king's and his company.

KING. I say they shall not come.

PRINCESS. Nay, my good lord, let me o'errule you now.
  That sport best pleases that doth least know how:
  Where zeal strives to content, and the contents
  Die in the zeal of those which it presents;
  Their form confounded makes most form in mirth,
  When great things labouring perish in their birth.
BEROWNE. A right description of our sport, my lord.

Enter Armado

ARMADO. Anointed, I implore so much expense of thy royal
  sweet breath as will utter a brace of words.

Armado converses with
the King, and delivers a paper to him

PRINCESS. Doth this man serve God?
BEROWNE. Why ask you?
PRINCESS. He speaks not like a man of God's making.
ARMADO. That 's all one, my fair, sweet, honey monarch;
  for, I protest, the schoolmaster is exceeding fantastical;
  too-too vain; too-too vain: but we will put it, as they say,
  to fortuna de la guerra. I wish you the peace of mind,
  most royal couplement!   *Exit*
KING. Here is like to be a good presence of Worthies. He
  presents Hector of Troy; the swain, Pompey the Great;
  the parish curate, Alexander; Armado's page, Hercules;
  the pedant, Judas Maccabæus:
  And if these four Worthies in their first show thrive,
  These four will change habits and present the other five.
BEROWNE. There is five in the first show.
KING. You are deceived, 'tis not so.
BEROWNE. The pedant, the braggart, the hedge-priest, the
  fool, and the boy:—
  Abate throw at novum, and the whole world again
  Cannot pick out five such, take each one in his vein.
KING. The ship is under sail, and here she comes amain.

Enter Costard armed, for Pompey

COSTARD. 'I Pompey am,'—
BOYET.   You lie, you are not he.
COSTARD. 'I Pompey am,'—
BOYET.   With libbard's head on knee.
BEROWNE. Well said, old mocker: I must needs be friends
  with thee.
COSTARD. 'I Pompey am, Pompey surnam'd the Big,'—
DUMAINE. 'The Great.'

COSTARD. It is 'Great,' sir; 'Pompey surnam'd the Great;
 That oft in field, with targe and shield, did make my foe
  to sweat:
 And travelling along this coast, I here am come by
  chance,
 And lay my arms before the legs of this sweet lass of
  France.'
If your ladyship would say, 'Thanks, Pompey,' I had done.
PRINCESS. Great thanks, great Pompey.
COSTARD. 'Tis not so much worth; but I hope I was perfect. I
 made a little fault in 'Great.'
BEROWNE. My hat to a halfpenny, Pompey proves the best
 Worthy.

   Enter Sir Nathaniel armed, for Alexander

NATHANIEL. 'When in the world I liv'd, I was the world's
 commander;
 By east, west, north, and south, I spread my conquering
  might:
 My scutcheon plain declares that I am Alisander,'—
BOYET. Your nose says, no, you are not; for it stands too
 right.
BEROWNE. Your nose smells 'no,' in this, most tender-smell-
 ing knight.
PRINCESS. The conqueror is dismay'd. Proceed, good Alex-
 ander.
NATHANIEL. 'When in the world I liv'd, I was the world's
 commander';—
BOYET. Most true; 'tis right: you were so, Alisander.
BEROWNE. Pompey the Great,—
COSTARD. Your servant, and Costard.
BEROWNE. Take away the conqueror, take away Alisander.
COSTARD. (*To Nathaniel*) O! sir, you have overthrown Alisander the conqueror! You will be scraped out of the
 painted cloth for this: your lion, that holds his poll-axe
 sitting on a close-stool, will be given to Ajax: he will be the
 ninth Worthy. A conqueror, and afeard to speak! run
 away for shame, Alisander! (*Nathaniel retires*) There, an
 't shall please you: a foolish mild man; an honest man,
 look you, and soon dashed! He is a marvellous good neighbour, faith, and a very good bowler; but, for Alisander,—
 alas, you see how 'tis,—a little o'erparted. But there are

Worthies a-coming will speak their mind in some other
sort.

PRINCESS. Stand aside, good Pompey.

Enter Holofernes armed,
for Judas; and Moth armed, for Hercules

HOLOFERNES. 'Great Hercules is presented by this imp,
 Whose club kill'd Cerberus, that three-headed canis;
And, when he was a babe, a child, a shrimp,
 Thus did he strangle serpents in his manus.
Quoniam, he seemeth in minority,
Ergo, I come with this apology.'
Keep some state in thy exit, and vanish.—   *Moth retires*
'Judas I am.'—

DUMAINE. A Judas!

HOLOFERNES. Not Iscariot, sir.

'Judas I am, ycleped Maccabæus.'

DUMAINE. Judas Maccabæus clipt is plain Judas.

BEROWNE. A kissing traitor. How art thou prov'd Judas?

HOLOFERNES. 'Judas I am.'—

DUMAINE. The more shame for you, Judas.

HOLOFERNES. What mean you, sir?

BOYET. To make Judas hang himself.

HOLOFERNES. Begin, sir; you are my elder.

BEROWNE. Well follow'd: Judas was hanged on an elder.

HOLOFERNES. I will not be put out of countenance.

BEROWNE. Because thou hast no face.

HOLOFERNES. What is this?

BOYET. A cittern-head.

DUMAINE. The head of a bodkin.

BEROWNE. A death's face in a ring.

LONGAVILLE. The face of an old Roman coin, scarce seen.

BOYET. The pommel of Cæsar's falchion.

DUMAINE. The carved-bone face on a flask.

BEROWNE. Saint George's half-cheek in a brooch.

DUMAINE. Ay, and in a brooch of lead.

BEROWNE. Ay, and worn in the cap of a tooth-drawer.
 And now forward; for we have put thee in countenance.

HOLOFERNES. You have put me out of countenance.

BEROWNE. False: we have given thee faces.

HOLOFERNES. But you have outfaced them all.

BEROWNE. An thou wert a lion, we would do so.

BOYET. Therefore, as he is an ass, let him go.

And so adieu, sweet Jude! nay, why dost thou stay?

DUMAINE. For the latter end of his name.

BEROWNE. For the ass to the Jude? give it him:—Judas,
away!

HOLOFERNES. This is not generous, not gentle, not humble.

BOYET. A light for Monsieur Judas! it grows dark, he may
stumble.

PRINCESS. Alas! poor Maccabæus, how hath he been baited.

Enter Armado armed, for Hector

BEROWNE. Hide thy head, Achilles: here comes Hector in
arms.

DUMAINE. Though my mocks come home by me, I will now
be merry.

KING. Hector was but a Troyan in respect of this.

BOYET. But is this Hector?

KING. I think Hector was not so clean-timbered.

LONGAVILLE. His calf is too big for Hector.

DUMAINE. More calf, certain.

BOYET. No; he is best indued in the small.

BEROWNE. This cannot be Hector.

DUMAINE. He's a god or a painter; for he makes faces.

ARMADO. 'The armipotent Mars, of lances the almighty,
    Gave Hector a gift,'—

DUMAINE. A gilt nutmeg.

BEROWNE. A lemon.

LONGAVILLE. Stuck with cloves.

DUMAINE. No, cloven.

ARMADO. Peace!
    'The armipotent Mars, of lances the almighty,
        Gave Hector a gift, the heir of Ilion;
    A man so breath'd, that certain he would fight ye
        From morn till night, out of his pavilion.
    I am that flower,'—

DUMAINE.   That mint.

LONGAVILLE.   That columbine.

ARMADO. Sweet Lord Longaville, rein thy tongue.

LONGAVILLE. I must rather give it the rein, for it runs against
Hector.

DUMAINE. Ay, and Hector's a greyhound.

ARMADO. The sweet war-man is dead and rotten; sweet
chucks, beat not the bones of the buried; when he
breathed, he was a man. But I will forward with my de-

vice. (*To the Princess*) Sweet royalty, bestow on me the
sense of hearing.

PRINCESS. Speak, brave Hector; we are much delighted.

ARMADO. I do adore thy sweet Grace's slipper.

BOYET. (*Aside to Dumaine*) Loves her by the foot.

DUMAINE. (*Aside to Boyet*) He may not by the yard.

ARMADO. 'This Hector far surmounted Hannibal,'—

COSTARD. The party is gone; fellow Hector, she is gone; she
is two months on her way.

ARMADO. What meanest thou?

COSTARD. Faith, unless you play the honest Troyan, the poor
wench is cast away: she 's quick; the child brags in her
belly already: 'tis yours.

ARMADO. Dost thou infamonize me among potentates? Thou
shalt die.

COSTARD. Then shall Hector be whipped for Jaquenetta that
is quick by him, and hanged for Pompey that is dead by
him.

DUMAINE. Most rare Pompey!

BOYET. Renowned Pompey!

BEROWNE. Greater than great, great, great, great Pompey!
Pompey the Huge!

DUMAINE. Hector trembles.

BEROWNE. Pompey is moved. More Ates, more Ates! stir
them on! stir them on!

DUMAINE. Hector will challenge him.

BEROWNE. Ay, if a' have no more man's blood in 's belly than
will sup a flea.

ARMADO. By the north pole, I do challenge thee.

COSTARD. I will not fight with a pole, like a northern man:
I 'll slash; I 'll do it by the sword. I bepray you, let me borrow my arms again.

DUMAINE. Room for the incensed Worthies!

COSTARD. I 'll do it in my shirt.

DUMAINE. Most resolute Pompey!

MOTH. Master, let me take you a button-hole lower. Do you
not see Pompey is uncasing for the combat? What mean
you? you will lose your reputation.

ARMADO. Gentlemen and soldiers, pardon me; I will not
combat in my shirt.

DUMAINE. You may not deny it; Pompey hath made the
challenge.

ARMADO. Sweet bloods, I both may and will.

BEROWNE. What reason have you for 't?

ARMADO. The naked truth of it is, I have no shirt. I go woolward for penance.

BOYET. True, and it was enjoined him in Rome for want of linen; since when, I 'll be sworn, he wore none but a dishclout of Jaquenetta's, and that a' wears next his heart for a favour.

Enter Monsieur Marcade, a Messenger

MARCADE. God save you, madam!

PRINCESS. Welcome, Marcade;
But that thou interrupt'st our merriment.

MARCADE. I am sorry, madam; for the news I bring
Is heavy in my tongue. The king your father—

PRINCESS. Dead, for my life!

MARCADE. Even so: my tale is told.

BEROWNE. Worthies, away! The scene begins to cloud.

ARMADO. For my own part, I breathe free breath. I have seen the day of wrong through the little hole of discretion, and I will right myself like a soldier.   *Exeunt Worthies*

KING. How fares your Majesty?

PRINCESS. Boyet, prepare: I will away to-night.

KING. Madam, not so: I do beseech you, stay.

PRINCESS. Prepare, I say. I thank you, gracious lords,
For all your fair endeavours; and entreat,
Out of a new-sad soul, that you vouchsafe
In your rich wisdom to excuse or hide
The liberal opposition of our spirits,
If over-boldly we have borne ourselves
In the converse of breath; your gentleness
Was guilty of it. Farewell, worthy lord!
A heavy heart bears not a nimble tongue,
Excuse me so, coming so short of thanks
For my great suit so easily obtain'd.

KING. The extreme part of time extremely forms
All causes to the purpose of his speed,
And often, at his very loose, decides
That which long process could not arbitrate:
And though the mourning brow of progeny
Forbid the smiling courtesy of love
The holy suit which fain it would convince;
Yet, since love's argument was first on foot,

Let not the cloud of sorrow justle it
From what it purpos'd; since, to wail friends lost
Is not by much so wholesome-profitable
As to rejoice at friends but newly found.

PRINCESS. I understand you not: my griefs are double.

BEROWNE. Honest plain words best pierce the ear of grief;
And by these badges understand the king.
For your fair sakes have we neglected time,
Play'd foul play with our oaths. Your beauty, ladies,
Hath much deform'd us, fashioning our humours
Even to the opposed end of our intents;
And what in us hath seem'd ridiculous,—
As love is full of unbefitting strains;
All wanton as a child, skipping and vain;
Form'd by the eye, and, therefore, like the eye,
Full of stray shapes, of habits and of forms,
Varying in subjects, as the eye doth roll
To every varied object in his glance:
Which parti-coated presence of loose love
Put on by us, if, in your heavenly eyes,
Have misbecome our oaths and gravities,
Those heavenly eyes, that look into these faults,
Suggested us to make. Therefore, ladies,
Our love being yours, the error that love makes
Is likewise yours: we to ourselves prove false,
By being once false for ever to be true
To those that make us both,—fair ladies, you:
And even that falsehood, in itself a sin,
Thus purifies itself and turns to grace.

PRINCESS. We have receiv'd your letters full of love;
Your favours, the embassadors of love;
And, in our maiden council, rated them
At courtship, pleasant jest, and courtesy,
As bombast and as lining to the time.
But more devout than this in our respects
Have we not been; and therefore met your loves
In their own fashion, like a merriment.

DUMAINE. Our letters, madam, show'd much more than jest.

LONGAVILLE. So did our looks.

ROSALINE.   We did not quote them so.

KING. Now, at the latest minute of the hour,
Grant us your loves.

PRINCESS. A time, methinks, too short
To make a world-without-end bargain in.
No, no, my lord, your Grace is perjur'd much,
Full of dear guiltiness; and therefore this:
If for my love,—as there is no such cause,—
You will do aught, this shall you do for me:
Your oath I will not trust; but go with speed
To some forlorn and naked hermitage,
Remote from all the pleasures of the world;
There stay, until the twelve celestial signs
Have brought about their annual reckoning.
If this austere insociable life
Change not your offer made in heat of blood;
If frosts and fasts, hard lodging and thin weeds,
Nip not the gaudy blossoms of your love,
But that it bear this trial and last love;
Then, at the expiration of the year,
Come challenge me, challenge me by these deserts,
And, by this virgin palm now kissing thine,
I will be thine; and, till that instant, shut
My woful self up in a mourning house,
Raining the tears of lamentation
For the remembrance of my father's death.
If this thou do deny, let our hands part;
Neither intitled in the other's heart.

KING. If this, or more than this, I would deny,
To flatter up these powers of mine with rest,
The sudden hand of death close up mine eye!
Hence ever then my heart is in thy breast.

BEROWNE. And what to me, my love? and what to me?

ROSALINE. You must be purged too, your sins are rack'd:
You are attaint with faults and perjury;
Therefore, if you my favour mean to get,
A twelvemonth shall you spend, and never rest,
But seek the weary beds of people sick.

DUMAINE. But what to me, my love? but what to me?

KATHARINE. A wife! A beard, fair health, and honesty;
With three-fold love I wish you all these three.

DUMAINE. O! shall I say, I thank you, gentle wife?

KATHARINE. Not so, my lord. A twelvemonth and a day
I 'll mark no words that smooth-fac'd wooers say:
Come when the king doth to my lady come;

Then, if I have much love, I 'll give you some.

DUMAINE. I 'll serve thee true and faithfully till then.

KATHARINE. Yet swear not, lest you be forsworn again.

LONGAVILLE. What says Maria?

MARIA.   At the twelvemonth's end
I 'll change my black gown for a faithful friend.

LONGAVILLE. I 'll stay with patience; but the time is long.

MARIA. The liker you; few taller are so young.

BEROWNE. Studies my lady? mistress, look on me.
Behold the window of my heart, mine eye,
What humble suit attends thy answer there;
Impose some service on me for thy love.

ROSALINE. Oft have I heard of you, my Lord Berowne,
Before I saw you, and the world's large tongue
Proclaims you for a man replete with mocks;
Full of comparisons and wounding flouts,
Which you on all estates will execute
That lie within the mercy of your wit:
To weed this wormwood from your fruitful brain,
And therewithal to win me, if you please,—
Without the which I am not to be won,—
You shall this twelvemonth term, from day to day,
Visit the speechless sick, and still converse
With groaning wretches; and your task shall be,
With all the fierce endeavour of your wit
To enforce the pained impotent to smile.

BEROWNE. To move wild laughter in the throat of death?
It cannot be; it is impossible:
Mirth cannot move a soul in agony.

ROSALINE. Why, that 's the way to choke a gibing spirit,
Whose influence is begot of that loose grace
Which shallow laughing hearers give to fools.
A jest's prosperity lies in the ear
Of him that hears it, never in the tongue
Of him that makes it: then, if sickly ears,
Deaf'd with the clamours of their own dear groans,
Will hear your idle scorns, continue them,
And I will have you and that fault withal;
But if they will not, throw away that spirit,
And I shall find you empty of that fault,
Right joyful of your reformation.

BEROWNE. A twelvemonth! well, befall what will befall,

I 'll jest a twelvemonth in a hospital.

PRINCESS. (*To the King*) Ay, sweet my lord; and so I take
    my leave.

KING. No, madam; we will bring you on your way.

BEROWNE. Our wooing doth not end like an old play;
    Jack hath not Jill; these ladies' courtesy
    Might well have made our sport a comedy.

KING. Come, sir, it wants a twelvemonth and a day,
    And then 'twill end.

BEROWNE.   That 's too long for a play.

Enter Armado

ARMADO. Sweet Majesty, vouchsafe me,—

PRINCESS. Was not that Hector?

DUMAINE. The worthy knight of Troy.

ARMADO. I will kiss thy royal finger, and take leave. I am a
    votary; I have vowed to Jaquenetta to hold the plough for
    her sweet love three years. But, most esteemed greatness,
    will you hear the dialogue that the two learned men have
    compiled in praise of the owl and the cuckoo? it should
    have followed in the end of our show.

KING. Call them forth quickly; we will do so.

ARMADO. Holla! approach.

Re-enter Holofernes,
Nathaniel, Moth, Costard, and others

This side is Hiems, Winter; this Ver, the Spring; the one
maintained by the owl, the other by the cuckoo. Ver, begin.

SPRING

I

When daisies pied and violets blue
    And lady-smocks all silver-white
And cuckoo-buds of yellow hue
    Do paint the meadows with delight,
The cuckoo then, on every tree,
Mocks married men; for thus sings he,
            Cuckoo;
Cuckoo, cuckoo: O, word of fear,
Unpleasing to a married ear!

II

When shepherds pipe on oaten straws,
    And merry larks are ploughmen's clocks,
When turtles tread, and rooks, and daws,
    And maidens bleach their summer smocks,
The cuckoo then, on every tree,
Mocks married men; for thus sings he,
                    Cuckoo;
Cuckoo, cuckoo: O, word of fear,
Unpleasing to a married ear!

WINTER

III

When icicles hang by the wall,
    And Dick the shepherd blows his nail,
And Tom bears logs into the hall,
    And milk comes frozen home in pail,
When blood is nipp'd, and ways be foul,
Then nightly sings the staring owl,
                    Tu-who;
Tu-whit, tu-who—a merry note,
While greasy Joan doth keel the pot.

IV

When all aloud the wind doth blow,
    And coughing drowns the parson's saw,
And birds sit brooding in the snow,
    And Marian's nose looks red and raw,
When roasted crabs hiss in the bowl,
Then nightly sings the staring owl,
                    Tu-who;
Tu-whit, tu-who—a merry note,
While greasy Joan doth keel the pot.

ARMADO. The words of Mercury are harsh after the songs of
    Apollo. You, that way: we, this way.   *Exeunt*

A MIDSUMMER-NIGHT'S DREAM

A MIDSUMMER-NIGHT'S

DREAM

CAST OF CHARACTERS

Theseus, Duke of Athens
Egeus, Father to Hermia
Lysander } in love with Hermia
Demetrius }
Philostrate, Master of the Revels to Theseus
Quince, a Carpenter
Snug, a Joiner
Bottom, a Weaver
Flute, a Bellows-mender
Snout, a Tinker
Starveling, a Tailor

Hippolyta, Queen of the Amazons, betrothed to Theseus
Hermia, Daughter to Egeus, in love with Lysander
Helena, in love with Demetrius

Oberon, King of the Fairies
Titania, Queen of the Fairies
Puck, or Robin Goodfellow
Peaseblossom }
Cobweb } Fairies
Moth }
Mustardseed }

Other Fairies attending their King and Queen
Attendants on Theseus and Hippolyta

SCENE
Athens, and a Wood near it

A MIDSUMMER-NIGHT'S DREAM

ACT ONE

SCENE ONE

Athens. The Palace of Theseus.

Enter Theseus, Hippolyta, Philostrate, and Attendants

THESEUS. Now, fair Hippolyta, our nuptial hour
Draws on apace: four happy days bring in
Another moon; but O! methinks how slow
This old moon wanes; she lingers my desires,
Like to a step-dame, or a dowager
Long withering out a young man's revenue.

HIPPOLYTA. Four days will quickly steep themselves in
night;
Four nights will quickly dream away the time;
And then the moon, like to a silver bow
New-bent in heaven, shall behold the night
Of our solemnities.

THESEUS.   Go, Philostrate,
Stir up the Athenian youth to merriments;
Awake the pert and nimble spirit of mirth;
Turn melancholy forth to funerals;
The pale companion is not for our pomp.   *Exit Philostrate*
Hippolyta, I woo'd thee with my sword,
And won thy love doing thee injuries;
But I will wed thee in another key,
With pomp, with triumph, and with revelling.

Enter Egeus, Hermia, Lysander, and Demetrius

EGEUS. Happy be Theseus, our renowned duke!

THESEUS. Thanks, good Egeus: what's the news with thee?

EGEUS. Full of vexation come I, with complaint

Against my child, my daughter Hermia.
Stand forth, Demetrius. My noble lord,
This man hath my consent to marry her.
Stand forth, Lysander: and, my gracious duke,
This man hath bewitch'd the bosom of my child:
Thou, thou, Lysander, thou hast given her rimes,
And interchang'd love-tokens with my child;
Thou hast by moonlight at her window sung,
With feigning voice, verses of feigning love;
And stol'n the impression of her fantasy
With bracelets of thy hair, rings, gawds, conceits,
Knacks, trifles, nosegays, sweetmeats, messengers
Of strong prevailment in unharden'd youth;
With cunning hast thou filch'd my daughter's heart;
Turn'd her obedience, which is due to me,
To stubborn harshness. And, my gracious duke,
Be it so she will not here before your Grace
Consent to marry with Demetrius,
I beg the ancient privilege of Athens,
As she is mine, I may dispose of her;
Which shall be either to this gentleman,
Or to her death, according to our law
Immediately provided in that case.

THESEUS. What say you, Hermia? Be advis'd, fair maid.
To you, your father should be as a god;
One that compos'd your beauties, yea, and one
To whom you are but as a form in wax
By him imprinted, and within his power
To leave the figure or disfigure it.
Demetrius is a worthy gentleman.

HERMIA. So is Lysander.

THESEUS.   In himself he is;
But, in this kind, wanting your father's voice,
The other must be held the worthier.

HERMIA. I would my father look'd but with my eyes.

THESEUS. Rather your eyes must with his judgment look.

HERMIA. I do entreat your Grace to pardon me.
I know not by what power I am made bold,
Nor how it may concern my modesty
In such a presence here to plead my thoughts;
But I beseech your Grace, that I may know
The worst that may befall me in this case,

If I refuse to wed Demetrius.

THESEUS. Either to die the death, or to abjure
Forever the society of men.
Therefore, fair Hermia, question your desires;
Know of your youth, examine well your blood,
Whether, if you yield not to your father's choice,
You can endure the livery of a nun,
For aye to be in shady cloister mew'd,
To live a barren sister all your life,
Chanting faint hymns to the cold fruitless moon.
Thrice blessed they that master so their blood,
To undergo such maiden pilgrimage;
But earthlier happy is the rose distill'd,
Than that which withering on the virgin thorn
Grows, lives, and dies, in single blessedness.

HERMIA. So will I grow, so live, so die, my lord,
Ere I will yield my virgin patent up
Unto his lordship, whose unwished yoke
My soul consents not to give sovereignty.

THESEUS. Take time to pause; and, by the next new moon,—
The sealing-day betwixt my love and me
For everlasting bond of fellowship,—
Upon that day either prepare to die
For disobedience to your father's will,
Or else to wed Demetrius, as he would;
Or on Diana's altar to protest
For aye austerity and single life.

DEMETRIUS. Relent, sweet Hermia; and, Lysander, yield
Thy crazed title to my certain right.

LYSANDER. You have her father's love, Demetrius;
Let me have Hermia's: do you marry him.

EGEUS. Scornful Lysander! true, he hath my love,
And what is mine my love shall render him;
And she is mine, and all my right of her
I do estate unto Demetrius.

LYSANDER. I am, my lord, as well deriv'd as he,
As well possess'd; my love is more than his;
My fortunes every way as fairly rank'd
If not with vantage, as Demetrius';
And, which is more than all these boasts can be,
I am belov'd of beauteous Hermia.
Why should not I then prosecute my right?

Demetrius, I 'll avouch it to his head,
Made love to Nedar's daughter, Helena.
And won her soul; and she, sweet lady, dotes,
Devoutly dotes, dotes in idolatry,
Upon this spotted and inconstant man.

THESEUS. I must confess that I have heard so much,
And with Demetrius thought to have spoke thereof;
But, being over-full of self-affairs,
My mind did lose it. But, Demetrius, come;
And come, Egeus; you shall go with me,
I have some private schooling for you both.
For you, fair Hermia, look you arm yourself
To fit your fancies to your father's will,
Or else the law of Athens yields you up,
Which by no means we may extenuate,
To death, or to a vow of single life.
Come, my Hippolyta: what cheer, my love?
Demetrius and Egeus, go along:
I must employ you in some business
Against our nuptial, and confer with you
Of something nearly that concerns yourselves.

EGEUS. With duty and desire we follow you.

Exeunt Theseus,
Hippolyta, Egeus, Demetrius, and Train

LYSANDER. How now, my love! Why is your cheek so pale?
How chance the roses there do fade so fast?

HERMIA. Belike for want of rain, which I could well
Beteem them from the tempest of mine eyes.

LYSANDER. Ay me! for aught that ever I could read,
Could ever hear by tale or history,
The course of true love never did run smooth;
But, either it was different in blood,—

HERMIA. O cross! too high to be enthrall'd to low.

LYSANDER. Or else misgraffed in respect of years,—

HERMIA. O spite! too old to be engag'd to young.

LYSANDER. Or else it stood upon the choice of friends,—

HERMIA. O hell! to choose love by another's eye.

LYSANDER. Or, if there were a sympathy in choice,
War, death, or sickness did lay siege to it,
Making it momentany as a sound,
Swift as a shadow, short as any dream,
Brief as the lightning in the collied night,

That, in a spleen, unfolds both heaven and earth,
And ere a man hath power to say, 'Behold!'
The jaws of darkness do devour it up:
So quick bright things come to confusion.

HERMIA. If then true lovers have been ever cross'd,
It stands as an edict in destiny:
Then let us teach our trial patience,
Because it is a customary cross,
As due to love as thoughts and dreams and sighs,
Wishes and tears, poor fancy's followers.

LYSANDER. A good persuasion: therefore, hear me, Hermia.
I have a widow aunt, a dowager
Of great revenue, and she hath no child:
From Athens is her house remote seven leagues;
And she respects me as her only son.
There, gentle Hermia, may I marry thee,
And to that place the sharp Athenian law
Cannot pursue us. If thou lov'st me then,
Steal forth thy father's house to-morrow night,
And in the wood, a league without the town,
Where I did meet thee once with Helena,
To do observance to a morn of May,
There will I stay for thee.

HERMIA.   My good Lysander!
I swear to thee by Cupid's strongest bow,
By his best arrow with the golden head,
By the simplicity of Venus' doves,
By that which knitteth souls and prospers loves,
And by that fire which burn'd the Carthage queen,
When the false Troyan under sail was seen,
By all the vows that ever men have broke,—
In number more than ever women spoke,—
In that same place thou hast appointed me,
To-morrow truly will I meet with thee.

LYSANDER. Keep promise, love. Look, here comes Helena.
                    Enter Helena

HERMIA. God speed fair Helena! Whither away?

HELENA. Call you me fair? That fair again unsay.
Demetrius loves your fair: O happy fair!
Your eyes are lode-stars! and your tongue's sweet air
More tuneable than lark to shepherd's ear,
When wheat is green, when hawthorn buds appear.

Sickness is catching: O! were favour so,
Yours would I catch, fair Hermia, ere I go;
My ear should catch your voice, my eye your eye,
My tongue should catch your tongue's sweet melody.
Were the world mine, Demetrius being bated,
The rest I'd give to be to you translated.
O! teach me how you look, and with what art
You sway the motion of Demetrius' heart.

HERMIA. I frown upon him, yet he loves me still.

HELENA. O! that your frowns would teach my smiles such
skill.

HERMIA. I give him curses, yet he gives me love.

HELENA. O! that my prayers could such affection move.

HERMIA. The more I hate, the more he follows me.

HELENA. The more I love, the more he hateth me.

HERMIA. His folly, Helena, is no fault of mine.

HELENA. None, but your beauty: would that fault were
mine!

HERMIA. Take comfort: he no more shall see my face;
Lysander and myself will fly this place.
Before the time I did Lysander see,
Seem'd Athens as a paradise to me:
O! then, what graces in my love do dwell,
That he hath turn'd a heaven unto a hell.

LYSANDER. Helen, to you our minds we will unfold.
To-morrow night, when Phœbe doth behold
Her silver visage in the watery glass,
Decking with liquid pearl the bladed grass,—
A time that lovers' flights doth still conceal,—
Through Athens' gates have we devis'd to steal.

HERMIA. And in the wood, where often you and I
Upon faint primrose-beds were wont to lie,
Emptying our bosoms of their counsel sweet,
There my Lysander and myself shall meet;
And thence from Athens turn away our eyes,
To seek new friends and stranger companies.
Farewell, sweet playfellow: pray thou for us;
And good luck grant thee thy Demetrius!
Keep word, Lysander: we must starve our sight
From lovers' food till morrow deep midnight.

LYSANDER. I will, my Hermia.—(*Exit Hermia*) Helena,
adieu:

As you on him, Demetrius dote on you!   *Exit*

HELENA. How happy some o'er other some can be!
　　Through Athens I am thought as fair as she;
　　But what of that? Demetrius thinks not so;
　　He will not know what all but he do know;
　　And as he errs, doting on Hermia's eyes,
　　So I, admiring of his qualities.
　　Things base and vile, holding no quantity,
　　Love can transpose to form and dignity.
　　Love looks not with the eyes, but with the mind,
　　And therefore is wing'd Cupid painted blind.
　　Nor hath Love's mind of any judgment taste;
　　Wings and no eyes figure unheedy haste:
　　And therefore is Love said to be a child,
　　Because in choice he is so oft beguil'd.
　　As waggish boys in game themselves forswear,
　　So the boy Love is perjur'd every where;
　　For ere Demetrius look'd on Hermia's eyne,
　　He hail'd down oaths that he was only mine;
　　And when this hail some heat from Hermia felt,
　　So he dissolv'd, and showers of oaths did melt.
　　I will go tell him of fair Hermia's flight:
　　Then to the wood will he to-morrow night
　　Pursue her; and for this intelligence
　　If I have thanks, it is a dear expense:
　　But herein mean I to enrich my pain,
　　To have his sight thither and back again.   *Exit*

SCENE TWO

The Same. A Room in Quince's House.

*Enter Quince, Snug, Bottom, Flute, Snout,
and Starveling*

QUINCE. Is all our company here?

BOTTOM. You were best to call them generally, man by man,
　　according to the scrip.

QUINCE. Here is the scroll of every man's name, which is
　　thought fit, through all Athens, to play in our interlude be-
　　fore the duke and the duchess on his wedding-day at
　　night.

BOTTOM. First, good Peter Quince, say what the play treats on; then read the names of the actors, and so grow to a point.

QUINCE. Marry, our play is, The most lamentable comedy, and most cruel death of Pyramus and Thisby.

BOTTOM. A very good piece of work, I assure you, and a merry. Now, good Peter Quince, call forth your actors by the scroll. Masters, spread yourselves.

QUINCE. Answer as I call you. Nick Bottom, the weaver.

BOTTOM. Ready. Name what part I am for, and proceed.

QUINCE. You, Nick Bottom, are set down for Pyramus.

BOTTOM. What is Pyramus? a lover, or a tyrant?

QUINCE. A lover, that kills himself most gallantly for love.

BOTTOM. That will ask some tears in the true performing of it: if I do it, let the audience look to their eyes; I will move storms, I will condole in some measure. To the rest: yet my chief humour is for a tyrant. I could play Ercles rarely, or a part to tear a cat in, to make all split.

> The raging rocks
> And shivering shocks
> Shall break the locks
>   Of prison gates:
> And Phibbus' car
> Shall shine from far
> And make and mar
>   The foolish Fates.

This was lofty! Now name the rest of the players. This is Ercles' vein, a tyrant's vein; a lover is more condoling.

QUINCE. Francis Flute, the bellows-mender.

FLUTE. Here, Peter Quince.

QUINCE. You must take Thisby on you.

FLUTE. What is Thisby? a wandering knight?

QUINCE. It is the lady that Pyramus must love.

FLUTE. Nay, faith, let not me play a woman; I have a beard coming.

QUINCE. That 's all one: you shall play it in a mask, and you may speak as small as you will.

BOTTOM. An I may hide my face, let me play Thisby too. I 'll speak in a monstrous little voice, 'Thisne, Thisne!' 'Ah, Pyramus, my lover dear; thy Thisby dear, and lady dear!'

QUINCE. No, no; you must play Pyramus; and Flute, you Thisby.

BOTTOM. Well, proceed.

QUINCE. Robin Starveling, the tailor.

STARVELING. Here, Peter Quince.

QUINCE. Robin Starveling, you must play Thisby's mother. Tom Snout, the tinker.

SNOUT. Here, Peter Quince.

QUINCE. You, Pyramus's father; myself, Thisby's father; Snug, the joiner, you the lion's part: and, I hope, here is a play fitted.

SNUG. Have you the lion's part written? pray you, if it be, give it me, for I am slow of study.

QUINCE. You may do it extempore, for it is nothing but roaring.

BOTTOM. Let me play the lion too. I will roar, that I will do any man's heart good to hear me; I will roar, that I will make the duke say, 'Let him roar again, let him roar again.'

QUINCE. An you should do it too terribly, you would fright the duchess and the ladies, that they would shriek; and that were enough to hang us all.

ALL. That would hang us, every mother's son.

BOTTOM. I grant you, friends, if that you should fright the ladies out of their wits, they would have no more discretion but to hang us; but I will aggravate my voice so that I will roar you as gently as any sucking dove; I will roar you as 'twere any nightingale.

QUINCE. You can play no part but Pyramus; for Pyramus is a sweet-faced man; a proper man, as one shall see in a summer's day; a most lovely, gentleman-like man; therefore, you must needs play Pyramus.

BOTTOM. Well, I will undertake it. What beard were I best to play it in?

QUINCE. Why, what you will.

BOTTOM. I will discharge it in either your straw-colour beard, your orange-tawny beard, your purple-ingrain beard, or your French-crown colour beard, your perfect yellow.

QUINCE. Some of your French crowns have no hair at all, and then you will play bare-faced. But masters, here are your parts; and I am to entreat you, request you, and desire you, to con them by to-morrow night, and meet me in the palace wood, a mile without the town, by moonlight:

there will we rehearse; for if we meet in the city, we shall be dogged with company, and our devices known. In the meantime I will draw a bill of properties, such as our play wants. I pray you, fail me not.

BOTTOM. We will meet; and there we may rehearse more obscenely and courageously. Take pains; be perfect; adieu.

QUINCE. At the duke's oak we meet.

BOTTOM. Enough; hold, or cut bow-strings.   *Exeunt*

ACT TWO

SCENE ONE

A Wood near Athens.

Enter a Fairy on one side, and Puck on the other

PUCK. How now, spirit! whither wander you?

FAIRY. Over hill, over dale,
　　　Thorough bush, thorough brier,
　　Over park, over pale,
　　　Thorough flood, thorough fire,
　　I do wander every where,
　　Swifter than the moone's sphere;
　　And I serve the fairy queen,
　　To dew her orbs upon the green:
　　The cowslips tall her pensioners be;
　　In their gold coats spots you see;
　　Those be rubies, fairy favours,
　　In those freckles live their savours:
　I must go seek some dew-drops here,
　And hang a pearl in every cowslip's ear.
　Farewell, thou lob of spirits: I 'll be gone;
　Our queen and all her elves come here anon.

PUCK. The king doth keep his revels here to-night:
　Take heed the queen come not within his sight;
　For Oberon is passing fell and wrath,
　Because that she as her attendant hath
　A lovely boy, stol'n from an Indian king;
　She never had so sweet a changeling;
　And jealous Oberon would have the child
　Knight of his train, to trace the forests wild;
　But she, perforce, withholds the loved boy,
　Crowns him with flowers, and makes him all her joy.
　And now they never meet in grove, or green,
　By fountain clear, or spangled starlight sheen,

But they do square; that all their elves, for fear,
Creep into acorn-cups and hide them there.

FAIRY. Either I mistake your shape and making quite,
Or else you are that shrewd and knavish sprite
Call'd Robin Goodfellow: are you not he
That frights the maidens of the villagery;
Skim milk, and sometimes labour in the quern,
And bootless make the breathless housewife churn;
And sometime make the drink to bear no barm;
Mislead night-wanderers, laughing at their harm?
Those that Hobgoblin call you and sweet Puck,
You do their work, and they shall have good luck:
Are you not he?

PUCK.   Fairy, thou speak'st aright;
I am that merry wanderer of the night.
I jest to Oberon, and make him smile
When I a fat and bean-fed horse beguile,
Neighing in likeness of a filly foal:
And sometime lurk I in a gossip's bowl,
In very likeness of a roasted crab;
And, when she drinks, against her lips I bob
And on her wither'd dewlap pour the ale.
The wisest aunt, telling the saddest tale,
Sometime for three-foot stool mistaketh me;
Then slip I from her bum, down topples she,
And 'tailor' cries, and falls into a cough;
And then the whole quire hold their hips and loff;
And waxen in their mirth, and neeze, and swear
A merrier hour was never wasted there.
But, room, fairy! here comes Oberon.

FAIRY. And here my mistress. Would that he were gone!

*Enter Oberon from one side,
with his Train; and Titania from the other, with hers*

OBERON. Ill met by moonlight, proud Titania.

TITANIA. What! jealous Oberon. Fairies, skip hence:
I have forsworn his bed and company.

OBERON. Tarry, rash wanton! am not I thy lord?

TITANIA. Then, I must be thy lady; but I know
When thou hast stol'n away from fairy land,
And in the shape of Corin sat all day,
Playing on pipes of corn, and versing love
To amorous Phillida. Why art thou here,

Come from the furthest steppe of India?
But that, forsooth, the bouncing Amazon,
Your buskin'd mistress and your warrior love,
To Theseus must be wedded, and you come
To give their bed joy and prosperity.

OBERON. How canst thou thus for shame, Titania,
Glance at my credit with Hippolyta,
Knowing I know thy love to Theseus?
Didst thou not lead him through the glimmering night
From Perigouna, whom he ravished?
And make him with fair Ægle break his faith,
With Ariadne, and Antiopa?

TITANIA. These are the forgeries of jealousy:
And never, since the middle summer's spring,
Met we on hill, in dale, forest, or mead,
By paved fountain, or by rushy brook,
Or in the beached margent of the sea,
To dance our ringlets to the whistling wind,
But with thy brawls thou hast disturb'd our sport.
Therefore the winds, piping to us in vain,
As in revenge, have suck'd up from the sea
Contagious fogs; which, falling in the land,
Have every pelting river made so proud
That they have overborne their continents:
The ox hath therefore stretch'd his yoke in vain,
The ploughman lost his sweat, and the green corn
Hath rotted ere his youth attain'd a beard:
The fold stands empty in the drowned field,
And crows are fatted with the murrion flock;
The nine men's morris is fill'd up with mud,
And the quaint mazes in the wanton green
For lack of tread are undistinguishable:
The human mortals want their winter here:
No night is now with hymn or carol blest:
Therefore the moon, the governess of floods,
Pale in her anger, washes all the air,
That rheumatic diseases do abound:
And thorough this distemperature we see
The seasons alter: hoary-headed frosts
Fall in the fresh lap of the crimson rose,
And on old Hiems' thin and icy crown
An odorous chaplet of sweet summer buds

Is, as in mockery, set. The spring, the summer,
The childing autumn, angry winter, change
Their wonted liveries, and the mazed world,
By their increase, now knows not which is which.
And this same progeny of evil comes
From our debate, from our dissension:
We are their parents and original.

OBERON. Do you amend it then; it lies in you.
Why should Titania cross her Oberon?
I do but beg a little changeling boy,
To be my henchman.

TITANIA.   Set your heart at rest;
The fairy land buys not the child of me.
His mother was a votaress of my order:
And, in the spiced Indian air, by night,
Full often hath she gossip'd by my side,
And sat with me on Neptune's yellow sands,
Marking the embarked traders on the flood;
When we have laugh'd to see the sails conceive
And grow big-bellied with the wanton wind;
Which she, with pretty and with swimming gait
Following,—her womb then rich with my young squire,—
Would imitate, and sail upon the land,
To fetch me trifles, and return again,
As from a voyage, rich with merchandise.
But she, being mortal, of that boy did die;
And for her sake I do rear up her boy,
And for her sake I will not part with him.

OBERON. How long within this wood intend you stay?

TITANIA. Perchance, till after Theseus' wedding-day.
If you will patiently dance in our round,
And see our moonlight revels, go with us;
If not, shun me, and I will spare your haunts.

OBERON. Give me that boy, and I will go with thee.

TITANIA. Not for thy fairy kingdom. Fairies, away!
We shall chide downright, if I longer stay.

                                        Exit Titania with her Train

OBERON. Well, go thy way: thou shalt not from this grove
Till I torment thee for this injury.
My gentle Puck, come hither. Thou remember'st
Since once I sat upon a promontory,
And heard a mermaid on a dolphin's back

Uttering such dulcet and harmonious breath,
That the rude sea grew civil at her song,
And certain stars shot madly from their spheres
To hear the sea-maid's music.

PUCK.   I remember.

OBERON. That very time I saw, but thou couldst not,
  Flying between the cold moon and the earth,
  Cupid all arm'd: a certain aim he took
  At a fair vestal throned by the west,
  And loos'd his love-shaft smartly from his bow,
  As it should pierce a hundred thousand hearts;
  But I might see young Cupid's fiery shaft
  Quench'd in the chaste beams of the watery moon,
  And the imperial votaress passed on,
  In maiden-meditation, fancy-free.
  Yet mark'd I where the bolt of Cupid fell:
  It fell upon a little western flower,
  Before milk-white, now purple with love's wound,
  And maidens call it, Love-in-idleness.
  Fetch me that flower; the herb I show'd thee once:
  The juice of it on sleeping eyelids laid
  Will make or man or woman madly dote
  Upon the next live creature that it sees.
  Fetch me this herb; and be thou here again
  Ere the leviathan can swim a league.

PUCK. I 'll put a girdle round about the earth
  In forty minutes.   *Exit*

OBERON.   Having once this juice
  I 'll watch Titania when she is asleep,
  And drop the liquor of it in her eyes:
· The next thing then she waking looks upon,
  Be it on lion, bear, or wolf, or bull,
  On meddling monkey, or on busy ape,
  She shall pursue it with the soul of love:
  And ere I take this charm off from her sight,
  As I can take it with another herb,
  I 'll make her render up her page to me.
  But who comes here? I am invisible,
  And I will overhear their conference.

          Enter Demetrius, Helena following him

DEMETRIUS. I love thee not, therefore pursue me not.
  Where is Lysander and fair Hermia?

The one I 'll slay, the other slayeth me.
Thou told'st me they were stol'n into this wood;
And here am I, and wood within this wood,
Because I cannot meet my Hermia.
Hence! get thee gone, and follow me no more.

HELENA. You draw me, you hard-hearted adamant:
But yet you draw not iron, for my heart
Is true as steel: leave you your power to draw,
And I shall have no power to follow you.

DEMETRIUS. Do I entice you? Do I speak you fair?
Or, rather, do I not in plainest truth
Tell you I do not nor I cannot love you?

HELENA. And even for that do I love you the more.
I am your spaniel; and, Demetrius,
The more you beat me, I will fawn on you:
Use me but as your spaniel, spurn me, strike me,
Neglect me, lose me; only give me leave,
Unworthy as I am, to follow you.
What worser place can I beg in your love,
And yet a place of high respect with me,
Than to be used as you use your dog?

DEMETRIUS. Tempt not too much the hatred of my spirit,
For I am sick when I do look on you.

HELENA. And I am sick when I look not on you.

DEMETRIUS. You do impeach your modesty too much,
To leave the city, and commit yourself
Into the hands of one that loves you not;
To trust the opportunity of night
And the ill counsel of a desert place
With the rich worth of your virginity.

HELENA. Your virtue is my privilege: for that
It is not night when I do see your face,
Therefore I think I am not in the night;
Nor doth this wood lack worlds of company,
For you in my respect are all the world:
Then how can it be said I am alone,
When all the world is here to look on me?

DEMETRIUS. I 'll run from thee and hide me in the brakes,
And leave thee to the mercy of wild beasts.

HELENA. The wildest hath not such a heart as you.
Run when you will, the story shall be chang'd;
Apollo flies, and Daphne holds the chase;

The dove pursues the griffin; the mild hind
Makes speed to catch the tiger: bootless speed,
When cowardice pursues and valour flies.

DEMETRIUS. I will not stay thy questions: let me go;
Or, if thou follow me, do not believe
But I shall do thee mischief in the wood.

HELENA. Ay, in the temple, in the town, the field,
You do me mischief. Fie, Demetrius!
Your wrongs do set a scandal on my sex.
We cannot fight for love, as men may do;
We should be woo'd and were not made to woo.

Exit Demetrius

I 'll follow thee and make a heaven of hell,
To die upon the hand I love so well.   *Exit*

OBERON. Fare thee well, nymph: ere he do leave this grove,
Thou shalt fly him, and he shall seek thy love.

Re-enter Puck

Hast thou the flower there? Welcome, wanderer.

PUCK. Ay, there it is.

OBERON.   I pray thee, give it me.
I know a bank whereon the wild thyme blows,
Where oxlips and the nodding violet grows
Quite over-canopied with luscious woodbine,
With sweet musk-roses, and with eglantine:
There sleeps Titania some time of the night,
Lull'd in these flowers with dances and delight;
And there the snake throws her enamell'd skin,
Weed wide enough to wrap a fairy in:
And with the juice of this I 'll streak her eyes,
And make her full of hateful fantasies.
Take thou some of it, and seek through this grove:
A sweet Athenian lady is in love
With a disdainful youth: anoint his eyes;
But do it when the next thing he espies
May be the lady. Thou shalt know the man
By the Athenian garments he hath on.
Effect it with some care, that he may prove
More fond on her than she upon her love.
And look thou meet me ere the first cock crow.

PUCK. Fear not, my lord, your servant shall do so.   *Exeunt*

SCENE TWO

Another Part of the Wood.

Enter Titania, with her Train

TITANIA. Come, now a roundel and a fairy song;
Then, for the third part of a minute, hence;
Some to kill cankers in the musk-rose buds,
Some war with rere-mice for their leathern wings,
To make my small elves coats, and some keep back
The clamorous owl, that nightly hoots, and wonders
At our quaint spirits. Sing me now asleep;
Then to your offices, and let me rest.

The Fairies sing

I.

You spotted snakes with double tongue,
    Thorny hedge-hogs, be not seen;
Newts, and blind-worms, do no wrong;
    Come not near our fairy queen.
        Philomel, with melody,
        Sing in our sweet lullaby;
Lulla, lulla, lullaby; lulla, lulla, lullaby:
        Never harm,
        Nor spell, nor charm,
    Come our lovely lady nigh;
So, good night, with lullaby.

II.

Weaving spiders come not here;
    Hence, you long-legg'd spinners, hence!
Beetles, black, approach not near;
    Worm nor snail, do no offence.

        Philomel, with melody, &c.

FAIRY. Hence, away! now all is well.
    One aloof stand sentinel.

Exeunt Fairies. Titania sleeps
Enter Oberon, and squeezes the flower on Titania's eyelids

OBERON. What thou seest when thou dost wake
   Do it for thy true-love take;
   Love and languish for his sake:
   Be it ounce, or cat, or bear,
   Pard, or boar with bristled hair,
   In thy eye that shall appear
   When thou wak'st, it is thy dear.
   Wake when some vile thing is near.   *Exit*

       Enter Lysander and Hermia

LYSANDER. Fair love, you faint with wandering in the wood;
   And to speak troth, I have forgot our way:
   We 'll rest us, Hermia, if you think it good,
   And tarry for the comfort of the day.
HERMIA. Be it so, Lysander: find you out a bed,
   For I upon this bank will rest my head.
LYSANDER. One turf shall serve as pillow for us both;
   One heart, one bed, two bosoms, and one troth.
HERMIA. Nay, good Lysander; for my sake, my dear,
   Lie further off yet, do not lie so near.
LYSANDER. O! take the sense, sweet, of my innocence,
   Love takes the meaning in love's conference.
   I mean that my heart unto yours is knit,
   So that but one heart we can make of it;
   Two bosoms interchained with an oath;
   So then two bosoms and a single troth.
   Then by your side no bed-room me deny,
   For, lying so, Hermia, I do not lie.
HERMIA. Lysander riddles very prettily:
   Now much beshrew my manners and my pride,
   If Hermia meant to say Lysander lied.
   But, gentle friend, for love and courtesy
   Lie further off; in human modesty,
   Such separation as may well be said
   Becomes a virtuous bachelor and a maid,
   So far be distant; and, good-night, sweet friend.
   Thy love ne'er alter till thy sweet life end!
LYSANDER. Amen, amen, to that fair prayer, say I;
   And then end life when I end loyalty!
       Retires a little distance
   Here is my bed: sleep give thee all his rest!
HERMIA. With half that wish the wisher's eyes be press'd!
       They sleep

Enter Puck

PUCK.   Through the forest have I gone,
           But Athenian found I none,
           On whose eyes I might approve
           This flower's force in stirring love.
           Night and silence! who is here?
           Weeds of Athens he doth wear:
           This is he, my master said,
           Despised the Athenian maid;
           And here the maiden, sleeping sound,
           On the dank and dirty ground.
           Pretty soul! she durst not lie
           Near this lack-love, this kill-courtesy.

                    Squeezes the flower on Lysander's eyelids

           Churl, upon thy eyes I throw
           All the power this charm doth owe.
           When thou wak'st, let love forbid
           Sleep his seat on thy eyelid:
           So awake when I am gone;
           For I must now to Oberon.   *Exit*

           Enter Demetrius and Helena, running

HELENA.   Stay, though thou kill me, sweet Demetrius.
DEMETRIUS. I charge thee, hence, and do not haunt me thus.
HELENA.   O! wilt thou darkling leave me? do not so.
DEMETRIUS. Stay, on thy peril: I alone will go.

                                    Exit Demetrius

HELENA.   O! I am out of breath in this fond chase.
           The more my prayer, the lesser is my grace.
           Happy is Hermia, wheresoe'er she lies;
           For she hath blessed and attractive eyes.
           How came her eyes so bright? Not with salt tears:
           If so, my eyes are oftener wash'd than hers.
           No, no, I am as ugly as a bear;
           For beasts that meet me run away for fear;
           Therefore no marvel though Demetrius
           Do, as a monster, fly my presence thus.
           What wicked and dissembling glass of mine
           Made me compare with Hermia's sphery eyne?
           But who is here? Lysander! on the ground!
           Dead? or asleep? I see no blood, no wound.
           Lysander, if you live, good sir, awake.
LYSANDER. (*Awaking*) And run through fire I will for thy
           sweet sake.

Transparent Helena! Nature shows art,
That through thy bosom makes me see thy heart.
Where is Demetrius? O! how fit a word
Is that vile name to perish on my sword.

HELENA. Do not say so, Lysander; say not so.
What though he love your Hermia? Lord! what though?
Yet Hermia still loves you: then be content.

LYSANDER. Content with Hermia! No: I do repent
The tedious minutes I with her have spent.
Not Hermia, but Helena I love:
Who will not change a raven for a dove?
The will of man is by his reason sway'd,
And reason says you are the worthier maid.
Things growing are not ripe until their season;
So I, being young, till now ripe not to reason;
And touching now the point of human skill,
Reason becomes the marshal to my will,
And leads me to your eyes; where I o'erlook
Love's stories written in love's richest book.

HELENA. Wherefore was I to this keen mockery born?
When at your hands did I deserve this scorn?
Is 't not enough, is 't not enough, young man,
That I did never, no, nor never can,
Deserve a sweet look from Demetrius' eye,
But you must flout my insufficiency?
Good troth, you do me wrong, good sooth, you do,
In such disdainful manner me to woo.
But fare you well: perforce I must confess
I thought you lord of more true gentleness.
O! that a lady of one man refus'd,
Should of another therefore be abus'd.   *Exit*

LYSANDER. She sees not Hermia. Hermia, sleep thou there;
And never mayst thou come Lysander near.
For, as a surfeit of the sweetest things
The deepest loathing to the stomach brings;
Or, as the heresies that men do leave
Are hated most of those they did deceive:
So thou, my surfeit and my heresy,
Of all be hated, but the most of me!
And, all my powers, address your love and might
To honour Helen, and to be her knight.   *Exit*

HERMIA. (*Awaking*) Help me, Lysander, help me! do thy
best

To pluck this crawling serpent from my breast.
Ay me, for pity! what a dream was here!
Lysander, look how I do quake with fear:
Methought a serpent eat my heart away,
And you sat smiling at his cruel prey.
Lysander! what! remov'd?—Lysander! lord!
What! out of hearing? gone? no sound, no word?
Alack! where are you? speak, an if you hear;
Speak, of all loves! I swound almost with fear.
No! then I well perceive you are not nigh:
Either death or you I 'll find immediately.   *Exit*

ACT THREE

SCENE ONE

A Wood. Titania lying asleep.

*Enter Quince, Snug, Bottom, Flute, Snout,
and Starveling*

BOTTOM. Are we all met?

QUINCE. Pat, pat; and here 's a marvellous convenient place
for our rehearsal. This green plot shall be our stage, this
hawthorn-brake our tiring-house; and we will do it in action as we will do it before the duke.

BOTTOM. Peter Quince,—

QUINCE. What sayst thou, bully Bottom?

BOTTOM. There are things in this comedy of Pyramus and
Thisby that will never please. First, Pyramus must draw
a sword to kill himself, which the ladies cannot abide.
How answer you that?

SNOUT. By 'r lakin, a parlous fear.

STARVELING. I believe we must leave the killing out, when
all is done.

BOTTOM. Not a whit: I have a device to make all well.
Write me a prologue; and let the prologue seem to say,
we will do no harm with our swords, and that Pyramus is
not killed indeed; and, for the more better assurance, tell
them that I, Pyramus, am not Pyramus, but Bottom the
weaver: this will put them out of fear.

QUINCE. Well, we will have such a prologue, and it shall be
written in eight and six.

BOTTOM. No, make it two more: let it be written in eight
and eight.

SNOUT. Will not the ladies be afeard of the lion?

STARVELING. I fear it, I promise you.

BOTTOM. Masters, you ought to consider with yourselves:
to bring in,—God shield us!—a lion among ladies, is a

most dreadful thing; for there is not a more fearful wild-fowl than your lion living, and we ought to look to it.

SNOUT. Therefore, another prologue must tell he is not a lion.

BOTTOM. Nay, you must name his name, and half his face must be seen through the lion's neck; and he himself must speak through, saying thus, or to the same defect, 'Ladies,' or 'Fair ladies,' 'I would wish you,' or, 'I would request you,' or, 'I would entreat you, not to fear, not to tremble: my life for yours. If you think I come hither as a lion, it were pity of my life: no, I am no such thing: I am a man as other men are': and there indeed let him name his name, and tell them plainly he is Snug the joiner.

QUINCE. Well, it shall be so. But there is two hard things, that is, to bring the moonlight into a chamber; for, you know, Pyramus and Thisby meet by moonlight.

SNUG. Doth the moon shine that night we play our play?

BOTTOM. A calendar, a calendar! look in the almanack; find out moonshine, find out moonshine.

QUINCE. Yes, it doth shine that night.

BOTTOM. Why, then may you leave a casement of the great chamber-window, where we play, open; and the moon may shine in at the casement.

QUINCE. Ay; or else one must come in with a bush of thorns and a lanthorn, and say he comes to disfigure, or to present, the person of Moonshine. Then, there is another thing: we must have a wall in the great chamber; for Pyramus and Thisby, says the story, did talk through the chink of a wall.

SNUG. You can never bring in a wall. What say you, Bottom?

BOTTOM. Some man or other must present Wall; and let him have some plaster, or some loam, or some rough-cast about him, to signify wall; and let him hold his fingers thus, and through that cranny shall Pyramus and Thisby whisper.

QUINCE. If that may be, then all is well. Come, sit down, every mother's son, and rehearse your parts. Pyramus, you begin: when you have spoken your speech, enter into that brake; and so every one according to his cue.

Enter Puck behind

PUCK. What hempen homespuns have we swaggering here,
So near the cradle of the fairy queen?
What! a play toward! I'll be an auditor;
An actor too perhaps, if I see cause.

QUINCE. Speak, Pyramus.—Thisby, stand forth.

BOTTOM. 'Thisby, the flowers have odious savours sweet'—

QUINCE. Odorous, odorous.

BOTTOM.—'odours savours sweet:

So hath thy breath, my dearest Thisby dear.

But hark, a voice! stay thou but here awhile,

And by and by I will to thee appear.'   *Exit*

PUCK. A stranger Pyramus than e'er play'd here!   *Exit*

FLUTE. Must I speak now?

QUINCE. Ay, marry, must you; for you must understand, he goes but to see a noise that he heard, and is to come again.

FLUTE. 'Most radiant Pyramus, most lily-white of hue,

Of colour like the red rose on triumphant brier,

Most brisky juvenal, and eke most lovely Jew,

As true as truest horse that yet would never tire,

I 'll meet thee, Pyramus, at Ninny's tomb.'

QUINCE. 'Ninus' tomb,' man. Why, you must not speak that yet; that you answer to Pyramus: you speak all your part at once, cues and all. Pyramus, enter: your cue is past; it is 'never tire.'

FLUTE. O!—'As true as truest horse, that yet would never tire.'

Re-enter Puck, and Bottom with an ass's head

BOTTOM. 'If I were fair, Thisby, I were only thine.'

QUINCE. O monstrous! O strange! we are haunted.

Pray, masters! fly, masters!—Help!   *Exeunt Clowns*

PUCK. I 'll follow you, I 'll lead you about a round,

Through bog, through bush, through brake, through brier:

Sometimes a horse I 'll be, sometime a hound,

A hog, a headless bear, sometime a fire;

And neigh, and bark, and grunt, and roar, and burn.

Like horse, hound, hog, bear, fire, at every turn.   *Exit*

BOTTOM. Why do they run away? this is a knavery of them to make me afeard.

Re-enter Snout

SNOUT. O Bottom, thou art changed! what do I see on thee?

BOTTOM. What do you see? you see an ass-head of your own, do you?   *Exit Snout*

Re-enter Quince

QUINCE. Bless thee, Bottom! bless thee! thou art translated.   *Exit*

BOTTOM. I see their knavery: this is to make an ass of me;
to fright me, if they could. But I will not stir from this
place, do what they can: I will walk up and down here,
and I will sing, that they shall hear I am not afraid.
(*Sings*)

> The ousel-cock, so black of hue,
> > With orange-tawny bill,
> The throstle with his note so true,
> > The wren with little quill.

TITANIA. (*Awaking*.) What angel wakes me from my flowery bed?

BOTTOM. (*Sings*) The finch, the sparrow, and the lark,
> > The plain-song cuckoo gray,
> Whose note full many a man doth mark,
> > And dares not answer, nay.

For indeed, who would set his wit to so foolish a bird?
Who would give a bird the lie, though he cry 'cuckoo'
never so?

TITANIA. I pray thee, gentle mortal, sing again:
Mine ear is much enamour'd of thy note;
So is mine eye enthralled to thy shape;
And thy fair virtue's force, perforce, doth move me,
On the first view, to say, to swear, I love thee.

BOTTOM. Methinks, mistress, you should have little reason
for that: and yet, to say the truth, reason and love keep
little company together now-a-days. The more the pity,
that some honest neighbours will not make them friends.
Nay, I can gleek upon occasion.

TITANIA. Thou art as wise as thou art beautiful.

BOTTOM. Not so, neither; but if I had wit enough to get out
of this wood, I have enough to serve mine own turn.

TITANIA. Out of this wood do not desire to go:
Thou shalt remain here, whe'r thou wilt or no.
I am a spirit of no common rate;
The summer still doth tend upon my state;
And I do love thee: therefore, go with me;
I'll give thee fairies to attend on thee,
And they shall fetch thee jewels from the deep,
And sing, while thou on pressed flowers dost sleep:
And I will purge thy mortal grossness so
That thou shalt like an airy spirit go.
Pease-blossom! Cobweb! Moth! and Mustard-seed!

Enter Four Fairies

PEASE-BLOSSOM. Ready.

COBWEB.   And I.

MUSTARD-SEED.   And I.

ALL FOUR.   Where shall we go?

TITANIA. Be kind and courteous to this gentleman;
  Hop in his walks, and gambol in his eyes;
  Feed him with apricocks and dewberries,
  With purple grapes, green figs, and mulberries.
  The honey-bags steal from the humble-bees,
  And for night-tapers crop their waxen thighs,
  And light them at the fiery glow-worm's eyes,
  To have my love to bed, and to arise;
  And pluck the wings from painted butterflies
  To fan the moonbeams from his sleeping eyes:
  Nod to him, elves, and do him courtesies.

PEASE-BLOSSOM. Hail, mortal!

COBWEB. Hail!

MOTH. Hail!

MUSTARD-SEED. Hail!

BOTTOM. I cry your worships mercy, heartily: I beseech
  your worship's name.

COBWEB. Cobweb.

BOTTOM. I shall desire you of more acquaintance, good
  Master Cobweb: if I cut my finger, I shall make bold
  with you. Your name, honest gentleman?

PEASE-BLOSSOM. Pease-blossom.

BOTTOM. I pray you, commend me to Mistress Squash, your
  mother, and to Master Peascod, your father. Good Master Pease-blossom, I shall desire you of more acquaintance too. Your name, I beseech you, sir?

MUSTARD-SEED. Mustard-seed.

BOTTOM. Good Master Mustard-seed, I know your patience
  well: that same cowardly, giant-like ox-beef hath de-
  voured many a gentleman of your house. I promise you,
  your kindred hath made my eyes water ere now. I desire
  you of more acquaintance, good Master Mustard-seed.

TITANIA. Come, wait upon him: lead him to my bower.
  The moon methinks, looks with a watery eye;
  And when she weeps, weeps every little flower,
  Lamenting some enforced chastity.
  Tie up my love's tongue, bring him silently.   *Exeunt*

SCENE TWO

Another Part of the Wood.

Enter Oberon

OBERON. I wonder if Titania be awak'd;
Then, what it was that next came in her eye,
Which she must dote on in extremity.
Here comes my messenger.

Enter Puck

How now, mad spirit!
What night-rule now about this haunted grove?

PUCK. My mistress with a monster is in love.
Near to her close and consecrated bower,
While she was in her dull and sleeping hour,
A crew of patches, rude mechanicals,
That work for bread upon Athenian stalls,
Were met together to rehearse a play
Intended for great Theseus' nuptial day.
The shallowest thick-skin of that barren sort,
Who Pyramus presented in their sport
Forsook his scene, and enter'd in a brake,
When I did him at this advantage take;
An ass's nowl I fixed on his head:
Anon his Thisby must be answered,
And forth my mimick comes. When they him spy,
As wild geese that the creeping fowler eye,
Or russet-pated choughs, many in sort,
Rising and cawing at the gun's report,
Sever themselves, and madly sweep the sky;
So, at his sight, away his fellows fly,
And, at our stamp, here o'er and o'er one falls;
He murder cries, and help from Athens calls.
Their sense thus weak, lost with their fears thus strong,
Made senseless things begin to do them wrong;
For briers and thorns at their apparel snatch;
Some sleeves, some hats, from yielders all things catch.
I led them on in this distracted fear,
And left sweet Pyramus translated there;

When in that moment, so it came to pass,
Titania wak'd and straightway lov'd an ass.

OBERON. This falls out better than I could devise.
But hast thou yet latch'd the Athenian's eyes
With the love-juice, as I did bid thee do?

PUCK. I took him sleeping,—that is finish'd too,—
And the Athenian woman by his side;
That, when he wak'd, of force she must be ey'd.

Enter Demetrius and Hermia

OBERON. Stand close: this is the same Athenian.

PUCK. This is the woman; but not this the man.

DEMETRIUS. O! why rebuke you him that loves you so?
Lay breath so bitter on your bitter foe.

HERMIA. Now I but chide; but I should use thee worse,
For thou, I fear, hast given me cause to curse.
If thou hast slain Lysander in his sleep,
Being o'er shoes in blood, plunge in knee deep,
And kill me too.
The sun was not so true unto the day
As he to me. Would he have stol'n away
From sleeping Hermia? I 'll believe as soon
This whole earth may be bor'd, and that the moon
May through the centre creep, and so displease
Her brother's noontide with the Antipodes.
It cannot be but thou hast murder'd him;
So should a murderer look, so dead, so grim.

DEMETRIUS. So should the murder'd look, and so should I,
Pierc'd through the heart with your stern cruelty;
Yet you, the murderer, look as bright, as clear,
As yonder Venus in her glimmering sphere.

HERMIA. What 's this to my Lysander? where is he?
Ah! good Demetrius, wilt thou give him me?

DEMETRIUS. I had rather give his carcass to my hounds.

HERMIA. Out, dog! out, cur! thou driv'st me past the bounds
Of maiden's patience. Hast thou slain him then?
Henceforth be never number'd among men!
O! once tell true, tell true, e'en for my sake;
Durst thou have look'd upon him being awake,
And hast thou kill'd him sleeping? O brave touch!
Could not a worm, an adder, do so much?
An adder did it; for with doubler tongue

Than thine, thou serpent, never adder stung.

DEMETRIUS. You spend your passion on a mispris'd mood:
I am not guilty of Lysander's blood,
Nor is he dead, for aught that I can tell.

HERMIA. I pray thee, tell me then that he is well.

DEMETRIUS. An if I could, what should I get therefore?

HERMIA. A privilege never to see me more.
And from thy hated presence part I so;
See me no more, whe'r he be dead or no.   *Exit*

DEMETRIUS. There is no following her in this fierce vein:
Here therefore for awhile I will remain.
So sorrow's heaviness doth heavier grow
For debt that bankrupt sleep doth sorrow owe
Which now in some slight measure it will pay,
If for his tender here I make some stay.

                              Lies down and sleeps

OBERON. What has thou done? thou hast mistaken quite,
And laid the love-juice on some true-love's sight:
Of thy misprision must perforce ensue
Some true-love turn'd, and not a false turn'd true.

PUCK. Then fate o'er-rules, that, one man holding troth,
A million fail, confounding oath on oath.

OBERON. About the wood go swifter than the wind,
And Helena of Athens look thou find:
All fancy-sick she is, and pale of cheer
With sighs of love, that cost the fresh blood dear.
By some illusion see thou bring her here:
I'll charm his eyes against she do appear.

PUCK. I go, I go; look how I go;
Swifter than arrow from the Tartar's bow.   *Exit*

OBERON.   Flower of this purple dye,
          Hit with Cupid's archery,
          Sink in apple of his eye.
          When his love he doth espy,
          Let her shine as gloriously
          As the Venus of the sky.
          When thou wak'st, if she be by,
          Beg of her for remedy.

                         Re-enter Puck

PUCK.   Captain of our fairy band,
          Helena is here at hand,
          And the youth, mistook by me,

Pleading for a lover's fee.
Shall we their fond pageant see?
Lord, what fools these mortals be!

OBERON. Stand aside: the noise they make
    Will cause Demetrius to awake.

PUCK. Then will two at once woo one;
    That must needs be sport alone;
    And those things do best please me
    That befall preposterously.

Enter Lysander and Helena

LYSANDER. Why should you think that I should woo in scorn?
  Scorn and derision never come in tears:
  Look, when I vow, I weep; and vows so born,
    In their nativity all truth appears.
  How can these things in me seem scorn to you,
  Bearing the badge of faith to prove them true?

HELENA. You do advance your cunning more and more.
    When truth kills truth, O devilish-holy fray!
  These vows are Hermia's: will you give her o'er?
    Weigh oath with oath, and you will nothing weigh:
  Your vows, to her and me, put in two scales,
  Will even weigh, and both as light as tales.

LYSANDER. I had no judgment when to her I swore.

HELENA. Nor none, in my mind, now you give her o'er.

LYSANDER. Demetrius loves her, and he loves not you.

DEMETRIUS. (*Awaking*) O Helen! goddess, nymph, perfect, divine!
  To what, my love, shall I compare thine eyne?
  Crystal is muddy. O! how ripe in show
  Thy lips, those kissing cherries, tempting grow;
  This pure congealed white, high Taurus' snow,
  Fann'd with the eastern wind, turns to a crow
  When thou hold'st up thy hand. O! let me kiss
  That princess of pure white, this seal of bliss.

HELENA. O spite! O hell! I see you all are bent
  To set against me for your merriment:
  If you were civil and knew courtesy,
  You would not do me thus much injury.
  Can you not hate me, as I know you do,
  But you must join in souls to mock me too?
  If you were men, as men you are in show,

You would not use a gentle lady so;
To vow, and swear, and superpraise my parts,
When I am sure you hate me with your hearts.
You both are rivals, and love Hermia,
And now both rivals, to mock Helena:
A trim exploit, a manly enterprise,
To conjure tears up in a poor maid's eyes
With your derision! none of noble sort
Would so offend a virgin, and extort
A poor soul's patience, all to make you sport.

LYSANDER. You are unkind, Demetrius; be not so;
For you love Hermia; this you know I know:
And here, with all good will, with all my heart,
In Hermia's love I yield you up my part;
And yours of Helena to me bequeath,
Whom I do love, and will do to my death.

HELENA. Never did mockers waste more idle breath.

DEMETRIUS. Lysander, keep thy Hermia; I will none:
If e'er I lov'd her, all that love is gone.
My heart with her but as guest-wise sojourn'd,
And now to Helen it is home return'd,
There to remain.

LYSANDER.   Helen, it is not so.

DEMETRIUS. Disparage not the faith thou dost not know,
Lest to thy peril thou aby it dear.
Look! where thy love comes: yonder is thy dear.

Re-enter Hermia

HERMIA. Dark night, that from the eye his function takes,
The ear more quick of apprehension makes;
Wherein it doth impair the seeing sense,
It pays the hearing double recompense.
Thou art not by mine eye, Lysander, found;
Mine ear, I thank it, brought me to thy sound.
But why unkindly didst thou leave me so?

LYSANDER. Why should he stay, whom love doth press to go?

HERMIA. What love could press Lysander from my side?

LYSANDER. Lysander's love, that would not let him bide,
Fair Helena, who more engilds the night
Than all yon fiery oes and eyes of light.
Why seek'st thou me? Could not this make thee know,
The hate I bear thee made me leave thee so?

HERMIA. You speak not as you think: it cannot be.

HELENA. Lo! she is one of this confederacy.
Now I perceive they have conjoin'd all three
To fashion this false sport in spite of me.
Injurious Hermia! most ungrateful maid!
Have you conspir'd, have you with these contriv'd
To bait me with this foul derision?
Is all the counsel that we two have shar'd,
The sister-vows, the hours that we have spent,
When we have chid the hasty-footed time
For parting us, O! is it all forgot?
All school-days' friendship, childhood innocence?
We, Hermia, like two artificial gods,
Have with our neelds created both one flower,
Both on one sampler, sitting on one cushion,
Both warbling of one song, both in one key,
As if our hands, our sides, voices, and minds,
Had been incorporate. So we grew together,
Like to a double cherry, seeming parted,
But yet an union in partition;
Two lovely berries moulded on one stem;
So, with two seeming bodies, but one heart;
Two of the first, like coats in heraldry,
Due but to one, and crowned with one crest.
And will you rent our ancient love asunder,
To join with men in scorning your poor friend?
It is not friendly, 'tis not maidenly:
Our sex, as well as I, may chide you for it,
Though I alone do feel the injury.

HERMIA. I am amazed at your passionate words.
I scorn you not: it seems that you scorn me.

HELENA. Have you not set Lysander, as in scorn,
To follow me and praise my eyes and face,
And made your other love, Demetrius,—
Who even but now did spurn me with his foot,—
To call me goddess, nymph, divine and rare,
Precious, celestial? Wherefore speaks he this
To her he hates? and wherefore doth Lysander
Deny your love, so rich within his soul,
And tender me, forsooth, affection,
But by your setting on, by your consent?
What though I be not so in grace as you,
So hung upon with love, so fortunate,

But miserable most to love unlov'd?

This you should pity rather than despise.

HERMIA. I understand not what you mean by this.

HELENA. Ay, do, persever, counterfeit sad looks,
Make mouths upon me when I turn my back;
Wink each at other; hold the sweet jest up:
This sport, well carried, shall be chronicled.
If you have any pity, grace, or manners,
You would not make me such an argument.
But, fare ye well: 'tis partly mine own fault,
Which death or absence soon shall remedy.

LYSANDER. Stay, gentle Helena! hear my excuse:
My love, my life, my soul, fair Helena!

HELENA. O excellent!

HERMIA.   Sweet, do not scorn her so.

DEMETRIUS. If she cannot entreat, I can compel.

LYSANDER. Thou canst compel no more than she entreat:
Thy threats have no more strength than her weak prayers.
Helen, I love thee; by my life, I do:
I swear by that which I will lose for thee,
To prove him false that says I love thee not.

DEMETRIUS. I say I love thee more than he can do.

LYSANDER. If thou say so, withdraw, and prove it too.

DEMETRIUS. Quick, come!

HERMIA.   Lysander, whereto tends all this?

LYSANDER. Away, you Ethiop!

DEMETRIUS.   No, no, sir! You
Seem to break loose; take on, as you would follow,
But yet come not: you are a tame man, go!

LYSANDER. (*To Hermia*) Hang off, thou cat, thou burr! vile
thing, let loose,
Or I will shake thee from me like a serpent.

HERMIA. Why are you grown so rude? what change is this,
Sweet love,—

LYSANDER.   Thy love! out, tawny Tartar, out!
Out, loathed medicine! hated poison, hence!

HERMIA. Do you not jest?

HELENA.   Yes, sooth; and so do you.

LYSANDER. Demetrius, I will keep my word with thee.

DEMETRIUS. I would I had your bond, for I perceive
A weak bond holds you: I'll not trust your word.

LYSANDER. What! should I hurt her, strike her, kill her dead?

Although I hate her, I 'll not harm her so.

HERMIA.   What! can you do me greater harm than hate?
  Hate me! wherefore? O me! what news, my love?
  Am not I Hermia? Are not you Lysander?
  I am as fair now as I was erewhile.
  Since night you lov'd me; yet, since night you left me:
  Why, then you left me,—O, the gods forbid!—
  In earnest, shall I say?

LYSANDER.   Ay, by my life;
  And never did desire to see thee more.
  Therefore be out of hope, of question, doubt;
  Be certain, nothing truer: 'tis no jest,
  That I do hate thee and love Helena.

HERMIA.   O me! you juggler! you canker-blossom!
  You thief of love! what! have you come by night
  And stol'n my love's heart from him?

HELENA.   Fine, i' faith!
  Have you no modesty, no maiden shame,
  No touch of bashfulness? What! will you tear
  Impatient answers from my gentle tongue?
  Fie, fie! you counterfeit, you puppet you!

HERMIA.   Puppet! why, so: ay, that way goes the game.
  Now I perceive that she hath made compare
  Between our statures: she hath urg'd her height;
  And with her personage, her tall personage,
  Her height, forsooth, she hath prevail'd with him.
  And are you grown so high in his esteem,
  Because I am so dwarfish and so low?
  How low am I, thou painted maypole? speak;
  How low am I? I am not yet so low
  But that my nails can reach unto thine eyes.

HELENA.   I pray you, though you mock me, gentlemen,
  Let her not hurt me: I was never curst;
  I have no gift at all in shrewishness;
  I am a right maid for my cowardice:
  Let her not strike me. You perhaps may think,
  Because she is something lower than myself,
  That I can match her.

HERMIA.   Lower! hark, again.

HELENA.   Good Hermia, do not be so bitter with me.
  I evermore did love you, Hermia,
  Did ever keep your counsels, never wrong'd you;

Save that, in love unto Demetrius,
I told him of your stealth unto this wood.
He follow'd you; for love I follow'd him;
But he hath chid me hence, and threaten'd me
To strike me, spurn me, nay, to kill me too:
And now, so you will let me quiet go,
To Athens will I bear my folly back,
And follow you no further: let me go:
You see how simple and how fond I am.

HERMIA. Why, get you gone. Who is 't that hinders you?
HELENA. A foolish heart, that I leave here behind.
HERMIA. What! with Lysander?
HELENA.   With Demetrius.
LYSANDER. Be not afraid: she shall not harm thee, Helena.
DEMETRIUS. No, sir; she shall not, though you take her part.
HELENA. O! when she 's angry, she is keen and shrewd.
  She was a vixen when she went to school:
  And though she be but little, she is fierce.
HERMIA. 'Little' again! nothing but 'low' and 'little'!
  Why will you suffer her to flout me thus?
  Let me come to her.
LYSANDER.   Get you gone, you dwarf;
  You minimus, of hindering knot-grass made;
  You bead, you acorn!
DEMETRIUS.   You are too officious
  In her behalf that scorns your services.
  Let her alone; speak not of Helena;
  Take not her part, for, if thou dost intend
  Never so little show of love to her,
  Thou shalt aby it.
LYSANDER.   Now she holds me not;
  Now follow, if thou dar'st, to try whose right,
  Or thine or mine, is most in Helena.
DEMETRIUS. Follow! nay, I 'll go with thee, cheek by jowl.
                    Exeunt Lysander and Demetrius
HERMIA. You, mistress, all this coil is 'long of you:
  Nay, go not back.
HELENA.   I will not trust you, I,
  Nor longer stay in your curst company.
  Your hands than mine are quicker for a fray,
  My legs are longer though, to run away.   *Exit*
HERMIA. I am amaz'd, and know not what to say.   *Exit*

OBERON. This is thy negligence: still thou mistak'st,
  Or else commit'st thy knaveries wilfully.
PUCK. Believe me, king of shadows, I mistook.
  Did not you tell me I should know the man
  By the Athenian garments he had on?
  And so far blameless proves my enterprise,
  That I have 'nointed an Athenian's eyes;
  And so far am I glad it so did sort,
  As this their jangling I esteem a sport.
OBERON. Thou see'st these lovers seek a place to fight:
  Hie therefore, Robin, overcast the night;
  The starry welkin cover thou anon
  With drooping fog as black as Acheron;
  And lead these testy rivals so astray,
  As one come not within another's way.
  Like to Lysander sometime frame thy tongue,
  Then stir Demetrius up with bitter wrong;
  And sometime rail thou like Demetrius;
  And from each other look thou lead them thus,
  Till o'er their brows death-counterfeiting sleep
  With leaden legs and batty wings doth creep:
  Then crush this herb into Lysander's eye;
  Whose liquor hath this virtuous property,
  To take from thence all error with his might,
  And make his eyeballs roll with wonted sight.
  When they next wake, all this derision
  Shall seem a dream and fruitless vision;
  And back to Athens shall the lovers wend,
  With league whose date till death shall never end
  Whiles I in this affair do thee employ,
  I 'll to my queen and beg her Indian boy;
  And then I will her charmed eye release
  From monster's view, and all things shall be peace.
PUCK. My fairy lord, this must be done with haste,
  For night's swift dragons cut the clouds full fast,
  And yonder shines Aurora's harbinger;
  At whose approach, ghosts, wandering here and there,
  Troop home to churchyards: damned spirits all,
  That in cross-ways and floods have burial,
  Already to their wormy beds are gone;
  For fear lest day should look their shames upon,
  They wilfully themselves exile from light,

And must for aye consort with black-brow'd night.   420]

OBERON. But we are spirits of another sort.

I with the morning's love have oft made sport;
And, like a forester, the groves may tread,
Even till the eastern gate, all fiery-red,
Opening on Neptune with fair blessed beams,
Turns into yellow gold his salt green streams.
But, notwithstanding, haste; make no delay:
We may effect this business yet ere day.   *Exit Oberon*

PUCK.   Up and down, up and down;
          I will lead them up and down:
          I am fear'd in field and town;
          Goblin, lead them up and down.
Here comes one.

Re-enter Lysander

LYSANDER. Where art thou, proud Demetrius? speak thou
now.

PUCK. Here, villain! drawn and ready. Where art thou?

LYSANDER. I will be with thee straight.

PUCK.   Follow me, then,
To plainer ground. *Exit Lysander, as following the voice*
              Re-enter Demetrius

DEMETRIUS.   Lysander! speak again.
Thou runaway, thou coward, art thou fled?
Speak! In some bush? Where dost thou hide thy head?

PUCK. Thou coward! art thou bragging to the stars,
Telling the bushes that thou look'st for wars,
And wilt not come? Come, recreant; come, thou child;
I 'll whip thee with a rod: he is defil'd
That draws a sword on thee.

DEMETRIUS.   Yea, art thou there?

PUCK. Follow my voice: we 'll try no manhood here. *Exeunt*
              Re-enter Lysander

LYSANDER. He goes before me and still dares me on:
When I come where he calls, then he is gone.
The villain is much lighter-heel'd than I:
I follow'd fast, but faster he did fly;
That fallen am I in dark uneven way,
And here will rest me. (*Lies down*) Come, thou gentle
day!
For if but once thou show me thy grey light,
I 'll find Demetrius and revenge this spite.   *Sleeps*

Re-enter Puck and Demetrius

PUCK. Ho! ho! ho! Coward, why com'st thou not?

DEMETRIUS. Abide me, if thou dar'st; for well I wot
   Thou runn'st before me, shifting every place,
   And dar'st not stand, nor look me in the face.
   Where art thou now?

PUCK.   Come hither: I am here.

DEMETRIUS. Nay then, thou mock'st me. Thou shalt buy
      this dear,
   If ever I thy face by daylight see:
   Now, go thy way. Faintness constraineth me
   To measure out my length on this cold bed:
   By day's approach look to be visited.
                              Lies down and sleeps
               Re-enter Helena

HELENA. O weary night! O long and tedious night,
   Abate thy hours! shine, comforts, from the east!
   That I may back to Athens by daylight,
      From these that my poor company detest:
   And sleep, that sometimes shuts up sorrow's eye,
   Steal me awhile from mine own company.
                              Lies down and sleeps

PUCK.   Yet but three? Come one more;
            Two of both kinds make up four.
            Here she comes, curst and sad:
            Cupid is a knavish lad,
            Thus to make poor females mad.
               Re-enter Hermia

HERMIA. Never so weary, never so in woe,
   Bedabbled with the dew and torn with briers,
   I can no further crawl, no further go;
      My legs can keep no pace with my desires.
   Here will I rest me till the break of day.
   Heavens shield Lysander, if they mean a fray!
                              Lies down and sleeps

PUCK.   On the ground
         Sleep sound:
         I 'll apply
         To your eye,
Gentle lover, remedy.

         Squeezing the juice on Lysander's eyes
         When thou wak'st,
         Thou tak'st
         True delight
         In the sight
Of thy former lady's eye:
And the country proverb known,
That every man should take his own,
In your waking shall be shown:
         Jack shall have Jill;
         Nought shall go ill;
The man shall have his mare again,
And all shall be well.   *Exit*

ACT FOUR

SCENE ONE

A Wood. Lysander,
Demetrius, Helena, and Hermia lying asleep.

Enter Titania and Bottom, Fairies attending;
Oberon behind unseen

TITANIA. Come, sit thee down upon this flowery bed,
   While I thy amiable cheeks do coy,
And stick musk-roses in thy sleek smooth head,
   And kiss thy fair large ears, my gentle joy.

BOTTOM. Where 's Pease-blossom?

PEASE-BLOSSOM. Ready.

BOTTOM. Scratch my head, Pease-blossom. Where 's Mounsieur Cobweb?

COBWEB. Ready.

BOTTOM. Mounsieur Cobweb, good mounsieur, get your
   weapons in your hand, and kill me a red-hipped humble-
   bee on the top of a thistle; and, good mounsieur, bring me
   the honey-bag. Do not fret yourself too much in the action, mounsieur; and, good mounsieur, have a care the
   honey-bag break not; I would be loath to have you over-
   flown with a honey-bag, signior. Where's Mounsieur Mustard-seed?

MUSTARD-SEED. Ready.

BOTTOM. Give me your neaf, Mounsieur Mustard-seed. Pray
   you, leave your curtsy, good mounsieur.

MUSTARD-SEED. What 's your will?

BOTTOM. Nothing, good mounsieur, but to help Cavalery
   Cobweb to scratch. I must to the barber's, mounsieur, for
   methinks I am marvellous hairy about the face; and I am
   such a tender ass, if my hair do but tickle me, I must
   scratch.

TITANIA. What, wilt thou hear some music, my sweet love?

BOTTOM. I have a reasonable good ear in music: let us have
   the tongs and the bones.

TITANIA. Or say, sweet love, what thou desir'st to eat.

BOTTOM. Truly, a peck of provender: I could munch your
good dry oats. Methinks I have a great desire to a bottle
of hay: good hay, sweet hay, hath no fellow.

TITANIA. I have a venturous fairy that shall seek
The squirrel's hoard, and fetch thee thence new nuts.

BOTTOM. I had rather have a handful or two of dried pease.
But, I pray you, let none of your people stir me: I have
an exposition of sleep come upon me.

TITANIA. Sleep thou, and I will wind thee in my arms.
Fairies, be gone, and be all ways away.   *Exeunt Fairies*
So doth the woodbine the sweet honeysuckle
Gently entwist; the female ivy so
Enrings the barky fingers of the elm.
O! how I love thee; how I dote on thee!   *They sleep*

Enter Puck

OBERON. (*Advancing*) Welcome, good Robin. See'st thou
this sweet sight?
Her dotage now I do begin to pity:
For, meeting her of late behind the wood,
Seeking sweet favours for this hateful fool,
I did upbraid her and fall out with her;
For she his hairy temples then had rounded
With coronet of fresh and fragrant flowers;
And that same dew, which sometime on the buds
Was wont to swell like round and orient pearls,
Stood now within the pretty flowerets' eyes
Like tears that did their own disgrace bewail.
When I had at my pleasure taunted her,
And she in mild terms begg'd my patience,
I then did ask of her her changeling child;
Which straight she gave me, and her fairy sent
To bear him to my bower in fairy land.
And now I have the boy, I will undo
This hateful imperfection of her eyes:
And, gentle Puck, take this transformed scalp
From off the head of this Athenian swain,
That he, awaking when the other do,
May all to Athens back again repair,
And think no more of this night's accidents
But as the fierce vexation of a dream.
But first I will release the fairy queen.
Touching her eyes with an herb

            Be as thou wast wont to be;
            See as thou wast wont to see:
            Dian's bud o'er Cupid's flower
            Hath such force and blessed power.
    Now, my Titania; wake you, my sweet queen.

TITANIA. My Oberon! what visions have I seen!
    Methought I was enamour'd of an ass.

OBERON. There lies your love.

TITANIA.   How came these things to pass?
    O! how mine eyes do loathe his visage now.

OBERON. Silence, awhile. Robin, take off this head.
    Titania, music call; and strike more dead
    Than common sleep of all these five the sense.

TITANIA. Music, ho! music! such as charmeth sleep.   *Music*

PUCK. When thou wak'st, with thine own fool's eyes peep.

OBERON. Sound, music! (*Still, music*) Come, my queen,
      take hands with me,
    And rock the ground whereon these sleepers be.   *Dance*
    Now thou and I are new in amity,
    And will to-morrow midnight solemnly
    Dance in Duke Theseus' house triumphantly,
    And bless it to all fair prosperity.
    There shall the pairs of faithful lovers be
    Wedded, with Theseus, all in jollity.

PUCK.   Fairy king, attend, and mark:
          I do hear the morning lark.

OBERON. Then, my queen, in silence sad,
          Trip we after the night's shade;
          We the globe can compass soon,
          Swifter than the wandering moon.

TITANIA. Come, my lord; and in our flight
          Tell me how it came this night
          That I sleeping here was found
          With these mortals on the ground.
               Exeunt. Horns winded within
     Enter Theseus, Hippolyta, Egeus, and Train

THESEUS. Go, one of you, find out the forester;
    For now our observation is perform'd;
    And since we have the vaward of the day,
    My love shall hear the music of my hounds.
    Uncouple in the western valley; let them go:
    Dispatch, I say, and find the forester.
    We will, fair queen, up to the mountain's top,

And mark the musical confusion
Of hounds and echo in conjunction.

HIPPOLYTA. I was with Hercules and Cadmus once,
When in a wood of Crete they bay'd the bear
With hounds of Sparta: never did I hear
Such gallant chiding; for, besides the groves,
The skies, the fountains, every region near
Seem'd all one mutual cry. I never heard
So musical a discord, such sweet thunder.

THESEUS. My hounds are bred out of the Spartan kind,
So flew'd, so sanded; and their heads are hung
With ears that sweep away the morning dew;
Crook-knee'd, and dew-lapp'd like Thessalian bulls;
Slow in pursuit, but match'd in mouth like bells,
Each under each. A cry more tuneable
Was never holla'd to, nor cheer'd with horn,
In Crete, in Sparta, nor in Thessaly:
Judge, when you hear. But, soft! what nymphs are these?

EGEUS. My lord, this is my daughter here asleep;
And this, Lysander; this Demetrius is;
This Helena, old Nedar's Helena:
I wonder of their being here together.

THESEUS. No doubt they rose up early to observe
The rite of May, and, hearing our intent,
Came here in grace of our solemnity.
But speak, Egeus, is not this the day
That Hermia should give answer of her choice?

EGEUS. It is, my lord.

THESEUS. Go, bid the huntsmen wake them with their horns.
                    Horns and shout within. Lysander,
            Demetrius, Hermia, and Helena, wake and start up
Good-morrow, friends. Saint Valentine is past:
Begin these wood-birds but to couple now?

LYSANDER. Pardon, my lord.   *He and the rest kneel*

THESEUS.   I pray you all, stand up.
I know you two are rival enemies:
How comes this gentle concord in the world,
That hatred is so far from jealousy,
To sleep by hate, and fear no enmity?

LYSANDER. My lord, I shall reply amazedly,
Half sleep, half waking: but as yet, I swear,
I cannot truly say how I came here;
But, as I think,—for truly would I speak,

And now I do bethink me, so it is,—
I came with Hermia hither: our intent
Was to be gone from Athens, where we might,
Without the peril of the Athenian law—

EGEUS. Enough, enough, my lord! you have enough:
I beg the law, the law, upon his head.
They would have stol'n away; they would, Demetrius,
Thereby to have defeated you and me;
You of your wife, and me of my consent,
Of my consent that she should be your wife.

DEMETRIUS. My lord, fair Helen told me of their stealth,
Of this their purpose hither, to this wood;
And I in fury hither follow'd them,
Fair Helena in fancy following me.
But, my good lord, I wot not by what power,—
But by some power it is,—my love to Hermia,
Melted as doth the snow, seems to me now
As the remembrance of an idle gaud
Which in my childhood I did dote upon;
And all the faith, the virtue of my heart,
The object and the pleasure of mine eye,
Is only Helena. To her, my lord,
Was I betroth'd ere I saw Hermia:
But, like in sickness, did I loathe this food;
But, as in health, come to my natural taste,
Now do I wish it, love it, long for it,
And will for evermore be true to it.

THESEUS. Fair lovers, you are fortunately met:
Of this discourse we more will hear anon.
Egeus, I will overbear your will,
For in the temple, by and by, with us,
These couples shall eternally be knit:
And, for the morning now is something worn,
Our purpos'd hunting shall be set aside.
Away with us, to Athens: three and three,
We'll hold a feast in great solemnity.
Come, Hippolyta.

                    Exeunt Theseus, Hippolyta, Egeus, and Train

DEMETRIUS. These things seem small and undistinguishable,
Like far-off mountains turned into clouds.

HERMIA. Methinks I see these things with parted eye,
When everything seems double.

HELENA.   So methinks:

And I have found Demetrius, like a jewel,
Mine own, and not mine own.

DEMETRIUS.   Are you sure
That we are awake? It seems to me
That yet we sleep, we dream. Do you not think
The duke was here, and bid us follow him?

HERMIA. Yea; and my father.

HELENA.   And Hippolyta.

LYSANDER. And he did bid us follow to the temple.

DEMETRIUS. Why then, we are awake. Let's follow him;
And by the way let us recount our dreams.   *Exeunt*

BOTTOM. (*Awaking*) When my cue comes, call me, and I
will answer: my next is, 'Most fair Pyramus.' Heigh-ho!
Peter Quince! Flute, the bellows-mender! Snout, the
tinker! Starveling! God's my life! Stolen hence, and left
me asleep! I have had a most rare vision. I have had a
dream, past the wit of man to say what dream it was: man
is but an ass, if he go about to expound this dream. Methought I was—there is no man can tell what. Methought I
was,—and methought I had,—but man is but a patched
fool, if he will offer to say what methought I had. The eye
of man hath not heard, the ear of man hath not seen, man's
hand is not able to taste, his tongue to conceive, nor his
heart to report, what my dream was. I will get Peter
Quince to write a ballad of this dream; it shall be called
Bottom's Dream, because it hath no bottom; and I will
sing it in the latter end of a play, before the duke: peradventure, to make it the more gracious, I shall sing it at her
death.   *Exit*

SCENE TWO

Athens. A Room in Quince's House.

Enter Quince, Flute, Snout, and Starveling

QUINCE. Have you sent to Bottom's house? is he come home
yet?

STARVELING. He cannot be heard of. Out of doubt he is
transported.

FLUTE. If he come not, then the play is marred: it goes not
forward, doth it?

QUINCE. It is not possible: you have not a man in all Athens
able to discharge Pyramus but he.

FLUTE. No; he hath simply the best wit of any handicraft
man in Athens.

QUINCE. Yea, and the best person too; and he is a very paramour for a sweet voice.

FLUTE. You must say, 'paragon': a paramour is, God bless
us! a thing of naught.

Enter Snug

SNUG. Masters, the duke is coming from the temple, and
there is two or three lords and ladies more married: if our
sport had gone forward, we had all been made men.

FLUTE. O sweet bully Bottom! Thus hath he lost sixpence a
day during his life; he could not have 'scaped sixpence a
day: an the duke had not given him sixpence a day for
playing Pyramus, I 'll be hanged; he would have deserved
it: sixpence a day in Pyramus, or nothing.

Enter Bottom

BOTTOM. Where are these lads? where are these hearts?

QUINCE. Bottom! O most courageous day! O most happy
hour!

BOTTOM. Masters, I am to discourse wonders: but ask me
not what; for if I tell you, I am no true Athenian. I will tell
you everything, right as it fell out.

QUINCE. Let us hear, sweet Bottom.

BOTTOM. Not a word of me. All that I will tell you is, that
the duke hath dined. Get your apparel together, good
strings to your beards, new ribbons to your pumps; meet
presently at the palace; every man look o'er his part; for
the short and the long is, our play is preferred. In any case,
let Thisby have clean linen; and let not him that plays the
lion pare his nails, for they shall hang out for the lion's
claws. And, most dear actors, eat no onions nor garlic, for
we are to utter sweet breath, and I do not doubt but to
hear them say, it is a sweet comedy. No more words:
away! go; away.   *Exeunt*

ACT FIVE

SCENE ONE

Athens. An Apartment in the Palace of Theseus.

Enter Theseus, Hippolyta, Philostrate, Lords,
and Attendants

HIPPOLYTA. 'Tis strange, my Theseus, that these lovers
  speak of.
THESEUS. More strange than true. I never may believe
  These antique fables, nor these fairy toys.
  Lovers and madmen have such seething brains,
  Such shaping fantasies, that apprehend
  More than cool reason ever comprehends.
  The lunatic, the lover, and the poet,
  Are of imagination all compact:
  One sees more devils than vast hell can hold,
  That is, the madman; the lover, all as frantic,
  Sees Helen's beauty in a brow of Egypt:
  The poet's eye, in a fine frenzy rolling,
  Doth glance from heaven to earth, from earth to heaven;
  And, as imagination bodies forth
  The forms of things unknown, the poet's pen
  Turns them to shapes, and gives to airy nothing
  A local habitation and a name.
  Such tricks hath strong imagination,
  That, if it would but apprehend some joy,
  It comprehends some bringer of that joy;
  Or in the night, imagining some fear,
  How easy is a bush suppos'd a bear!
HIPPOLYTA. But all the story of the night told over,
  And all their minds transfigur'd so together,
  More witnesseth than fancy's images,
  And grows to something of great constancy,
  But, howsoever, strange and admirable.

THESEUS. Here come the lovers, full of joy and mirth.
        Enter Lysander, Demetrius, Hermia, and Helena
    Joy, gentle friends! joy, and fresh days of love
    Accompany your hearts!
LYSANDER.   More than to us
    Wait in your royal walks, your board, your bed!
THESEUS. Come now; what masques, what dances shall we
    have,
    To wear away this long age of three hours
    Between our after-supper and bed-time?
    Where is our usual manager of mirth?
    What revels are in hand? Is there no play,
    To ease the anguish of a torturing hour?
    Call Philostrate.
PHILOSTRATE.   Here, mighty Theseus.
THESEUS. Say, what abridgment have you for this evening?
    What masque? what music? How shall we beguile
    The lazy time, if not with some delight?
PHILOSTRATE. There is a brief how many sports are ripe;
    Make choice of which your Highness will see first.
                                Gives a paper
THESEUS. 'The battle with the Centaurs, to be sung
    By an Athenian eunuch to the harp.'
    We 'll none of that: that have I told my love,
    In glory of my kinsman Hercules.
    'The riot of the tipsy Bacchanals,
    Tearing the Thracian singer in their rage.'
    That is an old device; and it was play'd
    When I from Thebes came last a conqueror.
    'The thrice three Muses mourning for the death
    Of Learning, late deceas'd in beggary.'
    That is some satire keen and critical,
    Not sorting with a nuptial ceremony.
    'A tedious brief scene of young Pyramus
    And his love Thisby; very tragical mirth.'
    Merry and tragical! tedious and brief!
    That is, hot ice and wonderous strange snow.
    How shall we find the concord of this discord?
PHILOSTRATE. A play there is, my lord, some ten words long,
    Which is as brief as I have known a play;
    But by ten words, my lord, it is too long,
    Which makes it tedious; for in all the play

There is not one word apt, one player fitted.
And tragical, my noble lord, it is;
For Pyramus therein doth kill himself.
Which when I saw rehears'd, I must confess,
Made mine eyes water; but more merry tears
The passion of loud laughter never shed.

THESEUS. What are they that do play it?

PHILOSTRATE. Hard-handed men, that work in Athens here,
Which never labour'd in their minds till now,
And now have toil'd their unbreath'd memories
With this same play, against your nuptial.

THESEUS. And we will hear it.

PHILOSTRATE.   No, my noble lord;
It is not for you: I have heard it over,
And it is nothing, nothing in the world;
Unless you can find sport in their intents,
Extremely stretch'd and conn'd with cruel pain,
To do you service.

THESEUS.   I will hear that play;
For never anything can be amiss,
When simpleness and duty tender it.
Go, bring them in: and take your places, ladies.

Exit Philostrate

HIPPOLYTA. I love not to see wretchedness o'ercharg'd,
And duty in his service perishing.

THESEUS. Why, gentle sweet, you shall see no such thing.

HIPPOLYTA. He says they can do nothing in this kind.

THESEUS. The kinder we, to give them thanks for nothing.
Our sport shall be to take what they mistake:
And what poor duty cannot do, noble respect
Takes it in might, not merit.
Where I have come, great clerks have purposed
To greet me with premeditated welcomes;
Where I have seen them shiver and look pale,
Make periods in the midst of sentences,
Throttle their practis'd accent in their fears,
And, in conclusion, dumbly have broke off,
Not paying me a welcome. Trust me, sweet,
Out of this silence yet I pick'd a welcome;
And in the modesty of fearful duty
I read as much as from the rattling tongue
Of saucy and audacious eloquence.

Love, therefore, and tongue-tied simplicity
In least speak most, to my capacity.

Re-enter Philostrate

PHILOSTRATE. So please your Grace, the Prologue is
address'd.

THESEUS. Let him approach.   *Flourish of trumpets*
Enter Quince for the Prologue

PROLOGUE. If we offend, it is with our good will.
That you should think, we come not to offend,
But with good will. To show our simple skill,
That is the true beginning of our end.
Consider then we come but in despite.
We do not come as minding to content you,
Our true intent is. All for your delight,
We are not here. That you should here repent you,
The actors are at hand; and, by their show,
You shall know all that you are like to know.

THESEUS. This fellow doth not stand upon points.

LYSANDER. He hath rid his prologue like a rough colt; he
knows not the stop. A good moral, my lord: it is not
enough to speak, but to speak true.

HIPPOLYTA. Indeed he hath played on his prologue like a
child on a recorder; a sound, but not in government.

THESEUS. His speech was like a tangled chain; nothing impaired, but all disordered. Who is next?

Enter Pyramus and Thisby,
Wall, Moonshine, and Lion, as in dumb show

PROLOGUE. Gentles, perchance you wonder at this show;
But wonder on, till truth make all things plain.
This man is Pyramus, if you would know;
This beauteous lady Thisby is, certain.
This man, with lime and rough-cast, doth present
Wall, that vile Wall which did these lovers sunder;
And through Wall's chink, poor souls, they are content
To whisper, at the which let no man wonder.
This man, with lanthorn, dog, and bush of thorn,
Presenteth Moonshine; for, if you will know,
By moonshine did these lovers think no scorn
To meet at Ninus' tomb, there, there to woo.
This grisly beast, which Lion hight by name,
The trusty Thisby, coming first by night,
Did scare away, or rather did affright;

And, as she fled, her mantle she did fall,
 Which Lion vile with bloody mouth did stain.
Anon comes Pyramus, sweet youth and tall,
 And finds his trusty Thisby's mantle slain:
Whereat, with blade, with bloody blameful blade,
 He bravely broach'd his boiling bloody breast;
And Thisby, tarrying in mulberry shade,
 His dagger drew, and died. For all the rest,
Let Lion, Moonshine, Wall, and lovers twain,
At large discourse, while here they do remain.
 Exeunt Prologue, Pyramus, Thisby, Lion, and Moonshine

THESEUS. I wonder, if the lion be to speak.

DEMETRIUS. No wonder, my lord: one lion may, when many
asses do.

WALL. In this same interlude it doth befall
 That I, one Snout by name, present a wall;
 And such a wall, as I would have you think,
 That had in it a crannied hole or chink,
 Through which the lovers, Pyramus and Thisby,
 Did whisper often very secretly.
 This loam, this rough-cast, and this stone doth show
 That I am that same wall; the truth is so;
 And this the cranny is, right and sinister,
 Through which the fearful lovers are to whisper.

THESEUS. Would you desire lime and hair to speak better?

DEMETRIUS. It is the wittiest partition that ever I heard discourse, my lord.

THESEUS. Pyramus draws near the wall: silence!
     Re-enter Pyramus

PYRAMUS. O grim-look'd night! O night with hue so black!
 O night, which ever art when day is not!
 O night! O night! alack, alack, alack!
  I fear my Thisby's promise is forgot.
 And thou, O wall! O sweet, O lovely wall!
 That stand'st between her father's ground and mine;
 Thou wall, O wall! O sweet, and lovely wall!
 Show me thy chink to blink through with mine eyne.
     Wall holds up his fingers
 Thanks, courteous wall: Jove shield thee well for this!
 But what see I? No Thisby do I see.
 O wicked wall! through whom I see no bliss;
 Curs'd be thy stones for thus deceiving me!

THESEUS. The wall, methinks, being sensible, should curse
   again.
PYRAMUS. No, in truth, sir, he should not. 'Deceiving me,' is
   Thisby's cue: she is to enter now, and I am to spy her
   through the wall. You shall see, it will fall pat as I told you.
   Yonder she comes.

Re-enter Thisby

THISBY. O wall! full often hast thou heard my moans,
      For parting my fair Pyramus and me:
   My cherry lips have often kiss'd thy stones,
      Thy stones with lime and hair knit up in thee.
PYRAMUS. I see a voice: now will I to the chink,
      To spy an I can hear my Thisby's face.
   Thisby!
THISBY. My love! thou art my love, I think.
PYRAMUS. Think what thou wilt, I am thy lover's grace;
      And, like Limander, am I trusty still.
THISBY. And I like Helen, till the Fates me kill.
PYRAMUS. Not Shafalus to Procrus was so true.
THISBY. As Shafalus to Procrus, I to you.
PYRAMUS. O! kiss me through the hole of this vile wall.
THISBY. I kiss the wall's hole, not your lips at all.
PYRAMUS. Wilt thou at Ninny's tomb meet me straightway?
THISBY. 'Tide life, 'tide death, I come without delay.

Exeunt Pyramus and Thisby

WALL. Thus have I, Wall, my part discharged so;
      And, being done, thus Wall away doth go.   *Exit*
THESEUS. Now is the mural down between the two neighbours.
DEMETRIUS. No remedy, my lord, when walls are so wilful
   to hear without warning.
HIPPOLYTA. This is the silliest stuff that ever I heard.
THESEUS. The best in this kind are but shadows, and the
   worst are no worse, if imagination amend them.
HIPPOLYTA. It must be your imagination then, and not
   theirs.
THESEUS. If we imagine no worse of them than they of themselves, they may pass for excellent men. Here come two
   noble beasts in, a man and a lion.

Re-enter Lion and Moonshine

LION. You, ladies, you, whose gentle hearts do fear
      The smallest monstrous mouse that creeps on floor,

May now perchance both quake and tremble here,   258]
  When lion rough in wildest rage doth roar.
Then know that I, one Snug the joiner, am
A lion-fell, nor else no lion's dam:
For, if I should as lion come in strife
Into this place, 'twere pity on my life.

THESEUS. A very gentle beast, and of a good conscience.

DEMETRIUS. The very best at a beast, my lord, that e'er I saw.

LYSANDER. This lion is a very fox for his valour.

THESEUS. True; and a goose for his discretion.

DEMETRIUS. Not so, my lord; for his valour cannot carry his discretion, and the fox carries the goose.

THESEUS. His discretion, I am sure, cannot carry his valour, for the goose carries not the fox. It is well: leave it to his discretion, and let us listen to the moon.

MOON. This lanthorn doth the horned moon present;—

DEMETRIUS. He should have worn the horns on his head.

THESEUS. He is no crescent, and his horns are invisible within the circumference.

MOON. This lanthorn doth the horned moon present;
  Myself the man i' the moon do seem to be.

THESEUS. This is the greatest error of all the rest. The man should be put into the lanthorn: how is it else the man i' the moon?

DEMETRIUS. He dares not come there for the candle; for, you see, it is already in snuff.

HIPPOLYTA. I am aweary of this moon: would he would change!

THESEUS. It appears, by his small light of discretion, that he is in the wane; but yet, in courtesy, in all reason, we must stay the time.

LYSANDER. Proceed, Moon.

MOON. All that I have to say, is, to tell you that the lanthorn is the moon; I, the man in the moon; this thorn-bush, my thorn-bush; and this dog, my dog.

DEMETRIUS. Why, all these should be in the lanthorn; for all these are in the moon. But, silence! here comes Thisby.

Re-enter Thisby

THISBY. This is old Ninny's tomb. Where is my love?

LION. (*Roaring*) Oh—.   *Thisby runs off*

DEMETRIUS. Well roared, Lion.

THESEUS. Well run, Thisby.

HIPPOLYTA. Well shone, Moon. Truly, the moon shines with
a good grace.

The Lion tears Thisby's mantle, and exit

THESEUS. Well moused, Lion.

DEMETRIUS. And then came Pyramus.

LYSANDER. And so the lion vanished.

Re-enter Pyramus

PYRAMUS. Sweet moon, I thank thee for thy sunny beams;
 I thank thee, moon, for shining now so bright,
For, by thy gracious, golden, glittering streams,
 I trust to taste of truest Thisby's sight.
    But stay, O spite!
    But mark, poor knight,
  What dreadful dole is here!
    Eyes, do you see?
    How can it be?
  O dainty duck! O dear!
    Thy Mantle good,
    What! stain'd with blood!
  Approach, ye Furies fell!
    O Fates, come, come,
    Cut thread and thrum;
  Quail, crush, conclude, and quell!

THESEUS. This passion, and the death of a dear friend, would
go near to make a man look sad.

HIPPOLYTA. Beshrew my heart, but I pity the man.

PYRAMUS. O! wherefore, Nature, didst thou lions frame?
Since lion vile hath here deflower'd my dear?
Which is—no, no—which was the fairest dame
 That liv'd, that lov'd, that lik'd, that look'd with cheer.
    Come tears, confound;
    Out, sword, and wound
  The pap of Pyramus:
    Ay, that left pap,
    Where heart doth hop:
  Thus die I, thus, thus, thus. *Stabs himself*
    Now am I dead,
    Now am I fled;
  My soul is in the sky:
    Tongue, lose thy light!
    Moon, take thy flight! *Exit Moonshine*
  Now die, die, die, die, die.   *Dies*

DEMETRIUS. No die, but an ace, for him; for he is but one.

LYSANDER. Less than an ace, man, for he is dead; he is nothing.

THESEUS. With the help of a surgeon, he might yet recover, and prove an ass.

HIPPOLYTA. How chance Moonshine is gone before Thisby comes back and finds her lover?

THESEUS. She will find him by starlight. Here she comes; and her passion ends the play.

Re-enter Thisby

HIPPOLYTA. Methinks she should not use a long one for such a Pyramus: I hope she will be brief.

DEMETRIUS. A mote will turn the balance, which Pyramus, which Thisby, is the better: he for a man, God warrant us; she for a woman, God bless us.

LYSANDER. She hath spied him already with those sweet eyes.

DEMETRIUS. And thus she moans, videlicet:—

THISBY.   Asleep, my love?
              What, dead, my dove?
         O Pyramus, arise!
              Speak, speak! Quite dumb?
              Dead, dead! A tomb
         Must cover thy sweet eyes.
              These lily lips,
              This cherry nose,
         These yellow cowslip cheeks,
              Are gone, are gone:
              Lovers, make moan!
         His eyes were green as leeks.
              O, Sisters Three,
              Come, come to me,
         With hands as pale as milk;
              Lay them in gore,
              Since you have shore
         With shears his thread of silk.
              Tongue, not a word:
              Come, trusty sword:
         Come, blade, my breast imbrue: *Stabs herself*
              And farewell, friends;
              Thus Thisby ends:
         Adieu, adieu, adieu.   *Dies*

THESEUS. Moonshine and Lion are left to bury the dead.

DEMETRIUS. Ay, and Wall too.

BOTTOM. No, I assure you; the wall is down that parted their
fathers. Will it please you to see the epilogue, or to hear a
Bergomask dance between two of our company?

THESEUS. No epilogue, I pray you; for your play needs no
excuse. Never excuse; for when the players are all dead,
there need none to be blamed. Marry, if he that writ it had
played Pyramus, and hanged himself in Thisby's garter, it
would have been a fine tragedy: and so it is, truly, and
very notably discharged. But come, your Bergomask: let
your epilogue alone.   *A dance*

The iron tongue of midnight hath told twelve;
Lovers, to bed; 'tis almost fairy time.
I fear we shall out-sleep the coming morn,
As much as we this night have overwatch'd,
This palpable-gross play hath well beguil'd
The heavy gait of night. Sweet friends, to bed.
A fortnight hold we this solemnity,
In nightly revels, and new jollity.   *Exeunt*

SCENE TWO

Enter Puck

PUCK.   Now the hungry lion roars,
  And the wolf behowls the moon;
 Whilst the heavy ploughman snores,
  All with weary task fordone.
 Now the wasted brands do glow,
  Whilst the screech-owl, screeching loud,
 Puts the wretch that lies in woe
  In remembrance of a shroud.
 Now it is the time of night
  That the graves, all gaping wide,
 Every one lets forth his sprite,
  In the church-way paths to glide:
 And we fairies, that do run
  By the triple Hecate's team,
 From the presence of the sun,
  Following darkness like a dream,
 Now are frolic; not a mouse
 Shall disturb this hallow'd house:
 I am sent with broom before,
 To sweep the dust behind the door.

Enter Oberon and Titania, with their Train

OBERON.   Through the house give glimmering light
  By the dead and drowsy fire;
 Every elf and fairy sprite
  Hop as light as bird from brier
 And this ditty after me
 Sing and dance it trippingly.

TITANIA.   First, rehearse your song by rote,
 To each word a warbling note:
 Hand in hand, with fairy grace,
 Will we sing, and bless this place.

       Song and dance

OBERON.   Now, until the break of day,
 Through this house each fairy stray.
 To the best bride-bed will we,
 Which by us shall blessed be;
 And the issue there create

Ever shall be fortunate.
So shall all the couples three
Ever true in loving be;
And the blots of Nature's hand
Shall not in their issue stand:
Never mole, hare-lip, nor scar,
Nor mark prodigious, such as are
Despised in nativity,
Shall upon their children be.
With this field-dew consecrate,
Every fairy take his gait,
And each several chamber bless,
Through this palace, with sweet peace;
Ever shall in safety rest,
And the owner of it blest.
　　　Trip away;
　　　Make no stay;
Meet me all by break of day.
　　　　　　Exeunt Oberon, Titania, and Train

PUCK.　If we shadows have offended,
Think but this, and all is mended,
That you have but slumber'd here
While these visions did appear.
And this weak and idle theme,
No more yielding but a dream,
Gentles, do not reprehend:
If you pardon, we will mend.
And, as I 'm an honest Puck,
If we have unearned luck
Now to 'scape the serpent's tongue,
We will make amends ere long;
Else the Puck a liar call:
So, good-night unto you all.
Give me your hands, if we be friends,
And Robin shall restore amends.　　　　*Exit*

Ever shall be fortunate.
So shall all the couples three
Ever true in loving be;
And the blots of Nature's hand
Shall not in their issue stand:
Never mole, hare-lip, nor scar,
Nor mark prodigious, such as are
Despised in nativity,
Shall upon their children be.
With this field-dew consecrate,
Every fairy take his gait;
And each several chamber bless,
Through this palace, with sweet peace;
Ever shall in safety rest,
And the owner of it blest.
            Trip away;
            Make no stay;
Meet me all by break of day.

Exeunt Oberon, Titania, and Train.

PUCK. If we shadows have offended,
Think but this, and all is mended,
That you have but slumber'd here
While these visions did appear.
And this weak and idle theme,
No more yielding but a dream,
Gentles, do not reprehend:
If you pardon, we will mend.
And, as I 'm an honest Puck,
If we have unearned luck
Now to 'scape the serpent's tongue,
We will make amends ere long;
Else the Puck a liar call:
So, good-night unto you all.
Give me your hands, if we be friends,
And Robin shall restore amends.

                    Exit.

THE MERCHANT OF VENICE

CAST OF CHARACTERS

DUKE OF VENICE

PRINCE OF MOROCCO ⎱ *Suitors to Portia*
PRINCE OF ARRAGON ⎰

ANTONIO, *a Merchant of Venice*
BASSANIO, *his Friend*

GRATIANO ⎱
SALANIO ⎰ *Friends to Antonio and Bassanio*
SALARINO

LORENZO, *in love with Jessica*
SHYLOCK, *a rich Jew*
TUBAL, *a Jew, his Friend*
LAUNCELOT GOBBO, *a Clown, Servant to Shylock*
OLD GOBBO, *Father to Launcelot*
LEONARDO, *Servant to Bassanio*

BALTHAZAR ⎱ *Servants to Portia*
STEPHANO ⎰

PORTIA, *a rich Heiress*
NERISSA, *her Waiting-maid*
JESSICA, *Daughter to Shylock*

Magnificoes of Venice, Officers of the Court of
Justice, Gaoler, Servants to Portia, and other Attendants

SCENE

*Partly at Venice, and partly at Belmont, the seat
of Portia, on the Continent*

THE MERCHANT OF VENICE

ACT ONE

SCENE ONE

Venice. A Street.

Enter Antonio, Salarino, and Salanio

ANTONIO. In sooth, I know not why I am so sad:
It wearies me; you say it wearies you;
But how I caught it, found it, or came by it,
What stuff 'tis made of, whereof it is born,
I am to learn;
And such a want-wit sadness makes of me,
That I have much ado to know myself.

SALARINO. Your mind is tossing on the ocean;
There, where your argosies with portly sail,—
Like signiors and rich burghers on the flood,
Or, as it were, the pageants of the sea,—
Do overpeer the petty traffickers,
That curtsy to them, do them reverence,
As they fly by them with their woven wings.

SALANIO. Believe me, sir, had I such venture forth,
The better part of my affections would
Be with my hopes abroad. I should be still
Plucking the grass to know where sits the wind;
Peering in maps for ports, and piers, and roads;
And every object that might make me fear
Misfortune to my ventures, out of doubt
Would make me sad.

SALARINO.   My wind, cooling my broth
Would blow me to an ague, when I thought
What harm a wind too great might do at sea.
I should not see the sandy hour-glass run
But I should think of shallows and of flats,

And see my wealthy Andrew dock'd in sand
Vailing her high-top lower than her ribs
To kiss her burial. Should I go to church
And see the holy edifice of stone,
And not bethink me straight of dangerous rocks,
Which touching but my gentle vessel's side
Would scatter all her spices on the stream,
Enrobe the roaring waters with my silks;
And, in a word, but even now worth this,
And now worth nothing? Shall I have the thought
To think on this, and shall I lack the thought
That such a thing bechanc'd would make me sad?
But tell not me: I know Antonio
Is sad to think upon his merchandise.

ANTONIO. Believe me, no: I thank my fortune for it,
My ventures are not in one bottom trusted,
Nor to one place; nor is my whole estate
Upon the fortune of this present year:
Therefore, my merchandise makes me not sad.

SALARINO. Why, then you are in love.

ANTONIO.   Fie, fie!

SALARINO. Not in love neither? Then let 's say you are sad,
Because you are not merry: and 'twere as easy
For you to laugh and leap, and say you are merry,
Because you are not sad. Now, by two-headed Janus,
Nature hath fram'd strange fellows in her time:
Some that will evermore peep through their eyes
And laugh like parrots at a bag-piper,
And other of such vinegar aspect
That they 'll not show their teeth in way of smile,
Though Nestor swear the jest be laughable.

Enter Bassanio, Lorenzo, and Gratiano

SALANIO. Here comes Bassanio, your most noble kinsman,
Gratiano, and Lorenzo. Fare ye well:
We leave you now with better company.

SALARINO. I would have stay'd till I had made you merry,
If worthier friends had not prevented me.

ANTONIO. Your worth is very dear in my regard.
I take it, your own business calls on you,
And you embrace the occasion to depart.

SALARINO. Good-morrow, my good lords.

BASSANIO. Good signiors both, when shall we laugh? say
    when?

    You grow exceeding strange: must it be so?

SALARINO. We 'll make our leisures to attend on yours.

                Exeunt Salarino and Salanio

LORENZO. My Lord Bassanio, since you have found Antonio,
    We too will leave you; but, at dinner-time,
    I pray you, have in mind where we must meet.

BASSANIO. I will not fail you.

GRATIANO. You look not well, Signior Antonio;
    You have too much respect upon the world:
    They lose it that do buy it with much care:
    Believe me, you are marvellously chang'd.

ANTONIO. I hold the world but as the world, Gratiano;
    A stage where every man must play a part,
    And mine a sad one.

GRATIANO.   Let me play the fool:
    With mirth and laughter let old wrinkles come,
    And let my liver rather heat with wine
    Than my heart cool with mortifying groans.
    Why should a man, whose blood is warm within,
    Sit like his grandsire cut in alabaster?
    Sleep when he wakes, and creep into the jaundice
    By being peevish? I tell thee what, Antonio—
    I love thee, and it is my love that speaks—
    There are a sort of men whose visages
    Do cream and mantle like a standing pond,
    And do a wilful stillness entertain,
    With purpose to be dress'd in an opinion
    Of wisdom, gravity, profound conceit;
    As who should say, 'I am Sir Oracle,
    And when I ope my lips let no dog bark!'
    O, my Antonio, I do know of these,
    That therefore only are reputed wise
    For saying nothing; when, I am very sure,
    If they should speak, would almost damn those ears
    Which, hearing them, would call their brothers fools.
    I 'll tell thee more of this another time:
    But fish not, with this melancholy bait,
    For this fool-gudgeon, this opinion.
    Come, good Lorenzo. Fare ye well awhile:
    I 'll end my exhortation after dinner.

LORENZO. Well, we will leave you then till dinner-time.
I must be one of these same dumb wise men,
For Gratiano never lets me speak.

GRATIANO. Well, keep me company but two years moe,
Thou shalt not know the sound of thine own tongue.

ANTONIO. Farewell: I 'll grow a talker for this gear.

GRATIANO. Thanks, i' faith; for silence is only commendable
In a neat's tongue dried and a maid not vendible.

Exeunt Gratiano and Lorenzo

ANTONIO. Is that any thing now?

BASSANIO. Gratiano speaks an infinite deal of nothing, more
than any man in all Venice. His reasons are as two grains
of wheat hid in two bushels of chaff: you shall seek all day
ere you find them, and, when you have them, they are not
worth the search.

ANTONIO. Well, tell me now, what lady is the same
To whom you swore a secret pilgrimage,
That you to-day promis'd to tell me of?

BASSANIO. 'Tis not unknown to you, Antonio,
How much I have disabled mine estate,
By something showing a more swelling port
Than my faint means would grant continuance:
Nor do I now make moan to be abridg'd
From such a noble rate; but my chief care
Is, to come fairly off from the great debts
Wherein my time, something too prodigal,
Hath left me gag'd. To you, Antonio,
I owe the most, in money and in love;
And from your love I have a warranty
To unburthen all my plots and purposes
How to get clear of all the debts I owe.

ANTONIO. I pray you, good Bassanio, let me know it;
And if it stand, as you yourself still do,
Within the eye of honour, be assur'd,
My purse, my person, my extremest means,
Lie all unlock'd to your occasions.

BASSANIO. In my school-days, when I had lost one shaft,
I shot his fellow of the self-same flight
The self-same way with more advised watch,
To find the other forth, and by adventuring both,
I oft found both. I urge this childhood proof,
Because what follows is pure innocence.

I owe you much, and, like a wilful youth,
That which I owe is lost; but if you please
To shoot another arrow that self way
Which you did shoot the first, I do not doubt,
As I will watch the aim, or to find both,
Or bring your latter hazard back again,
And thankfully rest debtor for the first.

ANTONIO. You know me well, and herein spend but time
To wind about my love with circumstance;
And out of doubt you do me now more wrong
In making question of my uttermost
Than if you had made waste of all I have:
Then do but say to me what I should do
That in your knowledge may by me be done,
And I am prest unto it: therefore speak.

BASSANIO. In Belmont is a lady richly left,
And she is fair, and, fairer than that word,
Of wondrous virtues: sometimes from her eyes
I did receive fair speechless messages:
Her name is Portia; nothing undervalu'd
To Cato's daughter, Brutus' Portia:
Nor is the wide world ignorant of her worth,
For the four winds blow in from every coast
Renowned suitors; and her sunny locks
Hang on her temples like a golden fleece;
Which makes her seat of Belmont Colchos' strond,
And many Jasons come in quest of her.
O my Antonio! had I but the means
To hold a rival place with one of them,
I have a mind presages me such thrift,
That I should questionless be fortunate.

ANTONIO. Thou knowest that all my fortunes are at sea;
Neither have I money, nor commodity
To raise a present sum: therefore go forth;
Try what my credit can in Venice do:
That shall be rack'd, even to the uttermost,
To furnish thee to Belmont, to fair Portia.
Go, presently inquire, and so will I,
Where money is, and I no question make
To have it of my trust or for my sake.   *Exeunt*

SCENE TWO

Belmont. A Room in Portia's House.

Enter Portia and Nerissa

PORTIA. By my troth, Nerissa, my little body is aweary of this great world.

NERISSA. You would be, sweet madam, if your miseries were in the same abundance as your good fortunes are: and yet, for aught I see, they are as sick that surfeit with too much as they that starve with nothing. It is no mean happiness therefore, to be seated in the mean: superfluity comes sooner by white hairs, but competency lives longer.

PORTIA. Good sentences and well pronounced.

NERISSA. They would be better if well followed.

PORTIA. If to do were as easy as to know what were good to do, chapels had been churches, and poor men's cottages princes' palaces. It is a good divine that follows his own instructions: I can easier teach twenty what were good to be done, than be one of the twenty to follow mine own teaching. The brain may devise laws for the blood, but a hot temper leaps o'er a cold decree: such a hare is madness the youth, to skip o'er the meshes of good counsel the cripple. But this reasoning is not in the fashion to choose me a husband. O me, the word 'choose'! I may neither choose whom I would nor refuse whom I dislike; so is the will of a living daughter curbed by the will of a dead father. Is it not hard, Nerissa, that I cannot choose one nor refuse none?

NERISSA. Your father was ever virtuous, and holy men at their death have good inspirations; therefore, the lottery that he hath devised in these three chests of gold, silver, and lead, whereof who chooses his meaning chooses you, will, no doubt, never be chosen by any rightly but one who you shall rightly love. But what warmth is there in your affection towards any of these princely suitors that are already come?

PORTIA. I pray thee, over-name them, and as thou namest them, I will describe them; and, according to my description, level at my affection.

NERISSA. First, there is the Neapolitan prince.

PORTIA. Ay, that 's a colt indeed, for he doth nothing but talk of his horse; and he makes it a great appropriation to his own good parts that he can shoe him himself. I am much afeard my lady his mother played false with a smith.

NERISSA. Then is there the County Palatine.

PORTIA. He doth nothing but frown, as who should say, 'An you will not have me, choose.' He hears merry tales, and smiles not: I fear he will prove the weeping philosopher when he grows old, being so full of unmannerly sadness in his youth. I had rather be married to a death's-head with a bone in his mouth than to either of these. God defend me from these two!

NERISSA. How say you by the French lord, Monsieur Le Bon?

PORTIA. God made him, and therefore let him pass for a man. In truth, I know it is a sin to be a mocker; but, he! why, he hath a horse better than the Neapolitan's, a better bad habit of frowning than the Count Palatine; he is every man in no man; if a throstle sing, he falls straight a-capering; he will fence with his own shadow: if I should marry him, I should marry twenty husbands. If he would despise me, I would forgive him, for if he love me to madness, I shall never requite him.

NERISSA. What say you, then, to Falconbridge, the young baron of England?

PORTIA. You know I say nothing to him, for he understands not me, nor I him: he hath neither Latin, French, nor Italian; and you will come into the court and swear that I have a poor pennyworth in the English. He is a proper man's picture, but, alas! who can converse with a dumb-show? How oddly he is suited! I think he bought his doublet in Italy, his round hose in France, his bonnet in Germany, and his behaviour everywhere.

NERISSA. What think you of the Scottish lord, his neighbour?

PORTIA. That he hath a neighbourly charity in him, for he borrowed a box of the ear of the Englishman, and swore he would pay him again when he was able: I think the Frenchman became his surety and sealed under for another.

NERISSA. How like you the young German, the Duke of Saxony's nephew?

PORTIA. Very vilely in the morning, when he is sober, and most vilely in the afternoon, when he is drunk: when he is best, he is a little worse than a man, and when he is worst, he is little better than a beast. An the worst fall that ever fell, I hope I shall make shift to go without him.

NERISSA. If he should offer to choose, and choose the right casket, you should refuse to perform your father's will, if you should refuse to accept him.

PORTIA. Therefore, for fear of the worst, I pray thee, set a deep glass of Rhenish wine on the contrary casket, for, if the devil be within and that temptation without, I know he will choose it. I will do anything, Nerissa, ere I will be married to a sponge.

NERISSA. You need not fear, lady, the having any of these lords: they have acquainted me with their determinations; which is, indeed, to return to their home and to trouble you with no more suit, unless you may be won by some other sort than your father's imposition depending on the caskets.

PORTIA. If I live to be as old as Sibylla, I will die as chaste as Diana, unless I be obtained by the manner of my father's will. I am glad this parcel of wooers are so reasonable, for there is not one among them but I dote on his very absence, and I pray God grant them a fair departure.

NERISSA. Do you not remember, lady, in your father's time, a Venetian, a scholar and a soldier, that came hither in the company of the Marquis of Montferrat?

PORTIA. Yes, yes: it was Bassanio; as I think, he was so called.

NERISSA. True, madam: he, of all the men that ever my foolish eyes looked upon, was the best deserving a fair lady.

PORTIA. I remember him well, and I remember him worthy of thy praise.

Enter a Servant

How now! what news?

SERVANT. The four strangers seek for you, madam, to take their leave; and there is a forerunner come from a fifth, the Prince of Morocco, who brings word the prince his master will be here to-night.

PORTIA. If I could bid the fifth welcome with so good heart as I can bid the other four farewell, I should be glad of his approach: if he have the condition of a saint and the com-

plexion of a devil, I had rather he should shrive me than
wive me. Come, Nerissa. Sirrah, go before.

Whiles we shut the gate upon one wooer, another knocks
at the door.   *Exeunt*

SCENE THREE

Venice. A public Place.

Enter Bassanio and Shylock

SHYLOCK. Three thousand ducats; well?

BASSANIO. Ay, sir, for three months.

SHYLOCK. For three months; well?

BASSANIO. For the which, as I told you, Antonio shall be
bound.

SHYLOCK. Antonio shall become bound; well?

BASSANIO. May you stead me? Will you pleasure me? Shall I
know your answer?

SHYLOCK. Three thousand ducats, for three months, and Antonio bound.

BASSANIO. Your answer to that.

SHYLOCK. Antonio is a good man.

BASSANIO. Have you heard any imputation to the contrary?

SHYLOCK. Ho, no, no, no, no: my meaning in saying he is a
good man is to have you understand me that he is sufficient. Yet his means are in supposition: he hath an argosy
bound to Tripolis, another to the Indies; I understand
moreover upon the Rialto, he hath a third at Mexico, a
fourth for England, and other ventures he hath, squandered abroad. But ships are but boards, sailors but men:
there be land-rats and water-rats, land-thieves, and water-
thieves,—I mean pirates,—and then there is the peril of
waters, winds, and rocks. The man is, notwithstanding,
sufficient. Three thousand ducats; I think, I may take his
bond.

BASSANIO. Be assured you may.

SHYLOCK. I will be assured I may; and, that I may be assured, I will bethink me. May I speak with Antonio?

BASSANIO. If it please you to dine with us.

SHYLOCK. Yes, to smell pork; to eat of the habitation which
your prophet the Nazarite conjured the devil into. I will

buy with you, sell with you, talk with you, walk with you,
and so following; but I will not eat with you, drink with
you, nor pray with you. What news on the Rialto? Who is
he comes here?

Enter Antonio

BASSANIO. This is Signior Antonio.

SHYLOCK. (*Aside*) How like a fawning publican he looks!
　I hate him for he is a Christian;
　But more for that in low simplicity
　He lends out money gratis, and brings down
　The rate of usance here with us in Venice.
　If I can catch him once upon the hip,
　I will feed fat the ancient grudge I bear him.
　He hates our sacred nation, and he rails,
　Even there where merchants most do congregate,
　On me, my bargains, and my well-won thrift,
　Which he calls interest. Cursed be my tribe,
　If I forgive him!

BASSANIO.　　　　Shylock, do you hear?

SHYLOCK. I am debating of my present store,
　And, by the near guess of my memory,
　I cannot instantly raise up the gross
　Of full three thousand ducats. What of that?
　Tubal, a wealthy Hebrew of my tribe,
　Will furnish me. But soft! how many months
　Do you desire? (*To Antonio*) Rest you fair, good signior;
　Your worship was the last man in our mouths.

ANTONIO. Shylock, albeit I neither lend nor borrow
　By taking nor by giving of excess,
　Yet, to supply the ripe wants of my friend,
　I 'll break a custom. (*To Bassanio*) Is he yet possess'd
　How much ye would?

SHYLOCK.　　　　Ay, ay, three thousand ducats.

ANTONIO. And for three months.

SHYLOCK. I had forgot; three months; you told me so.
　Well then, your bond; and let me see. But hear you:
　Methought you said you neither lend nor borrow
　Upon advantage.

ANTONIO.　　　　I do never use it.

SHYLOCK. When Jacob graz'd his uncle Laban's sheep,—
　This Jacob from our holy Abram was,
　As his wise mother wrought in his behalf,

The third possessor: ay, he was the third,—
ANTONIO. And what of him? Did he take interest?
SHYLOCK. No; not take interest; not, as you would say,
 Directly interest: mark what Jacob did.
 When Laban and himself were compromis'd,
 That all the eanlings that were streak'd and pied
 Should fall as Jacob's hire, the ewes, being rank,
 In end of autumn turned to the rams;
 And, when the work of generation was
 Between these woolly breeders in the act,
 The skilful shepherd peel'd me certain wands,
 And, in the doing of the deed of kind,
 He stuck them up before the fulsome ewes,
 Who, then conceiving, did in eaning time
 Fall parti-colour'd lambs, and those were Jacob's.
 This was a way to thrive, and he was blest:
 And thrift is blessing, if men steal it not.
ANTONIO. This was a venture, sir, that Jacob serv'd for;
 A thing not in his power to bring to pass,
 But sway'd and fashion'd by the hand of heaven.
 Was this inserted to make interest good?
 Or is your gold and silver ewes and rams?
SHYLOCK. I cannot tell; I make it breed as fast:
 But note me, signior.
ANTONIO.   Mark you this, Bassanio,
 The devil can cite Scripture for his purpose.
 An evil soul, producing holy witness,
 Is like a villain with a smiling cheek,
 A goodly apple rotten at the heart.
 O, what a goodly outside falsehood hath!
SHYLOCK. Three thousand ducats; 'tis a good round sum.
 Three months from twelve, then let me see the rate.
ANTONIO. Well, Shylock, shall we be beholding to you?
SHYLOCK. Signior Antonio, many a time and oft
 In the Rialto you have rated me
 About my moneys and my usances:
 Still have I borne it with a patient shrug,
 For sufferance is the badge of all our tribe.
 You call me misbeliever, cut-throat dog,
 And spet upon my Jewish gaberdine,
 And all for use of that which is mine own.
 Well then, it now appears you need my help:

Go to then; you come to me, and you say,
'Shylock, we would have moneys': you say so;
You, that did void your rheum upon my beard,
And foot me as you spurn a stranger cur
Over your threshold: moneys is your suit.
What should I say to you? Should I not say,
'Hath a dog money? Is it possible
A cur can lend three thousand ducats?' or
Shall I bend low, and in a bondman's key,
With bated breath, and whispering humbleness,
Say this:—
'Fair sir, you spet on me on Wednesday last;
You spurn'd me such a day; another time
You call'd me dog; and for these courtesies
I 'll lend you thus much moneys'?

ANTONIO. I am as like to call thee so again,
To spet on thee again, to spurn thee too.
If thou wilt lend this money, lend it not
As to thy friends,—for when did friendship take
A breed for barren metal of his friend?—
But lend it rather to thine enemy;
Who if he break, thou mayst with better face
Exact the penalty.

SHYLOCK.   Why, look you, how you storm!
I would be friends with you, and have your love,
Forget the shames that you have stain'd me with,
Supply your present wants, and take no doit
Of usance for my moneys, and you 'll not hear me:
This is kind I offer.

ANTONIO. This were kindness.

SHYLOCK.   This kindness will I show.
Go with me to a notary, seal me there
Your single bond; and, in a merry sport,
If you repay me not on such a day,
In such a place, such sum or sums as are
Express'd in the condition, let the forfeit
Be nominated for an equal pound
Of your fair flesh, to be cut off and taken
In what part of your body pleaseth me.

ANTONIO. Content, i' faith: I 'll seal to such a bond,
And say there is much kindness in the Jew.

BASSANIO. You shall not seal to such a bond for me:

I 'll rather dwell in my necessity.

ANTONIO. Why, fear not, man; I will not forfeit it:
Within these two months, that 's a month before
This bond expires, I do expect return
Of thrice three times the value of this bond.

SHYLOCK. O father Abram! what these Christians are,
Whose own hard dealing teaches them suspect
The thoughts of others. Pray you, tell me this;
If he should break his day, what should I gain
By the exaction of the forfeiture?
A pound of man's flesh, taken from a man,
Is not so estimable, profitable neither,
As flesh of muttons, beefs, or goats. I say,
To buy his favour, I extend this friendship:
If he will take it, so; if not, adieu;
And, for my love, I pray you wrong me not.

ANTONIO. Yes, Shylock, I will seal unto this bond.

SHYLOCK. Then meet me forthwith at the notary's;
Give him direction for this merry bond,
And I will go and purse the ducats straight,
See to my house, left in the fearful guard
Of an unthrifty knave, and presently
I will be with you.

ANTONIO.   Hie thee, gentle Jew.   *Exit Shylock*
This Hebrew will turn Christian: he grows kind.

BASSANIO. I like not fair terms and a villain's mind.

ANTONIO. Come on: in this there can be no dismay;
My ships come home a month before the day.   *Exeunt*

ACT TWO

SCENE ONE

Belmont. A Room in Portia's House.

Flourish of Cornets. Enter the Prince of Morocco, and his Followers; Portia, Nerissa, and Others of her Train.

MOROCCO. Mislike me not for my complexion,
  The shadow'd livery of the burnish'd sun,
  To whom I am a neighbour and near bred.
  Bring me the fairest creature northward born,
  Where Phœbus' fire scarce thaws the icicles,
  And let us make incision for your love,
  To prove whose blood is reddest, his or mine.
  I tell thee, lady, this aspect of mine
  Hath fear'd the valiant: by my love, I swear
  The best regarded virgins of our clime
  Have lov'd it too: I would not change this hue,
  Except to steal your thoughts, my gentle queen.
PORTIA. In terms of choice I am not solely led
  By nice direction of a maiden's eyes;
  Besides, the lottery of my destiny
  Bars me the right of voluntary choosing:
  But if my father had not scanted me
  And hedg'd me by his wit, to yield myself
  His wife who wins me by that means I told you,
  Yourself, renowned prince, then stood as fair
  As any comer I have look'd on yet
  For my affection.
MOROCCO.   Even for that I thank you:
  Therefore, I pray you, lead me to the caskets
  To try my fortune. By this scimitar,—
  That slew the Sophy, and a Persian prince
  That won three fields of Sultan Solyman,—
  I would outstare the sternest eyes that look,

Outbrave the heart most daring on the earth,
Pluck the young sucking cubs from the she-bear,
Yea, mock the lion when he roars for prey,
To win thee, lady. But, alas the while!
If Hercules and Lichas play at dice
Which is the better man, the greater throw
May turn by fortune from the weaker hand:
So is Alcides beaten by his page;
And so may I, blind fortune leading me,
Miss that which one unworthier may attain,
And die with grieving.

PORTIA.   You must take your chance;
And either not attempt to choose at all,
Or swear before you choose, if you choose wrong,
Never to speak to lady afterward
In way of marriage: therefore be advis'd.

MOROCCO. Nor will not: come, bring me unto my chance.

PORTIA. First, forward to the temple: after dinner
Your hazard shall be made.

MOROCCO.   Good fortune then!
To make me blest or cursed'st among men!

                              Cornets, and exeunt

SCENE TWO

Venice. A Street.

Enter Launcelot Gobbo

LAUNCELOT. Certainly my conscience will serve me to run
from this Jew my master. The fiend is at mine elbow, and
tempts me, saying to me, 'Gobbo, Launcelot Gobbo, good
Launcelot,' or 'good Gobbo,' or 'good Launcelot Gobbo,
use your legs, take the start, run away.' My conscience
says, 'No; take heed, honest Launcelot; take heed, honest
Gobbo'; or, as aforesaid, 'honest Launcelot Gobbo; do not
run; scorn running with thy heels.' Well, the most courageous fiend bids me pack: 'Via!' says the fiend; 'away!'
says the fiend; 'for the heavens, rouse up a brave mind,'
says the fiend, 'and run.' Well, my conscience, hanging
about the neck of my heart, says very wisely to me, 'My
honest friend Launcelot, being an honest man's son,'—or

rather an honest woman's son;—for, indeed, my father did something smack, something grow to, he had a kind of taste;—well, my conscience says, 'Launcelot, budge not.' 'Budge,' says the fiend. 'Budge not,' says my conscience. 'Conscience,' say I, 'you counsel well'; 'fiend,' say I, 'you counsel well': to be ruled by my conscience, I should stay with the Jew my master, who, God bless the mark! is a kind of devil; and, to run away from the Jew, I should be ruled by the fiend, who, saving your reverence, is the devil himself. Certainly, the Jew is the very devil incarnal; and, in my conscience, my conscience is but a kind of hard conscience, to offer to counsel me to stay with the Jew. The fiend gives the more friendly counsel: I will run, fiend; my heels are at your commandment; I will run.

Enter Old Gobbo, with a basket

GOBBO. Master young man, you; I pray you, which is the way to Master Jew's?

LAUNCELOT. (*Aside*) O heavens! this is my true-begotten father, who, being more than sand-blind, high-gravel blind, knows me not: I will try confusions with him.

GOBBO. Master young gentleman, I pray you, which is the way to Master Jew's?

LAUNCELOT. Turn up on your right hand at the next turning, but, at the next turning of all, on your left; marry, at the very next turning, turn of no hand, but turn down indirectly to the Jew's house.

GOBBO. By God's sonties, 'twill be a hard way to hit. Can you tell me whether one Launcelot, that dwells with him, dwell with him or no?

LAUNCELOT. Talk you of young Master Launcelot? (*Aside*) Mark me now; now will I raise the waters. Talk you of young Master Launcelot?

GOBBO. No master, sir, but a poor man's son: his father, though I say it, is an honest, exceeding poor man, and, God be thanked, well to live.

LAUNCELOT. Well, let his father be what a' will, we talk of young Master Launcelot.

GOBBO. Your worship's friend, and Launcelot, sir.

LAUNCELOT. But I pray you, ergo, old man, ergo, I beseech you, talk you of young Master Launcelot?

GOBBO. Of Launcelot, an 't please your mastership.

LAUNCELOT. Ergo, Master Launcelot. Talk not of Master

Launcelot, father; for the young gentleman,—according to Fates and Destinies and such odd sayings, the Sisters Three and such branches of learning,—is, indeed, deceased; or, as you would say in plain terms, gone to heaven.

GOBBO. Marry, God forbid! the boy was the very staff of my age, my very prop.

LAUNCELOT. (*Aside*) Do I look like a cudgel or a hovel-post, a staff or a prop? Do you know me, father?

GOBBO. Alack the day! I know you not, young gentleman: but I pray you, tell me, is my boy,—God rest his soul!— alive or dead?

LAUNCELOT. Do you not know me, father?

GOBBO. Alack, sir, I am sand-blind; I know you not.

LAUNCELOT. Nay, indeed, if you had your eyes, you might fail of the knowing me: it is a wise father that knows his own child. Well, old man, I will tell you news of your son. Give me your blessing; truth will come to light; murder cannot be hid long; a man's son may, but, in the end, truth will out.

GOBBO. Pray you, sir, stand up. I am sure you are not Launcelot, my boy.

LAUNCELOT. Pray you, let 's have no more fooling about it, but give me your blessing: I am Launcelot, your boy that was, your son that is, your child that shall be.

GOBBO. I cannot think you are my son.

LAUNCELOT. I know not what I shall think of that; but I am Launcelot, the Jew's man, and I am sure Margery your wife is my mother.

GOBBO. Her name is Margery, indeed: I 'll be sworn, if thou be Launcelot, thou art mine own flesh and blood. Lord worshipped might he be! what a beard hast thou got! thou hast got more hair on thy chin than Dobbin my thill-horse has on his tail.

LAUNCELOT. It should seem then that Dobbin's tail grows backward: I am sure he had more hair on his tail than I have on my face, when I last saw him.

GOBBO. Lord! how art thou changed. How dost thou and thy master agree? I have brought him a present. How 'gree you now?

LAUNCELOT. Well, well: but, for mine own part, as I have set up my rest to run away, so I will not rest till I have run

some ground. My master 's a very Jew: give him a present! give him a halter: I am famished in his service; you
may tell every finger I have with my ribs. Father, I am
glad you are come: give me your present to one Master
Bassanio, who, indeed, gives rare new liveries. If I serve
not him, I will run as far as God has any ground. O rare
fortune! here comes the man: to him, father; for I am a
Jew, if I serve the Jew any longer.

Enter Bassanio, with Leonardo, and other Followers

BASSANIO. You may do so; but let it be so hasted that supper be ready at the very furthest by five of the clock. See
these letters delivered; put the liveries to making; and desire Gratiano to come anon to my lodging. *Exit a Servant*

LAUNCELOT. To him, father.

GOBBO. God bless your worship!

BASSANIO. Gramercy! wouldst thou aught with me?

GOBBO. Here 's my son, sir, a poor boy,—

LAUNCELOT. Not a poor boy, sir, but the rich Jew's man;
that would, sir,—as my father shall specify,—

GOBBO. He hath a great infection, sir, as one would say, to
serve—

LAUNCELOT. Indeed, the short and the long is, I serve the
Jew, and have a desire, as my father shall specify,—

GOBBO. His master and he, saving your worship's reverence,
are scarce cater-cousins,—

LAUNCELOT. To be brief, the very truth is that the Jew having done me wrong, doth cause me,—as my father, being,
I hope, an old man, shall frutify unto you,—

GOBBO. I have here a dish of doves that I would bestow
upon your worship, and my suit is,—

LAUNCELOT. In very brief, the suit is impertinent to myself,
as your worship shall know by this honest old man; and,
though I say it, though old man, yet poor man, my father.

BASSANIO. One speak for both. What would you?

LAUNCELOT. Serve you, sir.

GOBBO. That is the very defect of the matter, sir.

BASSANIO. I know thee well; thou hast obtain'd thy suit:
Shylock thy master spoke with me this day
And hath preferr'd thee, if it be preferment
To leave a rich Jew's service, to become
The follower of so poor a gentleman.

LAUNCELOT. The old proverb is very well parted between

my master Shylock and you, sir: you have the grace of
God, sir, and he hath enough.

BASSANIO. Thou speak'st it well. Go, father, with thy son.
Take leave of thy old master, and inquire
My lodging out. (*To his Followers*) Give him a livery
More guarded than his fellows': see it done.

LAUNCELOT. Father, in. I cannot get a service, no; I have
ne'er a tongue in my head. Well, (*Looking on his palm*)
if any man in Italy have a fairer table which doth offer to
swear upon a book, I shall have good fortune. Go to;
here 's a simple line of life: here 's a small trifle of wives:
alas! fifteen wives is nothing: a 'leven widows and nine
maids is a simple coming-in for one man; and then to
'scape drowning thrice, and to be in peril of my life with
the edge of a feather-bed; here are simple 'scapes. Well,
if Fortune be a woman, she 's a good wench for this gear.
Father, come; I 'll take my leave of the Jew in the twinkling of an eye.   *Exeunt Launcelot and Old Gobbo*

BASSANIO. I pray thee, good Leonardo, think on this:
These things being bought, and orderly bestow'd,
Return in haste, for I do feast to-night
My best-esteem'd acquaintance: hie thee, go.

LEONARDO. My best endeavours shall be done herein.

Enter Gratiano

GRATIANO. Where is your master?

LEONARDO.   Yonder, sir, he walks.   *Exit*

GRATIANO. Signior Bassanio!—

BASSANIO. Gratiano!

GRATIANO. I have a suit to you.

BASSANIO.   You have obtain'd it.

GRATIANO. You must not deny me: I must go with you to
Belmont.

BASSANIO. Why, then you must. But hear thee, Gratiano;
Thou art too wild, too rude and bold of voice;
Parts that become thee happily enough,
And in such eyes as ours appear not faults;
But where thou art not known, why, there they show
Something too liberal. Pray thee, take pain
To allay with some cold drops of modesty
Thy skipping spirit, lest, through thy wild behaviour,
I be misconstru'd in the place I go to,
And lose my hopes.

GRATIANO.   Signior Bassanio, hear me:
  If I do not put on a sober habit,
  Talk with respect, and swear but now and then,
  Wear prayer-books in my pocket, look demurely,
  Nay more, while grace is saying, hood mine eyes
  Thus with my hat, and sigh, and say 'amen';
  Use all the observance of civility,
  Like one well studied in a sad ostent
  To please his grandam, never trust me more.
BASSANIO. Well, we shall see your bearing.
GRATIANO. Nay, but I bar to-night; you shall not gauge me
  By what we do to-night.
BASSANIO.   No, that were pity:
  I would entreat you rather to put on
  Your boldest suit of mirth, for we have friends
  That purpose merriment. But fare you well:
  I have some business.
GRATIANO. And I must to Lorenzo and the rest;
  But we will visit you at supper-time.   *Exeunt*

SCENE THREE

The Same. A Room in Shylock's House.

Enter Jessica and Launcelot

JESSICA. I am sorry thou wilt leave my father so:
  Our house is hell, and thou, a merry devil,
  Didst rob it of some taste of tediousness.
  But fare thee well; there is a ducat for thee:
  And, Launcelot, soon at supper shalt thou see
  Lorenzo, who is thy new master's guest:
  Give him this letter; do it secretly;
  And so farewell: I would not have my father
  See me in talk with thee.
LAUNCELOT. Adieu! tears exhibit my tongue. Most beauti-
  ful pagan, most sweet Jew! If a Christian did not play the
  knave and get thee, I am much deceived. But, adieu!
  these foolish drops do somewhat drown my manly spirit:
  adieu!
JESSICA. Farewell, good Launcelot.   *Exit Launcelot*
  Alack, what heinous sin is it in me

To be asham'd to be my father's child!
But though I am a daughter to his blood,
I am not to his manners. O Lorenzo!
If thou keep promise, I shall end this strife,
Become a Christian, and thy loving wife.   *Exit*

SCENE FOUR

The Same. A Street.

Enter Gratiano, Lorenzo, Salarino, and Salanio

LORENZO. Nay, we will slink away in supper-time,
  Disguise us at my lodging, and return
  All in an hour.

GRATIANO. We have not made good preparation.

SALARINO. We have not spoke us yet of torch-bearers.

SALANIO. 'Tis vile, unless it may be quaintly order'd,
  And better, in my mind, not undertook.

LORENZO. 'Tis now but four o'clock: we have two hours
  To furnish us.

        Enter Launcelot, with a letter
              Friend Launcelot, what 's the news?

LAUNCELOT. An it shall please you to break up this, it shall
  seem to signify.

LORENZO. I know the hand: in faith, 'tis a fair hand;
  And whiter than the paper it writ on
  Is the fair hand that writ.

GRATIANO.   Love news, in faith.

LAUNCELOT. By your leave, sir.

LORENZO. Whither goest thou?

LAUNCELOT. Marry, sir, to bid my old master, the Jew, to
  sup to-night with my new master, the Christian.

LORENZO. Hold there, take this: tell gentle Jessica
  I will not fail her; speak it privately.
  Go, gentlemen,   *Exit Launcelot*
  Will you prepare you for this masque to-night?
  I am provided of a torch-bearer.

SALARINO. Ay, marry, I 'll be gone about it straight.

SALANIO. And so will I.

LORENZO.   Meet me and Gratiano
  At Gratiano's lodging some hour hence.

SALARINO. 'Tis good we do so.

Exeunt Salarino and Salanio

GRATIANO. Was not that letter from fair Jessica?

LORENZO. I must needs tell thee all. She hath directed
How I shall take her from her father's house;
What gold and jewels she is furnish'd with;
What page's suit she hath in readiness.
If e'er the Jew her father come to heaven,
It will be for his gentle daughter's sake;
And never dare misfortune cross her foot,
Unless she do it under this excuse,
That she is issue to a faithless Jew.
Come, go with me: peruse this as thou goest.
Fair Jessica shall be my torch-bearer.   *Exeunt*

SCENE FIVE

The Same. Before Shylock's House.

Enter Shylock and Launcelot

SHYLOCK. Well, thou shalt see, thy eyes shall be thy judge,
The difference of old Shylock and Bassanio:—
What, Jessica!—thou shalt not gormandize,
As thou hast done with me;—What, Jessica!—
And sleep and snore, and rend apparel out—
Why, Jessica, I say!

LAUNCELOT.   Why, Jessica!

SHYLOCK. Who bids thee call? I do not bid thee call.

LAUNCELOT. Your worship was wont to tell me that I could
do nothing without bidding.

Enter Jessica

JESSICA. Call you? What is your will?

SHYLOCK. I am bid forth to supper, Jessica:
There are my keys. But wherefore should I go?
I am not bid for love; they flatter me:
But yet I 'll go in hate, to feed upon
The prodigal Christian. Jessica, my girl,
Look to my house. I am right loath to go:
There is some ill a-brewing towards my rest,
For I did dream of money-bags to-night.

LAUNCELOT. I beseech you, sir, go: my young master doth
expect your reproach.

SHYLOCK. So do I his.

LAUNCELOT. And they have conspired together: I will not
say you shall see a masque; but if you do, then it was not
for nothing that my nose fell a-bleeding on Black-Monday
last, at six o'clock i' the morning, falling out that year on
Ash-Wednesday was four year in the afternoon.

SHYLOCK. What! are there masques? Hear you me, Jessica:
Lock up my doors; and when you hear the drum,
And the vile squealing of the wry-neck'd fife,
Clamber not you up to the casements then,
Nor thrust your head into the public street
To gaze on Christian fools with varnish'd faces,
But stop my house's ears, I mean my casements;
Let not the sound of shallow foppery enter
My sober house. By Jacob's staff I swear
I have no mind of feasting forth to-night;
But I will go. Go you before me, sirrah;
Say I will come.

LAUNCELOT. I will go before, sir. Mistress, look out at window, for all this;
       There will come a Christian by,
       Will be worth a Jewess' eye.   *Exit Launcelot*

SHYLOCK. What says that fool of Hagar's offspring, ha?

JESSICA. His words were, 'Farewell, mistress'; nothing else.

SHYLOCK. The patch is kind enough, but a huge feeder;
Snail-slow in profit, and he sleeps by day
More than the wild cat: drones hive not with me;
Therefore I part with him, and part with him
To one that I would have him help to waste
His borrow'd purse. Well, Jessica, go in:
Perhaps I will return immediately:
Do as I bid you; shut doors after you:
'Fast bind, fast find,'
A proverb never stale in thrifty mind.   *Exit*

JESSICA. Farewell; and if my fortune be not crost,
I have a father, you a daughter, lost.   *Exit*

SCENE SIX

The Same.

Enter Gratiano and Salarino, masqued

GRATIANO. This is the penthouse under which Lorenzo
  Desir'd us to make stand.

SALARINO.   His hour is almost past.

GRATIANO. And it is marvel he out-dwells his hour,
  For lovers ever run before the clock.

SALARINO. O! ten times faster Venus' pigeons fly
  To seal love's bonds new-made, than they are wont
  To keep obliged faith unforfeited!

GRATIANO. That ever holds: who riseth from a feast
  With that keen appetite that he sits down?
  Where is the horse that doth untread again
  His tedious measures with the unbated fire
  That he did pace them first? All things that are,
  Are with more spirit chased than enjoy'd.
  How like a younker or a prodigal
  The scarfed bark puts from her native bay,
  Hugg'd and embraced by the strumpet wind!
  How like the prodigal doth she return,
  With over-weather'd ribs and ragged sails,
  Lean, rent, and beggar'd by the strumpet wind!

SALARINO. Here comes Lorenzo: more of this hereafter.

Enter Lorenzo

LORENZO. Sweet friends, your patience for my long abode;
  Not I, but my affairs, have made you wait:
  When you shall please to play the thieves for wives,
  I 'll watch as long for you then. Approach;
  Here dwells my father Jew. Ho! who 's within?

Enter Jessica above, in boy's clothes

JESSICA. Who are you? Tell me, for more certainty,
  Albeit I 'll swear that I do know your tongue.

LORENZO. Lorenzo, and thy love.

JESSICA. Lorenzo, certain; and my love indeed,
  For whom love I so much? And now who knows
  But you, Lorenzo, whether I am yours?

LORENZO. Heaven and thy thoughts are witness that thou
  art.

JESSICA. Here, catch this casket; it is worth the pains.
　I am glad 'tis night, you do not look on me,
　For I am much asham'd of my exchange;
　But love is blind, and lovers cannot see
　The pretty follies that themselves commit;
　For if they could, Cupid himself would blush
　To see me thus transformed to a boy.
LORENZO. Descend, for you must be my torch-bearer.
JESSICA. What! must I hold a candle to my shames?
　They in themselves, good sooth, are too-too light.
　Why, 'tis an office of discovery, love,
　And I should be obscur'd.
LORENZO.　　　　　　　So are you, sweet,
　Even in the lovely garnish of a boy.
　But come at once;
　For the close night doth play the runaway,
　And we are stay'd for at Bassanio's feast.
JESSICA. I will make fast the doors, and gild myself
　With some more ducats, and be with you straight.
　　　　　　　　　　　　　　　　　Exit above
GRATIANO. Now, by my hood, a Gentile, and no Jew.
LORENZO. Beshrew me, but I love her heartily;
　For she is wise, if I can judge of her,
　And fair she is, if that mine eyes be true,
　And true she is, as she hath prov'd herself;
　And therefore, like herself, wise, fair, and true,
　Shall she be placed in my constant soul.
　　　　　　　　　　Enter Jessica
　What, art thou come? On, gentlemen; away!
　Our masquing mates by this time for us stay.
　　　　　　　Exit with Jessica and Salarino
　　　　　　　Enter Antonio
ANTONIO. Who 's there?
GRATIANO. Signior Antonio!
ANTONIO. Fie, fie, Gratiano! where are all the rest?
　'Tis nine o'clock; our friends all stay for you.
　No masque to-night: the wind is come about;
　Bassanio presently will go aboard:
　I have sent twenty out to seek for you.
GRATIANO. I am glad on 't: I desire no more delight
　Than to be under sail and gone to-night.　　*Exeunt*

SCENE SEVEN

Belmont. A Room in Portia's House.

Flourish of Cornets. Enter Portia, with the Prince of Morocco, and their Trains

PORTIA. Go, draw aside the curtains, and discover
The several caskets to this noble prince.
Now make your choice.

MOROCCO. The first, of gold, which this inscription bears:
'Who chooseth me shall gain what many men desire.'
The second, silver, which this promise carries:
'Who chooseth me shall get as much as he deserves.'
This third, dull lead, with warning all as blunt:
'Who chooseth me must give and hazard all he hath.'
How shall I know if I do choose the right?

PORTIA. The one of them contains my picture, prince:
If you choose that, then I am yours withal.

MOROCCO. Some god direct my judgment! Let me see:
I will survey the inscriptions back again:
What says this leaden casket?
'Who chooseth me must give and hazard all he hath.'
Must give: For what? for lead? hazard for lead?
This casket threatens. Men that hazard all
Do it in hope of fair advantages:
A golden mind stoops not to shows of dross;
I 'll then nor give nor hazard aught for lead.
What says the silver with her virgin hue?
'Who chooseth me shall get as much as he deserves.'
As much as he deserves! Pause there, Morocco,
And weigh thy value with an even hand.
If thou be'st rated by thy estimation,
Thou dost deserve enough; and yet enough
May not extend so far as to the lady:
And yet to be afeard of my deserving
Were but a weak disabling of myself.
As much as I deserve! Why, that 's the lady:
I do in birth deserve her, and in fortunes,
In graces, and in qualities of breeding;
But more than these, in love I do deserve.

What if I stray'd no further, but chose here?
Let 's see once more this saying grav'd in gold:
'Who chooseth me shall gain what many men desire.'
Why, that 's the lady: all the world desires her;
From the four corners of the earth they come,
To kiss this shrine, this mortal-breathing saint:
The Hyrcanian deserts and the vasty wilds
Of wide Arabia are as throughfares now
For princes to come view fair Portia:
The watery kingdom, whose ambitious head
Spits in the face of heaven, is no bar
To stop the foreign spirits, but they come,
As o'er a brook, to see fair Portia.
One of these three contains her heavenly picture.
Is 't like that lead contains her? 'Twere damnation
To think so base a thought: it were too gross
To rib her cerecloth in the obscure grave.
Or shall I think in silver she 's immur'd,
Being ten times undervalu'd to tried gold?
O sinful thought! Never so rich a gem
Was set in worse than gold. They have in England
A coin that bears the figure of an angel
Stamped in gold, but that 's insculp'd upon;
But here an angel in a golden bed
Lies all within. Deliver me the key:
Here do I choose, and thrive I as I may!

PORTIA. There, take it, prince; and if my form lie there,
    Then I am yours. *He unlocks the golden casket*

MOROCCO.   O hell! what have we here?
A carrion Death, within whose empty eye
There is a written scroll. I 'll read the writing.

       'All that glisters is not gold;
       Often have you heard that told:
       Many a man his life hath sold
       But my outside to behold:
       Gilded tombs do worms infold.
       Had you been as wise as bold,
       Young in limbs, in judgment old,
       Your answer had not been inscroll'd:
       Fare you well; your suit is cold.'

    Cold, indeed; and labour lost:
Then, farewell, heat, and welcome, frost!

Portia, adieu. I have too griev'd a heart
To take a tedious leave: thus losers part.

Exit with his Train. Flourish of Cornets

PORTIA. A gentle riddance. Draw the curtains: go.
Let all of his complexion choose me so.   *Exeunt*

SCENE EIGHT

Venice. A Street.

Enter Salarino and Salanio

SALARINO. Why, man, I saw Bassanio under sail:
With him is Gratiano gone along;
And in their ship I 'm sure Lorenzo is not.

SALANIO. The villain Jew with outcries rais'd the duke,
Who went with him to search Bassanio's ship.

SALARINO. He came too late, the ship was under sail:
But there the duke was given to understand
That in a gondola were seen together
Lorenzo and his amorous Jessica.
Besides, Antonio certified the duke
They were not with Bassanio in his ship.

SALANIO. I never heard a passion so confus'd,
So strange, outrageous, and so variable,
As the dog Jew did utter in the streets:
'My daughter! O my ducats! O my daughter!
Fled with a Christian! O my Christian ducats!
Justice! the law! my ducats, and my daughter!
A sealed bag, two sealed bags of ducats,
Of double ducats, stol'n from me by my daughter!
And jewels! two stones, two rich and precious stones,
Stol'n by my daughter! Justice! find the girl!
She hath the stones upon her, and the ducats.'

SALARINO. Why, all the boys in Venice follow him,
Crying, his stones, his daughter, and his ducats.

SALANIO. Let good Antonio look he keep his day,
Or he shall pay for this.

SALARINO.   Marry, well remember'd.
I reason'd with a Frenchman yesterday,
Who told me,—in the narrow seas that part

The French and English,—there miscarried
A vessel of our country richly fraught.
I thought upon Antonio when he told me,
And wish'd in silence that it were not his.

SALANIO. You were best to tell Antonio what you hear;
    Yet do not suddenly, for it may grieve him.

SALARINO. A kinder gentleman treads not the earth.
    I saw Bassanio and Antonio part:
    Bassanio told him he would make some speed
    Of his return: he answer'd 'Do not so;
    Slubber not business for my sake, Bassanio,
    But stay the very riping of the time;
    And for the Jew's bond which he hath of me,
    Let it not enter in your mind of love:
    Be merry, and employ your chiefest thoughts
    To courtship and such fair ostents of love
    As shall conveniently become you there.'
    And even there, his eye being big with tears,
    Turning his face, he put his hand behind him,
    And with affection wondrous sensible
    He wrung Bassanio's hand; and so they parted.

SALANIO. I think he only loves the world for him.
    I pray thee, let us go and find him out,
    And quicken his embraced heaviness
    With some delight or other.

SALARINO.   Do we so.   *Exeunt*

SCENE NINE

Belmont. A Room in Portia's House.

Enter Nerissa, with a Servitor

NERISSA. Quick, quick, I pray thee; draw the curtain straight:
    The Prince of Arragon hath ta'en his oath
    And comes to his election presently.

            Flourish of Cornets. Enter the
        Prince of Arragon, Portia, and their Trains

PORTIA. Behold, there stands the caskets, noble prince:
    If you choose that wherein I am contain'd,
    Straight shall our nuptial rites be solemniz'd;

But if you fail, without more speech, my lord,
You must be gone from hence immediately.

ARRAGON. I am enjoin'd by oath to observe three things:
First, never to unfold to any one
Which casket 'twas I chose; next, if I fail
Of the right casket, never in my life
To woo a maid in way of marriage;
Lastly,
If I do fail in fortune of my choice,
Immediately to leave you and be gone.

PORTIA. To these injunctions every one doth swear
That comes to hazard for my worthless self.

ARRAGON. And so have I address'd me. Fortune now
To my heart's hope! Gold, silver, and base lead.
'Who chooseth me must give and hazard all he hath':
You shall look fairer, ere I give or hazard.
What says the golden chest? ha! let me see:
'Who chooseth me shall gain what many men desire.'
What many men desire! that 'many' may be meant
By the fool multitude, that choose by show,
Not learning more than the fond eye doth teach;
Which pries not to the interior, but, like the martlet,
Builds in the weather on the outward wall,
Even in the force and road of casualty.
I will not choose what many men desire,
Because I will not jump with common spirits
And rank me with the barbarous multitude.
Why, then to thee, thou silver treasure-house;
Tell me once more what title thou dost bear:
'Who chooseth me shall get as much as he deserves.'
And well said too; for who shall go about
To cozen fortune and be honourable
Without the stamp of merit? Let none presume
To wear an undeserved dignity.
O! that estates, degrees, and offices
Were not deriv'd corruptly, and that clear honour
Were purchas'd by the merit of the wearer.
How many then should cover that stand bare;
How many be commanded that command;
How much low peasantry would then be glean'd
From the true seed of honour; and how much honour
Pick'd from the chaff and ruin of the times

To be new varnish'd! Well, but to my choice:
'Who chooseth me shall get as much as he deserves.'
I will assume desert. Give me a key for this,
And instantly unlock my fortunes here.

He opens the silver casket

PORTIA. Too long a pause for that which you find there.

ARRAGON. What 's here? the portrait of a blinking idiot,
Presenting me a schedule! I will read it.
How much unlike art thou to Portia!
How much unlike my hopes and my deservings!
'Who chooseth me shall have as much as he deserves.'
Did I deserve no more than a fool's head?
Is that my prize? Are my deserts no better?

PORTIA. To offend, and judge, are distinct offices,
And of opposed natures.

ARRAGON.   What is here?
      'The fire seven times tried this:
      Seven times tried that judgment is
      That did never choose amiss.
      Some there be that shadows kiss;
      Such have but a shadow's bliss:
      There be fools alive, I wis,
      Silver'd o'er; and so was this.
      Take what wife you will to bed,
      I will ever be your head:
      So be gone, sir: you are sped.'
   Still more fool I shall appear
   By the time I linger here:
   With one fool's head I came to woo,
   But I go away with two.
   Sweet, adieu. I 'll keep my oath,
   Patiently to bear my wroth. *Exit Arragon with his Train*

PORTIA. Thus hath the candle sing'd the moth.
   O, these deliberate fools! When they do choose,
   They have the wisdom by their wit to loose.

NERISSA. The ancient saying is no heresy:
   'Hanging and wiving goes by destiny.'

PORTIA. Come, draw the curtain, Nerissa.

Enter a Servant

SERVANT. Where is my lady?

PORTIA.   Here; what would my lord?

SERVANT. Madam, there is alighted at your gate

A young Venetian, one that comes before
To signify the approaching of his lord;
From whom he bringeth sensible regreets,
To wit,—besides commends and courteous breath,—
Gifts of rich value. Yet I have not seen
So likely an ambassador of love.
A day in April never came so sweet,
To show how costly summer was at hand,
As this fore-spurrer comes before his lord.

PORTIA. No more, I pray thee: I am half afeard
Thou wilt say anon he is some kin to thee,
Thou spend'st such high-day wit in praising him.
Come, come, Nerissa; for I long to see
Quick Cupid's post that comes so mannerly.

NERISSA. Bassanio, Lord Love, if thy will it be!   *Exeunt*

ACT THREE

SCENE ONE

Venice. A Street.

Enter Salanio and Salarino

SALANIO. Now, what news on the Rialto?

SALARINO. Why, yet it lives there unchecked that Antonio
hath a ship of rich lading wracked on the narrow seas; the
Goodwins, I think they call the place; a very dangerous
flat, and fatal, where the carcasses of many a tall ship lie
buried, as they say, if my gossip Report be an honest
woman of her word.

SALANIO. I would she were as lying a gossip in that as ever
knapped ginger, or made her neighbours believe she wept
for the death of a third husband. But it is true,—without
any slips of prolixity or crossing the plain highway of talk,
—that the good Antonio, the honest Antonio,—O, that I
had a title good enough to keep his name company!—

SALARINO. Come, the full stop.

SALANIO. Ha! what sayst thou? Why, the end is, he hath lost
a ship.

SALARINO. I would it might prove the end of his losses.

SALANIO. Let me say 'amen' betimes, lest the devil cross my
prayer, for here he comes in the likeness of a Jew.

Enter Shylock

How now, Shylock! What news among the merchants?

SHYLOCK. You knew, none so well, none so well as you, of my
daughter's flight.

SALARINO. That 's certain: I, for my part, knew the tailor
that made the wings she flew withal.

SALANIO. And Shylock, for his own part, knew the bird was
fledged; and then it is the complexion of them all to leave
the dam.

SHYLOCK. She is damned for it.

SALARINO. That's certain, if the devil may be her judge.

SHYLOCK. My own flesh and blood to rebel!

SALANIO. Out upon it, old carrion! rebels it at these years?

SHYLOCK. I say my daughter is my flesh and blood.

SALARINO. There is more difference between thy flesh and hers than between jet and ivory; more between your bloods than there is between red wine and Rhenish. But tell us, do you hear whether Antonio have had any loss at sea or no?

SHYLOCK. There I have another bad match: a bankrupt, a prodigal, who dare scarce show his head on the Rialto; a beggar, that used to come so smug upon the mart; let him look to his bond: he was wont to call me usurer; let him look to his bond: he was wont to lend money for a Christian courtesy; let him look to his bond.

SALARINO. Why, I am sure, if he forfeit thou wilt not take his flesh: what's that good for?

SHYLOCK. To bait fish withal: if it will feed nothing else, it will feed my revenge. He hath disgraced me, and hindered me half a million, laughed at my losses, mocked at my gains, scorned my nation, thwarted my bargains, cooled my friends, heated mine enemies; and what's his reason? I am a Jew. Hath not a Jew eyes? hath not a Jew hands, organs, dimensions, senses, affections, passions? fed with the same food, hurt with the same weapons, subject to the same diseases, healed by the same means, warmed and cooled by the same winter and summer, as a Christian is? If you prick us, do we not bleed? if you tickle us, do we not laugh? if you poison us, do we not die? and if you wrong us, shall we not revenge? If we are like you in the rest, we will resemble you in that. If a Jew wrong a Christian, what is his humility? Revenge. If a Christian wrong a Jew, what should his sufferance be by Christian example? Why, revenge. The villany you teach me I will execute, and it shall go hard but I will better the instruction.

Enter a Servant

SERVANT. Gentlemen, my master Antonio is at his house, and desires to speak with you both.

SALARINO. We have been up and down to seek him.

Enter Tubal

SALANIO. Here comes another of the tribe: a third cannot be

matched, unless the devil himself turn Jew.

Exeunt Salanio, Salarino and Servant

SHYLOCK. How now, Tubal! What news from Genoa? Hast thou found my daughter?

TUBAL. I often came where I did hear of her, but cannot find her.

SHYLOCK. Why there, there, there, there! a diamond gone, cost me two thousand ducats in Frankfort! The curse never fell upon our nation till now; I never felt it till now: two thousand ducats in that; and other precious, precious jewels. I would my daughter were dead at my foot, and the jewels in her ear! Would she were hearsed at my foot, and the ducats in her coffin! No news of them? Why, so: and I know not what 's spent in the search: Why thou—loss upon loss! the thief gone with so much, and so much to find the thief; and no satisfaction, no revenge: nor no ill luck stirring but what lights on my shoulders; no sighs but of my breathing; no tears but of my shedding.

TUBAL. Yes, other men have ill luck too. Antonio, as I heard in Genoa,—

SHYLOCK. What, what, what? Ill luck, ill luck?

TUBAL. —hath an argosy cast away, coming from Tripolis.

SHYLOCK. I thank God! I thank God! Is it true? Is it true?

TUBAL. I spoke with some of the sailors that escaped the wrack.

SHYLOCK. I thank thee, good Tubal. Good news, good news! ha, ha! Where? in Genoa?

TUBAL. Your daughter spent in Genoa, as I heard, one night, fourscore ducats.

SHYLOCK. Thou stick'st a dagger in me: I shall never see my gold again: fourscore ducats at a sitting! fourscore ducats!

TUBAL. There came divers of Antonio's creditors in my company to Venice, that swear he cannot choose but break.

SHYLOCK. I am very glad of it: I 'll plague him; I 'll torture him: I am glad of it.

TUBAL. One of them showed me a ring that he had of your daughter for a monkey.

SHYLOCK. Out upon her! Thou torturest me, Tubal: it was my turquoise; I had it of Leah when I was a bachelor: I would not have given it for a wilderness of monkeys.

TUBAL. But Antonio is certainly undone.

SHYLOCK. Nay, that 's true, that 's very true. Go, Tubal, fee

me an officer; bespeak him a fortnight before. I will have
the heart of him, if he forfeit; for, were he out of Venice, I
can make what merchandise I will. Go, go, Tubal, and
meet me at our synagogue; go, good Tubal; at our synagogue, Tubal.   *Exeunt*

SCENE TWO

Belmont. A Room in Portia's House.

*Enter Bassanio, Portia, Gratiano, Nerissa,
and Attendants*

PORTIA. I pray you, tarry: pause a day or two
Before you hazard; for, in choosing wrong,
I lose your company: therefore, forbear awhile.
There 's something tells me, but it is not love,
I would not lose you; and you know yourself,
Hate counsels not in such a quality.
But lest you should not understand me well,—
And yet a maiden hath no tongue but thought,—
I would detain you here some month or two
Before you venture for me. I could teach you
How to choose right, but then I am forsworn;
So will I never be: so may you miss me;
But if you do, you 'll make me wish a sin,
That I had been forsworn. Beshrew your eyes,
They have o'erlook'd me and divided me:
One half of me is yours, the other half yours,
Mine own, I would say; but if mine, then yours,
And so all yours. O! these naughty times
Put bars between the owners and their rights;
And so, though yours, not yours. Prove it so,
Let fortune go to hell for it, not I.
I speak too long; but 'tis to peise the time,
To eke it and to draw it out in length,
To stay you from election.
BASSANIO.   Let me choose;
For as I am, I live upon the rack.
PORTIA. Upon the rack, Bassanio! Then confess
What treason there is mingled with your love.

BASSANIO. None but that ugly treason of mistrust,
  Which makes me fear th' enjoying of my love:
  There may as well be amity and life
  'Tween snow and fire, as treason and my love.
PORTIA. Ay, but I fear you speak upon the rack,
  Where men enforced do speak anything.
BASSANIO. Promise me life, and I 'll confess the truth.
PORTIA. Well then, confess, and live.
BASSANIO.   'Confess' and 'love'
  Had been the very sum of my confession:
  O happy torment, when my torturer
  Doth teach me answers for deliverance!
  But let me to my fortune and the caskets.
PORTIA. Away then! I am lock'd in one of them:
  If you do love me, you will find me out.
  Nerissa and the rest, stand all aloof.
  Let music sound while he doth make his choice;
  Then, if he lose, he makes a swan-like end,
  Fading in music: that the comparison
  May stand more proper, my eye shall be the stream
  And watery death-bed for him. He may win;
  And what is music then? Then music is
  Even as the flourish when true subjects bow
  To a new-crowned monarch: such it is
  As are those dulcet sounds in break of day
  That creep into the dreaming bridegroom's ear,
  And summon him to marriage. Now he goes,
  With no less presence, but with much more love,
  Than young Alcides, when he did redeem
  The virgin tribute paid by howling Troy
  To the sea-monster: I stand for sacrifice;
  The rest aloof are the Dardanian wives,
  With bleared visages, come forth to view
  The issue of the exploit. Go, Hercules!
  Live thou, I live: with much, much more dismay
  I view the fight than thou that mak'st the fray.

A Song, whilst Bassanio
comments on the caskets to himself

Tell me where is fancy bred,
Or in the heart or in the head?
How begot, how nourished?
  Reply, reply.

It is engender'd in the eyes,
With gazing fed; and fancy dies
In the cradle where it lies.
  Let us all ring fancy's knell:
  I 'll begin it.—Ding, dong, bell.

ALL. Ding, dong, bell.

BASSANIO. So may the outward shows be least themselves:
The world is still deceiv'd with ornament.
In law, what plea so tainted and corrupt
But, being season'd with a gracious voice,
Obscures the show of evil? In religion,
What damned error, but some sober brow
Will bless it and approve it with a text,
Hiding the grossness with fair ornament?
There is no vice so simple but assumes
Some mark of virtue on his outward parts.
How many cowards, whose hearts are all as false
As stairs of sand, wear yet upon their chins
The beards of Hercules and frowning Mars,
Who, inward search'd, have livers white as milk;
And these assume but valour's excrement
To render them redoubted! Look on beauty,
And you shall see 'tis purchas'd by the weight;
Which therein works a miracle in nature,
Making them lightest that wear most of it:
So are those crisped snaky golden locks
Which make such wanton gambols with the wind,
Upon supposed fairness, often known
To be the dowry of a second head,
The skull that bred them, in the sepulchre.
Thus ornament is but the guiled shore
To a most dangerous sea; the beauteous scarf
Veiling an Indian beauty; in a word,
The seeming truth which cunning times put on
To entrap the wisest. Therefore, thou gaudy gold,
Hard food for Midas, I will none of thee;

Nor none of thee, thou pale and common drudge
'Tween man and man: but thou, thou meagre lead,
Which rather threat'nest than dost promise aught,
Thy plainness moves me more than eloquence,
And here choose I: joy be the consequence!
PORTIA. (*Aside*) How all the other passions fleet to air,
As doubtful thoughts, and rash-embrac'd despair,
And shuddering fear, and green-ey'd jealousy.
O love! be moderate; allay thy ecstasy;
In measure rain thy joy; scant this excess;
I feel too much thy blessing; make it less,
For fear I surfeit!
BASSANIO.   What find I here?
                              Opening the leaden casket
Fair Portia's counterfeit! What demi-god
Hath come so near creation? Move these eyes?
Or whether, riding on the balls of mine,
Seem they in motion? Here are sever'd lips,
Parted with sugar breath; so sweet a bar
Should sunder such sweet friends. Here, in her hairs
The painter plays the spider, and hath woven
A golden mesh to entrap the hearts of men
Faster than gnats in cobwebs: but her eyes!—
How could he see to do them? Having made one,
Methinks it should have power to steal both his
And leave itself unfurnish'd: yet look, how far
The substance of my praise doth wrong this shadow
In underprizing it, so far this shadow
Doth limp behind the substance. Here 's the scroll,
The continent and summary of my fortune.

            'You that choose not by the view,
            Chance as fair and choose as true!
            Since this fortune falls to you,
            Be content and seek no new.
            If you be well pleas'd with this
            And hold your fortune for your bliss,
            Turn you where your lady is
            And claim her with a loving kiss.'

A gentle scroll. Fair lady, by your leave;   *Kissing her*
I come by note, to give and to receive.
Like one of two contending in a prize,
That thinks he hath done well in people's eyes,

Hearing applause and universal shout,
Giddy in spirit, still gazing in a doubt
Whether those peals of praise be his or no;
So, thrice-fair lady, stand I, even so,
As doubtful whether what I see be true,
Until confirm'd, sign'd, ratified by you.

PORTIA. You see me, Lord Bassanio, where I stand,
Such as I am: though for myself alone
I would not be ambitious in my wish,
To wish myself much better; yet, for you
I would be trebled twenty times myself;
A thousand times more fair, ten thousand times
More rich;
That only to stand high in your account,
I might in virtues, beauties, livings, friends,
Exceed account: but the full sum of me
Is sum of nothing; which, to term in gross,
Is an unlesson'd girl, unschool'd, unpractis'd;
Happy in this, she is not yet so old
But she may learn; happier than this,
She is not bred so dull but she can learn;
Happiest of all is that her gentle spirit
Commits itself to yours to be directed,
As from her lord, her governor, her king.
Myself and what is mine to you and yours
Is now converted: but now I was the lord
Of this fair mansion, master of my servants,
Queen o'er myself; and even now, but now,
This house, these servants, and this same myself
Are yours, my lord. I give them with this ring;
Which when you part from, lose, or give away,
Let it presage the ruin of your love,
And be my vantage to exclaim on you.

BASSANIO. Madam, you have bereft me of all words,
Only my blood speaks to you in my veins;
And there is such confusion in my powers,
As, after some oration fairly spoke
By a beloved prince, there doth appear
Among the buzzing pleased multitude;
Where every something, being blent together,
Turns to a wild of nothing, save of joy,
Express'd and not express'd. But when this ring

Parts from this finger, then parts life from hence:
O! then be bold to say Bassanio's dead.

NERISSA. My lord and lady, it is now our time,
That have stood by and seen our wishes prosper,
To cry, good joy. Good joy, my lord and lady!

GRATIANO. My Lord Bassanio and my gentle lady,
I wish you all the joy that you can wish;
For I am sure you can wish none from me:
And when your honours mean to solemnize
The bargain of your faith, I do beseech you,
Even at that time I may be married too.

BASSANIO. With all my heart, so thou canst get a wife.

GRATIANO. I thank your lordship, you have got me one.
My eyes, my lord, can look as swift as yours:
You saw the mistress, I beheld the maid;
You lov'd, I lov'd for intermission.
No more pertains to me, my lord, than you.
Your fortune stood upon the caskets there,
And so did mine too, as the matter falls;
For wooing here until I sweat again,
And swearing till my very roof was dry
With oaths of love, at last, if promise last,
I got a promise of this fair one here
To have her love, provided that your fortune
Achiev'd her mistress.

PORTIA.   Is this true, Nerissa?

NERISSA. Madam, it is, so you stand pleas'd withal.

BASSANIO. And do you, Gratiano, mean good faith?

GRATIANO. Yes, faith, my lord.

BASSANIO. Our feast shall be much honour'd in your marriage.

GRATIANO. We'll play with them the first boy for a thousand
ducats.

NERISSA. What! and stake down?

GRATIANO. No; we shall ne'er win at that sport, and stake
down.
But who comes here? Lorenzo and his infidel?
What! and my old Venetian friend, Salanio?

Enter Lorenzo, Jessica, and Salanio

BASSANIO. Lorenzo, and Salanio, welcome hither,
If that the youth of my new interest here
Have power to bid you welcome. By your leave,

I bid my very friends and countrymen,
Sweet Portia, welcome.

PORTIA.   So do I, my lord:
They are entirely welcome.

LORENZO. I thank your honour. For my part, my lord,
My purpose was not to have seen you here;
But meeting with Salanio by the way,
He did entreat me, past all saying nay,
To come with him along.

SALANIO.   I did, my lord,
And I have reason for it. Signior Antonio
Commends him to you.   *Gives Bassanio a letter*

BASSANIO.   Ere I ope his letter,
I pray you, tell me how my good friend doth.

SALANIO. Not sick, my lord, unless it be in mind;
Nor well, unless in mind: his letter there
Will show you his estate.

GRATIANO. Nerissa, cheer yon stranger; bid her welcome.
Your hand, Salanio. What 's the news from Venice?
How doth that royal merchant, good Antonio?
I know he will be glad of our success;
We are the Jasons, we have won the fleece.

SALANIO. I would you had won the fleece that he hath lost.

PORTIA. There are some shrewd contents in yon same paper,
That steal the colour from Bassanio's cheek:
Some dear friend dead, else nothing in the world
Could turn so much the constitution
Of any constant man. What, worse and worse!
With leave, Bassanio; I am half yourself,
And I must freely have the half of anything
That this same paper brings you.

BASSANIO.   O sweet Portia!
Here are a few of the unpleasant'st words
That ever blotted paper. Gentle lady,
When I did first impart my love to you,
I freely told you all the wealth I had
Ran in my veins, I was a gentleman:
And then I told you true; and yet, dear lady,
Rating myself at nothing, you shall see
How much I was a braggart. When I told you
My state was nothing, I should then have told you
That I was worse than nothing; for, indeed,

I have engag'd myself to a dear friend,
Engag'd my friend to his mere enemy,
To feed my means. Here is a letter, lady;
The paper as the body of my friend,
And every word in it a gaping wound,
Issuing life-blood. But is it true, Salanio?
Hath all his ventures fail'd? What, not one hit?
From Tripolis, from Mexico, and England,
From Lisbon, Barbary, and India?
And not one vessel 'scape the dreadful touch
Of merchant-marring rocks?

SALANIO.   Not one, my lord.
Besides, it should appear, that if he had
The present money to discharge the Jew,
He would not take it. Never did I know
A creature, that did bear the shape of man,
So keen and greedy to confound a man.
He plies the duke at morning and at night,
And doth impeach the freedom of the state,
If they deny him justice: twenty merchants,
The duke himself, and the magnificoes
Of greatest port, have all persuaded with him;
But none can drive him from the envious plea
Of forfeiture, of justice, and his bond.

JESSICA. When I was with him, I have heard him swear
To Tubal and to Chus, his countrymen,
That he would rather have Antonio's flesh
Than twenty times the value of the sum
That he did owe him; and I know, my lord,
If law, authority, and power deny not,
It will go hard with poor Antonio.

PORTIA. Is it your dear friend that is thus in trouble?

BASSANIO. The dearest friend to me, the kindest man,
The best-condition'd and unwearied spirit
In doing courtesies, and one in whom
The ancient Roman honour more appears
Than any that draws breath in Italy.

PORTIA. What sum owes he the Jew?

BASSANIO. For me, three thousand ducats.

PORTIA.   What, no more?
Pay him six thousand, and deface the bond;
Double six thousand, and then treble that,

Before a friend of this description
Shall lose a hair thorough Bassanio's fault.
First go with me to church and call me wife,
And then away to Venice to your friend;
For never shall you lie by Portia's side
With an unquiet soul. You shall have gold
To pay the petty debt twenty times over:
When it is paid, bring your true friend along.
My maid Nerissa and myself meantime,
Will live as maids and widows. Come, away!
For you shall hence upon your wedding-day.
Bid your friends welcome, show a merry cheer;
Since you are dear bought, I will love you dear.
But let me hear the letter of your friend.

BASSANIO. 'Sweet Bassanio, my ships have all miscarried, my
creditors grow cruel, my estate is very low, my bond to the
Jew is forfeit; and since, in paying it, it is impossible I
should live, all debts are cleared between you and I, if I
might but see you at my death. Notwithstanding, use your
pleasure: if your love do not persuade you to come, let
not my letter.'

PORTIA. O love, dispatch all business, and be gone!

BASSANIO. Since I have your good leave to go away,
    I will make haste; but, till I come again,
No bed shall e'er be guilty of my stay,
    Nor rest be interposer 'twixt us twain.   *Exeunt*

SCENE THREE

Venice. A Street.

Enter Shylock, Salarino, Antonio, and Gaoler

SHYLOCK. Gaoler, look to him: tell not me of mercy;
    This is the fool that lent out money gratis:
    Gaoler, look to him.

ANTONIO.   Hear me yet, good Shylock.

SHYLOCK. I 'll have my bond; speak not against my bond:
    I have sworn an oath that I will have my bond.
    Thou call'dst me dog before thou hadst a cause,
    But, since I am a dog, beware my fangs:
    The duke shall grant me justice. I do wonder,

Thou naughty gaoler, that thou art so fond
To come abroad with him at his request.

ANTONIO. I pray thee, hear me speak.

SHYLOCK. I 'll have my bond; I will not hear thee speak:
I 'll have my bond, and therefore speak no more.
I 'll not be made a soft and dull-eyed fool,
To shake the head, relent, and sigh, and yield
To Christian intercessors. Follow not;
I 'll have no speaking; I will have my bond.   *Exit*

SALARINO. It is the most impenetrable cur
That ever kept with men.

ANTONIO.   Let him alone:
I 'll follow him no more with bootless prayers.
He seeks my life; his reason well I know.
I oft deliver'd from his forfeitures
Many that have at times made moan to me;
Therefore he hates me.

SALARINO.   I am sure the duke
Will never grant this forfeiture to hold.

ANTONIO. The duke cannot deny the course of law:
For the commodity that strangers have
With us in Venice, if it be denied,
'Twill much impeach the justice of the state;
Since that the trade and profit of the city
Consisteth of all nations. Therefore, go:
These griefs and losses have so bated me,
That I shall hardly spare a pound of flesh
To-morrow to my bloody creditor.
Well, gaoler, on. Pray God, Bassanio come
To see me pay his debt, and then I care not!   *Exeunt*

SCENE FOUR

Belmont. A Room in Portia's House.

Enter Portia, Nerissa, Lorenzo, Jessica, and Balthazar

LORENZO. Madam, although I speak it in your presence,
You have a noble and a true conceit
Of god-like amity; which appears most strongly
In bearing thus the absence of your lord.
But if you knew to whom you show this honour,

How true a gentleman you send relief,
How dear a lover of my lord your husband,
I know you would be prouder of the work
Than customary bounty can enforce you.

PORTIA. I never did repent for doing good,
Nor shall not now: for in companions
That do converse and waste the time together,
Whose souls do bear an equal yoke of love,
There must be needs a like proportion
Of lineaments, of manners, and of spirit;
Which makes me think that this Antonio,
Being the bosom lover of my lord,
Must needs be like my lord. If it be so,
How little is the cost I have bestow'd
In purchasing the semblance of my soul
From out the state of hellish cruelty!
This comes too near the praising of myself;
Therefore, no more of it: hear other things.
Lorenzo, I commit into your hands
The husbandry and manage of my house
Until my lord's return: for mine own part,
I have toward heaven breath'd a secret vow
To live in prayer and contemplation,
Only attended by Nerissa here,
Until her husband and my lord's return.
There is a monastery two miles off,
And there will we abide. I do desire you
Not to deny this imposition,
The which my love and some necessity
Now lays upon you.

LORENZO.   Madam, with all my heart:
I shall obey you in all fair commands.

PORTIA. My people do already know my mind,
And will acknowledge you and Jessica
In place of Lord Bassanio and myself.
So fare you well till we shall meet again.

LORENZO. Fair thoughts and happy hours attend on you!

JESSICA. I wish your ladyship all heart's content.

PORTIA. I thank you for your wish, and am well pleas'd
To wish it back on you: fare you well, Jessica.

Exeunt Jessica and Lorenzo

Now, Balthazar,
As I have ever found thee honest-true,
So let me find thee still. Take this same letter,
And use thou all the endeavour of a man
In speed to Padua: see thou render this
Into my cousin's hand, Doctor Bellario;
And, look, what notes and garments he doth give thee,
Bring them, I pray thee, with imagin'd speed
Unto the traject, to the common ferry
Which trades to Venice. Waste no time in words,
But get thee gone: I shall be there before thee.

BALTHAZAR. Madam, I go with all convenient speed.   *Exit*

PORTIA. Come on, Nerissa: I have work in hand
That you yet know not of: we 'll see our husbands
Before they think of us.

NERISSA.   Shall they see us?

PORTIA. They shall, Nerissa; but in such a habit
That they shall think we are accomplished
With that we lack. I 'll hold thee any wager,
When we are both accoutred like young men,
I 'll prove the prettier fellow of the two,
And wear my dagger with the braver grace,
And speak between the change of man and boy
With a reed voice, and turn two mincing steps
Into a manly stride, and speak of frays
Like a fine bragging youth, and tell quaint lies,
How honourable ladies sought my love,
Which I denying, they fell sick and died:
I could not do withal; then I 'll repent,
And wish, for all that, that I had not kill'd them:
And twenty of these puny lies I 'll tell,
That men shall swear I have discontinu'd school
Above a twelvemonth. I have within my mind
A thousand raw tricks of these bragging Jacks,
Which I will practise.

NERISSA.   Why, shall we turn to men?

PORTIA. Fie, what a question 's that,
If thou wert near a lewd interpreter!
But come: I 'll tell thee all my whole device
When I am in my coach, which stays for us
At the park gate; and therefore haste away,
For we must measure twenty miles to-day.   *Exeunt*

SCENE FIVE

The Same. A Garden.

Enter Launcelot and Jessica

LAUNCELOT. Yes, truly; for, look you, the sins of the father are to be laid upon the children; therefore, I promise you, I fear you. I was always plain with you, and so now I speak my agitation of the matter: therefore be of good cheer; for, truly, I think you are damned. There is but one hope in it that can do you any good, and that is but a kind of bastard hope neither.

JESSICA. And what hope is that, I pray thee?

LAUNCELOT. Marry, you may partly hope that your father got you not, that you are not the Jew's daughter.

JESSICA. That were a kind of bastard hope, indeed: so the sins of my mother should be visited upon me.

LAUNCELOT. Truly then I fear you are damned both by father and mother: thus when I shun Scylla, your father, I fall into Charybdis, your mother: well, you are gone both ways.

JESSICA. I shall be saved by my husband; he hath made me a Christian.

LAUNCELOT. Truly the more to blame he: we were Christians enow before; e'en as many as could well live one by another. This making of Christians will raise the price of hogs: if we grow all to be pork-eaters, we shall not shortly have a rasher on the coals for money.

JESSICA. I 'll tell my husband, Launcelot, what you say: here he comes.

Enter Lorenzo

LORENZO. I shall grow jealous of you shortly, Launcelot, if you thus get my wife into corners.

JESSICA. Nay, you need not fear us, Lorenzo: Launcelot and I are out. He tells me flatly, there is no mercy for me in heaven, because I am a Jew's daughter: and he says you are no good member of the commonwealth, for, in converting Jews to Christians, you raise the price of pork.

LORENZO. I shall answer that better to the commonwealth

than you can the getting up of the negro's belly: the Moor
is with child by you, Launcelot.

LAUNCELOT. It is much that the Moor should be more than
reason; but if she be less than an honest woman, she is indeed more than I took her for.

LORENZO. How every fool can play upon the word! I think
the best grace of wit will shortly turn into silence, and discourse grow commendable in none only but parrots. Go
in, sirrah: bid them prepare for dinner.

LAUNCELOT. That is done, sir; they have all stomachs.

LORENZO. Goodly Lord, what a wit-snapper are you! Then
bid them prepare dinner.

LAUNCELOT. That is done too, sir; only, 'cover' is the word.

LORENZO. Will you cover, then, sir?

LAUNCELOT. Not so, sir, neither; I know my duty.

LORENZO. Yet more quarrelling with occasion! Wilt thou
show the whole wealth of thy wit in an instant? I pray
thee, understand a plain man in his plain meaning: go to
thy fellows; bid them cover the table, serve in the meat,
and we will come in to dinner.

LAUNCELOT. For the table, sir, it shall be served in; for the
meat, sir, it shall be covered; for your coming in to dinner,
sir, why, let it be as humours and conceits shall govern.

Exit

LORENZO. O dear discretion, how his words are suited!
The fool hath planted in his memory
An army of good words: and I do know
A many fools, that stand in better place,
Garnish'd like him, that for a tricksy word
Defy the matter. How cheer'st thou, Jessica?
And now, good sweet, say thy opinion;
How dost thou like the Lord Bassanio's wife?

JESSICA. Past all expressing. It is very meet,
The Lord Bassanio live an upright life,
For, having such a blessing in his lady,
He finds the joys of heaven here on earth;
And if on earth he do not mean it, then
In reason he should never come to heaven.
Why, if two gods should play some heavenly match,
And on the wager lay two earthly women,
And Portia one, there must be something else

Pawn'd with the other, for the poor rude world
Hath not her fellow.

LORENZO.   Even such a husband
Hast thou of me as she is for a wife.

JESSICA. Nay, but ask my opinion too of that.

LORENZO. I will anon; first, let us go to dinner.

JESSICA. Nay, let me praise you while I have a stomach.

LORENZO. No, pray thee, let it serve for table-talk;
    Then howsoe'er thou speak'st, 'mong other things
    I shall digest it.

JESSICA.   Well, I'll set you forth.   *Exeunt*

ACT FOUR

SCENE ONE

Venice. A Court of Justice.

*Enter the Duke: the Magnificoes; Antonio, Bassanio,
Gratiano, Salarino, Salanio, and Others*

DUKE. What, is Antonio here?

ANTONIO. Ready, so please your Grace.

DUKE. I am sorry for thee: thou art come to answer
A stony adversary, an inhuman wretch
Uncapable of pity, void and empty
From any dram of mercy.

ANTONIO.   I have heard
Your Grace hath ta'en great pains to qualify
His rigorous course; but since he stands obdurate,
And that no lawful means can carry me
Out of his envy's reach, I do oppose
My patience to his fury, and am arm'd
To suffer with a quietness of spirit
The very tyranny and rage of his.

DUKE. Go one, and call the Jew into the court.

SALARINO. He's ready at the door: he comes, my lord.

Enter Shylock

DUKE. Make room, and let him stand before our face.
Shylock, the world thinks, and I think so too,
That thou but lead'st this fashion of thy malice
To the last hour of act; and then 'tis thought
Thou 'lt show thy mercy and remorse more strange
Than is thy strange-apparent cruelty;
And where thou now exact'st the penalty,—
Which is a pound of this poor merchant's flesh,—
Thou wilt not only loose the forfeiture,
But, touch'd with human gentleness and love,
Forgive a moiety of the principal;

Glancing an eye of pity on his losses,
That have of late so huddled on his back,
Enow to press a royal merchant down,
And pluck commiseration of his state
From brassy bosoms and rough hearts of flint,
From stubborn Turks and Tartars, never train'd
To offices of tender courtesy.
We all expect a gentle answer, Jew.

SHYLOCK. I have possess'd your Grace of what I purpose;
And by our holy Sabbath have I sworn
To have the due and forfeit of my bond:
If you deny it, let the danger light
Upon your charter and your city's freedom.
You 'll ask me, why I rather choose to have
A weight of carrion flesh than to receive
Three thousand ducats: I 'll not answer that:
But say it is my humour: is it answer'd?
What if my house be troubled with a rat,
And I be pleas'd to give ten thousand ducats
To have it ban'd? What, are you answer'd yet?
Some men there are love not a gaping pig;
Some, that are mad if they behold a cat;
And others, when the bagpipe sings i' the nose,
Cannot contain their urine: for affection,
Mistress of passion, sways it to the mood
Of what it likes, or loathes. Now, for your answer
As there is no firm reason to be render'd,
Why he cannot abide a gaping pig;
Why he, a harmless necessary cat;
Why he, a wauling bagpipe; but of force
Must yield to such inevitable shame
As to offend, himself being offended;
So can I give no reason, nor I will not,
More than a lodg'd hate and a certain loathing
I bear Antonio, that I follow thus
A losing suit against him. Are you answer'd?

BASSANIO. This is no answer, thou unfeeling man,
To excuse the current of thy cruelty.

SHYLOCK. I am not bound to please thee with my answer.

BASSANIO. Do all men kill the things they do not love?

SHYLOCK. Hates any man the thing he would not kill?

BASSANIO. Every offence is not a hate at first.

SHYLOCK. What! wouldst thou have a serpent sting thee
  twice?

ANTONIO. I pray you, think you question with the Jew:
  You may as well go stand upon the beach,
  And bid the main flood bate his usual height;
  You may as well use question with the wolf,
  Why he hath made the ewe bleat for the lamb;
  You may as well forbid the mountain pines
  To wag their high tops, and to make no noise
  When they are fretted with the gusts of heaven;
  You may as well do anything most hard,
  As seek to soften that—than which what 's harder?—
  His Jewish heart: therefore, I do beseech you,
  Make no more offers, use no further means;
  But with all brief and plain conveniency,
  Let me have judgment, and the Jew his will.

BASSANIO. For thy three thousand ducats here is six.

SHYLOCK. If every ducat in six thousand ducats
  Were in six parts and every part a ducat,
  I would not draw them; I would have my bond.

DUKE. How shalt thou hope for mercy, rendering none?

SHYLOCK. What judgment shall I dread, doing no wrong?
  You have among you many a purchas'd slave,
  Which, like your asses and your dogs and mules,
  You use in abject and in slavish parts,
  Because you bought them: shall I say to you,
  Let them be free, marry them to your heirs?
  Why sweat they under burdens? Let their beds
  Be made as soft as yours, and let their palates
  Be season'd with such viands? You will answer:
  'The slaves are ours': so do I answer you:
  The pound of flesh which I demand of him,
  Is dearly bought; 'tis mine and I will have it.
  If you deny me, fie upon your law!
  There is no force in the decrees of Venice.
  I stand for judgment: answer; shall I have it?

DUKE. Upon my power I may dismiss this court,
  Unless Bellario, a learned doctor,
  Whom I have sent for to determine this,
  Come here to-day.

SALARINO.   My lord, here stays without
  A messenger with letters from the doctor,

New come from Padua.

DUKE. Bring us the letters: call the messenger.

BASSANIO. Good cheer, Antonio! What, man, courage yet!
The Jew shall have my flesh, blood, bones, and all,
Ere thou shalt lose for me one drop of blood.

ANTONIO. I am a tainted wether of the flock,
Meetest for death: the weakest kind of fruit
Drops earliest to the ground; and so let me:
You cannot better be employ'd, Bassanio,
Than to live still, and write mine epitaph.

Enter Nerissa, dressed like a lawyer's clerk

DUKE. Came you from Padua, from Bellario?

NERISSA. From both, my lord. Bellario greets your Grace.

Presents a letter

BASSANIO. Why dost thou whet thy knife so earnestly?

SHYLOCK. To cut the forfeiture from that bankrupt there.

GRATIANO. Not on thy sole, but on thy soul, harsh Jew,
Thou mak'st thy knife keen; but no metal can,
No, not the hangman's axe, bear half the keenness
Of thy sharp envy. Can no prayers pierce thee?

SHYLOCK. No, none that thou hast wit enough to make.

GRATIANO. O, be thou damn'd, inexecrable dog!
And for thy life let justice be accus'd.
Thou almost mak'st me waver in my faith
To hold opinion with Pythagoras,
That souls of animals infuse themselves
Into the trunks of men: thy currish spirit
Govern'd a wolf, who, hang'd for human slaughter,
Even from the gallows did his fell soul fleet,
And whilst thou lay'st in thy unhallow'd dam,
Infus'd itself in thee; for thy desires
Are wolfish, bloody, starv'd, and ravenous.

SHYLOCK. Till thou canst rail the seal from off my bond,
Thou but offend'st thy lungs to speak so loud:
Repair thy wit, good youth, or it will fall
To cureless ruin. I stand here for law.

DUKE. This letter from Bellario doth commend
A young and learned doctor to our court.
Where is he?

NERISSA.   He attendeth here hard by,
To know your answer, whether you 'll admit him.

DUKE. With all my heart: some three or four of you

Go give him courteous conduct to this place.
Meantime, the court shall hear Bellario's letter.

CLERK. (*Reads*) 'Your Grace shall understand that at the receipt of your letter I am very sick; but in the instant that your messenger came, in loving visitation was with me a young doctor of Rome; his name is Balthazar. I acquainted him with the cause in controversy between the Jew and Antonio the merchant: we turned o'er many books together: he is furnished with my opinion; which, bettered with his own learning,—the greatness whereof I cannot enough commend,—comes with him, at my importunity, to fill up your Grace's request in my stead. I beseech you, let his lack of years be no impediment to let him lack a reverend estimation, for I never knew so young a body with so old a head. I leave him to your gracious acceptance, whose trial shall better publish his commendation.'

DUKE. You hear the learn'd Bellario, what he writes:
And here, I take it, is the doctor come.

Enter Portia, dressed like a doctor of laws

Give me your hand. Came you from old Bellario?

PORTIA. I did, my lord.

DUKE.   You are welcome: take your place.
Are you acquainted with the difference
That holds this present question in the court?

PORTIA. I am informed throughly of the cause.
Which is the merchant here, and which the Jew?

DUKE. Antonio and old Shylock, both stand forth.

PORTIA. Is your name Shylock?

SHYLOCK.   Shylock is my name.

PORTIA. Of a strange nature is the suit you follow;
Yet in such rule that the Venetian law
Cannot impugn you as you do proceed.
(*To Antonio*) You stand within his danger, do you not?

ANTONIO. Ay, so he says.

PORTIA.   Do you confess the bond?

ANTONIO. I do.

PORTIA.   Then must the Jew be merciful.

SHYLOCK. On what compulsion must I? tell me that.

PORTIA. The quality of mercy is not strain'd,
It droppeth as the gentle rain from heaven
Upon the place beneath: it is twice bless'd;

It blesseth him that gives and him that takes:
'Tis mightiest in the mightiest; it becomes
The throned monarch better than his crown;
His sceptre shows the force of temporal power,
The attribute to awe and majesty,
Wherein doth sit the dread and fear of kings;
But mercy is above this sceptred sway,
It is enthroned in the hearts of kings,
It is an attribute to God himself,
And earthly power doth then show likest God's
When mercy seasons justice. Therefore, Jew,
Though justice be thy plea, consider this,
That in the course of justice none of us
Should see salvation: we do pray for mercy,
And that same prayer doth teach us all to render
The deeds of mercy. I have spoke thus much
To mitigate the justice of thy plea,
Which if thou follow, this strict court of Venice
Must needs give sentence 'gainst the merchant there.

SHYLOCK. My deeds upon my head! I crave the law,
The penalty and forfeit of my bond.

PORTIA. Is he not able to discharge the money?

BASSANIO. Yes, here I tender it for him in the court;
Yea, twice the sum: if that will not suffice,
I will be bound to pay it ten times o'er,
On forfeit of my hands, my head, my heart.
If this will not suffice, it must appear
That malice bears down truth. And, I beseech you,
Wrest once the law to your authority:
To do a great right, do a little wrong,
And curb this cruel devil of his will.

PORTIA. It must not be. There is no power in Venice
Can alter a decree established:
'Twill be recorded for a precedent,
And many an error by the same example
Will rush into the state. It cannot be.

SHYLOCK. A Daniel come to judgment! yea, a Daniel!
O wise young judge, how I do honour thee!

PORTIA. I pray you, let me look upon the bond.

SHYLOCK. Here 'tis, most reverend doctor; here it is.

PORTIA. Shylock, there 's thrice thy money offer'd thee.

SHYLOCK. An oath, an oath, I have an oath in heaven:

Shall I lay perjury upon my soul?
No, not for Venice.

PORTIA.   Why, this bond is forfeit;
And lawfully by this the Jew may claim
A pound of flesh to be by him cut off
Nearest the merchant's heart. Be merciful:
Take thrice thy money; bid me tear the bond.

SHYLOCK. When it is paid according to the tenour.
It doth appear you are a worthy judge;
You know the law, your exposition
Hath been most sound: I charge you by the law,
Whereof you are a well-deserving pillar,
Proceed to judgment: by my soul I swear
There is no power in the tongue of man
To alter me. I stay here on my bond.

ANTONIO. Most heartily I do beseech the court
To give the judgment.

PORTIA.   Why then, thus it is:
You must prepare your bosom for his knife.

SHYLOCK. O noble judge! O excellent young man!

PORTIA. For, the intent and purpose of the law
Hath full relation to the penalty,
Which here appeareth due upon the bond.

SHYLOCK. 'Tis very true! O wise and upright judge!
How much more elder art thou than thy looks!

PORTIA. Therefore lay bare your bosom.

SHYLOCK.   Ay, 'his breast':
So says the bond:—doth it not, noble judge?—
'Nearest his heart': those are the very words.

PORTIA. It is so. Are there balance here to weigh
The flesh?

SHYLOCK.   I have them ready.

PORTIA. Have by some surgeon, Shylock, on your charge,
To stop his wounds, lest he do bleed to death.

SHYLOCK. Is it so nominated in the bond?

PORTIA. It is not so express'd; but what of that?
'Twere good you do so much for charity.

SHYLOCK. I cannot find it: 'tis not in the bond.

PORTIA. You, merchant, have you any thing to say?

ANTONIO. But little: I am arm'd and well prepar'd.
Give me your hand, Bassanio: fare you well!
Grieve not that I am fallen to this for you;

For herein Fortune shows herself more kind
Than is her custom: it is still her use
To let the wretched man outlive his wealth,
To view with hollow eye and wrinkled brow
An age of poverty; from which lingering penance
Of such a misery doth she cut me off.
Commend me to your honourable wife:
Tell her the process of Antonio's end;
Say how I lov'd you, speak me fair in death;
And, when the tale is told, bid her be judge
Whether Bassanio had not once a love.
Repent not you that you shall lose your friend,
And he repents not that he pays your debt;
For if the Jew do cut but deep enough,
I 'll pay it instantly with all my heart.

BASSANIO. Antonio, I am married to a wife
Which is as dear to me as life itself;
But life itself, my wife, and all the world,
Are not with me esteem'd above thy life:
I would lose all, ay, sacrifice them all,
Here to this devil, to deliver you.

PORTIA. Your wife would give you little thanks for that,
If she were by to hear you make the offer.

GRATIANO. I have a wife, whom, I protest, I love:
I would she were in heaven, so she could
Entreat some power to change this currish Jew.

NERISSA. 'Tis well you offer it behind her back;
The wish would make else an unquiet house.

SHYLOCK. These be the Christian husbands! I have a daugh-
    ter;
Would any of the stock of Barabbas
Had been her husband rather than a Christian!
We trifle time; I pray thee, pursue sentence.

PORTIA. A pound of that same merchant's flesh is thine.
The court awards it, and the law doth give it.

SHYLOCK. Most rightful judge!

PORTIA. And you must cut this flesh from off his breast:
The law allows it, and the court awards it.

SHYLOCK. Most learned judge! A sentence! come, prepare!

PORTIA. Tarry a little: there is something else.
This bond doth give thee here no jot of blood;
The words expressly are 'a pound of flesh':

Then take thy bond, take thou thy pound of flesh;
But, in the cutting it, if thou dost shed
One drop of Christian blood, thy lands and goods
Are, by the laws of Venice, confiscate
Unto the state of Venice.

GRATIANO. O upright judge! Mark, Jew: O learned judge!

SHYLOCK. Is that the law?

PORTIA.   Thyself shalt see the act;
For, as thou urgest justice, be assur'd
Thou shalt have justice, more than thou desir'st.

GRATIANO. O learned judge! Mark, Jew: a learned judge!

SHYLOCK. I take this offer then: pay the bond thrice,
And let the Christian go.

BASSANIO.   Here is the money.

PORTIA. Soft!
The Jew shall have all justice; soft! no haste:—
He shall have nothing but the penalty.

GRATIANO. O Jew! an upright judge, a learned judge!

PORTIA. Therefore prepare thee to cut off the flesh.
Shed thou no blood; nor cut thou less, nor more,
But just a pound of flesh: if thou tak'st more,
Or less, than a just pound, be it but so much
As makes it light or heavy in the substance,
Or the division of the twentieth part
Of one poor scruple, nay, if the scale do turn
But in the estimation of a hair,
Thou diest and all thy goods are confiscate.

GRATIANO. A second Daniel, a Daniel, Jew!
Now, infidel, I have thee on the hip.

PORTIA. Why doth the Jew pause? Take thy forfeiture.

SHYLOCK. Give me my principal, and let me go.

BASSANIO. I have it ready for thee; here it is.

PORTIA. He hath refus'd it in the open court:
He shall have merely justice, and his bond.

GRATIANO. A Daniel, still say I; a second Daniel!
I thank thee, Jew, for teaching me that word.

SHYLOCK. Shall I not have barely my principal?

PORTIA. Thou shalt have nothing but the forfeiture,
To be so taken at thy peril, Jew.

SHYLOCK. Why, then the devil give him good of it!
I'll stay no longer question.

PORTIA.   Tarry, Jew:

The law hath yet another hold on you.
It is enacted in the laws of Venice,
If it be prov'd against an alien
That by direct or indirect attempts
He seek the life of any citizen,
The party 'gainst the which he doth contrive
Shall seize one half his goods; the other half
Comes to the privy coffer of the state;
And the offender's life lies in the mercy
Of the duke only, 'gainst all other voice.
In which predicament, I say, thou stand'st;
For it appears by manifest proceeding,
That indirectly and directly too
Thou hast contrived against the very life
Of the defendant; and thou hast incurr'd
The danger formerly by me rehears'd.
Down therefore and beg mercy of the duke.

GRATIANO. Beg that thou mayst have leave to hang thyself:
And yet, thy wealth being forfeit to the state,
Thou hast not left the value of a cord;
Therefore thou must be hang'd at the state's charge.

DUKE. That thou shalt see the difference of our spirits,
I pardon thee thy life before thou ask it.
For half thy wealth, it is Antonio's;
The other half comes to the general state,
Which humbleness may drive into a fine.

PORTIA. Ay, for the state; not for Antonio.

SHYLOCK. Nay, take my life and all; pardon not that:
You take my house when you do take the prop
That doth sustain my house; you take my life
When you do take the means whereby I live.

PORTIA. What mercy can you render him, Antonio?

GRATIANO. A halter gratis; nothing else, for God's sake!

ANTONIO. So please my lord the duke, and all the court,
To quit the fine for one half of his goods,
I am content; so he will let me have
The other half in use, to render it,
Upon his death, unto the gentleman
That lately stole his daughter:
Two things provided more, that, for this favour,
He presently become a Christian;
The other, that he do record a gift,

Here in the court, of all he dies possess'd,
Unto his son Lorenzo, and his daughter.
DUKE. He shall do this, or else I do recant
The pardon that I late pronounced here.
PORTIA. Art thou contented, Jew? what dost thou say?
SHYLOCK. I am content.
PORTIA.   Clerk, draw a deed of gift.
SHYLOCK. I pray you give me leave to go from hence:
I am not well. Send the deed after me,
And I will sign it.
DUKE.   Get thee gone, but do it.
GRATIANO. In christening thou shalt have two godfathers;
Had I been judge, thou shouldst have had ten more,
To bring thee to the gallows, not the font.   *Exit Shylock*
DUKE. Sir, I entreat you home with me to dinner.
PORTIA. I humbly do desire your Grace of pardon:
I must away this night toward Padua,
And it is meet I presently set forth.
DUKE. I am sorry that your leisure serves you not.
Antonio, gratify this gentleman,
For, in my mind, you are much bound to him.
                    Exeunt Duke, Magnificoes, and Train
BASSANIO. Most worthy gentleman, I and my friend
Have by your wisdom been this day acquitted
Of grievous penalties; in lieu whereof,
Three thousand ducats, due unto the Jew,
We freely cope your courteous pains withal.
ANTONIO. And stand indebted, over and above,
In love and service to you evermore.
PORTIA. He is well paid that is well satisfied;
And I, delivering you, am satisfied,
And therein do account myself well paid:
My mind was never yet more mercenary.
I pray you, know me when we meet again:
I wish you well, and so I take my leave.
BASSANIO. Dear sir, of force I must attempt you further:
Take some remembrance of us, as a tribute,
Not as a fee. Grant me two things, I pray you,
Not to deny me, and to pardon me.
PORTIA. You press me far, and therefore I will yield.
    (*To Antonio*) Give me your gloves, I 'll wear them for
    your sake;

(*To Bassanio*) And for your love, I 'll take this ring from
  you.
Do not draw back your hand; I 'll take no more;
And you in love shall not deny me this;

BASSANIO. This ring, good sir? alas! it is a trifle;
I will not shame myself to give you this.

PORTIA. I will have nothing else but only this;
And now methinks I have a mind to it.

BASSANIO. There 's more depends on this than on the value.
The dearest ring in Venice will I give you,
And find it out by proclamation:
Only for this, I pray you, pardon me.

PORTIA. I see, sir, you are liberal in offers:
You taught me first to beg, and now methinks
You teach me how a beggar should be answer'd.

BASSANIO. Good sir, this ring was given me by my wife;
And, when she put it on, she made me vow
That I should never sell nor give nor lose it.

PORTIA. That 'scuse serves many men to save their gifts.
An if your wife be not a mad-woman,
And know how well I have deserv'd the ring,
She would not hold out enemy for ever,
For giving it to me. Well, peace be with you.

                        Exeunt Portia and Nerissa

ANTONIO. My Lord Bassanio, let him have the ring:
Let his deservings and my love withal
Be valu'd 'gainst your wife's commandment.

BASSANIO. Go, Gratiano; run and overtake him;
Give him the ring, and bring him, if thou canst,
Unto Antonio's house. Away! make haste.   *Exit Gratiano*
Come, you and I will thither presently,
And in the morning early will we both
Fly toward Belmont. Come, Antonio.   *Exeunt*

SCENE TWO

The Same. A Street.

Enter Portia and Nerissa

PORTIA. Inquire the Jew's house out, give him this deed,
And let him sign it. We 'll away to-night,
And be a day before our husbands home:
This deed will be well welcome to Lorenzo.

Enter Gratiano

GRATIANO. Fair sir, you are well o'erta'en.
My Lord Bassanio upon more advice
Hath sent you here this ring, and doth entreat
Your company at dinner.

PORTIA.   That cannot be:
His ring I do accept most thankfully;
And so, I pray you, tell him: furthermore,
I pray you, show my youth old Shylock's house.

GRATIANO. That will I do.

NERISSA.   Sir, I would speak with you.
(*Aside to Portia*) I 'll see if I can get my husband's ring,
Which I did make him swear to keep for ever.

PORTIA. Thou mayst, I warrant. We shall have old swearing
That they did give the rings away to men;
But we 'll outface them, and outswear them too.
Away! make haste: thou know'st where I will tarry.

NERISSA. Come, good sir, will you show me to this house?

                                              Exeunt

ACT FIVE

SCENE ONE

Belmont. The Avenue to Portia's House.

Enter Lorenzo and Jessica

LORENZO. The moon shines bright: in such a night as this,
  When the sweet wind did gently kiss the trees
  And they did make no noise, in such a night
  Troilus methinks mounted the Troyan walls,
  And sigh'd his soul toward the Grecian tents,
  Where Cressid lay that night.

JESSICA.   In such a night
  Did Thisbe fearfully o'ertrip the dew,
  And saw the lion's shadow ere himself,
  And ran dismay'd away.

LORENZO.   In such a night
  Stood Dido with a willow in her hand
  Upon the wild sea-banks, and waft her love
  To come again to Carthage.

JESSICA.   In such a night
  Medea gather'd the enchanted herbs
  That did renew old Æson.

LORENZO.   In such a night
  Did Jessica steal from the wealthy Jew,
  And with an unthrift love did run from Venice,
  As far as Belmont.

JESSICA.   In such a night
  Did young Lorenzo swear he lov'd her well,
  Stealing her soul with many vows of faith—
  And ne'er a true one.

LORENZO.   In such a night
  Did pretty Jessica, like a little shrew,
  Slander her love, and he forgave it her.

JESSICA. I would out-night you, did no body come;

But, hark! I hear the footing of a man.

Enter Stephano

LORENZO. Who comes so fast in silence of the night?

STEPHANO. A friend.

LORENZO. A friend! What friend? your name, I pray you,
   friend.

STEPHANO. Stephano is my name; and I bring word
   My mistress will before the break of day
   Be here at Belmont. She doth stray about
   By holy crosses, where she kneels and prays
   For happy wedlock hours.

LORENZO.   Who comes with her?

STEPHANO. None, but a holy hermit and her maid.
   I pray you, is my master yet return'd?

LORENZO. He is not, nor we have not heard from him.
   But go we in, I pray thee, Jessica,
   And ceremoniously let us prepare
   Some welcome for the mistress of the house.

Enter Launcelot

LAUNCELOT. Sola, sola! wo ha, ho! sola, sola!

LORENZO. Who calls?

LAUNCELOT. Sola! did you see Master Lorenzo?
   Master Lorenzo! sola, sola!

LORENZO. Leave hollaing, man; here.

LAUNCELOT. Sola! where? where?

LORENZO. Here.

LAUNCELOT. Tell him there 's a post come from my master,
   with his horn full of good news: my master will be here
   ere morning.   *Exit*

LORENZO. Sweet soul, let 's in, and there expect their com-
   ing.
   And yet no matter; why should we go in?
   My friend Stephano, signify, I pray you,
   Within the house, your mistress is at hand;
   And bring your music forth into the air.   *Exit Stephano*
   How sweet the moonlight sleeps upon this bank!
   Here will we sit, and let the sounds of music
   Creep in our ears: soft stillness and the night
   Become the touches of sweet harmony.
   Sit, Jessica: look, how the floor of heaven
   Is thick inlaid with patines of bright gold:
   There 's not the smallest orb which thou behold'st

But in his motion like an angel sings,
Still quiring to the young-eyed cherubins;
Such harmony is in immortal souls;
But, whilst this muddy vesture of decay
Doth grossly close it in, we cannot hear it.

Enter Musicians

Come, ho! and wake Diana with a hymn:
With sweetest touches pierce your mistress' ear,
And draw her home with music.   *Music*

JESSICA. I am never merry when I hear sweet music.
LORENZO. The reason is, your spirits are attentive:
For do but note a wild and wanton herd,
Or race of youthful and unhandled colts,
Fetching mad bounds, bellowing and neighing loud,
Which is the hot condition of their blood;
If they but hear perchance a trumpet sound,
Or any air of music touch their ears,
You shall perceive them make a mutual stand,
Their savage eyes turn'd to a modest gaze
By the sweet power of music: therefore the poet
Did feign that Orpheus drew trees, stones, and floods;
Since naught so stockish, hard, and full of rage,
But music for the time doth change his nature,
The man that hath no music in himself,
Nor is not mov'd with concord of sweet sounds,
Is fit for treasons, stratagems, and spoils;
The motions of his spirit are dull as night,
And his affections dark as Erebus:
Let no such man be trusted. Mark the music.

Enter Portia and Nerissa, at a distance

PORTIA. That light we see is burning in my hall.
How far that little candle throws his beams!
So shines a good deed in a naughty world.
NERISSA. When the moon shone, we did not see the candle.
PORTIA. So doth the greater glory dim the less:
A substitute shines brightly as a king
Until a king be by, and then his state
Empties itself, as doth an inland brook
Into the main of waters. Music! hark!
NERISSA. It is your music, madam, of the house.
PORTIA. Nothing is good, I see, without respect:
Methinks it sounds much sweeter than by day.

NERISSA. Silence bestows that virtue on it, madam.

PORTIA. The crow doth sing as sweetly as the lark
When neither is attended, and I think
The nightingale, if she should sing by day,
When every goose is cackling, would be thought
No better a musician than the wren.
How many things by season season'd are
To their right praise and true perfection!
Peace, ho! the moon sleeps with Endymion,
And would not be awak'd!   *Music ceases*

LORENZO.   That is the voice,
Or I am much deceiv'd, of Portia.

PORTIA. He knows me, as the blind man knows the cuckoo,
By the bad voice.

LORENZO.   Dear lady, welcome home.

PORTIA. We have been praying for our husbands' welfare,
Which speed, we hope, the better for our words.
Are they return'd?

LORENZO.   Madam, they are not yet;
But there is come a messenger before,
To signify their coming.

PORTIA.   Go in, Nerissa:
Give order to my servants that they take
No note at all of our being absent hence;
Nor you, Lorenzo; Jessica, nor you.   *A tucket sounds*

LORENZO. Your husband is at hand; I hear his trumpet:
We are no tell-tales, madam; fear you not.

PORTIA. This night methinks is but the daylight sick;
It looks a little paler: 'tis a day,
Such as the day is when the sun is hid.

Enter Bassanio, Antonio, Gratiano, and their Followers

BASSANIO. We should hold day with the Antipodes,
If you would walk in absence of the sun.

PORTIA. Let me give light, but let me not be light;
For a light wife doth make a heavy husband,
And never be Bassanio so for me:
But God sort all! You are welcome home, my lord.

BASSANIO. I thank you, madam. Give welcome to my friend:
This is the man, this is Antonio,
To whom I am so infinitely bound.

PORTIA. You should in all sense be much bound to him,
For, as I hear, he was much bound for you.

ANTONIO. No more than I am well acquitted of.

PORTIA. Sir, you are very welcome to our house:
It must appear in other ways than words,
Therefore I scant this breathing courtesy.

GRATIANO. (*To Nerissa*) By yonder moon I swear you do
me wrong;
In faith, I gave it to the judge's clerk:
Would he were gelt that had it, for my part,
Since you do take it, love, so much at heart.

PORTIA. A quarrel, ho, already! what's the matter?

GRATIANO. About a hoop of gold, a paltry ring
That she did give me, whose posy was
For all the world like cutlers' poetry
Upon a knife, 'Love me, and leave me not.'

NERISSA. What talk you of the posy, or the value?
You swore to me, when I did give it you,
That you would wear it till your hour of death,
And that it should lie with you in your grave:
Though not for me, yet for your vehement oaths,
You should have been respective and have kept it.
Gave it a judge's clerk! no, God's my judge,
The clerk will ne'er wear hair on 's face that had it.

GRATIANO. He will, an if he live to be a man.

NERISSA. Ay, if a woman live to be a man.

GRATIANO. Now, by this hand, I gave it to a youth,
A kind of boy, a little scrubbed boy,
No higher than thyself, the judge's clerk.
A prating boy, that begg'd it as a fee:
I could not for my heart deny it him.

PORTIA. You were to blame,—I must be plain with you,—
To part so slightly with your wife's first gift;
A thing stuck on with oaths upon your finger,
And riveted so with faith unto your flesh.
I gave my love a ring and made him swear
Never to part with it; and here he stands,
I dare be sworn for him he would not leave it
Nor pluck it from his finger for the wealth
That the world masters. Now, in faith, Gratiano,
You give your wife too unkind a cause of grief:
An 'twere to me, I should be mad at it.

BASSANIO. (*Aside*) Why, I were best to cut my left hand off,
And swear I lost the ring defending it.

GRATIANO. My Lord Bassanio gave his ring away
  Unto the judge that begg'd it, and indeed
  Deserv'd it too; and then the boy, his clerk,
  That took some pains in writing, he begg'd mine;
  And neither man nor master would take aught
  But the two rings.

PORTIA.   What ring gave you, my lord?
  Not that, I hope, that you receiv'd of me.

BASSANIO. If I could add a lie unto a fault,
  I would deny it; but you see my finger
  Hath not the ring upon it; it is gone.

PORTIA. Even so void is your false heart of truth.
  By heaven, I will ne'er come in your bed
  Until I see the ring.

NERISSA.   Nor I in yours,
  Till I again see mine.

BASSANIO.   Sweet Portia,
  If you did know to whom I gave the ring,
  If you did know for whom I gave the ring,
  And would conceive for what I gave the ring,
  And how unwillingly I left the ring,
  When naught would be accepted but the ring,
  You would abate the strength of your displeasure.

PORTIA. If you had known the virtue of the ring,
  Or half her worthiness that gave the ring,
  Or your own honour to contain the ring,
  You would not then have parted with the ring.
  What man is there so much unreasonable,
  If you had pleas'd to have defended it
  With any terms of zeal, wanted the modesty
  To urge the thing held as a ceremony?
  Nerissa teaches me what to believe:
  I 'll die for 't but some woman had the ring.

BASSANIO. No, by my honour, madam, by my soul,
  No woman had it; but a civil doctor
  Which did refuse three thousand ducats of me,
  And begg'd the ring, the which I did deny him,
  And suffer'd him to go displeas'd away;
  Even he that did uphold the very life
  Of my dear friend. What should I say, sweet lady?
  I was enforc'd to send it after him;
  I was beset with shame and courtesy;

My honour would not let ingratitude
So much besmear it. Pardon me, good lady,
For, by these blessed candles of the night,
Had you been there, I think you would have begg'd
The ring of me to give the worthy doctor.

PORTIA. Let not that doctor e'er come near my house.
Since he hath got the jewel that I lov'd,
And that which you did swear to keep for me,
I will become as liberal as you;
I 'll not deny him any thing I have;
No, not my body, nor my husband's bed.
Know him I shall, I am well sure of it:
Lie not a night from home; watch me like Argus:
If you do not, if I be left alone,
Now by mine honour, which is yet mine own,
I 'll have that doctor for my bedfellow.

NERISSA. And I his clerk; therefore be well advis'd
How you do leave me to mine own protection.

GRATIANO. Well, do you so: let me not take him, then;
For if I do, I 'll mar the young clerk's pen.

ANTONIO. I am the unhappy subject of these quarrels.

PORTIA. Sir, grieve not you; you are welcome notwithstanding.

BASSANIO. Portia, forgive me this enforced wrong;
And in the hearing of these many friends,
I swear to thee, even by thine own fair eyes,
Wherein I see myself,—

PORTIA.   Mark you but that!
In both my eyes he doubly sees himself;
In each eye, one: swear by your double self,
And there 's an oath of credit.

BASSANIO.   Nay, but hear me:
Pardon this fault, and by my soul I swear
I never more will break an oath with thee.

ANTONIO. I once did lend my body for his wealth,
Which, but for him that had your husband's ring,
Had quite miscarried: I dare be bound again,
My soul upon the forfeit, that your lord
Will never more break faith advisedly.

PORTIA. Then you shall be his surety. Give him this,
And bid him keep it better than the other.

ANTONIO. Here, Lord Bassanio; swear to keep this ring.

BASSANIO. By heaven! it is the same I gave the doctor!

PORTIA. I had it of him: pardon me, Bassanio,
For, by this ring, the doctor lay with me.

NERISSA. And pardon me, my gentle Gratiano;
For that same scrubbed boy, the doctor's clerk,
In lieu of this last night did lie with me.

GRATIANO. Why, this is like the mending of high ways
In summer, where the ways are fair enough.
What! are we cuckolds ere we have deserv'd it?

PORTIA. Speak not so grossly. You are all amaz'd:
Here is a letter; read it at your leisure;
It comes from Padua, from Bellario:
There you shall find that Portia was the doctor,
Nerissa, there, her clerk: Lorenzo here
Shall witness I set forth as soon as you
And even but now return'd; I have not yet
Enter'd my house. Antonio, you are welcome;
And I have better news in store for you
Than you expect: unseal this letter soon;
There you shall find three of your argosies
Are richly come to harbour suddenly.
You shall not know by what strange accident
I chanced on this letter.

ANTONIO.   I am dumb.

BASSANIO. Were you the doctor and I knew you not?

GRATIANO. Were you the clerk that is to make me cuckold?

NERISSA. Ay; but the clerk that never means to do it,
Unless he live until he be a man.

BASSANIO. Sweet doctor, you shall be my bedfellow:
When I am absent, then, lie with my wife.

ANTONIO. Sweet lady, you have given me life and living;
For here I read for certain that my ships
Are safely come to road.

PORTIA.   How now, Lorenzo!
My clerk hath some good comforts too for you.

NERISSA. Ay, and I 'll give them him without a fee.
There do I give to you and Jessica,
From the rich Jew, a special deed of gift,
After his death, of all he dies possess'd of.

LORENZO. Fair ladies, you drop manna in the way
Of starved people.

PORTIA.   It is almost morning,

And yet I am sure you are not satisfied
Of these events at full. Let us go in;
And charge us there upon inter'gatories,
And we will answer all things faithfully.

GRATIANO. Let it be so: the first inter'gatory
That my Nerissa shall be sworn on is,
Whe'r till the next night she had rather stay,
Or go to bed now, being two hours to day:
But were the day come, I should wish it dark,
That I were couching with the doctor's clerk.
Well, while I live I 'll fear no other thing
So sore as keeping safe Nerissa's ring.   *Exeunt*

AS YOU LIKE IT

CAST OF CHARACTERS

DUKE, *living in exile*
FREDERICK, *his Brother, Usurper of his Dominions*

AMIENS
JAQUES
} *Lords attending upon the banished Duke*

LE BEAU, *a Courtier, attending upon Frederick*
CHARLES, *a Wrestler*

OLIVER
JAQUES
ORLANDO
} *Sons of Sir Rowland de Boys*

ADAM
DENNIS
} *Servants to Oliver*

TOUCHSTONE, *a Clown*
SIR OLIVER MARTEXT, *a Vicar*

CORIN
SILVIUS
} *Shepherds*

WILLIAM, *a Country Fellow, in love with Audrey*
A person representing Hymen

ROSALIND, *Daughter to the banished Duke*
CELIA, *Daughter to Frederick*
PHEBE, *a Shepherdess*
AUDREY, *a Country Wench*

Lords, Pages, Foresters, and Attendants

SCENE

First, Oliver's Orchard near his House; afterwards, in the Usurper's Court, and in the Forest of Arden

AS YOU LIKE IT

ACT ONE

SCENE ONE

An Orchard near Oliver's House.

Enter Orlando and Adam

ORLANDO. As I remember, Adam, it was upon this fashion:
he bequeathed me by will but poor a thousand crowns,
and, as thou sayest, charged my brother on his blessing,
to breed me well: and there begins my sadness. My
brother Jaques he keeps at school, and report speaks
goldenly of his profit. For my part, he keeps me rustically
at home, or, to speak more properly, stays me here at home
unkept; for call you that keeping for a gentleman of my
birth, that differs not from the stalling of an ox? His horses
are bred better; for, besides that they are fair with their
feeding, they are taught their manage, and to that end
riders dearly hired: but I, his brother, gain nothing under
him but growth, for the which his animals on his dung-
hills are as much bound to him as I. Besides this nothing
that he so plentifully gives me, the something that nature
gave me, his countenance seems to take from me. He lets
me feed with his hinds, bars me the place of a brother,
and, as much as in him lies, mines my gentility with my
education. This is it, Adam, that grieves me; and the spirit
of my father, which I think is within me, begins to mutiny
against this servitude. I will no longer endure it, though
yet I know no wise remedy how to avoid it.

ADAM. Yonder comes my master, your brother.

ORLANDO. Go apart, Adam, and thou shalt hear how he will
shake me up.

Enter Oliver

OLIVER. Now, sir! what make you here?

ORLANDO. Nothing. I am not taught to make anything.

OLIVER. What mar you then, sir.

ORLANDO. Marry, sir, I am helping you to mar that which God made, a poor unworthy brother of yours, with idleness.

OLIVER. Marry, sir, be better employed, and be naught awhile.

ORLANDO. Shall I keep your hogs, and eat husks with them? What prodigal portion have I spent, that I should come to such penury?

OLIVER. Know you where you are, sir?

ORLANDO. O! sir, very well: here in your orchard.

OLIVER. Know you before whom, sir?

ORLANDO. Ay, better than he I am before knows me. I know you are my eldest brother; and, in the gentle condition of blood, you should so know me. The courtesy of nations allows you my better, in that you are the first-born; but the same tradition takes not away my blood, were there twenty brothers betwixt us. I have as much of my father in me as you; albeit, I confess, your coming before me is nearer to his reverence.

OLIVER. What, boy!   *Strikes him*

ORLANDO. Come, come, elder brother, you are too young in this.   *Seizes him*

OLIVER. Wilt thou lay hands on me, villain?

ORLANDO. I am no villain; I am the youngest son of Sir Rowland de Boys; he was my father, and he is thrice a villain that says such a father begot villains. Wert thou not my brother, I would not take this hand from thy throat till this other had pulled out thy tongue for saying so: thou hast railed on thyself.

ADAM. (*Coming forward*) Sweet masters, be patient: for your father's remembrance, be at accord.

OLIVER. Let me go, I say.

ORLANDO. I will not, till I please: you shall hear me. My father charged you in his will to give me good education: you have trained me like a peasant, obscuring and hiding from me all gentleman-like qualities. The spirit of my father grows strong in me, and I will no longer endure it; therefore allow me such exercises as may become a gentleman, or give me the poor allottery my father left me by testament; with that I will go buy my fortunes.

                                                    Releases him

OLIVER. And what wilt thou do? beg, when that is spent? Well, sir, get you in: I will not long be troubled with you; you shall have some part of your will: I pray you, leave me.

ORLANDO. I will no further offend you than becomes me for my good.

OLIVER. Get you with him, you old dog.

ADAM. Is 'old dog' my reward? Most true, I have lost my teeth in your service. God be with my old master! he would not have spoke such a word.

                                    Exeunt Orlando and Adam

OLIVER. Is it even so? begin you to grow upon me? I will physic your rankness, and yet give no thousand crowns neither. Holla, Dennis!

                        Enter Dennis

DENNIS. Calls your worship?

OLIVER. Was not Charles the duke's wrestler here to speak with me?

DENNIS. So please you, he is here at the door, and importunes access to you.

OLIVER. Call him in. (*Exit Dennis*) 'Twill be a good way; and to-morrow the wrestling is.

                        Enter Charles

CHARLES. Good-morrow to your worship.

OLIVER. Good Monsieur Charles. What 's the new news at the new court?

CHARLES. There 's no news at the court, sir, but the old news: that is, the old duke is banished by his younger brother the new duke; and three or four loving lords have put themselves into voluntary exile with him, whose lands and revenues enrich the new duke; therefore he gives them good leave to wander.

OLIVER. Can you tell if Rosalind, the duke's daughter, be banished with her father?

CHARLES. O, no; for the duke's daughter, her cousin, so loves her,—being ever from their cradles bred together, —that she would have followed her exile, or have died to stay behind her. She is at the court, and no less beloved of her uncle than his own daughter; and never two ladies loved as they do.

OLIVER. Where will the old duke live?

CHARLES. They say he is already in the forest of Arden, and

a many merry men with him; and there they live like the
old Robin Hood of England. They say many young gentlemen flock to him every day, and fleet the time carelessly, as they did in the golden world.

OLIVER. What, you wrestle to-morrow before the new duke?

CHARLES. Marry, do I, sir; and I came to acquaint you with
a matter. I am given, sir, secretly to understand that your
younger brother Orlando hath a disposition to come in
disguised against me to try a fall. To-morrow, sir, I
wrestle for my credit, and he that escapes me without
some broken limb shall acquit him well. Your brother is
but young and tender; and, for your love, I would be
loath to foil him as I must, for my own honour, if he come
in: therefore, out of my love to you, I came hither to acquaint you withal, that either you might stay him from
his intendment, or brook such disgrace well as he shall
run into, in that it is a thing of his own search and altogether against my will.

OLIVER. Charles, I thank thee for thy love to me, which
thou shalt find I will most kindly requite. I had myself
notice of my brother's purpose herein, and have by un-
derhand means laboured to dissuade him from it, but he
is resolute. I 'll tell thee, Charles, it is the stubbornest
young fellow of France; full of ambition, an envious em-
ulator of every man's good parts, a secret and villanous
contriver against me his natural brother; therefore use
thy discretion. I had as lief thou didst break his neck as
his finger. And thou wert best look to 't; for if thou dost
him any slight disgrace, or if he do not mightily grace
himself on thee, he will practise against thee by poison,
entrap thee by some treacherous device, and never leave
thee till he hath ta'en thy life by some indirect means or
other; for, I assure thee,—and almost with tears I speak it,
—there is not one so young and so villanous this day living. I speak but brotherly of him; but should I anatomize
him to thee as he is, I must blush and weep, and thou
must look pale and wonder.

CHARLES. I am heartily glad I came hither to you. If he
come to-morrow, I 'll give him his payment: if ever he go
alone again, I 'll never wrestle for prize more; and so God
keep your worship!   *Exit*

OLIVER. Farewell, good Charles. Now will I stir this gamester. I hope I shall see an end of him; for my soul, yet I know not why, hates nothing more than he. Yet he 's gentle, never schooled and yet learned, full of noble device, of all sorts enchantingly beloved, and, indeed so much in the heart of the world, and especially of my own people, who best know him, that I am altogether misprised. But it shall not be so long; this wrestler shall clear all: nothing remains but that I kindle the boy thither, which now I 'll go about.

SCENE TWO

A Lawn before the Duke's Palace.

Enter Rosalind and Celia

CELIA. I pray thee, Rosalind, sweet my coz, be merry.

ROSALIND. Dear Celia, I show more mirth than I am mistress of, and would you yet I were merrier? Unless you could teach me to forget a banished father, you must not learn me how to remember any extraordinary pleasure.

CELIA. Herein I see thou lovest me not with the full weight that I love thee. If my uncle, thy banished father, had banished thy uncle, the duke my father, so thou hadst been still with me, I could have taught my love to take thy father for mine: so wouldst thou, if the truth of thy love to me were so righteously tempered as mine is to thee.

ROSALIND. Well, I will forget the condition of my estate, to rejoice in yours.

CELIA. You know my father hath no child but I, nor none is like to have; and, truly, when he dies, thou shalt be his heir: for what he hath taken away from thy father perforce, I will render thee again in affection; by mine honour, I will; and when I break that oath, let me turn monster. Therefore, my sweet Rose, my dear Rose, be merry.

ROSALIND. From henceforth I will, coz, and devise sports. Let me see; what think you of falling in love?

CELIA. Marry, I prithee, do, to make sport withal: but love no man in good earnest; nor no further in sport neither, than with safety of a pure blush thou mayst in honour come off again.

ROSALIND. What shall be our sport then?

CELIA. Let us sit and mock the good housewife Fortune from her wheel, that her gifts may henceforth be bestowed equally.

ROSALIND. I would we could do so, for her benefits are mightily misplaced, and the bountiful blind woman doth most mistake in her gifts to women.

CELIA. 'Tis true; for those that she makes fair she scarce makes honest, and those that she makes honest she makes very ill-favouredly.

ROSALIND. Nay, now thou goest from Fortune's office to Nature's: Fortune reigns in gifts of the world, not in the lineaments of Nature.

Enter Touchstone

CELIA. No? When Nature hath made a fair creature, may she not by Fortune fall into the fire? Though Nature hath given us wit to flout at Fortune, hath not Fortune sent in this fool to cut off the argument?

ROSALIND. Indeed, there is Fortune too hard for Nature, when Fortune makes Nature's natural the cutter-off of Nature's wit.

CELIA. Peradventure this is not Fortune's work neither, but Nature's; who, perceiving our natural wits too dull to reason of such goddesses, hath sent this natural for our whetstone: for always the dullness of the fool is the whetstone of the wits. How now, wit! Whither wander you?

TOUCHSTONE. Mistress, you must come away to your father.

CELIA. Were you made the messenger?

TOUCHSTONE. No, by mine honour; but I was bid to come for you.

ROSALIND. Where learned you that oath, fool?

TOUCHSTONE. Of a certain knight that swore by his honour they were good pancakes, and swore by his honour the mustard was naught. Now, I 'll stand to it, the pancakes were naught and the mustard was good, and yet was not the knight forsworn.

CELIA. How prove you that, in the great heap of your knowledge?

ROSALIND. Ay, marry: now unmuzzle your wisdom.

TOUCHSTONE. Stand you both forth now. Stroke your chins, and swear by your beards that I am a knave.

CELIA. By our beards, if we had them, thou art.

TOUCHSTONE. By my knavery, if I had it, then I were; but if you swear by that that is not, you are not forsworn: no more was this knight, swearing by his honour, for he never had any; or if he had, he had sworn it away before ever he saw those pancakes or that mustard.

CELIA. Prithee, who is 't that thou meanest?

TOUCHSTONE. One that old Frederick, your father, loves.

CELIA. My father's love is enough to honour him. Enough! speak no more of him; you 'll be whipped for taxation one of these days.

TOUCHSTONE. The more pity that fools may not speak wisely what wise men do foolishly.

CELIA. By my troth, thou sayest true; for since the little wit that fools have was silenced, the little foolery that wise men have makes a great show. Here comes Monsieur Le Beau.

ROSALIND. With his mouth full of news.

CELIA. Which he will put on us, as pigeons feed their young.

ROSALIND. Then we shall be news-cramm'd.

CELIA. All the better; we shall be more marketable.

Enter Le Beau

Bon jour, Monsieur Le Beau. What 's the news?

LE BEAU. Fair princess, you have lost much good sport.

CELIA. Sport! Of what colour?

LE BEAU. What colour, madam! How shall I answer you?

ROSALIND. As wit and fortune will.

TOUCHSTONE. Or as the Destinies decree.

CELIA. Well said! That was laid on with a trowel.

TOUCHSTONE. Nay, if I keep not my rank,—

ROSALIND. Thou losest thy old smell.

LE BEAU. You amaze me, ladies. I would have told you of good wrestling, which you have lost the sight of.

ROSALIND. Yet tell us the manner of the wrestling.

LE BEAU. I will tell you the beginning; and, if it please your ladyships, you may see the end, for the best is yet to do; and here, where you are, they are coming to perform it.

CELIA. Well, the beginning, that is dead and buried.

LE BEAU. There comes an old man and his three sons,—

CELIA. I could match this beginning with an old tale.

LE BEAU. Three proper young men, of excellent growth and presence;—

ROSALIND. With bills on their necks, 'Be it known unto all men by these presents.'

LE BEAU. The eldest of the three wrestled with Charles, the duke's wrestler; which Charles in a moment threw him and broke three of his ribs, that there is little hope of life in him. So he served the second, and so the third. Yonder they lie; the poor old man, their father, making such pitiful dole over them that all the beholders take his part with weeping.

ROSALIND. Alas!

TOUCHSTONE. But what is the sport, monsieur, that the ladies have lost?

LE BEAU. Why, this that I speak of.

TOUCHSTONE. Thus men may grow wiser every day. It is the first time that ever I heard breaking of ribs was sport for ladies.

CELIA. Or I, I promise thee.

ROSALIND. But is there any else longs to feel this broken music in his sides? Is there yet another dotes upon ribbreaking? Shall we see this wrestling, cousin?

LE BEAU. You must, if you stay here; for here is the place appointed for the wrestling, and they are ready to perform it.

CELIA. Yonder, sure, they are coming. Let us now stay and see it.

Flourish. Enter Duke Frederick,
Lords, Orlando, Charles, and Attendants

DUKE FREDERICK. Come on. Since the youth will not be entreated, his own peril on his forwardness.

ROSALIND. Is yonder the man?

LE BEAU. Even he, madam.

CELIA. Alas! he is too young: yet he looks successfully.

DUKE FREDERICK. How now, daughter and cousin! Are you crept hither to see the wrestling?

ROSALIND. Ay, my liege, so please you give us leave.

DUKE FREDERICK. You will take little delight in it, I can tell you, there is such odds in the man. In pity of the challenger's youth I would fain dissuade him, but he will not be entreated. Speak to him, ladies; see if you can move him.

CELIA. Call him hither, good Monsieur Le Beau.

DUKE FREDERICK. Do so. I 'll not be by.   *Duke goes apart*

LE BEAU. Monsieur the challenger, the princess calls for you.

ORLANDO. I attend them with all respect and duty.

ROSALIND. Young man, have you challenged Charles the wrestler?

ORLANDO. No, fair princess; he is the general challenger: I come but in, as others do, to try with him the strength of my youth.

CELIA. Young gentleman, your spirits are too bold for your years. You have seen cruel proof of this man's strength. If you saw yourself with your eyes or knew yourself with your judgment, the fear of your adventure would counsel you to a more equal enterprise. We pray you, for your own sake, to embrace your own safety and give over this attempt.

ROSALIND. Do, young sir. Your reputation shall not therefore be misprised. We will make it our suit to the duke that the wrestling might not go forward.

ORLANDO. I beseech you, punish me not with your hard thoughts, wherein I confess me much guilty, to deny so fair and excellent ladies anything. But let your fair eyes and gentle wishes go with me to my trial: wherein if I be foiled, there is but one shamed that was never gracious; if killed, but one dead that is willing to be so. I shall do my friends no wrong, for I have none to lament me; the world no injury, for in it I have nothing; only in the world I fill up a place, which may be better supplied when I have made it empty.

ROSALIND. The little strength that I have, I would it were with you.

CELIA. And mine, to eke out hers.

ROSALIND. Fare you well. Pray heaven I be deceived in you!

CELIA. Your heart's desires be with you!

CHARLES. Come, where is this young gallant that is so desirous to lie with his mother earth?

ORLANDO. Ready, sir; but his will hath in it a more modest working.

DUKE FREDERICK. You shall try but one fall.

CHARLES. No, I warrant your Grace, you shall not entreat him to a second, that have so mightily presuaded him from a first.

ORLANDO. You mean to mock me after; you should not have
  mocked me before: but come your ways.

ROSALIND. Now Hercules be thy speed, young man!

CELIA. I would I were invisible, to catch the strong fellow
  by the leg.   *Charles and Orlando wrestle*

ROSALIND. O excellent young man!

CELIA. If I had a thunderbolt in mine eye, I can tell who
  should down.   *Charles is thrown. Shout*

DUKE FREDERICK. No more, no more.

ORLANDO. Yes, I beseech your Grace. I am not yet well
  breathed.

DUKE FREDERICK. How dost thou, Charles?

LE BEAU. He cannot speak, my lord.

DUKE FREDERICK. Bear him away. What is thy name, young
  man?   *Charles is borne out*

ORLANDO. Orlando, my liege; the youngest son of Sir Rowland de Boys.

DUKE FREDERICK. I would thou hadst been son to some man
  else!
    The world esteem'd thy father honourable,
    But I did find him still mine enemy:
    Thou shouldst have better pleas'd me with this deed,
    Hadst thou descended from another house.
    But fare thee well; thou art a gallant youth:
    I would thou hadst told me of another father.
                       Exeunt Duke Frederick, Train, and Le Beau

CELIA. Were I my father, coz, would I do this?

ORLANDO. I am more proud to be Sir Rowland's son,
    His youngest son; and would not change that calling,
    To be adopted heir to Frederick.

ROSALIND. My father lov'd Sir Rowland as his soul,
    And all the world was of my father's mind:
    Had I before known this young man his son,
    I should have given him tears unto entreaties,
    Ere he should thus have ventur'd.

CELIA.   Gentle cousin,
    Let us go thank him and encourage him.
    My father's rough and envious disposition
    Sticks me at heart. Sir, you have well deserv'd.
    If you do keep your promises in love
    But justly, as you have exceeded all promise,
    Your mistress shall be happy.

ROSALIND.   Gentleman,
            Giving him a chain from her neck
  Wear this for me, one out of suits with fortune,
  That could give more, but that her hand lacks means.
  Shall we go, coz?

CELIA.   Ay. Fare you well, fair gentleman.

ORLANDO. Can I not say, I thank you? My better parts
  Are all thrown down, and that which here stands up
  Is but a quintain, a mere lifeless block.

ROSALIND. He calls us back. My pride fell with my fortunes;
  I 'll ask him what he would. Did you call, sir?
  Sir, you have wrestled well, and overthrown
  More than your enemies.

CELIA.   Will you go, coz?

ROSALIND. Have with you. Fare you well.

                    Exeunt Rosalind and Celia

ORLANDO. What passion hangs these weights upon my
      tongue?
  I cannot speak to her, yet she urg'd conference.
  O poor Orlando, thou art overthrown!
  Or Charles or something weaker masters thee.

                    Re-enter Le Beau

LE BEAU. Good sir, I do in friendship counsel you
  To leave this place. Albeit you have deserv'd
  High commendation, true applause and love,
  Yet such is now the duke's condition
  That he misconstrues all that you have done.
  The duke is humorous. What he is indeed,
  More suits you to conceive than I to speak of.

ORLANDO. I thank you, sir; and pray you, tell me this;
  Which of the two was daughter of the duke,
  That here was at the wrestling?

LE BEAU. Neither his daughter, if we judge by manners:
  But yet, indeed the smaller is his daughter:
  The other is daughter to the banish'd duke,
  And here detain'd by her usurping uncle,
  To keep his daughter company; whose loves
  Are dearer than the natural bond of sisters.
  But I can tell you that of late this duke
  Hath ta'en displeasure 'gainst his gentle niece,
  Grounded upon no other argument
  But that the people praise her for her virtues,

And pity her for her good father's sake;
And, on my life, his malice 'gainst the lady
Will suddenly break forth. Sir, fare you well.
Hereafter, in a better world than this,
I shall desire more love and knowledge of you.

ORLANDO. I rest much bounden to you. Fare you well.

Exit Le Beau

Thus must I from the smoke into the smother;
From tyrant duke unto a tyrant brother.
But heavenly Rosalind!   *Exit*

SCENE THREE

A Room in the Palace.

Enter Celia and Rosalind

CELIA. Why, cousin! why, Rosalind! Cupid have mercy!
Not a word?

ROSALIND. Not one to throw at a dog.

CELIA. No, thy words are too precious to be cast away upon
curs; throw some of them at me; come, lame me with reasons.

ROSALIND. Then there were two cousins laid up, when the
one should be lamed with reasons and the other mad
without any.

CELIA. But is all this for your father?

ROSALIND. No, some of it is for my child's father. O, how
full of briers is this working-day world!

CELIA. They are but burrs, cousin, thrown upon thee in
holiday foolery. If we walk not in the trodden paths, our
very petticoats will catch them.

ROSALIND. I could shake them off my coat. These burrs are
in my heart.

CELIA. Hem them away.

ROSALIND. I would try, if I could cry 'hem,' and have him.

CELIA. Come, come; wrestle with thy affections.

ROSALIND. O! they take the part of a better wrestler than
myself!

CELIA. O, a good wish upon you! You will try in time, in despite of a fall. But, turning these jests out of service, let
us talk in good earnest. Is it possible, on such a sudden,

you should fall into so strong a liking with old Sir Rowland's youngest son?

ROSALIND. The duke my father loved his father dearly.

CELIA. Doth it therefore ensue that you should love his son
dearly? By this kind of chase, I should hate him, for my
father hated his father dearly; yet I hate not Orlando.

ROSALIND. No, faith, hate him not, for my sake.

CELIA. Why should I not? Doth he not deserve well?

ROSALIND. Let me love him for that; and do you love him,
because I do. Look, here comes the duke.

CELIA. With his eyes full of anger.

Enter Duke Frederick, with Lords

DUKE FREDERICK. Mistress, dispatch you with your safest
    haste,
And get you from our court.

ROSALIND.   Me, uncle?

DUKE FREDERICK.   You, cousin.
Within these ten days if that thou be'st found
So near our public court as twenty miles,
Thou diest for it.

ROSALIND.   I do beseech your Grace,
Let me the knowledge of my fault bear with me.
If with myself I hold intelligence,
Or have acquaintance with mine own desires,
If that I do not dream or be not frantic,—
As I do trust I am not,—then, dear uncle,
Never so much as in a thought unborn
Did I offend your Highness.

DUKE FREDERICK.   Thus do all traitors.
If their purgation did consist in words,
They are as innocent as grace itself.
Let it suffice thee that I trust thee not.

ROSALIND. Yet your mistrust cannot make me a traitor.
Tell me whereon the likelihood depends.

DUKE FREDERICK. Thou art thy father's daughter; there 's
    enough.

ROSALIND. So was I when your Highness took his dukedom;
So was I when your Highness banish'd him.
Treason is not inherited, my lord;
Or, if we did derive it from our friends,
What 's that to me? My father was no traitor.
Then, good my liege, mistake me not so much

To think my poverty is treacherous.

CELIA. Dear sovereign, hear me speak.

DUKE FREDERICK. Ay, Celia; we stay'd her for your sake;
　　Else had she with her father rang'd along.

CELIA. I did not then entreat to have her stay:
　　It was your pleasure and your own remorse.
　　I was too young that time to value her;
　　But now I know her. If she be a traitor,
　　Why so am I; we still have slept together,
　　Rose at an instant, learn'd, play'd, eat together;
　　And wheresoe'er we went, like Juno's swans,
　　Still we went coupled and inseparable.

DUKE FREDERICK. She is too subtle for thee; and her smooth-
　　　　ness,
　　Her very silence and her patience,
　　Speak to the people, and they pity her.
　　Thou art a fool: she robs thee of thy name;
　　And thou wilt show more bright and seem more virtuous
　　When she is gone. Then open not thy lips.
　　Firm and irrevocable is my doom
　　Which I have pass'd upon her; she is banish'd.

CELIA. Pronounce that sentence then, on me, my liege:
　　I cannot live out of her company.

DUKE FREDERICK. You are a fool. You, niece, provide your-
　　　　self.
　　If you outstay the time, upon mine honour,
　　And in the greatness of my word, you die.

Exeunt Duke Frederick and Lords

CELIA. O my poor Rosalind! whither wilt thou go?
　　Wilt thou change fathers? I will give thee mine.
　　I charge thee, be not thou more griev'd than I am.

ROSALIND. I have more cause.

CELIA.　　　　　　　　　Thou hast not, cousin.
　　Prithee, be cheerful; know'st thou not, the duke
　　Hath banish'd me, his daughter?

ROSALIND.　　　　　　　　That he hath not.

CELIA. No, hath not? Rosalind lacks then the love
　　Which teacheth thee that thou and I am one.
　　Shall we be sunder'd? Shall we part, sweet girl?
　　No: let my father seek another heir.
　　Therefore devise with me how we may fly,
　　Whither to go, and what to bear with us:

And do not seek to take your change upon you,
To bear your griefs yourself and leave me out;
For, by this heaven, now at our sorrows pale,
Say what thou canst, I 'll go along with thee.

ROSALIND. Why, whither shall we go?

CELIA. To seek my uncle in the forest of Arden.

ROSALIND. Alas, what danger will it be to us,
Maids as we are, to travel forth so far!
Beauty provoketh thieves sooner than gold.

CELIA. I 'll put myself in poor and mean attire,
And with a kind of umber smirch my face;
The like do you. So shall we pass along
And never stir assailants.

ROSALIND.   Were it not better,
Because that I am more than common tall,
That I did suit me all points like a man?
A gallant curtle-axe upon my thigh,
A boar-spear in my hand; and,—in my heart
Lie there what hidden woman's fear there will,—
We 'll have a swashing and a martial outside,
As many other mannish cowards have
That do outface it with their semblances.

CELIA. What shall I call thee when thou art a man?

ROSALIND. I 'll have no worse a name than Jove's own page,
And therefore look you call me Ganymede.
But what will you be call'd?

CELIA. Something that hath a reference to my state:
No longer Celia, but Aliena.

ROSALIND. But, cousin, what if we assay'd to steal
The clownish fool out of your father's court?
Would he not be a comfort to our travel?

CELIA. He 'll go along o'er the wide world with me;
Leave me alone to woo him. Let 's away,
And get our jewels and our wealth together,
Devise the fittest time and safest way
To hide us from pursuit that will be made
After my flight. Now go we in content
To liberty and not to banishment.   *Exeunt*

ACT TWO

SCENE ONE

The Forest of Arden.

Enter Duke Senior, Amiens, and other Lords, like Foresters

DUKE SENIOR. Now, my co-mates and brothers in exile,
Hath not old custom made this life more sweet
Than that of painted pomp? Are not these woods
More free from peril than the envious court?
Here feel we but the penalty of Adam,
The seasons' difference; as, the icy fang
And churlish chiding of the winter's wind,
Which, when it bites and blows upon my body,
Even till I shrink with cold, I smile and say
'This is no flattery: these are counsellors
That feelingly persuade me what I am.'
Sweet are the uses of adversity,
Which like the toad, ugly and venomous,
Wears yet a precious jewel in his head;
And this our life exempt from public haunt,
Finds tongues in trees, books in the running brook,
Sermons in stones, and good in every thing.
I would not change it.

AMIENS.   Happy is your Grace,
That can translate the stubbornness of fortune
Into so quiet and so sweet a style.

DUKE SENIOR. Come, shall we go and kill us venison?
And yet it irks me, the poor dappled fools,
Being native burghers of this desert city,
Should in their own confines with forked heads
Have their round haunches gor'd.

FIRST LORD.   Indeed, my lord,
The melancholy Jaques grieves at that;
And, in that kind, swears you do more usurp
Than doth your brother that hath banish'd you.

To-day my Lord of Amiens and myself
Did steal behind him as he lay along
Under an oak whose antique root peeps out
Upon the brook that brawls along this wood;
To the which place a poor sequester'd stag,
That from the hunters' aim had ta'en a hurt,
Did come to languish; and, indeed, my lord,
The wretched animal heav'd forth such groans
That their discharge did stretch his leathern coat
Almost to bursting, and the big round tears
Cours'd one another down his innocent nose
In piteous chase; and thus the hairy fool,
Much marked of the melancholy Jaques,
Stood on the extremest verge of the swift brook,
Augmenting it with tears.

DUKE SENIOR.   But what said Jaques?
Did he not moralize this spectacle?

FIRST LORD. O, yes, into a thousand similes.
First, for his weeping into the needless stream;
'Poor deer,' quoth he, 'thou mak'st a testament
As worldlings do, giving thy sum of more
To that which had too much.' Then, being there alone,
Left and abandon'd of his velvet friends:
' 'Tis right,' quoth he; 'thus misery doth part
The flux of company.' Anon, a careless herd,
Full of the pasture, jumps along by him
And never stays to greet him. 'Ay,' quoth Jaques,
'Sweep on, you fat and greasy citizens;
'Tis just the fashion; wherefore do you look
Upon that poor and broken bankrupt there?'
Thus most invectively he pierceth through
The body of the country, city, court,
Yea, and of this our life, swearing that we
Are mere usurpers, tyrants, and what 's worse,
To fright the animals and to kill them up
In their assign'd and native dwelling-place.

DUKE SENIOR. And did you leave him in this contemplation?

SECOND LORD. We did, my lord, weeping and commenting
Upon the sobbing deer.

DUKE SENIOR.   Show me the place.
I love to cope him in these sullen fits,
For then he 's full of matter.

SECOND LORD. I 'll bring you to him straight.   *Exeunt*

SCENE TWO

A Room in the Palace.

Enter Duke Frederick, Lords, and Attendants

DUKE FREDERICK. Can it be possible that no man saw them?
  It cannot be. Some villains of my court
  Are of consent and sufferance in this.
FIRST LORD. I cannot hear of any that did see her.
  The ladies, her attendants of her chamber,
  Saw her a-bed; and, in the morning early
  They found the bed untreasur'd of their mistress.
SECOND LORD. My lord, the roynish clown, at whom so oft
  Your Grace was wont to laugh, is also missing.
  Hisperia, the princess' gentlewoman,
  Confesses that she secretly o'erheard
  Your daughter and her cousin much commend
  The parts and graces of the wrestler
  That did but lately foil the sinewy Charles;
  And she believes, wherever they are gone,
  That youth is surely in their company.
DUKE FREDERICK. Send to his brother; fetch that gallant hither;
  If he be absent, bring his brother to me;
  I 'll make him find him. Do this suddenly,
  And let not search and inquisition quail
  To bring again these foolish runaways.   *Exeunt*

SCENE THREE

Before Oliver's House.

Enter Orlando and Adam, meeting

ORLANDO. Who 's there?
ADAM. What! my young master? O my gentle master!
  O my sweet master! O you memory
  Of old Sir Rowland! Why, what make you here?
  Why are you virtuous? Why do people love you?
  And wherefore are you gentle, strong, and valiant?

Why would you be so fond to overcome
The bony priser of the humorous duke?
Your praise is come too swiftly home before you.
Know you not, master, to some kind of men
Their graces serve them but as enemies?
No more do yours. Your virtues, gentle master,
Are sanctified and holy traitors to you.
O, what a world is this, when what is comely
Envenoms him that bears it!

ORLANDO. Why, what 's the matter?
ADAM.   O unhappy youth!
Come not within these doors; within this roof
The enemy of all your graces lives.
Your brother,—no, no brother; yet the son,—
Yet not the son, I will not call him son
Of him I was about to call his father,—
Hath heard your praises, and this night he means
To burn the lodging where you use to lie,
And you within it. If he fail of that,
He will have other means to cut you off.
I overheard him and his practices.
This is no place; this house is but a butchery.
Abhor it, fear it, do not enter it.

ORLANDO. Why, whither, Adam, wouldst thou have me go?
ADAM. No matter whither, so you come not here.
ORLANDO. What! wouldst thou have me go and beg my
       food?
Or with a base and boisterous sword enforce
A thievish living on the common road?
This I must do, or know not what to do:
Yet this I will not do, do how I can;
I rather will subject me to the malice
Of a diverted and bloody brother.

ADAM. But do not so. I have five hundred crowns,
The thrifty hire I sav'd under your father,
Which I did store to be my foster-nurse
When service should in my old limbs lie lame,
And unregarded age in corners thrown.
Take that; and He that doth the ravens feed,
Yea, providently caters for the sparrow,
Be comfort to my age! Here is the gold;
All this I give you. Let me be your servant.

Though I look old, yet I am strong and lusty;
For in my youth I never did apply
Hot and rebellious liquors in my blood,
Nor did not with unbashful forehead woo
The means of weakness and debility;
Therefore my age is as a lusty winter,
Frosty, but kindly. Let me go with you;
I'll do the service of a younger man
In all your business and necessities.

ORLANDO. O good old man! how well in thee appears
The constant service of the antique world,
When service sweat for duty, not for meed!
Thou art not for the fashion of these times,
Where none will sweat but for promotion,
And having that, do choke their service up
Even with the having. It is not so with thee.
But, poor old man, thou prun'st a rotten tree,
That cannot so much as a blossom yield,
In lieu of all thy pains and husbandry.
But come thy ways, we'll go along together,
And ere we have thy youthful wages spent,
We'll light upon some settled low content.

ADAM. Master, go on, and I will follow thee
To the last gasp with truth and loyalty.
From seventeen years till now almost fourscore
Here lived I, but now live here no more.
At seventeen years many their fortunes seek;
But at fourscore it is too late a week:
Yet fortune cannot recompense me better
Than to die well and not my master's debtor.   *Exeunt*

SCENE FOUR

The Forest of Arden.

*Enter Rosalind in boy's clothes, Celia dressed like
a shepherdess, and Touchstone*

ROSALIND. O Jupiter! how weary are my spirits.

TOUCHSTONE. I care not for my spirits if my legs were not
weary.

ROSALIND. I could find it in my heart to disgrace my man's
apparel and to cry like a woman; but I must comfort the
weaker vessel, as doublet and hose ought to show itself
courageous to petticoat. Therefore, courage, good Aliena.

CELIA. I pray you, bear with me. I cannot go no further.

TOUCHSTONE. For my part, I had rather bear with you than
bear you; yet I should bear no cross if I did bear you, for I
think you have no money in your purse.

ROSALIND. Well, this is the forest of Arden.

TOUCHSTONE. Ay, now am I in Arden; the more fool I; when
I was at home, I was in a better place: but travellers must
be content.

ROSALIND. Ay, be so, good Touchstone. Look you, who
comes here; a young man and an old in solemn talk.

Enter Corin and Silvius

CORIN. That is the way to make her scorn you still.

SILVIUS. O Corin, that thou knew'st how I do love her!

CORIN. I partly guess, for I have lov'd ere now.

SILVIUS. No, Corin; being old, thou canst not guess,
  Though in thy youth thou wast as true a lover
  As ever sigh'd upon a midnight pillow.
  But if thy love were ever like to mine,—
  As sure I think did never man love so,—
  How many actions most ridiculous
  Hast thou been drawn to by thy fantasy?

CORIN. Into a thousand that I have forgotten.

SILVIUS. O! thou didst then ne'er love so heartily.
  If thou remember'st not the slightest folly
  That ever love did make thee run into,
  Thou hast not lov'd.
  Or if thou hast not sat as I do now,

Wearing thy hearer with thy mistress' praise,
Thou hast not lov'd:
Or if thou hast not broke from company
Abruptly, as my passion now makes me,
Thou hast not lov'd. O Phebe, Phebe, Phebe!   *Exit*

ROSALIND. Alas, poor shepherd! searching of thy wound,
I have by hard adventure found mine own.

TOUCHSTONE. And I mine. I remember, when I was in love I
broke my sword upon a stone, and bid him take that for
coming a-night to Jane Smile; and I remember the kissing
of her batler, and the cow's dugs that her pretty chopped
hands had milked; and I remember the wooing of a peascod instead of her, from whom I took two cods, and giving
her them again, said with weeping tears, 'Wear these for
my sake.' We that are true lovers run into strange capers;
but as all is mortal in nature, so is all nature in love mortal
in folly.

ROSALIND. Thou speakest wisér than thou art ware of.

TOUCHSTONE. Nay, I shall ne'er be ware of mine own wit till
I break my shins against it.

ROSALIND. Jove, Jove! this shepherd's passion
Is much upon my fashion.

TOUCHSTONE. And mine; but it grows something stale with me.

CELIA. I pray you, one of you question yond man,
If he for gold will give us any food:
I faint almost to death.

TOUCHSTONE.   Holla, you clown!

ROSALIND. Peace, fool: he 's not thy kinsman.

CORIN.   Who calls?

TOUCHSTONE. Your betters, sir.

CORIN.   Else are they very wretched.

ROSALIND. Peace, I say. Good even to you, friend.

CORIN. And to you, gentle sir, and to you all.

ROSALIND. I prithee, shepherd, if that love or gold
Can in this desert place buy entertainment,
Bring us where we may rest ourselves and feed.
Here 's a young maid with travel much oppress'd,
And faints for succour.

CORIN.   Fair sir, I pity her,
And wish, for her sake more than for mine own,
My fortunes were more able to relieve her;
But I am shepherd to another man,

And do not shear the fleeces that I graze:
My master is of churlish disposition
And little recks to find the way to heaven
By doing deeds of hospitality.
Besides, his cote, his flocks, and bounds of feed
Are now on sale; and at our sheepcote now,
By reason of his absence, there is nothing
That you will feed on; but what is, come see,
And in my voice most welcome shall you be.

ROSALIND.　What is he that shall buy his flock and pasture?

CORIN.　That young swain that you saw here but erewhile,
That little cares for buying any thing.

ROSALIND.　I pray thee, if it stand with honesty,
Buy thou the cottage, pasture, and the flock,
And thou shalt have to pay for it of us.

CELIA.　And we will mend thy wages. I like this place,
And willingly could waste my time in it.

CORIN.　Assuredly the thing is to be sold.
Go with me. If you like upon report
The soil, the profit, and this kind of life,
I will your very faithful feeder be,
And buy it with your gold right suddenly.　　　　*Exeunt*

SCENE FIVE

Another part of the Forest.

Enter Amiens, Jaques, and Others

SONG

AMIENS.　　　　Under the greenwood tree
　　　　　　Who loves to lie with me,
　　　　　　And turn his merry note
　　　　　　Unto the sweet bird's throat,
　　Come hither, come hither, come hither!
　　　　　　　Here shall he see
　　　　　　　No enemy
　　　　But winter and rough weather.

JAQUES.　More, more, I prithee, more.

AMIENS.　It will make you melancholy, Monsieur Jaques.

JAQUES.　I thank it. More! I prithee, more. I can suck melancholy out of a song as a weasel sucks eggs. More! I prithee,
more.

AMIENS. My voice is ragged; I know I cannot please you.

JAQUES. I do not desire you to please me; I do desire you to sing. Come, more; another stanzo. Call you them stanzos?

AMIENS. What you will, Monsieur Jaques.

JAQUES. Nay, I care not for their names; they owe me nothing. Will you sing?

AMIENS. More at your request than to please myself.

JAQUES. Well then, if ever I thank any man, I 'll thank you. But that they call compliment is like the encounter of two dog-apes, and when a man thanks me heartily, methinks I have given him a penny and he renders me the beggarly thanks. Come, sing; and you that will not, hold your tongues.

AMIENS. Well, I 'll end the song. Sirs, cover the while; the duke will drink under this tree. He hath been all this day to look you.

JAQUES. And I have been all this day to avoid him. He is too disputable for my company. I think of as many matters as he, but I give heaven thanks, and make no boast of them. Come, warble; come.

SONG

AMIENS.   Who doth ambition shun *All together here*
    And loves to live i' the sun,
    Seeking the food he eats,
    And pleas'd with what he gets,
  Come hither, come hither, come hither:
     Here shall he see
     No enemy
    But winter and rough weather.

JAQUES. I 'll give you a verse to this note, that I made yesterday in despite of my invention.

AMIENS. And I 'll sing it.

JAQUES. Thus it goes:

    If it do come to pass
    That any man turn ass,
    Leaving his wealth and ease,
    A stubborn will to please,
  Ducdame, ducdame, ducdame:
     Here shall he see
     Gross fools as he,
    And if he will come to me.

AMIENS. What's that 'ducdame'?

JAQUES. 'Tis a Greek invocation to call fools into a circle. I'll
go sleep if I can; if I cannot, I'll rail against all the first-
born of Egypt.

AMIENS. And I'll go seek the duke. His banquet is pre-
pared.   *Exeunt severally*

SCENE SIX

Another Part of the Forest.

Enter Orlando and Adam

ADAM. Dear master, I can go no further. O! I die for food.
Here lie I down, and measure out my grave. Farewell,
kind master.

ORLANDO. Why, how now, Adam! no greater heart in thee?
Live a little; comfort a little; cheer thyself a little. If this
uncouth forest yield anything savage, I will either be food
for it, or bring it for food to thee. Thy conceit is nearer
death than thy powers. For my sake be comfortable, hold
death awhile at the arm's end, I will here be with thee
presently, and if I bring thee not something to eat, I will
give thee leave to die; but if thou diest before I come, thou
art a mocker of my labour. Well said! thou lookest cheerly,
and I'll be with thee quickly. Yet thou liest in the bleak
air: come, I will bear thee to some shelter, and thou shalt
not die for lack of a dinner, if there live anything in this
desert. Cheerly, good Adam.   *Exeunt*

SCENE SEVEN

Another part of the Forest.

*A table set out. Enter Duke Senior, Amiens,
Lords like Outlaws*

DUKE SENIOR. I think he be transform'd into a beast,
For I can nowhere find him like a man.

FIRST LORD. My lord, he is but even now gone hence.
Here was he merry, hearing of a song.

DUKE SENIOR. If he, compact of jars, grow musical,

We shall have shortly discord in the spheres.
Go, seek him: tell him I would speak with him.
FIRST LORD. He saves my labour by his own approach.

Enter Jaques

DUKE SENIOR. Why, how now, monsieur! what a life is this,
That your poor friends must woo your company?
What, you look merrily!

JAQUES. A fool, a fool! I met a fool i' the forest,
A motley fool; a miserable world!
As I do live by food, I met a fool;
Who laid him down and bask'd him in the sun,
And rail'd on Lady Fortune in good terms,
In good set terms, and yet a motley fool.
'Good-morrow, fool,' quoth I. 'No, sir,' quoth he,
'Call me not fool till heaven hath sent me fortune.'
And then he drew a dial from his poke,
And, looking on it with lack-lustre eye,
Says very wisely, 'It is ten o'clock; ·
Thus may we see,' quoth he, 'how the world wags.
'Tis but an hour ago since it was nine,
And after one hour more 'twill be eleven;
And so, from hour to hour we ripe and ripe,
And then from hour to hour we rot and rot,
And thereby hangs a tale.' When I did hear
The motley fool thus moral on the time,
My lungs began to crow like chanticleer,
That fools should be so deep-contemplative,
And I did laugh sans intermission
An hour by his dial. O noble fool!
A worthy fool! Motley 's the only wear.

DUKE SENIOR. What fool is this?

JAQUES. O worthy fool! One that hath been a courtier,
And says, if ladies be but young and fair,
They have the gift to know it; and in his brain,—
Which is as dry as the remainder biscuit
After a voyage,—he hath strange places cramm'd
With observation, the which he vents
In mangled forms. O that I were a fool!
I am ambitious for a motley coat.

DUKE SENIOR. Thou shalt have one.

JAQUES.   It is my only suit;
Provided that you weed your better judgments

Of all opinion that grows rank in them
That I am wise. I must have liberty
Withal, as large a charter as the wind,
To blow on whom I please; for so fools have.
And they that are most galled with my folly,
They most must laugh. And why, sir, must they so?
The 'why' is plain as way to parish church:
He that a fool doth very wisely hit
Doth very foolishly, although he smart,
Not to seem senseless of the bob; if not,
The wise man's folly is anatomiz'd
Even by the squandering glances of the fool.
Invest me in my motley; give me leave
To speak my mind, and I will through and through
Cleanse the foul body of th' infected world,
If they will patiently receive my medicine.

DUKE SENIOR. Fie on thee! I can tell what thou wouldst do.

JAQUES. What, for a counter, would I do, but good?

DUKE SENIOR. Most mischievous foul sin, in chiding sin.
For thou thyself hast been a libertine,
As sensual as the brutish sting itself;
And all the embossed sores and headed evils,
That thou with licence of free foot hast caught,
Wouldst thou disgorge into the general world.

JAQUES. Why, who cries out on pride,
That can therein tax any private party?
Doth it not flow as hugely as the sea,
Till that the wearer's very means do ebb?
What woman in the city do I name,
When that I say the city-woman bears
The cost of princes on unworthy shoulders?
Who can come in and say that I mean her,
When such a one as she such is her neighbour?
Or what is he of basest function,
That says his bravery is not on my cost,—
Thinking that I mean him,—but therein suits
His folly to the mettle of my speech?
There then; how then? what then? Let me see wherein
My tongue hath wrong'd him: if it do him right,
Then he hath wrong'd himself; if he be free,
Why then, my taxing like a wild goose flies,
Unclaim'd of any man. But who comes here?

Enter Orlando, with his sword drawn

ORLANDO. Forbear, and eat no more.

JAQUES.   Why, I have eat none yet.

ORLANDO. Nor shalt not, till necessity be serv'd.

JAQUES. Of what kind should this cock come off?

DUKE SENIOR. Art thou thus bolden'd, man, by thy distress,
    Or else a rude despiser of good manners,
    That in civility thou seem'st so empty?

ORLANDO. You touch'd my vein at first: the thorny point
    Of bare distress hath ta'en from me the show
    Of smooth civility; yet I am inland bred
    And know some nurture. But forbear, I say:
    He dies that touches any of this fruit
    Till I and my affairs are answered.

JAQUES. An you will not be answered with reason,
    I must die.

DUKE SENIOR. What would you have? Your gentleness shall
        force
    More than your force move us to gentleness.

ORLANDO. I almost die for food; and let me have it.

DUKE SENIOR. Sit down and feed, and welcome to our table.

ORLANDO. Speak you so gently? Pardon me, I pray you:
    I thought that all things had been savage here,
    And therefore put I on the countenance
    Of stern commandment. But whate'er you are
    That in this desert inaccessible,
    Under the shade of melancholy boughs,
    Lose and neglect the creeping hours of time;
    If ever you have look'd on better days,
    If ever been where bells have knoll'd to church,
    If ever sat at any good man's feast,
    If ever from your eyelids wip'd a tear,
    And know what 'tis to pity, and be pitied,
    Let gentleness my strong enforcement be:
    In the which hope I blush, and hide my sword.

DUKE SENIOR. True is it that we have seen better days,
    And have with holy bell been knoll'd to church,
    And sat at good men's feasts, and wip'd our eyes
    Of drops that sacred pity hath engender'd;
    And therefore sit you down in gentleness
    And take upon command what help we have
    That to your wanting may be minister'd.

ORLANDO. Then but forbear your food a little while,
 Whiles, like a doe, I go to find my fawn
 And give it food. There is an old poor man,
 Who after me hath many a weary step
 Limp'd in pure love; till he be first suffic'd,
 Oppress'd with two weak evils, age and hunger,
 I will not touch a bit.

DUKE SENIOR.   Go find him out,
 And we will nothing waste till you return.

ORLANDO. I thank ye; and be bless'd for your good comfort!
                 Exit

DUKE SENIOR. Thou seest we are not all alone unhappy:
 This wide and universal theatre
 Presents more woful pageants than the scene
 Wherein we play in.

JAQUES.   All the world 's a stage,
 And all the men and women merely players.
 They have their exits and their entrances;
 And one man in his time plays many parts,
 His acts being seven ages. At first the infant,
 Mewling and puking in the nurse's arms.
 And then the whining school-boy, with his satchel,
 And shining morning face, creeping like snail
 Unwillingly to school. And then the lover,
 Sighing like furnace, with a woful ballad
 Made to his mistress' eyebrow. Then a soldier,
 Full of strange oaths, and bearded like the pard,
 Jealous in honour, sudden and quick in quarrel,
 Seeking the bubble reputation
 Even in the cannon's mouth. And then the justice,
 In fair round belly with good capon lin'd,
 With eyes severe, and beard of formal cut,
 Full of wise saws and modern instances;
 And so he plays his part. The sixth age shifts
 Into the lean and slipper'd pantaloon,
 With spectacles on nose and pouch on side,
 His youthful hose well sav'd a world too wide
 For his shrunk shank; and his big manly voice,
 Turning again toward childish treble, pipes
 And whistles in his sound. Last scene of all,
 That ends this strange eventful history,
 Is second childishness and mere oblivion,
 Sans teeth, sans eyes, sans taste, sans everything.

Re-enter Orlando, with Adam

DUKE SENIOR. Welcome. Set down your venerable burden,
  And let him feed.

ORLANDO.   I thank you most for him.

ADAM. So had you need:
  I scarce can speak to thank you for myself.

DUKE SENIOR. Welcome; fall to: I will not trouble you
  As yet, to question you about your fortunes.
  Give us some music; and, good cousin, sing.

SONG

AMIENS.   Blow, blow, thou winter wind,
                 Thou art not so unkind
                   As man's ingratitude;
               Thy tooth is not so keen,
               Because thou art not seen,
                 Although thy breath be rude.
      Heigh-ho! sing, heigh-ho! unto the green holly:
      Most friendship is feigning, most loving mere folly.
               Then heigh-ho! the holly!
                 This life is most jolly.

               Freeze, freeze, thou bitter sky,
                 That dost not bite so nigh
                   As benefits forgot:
               Though thou the waters warp,
               Thy sting is not so sharp
                 As friend remember'd not.
      Heigh-ho! sing, heigh-ho! unto the green holly:
      Most friendship is feigning, most loving mere folly.
               Then heigh-ho! the holly!
                 This life is most jolly.

DUKE SENIOR. If that you were the good Sir Rowland's son,
  As you have whisper'd faithfully you were,
  And as mine eye doth his effigies witness
  Most truly limn'd and living in your face,
  Be truly welcome hither. I am the duke
  That lov'd your father. The residue of your fortune,
  Go to my cave and tell me. Good old man,
  Thou art right welcome as thy master is.
  Support him by the arm. Give me your hand,
  And let me all your fortunes understand.   *Exeunt*

ACT THREE

SCENE ONE

A Room in the Palace.

Enter Duke Frederick, Oliver, Lords, and Attendants

DUKE FREDERICK. Not seen him since! Sir, sir, that cannot
    be:
  But were I not the better part made mercy,
  I should not seek an absent argument
  Of my revenge, thou present. But look to it:
  Find out thy brother, wheresoe'er he is;
  Seek him with candle; bring him, dead or living,
  Within this twelvemonth, or turn thou no more
  To seek a living in our territory.
  Thy lands and all things that thou dost call thine
  Worth seizure, do we seize into our hands,
  Till thou canst quit thee by thy brother's mouth
  Of what we think against thee.
OLIVER. O that your Highness knew my heart in this!
  I never lov'd my brother in my life.
DUKE FREDERICK. More villain thou. Well, push him out of
    doors;
  And let my officers of such a nature
  Make an extent upon his house and lands.
  Do this expediently and turn him going.   *Exeunt*

SCENE TWO

The Forest of Arden.

Enter Orlando, with a paper

ORLANDO. Hang there, my verse, in witness of my love:
    And thou, thrice-crowned queen of night, survey
With thy chaste eye, from thy pale sphere above,
    Thy huntress' name, that my full life doth sway.
O Rosalind! these trees shall be my books,
    And in their barks my thoughts I 'll character,
That every eye, which in this forest looks,
    Shall see thy virtue witness'd everywhere.
Run, run, Orlando: carve on every tree
The fair, the chaste, and unexpressive she.   *Exit*

Enter Corin and Touchstone

CORIN. And how like you this shepherd's life, Master Touchstone?

TOUCHSTONE. Truly, shepherd, in respect of itself, it is a
good life; but in respect that it is a shepherd's life, it is
naught. In respect that it is solitary, I like it very well; but
in respect that it is private, it is a very vile life. Now, in respect it is in the fields, it pleaseth me well; but in respect
it is not in the court, it is tedious. As it is a spare life, look
you, it fits my humour well; but as there is no more plenty
in it, it goes much against my stomach. Hast any philosophy in thee, shepherd?

CORIN. No more but that I know the more one sickens the
worse at ease he is; and that he that wants money, means,
and content, is without three good friends; that the property of rain is to wet, and fire to burn; that good pasture
makes fat sheep, and that a great cause of the night is lack
of the sun; that he that hath learned no wit by nature nor
art may complain of good breeding, or comes of a very
dull kindred.

TOUCHSTONE. Such a one is a natural philosopher. Wast ever
in court, shepherd?

CORIN. No, truly.

TOUCHSTONE. Then thou art damned.

CORIN. Nay, I hope.

TOUCHSTONE. Truly, thou art damned like an ill-roasted egg, all on one side.

CORIN. For not being at court? Your reason.

TOUCHSTONE. Why, if thou never wast at court, thou never sawest good manners; if thou never sawest good manners, then thy manners must be wicked; and wickedness is sin, and sin is damnation. Thou art in a parlous state, shepherd.

CORIN. Not a whit, Touchstone. Those that are good manners at the court are as ridiculous in the country as the behaviour of the country is most mockable at the court. You told me you salute not at the court, but you kiss your hands. That courtesy would be uncleanly if courtiers were shepherds.

TOUCHSTONE. Instance, briefly; come, instance.

CORIN. Why, we are still handling our ewes, and their fells, you know, are greasy.

TOUCHSTONE. Why, do not your courtier's hands sweat? and is not the grease of a mutton as wholesome as the sweat of a man? Shallow, shallow. A better instance, I say; come.

CORIN. Besides, our hands are hard.

TOUCHSTONE. Your lips will feel them the sooner: shallow again. A more sounder instance; come.

CORIN. And they are often tarred over with the surgery of our sheep; and would you have us kiss tar? The courtier's hands are perfumed with civet.

TOUCHSTONE. Most shallow man! Thou worms-meat, in respect of a good piece of flesh, indeed! Learn of the wise, and perpend. Civet is of a baser birth than tar, the very uncleanly flux of a cat. Mend the instance, shepherd.

CORIN. You have too courtly a wit for me. I 'll rest.

TOUCHSTONE. Wilt thou rest damned? God help thee, shallow man! God make incision in thee! thou art raw.

CORIN. Sir, I am a true labourer: I earn that I eat, get that I wear, owe no man hate, envy no man's happiness, glad of other men's good, content with my harm; and the greatest of my pride is to see my ewes graze and my lambs suck.

TOUCHSTONE. That is another simple sin in you, to bring the ewes and the rams together, and to offer to get your living by the copulation of cattle; to be bawd to a bell-wether, and to betray a she-lamb of a twelvemonth to a crooked-pated, old, cuckoldy ram, out of all reasonable match. If

thou be'st not damned for this, the devil himself will have
no shepherds: I cannot see else how thou shouldst 'scape.

CORIN. Here comes young Master Ganymede, my new mistress's brother.

Enter Rosalind, reading a paper

ROSALIND. 'From the east to western Ind,
No jewel is like Rosalind.
Her worth, being mounted on the wind,
Through all the world bears Rosalind.
All the pictures fairest lin'd
Are but black to Rosalind.
Let no face be kept in mind,
But the fair of Rosalind.'

TOUCHSTONE. I'll rime you so, eight years together, dinners
and suppers and sleeping hours excepted. It is the right
butter-women's rank to market.

ROSALIND. Out, fool!

TOUCHSTONE. For a taste:—
If a hart do lack a hind,
Let him seek out Rosalind.
If the cat will after kind,
So be sure will Rosalind.
Winter-garments must be lin'd,
So must slender Rosalind.
They that reap must sheaf and bind,
Then to cart with Rosalind.
Sweetest nut hath sourest rind,
Such a nut is Rosalind.
He that sweetest rose will find
Must find love's prick and Rosalind.
This is the very false gallop of verses. Why do you infect
yourself with them?

ROSALIND. Peace! you dull fool. I found them on a tree.

TOUCHSTONE. Truly the tree yields bad fruit.

ROSALIND. I'll graff it with you, and then I shall graff it with
a medlar: then it will be the earliest fruit i' the country;
for you'll be rotten ere you be half ripe, and that's the
right virtue of the medlar.

TOUCHSTONE. You have said; but whether wisely or no, let
the forest judge.

Enter Celia, reading a paper

ROSALIND. Peace!

Here comes my sister, reading: stand aside.

CELIA.
  'Why should this a desert be?
    For it is unpeopled? No;
  Tongues I 'll hang on every tree,
    That shall civil sayings show.
  Some, how brief the life of man
    Runs his erring pilgrimage,
  That the stretching of a span
    Buckles in his sum of age;
  Some, of violated vows
    'Twixt the souls of friend and friend:
  But upon the fairest boughs,
    Or at every sentence' end,
  Will I Rosalinda write;
    Teaching all that read to know
  The quintessence of every sprite
    Heaven would in little show.
  Therefore Heaven Nature charg'd
    That one body should be fill'd
  With all graces wide enlarg'd.
    Nature presently distill'd
  Helen's cheek, but not her heart,
    Cleopatra's majesty,
  Atalanta's better part,
    Sad Lucretia's modesty.
  Thus Rosalind of many parts
    By heavenly synod was devis'd,
  Of many faces, eyes, and hearts,
    To have the touches dearest priz'd.
  Heaven would that she these gifts should have,
  And I to live and die her slave.'

ROSALIND. O most gentle pulpiter! what tedious homily of love have you wearied your parishioners withal, and never cried, 'Have patience, good people!'

CELIA. How now! back, friends! Shepherd, go off a little. Go with him, sirrah.

TOUCHSTONE. Come, shepherd, let us make an honourable retreat; though not with bag and baggage, yet with scrip and scrippage.   *Exeunt Corin and Touchstone*

CELIA. Didst thou hear these verses?

ROSALIND. O, yes, I heard them all, and more too; for some of them had in them more feet than the verses would bear.

CELIA. That's no matter. The feet might bear the verses.

ROSALIND. Ay, but the feet were lame, and could not bear themselves without the verse, and therefore stood lamely in the verse.

CELIA. But didst thou hear without wondering, how thy name should be hanged and carved upon these trees?

ROSALIND. I was seven of the nine days out of the wonder before you came; for look here what I found on a palm-tree; I was never so be-rimed since Pythagoras' time, that I was an Irish rat, which I can hardly remember.

CELIA. Trow you who hath done this?

ROSALIND. Is it a man?

CELIA. And a chain, that you once wore, about his neck. Change you colour?

ROSALIND. I prithee, who?

CELIA. O Lord, Lord! it is a hard matter for friends to meet; but mountains may be removed with earthquakes, and so encounter.

ROSALIND. Nay, but who is it?

CELIA. Is it possible?

ROSALIND. Nay, I prithee now, with most petitionary vehemence, tell me who it is.

CELIA. O wonderful, wonderful, and most wonderful wonderful! and yet again wonderful! and after that, out of all whooping!

ROSALIND. Good my complexion! Dost thou think, though I am caparison'd like a man, I have a doublet and hose in my disposition? One inch of delay more is a South-sea of discovery; I prithee, tell me who is it quickly, and speak apace. I would thou couldst stammer, that thou mightst pour this concealed man out of thy mouth, as wine comes out of a narrow-mouth'd bottle; either too much at once, or none at all. I prithee, take the cork out of thy mouth, that I may drink thy tidings.

CELIA. So you may put a man in your belly.

ROSALIND. Is he of God's making? What manner of man? Is his head worth a hat, or his chin worth a beard?

CELIA. Nay, he hath but a little beard.

ROSALIND. Why, God will send more, if the man will be thankful. Let me stay the growth of his beard, if thou delay me not the knowledge of his chin.

CELIA. It is young Orlando, that tripped up the wrestler's

heels and your heart both, in an instant.

ROSALIND. Nay, but the devil take mocking. Speak, sad brow and true maid.

CELIA. I' faith, coz, 'tis he.

ROSALIND. Orlando?

CELIA. Orlando.

ROSALIND. Alas the day! what shall I do with my doublet and hose? What did he when thou sawest him? What said he? How looked he? Wherein went he? What makes he here? Did he ask for me? Where remains he? How parted he with thee, and when shalt thou see him again? Answer me in one word.

CELIA. You must borrow me Gargantua's mouth first: 'tis a word too great for any mouth of this age's size. To say ay and no to these particulars is more than to answer in a catechism.

ROSALIND. But doth he know that I am in this forest and in man's apparel? Looks he as freshly as he did the day he wrestled?

CELIA. It is as easy to count atomies as to resolve the propositions of a lover; but take a taste of my finding him, and relish it with good observance. I found him under a tree, like a dropped acorn.

ROSALIND. It may well be called Jove's tree, when it drops forth such fruit.

CELIA. Give me audience, good madam.

ROSALIND. Proceed.

CELIA. There lay he, stretch'd along like a wounded knight.

ROSALIND. Though it be pity to see such a sight, it well becomes the ground.

CELIA. Cry 'holla!' to thy tongue, I prithee; it curvets unseasonably. He was furnish'd like a hunter.

ROSALIND. O, ominous! he comes to kill my heart.

CELIA. I would sing my song without a burthen. Thou bringest me out of tune.

ROSALIND. Do you not know I am a woman? When I think, I must speak. Sweet, say on.

CELIA. You bring me out. Soft! comes he not here?

ROSALIND. 'Tis he! Slink by, and note him.

Enter Orlando and Jaques

JAQUES. I thank you for your company; but, good faith, I had as lief have been myself alone.

ORLANDO. And so had I; but yet, for fashion' sake, I thank you too for your society.

JAQUES. God be wi' you. Let 's meet as little as we can.

ORLANDO. I do desire we may be better strangers.

JAQUES. I pray you, mar no more trees with writing love-songs in their barks.

ORLANDO. I pray you mar no more of my verses with reading them ill-favouredly.

JAQUES. Rosalind is your love's name?

ORLANDO. Yes, just.

JAQUES. I do not like her name.

ORLANDO. There was no thought of pleasing you when she was christened.

JAQUES. What stature is she of?

ORLANDO. Just as high as my heart.

JAQUES. You are full of pretty answers. Have you not been acquainted with goldsmiths' wives, and conn'd them out of rings?

ORLANDO. Not so; but I answer you right painted cloth, from whence you have studied your questions.

JAQUES. You have a nimble wit. I think 'twas made of Atalanta's heels. Will you sit down with me? and we two will rail against our mistress the world, and all our misery.

ORLANDO. I will chide no breather in the world but myself, against whom I know most faults.

JAQUES. The worst fault you have is to be in love.

ORLANDO. 'Tis a fault I will not change for your best virtue. I am weary of you.

JAQUES. By my troth, I was seeking for a fool when I found you.

ORLANDO. He is drowned in the brook. Look but in, and you shall see him.

JAQUES. There I shall see mine own figure.

ORLANDO. Which I take to be either a fool or a cipher.

JAQUES. I 'll tarry no longer with you. Farewell, good Signior Love.

ORLANDO. I am glad of your departure. Adieu, good Monsieur Melancholy.   *Exit Jaques*

ROSALIND. I will speak to him like a saucy lackey, and under that habit play the knave with him. Do you hear, forester?

ORLANDO. Very well. What would you?

ROSALIND. I pray you, what is 't o'clock?

ORLANDO. You should ask me, what time o' day; there 's no clock in the forest.

ROSALIND. Then there is no true lover in the forest; else sighing every minute and groaning every hour would detect the lazy foot of Time as well as a clock.

ORLANDO. And why not the swift foot of Time? Had not that been as proper?

ROSALIND. By no means, sir. Time travels in divers paces with divers persons. I 'll tell you who Time ambles withal, who Time trots withal, who Time gallops withal, and who he stands still withal.

ORLANDO. I prithee, who doth he trot withal?

ROSALIND. Marry, he trots hard with a young maid between the contract of her marriage and the day it is solemnized; if the interim be but a se'nnight, Time's pace is so hard that it seems the length of seven year.

ORLANDO. Who ambles Time withal?

ROSALIND. With a priest that lacks Latin, and a rich man that hath not the gout; for the one sleeps easily because he cannot study, and the other lives merrily because he feels no pain; the one lacking the burden of lean and wasteful learning, the other knowing no burden of heavy tedious penury. These Time ambles withal.

ORLANDO. Who doth he gallop withal?

ROSALIND. With a thief to the gallows; for though he go as softly as foot can fall he thinks himself too soon there.

ORLANDO. Who stays it still withal?

ROSALIND. With lawyers in the vacation; for they sleep between term and term, and then they perceive not how Time moves.

ORLANDO. Where dwell you, pretty youth?

ROSALIND. With this shepherdess, my sister; here in the skirts of the forest, like fringe upon a petticoat.

ORLANDO. Are you native of this place?

ROSALIND. As the cony, that you see dwell where she is kindled.

ORLANDO. Your accent is something finer than you could purchase in so removed a dwelling.

ROSALIND. I have been told so of many: but indeed an old religious uncle of mine taught me to speak, who was in his youth an inland man; one that knew courtship too well, for there he fell in love. I have heard him read many lectures against it; and I thank God, I am not a woman, to be touched with so many giddy offences as he hath generally taxed their whole sex withal.

ORLANDO. Can you remember any of the principal evils that he laid to the charge of women?

ROSALIND. There were none principal; they were all like one another as half-pence are; every one fault seeming monstrous till his fellow fault came to match it.

ORLANDO. I prithee, recount some of them.

ROSALIND. No, I will not cast away my physic, but on those that are sick. There is a man haunts the forest, that abuses our young plants with carving 'Rosalind' on their barks; hangs odes upon hawthorns, and elegies on brambles; all, forsooth, deifying the name of Rosalind: if I could meet that fancy-monger, I would give him some good counsel, for he seems to have the quotidian of love upon him.

ORLANDO. I am he that is so love-shaked. I pray you, tell me your remedy.

ROSALIND. There is none of my uncle's marks upon you: he taught me how to know a man in love; in which cage of rushes I am sure you are not prisoner.

ORLANDO. What were his marks?

ROSALIND. A lean cheek, which you have not; a blue eye and sunken, which you have not; an unquestionable spirit, which you have not; a beard neglected, which you have not: but I pardon you for that, for, simply, your having in beard is a younger brother's revenue. Then, your hose should be ungartered, your bonnet unbanded, your sleeve unbuttoned, your shoe untied, and everything about you demonstrating a careless desolation. But you are no such man: you are rather point-device in your accoutrements; as loving yourself than seeming the lover of any other.

ORLANDO. Fair youth, I would I could make thee believe I love.

ROSALIND. Me believe it! You may as soon make her that you love believe it; which, I warrant, she is apter to do than to confess she does; that is one of the points in the which women still give the lie to their consciences. But, in good sooth, are you he that hangs the verses on the trees, wherein Rosalind is so admired?

ORLANDO. I swear to thee, youth, by the white hand of Rosalind, I am that he, that unfortunate he.

ROSALIND. But are you so much in love as your rimes speak?

ORLANDO. Neither rime nor reason can express how much.

ROSALIND. Love is merely a madness, and, I tell you, deserves as well a dark house and a whip as madmen do; and
the reason why they are not so punished and cured is, that
the lunacy is so ordinary that the whippers are in love too.
Yet I profess curing it by counsel.

ORLANDO. Did you ever cure any so?

ROSALIND. Yes, one; and in this manner. He was to imagine
me his love, his mistress; and I set him every day to woo
me. At which time would I, being but a moonish youth,
grieve, be effeminate, changeable, longing and liking;
proud, fantastical, apish, shallow, inconstant, full of tears,
full of smiles, for every passion something, and for no passion truly anything, as boys and women are, for the most
part, cattle of this colour; would now like him, now loathe
him; then entertain him, then forswear him; now weep for
him, then spit at him; that I drave my suitor from his mad
humour of love to a living humour of madness, which was,
to forswear the full stream of the world, and to live in a
nook merely monastic. And thus I cured him; and this way
will I take upon me to wash your liver as clean as a sound
sheep's heart, that there shall not be one spot of love in 't.

ORLANDO. I would not be cured, youth.

ROSALIND. I would cure you, if you would but call me Rosalind, and come every day to my cote and woo me.

ORLANDO. Now, by the faith of my love, I will. Tell me
where it is.

ROSALIND. Go with me to it and I 'll show it you; and by the
way you shall tell me where in the forest you live. Will you
go?

ORLANDO. With all my heart, good youth.

ROSALIND. Nay, you must call me Rosalind. Come, sister,
will you go?   *Exeunt*

SCENE THREE

Another Part of the Forest.

Enter Touchstone and Audrey; Jaques behind

TOUCHSTONE. Come apace, good Audrey. I will fetch up your goats, Audrey. And how, Audrey, am I the man yet? Doth my simple feature content you?

AUDREY. Your features! Lord warrant us! What features?

TOUCHSTONE. I am here with thee and thy goats, as the most capricious poet, honest Ovid, was among the Goths.

JAQUES. (*Aside*) O knowledge ill-inhabited, worse than Jove in a thatch'd house!

TOUCHSTONE. When a man's verses cannot be understood, nor a man's good wit seconded with the forward child Understanding, it strikes a man more dead than a great reckoning in a little room. Truly, I would the gods had made thee poetical.

AUDREY. I do not know what 'poetical' is. Is it honest in deed and word? Is it a true thing?

TOUCHSTONE. No, truly, for the truest poetry is the most feigning; and lovers are given to poetry, and what they swear in poetry may be said as lovers they do feign.

AUDREY. Do you wish then that the gods had made me poetical?

TOUCHSTONE. I do, truly; for thou swearest to me thou art honest: now, if thou wert a poet, I might have some hope thou didst feign.

AUDREY. Would you not have me honest?

TOUCHSTONE. No, truly, unless thou wert hard-favour'd; for honesty coupled to beauty is to have honey a sauce to sugar.

JAQUES. (*Aside*) A material fool.

AUDREY. Well, I am not fair, and therefore I pray the gods make me honest.

TOUCHSTONE. Truly, and to cast away honesty upon a foul slut were to put good meat into an unclean dish.

AUDREY. I am not a slut, though I thank the gods I am foul.

TOUCHSTONE. Well, praised be the gods for thy foulness! Sluttishness may come hereafter. But be it as it may be, I will marry thee; and to that end I have been with Sir Oliver Martext, the vicar of the next village, who hath promised to meet me in this place of the forest, and to couple us.

JAQUES. (*Aside*) I would fain see this meeting.

AUDREY. Well, the gods give us joy!

TOUCHSTONE. Amen. A man may, if he were of a fearful heart, stagger in this attempt; for here we have no temple but the wood, no assembly but horn-beasts. But what though? Courage! As horns are odious, they are necessary. It is said, 'many a man knows no end of his goods.' Right! Many a man has good horns, and knows no end of them. Well, that is the dowry of his wife; 'tis none of his own getting. Horns? Even so. Poor men alone? No, no; the noblest deer hath them as huge as the rascal. Is the single man therefore blessed? No: as a walled town is more worthier than a village, so is the forehead of a married man more honourable than the bare brow of a bachelor; and by how much defence is better than no skill, by so much is a horn more precious than to want. Here comes Sir Oliver.

Enter Sir Oliver Martext

Sir Oliver Martext, you are well met: will you dispatch us here under this tree, or shall we go with you to your chapel?

SIR OLIVER. Is there none here to give the woman?

TOUCHSTONE. I will not take her on gift of any man.

SIR OLIVER. Truly, she must be given, or the marriage is not lawful.

JAQUES. (*Coming forward*) Proceed, proceed! I'll give her.

TOUCHSTONE. Good even, good Master What-ye-call 't: how do you, sir? You are very well met: God 'ild you for your last company. I am very glad to see you. Even a toy in hand here, sir. Nay, pray be covered.

JAQUES. Will you be married, motley?

TOUCHSTONE. As the ox hath his bow, sir, the horse his curb, and the falcon her bells, so man hath his desires; and as pigeons bill, so wedlock would be nibbling.

JAQUES. And will you, being a man of your breeding, be married under a bush, like a beggar? Get you to church, and have a good priest that can tell you what marriage is. This fellow will but join you together as they join wainscot; then one of you will prove a shrunk panel, and like green timber, warp, warp.

TOUCHSTONE. (*Aside*) I am not in the mind but I were better to be married of him than of another: for he is not like to marry me well, and not being well married, it will be a good excuse for me hereafter to leave my wife.

JAQUES. Go thou with me, and let me counsel thee.

TOUCHSTONE. Come, sweet Audrey:
We must be married, or we must live in bawdry.
Farewell, good Master Oliver: not
                    O sweet Oliver!
                    O brave Oliver!
          Leave me not behind thee:
but,—
                    Wind away,
                    Begone, I say,
          I will not to wedding with thee.
                    Exeunt Jaques, Touchstone, and Audrey

SIR OLIVER. 'Tis no matter. Ne'er a fantastical knave of them all shall flout me out of my calling.   *Exit*

SCENE FOUR

Another Part of the Forest.

Enter Rosalind and Celia

ROSALIND. Never talk to me. I will weep.

CELIA. Do, I prithee; but yet have the grace to consider that tears do not become a man.

ROSALIND. But have I not cause to weep?

CELIA. As good cause as one would desire; therefore weep.

ROSALIND. His very hair is of the dissembling colour.

CELIA. Something browner than Judas's; marry, his kisses are Judas's own children.

ROSALIND. I' faith, his hair is of a good colour.

CELIA. An excellent colour. Your chestnut was ever the only colour.

ROSALIND. And his kissing is as full of sanctity as the touch of holy bread.

CELIA. He hath bought a pair of cast lips of Diana. A nun of winter's sisterhood kisses not more religiously; the very ice of chastity is in them.

ROSALIND. But why did he swear he would come this morning, and comes not?

CELIA. Nay, certainly, there is no truth in him.

ROSALIND. Do you think so?

CELIA. Yes: I think he is not a pick-purse nor a horse-stealer; but for his verity in love, I do think him as concave as a covered goblet or a worm-eaten nut.

ROSALIND. Not true in love?

CELIA. Yes, when he is in; but I think he is not in.

ROSALIND. You have heard him swear downright he was.

CELIA. 'Was' is not 'is.' Besides, the oath of a lover is no stronger than the word of a tapster; they are both the confirmers of false reckonings. He attends here in the forest on the duke your father.

ROSALIND. I met the duke yesterday and had much question with him. He asked me of what parentage I was; I told him, of as good as he; so he laughed, and let me go. But what talk we of fathers, when there is such a man as Orlando?

CELIA. O, that 's a brave man! He writes brave verses, speaks brave words, swears brave oaths, and breaks them bravely, quite traverse, athwart the heart of his lover; as a puisny tilter, that spurs his horse but on one side, breaks his staff like a noble goose. But all 's brave that youth mounts and folly guides. Who comes here?

Enter Corin

CORIN. Mistress and master, you have oft inquir'd
After the shepherd that complain'd of love,
Who you saw sitting by me on the turf,
Praising the proud disdainful shepherdess
That was his mistress.

CELIA.   Well, and what of him?

CORIN. If you will see a pageant truly play'd,
Between the pale complexion of true love
And the red glow of scorn and proud disdain,
Go hence a little, and I shall conduct you,
If you will mark it.

ROSALIND.   O! come, let us remove:
The sight of lovers feedeth those in love.
Bring us to this sight, and you shall say
I 'll prove a busy actor in their play.   *Exeunt*

SCENE FIVE

Another Part of the Forest.

Enter Silvius and Phebe

SILVIUS. Sweet Phebe, do not scorn me; do not, Phebe!
    Say that you love me not, but say not so
    In bitterness. The common executioner,
    Whose heart the accustom'd sight of death makes hard,
    Falls not the axe upon the humbled neck
    But first begs pardon: will you sterner be
    Than he that dies and lives by bloody drops?
        Enter Rosalind, Celia, and Corin, behind
PHEBE. I would not be thy executioner.
    I fly thee, for I would not injure thee.
    Thou tell'st me there is murder in mine eye:
    'Tis pretty, sure, and very probable,
    That eyes, that are the frail'st and softest things,
    Who shut their coward gates on atomies,
    Should be call'd tyrants, butchers, murderers!
    Now I do frown on thee with all my heart;
    And, if mine eyes can wound, now let them kill thee;
    Now counterfeit to swound; why now fall down;
    Or, if thou canst not, O! for shame, for shame,
    Lie not, to say mine eyes are murderers.
    Now show the wound mine eye hath made in thee;
    Scratch thee but with a pin, and there remains
    Some scar of it; lean but upon a rush,
    The cicatrice and capable impressure
    Thy palm some moment keeps; but now mine eyes,
    Which I have darted at thee, hurt thee not,
    Nor, I am sure, there is no force in eyes
    That can do hurt.
SILVIUS.   O dear Phebe,
    If ever,—as that ever may be near,—
    You meet in some fresh cheek the power of fancy,
    Then shall you know the wounds invisible
    That love's keen arrows make.
PHEBE.   But, till that time
    Come not thou near me; and, when that time comes,

Afflict me with thy mocks, pity me not;
As, till that time I shall not pity thee.
ROSALIND. (*Advancing*) And why, I pray you? Who might
    be your mother,
That you insult, exult, and all at once,
Over the wretched? What though you have no beauty,—
As by my faith, I see no more in you
Than without candle may go dark to bed,—
Must you be therefore proud and pitiless?
Why, what means this? Why do you look on me?
I see no more in you than in the ordinary
Of nature's sale-work. Od's my little life!
I think she means to tangle my eyes too.
No, faith, proud mistress, hope not after it.
'Tis not your inky brows, your black silk hair,
Your bugle eyeballs, nor your cheek of cream,
That can entame my spirits to your worship.
You foolish shepherd, wherefore do you follow her,
Like foggy south puffing with wind and rain?
You are a thousand times a properer man
Than she a woman. 'Tis such fools as you
That make the world full of ill-favour'd children:
'Tis not her glass, but you, that flatters her;
And out of you she sees herself more proper
Than any of her lineaments can show her.
But, mistress, know yourself. Down on your knees,
And thank heaven, fasting, for a good man's love:
For I must tell you friendly in your ear,
Sell when you can; you are not for all markets.
Cry the man mercy; love him; take his offer:
Foul is most foul, being foul to be a scoffer.
So take her to thee, shepherd. Fare you well.
PHEBE. Sweet youth, I pray you, chide a year together:
    I had rather hear you chide than this man woo.
ROSALIND. He's fallen in love with her foulness, and she'll
    fall in love with my anger. If it be so, as fast as she an-
    swers thee with frowning looks, I'll sauce her with bitter
    words. Why look you so upon me?
PHEBE. For no ill will I bear you.
ROSALIND. I pray you, do not fall in love with me,
    For I am falser than vows made in wine.
    Besides, I like you not. If you will know my house,

'Tis at the tuft of olives here hard by.
Will you go, sister? Shepherd, ply her hard.
Come, sister. Shepherdess, look on him better,
And be not proud: though all the world could see,
None could be so abus'd in sight as he.
Come, to our flock.   *Exeunt Rosalind, Celia, and Corin*

PHEBE. Dead shepherd, now I find thy saw of might;
'Who ever lov'd that lov'd not at first sight?'

SILVIUS. Sweet Phebe,—

PHEBE.   Ha! what sayst thou, Silvius?

SILVIUS. Sweet Phebe, pity me.

PHEBE. Why, I am sorry for thee, gentle Silvius.

SILVIUS. Wherever sorrow is, relief would be:
If you do sorrow at my grief in love,
By giving love your sorrow and my grief
Were both extermin'd.

PHEBE. Thou hast my love: is not that neighbourly?

SILVIUS. I would have you.

PHEBE.   Why, that were covetousness.
Silvius, the time was that I hated thee;
And yet it is not that I bear thee love:
But since that thou canst talk of love so well,
Thy company, which erst was irksome to me,
I will endure, and I 'll employ thee too;
But do not look for further recompense
Than thine own gladness that thou art employ'd.

SILVIUS. So holy and so perfect is my love,
And I in such a poverty of grace,
That I shall think it a most plenteous crop
To glean the broken ears after the man
That the main harvest reaps. Loose now and then
A scatter'd smile, and that I 'll live upon.

PHEBE. Know'st thou the youth that spoke to me erewhile?

SILVIUS. Not very well, but I have met him oft;
And he hath bought the cottage and the bounds
That the old carlot once was master of.

PHEBE. Think not I love him, though I ask for him.
'Tis but a peevish boy; yet he talks well;
But what care I for words? Yet words do well,
When he that speaks them pleases those that hear.
It is a pretty youth: not very pretty:
But sure, he 's proud; and yet his pride becomes him.

He 'll make a proper man. The best thing in him
Is his complexion; and faster than his tongue
Did make offence his eye did heal it up.
He is not very tall; yet for his years he 's tall.
His leg is but so so; and yet 'tis well.
There was a pretty redness in his lip,
A little riper and more lusty red
Than that mix'd in his cheek; 'twas just the difference
Betwixt the constant red and mingled damask.
There be some women, Silvius, had they mark'd him
In parcels as I did, would have gone near
To fall in love with him; but, for my part,
I love him not nor hate him not; and yet
Have more cause to hate him than to love him:
For what had he to do to chide at me?
He said mine eyes were black and my hair black;
And, now I am remember'd, scorn'd at me.
I marvel why I answer'd not again.
But that 's all one; omittance is no quittance.
I 'll write to him a very taunting letter,
And thou shalt bear it. Wilt thou, Silvius?

SILVIUS. Phebe, with all my heart.

PHEBE.   I 'll write it straight;
The matter 's in my head and in my heart:
I will be bitter with him and passing short.
Go with me, Silvius.   *Exeunt*

ACT FOUR

SCENE ONE

The Forest of Arden.

Enter Rosalind, Celia, and Jaques

JAQUES. I prithee, pretty youth, let me be better acquainted with thee.

ROSALIND. They say you are a melancholy fellow.

JAQUES. I am so; I do love it better than laughing.

ROSALIND. Those that are in extremity of either are abominable fellows, and betray themselves to every modern censure worse than drunkards.

JAQUES. Why, 'tis good to be sad and say nothing.

ROSALIND. Why, then, 'tis good to be a post.

JAQUES. I have neither the scholar's melancholy, which is emulation; nor the musician's, which is fantastical; nor the courtier's, which is proud; nor the soldier's, which is ambitious; nor the lawyer's, which is politic; nor the lady's, which is nice; nor the lover's, which is all these: but it is a melancholy of mine own, compounded of many simples, extracted from many objects, and indeed the sundry contemplation of my travels, which, by often rumination, wraps me in a most humorous sadness.

ROSALIND. A traveller! By my faith, you have great reason to be sad. I fear you have sold your own lands to see other men's; then, to have seen much and to have nothing, is to have rich eyes and poor hands.

JAQUES. Yes, I have gained my experience.

ROSALIND. And your experience makes you sad. I had rather have a fool to make me merry than experience to make me sad: and to travel for it too!

Enter Orlando

ORLANDO. Good day, and happiness, dear Rosalind!

JAQUES. Nay then, God be wi' you, an you talk in blank
verse.   *Exit*

ROSALIND. Farewell, Monsieur Traveller. Look you lisp, and
wear strange suits, disable all the benefits of your own
country, be out of love with your nativity, and almost
chide God for making you that countenance you are; or I
will scarce think you have swam in a gondola. Why, how
now, Orlando! Where have you been all this while? You a
lover! An you serve me such another trick, never come in
my sight more.

ORLANDO. My fair Rosalind, I come within an hour of my
promise.

ROSALIND. Break an hour's promise in love! He that will divide a minute into a thousand parts, and break but a part
of the thousandth part of a minute in the affairs of love,
it may be said of him that Cupid hath clapped him o' the
shoulder, but I 'll warrant him heart-whole.

ORLANDO. Pardon me, dear Rosalind.

ROSALIND. Nay, an you be so tardy, come no more in my
sight. I had as lief be wooed of a snail.

ORLANDO. Of a snail!

ROSALIND. Ay, of a snail; for though he comes slowly, he
carries his house on his head; a better jointure, I think,
than you make a woman. Besides, he brings his destiny
with him.

ORLANDO. What 's that?

ROSALIND. Why, horns; that such as you are fain to be beholding to your wives for: but he comes armed in his fortune and prevents the slander of his wife.

ORLANDO. Virtue is no horn-maker; and my Rosalind is virtuous.

ROSALIND. And I am your Rosalind?

CELIA. It pleases him to call you so; but he hath a Rosalind
of a better leer than you.

ROSALIND. Come, woo me, woo me; for now I am in a holiday humour, and like enough to consent. What would
you say to me now, an I were your very very Rosalind?

ORLANDO. I would kiss before I spoke.

ROSALIND. Nay, you were better speak first, and when you
were gravelled for lack of matter, you might take occasion
to kiss. Very good orators, when they are out, they will

spit; and for lovers lacking,—God warn us!—matter, the cleanliest shift is to kiss.

ORLANDO. How if the kiss be denied?

ROSALIND. Then she puts you to entreaty, and there begins new matter.

ORLANDO. Who could be out, being before his beloved mistress?

ROSALIND. Marry, that should you, if I were your mistress; or I should think my honesty ranker than my wit.

ORLANDO. What, of my suit?

ROSALIND. Not out of your apparel, and yet out of your suit. Am not I your Rosalind?

ORLANDO. I take some joy to say you are, because I would be talking of her.

ROSALIND. Well, in her person I say I will not have you.

ORLANDO. Then in mine own person I die.

ROSALIND. No, faith, die by attorney. The poor world is almost six thousand years old, and in all this time there was not any man died in his own person, videlicet, in a love-cause. Troilus had his brains dashed out with a Grecian club; yet he did what he could to die before, and he is one of the patterns of love. Leander, he would have lived many a fair year, though Hero had turned nun, if it had not been for a hot midsummer night; for, good youth, he went but forth to wash him in the Hellespont, and being taken with the cramp was drowned; and the foolish coroners of that age found it was 'Hero of Sestos.' But these are all lies; men have died from time to time, and worms have eaten them, but not for love.

ORLANDO. I would not have my right Rosalind of this mind; for, I protest, her frown might kill me.

ROSALIND. By this hand, it will not kill a fly. But come, now I will be your Rosalind in a more coming-on disposition; and ask me what you will, I will grant it.

ORLANDO. Then love me, Rosalind.

ROSALIND. Yes, faith will I, Fridays and Saturdays and all.

ORLANDO. And wilt thou have me?

ROSALIND. Ay, and twenty such.

ORLANDO. What sayest thou?

ROSALIND. Are you not good?

ORLANDO. I hope so.

ROSALIND. Why then, can one desire too much of a good

thing?—Come, sister, you shall be the priest and marry us.—Give me your hand, Orlando. What do you say, sister?

ORLANDO. Pray thee, marry us.

CELIA. I cannot say the words.

ROSALIND. You must begin,—'Will you, Orlando,'—

CELIA. Go to.—Will you, Orlando, have to wife this Rosalind?

ORLANDO. I will.

ROSALIND. Ay, but when?

ORLANDO. Why now; as fast as she can marry us.

ROSALIND. Then you must say, 'I take thee, Rosalind, for wife.'

ORLANDO. I take thee, Rosalind, for wife.

ROSALIND. I might ask you for your commission; but, I do take thee, Orlando, for my husband. There 's a girl goes before the priest; and, certainly, a woman's thought runs before her actions.

ORLANDO. So do all thoughts; they are winged.

ROSALIND. Now tell me how long you would have her after you have possessed her?

ORLANDO. For ever and a day.

ROSALIND. Say 'a day,' without the 'ever.' No, no, Orlando; men are April when they woo, December when they wed: maids are May when they are maids, but the sky changes when they are wives. I will be more jealous of thee than a Barbary cock-pigeon over his hen; more clamorous than a parrot against rain; more new-fangled than an ape; more giddy in my desires than a monkey: I will weep for nothing, like Diana in the fountain, and I will do that when you are disposed to be merry; I will laugh like a hyen, and that when thou art inclined to sleep.

ORLANDO. But will my Rosalind do so?

ROSALIND. By my life, she will do as I do.

ORLANDO. O! but she is wise.

ROSALIND. Or else she could not have the wit to do this: the wiser, the waywarder: make the doors upon a woman's wit, and it will out at the casement; shut that, and 'twill out at the key-hole; stop that, 'twill fly with the smoke out at the chimney.

ORLANDO. A man that hath a wife with such a wit, he might say, 'Wit, whither wilt?'

ROSALIND. Nay, you might keep that check for it till you met your wife's wit going to your neighbour's bed.

ORLANDO. And what wit could wit have to excuse that?

ROSALIND. Marry, to say she came to seek you there. You shall never take her without her answer, unless you take her without her tongue. O! that woman that cannot make her fault her husband's occasion, let her never nurse her child herself, for she will breed it like a fool.

ORLANDO. For these two hours, Rosalind, I will leave thee.

RÒSALIND. Alas! dear love, I cannot lack thee two hours.

ORLANDO. I must attend the duke at dinner. By two o'clock I will be with thee again.

ROSALIND. Ay, go your ways, go your ways; I knew what you would prove, my friends told me as much, and I thought no less. That flattering tongue of yours won me. 'Tis but one cast away, and so, come, death! Two o'clock is your hour?

ORLANDO. Ay, sweet Rosalind.

ROSALIND. By my troth, and in good earnest, and so God mend me, and by all pretty oaths that are not dangerous, if you break one jot of your promise or come one minute behind your hour, I will think you the most pathetical break-promise, and the most hollow lover, and the most unworthy of her you call Rosalind, that may be chosen out of the gross band of the unfaithful. Therefore, beware my censure, and keep your promise.

ORLANDO. With no less religion than if thou wert indeed my Rosalind: so, adieu.

ROSALIND. Well, Time is the old justice that examines all such offenders, and let Time try. Adieu.   *Exit Orlando*

CELIA. You have simply misused our sex in your love-prate. We must have your doublet and hose plucked over your head, and show the world what the bird hath done to her own nest.

ROSALIND. O coz, coz, coz, my pretty little coz, that thou didst know how many fathom deep I am in love! But it cannot be sounded. My affection hath an unknown bottom, like the bay of Portugal.

CELIA. Or rather, bottomless; that as fast as you pour affection in, it runs out.

ROSALIND. No; that same wicked bastard of Venus, that was begot of thought, conceived of spleen, and born of madness, that blind rascally boy that abuses every one's eyes because his own are out, let him be judge how deep I am in love. I 'll tell thee, Aliena, I cannot be out of the sight of Orlando. I 'll go find a shadow and sigh till he come.

CELIA. And I 'll sleep.   *Exeunt*

SCENE TWO

Another Part of the Forest.

Enter Jaques, Lords, and Foresters

JAQUES. Which is he that killed the deer?

FIRST LORD. Sir, it was I.

JAQUES. Let 's present him to the duke, like a Roman conqueror; and it would do well to set the deer's horns upon his head for a branch of victory. Have you no song, forester, for this purpose?

SECOND LORD. Yes, sir.

JAQUES. Sing it: 'tis no matter how it be in tune so it make noise enough.

SONG

What shall he have that kill'd the deer?
His leather skin and horns to wear.
    Then sing him home.   *The rest shall*
                                bear this burden

Take thou no scorn to wear the horn;
It was a crest ere thou wast born:
        Thy father's father wore it,
        And thy father bore it.
The horn, the horn, the lusty horn
Is not a thing to laugh to scorn.   *Exeunt*

SCENE THREE

Another Part of the Forest.

Enter Rosalind and Celia

ROSALIND. How say you now? Is it not past two o'clock?
     And here much Orlando!

CELIA. I warrant you, with pure love and a troubled brain,
     he hath ta'en his bow and arrows, and is gone forth to
     sleep. Look, who comes here.

Enter Silvius

SILVIUS. My errand is to you, fair youth.
     My gentle Phebe did bid me give you this. *Giving a letter*
     I know not the contents; but, as I guess
     By the stern brow and waspish action
     Which she did use as she was writing of it,
     It bears an angry tenour. Pardon me;
     I am but as a guiltless messenger.

ROSALIND. Patience herself would startle at this letter,
     And play the swaggerer. Bear this, bear all:
     She says I am not fair; that I lack manners;
     She calls me proud, and that she could not love me
     Were man as rare as phœnix. 'Od 's my will!
     Her love is not the hare that I do hunt.
     Why writes she so to me? Well, shepherd, well,
     This is a letter of your own device.

SILVIUS. No, I protest, I know not the contents.
     Phebe did write it.

ROSALIND.   Come, come, you are a fool,
     And turn'd into the extremity of love.
     I saw her hand: she has a leathern hand,
     A freestone-colour'd hand; I verily did think
     That her old gloves were on, but 'twas her hands.
     She has a housewife's hand; but that 's no matter.
     I say she never did invent this letter;
     This is a man's invention, and his hand.

SILVIUS. Sure, it is hers.

ROSALIND. Why, 'tis a boisterous and a cruel style,
     A style for challengers; why, she defies me,
     Like Turk to Christian! Woman's gentle brain

Could not drop forth such giant-rude invention,
Such Ethiop words, blacker in their effect
Than in their countenance. Will you hear the letter?

SILVIUS. So please you, for I never heard it yet;
Yet heard too much of Phebe's cruelty.

ROSALIND. She Phebes me. Mark how the tyrant writes.
    (*Reads*)
        'Art thou god to shepherd turn'd,
        That a maiden's heart hath burn'd?'
Can a woman rail thus?

SILVIUS. Call you this railing?

ROSALIND. (*Reads*)
        'Why, thy godhead laid apart,
        Warr'st thou with a woman's heart?'
Did you ever hear such railing?
        'Whiles the eye of man did woo me,
        That could do no vengeance to me.'
Meaning me a beast.
        'If the scorn of your bright eyne
        Have power to raise such love in mine,
        Alack! in me what strange effect
        Would they work in mild aspect.
        Whiles you chid me, I did love;
        How then might your prayers move!
        He that brings this love to thee
        Little knows this love in me;
        And by him seal up thy mind;
        Whether that thy youth and kind
        Will the faithful offer take
        Of me and all that I can make;
        Or else by him my love deny,
        And then I 'll study how to die.'

SILVIUS. Call you this chiding?

CELIA. Alas, poor shepherd!

ROSALIND. Do you pity him? No, he deserves no pity. Wilt
thou love such a woman? What, to make thee an instrument and play false strains upon thee! not to be endured!
Well, go your way to her, for I see love hath made thee a
tame snake, and say this to her: that if she love me, I
charge her to love thee: if she will not, I will never have
her, unless thou entreat for her. If you be a true lover,
hence, and not a word, for here comes more company.
                                        Exit Silvius

Enter Oliver

OLIVER. Good-morrow, fair ones. Pray you if you know,
 Where in the purlieus of this forest stands
 A sheepcote fenc'd about with olive-trees?
CELIA. West of this place, down in the neighbour bottom.
 The rank of osiers by the murmuring stream
 Left on your right hand brings you to the place.
 But at this hour the house doth keep itself;
 There 's none within.
OLIVER. If that an eye may profit by a tongue,
 Then should I know you by description;
 Such garments, and such years: 'The boy is fair,
 Of female favour, and bestows himself
 Like a ripe sister: but the woman low,
 And browner than her brother.' Are not you
 The owner of the house I did inquire for?
CELIA. It is no boast, being ask'd, to say, we are.
OLIVER. Orlando doth commend him to you both,
 And to that youth he calls his Rosalind
 He sends this bloody napkin. Are you he?
ROSALIND. I am. What must we understand by this?
OLIVER. Some of my shame; if you will know of me
 What man I am, and how, and why, and where
 This handkercher was stain'd.
CELIA.   I pray you, tell it.
OLIVER. When last the young Orlando parted from you
 He left a promise to return again
 Within an hour; and, pacing through the forest,
 Chewing the food of sweet and bitter fancy,
 Lo, what befell! he threw his eye aside,
 And mark what object did present itself:
 Under an oak, whose boughs were moss'd with age,
 And high top bald with dry antiquity,
 A wretched ragged man, o'ergrown with hair,
 Lay sleeping on his back: about his neck
 A green and gilded snake had wreath'd itself,
 Who with her head nimble in threats approach'd
 The opening of his mouth; but suddenly,
 Seeing Orlando, it unlink'd itself,
 And with indented glides did slip away
 Into a bush; under which bush's shade
 A lioness, with udders all drawn dry,

Lay couching, head on ground, with catlike watch,
When that the sleeping man should stir; for 'tis
The royal disposition of that beast
To prey on nothing that doth seem as dead:
This seen, Orlando did approach the man,
And found it was his brother, his elder brother.

CELIA. O! I have heard him speak of that same brother;
And he did render him the most unnatural
That liv'd 'mongst men.

OLIVER.   And well he might so do,
For well I know he was unnatural.

ROSALIND. But, to Orlando: did he leave him there,
Food to the suck'd and hungry lioness?

OLIVER. Twice did he turn his back and purpos'd so;
But kindness, nobler ever than revenge,
And nature, stronger than his just occasion,
Made him give battle to the lioness,
Who quickly fell before him: in which hurtling
From miserable slumber I awak'd.

CELIA. Are you his brother?

ROSALIND.   Was it you he rescu'd?

CELIA. Was 't you that did so oft contrive to kill him?

OLIVER. 'Twas I; but 'tis not I. I do not shame
To tell you what I was, since my conversion
So sweetly tastes, being the thing I am.

ROSALIND. But, for the bloody napkin?

OLIVER.   By and by.
When from the first to last, betwixt us two,
Tears our recountments had most kindly bath'd,
As how I came into that desert place:—
In brief, he led me to the gentle duke,
Who gave me fresh array and entertainment,
Committing me unto my brother's love;
Who led me instantly unto his cave,
There stripp'd himself; and here, upon his arm
The lioness had torn some flesh away,
Which all this while had bled; and now he fainted,
And cried, in fainting, upon Rosalind.
Brief, I recover'd him, bound up his wound;
And, after some small space, being strong at heart,
He sent me hither, stranger as I am,
To tell this story, that you might excuse

His broken promise; and to give this napkin,
Dy'd in his blood, unto the shepherd youth
That he in sport doth call his Rosalind.

CELIA. *(Rosalind swoons)* Why, how now, Ganymede!
sweet Ganymede!

OLIVER. Many will swoon when they do look on blood.

CELIA. There is more in it. Cousin! Ganymede!

OLIVER. Look, he recovers.

ROSALIND. I would I were at home.

CELIA.   We 'll lead you thither.
I pray you, will you take him by the arm?

OLIVER. Be of good cheer, youth. You a man! You lack a
man's heart.

ROSALIND. I do so, I confess it. Ah, sirrah! a body would
think this was well counterfeited. I pray you, tell your
brother how well I counterfeited. Heigh-ho!

OLIVER. This was not counterfeit. There is too great testimony in your complexion that it was a passion of earnest.

ROSALIND. Counterfeit, I assure you.

OLIVER. Well then, take a good heart and counterfeit to be a
man.

ROSALIND. So I do; but, i' faith, I should have been a woman
by right.

CELIA. Come; you look paler and paler. Pray you, draw
homewards. Good sir, go with us.

OLIVER. That will I, for I must bear answer back
How you excuse my brother, Rosalind.

ROSALIND. I shall devise something. But, I pray you, commend my counterfeiting to him. Will you go?   *Exeunt*

ACT FIVE

SCENE ONE

The Forest of Arden.

Enter Touchstone and Audrey

TOUCHSTONE. We shall find a time, Audrey. Patience, gentle Audrey.

AUDREY. Faith, the priest was good enough, for all the old gentleman's saying.

TOUCHSTONE. A most wicked Sir Oliver, Audrey; a most vile Martext. But, Audrey, there is a youth here in the forest lays claim to you.

AUDREY. Ay, I know who 'tis. He hath no interest in me in the world. Here comes the man you mean.

Enter William

TOUCHSTONE. It is meat and drink to me to see a clown. By my troth, we that have good wits have much to answer for. We shall be flouting; we cannot hold.

WILLIAM. Good even, Audrey.

AUDREY. God ye good even, William.

WILLIAM. And good even to you, sir.

TOUCHSTONE. Good even, gentle friend. Cover thy head, cover thy head; nay, prithee, be covered. How old are you, friend?

WILLIAM. Five-and-twenty, sir.

TOUCHSTONE. A ripe age. Is thy name William?

WILLIAM. William, sir.

TOUCHSTONE. A fair name. Wast born i' the forest here?

WILLIAM. Ay, sir, I thank God.

TOUCHSTONE. 'Thank God'; a good answer. Art rich?

WILLIAM. Faith, sir, so so.

TOUCHSTONE. 'So so,' is good, very good, very excellent good: and yet it is not; it is but so so. Art thou wise?

WILLIAM. Ay, sir, I have a pretty wit.

TOUCHSTONE. Why, thou sayest well. I do now remember a saying, 'The fool doth think he is wise, but the wise man knows himself to be a fool.' The heathen philosopher, when he had a desire to eat a grape, would open his lips when he put it into his mouth; meaning thereby that grapes were made to eat and lips to open. You do love this maid?

WILLIAM. I do, sir.

TOUCHSTONE. Give me your hand. Art thou learned?

WILLIAM. No, sir.

TOUCHSTONE. Then learn this of me: to have, is to have; for it is a figure in rhetoric, that drink, being poured out of a cup into a glass, by filling the one doth empty the other; for all your writers do consent that ipse is he: now, you are not ipse, for I am he.

WILLIAM. Which he, sir?

TOUCHSTONE. He, sir, that must marry this woman. Therefore, you clown, abandon,—which is in the vulgar, leave, —the society,—which in the boorish is, company,—of this female,—which in the common is, woman; which together is, abandon the society of this female, or, clown, thou perishest; or, to thy better understanding, diest; or, to wit, I kill thee, make thee away, translate thy life into death, thy liberty into bondage. I will deal in poison with thee, or in bastinado, or in steel; I will bandy with thee in faction; I will o'errun thee with policy; I will kill thee a hundred and fifty ways: therefore tremble, and depart.

AUDREY. Do, good William.

WILLIAM. God rest you merry, sir.   *Exit*

Enter Corin

CORIN. Our master and mistress seek you. Come, away, away!

TOUCHSTONE. Trip, Audrey! trip, Audrey! I attend, I attend.
                                                              Exeunt

SCENE TWO

Another Part of the Forest.

Enter Orlando and Oliver

ORLANDO. Is 't possible that on so little acquaintance you should like her? that, but seeing, you should love her? and, loving, woo? and, wooing, she should grant? and will you persever to enjoy her?

OLIVER. Neither call the giddiness of it in question, the poverty of her, the small acquaintance, my sudden wooing, nor her sudden consenting; but say with me, I love Aliena; say with her that she loves me; consent with both that we may enjoy each other: it shall be to your good; for my father's house and all the revenue that was old Sir Rowland's will I estate upon you, and here live and die a shepherd.

ORLANDO. You have my consent. Let your wedding be tomorrow. Thither will I invite the duke and all 's contented followers. Go you and prepare Aliena; for, look you, here comes my Rosalind.

Enter Rosalind

ROSALIND. God save you, brother.

OLIVER. And you, fair sister.   *Exit*

ROSALIND. O! my dear Orlando, how it grieves me to see thee wear thy heart in a scarf.

ORLANDO. It is my arm.

ROSALIND. I thought thy heart had been wounded with the claws of a lion.

ORLANDO. Wounded it is, but with the eyes of a lady.

ROSALIND. Did your brother tell you how I counterfeited to swound when he showed me your handkercher?

ORLANDO. Ay, and greater wonders than that.

ROSALIND. O! I know where you are. Nay, 'tis true. There was never anything so sudden but the fight of two rams, and Cæsar's thrasonical brag of 'I came, saw, and overcame': for your brother and my sister no sooner met, but they looked; no sooner looked but they loved; no sooner loved but they sighed; no sooner sighed but they asked one another the reason; no sooner knew the reason but they sought the remedy: and in these degrees have they made a pair of stairs to marriage which they will climb incontinent, or else be incontinent before marriage. They are in the very wrath of love, and they will together. Clubs cannot part them.

ORLANDO. They shall be married to-morrow, and I will bid the duke to the nuptial. But, O! how bitter a thing it is to look into happiness through another man's eyes. By so much the more shall I to-morrow be at the height of heart-heaviness, by how much I shall think my brother happy in having what he wishes for.

ROSALIND. Why then, to-morrow I cannot serve your turn for Rosalind?

ORLANDO. I can live no longer by thinking.

ROSALIND. I will weary you then no longer with idle talking. Know of me then,—for now I speak to some purpose,—that I know you are a gentleman of good conceit. I speak not this that you should bear a good opinion of my knowledge, insomuch I say I know you are; neither do I labour for a greater esteem than may in some little measure draw a belief from you, to do yourself good, and not to grace me. Believe then, if you please, that I can do strange things. I have, since I was three years old, conversed with a magician, most profound in his art and yet not damnable. If you do love Rosalind so near the heart as your gesture cries it out, when your brother marries Aliena, shall you marry her. I know into what straits of fortune she is driven; and it is not impossible to me, if it appear not inconvenient to you, to set her before your eyes to-morrow, human as she is, and without any danger.

ORLANDO. Speakest thou in sober meanings?

ROSALIND. By my life, I do; which I tender dearly, though I say I am a magician. Therefore, put you in your best array; bid your friends; for if you will be married to-morrow, you shall; and to Rosalind, if you will. Look, here comes a lover of mine, and a lover of hers.

Enter Silvius and Phebe

PHEBE. Youth, you have done me much ungentleness,
To show the letter that I writ to you.

ROSALIND. I care not if I have: it is my study
To seem despiteful and ungentle to you.
You are there follow'd by a faithful shepherd.
Look upon him, love him; he worships you.

PHEBE. Good shepherd, tell this youth what 'tis to love.

SILVIUS. It is to be all made of sighs and tears;
  And so am I for Phebe.

PHEBE. And I for Ganymede.

ORLANDO. And I for Rosalind.

ROSALIND. And I for no woman.

SILVIUS. It is to be all made of faith and service;
  And so am I for Phebe.

PHEBE. And I for Ganymede.

ORLANDO. And I for Rosalind.

ROSALIND. And I for no woman.

SILVIUS. It is to be all made of fantasy,
  All made of passion, and all made of wishes;
  All adoration, duty, and observance;
  All humbleness, all patience, and impatience;
  All purity, all trial, all obeisance;
  And so am I for Phebe.

PHEBE. And so am I for Ganymede.

ORLANDO. And so am I for Rosalind.

ROSALIND. And so am I for no woman.

PHEBE. (*To Rosalind*) If this be so, why blame you me to
  love you?

SILVIUS. (*To Phebe*) If this be so, why blame you me to love
  you?

ORLANDO. If this be so, why blame you me to love you?

ROSALIND. Who do you speak to, 'Why blame you me to love
  you'?

ORLANDO. To her that is not here, nor doth not hear.

ROSALIND. Pray you, no more of this: 'tis like the howling of
  Irish wolves against the moon. (*To Silvius*) I will help
  you, if I can. (*To Phebe*) I would love you, if I could. To-
  morrow meet me all together. (*To Phebe*) I will marry
  you, if ever I marry woman, and I 'll be married to-morrow. (*To Orlando*) I will satisfy you, if ever I satisfied
  man, and you shall be married to-morrow. (*To Silvius*) I
  will content you, if what pleases you contents you, and
  you shall be married to-morrow. (*To Orlando*) As you
  love Rosalind, meet. (*To Silvius*) As you love Phebe,
  meet: and as I love no woman, I 'll meet. So, fare you well.
  I have left you commands.

SILVIUS. I 'll not fail, if I live.

PHEBE. Nor I.

ORLANDO. Nor I.   *Exeunt*

SCENE THREE

Another Part of the Forest.

Enter Touchstone and Audrey

TOUCHSTONE. To-morrow is the joyful day, Audrey; to-morrow will we be married.

AUDREY. I do desire it with all my heart, and I hope it is no dishonest desire to desire to be a woman of the world. Here come two of the banished duke's pages.

Enter two Pages

FIRST PAGE. Well met, honest gentleman.

TOUCHSTONE. By my troth, well met. Come, sit, sit, and a song.

SECOND PAGE. We are for you: sit i' the middle.

FIRST PAGE. Shall we clap into 't roundly, without hawking or spitting, or saying we are hoarse, which are the only prologues to a bad voice?

SECOND PAGE. I' faith, i' faith; and both in a tune, like two gipsies on a horse.

SONG

It was a lover and his lass,
  With a hey, and a ho, and a hey nonino,
That o'er the green corn-field did pass,
  In the spring time, the only pretty ring time,
When birds do sing, hey ding a ding, ding;
  Sweet lovers love the spring.
Between the acres of the rye,
  With a hey, and a ho, and a hey nonino,
These pretty country folks would lie,
  In the spring time, &c.
This carol they began that hour,
  With a hey, and a ho, and a hey nonino,
How that a life was but a flower
  In the spring time, &c.
And therefore take the present time,
  With a hey, and a ho, and a hey nonino;
For love is crowned with the prime
  In the spring time, &c.

TOUCHSTONE. Truly, young gentlemen, though there was no
  great matter in the ditty, yet the note was very untuneable.

FIRST PAGE. You are deceived, sir. We kept time; we lost not
  our time.

TOUCHSTONE. By my troth, yes; I count it but time lost to
  hear such a foolish song. God be wi' you; and God mend
  your voices! Come, Audrey.   *Exeunt*

SCENE FOUR

Another Part of the Forest.

*Enter Duke Senior, Amiens, Jaques, Orlando, Oliver,
and Celia*

DUKE SENIOR. Dost thou believe, Orlando, that the boy
  Can do all this that he hath promised?

ORLANDO. I sometimes do believe, and sometimes do not;
  As those that fear they hope, and know they fear.
      Enter Rosalind, Silvius, and Phebe

ROSALIND. Patience once more, whiles our compact is urg'd.
  (*To the Duke*) You say, if I bring in your Rosalind,
  You will bestow her on Orlando here?

DUKE SENIOR. That would I, had I kingdoms to give with
  her.

ROSALIND. (*To Orlando*) And you say, you will have her
  when I bring her?

ORLANDO. That would I, were I of all kingdoms king.

ROSALIND. (*To Phebe*) You say, that you 'll marry me, if I be
  willing?

PHEBE. That will I, should I die the hour after.

ROSALIND. But if you do refuse to marry me,
  You 'll give yourself to this most faithful shepherd?

PHEBE. So is the bargain.

ROSALIND. (*To Silvius*) You say, that you 'll have Phebe, if
  she will?

SILVIUS. Though to have her and death were both one thing.

ROSALIND. I have promis'd to make all this matter even.
  Keep you your word, O duke, to give your daughter;
  You yours, Orlando, to receive his daughter;
  Keep your word, Phebe, that you 'll marry me,

Or else, refusing me, to wed this shepherd;
Keep your word, Silvius, that you 'll marry her,
If she refuse me: and from hence I go,
To make these doubts all even. *Exeunt Rosalind and Celia*

DUKE SENIOR. I do remember in this shepherd boy
Some lively touches of my daughter's favour.

ORLANDO. My lord, the first time that I ever saw him,
Methought he was a brother to your daughter;
But, my good lord, this boy is forest-born,
And hath been tutor'd in the rudiments
Of many desperate studies by his uncle,
Whom he reports to be a great magician,
Obscured in the circle of this forest.

Enter Touchstone and Audrey

JAQUES. There is, sure, another flood toward, and these
couples are coming to the ark. Here comes a pair of very
strange beasts, which in all tongues are called fools.

TOUCHSTONE. Salutation and greeting to you all!

JAQUES. Good my lord, bid him welcome. This is the motley-minded gentleman that I have so often met in the forest. He hath been a courtier, he swears.

TOUCHSTONE. If any man doubt that, let him put me to my
purgation. I have trod a measure; I have flattered a lady;
I have been politic with my friend, smooth with mine enemy; I have undone three tailors; I have had four quarrels,
and like to have fought one.

JAQUES. And how was that ta'en up?

TOUCHSTONE. Faith, we met, and found the quarrel was
upon the seventh cause.

JAQUES. How seventh cause? Good my lord, like this fellow.

DUKE SENIOR. I like him very well.

TOUCHSTONE. God 'ild you, sir; I desire you of the like. I
press in here, sir, amongst the rest of the country copulatives, to swear, and to forswear, according as marriage
binds and blood breaks. A poor virgin, sir, an ill-favoured
thing, sir, but mine own: a poor humour of mine, sir, to
take that that no man else will. Rich honesty dwells like a
miser, sir, in a poor house, as your pearl in your foul oyster.

DUKE SENIOR. By my faith, he is very swift and sententious.

TOUCHSTONE. According to the fool's bolt, sir, and such dulcet diseases.

JAQUES. But, for the seventh cause; how did you find the quarrel on the seventh cause?

TOUCHSTONE. Upon a lie seven times removed:—bear your body more seeming, Audrey:—as thus, sir. I did dislike the cut of a certain courtier's beard: he sent me word, if I said his beard was not cut well, he was in the mind it was: this is called 'the retort courteous.' If I sent him word again, it was not well cut, he would send me word, he cut it to please himself: this is called the 'quip modest.' If again, it was not well cut, he disabled my judgment: this is called the 'reply churlish.' If again, it was not well cut, he would answer, I spake not true: this is called the 'reproof valiant': if again, it was not well cut, he would say, I lie: this is called the 'countercheck quarrelsome': and so to the 'lie circumstantial,' and the 'lie direct.'

JAQUES. And how oft did you say his beard was not well cut?

TOUCHSTONE. I durst go no further than the 'lie circumstantial,' nor he durst not give me the 'lie direct': and so we measured swords and parted.

JAQUES. Can you nominate in order now the degrees of the lie?

TOUCHSTONE. O sir, we quarrel in print; by the book, as you have books for good manners: I will name you the degrees. The first, the 'retort courteous'; the second, the 'quip modest'; the third, the 'reply churlish'; the fourth, the 'reproof valiant'; the fifth, the 'countercheck quarrelsome'; the sixth, the 'lie with circumstance'; the seventh, the 'lie direct.' All these you may avoid but the lie direct; and you may avoid that too, with an 'if.' I knew when seven justices could not take up a quarrel; but when the parties were met themselves, one of them thought but of an 'if,' as 'If you said so, then I said so'; and they shook hands and swore brothers. Your 'if' is the only peacemaker; much virtue in 'if.'

JAQUES. Is not this a rare fellow, my lord? He 's as good at any thing, and yet a fool.

DUKE SENIOR. He uses his folly like a stalking-horse, and under the presentation of that he shoots his wit.

Enter Hymen, leading Rosalind in woman's clothes, and Celia

Still Music

HYMEN.   Then is there mirth in heaven,
              When earthly things made even
                  Atone together.
          Good duke, receive thy daughter;
          Hymen from heaven brought her;
                  Yea, brought her hither,
          That thou mightst join her hand with his,
              Whose heart within her bosom is.

ROSALIND. (*To Duke Senior*) To you I give myself, for I am
          yours.

          (*To Orlando*) To you I give myself, for I am yours.

DUKE SENIOR. If there be truth in sight, you are my daughter.

ORLANDO. If there be truth in sight, you are my Rosalind.

PHEBE.   If sight and shape be true,
          Why then, my love adieu!

ROSALIND. (*To Duke Senior*) I 'll have no father, if you be
          not he.

          (*To Orlando*) I 'll have no husband, if you be not he.

          (*To Phebe*) Nor ne'er wed woman, if you be not she.

HYMEN.   Peace, ho, ho! I bar confusion:
              'Tis I must make conclusion
                  Of these most strange events:
              Here 's eight that must take hands
              To join in Hymen's bands,
                  If truth holds true contents.
          (*To Orlando and Rosalind*) You and you no cross shall
          part.
          (*To Oliver and Celia*) You and you are heart in heart.
          (*To Phebe*) You to his love must accord,
          Or have a woman to your lord:
          (*To Touchstone and Audrey*) You and you are sure to-
          gether,
          As the winter to foul weather.
          Whiles a wedlock hymn we sing,
          Feed yourselves with questioning,
          That reason wonder may diminish,
          How thus we met, and these things finish.

                          SONG

              Wedding is great Juno's crown:
                  O blessed bond of board and bed!
              'Tis Hymen peoples every town;
                  High wedlock then be honoured.

Honour, high honour, and renown,
To Hymen, god of every town!

DUKE SENIOR.　O my dear niece! welcome thou art to me.
Even daughter, welcome in no less degree.

PHEBE.　*(To Silvius)* I will not eat my word, now thou art
mine;
Thy faith my fancy to thee doth combine.

Enter Jaques de Boys

JAQUES DE BOYS.　Let me have audience for a word or two:
I am the second son of old Sir Rowland,
That bring these tidings to this fair assembly.
Duke Frederick, hearing how that every day
Men of great worth resorted to this forest,
Address'd a mighty power, which were on foot
In his own conduct, purposely to take
His brother here and put him to the sword:
And to the skirts of this wild wood he came,
Where, meeting with an old religious man,
After some question with him, was converted
Both from his enterprise and from the world;
His crown bequeathing to his banish'd brother,
And all their lands restor'd to them again
That were with him exil'd. This to be true,
I do engage my life.

DUKE SENIOR.　　　　Welcome, young man;
Thou offer'st fairly to thy brothers' wedding:
To one, his lands withheld; and to the other
A land itself at large, a potent dukedom.
First, in this forest, let us do those ends
That here were well begun and well begot;
And after, every of this happy number
That have endur'd shrewd days and nights with us,
Shall share the good of our returned fortune,
According to the measure of their states.
Meantime, forget this new-fall'n dignity,
And fall into our rustic revelry.
Play, music! and you, brides and bridegrooms all,
With measure heap'd in joy, to the measures fall.

JAQUES.　Sir, by your patience. If I heard you rightly,
The duke hath put on a religious life,
And thrown into neglect the pompous court?

JAQUES DE BOYS.　He hath.

JAQUES. To him will I. Out of these convertites
There is much matter to be heard and learn'd.
(To Duke Senior) You to your former honour I bequeath;
Your patience and your virtue well deserve it.
(To Orlando) You to a love that your true faith doth
    merit:
(To Oliver) You to your land, and love, and great allies:
(To Silvius) You to a long and well-deserved bed:
(To Touchstone) And you to wrangling; for thy loving
    voyage
Is but for two months victual'd. So, to your pleasures!
I am for other than for dancing measures.
DUKE SENIOR. Stay, Jaques, stay.
JAQUES. To see no pastime, I! What you would have
I 'll stay to know at your abandon'd cave.   *Exit*
DUKE SENIOR. Proceed, proceed. We will begin these rites,
As we do trust they 'll end, in true delights.

                              A dance. Exeunt

EPILOGUE

Spoken by Rosalind

It is not the fashion to see the lady the epilogue; but it
is no more unhandsome than to see the lord the prologue.
If it be true that good wine needs no bush, 'tis true that a
good play needs no epilogue; yet to good wine they do use
good bushes, and good plays prove the better by the help
of good epilogues. What a case am I in then, that am
neither a good epilogue, nor cannot insinuate with you in
the behalf of a good play! I am not furnished like a beggar,
therefore to beg will not become me. My way is, to conjure
you; and I 'll begin with the women. I charge you, O
women! for the love you bear to men, to like as much of
this play as please you: and I charge you, O men! for the
love you bear to women,—as I perceive by your simper-
ing none of you hate them,—that between you and the
women, the play may please. If I were a woman I would
kiss as many of you as had beards that pleased me, complexions that liked me, and breaths that I defied not; and,
I am sure, as many as have good beards, or good faces, or
sweet breaths, will, for my kind offer, when I make curtsy,
bid me farewell.   *Exeunt*

THE TAMING OF THE SHREW

CAST OF CHARACTERS

A Lord

CHRISTOPHER SLY, *a Tinker* ⎫
Hostess, Page, Players, Hunts-   ⎬ *Persons in the Induction*
   men, and Servants ⎭

BAPTISTA, *a rich Gentleman of Padua*
VINCENTIO, *an old Gentleman of Pisa*
LUCENTIO, *son to Vincentio; in love with Bianca*
PETRUCHIO, *a Gentleman of Verona; Suitor to Katharina*

GREMIO ⎫
HORTENSIO ⎬ *Suitors to Bianca*

TRANIO ⎫
BIONDELLO ⎬ *Servants to Lucentio*

GRUMIO ⎫
CURTIS ⎬ *Servants to Petruchio*

Pedant, set up to personate Vincentio

KATHARINA, *the Shrew* ⎫
BIANCA ⎬ *Daughters to Baptista*

Widow

Tailor, Haberdasher, and Servants attending on Baptista and Petruchio

SCENE

Padua; and in Petruchio's House in the Country

THE TAMING OF THE SHREW

INDUCTION

SCENE ONE

Before an Alehouse on a Heath.

Enter Hostess and Sly

SLY. I 'll pheeze you, in faith.

HOSTESS. A pair of stocks, you rogue!

SLY. Y' are a baggage: the Slys are no rogues; look in the chronicles; we came in with Richard Conqueror. Therefore, paucas pallabris; let the world slide. Sessa!

HOSTESS. You will not pay for the glasses you have burst?

SLY. No, not a denier. Go by, Jeronimy, go to thy cold bed, and warm thee.

HOSTESS. I know my remedy: I must go fetch the third-borough.   *Exit*

SLY. Third, or fourth, or fifth borough, I 'll answer him by law. I 'll not budge an inch, boy: let him come, and kindly.

Lies down on the ground, and falls asleep
Horns winded. Enter a
Lord from hunting, with Huntsmen and Servants

LORD. Huntsman, I charge thee, tender well my hounds:
Brach Merriman, the poor cur is emboss'd,
And couple Clowder with the deep-mouth'd brach.
Saw'st thou not, boy, how Silver made it good
At the hedge-corner, in the coldest fault?
I would not lose the dog for twenty pound.

FIRST HUNTSMAN. Why, Bellman is as good as he, my lord;
He cried upon it at the merest loss,
And twice to-day pick'd out the dullest scent:
Trust me, I take him for the better dog.

LORD. Thou art a fool: if Echo were as fleet,

I would esteem him worth a dozen such.
But sup them well, and look unto them all:
To-morrow I intend to hunt again.
FIRST HUNTSMAN. I will, my lord.
LORD. (*Sees Sly*) What's here? one dead, or drunk? See,
    doth he breathe?
SECOND HUNTSMAN. He breathes, my lord. Were he not
    warm'd with ale,
This were a bed but cold to sleep so soundly.
LORD. O monstrous beast! how like a swine he lies!
Grim death, how foul and loathsome is thine image!
Sirs, I will practise on this drunken man.
What think you, if he were convey'd to bed,
Wrapp'd in sweet clothes, rings put upon his fingers,
A most delicious banquet by his bed,
And brave attendants near him when he wakes,
Would not the beggar then forget himself?
FIRST HUNTSMAN. Believe me, lord, I think he cannot choose.
SECOND HUNTSMAN. It would seem strange unto him when
    he wak'd.
LORD. Even as a flattering dream or worthless fancy.
Then take him up and manage well the jest.
Carry him gently to my fairest chamber,
And hang it round with all my wanton pictures;
Balm his foul head in warm distilled waters,
And burn sweet wood to make the lodging sweet.
Procure me music ready when he wakes,
To make a dulcet and a heavenly sound;
And if he chance to speak, be ready straight,
And with a low submissive reverence
Say, 'What is it your honour will command?'
Let one attend him with a silver basin
Full of rose-water, and bestrew'd with flowers;
Another bear the ewer, the third a diaper,
And say, 'Will 't please your lordship cool your hands?'
Some one be ready with a costly suit,
And ask him what apparel he will wear;
Another tell him of his hounds and horse,
And that his lady mourns at his disease.
Persuade him that he hath been lunatic;
And, when he says he is——say that he dreams,
For he is nothing but a mighty lord.

This do, and do it kindly, gentle sirs:
It will be pastime passing excellent,
If it be husbanded with modesty.

FIRST HUNTSMAN. My lord, I warrant you we will play our
     part,
    As he shall think, by our true diligence,
    He is no less than what we say he is.

LORD. Take him up gently, and to bed with him,
    And each one to his office when he wakes.

                  Sly is borne out. A trumpet sounds
    Sirrah, go see what trumpet 'tis that sounds: *Exit Servant*
    Belike, some noble gentleman that means,
    Travelling some journey, to repose him here.

                  Re-enter Servant
    How now! who is it?

SERVANT.   An it please your honour,
    Players that offer service to your lordship.

LORD. Bid them come near.

                  Enter Players
               Now, fellows, you are welcome.

PLAYERS. We thank your honour.

LORD. Do you intend to stay with me to-night?

A PLAYER. So please your lordship to accept our duty.

LORD. With all my heart. This fellow I remember,
    Since once he play'd a farmer's eldest son:
    'Twas where you woo'd the gentlewoman so well.
    I have forgot your name; but, sure, that part
    Was aptly fitted and naturally perform'd.

A PLAYER. I think 'twas Soto that your honour means.

LORD. 'Tis very true: thou didst it excellent.
    Well, you are come to me in happy time,
    The rather for I have some sport in hand
    Wherein your cunning can assist me much.
    There is a lord will hear you play to-night;
    But I am doubtful of your modesties,
    Lest, over-eyeing of his odd behaviour,—
    For yet his honour never heard a play,—
    You break into some merry passion
    And so offend him; for I tell you, sirs,
    If you should smile he grows impatient.

A PLAYER. Fear not, my lord: we can contain ourselves
    Were he the veriest antick in the world.

LORD. Go, sirrah, take them to the buttery,
And give them friendly welcome every one:
Let them want nothing that my house affords.

Exeunt one with the Players

Sirrah, go you to Barthol'mew my page,
And see him dress'd in all suits like a lady:
That done, conduct him to the drunkard's chamber;
And call him 'madam,' do him obeisance.
Tell him from me,—as he will win my love,—
He bear himself with honourable action,
Such as he hath observ'd in noble ladies
Unto their lords, by them accomplished:
Such duty to the drunkard let him do
With soft low tongue and lowly courtesy;
And say, 'What is 't your honour will command,
Wherein your lady and your humble wife
May show her duty, and make known her love?'
And then, with kind embracements, tempting kisses,
And with declining head into his bosom,
Bid him shed tears, as being overjoy'd
To see her noble lord restor'd to health,
Who for this seven years hath esteemed him
No better than a poor and loathsome beggar.
And if the boy have not a woman's gift
To rain a shower of commanded tears,
An onion will do well for such a shift,
Which in a napkin being close convey'd,
Shall in despite enforce a watery eye.
See this dispatch'd with all the haste thou canst:
Anon I 'll give thee more instructions.   *Exit Servant*
I know the boy will well usurp the grace,
Voice, gait, and action of a gentlewoman:
I long to hear him call the drunkard husband,
And how my men will stay themselves from laughter
When they do homage to this simple peasant.
I 'll in to counsel them: haply, my presence
May well abate the over merry spleen
Which otherwise would grow into extremes.   *Exeunt*

SCENE TWO

A Bedchamber in the Lord's House.

Sly is discovered in a rich nightgown, with Attendants: some with apparel, others with basin, ewer, and other appurtenances; and Lord, dressed like a servant

SLY. For God's sake! a pot of small ale.

FIRST SERVANT. Will 't please your lordship drink a cup of sack?

SECOND SERVANT. Will 't please your honour taste of these conserves?

THIRD SERVANT. What raiment will your honour wear today?

SLY. I am Christophero Sly; call not me honour, nor lordship: I ne'er drank sack in my life; and if you give me any conserves, give me conserves of beef. Ne'er ask me what raiment I 'll wear, for I have no more doublets than backs, no more stockings than legs, nor no more shoes than feet: nay, sometime more feet than shoes, or such shoes as my toes look through the over-leather.

LORD. Heaven cease this idle humour in your honour!
O, that a mighty man, of such descent,
Of such possessions, and so high esteem,
Should be infused with so foul a spirit!

SLY. What! would you make me mad? Am not I Christopher Sly, old Sly's son, of Burton-heath; by birth a pedlar, by education a card-maker, by transmutation a bear-herd, and now by present profession a tinker? Ask Marian Hacket, the fat ale-wife of Wincot, if she know me not: if she say I am not fourteen pence on the score for sheer ale, score me up for the lyingest knave in Christendom. What! I am not bestraught: here 's—

FIRST SERVANT. O! this it is that makes your lady mourn.

SECOND SERVANT. O! this it is that makes your servants droop.

LORD. Hence comes it that your kindred shuns your house,
As beaten hence by your strange lunacy.
O noble lord, bethink thee of thy birth,
Call home thy ancient thoughts from banishment,
And banish hence these abject lowly dreams.

Look how thy servants do attend on thee,
Each in his office ready at thy beck:
Wilt thou have music? hark! Apollo plays,   *Music*
And twenty caged nightingales do sing:
Or wilt thou sleep? We 'll have thee to a couch
Softer and sweeter than the lustful bed
On purpose trimm'd up for Semiramis.
Say thou wilt walk, we will bestrew the ground:
Or wilt thou ride? Thy horses shall be trapp'd,
Their harness studded all with gold and pearl.
Dost thou love hawking? Thou hast hawks will soar
Above the morning lark: or wilt thou hunt?
Thy hounds shall make the welkin answer them,
And fetch shrill echoes from the hollow earth.

FIRST SERVANT. Say thou wilt course; thy greyhounds are as
    swift
As breathed stags, ay, fleeter than the roe.

SECOND SERVANT. Dost thou love pictures? we will fetch
    thee straight
Adonis painted by a running brook,
And Cytherea all in sedges hid,
Which seem to move and wanton with her breath,
Even as the waving sedges play with wind.

LORD. We 'll show thee Io as she was a maid,
And how she was beguiled and surpris'd,
As lively painted as the deed was done.

THIRD SERVANT. Or Daphne roaming through a thorny wood,
Scratching her legs that one shall swear she bleeds;
And at that sight shall sad Apollo weep,
So workmanly the blood and tears are drawn.

LORD. Thou art a lord and nothing but a lord:
Thou hast a lady far more beautiful
Than any woman in this waning age.

FIRST SERVANT. And till the tears that she hath shed for thee
Like envious floods o'er-run her lovely face,
She was the fairest creature in the world;
And yet she is inferior to none.

SLY. Am I a lord? and have I such a lady?
Or do I dream? or have I dream'd till now?
I do not sleep; I see, I hear, I speak;
I smell sweet savours, and I feel soft things:
Upon my life, I am a lord indeed;

And not a tinker, nor Christophero Sly.

Well, bring our lady hither to our sight;
And once again, a pot o' the smallest ale.

SECOND SERVANT. Will 't please your mightiness to wash
your hands? *Servants present a ewer, basin, and napkin*
O, how we joy to see your wit restor'd!
O, that once more you knew but what you are!
These fifteen years you have been in a dream,
Or, when you wak'd, so wak'd as if you slept.

SLY. These fifteen years! by my fay, a goodly nap.
But did I never speak of all that time?

FIRST SERVANT. O! yes, my lord, but very idle words;
For though you lay here in this goodly chamber,
Yet would you say ye were beaten out of door,
And rail upon the hostess of the house,
And say you would present her at the leet,
Because she brought stone jugs and no seal'd quarts.
Sometimes you would call out for Cicely Hacket.

SLY. Ay, the woman's maid of the house.

THIRD SERVANT. Why, sir, you know no house, nor no such
maid,
Nor no such men as you have reckon'd up,
As Stephen Sly, and old John Naps of Greece,
And Peter Turf, and Henry Pimpernell,
And twenty more such names and men as these,
Which never were nor no man ever saw.

SLY. Now, Lord be thanked for my good amends!

ALL. Amen.

SLY. I thank thee; thou shalt not lose by it.
Enter the Page, as a lady, with Attendants

PAGE. How fares my noble lord?

SLY. Marry, I fare well, for here is cheer enough.
Where is my wife?

PAGE. Here, noble lord: what is thy will with her?

SLY. Are you my wife, and will not call me husband?
My men should call me lord: I am your goodman.

PAGE. My husband and my lord, my lord and husband;
I am your wife in all obedience.

SLY. I know it well. What must I call her?

LORD. Madam.

SLY. Al'ce madam, or Joan madam?

LORD. Madam, and nothing else: so lords call ladies.

SLY. Madam wife, they say that I have dream'd
    And slept above some fifteen year or more.
PAGE. Ay, and the time seems thirty unto me,
    Being all this time abandon'd from your bed.
SLY. 'Tis much. Servants, leave me and her alone.
    Madam, undress you, and come now to bed.
PAGE. Thrice noble lord, let me entreat of you
    To pardon me yet for a night or two,
    Or, if not so, until the sun be set:
    For your physicians have expressly charg'd,
    In peril to incur your former malady,
    That I should yet absent me from your bed:
    I hope this reason stands for my excuse.
SLY. Ay, it stands so, that I may hardly tarry so long; but I
    would be loath to fall into my dreams again: I will there-
    fore tarry, in spite of the flesh and the blood.

Enter a Servant

SERVANT. Your honour's players, hearing your amendment,
    Are come to play a pleasant comedy;
    For so your doctors hold it very meet,
    Seeing too much sadness hath congeal'd your blood,
    And melancholy is the nurse of frenzy:
    Therefore they thought it good you hear a play,
    And frame your mind to mirth and merriment,
    Which bars a thousand harms and lengthens life.
SLY. Marry, I will; let them play it. Is not a commonty a
    Christmas gambold or a tumbling-trick?
PAGE. No, my good lord; it is more pleasing stuff.
SLY. What! household stuff?
PAGE. It is a kind of history.
SLY. Well, we 'll see 't. Come, madam wife, sit by my side,
    And let the world slip: we shall ne'er be younger.

Flourish

ACT ONE

SCENE ONE

Padua. A public Place.

Enter Lucentio and Tranio

LUCENTIO. Tranio, since for the great desire I had
　　To see fair Padua, nursery of arts,
　　I am arriv'd for fruitful Lombardy,
　　The pleasant garden of great Italy;
　　And by my father's love and leave am arm'd
　　With his good will and thy good company,
　　My trusty servant well approv'd in all,
　　Here let us breathe, and haply institute
　　A course of learning and ingenious studies.
　　Pisa, renowned for grave citizens,
　　Gave me my being and my father first,
　　A merchant of great traffic through the world,
　　Vincentio, come of the Bentivolii.
　　Vincentio's son, brought up in Florence,
　　It shall become to serve all hopes conceiv'd,
　　To deck his fortune with his virtuous deeds:
　　And therefore, Tranio, for the time I study,
　　Virtue and that part of philosophy
　　Will I apply that treats of happiness
　　By virtue specially to be achiev'd.
　　Tell me thy mind; for I have Pisa left
　　And am to Padua come, as he that leaves
　　A shallow plash to plunge him in the deep,
　　And with satiety seeks to quench his thirst.
TRANIO. Mi perdonate, gentle master mine,
　　I am in all affected as yourself,
　　Glad that you thus continue your resolve
　　To suck the sweets of sweet philosophy.
　　Only, good master, while we do admire

This virtue and this moral discipline,
Let 's be no stoics nor no stocks, I pray;
Or so devote to Aristotle's checks
As Ovid be an outcast quite abjur'd.
Balk logic with acquaintance that you have,
And practise rhetoric in your common talk;
Music and poesy use to quicken you;
The mathematics and the metaphysics,
Fall to them as you find your stomach serves you:
No profit grows where is no pleasure ta'en;
In brief, sir, study what you most affect.

LUCENTIO. Gramercies, Tranio, well dost thou advise.
If, Biondello, thou wert come ashore,
We could at once put us in readiness,
And take a lodging fit to entertain
Such friends as time in Padua shall beget.
But stay awhile: what company is this?

TRANIO. Master, some show to welcome us to town.

Enter Baptista, Katharina, Bianca,
Gremio, and Hortensio. Lucentio and Tranio stand aside

BAPTISTA. Gentlemen, importune me no further,
For how I firmly am resolv'd you know;
That is, not to bestow my youngest daughter
Before I have a husband for the elder.
If either of you both love Katharina,
Because I know you well and love you well,
Leave shall you have to court her at your pleasure.

GREMIO. To cart her rather: she 's too rough for me.
There, there, Hortensio, will you any wife?

KATHARINA. (*To Baptista*) I pray you, sir, is it your will
To make a stale of me amongst these mates?

HORTENSIO. Mates, maid! how mean you that? no mates for
you,
Unless you were of gentler, milder mould.

KATHARINA. I' faith, sir, you shall never need to fear:
I wis it is not half way to her heart;
But if it were, doubt not her care should be
To comb your noddle with a three-legg'd stool,
And paint your face, and use you like a fool.

HORTENSIO. From all such devils, good Lord deliver us!

GREMIO. And me too, good Lord!

TRANIO. Hush, master! here is some good pastime toward:

That wench is stark mad or wonderful froward.

LUCENTIO. But in the other's silence do I see

Maid's mild behaviour and sobriety.

Peace, Tranio!

TRANIO. Well said, master; mum! and gaze your fill.

BAPTISTA. Gentlemen, that I may soon make good

What I have said,—Bianca, get you in:

And let it not displease thee, good Bianca,

For I will love thee ne'er the less, my girl.

KATHARINA. A pretty peat! it is best

Put finger in the eye, an she knew why.

BIANCA. Sister, content you in my discontent.

Sir, to your pleasure humbly I subscribe:

My books and instruments shall be my company,

On them to look and practise by myself.

LUCENTIO. Hark, Tranio! thou mayst hear Minerva speak.

HORTENSIO. Signior Baptista, will you be so strange?

Sorry am I that our good will effects

Bianca's grief.

GREMIO.   Why will you mew her up,

Signior Baptista, for this fiend of hell,

And make her bear the penance of her tongue?

BAPTISTA. Gentlemen, content ye; I am resolv'd.

Go in, Bianca.   *Exit Bianca*

And for I know she taketh most delight

In music, instruments, and poetry,

Schoolmasters will I keep within my house,

Fit to instruct her youth. If you, Hortensio,

Or Signior Gremio, you, know any such,

Prefer them hither; for to cunning men

I will be very kind, and liberal

To mine own children in good bringing up;

And so, farewell. Katharina, you may stay;

For I have more to commune with Bianca.   *Exit*

KATHARINA. Why, and I trust I may go too; may I not?

What! shall I be appointed hours, as though, belike,

I knew not what to take, and what to leave? Ha! *Exit*

GREMIO. You may go to the devil's dam: your gifts are so

good, here's none will hold you. Their love is not so great,

Hortensio, but we may blow our nails together, and fast it

fairly out: our cake's dough on both sides. Farewell: yet,

for the love I bear my sweet Bianca, if I can by any means

light on a fit man to teach her that wherein she delights, I
will wish him to her father.

HORTENSIO. So will I, Signior Gremio: but a word, I pray.
Though the nature of our quarrel yet never brooked parle,
know now, upon advice, it toucheth us both,—that we may
yet again have access to our fair mistress and be happy
rivals in Bianca's love,—to labour and effect one thing
specially.

GREMIO. What's that, I pray?

HORTENSIO. Marry, sir, to get a husband for her sister.

GREMIO. A husband! a devil.

HORTENSIO. I say, a husband.

GREMIO. I say, a devil. Thinkest thou, Hortensio, though her
father be very rich, any man is so very a fool to be married
to hell?

HORTENSIO. Tush, Gremio! though it pass your patience and
mine to endure her loud alarums, why, man, there be good
fellows in the world, an a man could light on them, would
take her with all faults, and money enough.

GREMIO. I cannot tell; but I had as lief take her dowry with
this condition, to be whipped at the high-cross every
morning.

HORTENSIO. Faith, as you say, there's small choice in rotten
apples. But, come; since this bar in law makes us friends,
it shall be so far forth friendly maintained, till by helping
Baptista's eldest daughter to a husband, we set his youngest free for a husband, and then have to 't afresh. Sweet
Bianca! Happy man be his dole! He that runs fastest gets
the ring. How say you, Signior Gremio?

GREMIO. I am agreed: and would I had given him the best
horse in Padua to begin his wooing, that would thoroughly
woo her, wed her, and bed her, and rid the house of her.
Come on.   *Exeunt Gremio and Hortensio*

TRANIO. I pray, sir, tell me, is it possible
That love should of a sudden take such hold?

LUCENTIO. O Tranio! till I found it to be true,
I never thought it possible or likely;
But see, while idly I stood looking on,
I found the effect of love in idleness;
And now in plainness do confess to thee,
That art to me as secret and as dear
As Anna to the Queen of Carthage was,

Tranio, I burn, I pine, I perish, Tranio,
If I achieve not this young modest girl.
Counsel me, Tranio, for I know thou canst:
Assist me, Tranio, for I know thou wilt.

TRANIO. Master, it is no time to chide you now;
Affection is not rated from the heart:
If love have touch'd you, nought remains but so,
Redime te captum, quam queas minimo.

LUCENTIO. Gramercies, lad; go forward: this contents:
The rest will comfort, for thy counsel's sound.

TRANIO. Master, you look'd so longly on the maid,
Perhaps you mark'd not what's the pith of all.

LUCENTIO. O yes, I saw sweet beauty in her face,
Such as the daughter of Agenor had,
That made great Jove to humble him to her hand,
When with his knees he kiss'd the Cretan strand.

TRANIO. Saw you no more? Mark'd you not how her sister
Began to scold and raise up such a storm
That mortal ears might hardly endure the din?

LUCENTIO. Tranio, I saw her coral lips to move,
And with her breath she did perfume the air;
Sacred and sweet was all I saw in her.

TRANIO. Nay, then, 'tis time to stir him from his trance.
I pray, awake, sir: if you love the maid,
Bend thoughts and wits to achieve her. Thus it stands:
Her elder sister is so curst and shrewd,
That till the father rid his hands of her,
Master, your love must live a maid at home;
And therefore has he closely mew'd her up,
Because she will not be annoy'd with suitors.

LUCENTIO. Ah, Tranio, what a cruel father's he!
But art thou not advis'd he took some care
To get her cunning schoolmasters to instruct her?

TRANIO. Ay, marry, am I, sir; and now 'tis plotted.

LUCENTIO. I have it, Tranio.

TRANIO.   Master, for my hand,
Both our inventions meet and jump in one.

LUCENTIO. Tell me thine first.

TRANIO.   You will be schoolmaster,
And undertake the teaching of the maid:
That's your device.

LUCENTIO.   It is: may it be done?

TRANIO. Not possible; for who shall bear your part,
And be in Padua here Vincentio's son?
Keep house and ply his book, welcome his friends,
Visit his countrymen, and banquet them?

LUCENTIO. Basta; content thee; for I have it full.
We have not yet been seen in any house,
Nor can we be distinguish'd by our faces
For man, or master: then, it follows thus:
Thou shalt be master, Tranio, in my stead,
Keep house, and port, and servants, as I should:
I will some other be; some Florentine,
Some Neapolitan, or meaner man of Pisa.
'Tis hatch'd and shall be so: Tranio, at once
Uncase thee, take my colour'd hat and cloak:
When Biondello comes, he waits on thee;
But I will charm him first to keep his tongue.

                                    They exchange habits

TRANIO. So had you need.
In brief then, sir, sith it your pleasure is,
And I am tied to be obedient;
For so your father charg'd me at our parting,
'Be serviceable to my son,' quoth he,
Although I think 'twas in another sense:
I am content to be Lucentio,
Because so well I love Lucentio.

LUCENTIO. Tranio, be so, because Lucentio loves;
And let me be a slave, to achieve that maid
Whose sudden sight hath thrall'd my wounded eye.
Here comes the rogue.

                            Enter Biondello

                            Sirrah, where have you been?

BIONDELLO. Where have I been! Nay, how now! where are
you?
Master, has my fellow Tranio stol'n your clothes,
Or you stol'n his? or both? pray, what's the news?

LUCENTIO. Sirrah, come hither: 'tis no time to jest,
And therefore frame your manners to the time.
Your fellow Tranio, here, to save my life,
Puts my apparel and my countenance on,
And I for my escape have put on his;
For in a quarrel since I came ashore
I kill'd a man, and fear I was descried.

Wait you on him, I charge you, as becomes,
While I make way from hence to save my life:
You understand me?

BIONDELLO.   I, sir! Ne'er a whit.

LUCENTIO. And not a jot of Tranio in your mouth:
Tranio is changed to Lucentio.

BIONDELLO. The better for him: would I were so too!

TRANIO. So would I, faith, boy, to have the next wish after,
That Lucentio indeed had Baptista's youngest daughter.
But, sirrah, not for my sake, but your master's, I advise
You use your manners discreetly in all kind of companies:
When I am alone, why, then I am Tranio;
But in all places else your master, Lucentio.

LUCENTIO. Tranio, let 's go. One thing more rests, that thyself execute, to make one among these wooers: if thou ask
me why, sufficeth my reasons are both good and weighty.
                                                            Exeunt

The Presenters above speak

FIRST SERVANT. My lord, you nod; you do not mind the play.

SLY. Yes, by Saint Anne, I do. A good matter, surely: comes
there any more of it?

PAGE. My lord, 'tis but begun.

SLY. 'Tis a very excellent piece of work, madam lady: would
'twere done!   *They sit and mark*

SCENE TWO

The Same. Before Hortensio's House.

Enter Petruchio and Grumio

PETRUCHIO. Verona, for awhile I take my leave,
To see my friends in Padua; but, of all
My best beloved and approved friend,
Hortensio; and I trow this is his house.
Here, sirrah Grumio; knock, I say.

GRUMIO. Knock, sir! Whom should I knock? Is there any
man has rebused your worship?

PETRUCHIO. Villain, I say, knock me here soundly.

GRUMIO. Knock you here, sir! Why, sir, what am I, sir, that I
should knock you here, sir?

PETRUCHIO. Villain, I say, knock me at this gate;
And rap me well, or I 'll knock your knave's pate.

GRUMIO. My master is grown quarrelsome. I should knock
you first,
And then I know after who comes by the worst.

PETRUCHIO. Will it not be?
Faith, sirrah, and you 'll not knock, I 'll ring it;
I 'll try how you can sol, fa, and sing it.

He wrings Grumio by the ears

GRUMIO. Help, masters, help! My master is mad.

PETRUCHIO. Now, knock when I bid you, sirrah villain!

Enter Hortensio

HORTENSIO. How now! what 's the matter? My old friend
Grumio! and my good friend Petruchio! How do you all at
Verona?

PETRUCHIO. Signior Hortensio, come you to part the fray?
Con tutto il cuore ben trovato, may I say.

HORTENSIO. Alla nostra casa ben venuto; molto honorato signior mio Petruchio.
Rise, Grumio, rise: we will compound this quarrel.

GRUMIO. Nay, 'tis no matter, sir, what he 'leges in Latin. If
this be not a lawful cause for me to leave his service, look
you, sir, he bid me knock him and rap him soundly, sir:
well, was it fit for a servant to use his master so; being,
perhaps, for aught I see, two-and-thirty, a pip out?
Whom would to God, I had well knock'd at first,
Then had not Grumio come by the worst.

PETRUCHIO. A senseless villain! Good Hortensio,
I bade the rascal knock upon your gate,
And could not get him for my heart to do it.

GRUMIO. Knock at the gate! O heavens! Spake you not these
words plain, 'Sirrah, knock me here, rap me here, knock
me well, and knock me soundly'? And come you now with
'knocking at the gate'?

PETRUCHIO. Sirrah, be gone, or talk not, I advise you.

HORTENSIO. Petruchio, patience; I am Grumio's pledge.
Why, this 's a heavy chance 'twixt him and you,
Your ancient, trusty, pleasant servant Grumio.
And tell me now, sweet friend, what happy gale
Blows you to Padua here from old Verona?

PETRUCHIO. Such wind as scatters young men through the
world

To seek their fortunes further than at home,
Where small experience grows. But in a few,
Signior Hortensio, thus it stands with me:
Antonio, my father, is deceas'd,
And I have thrust myself into this maze,
Haply to wive and thrive as best I may.
Crowns in my purse I have and goods at home,
And so am come abroad to see the world.

HORTENSIO. Petruchio, shall I then come roundly to thee,
And wish thee to a shrewd ill-favour'd wife?
Thou 'dst thank me but a little for my counsel;
And yet I 'll promise thee she shall be rich,
And very rich: but thou 'rt too much my friend,
And I 'll not wish thee to her.

PETRUCHIO. Signior Hortensio, 'twixt such friends as we,
Few words suffice; and therefore, if thou know
One rich enough to be Petruchio's wife,
As wealth is burden of my wooing dance,
Be she as foul as was Florentius' love,
As old as Sibyl, and as curst and shrewd
As Socrates' Xanthippe, or a worse,
She moves me not, or not removes, at least,
Affection's edge in me, were she as rough
As are the swelling Adriatic seas:
I come to wive it wealthily in Padua;
If wealthily, then happily in Padua.

GRUMIO. Nay, look you, sir, he tells you flatly what his mind
is: why, give him gold enough and marry him to a puppet
or an aglet-baby; or an old trot with ne'er a tooth in her
head, though she have as many diseases as two-and-fifty
horses: why, nothing comes amiss, so money comes withal.

HORTENSIO. Petruchio, since we are stepp'd thus far in,
I will continue that I broach'd in jest.
I can, Petruchio, help thee to a wife
With wealth enough, and young and beauteous,
Brought up as best becomes a gentlewoman:
Her only fault,—and that is faults enough,—
Is, that she is intolerable curst
And shrewd and froward, so beyond all measure,
That, were my state far worser than it is,
I would not wed her for a mine of gold.

PETRUCHIO. Hortensio, peace! thou know'st not gold's
    effect:
    Tell me her father's name, and 'tis enough;
    For I will board her, though she chide as loud
    As thunder when the clouds in autumn crack.
HORTENSIO. Her father is Baptista Minola,
    An affable and courteous gentleman;
    Her name is Katharina Minola,
    Renown'd in Padua for her scolding tongue.
PETRUCHIO. I know her father, though I know not her;
    And he knew my deceased father well.
    I will not sleep, Hortensio, till I see her;
    And therefore let me be thus bold with you,
    To give you over at this first encounter,
    Unless you will accompany me thither.
GRUMIO. I pray you, sir, let him go while the humour lasts.
    O' my word, an she knew him as well as I do, she would
    think scolding would do little good upon him. She may,
    perhaps, call him half a score knaves or so: why, that's
    nothing: an he begin once, he 'll rail in his rope-tricks. I 'll
    tell you what, sir, an she stand him but a little, he will
    throw a figure in her face, and so disfigure her with it that
    she shall have no more eyes to see withal than a cat. You
    know him not, sir.
HORTENSIO. Tarry, Petruchio, I must go with thee,
    For in Baptista's keep my treasure is:
    He hath the jewel of my life in hold,
    His youngest daughter, beautiful Bianca,
    And her withholds from me and other more,
    Suitors to her and rivals in my love;
    Supposing it a thing impossible,
    For those defects I have before rehears'd,
    That ever Katharina will be woo'd;
    Therefore this order hath Baptista ta'en,
    That none shall have access unto Bianca,
    Till Katharine the curst have got a husband.
GRUMIO. Katharine the curst!
    A title for a maid of all titles the worst.
HORTENSIO. Now shall my friend Petruchio do me grace,
    And offer me, disguis'd in sober robes,
    To old Baptista as a schoolmaster
    Well seen in music, to instruct Bianca;

That so I may, by this device at least
Have leave and leisure to make love to her,
And unsuspected court her by herself.

GRUMIO. Here 's no knavery! See, to beguile the old folks,
how the young folks lay their heads together!

*Enter Gremio, and
Lucentio disguised, with books under his arm*

Master, master, look about you: who goes there, ha?

HORTENSIO. Peace, Grumio! 'tis the rival of my love.
Petruchio, stand by awhile.

GRUMIO. A proper stripling, and an amorous!

GREMIO. O! very well; I have perus'd the note.
Hark you, sir; I 'll have them very fairly bound:
All books of love, see that at any hand,
And see you read no other lectures to her.
You understand me. Over and beside
Signior Baptista's liberality,
I 'll mend it with a largess. Take your papers too,
And let me have them very well perfum'd;
For she is sweeter than perfume itself
To whom they go to. What will you read to her?

LUCENTIO. Whate'er I read to her, I 'll plead for you,
As for my patron, stand you so assur'd,
As firmly as yourself were still in place;
Yea, and perhaps with more successful words
Than you, unless you were a scholar, sir.

GREMIO. O! this learning, what a thing it is.

GRUMIO. O! this woodcock, what an ass it is.

PETRUCHIO. Peace, sirrah!

HORTENSIO. Grumio, mum! God save you, Signior Gremio!

GREMIO. And you 're well met, Signior Hortensio.
Trow you whither I am going? To Baptista Minola.
I promis'd to inquire carefully
About a schoolmaster for the fair Bianca;
And, by good fortune, I have lighted well
On this young man; for learning and behaviour
Fit for her turn; well read in poetry
And other books, good ones, I warrant ye.

HORTENSIO. 'Tis well: and I have met a gentleman
Hath promis'd me to help me to another,
A fine musician to instruct our mistress:
So shall I no whit be behind in duty

To fair Bianca, so belov'd of me.

GREMIO. Belov'd of me, and that my deeds shall prove.

GRUMIO. (*Aside*) And that his bags shall prove.

HORTENSIO. Gremio, 'tis now no time to vent our love:
    Listen to me, and if you speak me fair,
    I 'll tell you news indifferent good for either.
    Here is a gentleman whom by chance I met,
    Upon agreement from us to his liking,
    Will undertake to woo curst Katharine;
    Yea, and to marry her, if her dowry please.

GREMIO. So said, so done, is well.
    Hortensio, have you told him all her faults?

PETRUCHIO. I know she is an irksome, brawling scold:
    If that be all, masters, I hear no harm.

GREMIO. No, sayst me so, friend? What countryman?

PETRUCHIO. Born in Verona, old Antonio's son:
    My father dead, my fortune lives for me;
    And I do hope good days and long to see.

GREMIO. O, sir, such a life, with such a wife, were strange!
    But if you have a stomach, to 't i' God's name:
    You shall have me assisting you in all.
    But will you woo this wild-cat?

PETRUCHIO.   Will I live?

GRUMIO. Will he woo her? ay, or I 'll hang her.

PETRUCHIO. Why came I hither but to that intent?
    Think you a little din can daunt mine ears?
    Have I not in my time heard lions roar?
    Have I not heard the sea, puff'd up with winds,
    Rage like an angry boar chafed with sweat?
    Have I not heard great ordnance in the field,
    And heaven's artillery thunder in the skies?
    Have I not in a pitched battle heard
    Loud 'larums, neighing steeds, and trumpets' clang?
    And do you tell me of a woman's tongue,
    That gives not half so great a blow to hear
    As will a chestnut in a farmer's fire?
    Tush, tush! fear boys with bugs.

GRUMIO.   (*Aside*) For he fears none.

GREMIO. Hortensio, hark:
    This gentleman is happily arriv'd,
    My mind presumes, for his own good and ours.

HORTENSIO. I promis'd we would be contributors,

And bear his charge of wooing, whatsoe'er.

GREMIO. And so we will, provided that he win her.

GRUMIO. (*Aside*) I would I were as sure of a good dinner.

Enter Tranio, bravely apparelled; and Biondello

TRANIO. Gentlemen, God save you! If I may be bold,
Tell me, I beseech you, which is the readiest way
To the house of Signior Baptista Minola?

BIONDELLO. He that has the two fair daughters: is 't he you
mean?

TRANIO. Even he, Biondello!

GREMIO. Hark you, sir; you mean not her to—

TRANIO. Perhaps, him and her, sir: what have you to do?

PETRUCHIO. Not her that chides, sir, at any hand, I pray.

TRANIO. I love no chiders, sir. Biondello, let 's away.

LUCENTIO. (*Aside*) Well begun, Tranio.

HORTENSIO.   Sir, a word ere you go.
Are you a suitor to the maid you talk of, yea or no?

TRANIO. And if I be, sir, is it any offence?

GREMIO. No; if without more words you will get you hence.

TRANIO. Why, sir, I pray, are not the streets as free
For me as for you?

GREMIO.   But so is not she.

TRANIO. For what reason, I beseech you?

GREMIO. For this reason, if you 'll know,
That she 's the choice love of Signior Gremio.

HORTENSIO. That she 's the chosen of Signior Hortensio.

TRANIO. Softly, my masters! if you be gentlemen,
Do me this right; hear me with patience.
Baptista is a noble gentleman,
To whom my father is not all unknown;
And were his daughter fairer than she is,
She may more suitors have, and me for one.
Fair Leda's daughter had a thousand wooers;
Then well one more may fair Bianca have,
And so she shall; Lucentio shall make one,
Though Paris came in hope to speed alone.

GREMIO. What! this gentleman will out-talk us all.

LUCENTIO. Sir, give him head: I know he 'll prove a jade.

PETRUCHIO. Hortensio, to what end are all these words?

HORTENSIO. Sir, let me be so bold as ask you,
Did you yet ever see Baptista's daughter?

TRANIO. No, sir; but hear I do that he hath two,

The one as famous for a scolding tongue
As is the other for beauteous modesty.

PETRUCHIO. Sir, sir, the first 's for me; let her go by.

GREMIO. Yea, leave that labour to great Hercules,
And let it be more than Alcides' twelve.

PETRUCHIO. Sir, understand you this of me in sooth:
The youngest daughter, whom you hearken for,
Her father keeps from all access of suitors,
And will not promise her to any man
Until the elder sister first be wed;
The younger then is free, and not before.

TRANIO. If it be so, sir, that you are the man
Must stead us all, and me among the rest;
And if you break the ice, and do this feat,
Achieve the elder, set the younger free
For our access, whose hap shall be to have her
Will not so graceless be to be ingrate.

HORTENSIO. Sir, you say well, and well you do conceive;
And since you do profess to be a suitor,
You must, as we do, gratify this gentleman,
To whom we all rest generally beholding.

TRANIO. Sir, I shall not be slack: in sign whereof,
Please ye we may contrive this afternoon,
And quaff carouses to our mistress' health,
And do as adversaries do in law,
Strive mightily, but eat and drink as friends.

GRUMIO. ⎫
BIONDELLO. ⎬ O excellent motion! Fellows, let 's be gone.

HORTENSIO. The motion 's good indeed, and be it so:—
Petruchio, I shall be your ben venuto.   *Exeunt*

ACT TWO

SCENE ONE

Padua. A Room in Baptista's House.

Enter Katharina and Bianca

BIANCA. Good sister, wrong me not, nor wrong yourself,
  To make a bondmaid and a slave of me;
  That I disdain: but for these other gawds,
  Unbind my hands, I 'll pull them off myself,
  Yea, all my raiment, to my petticoat;
  Or what you will command me will I do,
  So well I know my duty to my elders.

KATHARINA. Of all thy suitors, here I charge thee, tell
  Whom thou lov'st best: see thou dissemble not.

BIANCA. Believe me, sister, of all the men alive
  I never yet beheld that special face
  Which I could fancy more than any other.

KATHARINA. Minion, thou liest. Is 't not Hortensio?

BIANCA. If you affect him, sister, here I swear
  I 'll plead for you myself, but you shall have him.

KATHARINA. O! then, belike, you fancy riches more:
  You will have Gremio to keep you fair.

BIANCA. Is it for him you do envy me so?
  Nay, then you jest; and now I well perceive
  You have but jested with me all this while:
  I prithee, sister Kate, untie my hands.

KATHARINA. If that be jest, then all the rest was so.

                                    Strikes her
                     Enter Baptista

BAPTISTA. Why, how now, dame! whence grows this inso-
    lence?
  Bianca, stand aside. Poor girl! she weeps.
  Go ply thy needle; meddle not with her.
  For shame, thou hilding of a devilish spirit,

Why dost thou wrong her that did ne'er wrong thee?
When did she cross thee with a bitter word?

KATHARINA. Her silence flouts me, and I 'll be reveng'd.

Flies after Bianca

BAPTISTA. What! in my sight? Bianca, get thee in.

Exit Bianca

KATHARINA. What! will you not suffer me? Nay, now I see
She is your treasure, she must have a husband;
I must dance bare-foot on her wedding-day,
And, for your love to her, lead apes in hell.
Talk not to me: I will go sit and weep
Till I can find occasion of revenge.   *Exit*

BAPTISTA. Was ever gentleman thus griev'd as I?
But who comes here?

Enter Gremio, with Lucentio in the habit
of a mean man; Petruchio, with Hortensio as a Musician; and
Tranio, with Biondello bearing a lute and books

GREMIO. Good-morrow, neighbour Baptista.

BAPTISTA. Good-morrow, neighbour Gremio. God save you,
gentlemen!

PETRUCHIO. And you, good sir. Pray, have you not a daughter
Call'd Katharina, fair and virtuous?

BAPTISTA. I have a daughter, sir, call'd Katharina.

GREMIO. You are too blunt: go to it orderly.

PETRUCHIO. You wrong me, Signior Gremio: give me leave.
I am a gentleman of Verona, sir,
That, hearing of her beauty and her wit,
Her affability and bashful modesty,
Her wondrous qualities and mild behaviour,
Am bold to show myself a forward guest
Within your house, to make mine eye the witness
Of that report which I so oft have heard.
And, for an entrance to my entertainment,
I do present you with a man of mine, *Presenting Hortensio*
Cunning in music and the mathematics,
To instruct her fully in those sciences,
Whereof I know she is not ignorant.
Accept of him, or else you do me wrong:
His name is Licio, born in Mantua.

BAPTISTA. You 're welcome, sir; and he, for your good sake.
But for my daughter Katharine, this I know,

She is not for your turn, the more my grief.

PETRUCHIO. I see you do not mean to part with her,
Or else you like not of my company.

BAPTISTA. Mistake me not; I speak but as I find.
Whence are you, sir? What may I call your name?

PETRUCHIO. Petruchio is my name; Antonio's son;
A man well known throughout all Italy.

BAPTISTA. I know him well: you are welcome for his sake.

GREMIO. Saving your tale, Petruchio, I pray,
Let us, that are poor petitioners, speak too.
Backare! you are marvellous forward.

PETRUCHIO. O, pardon me, Signior Gremio; I would fain be
doing.

GREMIO. I doubt it not, sir; but you will curse your wooing.
Neighbour, this is a gift very grateful, I am sure of it. To
express the like kindness, myself, that have been more
kindly beholding to you than any, freely give unto you this
young scholar, (*Presenting Lucentio*) that has been long
studying at Rheims; as cunning in Greek, Latin, and other
languages, as the other in music and mathematics. His
name is Cambio; pray accept his service.

BAPTISTA. A thousand thanks, Signior Gremio; welcome,
good Cambio.— (*To Tranio*) But, gentle sir, methinks
you walk like a stranger: may I be so bold to know the
cause of your coming?

TRANIO. Pardon me, sir, the boldness is mine own,
That, being a stranger in this city here,
Do make myself a suitor to your daughter,
Unto Bianca, fair and virtuous.
Nor is your firm resolve unknown to me,
In the preferment of the eldest sister.
This liberty is all that I request,
That, upon knowledge of my parentage,
I may have welcome 'mongst the rest that woo,
And free access and favour as the rest:
And, toward the education of your daughters,
I here bestow a simple instrument,
And this small packet of Greek and Latin books:
If you accept them, then their worth is great.

BAPTISTA. Lucentio is your name, of whence, I pray?

TRANIO. Of Pisa, sir; son to Vincentio.

BAPTISTA. A mighty man of Pisa; by report

I know him well: you are very welcome, sir.

(*To Hortensio*) Take you the lute, (*To Lucentio*) and
you the set of books;

You shall go see your pupils presently.

Holla, within!

Enter a Servant

Sirrah, lead these gentlemen

To my two daughters, and then tell them both

These are their tutors: bid them use them well.

Exit Servant, with Hortensio, Lucentio, and Biondello

We will go walk a little in the orchard,

And then to dinner. You are passing welcome,

And so I pray you all to think yourselves.

PETRUCHIO. Signior Baptista, my business asketh haste,

And every day I cannot come to woo.

You knew my father well, and in him me,

Left solely heir to all his lands and goods,

Which I have better'd rather than decreas'd:

Then tell me, if I get your daughter's love,

What dowry shall I have with her to wife?

BAPTISTA. After my death the one half of my lands,

And in possession twenty thousand crowns.

PETRUCHIO. And, for that dowry, I 'll assure her of

Her widowhood, be it that she survive me,

In all my lands and leases whatsoever.

Let specialties be therefore drawn between us,

That covenants may be kept on either hand.

BAPTISTA. Ay, when the special thing is well obtain'd,

That is, her love; for that is all in all.

PETRUCHIO. Why, that is nothing; for I tell you, father,

I am as peremptory as she proud-minded;

And where two raging fires meet together

They do consume the thing that feeds their fury:

Though little fire grows great with little wind,

Yet extreme gusts will blow out fire and all;

So I to her, and so she yields to me;

For I am rough and woo not like a babe.

BAPTISTA. Well mayst thou woo, and happy be thy speed!

But be thou arm'd for some unhappy words.

PETRUCHIO. Ay, to the proof; as mountains are for winds,

That shake not, though they blow perpetually.

Re-enter Hortensio, with his head broke

BAPTISTA. How now, my friend! Why dost thou look so pale?

HORTENSIO. For fear, I promise you, if I look pale.

BAPTISTA. What, will my daughter prove a good musician?

HORTENSIO. I think she 'll sooner prove a soldier:
Iron may hold with her, but never lutes.

BAPTISTA. Why, then thou canst not break her to the lute?

HORTENSIO. Why, no; for she hath broke the lute to me.
I did but tell her she mistook her frets,
And bow'd her hand to teach her fingering;
When, with a most impatient devilish spirit,
'Frets, call you these?' quoth she; 'I 'll fume with them';
And, with that word, she struck me on the head,
And through the instrument my pate made way;
And there I stood amazed for a while,
As on a pillory, looking through the lute;
While she did call me rascal fiddler,
And twangling Jack; with twenty such vile terms
As she had studied to misuse me so.

PETRUCHIO. Now, by the world, it is a lusty wench!
I love her ten times more than e'er I did:
O! how I long to have some chat with her!

BAPTISTA. (To Hortensio) Well, go with me, and be not so discomfited:
Proceed in practice with my younger daughter;
She 's apt to learn, and thankful for good turns.
Signior Petruchio, will you go with us,
Or shall I send my daughter Kate to you?

PETRUCHIO. I pray you do; I will attend her here,
         Exeunt Baptista, Gremio, Tranio, and Hortensio
And woo her with some spirit when she comes.
Say that she rail; why then I 'll tell her plain
She sings as sweetly as a nightingale:
Say that she frown; I 'll say she looks as clear
As morning roses newly wash'd with dew:
Say she be mute and will not speak a word;
Then I 'll commend her volubility,
And say she uttereth piercing eloquence:
If she do bid me pack, I 'll give her thanks,
As though she bid me stay by her a week:
If she deny to wed, I 'll crave the day
When I shall ask the banns, and when be married.
But here she comes; and now, Petruchio, speak.

Enter Katharina

Good-morrow, Kate; for that 's your name, I hear.

KATHARINA. Well have you heard, but something hard of
hearing:

They call me Katharine that do talk of me.

PETRUCHIO. You lie, in faith; for you are call'd plain Kate,
And bonny Kate, and sometimes Kate the curst;
But, Kate, the prettiest Kate in Christendom;
Kate of Kate-Hall, my super-dainty Kate,
For dainties are all cates: and therefore, Kate,
Take this of me, Kate of my consolation;
Hearing thy mildness prais'd in every town,
Thy virtues spoke of, and thy beauty sounded,—
Yet not so deeply as to thee belongs,—
Myself am mov'd to woo thee for my wife.

KATHARINA. Mov'd! in good time: let him that mov'd you
hither

Remove you hence. I knew you at the first,
You were a moveable.

PETRUCHIO.   Why, what 's a moveable?

KATHARINA. A joint-stool.

PETRUCHIO.   Thou hast hit it: come, sit on me.

KATHARINA. Asses are made to bear, and so are you.

PETRUCHIO. Women are made to bear, and so are you.

KATHARINA. No such jade as bear you, if me you mean.

PETRUCHIO. Alas! good Kate, I will not burden thee;
For, knowing thee to be but young and light,—

KATHARINA. Too light for such a swain as you to catch,
And yet as heavy as my weight should be.

PETRUCHIO. Should be! should buzz!

KATHARINA.   Well ta'en, and like a buzzard.

PETRUCHIO. O slow-wing'd turtle! shall a buzzard take thee?

KATHARINA. Ay, for a turtle, as he takes a buzzard.

PETRUCHIO. Come, come, you wasp; i' faith you are too
angry.

KATHARINA. If I be waspish, best beware my sting.

PETRUCHIO. My remedy is, then, to pluck it out.

KATHARINA. Ay, if the fool could find it where it lies.

PETRUCHIO. Who knows not where a wasp does wear his
sting?
In his tail.

KATHARINA. In his tongue.

PETRUCHIO.   Whose tongue?

KATHARINA. Yours, if you talk of tails; and so farewell.

PETRUCHIO. What! with my tongue in your tail? nay, come
again.
Good Kate, I am a gentleman.

KATHARINA.   That I'll try. *Striking him*

PETRUCHIO. I swear I'll cuff you if you strike again.

KATHARINA. So may you lose your arms:
If you strike me, you are no gentleman;
And if no gentleman, why then no arms.

PETRUCHIO. A herald, Kate? O! put me in thy books.

KATHARINA. What is your crest? a coxcomb?

PETRUCHIO. A combless cock, so Kate will be my hen.

KATHARINA. No cock of mine; you crow too like a craven.

PETRUCHIO. Nay, come, Kate, come; you must not look so
sour.

KATHARINA. It is my fashion when I see a crab.

PETRUCHIO. Why, here's no crab, and therefore look not
sour.

KATHARINA. There is, there is.

PETRUCHIO. Then show it me.

KATHARINA.   Had I a glass, I would.

PETRUCHIO. What, you mean my face?

KATHARINA.   Well aim'd of such a young one.

PETRUCHIO. Now, by Saint George, I am too young for you.

KATHARINA. Yet you are wither'd.

PETRUCHIO.   'Tis with cares.

KATHARINA.   I care not.

PETRUCHIO. Nay, hear you, Kate: in sooth, you 'scape not so.

KATHARINA. I chafe you, if I tarry: let me go.

PETRUCHIO. No, not a whit: I find you passing gentle.
'Twas told me you were rough and coy and sullen,
And now I find report a very liar;
For thou art pleasant, gamesome, passing courteous,
But slow in speech, yet sweet as spring-time flowers:
Thou canst not frown, thou canst not look askance,
Nor bite the lip, as angry wenches will;
Nor hast thou pleasure to be cross in talk;
But thou with mildness entertain'st thy wooers,
With gentle conference, soft and affable.
Why does the world report that Kate doth limp?
O slanderous world! Kate, like the hazel-twig,

Is straight and slender, and as brown in hue
As hazel-nuts, and sweeter than the kernels.
O! let me see thee walk: thou dost not halt.

KATHARINA. Go, fool, and whom thou keep'st command.

PETRUCHIO. Did ever Dian so become a grove
As Kate this chamber with her princely gait?
O! be thou Dian, and let her be Kate,
And then let Kate be chaste, and Dian sportful!

KATHARINA. Where did you study all this goodly speech?

PETRUCHIO. It is extempore, from my mother-wit.

KATHARINA. A witty mother! witless else her son.

PETRUCHIO. Am I not wise?

KATHARINA.   Yes; keep you warm.

PETRUCHIO. Marry, so I mean, sweet Katharine, in thy bed:
And therefore, setting all this chat aside,
Thus in plain terms: your father hath consented
That you shall be my wife; your dowry 'greed on;
And will you, nill you, I will marry you.
Now, Kate, I am a husband for your turn;
For, by this light, whereby I see thy beauty,—
Thy beauty that doth make me like thee well,—
Thou must be married to no man but me:
For I am he am born to tame you, Kate;
And bring you from a wild Kate to a Kate
Conformable as other household Kates.
Here comes your father: never make denial;
I must and will have Katharine to my wife.

            Re-enter Baptista, Gremio, and Tranio

BAPTISTA. Now, Signior Petruchio, how speed you with my
    daughter?

PETRUCHIO. How but well, sir? how but well?
It were impossible I should speed amiss.

BAPTISTA. Why, how now, daughter Katharine! in your
    dumps?

KATHARINA. Call you me daughter? Now, I promise you
You have show'd a tender fatherly regard,
To wish me wed to one half lunatic;
A mad-cap ruffian and a swearing Jack,
That thinks with oaths to face the matter out.

PETRUCHIO. Father, 'tis thus: yourself and all the world,
That talk'd of her, have talk'd amiss of her:
If she be curst, it is for policy,

For she 's not froward, but modest as the dove;
She is not hot, but temperate as the morn;
For patience she will prove a second Grissel,
And Roman Lucrece for her chastity;
And to conclude, we have 'greed so well together,
That upon Sunday is the wedding-day.

KATHARINA. I 'll see thee hang'd on Sunday first.

GREMIO. Hark, Petruchio: she says she 'll see thee hang'd
first.

TRANIO. Is this your speeding? Nay then, good-night our
part!

PETRUCHIO. Be patient, gentlemen; I choose her for myself:
If she and I be pleas'd, what 's that to you?
'Tis bargain'd 'twixt us twain, being alone,
That she shall still be curst in company.
I tell you, 'tis incredible to believe
How much she loves me: O! the kindest Kate!
She hung about my neck, and kiss on kiss
She vied so fast, protesting oath on oath,
That in a twink she won me to her love.
O! you are novices: 'tis a world to see,
How tame, when men and women are alone,
A meacock wretch can make the curstest shrew.
Give me thy hand, Kate: I will unto Venice
To buy apparel 'gainst the wedding-day.
Provide the feast, father, and bid the guests;
I will be sure my Katharine shall be fine.

BAPTISTA. I know not what to say; but give me your hands.
God send you joy, Petruchio! 'tis a match.

GREMIO. }
TRANIO. } Amen, say we: we will be witnesses.

PETRUCHIO. Father, and wife, and gentlemen, adieu.
I will to Venice; Sunday comes apace:
We will have rings, and things, and fine array;
And, kiss me, Kate, we will be married o' Sunday.
                    Exeunt Petruchio and Katharina, severally

GREMIO. Was ever match clapp'd up so suddenly?

BAPTISTA. Faith, gentlemen, now I play a merchant's part,
And venture madly on a desperate mart.

TRANIO. 'Twas a commodity lay fretting by you:
'Twill bring you gain, or perish on the seas.

BAPTISTA. The gain I seek is, quiet in the match.

GREMIO. No doubt but he hath got a quiet catch.
    But now, Baptista, to your younger daughter:
    Now is the day we long have looked for:
    I am your neighbour, and was suitor first.
TRANIO. And I am one that love Bianca more
    Than words can witness, or your thoughts can guess.
GREMIO. Youngling, thou canst not love so dear as I.
TRANIO. Greybeard, thy love doth freeze.
GREMIO.   But thine doth fry.
    Skipper, stand back: 'tis age that nourisheth.
TRANIO. But youth in ladies' eyes that flourisheth.
BAPTISTA. Content you, gentlemen; I 'll compound this
        strife:
    'Tis deeds must win the prize; and he, of both
    That can assure my daughter greatest dower
    Shall have my Bianca's love.
    Say, Signior Gremio, what can you assure her?
GREMIO. First, as you know, my house within the city
    Is richly furnished with plate and gold:
    Basins and ewers to lave her dainty hands;
    My hangings all of Tyrian tapestry;
    In ivory coffers I have stuff'd my crowns;
    In cypress chests my arras counterpoints,
    Costly apparel, tents, and canopies,
    Fine linen, Turkey cushions boss'd with pearl,
    Valance of Venice gold in needle-work,
    Pewter and brass, and all things that belong
    To house or housekeeping: then, at my farm
    I have a hundred milch-kine to the pail,
    Six score fat oxen standing in my stalls,
    And all things answerable to this portion.
    Myself am struck in years, I must confess;
    And if I die to-morrow, this is hers,
    If whilst I live she will be only mine.
TRANIO. That 'only' came well in. Sir, list to me:
    I am my father's heir and only son:
    If I may have your daughter to my wife,
    I 'll leave her houses three or four as good,
    Within rich Pisa walls, as any one
    Old Signior Gremio has in Padua;
    Besides two thousand ducats by the year
    Of fruitful land, all of which shall be her jointure.

What, have I pinch'd you, Signior Gremio?

GREMIO. Two thousand ducats by the year of land!
My land amounts not to so much in all:
That she shall have; besides an argosy
That now is lying in Marseilles' road.
What, have I chok'd you with an argosy?

TRANIO. Gremio, 'tis known my father hath no less
Than three great argosies, besides two galliasses,
And twelve tight galleys; these I will assure her,
And twice as much, whate'er thou offer'st next.

GREMIO. Nay, I have offer'd all, I have no more;
And she can have no more than all I have:
If you like me, she shall have me and mine.

TRANIO. Why, then the maid is mine from all the world,
By your firm promise. Gremio is out-vied.

BAPTISTA. I must confess your offer is the best;
And, let your father make her the assurance,
She is your own; else, you must pardon me:
If you should die before him, where 's her dower?

TRANIO. That 's but a cavil: he is old, I young.

GREMIO. And may not young men die as well as old?

BAPTISTA. Well, gentlemen,
I am thus resolv'd. On Sunday next, you know,
My daughter Katharine is to be married:
Now, on the Sunday following, shall Bianca
Be bride to you, if you make this assurance;
If not, to Signior Gremio:
And so, I take my leave, and thank you both.

GREMIO. Adieu, good neighbour. (*Exit Baptista*) Now I
    fear thee not:
Sirrah young gamester, your father were a fool
To give thee all, and in his waning age
Set foot under thy table. Tut! a toy!
An old Italian fox is not so kind, my boy.   *Exit*

TRANIO. A vengeance on your crafty wither'd hide!
Yet I have fac'd it with a card of ten.
'Tis in my head to do my master good:
I see no reason, but suppos'd Lucentio
Must get a father, called 'suppos'd Vincentio';
And that 's a wonder: fathers, commonly,
Do get their children; but in this case of wooing,
A child shall get a sire, if I fail not of my cunning.   *Exit*

ACT THREE

SCENE ONE

Padua. A Room in Baptista's House.

Enter Lucentio, Hortensio, and Bianca

LUCENTIO. Fiddler, forbear; you grow too forward, sir:
Have you so soon forgot the entertainment
Her sister Katharine welcom'd you withal?

HORTENSIO. But, wrangling pedant, this is
The patroness of heavenly harmony:
Then give me leave to have prerogative;
And when in music we have spent an hour,
Your lecture shall have leisure for as much.

LUCENTIO. Preposterous ass, that never read so far
To know the cause why music was ordain'd!
Was it not to refresh the mind of man
After his studies or his usual pain?
Then give me leave to read philosophy,
And while I pause, serve in your harmony.

HORTENSIO. Sirrah, I will not bear these braves of thine.

BIANCA. Why, gentlemen, you do me double wrong,
To strive for that which resteth in my choice.
I am no breeching scholar in the schools;
I 'll not be tied to hours nor 'pointed times,
But learn my lessons as I please myself.
And, to cut off all strife, here sit we down:
Take you your instrument, play you the whiles;
His lecture will be done ere you have tun'd.

HORTENSIO. You 'll leave his lecture when I am in tune?

Retires

LUCENTIO. That will be never: tune your instrument.

BIANCA. Where left we last?

LUCENTIO. Here, madam:—

     Hic ibat Simois; hic est Sigeia tellus;
     Hic steterat Priami regia celsa senis.

BIANCA. Construe them.

LUCENTIO. 'Hic ibat,' as I told you before, 'Simois,' I am
     Lucentio, 'hic est,' son unto Vincentio of Pisa, 'Sigeia
     tellus,' disguised thus to get your love; 'Hic steterat,' and
     that Lucentio that comes a-wooing, 'Priami,' is my man
     Tranio, 'regia,' bearing my port, 'celsa senis,' that we
     might beguile the old pantaloon.

HORTENSIO. (*Returning*) Madam, my instrument 's in tune.

BIANCA. Let's hear.—   *Hortensio plays*
     O fie! the treble jars.

LUCENTIO. Spit in the hole, man, and tune again.

BIANCA. Now let me see if I can construe it: 'Hic ibat Si-
     mois,' I know you not, 'hic est Sigeia tellus,' I trust you
     not; 'Hic steterat Priami,' take heed he hear us not, 'regia,'
     presume not; 'celsa senis,' despair not.

HORTENSIO. Madam, 'tis now in tune.

LUCENTIO.   All but the base.

HORTENSIO. The base is right; 'tis the base knave that jars.
     How fiery and forward our pedant is!
     (*Aside*) Now, for my life, the knave doth court my love:
     Pedascule, I 'll watch you better yet.

BIANCA. In time I may believe, yet I mistrust.

LUCENTIO. Mistrust it not; for, sure, Æacides
     Was Ajax, call'd so from his grandfather.

BIANCA. I must believe my master; else, I promise you,
     I should be arguing still upon that doubt:
     But let it rest. Now, Licio, to you.
     Good masters, take it not unkindly, pray,
     That I have been thus pleasant with you both.

HORTENSIO. (*To Lucentio*) You may go walk, and give me
     leave a while:
     My lessons make no music in three parts.

LUCENTIO. Are you so formal, sir? (*Aside*) Well, I must
     wait,
     And watch withal; for, but I be deceiv'd,
     Our fine musician groweth amorous.

HORTENSIO. Madam, before you touch the instrument,
     To learn the order of my fingering,
     I must begin with rudiments of art;
     To teach you gamut in a briefer sort,

More pleasant, pithy, and effectual,
Than hath been taught by any of my trade:
And there it is in writing, fairly drawn.

BIANCA. Why, I am past my gamut long ago.

HORTENSIO. Yet read the gamut of Hortensio.

BIANCA.

    ' "Gamut" I am, the ground of all accord,
       "A re," to plead Hortensio's passion;
    "B mi," Bianca, take him for thy lord,
       "C fa ut," that loves with all affection:
    "D sol re," one clef, two notes have I;
       "E la mi," show pity, or I die.'
Call you this gamut? Tut, I like it not:
Old fashions please me best; I am not so nice,
To change true rules for odd inventions.

Enter a Servant

SERVANT. Mistress, your father prays you leave your books,
And help to dress your sister's chamber up:
You know to-morrow is the wedding-day.

BIANCA. Farewell, sweet masters both: I must be gone.

Exeunt Bianca and Servant

LUCENTIO. Faith, mistress, then I have no cause to stay. *Exit*

HORTENSIO. But I have cause to pry into this pedant:
Methinks he looks as though he were in love.
Yet if thy thoughts, Bianca, be so humble
To cast thy wandering eyes on every stale,
Seize thee that list: if once I find thee ranging,
Hortensio will be quit with thee by changing.   *Exit*

SCENE TWO

The Same. Before Baptista's House.

*Enter Baptista, Gremio, Tranio, Katharina, Bianca,
Lucentio, and Attendants*

BAPTISTA. (*To Tranio*) Signior Lucentio, this is the 'pointed
    day
That Katharine and Petruchio should be married,
And yet we hear not of our son-in-law.
What will be said? What mockery will it be
To want the bridegroom when the priest attends

To speak the ceremonial rites of marriage!
What says Lucentio to this shame of ours?

KATHARINA. No shame but mine: I must, forsooth, be forc'd
To give my hand oppos'd against my heart
Unto a mad-brain rudesby, full of spleen;
Who woo'd in haste and means to wed at leisure.
I told you, I, he was a frantic fool,
Hiding his bitter jests in blunt behaviour;
And to be noted for a merry man,
He 'll woo a thousand, 'point the day of marriage,
Make friends invite, and proclaim the banns;
Yet never means to wed where he hath woo'd.
Now must the world point at poor Katharine,
And say, 'Lo! there is mad Petruchio's wife,
If it would please him come and marry her.'

TRANIO. Patience, good Katharine, and Baptista too.
Upon my life, Petruchio means but well,
Whatever fortune stays him from his word:
Though he be blunt, I know him passing wise;
Though he be merry, yet withal he 's honest.

KATHARINA. Would Katharine had never seen him though!
            Exit weeping, followed by Bianca and others

BAPTISTA. Go, girl: I cannot blame thee now to weep,
For such an injury would vex a very saint,
Much more a shrew of thy impatient humour.
                    Enter Biondello

BIONDELLO. Master, master! news! old news, and such news
as you never heard of!

BAPTISTA. Is it new and old too? How may that be?

BIONDELLO. Why, is it not news to hear of Petruchio's coming?

BAPTISTA. Is he come?

BIONDELLO. Why, no, sir.

BAPTISTA. What then?

BIONDELLO. He is coming.

BAPTISTA. When will he be here?

BIONDELLO. When he stands where I am and sees you there.

TRANIO. But, say, what to thine old news?

BIONDELLO. Why, Petruchio is coming, in a new hat and an
old jerkin; a pair of old breeches thrice turned; a pair of
boots that have been candle-cases, one buckled, another
laced; an old rusty sword ta'en out of the town-armoury,

with a broken hilt, and chapeless; with two broken points:
his horse hipped with an old mothy saddle and stirrups of
no kindred; besides, possessed with the glanders and like
to mose in the chine; troubled with the lampass, infected
with the fashions, full of windgalls, sped with spavins,
rayed with the yellows, past cure of the fives, stark spoiled
with the staggers, begnawn with the bots, swayed in the
back, and shoulder-shotten; near-legged before, and with
a half-checked bit, and a head-stall of sheep's leather,
which, being restrained to keep him from stumbling, hath
been often burst and now repaired with knots; one girth
six times pieced, and a woman's crupper of velure, which
hath two letters for her name fairly set down in studs, and
here and there pieced with packthread.

BAPTISTA. Who comes with him?

BIONDELLO. O, sir! his lackey, for all the world caparisoned
like the horse; with a linen stock on one leg and a kersey
boot-hose on the other, gartered with a red and blue list;
an old hat, and the 'humour of forty fancies' pricked in 't
for a feather: a monster, a very monster in apparel, and
not like a Christian footboy or a gentleman's lackey.

TRANIO. 'Tis some odd humour pricks him to this fashion;
Yet oftentimes he goes but mean-apparell'd.

BAPTISTA. I am glad he is come, howsoe'er he comes.

BIONDELLO. Why, sir, he comes not.

BAPTISTA. Didst thou not say he comes?

BIONDELLO. Who? that Petruchio came?

BAPTISTA. Ay, that Petruchio came..

BIONDELLO. No, sir; I say his horse comes, with him on his
back.

BAPTISTA. Why, that 's all one.

BIONDELLO.   Nay, by Saint Jamy,
          I hold you a penny,
          A horse and a man
          Is more than one,
          And yet not many.

Enter Petruchio and Grumio

PETRUCHIO. Come, where be these gallants? Who is at
home?

BAPTISTA. You are welcome, sir.

PETRUCHIO.   And yet I come not well.

BAPTISTA. And yet you halt not.

TRANIO.   Not so well apparell'd
    As I wish you were. Were it better, I should rush in thus.

PETRUCHIO. Were it better, I should rush in thus.
    But where is Kate? where is my lovely bride?
    How does my father? Gentles, methinks you frown:
    And wherefore gaze this goodly company,
    As if they saw some wondrous monument,
    Some comet, or unusual prodigy?

BAPTISTA. Why, sir, you know this is your wedding-day:
    First were we sad, fearing you would not come;
    Now sadder, that you come so unprovided.
    Fie! doff this habit, shame to your estate,
    An eye-sore to our solemn festival.

TRANIO. And tell us what occasion of import
    Hath all so long detain'd you from your wife,
    And sent you hither so unlike yourself?

PETRUCHIO. Tedious it were to tell, and harsh to hear:
    Sufficeth, I am come to keep my word,
    Though in some part enforced to digress;
    Which, at more leisure, I will so excuse
    As you shall well be satisfied withal.
    But where is Kate? I stay too long from her:
    The morning wears, 'tis time we were at church.

TRANIO. See not your bride in these unreverent robes:
    Go to my chamber; put on clothes of mine.

PETRUCHIO. Not I, believe me: thus I 'll visit her.

BAPTISTA. But thus, I trust, you will not marry her.

PETRUCHIO. Good sooth, even thus; therefore ha' done with
    words:
    To me she 's married, not unto my clothes.
    Could I repair what she will wear in me
    As I can change these poor accoutrements,
    'Twere well for Kate and better for myself.
    But what a fool am I to chat with you
    When I should bid good-morrow to my bride,
    And seal the title with a lovely kiss!
               Exeunt Petruchio, Grumio, and Biondello

TRANIO. He hath some meaning in his mad attire.
    We will persuade him, be it possible,
    To put on better ere he go to church.

BAPTISTA. I 'll after him, and see the event of this.
               Exeunt Baptista, Gremio, and Attendants

TRANIO. But to her love concerneth us to add
    Her father's liking: which to bring to pass,
    As I before imparted to your worship,
    I am to get a man,—whate'er he be
    It skills not much, we 'll fit him to our turn,—
    And he shall be Vincentio of Pisa,
    And make assurance here in Padua,
    Of greater sums than I have promised.
    So shall you quietly enjoy your hope,
    And marry sweet Bianca with consent.
LUCENTIO. Were it not that my fellow schoolmaster
    Doth watch Bianca's steps so narrowly,
    'Twere good, methinks, to steal our marriage;
    Which once perform'd, let all the world say no,
    I 'll keep mine own, despite of all the world.
TRANIO. That by degrees we mean to look into,
    And watch our vantage in this business.
    We 'll over-reach the greybeard, Gremio,
    The narrow-prying father, Minola,
    The quaint musician, amorous Licio;
    All for my master's sake, Lucentio.

Re-enter Gremio

    Signior Gremio, came you from the church?
GREMIO. As willingly as e'er I came from school.
TRANIO. And is the bride and bridegroom coming home?
GREMIO. A bridegroom say you? 'Tis a groom indeed,
    A grumbling groom, and that the girl shall find.
TRANIO. Curster than she? Why, 'tis impossible.
GREMIO. Why, he 's a devil, a devil, a very fiend.
TRANIO. Why, she 's a devil, a devil, the devil's dam.
GREMIO. Tut! she 's a lamb, a dove, a fool to him.
    I 'll tell you, Sir Lucentio: when the priest
    Should ask, if Katharine should be his wife,
    'Ay, by gogs-wouns!' quoth he; and swore so loud,
    That, all amaz'd, the priest let fall the book;
    And, as he stoop'd again to take it up,
    The mad-brain'd bridegroom took him such a cuff
    That down fell priest and book and book and priest:
    'Now take them up,' quoth he, 'if any list.'
TRANIO. What said the wench when he arose again?
GREMIO. Trembled and shook; for why, he stampt and
    swore,

As if the vicar meant to cozen him.
But after many ceremonies done,
He calls for wine: 'A health!' quoth he; as if
He had been aboard, carousing to his mates
After a storm; quaff'd off the muscadel,
And threw the sops all in the sexton's face;
Having no other reason
But that his beard grew thin and hungerly,
And seem'd to ask him sops as he was drinking.
This done, he took the bride about the neck,
And kiss'd her lips with such a clamorous smack
That at the parting all the church did echo:
And I, seeing this, came thence for very shame;
And after me, I know, the rout is coming.
Such a mad marriage never was before.
Hark, hark! I hear the minstrels play.   *Music*

Re-enter Petruchio, Katharina,
Bianca, Baptista, Hortensio, Grumio, and Train

PETRUCHIO. Gentlemen and friends, I thank you for your
    pains:
  I know you think to dine with me to-day,
  And have prepar'd great store of wedding cheer;
  But so it is, my haste doth call me hence,
  And therefore here I mean to take my leave.

BAPTISTA. Is 't possible you will away to-night?

PETRUCHIO. I must away to-day, before night come.
  Make it no wonder: if you knew my business,
  You would entreat me rather go than stay.
  And, honest company, I thank you all,
  That have beheld me give away myself
  To this most patient, sweet, and virtuous wife.
  Dine with my father, drink a health to me,
  For I must hence; and farewell to you all.

TRANIO. Let us entreat you stay till after dinner.

PETRUCHIO. It may not be.

GREMIO.   Let me entreat you.

PETRUCHIO. It cannot be.

KATHARINA.   Let me entreat you.

PETRUCHIO. I am content.

KATHARINA.   Are you content to stay?

PETRUCHIO. I am content you shall entreat me stay,
  But yet not stay, entreat me how you can.

KATHARINA. Now, if you love me, stay.

PETRUCHIO.   Grumio, my horse!

GRUMIO. Ay, sir, they be ready: the oats have eaten the
    horses.

KATHARINA. Nay, then,
    Do what thou canst, I will not go to-day;
    No, nor to-morrow, nor till I please myself.
    The door is open, sir, there lies your way;
    You may be jogging whiles your boots are green;
    For me, I 'll not be gone till I please myself.
    'Tis like you 'll prove a jolly surly groom,
    That take it on you at the first so roundly.

PETRUCHIO. O Kate! content thee: prithee, be not angry.

KATHARINA. I will be angry: what hast thou to do?
    Father, be quiet; he shall stay my leisure.

GREMIO. Ay, marry, sir, now it begins to work.

KATHARINA. Gentlemen, forward to the bridal dinner:
    I see a woman may be made a fool,
    If she had not a spirit to resist.

PETRUCHIO. They shall go forward, Kate, at thy command.
    Obey the bride, you that attend on her;
    Go to the feast, revel and domineer,
    Carouse full measure to her maidenhead,
    Be mad and merry, or go hang yourselves:
    But for my bonny Kate, she must with me.
    Nay, look not big, nor stamp, nor stare, nor fret;
    I will be master of what is mine own.
    She is my goods, my chattels; she is my house,
    My household stuff, my field, my barn,
    My horse, my ox, my ass, my any thing;
    And here she stands, touch her whoever dare;
    I 'll bring mine action on the proudest he
    That stops my way in Padua. Grumio,
    Draw forth thy weapon, we 're beset with thieves;
    Rescue thy mistress, if thou be a man.
    Fear not, sweet wench; they shall not touch thee, Kate:
    I 'll buckler thee against a million.

              Exeunt Petruchio, Katharina, and Grumio

BAPTISTA. Nay, let them go, a couple of quiet ones.

GREMIO. Went they not quickly I should die with laughing.

TRANIO. Of all mad matches never was the like.

LUCENTIO. Mistress, what 's your opinion of your sister?

BIANCA. That, being mad herself, she 's madly mated.

GREMIO. I warrant him, Petruchio is Kated.

BAPTISTA. Neighbours and friends, though bride and bride-
   groom wants
   For to supply the places at the table,
   You know there wants no junkets at the feast.
   Lucentio, you shall supply the bridegroom's place,
   And let Bianca take her sister's room.

TRANIO. Shall sweet Bianca practise how to bride it?

BAPTISTA. She shall, Lucentio. Come, gentlemen, let 's go.

                                        Exeunt

ACT FOUR

SCENE ONE

A Hall in Petruchio's Country House.

Enter Grumio

GRUMIO. Fie, fie, on all tired jades, on all mad masters
all foul ways! Was ever man so beaten? Was ever m
rayed? Was ever man so weary? I am sent before to
a fire, and they are coming after to warm them. Now,
not I a little pot and soon hot, my very lips might free
my teeth, my tongue to the roof of my mouth, my he
my belly, ere I should come by a fire to thaw me; I
with blowing the fire, shall warm myself; for, consid
the weather, a taller man than I will take cold. Holl
Curtis.

Enter Curtis

CURTIS. Who is that calls so coldly?

GRUMIO. A piece of ice: if thou doubt it, thou mayst
from my shoulder to my heel with no greater a run b
head and my neck. A fire, good Curtis.

CURTIS. Is my master and his wife coming, Grumio?

GRUMIO. O, ay! Curtis, ay; and therefore fire, fire; cast
water.

CURTIS. Is she so hot a shrew as she 's reported?

GRUMIO. She was, good Curtis, before this frost; but,
knowest, winter tames man, woman, and beast; for it
tamed my old master, and my new mistress, and m
fellow Curtis.

CURTIS. Away, you three-inch fool! I am no beast.

GRUMIO. Am I but three inches? Why, thy horn is a foot
so long am I at the least. But wilt thou make a fire, or
I complain on thee to our mistress, whose hand,—sh
ing now at hand,—thou shalt soon feel, to thy cold
fort, for being slow in thy hot office?

CURTIS. I prithee, good Grumio, tell me, how goes the world?

GRUMIO. A cold world, Curtis, in every office but thine; and therefore, fire. Do thy duty, and have thy duty, for my master and mistress are almost frozen to death.

CURTIS. There 's fire ready; and therefore, good Grumio, the news?

GRUMIO. Why, 'Jack, boy! ho, boy!' and as much news as thou wilt.

CURTIS. Come, you are so full of cony-catching.

GRUMIO. Why, therefore fire: for I have caught extreme cold. Where 's the cook? Is supper ready, the house trimmed, rushes strewed, cobwebs swept; the serving-men in their new fustian, their white stockings, and every officer his wedding-garment on? Be the Jacks fair within, the Jills fair without, and carpets laid, and everything in order?

CURTIS. All ready; and therefore, I pray thee, news?

GRUMIO. First, know, my horse is tired; my master and mistress fallen out.

CURTIS. How?

GRUMIO. Out of their saddles into the dirt; and thereby hangs a tale.

CURTIS. Let 's ha 't, good Grumio.

GRUMIO. Lend thine ear.

CURTIS. Here.

GRUMIO. (Striking him) There.

CURTIS. This is to feel a tale, not to hear a tale.

GRUMIO. And therefore it is called a sensible tale; and this cuff was but to knock at your ear and beseech listening. Now I begin: Imprimis, we came down a foul hill, my master riding behind my mistress,—

CURTIS. Both of one horse?

GRUMIO. What 's that to thee?

CURTIS. Why, a horse.

GRUMIO. Tell thou the tale: but hadst thou not crossed me thou shouldst have heard how her horse fell, and she under her horse; thou shouldst have heard in how miry a place, how she was bemoiled; how he left her with the horse upon her; how he beat me because her horse stumbled; how she waded through the dirt to pluck him off me: how he swore; how she prayed, that never prayed before;

how I cried; how the horses ran away; how her bridle was
burst; how I lost my crupper; with many things of worthy
memory, which now shall die in oblivion, and thou return
unexperienced to thy grave.

CURTIS. By this reckoning he is more shrew than she.

GRUMIO. Ay; and that, thou and the proudest of you all shall
find when he comes home. But what talk I of this? Call
forth Nathaniel, Joseph, Nicholas, Philip, Walter, Sugar-
sop, and the rest: let their heads be sleekly combed, their
blue coats brushed, and their garters of an indifferent knit:
let them curtsy with their left legs, and not presume to
touch a hair of my master's horsetail till they kiss their
hands. Are they all ready?

CURTIS. They are.

GRUMIO. Call them forth.

CURTIS. Do you hear? ho! you must meet my master to countenance my mistress.

GRUMIO. Why, she hath a face of her own.

CURTIS. Who knows not that?

GRUMIO. Thou, it seems, that callest for company to countenance her.

CURTIS. I call them forth to credit her.

GRUMIO. Why, she comes to borrow nothing of them.

Enter several Servants

NATHANIEL. Welcome home, Grumio!

PHILIP. How now, Grumio?

JOSEPH. What, Grumio!

NICHOLAS. Fellow Grumio!

NATHANIEL. How now, old lad!

GRUMIO. Welcome, you; how now, you; what, you; fellow,
you; and thus much for greeting. Now, my spruce companions, is all ready, and all things neat?

NATHANIEL. All things is ready. How near is our master?

GRUMIO. E'en at hand, alighted by this; and therefore be
not,—Cock's passion, silence! I hear my master.

Enter Petruchio and Katharina

PETRUCHIO. Where be these knaves? What! no man at door
To hold my stirrup nor to take my horse?
Where is Nathaniel, Gregory, Philip?—

ALL SERVANTS. Here, here, sir; here, sir.

PETRUCHIO. Here, sir! here, sir! here, sir! here, sir!
You logger-headed and unpolish'd grooms!

What, no attendance? no regard? no duty?
Where is the foolish knave I sent before?

GRUMIO. Here, sir; as foolish as I was before.

PETRUCHIO. You peasant swain! you whoreson malt-horse
  drudge!
Did I not bid thee meet me in the park,
And bring along these rascal knaves with thee?

GRUMIO. Nathaniel's coat, sir, was not fully made,
And Gabriel's pumps were all unpink'd i' the heel,
There was no link to colour Peter's hat,
And Walter's dagger was not come from sheathing,
There was none fine but Adam, Ralph, and Gregory;
The rest were ragged, old, and beggarly;
Yet, as they are, here are they come to meet you.

PETRUCHIO. Go, rascals, go, and fetch my supper in.

                                    Exeunt some of the Servants
'Where is the life that late I led?'
Where are those—? Sit down, Kate, and welcome.
Soud, soud, soud, soud!

            Re-enter Servants with supper
Why, when, I say?—Nay, good sweet Kate, be merry.—
Off with my boots, you rogues! you villains! When?
          It was the friar of orders grey,
          As he forth walked on his way:
Out, you rogue! you pluck my foot awry: *Strikes him*
Take that, and mend the plucking off the other.
Be merry, Kate. Some water, here; what, ho!
Where's my spaniel Troilus? Sirrah, get you hence
And bid my cousin Ferdinand come hither: *Exit Servant*
One, Kate, that you must kiss, and be acquainted with.
Where are my slippers? Shall I have some water?
Come, Kate, and wash, and welcome heartily.—
          Servant lets the ewer fall. Petruchio strikes him
You whoreson villain! will you let it fall?

KATHARINA. Patience, I pray you; 'twas a fault unwilling.

PETRUCHIO. A whoreson, beetle-headed, flap-ear'd knave!
Come, Kate, sit down; I know you have a stomach.
Will you give thanks, sweet Kate, or else shall I?—
What's this? mutton?

FIRST SERVANT.   Ay.

PETRUCHIO.   Who brought it?

FIRST SERVANT.   I.

PETRUCHIO. 'Tis burnt; and so is all the meat.
What dogs are these! Where is the rascal cook?
How durst you, villains, bring it from the dresser,
And serve it thus to me that love it not?

Throws the meat, &c., at

There, take it to you, trenchers, cups, and all.
You heedless joltheads and unmanner'd slaves!
What! do you grumble? I 'll be with you straight.

KATHARINA. I pray you, husband, be not so disquiet:
The meat was well if you were so contented.

PETRUCHIO. I tell thee, Kate, 'twas burnt and dried awa
And I expressly am forbid to touch it,
For it engenders choler, planteth anger;
And better 'twere that both of us did fast,
Since, of ourselves, ourselves are choleric,
Than feed it with such over-roasted flesh.
Be patient; to-morrow 't shall be mended,
And for this night we 'll fast for company:
Come, I will bring thee to thy bridal chamber.

Exeunt Petruchio, Katharina, and C

NATHANIEL. Peter, didst ever see the like?

PETER. He kills her in her own humour.

Re-enter Curtis

GRUMIO. Where is he?

CURTIS. In her chamber, making a sermon of continen
her;
And rails, and swears, and rates, that she, poor soul,
Knows not which way to stand, to look, to speak,
And sits as one new-risen from a dream.
Away, away! for he is coming hither.   E*

Re-enter Petruchio

PETRUCHIO. Thus have I politicly begun my reign,
And 'tis my hope to end successfully.
My falcon now is sharp and passing empty,
And till she stoop she must not be full-gorg'd,
For then she never looks upon her lure.
Another way I have to man my haggard,
To make her come and know her keeper's call;
That is, to watch her, as we watch these kites
That bate and beat and will not be obedient.
She eat no meat to-day, nor none shall eat;
Last night she slept not, nor to-night she shall not:

As with the meat, some undeserved fault
I 'll find about the making of the bed;
And here I 'll fling the pillow, there the bolster,
This way the coverlet, another way the sheets:
Ay, and amid this hurly I intend
That all is done in reverend care of her;
And in conclusion she shall watch all night:
And if she chance to nod I 'll rail and brawl,
And with the clamour keep her still awake.
This is a way to kill a wife with kindness;
And thus I 'll curb her mad and headstrong humour.
He that knows better how to tame a shrew,
Now let him speak: 'tis charity to show.   *Exit*

SCENE TWO

Padua. Before Baptista's House.

Enter Tranio and Hortensio

TRANIO. Is 't possible, friend Licio, that Mistress Bianca
    Doth fancy any other but Lucentio?
    I tell you, sir, she bears me fair in hand.
HORTENSIO. Sir, to satisfy you in what I have said,
    Stand by, and mark the manner of his teaching.
                                        They stand aside
Enter Bianca and Lucentio
LUCENTIO. Now, mistress, profit you in what you read?
BIANCA. What, master, read you? First resolve me that.
LUCENTIO. I read that I profess, the Art to Love.
BIANCA. And may you prove, sir, master of your art!
LUCENTIO. While you, sweet dear, prove mistress of my
    heart.   *They retire*
HORTENSIO. Quick proceeders, marry! Now, tell me, I pray,
    You that durst swear that your mistress Bianca
    Lov'd none in the world so well as Lucentio.
TRANIO. O despiteful love! unconstant womankind!
    I tell thee, Licio, this is wonderful.
HORTENSIO. Mistake no more: I am not Licio,
    Nor a musician, as I seem to be;
    But one that scorns to live in this disguise,
    For such a one as leaves a gentleman,

And makes a god of such a cullion:
Know, sir, that I am call'd Hortensio.

TRANIO. Signior Hortensio, I have often heard
Of your entire affection to Bianca;
And since mine eyes are witness of her lightness,
I will with you, if you be so contented,
Forswear Bianca and her love for ever.

HORTENSIO. See, how they kiss and court! Signior **Lucentio**,
Here is my hand, and here I firmly vow
Never to woo her more; but do forswear her,
As one unworthy all the former favours
That I have fondly flatter'd her withal.

TRANIO. And here I take the like unfeigned oath,
Never to marry with her though she would entreat.
Fie on her! See how beastly she doth court him.

HORTENSIO. Would all the world, but he had quite forsworn!
For me, that I may surely keep mine oath,
I will be married to a wealthy widow
Ere three days pass, which hath as long lov'd me
As I have lov'd this proud disdainful haggard.
And so farewell, Signior Lucentio.
Kindness in women, not their beauteous looks,
Shall win my love: and so I take my leave,
In resolution as I swore before.

                    Exit Hortensio. Lucentio and Bianca advance

TRANIO. Mistress Bianca, bless you with such grace
As 'longeth to a lover's blessed case!
Nay, I have ta'en you napping, gentle love,
And have forsworn you with Hortensio.

BIANCA. Tranio, you jest. But have you both forsworn me?

TRANIO. Mistress, we have.

LUCENTIO.   Then we are rid of Licio.

TRANIO. I' faith, he 'll have a lusty widow now,
That shall be woo'd and wedded in a day.

BIANCA. God give him joy!

TRANIO. Ay, and he 'll tame her.

BIANCA.   He says so, Tranio.

TRANIO. Faith, he is gone unto the taming-school.

BIANCA. The taming-school! what, is there such a place?

TRANIO. Ay, mistress, and Petruchio is the master;
That teacheth tricks eleven and twenty long,
To tame a shrew, and charm her chattering tongue.

Enter Biondello, running

BIONDELLO. O master, master! I have watch'd so long
  That I 'm dog-weary; but at last I spied
  An ancient angel coming down the hill
  Will serve the turn.

TRANIO.   What is he, Biondello?

BIONDELLO. Master, a mercatante, or a pedant,
  I know not what; but formal in apparel,
  In gait and countenance surely like a father.

LUCENTIO. And what of him, Tranio?

TRANIO. If he be credulous and trust my tale,
  I 'll make him glad to seem Vincentio,
  And give assurance to Baptista Minola,
  As if he were the right Vincentio.
  Take in your love, and then let me alone.

                      Exeunt Lucentio and Bianca
                        Enter a Pedant

PEDANT. God save you, sir!

TRANIO.   And you, sir! you are welcome.
  Travel you far on, or are you at the farthest?

PEDANT. Sir, at the farthest for a week or two;
  But then up farther, and as far as Rome;
  And so to Tripoli, if God lend me life.

TRANIO. What countryman, I pray?

PEDANT.   Of Mantua.

TRANIO. Of Mantua, sir! marry, God forbid!
  And come to Padua, careless of your life?

PEDANT. My life, sir! How, I pray? For that goes hard.

TRANIO. 'Tis death for any one in Mantua
  To come to Padua. Know you not the cause?
  Your ships are stay'd at Venice; and the duke,—
  For private quarrel 'twixt your duke and him,—
  Hath publish'd and proclaim'd it openly.
  'Tis marvel, but that you are but newly come,
  You might have heard it else proclaim'd about.

PEDANT. Alas, sir! it is worse for me than so;
  For I have bills for money by exchange
  From Florence, and must here deliver them.

TRANIO. Well, sir, to do you courtesy,
  This will I do, and this I will advise you:
  First, tell me, have you ever been at Pisa?

PEDANT. Ay, sir, in Pisa have I often been;

Pisa, renowned for grave citizens.

TRANIO. Among them, know you one Vincentio?

PEDANT. I know him not, but I have heard of him;
A merchant of incomparable wealth.

TRANIO. He is my father, sir; and, sooth to say,
In countenance somewhat doth resemble you.

BIONDELLO. (*Aside*) As much as an apple doth an oyster,
and all one.

TRANIO. To save your life in this extremity,
This favour will I do you for his sake;
And think it not the worst of all your fortunes
That you are like to Sir Vincentio.
His name and credit shall you undertake,
And in my house you shall be friendly lodg'd,
Look that you take upon you as you should!
You understand me, sir; so shall you stay
Till you have done your business in the city.
If this be courtesy, sir, accept of it.

PEDANT. O sir, I do; and will repute you ever
The patron of my life and liberty.

TRANIO. Then go with me to make the matter good.
This, by the way, I let you understand:
My father is here look'd for every day,
To pass assurance of a dower in marriage
'Twixt me and one Baptista's daughter here:
In all these circumstances I 'll instruct you.
Go with me to clothe you as becomes you.   *Exeunt*

SCENE THREE

A Room in Petruchio's House.

Enter Katharina and Grumio

GRUMIO. No, no, forsooth; I dare not, for my life.

KATHARINA. The more my wrong the more his spite appears.
What, did he marry me to famish me?
Beggars, that come unto my father's door,
Upon entreaty have a present alms;
If not, elsewhere they meet with charity:
But I, who never knew how to entreat,
Nor never needed that I should entreat,

Am starv'd for meat, giddy for lack of sleep;
With oaths kept waking, and with brawling fed.
And that which spites me more than all these wants,
He does it under name of perfect love;
As who should say, if I should sleep or eat
'Twere deadly sickness, or else present death.
I prithee go and get me some repast;
I care not what, so it be wholesome food.

GRUMIO. What say you to a neat's foot?

KATHARINA. 'Tis passing good: I prithee let me have it.

GRUMIO. I fear it is too choleric a meat.
How say you to a fat tripe finely broil'd?

KATHARINA. I like it well: good Grumio, fetch it me.

GRUMIO. I cannot tell; I fear 'tis choleric.
What say you to a piece of beef and mustard?

KATHARINA. A dish that I do love to feed upon.

GRUMIO. Ay, but the mustard is too hot a little.

KATHARINA. Why, then the beef, and let the mustard rest.

GRUMIO. Nay, then I will not: you shall have the mustard,
Or else you get no beef of Grumio.

KATHARINA. Then both, or one, or anything thou wilt.

GRUMIO. Why then, the mustard without the beef.

KATHARINA. Go, get thee gone, thou false deluding slave,

Beats him

That feed'st me with the very name of meat.
Sorrow on thee and all the pack of you,
That triumph thus upon my misery!
Go, get thee gone, I say.

Enter Petruchio with a dish of meat; and Hortensio

PETRUCHIO. How fares my Kate? What, sweeting, all amort?

HORTENSIO. Mistress, what cheer?

KATHARINA.   Faith, as cold as can be.

PETRUCHIO. Pluck up thy spirits; look cheerfully upon me.
Here, love; thou seest how diligent I am,
To dress thy meat myself and bring it thee:

Sets the dish on a table

I am sure, sweet Kate, this kindness merits thanks.
What! not a word? Nay then, thou lov'st it not,
And all my pains is sorted to no proof.
Here, take away this dish.

KATHARINA.   I pray you, let it stand.

PETRUCHIO. The poorest service is repaid with thanks,

And so shall mine, before you touch the meat.

KATHARINA. I thank you, sir.

HORTENSIO. Signior Petruchio, fie! you are to blame.

Come, Mistress Kate, I 'll bear you company.

PETRUCHIO. (*Aside*) Eat it up all, Hortensio, if thou lov'st
    me.

Much good do it unto thy gentle heart!

Kate, eat apace: and now, my honey love,

Will we return unto thy father's house,

And revel it as bravely as the best,

With silken coats and caps and golden rings,

With ruffs and cuffs and farthingales and things;

With scarfs and fans and double change of bravery,

With amber bracelets, beads and all this knavery.

What! hast thou din'd? The tailor stays thy leisure,

To deck thy body with his ruffling treasure.

Enter Tailor

Come, tailor, let us see these ornaments;

Lay forth the gown.—

Enter Haberdasher

                    What news with you, sir?

HABERDASHER. Here is the cap your worship did bespeak.

PETRUCHIO. Why, this was moulded on a porringer;

A velvet dish: fie, fie! 'tis lewd and filthy:

Why, 'tis a cockle or a walnut-shell,

A knack, a toy, a trick, a baby's cap:

Away with it! Come, let me have a bigger.

KATHARINA. I 'll have no bigger: this doth fit the time,

And gentlewomen wear such caps as these.

PETRUCHIO. When you are gentle, you shall have one too;

And not till then.

HORTENSIO. (*Aside*) That will not be in haste.

KATHARINA. Why, sir, I trust I may have leave to speak,

And speak I will; I am no child, no babe:

Your betters have endur'd me say my mind,

And if you cannot, best you stop your ears.

My tongue will tell the anger of my heart,

Or else my heart, concealing it, will break:

And rather than it shall, I will be free

Even to the uttermost, as I please, in words.

PETRUCHIO. Why, thou sayst true; it is a paltry cap,

A custard-coffin, a bauble, a silken pie.

I love thee well in that thou lik'st it not.

KATHARINA. Love me or love me not, I like the cap,
And it I will have, or I will have none.   *Exit Haberdasher*

PETRUCHIO. Thy gown? why, ay: come, tailor, let us see 't.
O mercy, God! what masquing stuff is here?
What 's this? a sleeve? 'Tis like a demi-cannon:
What! up and down, carv'd like an apple-tart?
Here 's snip and nip and cut and slish and slash,
Like to a censer in a barber's shop.
Why, what, i' devil's name, tailor, call'st thou this?

HORTENSIO. (*Aside*) I see, she's like to have neither cap nor
gown.

TAILOR. You bid me make it orderly and well,
According to the fashion and the time.

PETRUCHIO. Marry, and did: but if you be remember'd,
I did not bid you mar it to the time.
Go, hop me over every kennel home,
For you shall hop without my custom, sir.
I 'll none of it: hence! make your best of it.

KATHARINA. I never saw a better-fashion'd gown,
More quaint, more pleasing, nor more commendable.
Belike you mean to make a puppet of me.

PETRUCHIO. Why, true; he means to make a puppet of thee.

TAILOR. She says your worship means to make a puppet of
her.

PETRUCHIO. O monstrous arrogance! Thou liest, thou thread,
Thou thimble,
Thou yard, three-quarters, half-yard, quarter, nail!
Thou flea, thou nit, thou winter-cricket thou!
Brav'd in mine own house with a skein of thread!
Away! thou rag, thou quantity, thou remnant,
Or I shall so be-mete thee with thy yard
As thou shalt think on prating whilst thou liv'st!
I tell thee, I, that thou hast marr'd her gown.

TAILOR. Your worship is deceiv'd: the gown is made
Just as my master had direction.
Grumio gave order how it should be done.

GRUMIO. I gave him no order; I gave him the stuff.

TAILOR. But how did you desire it should be made?

GRUMIO. Marry, sir, with needle and thread.

TAILOR. But did you not request to have it cut?

GRUMIO. Thou hast faced many things.

TAILOR. I have.

GRUMIO. Face not me: thou hast braved many men; brave not me: I will neither be faced nor braved. I say unto thee, I bid thy master cut out the gown; but I did not bid him cut it to pieces: ergo, thou liest.

TAILOR. Why, here is the note of the fashion to testify.

PETRUCHIO. Read it.

GRUMIO. The note lies in 's throat if he say I said so.

TAILOR. 'Imprimis. A loose-bodied gown.'

GRUMIO. Master, if ever I said loose-bodied gown, sew me in the skirts of it, and beat me to death with a bottom of brown thread. I said, a gown.

PETRUCHIO. Proceed.

TAILOR. 'With a small compassed cape.'

GRUMIO. I confess the cape.

TAILOR. 'With a trunk sleeve.'

GRUMIO. I confess two sleeves.

TAILOR. 'The sleeves curiously cut.'

PETRUCHIO. Ay, there 's the villany.

GRUMIO. Error i' the bill, sir; error i' the bill. I commanded the sleeves should be cut out and sewed up again; and that I 'll prove upon thee, though thy little finger be armed in a thimble.

TAILOR. This is true that I say: an I had thee in place where thou shouldst know it.

GRUMIO. I am for thee straight: take thou the bill, give me thy mete-yard, and spare not me.

HORTENSIO. God-a-mercy, Grumio! then he shall have no odds.

PETRUCHIO. Well, sir, in brief, the gown is not for me.

GRUMIO. You are i' the right, sir; tis for my mistress.

PETRUCHIO. Go, take it up unto thy master's use.

GRUMIO. Villain, not for thy life! take up my mistress' gown for thy master's use!

PETRUCHIO. Why, sir, what 's your conceit in that?

GRUMIO. O, sir, the conceit is deeper than you think for.
Take up my mistress' gown to his master's use!
O, fie, fie, fie!

PETRUCHIO. (Aside) Hortensio, say thou wilt see the tailor paid.
(To Tailor) Go take it hence; be gone, and say no more.

HORTENSIO. *(Aside to Tailor)* Tailor, I 'll pay thee for thy
    gown to-morrow:
    Take no unkindness of his hasty words.
    Away! I say; commend me to thy master.   *Exit Tailor*
PETRUCHIO. Well, come, my Kate; we will unto your fa-
    ther's,
    Even in these honest mean habiliments.
    Our purses shall be proud, our garments poor;
    For 'tis the mind that makes the body rich;
    And as the sun breaks through the darkest clouds,
    So honour peereth in the meanest habit.
    What is the jay more precious than the lark
    Because his feathers are more beautiful?
    Or is the adder better than the eel
    Because his painted skin contents the eye?
    O, no, good Kate; neither art thou the worse
    For this poor furniture and mean array.
    If thou account'st it shame, lay it on me;
    And therefore frolic: we will hence forthwith,
    To feast and sport us at thy father's house.
    Go, call my men, and let us straight to him;
    And bring our horses unto Long-lane end;
    There will we mount, and thither walk on foot.
    Let 's see; I think 'tis now some seven o'clock,
    And well we may come there by dinner-time.
KATHARINA. I dare assure you, sir, 'tis almost two;
    And 'twill be supper-time ere you come there.
PETRUCHIO. It shall be seven ere I go to horse.
    Look, what I speak, or do, or think to do,
    You are still crossing it. Sirs, let 't alone:
    I will not go to-day; and ere I do,
    It shall be what o'clock I say it is.
HORTENSIO. Why, so this gallant will command the sun.
                               Exeunt

SCENE FOUR

Padua. Before Baptista's House.

Enter Tranio, and the Pedant dressed like Vincentio

TRANIO. Sir, this is the house: please it you that I call?

PEDANT. Ay, what else? and, but I be deceived,
    Signior Baptista may remember me,
    Near twenty years ago, in Genoa,
    Where we were lodgers at the Pegasus.

TRANIO. 'Tis well; and hold your own, in any case,
    With such austerity as 'longeth to a father.

PEDANT. I warrant you. But, sir, here comes your boy;
    'Twere good he were school'd.

Enter Biondello

TRANIO. Fear you not him. Sirrah Biondello,
    Now do your duty throughly, I advise you:
    Imagine 'twere the right Vincentio.

BIONDELLO. Tut! fear not me.

TRANIO. But hast thou done thy errand to Baptista?

BIONDELLO. I told him that your father was at Venice,
    And that you look'd for him this day in Padua.

TRANIO. Thou 'rt a tall fellow: hold thee that to drink.
    Here comes Baptista. Set your countenance, sir.

Enter Baptista and Lucentio

    Signior Baptista, you are happily met.
    (*To the Pedant*) Sir, this is the gentleman I told you of:
    I pray you, stand good father to me now,
    Give me Bianca for my patrimony.

PEDANT. Soft, son!
    Sir, by your leave: having come to Padua
    To gather in some debts, my son Lucentio
    Made me acquainted with a weighty cause
    Of love between your daughter and himself:
    And,—for the good report I hear of you,
    And for the love he beareth to your daughter,
    And she to him,—to stay him not too long,
    I am content, in a good father's care,
    To have him match'd; and, if you please to like
    No worse than I, upon some agreement

Me shall you find ready and willing
With one consent to have her so bestow'd;
For curious I cannot be with you,
Signior Baptista, of whom I hear so well.

BAPTISTA. Sir, pardon me in what I have to say:
Your plainness and your shortness please me well.
Right true it is, your son Lucentio here
Doth love my daughter and she loveth him,
Or both dissemble deeply their affections:
And therefore, if you say no more than this,
That like a father you will deal with him
And pass my daughter a sufficient dower,
The match is made, and all is done:
Your son shall have my daughter with consent.

TRANIO. I thank you, sir. Where, then, do you know best
We be affied and such assurance ta'en
As shall with either part's agreement stand?

BAPTISTA. Not in my house, Lucentio; for, you know,
Pitchers have ears, and I have many servants.
Besides, old Gremio is hearkening still,
And happily we might be interrupted.

TRANIO. Then at my lodging, an it like you:
There doth my father lie, and there this night
We 'll pass the business privately and well.
Send for your daughter by your servant here;
My boy shall fetch the scrivener presently.
The worst is this, that, at so slender warning,
You're like to have a thin and slender pittance.

BAPTISTA. It likes me well. Cambio, hie you home,
And bid Bianca make her ready straight;
And, if you will, tell what hath happened:
Lucentio's father is arriv'd in Padua,
And how she 's like to be Lucentio's wife.

LUCENTIO. I pray the gods she may with all my heart!

TRANIO. Dally not with the gods, but get thee gone.
Signior Baptista, shall I lead the way?
Welcome! one mess is like to be your cheer.
Come, sir; we will better it in Pisa.

BAPTISTA. I follow you.

Exeunt Tranio, Pedant, and Baptista

BIONDELLO. Cambio!

LUCENTIO. What sayst thou, Biondello?

BIONDELLO. You saw my master wink and laugh upon you?

LUCENTIO. Biondello, what of that?

BIONDELLO. Faith, nothing; but he has left me here behind to expound the meaning or moral of his signs and tokens.

LUCENTIO. I pray thee, moralize them.

BIONDELLO. Then thus. Baptista is safe, talking with the deceiving father of a deceitful son.

LUCENTIO. And what of him?

BIONDELLO. His daughter is to be brought by you to the supper.

LUCENTIO. And then?

BIONDELLO. The old priest at Saint Luke's church is at your command at all hours.

LUCENTIO. And what of all this?

BIONDELLO. I cannot tell, expect they are busied about a counterfeit assurance: take you assurance of her, cum privilegio ad imprimendum solum. To the church! Take the priest, clerk, and some sufficient honest witnesses.
      If this be not that you look for, I have no more to say,
      But bid Bianca farewell for ever and a day.   *Going*

LUCENTIO. Hearest thou, Biondello?

BIONDELLO. I cannot tarry: I knew a wench married in an afternoon as she went to the garden for parsley to stuff a rabbit; and so may you, sir; and so, adieu, sir. My master hath appointed me to go to Saint Luke's, to bid the priest be ready to come against you come with your appendix.

Exit

LUCENTIO. I may, and will, if she be so contented:
      She will be pleas'd; then wherefore should I doubt?
      Hap what hap may, I 'll roundly go about her:
      It shall go hard if Cambio go without her.   *Exit*

SCENE FIVE

A public Road.

Enter Petruchio, Katharina, Hortensio, and Servants

PETRUCHIO. Come on, i' God's name; once more toward our father's.
      Good Lord, how bright and goodly shines the moon!

KATHARINA. The moon! the sun: it is not moonlight now.

PETRUCHIO. I say it is the moon that shines so bright.

KATHARINA. I know it is the sun that shines so bright.

PETRUCHIO. Now, by my mother's son, and that 's myself,
 It shall be moon, or star, or what I list,
 Or ere I journey to your father's house.
 Go one and fetch our horses back again.
 Evermore cross'd and cross'd; nothing but cross'd!

HORTENSIO. Say as he says, or we shall never go.

KATHARINA. Forward, I pray, since we have come so far,
 And be it moon, or sun, or what you please.
 An if you please to call it a rush-candle,
 Henceforth I vow it shall be so for me.

PETRUCHIO. I say it is the moon.

KATHARINA.   I know it is the moon.

PETRUCHIO. Nay, then you lie; it is the blessed sun.

KATHARINA. Then God be bless'd, it is the blessed sun:
 But sun it is not when you say it is not,
 And the moon changes even as your mind.
 What you will have it nam'd, even that it is;
 And so, it shall be so for Katharine.

HORTENSIO. Petruchio, go thy ways; the field is won.

PETRUCHIO. Well, forward, forward! thus the bowl should
   run,
 And not unluckily against the bias.
 But soft! what company is coming here?

          Enter Vincentio, in a travelling dress

 (*To Vincentio*) Good-morrow, gentle mistress: where
   away?
 Tell me, sweet Kate, and tell me truly too,
 Hast thou beheld a fresher gentlewoman?
 Such war of white and red within her cheeks!
 What stars do spangle heaven with such beauty,
 As those two eyes become that heavenly face?
 Fair lovely maid, once more good day to thee.
 Sweet Kate, embrace her for her beauty's sake.

HORTENSIO. A' will make the man mad, to make a woman of
 him.

KATHARINA. Young budding virgin, fair and fresh and sweet,
 Whither away, or where is thy abode?
 Happy the parents of so fair a child;
 Happier the man, whom favourable stars
 Allot thee for his lovely bed-fellow!

PETRUCHIO. Why, how now, Kate! I hope thou art not mad:
    This is a man, old, wrinkled, faded, wither'd,
    And not a maiden, as thou sayst he is.

KATHARINA. Pardon, old father, my mistaking eyes,
    That have been so bedazzled with the sun
    That everything I look on seemeth green:
    Now I perceive thou art a reverend father;
    Pardon, I pray thee, for my mad mistaking.

PETRUCHIO. Do, good old grandsire; and withal make known
    Which way thou travellest: if along with us,
    We shall be joyful of thy company.

VINCENTIO. Fair sir, and you my merry mistress,
    That with your strange encounter much amaz'd me,
    My name is called Vincentio; my dwelling, Pisa;
    And bound I am to Padua, there to visit
    A son of mine, which long I have not seen.

PETRUCHIO. What is his name?

VINCENTIO.   Lucentio, gentle sir.

PETRUCHIO. Happily met; the happier for thy son.
    And now by law, as well as reverend age,
    I may entitle thee my loving father:
    The sister to my wife, this gentlewoman,
    Thy son by this hath married. Wonder not,
    Nor be not griev'd: she is of good esteem,
    Her dowry wealthy, and of worthy birth;
    Beside, so qualified as may beseem
    The spouse of any noble gentleman.
    Let me embrace with old Vincentio;
    And wander we to see thy honest son,
    Who will of thy arrival be full joyous.

VINCENTIO. But is this true? or is it else your pleasure,
    Like pleasant travellers, to break a jest
    Upon the company you overtake?

HORTENSIO. I do assure thee, father, so it is.

PETRUCHIO. Come, go along, and see the truth hereof;
    For our first merriment hath made thee jealous.
                   Exeunt all but Hortensio

HORTENSIO. Well, Petruchio, this has put me in heart.
    Have to my widow! and if she be froward,
    Then hast thou taught Hortensio to be untoward.   *Exit*

ACT FIVE

SCENE ONE

Padua. Before Lucentio's House.

Enter on one side Biondello, Lucentio, and Bianca;
Gremio walking on the other side

BIONDELLO. Softly and swiftly, sir, for the priest is ready.

LUCENTIO. I fly, Biondello: but they may chance to need
thee at home; therefore leave us.

BIONDELLO. Nay, faith, I 'll see the church o' your back; and
then come back to my master as soon as I can.

Exeunt Lucentio, Bianca, and Biondello

GREMIO. I marvel Cambio comes not all this while.

Enter Petruchio, Katharina, Vincentio, and Attendants

PETRUCHIO. Sir, here 's the door, this is Lucentio's house:
My father's bears more toward the market-place;
Thither must I, and here I leave you, sir.

VINCENTIO. You shall not choose but drink before you go.
I think I shall command your welcome here,
And, by all likelihood, some cheer is toward.   *Knocks*

GREMIO. They 're busy within; you were best knock louder.

Enter Pedant above, at a window

PEDANT. What 's he that knocks as he would beat down the
gate?

VINCENTIO. Is Signior Lucentio within, sir?

PEDANT. He 's within, sir, but not to be spoken withal.

VINCENTIO. What if a man bring him a hundred pound or
two, to make merry withal?

PEDANT. Keep your hundred pounds to yourself: he shall
need none so long as I live.

PETRUCHIO. Nay, I told you your son was well beloved in
Padua. Do you hear, sir? To leave frivolous circumstances,
I pray you, tell Signior Lucentio that his father is come
from Pisa, and is here at the door to speak with him.

PEDANT. Thou liest: his father is come from Padua, and here looking out at the window.

VINCENTIO. Art thou his father?

PEDANT. Ay, sir; so his mother says, if I may believe her.

PETRUCHIO. (*To Vincentio*) Why, how now, gentleman! why, this is flat knavery, to take upon you another man's name.

PEDANT. Lay hands on the villain: I believe, a' means to cozen somebody in this city under my countenance.

Re-enter Biondello

BIONDELLO. I have seen them in the church together: God send 'em good shipping! But who is here? Mine old master, Vincentio! Now we are undone and brought to nothing.

VINCENTIO. (*Seeing Biondello*) Come hither, crack-hemp.

BIONDELLO. I hope I may choose, sir.

VINCENTIO. Come hither, you rogue. What, have you forgot me?

BIONDELLO. Forgot you! no, sir: I could not forget you, for I never saw you before in all my life.

VINCENTIO. What, you notorious villain! Didst thou never see thy master's father, Vincentio?

BIONDELLO. What, my old, worshipful old master? Yes, marry, sir. See where he looks out of the window.

VINCENTIO. Is 't so, indeed?   *Beats Biondello*

BIONDELLO. Help, help, help! Here 's a madman will murder me.   *Exit*

PEDANT. Help, son! Help, Signior Baptista!

Exit from the window

PETRUCHIO. Prithee, Kate, let 's stand aside, and see the end of this controversy.   *They retire*

Re-enter Pedant below; Baptista, Tranio, and Servants

TRANIO. Sir, what are you that offer to beat my servant?

VINCENTIO. What am I, sir! nay, what are you, sir? O immortal gods! O fine villain! A silken doublet! a velvet hose! a scarlet cloak! and a copatain hat! O, I am undone! I am undone! while I play the good husband at home, my son and my servant spend all at the university.

TRANIO. How now! What 's the matter?

BAPTISTA. What, is the man lunatic?

TRANIO. Sir, you seem a sober ancient gentleman by your habit, but your words show you a madman. Why, sir, what

'cerns it you if I wear pearl and gold? I thank my good
father, I am able to maintain it.

VINCENTIO. Thy father! O villain! He is a sailmaker in Bergamo.

BAPTISTA. You mistake, sir, you mistake, sir. Pray, what do
you think is his name?

VINCENTIO. His name! As if I knew not his name: I have
brought him up ever since he was three years old, and his
name is Tranio.

PEDANT. Away, away, mad ass! His name is Lucentio; and
he is mine only son, and heir to the lands of me, Signior
Vincentio.

VINCENTIO. Lucentio! O! he hath murdered his master. Lay
hold on him, I charge you in the duke's name. O my son,
my son! tell me, thou villain, where is my son Lucentio?

TRANIO. Call forth an officer.

Enter one with an Officer

Carry this mad knave to the gaol. Father Baptista,
I charge you see that he be forthcoming.

VINCENTIO. Carry me to the gaol!

GREMIO. Stay, officer: he shall not go to prison.

BAPTISTA. Talk not, Signior Gremio: I say he shall go to
prison.

GREMIO. Take heed, Signior Baptista, lest you be conycatched in this business: I dare swear this is the right Vincentio.

PEDANT. Swear, if thou darest.

GREMIO. Nay, I dare not swear it.

TRANIO. Then thou wert best say that I am not Lucentio.

GREMIO. Yes, I know thee to be Signior Lucentio.

BAPTISTA. Away with the dotard! To the gaol with him!

VINCENTIO. Thus strangers may be haled and abused:
O monstrous villain!

Re-enter Biondello, with Lucentio and Bianca

BIONDELLO. O! we are spoiled; and yonder he is: deny him,
forswear him, or else we are all undone.

LUCENTIO. (*Kneeling*) Pardon, sweet father.

VINCENTIO.   Lives my sweetest son?

                    Biondello, Tranio, and Pedant run out

BIANCA. (*Kneeling*) Pardon, dear father.

BAPTISTA.   How hast thou offended?
Where is Lucentio?

LUCENTIO.   Here 's Lucentio,
  Right son to the right Vincentio;
  That have by marriage made thy daughter mine,
  While counterfeit supposes blear'd thine eyne.
GREMIO. Here 's packing, with a witness, to deceive us all!
VINCENTIO. Where is that damned villain Tranio,
  That fac'd and brav'd me in this matter so?
BAPTISTA. Why, tell me, is not this my Cambio?
BIANCA. Cambio is chang'd into Lucentio.
LUCENTIO. Love wrought these miracles. Bianca's love
  Made me exchange my state with Tranio,
  While he did bear my countenance in the town;
  And happily I have arriv'd at last
  Unto the wished haven of my bliss.
  What Tranio did, myself enforc'd him to;
  Then pardon him, sweet father, for my sake.
VINCENTIO. I 'll slit the villain's nose, that would have sent
  me to the gaol.
BAPTISTA. (*To Lucentio*) But do you hear, sir?
  Have you married my daughter without asking my good
  will?
VINCENTIO. Fear not, Baptista; we will content you, go to:
  but I will in, to be revenged for this villany.   *Exit*
BAPTISTA. And I, to sound the depth of this knavery.   *Exit*
LUCENTIO. Look not pale, Bianca; thy father will not frown.
                              Exeunt Lucentio and Bianca
GREMIO. My cake is dough; but I 'll in among the rest,
  Out of hope of all, but my share of the feast.   *Exit*
             Petruchio and Katharina advance
KATHARINA. Husband, let 's follow, to see the end of this
  ado.
PETRUCHIO. First kiss me, Kate, and we will.
KATHARINA. What! in the midst of the street?
PETRUCHIO. What! art thou ashamed of me?
KATHARINA. No, sir, God forbid; but ashamed to kiss.
PETRUCHIO. Why, then let 's home again. Come, sirrah, let 's
  away.
KATHARINA. Nay, I will give thee a kiss: now pray thee, love,
  stay.
PETRUCHIO. Is not this well? Come, my sweet Kate:
  Better once than never, for never too late.   *Exeunt*

SCENE TWO

A Room in Lucentio's House.

*A Banquet set out. Enter Baptista, Vincentio, Gremio, the
Pedant, Lucentio, Bianca, Petruchio, Katharina, Hortensio,
and Widow. Tranio, Biondello, Grumio,
and Others, attending*

LUCENTIO. At last, though long, our jarring notes agree:
　And time it is, when raging war is done,
　To smile at 'scapes and perils overblown.
　My fair Bianca, bid my father welcome,
　While I with self-same kindness welcome thine.
　Brother Petruchio, sister Katharina,
　And thou, Hortensio, with thy loving widow,
　Feast with the best, and welcome to my house:
　My banquet is to close our stomachs up,
　After our great good cheer. Pray you, sit down;
　For now we sit to chat as well as eat.　　*They sit at table*

PETRUCHIO. Nothing but sit and sit, and eat and eat!

BAPTISTA. Padua affords this kindness, son Petruchio.

PETRUCHIO. Padua affords nothing but what is kind.

HORTENSIO. For both our sakes I would that word were true.

PETRUCHIO. Now, for my life, Hortensio fears his widow.

WIDOW. Then never trust me, if I be afeard.

PETRUCHIO. You are very sensible, and yet you miss my
　sense:
　I mean, Hortensio is afeard of you.

WIDOW. He that is giddy thinks the world turns round.

PETRUCHIO. Roundly replied.

KATHARINA.　　　　　　　　Mistress, how mean you that?

WIDOW. Thus I conceive by him.

PETRUCHIO. Conceives by me! How likes Hortensio that?

HORTENSIO. My widow says, thus she conceives her tale.

PETRUCHIO. Very well mended. Kiss him for that, good
　widow.

KATHARINA. 'He that is giddy thinks the world turns round':
　I pray you, tell me what you meant by that.

WIDOW. Your husband, being troubled with a shrew,
　Measures my husband's sorrow by his woe:

And now you know my meaning.

KATHARINA. A very mean meaning.

WIDOW.   Right, I mean you.

KATHARINA. And I am mean, indeed, respecting you.

PETRUCHIO. To her, Kate!

HORTENSIO. To her, widow!

PETRUCHIO. A hundred marks, my Kate does put her down.

HORTENSIO. That's my office.

PETRUCHIO. Spoke like an officer: ha' to thee, lad.

Drinks to Hortensio

BAPTISTA. How likes Gremio these quick-witted folks?

GREMIO. Believe me, sir, they butt together well.

BIANCA. Head and butt! a hasty-witted body
Would say your head and butt were head and horn.

VINCENTIO. Ay, mistress bride, hath that awaken'd you?

BIANCA. Ay, but not frighted me; therefore I'll sleep again.

PETRUCHIO. Nay, that you shall not; since you have begun,
Have at you for a bitter jest or two.

BIANCA. Am I your bird? I mean to shift my bush;
And then pursue me as you draw your bow.
You are welcome all.

Exeunt Bianca, Katharina, and Widow

PETRUCHIO. She hath prevented me. Here, Signior Tranio;
This bird you aim'd at, though you hit her not:
Therefore a health to all that shot and miss'd.

TRANIO. O sir! Lucentio slipp'd me, like his greyhound,
Which runs himself, and catches for his master.

PETRUCHIO. A good swift simile, but something currish.

TRANIO. 'Tis well, sir, that you hunted for yourself:
'Tis thought your deer does hold you at a bay.

BAPTISTA. O ho, Petruchio! Tranio hits you now.

LUCENTIO. I thank thee for that gird, good Tranio.

HORTENSIO. Confess, confess, hath he not hit you here?

PETRUCHIO. A' has a little gall'd me, I confess;
And, as the jest did glance away from me,
'Tis ten to one it maim'd you two outright.

BAPTISTA. Now, in good sadness, son Petruchio,
I think thou hast the veriest shrew of all.

PETRUCHIO. Well, I say no: and therefore, for assurance,
Let's each one send unto his wife;
And he whose wife is most obedient
To come at first when he doth send for her,

Shall win the wager which we will propose.

HORTENSIO. Content. What is the wager?

LUCENTIO.   Twenty crowns.

PETRUCHIO. Twenty crowns!

   I 'll venture so much of my hawk or hound,

   But twenty times so much upon my wife.

LUCENTIO. A hundred then.

HORTENSIO.   Content.

PETRUCHIO.   A match! 'tis done.

HORTENSIO. Who shall begin?

LUCENTIO.   That will I.

   Go, Biondello, bid your mistress come to me.

BIONDELLO. I go.   *Exit*

BAPTISTA. Son, I will be your half, Bianca comes.

LUCENTIO. I 'll have no halves; I 'll bear it all myself.

                  Re-enter Biondello

   How now! what news?

BIONDELLO.   Sir, my mistress sends you word

   That she is busy and she cannot come.

PETRUCHIO. How! she is busy, and she cannot come!

   Is that an answer?

GREMIO.   Ay, and a kind one too:

   Pray God, sir, your wife send you not a worse.

PETRUCHIO. I hope, better.

HORTENSIO. Sirrah Biondello, go and entreat my wife

   To come to me forthwith.   *Exit Biondello*

PETRUCHIO.   O ho! entreat her!

   Nay, then she must needs come.

HORTENSIO.   I am afraid, sir,

   Do what you can, yours will not be entreated.

                  Re-enter Biondello

   Now, where 's my wife?

BIONDELLO. She says you have some goodly jest in hand:

   She will not come: she bids you come to her.

PETRUCHIO. Worse and worse; she will not come! O vile,

   Intolerable, not to be endur'd!

   Sirrah Grumio, go to your mistress; say,

   I command her come to me.   *Exit Grumio*

HORTENSIO.   I know her answer.

PETRUCHIO. What?

HORTENSIO. She will not.

PETRUCHIO. The fouler fortune mine, and there an end.

Re-enter Katharina

BAPTISTA. Now, by my holidame, here comes Katharina!

KATHARINA. What is your will, sir, that you send for me?

PETRUCHIO. Where is your sister, and Hortensio's wife?

KATHARINA. They sit conferring by the parlour fire.

PETRUCHIO. Go, fetch them hither: if they deny to come,
Swinge me them soundly forth unto their husbands.
Away, I say, and bring them hither straight.

Exit Katharina

LUCENTIO. Here is a wonder, if you talk of a wonder.

HORTENSIO. And so it is. I wonder what it bodes.

PETRUCHIO. Marry, peace it bodes, and love, and quiet life,
An awful rule and right supremacy;
And, to be short, what not that 's sweet and happy.

BAPTISTA. Now fair befall thee, good Petruchio!
The wager thou hast won; and I will add
Unto their losses twenty thousand crowns;
Another dowry to another daughter,
For she is chang'd, as she had never been.

PETRUCHIO. Nay, I will win my wager better yet,
And show more sign of her obedience,
Her new-built virtue and obedience.
See where she comes, and brings your froward wives
As prisoners to her womanly persuasion.

Re-enter Katharina, with Bianca and Widow

Katharine, that cap of yours becomes you not:
Off with that bauble, throw it under foot.

Katharina pulls off her cap and throws it down

WIDOW. Lord! let me never have a cause to sigh,
Till I be brought to such a silly pass!

BIANCA. Fie! what a foolish duty call you this?

LUCENTIO. I would your duty were as foolish too:
The wisdom of your duty, fair Bianca,
Hath cost me an hundred crowns since supper-time.

BIANCA. The more fool you for laying on my duty.

PETRUCHIO. Katharine, I charge thee, tell these headstrong
women
What duty they do owe their lords and husbands.

WIDOW. Come, come, you 're mocking: we will have no telling.

PETRUCHIO. Come on, I say; and first begin with her.

WIDOW. She shall not.

PETRUCHIO. I say she shall: and first begin with her.

KATHARINA. Fie, fie! unknit that threatening unkind brow,
  And dart not scornful glances from those eyes,
  To wound thy lord, thy king, thy governor:
  It blots thy beauty as frosts do bite the meads,
  Confounds thy fame as whirlwinds shake fair buds,
  And in no sense is meet or amiable.
  A woman mov'd is like a fountain troubled,
  Muddy, ill-seeming, thick, bereft of beauty;
  And while it is so, none so dry or thirsty
  Will deign to sip or touch one drop of it.
  Thy husband is thy lord, thy life, thy keeper,
  Thy head, thy sovereign; one that cares for thee,
  And for thy maintenance commits his body
  To painful labour both by sea and land,
  To watch the night in storms, the day in cold,
  Whilst thou liest warm at home, secure and safe;
  And craves no other tribute at thy hands
  But love, fair looks, and true obedience;
  Too little payment for so great a debt.
  Such duty as the subject owes the prince,
  Even such a woman oweth to her husband;
  And when she 's froward, peevish, sullen, sour,
  And not obedient to his honest will,
  What is she but a foul contending rebel,
  And graceless traitor to her loving lord?—
  I am asham'd that women are so simple
  To offer war where they should kneel for peace,
  Or seek for rule, supremacy, and sway,
  When they are bound to serve, love, and obey.
  Why are our bodies soft, and weak, and smooth,
  Unapt to toil and trouble in the world,
  But that our soft conditions and our hearts
  Should well agree with our external parts?
  Come, come, you froward and unable worms!
  My mind hath been as big as one of yours,
  My heart as great, my reason haply more,
  To bandy word for word and frown for frown;
  But now I see our lances are but straws,
  Our strength as weak, our weakness past compare,
  That seeming to be most which we indeed least are.
  Then vail your stomachs, for it is no boot,

And place your hands below your husband's foot:
In token of which duty, if he please,
My hand is ready; may it do him ease.

PETRUCHIO. Why, there's a wench! Come on, and kiss me, Kate.

LUCENTIO. Well, go thy ways, old lad, for thou shalt ha 't.

VINCENTIO. 'Tis a good hearing when children are toward.

LUCENTIO. But a harsh hearing when women are froward.

PETRUCHIO. Come, Kate, we'll to bed.
We three are married, but you two are sped.
'Twas I won the wager, (*To Lucentio*) though you hit the white;
And, being a winner, God give you good night!

Exeunt Petruchio and Katharina

HORTENSIO. Now, go thy ways; thou hast tam'd a curst shrew.

LUCENTIO. 'Tis a wonder, by your leave, she will be tam'd so.

Exeunt

ALL'S WELL THAT ENDS WELL

ALL'S WELL THAT ENDS WELL

CAST OF CHARACTERS

King of France
Duke of Florence
Bertram, Count of Rousillon
Lafeu, an old Lord
Parolles, a follower of Bertram
Steward to the Countess of Rousillon
Lavache, a Clown in the Household
A Page

Countess of Rousillon, Mother to Bertram
Helena, a Gentlewoman protected by the Countess
An Old Widow of Florence
Diana, Daughter to the Widow

Violenta }
Mariana } Neighbours and Friends to the Widow

Lords, Officers, Soldiers, &c., French and Florentine.

SCENE

Rousillon, Paris, Florence, Marseilles

ALL'S WELL THAT ENDS WELL

ACT ONE

SCENE ONE

Rousillon. A Room in the Countess's Palace.

Enter Bertram, the Countess of Rousillon, Helena, and Lafeu, all in black

COUNTESS. In delivering my son from me, I bury a second husband.

BERTRAM. And I, in going, madam, weep o'er my father's death anew; but I must attend his Majesty's command, to whom I am now in ward, evermore in subjection.

LAFEU. You shall find of the king a husband, madam; you, sir, a father. He that so generally is at all times good, must of necessity hold his virtue to you, whose worthiness would stir it up where it wanted rather than lack it where there is such abundance.

COUNTESS. What hope is there of his Majesty's amendment?

LAFEU. He hath abandoned his physicians, madam; under whose practices he hath persecuted time with hope, and finds no other advantage in the process but only the losing of hope by time.

COUNTESS. This young gentlewoman had a father,—O, that 'had'! how sad a passage 'tis!—whose skill was almost as great as his honesty; had it stretched so far, would have made nature immortal, and death should have play for lack of work. Would, for the king's sake, he were living! I think it would be the death of the king's disease.

LAFEU. How called you the man you speak of, madam?

COUNTESS. He was famous, sir, in his profession, and it was his great right to be so: Gerard de Narbon.

LAFEU. He was excellent indeed, madam: the king very
lately spoke of him admiringly and mourningly. He was
skilful enough to have lived still, if knowledge could be set
up against mortality.

BERTRAM. What is it, my good lord, the king languishes of?

LAFEU. A fistula, my lord.

BERTRAM. I heard not of it before.

LAFEU. I would it were not notorious. Was this gentlewoman the daughter of Gerard de Narbon?

COUNTESS. His sole child, my lord; and bequeathed to my
overlooking. I have those hopes of her good that her education promises: her dispositions she inherits, which
makes fair gifts fairer; for where an unclean mind carries
virtuous qualities, there commendations go with pity; they
are virtues and traitors too: in her they are the better for
their simpleness; she derives her honesty and achieves her
goodness.

LAFEU. Your commendations, madam, get from her tears.

COUNTESS. 'Tis the best brine a maiden can season her praise
in. The remembrance of her father never approaches her
heart but the tyranny of her sorrows takes all livelihood
from her cheek. No more of this, Helena, go to, no more;
lest it be rather thought you affect a sorrow, than have it.

HELENA. I do affect a sorrow indeed, but I have it too.

LAFEU. Moderate lamentation is the right of the dead, excessive grief the enemy to the living.

HELENA. If the living be enemy to the grief, the excess
makes it soon mortal.

BERTRAM. Madam, I desire your holy wishes.

LAFEU. How understand we that?

COUNTESS. Be thou blest, Bertram; and succeed thy father
In manners, as in shape! Thy blood and virtue
Contend for empire in thee; and thy goodness
Share with thy birthright! Love all, trust a few,
Do wrong to none: be able for thine enemy
Rather in power than use, and keep thy friend
Under thy own life's key: be check'd for silence,
But never tax'd for speech. What heaven more will
That thee may furnish, and my prayers pluck down,
Fall on thy head! Farewell, my lord;
'Tis an unseason'd courtier; good my lord,
Advise him.

LAFEU. He cannot want the best
That shall attend his love.

COUNTESS. Heaven bless him! Farewell, Bertram. *Exit*

BERTRAM. (*To Helena*) The best wishes that can be forged
in your thoughts be servants to you! Be comfortable to my
mother, your mistress, and make much of her.

LAFEU. Farewell, pretty lady: you must hold the credit of
your father. *Exeunt Bertram and Lafeu*

HELENA. O! were that all. I think not on my father;
And these great tears grace his remembrance more
Than those I shed for him. What was he like?
I have forgot him: my imagination
Carries no favour in 't but Bertram's.
I am undone: there is no living, none,
If Bertram be away. It were all one
That I should love a bright particular star
And think to wed it, he is so above me:
In his bright radiance and collateral light
Must I be comforted, not in his sphere.
The ambition in my love thus plagues itself:
The hind that would be mated by the lion
Must die for love. 'Twas pretty, though a plague,
To see him every hour; to sit and draw
His arched brows, his hawking eye, his curls,
In our heart's table; heart too capable
Of every line and trick of his sweet favour:
But now he 's gone, and my idolatrous fancy
Must sanctify his reliques. Who comes here?
One that goes with him; I love him for his sake;
And yet I know him a notorious liar,
Think him a great way fool, solely a coward;
Yet these fix'd evils sit so fit in him,
That they take place, when virtue's steely bones
Look bleak in the cold wind: withal, full oft we see
Cold wisdom waiting on superfluous folly.

Enter Parolles

PAROLLES. Save you, fair queen!

HELENA. And you, monarch!

PAROLLES. No.

HELENA. And no.

PAROLLES. Are you meditating on virginity?

HELENA. Ay. You have some stain of soldier in you; let me

ask you a question. Man is enemy to virginity;
how may we barricade it against him?

PAROLLES. Keep him out.

HELENA. But he assails; and our virginity, though valiant in
the defence, yet is weak. Unfold to us some warlike resistance.

PAROLLES. There is none: man, sitting down before you, will
undermine you and blow you up.

HELENA. Bless our poor virginity from underminers and
blowers up! Is there no military policy, how virgins might
blow up men?

PAROLLES. Virginity being blown down, man will quicklier
be blown up: marry, in blowing him down again, with the
breach yourselves made, you lose your city. It is not politic
in the commonwealth of nature to preserve virginity. Loss
of virginity is rational increase, and there was never virgin
got till virginity was first lost. That you were made of is
metal to make virgins. Virginity, by being once lost, may
be ten times found: by being ever kept, it is ever lost. 'Tis
too cold a companion: away with 't!

HELENA. I will stand for 't a little, though therefore I die a
virgin.

PAROLLES. There's little can be said in 't; 'tis against the rule
of nature. To speak on the part of virginity is to accuse
your mothers, which is most infallible disobedience. He
that hangs himself is a virgin: virginity murders itself, and
should be buried in highways, out of all sanctified limit, as
a desperate offendress against nature. Virginity breeds
mites, much like a cheese, consumes itself to the very paring, and so dies with feeding his own stomach. Besides,
virginity is peevish, proud, idle, made of self-love, which
is the most inhibited sin in the canon. Keep it not; you cannot choose but lose by 't! Out with 't! within the year it
will make itself two, which is a goodly increase, and the
principal itself not much the worse. Away with 't!

HELENA. How might one do, sir, to lose it to her own liking?

PAROLLES. Let me see: marry, ill, to like him that ne'er it
likes. 'Tis a commodity that will lose the gloss with lying;
the longer kept, the less worth: off with 't, while 'tis vendible; answer the time of request. Virginity, like an old
courtier, wears her cap out of fashion; richly suited, but
unsuitable: just like the brooch and the tooth-pick, which

wear not now. Your date is better in your pie and your porridge than in your cheek: and your virginity, your old virginity, is like one of our French withered pears; it looks ill, it eats drily; marry, 'tis a withered pear; it was formerly better; marry, yet 'tis a withered pear. Will you anything with it?

HELENA. Not my virginity yet.
There shall your master have a thousand loves,
A mother, and a mistress, and a friend,
A phœnix, captain, and an enemy,
A guide, a goddess, and a sovereign,
A counsellor, a traitress, and a dear;
His humble ambition, proud humility,
His jarring concord, and his discord dulcet,
His faith, his sweet disaster; with a world
Of pretty, fond, adoptious christendoms,
That blinking Cupid gossips. Now shall he—
I know not what he shall. God send him well!
The court's a learning-place, and he is one—

PAROLLES. What one, i' faith?

HELENA. That I wish well. 'Tis pity—

PAROLLES. What's pity?

HELENA. That wishing well had not a body in 't,
Which might be felt; that we, the poorer born,
Whose baser stars do shut us up in wishes,
Might with effects of them follow our friends,
And show what we alone must think, which never
Returns us thanks.

Enter a Page

PAGE. Monsieur Parolles, my lord calls for you.

PAROLLES. Little Helen, farewell: if I can remember thee, I will think of thee at court.

HELENA. Monsieur Parolles, you were born under a charitable star.

PAROLLES. Under Mars, I.

HELENA. I especially think, under Mars.

PAROLLES. Why under Mars?

HELENA. The wars have so kept you under that you must needs be born under Mars.

PAROLLES. When he was predominant.

HELENA. When he was retrograde, I think rather.

PAROLLES. Why think you so?

HELENA. You go so much backward when you fight.

PAROLLES. That's for advantage.

HELENA. So is running away, when fear proposes the safety:
but the composition that your valour and fear makes in
you is a virtue of a good wing, and I like the wear well.

PAROLLES. I am so full of businesses I cannot answer thee
acutely. I will return perfect courtier; in the which, my instruction shall serve to naturalize thee, so thou wilt be
capable of a courtier's counsel, and understand what advice shall thrust upon thee; else thou diest in thine un-
thankfulness, and thine ignorance makes thee away: farewell. When thou hast leisure, say thy prayers; when thou
hast none, remember thy friends. Get thee a good husband, and use him as he uses thee: so, farewell.   *Exit*

HELENA. Our remedies oft in ourselves do lie
Which we ascribe to heaven: the fated sky
Gives us free scope; only doth backward pull
Our slow designs when we ourselves are dull.
What power is it which mounts my love so high;
That makes me see, and cannot feed mine eye?
The mightiest space in fortune nature brings
To join like likes, and kiss like native things.
Impossible be strange attempts to those
That weigh their pains in sense, and do suppose
What hath been cannot be: who ever strove
To show her merit, that did miss her love?
The king's disease,—my project may deceive me,
But my intents are fix'd and will not leave me.   *Exit*

SCENE TWO

Paris. A Room in the King's Palace.

*Flourish of Cornets. Enter the King of France, with letters;
Lords and Others Attending.*

KING. The Florentines and Senoys are by the ears;
Have fought with equal fortune, and continue
A braving war.

FIRST LORD.   So 'tis reported, sir.

KING. Nay, 'tis most credible: we here receive it
A certainty, vouch'd from our cousin Austria,

With caution that the Florentine will move us
For speedy aid; wherein our dearest friend
Prejudicates the business, and would seem
To have us make denial.

FIRST LORD.   His love and wisdom,
Approv'd so to your Majesty, may plead
For amplest credence.

KING.   He hath arm'd our answer,
And Florence is denied before he comes:
Yet, for our gentlemen that mean to see
The Tuscan service, freely have they leave
To stand on either part.

SECOND LORD.   It well may serve
A nursery to our gentry, who are sick
For breathing and exploit.

KING.   What 's he comes here?
Enter Bertram, Lafeu, and Parolles

FIRST LORD. It is the Count Rousillon, my good lord,
Young Bertram.

KING.   Youth, thou bear'st thy father's face;
Frank nature, rather curious than in haste,
Hath well compos'd thee. Thy father's moral parts
Mayst thou inherit too! Welcome to Paris.

BERTRAM. My thanks and duty are your Majesty's.

KING. I would I had that corporal soundness now,
As when thy father and myself in friendship
First tried our soldiership! He did look far
Into the service of the time and was
Discipled of the bravest: he lasted long;
But on us both did haggish age steal on,
And wore us out of act. It much repairs me
To talk of your good father. In his youth
He had the wit which I can well observe
To-day in our young lords; but they may jest
Till their own scorn return to them unnoted
Ere they can hide their levity in honour.
So like a courtier, contempt nor bitterness
Were in his pride or sharpness; if they were,
His equal had awak'd them; and his honour,
Clock to itself, knew the true minute when
Exception bid him speak, and at this time
His tongue obey'd his hand: who were below him

He us'd as creatures of another place,
And bow'd his eminent top to their low ranks,
Making them proud of his humility,
In their poor praise he humbled. Such a man
Might be a copy to these younger times,
Which, follow'd well, would demonstrate them now
But goers backward.

BERTRAM.   His good remembrance, sir,
Lies richer in your thoughts than on his tomb;
So in approof lives not his epitaph
As in your royal speech.

KING. Would I were with him! He would always say,—
Methinks I hear him now: his plausive words
He scatter'd not in ears, but grafted them,
To grow there and to bear. 'Let me not live,'—
Thus his good melancholy oft began,
On the catastrophe and heel of pastime,
When it was out,—'Let me not live,' quoth he,
'After my flame lacks oil, to be the snuff
Of younger spirits, whose apprehensive senses
All but new things disdain; whose judgments are
Mere fathers of their garments; whose constancies
Expire before their fashions.' This he wish'd:
I, after him, do after him wish too,
Since I nor wax nor honey can bring home,
I quickly were dissolved from my hive,
To give some labourers room.

SECOND LORD.   You are lov'd, sir;
They that least lend it you shall lack you first.

KING. I fill a place, I know 't. How long is 't, count,
Since the physician at your father's died?
He was much fam'd.

BERTRAM.   Some six months since, my lord.

KING. If he were living, I would try him yet:
Lend me an arm: the rest have worn me out
With several applications: nature and sickness
Debate it at their leisure. Welcome, count;
My son 's no dearer.

BERTRAM.   Thank your Majesty.   *Exeunt. Flourish*

SCENE THREE

Rousillon. A Room in the Countess's Palace.

Enter Countess, Steward, and Clown

COUNTESS. I will now hear: what say you of this gentle-woman?

STEWARD. Madam, the care I have had to even your content, I wish might be found in the calendar of my past endeavours; for then we wound our modesty and make foul the clearness of our deservings, when of ourselves we publish them.

COUNTESS. What does this knave here? Get you gone, sirrah: the complaints I have heard of you I do not all believe: 'tis my slowness that I do not; for I know you lack not folly to commit them, and have ability enough to make such knaveries yours.

CLOWN. 'Tis not unknown to you, madam, I am a poor fellow.

COUNTESS. Well, sir.

CLOWN. No, madam, 'tis not so well that I am poor, though many of the rich are damned. But, if I may have your ladyship's good will to go to the world, Isbel the woman and I will do as we may.

COUNTESS. Wilt thou needs be a beggar?

CLOWN. I do beg your good will in this case.

COUNTESS. In what case?

CLOWN. In Isbel's case and mine own. Service is no heritage; and I think I shall never have the blessing of God till I have issue o' my body, for they say barnes are blessings.

COUNTESS. Tell me thy reason why thou wilt marry.

CLOWN. My poor body, madam, requires it: I am driven on by the flesh; and he must needs go that the devil drives.

COUNTESS. Is this all your worship's reason?

CLOWN. Faith, madam, I have other holy reasons, such as they are.

COUNTESS. May the world know them?

CLOWN. I have been, madam, a wicked creature, as you and all flesh and blood are; and, indeed, I do marry that I may repent.

COUNTESS. Thy marriage, sooner than thy wickedness.

CLOWN. I am out o' friends, madam; and I hope to have friends for my wife's sake.

COUNTESS. Such friends are thine enemies, knave.

CLOWN. You 're shallow, madam, in great friends; for the knaves come to do that for me which I am aweary of. He that ears my land spares my team, and gives me leave to in the crop: if I be his cuckold, he 's my drudge. He that comforts my wife is the cherisher of my flesh and blood; he that cherishes my flesh and blood loves my flesh and blood; he that loves my flesh and blood is my friend: ergo, he that kisses my wife is my friend. If men could be contented to be what they are, there were no fear in marriage; for young Charbon the puritan, and old Poysam the papist, howsome'er their hearts are severed in religion, their heads are both one; they may joul horns together like any deer i' the herd.

COUNTESS. Wilt thou ever be a foul-mouthed and calumnious knave?

CLOWN. A prophet I, madam; and I speak the truth the next way:

> For I the ballad will repeat,
>   Which men full true shall find;
> Your marriage comes by destiny,
>   Your cuckoo sings by kind.

COUNTESS. Get you gone, sir: I 'll talk with you more anon.

STEWARD. May it please you, madam, that he bid Helen come to you: of her I am to speak.

COUNTESS. Sirrah, tell my gentlewoman I would speak with her; Helen I mean.

CLOWN.   Was this fair face the cause, quoth she,
>   Why the Grecians sacked Troy?
>   Fond done, done fond,
>   Was this King Priam's joy?
>   With that she sighed as she stood,
>   With that she sighed as she stood
>   And gave this sentence then;
>   Among nine bad if one be good,
>   Among nine bad if one be good,
>   There 's yet one good in ten.

COUNTESS. What! one good in ten? You corrupt the song, sirrah.

CLOWN. One good woman in ten, madam; which is a purify-
ing o' the song. Would God would serve the world so all
the year! We 'd find no fault with the tithe-woman if I
were the parson. One in ten, quoth a'! An we might have a
good woman born but for every blazing star, or at an earthquake, 'twould mend the lottery well: a man may draw his
heart out ere a' pluck one.

COUNTESS. You 'll be gone, sir knave, and do as I command
you!

CLOWN. That man should be at woman's command, and yet
no hurt done! Though honesty be no puritan, yet it will do
no hurt; it will wear the surplice of humility over the black
gown of a big heart. I am going, forsooth: the business is
for Helen to come hither.   *Exit*

COUNTESS. Well, now.

STEWARD. I know, madam, you love your gentlewoman entirely.

COUNTESS. Faith, I do: her father bequeathed her to me: and
she herself, without other advantage, may lawfully make
title to as much love as she finds: there is more owing her
than is paid, and more shall be paid her than she 'll demand.

STEWARD. Madam, I was very late more near her than I
think she wished me: alone she was, and did communicate
to herself her own words to her own ears; she thought, I
dare vow for her, they touched not any stranger sense. Her
matter was, she loved your son: Fortune, she said, was no
goddess, that had put such difference betwixt their two
estates: Love no god, that would not extend his might,
only where qualities were level; Dian no queen of virgins,
that would suffer her poor knight surprised, without rescue in the first assault or ransom afterward. This she delivered in the most bitter touch of sorrow that e'er I heard
virgin exclaim in; which I held my duty speedily to acquaint you withal, sithence in the loss that may happen, it
concerns you something to know it.

COUNTESS. You have discharged this honestly: keep it to
yourself. Many likelihoods informed me of this before,
which hung so tottering in the balance that I could neither
believe nor misdoubt. Pray you, leave me: stall this in your
bosom; and I thank you for your honest care. I will speak
with you further anon.   *Exit Steward*

Enter Helena

Even so it was with me when I was young:
      If ever we are nature's, these are ours; this thorn
Doth to our rose of youth rightly belong;
      Our blood to us, this to our blood is born:
It is the show and seal of nature's truth,
Where love's strong passion is impress'd in youth:
By our remembrances of days foregone,
Such were our faults; or then we thought them none.
Her eye is sick on 't: I observe her now.

HELENA. What is your pleasure, madam?

COUNTESS.   You know, Helen,
I am a mother to you.

HELENA. Mine honourable mistress.

COUNTESS.   Nay, a mother:
Why not a mother? When I said, 'a mother,'
Methought you saw a serpent: what 's in 'mother'
That you start at it? I say, I am your mother;
And put you in the catalogue of those
That were enwombed mine: 'tis often seen
Adoption strives with nature, and choice breeds
A native slip to us from foreign seeds;
You ne'er oppress'd me with a mother's groan,
Yet I express to you a mother's care.
God's mercy, maiden! does it curd thy blood
To say I am thy mother? What 's the matter,
That this distemper'd messenger of wet,
The many-colour'd Iris, rounds thine eye?
Why? that you are my daughter?

HELENA.   That I am not.

COUNTESS. I say, I am your mother.

HELENA.   Pardon, madam;
The Count Rousillon cannot be my brother:
I am from humble, he from honour'd name;
No note upon my parents, his all noble:
My master, my dear lord he is; and I
His servant live, and will his vassal die.
He must not be my brother.

COUNTESS.   Nor I your mother?

HELENA. You are my mother, madam: would you were,—
So that my lord your son were not my brother,—
Indeed my mother! or were you both our mothers,

I care no more for than I do for heaven,
So I were not his sister. Can 't no other,
But, I your daughter, he must be my brother?

COUNTESS. Yes, Helen, you might be my daughter-in-law:
God shield you mean it not! daughter and mother
So strive upon your pulse. What, pale again?
My fear hath catch'd your fondness: now I see
The mystery of your loneliness, and find
Your salt tears' head: now to all sense 'tis gross
You love my son: invention is asham'd
Against the proclamation of thy passion,
To say thou dost not: therefore tell me true;
But tell me then, 'tis so; for, look, thy cheeks
Confess it, th' one to th' other; and thine eyes
See it so grossly shown in thy behaviours
That in their kind they speak it: only sin
And hellish obstinacy tie thy tongue,
That truth should be suspected. Speak, is 't so?
If it be so, you have wound a goodly clew;
If it be not, forswear 't: howe'er, I charge thee,
As heaven shall work in me for thine avail,
To tell me truly.

HELENA.   Good madam, pardon me!

COUNTESS. Do you love my son?

HELENA.   Your pardon, noble mistress!

COUNTESS. Love you my son?

HELENA.   Do not you love him, madam?

COUNTESS. Go not about; my love hath in 't a bond
Whereof the world takes note: come, come, disclose
The state of your affection, for your passions
Have to the full appeach'd.

HELENA.   Then, I confess,
Here on my knee, before high heaven and you,
That before you, and next unto high heaven,
I love your son.
My friends were poor, but honest; so 's my love:
Be not offended, for it hurts not him
That he is lov'd of me: I follow him not
By any token of presumptuous suit;
Nor would I have him till I do deserve him;
Yet never know how that desert should be.
I know I love in vain, strive against hope;

Yet, in this captious and intenible sieve
I still pour in the waters of my love,
And lack not to lose still. Thus, Indian-like,
Religious in mine error, I adore
The sun, that looks upon his worshipper,
But knows of him no more. My dearest madam,
Let not your hate encounter with my love
For loving where you do: but, if yourself,
Whose aged honour cites a virtuous youth,
Did ever in so true a flame of liking
Wish chastely and love dearly, that your Dian
Was both herself and Love; O! then, give pity
To her, whose state is such that cannot choose
But lend and give where she is sure to lose;
That seeks not to find that her search implies,
But, riddle-like, lives sweetly where she dies.

COUNTESS. Had you not lately an intent, speak truly,
    To go to Paris?

HELENA.   Madam, I had.

COUNTESS.   Wherefore? tell true.

HELENA. I will tell truth; by grace itself I swear.
You know my father left me some prescriptions
Of rare and prov'd effects, such as his reading
And manifest experience had collected
For general sovereignty; and that he will'd me
In heedfull'st reservation to bestow them,
As notes whose faculties inclusive were
More than they were in note. Amongst the rest,
There is a remedy, approv'd, set down
To cure the desperate languishings whereof
The king is render'd lost.

COUNTESS.   This was your motive
    For Paris, was it? Speak.

HELENA. My lord your son made me to think of this;
Else Paris, and the medicine, and the king,
Had from the conversation of my thoughts
Haply been absent then.

COUNTESS.   But think you, Helen,
If you should tender your supposed aid,
He would receive it? He and his physicians
Are of a mind; he, that they cannot help him,
They, that they cannot help. How shall they credit

A poor unlearned virgin, when the schools,
Embowell'd of their doctrine, have left off
The danger to itself?

HELENA.   There 's something in 't,
More than my father's skill, which was the great'st
Of his profession, that his good receipt
Shall for my legacy be sanctified
By the luckiest stars in heaven: and, would your honour
But give me leave to try success, I 'd venture
The well-lost life of mine on his Grace's cure,
By such a day, and hour.

COUNTESS.   Dost thou believe 't?

HELENA. Ay, madam, knowingly.

COUNTESS. Why, Helen, thou shalt have my leave and love,
Means, and attendants, and my loving greetings
To those of mine in court. I 'll stay at home
And pray God's blessing into thy attempt.
Be gone to-morrow; and be sure of this,
What I can help thee to thou shalt not miss.   *Exeunt*

ACT TWO

SCENE ONE

Paris. A Room in the King's Palace.

Flourish. Enter the King, with divers young Lords taking leave for the Florentine War; Bertram, Parolles, and Attendants

KING. Farewell, young lords: these warlike principles
    Do not throw from you: and you, my lords, farewell;
    Share the advice betwixt you; if both gain, all
    The gift doth stretch itself as 'tis receiv'd,
    And is enough for both.

FIRST LORD.   'Tis our hope, sir,
    After well enter'd soldiers, to return
    And find your Grace in health.

KING. No, no, it cannot be; and yet my heart
    Will not confess he owes the malady
    That doth my life besiege. Farewell, young lords;
    Whether I live or die, be you the sons
    Of worthy Frenchmen: let higher Italy—
    Those bated that inherit but the fall
    Of the last monarchy—see that you come
    Not to woo honour, but to wed it; when
    The bravest questant shrinks, find what you seek,
    That fame may cry you loud: I say, farewell.

SECOND LORD. Health, at your bidding, serve your Majesty!

KING. Those girls of Italy, take heed of them:
    They say, our French lack language to deny
    If they demand: beware of being captives,
    Before your serve.

BOTH LORDS.   Our hearts receive your warnings.

KING. Farewell. Come hither to me.   *Exit, attende[e]*

FIRST LORD. O my sweet lord, that you will stay behind us!

PAROLLES. 'Tis not his fault, the spark.

SECOND LORD.   O! 'tis brave wars.

PAROLLES. Most admirable: I have seen those wars.

BERTRAM. I am commanded here, and kept a coil with
'Too young,' and 'the next year,' and ' 'tis too early.'

PAROLLES. An thy mind stand to 't, boy, steal away bravely.

BERTRAM. I shall stay here the forehorse to a smock,
Creaking my shoes on the plain masonry,
Till honour be bought up and no sword worn
But one to dance with! By heaven! I 'll steal away.

FIRST LORD. There 's honour in the theft.

PAROLLES.   Commit it, count.

SECOND COUNT. I am your accessory; and so farewell.

BERTRAM. I grow to you, and our parting is a tortured body.

FIRST LORD. Farewell, captain.

SECOND LORD. Sweet Monsieur Parolles!

PAROLLES. Noble heroes, my sword and yours are kin. Good
sparks and lustrous, a word, good metals: you shall find in
the regiment of the Spinii, one Captain Spurio, with his
cicatrice, an emblem of war, here on his sinister cheek: it
was this very sword entrenched it: say to him, I live, and
observe his reports for me.

SECOND LORD. We shall, noble captain.   *Exeunt Lords*

PAROLLES. Mars dote on you for his novices! What will ye
do?

BERTRAM. Stay; the king.

Re-enter King; Parolles and Bertram retire

PAROLLES. Use a more spacious ceremony to the noble lords;
you have restrained yourself within the list of too cold an
adieu: be more expressive to them; for they wear themselves in the cap of the time, there do muster true gait,
eat, speak, and move under the influence of the most received star; and though the devil lead the measure, such
are to be followed. After them, and take a more dilated
farewell.

BERTRAM. And I will do so.

PAROLLES. Worthy fellows; and like to prove most sinewy
swordmen.   *Exeunt Bertram and Parolles*

Enter Lafeu

LAFEU. (*Kneeling*) Pardon, my lord, for me and for my tidings.

KING. I 'll fee thee to stand up.

LAFEU. Then here 's a man stands that has brought his par-
don.
  I would you had kneel'd, my lord, to ask me mercy,
  And that at my bidding you could so stand up.

KING. I would I had; so I had broke thy pate,
  And ask'd thee mercy for 't.

LAFEU. Good faith, across: but, my good lord, 'tis thus;
  Will you be cur'd of your infirmity?

KING. No.

LAFEU. O! will you eat no grapes, my royal fox?
  Yes, but you will my noble grapes an if
  My royal fox could reach them. I have seen a medicine
  That 's able to breathe life into a stone,
  Quicken a rock, and make you dance canary
  With spritely fire and motion; whose simple touch
  Is powerful to araise King Pepin, nay,
  To give great Charlemain a pen in 's hand
  And write to her a love-line.

KING.   What 'her' is this?

LAFEU. Why, Doctor She. My lord, there 's one arriv'd
  If you will see her: now, by my faith and honour,
  If seriously I may convey my thoughts
  In this my light deliverance, I have spoke
  With one, that in her sex, her years, profession,
  Wisdom, and constancy, hath amaz'd me more
  Than I dare blame my weakness. Will you see her,
  For that is her demand, and know her business?
  That done, laugh well at me.

KING.   Now, good Lafeu,
  Bring in the admiration, that we with thee
  May spend our wonder too, or take off thine
  By wondering how thou took'st it.

LAFEU.   Nay, I 'll fit you,
  And not be all day neither.   *Exit*

KING. Thus he his special nothing ever prologues.
                Re-enter Lafeu, with Helena

LAFEU. Nay, come your ways.

KING.   This haste hath wings indeed.

LAFEU. Nay, come your ways;
  This is his Majesty, say your mind to him:
  A traitor you do look like; but such traitors
  His Majesty seldom fears: I am Cressid's uncle,

That dare leave two together. Fare you well.   • *Exit*

KING. Now, fair one, does your business follow us?

HELENA. Ay, my good lord.
      Gerard de Narbon was my father;
      In what he did profess well found.

KING.   I knew him.

HELENA. The rather will I spare my praises towards him;
      Knowing him is enough. On 's bed of death
      Many receipts he gave me; chiefly one,
      Which, as the dearest issue of his practice,
      And of his old experience the only darling,
      He bade me store up as a triple eye,
      Safer than mine own two, more dear. I have so;
      And, hearing your high Majesty is touch'd
      With that malignant cause wherein the honour
      Of my dear father's gift stands chief in power,
      I come to tender it and my appliance,
      With all bound humbleness.

KING.   We thank you, maiden;
      But may not be so credulous of cure,
      When our most learned doctors leave us, and
      The congregated college have concluded
      That labouring art can never ransom nature
      From her inaidable estate; I say we must not
      So stain our judgment, or corrupt our hope,
      To prostitute our past-cure malady
      To empirics, or to dissever so
      Our great self and our credit, to esteem
      A senseless help when help past sense we deem.

HELENA. My duty then, shall pay me for my pains:
      I will no more enforce mine office on you;
      Humbly entreating from your royal thoughts
      A modest one, to bear me back again.

KING. I cannot give thee less, to be call'd grateful.
      Thou thought'st to help me, and such thanks I give
      As one near death to those that wish him live;
      But what at full I know, thou know'st no part,
      I knowing all my peril, thou no art.

HELENA. What I can do can do no hurt to try,
      Since you set up your rest 'gainst remedy.
      He that of greatest works is finisher
      Oft does them by the weakest minister:

So holy writ in babes hath judgment shown,
When judges have been babes; great floods have flown
From simple sources; and great seas have dried
When miracles have by the greatest been denied.
Oft expectation fails, and most oft there
Where most it promises; and oft it hits
Where hope is coldest and despair most fits.

KING. I must not hear thee: fare thee well, kind maid.
Thy pains, not us'd, must by thyself be paid:
Proffers not took reap thanks for their reward.

HELENA. Inspired merit so by breath is barr'd.
It is not so with Him that all things knows,
As 'tis with us that square our guess by shows;
But most it is presumption in us when
The help of heaven we count the act of men.
Dear sir, to my endeavours give consent;
Of heaven, not me, make an experiment.
I am not an impostor that proclaim
Myself against the level of mine aim;
But know I think, and think I know most sure,
My art is not past power nor you past cure.

KING. Art thou so confident? Within what space
Hop'st thou my cure?

HELENA.   The great'st grace lending grace,
Ere twice the horses of the sun shall bring
Their fiery torcher his diurnal ring,
Ere twice in murk and occidental damp
Moist Hesperus hath quench'd his sleepy lamp,
Or four and twenty times the pilot's glass
Hath told the thievish minutes how they pass,
What is infirm from your sound parts shall fly,
Health shall live free, and sickness freely die.

KING. Upon thy certainty and confidence
What dar'st thou venture?

HELENA.   Tax of impudence,
A strumpet's boldness, a divulged shame,
Traduc'd by odious ballads: my maiden's name
Sear'd otherwise; nay worse—if worse—extended
With vilest torture let my life be ended.

KING. Methinks in thee some blessed spirit doth speak,
His powerful sound within an organ weak;
And what impossibility would slay

In common sense, sense saves another way.
Thy life is dear; for all that life can rate
Worth name of life in thee hath estimate;
Youth, beauty, wisdom, courage, virtue, all
That happiness and prime can happy call:
Thou this to hazard needs must intimate
Skill infinite or monstrous desperate.
Sweet practiser, thy physic I will try,
That ministers thine own death if I die.

HELENA. If I break time, or flinch in property
Of what I spoke, unpitied let me die,
And well deserv'd. Not helping, death 's my fee;
But, if I help, what do you promise me?

KING. Make thy demand.

HELENA.   But will you make it even?

KING. Ay, be my sceptre, and my hopes of heaven.

HELENA. Then shalt thou give me with thy kingly hand
What husband in thy power I will command.
Exempted be from me the arrogance
To choose from forth the royal blood of France,
My low and humble name to propagate
With any branch or image of thy state;
But such a one, thy vassal, whom I know
Is free for me to ask, thee to bestow.

KING. Here is my hand; the premises observ'd,
Thy will by my performance shall be serv'd:
So make the choice of thy own time, for I,
Thy resolv'd patient, on thee still rely.
More should I question thee, and more I must,
Though more to know could not be more to trust,
From whence thou cam'st, how tended on; but rest
Unquestion'd welcome and undoubted blest.
Give me some help here, ho! If thou proceed
As high as word, my deed shall match thy deed.
                              Flourish. Exeunt

SCENE TWO

Rousillon. A Room in the Countess's Palace.

Enter Countess and Clown

COUNTESS. Come on, sir; I shall now put you to the height of your breeding.

CLOWN. I will show myself highly fed and lowly taught. I know my business is but to the court.

COUNTESS. To the court! Why, what place make you special, when you put off that with such contempt? 'But to the court'!

CLOWN. Truly, madam, if God have lent a man any manners, he may easily put it off at court: he that cannot make a leg, put off 's cap, kiss his hand, and say nothing, has neither leg, hands, lip, nor cap; and indeed such a fellow, to say precisely, were not for the court. But, for me, I have an answer will serve all men.

COUNTESS. Marry, that 's a bountiful answer that fits all questions.

CLOWN. It is like a barber's chair that fits all buttocks; the pin-buttock, the quatch-buttock, the brawn-buttock, or any buttock.

COUNTESS. Will your answer serve fit to all questions?

CLOWN. As fit as ten groats is for the hand of an attorney, as your French crown for your taffeta punk, as Tib's rush for Tom's forefinger, as a pancake for Shrove-Tuesday, a morris for May-day, as the nail to his hole, the cuckold to his horn, as a scolding quean to a wrangling knave, as the nun's lip to the friar's mouth; nay, as the pudding to his skin.

COUNTESS. Have you, I say, an answer of such fitness for all questions?

CLOWN. From below your duke to beneath your constable, it will fit any question.

COUNTESS. It must be an answer of most monstrous size that must fit all demands.

CLOWN. But a trifle neither, in good faith, if the learned should speak truth of it. Here it is, and all that belongs

to 't: ask me if I am a courtier; it shall do you no harm to
learn.

COUNTESS. To be young again, if we could. I will be a fool in
question, hoping to be the wiser by your answer. I pray
you, sir, are you a courtier?

CLOWN. O Lord, sir! There 's a simple putting off. More,
more, a hundred of them.

COUNTESS. Sir, I am a poor friend of yours, that loves you.

CLOWN. O Lord, sir! Thick, thick, spare not me.

COUNTESS. I think, sir, you can eat none of this homely meat.

CLOWN. O Lord, sir! Nay, put me to 't, I warrant you.

COUNTESS. You were lately whipped, sir, as I think.

CLOWN. O Lord, sir! Spare not me.

COUNTESS. Do you cry, 'O Lord, sir!' at your whipping, and
'Spare not me'? Indeed your 'O Lord, sir!' is very sequent
to your whipping: you would answer very well to a whipping, if you were but bound to 't.

CLOWN. I ne'er had worse luck in my life in my 'O Lord, sir!'
I see things may serve long, but not serve ever.

COUNTESS. I play the noble housewife with the time,
To entertain 't so merrily with a fool.

CLOWN. O Lord, sir! why, there 't serves well again.

COUNTESS. An end, sir: to your business. Give Helen this,
And urge her to a present answer back:
Commend me to my kinsmen and my son.
This is not much.

CLOWN. Not much commendation to them.

COUNTESS. Not much employment for you: you understand
me?

CLOWN. Most fruitfully: I am there before my legs.

COUNTESS. Haste you again.   *Exeunt severally*

SCENE THREE

Paris. A Room in the King's Palace.

Enter Bertram, Lafeu, and Parolles

LAFEU. They say miracles are past; and we have our philo-
sophical persons, to make modern and familiar, things su-
pernatural and causeless. Hence is it that we make trifles
of terrors, ensconcing ourselves into seeming knowledge,

when we should submit ourselves to an unknown fear.

PAROLLES. Why, 'tis the rarest argument of wonder that hath shot out in our latter times.

BERTRAM. And so 'tis.

LAFEU. To be relinquished of the artists,—

PAROLLES. So I say.

LAFEU. Both of Galen and Paracelsus.

PAROLLES. So I say.

LAFEU. Of all the learned and authentic fellows,—

PAROLLES. Right; so I say.

LAFEU. That gave him out incurable,—

PAROLLES. Why, there 'tis; so say I too.

LAFEU. Not to be helped,—

PAROLLES. Right; as 'twere, a man assured of a—

LAFEU. Uncertain life, and sure death.

PAROLLES. Just, you say well: so would I have said.

LAFEU. I may truly say it is a novelty to the world.

PAROLLES. It is, indeed: if you will have it in showing, you shall read it in—what do you call there—

LAFEU. A showing of a heavenly effect in an earthly actor.

PAROLLES. That 's it I would have said; the very same.

LAFEU. Why, your dolphin is not lustier: 'fore me, I speak in respect—

PAROLLES. Nay, 'tis strange, tis very strange, that is the brief and the tedious of it; and he is of a most facinorous spirit, that will not acknowledge it to be the—

LAFEU. Very hand of heaven—

PAROLLES. Ay, so I say.

LAFEU. In a most weak and debile minister, great power, great transcendence: which should, indeed, give us a further use to be made than alone the recovery of the king, as to be generally thankful.

PAROLLES. I would have said it; you say well.
    Here comes the king.

Enter King, Helena, and Attendants

LAFEU. Lustig, as the Dutchman says: I 'll like a maid the better, whilst I have a tooth in my head. Why, he 's able to lead her a coranto.

PAROLLES. Mort du vinaigre! Is not this Helen?

LAFEU. 'Fore God, I think so.

KING. Go, call before me all the lords in court.
                                    Exit an Attendant

Sit, my preserver, by thy patient's side:
And with this healthful hand, whose banish'd sense
Thou hast repeal'd, a second time receive
The confirmation of my promis'd gift,
Which but attends thy naming.

Enter several Lords

Fair maid, send forth thine eye: this youthful parcel
Of noble bachelors stand at my bestowing,
O'er whom both sovereign power and father's voice
I have to use: thy frank election make;
Thou hast power to choose, and they none to forsake.

HELENA. To each of you one fair and virtuous mistress
Fall, when Love please! marry, to each, but one.

LAFEU. I 'd give bay Curtal, and his furniture,
My mouth no more were broken than these boys'
And writ as little beard.

KING.   Peruse them well:
Not one of those but had a noble father.

HELENA. Gentlemen,
Heaven hath through me restor'd the king to health.

ALL. We understand it, and thank heaven for you.

HELENA. I am a simple maid; and therein wealthiest
That I protest I simply am a maid.
Please it your Majesty, I have done already:
The blushes in my cheeks thus whisper me,
'We blush, that thou shouldst choose; but, be refus'd,
Let the white death sit on thy cheek for ever;
We 'll ne'er come there again.'

KING.   Make choice; and see,
Who shuns thy love, shuns all his love in me.

HELENA. Now, Dian, from thy altar do I fly,
And to imperial Love, that god most high,
Do my sighs stream. Sir, will you hear my suit?

FIRST LORD. And grant it.

HELENA.   Thanks, sir; all the rest is mute.

LAFEU. I had rather be in this choice than throw ames-ace
for my life.

HELENA. The honour, sir, that flames in your fair eyes,
Before I speak, too threateningly replies:
Love make your fortunes twenty times above
Her that so wishes, and her humble love!

SECOND LORD. No better, if you please.

HELENA.   My wish receive,
 Which great Love grant! and so I take my leave.

LAFEU. Do all they deny her? An they were sons of mine,
 I'd have them whipp'd or I would send them to the Turk
 to make eunuchs of.

HELENA. *(To third Lord)* Be not afraid that I your hand
     should take;
 I'll never do you wrong for your own sake:
 Blessing upon your vows! and in your bed
 Find fairer fortune, if you ever wed!

LAFEU. These boys are boys of ice, they'll none have her:
 sure, they are bastards to the English; the French ne'er
 got 'em.

HELENA. You are too young, too happy, and too good,
 To make yourself a son out of my blood.

FOURTH LORD. Fair one, I think not so.

LAFEU. There's one grape yet. I am sure thy father drunk
 wine. But if thou be'st not an ass, I am a youth of fourteen:
 I have known thee already.

HELENA. *(To Bertram)* I dare not say I take you; but I give
 Me and my service, ever whilst I live,
 Into your guiding power. This is the man.

KING. Why then, young Bertram, take her; she's thy wife.

BERTRAM. My wife, my liege! I shall beseech your Highness
 In such a business give me leave to use
 The help of mine own eyes.

KING.   Know'st thou not, Bertram,
 What she has done for me?

BERTRAM.   Yes, my good lord;
 But never hope to know why I should marry her.

KING. Thou know'st she has rais'd me from my sickly bed.

BERTRAM. But follows it, my lord, to bring me down
 Must answer for your raising? I know her well:
 She had her breeding at my father's charge.
 A poor physician's daughter my wife! Disdain
 Rather corrupt me ever!

KING. 'Tis only title thou disdain'st in her, the which
 I can build up. Strange is it that our bloods,
 Of colour, weight, and heat, pour'd all together,
 Would quite confound distinction, yet stand off
 In differences so mighty. If she be
 All that is virtuous, save what thou dislik'st,

A poor physician's daughter, thou dislik'st
Of virtue for the name; but do not so:
From lowest place when virtuous things proceed,
The place is dignified by the doer's deed:
Where great additions swell 's, and virtue none,
It is a dropsied honour. Good alone
Is good without a name: vileness is so:
The property by what it is should go,
Not by the title. She is young, wise, fair;
In these to nature she 's immediate heir,
And these breed honour: that is honour's scorn
Which challenges itself as honour's born,
And is not like the sire: honours thrive
When rather from our acts we them derive
Than our foregoers. The mere word 's a slave,
Debosh'd on every tomb, on every grave
A lying trophy, and as oft is dumb
Where dust and damn'd oblivion is the tomb
Of honour'd bones indeed. What should be said?
If thou canst like this creature as a maid,
I can create the rest: virtue and she
Is her own dower; honour and wealth from me.

BERTRAM. I cannot love her, nor will strive to do 't.

KING. Thou wrong'st thyself if thou shouldst strive to choose.

HELENA. That you are well restor'd, my lord, I 'm glad:
Let the rest go.

KING. My honour 's at the stake, which to defeat
I must produce my power. Here, take her hand,
Proud scornful boy, unworthy this good gift,
That dost in vile misprision shackle up
My love and her desert; thou canst not dream
We, poising us in her defective scale,
Shall weigh thee to the beam; that wilt not know,
It is in us to plant thine honour where
We please to have it grow. Check thy contempt:
Obey our will, which travails in thy good:
Believe not thy disdain, but presently
Do thine own fortunes that obedient right
Which both thy duty owes and our power claims;
Or I will throw thee from my care for ever
Into the staggers and the careless lapse
Of youth and ignorance; both my revenge and hate

Loosing upon thee, in the name of justice,
Without all terms of pity. Speak; thine answer.

BERTRAM. Pardon, my gracious lord; for I submit
My fancy to your eyes. When I consider
What great creation and what dole of honour
Flies where you bid it, I find that she, which late
Was in my nobler thoughts most base, is now
The praised of the king; who, so ennobled,
Is, as 'twere, born so.

KING.   Take her by the hand,
And tell her she is thine: to whom I promise
A counterpoise, if not to thy estate
A balance more replete.

BERTRAM.   I take her hand.

KING. Good fortune and the favour of the king
  Smile upon this contract; whose ceremony
  Shall seem expedient on the now-born brief,
  And be perform'd to-night: the solemn feast
  Shall more attend upon the coming space,
  Expecting absent friends. As thou lov'st her,
  Thy love 's to me religious; else, does err.

        Exeunt King, Bertram, Helena, Lords and Attendants

LAFEU. Do you hear, monsieur? A word with you.

PAROLLES. Your pleasure, sir?

LAFEU. Your lord and master did well to make his recantation.

PAROLLES. Recantation! My lord! My master!

LAFEU. Ay; is it not a language I speak?

PAROLLES. A most harsh one, and not to be understood without bloody succeeding. My master!

LAFEU. Are you companion to the Count Rousillon?

PAROLLES. To any count; to all counts; to what is man.

LAFEU. To what is count's man: count's master is of another
style.

PAROLLES. You are too old, sir; let it satisfy you, you are too
old.

LAFEU. I must tell thee, sirrah, I write man; to which title
age cannot bring thee.

PAROLLES. What I dare too well do, I dare not do.

LAFEU. I did think thee, for two ordinaries, to be a pretty
wise fellow: thou didst make tolerable vent of thy travel;
it might pass: yet the scarfs and the bannerets about thee

did manifoldly dissuade me from believing thee a vessel of too great a burden. I have now found thee; when I lose thee again, I care not; yet art thou good for nothing but taking up, and that thou'rt scarce worth.

PAROLLES. Hadst thou not the privilege of antiquity upon thee,—

LAFEU. Do not plunge thyself too far in anger, lest thou hasten thy trial; which if—Lord have mercy on thee for a hen! So, my good window of lattice, fare thee well: thy casement I need not open, for I look through thee. Give me thy hand.

PAROLLES. My lord, you give me most egregious indignity.

LAFEU. Ay, with all my heart; and thou art worthy of it.

PAROLLES. I have not, my lord, deserved it.

LAFEU. Yes, good faith, every dram of it; and I will not bate thee a scruple.

PAROLLES. Well, I shall be wiser.

LAFEU. E'en as soon as thou canst, for thou hast to pull at a smack o' the contrary. If ever thou be'st bound in thy scarf and beaten, thou shalt find what it is to be proud of thy bondage. I have a desire to hold my acquaintance with thee, or rather my knowledge, that I may say in the default, he is a man I know.

PAROLLES. My lord, you do me most insupportable vexation.

LAFEU. I would it were hell-pains for thy sake, and my poor doing eternal: for doing I am past; as I will by thee, in what motion age will give me leave. *Exit*

PAROLLES. Well, thou hast a son shall take this disgrace off me; scurvy, old, filthy, scurvy lord! Well, I must be patient; there is no fettering of authority. I 'll beat him, by my life, if I can meet him with any convenience, an he were double and double a lord. I 'll have no more pity of his age than I would have of—I 'll beat him, an if I could but meet him again!

Re-enter Lafeu

LAFEU. Sirrah, your lord and master 's married; there 's news for you: you have a new mistress.

PAROLLES. I most unfeignedly beseech your lordship to make some reservation of your wrongs: he is my good lord: whom I serve above is my master.

LAFEU. Who? God?

PAROLLES. Ay, sir.

LAFEU. The devil it is that 's thy master. Why dost thou
  garter up thy arms o' this fashion? dost make hose of thy
  sleeves? do other servants so? Thou wert best set thy lower
  part where thy nose stands. By mine honour, if I were but
  two hours younger, I 'd beat thee: methinks thou art a general offence, and every man should beat thee: I think thou
  wast created for men to breathe themselves upon thee.

PAROLLES. This is hard and undeserved measure, my lord.

LAFEU. Go to, sir; you were beaten in Italy for picking a kernel out of a pomegranate; you are a vagabond and no true
  traveller: you are more saucy with lords and honourable
  personages than the heraldry of your birth and virtue
  gives you commission. You are not worth another word,
  else I 'd call you knave. I leave you.   *Exit*

PAROLLES. Good, very good; it is so then: good, very good.
  Let it be concealed awhile.

                    Re-enter Bertram

BERTRAM. Undone, and forfeited to cares for ever!

PAROLLES. What is the matter, sweet heart?

BERTRAM. Although before the solemn priest I have sworn,
  I will not bed her.

PAROLLES. What, what, sweet heart?

BERTRAM. O my Parolles, they have married me!
  I 'll to the Tuscan wars, and never bed her.

PAROLLES. France is a dog-hole, and it no more merits
  The tread of a man's foot. To the wars!

BERTRAM. There's letters from my mother: what the
      import is
  I know not yet.

PAROLLES. Ay, that would be known. To the wars, my boy!
      to the wars!
  He wears his honour in a box, unseen,
  That hugs his kicky-wicky here at home,
  Spending his manly marrow in her arms,
  Which should sustain the bound and high curvet
  Of Mars's fiery steed. To other regions!
  France is a stable; we that dwell in 't jades;
  Therefore, to the war!

BERTRAM. It shall be so: I 'll send her to my house,
  Acquaint my mother with my hate to her,
  And wherefore I am fled; write to the king
  That which I durst not speak: his present gift

  Shall furnish me to those Italian fields,
  Where noble fellows strike. War is no strife
  To the dark house and the detested wife.

PAROLLES. Will this capriccio hold in thee? art sure?

BERTRAM. Go with me to my chamber, and advise me.
  I'll send her straight away: to-morrow
  I'll to the wars, she to her single sorrow.

PAROLLES. Why, these balls bound; there's noise in it. 'Tis
  hard:
  A young man married is a man that's marr'd:
  Therefore away, and leave her bravely; go:
  The king has done you wrong: but, hush! 'tis so.   *Exeunt*

SCENE FOUR

The Same. Another Room in the Palace.

Enter Helena and Clown

HELENA. My mother greets me kindly: is she well?

CLOWN. She is not well; but yet she has her health; she's
  very merry; but yet she is not well: but thanks be given,
  she's very well, and wants nothing i' the world; but yet
  she is not well.

HELENA. If she be very well, what does she ail that she's not
  very well?

CLOWN. Truly, she's very well indeed, but for two things.

HELENA. What two things?

CLOWN. One, that she's not in heaven, whither God send
  her quickly! the other, that she's in earth, from whence
  God send her quickly!

Enter Parolles

PAROLLES. Bless you, my fortunate lady!

HELENA. I hope, sir, I have your good will to have mine own
  good fortunes.

PAROLLES. You had my prayers to lead them on; and to keep
  them on, have them still. O! my knave, how does my old
  lady?

CLOWN. So that you had her wrinkles, and I her money, I
  would she did as you say.

PAROLLES. Why, I say nothing.

CLOWN. Marry, you are the wiser man; for many a man's

tongue shakes out his master's undoing. To say nothing, to
do nothing, to know nothing, and to have nothing, is to be
a great part of your title; which is within a very little of
nothing.

PAROLLES. Away! thou 'rt a knave.

CLOWN. You should have said, sir, before a knave thou 'rt a
knave; that is before me thou 'rt a knave: this had been
truth, sir.

PAROLLES. Go to, thou art a witty fool; I have found thee.

CLOWN. Did you find me in yourself, sir? or were you taught
to find me? The search, sir, was profitable; and much fool
may you find in you, even to the world's pleasure and the
increase of laughter.

PAROLLES. A good knave, i' faith, and well fed.
Madam, my lord will go away to-night;
A very serious business calls on him.
The great prerogative and rite of love,
Which, as your due, time claims, he does acknowledge,
But puts it off to a compell'd restraint;
Whose want, and whose delay, is strew'd with sweets,
Which they distil now in the curbed time,
To make the coming hour o'erflow with joy,
And pleasure drown the brim.

HELENA.   What 's his will else?

PAROLLES. That you will take your instant leave o' the king,
And make this haste as your own good proceeding,
Strengthen'd with what apology you think
May make it probable need.

HELENA.   What more commands he?

PAROLLES. That, having this obtain'd, you presently
Attend his further pleasure.

HELENA. In everything I wait upon his will.

PAROLLES. I shall report it so.

HELENA.   I pray you. Come, sirrah.

                                           Exeunt

SCENE FIVE

Another Room in the Same.

Enter Lafeu and Bertram

LAFEU. But I hope your lordship thinks not him a soldier.

BERTRAM. Yes, my lord, and of very valiant approof.

LAFEU. You have it from his own deliverance.

BERTRAM. And by other warranted testimony.

LAFEU. Then my dial goes not true: I took this lark for a bunting.

BERTRAM. I do assure you, my lord, he is very great in knowledge, and accordingly valiant.

LAFEU. I have then sinned against his experience and transgressed against his valour; and my state that way is dangerous, since I cannot yet find in my heart to repent. Here he comes; I pray you, make us friends; I will pursue the amity.

Enter Parolles

PAROLLES. (*To Bertram*) These things shall be done, sir.

LAFEU. Pray you, sir, who 's his tailor?

PAROLLES. Sir?

LAFEU. O! I know him well. Ay, sir; he, sir, is a good workman, a very good tailor.

BERTRAM. (*Aside to Parolles*) Is she gone to the king?

PAROLLES. She is.

BERTRAM. Will she away to-night?

PAROLLES. As you 'll have her.

BERTRAM. I have writ my letters, casketed my treasure,
Given orders for our horses; and to-night,
When I should take possession of the bride,
End ere I do begin.

LAFEU. A good traveller is something at the latter end of a dinner; but one that lies three thirds, and uses a known truth to pass a thousand nothings with, should be once heard and thrice beaten. God save you, captain.

BERTRAM. Is there any unkindness between my lord and you, monsieur?

PAROLLES. I know not how I have deserved to run into my lord's displeasure.

LAFEU. You have made shift to run into 't, boots and spurs
and all, like him that leaped into the custard; and out of it
you 'll run again, rather than suffer question for your residence.

BERTRAM. It may be you have mistaken him, my lord.

LAFEU. And shall do so ever, though I took him at his prayers. Fare you well, my lord; and believe this of me, there
can be no kernel in this light nut; the soul of this man is his
clothes. Trust him not in matter of heavy consequence; I
have kept of them tame, and know their natures. Farewell,
monsieur: I have spoken better of you than you have or
will to deserve at my hand; but we must do good against
evil.   *Exit*

PAROLLES. An idle lord, I swear.

BERTRAM. I think not so.

PAROLLES. Why, do you not know him?

BERTRAM. Yes, I do know him well; and common speech
Gives him a worthy pass. Here comes my clog.

Enter Helena

HELENA. I have, sir, as I was commanded from you,
Spoke with the king, and have procur'd his leave
For present parting; only, he desires
Some private speech with you.

BERTRAM.   I shall obey his will.
You must not marvel, Helen, at my course,
Which holds not colour with the time, nor does
The ministration and required office
On my particular: prepar'd I was not
For such a business; therefore am I found
So much unsettled. This drives me to entreat you
That presently you take your way for home;
And rather muse than ask why I entreat you;
For my respects are better than they seem,
And my appointments have in them a need
Greater than shows itself at the first view
To you that know them not. This to my mother.

                                              Giving a letter

'Twill be two days ere I shall see you, so
I leave you to your wisdom.

HELENA.   Sir, I can nothing say,
But that I am your most obedient servant.

BERTRAM. Come, come, no more of that.

HELENA.   And ever shall
    With true observance seek to eke out that
    Wherein toward me my homely stars have fail'd
    To equal my great fortune.

BERTRAM.   Let that go:
    My haste is very great. Farewell: hie home.

HELENA.   Pray sir, your pardon.

BERTRAM.   Well, what would you say?

HELENA.   I am not worthy of the wealth I owe,
    Nor dare I say 'tis mine, and yet it is;
    But, like a timorous thief, most fain would steal
    What law does vouch mine own.

BERTRAM.   What would you have?

HELENA.   Something, and scarce so much: nothing indeed.
    I would not tell you what I would, my lord:—
    Faith, yes;
    Strangers and foes do sunder, and not kiss.

BERTRAM.   I pray you, stay not, but in haste to horse.

HELENA.   I shall not break your bidding, good my lord.

BERTRAM.   (*To Parolles*) Where are my other men, mon-
     sieur? (*To Helena*) Farewell.   *Exit Helena*
    Go thou toward home; where I will never come
    Whilst I can shake my sword or hear the drum.
    Away! and for our flight.

PAROLLES.   Bravely, coragio!   *Exeunt*

ACT THREE

SCENE ONE

Florence. A Room in the Duke's Palace.

Flourish. Enter the Duke, attended; two French Lords, and Soldiers

DUKE. So that from point to point now have you heard
The fundamental reasons of this war,
Whose great decision hath much blood let forth,
And more thirsts after.

FIRST LORD.   Holy seems the quarrel
Upon your Grace's part; black and fearful
On the opposer.

DUKE. Therefore we marvel much our cousin France
Would in so just a business shut his bosom
Against our borrowing prayers.

FIRST LORD.   Good my lord,
The reasons of our state I cannot yield,
But like a common and an outward man,
That the great figure of a council frames
By self-unable motion: therefore dare not
Say what I think of it, since I have found
Myself in my incertain grounds to fail
As often as I guess'd.

DUKE.   Be it his pleasure.

SECOND LORD. But I am sure the younger of our nature,
That surfeit on their ease, will day by day
Come here for physic.

DUKE.   Welcome shall they be,
And all the honours that can fly from us
Shall on them settle. You know your places well;
When better fall, for your avails they fell.
To-morrow to the field.   *Flourish. Exeunt*

SCENE TWO

Rousillon. A Room in the Countess's Palace.

Enter Countess and Clown

COUNTESS. It hath happened all as I would have had it, save that he comes not along with her.

CLOWN. By my troth, I take my young lord to be a very melancholy man.

COUNTESS. By what observance, I pray you?

CLOWN. Why, he will look upon his boot and sing; mend the ruff and sing; ask questions and sing; pick his teeth and sing. I know a man that had this trick of melancholy sold a goodly manor for a song.

COUNTESS. (*Opening a letter*) Let me see what he writes, and when he means to come.

CLOWN. I have no mind to Isbel since I was at court. Our old ling and our Isbels o' the country are nothing like your old ling and your Isbels o' the court: the brains of my Cupid's knocked out, and I begin to love, as an old man loves money, with no stomach.

COUNTESS. What have we here?

CLOWN. E'n that you have there.   *Exit*

COUNTESS. 'I have sent you a daughter-in-law: she hath recovered the king, and undone me. I have wedded her, not bedded her; and sworn to make the "not" eternal. You shall hear I am run away: know it before the report come. If there be breadth enough in the world, I will hold a long distance. My duty to you.

                         Your unfortunate son,
                                        'Bertram.'

This is not well: rash and unbridled boy,
To fly the favours of so good a king!
To pluck his indignation on thy head
By the misprising of a maid too virtuous
For the contempt of empire!

Re-enter Clown

CLOWN. O madam! yonder is heavy news within between two soldiers and my young lady.

COUNTESS. What is the matter?

CLOWN. Nay, there is some comfort in the news, some comfort; your son will not be killed so soon as I thought he would.

COUNTESS. Why should he be killed?

CLOWN. So say I, madam, if he run away, as I hear he does: the danger is in standing to 't; that 's the loss of men, though it be the getting of children. Here they come will tell you more; for my part, I only hear your son was run away. *Exit*

Enter Helena and two Gentlemen

FIRST GENTLEMAN. Save you, good madam.

HELENA. Madam, my lord is gone, for ever gone.

SECOND GENTLEMAN. Do not say so.

COUNTESS. Think upon patience. Pray you, gentlemen,
I have felt so many quirks of joy and grief,
That the first face of neither, on the start,
Can woman me unto 't. Where is my son, I pray you?

SECOND GENTLEMAN. Madam, he 's gone to serve the Duke
of Florence:
We met him thitherward; for thence we came,
And, after some dispatch in hand at court,
Thither we bend again.

HELENA. Look on his letter, madam; here 's my passport.
'When thou canst get the ring upon my finger, which
never shall come off, and show me a child begotten of thy
body that I am father to, then call me husband: but in
such a "then" I write a "never."'
This is a dreadful sentence.

COUNTESS. Brought you this letter, gentlemen?

FIRST GENTLEMAN.   Ay, madam;
And for the contents' sake are sorry for our pains.

COUNTESS. I prithee, lady, have a better cheer;
If thou engrossest all the griefs are thine,
Thou robb'st me of a moiety: he was my son,
But I do wash his name out of my blood,
And thou art all my child. Towards Florence is he?

SECOND GENTLEMAN. Ay, madam.

COUNTESS.   And to be a soldier?

SECOND GENTLEMAN. Such is his noble purpose; and, believe 't,
The duke will lay upon him all the honour
That good convenience claims.

COUNTESS.   Return you thither?

FIRST GENTLEMAN. Ay, madam, with the swiftest wing of
 speed.

HELENA. 'Till I have no wife, I have nothing in France.'
 'Tis bitter.

COUNTESS. Find you that there?

HELENA.   Ay, madam.

FIRST GENTLEMAN. 'Tis but the boldness of his hand, haply,
 which his heart was not consenting to.

COUNTESS. Nothing in France until he have no wife!
 There's nothing here that is too good for him
 But only she; and she deserves a lord
 That twenty such rude boys might tend upon,
 And call her hourly mistress. Who was with him?

FIRST GENTLEMAN. A servant only, and a gentleman
 Which I have sometime known.

COUNTESS.   Parolles, was it not?

FIRST GENTLEMAN. Ay, my good lady, he.

COUNTESS. A very tainted fellow, and full of wickedness.
 My son corrupts a well-derived nature
 With his inducement.

FIRST GENTLEMAN.   Indeed, good lady,
 The fellow has a deal of that too much,
 Which holds him much to have.

COUNTESS. Y' are welcome, gentlemen.
 I will entreat you, when you see my son,
 To tell him that his sword can never win
 The honour that he loses: more I'll entreat you
 Written to bear along.

SECOND GENTLEMAN. We serve you, madam,
 In that and all your worthiest affairs.

COUNTESS. Not so, but as we change our courtesies.
 Will you draw near? *Exeunt Countess and Gentlemen*

HELENA. 'Till I have no wife, I have nothing in France.'
 Nothing in France until he has no wife!
 Thou shalt have none, Rousillon, none in France;
 Then hast thou all again. Poor lord! is 't I
 That chase thee from thy country, and expose
 Those tender limbs of thine to the event
 Of the none-sparing war? and is it I
 That drive thee from the sportive court, where thou
 Wast shot at with fair eyes, to be the mark
 Of smoky muskets? O you leaden messengers,
 That ride upon the violent speed of fire,

Fly with false aim; move the still-piecing air,
That sings with piercing; do not touch my lord!
Whoever shoots at him, I set him there;
Whoever charges on his forward breast,
I am the caitiff that do hold him to 't;
And, though I kill him not, I am the cause
His death was so effected: better 'twere
I met the ravin lion when he roar'd
With sharp constraint of hunger; better 'twere
That all the miseries which nature owes
Were mine at once. No, come thou home, Rousillon,
Whence honour but of danger wins a scar,
As oft it loses all: I will be gone;
My being here it is that holds thee hence:
Shall I stay here to do 't? No, no, although
The air of paradise did fan the house,
And angels offic'd all: I will be gone,
That pitiful rumour may report my flight,
To consolate thine ear. Come, night; end, day!
For with the dark, poor thief, I 'll steal away.   *Exit*

SCENE THREE

Florence. Before the Duke's Palace.

*Flourish. Enter Duke, Bertram, Parolles, Soldiers.
Drum and Trumpets.*

DUKE. The general of our horse thou art; and we,
  Great in our hope, lay our best love and credence
  Upon thy promising fortune.
BERTRAM.   Sir, it is
  A charge too heavy for my strength, but yet
  We 'll strive to bear it for your worthy sake
  To the extreme edge of hazard.
DUKE.   Then go thou forth,
  And fortune play upon thy prosperous helm
  As thy auspicious mistress!
BERTRAM.   This very day,
  Great Mars, I put myself into thy file:
  Make me but like my thoughts, and I shall prove
  A lover of thy drum, hater of love.   *Exeunt*

SCENE FOUR

Rousillon. A Room in the Countess's Palace.

Enter Countess and Steward

COUNTESS. Alas! and would you take the letter of her?
　Might you not know she would do as she has done,
　By sending me a letter? Read it again.
STEWARD. 'I am Saint Jaques' pilgrim, thither gone:
　　Ambitious love hath so in me offended
　That bare-foot plod I the cold ground upon
　　With sainted vow my faults to have amended.
　Write, write, that from the bloody course of war,
　　My dearest master, your dear son, may hie:
　Bless him at home in peace, whilst I from far
　　His name with zealous fervour sanctify:
　His taken labours bid him me forgive;
　　I, his despiteful Juno, sent him forth
　From courtly friends, with camping foes to live,
　　Where death and danger dog the heels of worth:
　He is too good and fair for Death and me;
　　Whom I myself embrace, to set him free.'
COUNTESS. Ah, what sharp stings are in her mildest words!
　Rinaldo, you did never lack advice so much,
　As letting her pass so: had I spoke with her,
　I could have well diverted her intents,
　Which thus she hath prevented.
STEWARD. 　　　　　　　Pardon me, madam:
　If I had given you this at over-night
　She might have been o'erta'en; and yet she writes,
　Pursuit would be but vain.
COUNTESS. 　　　　　　What angel shall
　Bless this unworthy husband? He cannot thrive,
　Unless her prayers, whom heaven delights to hear,
　And loves to grant, reprieve him from the wrath
　Of greatest justice. Write, write, Rinaldo,
　To this unworthy husband of his wife;
　Let every word weigh heavy of her worth
　That he does weigh too light: my greatest grief,
　Though little he do feel it, set down sharply.

Dispatch the most convenient messenger:
When haply he shall hear that she is gone,
He will return; and hope I may that she,
Hearing so much, will speed her foot again,
Led hither by pure love. Which of them both
Is dearest to me I have no skill in sense
To make distinction. Provide this messenger.
My heart is heavy and mine age is weak;
Grief would have tears, and sorrow bids me speak. *Exeunt*

SCENE FIVE

Without the Walls of Florence.

*A tucket afar off. Enter a Widow of Florence, Diana,
Violenta, Mariana, and other Citizens*

WIDOW. Nay, come; for if they do approach the city we shall
lose all the sight.

DIANA. They say the French Count has done most honourable service.

WIDOW. It is reported that he has taken their greatest commander, and that with his own hand he slew the duke's
brother. We have lost our labour; they are gone a contrary way. Hark! you may know by their trumpets.

MARIANA. Come; let 's return again, and suffice ourselves
with the report of it. Well, Diana, take heed of this French
earl: the honour of a maid is her name, and no legacy is so
rich as honesty.

WIDOW. I have told my neighbour how you have been so-
licited by a gentleman his companion.

MARIANA. I know that knave; hang him! one Parolles: a
filthy officer he is in those suggestions for the young
earl. Beware of them, Diana; their promises, enticements,
oaths, tokens, and all these engines of lust, are not the
things they go under: many a maid hath been seduced by
them; and the misery is, example, that so terrible shows in
the wrack of maidenhood, cannot for all that dissuade succession, but that they are limed with the twigs that
threaten them. I hope I need not to advise you further;
but I hope your own grace will keep you where you are,

though there were no further danger known but the modesty which is so lost.

DIANA. You shall not need to fear me.

WIDOW. I hope so. Look, here comes a pilgrim: I know she
will lie at my house; thither they send one another. I 'll
question her.

Enter Helena in the dress of a Pilgrim

God save you, pilgrim! Whither are you bound?

HELENA. To Saint Jaques le Grand.
Where do the palmers lodge, I do beseech you?

WIDOW. At the Saint Francis, here beside the port.

HELENA. Is this the way?

WIDOW.   Ay, marry, is 't. Hark you!

A march afar off

They come this way. If you will tarry, holy pilgrim,
But till the troops come by,
I will conduct you where you shall be lodg'd:
The rather, for I think I know your hostess
As ample as myself.

HELENA.   Is it yourself?

WIDOW. If you shall please so, pilgrim.

HELENA. I thank you, and will stay upon your leisure.

WIDOW. You came, I think, from France?

HELENA.   I did so.

WIDOW. Here you shall see a countryman of yours
That has done worthy service.

HELENA.   His name, I pray you.

DIANA. The Count Rousillon: know you such a one?

HELENA. But by the ear, that hears most nobly of him;
His face I know not.

DIANA.   Whatsoe'er he is,
He 's bravely taken here. He stole from France,
As 'tis reported, for the king had married him
Against his liking. Think you it is so?

HELENA. Ay, surely, mere the truth: I know his lady.

DIANA. There is a gentleman that serves the count
Reports but coarsely of her.

HELENA.   What 's his name?

DIANA. Monsieur Parolles.

HELENA.   O! I believe with him,
In argument of praise, or to the worth
Of the great count himself, she is too mean

To have her name repeated: all her deserving
Is a reserved honesty, and that
I have not heard examin'd.

DIANA.   Alas, poor lady!
'Tis a hard bondage to become the wife
Of a detesting lord.

WIDOW. Ay, right; good creature, wheresoe'er she is,
Her heart weighs sadly. This young maid might do her
A shrewd turn if she pleas'd.

HELENA.   How do you mean?
May be the amorous count solicits her
In the unlawful purpose.

WIDOW.   He does, indeed;
And brokes with all that can in such a suit
Corrupt the tender honour of a maid:
But she is arm'd for him and keeps her guard
In honestest defence.

MARIANA.   The gods forbid else!

Enter, with drum and colours,
a party of the Florentine army, Bertram and Parolles

WIDOW. So, now they come.
That is Antonio, the duke's eldest son;
That, Escalus.

HELENA.   Which is the Frenchman?

DIANA.   He;
That with the plume: 'tis a most gallant fellow;
I would he lov'd his wife. If he were honester,
He were much goodlier; is 't not a handsome gentleman?

HELENA. I like him well.

DIANA. 'Tis pity he is not honest. Yond 's that same knave
That leads him to these places: were I his lady
I would poison that vile rascal.

HELENA.   Which is he?

DIANA. That jack-an-apes with scarfs. Why is he melancholy?

HELENA. Perchance he 's hurt i' the battle.

PAROLLES. Lose our drum! well.

MARIANA. He 's shrewdly vexed at something. Look, he has
spied us.

WIDOW. Marry, hang you!

MARIANA. And your courtesy, for a ring-carrier!

Exeunt Bertram, Parolles, Officers, and Soldiers

WIDOW. The troop is past. Come, pilgrim, I will bring you
　　Where you shall host: of enjoin'd penitents
　　There 's four or five, to great Saint Jaques bound,
　　Already at my house.

HELENA.　　　　　　　　I humbly thank you.
　　Please it this matron and this gentle maid
　　To eat with us to-night, the charge and thanking
　　Shall be for me; and, to requite you further,
　　I will bestow some precepts of this virgin
　　Worthy the note.

BOTH.　　　　　　　We 'll take your offer kindly.　　*Exeunt*

SCENE SIX

Camp before Florence.

Enter Bertram and the two French Lords

FIRST LORD. Nay, good my lord, put him to 't: let him have
　　his way.

SECOND LORD. If your lordship find him not a hilding, hold
　　me no more in your respect.

FIRST LORD. On my life, my lord, a bubble.

BERTRAM. Do you think I am so far deceived in him?

FIRST LORD. Believe it, my lord, in mine own direct knowl-
　　edge, without any malice, but to speak of him as my kins-
　　man, he 's a most notable coward, an infinite and endless
　　liar, an hourly promise-breaker, the owner of no one good
　　quality worthy your lordship's entertainment.

SECOND LORD. It were fit you knew him; lest, reposing too
　　far in his virtue, which he hath not, he might at some great
　　and trusty business in a main danger fail you.

BERTRAM. I would I knew in what particular action to try
　　him.

SECOND LORD. None better than to let him fetch off his drum,
　　which you hear him so confidently undertake to do.

FIRST LORD. I, with a troop of Florentines, will suddenly sur-
　　prise him: such I will have whom I am sure he knows not
　　from the enemy. We will bind and hoodwink him so, that
　　he shall suppose no other but that he is carried into the
　　leaguer of the adversaries, when we bring him to our own
　　tents. Be but your lordship present at his examination: if

he do not, for the promise of his life and in the highest compulsion of base fear, offer to betray you and deliver all the intelligence in his power against you, and that with the divine forfeit of his soul upon oath, never trust my judgment in anything.

SECOND LORD. O! for the love of laughter, let him fetch his drum: he says he has a stratagem for 't. When your lordship sees the bottom of his success in 't, and to what metal this counterfeit lump of ore will be melted, if you give him not John Drum's entertainment, your inclining cannot be removed. Here he comes.

FIRST LORD. O! for the love of laughter, hinder not the honour of his design: let him fetch off his drum in any hand.

Enter Parolles

BERTRAM. How now, monsieur! This drum sticks sorely in your disposition.

SECOND LORD. A pox on 't! let it go: 'tis but a drum.

PAROLLES. 'But a drum'! Is 't 'but a drum'? A drum so lost! There was excellent command, to charge in with our horse upon our own wings, and to rend our own soldiers!

SECOND LORD. That was not to be blamed in the command of the service: it was a disaster of war that Cæsar himself could not have prevented if he had been there to command.

BERTRAM. Well, we cannot greatly condemn our success: some dishonour we had in the loss of that drum; but it is not to be recovered.

PAROLLES. It might have been recovered.

BERTRAM. It might; but it is not now.

PAROLLES. It is to be recovered. But that the merit of service is seldom attributed to the true and exact performer, I would have that drum or another, or hic jacet.

BERTRAM. Why, if you have a stomach to 't, monsieur, if you think your mystery in stratagem can bring this instrument of honour again into its native quarter, be magnanimous in the enterprise and go on; I will grace the attempt for a worthy exploit: if you speed well in it, the duke shall both speak of it, and extend to you what further becomes his greatness, even to the utmost syllable of your worthiness.

PAROLLES. By the hand of a soldier, I will undertake it.

BERTRAM. But you must not now slumber in it.

PAROLLES. I 'll about it this evening: and I will presently pen

down my dilemmas, encourage myself in my certainty,
put myself into my mortal preparation, and by midnight
look to hear further from me.

BERTRAM. May I be bold to acquaint his Grace you are gone
about it?

PAROLLES. I know not what the success will be, my lord; but
the attempt I vow.

BERTRAM. I know thou 'rt valiant; and, to the possibility of
thy soldiership will subscribe for thee. Farewell.

PAROLLES. I love not many words.   *Exit*

FIRST LORD. No more than a fish loves water. Is not this a
strange fellow, my lord, that so confidently seems to undertake this business, which he knows is not to be done;
damns himself to do, and dares better be damned than to
do 't?

SECOND LORD. You do not know him, my lord, as we do: certain it is, that he will steal himself into a man's favour, and
for a week escape a great deal of discoveries; but when
you find him out you have him ever after.

BERTRAM. Why, do you think he will make no deed at all of
this that so seriously he does address himself unto?

FIRST LORD. None in the world; but return with an invention
and clap upon you two or three probable lies. But we have
almost embossed him, you shall see his fall to-night; for,
indeed, he is not for your lordship's respect.

SECOND LORD. We 'll make you some sport with the fox ere
we case him. He was first smoked by the old Lord Lafeu:
when his disguise and he is parted, tell me what a sprat
you shall find him; which you shall see this very night.

FIRST LORD. I must go look my twigs: he shall be caught.

BERTRAM. Your brother, he shall go along with me.

FIRST LORD. As 't please your lordship: I 'll leave you. *Exit*

BERTRAM. Now will I lead you to the house, and show you
The lass I spoke of.

SECOND LORD.   But you say she 's honest.

BERTRAM. That 's all the fault. I spoke with her but once,
And found her wondrous cold; but I sent to her,
By this same coxcomb that we have i' the wind,
Tokens and letters which she did re-send;
And this is all I have done. She 's a fair creature;
Will you go see her?

SECOND LORD.   With all my heart, my lord. *Exeunt*

SCENE SEVEN

Florence. A Room in the Widow's House.

Enter Helena and Widow

HELENA. If you misdoubt me that I am not she,
  I know not how I shall assure you further,
  But I shall lose the grounds I work upon.

WIDOW. Though my estate be fall'n, I was well born,
  Nothing acquainted with these businesses;
  And would not put my reputation now
  In any staining act.

HELENA.   Nor would I wish you.
  First, give me trust, the county is my husband,
  And what to your sworn counsel I have spoken
  Is so from word to word; and then you cannot,
  By the good aid that I of you shall borrow,
  Err in bestowing it.

WIDOW.   I should believe you:
  For you have show'd me that which well approves
  You 're great in fortune.

HELENA.   Take this purse of gold,
  And let me buy your friendly help thus far,
  Which I will over-pay and pay again
  When I have found it. The county woos your daughter,
  Lays down his wanton siege before her beauty
  Resolv'd to carry her: let her in fine consent,
  As we 'll direct her how 'tis best to bear it.
  Now, his important blood will naught deny
  That she 'll demand: a ring the county wears,
  That downward hath succeeded in his house
  From son to son, some four or five descents
  Since the first father wore it: this ring he holds
  In most rich choice; yet, in his idle fire,
  To buy his will, it would not seem too dear,
  Howe'er repented after.

WIDOW.   Now I see
  The bottom of your purpose.

HELENA. You see it lawful then. It is no more,
  But that your daughter, ere she seems as won,

Desires this ring, appoints him an encounter,
In fine, delivers me to fill the time,
Herself most chastely absent. After this,
To marry her, I 'll add three thousand crowns
To what is past already.

WIDOW.   I have yielded.
Instruct my daughter how she shall persever,
That time and place with this deceit so lawful
May prove coherent. Every night he comes
With musics of all sorts and songs compos'd
To her unworthiness: it nothing steads us
To chide him from our eaves, for he persists
As if his life lay on 't.

HELENA.   Why then to-night
Let us assay our plot; which, if it speed,
Is wicked meaning in a lawful deed,
And lawful meaning in a lawful act,
Where both not sin, and yet a sinful fact.
But let 's about it.   *Exeunt*

ACT FOUR

SCENE ONE

Without the Florentine Camp.

Enter First French Lord, with five or six Soldiers in ambush

FIRST LORD. He can come no other way but by this hedge-corner. When you sally upon him, speak what terrible language you will: though you understand it not yourselves, no matter; for we must not seem to understand him, unless some one among us, whom we must produce for an interpreter.

FIRST SOLDIER. Good captain, let me be the interpreter.

FIRST LORD. Art not acquainted with him? Knows he not thy voice?

FIRST SOLDIER. No, sir, I warrant you.

FIRST LORD. But what linsey-woolsey hast thou to speak to us again?

FIRST SOLDIER. Even such as you speak to me.

FIRST LORD. He must think us some band of strangers i' the adversary's entertainment. Now, he hath a smack of all neighbouring languages; therefore we must every one be a man of his own fancy, not to know what we speak one to another; so we seem to know, is to know straight our purpose: chough's language, gabble enough, and good enough. As for you, interpreter, you must seem very politic. But couch, ho! here he comes, to beguile two hours in a sleep, and then to return and swear the lies he forges.

Enter Parolles

PAROLLES. Ten o'clock: within these three hours 'twill be time enough to go home. What shall I say I have done? It must be a very plausive invention that carries it. They begin to smoke me, and disgraces have of late knocked too often at my door. I find my tongue is too foolhardy; but my

heart hath the fear of Mars before it and of his creatures,
not daring the reports of my tongue.

FIRST LORD. This is the first truth that e'er thine own tongue
was guilty of.

PAROLLES. What the devil should move me to undertake the
recovery of this drum, being not ignorant of the impossibility, and knowing I had no such purpose? I must give
myself some hurts and say I got them in exploit. Yet slight
ones will not carry it: they will say, 'Came you off with so
little?' and great ones I dare not give. Wherefore, what 's
the instance. Tongue, I must put you into a butter-wom-
an's mouth, and buy myself another Bajazet's mule, if you
prattle me into these perils.

FIRST LORD. Is it possible he should know what he is, and be
that he is?

PAROLLES. I would the cutting of my garments would serve
the turn or the breaking of my Spanish sword.

FIRST LORD. We cannot afford you so.

PAROLLES. Or the baring of my beard, and to say it was in
stratagem.

FIRST LORD. 'Twould not do.

PAROLLES. Or to drown my clothes, and say I was stripped.

FIRST LORD. Hardly serve.

PAROLLES. Though I swore I leaped from the window of the
citadel—

FIRST LORD. How deep?

PAROLLES. Thirty fathom.

FIRST LORD. Three great oaths would scarce make that be believed.

PAROLLES. I would I had any drum of the enemy's: I would
swear I recovered it.

FIRST LORD. Thou shalt hear one anon.

PAROLLES. A drum now of the enemy's! *Alarum within*

FIRST LORD. Throca movousus, cargo, cargo, cargo.

ALL. Cargo, cargo, villianda par corbo, cargo.

They seize and blindfold him

PAROLLES. O! ransom, ransom! Do not hide mine eyes.

FIRST SOLDIER. Boskos thromuldo boskos.

PAROLLES. I know you are the Muskos' regiment;
And I shall lose my life for want of language.
If there be here German, or Dane, low Dutch,

Italian, or French, let him speak to me:
I will discover that which shall undo
The Florentine.

FIRST SOLDIER.   Boskos vauvado:
I understand thee, and can speak thy tongue:
Kerelybonto: Sir,
Betake thee to thy faith, for seventeen poniards
Are at thy bosom.

PAROLLES.   O!

FIRST SOLDIER.   O! pray, pray, pray.
Manka revania dulche.

FIRST LORD.   Oscorbidulchos volivorco.

FIRST SOLDIER.   The general is content to spare thee yet;
And, hoodwink'd as thou art, will lead thee on
To gather from thee: haply thou may'st inform
Something to save thy life.

PAROLLES.   O! let me live,
And all the secrets of our camp I'll show,
Their force, their purposes; nay, I'll speak that
Which you will wonder at.

FIRST SOLDIER.   But wilt thou faithfully?

PAROLLES.   If I do not, damn me.

FIRST SOLDIER.   Acordo linta.
Come on; thou art granted space.

        Exit, with Parolles guarded. A short alarum within

FIRST LORD.   Go, tell the Count Rousillon, and my brother,
We have caught the woodcock, and will keep him muffled
Till we do hear from them.

SECOND SOLDIER.   Captain, I will.

FIRST LORD.   A' will betray us all unto ourselves:
Inform on that.

SECOND SOLDIER.   So I will, sir.

FIRST LORD.   Till then, I'll keep him dark and safely lock'd.

                                Exeunt

SCENE TWO

Florence. A Room in the Widow's House.

Enter Bertram and Diana

BERTRAM. They told me that your name was Fontibell.

DIANA. No, my good lord, Diana.

BERTRAM.   Titled goddess;
And worth it, with addition! But, fair soul,
In your fine frame hath love no quality?
If the quick fire of youth light not your mind,
You are no maiden, but a monument:
When you are dead, you should be such a one
As you are now, for you are cold and stern;
And now you should be as your mother was
When your sweet self was got.

DIANA. She then was honest.

BERTRAM.   So should you be.

DIANA.   No:
My mother did but duty; such, my lord,
As you owe to your wife.

BERTRAM.   No more o' that!
I prithee do not strive against my vows.
I was compell'd to her; but I love thee
By love's own sweet constraint, and will for ever
Do thee all rights of service.

DIANA.   Ay, so you serve us
Till we serve you; but when you have our roses,
You barely leave our thorns to prick ourselves
And mock us with our bareness.

BERTRAM.   How have I sworn!

DIANA. 'Tis not the many oaths that make the truth,
But the plain single vow that is vow'd true.
What is not holy, that we swear not by,
But take the Highest to witness: then, pray you, tell me,
If I should swear by God's great attributes
I lov'd you dearly, would you believe my oaths,
When I did love you ill? This has no holding,
To swear by him whom I protest to love,
That I will work against him: therefore your oaths

Are words and poor conditions, but unseal'd;
At least in my opinion.

BERTRAM. Change it, change it.
Be not so holy-cruel: love is holy;
And my integrity ne'er knew the crafts
That you do charge men with. Stand no more off,
But give thyself unto my sick desires,
Who then recover: say thou art mine, and ever
My love as it begins shall so persever.

DIANA. I see that men make ropes in such a scarr
That we 'll forsake ourselves. Give me that ring.

BERTRAM. I 'll lend it thee, my dear; but have no power
To give it from me.

DIANA. Will you not, my lord?

BERTRAM. It is an honour 'longing to our house,
Bequeathed down from many ancestors,
Which were the greatest obloquy i' the world
In me to lose.

DIANA. Mine honour 's such a ring:
My chastity 's the jewel of our house,
Bequeathed down from many ancestors,
Which were the greatest obloquy i' the world
In me to lose. Thus your own proper wisdom
Brings in the champion honour on my part
Against your vain assault.

BERTRAM. Here, take my ring:
My house, mine honour, yea, my life, be thine,
And I 'll be bid by thee.

DIANA. When midnight comes, knock at my chamber-
window:
I 'll order take my mother shall not hear.
Now will I charge you in the band of truth,
When you have conquer'd my yet maiden bed,
Remain there but an hour, nor speak to me.
My reasons are most strong; and you shall know them
When back again this ring shall be deliver'd:
And on your finger in the night I 'll put
Another ring, that what in time proceeds
May token to the future our past deeds.
Adieu, till then; then, fail not. You have won
A wife of me, though there my hope be done.

BERTRAM. A heaven on earth I have won by wooing thee.

Exit

DIANA. For which live long to thank both heaven and me!
You may so in the end.
My mother told me just how he would woo
As if she sat in 's heart; she says all men
Have the like oaths: he had sworn to marry me
When his wife 's dead; therefore I 'll lie with him
When I am buried. Since Frenchmen are so braid,
Marry that will, I live and die a maid:
Only in this disguise I think 't no sin
To cozen him that would unjustly win.   *Exit*

SCENE THREE

The Florentine Camp.

Enter the two French Lords, and two or three Soldiers

FIRST LORD. You have not given him his mother's letter?

SECOND LORD. I have delivered it an hour since: there is
something in 't that stings his nature, for on the reading it
he changed almost into another man.

FIRST LORD. He has much worthy blame laid upon him for
shaking off so good a wife and so sweet a lady.

SECOND LORD. Especially he hath incurred the everlasting
displeasure of the king, who had even tuned his bounty to
sing happiness to him. I will tell you a thing, but you shall
let it dwell darkly with you.

FIRST LORD. When you have spoken it, 'tis dead, and I am
the grave of it.

SECOND LORD. He hath perverted a young gentle-woman
here in Florence, of a most chaste renown; and this night
he fleshes his will in the spoil of her honour: he hath given
her his monumental ring, and thinks himself made in the
unchaste composition.

FIRST LORD. Now, God delay our rebellion! As we are ourselves, what things are we!

SECOND LORD. Merely our own traitors: and as in the common course of all treasons, we still see them reveal themselves, till they attain to their abhorred ends, so he that in

this action contrives against his own nobility, in his proper stream o'erflows himself.

FIRST LORD. Is it not most damnable in us, to be trumpeters of our unlawful intents? We shall not then have his company to-night?

SECOND LORD. Not till after midnight, for he is dieted to his hour.

FIRST LORD. That approaches apace: I would gladly have him see his company anatomized, that he might take a measure of his own judgments, wherein so curiously he had set this counterfeit.

SECOND LORD. We will not meddle with him till he come, for his presence must be the whip of the other.

FIRST LORD. In the meantime what hear you of these wars?

SECOND LORD. I hear there is an overture of peace.

FIRST LORD. Nay, I assure you, a peace concluded.

SECOND LORD. What will Count Rousillon do then? Will he travel higher, or return again into France?

FIRST LORD. I perceive by this demand, you are not altogether of his council.

SECOND LORD. Let it be forbid, sir; so should I be a great deal of his act.

FIRST LORD. Sir, his wife some two months since fled from his house: her pretence is a pilgrimage to Saint Jaques le Grand; which holy undertaking with most austere sanctimony she accomplished; and, there residing, the tenderness of her nature became as a prey to her grief; in fine, made a groan of her last breath, and now she sings in heaven.

SECOND LORD. How is this justified?

FIRST LORD. The stronger part of it by her own letters, which make her story true, even to the point of her death: her death itself, which could not be her office to say is come, was faithfully confirmed by the rector of the place.

SECOND LORD. Hath the count all this intelligence?

FIRST LORD. Ay, and the particular confirmations, point from point, to the full arming of the verity.

SECOND LORD. I am heartily sorry that he'll be glad of this.

FIRST LORD. How mightily sometimes we make us comforts of our losses!

SECOND LORD. And how mightily some other times we drown our gain in tears! The great dignity that his valour hath

here acquired for him shall at home be encountered with a
shame as ample.

FIRST LORD. The web of our life is of a mingled yarn, good
and ill together: our virtues would be proud if our faults
whipped them not; and our crimes would despair if they
were not cherished by our virtues.

Enter a Servant

How now! where 's your master?

SERVANT. He met the duke in the street, sir, of whom he hath
taken a solemn leave: his lordship will next morning for
France. The duke hath offered him letters of commendations to the king.

SECOND LORD. They shall be no more than needful there, if
they were more than they can commend.

FIRST LORD. They cannot be too sweet for the king's tartness.
Here 's his lordship now.

Enter Bertram

How now, my lord: is 't not after midnight?

BERTRAM. I have to-night dispatched sixteen businesses, a
month's length a-piece, by an abstract of success: I have
conge'd with the duke, done my adieu with his nearest,
buried a wife, mourned for her, writ to my lady mother I
am returning, entertained my convoy; and between these
main parcels of dispatch effected many nicer needs: the
last was the greatest, but that I have not ended yet.

SECOND LORD. If the business be of any difficulty, and this
morning your departure hence, it requires haste of your
lordship.

BERTRAM. I mean, the business is not ended, as fearing to
hear of it hereafter. But shall we have this dialogue between the fool and the soldier? Come, bring forth this
counterfeit model: he has deceived me, like a double-
meaning prophesier.

SECOND LORD. Bring him forth. (*Exeunt Soldiers*) Has sat i'
the stocks all night, poor gallant knave.

BERTRAM. No matter; his heels have deserved it, in usurping
his spurs so long. How does he carry himself?

FIRST LORD. I have told your lordship already, the stocks
carry him. But to answer you as you would be understood;
he weeps like a wench that had shed her milk: he hath
confessed himself to Morgan,—whom he supposes to be a
friar,—from the time of his remembrance to this very in-

stant disaster of his setting i' the stocks: and
what think you he hath confessed?

BERTRAM. Nothing of me, has a'?

SECOND LORD. His confession is taken, and it shall be read to
his face: if your lordship be in 't, as I believe you are, you
must have the patience to hear it.

Re-enter Soldiers with Parolles

BERTRAM. A plague upon him! muffled! he can say nothing
of me: hush! hush!

FIRST LORD. Hoodman comes! Porto tartarossa.

FIRST SOLDIER. He calls for the tortures: what will you say
without 'em?

PAROLLES. I will confess what I know without constraint: if
ye pinch me like a pasty, I can say no more.

FIRST SOLDIER. Bosko chimurcho.

FIRST LORD. Boblibindo chicurmurco.

FIRST SOLDIER. You are a merciful general. Our general bids
you answer to what I shall ask you out of a note.

PAROLLES. And truly, as I hope to live.

FIRST SOLDIER. 'First, demand of him how many horse the
duke is strong.' What say you to that?

PAROLLES. Five or six thousand; but very weak and unserv-
iceable: the troops are all scattered, and the commanders
very poor rogues, upon my reputation and credit, and as I
hope to live.

FIRST SOLDIER. Shall I set down your answer so?

PAROLLES. Do: I 'll take the sacrament on 't, how and which
way you will.

BERTRAM. All 's one to him. What a past-saving slave is this!

FIRST LORD. You are deceived, my lord: this is Monsieur
Parolles, the gallant militarist,—that was his own phrase,—
that had the whole theorick of war in the knot of his scarf,
and the practice in the chape of his dagger.

SECOND LORD. I will never trust a man again for keeping his
sword clean; nor believe he can have everything in him by
wearing his apparel neatly.

FIRST SOLDIER. Well, that 's set down.

PAROLLES. Five or six thousand horse, I said,—I will say true,
—or thereabouts, set down, for I 'll speak truth.

FIRST LORD. He 's very near the truth in this.

BERTRAM. But I con him no thanks for 't, in the nature he delivers it.

PAROLLES. Poor rogues, I pray you, say.

FIRST SOLDIER. Well, that 's set down.

PAROLLES. I humbly thank you, sir. A truth 's a truth; the rogues are marvellous poor.

FIRST SOLDIER. 'Demand of him, of what strength they are a-foot.' What say you to that?

PAROLLES. By my troth, sir, if I were to live this present hour, I will tell true. Let me see: Spurio, a hundred and fifty; Sebastian, so many; Corambus, so many; Jaques, so many; Guiltian, Cosmo, Lodowick, and Gratii, two hundred fifty each; mine own company, Chitopher, Vaumond, Bentii, two hundred fifty each: so that the muster-file, rotten and sound, upon my life, amounts not to fifteen thousand poll; half of the which dare not shake the snow from off their cassocks, lest they shake themselves to pieces.

BERTRAM. What shall be done to him?

FIRST LORD. Nothing, but let him have thanks. Demand of him my condition, and what credit I have with the duke.

FIRST SOLDIER. Well, that 's set down. 'You shall demand of him, whether one Captain Dumain be i' the camp, a Frenchman; what his reputation is with the duke; what his valour, honesty, and expertness in wars; or whether he thinks it were not possible, with well-weighing sums of gold, to corrupt him to a revolt.' What say you to this? What do you know of it?

PAROLLES. I beseech you, let me answer to the particular of the inter'gatories: demand them singly.

FIRST SOLDIER. Do you know this Captain Dumain?

PAROLLES. I know him: a' was a botcher's 'prentice in Paris, from whence he was whipped for getting the shrieve's fool with child; a dumb innocent, that could not say him nay.

Dumain lifts up his hand in anger

BERTRAM. Nay, by your leave, hold your hands; though I know his brains are forfeit to the next tile that falls.

FIRST SOLDIER. Well, is this captain in the Duke of Florence's camp?

PAROLLES. Upon my knowledge he is, and lousy.

FIRST LORD. Nay, look not so upon me; we shall hear of your lordship anon.

FIRST SOLDIER. What is his reputation with the duke?

PAROLLES. The duke knows him for no other but a poor officer of mine, and writ to me this other day to turn him out o' the band: I think I have his letter in my pocket.

FIRST SOLDIER. Marry, we 'll search.

PAROLLES. In good sadness, I do not know: either it is there, or it is upon a file with the duke's other letters in my tent.

FIRST SOLDIER. Here 'tis; here 's a paper; shall I read it to you?

PAROLLES. I do not know if it be it or no.

BERTRAM. Our interpreter does it well.

FIRST LORD. Excellently.

FIRST SOLDIER. 'Dian, the count 's a fool, and full of gold'—

PAROLLES. That is not the duke's letter, sir; that is an advertisement to a proper maid in Florence, one Diana, to take heed of the allurement of one Count Rousillon, a foolish idle boy, but for all that very ruttish. I pray you, sir, put it up again.

FIRST SOLDIER. Nay, I 'll read it first, by your favour.

PAROLLES. My meaning in 't, I protest, was very honest in the behalf of the maid; for I knew the young count to be a dangerous and lascivious boy, who is a whale to virginity, and devours up all the fry it finds.

BERTRAM. Damnable both-sides rogue!

FIRST SOLDIER. 'When he swears oaths, bid him drop gold
    and take it;
After he scores, he never pays the score:
Half won is match well made; match, and well make it;
He ne'er pays after-debts; take it before,
And say a soldier, Dian, told thee this,
Men are to mell with, boys are not to kiss;
For count of this, the count 's a fool, I know it,
Who pays before, but not when he does owe it.
    Thine, as he vow'd to thee in thine ear,   Parolles.'

BERTRAM. He shall be whipped through the army with this rime in 's forehead.

FIRST LORD. This is your devoted friend, sir; the manifold linguist and the armipotent soldier.

BERTRAM. I could endure anything before but a cat, and now he 's a cat to me.

FIRST SOLDIER. I perceive, sir, by our general's looks, we shall be fain to hang you.

PAROLLES. My life, sir, in any case! Not that I am afraid to die; but that, my offences being many, I would repent out

the remainder of nature. Let me live, sir, in a dungeon, i'
the stocks, or anywhere, so I may live.

FIRST SOLDIER. We 'll see what may be done, so you confess
freely: therefore, once more to this Captain Dumain. You
have answered to his reputation with the duke and to his
valour: what is his honesty?

PAROLLES. He will steal, sir, an egg out of a cloister; for
rapes and ravishments he parallels Nessus; he professes
not keeping of oaths; in breaking 'em he is stronger than
Hercules; he will lie, sir, with such volubility, that you
would think truth were a fool; drunkenness is his best virtue, for he will be swine-drunk, and in his sleep he does
little harm, save to his bed-clothes about him; but they
know his conditions, and lay him in straw. I have but little
more to say, sir, of his honesty: he has everything that an
honest man should not have; what an honest man should
have, he has nothing.

FIRST LORD. I begin to love him for this.

BERTRAM. For this description of thine honesty? A pox upon
him for me! He is more and more a cat.

FIRST SOLDIER. What say you to his expertness in war?

PAROLLES. Faith, sir, he has led the drum before the English
tragedians,—to belie him I will not,—and more of his soldiership I know not; except, in that country, he had the
honour to be the officer at a place there called Mile-end, to
instruct for the doubling of files: I would do the man what
honour I can, but of this I am not certain.

FIRST LORD. He hath out-villained villany so far, that the
rarity redeems him.

BERTRAM. A pox on him! He 's a cat still.

FIRST SOLDIER. His qualities being at this poor price, I need
not ask you, if gold will corrupt him to revolt.

PAROLLES. Sir, for a cardecu he will sell the fee-simple of his
salvation, the inheritance of it; and cut the entail from all
remainders, and a perpetual succession for it perpetually.

FIRST SOLDIER. What 's his brother, the other Captain Dumain?

SECOND LORD. Why does he ask him of me?

FIRST SOLDIER. What 's he?

PAROLLES. E'en a crow o' the same nest; not altogether so
great as the first in goodness, but greater a great deal in
evil. He excels his brother for a coward, yet his brother is

reputed one of the best that is. In a retreat he out-
runs any lackey; marry, in coming on he has the cramp.

FIRST SOLDIER. If your life be saved, will you undertake to
betray the Florentine?

PAROLLES. Ay, and the captain of his horse, Count Rousillon.

FIRST SOLDIER. I 'll whisper with the general, and know his
pleasure.

PAROLLES. (*Aside*) I 'll no more drumming; a plague of all
drums! Only to seem to deserve well, and to beguile the
supposition of that lascivious young boy the count, have I
run into this danger. Yet who would have suspected an
ambush where I was taken?

FIRST SOLDIER. There is no remedy, sir, but you must die.
The general says, you, that have so traitorously discovered
the secrets of your army, and made such pestiferous reports of men very nobly held, can serve the world for no
honest use; therefore you must die. Come, headsman, off
with his head.

PAROLLES. O Lord, sir, let me live, or let me see my death!

FIRST SOLDIER. That shall you, and take your leave of all
your friends.   *Unmuffling him*
So, look about you: know you any here?

BERTRAM. Good-morrow, noble captain.

SECOND LORD. God bless you, Captain Parolles.

FIRST LORD. God save you, noble captain.

SECOND LORD. Captain, what greeting will you to my Lord
Lafeu? I am for France.

FIRST LORD. Good captain, will you give me a copy of the
sonnet you writ to Diana in behalf of the Count Rousillon?
An I were not a very coward I 'd compel it of you; but fare
you well.   *Exeunt Bertram and Lords*

FIRST SOLDIER. You are undone, captain; all but your scarf;
that has a knot on 't yet.

PAROLLES. Who cannot be crushed with a plot?

FIRST SOLDIER. If you could find out a country where but
women were that had received so much shame, you might
begin an impudent nation. Fare ye well, sir; I am for
France too: we shall speak of you there.   *Exit*

PAROLLES. Yet am I thankful: if my heart were great
'Twould burst at this. Captain I 'll be no more;
But I will eat and drink, and sleep as soft
As captain shall: simply the thing I am

Shall make me live. Who knows himself a braggart,
Let him fear this; for it will come to pass
That every braggart shall be found an ass.
Rust, sword! cool, blushes! and Parolles, live
Safest in shame! being fool'd, by foolery thrive!
There 's place and means for every man alive.
I 'll after them.   *Exit*

SCENE FOUR

Florence. A Room in the Widow's House.

Enter Helena, Widow, and Diana

HELENA. That you may well perceive I have not wrong'd
          you,
One of the greatest in the Christian world
Shall be my surety; 'fore whose throne 'tis needful,
Ere I can perfect mine intents, to kneel.
Time was I did him a desired office,
Dear almost as his life; which gratitude
Through flinty Tartar's bosom would peep forth,
And answer, thanks. I duly am inform'd
His Grace is at Marseilles; to which place
We have convenient convoy. You must know,
I am supposed dead: the army breaking,
My husband hies him home; where, heaven aiding,
And by the leave of my good lord the king,
We 'll be before our welcome.
WIDOW.   Gentle madam,
You never had a servant to whose trust
Your business was more welcome.
HELENA.   Nor you, mistress,
Ever a friend whose thoughts more truly labour
To recompense your love. Doubt not but heaven
Hath brought me up to be your daughter's dower,
As it hath fated her to be my motive
And helper to a husband. But, O strange men!
That can such sweet use make of what they hate,
When saucy trusting of the cozen'd thoughts
Defiles the pitchy night: so lust doth play
With what it loathes for that which is away.

But more of this hereafter. You, Diana,
Under my poor instructions yet must suffer
Something in my behalf.

DIANA.   Let death and honesty
Go with your impositions, I am yours
Upon your will to suffer.

HELENA.   Yet, I pray you:
But with the word the time will bring on summer,
When briers shall have leaves as well as thorns,
And be as sweet as sharp. We must away;
Our waggon is prepar'd, and time revives us:
All's well that ends well: still the fine's the crown;
Whate'er the course, the end is the renown.   *Exeunt*

SCENE FIVE

Rousillon. A Room in the Countess's Palace.

Enter Countess, Lafeu, and Clown

LAFEU. No, no, no; your son was misled with a snipt-taffeta
fellow there, whose villanous saffron would have made all
the unbaked and doughy youth of a nation in his colour:
your daughter-in-law had been alive at this hour, and your
son here at home, more advanced by the king than by that
red-tailed humble-bee I speak of.

COUNTESS. I would I had not known him; it was the death of
the most virtuous gentlewoman that ever nature had
praise for creating. If she had partaken of my flesh, and
cost me the dearest groans of a mother, I could not have
owed her a more rooted love.

LAFEU. 'Twas a good lady, 'twas a good lady: we may pick a
thousand salads ere we light on such another herb.

CLOWN. Indeed, sir, she was the sweet-marjoram of the sal-
ad, or, rather the herb of grace.

LAFEU. They are not salad-herbs, you knave; they are nose-
herbs.

CLOWN. I am no great Nebuchadnezzar, sir; I have not much
skill in grass.

LAFEU. Whether dost thou profess thyself, a knave, or a
fool?

CLOWN. A fool, sir, at a woman's service, and a knave at a man's.

LAFEU. Your distinction?

CLOWN. I would cozen the man of his wife, and do his service.

LAFEU. So you were a knave at his service, indeed.

CLOWN. And I would give his wife my bauble, sir, to do her service.

LAFEU. I will subscribe for thee, thou art both knave and fool.

CLOWN. At your service.

LAFEU. No, no, no.

CLOWN. Why, sir, if I cannot serve you, I can serve as great a prince as you are.

LAFEU. Who's that? a Frenchman?

CLOWN. Faith, sir, a' has an English name; but his phisnomy is more hotter in France than there.

LAFEU. What prince is that?

CLOWN. The black prince, sir; alias, the prince of darkness; alias, the devil.

LAFEU. Hold thee, there's my purse. I give thee not this to suggest thee from thy master thou talkest of: serve him still.

CLOWN. I am a woodland fellow, sir, that always loved a great fire; and the master I speak of, ever keeps a good fire. But, sure, he is the prince of the world; let his nobility remain in's court. I am for the house with the narrow gate, which I take to be too little for pomp to enter: some that humble themselves may; but the many will be too chill and tender, and they'll be for the flowery way that leads to the broad gate and the great fire.

LAFEU. Go thy ways, I begin to be aweary of thee; and I tell thee so before, because I would not fall out with thee. Go thy ways: let my horses be well looked to, without any tricks.

CLOWN. If I put any tricks upon 'em, sir, they shall be jades' tricks, which are their own right by the law of nature.

Exit

LAFEU. A shrewd knave and an unhappy.

COUNTESS. So he is. My lord that's gone made himself much sport out of him: by his authority he remains here, which he thinks is a patent for his sauciness; and, indeed, he has no pace, but runs where he will.

LAFEU. I like him well; 'tis not amiss. And I was about to tell you, since I heard of the good lady's death, and that my lord your son was upon his return home, I moved the king my master to speak in the behalf of my daughter; which, in the minority of them both, his Majesty, out of a self-gracious remembrance, did first propose. His Highness hath promised me to do it; and to stop up the displeasure he hath conceived against your son, there is no fitter matter. How does your ladyship like it?

COUNTESS. With very much content, my lord; and I wish it happily effected.

LAFEU. His Highness comes post from Marseilles, of as able body as when he numbered thirty: he will be here to-morrow, or I am deceived by him that in such intelligence hath seldom failed.

COUNTESS. It rejoices me that I hope I shall see him ere I die. I have letters that my son will be here to-night: I shall beseech your lordship to remain with me till they meet together.

LAFEU. Madam, I was thinking with what manners I might safely be admitted.

COUNTESS. You need but plead your honourable privilege.

LAFEU. Lady, of that I have made a bold charter; but I thank my God it holds yet.

Re-enter Clown

CLOWN. O madam! yonder 's my lord your son with a patch of velvet on 's face: whether there be a scar under it or no, the velvet knows; but 'tis a goodly patch of velvet. His left cheek is a cheek of two pile and a half, but his right cheek is worn bare.

LAFEU. A scar nobly got, or a noble scar, is a good livery of honour; so belike is that.

CLOWN. But it is your carbonadoed face.

LAFEU. Let us go see your son, I pray you: I long to talk with the young noble soldier.

CLOWN. Faith, there 's a dozen of 'em, with delicate fine hats and most courteous feathers, which bow the head and nod at every man.   *Exeunt*

ACT FIVE

SCENE ONE

Marseilles. A Street.

Enter Helena, Widow, and Diana, with two Attendants

HELENA. But this exceeding posting, day and night,
Must wear your spirits low; we cannot help it:
But since you have made the days and nights as one,
To wear your gentle limbs in my affairs,
Be bold you do so grow in my requital
As nothing can unroot you. In happy time;
                    Enter a gentle Astringer
This man may help me to his Majesty's ear,
If he would spend his power. God save you, sir.

ASTRINGER. And you.

HELENA. Sir, I have seen you in the court of France.

ASTRINGER. I have been sometimes there.

HELENA. I do presume, sir, that you are not fallen
From the report that goes upon your goodness;
And therefore, goaded with most sharp occasions,
Which lay nice manners by, I put you to
The use of your own virtues, for the which
I shall continue thankful.

ASTRINGER.   What 's your will?

HELENA. That it will please you
To give this poor petition to the king,
And aid me with that store of power you have
To come into his presence.

ASTRINGER. The king 's not here.

HELENA.   Not here, sir!

ASTRINGER.   Not, indeed:
He hence remov'd last night, and with more haste
Than is his use.

WIDOW.   Lord, how we lose our pains!

HELENA. All 's well that ends well yet,
Though time seems so adverse and means unfit.
I do beseech you, whither is he gone?

ASTRINGER. Marry, as I take it, to Rousillon;
Whither I am going.

HELENA.   I do beseech you, sir,
Since you are like to see the king before me,
Commend the paper to his gracious hand;
Which I presume shall render you no blame
But rather make you thank your pains for it.
I will come after you with what good speed
Our means will make us means.

ASTRINGER.   This I 'll do for you.

HELENA. And you shall find yourself to be well thank'd,
Whate'er falls more. We must to horse again:
Go, go, provide.   *Exeunt*

SCENE TWO

Rousillon. The inner Court of the Countess's Palace.

Enter Clown and Parolles

PAROLLES. Good Monsieur Lavache, give my Lord Lafeu
this letter. I have ere now, sir, been better known to you,
when I have held familiarity with fresher clothes; but I am
now, sir, muddied in Fortune's mood, and smell somewhat
strong of her strong displeasure.

CLOWN. Truly, Fortune's displeasure is but sluttish if it smell
so strongly as thou speakest of: I will henceforth eat no
fish of Fortune's buttering. Prithee, allow the wind.

PAROLLES. Nay, you need not to stop your nose, sir: I spake
but by a metaphor.

CLOWN. Indeed, sir, if your metaphor stink, I will stop my
nose; or against any man's metaphor. Prithee, get thee further.

PAROLLES. Pray you, sir, deliver me this paper.

CLOWN. Foh! prithee, stand away: a paper from Fortune's
close-stool to give to a nobleman! Look, here he comes
himself.

Enter Lafeu

Here is a purr of Fortune's, sir, or of Fortune's cat—but not a musk-cat—that has fallen into the unclean fishpond of her displeasure, and, as he says, is muddied withal. Pray you, sir, use the carp as you may, for he looks like a poor, decayed, ingenious, foolish, rascally knave. I do pity his distress in my similes of comfort, and leave him to your lordship.   *Exit*

PAROLLES. My lord, I am a man whom Fortune hath cruelly scratched.

LAFEU. And what would you have me to do? 'Tis too late to pare her nails now. Wherein have you played the knave with Fortune that she should scratch you, who of herself is a good lady, and would not have knaves thrive long under her? There 's a cardecu for you. Let the justices make you and Fortune friends; I am for other business.

PAROLLES. I beseech your honour to hear me one single word.

LAFEU. You beg a single penny more: come, you shall ha 't; save your word.

PAROLLES. My name, my good lord, is Parolles.

LAFEU. You beg more than one word then. Cox my passion! Give me your hand. How does your drum?

PAROLLES. O, my good lord! You were the first that found me.

LAFEU. Was I, in sooth? And I was the first that lost thee.

PAROLLES. It lies in you, my lord, to bring me in some grace, for you did bring me out.

LAFEU. Out upon thee, knave! Dost thou put upon me at once both the office of God and the devil? One brings thee in grace and the other brings thee out. (*Trumpets sound*) The king 's coming; I know by his trumpets. Sirrah, inquire further after me; I had talk of you last night: though you are a fool and a knave, you shall eat: go to, follow.

PAROLLES. I praise God for you.   *Exeunt*

SCENE THREE

The Same. A Room in the Countess's Palace.

Flourish. Enter King, Countess, Lafeu, Lords,
Gentlemen, Guards, &c.

KING. We lost a jewel of her, and our esteem
Was made much poorer by it: but your son,
As mad in folly, lack'd the sense to know
Her estimation home.

COUNTESS.   'Tis past, my liege;
And I beseech your Majesty to make it
Natural rebellion, done i' the blaze of youth;
When oil and fire, too strong for reason's force,
O'erbears it and burns on.

KING.   My honour'd lady,
I have forgiven and forgotten all,
Though my revenges were high bent upon him,
And watch'd the time to shoot.

LAFEU.   This I must say,—
But first I beg my pardon,—the young lord
Did to his Majesty, his mother, and his lady,
Offence of mighty note, but to himself
The greatest wrong of all: he lost a wife
Whose beauty did astonish the survey
Of richest eyes, whose words all ears took captive,
Whose dear perfection hearts that scorn'd to serve
Humbly call'd mistress.

KING.   Praising what is lost
Makes the remembrance dear. Well, call him hither;
We are reconcil'd, and the first view shall kill
All repetition. Let him not ask our pardon:
The nature of his great offence is dead,
And deeper than oblivion we do bury
The incensing relics of it: let him approach,
A stranger, no offender; and inform him
So 'tis our will he should.

GENTLEMAN.   I shall, my liege.   *Exit*

KING. What says he to your daughter? have you spoke?

LAFEU. All that he is hath reference to your Highness.

KING. Then shall we have a match. I have letters sent me,
    That set him high in fame.

Enter Bertram

LAFEU.   He looks well on 't.
KING. I am not a day of season,
    For thou mayst see a sunshine and a hail
    In me at once; but to the brightest beams
    Distracted clouds give way: so stand thou forth;
    The time is fair again.
BERTRAM.   My high-repented blames,
    Dear sovereign, pardon to me.
KING.   All is whole;
    Not one word more of the consumed time.
    Let 's take the instant by the forward top,
    For we are old, and on our quick'st decrees
    The inaudible and noiseless foot of time
    Steals ere we can effect them. You remember
    The daughter of this lord?
BERTRAM. Admiringly, my liege:
    At first I stuck my choice upon her, ere my heart
    Durst make too bold a herald of my tongue,
    Where the impression of mine eye infixing,
    Contempt his scornful perspective did lend me,
    Which warp'd the line of every other favour;
    Scorn'd a fair colour, or express'd it stolen;
    Extended or contracted all proportions
    To a most hideous object: thence it came
    That she, whom all men prais'd, and whom myself,
    Since I have lost, have lov'd, was in mine eye
    The dust that did offend it.
KING.   Well excus'd:
    That thou didst love her, strikes some scores away
    From the great compt. But love that comes too late,
    Like a remorseful pardon slowly carried,
    To the great sender turns a sour offence,
    Crying, 'That 's good that 's gone.' Our rasher faults
    Make trivial price of serious things we have,
    Not knowing them until we know their grave:
    Oft our displeasures, to ourselves unjust,
    Destroy our friends and after weep their dust:
    Our own love waking cries to see what 's done,
    While shameful hate sleeps out the afternoon.

Be this sweet Helen's knell, and now forget her.
Send forth your amorous token for fair Maudlin:
The main consents are had; and here we 'll stay
To see our widower's second marriage-day.

COUNTESS. Which better than the first, O dear heaven, bless!
Or, ere they meet, in me, O nature, cesse!

LAFEU. Come on, my son, in whom my house's name
Must be digested, give a favour from you
To sparkle in the spirits of my daughter,
That she may quickly come.   *Bertram gives a ring*
                    By my old beard,
And every hair that 's on 't, Helen, that 's dead,
Was a sweet creature; such a ring as this,
The last that e'er I took her leave at court,
I saw upon her finger.

BERTRAM.   Hers it was not.

KING. Now, pray you, let me see it; for mine eye,
While I was speaking, oft was fasten'd to 't.—
This ring was mine; and, when I gave it Helen,
I bade her, if her fortunes ever stood
Necessitied to help, that by this token
I would relieve her. Had you that craft to reave her
Of what should stead her most?

BERTRAM.   My gracious sovereign,
Howe'er it pleases you to take it so,
The ring was never hers.

COUNTESS.   Son, on my life,
I have seen her wear it; and she reckon'd it
At her life's rate.

LAFEU.   I am sure I saw her wear it.

BERTRAM. You are deceiv'd, my lord, she never saw it:
In Florence was it from a casement thrown me,
Wrapp'd in a paper, which contain'd the name
Of her that threw it. Noble she was, and thought
I stood engag'd: but when I had subscrib'd
To mine own fortune, and inform'd her fully
I could not answer in that course of honour
As she had made the overture, she ceas'd,
In heavy satisfaction, and would never
Receive the ring again.

KING.   Plutus himself,
That knows the tinct and multiplying medicine,

Hath not in nature's mystery more science
Than I have in this ring: 'twas mine, 'twas Helen's,
Whoever gave it you. Then, if you know
That you are well acquainted with yourself,
Confess 'twas hers, and by what rough enforcement
You got it from her. She call'd the saints to surety,
That she would never put it from her finger
Unless she gave it to yourself in bed,
Where you have never come, or sent it us
Upon her great disaster.

BERTRAM.   She never saw it.

KING. Thou speak'st it falsely, as I love mine honour;
And mak'st conjectural fears to come into me
Which I would fain shut out. If it should prove
That thou art so inhuman,—'twill not prove so;—
And yet I know not: thou didst hate her deadly,
And she is dead; which nothing, but to close
Her eyes myself, could win me to believe,
More than to see this ring. Take him away.

                              Guards seize Bertram

My fore-past proofs, howe'er the matter fall,
Shall tax my fears of little vanity,
Having vainly fear'd too little. Away with him!
We 'll sift this matter further.

BERTRAM.   If you shall prove
This ring was ever hers, you shall as easy
Prove that I husbanded her bed in Florence,
Where yet she never was.   *Exit guarded*

KING. I am wrapp'd in dismal thinkings.

                    Enter the gentle Astringer

ASTRINGER.   Gracious sovereign,
Whether I have been to blame or no, I know not:
Here 's a petition from a Florentine,
Who hath, for four or five removes, come short
To tender it herself. I undertook it,
Vanquish'd thereto by the fair grace and speech
Of the poor suppliant, who by this I know
Is here attending: her business looks in her
With an importing visage, and she told me,
In a sweet verbal brief, it did concern
Your Highness with herself.

KING. 'Upon his many protestations to marry me when his

wife was dead, I blush to say it, he won me. Now is the
Count Rousillon a widower: his vows are forfeited to me,
and my honour's paid to him. He stole from Florence, taking no leave, and I follow him to his country for justice.
Grant it me, O king! In you it best lies; otherwise a seducer
flourishes, and a poor maid is undone.

> 'Diana Capilet.'

LAFEU. I will buy me a son-in-law in a fair, and toll for this:
I 'll none of him.

KING. The heavens have thought well on thee, Lafeu,
To bring forth this discovery. Seek these suitors:
Go speedily and bring again the count.

Exeunt the gentle Astringer, and some Attendants

I am afeard the life of Helen, lady,
Was foully snatch'd.

COUNTESS. Now, justice on the doers!

Re-enter Bertram, guarded

KING. I wonder, sir, sith wives are monsters to you,
And that you fly them as you swear them lordship,
Yet you desire to marry.

Re-enter the gentle Astringer, with Widow and Diana
What woman 's that?

DIANA. I am, my lord, a wretched Florentine,
Derived from the ancient Capilet:
My suit, as I do understand, you know,
And therefore know how far I may be pitied.

WIDOW. I am her mother, sir, whose age and honour
Both suffer under this complaint we bring,
And both shall cease, without your remedy.

KING. Come hither, county; do you know these women?

BERTRAM. My lord, I neither can nor will deny
But that I know them: do they charge me further?

DIANA. Why do you look so strange upon your wife?

BERTRAM. She 's none of mine, my lord.

DIANA. If you shall marry,
You give away this hand, and that is mine;
You give away heaven's vows, and those are mine;
You give away myself, which is known mine;
For I by vow am so embodied yours
That she which marries you must marry me;
Either both or none.

LAFEU. (*To Bertram*) Your reputation comes too short for

my daughter: you are no husband for her.

BERTRAM. My lord, this is a fond and desperate creature,
    Whom sometime I have laugh'd with: let your Highness
    Lay a more noble thought upon mine honour
    Than for to think that I would sink it here.

KING. Sir, for my thoughts, you have them ill to friend,
    Till your deeds gain them: fairer prove your honour,
    Than in my thought it lies.

DIANA.   Good my lord,
    Ask him upon his oath, if he does think
    He had not my virginity.

KING. What sayst thou to her?

BERTRAM.   She 's impudent, my lord;
    And was a common gamester to the camp.

DIANA. He does me wrong, my lord; if I were so,
    He might have bought me at a common price:
    Do not believe him. O! behold this ring,
    Whose high respect and rich validity
    Did lack a parallel; yet for all that
    He gave it to a commoner o' the camp,
    If I be one.

COUNTESS.   He blushes, and 'tis it:
    Of six preceding ancestors, that gem
    Conferr'd by testament to the sequent issue,
    Hath it been ow'd and worn. This is his wife:
    That ring 's a thousand proofs.

KING.   Methought you said
    You saw one here in court could witness it.

DIANA. I did, my lord, but loath am to produce
    So bad an instrument: his name 's Parolles.

LAFEU. I saw the man to-day, if man he be.

KING. Find him, and bring him hither.   *Exit an Attendant*

BERTRAM.   What of him?
    He 's quoted for a most perfidious slave,
    With all the spots of the world tax'd and debosh'd,
    Whose nature sickens but to speak a truth.
    Am I or that or this for what he 'll utter,
    That will speak anything?

KING.   She hath that ring of yours.

BERTRAM. I think she has: certain it is I lik'd her,
    And boarded her i' the wanton way of youth.
    She knew her distance and did angle for me,

Madding my eagerness with her restraint,
As all impediments in fancy's course
Are motives of more fancy; and, in fine,
Her infinite cunning, with her modern grace,
Subdued me to her rate: she got the ring,
And I had that which any inferior might
At market-price have bought.

DIANA.   I must be patient;
You, that have turn'd off a first so noble wife,
May justly diet me. I pray you yet,—
Since you lack virtue I will lose a husband,—
Send for your ring; I will return it home,
And give me mine again.

BERTRAM.   I have it not.

KING. What ring was yours, I pray you?

DIANA.   Sir, much like
The same upon your finger.

KING. Know you this ring? This ring was his of late.

DIANA. And this was it I gave him, being a-bed.

KING. The story then goes false you threw it him
Out of a casement.

DIANA.   I have spoke the truth.

Re-enter Attendant with Parolles

BERTRAM. My lord, I do confess the ring was hers.

KING. You boggle shrewdly, every feather starts you.
Is this the man you speak of?

DIANA.   Ay, my lord.

KING. Tell me, sirrah, but tell me true, I charge you,
Not fearing the displeasure of your master,—
Which, on your just proceeding I 'll keep off,—
By him and by this woman here what know you?

PAROLLES. So please your Majesty, my master hath been an
honourable gentleman: tricks he hath had in him, which
gentlemen have.

KING. Come, come, to the purpose: did he love this woman?

PAROLLES. Faith, sir, he did love her; but how?

KING. How, I pray you?

PAROLLES. He did love her, sir, as a gentleman loves a
woman.

KING. How is that?

PAROLLES. He loved her, sir, and loved her not.

KING. As thou art a knave, and no knave.

KING. Let us from point to point this story know,
    To make the even truth in pleasure flow.
    (*To Diana*) If thou be'st yet a fresh uncropped flower,
    Choose thou thy husband, and I 'll pay thy dower;
    For I can guess that by thy honest aid
    Thou keptst a wife herself, thyself a maid.
    Of that, and all the progress, more and less,
    Resolvedly more leisure shall express:
    All yet seems well; and if it end so meet,
    The bitter past, more welcome is the sweet.
                                    Flourish. Exeunt

EPILOGUE

Spoken by the King

The king's a beggar, now the play is done:
All is well ended if this suit be won,
That you express content; which we will pay,
With strife to please you, day exceeding day:
Ours be your patience then, and yours our parts;
Your gentle hands lend us, and take our hearts.   *Exeunt*

TWELFTH-NIGHT; OR, WHAT YOU WILL

CAST OF CHARACTERS

ORSINO, *Duke of Illyria*
SEBASTIAN, *Brother to Viola*
ANTONIO, *a Sea Captain, Friend to Sebastian*
A Sea Captain, *Friend to Viola*
VALENTINE ⎫
CURIO ⎬ *Gentlemen attending on the Duke*

SIR TOBY BELCH, *Uncle to Olivia*
SIR ANDREW AGUECHEEK
MALVOLIO, *Steward to Olivia*
FABIAN ⎫
FESTE, *a Clown* ⎬ *Servants to Olivia*

OLIVIA, *a rich Countess*
VIOLA, *in love with the Duke*
MARIA, *Olivia's Woman*

Lords, Priests, Sailors, Officers, Musicians, and other Attendants

SCENE
A City in Illyria; and the Sea-coast near it

TWELFTH-NIGHT;
OR, WHAT YOU WILL

ACT ONE

SCENE ONE

A Room in the Duke's Palace.

Enter Duke, Curio, Lords; Musicians attending

DUKE. If music be the food of love, play on;
    Give me excess of it, that, surfeiting,
    The appetite may sicken, and so die.
    That strain again! It had a dying fall:
    O! it came o'er my ear like the sweet sound
    That breathes upon a bank of violets,
    Stealing and giving odour. Enough! no more:
    'Tis not so sweet now as it was before.
    O spirit of love! how quick and fresh art thou,
    That, notwithstanding thy capacity
    Receiveth as the sea, naught enters there,
    Of what validity and pitch soe'er,
    But falls into abatement and low price,
    Even in a minute: so full of shapes is fancy,
    That it alone is high fantastical.
CURIO. Will you go hunt, my lord?
DUKE.   What, Curio?
CURIO. The hart.
DUKE. Why, so I do, the noblest that I have.
    O! when mine eyes did see Olivia first,
    Methought she purg'd the air of pestilence.
    That instant was I turn'd into a hart,
    And my desires, like fell and cruel hounds,
    E'er since pursue me.
               Enter Valentine

How now! what news from her?

VALENTINE. So please my lord, I might not be admitted;
But from her handmaid to return this answer:
The element itself, till seven years' heat,
Shall not behold her face at ample view;
But, like a cloistress, she will veiled walk,
And water once a day her chamber round
With eye-offending brine: all this, to season
A brother's dead love, which she would keep fresh
And lasting in her sad remembrance.

DUKE. O! she that hath a heart of that fine frame
To pay this debt of love but to a brother,
How will she love, when the rich golden shaft
Hath kill'd the flock of all affections else
That live in her; when liver, brain, and heart,
These sovereign thrones, are all supplied, and fill'd
Her sweet perfections with one self king.
Away before me to sweet beds of flowers;
Love-thoughts lie rich when canopied with bowers.

Exeunt

SCENE TWO

The Sea-coast.

Enter Viola, Captain, and Sailors

VIOLA. What country, friends, is this?
CAPTAIN.　　　　　　　　　　　　　This is Illyria, lady.
VIOLA. And what should I do in Illyria?
My brother he is in Elysium.
Perchance he is not drown'd. What think you sailors?
CAPTAIN. It is perchance that you yourself were sav'd.
VIOLA. O my poor brother! and so perchance may he be.
CAPTAIN. True, madam: and, to comfort you with chance,
Assure yourself, after our ship did split,
When you and those poor number sav'd with you
Hung on our driving boat, I saw your brother,
Most provident in peril, bind himself,—
Courage and hope both teaching him the practice,—
To a strong mast that liv'd upon the sea;
Where, like Arion on the dolphin's back,

I saw him hold acquaintance with the waves
So long as I could see.

VIOLA.   For saying so there 's gold.
Mine own escape unfoldeth to my hope,
Whereto thy speech serves for authority,
The like of him. Know'st thou this country?

CAPTAIN. Ay, madam, well; for I was bred and born
Not three hours' travel from this very place.

VIOLA. Who governs here?

CAPTAIN. A noble duke, in nature as in name.

VIOLA. What is his name?

CAPTAIN. Orsino.

VIOLA. Orsino! I have heard my father name him:
He was a bachelor then.

CAPTAIN. And so is now, or was so very late;
For but a month ago I went from hence,
And then 'twas fresh in murmur,—as, you know,
What great ones do the less will prattle of,—
That he did seek the love of fair Olivia.

VIOLA. What 's she?

CAPTAIN. A virtuous maid, the daughter of a count
That died some twelvemonth since; then leaving her
In the protection of his son, her brother,
Who shortly also died: for whose dear love,
They say she hath abjur'd the company
And sight of men.

VIOLA.   O! that I serv'd that lady,
And might not be deliver'd to the world,
Till I had made mine own occasion mellow,
What my estate is.

CAPTAIN.   That were hard to compass,
Because she will admit no kind of suit,
No, not the duke's.

VIOLA. There is a fair behaviour in thee, captain;
And though that nature with a beauteous wall
Doth oft close in pollution, yet of thee
I will believe thou hast a mind that suits
With this thy fair and outward character.
I prithee,—and I 'll pay thee bounteously,—
Conceal me what I am, and be my aid
For such disguise as haply shall become
The form of my intent. I 'll serve this duke:

Thou shall present me as a eunuch to him:
It may be worth thy pains; for I can sing
And speak to him in many sorts of music
That will allow me very worth his service.
What else may hap to time I will commit;
Only shape thou thy silence to my wit.

CAPTAIN. Be you his eunuch, and your mute I 'll be:
When my tongue blabs, then let mine eyes not see.

VIOLA. I thank thee: lead me on.   *Exeunt*

SCENE THREE

A Room in Olivia's House.

Enter Sir Toby Belch and Maria

SIR TOBY. What a plague means my niece, to take the death
of her brother thus? I am sure care 's an enemy to life.

MARIA. By my troth, Sir Toby, you must come in earlier o'
nights: your cousin, my lady, takes great exceptions to
your ill hours.

SIR TOBY. Why, let her except before excepted.

MARIA. Ay, but you must confine yourself within the modest
limits of order.

SIR TOBY. Confine! I 'll confine myself no finer than I am.
These clothes are good enough to drink in, and so be these
boots too: an they be not, let them hang themselves in
their own straps.

MARIA. That quaffing and drinking will undo you: I heard
my lady talk of it yesterday; and of a foolish knight that
you brought in one night here to be her wooer.

SIR TOBY. Who? Sir Andrew Aguecheek?

MARIA. Ay, he.

SIR TOBY. He 's as tall a man as any 's in Illyria.

MARIA. What 's that to the purpose?

SIR TOBY. Why, he has three thousand ducats a year.

MARIA. Ay, but he 'll have but a year in all these ducats: he 's
a very fool and a prodigal.

SIR TOBY. Fie, that you 'll say so! He plays o' the viol-de-
gamboys, and speaks three or four languages word for
word without book, and hath all the good gifts of nature.

MARIA. He hath indeed, almost natural; for, besides that he's a fool, he's a great quarreller; and but that he hath the gift of a coward to allay the gust he hath in quarrelling, 'tis thought among the prudent he would quickly have the gift of a grave.

SIR TOBY. By this hand, they are scoundrels and substractors that say so of him. Who are they?

MARIA. They that add, moreover, he's drunk nightly in your company.

SIR TOBY. With drinking healths to my niece. I'll drink to her as long as there is a passage in my throat and drink in Illyria. He's a coward and a coystril, that will not drink to my niece till his brains turn o' the toe like a parish-top. What, wench! Castiliano vulgo! for here comes Sir Andrew Agueface.

Enter Sir Andrew Aguecheek

SIR ANDREW. Sir Toby Belch! How now, Sir Toby Belch!

SIR TOBY. Sweet Sir Andrew!

SIR ANDREW. Bless you, fair shrew.

MARIA. And you too, sir.

SIR TOBY. Accost, Sir Andrew, accost.

SIR ANDREW. What's that?

SIR TOBY. My niece's chambermaid.

SIR ANDREW. Good Mistress Accost, I desire better acquaintance.

MARIA. My name is Mary, sir.

SIR ANDREW. Good Mistress Mary Accost,—

SIR TOBY. You mistake, knight: 'accost' is, front her, board her, woo her, assail her.

SIR ANDREW. By my troth, I would not undertake her in this company. Is that the meaning of 'accost'?

MARIA. Fare you well, gentlemen.

SIR TOBY. An thou let her part so, Sir Andrew, would thou mightst never draw sword again!

SIR ANDREW. An you part so, mistress, I would I might never draw sword again. Fair lady, do you think you have fools in hand?

MARIA. Sir, I have not you by the hand.

SIR ANDREW. Marry, but you shall have; and here's my hand.

MARIA. Now, sir, 'thought is free': I pray you, bring your hand to the buttery-bar and let it drink.

SIR ANDREW. Wherefore, sweetheart? What 's your metaphor?

MARIA. It 's dry, sir.

SIR ANDREW. Why, I think so: I am not such an ass but I can keep my hand dry. But what 's your jest?

MARIA. A dry jest, sir.

SIR ANDREW. Are you full of them?

MARIA. Ay, sir, I have them at my fingers' ends: marry, now I let go your hand, I am barren. *Exit*

SIR TOBY. O knight! thou lackest a cup of canary: when did I see thee so put down?

SIR ANDREW. Never in your life, I think; unless you see canary put me down. Methinks sometimes I have no more wit than a Christian or an ordinary man has; but I am a great eater of beef, and I believe that does harm to my wit.

SIR TOBY. No question.

SIR ANDREW. An I thought that, I 'd forswear it. I 'll ride home to-morrow, Sir Toby.

SIR TOBY. Pourquoi, my dear knight?

SIR ANDREW. What is 'pourquoi'? Do or not do? I would I had bestowed that time in the tongues that I have in fencing, dancing, and bear-baiting. O! had I but followed the arts!

SIR TOBY. Then hadst thou had an excellent head of hair.

SIR ANDREW. Why, would that have mended my hair?

SIR TOBY. Past question; for thou seest it will not curl by nature.

SIR ANDREW. But it becomes me well enough, does 't not?

SIR TOBY. Excellent; it hangs like flax on a distaff, and I hope to see a housewife take thee between her legs, and spin it off.

SIR ANDREW. Faith, I 'll home to-morrow, Sir Toby: your niece will not be seen; or if she be, it 's four to one she 'll none of me. The count himself here hard by woos her.

SIR TOBY. She 'll none o' the count; she 'll not match above her degree, neither in estate, years, nor wit; I have heard her swear it. Tut, there 's life in 't, man.

SIR ANDREW. I 'll stay a month longer. I am a fellow o' the strangest mind i' the world; I delight in masques and revels sometimes altogether.

SIR TOBY. Art thou good at these kickchawses, knight?

SIR ANDREW. As any man in Illyria, whatsoever he be, under

the degree of my betters: and yet I will not compare with an old man.

SIR TOBY. What is thy excellence in a galliard, knight?

SIR ANDREW. Faith, I can cut a caper.

SIR TOBY. And I can cut the mutton to 't.

SIR ANDREW. And I think I have the back-trick simply as strong as any man in Illyria.

SIR TOBY. Wherefore are these things hid? Wherefore have these gifts a curtain before 'em? Are they like to take dust, like Mistress Mall's picture? Why dost thou not go to church in a galliard, and come home in a coranto? My very walk should be a jig: I would not so much as make water but in a sink-a-pace. What dost thou mean? Is it a world to hide virtues in? I did think, by the excellent constitution of thy leg, it was formed under the star of a galliard.

SIR ANDREW. Ay, 'tis strong, and it does indifferent well in a flame-coloured stock. Shall we set about some revels?

SIR TOBY. What shall we do else? Were we not born under Taurus?

SIR ANDREW. Taurus! that 's sides and heart.

SIR TOBY. No, sir, it is legs and thighs. Let me see thee caper. Ha! higher: ha, ha! excellent!   *Exeunt*

SCENE FOUR

A Room in the Duke's Palace.

Enter Valentine, and Viola in man's attire

VALENTINE. If the duke continue these favours towards you, Cesario, you are like to be much advanced: he hath known you but three days, and already you are no stranger.

VIOLA. You either fear his humour or my negligence, that you call in question the continuance of his love. Is he inconstant, sir, in his favours?

VALENTINE. No, believe me.

VIOLA. I thank you. Here comes the count.

Enter Duke, Curio, and Attendants

DUKE. Who saw Cesario? ho!

VIOLA. On your attendance, my lord; here.

DUKE. Stand you awhile aloof. Cesario,
Thou know'st no less but all; I have unclasp'd

To thee the book even of my secret soul:
Therefore, good youth, address thy gait unto her,
Be not denied access, stand at her doors,
And tell them, there thy fixed foot shall grow
Till thou have audience.

VIOLA.   Sure, my noble lord,
If she be so abandon'd to her sorrow
As it is spoke, she never will admit me.

DUKE. Be clamorous and leap all civil bounds
Rather than make unprofited return.

VIOLA. Say I do speak with her, my lord, what then?

DUKE. O! then unfold the passion of my love;
Surprise her with discourse of my dear faith:
It shall become thee well to act my woes;
She will attend it better in thy youth
Than in a nuncio of more grave aspect.

VIOLA. I think not so, my lord.

DUKE.   Dear lad, believe it;
For they shall yet belie thy happy years
That say thou art a man: Diana's lip
Is not more smooth and rubious; thy small pipe
Is as the maiden's organ, shrill and sound;
And all is semblative a woman's part.
I know thy constellation is right apt
For this affair. Some four or five attend him;
All, if you will; for I myself am best
When least in company. Prosper well in this,
And thou shalt live as freely as thy lord,
To call his fortunes thine.

VIOLA.   I 'll do my best
To woo your lady: (Aside) yet, a barful strife!
Whoe'er I woo, myself would be his wife.   Exeunt

SCENE FIVE

A Room in Olivia's House.

Enter Maria and Clown

MARIA. Nay, either tell me where thou hast been, or I will
not open my lips so wide as a bristle may enter in way of
thy excuse. My lady will hang thee for thy absence.

CLOWN. Let her hang me: he that is well hanged in this
world needs to fear no colours.

MARIA. Make that good.

CLOWN. He shall see none to fear.

MARIA. A good lenten answer: I can tell thee where that saying was born, of 'I fear no colours.'

CLOWN. Where, good Mistress Mary?

MARIA. In the wars; and that may you be bold to say in your
foolery.

CLOWN. Well, God give them wisdom that have it; and those
that are fools, let them use their talents.

MARIA. Yet you will be hanged for being so long absent; or,
to be turned away, is not that as good as a hanging to you?

CLOWN. Many a good hanging prevents a bad marriage;
and, for turning away, let summer bear it out.

MARIA. You are resolute then?

CLOWN. Not so, neither; but I am resolved on two points.

MARIA. That if one break, the other will hold; or, if both
break, your gaskins fall.

CLOWN. Apt, in good faith; very apt. Well, go thy way: if
Sir Toby would leave drinking, thou wert as witty a piece
of Eve's flesh as any in Illyria.

MARIA. Peace, you rogue, no more o' that. Here comes my
lady: make your excuse wisely, you were best.   *Exit*

CLOWN. Wit, an 't be thy will, put me into good fooling!
Those wits that think they have thee, do very oft prove
fools; and I, that am sure I lack thee, may pass for a wise
man: for what says Quinapalus? 'Better a witty fool than
a foolish wit.'

Enter Olivia with Malvolio

God bless thee, lady!

OLIVIA. Take the fool away.

CLOWN. Do you not hear, fellows? Take away the lady.

OLIVIA. Go to, you're a dry fool; I'll no more of you: besides, you grow dishonest.

CLOWN. Two faults, madonna, that drink and good counsel will amend: for give the dry fool drink, then is the fool not dry; bid the dishonest man mend himself: if he mend, he is no longer dishonest; if he cannot, let the botcher mend him. Anything that's mended is but patched: virtue that transgresses is but patched with sin; and sin that amends is but patched with virtue. If that this simple syllogism will serve, so; if it will not, what remedy? As there is no true cuckold but calamity, so beauty's a flower. The lady bade take away the fool; therefore, I say again, take her away.

OLIVIA. Sir, I bade them take away you.

CLOWN. Misprision in the highest degree! Lady, cucullus non facit monachum; that's as much to say as I wear not motley in my brain. Good madonna, give me leave to prove you a fool.

OLIVIA. Can you do it?

CLOWN. Dexteriously, good madonna.

OLIVIA. Make your proof.

CLOWN. I must catechise you for it, madonna: good my mouse of virtue, answer me.

OLIVIA. Well, sir, for want of other idleness, I'll bide your proof.

CLOWN. Good madonna, why mournest thou?

OLIVIA. Good fool, for my brother's death.

CLOWN. I think his soul is in hell, madonna.

OLIVIA. I know his soul is in heaven, fool.

CLOWN. The more fool, madonna, to mourn for your brother's soul being in heaven. Take away the fool, gentlemen.

OLIVIA. What think you of this fool, Malvolio? Doth he not mend?

MALVOLIO. Yes, and shall do, till the pangs of death shake him: infirmity, that decays the wise, doth ever make the better fool.

CLOWN. God send you, sir, a speedy infirmity, for the better increasing your folly! Sir Toby will be sworn that I am no fox, but he will not pass his word for two pence that you are no fool.

OLIVIA. How say you to that, Malvolio?

MALVOLIO. I marvel your ladyship takes delight in such a barren rascal: I saw him put down the other day with an ordinary fool that has no more brain than a stone. Look you now, he 's out of his guard already; unless you laugh and minister occasion to him, he is gagged. I protest, I take these wise men, that crow so at these set kind of fools, no better than the fools' zanies.

OLIVIA. O! you are sick of self-love, Malvolio, and taste with a distempered appetite. To be generous, guiltless, and of free disposition, is to take those things for bird-bolts that you deem cannon-bullets. There is no slander in an allowed fool, though he do nothing but rail; nor no railing in a known discreet man, though he do nothing but reprove.

CLOWN. Now, Mercury endue thee with leasing, for thou speakest well of fools!

Re-enter Maria

MARIA. Madam, there is at the gate a young gentleman much desires to speak with you.

OLIVIA. From the Count Orsino, is it?

MARIA. I know not, madam: 'tis a fair young man, and well attended.

OLIVIA. Who of my people hold him in delay?

MARIA. Sir Toby, madam, your kinsman.

OLIVIA. Fetch him off, I pray you: he speaks nothing but madman. Fie on him! (*Exit Maria*) Go you, Malvolio: if it be a suit from the count, I am sick, or not at home; what you will, to dismiss it. (*Exit Malvolio*) Now you see, sir, how your fooling grows old, and people dislike it.

CLOWN. Thou hast spoken for us, madonna, as if thy eldest son should be a fool; whose skull Jove cram with brains! for here comes one of thy kin has a most weak pia mater.

Enter Sir Toby Belch

OLIVIA. By mine honour, half drunk. What is he at the gate, cousin?

SIR TOBY. A gentleman.

OLIVIA. A gentleman! What gentleman?

SIR TOBY. 'Tis a gentleman here,—a plague o' these pickle herring! How now, sot!

CLOWN. Good Sir Toby.

OLIVIA. Cousin, cousin, how have you come so early by this lethargy?

SIR TOBY. Lechery! I defy lechery! There's one at the gate.

CLOWN. Ay, marry, what is he?

SIR TOBY. Let him be the devil, an he will, I care not: give me faith, say I. Well, it's all one.   *Exit*

OLIVIA. What's a drunken man like, fool?

CLOWN. Like a drowned man, a fool, and a madman: one draught above heat makes him a fool, the second mads him, and a third drowns him.

OLIVIA. Go thou and seek the crowner, and let him sit o' my coz; for he's in the third degree of drink, he's drowned: go, look after him.

CLOWN. He is but mad yet, madonna; and the fool shall look to the madman.   *Exit*

Re-enter Malvolio

MALVOLIO. Madam, yond young fellow swears he will speak with you. I told him you were sick: he takes on him to understand so much, and therefore comes to speak with you. I told him you were asleep: he seems to have a foreknowledge of that too, and therefore comes to speak with you. What is to be said to him, lady? He's fortified against any denial.

OLIVIA. Tell him he shall not speak with me.

MALVOLIO. Has been told so; and he says, he'll stand at your door like a sheriff's post, and be the supporter to a bench, but he'll speak with you.

OLIVIA. What kind o' man is he?

MALVOLIO. Why, of mankind.

OLIVIA. What manner of man?

MALVOLIO. Of very ill manner. He'll speak with you, will you or no.

OLIVIA. Of what personage and years is he?

MALVOLIO. Not yet old enough for a man, nor young enough for a boy; as a squash is before 'tis a peascod, or a codling when 'tis almost an apple: 'tis with him in standing water, between boy and man. He is very well-favoured, and he speaks very shrewishly: one would think his mother's milk were scarce out of him.

OLIVIA. Let him approach. Call in my gentlewoman.

MALVOLIO. Gentlewoman, my lady calls.   *Exit*

Re-enter Maria

OLIVIA. Give me my veil: come, throw it o'er my face. We'll once more hear Orsino's embassy.

Enter Viola and Attendants

VIOLA. The honourable lady of the house, which is she?

OLIVIA. Speak to me; I shall answer for her. Your will?

VIOLA. Most radiant, exquisite, and unmatchable beauty,—
I pray you tell me if this be the lady of the house, for I
never saw her: I would be loath to cast away my speech;
for, besides that it is excellently well penned, I have taken
great pains to con it. Good beauties, let me sustain no
scorn; I am very comptible, even to the least sinister usage.

OLIVIA. Whence came you, sir?

VIOLA. I can say little more than I have studied, and that
question's out of my part. Good gentle one, give me modest assurance if you be the lady of the house, that I may
proceed in my speech.

OLIVIA. Are you a comedian?

VIOLA. No, my profound heart; and yet, by the very fangs of
malice I swear I am not that I play. Are you the lady of
the house?

OLIVIA. If I do not usurp myself, I am.

VIOLA. Most certain, if you are she, you do usurp yourself;
for, what is yours to bestow is not yours to reserve. But this
is from my commission: I will on with my speech in your
praise, and then show you the heart of my message.

OLIVIA. Come to what is important in 't: I forgive you the
praise.

VIOLA. Alas! I took great pains to study it, and 'tis poetical.

OLIVIA. It is the more like to be feigned: I pray you keep it
in. I heard you were saucy at my gates, and allowed your
approach rather to wonder at you than to hear you. If you
be not mad, be gone; if you have reason, be brief: 'tis not
that time of moon with me to make one in so skipping a
dialogue.

MARIA. Will you hoist sail, sir? Here lies your way.

VIOLA. No, good swabber; I am to hull here a little longer.
Some mollification for your giant, sweet lady.

OLIVIA. Tell me your mind.

VIOLA. I am a messenger.

OLIVIA. Sure, you have some hideous matter to deliver, when
the courtesy of it is so fearful. Speak your office.

VIOLA. It alone concerns your ear. I bring no overture of

war, no taxation of homage: I hold the olive in my hand;
my words are as full of peace as matter.

OLIVIA. Yet you began rudely. What are you? What would
you?

VIOLA. The rudeness that hath appear'd in me have I learn'd
from my entertainment. What I am, and what I would, are
as secret as maidenhead; to your ears, divinity; to any
other's, profanation.

OLIVIA. Give us the place alone: we will hear this divinity.
(*Exit Maria and attendants*) Now, sir; what is your text?

VIOLA. Most sweet lady,—

OLIVIA. A comfortable doctrine, and much may be said of it.
Where lies your text?

VIOLA. In Orsino's bosom.

OLIVIA. In his bosom! In what chapter of his bosom?

VIOLA. To answer by the method, in the first of his heart.

OLIVIA. O! I have read it: it is heresy. Have you no more to
say?

VIOLA. Good madam, let me see your face.

OLIVIA. Have you any commission from your lord to negotiate with my face? You are now out of your text: but we
will draw the curtain and show you the picture. (*Unveiling*) Look you, sir, such a one I was as this present: is 't
not well done?

VIOLA. Excellently done, if God did all.

OLIVIA. 'Tis in grain, sir; 'twill endure wind and weather.

VIOLA. 'Tis beauty truly blent, whose red and white
Nature's own sweet and cunning hand laid on:
Lady, you are the cruell'st she alive,
If you will lead these graces to the grave
And leave the world no copy.

OLIVIA. O! sir, I will not be so hard-hearted; I will give out
divers schedules of my beauty: it shall be inventoried, and
every particle and utensil labelled to my will: as Item,
Two lips, indifferent red; Item, Two grey eyes, with lids to
them; Item, One neck, one chin, and so forth. Were you
sent hither to praise me?

VIOLA. I see you what you are: you are too proud;
But, if you were the devil, you are fair.
My lord and master loves you: O! such love
Could be but recompens'd, though you were crown'd
The nonpareil of beauty.

OLIVIA.   How does he love me?

VIOLA. With adorations, with fertile tears,
With groans that thunder love, with sighs of fire.

OLIVIA. Your lord does know my mind; I cannot love him;
Yet I suppose him virtuous, know him noble,
Of great estate, of fresh and stainless youth;
In voices well divulg'd, free, learn'd, and valiant;
And, in dimension and the shape of nature
A gracious person; but yet I cannot love him:
He might have took his answer long ago.

VIOLA. If I did love you in my master's flame,
With such a suffering, such a deadly life,
In your denial I would find no sense;
I would not understand it.

OLIVIA.   Why, what would you?

VIOLA. Make me a willow cabin at your gate,
And call upon my soul within the house;
Write loyal cantons of contemned love,
And sing them loud even in the dead of night;
Holla your name to the reverberate hills,
And make the babbling gossip of the air
Cry out, 'Olivia!' O! you should not rest
Between the elements of air and earth,
But you should pity me!

OLIVIA. You might do much. What is your parentage?

VIOLA. Above my fortunes, yet my state is well:
I am a gentleman.

OLIVIA.   Get you to your lord:
I cannot love him. Let him send no more,
Unless, perchance, you come to me again,
To tell me how he takes it. Fare you well:
I thank you for your pains: spend this for me.

VIOLA. I am no fee'd post, lady; keep your purse:
My master, not myself, lacks recompense.
Love make his heart of flint that you shall love,
And let your fervour, like my master's, be
Plac'd in contempt! Farewell, fair cruelty.   *Exit*

OLIVIA. 'What is your parentage?'
'Above my fortunes, yet my state is well:
I am a gentleman.' I 'll be sworn thou art:
Thy tongue, thy face, thy limbs, actions, and spirit,
Do give thee five-fold blazon. Not too fast: soft! soft!

Unless the master were the man. How now?
Even so quickly may one catch the plague?
Methinks I feel this youth's perfections
With an invisible and subtle stealth
To creep in at mine eyes. Well, let it be.
What, ho! Malvolio!

Re-enter Malvolio

MALVOLIO.   Here, madam, at your service.
OLIVIA. Run after that same peevish messenger,
    The county's man: he left this ring behind him,
    Would I, or not: tell him I 'll none of it.
    Desire him not to flatter with his lord,
    Nor hold him up with hopes: I 'm not for him.
    If that the youth will come this way to-morrow,
    I 'll give him reasons for 't. Hie thee, Malvolio.
MALVOLIO. Madam, I will.   *Exit*
OLIVIA. I do I know not what, and fear to find
    Mine eye too great a flatterer for my mind.
    Fate, show thy force: ourselves we do not owe;
    What is decreed must be, and be this so!   *Exit*

ACT TWO

SCENE ONE

The Sea-coast.

Enter Antonio and Sebastian

ANTONIO. Will you stay no longer? nor will you not that I go
with you?

SEBASTIAN. By your patience, no. My stars shine darkly over
me; the malignancy of my fate might, perhaps, distemper
yours; therefore I shall crave of you your leave that I may
bear my evils alone. It were a bad recompense for your
love to lay any of them on you.

ANTONIO. Let me yet know of you whither you are bound.

SEBASTIAN. No, sooth, sir: my determinate voyage is mere
extravagancy. But I perceive in you so excellent a touch
of modesty that you will not extort from me what I am
willing to keep in; therefore, it charges me in manners the
rather to express myself. You must know of me then, Antonio, my name is Sebastian, which I called Roderigo. My
father was that Sebastian of Messaline, whom I know you
have heard of. He left behind him myself and a sister, both
born in an hour: if the heavens had been pleased, would
we had so ended! but you, sir, altered that; for some hour
before you took me from the breach of the sea was my sister drowned.

ANTONIO. Alas the day!

SEBASTIAN. A lady, sir, though it was said she much re-
sembled me, was yet of many accounted beautiful: but,
though I could not with such estimable wonder overfar
believe that, yet thus far I will boldly publish her: she
bore a mind that envy could not but call fair. She is
drowned already, sir, with salt water, though I seem to
drown her remembrance again with more.

ANTONIO. Pardon me, sir, your bad entertainment.

SEBASTIAN. O good Antonio! forgive me your trouble!

ANTONIO. If you will not murder me for my love, let me be your servant.

SEBASTIAN. If you will not undo what you have done, that is, kill him whom you have recovered, desire it not. Fare ye well at once: my bosom is full of kindness; and I am yet so near the manners of my mother, that upon the least occasion more mine eyes will tell tales of me. I am bound to the Count Orsino's court: farewell.   *Exit*

ANTONIO. The gentleness of all the gods go with thee!
I have many enemies in Orsino's court,
Else would I very shortly see thee there;
But, come what may, I do adore thee so,
That danger shall seem sport, and I will go.   *Exit*

SCENE TWO

A Street.

Enter Viola; Malvolio following

MALVOLIO. Were not you even now with the Countess Olivia?

VIOLA. Even now, sir: on a moderate pace I have since arrived but hither.

MALVOLIO. She returns this ring to you, sir: you might have saved me my pains, to have taken it away yourself. She adds, moreover, that you should put your lord into a desperate assurance she will none of him. And one thing more; that you be never so hardy to come again in his affairs, unless it be to report your lord's taking of this. Receive it so.

VIOLA. She took the ring of me; I 'll none of it.

MALVOLIO. Come, sir, you peevishly threw it to her; and her will is it should be so returned: if it be worth stooping for, there it lies in your eye; if not, be it his that finds it.   *Exit*

VIOLA. I left no ring with her: what means this lady?
Fortune forbid my outside have not charm'd her!
She made good view of me; indeed, so much,
That sure methought her eyes had lost her tongue,
For she did speak in starts distractedly.
She loves me, sure; the cunning of her passion

Invites me in this churlish messenger.
None of my lord's ring! why, he sent her none.
I am the man: if it be so, as 'tis,
Poor lady, she were better love a dream.
Disguise, I see, thou art a wickedness,
Wherein the pregnant enemy does much.
How easy is it for the proper-false
In women's waxen hearts to set their forms!
Alas! our frailty is the cause, not we!
For such as we are made of, such we be.
How will this fadge? My master loves her dearly;
And I, poor monster, fond as much on him;
And she, mistaken, seems to dote on me.
What will become of this? As I am man,
My state is desperate for my master's love;
As I am woman,—now alas the day!—
What thriftless sighs shall poor Olivia breathe!
O time! thou must untangle this, not I;
It is too hard a knot for me to untie.　　　　　　*Exit*

SCENE THREE

A Room in Olivia's House.

Enter Sir Toby Belch and Sir Andrew Aguecheek

SIR TOBY. Approach, Sir Andrew: not to be a-bed after midnight is to be up betimes; and *diluculo surgere,* thou
knowest,—

SIR ANDREW. Nay, by my troth, I know not; but I know, to be
up late is to be up late.

SIR TOBY. A false conclusion: I hate it as an unfilled can. To
be up after midnight and to go to bed then, is early; so that
to go to bed after midnight is to go to bed betimes. Does
not our life consist of the four elements?

SIR ANDREW. Faith, so they say; but, I think, it rather consists of eating and drinking.

SIR TOBY. Thou art a scholar; let us therefore eat and drink.
Marian, I say! a stoup of wine!

Enter Clown

SIR ANDREW. Here comes the fool, i' faith.

CLOWN. How now, my hearts! Did you never see the picture of 'we three'?

SIR TOBY. Welcome, ass. Now let 's have a catch.

SIR ANDREW. By my troth, the fool has an excellent breast. I had rather than forty shillings I had such a leg, and so sweet a breath to sing, as the fool has. In sooth, thou wast in very gracious fooling last night, when thou spokest of Pigrogromitus, of the Vapians passing the equinoctial of Queubus: 'twas very good, i' faith. I sent thee sixpence for thy leman: hadst it?

CLOWN. I did impeticos thy gratillity; for Malvolio's nose is no whipstock: my lady has a white hand, and the Myrmidons are not bottle-ale houses.

SIR ANDREW. Excellent! Why, this is the best fooling, when all is done. Now, a song.

SIR TOBY. Come on; there is sixpence for you: let 's have a song.

SIR ANDREW. There 's a testril of me too: if one knight give a—

CLOWN. Would you have a love-song, or a song of good life?

SIR TOBY. A love-song, a love-song.

SIR ANDREW. Ay, ay; I care not for good life.

CLOWN.   O mistress mine! where are you roaming?
        O! stay and hear; your true love 's coming,
           That can sing both high and low.
        Trip no further, pretty sweeting;
        Journeys end in lovers meeting,
           Every wise man's son doth know.

SIR ANDREW. Excellent good, i' faith.

SIR TOBY. Good, good.

CLOWN.   What is love? 'Tis not hereafter;
        Present mirth hath present laughter;
           What 's to come is still unsure:
        In delay there lies no plenty;
        Then come kiss me, sweet and twenty,
           Youth 's a stuff will not endure.

SIR ANDREW. A mellifluous voice, as I am true knight.

SIR TOBY. A contagious breath.

SIR ANDREW. Very sweet and contagious, i' faith.

SIR TOBY. To hear by the nose, it is dulcet in contagion. But shall we make the welkin dance indeed? Shall we rouse

the night-owl in a catch that will draw three souls out of
one weaver? Shall we do that?

SIR ANDREW. An you love me, let 's do 't: I am dog at a catch.

CLOWN. By 'r lady, sir, and some dogs will catch well.

SIR ANDREW. Most certain. Let our catch be, 'Thou knave.'

CLOWN. 'Hold thy peace, thou knave,' knight? I shall be constrain'd in 't to call thee knave, knight.

SIR ANDREW. 'Tis not the first time I have constrained one to
call me knave. Begin, fool: it begins, 'Hold thy peace.'

CLOWN. I shall never begin if I hold my peace.

SIR ANDREW. Good, i' faith. Come, begin.   *They sing a catch*
Enter Maria

MARIA. What a caterwauling do you keep here! If my lady
have not called up her steward Malvolio and bid him turn
you out of doors, never trust me.

SIR TOBY. My lady 's a Cataian; we are politicians; Malvolio 's a Peg-a-Ramsey, and 'Three merry men be we.'
Am not I consanguineous? Am I not of her blood? Tillyvally, lady!
'There dwelt a man in Babylon, lady, lady!'

CLOWN. Beshrew me, the knight 's in admirable fooling.

SIR ANDREW. Ay, he does well enough if he be disposed, and
so do I too: he does it with a better grace, but I do it more
natural.

SIR TOBY. 'O! the twelfth day of December,'—

MARIA. For the love o' God, peace!
Enter Malvolio

MALVOLIO. My masters, are you mad? or what are you?
Have you no wit, manners, nor honesty, but to gabble like
tinkers at this time of night? Do ye make an alehouse of
my lady's house, that ye squeak out your coziers' catches
without any mitigation or remorse of voice? Is there no respect of place, persons, nor time, in you?

SIR TOBY. We did keep time, sir, in our catches. Sneck up!

MALVOLIO. Sir Toby, I must be round with you. My lady
bade me tell you, that, though she harbours you as her
kinsman, she 's nothing allied to your disorders. If you can
separate yourself and your misdemeanours, you are welcome to the house; if not, an it would please you to take
leave of her, she is very willing to bid you farewell.

SIR TOBY. 'Farewell, dear heart, since I must needs be gone.'

MARIA. Nay, good Sir Toby.

CLOWN. 'His eyes do show his days are almost done.'

MALVOLIO. Is 't even so?

SIR TOBY. 'But I will never die.'

CLOWN. Sir Toby, there you lie.

MALVOLIO. This is much credit to you.

SIR TOBY. 'Shall I bid him go?'

CLOWN. 'What an if you do?'

SIR TOBY. 'Shall I bid him go, and spare not?'

CLOWN. 'O! no, no, no, no, you dare not.'

SIR TOBY. 'Out o' time!' Sir, ye lie. Art any more than a steward? Dost thou think, because thou art virtuous, there shall be no more cakes and ale?

CLOWN. Yes, by Saint Anne; and ginger shall be hot i' the mouth too.

SIR TOBY. Thou 'rt i' the right. Go, sir, rub your chain with crumbs. A stoup of wine, Maria!

MALVOLIO. Mistress Mary, if you prized my lady's favour at anything more than contempt, you would not give means for this uncivil rule: she shall know of it, by this hand. *Exit*

MARIA. Go shake your ears.

SIR ANDREW. 'Twere as good a deed as to drink when a man 's a-hungry, to challenge him the field, and then to break promise with him and make a fool of him.

SIR TOBY. Do 't, knight: I 'll write thee a challenge; or I 'll deliver thy indignation to him by word of mouth.

MARIA. Sweet Sir Toby, be patient for to-night: since the youth of the count's was to-day with my lady, she is much out of quiet. For Monsieur Malvolio, let me alone with him: if I do not gull him into a nayword, and make him a common recreation, do not think I have wit enough to lie straight in my bed. I know I can do it.

SIR TOBY. Possess us, possess us; tell us something of him.

MARIA. Marry, sir, sometimes he is a kind of puritan.

SIR ANDREW. O! if I thought that, I 'd beat him like a dog.

SIR TOBY. What, for being a puritan? Thy exquisite reason, dear knight?

SIR ANDREW. I have no exquisite reason for 't, but I have reason good enough.

MARIA. The devil a puritan that he is, or anything constantly but a time-pleaser; an affectioned ass, that cons state without book, and utters it by great swarths: the best persuaded of himself; so crammed, as he thinks, with excel-

lences, that it is his ground of faith that all that look on
him love him; and on that vice in him will my revenge find
notable cause to work.

SIR TOBY. What wilt thou do?

MARIA. I will drop in his way some obscure epistles of love;
wherein, by the colour of his beard, the shape of his leg,
the manner of his gait, the expressure of his eye, forehead,
and complexion, he shall find himself most feelingly per-
sonated. I can write very like my lady your niece; on a forgotten matter we can hardly make distinction of our
hands.

SIR TOBY. Excellent! I smell a device.

SIR ANDREW. I have 't in my nose too.

SIR TOBY. He shall think, by the letters that thou wilt drop,
that they come from my niece, and that she is in love with
him.

MARIA. My purpose is, indeed, a horse of that colour.

SIR ANDREW. And your horse now would make him an ass.

MARIA. Ass, I doubt not.

SIR ANDREW. O! 'twill be admirable.

MARIA. Sport royal, I warrant you: I know my physic will
work with him. I will plant you two, and let the fool make
a third, where he shall find the letter: observe his construction of it. For this night, to bed, and dream on the event.
Farewell.   *Exit*

SIR TOBY. Good night, Penthesilea.

SIR ANDREW. Before me, she 's a good wench.

SIR TOBY. She 's a beagle, true-bred, and one that adores me:
what o' that?

SIR ANDREW. I was adored once too.

SIR TOBY. Let 's to bed, knight. Thou hadst need send for
more money.

SIR ANDREW. If I cannot recover your niece, I am a foul way
out.

SIR TOBY. Send for money, knight: if thou hast her not i' the
end, call me cut.

SIR ANDREW. If I do not, never trust me, take it how you will.

SIR TOBY. Come, come: I 'll go burn some sack; 'tis too late to
go to bed now. Come, knight; come, knight.   *Exeunt*

SCENE FOUR

A Room in the Duke's Palace.

Enter Duke, Viola, Curio, and Others

DUKE. Give me some music. Now, good-morrow, friends:
  Now, good Cesario, but that piece of song,
  That old and antique song we heard last night;
  Methought it did relieve my passion much,
  More than light airs and recollected terms
  Of these most brisk and giddy-paced times:
  Come; but one verse.

CURIO. He is not here, so please your lordship, that should
  sing it.

DUKE. Who was it?

CURIO. Feste, the jester, my lord; a fool that the Lady
  Olivia's father took much delight in. He is about the house.

DUKE. Seek him out, and play the tune the while.

Exit Curio. Music

Come hither, boy: if ever thou shalt love,
  In the sweet pangs of it remember me;
  For such as I am all true lovers are:
  Unstaid and skittish in all motions else
  Save in the constant image of the creature
  That is belov'd. How dost thou like this tune?

VIOLA. It gives a very echo to the seat
  Where love is thron'd.

DUKE.   Thou dost speak masterly.
  My life upon 't, young though thou art, thine eye
  Hath stay'd upon some favour that it loves;
  Hath it not, boy?

VIOLA.   A little, by your favour.

DUKE. What kind of woman is 't?

VIOLA.   Of your complexion.

DUKE. She is not worth thee, then. What years, i' faith?

VIOLA. About your years, my lord.

DUKE. Too old, by heaven. Let still the woman take
  An elder than herself, so wears she to him,
  So sways she level in her husband's heart:
  For, boy, however we do praise ourselves,

Our fancies are more giddy and unfirm,
More longing, wavering, sooner lost and worn,
Than women's are.

VIOLA.   I think it well, my lord.

DUKE. Then, let thy love be younger than thyself,
    Or thy affection cannot hold the bent;
    For women are as roses, whose fair flower
    Being once display'd, doth fall that very hour.

VIOLA. And so they are: alas, that they are so;
    To die, even when they to perfection grow!

                    Re-enter Curio with Clown

DUKE. O, fellow! come, the song we had last night.
    Mark it, Cesario; it is old and plain;
    The spinsters and the knitters in the sun,
    And the free maids that weave their thread with bones,
    Do use to chant it: it is silly sooth,
    And dallies with the innocence of love,
    Like the old age.

CLOWN. Are you ready, sir?

DUKE. Ay; prithee, sing.   *Music*

CLOWN.   Come away, come away, death,
            And in sad cypress let me be laid;
         Fly away, fly away, breath;
            I am slain by a fair cruel maid.
         My shroud of white, stuck all with yew,
                O! prepare it.
         My part of death, no one so true
                Did share it.

         Not a flower, not a flower sweet,
            On my black coffin let there be strown;
         Not a friend, not a friend greet
            My poor corse, where my bones shall be thrown.
         A thousand thousand sighs to save,
                Lay me, O! where
         Sad true lover never find my grave,
                To weep there.

DUKE. There's for thy pains.

CLOWN. No pains, sir; I take pleasure in singing, sir.

DUKE. I'll pay thy pleasure then.

CLOWN. Truly, sir, and pleasure will be paid, one time or
    another.

DUKE. Give me now leave to leave thee.

CLOWN. Now, the melancholy god protect thee, and the
   tailor make thy doublet of changeable taffeta, for thy mind
   is a very opal! I would have men of such constancy put to
   sea, that their business might be every thing and their intent everywhere; for that 's it that always makes a good
   voyage of nothing. Farewell.   *Exit*

DUKE. Let all the rest give place.
                                   Exeunt Curio and attendants
                                   Once more, Cesario,
   Get thee to yond same sovereign cruelty:
   Tell her, my love, more noble than the world,
   Prizes not quantity of dirty lands;
   The parts that fortune hath bestow'd upon her,
   Tell her, I hold as giddily as fortune;
   But 'tis that miracle and queen of gems
   That nature pranks her in attracts my soul.

VIOLA. But if she cannot love you, sir?

DUKE. I cannot be so answer'd.

VIOLA.   Sooth, but you must.
   Say that some lady, as perhaps there is,
   Hath for your love as great a pang of heart
   As you have for Olivia: you cannot love her;
   You tell her so; must she not then be answer'd?

DUKE. There is no woman's sides
   Can bide the beating of so strong a passion
   As love doth give my heart; no woman's heart
   So big, to hold so much; they lack retention.
   Alas! their love may be call'd appetite,
   No motion of the liver, but the palate,
   That suffer surfeit, cloyment, and revolt;
   But mine is all as hungry as the sea,
   And can digest as much. Make no compare
   Between that love a woman can bear me
   And that I owe Olivia.

VIOLA.   Ay, but I know,—

DUKE. What dost thou know?

VIOLA. Too well what love women to men may owe:
   In faith, they are as true of heart as we.
   My father had a daughter lov'd a man,
   As it might be, perhaps, were I a woman,
   I should your lordship.

DUKE.   And what 's her history?

VIOLA. A blank, my lord. She never told her love,
But let concealment, like a worm i' the bud,
Feed on her damask cheek: she pin'd in thought,
And with a green and yellow melancholy,
She sat like Patience on a monument,
Smiling at grief. Was not this love indeed?
We men may say more, swear more; but indeed
Our shows are more than will, for still we prove
Much in our vows, but little in our love.

DUKE. But died thy sister of her love, my boy?

VIOLA. I am all the daughters of my father's house,
And all the brothers too; and yet I know not.
Sir, shall I to this lady?

DUKE.   Ay, that 's the theme.
To her in haste; give her this jewel; say
My love can give no place, bide no denay.   *Exeunt*

SCENE FIVE

Olivia's Garden.

Enter Sir Toby Belch, Sir Andrew Aguecheek, and Fabian

SIR TOBY. Come thy ways, Signior Fabian.

FABIAN. Nay, I 'll come: if I lose a scruple of this sport, let
me be boiled to death with melancholy.

SIR TOBY. Wouldst thou not be glad to have the niggardly
rascally sheep-biter come by some notable shame?

FABIAN. I would exult, man: you know he brought me out o'
favour with my lady about a bear-baiting here.

SIR TOBY. To anger him we 'll have the bear again; and we
will fool him black and blue. Shall we not, Sir Andrew?

SIR ANDREW. An we do not, it is pity of our lives.

SIR TOBY. Here comes the little villain.

Enter Maria

How now, my metal of India!

MARIA. Get ye all three into the box-tree. Malvolio's coming
down this walk: he has been yonder i' the sun practising
behaviour to his own shadow this half-hour. Observe him,
for the love of mockery; for I know this letter will make a
contemplative idiot of him. Close, in the name of jesting!

Lie thou there: (*Throws down a letter*) for here comes
the trout that must be caught with tickling.   *Exit*

Enter Malvolio

MALVOLIO. 'Tis but fortune; all is fortune. Maria once told
me she did affect me; and I have heard herself come thus
near, that should she fancy, it should be one of my complexion. Besides, she uses me with a more exalted respect
than anyone else that follows her. What should I think
on 't?

SIR TOBY. Here's an over-weening rogue!

FABIAN. O, peace! Contemplation makes a rare turkey-cock
of him: how he jets under his advanced plumes!

SIR ANDREW. 'Slight, I could so beat the rogue!

SIR TOBY. Peace! I say.

MALVOLIO. To be Count Malvolio!

SIR TOBY. Ah, rogue!

SIR ANDREW. Pistol him, pistol him.

SIR TOBY. Peace! peace!

MALVOLIO. There is example for 't: the lady of the Strachy
married the yeoman of the wardrobe.

SIR ANDREW. Fie on him, Jezebel!

FABIAN. O, peace! now he's deeply in; look how imagination
blows him.

MALVOLIO. Having been three months married to her, sitting
in my state,—

SIR TOBY. O! for a stone-bow, to hit him in the eye!

MALVOLIO. Calling my officers about me, in my branched
velvet gown; having come from a day-bed, where I have
left Olivia sleeping,—

SIR TOBY. Fire and brimstone!

FABIAN. O, peace! peace!

MALVOLIO. And then to have the humour of state: and after
a demure travel of regard, telling them I know my place,
as I would they should do theirs, to ask for my kinsman
Toby,—

SIR TOBY. Bolts and shackles!

FABIAN. O, peace, peace, peace! now, now.

MALVOLIO. Seven of my people, with an obedient start,
make out for him. I frown the while; and perchance wind
up my watch, or play with my—some rich jewel. Toby approaches; curtsies there to me,—

SIR TOBY. Shall this fellow live?

FABIAN. Though our silence be drawn from us with ears, yet peace!

MALVOLIO. I extend my hand to him thus, quenching my familiar smile with an austere regard of control,—

SIR TOBY. And does not Toby take you a blow o' the lips then?

MALVOLIO. Saying, 'Cousin Toby, my fortunes having cast me on your niece give me this prerogative of speech,'—

SIR TOBY. What, what?

MALVOLIO. 'You must amend your drunkenness.'

SIR TOBY. Out, scab!

FABIAN. Nay, patience, or we break the sinews of our plot.

MALVOLIO. 'Besides, you waste the treasure of your time with a foolish knight,'—

SIR ANDREW. That's me, I warrant you.

MALVOLIO. 'One Sir Andrew,'—

SIR ANDREW. I knew 'twas I; for many do call me fool.

MALVOLIO. (Seeing the letter) What employment have we here?

FABIAN. Now is the woodcock near the gin.

SIR TOBY. O, peace! and the spirit of humours intimate reading aloud to him!

MALVOLIO. (Taking up the letter) By my life, this is my lady's hand! These be her very C's, her U's, and her T's; and thus makes she her great P's. It is, in contempt of question, her hand.

SIR ANDREW. Her C's, her U's, and her T's: why that—

MALVOLIO. (Reads) 'To the unknown beloved, this and my good wishes.' Her very phrases! By your leave, wax. Soft! and the impressure her Lucrece, with which she uses to seal: 'tis my lady. To whom should this be?

FABIAN. This wins him, liver and all.

MALVOLIO.   'Jove knows I love;
                              But who?
                         Lips, do not move:
                         No man must know.'

'No man must know.' What follows? the numbers altered.
'No man must know': if this should be thee, Malvolio!

SIR TOBY. Marry, hang thee, brock!

MALVOLIO. (*Reads*)
> 'I may command where I adore;
>   But silence, like a Lucrece knife,
> With bloodless stroke my heart doth gore:
>   M, O, A, I, doth sway my life.'

FABIAN. A fustian riddle!

SIR TOBY. Excellent wench, say I.

MALVOLIO. 'M, O, A, I, doth sway my life.' Nay, but first, let me see, let me see, let me see.

FABIAN. What dish o' poison has she dressed him!

SIR TOBY. And with what wing the staniel checks at it!

MALVOLIO. 'I may command where I adore.' Why, she may command me: I serve her; she is my lady. Why, this is evident to any formal capacity; there is no obstruction in this. And the end, what should that alphabetical position portend? if I could make that resemble something in me,— Softly!—M, O, A, I,—

SIR TOBY. O! ay, make up that: he is now at a cold scent.

FABIAN. Sowter will cry upon 't, for all this, though it be as rank as a fox.

MALVOLIO. M, Malvolio; M, why, that begins my name.

FABIAN. Did not I say he would work it out? The cur is excellent at faults.

MALVOLIO. M,—But then there is no consonancy in the sequel; that suffers under probation: A should follow, but O does.

FABIAN. And O shall end, I hope.

SIR TOBY. Ay, or I 'll cudgel him, and make him cry, O!

MALVOLIO. And then I comes behind.

FABIAN. Ay, an you had any eye behind you, you might see more detraction at your heels than fortunes before you.

MALVOLIO. M, O, A, I; this simulation is not as the former. and yet, to crush this a little, it would bow to me, for every one of these letters are in my name. Soft! here follows prose.

  (*Reads*) 'If this fall into thy hand, revolve. In my stars I am above thee; but be not afraid of greatness: some are born great, some achieve greatness, and some have greatness thrust upon them. Thy Fates open their hands; let thy blood and spirit embrace them; and to inure thyself to what thou art like to be, cast thy humble slough, and appear fresh. Be opposite with a kinsman, surly with serv-

ants; let thy tongue tang arguments of state; put thyself
into the trick of singularity. She thus advises thee that
sighs for thee. Remember who commended thy yellow
stockings, and wished to see thee ever cross-gartered: I
say, remember. Go to, thou art made, if thou desirest to be
so; if not, let me see thee a steward still, the fellow of servants, and not worthy to touch Fortune's fingers. Farewell.
She that would alter services with thee,

> 'The Fortunate-Unhappy.'

Daylight and champian discovers not more: this is open. I
will be proud, I will read politic authors, I will baffle Sir
Toby, I will wash off gross acquaintance, I will be point-
devise the very man. I do not now fool myself, to let imagination jade me, for every reason excites to this, that my
lady loves me. She did commend my yellow stockings of
late, she did praise my leg being cross-gartered; and in this
she manifests herself to my love, and, with a kind of injunction drives me to these habits of her liking. I thank my
stars I am happy. I will be strange, stout, in yellow stockings, and cross-gartered, even with the swiftness of putting on. Jove and my stars be praised! Here is yet a post-
script.

'Thou canst not choose but know who I am. If thou en-
tertainest my love, let it appear in thy smiling; thy smiles
become thee well; therefore in my presence still smile,
dear my sweet, I prithee.'

Jove, I thank thee. I will smile: I will do everything that
thou wilt have me.   *Exit*

FABIAN. I will not give my part of this sport for a pension of
thousands to be paid from the Sophy.

SIR TOBY. I could marry this wench for this device.

SIR ANDREW. So could I too.

SIR TOBY. And ask no other dowry with her but such another
jest.

SIR ANDREW. Nor I neither.

FABIAN. Here comes my noble gull-catcher.

Re-enter Maria

SIR TOBY. Wilt thou set thy foot 'o my neck?

SIR ANDREW. Or o' mine either?

SIR TOBY. Shall I play my freedom at tray-trip, and become
thy bond-slave?

SIR ANDREW. I' faith, or I either?

SIR TOBY. Why, thou hast put him in such a dream, that
   when the image of it leaves him he must run mad.

MARIA. Nay, but say true; does it work upon him?

SIR TOBY. Like aqua-vitæ with a midwife.

MARIA. If you will, then, see the fruits of the sport, mark his
   first approach before my lady; he will come to her in yellow stockings, and 'tis a colour she abhors; and cross-
   gartered, a fashion she detests; and he will smile upon her,
   which will now be so unsuitable to her disposition, being
   addicted to a melancholy as she is, that it cannot but turn
   him into a notable contempt. If you will see it, follow me.

SIR TOBY. To the gates of Tartar, thou most excellent devil of
   wit!

SIR ANDREW. I 'll make one too.   *Exeunt*

ACT THREE

SCENE ONE

Olivia's Garden.

Enter Viola, and Clown with a tabor

VIOLA. Save thee, friend, and thy music. Dost thou live by thy tabor?

CLOWN. No, sir, I live by the church.

VIOLA. Art thou a churchman?

CLOWN. No such matter, sir: I do live by the church; for I do live at my house, and my house doth stand by the church.

VIOLA. So thou mayst say, the king lies by a beggar, if a beggar dwell near him; or, the church stands by thy tabor, if thy tabor stand by the church.

CLOWN. You have said, sir. To see this age! A sentence is but a cheveril glove to a good wit: how quickly the wrong side may be turned outward!

VIOLA. Nay, that's certain: they that dally nicely with words may quickly make them wanton.

CLOWN. I would therefore my sister had had no name, sir.

VIOLA. Why, man?

CLOWN. Why, sir, her name's a word; and to dally with that word might make my sister wanton. But indeed, words are very rascals since bonds disgraced them.

VIOLA. Thy reason, man?

CLOWN. Troth, sir, I can yield you none without words; and words are grown so false, I am loath to prove reason with them.

VIOLA. I warrant thou art a merry fellow, and carest for nothing.

CLOWN. Not so, sir, I do care for something; but in my conscience, sir, I do not care for you: if that be to care for nothing, sir, I would it would make you invisible.

VIOLA. Art not thou the Lady Olivia's fool?

CLOWN. No, indeed, sir; the Lady Olivia has no folly: she
    will keep no fool, sir, till she be married; and fools are as
    like husbands as pilchards are to herrings—the husband 's
    the bigger. I am indeed not her fool, but her corrupter of
    words.

VIOLA. I saw thee late at the Count Orsino's.

CLOWN. Foolery, sir, does walk about the orb like the sun; it
    shines everywhere. I would be sorry, sir, but the fool
    should be as oft with your master as with my mistress. I
    think I saw your wisdom there.

VIOLA. Nay, an thou pass upon me, I 'll no more with thee.
    Hold, there 's sixpence for thee.   *Gives a piece of money*

CLOWN. Now Jove, in his next commodity of hair, send thee
    a beard!

VIOLA. By my troth, I 'll tell thee, I am almost sick for one,
    though I would not have it grow on my chin. Is thy lady
    within?

CLOWN. (*Pointing to the coin*) Would not a pair of these
    have bred, sir?

VIOLA. Yes, being kept together and put to use.

CLOWN. I would play Lord Pandarus of Phrygia, sir, to bring
    a Cressida to this Troilus.

VIOLA. I understand you, sir; 'tis well begg'd.

CLOWN. The matter, I hope, is not great, sir, begging but a
    beggar: Cressida was a beggar. My lady is within, sir. I
    will conster to them whence you come; who you are and
    what you would are out of my welkin; I might say 'ele-
    ment,' but the word is overworn.   *Exit*

VIOLA. This fellow 's wise enough to play the fool,
    And to do that well craves a kind of wit:
    He must observe their mood on whom he jests,
    The quality of persons, and the time,
    And, like the haggard, check at every feather
    That comes before his eye. This is a practice
    As full of labour as a wise man's art;
    For folly that he wisely shows is fit;
    But wise men folly-fall'n, quite taint their wit.
        Enter Sir Toby Belch and Sir Andrew Aguecheek

SIR TOBY. Save you, gentleman.

VIOLA. And you, sir.

SIR ANDREW. Dieu vous garde, monsieur.

VIOLA. Et vous aussi; votre serviteur.

SIR ANDREW. I hope, sir, you are; and I am yours.

SIR TOBY. Will you encounter the house? My niece is desirous you should enter, if your trade be to her.

VIOLA. I am bound to your niece, sir: I mean, she is the list of
my voyage.

SIR TOBY. Taste your legs, sir: put them to motion.

VIOLA. My legs do better understand me, sir, than I understand what you mean by bidding me taste my legs.

SIR TOBY. I mean, to go, sir, to enter.

VIOLA. I will answer you with gait and entrance. But we are
prevented.

              Enter Olivia and Maria

Most excellent accomplished lady, the heavens rain odours
on you!

SIR ANDREW. That youth 's a rare courtier. 'Rain odours'!
well.

VIOLA. My matter hath no voice, lady, but to your own most
pregnant and vouchsafed ear.

SIR ANDREW. 'Odours,' 'pregnant,' and 'vouchsafed.' I 'll get
'em all three all ready.

OLIVIA. Let the garden door be shut, and leave me to my
hearing.   *Exeunt Sir Toby, Sir Andrew, and Maria*
Give me your hand, sir.

VIOLA. My duty, madam, and most humble service.

OLIVIA. What is your name?

VIOLA. Cesario is your servant's name, fair princess.

OLIVIA. My servant, sir! 'Twas never merry world
Since lowly feigning was call'd compliment.
You 're servant to the Count Orsino, youth.

VIOLA. And he is yours, and his must needs be yours:
Your servant's servant is your servant, madam.

OLIVIA. For him, I think not on him: for his thoughts,
Would they were blanks rather than fill'd with me!

VIOLA. Madam, I come to whet your gentle thoughts
On his behalf.

OLIVIA.   O! by your leave, I pray you,
I bade you never speak again of him:
But, would you undertake another suit,
I had rather hear you to solicit that
Than music from the spheres.

VIOLA. Dear lady,—

OLIVIA. Give me leave, beseech you. I did send,

After the last enchantment you did here,
A ring in chase of you: so did I abuse
Myself, my servant, and, I fear me, you:
Under your hard construction must I sit,
To force that on you, in a shameful cunning,
Which you knew none of yours: what might you think?
Have you not set mine honour at the stake,
And baited it with all th' unmuzzled thoughts
That tyrannous heart can think? To one of your receiving
Enough is shown; a cypress, not a bosom,
Hideth my heart. So, let me hear you speak.

VIOLA. I pity you.

OLIVIA. That's a degree to love.

VIOLA. No, not a grize; for 'tis a vulgar proof
That very oft we pity enemies.

OLIVIA. Why, then methinks 'tis time to smile again.
O world! how apt the poor are to be proud.
If one should be a prey, how much the better
To fall before the lion than the wolf!   *Clock strikes*
The clock upbraids me with the waste of time.
Be not afraid, good youth, I will not have you:
And yet, when wit and youth is come to harvest,
Your wife is like to reap a proper man:
There lies your way, due west.

VIOLA.   Then westward-ho!
Grace and good disposition attend your ladyship!
You 'll nothing, madam, to my lord by me?

OLIVIA. Stay:
I prithee, tell me what thou think'st of me.

VIOLA. That you do think you are not what you are.

OLIVIA. If I think so, I think the same of you.

VIOLA. Then think you right: I am not what I am.

OLIVIA. I would you were as I would have you be!

VIOLA. Would it be better, madam, than I am?
I wish it might, for now I am your fool.

OLIVIA. O! what a deal of scorn looks beautiful
In the contempt and anger of his lip.
A murderous guilt shows not itself more soon
Than love that would seem hid; love's night is noon.
Cesario, by the roses of the spring,
By maidhood, honour, truth, and every thing,
I love thee so, that, maugre all thy pride,

Nor wit nor reason can my passion hide.
Do not extort thy reasons from this clause,
For that I woo, thou therefore hast no cause;
But rather reason thus with reason fetter,
Love sought is good, but giv'n unsought is better.

VIOLA. By innocence I swear, and by my youth,
I have one heart, one bosom, and one truth,
And that no woman has; nor never none
Shall mistress be of it, save I alone.
And so adieu, good madam: never more
Will I my master's tears to you deplore.

OLIVIA. Yet come again, for thou perhaps mayst move
That heart, which now abhors, to like his love.   *Exeunt*

SCENE TWO

A Room in Olivia's House.

Enter Sir Toby Belch, Sir Andrew Aguecheek,
and Fabian

SIR ANDREW. No, faith, I 'll not stay a jot longer.

SIR TOBY. Thy reason, dear venom; give thy reason.

FABIAN. You must needs yield your reason, Sir Andrew.

SIR ANDREW. Marry, I saw your niece do more favours to the
count's serving-man than ever she bestowed upon me; I
saw 't i' the orchard.

SIR TOBY. Did she see thee the while, old boy? Tell me that.

SIR ANDREW. As plain as I see you now.

FABIAN. This was a great argument of love in her toward
you.

SIR ANDREW. 'Slight! will you make an ass o' me?

FABIAN. I will prove it legitimate, sir, upon the oaths of judgment and reason.

SIR TOBY. And they have been grand-jurymen since before
Noah was a sailor.

FABIAN. She did show favour to the youth in your sight only
to exasperate you, to awake your dormouse valour, to put
fire in your heart, and brimstone in your liver. You should
then have accosted her, and with some excellent jests, fire-
new from the mint, you should have banged the youth into
dumbness. This was looked for at your hand, and this was

balked: the double gilt of this opportunity you let time
wash off, and you are now sailed into the north of my
lady's opinion; where you will hang like an icicle on a
Dutchman's beard, unless you do redeem it by some laud-
able attempt, either of valour or policy.

SIR ANDREW. An 't be any way, it must be with valour, for
policy I hate: I had as lief be a Brownist as a politician.

SIR TOBY. Why, then, build me thy fortunes upon the basis of
valour: challenge me the count's youth to fight with him;
hurt him in eleven places: my niece shall take note of it;
and assure thyself, there is no love-broker in the world can
more prevail in man's commendation with woman than report of valour.

FABIAN. There is no way but this, Sir Andrew.

SIR ANDREW. Will either of you bear me a challenge to him?

SIR TOBY. Go, write it in a martial hand; be curst and brief;
it is no matter how witty, so it be eloquent, and full of invention: taunt him with the licence of ink: if thou thou'st
him some thrice, it shall not be amiss; and as many lies as
will lie in thy sheet of paper, although the sheet were big
enough for the bed of Ware in England, set 'em down: go,
about it. Let there be gall enough in thy ink, though thou
write with a goose-pen, no matter: about it.

SIR ANDREW. Where shall I find you?

SIR TOBY. We 'll call thee at the cubiculo: go.

Exit Sir Andrew

FABIAN. This is a dear manikin to you, Sir Toby.

SIR TOBY. I have been dear to him, lad, some two thousand
strong, or so.

FABIAN. We shall have a rare letter from him; but you 'll not
deliver it.

SIR TOBY. Never trust me, then; and by all means stir on the
youth to an answer. I think oxen and wain-ropes cannot
hale them together. For Andrew, if he were opened, and
you find so much blood in his liver as will clog the foot of a
flea, I 'll eat the rest of the anatomy.

FABIAN. And his opposite, the youth, bears in his visage no
great presage of cruelty.

SIR TOBY. Look, where the youngest wren of nine comes.

Enter Maria

MARIA. If you desire the spleen, and will laugh yourselves
into stitches, follow me. Yond gull Malvolio is turned

heathen, a very renegado; for there is no Christian, that
means to be saved by believing rightly, can ever believe
such impossible passages of grossness. He 's in yellow
stockings.

SIR TOBY. And cross-gartered?

MARIA. Most villanously; like a pedant that keeps a school i'
the church. I have dogged him like his murderer. He does
obey every point of the letter that I dropped to betray
him: he does smile his face into more lines than are in the
new map with the augmentation of the Indies. You have
not seen such a thing as 'tis; I can hardly forbear hurling
things at him. I know my lady will strike him: if she do,
he 'll smile and take 't for a great favour.

SIR TOBY. Come, bring us, bring us where he is.   *Exeunt*

SCENE THREE

A Street.

Enter Sebastian and Antonio

SEBASTIAN. I would not by my will have troubled you;
But since you make your pleasure of your pains,
I will no further chide you.

ANTONIO. I could not stay behind you: my desire,
More sharp than filed steel, did spur me forth;
And not all love to see you,—though so much
As might have drawn one to a longer voyage,—
But jealousy what might befall your travel,
Being skilless in these parts; which to a stranger,
Unguided and unfriended, often prove
Rough and unhospitable: my willing love,
The rather by these arguments of fear,
Set forth in your pursuit.

SEBASTIAN.   My kind Antonio,
I can no other answer make but thanks,
And thanks, and ever thanks; for oft good turns
Are shuffled off with such uncurrent pay:
But, were my worth, as is my conscience, firm,
You should find better dealing. What 's to do?
Shall we go see the reliques of this town?

ANTONIO. To-morrow, sir: best first go see your lodging.

SEBASTIAN. I am not weary, and 'tis long to night:
  I pray you, let us satisfy our eyes
  With the memorials and the things of fame
  That do renown this city.

ANTONIO.   Would you 'd pardon me;
  I do not without danger walk these streets:
  Once, in a sea-fight 'gainst the Count his galleys,
  I did some service; of such note indeed,
  That were I ta'en here it would scarce be answer'd.

SEBASTIAN. Belike you slew great number of his people?

ANTONIO. The offence is not of such a bloody nature,
  Albeit the quality of the time and quarrel
  Might well have given us bloody argument.
  It might have since been answer'd in repaying
  What we took from them; which, for traffic's sake,
  Most of our city did: only myself stood out;
  For which, if I be lapsed in this place,
  I shall pay dear.

SEBASTIAN.   Do not then walk too open.

ANTONIO. It doth not fit me. Hold, sir; here 's my purse.
  In the south suburbs, at the Elephant,
  Is best to lodge: I will bespeak our diet,
  Whiles you beguile the time and feed your knowledge
  With viewing of the town: there shall you have me.

SEBASTIAN. Why I your purse?

ANTONIO. Haply your eye shall light upon some toy
  You have desire to purchase; and your store,
  I think, is not for idle markets, sir.

SEBASTIAN. I 'll be your purse-bearer and leave you for an
  hour.

ANTONIO. To the Elephant.

SEBASTIAN. I do remember.   *Exeunt*

SCENE FOUR

Olivia's Garden.

Enter Olivia and Maria

OLIVIA. I have sent after him: he says he 'll come;
　How shall I feast him? what bestow of him?
　For youth is bought more oft than begg'd or borrow'd.
　I speak too loud.
　Where is Malvolio? He is sad, and civil,
　And suits well for a servant with my fortunes:
　Where is Malvolio?

MARIA. He 's coming, madam; but in very strange manner.
　He is sure possess'd, madam.

OLIVIA. Why, what 's the matter? Does he rave?

MARIA. No, madam; he does nothing but smile: your lady-
　ship were best to have some guard about you if he come,
　for sure the man is tainted in 's wits.

OLIVIA. Go call him hither.　　　　　　　　*Exit Maria*
　I am as mad as he,
　If sad and merry madness equal me.
　　　　　Re-enter Maria, with Malvolio
　How now, Malvolio!

MALVOLIO. Sweet lady, ho, ho.

OLIVIA. Smil'st thou?
　I sent for thee upon a sad occasion.

MALVOLIO. Sad, lady! I could be sad: this does make some
　obstruction in the blood, this cross-gartering; but what of
　that? If it please the eye of one, it is with me as the very
　true sonnet is, 'Please one and please all.'

OLIVIA. Why, how dost thou, man? What is the matter with
　thee?

MALVOLIO. Not black in my mind, though yellow in my legs.
　It did come to his hands, and commands shall be exe-
　cuted: I think we do know the sweet Roman hand.

OLIVIA. Wilt thou go to bed, Malvolio?

MALVOLIO. To bed! ay, sweetheart; and I 'll come to thee.

OLIVIA. God comfort thee! Why dost thou smile so and kiss
　thy hand so oft?

MARIA. How do you, Malvolio?

MALVOLIO. At your request! Yes; nightingales answer daws.

MARIA. Why appear you with this ridiculous boldness before my lady?

MALVOLIO. 'Be not afraid of greatness': 'Twas well writ.

OLIVIA. What meanest thou by that, Malvolio?

MALVOLIO. 'Some are born great,'—

OLIVIA. Ha!

MALVOLIO. 'Some achieve greatness,'—

OLIVIA. What sayst thou?

MALVOLIO. 'And some have greatness thrust upon them.'

OLIVIA. Heaven restore thee!

MALVOLIO. 'Remember who commended thy yellow stockings,'—

OLIVIA. Thy yellow stockings!

MALVOLIO. 'And wished to see thee cross-gartered.'

OLIVIA. Cross-gartered!

MALVOLIO. 'Go to, thou art made, if thou desirest to be so,'—

OLIVIA. Am I made?

MALVOLIO. 'If not, let me see thee a servant still.'

OLIVIA. Why, this is very midsummer madness.

Enter Servant

SERVANT. Madam, the young gentleman of the Count Orsino's is returned. I could hardly entreat him back: he attends your ladyship's pleasure.

OLIVIA. I 'll come to him. (*Exit Servant*) Good Maria, let this fellow be looked to. Where 's my cousin Toby? Let some of my people have a special care of him: I would not have him miscarry for the half of my dowry.

Exeunt Olivia and Maria

MALVOLIO. Oh, ho! do you come near me now? No worse man than Sir Toby to look to me! This concurs directly with the letter: she sends him on purpose, that I may appear stubborn to him; for she incites me to that in the letter. 'Cast thy humble slough,' says she; 'be opposite with a kinsman, surly with servants; let thy tongue tang with arguments of state; put thyself into the trick of singularity'; and consequently sets down the manner how; as, a sad face, a reverend carriage, a slow tongue, in the habit of some sir of note, and so forth. I have limed her; but it is Jove's doing, and Jove make me thankful! And when she went away now, 'Let this fellow be looked to'; fellow! not Malvolio, nor after my degree, but 'fellow.' Why, every-

thing adheres together, that no dram of a scruple, no
scruple of a scruple, no obstacle, no incredulous or unsafe
circumstance—What can be said? Nothing that can be can
come between me and the full prospect of my hopes. Well,
Jove, not I, is the doer of this, and he is to be thanked.

Re-enter Maria, with Sir Toby Belch and Fabian

SIR TOBY. Which way is he, in the name of sanctity? If all the
devils in hell be drawn in little, and Legion himself possess'd him, yet I 'll speak to him.

FABIAN. Here he is, here he is. How is 't with you, sir? How
is 't with you, man?

MALVOLIO. Go off; I discard you. Let me enjoy my private;
go off.

MARIA. Lo, how hollow the fiend speaks within him! Did not
I tell you? Sir Toby, my lady prays you to have a care of
him.

MALVOLIO. Ah, ha! does she so?

SIR TOBY. Go to, go to: peace! peace! we must deal gently
with him; let me alone. How do you, Malvolio? How is 't
with you? What, man! defy the devil: consider, he 's an
enemy to mankind.

MALVOLIO. Do you know what you say?

MARIA. La you! an you speak ill of the devil, how he takes it
at heart. Pray God, he be not bewitched!

FABIAN. Carry his water to the wise-woman.

MARIA. Marry, and it shall be done to-morrow morning, if I
live. My lady would not lose him for more than I 'll say.

MALVOLIO. How now, mistress!

MARIA. O Lord!

SIR TOBY. Prithee, hold thy peace; this is not the way: do you
not see you move him? Let me alone with him.

FABIAN. No way but gentleness; gently, gently: the fiend is
rough, and will not be roughly used.

SIR TOBY. Why, how now, my bawcock! How dost thou,
chuck?

MALVOLIO. Sir!

SIR TOBY. Ay, Biddy, come with me. What, man! 'tis not for
gravity to play at cherry-pit with Satan. Hang him, foul
collier!

MARIA. Get him to say his prayers, good Sir Toby, get him to
pray.

MALVOLIO. My prayers, minx!

MARIA. No, I warrant you, he will not hear of godliness.

MALVOLIO. Go, hang yourselves all! You are idle shallow things: I am not of your element. You shall know more hereafter.   *Exit*

SIR TOBY. Is 't possible?

FABIAN. If this were played upon a stage now, I could condemn it as an improbable fiction.

SIR TOBY. His very genius hath taken the infection of the device, man.

MARIA. Nay, pursue him now, lest the device take air, and taint.

FABIAN. Why, we shall make him mad indeed.

MARIA. The house will be the quieter.

SIR TOBY. Come, we 'll have him in a dark room, and bound. My niece is already in the belief that he 's mad: we may carry it thus, for our pleasure and his penance, till our very pastime, tired out of breath, prompt us to have mercy on him; at which time we will bring the device to the bar, and crown thee for a finder of madmen. But see, but see.

Enter Sir Andrew Aguecheek

FABIAN. More matter for a May morning.

SIR ANDREW. Here 's the challenge; read it: I warrant there 's vinegar and pepper in 't.

FABIAN. Is 't so saucy?

SIR ANDREW. Ay, is 't, I warrant him. Do but read.

SIR TOBY. Give me. 'Youth, whatsoever thou art, thou art but a scurvy fellow.'

FABIAN. Good, and valiant.

SIR TOBY. 'Wonder not, nor admire not in thy mind, why I do call thee so, for I will show thee no reason for 't.'

FABIAN. A good note, that keeps you from the blow of the law.

SIR TOBY. 'Thou comest to the Lady Olivia, and in my sight she uses thee kindly: but thou liest in thy throat; that is not the matter I challenge thee for.'

FABIAN. Very brief, and to exceeding good sense—less.

SIR TOBY. 'I will waylay thee going home; where, if it be thy chance to kill me,'—

FABIAN. Good.

SIR TOBY. 'Thou killest me like a rogue and a villain.'

FABIAN. Still you keep o' the windy side of the law: good.

SIR TOBY. 'Fare thee well; and God have mercy upon one of

our souls! He may have mercy upon mine, but my hope is
better; and so look to thyself. Thy friend, as thou usest
him, and thy sworn enemy,
                                'Andrew Aguecheek.'
If this letter move him not, his legs cannot. I 'll give 't him.

MARIA. You may have very fit occasion for 't: he is now in
some commerce with my lady, and will by and by depart.

SIR TOBY. Go, Sir Andrew; scout me for him at the corner of
the orchard like a bum-baily: so soon as ever thou seest
him, draw; and, as thou drawest, swear horrible; for it
comes to pass oft that a terrible oath, with a swaggering
accent sharply twanged off, gives manhood more approbation than ever proof itself would have earned him. Away!

SIR ANDREW. Nay, let me alone for swearing.   *Exit*

SIR TOBY. Now will not I deliver his letter: for the behaviour
of the young gentleman gives him out to be of good capacity and breeding; his employment between his lord and
my niece confirms no less: therefore this letter, being so
excellently ignorant, will breed no terror in the youth: he
will find it comes from a clodpole. But, sir, I will deliver
his challenge by word of mouth; set upon Aguecheek a
notable report of valour; and drive the gentleman,—as I
know his youth will aptly receive it,—into a most hideous
opinion of his rage, skill, fury, and impetuosity. This will
so fright them both that they will kill one another by the
look, like cockatrices.

FABIAN. Here he comes with your niece: give them way till
he take leave, and presently after him.

SIR TOBY. I will meditate the while upon some horrid message for a challenge.
                    Exeunt Sir Toby, Fabian, and Maria
                    Re-enter Olivia, with Viola

OLIVIA. I have said too much unto a heart of stone,
   And laid mine honour too unchary out:
   There 's something in me that reproves my fault,
   But such a headstrong potent fault it is
   That it but mocks reproof.

VIOLA. With the same haviour that your passion bears
   Goes on my master's griefs.

OLIVIA. Here; wear this jewel for me, 'tis my picture;
   Refuse it not; it hath no tongue to vex you;
   And I beseech you come again to-morrow.

What shall you ask of me that I 'll deny,
     That honour sav'd may upon asking give?

VIOLA. Nothing but this; your true love for my master.

OLIVIA. How with mine honour may I give him that
     Which I have given to you?

VIOLA.   I will acquit you.

OLIVIA. Well, come again to-morrow: fare thee well:
     A fiend like thee might bear my soul to hell.   *Exit*
          Re-enter Sir Toby Belch and Fabian

SIR TOBY. Gentleman, God save thee.

VIOLA. And you, sir.

SIR TOBY. That defence thou hast, betake thee to 't: of what
     nature the wrongs are thou hast done him, I know not; but
     thy intercepter, full of despite, bloody as the hunter, at-
     tends thee at the orchard-end. Dismount thy tuck, be yare
     in thy preparation, for thy assailant is quick, skilful, and
     deadly.

VIOLA. You mistake, sir: I am sure no man hath any quarrel
     to me: my remembrance is very free and clear from any
     image of offence done to any man.

SIR TOBY. You 'll find it otherwise, I assure you: therefore, if
     you hold your life at any price, betake you to your guard;
     for your opposite hath in him what youth, strength, skill,
     and wrath, can furnish man withal.

VIOLA. I pray you, sir, what is he?

SIR TOBY. He is knight dubbed with unhatched rapier, and
     on carpet consideration; but he is a devil in private brawl:
     souls and bodies hath he divorced three, and his incense-
     ment at this moment is so implacable that satisfaction can
     be none but by pangs of death and sepulchre. Hob, nob, is
     his word: give 't or take 't.

VIOLA. I will return again into the house and desire some
     conduct of the lady: I am no fighter. I have heard of some
     kind of men that put quarrels purposely on others to taste
     their valour; belike this is a man of that quirk.

SIR TOBY. Sir, no; his indignation derives itself out of a very
     competent injury: therefore get you on and give him his
     desire. Back you shall not to the house, unless you under-
     take that with me which with as much safety you might
     answer him: therefore, on, or strip your sword stark
     naked; for meddle you must, that 's certain, or forswear to
     wear iron about you.

VIOLA. This is as uncivil as strange. I beseech you, do me this courteous office, as to know of the knight what my offence to him is: it is something of my negligence, nothing of my purpose.

SIR TOBY. I will do so. Signior Fabian, stay you by this gentleman till my return.   *Exit*

VIOLA. Pray you, sir, do you know of this matter?

FABIAN. I know the knight is incensed against you, even to a mortal arbitrement, but nothing of the circumstance more.

VIOLA. I beseech you, what manner of man is he?

FABIAN. Nothing of that wonderful promise, to read him by his form, as you are like to find him in the proof of his valour. He is, indeed, sir, the most skilful, bloody, and fatal opposite that you could possibly have found in any part of Illyria. Will you walk towards him? I will make your peace with him if I can.

VIOLA. I shall be much bound to you for 't: I am one that had rather go with sir priest than sir knight: I care not who knows so much of my mettle.   *Exeunt*

Re-enter Sir Toby, with Sir Andrew

SIR TOBY. Why, man, he 's a very devil: I have not seen such a firago. I had a pass with him, rapier, scabbard and all, and he gives me the stuck in with such a mortal motion that it is inevitable; and on the answer, he pays you as surely as your feet hit the ground they step on. They say he has been fencer to the Sophy.

SIR ANDREW. Pox on 't, I 'll not meddle with him.

SIR TOBY. Ay, but he will not now be pacified: Fabian can scarce hold him yonder.

SIR ANDREW. Plague on 't; an I thought he had been valiant and so cunning in fence I 'd have seen him damned ere I 'd have challenged him. Let him let the matter slip, and I 'll give him my horse, grey Capilet.

SIR TOBY. I 'll make the motion. Stand here; make a good show on 't: this shall end without the perdition of souls.—
(*Aside*) Marry, I 'll ride your horse as well as I ride you.

Re-enter Fabian and Viola

(*To Fabian*) I have his horse to take up the quarrel. I have persuaded him the youth 's a devil.

FABIAN. He is as horribly conceited of him; and pants and looks pale, as if a bear were at his heels.

SIR TOBY. There 's no remedy, sir: he will fight with you for his oath's sake. Marry, he hath better bethought him of his quarrel, and he finds that now scarce to be worth talking of: therefore draw for the supportance of his vow: he protests he will not hurt you.

VIOLA. (*Aside*) Pray God defend me! A little thing would make me tell them how much I lack of a man.

FABIAN. Give ground, if you see him furious.

SIR TOBY. Come, Sir Andrew, there's no remedy: the gentleman will, for his honour's sake, have one bout with you; he cannot by the duello avoid it: but he has promised me, as he is a gentleman and a soldier, he will not hurt you. Come on; to 't.

SIR ANDREW. Pray God, he keep his oath!   *Draws*

VIOLA. I do assure you, 'tis against my will.   *Draws*

Enter Antonio

ANTONIO. Put up your sword. If this young gentleman
Have done offence, I take the fault on me:
If you offend him, I for him defy you.   *Drawing*

SIR TOBY. You, sir! Why, what are you?

ANTONIO. One, sir, that for his love dares yet do more
Than you have heard him brag to you he will.

SIR TOBY. Nay, if you be an undertaker, I am for you. *Draws*

FABIAN. O, good sir Toby, hold! Here come the officers.

SIR TOBY. I 'll be with you anon.

VIOLA. (*To Sir Andrew*) Pray, sir, put your sword up, if you please.

SIR ANDREW. Marry, will I, sir; and, for that I promised you, I 'll be as good as my word. He will bear you easily and reins well.

Enter two Officers

FIRST OFFICER. This is the man; do thy office.

SECOND OFFICER. Antonio, I arrest thee at the suit
Of Count Orsino.

ANTONIO.   You do mistake me, sir.

FIRST OFFICER. No, sir, no jot: I know your favour well,
Though now you have no sea-cap on your head.
Take him away: he knows I know him well.

ANTONIO. I must obey.—(*To Viola*) This comes with seeking you:
But there's no remedy: I shall answer it.
What will you do, now my necessity
Makes me to ask you for my purse? It grieves me

Much more for what I cannot do for you
Than what befalls myself. You stand amaz'd:
But be of comfort.

SECOND OFFICER. Come, sir, away.

ANTONIO. I must entreat of you some of that money.

VIOLA. What money, sir?
For the fair kindness you have show'd me here,
And part, being prompted by your present trouble,
Out of my lean and low ability
I 'll lend you something: my having is not much:
I 'll make division of my present with you.
Hold, there is half my coffer.

ANTONIO.   Will you deny me now?
Is 't possible that my deserts to you
Can lack persuasion? Do not tempt my misery,
Lest that it make me so unsound a man
As to upbraid you with those kindnesses
That I have done for you.

VIOLA.   I know of none;
Nor know I you by voice or any feature.
I hate ingratitude more in a man
Than lying, vainness, babbling drunkenness,
Or any taint of vice whose strong corruption
Inhabits our frail blood.

ANTONIO.   O heavens themselves!

SECOND OFFICER. Come, sir: I pray you, go.

ANTONIO. Let me speak a little. This youth that you see here
I snatch'd one-half out of the jaws of death,
Reliev'd him with such sanctity of love,
And to his image, which methought did promise
Most venerable worth, did I devotion.

FIRST OFFICER. What 's that to us? The time goes by: away!

ANTONIO. But O! how vile an idol proves this god.
Thou hast, Sebastian, done good feature shame.
In nature there 's no blemish but the mind;
None can be call'd deform'd but the unkind:
Virtue is beauty, but the beauteous evil
Are empty trunks o'erflourish'd by the devil.

FIRST OFFICER. The man grows mad: away with him! Come,
come, sir.

ANTONIO. Lead me on.   *Exeunt Officers with Antonio*

VIOLA. Methinks his words do from such passion fly,

That he believes himself; so do not I.
Prove true, imagination, O, prove true,
That I, dear brother, be now ta'en for you!

SIR TOBY. Come hither, knight; come hither, Fabian: we 'll
whisper o'er a couplet or two of most sage saws.

VIOLA. He nam'd Sebastian: I my brother know
Yet living in my glass; even such and so
In favour was my brother; and he went
Still in this fashion, colour, ornament,
For him I imitate. O! if it prove,
Tempests are kind, and salt waves fresh in love!   *Exit*

SIR TOBY. A very dishonest paltry boy, and more a coward
than a hare. His dishonesty appears in leaving his friend
here in necessity, and denying him; and for his coward-
ship, ask Fabian.

FABIAN. A coward, a most devout coward, religious in it.

SIR ANDREW. 'Slid, I 'll after him again and beat him.

SIR TOBY. Do; cuff him soundly, but never draw thy sword.

SIR ANDREW. An I do not,—   *Exit*

FABIAN. Come, let 's see the event.

SIR TOBY. I dare lay any money 'twill be nothing yet.   *Exeunt*

ACT FOUR

SCENE ONE

The Street adjoining Olivia's House.

Enter Sebastian and Clown

CLOWN. Will you make me believe that I am not sent for you?

SEBASTIAN. Go to, go to; thou art a foolish fellow: Let me be clear of thee.

CLOWN. Well held out, i' faith! No, I do not know you; nor I am not sent to you by my lady to bid you come speak with her; nor your name is not Master Cesario; nor this is not my nose neither. Nothing that is so is so.

SEBASTIAN. I prithee, vent thy folly somewhere else. Thou know'st not me.

CLOWN. Vent my folly! He has heard that word of some great man, and now applies it to a fool. Vent my folly! I am afraid this great lubber, the world, will prove a cockney. I prithee now, ungird thy strangeness and tell me what I shall vent to my lady. Shall I vent to her that thou art coming?

SEBASTIAN. I prithee, foolish Greek, depart from me: There 's money for thee: if you tarry longer I shall give worse payment.

CLOWN. By my troth, thou hast an open hand. These wise men that give fools money get themselves a good report after fourteen years' purchase.

Enter Sir Andrew

SIR ANDREW. Now, sir, have I met you again? There 's for you.   *Striking Sebastian*

SEBASTIAN. Why, there 's for thee, and there, and there, and there!   *Beating Sir Andrew*
Are all the people mad?

Enter Sir Toby and Fabian

SIR TOBY. Hold, sir, or I 'll throw your dagger o'er the house.

CLOWN. This will I tell my lady straight. I would not be in
some of your coats for twopence.   *Exit*

SIR TOBY. (*Holding Sebastian*) Come on, sir: hold.

SIR ANDREW. Nay, let him alone; I 'll go another way to work
with him: I 'll have an action of battery against him if there
be any law in Illyria. Though I struck him first, yet it 's no
matter for that.

SEBASTIAN. Let go thy hand.

SIR TOBY. Come, sir, I will not let you go. Come, my young
soldier, put up your iron: you are well fleshed; come on.

SEBASTIAN. I will be free from thee. (*Disengaging himself*)
What wouldst thou now?
If thou dar'st tempt me further, draw thy sword.

SIR TOBY. What, what! Nay then, I must have an ounce or
two of this malapert blood from you.   *Draws*

Enter Olivia

OLIVIA. Hold, Toby! On thy life I charge thee, hold!

SIR TOBY. Madam!

OLIVIA. Will it be ever thus? Ungracious wretch!
Fit for the mountains and the barbarous caves,
Where manners ne'er were preach'd. Out of my sight!
Be not offended, dear Cesario.
Rudesby, be gone!

          Exeunt Sir Toby, Sir Andrew, and Fabian
          I prithee, gentle friend,
Let thy fair wisdom, not thy passion, sway
In this uncivil and unjust extent
Against thy peace. Go with me to my house,
And hear thou there how many fruitless pranks
This ruffian hath botch'd up, that thou thereby
Mayst smile at this. Thou shalt not choose but go:
Do not deny. Beshrew his soul for me,
He started one poor heart of mine in thee.

SEBASTIAN. What relish is in this? How runs the stream?
Or I am mad, or else this is a dream:
Let fancy still my sense in Lethe steep;
If it be thus to dream, still let me sleep!

OLIVIA. Nay; come, I prithee. Would thou'dst be rul'd by
me!

SEBASTIAN. Madam, I will.

OLIVIA.   O! say so, and so be!   *Exeunt*

SCENE TWO

A Room in Olivia's House.

*Enter Maria and Clown; Malvolio in a dark
chamber adjoining*

MARIA. Nay, I prithee, put on this gown and this beard;
make him believe thou art Sir Topas the curate: do it
quickly; I 'll call Sir Toby the whilst.   *Exit*

CLOWN. Well, I 'll put it on and I will dissemble myself in 't:
and I would I were the first that ever dissembled in such a
gown. I am not tall enough to become the function well,
nor lean enough to be thought a good student; but to be
said an honest man and a good housekeeper goes as fairly
as to say a careful man and a great scholar. The competitors enter.

Enter Sir Toby Belch and Maria

SIR TOBY. God bless thee, Master parson.

CLOWN. Bonos dies, Sir Toby: for, as the old hermit of
Prague, that never saw pen and ink, very wittily said to a
niece of King Gorboduc, 'That, that is, is'; so I, being Master parson, am Master parson; for, what is 'that,' but 'that,'
and 'is,' but 'is'?

SIR TOBY. To him, Sir Topas.

CLOWN. What ho! I say. Peace in this prison!

SIR TOBY. The knave counterfeits well; a good knave.

MALVOLIO. *(Within)* Who calls there?

CLOWN. Sir Topas, the curate, who comes to visit Malvolio
the lunatic.

MALVOLIO. Sir Topas, Sir Topas, good Sir Topas, go to my
lady.

CLOWN. Out, hyperbolical fiend! How vexest thou this man!
Talkest thou nothing but of ladies?

SIR TOBY. Well said, Master Parson.

MALVOLIO. *(Within)* Sir Topas, never was man thus
wronged. Good Sir Topas, do not think I am mad. They
have laid me here in hideous darkness.

CLOWN. Fie, thou dishonest Satan! I call thee by the most
modest terms; for I am one of those gentle ones that will

use the devil himself with courtesy. Sayst thou that house is dark?

MALVOLIO. As hell, Sir Topas.

CLOWN. Why, it hath bay-windows transparent as barricadoes, and the clerestories toward the south-north are as lustrous as ebony; and yet complainest thou of obstruction?

MALVOLIO. I am not mad, Sir Topas. I say to you, this house is dark.

CLOWN. Madman, thou errest. I say, there is no darkness but ignorance, in which thou art more puzzled than the Egyptians in their fog.

MALVOLIO. I say this house is as dark as ignorance, though ignorance were as dark as hell; and I say, there was never man thus abused. I am no more mad than you are. Make the trial of it in any constant question.

CLOWN. What is the opinion of Pythagoras concerning wild fowl?

MALVOLIO. That the soul of our grandam might haply inhabit a bird.

CLOWN. What thinkest thou of his opinion?

MALVOLIO. I think nobly of the soul, and no way approve his opinion.

CLOWN. Fare thee well. Remain thou still in darkness. Thou shalt hold the opinion of Pythagoras ere I will allow of thy wits, and fear to kill a woodcock, lest thou dispossess the soul of thy grandam. Fare thee well.

MALVOLIO. Sir Topas! Sir Topas!

SIR TOBY. My most exquisite Sir Topas!

CLOWN. Nay, I am for all waters.

MARIA. Thou mightst have done this without thy beard and gown. He sees thee not.

SIR TOBY. To him in thine own voice, and bring me word how thou findest him: I would we were well rid of this knavery. If he may be conveniently delivered, I would he were; for I am now so far in offence with my niece that I cannot pursue with any safety this sport to the upshot. Come by and by to my chamber.

Exeunt Sir Toby and Maria

CLOWN. Hey Robin, jolly Robin,
        Tell me how thy lady does.

MALVOLIO. Fool!

CLOWN. 'My lady is unkind, perdy!'

MALVOLIO. Fool!

CLOWN. 'Alas, why is she so?'

MALVOLIO. Fool, I say!

CLOWN. 'She loves another.'
   Who calls, ha?

MALVOLIO. Good fool, as ever thou wilt deserve well at my
   hand, help me to a candle, and pen, ink, and paper. As I
   am a gentleman, I will live to be thankful to thee for 't.

CLOWN. Master Malvolio!

MALVOLIO. Ay, good fool.

CLOWN. Alas, sir, how fell you beside your five wits?

MALVOLIO. Fool, there was never man so notoriously abused.
   I am as well in my wits, fool, as thou art.

CLOWN. But as well? Then you are mad indeed, if you be no
   better in your wits than a fool.

MALVOLIO. They have here propertied me; keep me in darkness, send ministers to me, asses! and do all they can to
   face me out of my wits.

CLOWN. Advise you what you say. The minister is here. Malvolio, Malvolio, thy wits the heavens restore! Endeavour
   thyself to sleep, and leave thy vain bibble-babble.

MALVOLIO. Sir Topas!

CLOWN. Maintain no words with him, good fellow.—Who, I,
   sir? not I, sir. God be wi' you, good Sir Topas. Marry,
   amen. I will, sir, I will.

MALVOLIO. Fool, fool, fool, I say!

CLOWN. Alas, sir, be patient. What say you, sir? I am shent
   for speaking to you.

MALVOLIO. Good fool, help me to some light and some paper: I tell thee I am as well in my wits as any man in Illyria.

CLOWN. Well-a-day, that you were, sir!

MALVOLIO. By this hand, I am. Good fool, some ink, paper,
   and light; and convey what I will set down to my lady: it
   shall advantage thee more than ever the bearing of letter
   did.

CLOWN. I will help you to 't. But tell me true, are you not
   mad indeed? or do you but counterfeit?

MALVOLIO. Believe me, I am not: I tell thee true.

CLOWN. Nay, I 'll ne'er believe a madman till I see his brains.
   I will fetch you light and paper and ink.

MALVOLIO. Fool, I 'll requite it in the highest degree: I
    prithee, be gone.
CLOWN. (*Sings*) I am gone, sir,
                And anon, sir,
          I 'll be with you again
                In a trice,
                Like to the old Vice,
          Your need to sustain;
          Who with dagger of lath,
          In his rage and his wrath,
                Cries, Ah, ah! to the devil:
          Like a mad lad,
          Pare thy nails, dad;
                Adieu, goodman drivel.   *Exit*

SCENE THREE

Olivia's Garden.

Enter Sebastian

SEBASTIAN. This is the air; that is the glorious sun;
    This pearl she gave me, I do feel 't and see 't;
    And though 'tis wonder that enwraps me thus,
    Yet 'tis not madness. Where 's Antonio then?
    I could not find him at the Elephant;
    Yet there he was, and there I found this credit,
    That he did range the town to seek me out.
    His counsel now might do me golden service;
    For though my soul disputes well with my sense
    That this may be some error, but no madness,
    Yet doth this accident and flood of fortune
    So far exceed all instance, all discourse,
    That I am ready to distrust mine eyes,
    And wrangle with my reason that persuades me
    To any other trust but that I am mad
    Or else the lady 's mad: yet, if 'twere so,
    She could not sway her house, command her followers,
    Take and give back affairs and their dispatch
    With such a smooth, discreet, and stable bearing
    As I perceive she does. There 's something in 't
    That is deceivable. But here the lady comes.

Enter Olivia and a Priest

OLIVIA. Blame not this haste of mine. If you mean well,
    Now go with me and with this holy man
    Into the chantry by; there, before him,
    And underneath that consecrated roof,
    Plight me the full assurance of your faith;
    That my most jealous and too doubtful soul
    May live at peace. He shall conceal it
    Whiles you are willing it shall come to note,
    What time we will our celebration keep
    According to my birth. What do you say?

SEBASTIAN. I 'll follow this good man, and go with you;
    And, having sworn truth, ever will be true.

OLIVIA. Then lead the way, good father; and heavens so
        shine
    That they may fairly note this act of mine!   *Exeunt*

ACT FIVE

SCENE ONE

The Street before Olivia's House.

Enter Clown and Fabian

FABIAN. Now, as thou lovest me, let me see his letter.

CLOWN. Good Master Fabian, grant me another request.

FABIAN. Anything.

CLOWN. Do not desire to see this letter.

FABIAN. This is, to give a dog, and, in recompense desire my dog again.

Enter Duke, Viola, Curio, and Attendants

DUKE. Belong you to the Lady Olivia, friends?

CLOWN. Ay, sir; we are some of her trappings.

DUKE. I know thee well. How dost thou, my good fellow?

CLOWN. Truly, sir, the better for my foes and the worse for my friends.

DUKE. Just the contrary; the better for thy friends.

CLOWN. No, sir, the worse.

DUKE. How can that be?

CLOWN. Marry, sir, they praise me and make an ass of me; now my foes tell me plainly I am an ass: so that by my foes, sir, I profit in the knowledge of myself, and by my friends I am abused: so that, conclusions to be as kisses, if your four negatives make your two affirmatives, why then, the worse for my friends and the better for my foes.

DUKE. Why, this is excellent.

CLOWN. By my troth, sir, no; though it please you to be one of my friends.

DUKE. Thou shalt not be the worse for me. There 's gold.

CLOWN. But that it would be double-dealing, sir, I would you could make it another.

DUKE. O, you give me ill counsel.

CLOWN. Put your grace in your pocket, sir, for this once, and
let your flesh and blood obey it.

DUKE. Well, I will be so much a sinner to be a double-dealer:
there's another.

CLOWN. Primo, secundo, tertio, is a good play; and the old
saying is, 'the third pays for all': the triplex, sir, is a good
tripping measure; or the bells of Saint Bennet, sir, may put
you in mind; one, two, three.

DUKE. You can fool no more money out of me at this throw.
If you will let your lady know I am here to speak with her,
and bring her along with you, it may awake my bounty
further.

CLOWN. Marry, sir, lullaby to your bounty till I come again.
I go, sir; but I would not have you to think that my desire
of having is the sin of covetousness; but as you say, sir, let
your bounty take a nap, I will awake it anon.   *Exit*

VIOLA. Here comes the man, sir, that did rescue me.
                Enter Antonio and Officers

DUKE. That face of his I do remember well;
Yet when I saw it last, it was besmear'd
As black as Vulcan in the smoke of war.
A bawbling vessel was he captain of,
For shallow draught and hulk unprizable;
With which such scathful grapple did he make
With the most noble bottom of our fleet,
That very envy and the tongue of loss
Cried fame and honour on him. What's the matter?

FIRST OFFICER. Orsino, this is that Antonio
That took the Phœnix and her fraught from Candy;
And this is he that did the Tiger board,
When your young nephew Titus lost his leg.
Here in the streets, desperate of shame and state,
In private brabble did we apprehend him.

VIOLA. He did me kindness, sir, drew on my side;
But in conclusion put strange speech upon me:
I know not what 'twas but distraction.

DUKE. Notable pirate! thou salt-water thief!
What foolish boldness brought thee to their mercies
Whom thou, in terms so bloody and so dear,
Hast made thine enemies?

ANTONIO.   Orsino, noble sir,
Be pleas'd that I shake off these names you give me:

Antonio never yet was thief or pirate,
Though I confess, on base and ground enough,
Orsino's enemy. A witchcraft drew me hither:
That most ingrateful boy there by your side,
From the rude sea 's enrag'd and foamy mouth
Did I redeem; a wrack past hope he was:
His life I gave him, and did thereto add
My love, without retention or restraint,
All his in dedication; for his sake
Did I expose myself, pure for his love,
Into the danger of this adverse town;
Drew to defend him when he was beset:
Where being apprehended, his false cunning,
Not meaning to partake with me in danger,
Taught him to face me out of his acquaintance,
And grew a twenty years removed thing
While one would wink, denied me mine own purse,
Which I had recommended to his use
Not half an hour before.

VIOLA.   How can this be?

DUKE.   When came he to this town?

ANTONIO.   To-day, my lord; and for three months before,—
No interim, not a minute's vacancy,—
Both day and night did we keep company.

Enter Olivia and Attendants

DUKE.   Here comes the countess: now heaven walks on earth!
But for thee, fellow; fellow, thy words are madness:
Three months this youth hath tended upon me;
But more of that anon. Take him aside.

OLIVIA.   What would my lord, but that he may not have,
Wherein Olivia may seem serviceable?
Cesario, you do not keep promise with me.

VIOLA.   Madam!

DUKE.   Gracious Olivia.—

OLIVIA.   What do you say, Cesario? Good my lord,—

VIOLA.   My lord would speak; my duty hushes me.

OLIVIA.   If it be aught to the old tune, my lord,
It is as fat and fulsome to mine ear
As howling after music.

DUKE.   Still so cruel?

OLIVIA.   Still so constant, lord.

DUKE.   What, to perverseness? You uncivil lady,

To whose ingrate and unauspicious altars
My soul the faithfull'st offerings hath breath'd out
That e'er devotion tender'd! What shall I do?

OLIVIA. Even what it please my lord, that shall become him.

DUKE. Why should I not, had I the heart to do it,
Like to the Egyptian thief at point of death,
Kill what I love?—a savage jealousy
That sometimes savours nobly. But hear me this:
Since you to non-regardance cast my faith,
And that I partly know the instrument
That screws me from my true place in your favour,
Live you, the marble-breasted tyrant still;
But this your minion, whom I know you love,
And whom, by heaven I swear, I tender dearly,
Him will I tear out of that cruel eye,
Where he sits crowned in his master's spite.
Come, boy, with me; my thoughts are ripe in mischief;
I 'll sacrifice the lamb that I do love,
To spite a raven's heart within a dove.   *Going*

VIOLA. And I, most jocund, apt, and willingly,
To do you rest, a thousand deaths would die.   *Following*

OLIVIA. Where goes Cesario?

VIOLA.   After him I love
More than I love these eyes, more than my life,
More, by all mores, than e'er I shall love wife.
If I do feign, you witnesses above
Punish my life for tainting of my love!

OLIVIA. Ah me, detested! How am I beguil'd!

VIOLA. Who does beguile you? Who does do you wrong?

OLIVIA. Hast thou forgot thyself? Is it so long?
Call forth the holy father.   *Exit an Attendant*

DUKE.   (*To Viola*) Come away.

OLIVIA. Whither, my lord? Cesario, husband, stay.

DUKE. Husband?

OLIVIA.   Ay, husband: can he that deny?

DUKE. Her husband, sirrah?

VIOLA.   No, my lord, not I.

OLIVIA. Alas! it is the baseness of thy fear
That makes thee strangle thy propriety.
Fear not, Cesario; take thy fortunes up;
Be that thou know'st thou art, and then thou art
As great as that thou fear'st.

Enter Priest

O, welcome, father!
Father, I charge thee, by thy reverence,
Here to unfold,—though lately we intended
To keep in darkness what occasion now
Reveals before 'tis ripe,—what thou dost know
Hath newly pass'd between this youth and me.

PRIEST. A contract of eternal bond of love,
Confirm'd by mutual joinder of your hands,
Attested by the holy close of lips,
Strengthen'd by interchangement of your rings;
And all the ceremony of this compact
Seal'd in my function, by my testimony:
Since when, my watch hath told me, toward my grave
I have travell'd but two hours.

DUKE. O, thou dissembling cub! What wilt thou be
When time hath sow'd a grizzle on thy case?
Or will not else thy craft so quickly grow
That thine own trip shall be thine overthrow?
Farewell, and take her; but direct thy feet
Where thou and I henceforth may never meet.

VIOLA. My lord, I do protest,—

OLIVIA.   O! do not swear:
Hold little faith, though thou hast too much fear.

Enter Sir Andrew Aguecheek, with his head broken

SIR ANDREW. For the love of God, a surgeon! Send one presently to Sir Toby.

OLIVIA. What 's the matter?

SIR ANDREW. He has broke my head across, and has given
Sir Toby a bloody coxcomb too. For the love of God, your
help! I had rather than forty pound I were at home.

OLIVIA. Who has done this, Sir Andrew?

SIR ANDREW. The count's gentleman, one Cesario: we took
him for a coward, but he 's the very devil incardinate.

DUKE. My gentleman, Cesario?

SIR ANDREW. Od's lifelings! here he is. You broke my head
for nothing! and that that I did, I was set on to do 't by Sir
Toby.

VIOLA. Why do you speak to me? I never hurt you:
You drew your sword upon me without cause;
But I bespake you fair, and hurt you not.

SIR ANDREW. If a bloody coxcomb be a hurt, you have hurt

me: I think you set nothing by a bloody coxcomb. Here
comes Sir Toby halting;

Enter Sir Toby Belch, drunk, led by the Clown

you shall hear more: but if he had not been in drink he
would have tickled you othergates than he did.

DUKE. How now, gentleman! How is 't with you?

SIR TOBY. That 's all one: he has hurt me, and there 's the
end on 't. Sot, didst see Dick Surgeon, sot?

CLOWN. O! he 's drunk, Sir Toby, an hour agone: his eyes
were set at eight i' the morning.

SIR TOBY. Then he 's a rogue, and a passy-measures pavin. I
hate a drunken rogue.

OLIVIA. Away with him! Who hath made this havoc with
them?

SIR ANDREW. I 'll help you, Sir Toby, because we 'll be
dressed together.

SIR TOBY. Will you help? An ass-head and a coxcomb and a
knave, a thin-faced knave, a gull!

OLIVIA. Get him to bed, and let his hurt be look'd to.

Exeunt Clown, Fabian, Sir Toby, and Sir Andrew
Enter Sebastian

SEBASTIAN. I am sorry, madam, I have hurt your kinsman;
But, had it been the brother of my blood,
I must have done no less with wit and safety.
You throw a strange regard upon me, and by that
I do perceive it hath offended you:
Pardon me, sweet one, even for the vows
We made each other but so late ago.

DUKE. One face, one voice, one habit, and two persons;
A natural perspective, that is, and is not!

SEBASTIAN. Antonio! O my dear Antonio!
How have the hours rack'd and tortur'd me
Since I have lost thee!

ANTONIO. Sebastian are you?

SEBASTIAN.   Fear'st thou that, Antonio?

ANTONIO. How have you made division of yourself?
An apple cleft in two is not more twin
Than these two creatures. Which is Sebastian?

OLIVIA. Most wonderful!

SEBASTIAN. Do I stand there? I never had a brother;
Nor can there be that deity in my nature,
Of here and every where. I had a sister,

  Whom the blind waves and surges have devour'd.
  Of charity, what kin are you to me?
  What countryman? what name? what parentage?
VIOLA. Of Messaline: Sebastian was my father;
  Such a Sebastian was my brother too,
  So went he suited to his watery tomb.
  If spirits can assume both form and suit
  You come to fright us.
SEBASTIAN.   A spirit I am indeed;
  But am in that dimension grossly clad
  Which from the womb I did participate.
  Were you a woman, as the rest goes even,
  I should my tears let fall upon your cheek,
  And say, 'Thrice welcome, drowned Viola!'
VIOLA. My father had a mole upon his brow.
SEBASTIAN. And so had mine.
VIOLA. And died that day when Viola from her birth
  Had number'd thirteen years.
SEBASTIAN. O! that record is lively in my soul.
  He finished indeed his mortal act
  That day that made my sister thirteen years.
VIOLA. If nothing lets to make us happy both
  But this my masculine usurp'd attire,
  Do not embrace me till each circumstance
  Of place, time, fortune, do cohere and jump
  That I am Viola: which to confirm,
  I 'll bring you to a captain in this town,
  Where lie my maiden weeds: by whose gentle help
  I was preserv'd to serve this noble count.
  All the occurrence of my fortune since
  Hath been between this lady and this lord.
SEBASTIAN. (*To Olivia*) So comes it, lady, you have been
   mistook:
  But nature to her bias drew in that.
  You would have been contracted to a maid;
  Nor are you therein, by my life, deceiv'd,
  You are betroth'd both to a maid and man.
DUKE. Be not amaz'd; right noble is his blood.
  If this be so, as yet the glass seems true,
  I shall have share in this most happy wrack.
  (*To Viola*) Boy, thou hast said to me a thousand times
  Thou never shouldst love woman like to me.

VIOLA. And all those sayings will I over-swear,
And all those swearings keep as true in soul
As doth that orbed continent the fire
That severs day from night.

DUKE.   Give me thy hand;
And let me see thee in thy woman's weeds. •

VIOLA. The captain that did bring me first on shore
Hath my maid's garments: he upon some action
Is now in durance at Malvolio's suit,
A gentleman and follower of my lady's.

OLIVIA. He shall enlarge him. Fetch Malvolio hither.
And yet, alas, now I remember me,
They say, poor gentleman, he 's much distract.
A most extracting frenzy of mine own
From my remembrance clearly banish'd his.

          Re-enter Clown with a letter, and Fabian
How does he, sirrah?

CLOWN. Truly, madam, he holds Belzebub at the stave's end
as well as a man in his case may do. He has here writ a letter to you: I should have given it to you to-day morning;
but as a madman's epistles are no gospels, so it skills not
much when they are delivered.

OLIVIA. Open it, and read it.

CLOWN. Look then to be well edified, when the fool delivers
the madman.
'By the Lord, madam,'—

OLIVIA. How now! Art thou mad?

CLOWN. No, madam, I do but read madness: an your ladyship will have it as it ought to be, you must allow vox.

OLIVIA. Prithee, read i' thy right wits.

CLOWN. So I do, madonna; but to read his right wits is to
read thus: therefore perpend, my princess, and give ear.

OLIVIA. (*To Fabian*) Read it you, sirrah.

FABIAN. (*Reads*) 'By the Lord, madam, you wrong me, and
the world shall know it: though you have put me into
darkness, and given your drunken cousin rule over me, yet
have I the benefit of my senses as well as your ladyship. I
have your own letter that induced me to the semblance I
put on; with the which I doubt not but to do myself much
right, or you much shame. Think of me as you please. I
leave my duty a little unthought of, and speak out of my
injury.
          'The madly-used Malvolio.'

OLIVIA. Did he write this?

CLOWN. Ay, madam.

DUKE. This savours not much of distraction.

OLIVIA. See him deliver'd, Fabian; bring him hither.

Exit Fabian

My lord, so please you, these things further thought on,
To think me as well a sister as a wife,
One day shall crown the alliance on 't, so please you,
Here at my house and at my proper cost.

DUKE. Madam, I am most apt to embrace your offer.
 (*To Viola*) Your master quits you; and, for your service
   done him,
So much against the mettle of your sex,
So far beneath your soft and tender breeding;
And since you call'd me master for so long,
Here is my hand: you shall from this time be
Your master's mistress.

OLIVIA.   A sister! you are she.

Re-enter Fabian, with Malvolio

DUKE. Is this the madman?

OLIVIA.   Ay, my lord, this same.
How now, Malvolio!

MALVOLIO.   Madam, you have done me wrong,
Notorious wrong.

OLIVIA.   Have I, Malvolio? No.

MALVOLIO. Lady, you have. Pray you peruse that letter.
You must not now deny it is your hand:
Write from it, if you can, in hand or phrase,
Or say 'tis not your seal nor your invention:
You can say none of this. Well, grant it then,
And tell me, in the modesty of honour,
Why you have given me such clear lights of favour,
Bade me come smiling and cross-garter'd to you,
To put on yellow stockings, and to frown
Upon Sir Toby and the lighter people;
And, acting this in an obedient hope,
Why have you suffer'd me to be imprison'd,
Kept in a dark house, visited by the priest,
And made the most notorious geck and gull
That e'er invention play'd on? Tell me why.

OLIVIA. Alas! Malvolio, this is not my writing,
Though, I confess, much like the character;

But, out of question, 'tis Maria's hand:
And now I do bethink me, it was she
First told me thou wast mad; then cam'st in smiling,
And in such forms which here were presuppos'd
Upon thee in the letter. Prithee, be content:
This practice hath most shrewdly pass'd upon thee;
But when we know the grounds and authors of it,
Thou shalt be both the plaintiff and the judge
Of thine own cause.

FABIAN.   Good madam, hear me speak,
And let no quarrel nor no brawl to come
Taint the condition of this present hour,
Which I have wonder'd at. In hope it shall not,
Most freely I confess, myself and Toby
Set this device against Malvolio here,
Upon some stubborn and uncourteous parts
We had conceiv'd against him. Maria writ
The letter at Sir Toby's great importance;
In recompense whereof he hath married her.
How with a sportful malice it was follow'd,
May rather pluck on laughter than revenge,
If that the injuries be justly weigh'd
That have on both sides past.

OLIVIA. Alas, poor fool, how have they baffled thee!

CLOWN. Why, 'some are born great, some achieve greatness,
and some have greatness thrown upon them.' I was one,
sir, in this interlude; one Sir Topas, sir; but that 's all one.
'By the Lord, fool, I am not mad': But do you remember?
'Madam, why laugh you at such a barren rascal? An you
smile not, he 's gagged': and thus the whirligig of time
brings in his revenges.

MALVOLIO. I 'll be reveng'd on the whole pack of you. *Exit*

OLIVIA. He hath been most notoriously abus'd.

DUKE. Pursue him, and entreat him to a peace;—
He hath not told us of the captain yet:
When that is known and golden time convents,
A solemn combination shall be made
Of our dear souls. Meantime, sweet sister,
We will not part from hence. Cesario, come;
For so you shall be, while you are a man;
But when in other habits you are seen,
Orsino's mistress, and his fancy's queen.
                              Exeunt all except Clown

SONG

CLOWN. When that I was and a little tiny boy,
            With hey, ho, the wind and the rain;
        A foolish thing was but a toy,
            For the rain it raineth every day.

        But when I came to man's estate,
            With hey, ho, the wind and the rain;
        'Gainst knaves and thieves men shut their gates,
            For the rain it raineth every day.

        But when I came, alas! to wive,
            With hey, ho, the wind and the rain;
        By swaggering could I never thrive,
            For the rain it raineth every day.

        But when I came unto my beds,
            With hey, ho, the wind and the rain;
        With toss-pots still had drunken heads,
            For the rain it raineth every day.

        A great while ago the world begun,
            With hey, ho, the wind and the rain;
        But that 's all one, our play is done,
            And we 'll strive to please you every day.   *Exit*

THE WINTER'S TALE

CAST OF CHARACTERS

LEONTES, King of Sicilia.
MAMILLIUS, young Prince of Sicilia

CAMILLO
ANTIGONUS } Lords of Sicilia
CLEOMENES
DION

POLIXENES, King of Bohemia
FLORIZEL, his Son
ARCHIDAMUS, a Lord of Bohemia

A Mariner
A Gaoler
An old Shepherd, reputed Father of Perdita
Clown, his Son
Servant to the old Shepherd
AUTOLYCUS, a Rogue

HERMIONE, Queen to Leontes
PERDITA, Daughter to Leontes and Hermione
PAULINA, Wife to Antigonus

EMILIA, a Lady } attending the Queen
Other Ladies

MOPSA   } Shepherdesses
DORCAS

Sicilian Lords and Ladies, Attendants, Guards,
Satyrs, Shepherds, Shepherdesses, &c.

Time, as Chorus

SCENE

Sometimes in Sicilia, sometimes in Bohemia

THE WINTER'S TALE

ACT ONE

SCENE ONE

Sicilia. An Antechamber in Leontes' Palace.

Enter Camillo and Archidamus

ARCHIDAMUS. If you shall chance, Camillo, to visit Bohemia,
on the like occasion whereon my services are now on foot,
you shall see, as I have said, great difference betwixt our
Bohemia and your Sicilia.

CAMILLO. I think, this coming summer, the King of Sicilia
means to pay Bohemia the visitation which he justly owes
him.

ARCHIDAMUS. Wherein our entertainment shall shame us we
will be justified in our loves: for, indeed,—

CAMILLO. Beseech you,—

ARCHIDAMUS. Verily, I speak it in the freedom of my knowledge: we cannot with such magnificence—in so rare—I
know not what to say. We will give you sleepy drinks, that
your senses, unintelligent of our insufficience, may, though
they cannot praise us, as little accuse us.

CAMILLO. You pay a great deal too dear for what 's given
freely.

ARCHIDAMUS. Believe me, I speak as my understanding instructs me, and as mine honesty puts it to utterance.

CAMILLO. Sicilia cannot show himself over-kind to Bohemia.
They were trained together in their childhoods; and there
rooted betwixt them then such an affection which cannot
choose but branch now. Since their more mature dignities
and royal necessities made separation of their society,
their encounters, though not personal, have been royally
attorneyed with interchange of gifts, letters, loving em-

bassies; that they have seemed to be together, though absent, shook hands, as over a vast, and embraced, as it were, from the ends of opposed winds. The heavens continue their loves!

ARCHIDAMUS. I think there is not in the world either malice or matter to alter it. You have an unspeakable comfort of your young Prince Mamillius: it is a gentleman of the greatest promise that ever came into my note.

CAMILLO. I very well agree with you in the hopes of him. It is a gallant child; one that indeed physics the subject, makes old hearts fresh; they that went on crutches ere he was born desire yet their life to see him a man.

ARCHIDAMUS. Would they else be content to die?

CAMILLO. Yes; if there were no other excuse why they should desire to live.

ARCHIDAMUS. If the king had no son, they would desire to live on crutches till he had one.   *Exeunt*

SCENE TWO

The Same. A Room of State in the Palace.

Enter Leontes, Polixenes, Hermione, Mamillius, Camillo, and Attendants

POLIXENES. Nine changes of the watery star have been
The shepherd's note since we have left our throne
Without a burden. Time as long again
Would be fill'd up, my brother, with our thanks;
And yet we should for perpetuity
Go hence in debt: and therefore, like a cipher,
Yet standing in rich place, I multiply
With one 'We thank you' many thousands moe
That go before it.

LEONTES.   Stay your thanks awhile,
And pay them when you part.

POLIXENES.   Sir, that 's to-morrow.
I am question'd by my fears, of what may chance
Or breed upon our absence; that may blow
No sneaping winds at home, to make us say,
'This is put forth too truly!' Besides, I have stay'd
To tire your royalty.

LEONTES.   We are tougher, brother,
   Than you can put us to 't.
POLIXENES.   No longer stay.
LEONTES. One seven-night longer.
POLIXENES.   Very sooth, to-morrow.
LEONTES. We 'll part the time between 's then; and in that
   I 'll no gainsaying.
POLIXENES.   Press me not, beseech you, so.
   There is no tongue that moves, none, none i' the world,
   So soon as yours could win me: so it should now,
   Were there necessity in your request, although
   'Twere needful I denied it. My affairs
   Do even drag me homeward; which to hinder
   Were in your love a whip to me; my stay
   To you a charge and trouble: to save both,
   Farewell, our brother.
LEONTES.   Tongue-tied, our queen? Speak you.
HERMIONE. I had thought, sir, to have held my peace until
   You had drawn oaths from him not to stay. You, sir,
   Charge him too coldly: tell him, you are sure
   All in Bohemia 's well: this satisfaction
   The by-gone day proclaim'd: say this to him,
   He 's beat from his best ward.
LEONTES.   Well said, Hermione.
HERMIONE. To tell he longs to see his son were strong:
   But let him say so then, and let him go;
   But let him swear so, and he shall not stay,
   We 'll thwack him hence with distaffs.
   (*To Polixenes*) Yet of your royal presence I 'll adventure
   The borrow of a week. When at Bohemia
   You take my lord, I 'll give him my commission
   To let him there a month behind the gest
   Prefix'd for 's parting: yet, good deed, Leontes,
   I love thee not a jar o' the clock behind
   What lady she her lord. You 'll stay?
POLIXENES.   No, madam.
HERMIONE. Nay, but you will?
POLIXENES.   I may not, verily.
HERMIONE. Verily!
   You put me off with limber vows; but I,
   Though you would seek to unsphere the stars with oaths,
   Should yet say, 'Sir, no going.' Verily,

You shall not go: a lady's 'verily' 's
As potent as a lord's. Will you go yet?
Force me to keep you as a prisoner,
Not like a guest; so you shall pay your fees
When you depart, and save your thanks. How say you?
My prisoner, or my guest? By your dread 'verily,'
One of them you shall be.

POLIXENES.   Your guest, then, madam:
To be your prisoner should import offending;
Which is for me less easy to commit
Than you to punish.

HERMIONE.   Not your gaoler then,
But your kind hostess. Come, I'll question you
Of my lord's tricks and yours when you were boys.
You were pretty lordings then?

POLIXENES.   We were, fair queen,
Two lads that thought there was no more behind
But such a day to-morrow as to-day,
And to be boy eternal.

HERMIONE. Was not my lord the verier wag o' the two?

POLIXENES. We were as twinn'd lambs that did frisk i' the
      sun,
And bleat the one at the other: what we chang'd
Was innocence for innocence; we knew not
The doctrine of ill-doing, nor dream'd
That any did. Had we pursu'd that life,
And our weak spirits ne'er been higher rear'd
With stronger blood, we should have answer'd heaven
Boldly, 'not guilty'; the imposition clear'd
Hereditary ours.

HERMIONE.   By this we gather
You have tripp'd since.

POLIXENES.   O! my most sacred lady,
Temptations have since then been born to 's; for
In those unfledg'd days was my wife a girl;
Your precious self had then not cross'd the eyes
Of my young playfellow.

HERMIONE.   Grace to boot!
Of this make no conclusion, lest you say
Your queen and I are devils; yet go on:
The offences we have made you do we'll answer;
If you first sinn'd with us, and that with us

You did continue fault, and that you slipp'd not
With any but with us.

LEONTES.   Is he won yet?

HERMIONE. He 'll stay, my lord.

LEONTES.   At my request he would not.
Hermione, my dearest, thou never spok'st
To better purpose.

HERMIONE.   Never?

LEONTES.   Never, but once.

HERMIONE. What! have I twice said well? When was 't
    before?
I prithee tell me; cram 's with praise, and make 's
As fat as tame things: one good deed, dying tongueless,
Slaughters a thousand waiting upon that.
Our praises are our wages: you may ride 's
With one soft kiss a thousand furlongs ere
With spur we heat an acre. But to the goal:
My last good deed was to entreat his stay:
What was my first? It has an elder sister,
Or I mistake you: O! would her name were Grace.
But once before I spoke to the purpose. When?
Nay, let me have 't; I long.

LEONTES.   Why, that was when
Three crabbed months had sour'd themselves to death,
Ere I could make thee open thy white hand
And clap thyself my love: then didst thou utter,
'I am yours for ever.'

HERMIONE.   'Tis grace indeed.
Why, lo you now, I have spoke to the purpose twice.
The one for ever earn'd a royal husband,
The other for some while a friend.

                    Giving her hand to Polixenes

LEONTES. (*Aside*) Too hot, too hot!
To mingle friendship far is mingling bloods.
I have tremor cordis on me: my heart dances;
But not for joy; not joy. This entertainment
May a free face put on, derive a liberty
From heartiness, from bounty, fertile bosom,
And well become the agent: 't may I grant:
But to be paddling palms and pinching fingers,
As now they are, and making practis'd smiles,
As in a looking-glass; and then to sigh, as 'twere

The mort o' the deer; O! that is entertainment
My bosom likes not, nor my brows. Mamillius,
Art thou my boy?

MAMILLIUS.   Ay, my good lord.

LEONTES.   I' fecks?
Why, that 's my bawcock. What! hast smutch'd thy nose?
They say it is a copy out of mine. Come, captain,
We must be neat; not neat, but cleanly, captain:
And yet the steer, the heifer, and the calf,
Are all call'd neat. Still virginalling
Upon his palm! How now, you wanton calf!
Art thou my calf?

MAMILLIUS.   Yes, if you will, my lord.

LEONTES. Thou want'st a rough pash and the shoots that I
    have,
To be full like me: yet they say we are
Almost as like as eggs; women say so,
That will say anything: but were they false
As o'er-dy'd blacks, as wind, as waters, false
As dice are to be wish'd by one that fixes
No bourn 'twixt his and mine, yet were it true
To say this boy were like me. Come, sir page,
Look on me with your welkin eye: sweet villain!
Most dear'st! my collop! Can thy dam?—may 't be?—
Affection! thy intention stabs the centre:
Thou dost make possible things not so held,
Communicat'st with dreams;—how can this be?—
With what 's unreal thou co-active art,
And fellow'st nothing: then, 'tis very credent
Thou mayst co-join with something; and thou dost,
And that beyond commission, and I find it,
And that to the infection of my brains
And hardening of my brows.

POLIXENES.   What means Sicilia?

HERMIONE. He something seems unsettled.

POLIXENES.   How, my lord!
What cheer? how is 't with you, best brother?

HERMIONE.   You look
As if you held a brow of much distraction:
Are you mov'd, my lord?

LEONTES.   No, in good earnest.
How sometimes nature will betray its folly,

Its tenderness, and make itself a pastime
To harder bosoms! Looking on the lines
Of my boy's face, methoughts I did recoil
Twenty-three years, and saw myself unbreech'd,
In my green velvet coat, my dagger muzzled,
Lest it should bite its master, and so prove,
As ornaments oft do, too dangerous:
How like, methought, I then was to this kernel,
This squash, this gentleman. Mine honest friend,
Will you take eggs for money?

MAMILLIUS.   No, my lord, I 'll fight.

LEONTES. You will? Why, happy man be his dole! My
     brother,
Are you so fond of your young prince as we
Do seem to be of ours?

POLIXENES.   If at home, sir,
He 's all my exercise, my mirth, my matter,
Now my sworn friend and then mine enemy;
My parasite, my soldier, statesman, all:
He makes a July's day short as December,
And with his varying childness cures in me
Thoughts that would thick my blood.

LEONTES.   So stands this squire
Offic'd with me. We two will walk, my lord,
And leave you to your graver steps. Hermione,
How thou lov'st us, show in our brother's welcome:
Let what is dear in Sicily be cheap:
Next to thyself and my young rover, he 's
Apparent to my heart.

HERMIONE.   If you would seek us,
We are yours i' the garden: shall 's attend you there?

LEONTES. To your own bents dispose you: you 'll be found,
Be you beneath the sky.—(*Aside*) I am angling now,
Though you perceive me not how I give line.
Go to, go to!
How she holds up the neb, the bill to him!
And arms her with the boldness of a wife
To her allowing husband!

                    Exeunt Polixenes, Hermione, and Attendants
                         Gone already!
Inch-thick, knee-deep, o'er head and ears a fork'd one!
Go play, boy, play; thy mother plays, and I

Play too, but so disgrac'd a part, whose issue
Will hiss me to my grave: contempt and clamour
Will be my knell. Go play, boy, play. There have been,
Or I am much deceiv'd, cuckolds ere now;
And many a man there is even at this present,
Now, while I speak this, holds his wife by the arm,
That little thinks she has been sluic'd in 's absence,
And his pond fish'd by his next neighbour, by
Sir Smile, his neighbour: nay, there 's comfort in 't,
Whiles other men have gates, and those gates open'd,
As mine, against their will. Should all despair
That have revolted wives, the tenth of mankind
Would hang themselves. Physic for 't there is none;
It is a bawdy planet, that will strike
Where 'tis predominant; and 'tis powerful, think it,
From east, west, north, and south: be it concluded,
No barricado for a belly: know 't;
It will let in and out the enemy
With bag and baggage. Many a thousand on 's
Have the disease, and feel 't not. How now, boy!

MAMILLIUS. I am like you, they say.

LEONTES.   Why, that 's some comfort.
What! Camillo there?

CAMILLO. Ay, my good lord.

LEONTES. Go play, Mamillius; thou 'rt an honest man.

Exit Mamillius

Camillo, this great sir will yet stay longer.

CAMILLO. You had much ado to make his anchor hold:
When you cast out, it still came home.

LEONTES.   Didst note it?

CAMILLO. He would not stay at your petitions; made
His business more material.

LEONTES.   Didst perceive it?
    (*Aside*) They 're here with me already, whispering,
        rounding
'Sicilia is a so-forth.' 'Tis far gone,
When I shall gust it last. How came 't, Camillo,
That he did stay?

CAMILLO.   At the good queen's entreaty.

LEONTES. At the queen's, be 't: 'good' should be pertinent;
But so it is, it is not. Was this taken
By any understanding pate but thine?

For thy conceit is soaking; will draw in
More than the common blocks. Not noted, is 't,
But of the finer natures? by some severals
Of head-piece extraordinary? Lower messes
Perchance are to this business purblind? Say.

CAMILLO. Business, my lord! I think most understand
Bohemia stays here longer.

LEONTES.   Ha!

CAMILLO.   Stays here longer.

LEONTES. Ay, but why?

CAMILLO. To satisfy your Highness and the entreaties
Of our most gracious mistress.

LEONTES.   Satisfy!
The entreaties of your mistress! satisfy!
Let that suffice. I have trusted thee, Camillo,
With all the nearest things to my heart, as well
My chamber-councils, wherein, priest-like, thou
Hast cleans'd my bosom: I from thee departed
Thy penitent reform'd; but we have been
Deceiv'd in thy integrity, deceiv'd
In that which seems so.

CAMILLO.   Be it forbid, my lord!

LEONTES. To bide upon 't, thou art not honest; or,
If thou inclin'st that way, thou art a coward,
Which hoxes honesty behind, restraining
From course requir'd; or else thou must be counted
A servant grafted in my serious trust,
And therein negligent; or else a fool
That seest a game play'd home, the rich stake drawn,
And tak'st it all for jest.

CAMILLO.   My gracious lord,
I may be negligent, foolish, and fearful;
In every one of these no man is free,
But that his negligence, his folly, fear,
Among the infinite doings of the world,
Sometime puts forth. In your affairs, my lord,
If ever I were wilful-negligent,
It was my folly; if industriously
I play'd the fool, it was my negligence,
Not weighing well the end; if ever fearful
To do a thing, where I the issue doubted,
Whereof the execution did cry out

Against the non-performance, 'twas a fear
Which oft infects the wisest: these, my lord,
Are such allow'd infirmities that honesty
Is never free of: but, beseech your Grace,
Be plainer with me; let me know my trespass
By its own visage; if I then deny it,
'Tis none of mine.

LEONTES.   Ha' not you seen, Camillo,—
But that's past doubt; you have, or your eye-glass
Is thicker than a cuckold's horn,—or heard,—
For to a vision so apparent rumour
Cannot be mute,—or thought,—for cogitation
Resides not in that man that does not think,—
My wife is slippery? If thou wilt confess,—
Or else be impudently negative,
To have nor eyes, nor ears, nor thought,—then say
My wife's a hobby-horse; deserves a name
As rank as any flax-wench that puts to
Before her troth-plight: say't and justify't.

CAMILLO. I would not be a stander-by, to hear
My sovereign mistress clouded so, without
My present vengeance taken: 'shrew my heart,
You never spoke what did become you less
Than this; which to reiterate were sin
As deep as that, though true.

LEONTES.   Is whispering nothing?
Is leaning cheek to cheek? Is meeting noses?
Kissing with inside lip? stopping the career
Of laughter with a sigh?—a note infallible
Of breaking honesty,—horsing foot on foot?
Skulking in corners? wishing clocks more swift?
Hours, minutes? noon, midnight? and all eyes
Blind with the pin and web but theirs, theirs only,
That would unseen be wicked? Is this nothing?
Why, then the world and all that's in't is nothing;
The covering sky is nothing; Bohemia nothing;
My wife is nothing; nor nothing have these nothings,
If this be nothing.

CAMILLO.   Good my lord, be cur'd
Of this diseas'd opinion, and betimes;
For 'tis most dangerous.

LEONTES.   Say it be, 'tis true.

CAMILLO. No, no, my lord.

LEONTES.   It is; you lie, you lie:
  I say thou liest, Camillo, and I hate thee;
  Pronounce thee a gross lout, a mindless slave,
  Or else a hovering temporizer, that
  Canst with thine eyes at once see good and evil,
  Inclining to them both: were my wife's liver
  Infected as her life, she would not live
  The running of one glass.

CAMILLO.   Who does infect her?

LEONTES. Why, he that wears her like her medal, hanging
  About his neck, Bohemia: who, if I
  Had servants true about me, that bare eyes
  To see alike mine honour as their profits,
  Their own particular thrifts, they would do that
  Which should undo more doing: ay, and thou,
  His cup-bearer,—whom I from meaner form
  Have bench'd and rear'd to worship, who mayst see
  Plainly, as heaven sees earth, and earth sees heaven,
  How I am galled,—mightst bespice a cup,
  To give mine enemy a lasting wink;
  Which draught to me were cordial.

CAMILLO.   Sir, my lord,
  I could do this, and that with no rash potion,
  But with a lingering dram that should not work
  Maliciously like poison: but I cannot
  Believe this crack to be in my dread mistress,
  So sovereignly being honourable.
  I have lov'd thee,—

LEONTES.   Make that thy question, and go rot!
  Dost think I am so muddy, so unsettled,
  To appoint myself in this vexation; sully
  The purity and whiteness of my sheets,
  Which to preserve is sleep; which being spotted
  Is goads, thorns, nettles, tails of wasps?
  Give scandal to the blood o' the prince my son,
  Who I do think is mine, and love as mine,
  Without ripe moving to 't? Would I do this?
  Could man so blench?

CAMILLO.   I must believe you, sir:
  I do; and will fetch off Bohemia for 't;
  Provided that when he 's remov'd, your Highness

Will take again your queen as yours at first,
Even for your son's sake; and thereby for sealing
The injury of tongues in courts and kingdoms
Known and allied to yours.

LEONTES.   Thou dost advise me
Even so as I mine own course have set down:
I 'll give no blemish to her honour, none.

CAMILLO. My lord,
Go then; and with a countenance as clear
As friendship wears at feasts, keep with Bohemia,
And with your queen. I am his cup-bearer;
If from me he have wholesome beverage,
Account me not your servant.

LEONTES.   This is all:
Do 't, and thou hast the one half of my heart;
Do 't not, thou split'st thine own.

CAMILLO.   I 'll do 't, my lord.

LEONTES. I will seem friendly, as thou hast advis'd me.   *Exit*

CAMILLO. O miserable lady! But, for me,
What case stand I in? I must be the poisoner
Of good Polixenes; and my ground to do 't
Is the obedience to a master; one
Who, in rebellion with himself will have
All that are his so too. To do this deed
Promotion follows. If I could find example
Of thousands that had struck anointed kings,
And flourish'd after, I 'd not do 't; but since
Nor brass nor stone nor parchment bears not one,
Let villany itself forswear 't. I must
Forsake the court: to do 't, or no, is certain
To me a break-neck. Happy star reign now!
Here comes Bohemia.

                    Re-enter Polixenes

POLIXENES.   This is strange: methinks
My favour here begins to warp. Not speak?—
Good day, Camillo.

CAMILLO.   Hail, most royal sir!

POLIXENES. What is the news i' the court?

CAMILLO.   None rare, my lord.

POLIXENES. The king hath on him such a countenance
As he had lost some province and a region
Lov'd as he loves himself: even now I met him

With customary compliment, when he,
Wafting his eyes to the contrary, and falling
A lip of much contempt, speeds from me and
So leaves me to consider what is breeding
That changes thus his manners.

CAMILLO. I dare not know, my lord.

POLIXENES. How! dare not! do not! Do you know, and dare
not
Be intelligent to me? 'Tis thereabouts;
For, to yourself, what you do know, you must,
And cannot say you dare not. Good Camillo,
Your chang'd complexions are to me a mirror
Which shows me mine chang'd too; for I must be
A party in this alteration, finding
Myself thus alter'd with 't.

CAMILLO.   There is a sickness
Which puts some of us in distemper; but
I cannot name the disease, and it is caught
Of you that yet are well.

POLIXENES.   How! caught of me?
Make me not sighted like the basilisk:
I have look'd on thousands, who have sped the better
By my regard, but kill'd none so. Camillo,—
As you are certainly a gentleman, thereto
Clerk-like experienc'd, which no less adorns
Our gentry than our parents' noble names,
In whose success we are gentle,—I beseech you,
If you know aught which does behove my knowledge
Thereof to be inform'd, imprison it not
In ignorant concealment.

CAMILLO.   I may not answer.

POLIXENES. A sickness caught of me, and yet I well!
I must be answer'd. Dost thou hear, Camillo;
I conjure thee, by all the parts of man
Which honour does acknowledge,—whereof the least
Is not this suit of mine,—that thou declare
What incidency thou dost guess of harm
Is creeping toward me; how far off, how near;
Which way to be prevented if to be;
If not, how best to bear it.

CAMILLO.   Sir, I will tell you;
Since I am charg'd in honour and by him

That I think honourable. Therefore mark my counsel,
Which must be even as swiftly follow'd as
I mean to utter it, or both yourself and me
Cry 'lost,' and so good-night!

POLIXENES.   On, good Camillo.

CAMILLO. I am appointed him to murder you.

POLIXENES. By whom, Camillo?

CAMILLO.   By the king.

POLIXENES.   For what?

CAMILLO. He thinks, nay, with all confidence he swears,
As he had seen 't or been an instrument
To vice you to 't, that you have touch'd his queen
Forbiddenly.

POLIXENES.   O, then my best blood turn
To an infected jelly, and my name
Be yok'd with his that did betray the Best!
Turn then my freshest reputation to
A savour, that may strike the dullest nostril
Where I arrive; and my approach be shunn'd,
Nay, hated too, worse than the great'st infection
That e'er was heard or read!

CAMILLO.   Swear his thought over
By each particular star in heaven and
By all their influences, you may as well
Forbid the sea for to obey the moon
As or by oath remove or counsel shake
The fabric of his folly, whose foundation
Is pil'd upon his faith, and will continue
The standing of his body.

POLIXENES.   How should this grow?

CAMILLO. I know not: but I am sure 'tis safer to
Avoid what 's grown than question how 'tis born.
If therefore you dare trust my honesty,
That lies enclosed in this trunk, which you
Shall bear along impawn'd, away to-night!
Your followers I will whisper to the business,
And will by twos and threes at several posterns
Clear them o' the city. For myself, I 'll put
My fortunes to your service, which are here
By this discovery lost. Be not uncertain;
For, by the honour of my parents, I
Have utter'd truth, which, if you seek to prove,

    I dare not stand by; nor shall you be safer
    Than one condemn'd by the king's own mouth, thereon
    His execution sworn.

POLIXENES.   I do believe thee:
    I saw his heart in 's face. Give me thy hand:
    Be pilot to me and thy places shall
    Still neighbour mine. My ships are ready and
    My people did expect my hence departure
    Two days ago. This jealousy
    Is for a precious creature: as she 's rare
    Must it be great, and, as his person 's mighty
    Must it be violent, and, as he does conceive
    He is dishonour'd by a man which ever
    Profess'd to him, why, his revenges must
    In that be made more bitter. Fear o'ershades me:
    Good expedition be my friend, and comfort
    The gracious queen, part of his theme, but nothing
    Of his ill-ta'en suspicion! Come, Camillo;
    I will respect thee as a father if
    Thou bear'st my life off hence: let us avoid.

CAMILLO. It is in mine authority to command
    The keys of all the posterns: please your Highness
    To take the urgent hour. Come, sir, away!   *Exeunt*

ACT TWO

SCENE ONE

Sicilia. A Room in the Palace.

Enter Hermione, Mamillius, and Ladies

HERMIONE. Take the boy to you: he so troubles me,
  'Tis past enduring.
FIRST LADY.   Come, my gracious lord,
  Shall I be your playfellow?
MAMILLIUS.   No, I 'll none of you.
FIRST LADY. Why, my sweet lord?
MAMILLIUS. You 'll kiss me hard and speak to me as if
  I were a baby still. I love you better.
SECOND LADY. And why so, my lord?
MAMILLIUS.   Not for because
  Your brows are blacker; yet black brows, they say,
  Become some women best, so that there be not
  Too much hair there, but in a semicircle,
  Or a half-moon made with a pen.
SECOND LADY.   Who taught you this?
MAMILLIUS. I learn'd it out of women's faces. Pray now,
  What colour are your eyebrows?
FIRST LADY.   Blue, my lord.
MAMILLIUS. Nay, that 's a mock: I have seen a lady's nose
  That has been blue, but not her eyebrows.
SECOND LADY.   Hark ye;
  The queen your mother rounds apace: we shall
  Present our services to a fine new prince
  One of these days; and then you 'd wanton with us,
  If we would have you.
FIRST LADY.   She is spread of late
  Into a goodly bulk: good time encounter her!
HERMIONE. What wisdom stirs amongst you? Come sir, now
  I am for you again: pray you, sit by us,

And tell 's a tale.

MAMILLIUS.   Merry or sad shall 't be?

HERMIONE. As merry as you will.

MAMILLIUS.   A sad tale 's best for winter.
I have one of sprites and goblins.

HERMIONE.   Let 's have that, good sir.
Come on, sit down: come on, and do your best
To fright me with your sprites; you 're powerful at it.

MAMILLIUS. There was a man,—

HERMIONE.   Nay, come, sit down; then on.

MAMILLIUS. Dwelt by a churchyard. I will tell it softly;
Yond crickets shall not hear it.

HERMIONE.   Come on then,
And give 't me in mine ear.

Enter Leontes, Antigonus, Lords, and Others

LEONTES. Was he met there? his train? Camillo with him?

FIRST LORD. Behind the tuft of pines I met them: never
Saw I men scour so on their way: I ey'd them
Even to their ships.

LEONTES.   How blest am I
In my just censure, in my true opinion!
Alack, for lesser knowledge! How accurs'd
In being so blest! There may be in the cup
A spider steep'd, and one may drink, depart,
And yet partake no venom, for his knowledge
Is not infected; but if one present
The abhorr'd ingredient to his eye, make known
How he hath drunk, he cracks his gorge, his sides,
With violent hefts. I have drunk, and seen the spider.
Camillo was his help in this, his pandar:
There is a plot against my life, my crown;
All 's true that is mistrusted: that false villain
Whom I employ'd was pre-employ'd by him:
He has discover'd my design, and I
Remain a pinch'd thing; yea, a very trick
For them to play at will. How came the posterns
So easily open?

FIRST LORD.   By his great authority;
Which often hath no less prevail'd than so
On your command.

LEONTES.   I know 't too well.

(*To Hermione*) Give me the boy: I am glad you did not
   nurse him:
Though he does bear some signs of me, yet you
Have too much blood in him.

HERMIONE.   What is this? sport?

LEONTES. Bear the boy hence; he shall not come about her;
   Away with him!—(*Exit Mamillius, attended*) and let her
      sport herself
With that she 's big with; for 'tis Polixenes
Has made thee swell thus.

HERMIONE.   But I 'd say he had not,
And I 'll be sworn you would believe my saying,
Howe'er you lean to the nayward.

LEONTES.   You, my lords,
Look on her, mark her well; be but about
To say, 'she is a goodly lady,' and
The justice of your hearts will thereto add
' 'Tis pity she 's not honest, honourable':
Praise her but for this her without-door form,—
Which on my faith deserves high speech,—and straight
The shrug, the hum or ha, these petty brands
That calumny doth use,—O, I am out!—
That mercy does, for calumny will sear
Virtue itself: these shrugs, these hums and ha's,
When you have said 'she 's goodly,' come between
Ere you can say 'she 's honest.' But be 't known,
From him that has most cause to grieve it should be,
She 's an adulteress.

HERMIONE.   Should a villain say so,
The most replenish'd villain in the world,
He were as much more villain: you, my lord,
Do but mistake.

LEONTES.   You have mistook, my lady,
Polixenes for Leontes. O thou thing!
Which I 'll not call a creature of thy place,
Lest barbarism, making me the precedent,
Should a like language use to all degrees,
And mannerly distinguishment leave out
Betwixt the prince and beggar: I have said
She 's an adulteress; I have said with whom:
More, she 's a traitor, and Camillo is
A federary with her, and one that knows

What she should shame to know herself
But with her most vile principal, that she 's
A bed-swerver, even as bad as those
That vulgars give bold'st titles; ay, and privy
To this their late escape.

HERMIONE.   No, by my life,
Privy to none of this. How will this grieve you
When you shall come to clearer knowledge that
You thus have publish'd me! Gentle my lord,
You scarce can right me throughly then to say
You did mistake.

LEONTES.   No; if I mistake
In those foundations which I build upon,
The centre is not big enough to bear
A schoolboy's top. Away with her to prison!
He who shall speak for her is afar off guilty
But that he speaks.

HERMIONE.   There 's some ill planet reigns:
I must be patient till the heavens look
With an aspect more favourable. Good my lords,
I am not prone to weeping, as our sex
Commonly are; the want of which vain dew
Perchance shall dry your pities; but I have
That honourable grief lodg'd here which burns
Worse than tears drown. Beseech you all, my lords,
With thoughts so qualified as your charities
Shall best instruct you, measure me; and so
The king's will be perform'd!

LEONTES.   (To the Guards) Shall I be heard?

HERMIONE. Who is 't that goes with me? Beseech your High-
ness,
My women may be with me; for you see
My plight requires it. Do not weep, good fools;
There is no cause: when you shall know your mistress
Has deserv'd prison, then abound in tears
As I come out: this action I now go on
Is for my better grace. Adieu, my lord:
I never wish'd to see you sorry; now
I trust I shall. My women, come; you have leave.

LEONTES. Go, do our bidding: hence!

                    Exeunt Queen guarded, and Ladies

FIRST LORD. Beseech your Highness call the queen again.

ANTIGONUS. Be certain what you do, sir, lest your justice
  Prove violence: in the which three great ones suffer,
  Yourself, your queen, your son.

FIRST LORD.   For her, my lord,
  I dare my life lay down, and will do 't, sir,
  Please you to accept it,—that the queen is spotless
  I' the eyes of heaven and to you: I mean,
  In this which you accuse her.

ANTIGONUS.   If it prove
  She 's otherwise, I 'll keep my stables where
  I lodge my wife; I 'll go in couples with her;
  Than when I feel and see her no further trust her;
  For every inch of woman in the world,
  Ay, every dram of woman's flesh is false,
  If she be.

LEONTES. Hold your peaces!

FIRST LORD.   Good my lord,—

ANTIGONUS. It is for you we speak, not for ourselves.
  You are abus'd, and by some putter-on
  That will be damn'd for 't; would I knew the villain,
  I would land-damn him. Be she honour-flaw'd,—
  I have three daughters; the eldest is eleven,
  The second and the third, nine and some five;
  If this prove true, they 'll pay for 't: by mine honour,
  I 'll geld thee all; fourteen they shall not see,
  To bring false generations: they are co-heirs;
  And I had rather glib myself than they
  Should not produce fair issue.

LEONTES.   Cease! no more.
  You smell this business with a sense as cold
  As is a dead man's nose; but I do see 't and feel 't,
  As you feel doing thus, and see withal
  The instruments that feel.

ANTIGONUS.   If it be so,
  We need no grave to bury honesty:
  There 's not a grain of it the face to sweeten
  Of the whole dungy earth.

LEONTES.   What! lack I credit?

FIRST LORD. I had rather you did lack than I, my lord,
  Upon this ground; and more it would content me
  To have her honour true than your suspicion,
  Be blam'd for 't how you might.

LEONTES.   Why, what need we
   Commune with you of this, but rather follow
   Our forceful instigation? Our prerogative
   Calls not your counsels, but our natural goodness
   Imparts this; which, if you,—or stupefied
   Or seeming so in skill,—cannot or will not
   Relish a truth like us, inform yourselves
   We need no more of your advice: the matter,
   The loss, the gain, the ordering on 't, is all
   Properly ours.

ANTIGONUS.   And I wish, my liege,
   You had only in your silent judgment tried it,
   Without more overture.

LEONTES.   How could that be?
   Either thou art most ignorant by age,
   Or thou wert born a fool. Camillo's flight,
   Added to their familiarity,
   Which was as gross as ever touch'd conjecture,
   That lack'd sight only, naught for approbation
   But only seeing, all other circumstances
   Made up to the deed, doth push on this proceeding:
   Yet, for a greater confirmation,—
   For in an act of this importance 'twere
   Most piteous to be wild,—I have dispatch'd in post
   To sacred Delphos, to Apollo's temple,
   Cleomenes and Dion, whom you know
   Of stuff'd sufficiency. Now, from the oracle
   They will bring all; whose spiritual counsel had,
   Shall stop or spur me. Have I done well?

FIRST LORD. Well done, my lord.

LEONTES. Though I am satisfied and need no more
   Than what I know, yet shall the oracle
   Give rest to the minds of others, such as he
   Whose ignorant credulity will not
   Come up to the truth. So have we thought it good
   From our free person she should be confin'd,
   Lest that the treachery of the two fled hence
   Be left her to perform. Come, follow us:
   We are to speak in public; for this business
   Will raise us all.

ANTIGONUS. (*Aside*) To laughter, as I take it,
   If the good truth were known.   *Exeunt*

SCENE TWO

The Same. The outer Room of a Prison.

Enter Paulina and Attendants

PAULINA. The keeper of the prison, call to him;
Let him have knowledge who I am.—*Exit an Attendant*
Good lady,
No court in Europe is too good for thee;
What dost thou then in prison?
            Re-enter Attendant, with the Gaoler
                         Now, good sir,
You know me, do you not?
GAOLER.   For a worthy lady
And one whom much I honour.
PAULINA.   Pray you then,
Conduct me to the queen.
GAOLER. I may not, madam: to the contrary
I have express commandment.
PAULINA.   Here's ado,
To lock up honesty and honour from
The access of gentle visitors! Is 't lawful, pray you,
To see her women? any of them? Emilia?
GAOLER. So please you, madam,
To put apart these your attendants, I
Shall bring Emilia forth.
PAULINA.   I pray now, call her.
Withdraw yourselves.   *Exeunt Attendants*
GAOLER.   And, madam,
I must be present at your conference.
PAULINA. Well, be 't so, prithee.   *Exit Gaoler*
Here's such ado to make no stain a stain,
As passes colouring.
            Re-enter Gaoler, with Emilia
                 Dear gentlewoman,
How fares our gracious lady?
EMILIA. As well as one so great and so forlorn
May hold together. On her frights and griefs,—
Which never tender lady hath borne greater,—
She is something before her time deliver'd.

PAULINA. A boy?

EMILIA.   A daughter; and a goodly babe,
Lusty and like to live: the queen receives
Much comfort in 't; says, 'My poor prisoner,
I am innocent as you.'

PAULINA.   I dare be sworn:
These dangerous unsafe lunes i' the king, beshrew them!
He must be told on 't, and he shall: the office
Becomes a woman best; I 'll take 't upon me.
If I prove honey-mouth'd, let my tongue blister,
And never to my red-look'd anger be
The trumpet any more. Pray you, Emilia,
Commend my best obedience to the queen.
If she dares trust me with her little babe,
I 'll show it to the king and undertake to be
Her advocate to the loud'st. We do not know
How he may soften at the sight of the child.
The silence often of pure innocence
Persuades when speaking fails.

EMILIA.   Most worthy madam,
Your honour and your goodness is so evident
That your free undertaking cannot miss
A thriving issue: there is no lady living
So meet for this great errand. Please your ladyship
To visit the next room, I 'll presently
Acquaint the queen of your most noble offer,
Who but to-day hammer'd of this design,
But durst not tempt a minister of honour,
Lest she should be denied.

PAULINA.   Tell her, Emilia,
I 'll use that tongue I have: if wit flow from 't
As boldness from my bosom, let it not be doubted
I shall do good.

EMILIA.   Now be you blest for it!
I 'll to the queen. Please you, come something nearer.

GAOLER. Madam, if 't please the queen to send the babe,
I know not what I shall incur to pass it,
Having no warrant.

PAULINA.   You need not fear it, sir:
The child was prisoner to the womb, and is
By law and process of great nature thence
Freed and enfranchis'd; not a party to

The anger of the king, nor guilty of,
If any be, the trespass of the queen.

GAOLER. I do believe it.

PAULINA. Do not you fear: upon mine honour, I
Will stand betwixt you and danger.   *Exeunt*

SCENE THREE

The Same. A Room in the Palace.

Enter Leontes, Antigonus, Lords, and other Attendants

LEONTES. Nor night, nor day, no rest; it is but weakness
To bear the matter thus; mere weakness. If
The cause were not in being,—part o' the cause,
She the adultress; for the harlot king
Is quite beyond mine arm, out of the blank
And level of my brain, plot-proof; but she
I can hook to me: say, that she were gone,
Given to the fire, a moiety of my rest
Might come to me again. Who's there?

FIRST ATTENDANT.   (*Advancing*) My lord?

LEONTES. How does the boy?

FIRST ATTENDANT. He took good rest to-night;
'Tis hop'd his sickness is discharg'd.

LEONTES.   To see his nobleness!
Conceiving the dishonour of his mother,
He straight declin'd, droop'd, took it deeply,
Fasten'd and fix'd the shame on 't in himself,
Threw off his spirit, his appetite, his sleep,
And downright languish'd. Leave me solely: go,
See how he fares. (*Exit Attendant*)—Fie, fie! no thought
    of him;
The very thought of my revenges that way
Recoil upon me: in himself too mighty,
And in his parties, his alliance; let him be
Until a time may serve: for present vengeance,
Take it on her. Camillo and Polixenes
Laugh at me; make their pastime at my sorrow:
They should not laugh, if I could reach them, nor
Shall she within my power.

                    Enter Paulina, with a Child

FIRST LORD.   You must not enter.

PAULINA. Nay, rather, good my lords, be second to me:
　　Fear you his tyrannous passion more, alas,
　　Than the queen's life? a gracious innocent soul,
　　More free than he is jealous.

ANTIGONUS.   That's enough.

SECOND ATTENDANT. Madam, he hath not slept to-night;
　　　commanded
　　None should come at him.

PAULINA.   Not so hot, good sir;
　　I come to bring him sleep. 'Tis such as you,
　　That creep like shadows by him and do sigh
　　At each his needless heavings, such as you
　　Nourish the cause of his awaking. I
　　Do come with words as med'cinal as true,
　　Honest as either, to purge him of that humour
　　That presses him from sleep.

LEONTES.   What noise there, ho?

PAULINA. No noise, my lord; but needful conference
　　About some gossips for your Highness.

LEONTES.   How!
　　Away with that audacious lady! Antigonus,
　　I charg'd thee that she should not come about me.
　　I knew she would.

ANTIGONUS.   I told her so, my lord,
　　On your displeasure's peril, and on mine,
　　She should not visit you.

LEONTES.   What! canst not rule her?

PAULINA. From all dishonesty he can: in this,
　　Unless he take the course that you have done,
　　Commit me for committing honour, trust it,
　　He shall not rule me.

ANTIGONUS.   La you now! you hear;
　　When she will take the rein I let her run;
　　But she'll not stumble.

PAULINA.   Good my liege, I come,
　　And I beseech you, hear me, who professes
　　Myself your loyal servant, your physician,
　　Your most obedient counsellor, yet that dares
　　Less appear so in comforting your evils
　　Than such as most seem yours. I say, I come
　　From your good queen.

LEONTES.   Good queen!

PAULINA. Good queen, my lord, good queen; I say, good
    queen;
    And would by combat make her good, so were I
    A man, the worst about you.

LEONTES.   Force her hence.

PAULINA. Let him that makes but trifles of his eyes
    First hand me: on mine own accord I 'll off;
    But first I 'll do my errand. The good queen,
    For she is good, hath brought you forth a daughter:
    Here 'tis; commends it to your blessing.

                                    Laying down the Child

LEONTES.   Out!
    A mankind witch! Hence with her, out o' door:
    A most intelligencing bawd!

PAULINA.   Not so;
    I am as ignorant in that as you
    In so entitling me, and no less honest
    Than you are mad; which is enough, I 'll warrant,
    As this world goes, to pass for honest.

LEONTES.   Traitors!
    Will you not push her out? Give her the bastard.
    (*To Antigonus*) Thou dotard! thou art woman-tir'd, un-
    roosted
    By thy dame Partlet here. Take up the bastard;
    Take 't up, I say; give 't to thy crone.

PAULINA.   For ever
    Unvenerable be thy hands, if thou
    Tak'st up the princess by that forced baseness
    Which he has put upon 't!

LEONTES.   He dreads his wife.

PAULINA. So I would you did; then, 'twere past all doubt,
    You 'd call your children yours.

LEONTES.   A nest of traitors!

ANTIGONUS. I am none, by this good light.

PAULINA.   Nor I; nor any
    But one that 's here, and that 's himself; for he
    The sacred honour of himself, his queen's,
    His hopeful son's, his babe's, betrays to slander,
    Whose sting is sharper than the sword's; and will not,—
    For, as the case now stands, it is a curse
    He cannot be compell'd to 't,—once remove

The root of his opinion, which is rotten
As ever oak or stone was sound.

LEONTES.   A callat
Of boundless tongue, who late hath beat her husband
And now baits me! This brat is none of mine;
It is the issue of Polixenes:
Hence with it; and, together with the dam
Commit them to the fire!

PAULINA.   It is yours;
And, might we lay the old proverb to your charge,
'So like you, 'tis the worse.' Behold, my lords,
Although the print be little, the whole matter
And copy of the father; eye, nose, lip,
The trick of 's frown, his forehead, nay, the valley,
The pretty dimples of his chin and cheek, his smiles,
The very mould and frame of hand, nail, finger:
And thou, good goddess Nature, which hast made it
So like to him that got it, if thou hast
The ordering of the mind too, 'mongst all colours
No yellow in 't; lest she suspect, as he does,
Her children not her husband's.

LEONTES.   A gross hag!
And, lozel, thou art worthy to be hang'd,
That wilt not stay her tongue.

ANTIGONUS.   Hang all the husbands
That cannot do that feat, you 'll leave yourself
Hardly one subject.

LEONTES.   Once more, take her hence.

PAULINA. A most unworthy and unnatural lord
Can do no more.

LEONTES.   I 'll ha' thee burn'd.

PAULINA.   I care not:
It is a heretic that makes the fire,
Not she which burns in 't. I 'll not call you tyrant;
But this most cruel usage of your queen,—
Not able to produce more accusation
Than your own weak-hing'd fancy,—something savours
Of tyranny, and will ignoble make you,
Yea, scandalous to the world.

LEONTES.   On your allegiance,
Out of the chamber with her! Were I a tyrant,
Where were her life? She durst not call me so

If she did know me one. Away with her!

PAULINA. I pray you do not push me; I 'll be gone.
Look to your babe, my lord; 'tis yours. Jove send her
A better guiding spirit! What need these hands?
You, that are thus so tender o'er his follies,
Will never do him good, not one of you.
So, so: farewell; we are gone.   *Exit*

LEONTES. Thou, traitor, hast set on thy wife to this.
My child! away with 't!—even thou, that hast
A heart so tender o'er it, take it hence
And see it instantly consum'd with fire.
Even thou and none but thou. Take it up straight!
Within this hour bring me word 'tis done,—
And by good testimony,—or I 'll seize thy life,
With what thou else call'st thine. If thou refuse
And wilt encounter with my wrath, say so;
The bastard brains with these my proper hands
Shall I dash out. Go, take it to the fire:
For thou sett'st on thy wife.

ANTIGONUS.   I did not, sir:
These lords, my noble fellows, if they please,
Can clear me in 't.

FIRST LORD.   We can, my royal liege,
He is not guilty of her coming hither.

LEONTES. You are liars all.

FIRST LORD. Beseech your Highness, give us better credit:
We have always truly serv'd you, and beseech you
So to esteem of us; and on our knees we beg,
As recompense of our dear services
Past and to come, that you do change this purpose,
Which being so horrible, so bloody, must
Lead on to some foul issue. We all kneel.

LEONTES. I am a feather for each wind that blows.
Shall I live on to see this bastard kneel
And call me father? Better burn it now
Than curse it then. But, be it; let it live:
It shall not neither.—(*To Antigonus*) You, sir, come you
    hither;
You that have been so tenderly officious
With Lady Margery, your midwife there,
To save this bastard's life,—for 'tis a bastard,
So sure as thy beard 's grey,—what will you adventure

    To save this brat's life?

ANTIGONUS.   Any thing, my lord,
  That my ability may undergo,
  And nobleness impose: at least, thus much:
  I 'll pawn the little blood which I have left,
  To save the innocent: any thing possible.

LEONTES. It shall be possible. Swear by this sword
  Thou wilt perform my bidding.

ANTIGONUS.   I will, my lord.

LEONTES. Mark and perform it,—seest thou!—for the fail
  Of any point in 't shall not only be
  Death to thyself, but to thy lewd-tongu'd wife,
  Whom for this time we pardon. We enjoin thee,
  As thou art liegeman to us, that thou carry
  This female bastard hence; and that thou bear it
  To some remote and desert place quite out
  Of our dominions; and that there thou leave it,
  Without more mercy, to its own protection,
  And favour of the climate. As by strange fortune
  It came to us, I do in justice charge thee,
  On thy soul's peril and thy body's torture,
  That thou commend it strangely to some place,
  Where chance may nurse or end it. Take it up.

ANTIGONUS. I swear to do this, though a present death
  Had been more merciful. Come on, poor babe:
  Some powerful spirit instruct the kites and ravens
  To be thy nurses! Wolves and bears, they say,
  Casting their savageness aside have done
  Like offices of pity. Sir, be prosperous
  In more than this deed doth require! And blessing
  Against this cruelty fight on thy side,
  Poor thing, condemn'd to loss!   *Exit with the Child*

LEONTES.   No; I 'll not rear
  Another's issue.

             Enter a Servant

SERVANT.   Please your Highness, posts
  From those you sent to the oracle are come
  An hour since: Cleomenes and Dion,
  Being well arriv'd from Delphos, are both landed,
  Hasting to the court.

FIRST LORD.   So please you, sir, their speed
  Hath been beyond account.

LEONTES.   Twenty-three days
They have been absent: 'tis good speed; foretells
The great Apollo suddenly will have
The truth of this appear. Prepare you, lords;
Summon a session, that we may arraign
Our most disloyal lady; for, as she hath
Been publicly accus'd, so shall she have
A just and open trial. While she lives
My heart will be a burden to me. Leave me,
And think upon my bidding.   *Exeunt*

ACT THREE

SCENE ONE

A Sea-port in Sicilia.

Enter Cleomenes and Dion

CLEOMENES. The climate 's delicate, the air most sweet,
Fertile the isle, the temple much surpassing
The common praise it bears.

DION.   I shall report,
For most it caught me, the celestial habits,—
Methinks I so should term them,—and the reverence
Of the grave wearers. O, the sacrifice!
How ceremonious, solemn, and unearthly
It was i' the offering!

CLEOMENES.   But of all, the burst
And the ear-deafening voice o' the oracle,
Kin to Jove's thunder, so surpris'd my sense,
That I was nothing.

DION.   If the event o' the journey
Prove as successful to the queen,—O, be 't so!—
As it hath been to us rare, pleasant, speedy,
The time is worth the use on 't.

CLEOMENES.   Great Apollo
Turn all to the best! These proclamations,
So forcing faults upon Hermione,
I little like.

DION.   The violent carriage of it
Will clear or end the business: when the oracle,
Thus by Apollo's great divine seal'd up,
Shall the contents discover, something rare
Even then will rush to knowledge.—Go:—fresh horses!
And gracious be the issue!   *Exeunt*

SCENE TWO

Sicilia. A Court of Justice.

Leontes, Lords, and Officers

LEONTES. This sessions, to our great grief we pronounce,
    Even pushes 'gainst our heart: the party tried
    The daughter of a king, our wife, and one
    Of us too much belov'd. Let us be clear'd
    Of being tyrannous, since we so openly
    Proceed in justice, which shall have due course,
    Even to the guilt or the purgation.
    Produce the prisoner.
OFFICER. It is his Highness' pleasure that the queen
    Appear in person here in court. Silence!
    Enter Hermione guarded; Paulina and Ladies attending
LEONTES. Read the indictment.
OFFICER. (*Reads*) 'Hermione, queen to the worthy Leontes,
    King of Sicilia, thou art here accused and arraigned of
    high treason, in committing adultery with Polixenes, King
    of Bohemia, and conspiring with Camillo to take away the
    life of our sovereign lord the king, thy royal husband: the
    pretence whereof being by circumstances partly laid open,
    thou, Hermione, contrary to the faith and allegiance of a
    true subject, didst counsel and aid them, for their better
    safety, to fly away by night.'
HERMIONE. Since what I am to say must be but that
    Which contradicts my accusation, and
    The testimony on my part no other
    But what comes from myself, it shall scarce boot me
    To say 'Not guilty': mine integrity
    Being counted falsehood, shall, as I express it,
    Be so receiv'd. But thus: if powers divine
    Behold our human actions, as they do,
    I doubt not then but innocence shall make
    False accusation blush, and tyranny
    Tremble at patience. You, my lord, best know,—
    Who least will seem to do so,—my past life
    Hath been as continent, as chaste, as true,
    As I am now unhappy; which is more

Than history can pattern, though devis'd
And play'd to take spectators. For behold me,
A fellow of the royal bed, which owe
A moiety of the throne, a great king's daughter,
The mother to a hopeful prince, here standing
To prate and talk for life and honour 'fore
Who please to come and hear. For life, I prize it
As I weigh grief, which I would spare: for honour,
'Tis a derivative from me to mine,
And only that I stand for. I appeal
To your own conscience, sir, before Polixenes
Came to your court, how I was in your grace,
How merited to be so; since he came,
With what encounter so uncurrent I
Have strain'd, to appear thus: if one jot beyond
The bound of honour, or in act or will
That way inclining, harden'd be the hearts
Of all that hear me, and my near'st of kin
Cry fie upon my grave!

LEONTES.   I ne'er heard yet
That any of these bolder vices wanted
Less impudence to gainsay what they did
Than to perform it first.

HERMIONE.   That 's true enough;
Though 'tis a saying, sir, not due to me.

LEONTES. You will not own it.

HERMIONE.   More than mistress of
Which comes to me in name of fault, I must not
At all acknowledge. For Polixenes,—
With whom I am accus'd,—I do confess
I lov'd him as in honour he requir'd,
With such a kind of love as might become
A lady like me; with a love even such,
So and no other, as yourself commanded:
Which not to have done I think had been in me
Both disobedience and ingratitude
To you and toward your friend, whose love had spoke,
Even since it could speak, from an infant, freely
That it was yours. Now, for conspiracy,
I know not how it tastes, though it be dish'd
For me to try how: all I know of it
Is that Camillo was an honest man;

And why he left your court, the gods themselves,
Wotting no more than I, are ignorant.

LEONTES. You knew of his departure, as you know
What you have underta'en to do in 's absence.

HERMIONE. Sir,
You speak a language that I understand not:
My life stands in the level of your dreams,
Which I 'll lay down.

LEONTES.   Your actions are my dreams:
You had a bastard by Polixenes,
And I but dream'd it. As you were past all shame,—
Those of your fact are so,—so past all truth:
Which to deny concerns more than avails; for as
Thy brat hath been cast out, like to itself,
No father owning it,—which is, indeed,
More criminal in thee than it,—so thou
Shalt feel our justice, in whose easiest passage
Look for no less than death.

HERMIONE.   Sir, spare your threats:
The bug which you would fright me with I seek.
To me can life be no commodity:
The crown and comfort of my life, your favour,
I do give lost; for I do feel it gone,
But know not how it went. My second joy,
And first-fruits of my body, from his presence
I am barr'd, like one infectious. My third comfort,
Starr'd most unluckily, is from my breast,
The innocent milk in its most innocent mouth,
Hal'd out to murder: myself on every post
Proclaim'd a strumpet: with immodest hatred
The child-bed privilege denied, which 'longs
To women of all fashion: lastly, hurried
Here to this place, i' the open air, before
I have got strength of limit. Now, my liege,
Tell me what blessings I have here alive,
That I should fear to die? Therefore proceed.
But yet hear this; mistake me not; no life,
I prize it not a straw:—but for mine honour,
Which I would free, if I shall be condemn'd
Upon surmises, all proofs sleeping else
But what your jealousies awake, I tell you
'Tis rigour and not law. Your honours all,

I do refer me to the oracle:
Apollo be my judge!

FIRST LORD.   This your request
Is altogether just: therefore, bring forth,
And in Apollo's name, his oracle.   *Exeunt certain Officers*

HERMIONE. The Emperor of Russia was my father.
O! that he were alive, and here beholding
His daughter's trial; that he did but see
The flatness of my misery; yet with eyes
Of pity, not revenge!

Re-enter Officers, with Cleomenes and Dion

OFFICER. You here shall swear upon this sword of justice,
That you, Cleomenes and Dion, have
Been both at Delphos, and from thence have brought
This seal'd-up oracle, by the hand deliver'd
Of great Apollo's priest, and that since then
You have not dar'd to break the holy seal,
Nor read the secrets in 't.

CLEOMENES. }
DION.   }   All this we swear.

LEONTES. Break up the seals, and read.

OFFICER. 'Hermione is chaste; Polixenes blameless; Camillo
a true subject; Leontes a jealous tyrant; his innocent babe
truly begotten; and the king shall live without an heir if
that which is lost be not found!'

LORDS. Now blessed be the great Apollo!

HERMIONE.   Praised!

LEONTES. Hast thou read truth?

OFFICER.   Ay, my lord; even so
As it is here set down.

LEONTES. There is no truth at all i' the oracle:
The sessions shall proceed. This is mere falsehood!

Enter a Servant

SERVANT. My lord the king, the king!

LEONTES.   What is the business?

SERVANT. O sir! I shall be hated to report it:
The prince your son, with mere conceit and fear
Of the queen's speed, is gone.

LEONTES.   How! gone!

SERVANT.   Is dead.

LEONTES. Apollo 's angry; and the heavens themselves
Do strike at my injustice.   *Hermione swoons*

How now, there!

PAULINA. This news is mortal to the queen:—look down,
And see what death is doing.

LEONTES.   Take her hence:
Her heart is but o'ercharg'd; she will recover:
I have too much believ'd mine own suspicion:
Beseech you, tenderly apply to her
Some remedies for life.—

Exeunt Paulina and Ladies, with Hermione

Apollo, pardon
My great profaneness 'gainst thine oracle!
I 'll reconcile me to Polixenes,
New woo my queen, recall the good Camillo,
Whom I proclaim a man of truth, of mercy;
For, being transported by my jealousies
To bloody thoughts and to revenge, I chose
Camillo for the minister to poison
My friend Polixenes: which had been done,
But that the good mind of Camillo tardied
My swift command; though I with death and with
Reward did threaten and encourage him,
Not doing it, and being done: he, most humane
And fill'd with honour, to my kingly guest
Unclasp'd my practice, quit his fortunes here,
Which you knew great, and to the certain hazard
Of all incertainties himself commended,
No richer than his honour: how he glisters
Thorough my rust! and how his piety
Does my deeds make the blacker!

Re-enter Paulina

PAULINA.   Woe the while!
O, cut my lace, lest my heart, cracking it,
Break too!

FIRST LORD. What fit is this, good lady?

PAULINA. What studied torments, tyrant, hast for me?
What wheels? racks? fires? What flaying? or what boiling
In leads, or oils? What old or newer torture
Must I receive, whose every word deserves
To taste of thy most worst? Thy tyranny,
Together working with thy jealousies,
Fancies too weak for boys, too green and idle
For girls of nine, O! think what they have done,

And then run mad indeed, stark mad; for all
Thy by-gone fooleries were but spices of it.
That thou betray'dst Polixenes, 'twas nothing;
That did but show thee of a fool, inconstant
And damnable ingrateful; nor was 't much
Thou wouldst have poison'd good Camillo's honour
To have him kill a king; poor trespasses,
More monstrous standing by: whereof I reckon
The casting forth to crows thy baby daughter
To be or none or little; though a devil
Would have shed water out of fire ere done 't:
Nor is 't directly laid to thee, the death
Of the young prince, whose honourable thoughts,—
Thoughts high for one so tender,—cleft the heart
That could conceive a gross and foolish sire
Blemish'd his gracious dam: this is not, no,
Laid to thy answer: but the last,—O lords!
When I have said, cry, 'woe!'—the queen, the queen,
The sweetest, dearest creature 's dead, and vengeance
    for 't
Not dropp'd down yet.

FIRST LORD.   The higher powers forbid!

PAULINA. I say she 's dead; I 'll swear it: if word nor oath
Prevail not, go and see: if you can bring
Tincture or lustre in her lip, her eye,
Heat outwardly, or breath within, I 'll serve you
As I would do the gods. But, O thou tyrant!
Do not repent these things, for they are heavier
Than all thy woes can stir; therefore betake thee
To nothing but despair. A thousand knees
Ten thousand years together, naked, fasting,
Upon a barren mountain, and still winter
In storm perpetual, could not move the gods
To look that way thou wert.

LEONTES.   Go on, go on;
Thou canst not speak too much: I have deserv'd
All tongues to talk their bitterest.

FIRST LORD.   Say no more:
Howe'er the business goes, you have made fault
I' the boldness of your speech.

PAULINA.   I am sorry for 't:
All faults I make, when I shall come to know them,

I do repent. Alas! I have show'd too much
The rashness of a woman: he is touch'd
To the noble heart. What 's gone and what 's past help
Should be past grief: do not receive affliction
At my petition; I beseech you, rather
Let me be punish'd, that have minded you
Of what you should forget. Now, good my liege,
Sir, royal sir, forgive a foolish woman:
The love I bore your queen,—lo, fool again!—
I 'll speak of her no more, nor of your children;
I 'll not remember you of my own lord,
Who is lost too: take your patience to you,
And I 'll say nothing.

LEONTES.   Thou didst speak but well,
When most the truth, which I receive much better
Than to be pitied of thee. Prithee, bring me
To the dead bodies of my queen and son:
One grave shall be for both: upon them shall
The causes of their death appear, unto
Our shame perpetual. Once a day I 'll visit
The chapel where they lie, and tears shed there
Shall be my recreation: so long as nature
Will bear up with this exercise, so long
I daily vow to use it. Come and lead me
Unto these sorrows.   *Exeunt*

SCENE THREE

Bohemia. A desert Country near the Sea.

Enter Antigonus, with the Child; and a Mariner

ANTIGONUS. Thou art perfect, then, our ship hath touch'd
    upon
    The deserts of Bohemia?
MARINER.   Ay, my lord; and fear
    We have landed in ill time: the skies look grimly
    And threaten present blusters. In my conscience,
    The heavens with that we have in hand are angry,
    And frown upon 's.
ANTIGONUS. Their sacred wills be done! Go, get aboard;
    Look to thy bark: I 'll not be long before

I call upon thee.

MARINER.   Make your best haste, and go not
Too far i' the land: 'tis like to be loud weather;
Besides, this place is famous for the creatures
Of prey that keep upon 't.

ANTIGONUS.   Go thou away:
I 'll follow instantly.

MARINER.   I am glad at heart
To be so rid of the business.   *Exit*

ANTIGONUS.   Come, poor babe:
I have heard, but not believ'd, the spirits o' the dead
May walk again: if such thing be, thy mother
Appear'd to me last night, for ne'er was dream
So like a waking. To me comes a creature,
Sometimes her head on one side, some another;
I never saw a vessel of like sorrow,
So fill'd, and so becoming: in pure white robes,
Like very sanctity, she did approach
My cabin where I lay; thrice bow'd before me,
And, gasping to begin some speech, her eyes
Became two spouts: the fury spent, anon
Did this break from her: 'Good Antigonus,
Since fate, against thy better disposition,
Hath made thy person for the thrower-out
Of my poor babe, according to thine oath,
Places remote enough are in Bohemia,
There weep and leave it crying; and, for the babe
Is counted lost for ever, Perdita,
I prithee, call 't: for this ungentle business,
Put on thee by my lord, thou ne'er shalt see
Thy wife Paulina more': and so, with shrieks,
She melted into air. Affrighted much,
I did in time collect myself, and thought
This was so and no slumber. Dreams are toys;
Yet for this once, yea, superstitiously,
I will be squar'd by this. I do believe
Hermione hath suffer'd death; and that
Apollo would, this being indeed the issue
Of King Polixenes, it should here be laid,
Either for life or death, upon the earth
Of its right father. Blossom, speed thee well!
                         Laying down the Child

There lie; and there thy character: there these;

Laying down a bundle

Which may, if fortune please, both breed thee, pretty,
And still rest thine. The storm begins: poor wretch!
That for thy mother's fault art thus expos'd
To loss and what may follow. Weep I cannot,
But my heart bleeds, and most accurs'd am I
To be by oath enjoin'd to this. Farewell!
The day frowns more and more: thou art like to have
A lullaby too rough. I never saw
The heavens so dim by day. A savage clamour!
Well may I get aboard! This is the chase.
I am gone for ever.   *Exit, pursued by a bear*

Enter a Shepherd

SHEPHERD. I would there were no age between sixteen and
three-and-twenty, or that youth would sleep out the rest;
for there is nothing in the between but getting wenches
with child, wronging the ancientry, stealing, fighting.
Hark you now! Would any but these boiled brains of nineteen and two-and-twenty hunt this weather? They have
scared away two of my best sheep; which I fear the wolf
will sooner find than the master: if anywhere I have them,
'tis by the sea-side, browsing of ivy. Good luck, an 't be
thy will! what have we here? (*Taking up the Child*)
Mercy on 's, a barne; a very pretty barne! A boy or a
child, I wonder? A pretty one; a very pretty one; sure
some scape: though I am not bookish, yet I can read
waiting-gentlewoman in the scape. This has been some
stair-work, some trunk-work, some behind-door-work;
they were warmer that got this than the poor thing is
here. I 'll take it up for pity; yet I 'll tarry till my son
come; he hollaed but even now. Whoa, ho, hoa!

Enter Clown

CLOWN. Hilloa, loa!

SHEPHERD. What! art so near? If thou 'lt see a thing to talk
on when thou art dead and rotten, come hither. What ail-
est thou, man?

CLOWN. I have seen two such sights by sea and by land! But
I am not to say it is a sea, for it is now the sky: betwixt the
firmament and it you cannot thrust a bodkin's point.

SHEPHERD. Why, boy, how is it?

CLOWN. I would you did but see how it chafes, how it rages,

how it takes up the shore! But that 's not to the point. O! the most piteous cry of the poor souls; sometimes to see 'em, and not to see 'em; now the ship boring the moon with her mainmast, and anon swallowed with yeast and froth, as you'd thrust a cork into a hogshead. And then for the land-service: to see how the bear tore out his shoulder-bone; how he cried to me for help and said his name was Antigonus, a nobleman. But to make an end of the ship: to see how the sea flapdragoned it: but, first, how the poor souls roared, and the sea mocked them; and how the poor gentleman roared, and the bear mocked him, both roaring louder than the sea or weather.

SHEPHERD. Name of mercy! when was this, boy?

CLOWN. Now, now; I have not winked since I saw these sights: the men are not yet cold under water, nor the bear half dined on the gentleman: he 's at it now.

SHEPHERD. Would I had been by, to have helped the old man!

CLOWN. I would you had been by the ship's side, to have helped her: there your charity would have lacked footing.

SHEPHERD. Heavy matters! heavy matters! But look thee here, boy. Now bless thyself: thou mettest with things dying, I with things new born. Here 's a sight for thee; look thee, a bearing-cloth for a squire's child! Look thee here: take up, take up, boy; open 't. So, let 's see: it was told me, I should be rich by the fairies: this is some changeling.— Open 't. What 's within, boy?

CLOWN. You 're a made old man: if the sins of your youth are forgiven you, you 're well to live. Gold! all gold!

SHEPHERD. This is fairy gold, boy, and 'twill prove so: up with 't, keep it close: home, home, the next way. We are lucky, boy; and to be so still requires nothing but secrecy. Let my sheep go. Come, good boy, the next way home.

CLOWN. Go you the next way with your findings. I 'll go see if the bear be gone from the gentleman, and how much he hath eaten: they are never curst but when they are hungry. If there be any of him left, I 'll bury it.

SHEPHERD. That 's a good deed. If thou mayst discern by that which is left of him what he is, fetch me to the sight of him.

CLOWN. Marry, will I; and you shall help to put him i' the ground.

SHEPHERD. 'Tis a lucky day, boy, and we 'll do good deeds on 't.   *Exeunt*

ACT FOUR

Enter Time, the Chorus

TIME. I, that please some, try all, both joy and terror
　　Of good and bad, that make and unfold error,
　　Now take upon me, in the name of Time,
　　To use my wings. Impute it not a crime
　　To me or my swift passage, that I slide
　　O'er sixteen years, and leave the growth untried
　　Of that wide gap; since it is in my power
　　To o'erthrow law, and in one self-born hour
　　To plant and o'erwhelm custom. Let me pass
　　The same I am, ere ancient'st order was
　　Or what is now receiv'd: I witness to
　　The times that brought them in; so shall I do
　　To the freshest things now reigning, and make stale
　　The glistering of this present, as my tale
　　Now seems to it. Your patience this allowing,
　　I turn my glass and give my scene such growing
　　As you had slept between. Leontes leaving,—
　　The effects of his fond jealousies so grieving,
　　That he shuts up himself,—imagine me,
　　Gentle spectators, that I now may be
　　In fair Bohemia; and remember well,
　　I mention'd a son o' the king's, which Florizel
　　I now name to you; and with speed so pace
　　To speak of Perdita, now grown in grace
　　Equal with wondering. What of her ensues
　　I list not prophesy; but let Time's news
　　Be known when 'tis brought forth. A shepherd's daughter,
　　And what to her adheres, which follows after,
　　Is th' argument of Time. Of this allow,
　　If ever you have spent time worse ere now:
　　If never, yet that Time himself doth say
　　He wishes earnestly you never may.   *Exit*

SCENE ONE

Bohemia. A Room in the Palace of Polixenes.

Enter Polixenes and Camillo

POLIXENES. I pray thee, good Camillo, be no more importunate; 'tis a sickness denying thee any thing; a death to
grant this.

CAMILLO. It is fifteen years since I saw my country: though
I have for the most part been aired abroad, I desire to lay
my bones there. Besides, the penitent king, my master,
hath sent for me; to whose feeling sorrows I might be some
allay, or I o'erween to think so, which is another spur to
my departure.

POLIXENES. As thou lovest me, Camillo, wipe not out the rest
of thy services by leaving me now. The need I have of thee
thine own goodness hath made. Better not to have had ·
thee than thus to want thee. Thou, having made me businesses which none without thee can sufficiently manage,
must either stay to execute them thyself or take away with
thee the very services thou hast done; which if I have not
enough considered,—as too much I cannot,—to be more
thankful to thee shall be my study, and my profit therein,
the heaping friendships. Of that fatal country, Sicilia,
prithee speak no more, whose very naming punishes me
with the remembrance of that penitent, as thou callest
him, and reconciled king, my brother; whose loss of his
most precious queen and children are even now to be
afresh lamented. Say to me, when sawest thou the Prince
Florizel, my son? Kings are no less unhappy, their issue
not being gracious, than they are in losing them when they
have approved their virtues.

CAMILLO. Sir, it is three days since I saw the prince. What
his happier affairs may be, are to me unknown; but I have
missingly noted he is of late much retired from court, and
is less frequent to his princely exercises than formerly he
hath appeared.

POLIXENES. I have considered so much, Camillo, and with
some care; so far, that I have eyes under my service which
look upon his removedness; from whom I have this intelli-

gence, that he is seldom from the house of a most homely
shepherd; a man, they say, that from very nothing, and
beyond the imagination of his neighbours, is grown into an
unspeakable estate.

CAMILLO. I have heard, sir, of such a man, who hath a
daughter of most rare note. The report of her is extended
more than can be thought to begin from such a cottage.

POLIXENES. That 's likewise part of my intelligence; but, I
fear, the angle that plucks our son thither. Thou shalt accompany us to the place; where we will, not appearing
what we are, have some question with the shepherd; from
whose simplicity I think it not uneasy to get the cause of
my son's resort thither. Prithee, be my present partner in
this business, and lay aside the thoughts of Sicilia.

CAMILLO. I willingly obey your command.

POLIXENES. My best Camillo!—We must disguise ourselves.

Exeunt

SCENE TWO

The Same. A Road near the Shepherd's Cottage.

Enter Autolycus, singing

When daffodils begin to peer,
    With heigh! the doxy, over the dale,
Why, then comes in the sweet o' the year;
    For the red blood reigns in the winter's pale.
The white sheet bleaching on the hedge,
    With heigh! the sweet birds, O, how they sing!
Doth set my pugging tooth on edge;
    For a quart of ale is a dish for a king.
The lark, that tirra-lirra chants,
    With heigh! with heigh! the thrush and the jay,
Are summer songs for me and my aunts,
    While we lie tumbling in the hay.

I have served Prince Florizel, and in my time wore three-
pile; but now I am out of service:
        But shall I go mourn for that, my dear?
            The pale moon shines by night;
        And when I wander here and there,
            I then do most go right.

      If tinkers may have leave to live,
        And bear the sow-skin budget,
      Then my account I well may give,
        And in the stocks avouch it.

My traffic is sheets; when the kite builds, look to lesser linen. My father named me Autolycus; who being, as I am, littered under Mercury, was likewise a snapper-up of unconsidered trifles. With die and drab I purchased this caparison, and my revenue is the silly cheat. Gallows and knock are too powerful on the highway: beating and hanging are terrors to me: for the life to come, I sleep out the thought of it. A prize! a prize!

Enter Clown

CLOWN. Let me see: every 'leven wether tods; every tod yields pound and odd shilling: fifteen hundred shorn, what comes the wool to?

AUTOLYCUS. (*Aside*) If the springe hold, the cock 's mine.

CLOWN. I cannot do 't without compters. Let me see; what am I to buy for our sheep-shearing feast? 'Three pound of sugar; five pound of currants; rice,' what will this sister of mine do with rice? But my father hath made her mistress of the feast, and she lays it on. She hath made me four-and-twenty nosegays for the shearers, three-man song-men all, and very good ones; but they are most of them means and bases: but one puritan amongst them, and he sings psalms to hornpipes. I must have saffron, to colour the warden pies; mace, dates,—none; that 's out of my note:—nutmegs seven; a race or two of ginger,—but that I may beg;—four pound of prunes, and as many of raisins o' the sun.

AUTOLYCUS. O! that ever I was born!

Grovelling on the ground

CLOWN. I' the name of me!—

AUTOLYCUS. O! help me, help me! Pluck but off these rags, and then death, death!

CLOWN. Alack, poor soul! thou hast need of more rags to lay on thee, rather than have these off.

AUTOLYCUS. O, sir! the loathsomeness of them offends me more than the stripes I have received, which are mighty ones and millions.

CLOWN. Alas, poor man! A million of beating may come to a great matter.

AUTOLYCUS. I am robbed, sir, and beaten; my money and apparel ta'en from me, and these detestable things put upon me.

CLOWN. What, by a horseman or a footman?

AUTOLYCUS. A footman, sweet sir, a footman.

CLOWN. Indeed, he should be a footman, by the garments he hath left with thee: if this be a horseman's coat, it hath seen very hot service. Lend me thy hand, I 'll help thee: come, lend me thy hand.   *Helping him up*

AUTOLYCUS. O! good sir, tenderly, O!

CLOWN. Alas, poor soul!

AUTOLYCUS. O! good sir; softly, good sir! I fear, sir, my shoulder-blade is out.

CLOWN. How now! Canst stand?

AUTOLYCUS. Softly, dear sir; (*Picks his pocket*) good sir, softly. You ha' done me a charitable office.

CLOWN. Dost lack any money? I have a little money for thee.

AUTOLYCUS. No, good sweet sir: no, I beseech you, sir. I have a kinsman not past three-quarters of a mile hence, unto whom I was going: I shall there have money, or any thing I want. Offer me no money, I pray you! that kills my heart.

CLOWN. What manner of fellow was he that robbed you?

AUTOLYCUS. A fellow, sir, that I have known to go about with trol-my-dames: I knew him once a servant of the prince. I cannot tell, good sir, for which of his virtues it was, but he was certainly whipped out of the court.

CLOWN. His vices, you would say. There 's no virtue whipped out of the court. They cherish it, to make it stay there, and yet it will no more but abide.

AUTOLYCUS. Vices, I would say, sir. I know this man well. He hath been since an ape-bearer; then a process-server, a bailiff; then he compassed a motion of the Prodigal Son, and married a tinker's wife within a mile where my land and living lies; and having flown over many knavish professions, he settled only in rogue. Some call him Autolycus.

CLOWN. Out upon him! Prig, for my life, prig! He haunts wakes, fairs, and bear-baitings.

AUTOLYCUS. Very true, sir; he, sir, he. That 's the rogue that put me into this apparel.

CLOWN. Not a more cowardly rogue in all Bohemia. If you had but looked big and spit at him, he 'd have run.

AUTOLYCUS. I must confess to you, sir, I am no fighter. I am
    false of heart that way, and that he knew, I warrant him.

CLOWN. How do you now?

AUTOLYCUS. Sweet sir, much better than I was. I can stand
    and walk. I will even take my leave of you, and pace softly
    towards my kinsman's.

CLOWN. Shall I bring thee on the way?

AUTOLYCUS. No, good-faced sir; no, sweet sir.

CLOWN. Then fare thee well. I must go buy spices for our
    sheep-shearing.

AUTOLYCUS. Prosper you, sweet sir!—(*Exit Clown*) Your
    purse is not hot enough to purchase your spice. I'll be with
    you at your sheep-shearing too. If I make not this cheat
    bring out another, and the shearers prove sheep, let me be
    unrolled, and my name put in the book of virtue.

> Jog on, jog on, the footpath way,
>   And merrily hent the stile-a:
> A merry heart goes all the day,
>   Your sad tires in a mile-a.   *Exit*

SCENE THREE

The Same. A Lawn before the Shepherd's Cottage.

Enter Florizel and Perdita

FLORIZEL. These your unusual weeds to each part of you
    Do give a life: no shepherdess, but Flora
    Peering in April's front. This your sheep-shearing
    Is as a meeting of the petty gods,
    And you the queen on 't.

PERDITA.   Sir, my gracious lord,
    To chide at your extremes it not becomes me:
    O! pardon, that I name them. Your high self,
    The gracious mark o' the land, you have obscur'd
    With a swain's wearing, and me, poor lowly maid,
    Most goddess-like prank'd up. But that our feasts
    In every mess have folly, and the feeders
    Digest it with a custom, I should blush
    To see you so attired,—swoon, I think,
    To show myself a glass.

FLORIZEL.   I bless the time

When my good falcon made her flight across
Thy father's ground.

PERDITA.   Now, Jove afford you cause!
To me the difference forges dread; your greatness
Hath not been us'd to fear. Even now I tremble
To think, your father, by some accident,
Should pass this way as you did. O, the Fates!
How would he look, to see his work, so noble,
Vilely bound up? What would he say? Or how
Should I, in these my borrow'd flaunts, behold
The sternness of his presence?

FLORIZEL.   Apprehend
Nothing but jollity. The gods themselves,
Humbling their deities to love, have taken
The shapes of beasts upon them: Jupiter
Became a bull, and bellow'd; the green Neptune
A ram, and bleated; and the fire-rob'd god,
Golden Apollo, a poor humble swain,
As I seem now. Their transformations
Were never for a piece of beauty rarer,
Nor in a way so chaste, since my desires
Run not before mine honour, nor my lusts
Burn hotter than my faith.

PERDITA.   O! but, sir,
Your resolution cannot hold, when 'tis
Oppos'd, as it must be, by the power of the king.
One of these two must be necessities,
Which then will speak, that you must change this purpose,
Or I my life.

FLORIZEL.   Thou dearest Perdita,
With these forc'd thoughts, I prithee, darken not
The mirth o' the feast: or I 'll be thine, my fair,
Or not my father's; for I cannot be
Mine own, nor any thing to any, if
I be not thine: to this I am most constant,
Though destiny say no. Be merry, gentle;
Strangle such thoughts as these with any thing
That you behold the while. Your guests are coming:
Lift up your countenance, as it were the day
Of celebration of that nuptial which
We two have sworn shall come.

PERDITA.   O lady Fortune,

Stand you auspicious!

FLORIZEL.   See, your guests approach:
Address yourself to entertain them sprightly.
And let 's be red with mirth.

        Enter Shepherd, with Polixenes and
Camillo disguised; Clown, Mopsa, Dorcas, and Others

SHEPHERD. Fie, daughter! When my old wife liv'd, upon
This day she was both pantler, butler, cook;
Both dame and servant; welcom'd all, serv'd all,
Would sing her song and dance her turn; now here,
At upper end o' the table, now i' the middle;
On his shoulder, and his; her face o' fire
With labour and the thing she took to quench it,
She would to each one sip. You are retir'd,
As if you were a feasted one and not
The hostess of the meeting. Pray you, bid
These unknown friends to 's welcome; for it is
A way to make us better friends, more known.
Come, quench your blushes and present yourself
That which you are, mistress o' the feast: come on,
And bid us welcome to your sheep-shearing,
As your good flock shall prosper.

PERDITA.   (*To Polixenes*) Sir, welcome:
It is my father's will I should take on me
The hostess-ship o' the day. (*To Camillo*) You 're wel-
    come, sir.
Give me those flowers there, Dorcas. Reverend sirs,
For you there 's rosemary and rue; these keep
Seeming and savour all the winter long.
Grace and remembrance be to you both,
And welcome to our shearing!

POLIXENES.   Shepherdess,—
A fair one are you,—well you fit our ages
With flowers of winter.

PERDITA.   Sir, the year growing ancient,
Not yet on summer's death, nor on the birth
Of trembling winter, the fairest flowers o' the season
Are our carnations, and streak'd gillyvors,
Which some call nature's bastards: of that kind
Our rustic garden 's barren, and I care not
To get slips of them.

POLIXENES.   Wherefore, gentle maiden,

Do you neglect them?

PERDITA.   For I have heard it said
There is an art which in their piedness shares
With great creating nature.

POLIXENES.   Say there be;
Yet nature is made better by no mean
But nature makes that mean: so, over that art,
Which you say adds to nature, is an art
That nature makes. You see, sweet maid, we marry
A gentler scion to the wildest stock,
And make conceive a bark of baser kind
By bud of nobler race. This is an art
Which does mend nature, change it rather, but
The art itself is nature.

PERDITA.   So it is.

POLIXENES. Then make your garden rich in gillyvors,
And do not call them bastards.

PERDITA.   I 'll not put
The dibble in earth to set one slip of them;
No more than, were I painted, I would wish
This youth should say, 'twere well, and only therefore
Desire to breed by me. Here 's flowers for you;
Hot lavender, mints, savory, marjoram;
The marigold, that goes to bed wi' the sun,
And with him rises weeping: these are flowers
Of middle summer, and I think they are given
To men of middle age. You 're very welcome.

CAMILLO. I should leave grazing, were I of your flock,
And only live by gazing.

PERDITA.   Out, alas!
You 'd be so lean, that blasts of January
Would blow you through and through. Now, my fair'st
        friend,
I would I had some flower's o' the spring that might
Become your time of day; and yours, and yours,
That wear upon your virgin branches yet
Your maidenheads growing: O Proserpina!
For the flowers now that frighted thou let'st fall
From Dis's waggon! daffodils,
That come before the swallow dares, and take
The winds of March with beauty; violets dim,
But sweeter than the lids of Juno's eyes

Or Cytherea's breath; pale prime-roses,
That die unmarried, ere they can behold
Bright Phœbus in his strength, a malady
Most incident to maids; bold oxlips and
The crown imperial; lilies of all kinds,
The flower-de-luce being one. O! these I lack
To make you garlands of, and my sweet friend,
To strew him o'er and o'er!

FLORIZEL.   What! like a corse?

PERDITA. No, like a bank for love to lie and play on;
Not like a corse; or if,—not to be buried,
But quick and in mine arms. Come, take your flowers:
Methinks I play as I have seen them do
In Whitsun pastorals: sure this robe of mine
Does change my disposition.

FLORIZEL.   What you do
Still betters what is done. When you speak, sweet,
I 'd have you do it ever: when you sing,
I 'd have you buy and sell so; so give alms;
Pray so; and, for the ordering your affairs,
To sing them too: when you do dance, I wish you
A wave o' the sea, that you might ever do
Nothing but that; move still, still so,
And own no other function: each your doing,
So singular in each particular,
Crowns what you are doing in the present deed,
That all your acts are queens.

PERDITA.   O Doricles!
Your praises are too large: but that your youth,
And the true blood which fairly peeps through it,
Do plainly give you out an unstain'd shepherd,
With wisdom I might fear, my Doricles,
You woo'd me the false way.

FLORIZEL.   I think you have
As little skill to fear as I have purpose
To put you to 't. But, come; our dance, I pray.
Your hand, my Perdita. So turtles pair
That never mean to part.

PERDITA.   I 'll swear for 'em.

POLIXENES. This is the prettiest low-born lass that ever
Ran on the greensward: nothing she does or seems
But smacks of something greater than herself;

Too noble for this place.

CAMILLO.　　　　　　　　He tells her something
That makes her blood look out. Good sooth, she is
The queen of curds and cream.

CLOWN.　　　　　　　　　　Come on, strike up.

DORCAS. Mopsa must be your mistress: marry, garlic,
To mend her kissing with.

MOPSA.　　　　　　　Now, in good time!

CLOWN. Not a word, a word: we stand upon our manners.
Come, strike up.　　　　　*Music. Here a dance*
　　　　　　　　　　of Shepherds and Shepherdesses

POLIXENES. Pray, good shepherd, what fair swain is this
Which dances with your daughter?

SHEPHERD. They call him Doricles, and boasts himself
To have a worthy feeding; but I have it
Upon his own report and I believe it:
He looks like sooth. He says he loves my daughter:
I think so too; for never gaz'd the moon
Upon the water as he 'll stand and read
As 'twere my daughter's eyes; and, to be plain,
I think there is not half a kiss to choose
Who loves another best.

POLIXENES.　　　　　　She dances featly.

SHEPHERD. So she does any thing, though I report it
That should be silent. If young Doricles
Do light upon her, she shall bring him that
Which he not dreams of.

Enter a Servant

SERVANT. O master! if you did but hear the pedlar at the
door, you would never dance again after a tabor and pipe;
no, the bagpipe could not move you. He sings several
tunes faster than you 'll tell money; he utters them as he
had eaten ballads and all men's ears grew to his tunes.

CLOWN. He could never come better. He shall come in. I
love a ballad but even too well, if it be doleful matter merrily set down, or a very pleasant thing indeed and sung
lamentably.

SERVANT. He hath songs for man or woman, of all sizes; no
milliner can so fit his customers with gloves: he has the
prettiest love-songs for maids; so without bawdry, which
is strange; with such delicate burthens of dildos and fad-
ings, 'jump her and thump her'; and where some stretch-

mouthed rascal would, as it were, mean mischief and
break a foul gap into the matter, he makes the maid to
answer, 'Whoop, do me no harm, good man'; puts him off,
slights him with 'Whoop, do me no harm, good man.'

POLIXENES. This is a brave fellow.

CLOWN. Believe me, thou talkest of an admirable conceited
fellow. Has he any unbraided wares?

SERVANT. He hath ribands of all the colours i' the rainbow;
points more than all the lawyers in Bohemia can learnedly
handle, though they come to him by the gross; inkles, cad-
disses, cambrics, lawns. Why, he sings 'em over, as they
were gods or goddesses. You would think a smock were a
she-angel, he so chants to the sleevehand and the work
about the square on 't.

CLOWN. Prithee, bring him in, and let him approach singing.

PERDITA. Forewarn him that he use no scurrilous words in 's
tunes.   *Exit Servant*

CLOWN. You have of these pedlars that have more in them
than you 'd think, sister.

PERDITA. Ay, good brother, or go about to think.

Enter Autolycus, singing

    Lawn as white as driven snow;
    Cyprus black as e'er was crow;
    Gloves as sweet as damask roses;
    Masks for faces and for noses;
    Bugle-bracelet, necklace-amber,
    Perfume for a lady's chamber;
    Golden quoifs and stomachers,
    For my lads to give their dears;
    Pins and poking-sticks of steel;
    What maids lack from head to heel:
    Come buy of me, come; come buy, come buy;
    Buy, lads, or else your lasses cry:
    Come buy.

CLOWN. If I were not in love with Mopsa, thou shouldst take
no money of me; but being enthralled as I am, it will also
be the bondage of certain ribands and gloves.

MOPSA. I was promised them against the feast; but they
come not too late now.

DORCAS. He hath promised you more than that, or there be
liars.

MOPSA. He hath paid you all he promised you. May be he

has paid you more, which will shame you to give him again.

CLOWN. Is there no manners left among maids? Will they wear their plackets where they should bear their faces? Is there not milking-time, when you are going to bed, or kiln-hole, to whistle off these secrets, but you must be tittle-tattling before all our guests? 'Tis well they are whispering. Clamour your tongues, and not a word more.

MOPSA. I have done. Come, you promised me a tawdry lace and a pair of sweet gloves.

CLOWN. Have I not told thee how I was cozened by the way, and lost all my money?

AUTOLYCUS. And indeed, sir, there are cozeners abroad; therefore it behoves men to be wary.

CLOWN. Fear not thou, man, thou shalt lose nothing here.

AUTOLYCUS. I hope so, sir; for I have about me many parcels of charge.

CLOWN. What hast here? ballads?

MOPSA. Pray now, buy some. I love a ballad in print, a-life, for then we are sure they are true.

AUTOLYCUS. Here 's one to a very doleful tune, how a usurer's wife was brought to bed of twenty money-bags at a burden; and how she longed to eat adders' heads and toads carbonadoed.

MOPSA. Is it true too, think you?

AUTOLYCUS. Very true, and but a month old.

DORCAS. Bless me from marrying a usurer!

AUTOLYCUS. Here 's the midwife's name to 't, one Mistress Taleporter, and five or six honest wives' that were present. Why should I carry lies abroad?

MOPSA. Pray you now, buy it.

CLOWN. Come on, lay it by: and let 's first see moe ballads; we 'll buy the other things anon.

AUTOLYCUS. Here 's another ballad of a fish that appeared upon the coast on Wednesday the fourscore of April, forty thousand fathom above water, and sung this ballad against the hard hearts of maids. It was thought she was a woman and was turned into a cold fish for she would not exchange flesh with one that loved her. The ballad is very pitiful and as true.

DORCAS. Is it true too, think you?

AUTOLYCUS. Five justices' hands at it, and witnesses more than my pack will hold.

CLOWN. Lay it by too. Another.

AUTOLYCUS. This is a merry ballad, but a very pretty one.

MOPSA. Let 's have some merry ones.

AUTOLYCUS. Why, this is a passing merry one, and goes to the tune of 'Two maids wooing a man.' There 's scarce a maid westward but she sings it. 'Tis in request, I can tell you.

MOPSA. We can both sing it. If thou 'lt bear a part thou shalt hear; 'tis in three parts.

DORCAS. We had the tune on 't a month ago.

AUTOLYCUS. I can bear my part; you must know 'tis my occupation. Have at it with you!

AUTOLYCUS. Get you hence, for I must go,
Where it fits not you to know.

DORCAS. Whither?

MOPSA. O! whither?

DORCAS. Whither?

MOPSA. It becomes thy oath full well,
Thou to me thy secrets tell.

DORCAS. Me too: let me go thither.

MOPSA. Or thou go'st to the grange or mill.

DORCAS. If to either, thou dost ill.

AUTOLYCUS. Neither.

DORCAS. What, neither?

AUTOLYCUS. Neither.

DORCAS. Thou hast sworn my love to be.

MOPSA. Thou hast sworn it more to me:
Then whither go'st? Say, whither?

CLOWN. We 'll have this song out anon by ourselves. My father and the gentlemen are in sad talk, and we 'll not trouble them. Come, bring away thy pack after me. Wenches, I 'll buy for you both. Pedlar, let 's have the first choice. Follow me, girls.   *Exit with Dorcas and Mopsa*

AUTOLYCUS. And you shall pay well for 'em.
Will you buy any tape,
Or lace for your cape,
My dainty duck, my dear-a?
Any silk, any thread,
Any toys for your head,
Of the new'st and fin'st, fin'st wear-a?
Come to the pedlar;
Money 's a meddler,
That doth utter all men's ware-a.   *Exit*

Re-enter Servant

SERVANT. Master, there is three carters, three shepherds,
three neat-herds, three swine-herds, that have made themselves all men of hair; they call themselves Saltiers; and
they have a dance which the wenches say is a gallimaufry
of gambols, because they are not in 't; but they themselves
are o' the mind,—if it be not too rough for some that know
little but bowling,—it will please plentifully.

SHEPHERD. Away! we 'll none on 't. Here has been too much
homely foolery already. I know, sir, we weary you.

POLIXENES. You weary those that refresh us. Pray let 's see
these four threes of herdsmen.

SERVANT. One three of them, by their own report, sir, hath
danced before the king; and not the worst of the three but
jumps twelve foot and a half by the squire.

SHEPHERD. Leave your prating. Since these good men are
pleased, let them come in: but quickly now.

SERVANT. Why, they stay at door, sir.   *Exit*

*Re-enter Servant, with twelve Rustics
habited like Satyrs. They dance, and then exeunt*

POLIXENES. (*To Shepherd*) O, father! you 'll know more of
that hereafter.

(*To Camillo*) Is it not too far gone? 'Tis time to part them.
He 's simple and tells much. (*To Florizel*) How now, fair
shepherd!
Your heart is full of something that does take
Your mind from feasting. Sooth, when I was young,
And handed love as you do, I was wont
To load my she with knacks. I would have ransack'd
The pedlar's silken treasury and have pour'd it
To her acceptance. You have let him go
And nothing marted with him. If your lass
Interpretation should abuse and call this
Your lack of love or bounty, you were straited
For a reply, at least if you make a care
Of happy holding her.

FLORIZEL.   Old sir, I know
She prizes not such trifles as these are.
The gifts she looks from me are pack'd and lock'd
Up in my heart, which I have given already,
But not deliver'd. O! hear me breathe my life
Before this ancient sir, who, it should seem,

Hath sometime lov'd. I take thy hand; this hand,
As soft as dove's down, and as white as it,
Or Ethiopian's tooth, or the fann'd snow
That 's bolted by the northern blasts twice o'er.

POLIXENES. What follows this?
How prettily the young swain seems to wash
The hand was fair before! I have put you out:
But to your protestation: let me hear
What you profess.

FLORIZEL.   Do, and be witness to 't.

POLIXENES. And this my neighbour too?

FLORIZEL.   And he, and more
Than he, and men, the earth, the heavens, and all;
That, were I crown'd the most imperial monarch,
Thereof most worthy, were I the fairest youth
That ever made eye swerve, had force and knowledge
More than was ever man's I would not prize them
Without her love: for her employ them all;
Commend them and condemn them to her service
Or to their own perdition.

POLIXENES.   Fairly offer'd.

CAMILLO. This shows a sound affection.

SHEPHERD.   But, my daughter,
Say you the like to him?

PERDITA.   I cannot speak
So well, nothing so well; no, nor mean better.
By the pattern of mine own thoughts I cut out
The purity of his.

SHEPHERD.   Take hands; a bargain;
And, friends unknown, you shall bear witness to 't:
I give my daughter to him, and will make
Her portion equal his.

FLORIZEL.   O! that must be
I' the virtue of your daughter: one being dead,
I shall have more than you can dream of yet;
Enough then for your wonder. But, come on;
Contract us 'fore these witnesses.

SHEPHERD.   Come, your hand;
And, daughter, yours.

POLIXENES.   Soft, swain, awhile, beseech you.
Have you a father?

FLORIZEL.   I have; but what of him?

POLIXENES. Knows he of this?

FLORIZEL.   He neither does nor shall.

POLIXENES. Methinks a father
    Is, at the nuptial of his son, a guest
    That best becomes the table. Pray you, once more,
    Is not your father grown incapable
    Of reasonable affairs? Is he not stupid
    With age and altering rheums? can he speak? hear?
    Know man from man? dispute his own estate?
    Lies he not bed-rid? And again does nothing
    But what he did being childish?

FLORIZEL.   No, good sir:
    He has his health and ampler strength indeed
    Than most have of his age.

POLIXENES.   By my white beard,
    You offer him, if this be so, a wrong
    Something unfilial. Reason my son
    Should choose himself a wife, but as good reason
    The father,—all whose joy is nothing else
    But fair posterity,—should hold some counsel
    In such a business.

FLORIZEL.   I yield all this;
    But for some other reasons, my grave sir,
    Which 'tis not fit you know, I not acquaint
    My father of this business.

POLIXENES.   Let him know 't.

FLORIZEL. He shall not.

POLIXENES.   Prithee, let him.

FLORIZEL.   No, he must not.

SHEPHERD. Let him, my son: he shall not need to grieve
    At knowing of thy choice.

FLORIZEL.   Come, come, he must not.
    Mark our contract.

POLIXENES.   Mark your divorce, young sir,
                                                  Discovering himself
    Whom son I dare not call: thou art too base
    To be acknowledged: thou a sceptre's heir,
    That thus affect'st a sheep-hook! Thou old traitor,
    I am sorry that by hanging thee I can
    But shorten thy life one week. And thou, fresh piece
    Of excellent witchcraft, who of force must know

The royal fool thou cop'st with,—

SHEPHERD.   O, my heart!

POLIXENES. I 'll have thy beauty scratch'd with briers, and made
    More homely than thy state. For thee, fond boy,
    If I may ever know thou dost but sigh
    That thou no more shalt see this knack,—as never
    I mean thou shalt,—we 'll bar thee from succession;
    Not hold thee of our blood, no, not our kin,
    Far than Deucalion off: mark thou my words:
    Follow us to the court. Thou, churl, for this time,
    Though full of our displeasure, yet we free thee
    From the dead blow of it. And you, enchantment,—
    Worthy enough a herdsman; yea, him too,
    That makes himself, but for our honour therein,
    Unworthy thee,—if ever henceforth thou
    These rural latches to his entrance open,
    Or hoop his body more with thy embraces,
    I will devise a death as cruel for thee
    As thou art tender to 't.   *Exit*

PERDITA.   Even here undone!
    I was not much afeard; for once or twice
    I was about to speak and tell him plainly,
    The self-same sun that shines upon his court
    Hides not his visage from our cottage, but
    Looks on alike. Will 't please you, sir, be gone?
    I told you what would come of this: beseech you,
    Of your own state take care: this dream of mine—
    Being now awake, I 'll queen it no inch farther,
    But milk my ewes and weep.

CAMILLO.   Why, how now, father!
    Speak, ere thou diest.

SHEPHERD.   I cannot speak, nor think,
    Nor dare to know that which I know. O sir!
    You have undone a man of fourscore three,
    That thought to fill his grave in quiet, yea,
    To die upon the bed my father died,
    To lie close by his honest bones: but now
    Some hangman must put on my shroud and lay me
    Where no priest shovels in dust. O cursed wretch!
    That knew'st this was the prince, and wouldst adventure

To mingle faith with him. Undone! undone!
If I might die within this hour, I have liv'd
To die when I desire.   *Exit*

FLORIZEL.   Why look you so upon me?
I am but sorry, not afeard; delay'd,
But nothing alter'd. What I was, I am:
More straining on for plucking back; not following
My leash unwillingly.

CAMILLO.   Gracious my lord,
You know your father's temper: at this time
He will allow no speech, which I do guess
You do not purpose to him; and as hardly
Will he endure your sight as yet, I fear:
Then, till the fury of his Highness settle,
Come not before him.

FLORIZEL.   I not purpose it.
I think, Camillo?

CAMILLO.   Even he, my lord.

PERDITA.   How often have I told you 'twould be thus!
How often said my dignity would last
But till 'twere known!

FLORIZEL.   It cannot fail but by
The violation of my faith; and then
Let nature crush the sides o' the earth together
And mar the seeds within! Lift up thy looks:
From my succession wipe me, father; I
Am heir to my affection.

CAMILLO.   Be advis'd.

FLORIZEL.   I am; and by my fancy: if my reason
Will thereto be obedient, I have reason;
If not, my senses, better pleas'd with madness,
Do bid it welcome.

CAMILLO.   This is desperate, sir.

FLORIZEL.   So call it; but it does fulfil my vow,
I needs must think it honesty. Camillo,
Not for Bohemia, nor the pomp that may
Be thereat glean'd, for all the sun sees or
The close earth wombs or the profound sea hides
In unknown fathoms, will I break my oath
To this my fair belov'd. Therefore, I pray you,
As you have ever been my father's honour'd friend,

When he shall miss me,—as, in faith, I mean not
To see him any more,—cast your good counsels
Upon his passion: let myself and fortune
Tug for the time to come. This you may know
And so deliver, I am put to sea
With her whom here I cannot hold on shore;
And most opportune to our need, I have
A vessel rides fast by, but not prepar'd
For this design. What course I mean to hold
Shall nothing benefit your knowledge, nor
Concern me the reporting.

CAMILLO.   O my lord!
I would your spirit were easier for advice,
Or stronger for your need.

FLORIZEL.   Hark, Perdita. *Takes her aside*
(*To Camillo*) I'll hear you by and by.

CAMILLO.   He's irremovable,
Resolv'd for flight. Now were I happy if
His going I could frame to serve my turn,
Save him from danger, do him love and honour,
Purchase the sight again of dear Sicilia
And that unhappy king, my master, whom
I so much thirst to see.

FLORIZEL.   Now, good Camillo,
I am so fraught with curious business that
I leave out ceremony.

CAMILLO.   Sir, I think
You have heard of my poor services, i' the love
That I have borne your father?

FLORIZEL.   Very nobly
Have you deserv'd: it is my father's music
To speak your deeds, not little of his care
To have them recompens'd as thought on.

CAMILLO.   Well, my lord,
If you may please to think I love the king
And through him what's nearest to him, which is
Your gracious self, embrace but my direction.
If your more ponderous and settled project
May suffer alteration, on mine honour
I'll point you where you shall have such receiving
As shall become your Highness; where you may
Enjoy your mistress,—from the whom, I see,

There 's no disjunction to be made, but by,
As, heavens forfend! your ruin,—marry her;
And with my best endeavours in your absence
Your discontenting father strive to qualify,
And bring him up to liking.

FLORIZEL.   How, Camillo,
May this, almost a miracle, be done?
That I may call thee something more than man,
And after that trust to thee.

CAMILLO.   Have you thought on
A place whereto you 'll go?

FLORIZEL.   Not any yet;
But as the unthought-on accident is guilty
To what we wildly do, so we profess
Ourselves to be the slaves of chance and flies
Of every wind that blows.

CAMILLO.   Then list to me:
This follows; if you will not change your purpose
But undergo this flight, make for Sicilia,
And there present yourself and your fair princess,—
For so, I see, she must be,—'fore Leontes;
She shall be habited as it becomes
The partner of your bed. Methinks I see
Leontes opening his free arms and weeping
His welcomes forth; asks thee, the son, forgiveness
As 'twere i' the father's person; kisses the hands
Of your fresh princess; o'er and o'er divides him
'Twixt his unkindness and his kindness: the one
He chides to hell, and bids the other grow
Faster than thought or time.

FLORIZEL.   Worthy Camillo,
What colour for my visitation shall I
Hold up before him?

CAMILLO.   Sent by the king your father
To greet him and to give him comforts. Sir,
The manner of your bearing towards him, with
What you as from your father shall deliver,
Things known betwixt us three, I 'll write you down:
The which shall point you forth at every sitting
What you must say; that he shall not perceive
But that you have your father's bosom there
And speak his very heart.

FLORIZEL.   I am bound to you.
There is some sap in this.
CAMILLO.   A course more promising
Than a wild dedication of yourselves
To unpath'd waters, undream'd shores, most certain
To miseries enough: no hope to help you,
But as you shake off one to take another;
Nothing so certain as your anchors, who
Do their best office, if they can but stay you
Where you 'll be loath to be. Besides, you know
Prosperity 's the very bond of love,   .
Whose fresh complexion and whose heart together
Affliction alters.
PERDITA.   One of these is true:
I think affliction may subdue the cheek,
But not take in the mind.
CAMILLO.   Yea, say you so?
There shall not at your father's house these seven years
Be born another such.
FLORIZEL.   My good Camillo,
She is as forward of her breeding as
She is i' the rear o' her birth.
CAMILLO.   I cannot say 'tis pity
She lacks instructions, for she seems a mistress
To most that teach.
PERDITA.   Your pardon, sir; for this
I 'll blush you thanks.
FORIZEL.   My prettiest Perdita!
But O! the thorns we stand upon. Camillo,
Preserver of my father, now of me,
The medicine of our house, how shall we do?
We are not furnish'd like Bohemia's son,
Nor shall appear in Sicilia.
CAMILLO.   My lord,
Fear none of this: I think you know my fortunes
Do all lie there. It shall be so my care
To have you royally appointed as if
The scene you play were mine. For instance, sir,
That you may know you shall not want, one word.
                                   They talk aside
              Enter Autolycus
AUTOLYCUS. Ha, ha! what a fool Honesty is! and Trust, his

sworn brother, a very simple gentleman! I have sold all my
trumpery: not a counterfeit stone, not a riband, glass, pomander, brooch, table-book, ballad, knife, tape, glove,
shoe-tie, bracelet, horn-ring, to keep my pack from fasting; they throng who should buy first, as if my trinkets had
been hallowed and brought a benediction to the buyer: by
which means I saw whose purse was best in picture; and
what I saw, to my good use I remembered. My clown,—
who wants but something to be a reasonable man,—grew
so in love with the wenches' song that he would not stir
his pettitoes till he had both tune and words; which so
drew the rest of the herd to me that all their other senses
stuck in ears: you might have pinched a placket, it was
senseless; 'twas nothing to geld a codpiece of a purse; I
would have filed keys off that hung in chains: no hearing,
no feeling, but my sir's song, and admiring the nothing of
it; so that, in this time of lethargy I picked and cut most of
their festival purses; and had not the old man come in with
a whoo-bub against his daughter and the king's son, and
scared my choughs from the chaff, I had not left a purse
alive in the whole army.

Camillo, Florizel, and Perdita come forward

CAMILLO.　Nay, but my letters, by this means being there
So soon as you arrive, shall clear that doubt.

FLORIZEL.　And those that you 'll procure from King
　Leontes—

CAMILLO.　Shall satisfy your father.

PERDITA.　　　　　　　　　　　　　Happy be you!
All that you speak shows fair.

CAMILLO.　(*Seeing Autolycus*) Whom have we here?
We 'll make an instrument of this: omit
Nothing may give us aid.

AUTOLYCUS.　(*Aside*) If they have overheard me now, why,
hanging.

CAMILLO.　How now, good fellow! Why shakest thou so?
Fear not, man; here 's no harm intended to thee.

AUTOLYCUS.　I am a poor fellow, sir.

CAMILLO.　Why, be so still. Here 's nobody will steal that
from thee; yet, for the outside of thy poverty we must
make an exchange; therefore, discase thee instantly,—thou
must think, there 's a necessity in 't,—and change garments
with this gentleman: though the pennyworth on his side

be the worst, yet hold thee, there's some boot.

AUTOLYCUS. I am a poor fellow, sir.—(*Aside*) I know ye well
  enough.

CAMILLO. Nay, prithee, dispatch: the gentleman is half
  flayed already.

AUTOLYCUS. Are you in earnest, sir? (*Aside*) I smell the
  trick on 't.

FLORIZEL. Dispatch, I prithee.

AUTOLYCUS. Indeed, I have had earnest; but I cannot with
  conscience take it.

CAMILLO. Unbuckle, unbuckle.—

> *Florizel and Autolycus exchange garments*

Fortunate mistress,—let my prophecy
Come home to ye!—you must retire yourself
Into some covert: take your sweetheart's hat
And pluck it o'er your brows; muffle your face;
Dismantle you, and, as you can, disliken
The truth of your own seeming; that you may,—
For I do fear eyes over you,—to shipboard
Get undescried.

PERDITA.   I see the play so lies
That I must bear a part.

CAMILLO.   No remedy.
Have you done there?

FLORIZEL.   Should I now meet my father
He would not call me son.

CAMILLO.   Nay, you shall have no hat.

> *Giving it to Perdita*

Come, lady, come. Farewell, my friend.

AUTOLYCUS.   Adieu, sir.

FLORIZEL. O Perdita, what have we twain forgot!
Pray you, a word.   *They converse apart*

CAMILLO. (*Aside*) What I do next shall be to tell the king
Of this escape, and whither they are bound;
Wherein my hope is I shall so prevail
To force him after: in whose company
I shall review Sicilia, for whose sight
I have a woman's longing.

FLORIZEL.   Fortune speed us!
Thus we set on, Camillo, to the sea-side.

CAMILLO. The swifter speed the better.

> *Exeunt Florizel, Perdita, and Camillo*

AUTOLYCUS. I understand the business; I hear it. To have an open ear, a quick eye, and a nimble hand, is necessary for a cut-purse: a good nose is requisite also, to smell out work for the other senses. I see this is the time that the unjust man doth thrive. What an exchange had this been without boot! What a boot is here with this exchange! Sure, the gods do this year connive at us, and we may do anything extempore. The prince himself is about a piece of iniquity; stealing away from his father with his clog at his heels. If I thought it were a piece of honesty to acquaint the king withal, I would not do 't. I hold it the more knavery to conceal it, and therein am I constant to my profession. Aside, aside! Here is more matter for a hot brain. Every lane's end, every shop, church, session, hanging, yields a careful man work.

Re-enter Clown and Shepherd

CLOWN. See, see, what a man you are now! There is no other way but to tell the king she 's a changeling and none of your flesh and blood.

SHEPHERD. Nay, but hear me.

CLOWN. Nay, but hear me.

SHEPHERD. Go to, then.

CLOWN. She being none of your flesh and blood, your flesh and blood has not offended the king; and so your flesh and blood is not to be punished by him. Show those things you found about her; those secret things, all but what she has with her. This being done, let the law go whistle: I warrant you.

SHEPHERD. I will tell the king all, every word, yea, and his son's pranks too; who, I may say, is no honest man neither to his father nor to me, to go about to make me the king's brother-in-law.

CLOWN. Indeed, brother-in-law was the furthest off you could have been to him, and then your blood had been the dearer by I know not how much an ounce.

AUTOLYCUS. (*Aside*) Very wisely, puppies!

SHEPHERD. Well, let us to the king. There is that in this fardel will make him scratch his beard.

AUTOLYCUS. (*Aside*) I know not what impediment this complaint may be to the flight of my master.

CLOWN. Pray heartily he be at palace.

AUTOLYCUS. (*Aside*) Though I am not naturally honest, I am

so sometimes by chance. Let me pocket up my pedlar's excrement. (*Takes off his false beard*) How now, rustics!
Whither are you bound?

SHEPHERD. To the palace, an it like your worship.

AUTOLYCUS. Your affairs there, what, with whom, the condition of that fardel, the place of your dwelling, your names,
your ages, of what having, breeding, and anything that is
fitting to be known, discover.

CLOWN. We are but plain fellows, sir.

AUTOLYCUS. A lie! You are rough and hairy. Let me have no
lying; it becomes none but tradesmen, and they often give
us soldiers the lie; but we pay them for it with stamped
coin, not stabbing steel; therefore they do not give us the
lie.

CLOWN. Your worship had like to have given us one, if you
had not taken yourself with the manner.

SHEPHERD. Are you a courtier, an 't like you, sir?

AUTOLYCUS. Whether it like me or no, I am a courtier. Seest
thou not the air of the court in these enfoldings? Hath not
my gait in it the measure of the court? Receives not thy
nose court-odour from me? Reflect I not on thy baseness
court-contempt? Think'st thou, for that I insinuate, or
toaze from thee thy business, I am therefore no courtier? I
am courtier, cap-a-pe, and one that will either push on or
pluck back thy business there. Whereupon I command
thee to open thy affair.

SHEPHERD. My business, sir, is to the king.

AUTOLYCUS. What advocate hast thou to him?

SHEPHERD. I know not, an 't like you.

CLOWN. Advocate 's the court-word for a pheasant. Say you
have none.

SHEPHERD. None, sir; I have no pheasant, cock nor hen.

AUTOLYCUS. How bless'd are we that are not simple men!
Yet nature might have made me as these are,
Therefore I 'll not disdain.

CLOWN. This cannot be but a great courtier.

SHEPHERD. His garments are rich, but he wears them not
handsomely.

CLOWN. He seems to be the more noble in being fantastical:
a great man, I 'll warrant; I know by the picking on 's
teeth.

AUTOLYCUS. The fardel there? What 's i' the fardel? Wherefore that box?

SHEPHERD. Sir, there lies such secrets in this fardel and box
which none must know but the king; and which he shall
know within this hour if I may come to the speech of him.

AUTOLYCUS. Age, thou hast lost thy labour.

SHEPHERD. Why, sir?

AUTOLYCUS. The king is not at the palace; he is gone aboard
a new ship to purge melancholy and air himself: for, if
thou be'st capable of things serious, thou must know the
king is full of grief.

SHEPHERD. So 'tis said, sir, about his son, that should have
married a shepherd's daughter.

AUTOLYCUS. If that shepherd be not now in handfast, let him
fly. The curses he shall have, the torture he shall feel, will
break the back of man, the heart of monster.

CLOWN. Think you so, sir?

AUTOLYCUS. Not he alone shall suffer what wit can make
heavy and vengeance bitter; but those that are germane to
him, though removed fifty times, shall all come under the
hangman: which though it be great pity, yet it is necessary. An old sheep-whistling rogue, a ram-tender, to offer
to have his daughter come into grace! Some say he shall be
stoned; but that death is too soft for him, say I: draw our
throne into a sheep-cote! All deaths are too few, the sharp-
est too easy.

CLOWN. Has the old man e'er a son, sir, do you hear, an 't like
you, sir?

AUTOLYCUS. He has a son, who shall be flayed alive; then
'nointed over with honey, set on the head of a wasp's nest;
then stand till he be three quarters and a dram dead; then
recovered again with aqua-vitæ or some other hot infusion; then, raw as he is, and in the hottest day prognosti-
cation proclaims, shall he be set against a brick-wall, the
sun looking with a southward eye upon him, where he is to
behold him with flies blown to death. But what talk we of
these traitorly rascals, whose miseries are to be smiled at,
their offences being so capital? Tell me,—for you seem to
be honest plain men,—what you have to the king. Being
something gently considered, I 'll bring you where he is
aboard, tender your persons to his presence, whisper him
in your behalfs; and if it be in man besides the king to effect your suits, here is a man shall do it.

CLOWN. He seems to be of great authority. Close with him,

give him gold; and though authority be a stubborn bear,
yet he is oft led by the nose with gold. Show the inside of
your purse to the outside of his hand, and no more ado.
Remember, 'stoned,' and 'flayed alive'!

SHEPHERD. An 't please you, sir, to undertake the business
for us, here is that gold I have. I 'll make it as much more
and leave this young man in pawn till I bring it you.

AUTOLYCUS. After I have done what I promised?

SHEPHERD. Ay, sir.

AUTOLYCUS. Well, give me the moiety. Are you a party in
this business?

CLOWN. In some sort, sir: but though my case be a pitiful
one, I hope I shall not be flayed out of it.

AUTOLYCUS. O! that 's the case of the shepherd's son. Hang
him, he 'll be made an example.

CLOWN. Comfort, good comfort! we must to the king and
show our strange sights. He must know 'tis none of your
daughter nor my sister; we are gone else. Sir, I will give
you as much as this old man does when the business is performed; and remain, as he says, your pawn till it be
brought you.

AUTOLYCUS. I will trust you. Walk before toward the sea-
side; go on the right hand; I will but look upon the hedge
and follow you.

CLOWN. We are blessed in this man, as I may say, even
blessed.

SHEPHERD. Let 's before as he bids us. He was provided to do
us good.   *Exeunt Shepherd and Clown*

AUTOLYCUS. If I had a mind to be honest I see Fortune
would not suffer me: she drops booties in my mouth. I am
courted now with a double occasion, gold, and a means to
do the prince my master good; which who knows how that
may turn back to my advancement? I will bring these two
moles, these blind ones, aboard him. If he think it fit to
shore them again, and that the complaint they have to the
king concerns him nothing, let him call me rogue for being
so far officious; for I am proof against that title and what
shame else belongs to 't. To him will I present them: there
may be matter in it.   *Exit*

ACT FIVE

SCENE ONE

Sicilia. A Room in the Palace of Leontes.

Enter Leontes, Cleomenes, Dion, Paulina, and Others

CLEOMENES. Sir, you have done enough, and have per-
      form'd,
    A saint-like sorrow. No fault could you make
    Which you have not redeem'd; indeed, paid down
    More penitence than done trespass. At the last,
    Do as the heavens have done, forget your evil;
    With them forgive yourself.

LEONTES.   Whilst I remember
    Her and her virtues, I cannot forget
    My blemishes in them, and so still think of
    The wrong I did myself; which was so much,
    That heirless it hath made my kingdom, and
    Destroy'd the sweet'st companion that e'er man
    Bred his hopes out of.

PAULINA.   True, too true, my lord;
    If one by one you wedded all the world,
    Or from the all that are took something good,
    To make a perfect woman, she you kill'd
    Would be unparallel'd.

LEONTES.   I think so. Kill'd!
    She I kill'd! I did so; but thou strik'st me
    Sorely to say I did. It is as bitter
    Upon thy tongue as in my thought. Now, good now,
    Say so but seldom.

CLEOMENES.   Not at all, good lady.
    You might have spoken a thousand things that would
    Have done the time more benefit, and grac'd
    Your kindness better.

PAULINA.   You are one of those

Would have him wed again.

DION.　　　　　　　　　If you would not so,
You pity not the state, nor the remembrance
Of his most sovereign name; consider little
What dangers, by his Highness' fail of issue,
May drop upon his kingdom and devour
Incertain lookers-on. What were more holy
Than to rejoice the former queen is well?
What holier than for royalty's repair,
For present comfort, and for future good,
To bless the bed of majesty again
With a sweet fellow to 't?

PAULINA.　　　　　　　There is none worthy,
Respecting her that 's gone. Besides, the gods
Will have fulfill'd their secret purposes;
For has not the divine Apollo said,
Is 't not the tenour of his oracle,
That King Leontes shall not have an heir
Till his lost child be found? Which that it shall,
Is all as monstrous to our human reason
As my Antigonus to break his grave
And come again to me; who, on my life,
Did perish with the infant. 'Tis your counsel
My lord should to the heavens be contrary,
Oppose against their wills.—(*To Leontes*) Care not for
　issue;
The crown will find an heir. Great Alexander
Left his to the worthiest, so his successor
Was like to be the best.

LEONTES.　　　　　　　Good Paulina,
Who hast the memory of Hermione,
I know, in honour; O! that ever I
Had squar'd me to thy counsel! Then, even now,
I might have look'd upon my queen's full eyes,
Have taken treasure from her lips,—

PAULINA.　　　　　　　　　And left them
More rich, for what they yielded.

LEONTES.　　　　　　　　Thou speak'st truth.
No more such wives; therefore, no wife: one worse,
And better us'd, would make her sainted spirit
Again possess her corpse and on this stage,—
Where we 're offenders now,—appear soul-vex'd,

And begin, 'Why to me?'

PAULINA. Had she such power,
She had just cause.

LEONTES. She had; and would incense me
To murder her I married.

PAULINA. I should so.
Were I the ghost that walk'd I 'd bid you mark
Her eye, and tell me for what dull part in 't
You chose her; then I 'd shriek, that even your ears
Should rift to hear me; and the words that follow'd
Should be 'Remember mine.'

LEONTES. Stars, stars!
And all eyes else dead coals. Fear thou no wife;
I 'll have no wife, Paulina.

PAULINA. Will you swear
Never to marry but by my free leave?

LEONTES. Never, Paulina: so be bless'd my spirit!

PAULINA. Then, good my lords, bear witness to his oath.

CLEOMENES. You tempt him over much.

PAULINA. Unless another,
As like Hermione as is her picture,
Affront his eye.

CLEOMENES. Good madam,—

PAULINA. I have done.
Yet, if my lord will marry,—if you will, sir,
No remedy, but you will,—give me the office
To choose you a queen, she shall not be so young
As was your former; but she shall be such
As, walk'd your first queen's ghost, it should take joy
To see her in your arms.

LEONTES. My true Paulina,
We shall not marry till thou bidd'st us.

PAULINA. That
Shall be when your first queen 's again in breath;
Never till then.

Enter a Gentleman

GENTLEMAN. One that gives out himself Prince Florizel,
Son of Polixenes, with his princess,—she
The fairest I have yet beheld,—desires access
To your high presence.

LEONTES. What with him? He comes not
Like to his father's greatness; his approach,

So out of circumstance and sudden, tells us
'Tis not a visitation fram'd, but forc'd
By need and accident. What train?

GENTLEMAN.   But few,
And those but mean.

LEONTES.   His princess, say you, with him?

GENTLEMAN. Ay, the most peerless piece of earth, I think,
That e'er the sun shone bright on.

PAULINA.   O Hermione!
As every present time doth boast itself
Above a better gone, so must thy grave
Give way to what 's seen now. Sir, you yourself
Have said and writ so,—but your writing now
Is colder than that theme,—'She had not been,
Nor was not to be equall'd'; thus your verse
Flow'd with her beauty once: 'tis shrewdly ebb'd
To say you have seen a better.

GENTLEMAN.   Pardon, madam:
The one I have almost forgot—your pardon—
The other, when she has obtain'd your eye,
Will have your tongue too. This is a creature,
Would she begin a sect, might quench the zeal
Of all professors else, make proselytes
Of who she but bid follow.

PAULINA.   How! not women?

GENTLEMAN. Women will love her, that she is a woman
More worth than any man; men, that she is
The rarest of all women.

LEONTES.   Go, Cleomenes;
Yourself, assisted with your honour'd friends,
Bring them to our embracement. Still 'tis strange,
                    Exeunt Cleomenes, Lords, and Gentleman
He thus should steal upon us.

PAULINA.   Had our prince—
Jewel of children—seen this hour, he had pair'd
Well with this lord. There was not full a month
Between their births.

LEONTES. Prithee, no more: cease! Thou know'st
He dies to me again when talk'd of. Sure,
When I shall see this gentleman, thy speeches
Will bring me to consider that which may
Unfurnish me of reason. They are come.

Re-enter Cleomenes, with Florizel, Perdita, and Others

Your mother was most true to wedlock, prince;
For she did print your royal father off,
Conceiving you. Were I but twenty-one,
Your father's image is so hit in you,
His very air, that I should call you brother,
As I did him; and speak of something wildly
By us perform'd before. Most dearly welcome!
And you, fair princess,—goddess! O, alas!
I lost a couple, that 'twixt heaven and earth
Might thus have stood begetting wonder as
You, gracious couple, do: and then I lost—
All mine own folly—the society,
Amity too, of your brave father, whom,
Though bearing misery, I desire my life
Once more to look on him.

FLORIZEL.   By his command
Have I here touch'd Sicilia; and from him
Give you all greetings that a king, at friend,
Can send his brother: and, but infirmity,—
Which waits upon worn times,—hath something seiz'd
His wish'd ability, he had himself
The land and waters 'twixt your throne and his
Measur'd to look upon you, whom he loves—
He bade me say so—more than all the sceptres
And those that bear them living.

LEONTES.   O, my brother!—
Good gentleman,—the wrongs I have done thee stir
Afresh within me, and these thy offices
So rarely kind, are as interpreters
Of my behind-hand slackness! Welcome hither,
As is the spring to the earth. And hath he too
Expos'd this paragon to the fearful usage—
At least ungentle—of the dreadful Neptune,
To greet a man not worth her pains, much less
The adventure of her person?

FLORIZEL.   Good my lord,
She came from Libya.

LEONTES.   Where the war-like Smalus,
That noble honour'd lord, is fear'd and lov'd?

FLORIZEL. Most royal sir, from thence; from him, whose
    daughter

His tears proclaim'd his, parting with her: thence—
A prosperous south-wind friendly—we have cross'd,
To execute the charge my father gave me
For visiting your Highness. My best train
I have from your Sicilian shores dismiss'd;
Who for Bohemia bend, to signify
Not only my success in Libya, sir,
But my arrival and my wife's, in safety
Here where we are.

LEONTES.   The blessed gods
Purge all infection from our air whilst you
Do climate here! You have a holy father,
A graceful gentleman; against whose person,
So sacred as it is, I have done sin:
For which the heavens, taking angry note,
Have left me issueless; and your father 's bless'd—
As he from heaven merits it—with you,
Worthy his goodness. What might I have been,
Might I a son and daughter now have look'd on,
Such goodly things as you!

Enter a Lord

LORD.   Most noble sir,
That which I shall report will bear no credit,
Were not the proof so nigh. Please you, great sir,
Bohemia greets you from himself by me;
Desires you to attach his son, who has—
His dignity and duty both cast off—
Fled from his father, from his hopes, and with
A shepherd's daughter.

LEONTES.   Where 's Bohemia? Speak.

LORD. Here in your city; I now came from him:
I speak amazedly, and it becomes
My marvel and my message. To your court
Whiles he was hastening,—in the chase it seems
Of this fair couple,—meets he on the way
The father of this seeming lady and
Her brother, having both their country quitted
With this young prince.

FLORIZEL.   Camillo has betray'd me;
Whose honour and whose honesty till now
Endur'd all weathers.

LORD.   Lay 't so to his charge.

He 's with the king your father.

LEONTES.   Who? Camillo?

LORD. Camillo, sir. I spake with him, who now
Has these poor men in question. Never saw I
Wretches so quake. They kneel, they kiss the earth,
Forswear themselves as often as they speak.
Bohemia stops his ears, and threatens them
With divers deaths in death.

PERDITA.   O my poor father!
The heaven sets spies upon us, will not have
Our contract celebrated.

LEONTES.   You are married?

FLORIZEL. We are not, sir, nor are we like to be;
The stars, I see, will kiss the valleys first.
The odds for high and low 's alike.

LEONTES.   My lord,
Is this the daughter of a king?

FLORIZEL.   She is,
When once she is my wife.

LEONTES. That 'once,' I see, by your good father's speed,
Will come on very slowly. I am sorry,
Most sorry, you have broken from his liking
Where you were tied in duty; and as sorry
Your choice is not so rich in worth as beauty,
That you might well enjoy her.

FLORIZEL.   Dear, look up:
Though Fortune, visible an enemy,
Should chase us with my father, power no jot
Hath she to change our loves. Beseech you, sir,
Remember since you ow'd no more to time
Than I do now; with thought of such affections,
Step forth mine advocate; at your request
My father will grant precious things as trifles.

LEONTES. Would he do so, I 'd beg your precious mistress,
Which he counts but a trifle.

PAULINA.   Sir, my liege,
Your eye hath too much youth in 't. Not a month
'Fore your queen died, she was more worth such gazes
Than what you look on now.

LEONTES.   I thought of her,
Even in these looks I made. (*To Florizel*) But your petition

Is yet unanswer'd. I will to your father.
Your honour not o'erthrown by your desires,
I am friend to them and you; upon which errand
I now go toward him. Therefore follow me,
And mark what way I make. Come, my lord.   *Exeunt*

SCENE TWO

The Same. Before the Palace.

Enter Autolycus and a Gentleman

AUTOLYCUS. Beseech you, sir, were you present at this relation?

GENTLEMAN. I was by at the opening of the fardel, heard the old shepherd deliver the manner how he found it: whereupon, after a little amazedness, we were all commanded out of the chamber. Only this methought I heard the shepherd say; he found the child.

AUTOLYCUS. I would most gladly know the issue of it.

GENTLEMAN. I make a broken delivery of the business; but the changes I perceived in the king and Camillo were very notes of admiration. They seemed almost, with staring on one another, to tear the cases of their eyes; there was speech in their dumbness, language in their very gesture; they looked as they had heard of a world ransomed, or one destroyed. A notable passion of wonder appeared in them; but the wisest beholder, that knew no more but seeing, could not say if the importance were joy or sorrow; but in the extremity of the one it must needs be.

Enter another Gentleman

Here comes a gentleman that haply knows more. The news, Rogero?

SECOND GENTLEMAN. Nothing but bonfires. The oracle is fulfilled; the king's daughter is found. Such a deal of wonder is broken out within this hour that ballad-makers cannot be able to express it.

Enter a third Gentleman

Here comes the Lady Paulina's steward: he can deliver you more. How goes it now, sir? This news which is called true is so like an old tale that the verity of it is in strong suspicion. Has the king found his heir?

THIRD GENTLEMAN. Most true, if ever truth were pregnant
by circumstance. That which you hear you 'll swear you
see, there is such unity in the proofs. The mantle of Queen
Hermione, her jewel about the neck of it, the letters of
Antigonus found with it, which they know to be his character; the majesty of the creature in resemblance of the
mother, the affection of nobleness which nature shows
above her breeding, and many other evidences proclaim
her with all certainty to be the king's daughter. Did you
see the meeting of the two kings?

SECOND GENTLEMAN. No.

THIRD GENTLEMAN. Then have you lost a sight, which was to
be seen, cannot be spoken of. There might you have beheld one joy crown another, so, and in such manner that,
it seemed, sorrow wept to take leave of them, for their joy
waded in tears. There was casting up of eyes, holding up
of hands, with countenances of such distraction that they
were to be known by garment, not by favour. Our king,
being ready to leap out of himself for joy of his found
daughter, as if that joy were now become a loss, cries, 'O,
thy mother, thy mother!' then asks Bohemia forgiveness;
then embraces his son-in-law; then again worries he his
daughter with clipping her; now he thanks the old shepherd, which stands by like a weather-bitten conduit of
many kings' reigns. I never heard of such another encounter, which lames report to follow it and undoes description to do it.

SECOND GENTLEMAN. What, pray you, became of Antigonus
that carried hence the child?

THIRD GENTLEMAN. Like an old tale still, which will have
matter to rehearse, though credit be asleep and not an ear
open. He was torn to pieces with a bear. This avouches the
shepherd's son, who has not only his innocence—which
seems much—to justify him, but a handkerchief and rings
of his that Paulina knows.

FIRST GENTLEMAN. What became of his bark and his followers?

THIRD GENTLEMAN. Wracked, the same instant of their master's death, and in the view of the shepherd: so that all the
instruments which aided to expose the child were even
then lost when it was found. But, O! the noble combat that
'twixt joy and sorrow was fought in Paulina. She had one

eye declined for the loss of her husband, another elevated
that the oracle was fulfilled. She lifted the princess from
the earth, and so locks her in embracing, as if she would
pin her to her heart that she might no more be in danger of
losing.

FIRST GENTLEMAN. The dignity of this act was worth the
audience of kings and princes, for by such was it acted.

THIRD GENTLEMAN. One of the prettiest touches of all, and
that which angled for mine eyes,—caught the water
though not the fish,—was when at the relation of the
queen's death, with the manner how she came to it,—
bravely confessed and lamented by the king,—how atten-
tiveness wounded his daughter; till, from one sign of
dolour to another, she did, with an 'alas!' I would fain say,
bleed tears, for I am sure my heart wept blood. Who was
most marble there changed colour; some swounded, all
sorrowed. If all the world could have seen 't, the woe had
been universal.

FIRST GENTLEMAN. Are they returned to the court?

THIRD GENTLEMAN. No; the princess hearing of her mother's
statue, which is in the keeping of Paulina—a piece many
years in doing, and now newly performed by that rare
Italian master, Julio Romano; who, had he himself eternity
and could put breath into his work, would beguile Nature
of her custom, so perfectly he is her ape: he so near to
Hermione hath done Hermione that they say one would
speak to her and stand in hope of answer. Thither with all
greediness of affection are they gone, and there they intend to sup.

SECOND GENTLEMAN. I thought she had some great matter
there in hand, for she hath privately, twice or thrice a day,
ever since the death of Hermione, visited that removed
house. Shall we thither and with our company piece the
rejoicing?

FIRST GENTLEMAN. Who would be thence that has the benefit of access? Every wink of an eye some new grace will be
born. Our absence makes us unthrifty to our knowledge.
Let 's along.   *Exeunt Gentlemen*

AUTOLYCUS. Now, had I not the dash of my former life in me,
would preferment drop on my head. I brought the old man
and his son aboard the prince; told him I heard them talk
of a fardel and I know not what; but he at that time, over-

fond of the shepherd's daughter,—so he then took her to
be,—who began to be much sea-sick, and himself little better, extremity of weather continuing, this mystery remained undiscovered. But 'tis all one to me; for had I been
the finder out of this secret, it would not have relished
among my other discredits. Here come those I have done
good to against my will, and already appearing in the blossoms of their fortune.

Enter Shepherd and Clown

SHEPHERD. Come, boy; I am past moe children, but thy sons
and daughters will be all gentlemen born.

CLOWN. You are well met, sir. You denied to fight with me
this other day, because I was no gentleman born. See you
these clothes? Say you see them not and think me still no
gentleman born. You were best say these robes are not
gentlemen born. Give me the lie, do, and try whether I am
not now gentleman born.

AUTOLYCUS. I know you are now, sir, a gentleman born.

CLOWN. Ay, and have been so any time these four hours.

SHEPHERD. And so have I, boy.

CLOWN. So you have. But I was a gentleman born before my
father; for the king's son took me by the hand and called
me brother; and then the two kings called my father
brother; and then the prince my brother and the princess
my sister called my father father; and so we wept: and
there was the first gentleman-like tears that ever we shed.

SHEPHERD. We may live, son, to shed many more.

CLOWN. Ay; or else 'twere hard luck, being in so preposterous estate as we are.

AUTOLYCUS. I humbly beseech you, sir, to pardon me all the
faults I have committed to your worship, and to give me
your good report to the prince my master.

SHEPHERD. Prithee, son, do; for we must be gentle, now we
are gentlemen.

CLOWN. Thou wilt amend thy life?

AUTOLYCUS. Ay, an it like your good worship.

CLOWN. Give me thy hand. I will swear to the prince thou
art as honest a true fellow as any is in Bohemia.

SHEPHERD. You may say it, but not swear it.

CLOWN. Not swear it, now I am a gentleman? Let boors and
franklins say it, I 'll swear it.

SHEPHERD. How if it be false, son?

CLOWN. If it be ne'er so false, a true gentleman may swear it
   in the behalf of his friend. And I 'll swear to the prince
   thou art a tall fellow of thy hands and that thou wilt not be
   drunk; but I know thou art no tall fellow of thy hands and
   that thou wilt be drunk. But I 'll swear it, and I would thou
   wouldst be a tall fellow of thy hands.

AUTOLYCUS. I will prove so, sir, to my power.

CLOWN. Ay, by any means prove a tall fellow. If I do not
   wonder how thou darest venture to be drunk, not being a
   tall fellow, trust me not. Hark! the kings and the princes,
   our kindred, are going to see the queen's picture. Come,
   follow us. We 'll be thy good masters.   *Exeunt*

SCENE THREE

The Same. A Chapel in Paulina's House.

*Enter Leontes, Polixenes, Florizel, Perdita, Camillo,
Paulina, Lords, and Attendants*

LEONTES. O grave and good Paulina, the great comfort
   That I have had of thee!

PAULINA.   What, sovereign sir,
   I did not well, I meant well. All my services
   You have paid home; but that you have vouchsaf'd,
   With your crown'd brother and these your contracted
   Heirs of your kingdoms, my poor house to visit,
   It is a surplus of your grace, which never
   My life may last to answer.

LEONTES.   O Paulina!
   We honour you with trouble. But we came
   To see the statue of our queen. Your gallery
   Have we pass'd through, not without much content
   In many singularities, but we saw not
   That which my daughter came to look upon,
   The statue of her mother.

PAULINA.   As she liv'd peerless,
   So her dead likeness, I do well believe,
   Excels whatever yet you look'd upon
   Or hand of man hath done; therefore I keep it
   Lonely, apart. But here it is. Prepare
   To see the life as lively mock'd as ever

Still sleep mock'd death. Behold! and say 'tis well.

Paulina draws back
a curtain, and discovers Hermione as a statue

I like your silence: it the more shows off
Your wonder; but yet speak: first you, my liege.
Comes it not something near?

LEONTES.   Her natural posture!
Chide me, dear stone, that I may say, indeed
Thou art Hermione; or rather, thou art she
In thy not chiding, for she was as tender
As infancy and grace. But yet, Paulina,
Hermione was not so much wrinkled; nothing
So aged as this seems.

POLIXENES.   O! not by much.

PAULINA. So much the more our carver's excellence;
Which lets go by some sixteen years and makes her
As she liv'd now.

LEONTES.   As now she might have done,
So much to my good comfort, as it is
Now piercing to my soul. O! thus she stood,
Even with such life of majesty,—warm life,
As now it coldly stands,—when first I woo'd her.
I am asham'd. Does not the stone rebuke me
For being more stone than it? O royal piece!
There 's magic in thy majesty, which has
My evils conjur'd to remembrance, and
From thy admiring daughter took the spirits,
Standing like stone with thee.

PERDITA.   And give me leave,
And do not say 'tis superstition, that
I kneel and then implore her blessing. Lady,
Dear queen, that ended when I but began,
Give me that hand of yours to kiss.

PAULINA.   O, patience!
The statue is but newly fix'd, the colour 's
Not dry.

CAMILLO. My lord, your sorrow was too sore laid on,
Which sixteen winters cannot blow away,
So many summers dry. Scarce any joy
Did ever so long live; no sorrow
But kill'd itself much sooner.

POLIXENES.   Dear my brother,

Let him that was the cause of this have power
To take off so much grief from you as he
Will piece up in himself.

PAULINA.   Indeed, my lord,
If I had thought the sight of my poor image
Would thus have wrought you,—for the stone is mine,—
I 'd not have show'd it.

LEONTES.   Do not draw the curtain.

PAULINA. No longer shall you gaze on 't, lest your fancy
May think anon it moves.

LEONTES.   Let be, let be!
Would I were dead, but that, methinks, already—
What was he that did make it? See, my lord,
Would you not deem it breath'd, and that those veins
Did verily bear blood?

POLIXENES.   Masterly done!
The very life seems warm upon her lip.

LEONTES. The fixture of her eye has motion in 't,
As we are mock'd with art.

PAULINA.   I 'll draw the curtain;
My lord 's almost so far transported that
He 'll think anon it lives.

LEONTES.   O sweet Paulina!
Make me to think so twenty years together!
No settled senses of the world can match
The pleasure of that madness. Let 't alone.

PAULINA. I am sorry, sir, I have thus far stirr'd you: but
I could afflict you further.

LEONTES.   Do, Paulina;
For this affliction has a taste as sweet
As any cordial comfort. Still, methinks,
There is an air comes from her. What fine chisel
Could ever yet cut breath? Let no man mock me,
For I will kiss her.

PAULINA.   Good my lord, forbear.
The ruddiness upon her lip is wet.
You 'll mar it if you kiss it; stain your own
With oily painting. Shall I draw the curtain?

LEONTES. No, not these twenty years.

PERDITA.   So long could I
Stand by, a looker-on.

PAULINA.   Either forbear,

Quit presently the chapel, or resolve you
For more amazement. If you can behold it,
I 'll make the statue move indeed, descend,
And take you by the hand; but then you 'll think,—
Which I protest against,—I am assisted
By wicked powers.

LEONTES.   What you can make her do,
I am content to look on: what to speak,
I am content to hear; for 'tis as easy
To make her speak as move.

PAULINA.   It is requir'd
You do awake your faith. Then, all stand still;
Or those that think it is unlawful business
I am about, let them depart.

LEONTES.   Proceed:
No foot shall stir.

PAULINA.   Music, awake her! Strike!   *Music*
'Tis time; descend; be stone no more: approach;
Strike all that look upon with marvel. Come;
I 'll fill your grave up: stir; nay, come away;
Bequeath to death your numbness, for from him
Dear life redeems you. You perceive she stirs:

                    Hermione comes down

Start not; her actions shall be holy as
You hear my spell is lawful. Do not shun her
Until you see her die again, for then
You kill her double. Nay, present your hand.
When she was young you woo'd her; now in age
Is she become the suitor!

LEONTES. (*Embracing her*) O! she 's warm.
If this be magic, let it be an art
Lawful as eating.

POLIXENES.   She embraces him.

CAMILLO. She hangs about his neck.
If she pertain to life let her speak too.

POLIXENES. Ay; and make 't manifest where she has lived,
Or how stolen from the dead.

PAULINA.   That she is living,
Were it but told you, should be hooted at
Like an old tale; but it appears she lives,
Though yet she speak not. Mark a little while.
Please you to interpose, fair madam: kneel

And pray your mother's blessing. Turn, good lady;
Our Perdita is found.

Presenting Perdita, who kneels to Hermione

HERMIONE.   You gods, look down,
And from your sacred vials pour your graces
Upon my daughter's head! Tell me, mine own,
Where hast thou been preserved? where liv'd? how found
Thy father's court? For thou shalt hear that I,
Knowing by Paulina that the oracle
Gave hope thou wast in being, have preserv'd
Myself to see the issue.

PAULINA.   There's time enough for that;
Lest they desire upon this push to trouble
Your joys with like relation. Go together,
You precious winners all: your exultation
Partake to every one. I, an old turtle,
Will wing me to some wither'd bough, and there
My mate, that's never to be found again,
Lament till I am lost.

LEONTES.   O! peace, Paulina.
Thou shouldst a husband take by my consent,
As I by thine a wife. This is a match,
And made between's by vows. Thou hast found mine;
But how, is to be question'd; for I saw her,
As I thought, dead, and have in vain said many
A prayer upon her grave. I'll not seek far,—
For him, I partly know his mind,—to find thee
An honourable husband. Come, Camillo,
And take her by the hand; whose worth and honesty
Is richly noted, and here justified
By us, a pair of kings. Let's from this place.
What! look upon my brother. Both your pardons,
That e'er I put between your holy looks
My ill suspicion. This' your son-in-law,
And son unto the king,—whom heavens directing,
Is troth-plight to your daughter. Good Paulina,
Lead us from hence, where we may leisurely
Each one demand and answer to his part
Perform'd in this wide gap of time since first
We were dissever'd. Hastily lead away.   *Exeunt*

NOTES

THE TEMPEST

I. i. 60. '*long heath, brown furze*'; so the Folios; Hammer's emendation has been generally accepted:—'*ling, heath, broom, furze.*'

I. ii. 100. '*Who having into truth*'; 'into,' used in the sense of 'unto,' and so emended in most editions; the sentence though very involved is intelligible without any alteration; '*into truth*' depends upon '*a sinner*'; and '*it*' refers vaguely to '*his own lie*'; '*to credit*' = 'as to credit.'

I. ii. 169. '*Now I arise*'; probably derived from astrology; 'now my star is in the ascendent;' it should be noted that the stage direction 'Resumes his mantle' is not in the Folios.

I. ii. 266. '*for one thing she did*'; Shakespeare does not tell us what he refers to here; perhaps he merely added the point in order to account for her preservation, or the incident may have been mentioned in his original.

I. ii. 379-380. '*Kiss'd the wild waves*'; so the Folios, *i.e.*, 'Kissed the wild waves into silence;' often printed with a comma after 'kissed.'

II. i. 5. '*The masters of some merchant*'; *i.e.*, 'the owners of some merchantman'; Steevens suggested '*mistress* (old spelling '*maistres*'); the Cambridge editors '*master's*' (*i.e.*, 'master's wife').

II. i. 28. '*which, of he or Adrian*'; 'he' for 'him,' used somewhat substantively, probably owing to the use of the word in the previous sentence, '*he will be talking.*'

II. i. 36. The Folios read: 'Seb. *Ha, ha, ha!* Ant. *So you're paid.*' Theobald gives the whole line to Sebastian; and his reading is adopted by the Camb. ed. Possibly a better emendation is the transposition of the prefixes to the speeches; the point of the quibble is no doubt the old proverb 'let them laugh that win.' Capell ingeniously suggested that the Folio reading should stand with the slight change of '*you've paid*' for '*you're paid.*'

II. i. 123. '*who hath cause*'; the antecedent of 'who' is most probably '*she*'; some make the relative refer to '*eye*,' *i.e.* 'which hath cause to weep.'

II. i. 127. '*should bow*'; so Folios; seemingly unnecessary corrections have been made, *e.g.* '*she'd bow*'; '*which end the beam should bow*'; the omission of the pronoun 'it' or 'she' before 'should' can easily be paralleled in Shakespeare.

II. i. 238. '*But doubt discovery there*'; *i.e.* 'Cannot but doubt that anything can be discovered there.'

II. i. 245. '*She that from whom*'; the unnecessary 'that' is perhaps intentionally repeated, owing to the previous repetition of 'she that.'

II. i. 274. '*candied*'; generally explained as 'sugared over, and so insensible'; perhaps a better interpretation is 'made sweet as sugar,' as in the phrase 'the candied tongue.' Is Antonio possibly playing on 'candied' and 'candid' (a word not yet fully naturalised in the language, but probably familiar)?

II. ii. 74-75. '*I will not take too much for him*'; *i.e.* 'I will take as much as I can possibly get.'

II. ii. 167. '*Scamels*'; not found elsewhere in Shakespeare. Many emendations have been made; staniel (a species of hawk) has been adopted by some editors; the word occurs probably in *Twelfth Night* (II. v. 106), though the editions read 'stallion.' 'Scamel' is evidently the name of a rock-breeding bird; Mr. Wright has pointed out that, according to Stevenson's "Birds of Norfolk," "the female Bar-tailed God-wit is called a 'Scamell' by the gunners of Blakeney."

III. i. 15. '*Most busy lest, when I do it*'; so the first Folio. Various readings have been suggested; Pope, '*least busy when I do it*'; Theobald, '*most busie-less when I do it*'; Holt, '*most busiest, when I do it*'; Spedding, '*most busiest when idlest*,' &c., &c. It seems likely that the reading of the second, third, and fourth Folios throws light on the real meaning of the line —'*most busy least, when I do it*'; *i.e.*, 'most busy when I indulge my thoughts, least busy when I am actually at work.' A comma after 'busy' instead of after 'least' would simplify this reading, but it is possible to understand it as punctuated in the Folios; Shakespeare probably wished to make the superlatives as antithetical as possible; perhaps we should read 'labour' for 'labours.'

III. iii. 39. '*Praise in departing*'; a proverbial expression; "stay your praises till you see how your entertainment will end."

IV. i. 64. '*pioned and twilled*'; various emendations have been suggested for these difficult words of the Folio:—'*peonied and lilied*,' '*tulip'd*,' '*tilled*,' &c. It is noted that 'piony' is an old spelling of 'peony,' and that the flower was formerly spoken of as 'the mayden piony' and 'virgin peonie.' In all probability the meaning of the words has not yet been discovered; they are evidently technical terms of horticulture. (*Cp.* Glossary.)

IV. i. 110. Mr. Wright suggests that '*earths*' should be read as a dissyllable, 'earthes'; the second, third, and fourth Folios read '*and*' before '*foison*.'

IV. i. 147. &c. In *The Tragedy of Darius*, by William Alexander, afterwards Earl of Sterling, published in the year 1603, occurs the following passage, which, according to Steevens, may have been the original of Shakespeare's Speech:

> "Let greatnesse of her glascie sceptre vaunt:
> Not scepters, no, but reeds, soone brus'd, soone broken
> And let this worldlie pomp our wits inchant.
> All fades, and scarcelie leaues behind a token.
> Those golden pallaces, those gorgeous halles
> With fourniture superfluouslie faire:
> Those statelie courts, those sky-encountering walles
> Euanish all like vapours in the aire."

IV. i. 195. The Folios read 'hang on them.'

IV. i. 224. 'O King Stephano! O Peer!' an allusion to the old song, often referred to in Elizabethan literature, "Take thy old cloak about thee":—

> "King Stephen was a worthy peere,
> His breeches cost him but a crowne,
> He held them sixpence all too deere;
> Therefore he called the taylor Lowne."

The ballad is printed in Percy's Reliques; Shakespeare quotes it also in Othello, II, iii. 84.

IV. i. 233. 'Let's alone'; some verb of motion must be understood, i.e., 'let us go alone' (leaving Trinculo behind); 'alone' is possibly an error of the Folios for 'along,' as suggested by Theobald.

IV. i. 239. "An allusion to what often happens to people who pass the line. The violent fevers which they contract in that hot climate make them lose their hair."—Steevens.

V. i. 23-24. The first and second Folios place a comma after 'sharply,' making 'passion' a verb; the comma is omitted in the third and fourth Folios.

V. i. 310. The line is to be read, according to the Folios, 'to see our dear belov'd solémnizéd.'

THE TWO GENTLEMEN
OF VERONA

DRAMATIS PERSONÆ. 'The names of all the actors' are given at the end of the play in the Folios; the form 'Protheus' is invariably used for 'Proteus,' 'Athonio' for 'Antonio,' and 'Panthion' for 'Panthino.'

I. i. 19. 'On a love-book pray for my success;' an allusion to the Roman Catholic custom of placing the beads on the prayer-book, and of counting the beads with the prayers. 'The love-book' is in this case to take the place of the prayer-book; some have supposed that Shakespeare is here referring to Marlowe's Hero and Leander, which however, though entered on the

Stationers' Registers in 1593, was not printed till 1598, after which date many references occur to it in contemporary literature; Shakespeare directly quotes from it in *As You Like It*, IV. i. 100.

I. ii. 51. '*What fool is she;*' the first three Folios read '*what 'fool is she,*' indicating the omission of the indefinite article, a not uncommon Elizabethan idiom.

I. ii. 134. '*I see you have a month's mind to them;*' Schmidt in his 'Shakespeare Lexicon' explains the phrase 'month's mind' as 'a woman's longing,' as though the expression had its origin in the longing for particular articles of food shown by women, but this interpretation seems to have no authority. Johnson rightly remarks on this passage:—'*A month's mind*, in the ritual sense, signifies not desire or inclination, but remembrance; yet I suppose this is the true original of expression.'

I. iii. 27. "Shakespeare has been guilty of no mistake in placing the emperor's court at Milan. Several of the first German Emperors held their courts there occasionally, it being at that time their immediate property, and the chief town of their Italian dominions." Steevens.

II. i. 34. '*none else would;*' *i.e.* 'no one else would perceive them.'

II. i. 71. '*to put on your hose;*' various suggestions have been made for the emendation of these words:—'*to beyond your nose,*' '*to put spectacles on your nose,*' '*to put on your shoes,*' '*to button your hose.*' It is not certain that a rhyming couplet was intended. Probably 'unable to see to put on one's hose' was a proverbial expression meaning 'unable to tell which leg to put into one's hose first,' *i.e.* 'not to have one's wits about one.'

II. i. 154. '*for in print I found it.*' Probably these lines are quoted from some old ballad or play, though their source has not yet been found. One cannot help thinking that Shakespeare is quoting from some play of the *Two Italian Gentlemen* type; the reprinted extracts contain passages strongly reminding one of these lines.

II. iii. 26. '*a wood woman*'; the Folios read '*a would woman*'; Theobald first changed '*would*' into '*wood*' (*i.e.* mad); others '*an ould* (*i.e.* old) *woman.*'

II. iv. 112. The Folios give this line to Thurio;' if the reading be right, he must have quitted the stage during the scene, probably immediately before the entrance of Proteus, after line 99.

II. iv. 126. *Whose high imperious thoughts have punished me;*' Johnson proposed to read '*those*' for '*whose,*' as if the imperious '*thoughts*' are Valentine's and not '*Love's*'; the word '*thoughts*' certainly presents a difficulty, being used here probably in the sense of 'dispositions of the mind.'

II. iv. 193. '*Is it mine, or Valentine's praise;*' the first Folio reads, '*It is mine or Valentine's praise*'; the later Folios, '*Is it mine then, or Valentineans praise?*' Theobald's suggestion '*mine eye,*' has been generally adopted; 'if· this were unsatisfactory,' the Camb. editors remark, 'another guess might be hazarded:— '*Is it mine unstaid mind or Valentine's praise.*'

In the latter case 'Valentine's' must be read as a dissyllable; in the former as a quadrisyllable; it is not necessary to read, as has been proposed, 'Valentino's' or 'Valentinus'.' Two other ingenious emendations are noteworthy:—'*her mien,*' '*mine eyne,*' ('*thine eyne*' occurs as a rhyme in *A Midsummer-Night's Dream,* III. ii. 138).

II. v. 1; III. i. 81; V. iv. 129. The Cambridge editors have retained the reading of the Folios in these lines, 'Padua' in the first passage, and 'Verona' in the second and third, 'because it is impossible that the words can be a mere printer's, or transcriber's error. These inaccuracies are interesting as showing that Shakespeare had written the whole of the play before he had finally determined where the scene was to be laid'; the scene is in each case undoubtedly Milan (perhaps 'Milano,' *metri causa*).

III. i. 271. '*Condition;*' so the first three Folios; the fourth Folio reads '*conditions,*' adopted in many editions; '*condition*' is generally used by Shakespeare in the sense of 'temper,' 'quality.'

III. ii. 77. Malone suggests that some such line as the following has been lost after 'integrity':—'*as her obdurate heart may penetrate,*' but the meaning is perhaps rightly explained by Steevens:—"such ardour and sincerity as would be manifested by practising the directions given in the four preceding lines."

IV. i. 36. '*Robin Hood's fat friar,*' *i.e.* Friar Tuck. This allusion to 'Robin Hood's friar' by the Italian outlaw is somewhat unexpected; in the later play of *As You Like It* there is also an allusion to 'Robin Hood,' but Shakespeare is careful to add 'of England' ('*they live like the old Robin Hood of England,*' I. i. 115).

IV. i. 49. '*An heir, and near allied;*' the Folios read '*niece,*' for which Theobald suggested '*near,*' a reading generally accepted; possibly, but doubtfully, 'niece' may after all be correct, being used occasionally by Elizabethan writers to signify almost any relationship.

IV. iv. 53. '*Hangman boys;*' the Folios read '*hangman's boys;*' the reading in the text was given by Singer from a MS. note in a copy of the second Folio in his possession.

IV. iv. 71. The first Folio misprints, '*not leave her token.*'

V. iv. 2. Probably a better reading than the Folio is that generally adopted, due to Collier's MS.:—

'*these shadowy, desert, unfrequented woods.*'

V. iv. 47-50. '*Rend thy faith . . . perjury, to love me. Thou . . .*' The lines seem clear as they stand; a suggestion by Mr. Daniel is perhaps worthy of mention:—'*rain . . . perjury. To love me Thou,*' or '*hail . . . Discandied into perjury. To love me Thou . . .*'

V. iv. 71. A difficult line to scan; Johnson proposed '*O time most curst*'; others omit '*most*' or '*O*'; perhaps we have here an Alexandrine, '*O*' counting as a monosyllabic foot; the second syllable of '*deepest*' being an extra syllable before the pause:—

The pri'/vate wou'nd/ is de'epest;|| O'-/ time mo'st/ accur'st,/

THE MERRY WIVES OF WINDSOR

I. i. 19-20. '*The luce is the fresh fish; the salt fish is an old coat.*' No satisfactory explanation of this passage has as yet been offered; various suggestions have been made, *e.g.* 'salt-fish' = the hake borne by the stockfishmongers; 'same' for 'salt'; ' 'tis ott fish' (assigned to Evans), &c. May not, however, the whole point of the matter lie in Shallow's use of 'salt' in the sense of 'saltant,' the heraldic term, used especially for vermin? If so, 'salt fish' = 'the leaping louse,' with a quibble on 'salt' as opposed to 'fresh fish.' There is further allusion to the proverbial predilection of vermin for 'old coats,' used quibblingly in the sense of 'coat-of-arms.'

I. i. 81. '*Outrun on Cotsall,*' *i.e.* on the Cotswold hills (in Gloucestershire); probably an allusion to the famous Cotswold Games, which were revived at the beginning of the seventeenth century, though evidently instituted earlier; the allusion does not occur in the first and second Quartos.

I. i. 155. '*Scarlet and John*'; Robin Hood's boon companions; an allusion to Bardolph's red face.

I. iii. 25. '*A minute's rest*'; "*a minim's rest*" is the ingenious suggestion of Bennet Langton; *cp. Romeo and Juliet,* II. iv. 22, "*rests me his minim rest.*"

I. iii. 41. '*Carves*'; probably used here in the sense of 'to show favour by expressive gestures'; *cp.* "A carver: chironomus . . . one that useth apish motions with his hands."—Littleton's *Latin-English Dictionary* (1675).

I. iii. 61-62. '*Region of Guiana.*' Sir Walter Raleigh returned from his expedition to South America in 1596, and published his book on "The Discovery of the large, rich, and beautiful Empire of Guiana" in the same year.

I. iii. 85. '*By welkin and her star.*' This is no doubt the correct reading of the line, and there is no need to read *stars*, as has been suggested; 'star' is obviously used here for 'the sun'; the Quartos read 'fairies.'

II. i. 4, 5. '*Though Love use Reason for his physician.*' The Folios read '*precisian*'; the emendation adopted in the text was first suggested by Johnson, and has been generally accepted; *cp.* Sonnet CXLVII.: "*My reason the physician to my love.*"

II. i. 191, 193. In the Folios the name '*Broome*' is given instead of '*Brooke*'; but Falstaff's pun, "*Such Brooks are welcome to me, that overflow with liquor*," removes all doubt as to the correct reading, which is actually found in the Quartos.

II. i. 194. '*Will you go, An-hires?*' so the Folios and Quartos; Theobald's correction '*mynheers*' has been adopted by many modern editors. Other suggestions are "*on, here;*" "*on, hearts;*" "*on, heroes;*" "*cavaleires;*" &c.

II. iii. 75-76. '*Cried I aim?*' The Folios and Quartos read '*cried game*'; the ingenious emendation, due to Douce, was first adopted by Dyce.

III. i. 15, &c. Sir Hugh oddly confuses Marlowe's famous ditty, "*Come live with me and be my love*," and the old version of the 137th Psalm, "*When we did sit in Babylon.*"

III. i. 86. '*Gallia and Gaul*'; so the Folios; the first and second Quartos read '*Gawle and Gawlia*;' Farmer's conjecture "*Gaullia and Gaul*" was adopted by Malone and other editors. *Gallia =* Wales.

III. ii. 66. '*He shall not knit a knot in his fortunes*' (which are now as it were unravelled).

III. iii. 36. '*Have I caught thee*'; probably the reading of the Quarto which omits 'thee' is the more correct; Falstaff quotes from the second song in Sydney's *Astrophel and Stella:—*

> "*Have I caught my heav'nly jewell,*
> *Teaching sleep most faire to be?*
> *Now will I teach her that she*
> *When she wakes is too-too cruell.*"

III. v. 4. The reading of the Quartos is seemingly preferable: —'*Have I lived to be carried in a basket, and thrown into the Thames like a barrow of butcher's offal.*'

III. v. 8. '*The rogues slighted me into the river,*' *i.e.* 'Threw me in contemptuously;' the Quartos read '*slided me in.*'

IV. i. 41. '*Hang-hog is Latin for bacon*'; probably suggested by the famous story told of Sir Nicholas Bacon. A prisoner named Hog, who had been condemned to death, prayed for mercy on the score of kindred. "Aye but," replied the judge, "you and I cannot be of kindred unless you are hanged; for Hog is not Bacon till it be well hanged" (Bacon's *Apophthegms*).

IV. ii. 17. *'Old lunes'*; the Folios and third Quarto read *'lines;'* the first and second Quartos *'vaine;'* the correction is Theobald's; the same error occurs in *Troilus and Cressida*, II. iii. 128.

IV. ii. 84. *'The witch of Brentford'*; an actual personage of the sixteenth century. A tract is extant entitled "Jyl of Breyntford's Testament," whence it appears that the witch kept a tavern at Brentford; in Dekker & Webster's *Westward Ho* the following allusion is found:—"I doubt that old hag Gillian of Brainford has bewitched me."

IV. iv. 40. *'That Falstaff at that oak shall meet with us.'* After this line the following words from the Quartos have been added in many editions:—

"*We'll send him word to meet us in the field,*
   Disguised like Horne with huge horns on his head."

IV. iv. 56. *'To pinch'*; probably the correct reading should be 'to-pinch,' where 'to' is the intensive prefix so common in old English, though it is possible to explain it as the ordinary infinitive prefix, omitted in the case of the former verb in the sentence.

IV. iv. 81. *'Send quickly to Sir John.'* Theobald ingeniously suggested *'Quickly'* for *'quickly.'*

IV. v. 68. *'Cozen-germans'*; the first Quarto reads:—

"*For there is three sorts of cosen garmombles,*
   Is cosen all the Host of Maidenhead and Readings,"

where 'garmombles' is very possibly a perversion of Mömpelgard; Count Frederick of Mömpelgard visited Windsor in 1592; free post-horses were granted him by a passport of Lord Howard.

The Count became a "Duke of Jamany" (Wirtemberg) in 1593; considerable interest must have been taken in the Duke about 1598. A letter to the Queen, dated August 14, 1598, is extant, in which the following passage occurs:—"I have heard with extreme regret that some of my enemies endeavour to calumniate me and prejudice your majesty against me. I have given them no occasion for this. I hope that when your majesty has discovered this report to be false, you will have greater reason to continue your affection towards me, and give neither faith nor credit to such vipers." In the year 1602 appeared "An Account of the Duke's Bathing Excursion to the far-famed Kingdom of England" (*vide* Rye's *England as seen by Foreigners*).

V. v. 22. *'Bribe buck'*; the Folios read *'brib'd buck,'* which is probably the right reading: 'a bribed buck' was a buck cut up into portions (Old French *bribes* = 'portions of meat to be given away').

V. v. 37. *'Orphan heirs.'* Theobald suggested *'ouphen'* (elvish) for 'orphan,' and he has been followed by many editors, but the change is unnecessary. Cp. *'unfather'd heirs'* 2 *Henry IV*. iv. 122.

V. v. 40, 42. *'Toys,'* evidently to be read 'toyës,' rhyming with *'O-yes'* in the previous line; similarly *'unswept'* should probably be *'unswep'* rhyming with *'leap.'*

V. v. 105. *'These fair yokes'*; the first Folio reads *'yoakes,'* the second *'okes.' 'Yokes'* must refer to the resemblance of the buck's horns to a yoke; a sort of sense can be got out of *'oaks,'* the antlers resembling the branches of oaks, but the first Folio reading seems preferable.

MEASURE FOR MEASURE

I. i. 8. There is no gap in the Folios, which is due to Theobald's plausible theory that the obscurity of the passage is due to some careless omission on the part of the printers. Various attempts have been made to explain the lines, *e.g. "But that to your sufficiencies your worth is abled"* (Johnson); *"But your sufficiency as worth is able"* (Farmer); Theobald supplied the missing words thus—

> *"But that to your sufficiency you add*
> *Due diligency as your worth is able."*

I. i. 42. *'Hold therefore, Angelo;'* the Duke probably says these words on tendering commission to Angelo.

I. ii. 27-28. *'There went but a pair of shears between us;'* i.e. 'we are of one piece.'

I. ii. 116. *Cp. St. Paul to the Romans* ix. 15, 18: "For He saith to Moses, I will have mercy *on whom I will* have mercy," and again, "Therefore hath He mercy *on whom He will* have mercy, and *whom He will* He hardeneth."

I. ii. 127. *'Morality;'* the Folios misprint *'mortality.'*

I. ii. 143. *'Propagation;'* Folio 1 reads *propogation,* corrected in Folio 2; *prorogation, procuration, preservation,* have been suggested by various editors, but the text as it stands is probably correct, though not altogether clear; *'propagation'* = 'increase;' perhaps the word implies 'increase of interest,' and *'for propogation'* = 'that she might continue to receive the interest, which was to be hers while she remained unmarried.'

I. iii. 43. *'To do in slander;'* so the Folios; *'me'* and *'it'* have been suggested for *'in,'* but no change is necessary; *'do in'* = 'bring in, bring upon me.'

II. i. 39. *'Some run from brakes of ice, and answer none;'* the line as it stands in the Folios is obviously corrupt, and has occasioned much discussion. Shakespeare probably wrote *'brakes of vice;' brakes* = thickets, hence 'entanglements'; *'brakes of vice'* is antithetical to *'a fault alone,'* cp. *Henry VIII.* I. ii. 75—

> "the rough brake
> That virtue must go through."

The line therefore means 'some escape from whole thickets of sin, and pay no penalty.' Judging by the passage in *Henry VIII*, *through* for *from* would perhaps be an improvement.

II. i. 124. '*An open room;*' Schmidt, "*public room;*" perhaps it means 'open to sun, light, cheerful.'

II. ii. 80. '*Like man new made;*' commentators are strongly tempted to refer the words to '*new made man*,' *i.e.* Adam; Holt White paraphrased thus:—"And you, Angelo, will breathe new life into Claudio, as the Creator animated Adam, by breathing into his nostrils the breath of life." Malone explains:—"You will then appear as tender-hearted and merciful as the first man was in his days of innocence, immediately after his creation." Schmidt and others, "like man redeemed and regenerated by divine grace." The lines are perhaps capable of this interpretation:—"And mercy will breathe within your lips, even as Mercy (*i.e.* God) breathed within the lips of new made man."

II. ii. 91. "*Dormiunt aliquando leges, moriuntur nunquam,*" is a well-known maxim in law (Holt White).

II. ii. 160. '*Where prayers cross*,' *i.e.* where his prayer to possess Isabella crosses with hers, "Heaven keep your *honour* safe!"

II. iii. 11. '*The flaws of her own youth;*' possibly Warburton's correction "*flames*" should be adopted; *cp.*

'*To flaming youth let virtue be as wax,*
And melt in her own fire.'
          —HAMLET, III. iv. 84, 85.

II. iii. 40. '*O injurious love*' (Folios 'loue'); Hanmer's sugges- tion, "*law*" for "*loue*," has been generally accepted; the law re- spited her 'a life whose very comfort' was 'a dying horror.'

II. iv. 9. '*Feared;*' probably an error of '*feared,*' *i.e.* '*seared,*' which, according to Collier, is the reading of Lord Ellesmere's copy of the first Folio.

II. iv. 104. '*That longing have been sick for*,' Rowe suggested "*I've been sick for.*"

II. iv. 173. '*O perilous mouths;*' the line is defective as it stands (?) "*O pernicious mouths*" (Walker), or "*these perilous*" (Seymour).

III. i. 92, 95. '*Prenzie!*' the source of this strange word has baffled students; it seems identical with the Scottish *primsie*, 'de- mure, precise,' which in its turn is connected with *prim* (in Old French *prin, pren*): under any circumstances there is no reason why the word should be changed, as has been proposed, to '*princely,*' the reading of the second Folio, or '*priestly,*' '*pensive,*' &c.

III. ii. 8. "The passage seems to us to imply, furred (that is, lined with lamb-skin fur inside, and trimmed with fox-skin fur outside) with both kinds of fur, to show that craft (fox-skin),

being richer than innocency (lamb-skin), is used for decoration"
(Clarke).

III. ii. 10, 11. *'Good father friar'* . . . *'good brother father;'*
the joke, as Tyrwhitt pointed out, would be clearer in French,
'mon père frère' . . . *'mon frère père.'*

III. ii. 37. *'From our faults, as faults from seeming, free!'* So
Folio 1, Folio 2 and Folio 3, *'Free from our faults,'* &c.; Hanmer
corrects the latter part of the line, *'As from faults seeming free.'*
As it stands in the text, it would seem to mean "Would that we
were as free from faults, as our faults are from seeming (hypocrisy)." One feels inclined to hazard—

'Free from our faults, as from false seeming, free!'
(*Cp.* II. iv. 15. *'thy false seeming.'*)

III. ii. 212, 213. *'Security enough to make fellowships accurst;'*
cp. *Prov.* xi. 15.

III. ii. 241-262. These lines are in all probability not Shakespeare's, but by another hand.

III. ii. 244. *'Grace to stand, and virtue go;'* i.e. 'To have grace
to stand firm, and virtue to go forward.'

III. ii. 253-256. *'How may likeness made in crimes,'* &c.; these
lines do not readily admit of interpretation, and some corruption
has probably crept into the text; Malone suggested *wade* for
made, i.e. "How may hypocrisy wade in crimes;" Hanmer, "*that
likeness shading crimes,*" &c. None of the suggestions seems very
satisfactory. Perhaps *'to draw'* = *'to-draw,' i.e.* 'pull to pieces' (?).

IV. i. This song appears in Beaumont and Fletcher's *Bloody
Brother*, with the addition of the following stanza, assuredly not
Shakespeare's, though found in the spurious edition of his poems,
(1640)—

> "Hide, O hide those hills of snow
>   Which thy frozen bosom bears,
> On whose tops the pinks that grow
>   Are of those that April wears;
> But first set my poor heart free,
>   Bound by those icy chains by thee."

IV. i. 13. "Though the music soothed my sorrows, it had no
tendency to produce light merriment" (Johnson).

IV. ii. 41, 42. *'If it be too little—thief;'* the Folios give this to
Clo. (Pompey); Capell first transferred it to Abhorson, and he
has been followed by most editors. Cowden Clarke defends the
Folio arrangement; among other arguments he maintains that
"the speech is much more in character with the clown's snip-snap
style of chop-logic than with Abhorson's manner, which is remarkably curt and bluff."

IV. iv. 5. *'redeliver;'* Folio 1, *'re-liuer;'* Folio 2, *'deliuer;'* Capell first suggested *'redeliver.'*

IV. iv. 25. *'bears of a credent bulk;'* so Folios 1, 2, 3; many emendations have been proposed; Dyce's seems the most plausible—'*bears so credent bulk;*' '*credent bulk*' = 'weight of credit.'

V. i. 64. '*Do not banish reason, For inequality;*' *i.e.* because of 'improbability,' 'incongruity,' or, according to some, 'partiality.'

V. i. 315. "These shops," according to Nares, "were places of great resort, for passing away time in an idle manner. By way of enforcing some kind of regularity, and perhaps at least as much to promote drinking, certain laws were usually hung up, the transgression of which was to be punished by specific *forfeitures.* It is not to be wondered, that laws of that nature were as often laughed at as obeyed."

V. i. 347. '*be hanged an hour*' seems to have been a cant phrase, meaning little more than 'be hanged!'

V. i. 494. '*Give me your hand;*' *i.e.* 'if you give me your hand.'

THE COMEDY OF ERRORS

I. i. 78. '*The latter-born;*' line 125 below seems to imply that this should be 'elder-born,' a change adopted by Rowe; but probably 'the children became exchanged in the confusion during the breaking-up of the ship.'

I. ii. 41. '*The almanac of my true date,*' because both were born in the same hour.

I. ii. 64. '*I shall be post indeed;*' a post stood in the middle of the shop, on which the scores of the customers were *scored,* or marked with chalk or notches.

I. ii. 66. '*Clock;*' Pope's emendation for '*cook,*' the reading of the Folios.

II. i. 109-113. These lines read as follows in the Folio:—

'*I see the Iewell best enameled
Will loose his lustre; yet the gold bides still
That others touch, and often touching will,
Where gold and no man that hath a name,*' &c.

The change of *where* to *wear* in the last line has been generally accepted, as also *and though* for *yet* in the second line; *yet* for *and* in the third; *and so a man* for *and no man* in the fourth; Warburton paraphrases this passage thus emended:—"Gold, indeed, will long bear the handling; however, often *touching* (*i.e.* assaying) will wear even gold: just so the greatest character, though as pure as gold itself, may in time be injured by the repeated attacks of falsehood and corruption." The Cambridge editors wisely abstain from these wholesale emendations, though so far no satisfactory explanation has been given of the lines. May not the meaning of the passage depend on some such interpretation as this:—The wife (the jewel) soon loses her beauty and

ceases to attract, but man (the gold) still stands the test, assayed
by other women, and although gold wears out if assayed too
often, yet a man of good reputation is not shamed by his falsehood and corruption. 'Wherefore,' says Adriana, 'since I (the
jewel) cannot please his eye, I'll weep what's left away,' &c.

II. ii. 90. '*Jollity;*' Staunton suggested that the reading is an
error for '*policy,*' and the reading has been adopted by some
modern editors.

II. ii. 119. As the line stands, it reads as an Alexandrine.
Walker suggested *carv'd thee* for *carved to thee*; others propose
the omission of *to thee;* neither change seems desirable.

II. ii. 147. '*I live distain'd, thou undishonoured;*' so read the
Folios; *distain'd* has been changed to *unstain'd* in most modern
editions; Heath proposed '*I live distained, thou dishonoured.*'
The line as it stands in the text seems to mean, 'I live distained
(*i.e.* stained), if untrue to my marriage vows; you, however, live
undishonoured, however false you may be.'

II. ii. 186. '*this sure uncertainty,*' *i.e.* 'This to her surely a
thing uncertain.'

II. ii. 191. The second Folio reads '*and Elves Sprites,*' which
Rowe altered to '*Elvish sprites,*' a reading adopted by most editors. Theobald proposed to change *owls* to *ouphes.*

II. ii. 200. ' '*tis to an ass;*' the words remind one of Bottom's
transformation in the *Midsummer-Night's Dream.*

III. i. 53. '*If thy name be called Luce*': '*Luce*' = 'pike;' there is
perhaps a play upon 'pike' in the sense of 'spear,' *cp.* '*Shall I set
in my staff?*' line 51.

III. ii. 66. '*I am thee;*' this reading of the Folio may surely,
without risk, be emended:—'*I am thee,*' *i.e.* '*I aim at thee;*' the
transitive use of *aim* is found in Elizabethan writers.

III. ii. 125-126. '*armed and reverted, making war against her
heir;*' Folio 2 substituted *hair* for *heir,* but the play upon words
is the whole point of the passage, an allusion being intended to
the War of the League against Henry of Navarre, the heir of
Henry III. of France, whose cause was supported by Elizabeth;
in 1591 she sent a body of 4000 men under Essex to help him.
"Mistress Nell's brazen forehead seemed to push back her rough
and rebellious hair, as France resisted the claim of the Protestant
heir to the throne" (Clarke).

English enthusiasm for Henry of Navarre found expression,
too, in Shakespeare's *Love's Labour's Lost.*

As regards the peculiar use of *reverted,* *i.e.* 'turned back,'
Schmidt suggests that there may be a play upon the sense of
'fallen to another proprietor.'

IV. i. 21. '*I buy a thousand pound a year;*' some point in these
words, familiar to Shakespeare's audience, is lost to us, and no
satisfactory explanation has as yet been given, though Halliwell's

comparison of the line with 3 *Henry VI*. II. ii. 144, is noteworthy:—

> "A wisp of straw were worth a thousand crowns,
> To make this shameless callet know herself."

IV. ii. 35. 'A fiend, a fury;' the Folios read 'fairy,' corrected by Theobald, who has been followed by most editors, including the Cambridge editors; a strong case can, however, be made for the original reading (*e.g. cp. Hamlet* I. i. 161-163).

IV. ii. 61. '*If Time be in debt;*' the Folios read '*If I,*' where *I* is probably an error for '*a* (*i.e. he*) or *he*; the reading in the text is Rowe's emendation.

IV. iii. 13. '*What, have you got the picture of old Adam new-apparelled?*' 'The picture of old Adam' = the sergeant, who was clad '*in buff*'; in Elizabethan slang this latter phrase was used in the sense of 'bare skin,' *i.e.* 'naked'; hence the quibble. *New-apparelled* offers some difficulty, and depends on the general construction of the whole line. It has been ingeniously suggested that the idea is 'got him a new *suit*,' *i.e.* 'got rid of him.' On the other hand, there is a possibility that the phrase '*What have you got?*' is a vulgarism for '*What have you done with?*' Theobald proposed to read '*What, have you got rid of the picture,*' &c. In the latter cases *new-apparelled* must be regarded as merely a descriptive epithet, the whole phrase '*the picture of old Adam new-apparelled*' being an elaborate circumlocution for 'sergeant.'

IV. iii. 57. '*We'll mend our dinner,*' *i.e.* 'we'll buy something more for our dinner.'

IV. iv. 41-42. '*The prophecy like the parrot, beware the rope's-end;*' the Cambridge editors most ingeniously conjecture that we should read:—

> "or, rather, '*prospice funem,*' beware the rope's end.
> Antipholus of E. *Wilt thou still talk like the parrot?*"

Dyce proposed, '*or, rather, to prophecy, like,*' &c.

Parrots were taught uncomplimentary remarks in Elizabethan times, as they are at present; there are many allusions to the very phrase in the text: Ralpho, in Butler's *Hudibras*,

> "Could tell what subtlest parrots mean,
> That speak, but think contrary clean;
> What member 't is of whom they talk,
> When they cry rope, and walk, knave, walk."

V. i. 46. '*And much different,*' &c., the second Folio, for the sake of the metre, reads *much much*; a reading which does not commend itself; *too much* has been conjectured. The line as it stands is certainly doubtful: *différent* does not occur in Shakespeare.

V. i. 66. '*Glanced it;*' Pope's conjectural *at it* is unnecessary, though *glance* in the sense *to hint*, used transitively, does not otherwise occur; Folio 1 does not elide the *ed* of *glanced*.

V. i. 79. 'But moody and dull melancholy;' something is obviously amiss with the line; moody moping has been suggested. Kinsman in the next line is used in its general sense of akin, which some editors have unnecessarily substituted; it has even been changed to kinswoman.

V. i. 170. 'Beaten the maids,' &c. i.e. have beaten; but the previous verb has are,—a confusion of constructions which causes little difficulty, and fairly common in Elizabethan English.

V. i. 312. 'My feeble key of untuned cares;' i.e. 'the feeble tone of my voice, which gives utterance to nothing but unharmonious grief.'

V. i. 390. 'These ERRORS are arose,' so the Folios; are has been variously changed by scholars into all, rare, but no change is necessary; as far as rhythm is concerned the Folio reading is certainly preferable

V. i. 403. 'Thirty-three years;' this reading of the Folios has been changed to twenty-five by most editors, following Theobald, who calculates the age of the twins by putting together what Ægeon says in Act I. i. 126 and in line 319 of Act V. Capell suggested twenty-three, from Act I. i. line 126 and line 133. On the other hand, the Duke states in line 325 of the present Act that he has been patron to Antipholus for 'twenty years'; it looks as though Shakespeare changed his idea as to the age of the twins towards the end of the play, without troubling to make all his references fit in with one another.

V. i. 407. 'And you the calendars of their nativity;' i.e., the two Dromios; cp. 'Here comes the almanac of my true date,' I. ii. 41.

V. i. 409. 'After so long grief, such nativity;' the labouring line harmonises well with the emotion of the speaker; the line is evidently intended to be read as follows:—

'After | so long | grief, súch | nativ | ity.'

There seems no reason for changing nativity, though Hanmer's conjecture felicity has been accepted by most editors; Johnson proposed festivity.

MUCH ADO ABOUT NOTHING

I. i. 192-193. The English story of "Mr. Fox" alluded to here was first written down by Blakeway, who contributed to Malone's Variorum Edition a version of the tale he had heard from an old aunt (cp. Jacobs' English Fairy Tales).

II. i. 193-194. 'As melancholy as a lodge in a warren': the phrase suggests "The daughter of Zion is left as a cottage in a vineyard, as a lodge in a garden of cucumbers." Isaiah i. 8.

II. ii. 39. Some editors substitute 'Borachio' for 'Claudio' in order to relieve the difficulty here, but, as the Cambridge editors point out, "Hero's supposed offence would not be enhanced by calling one lover by the name of the other. . . . Perhaps the author meant that Borachio should persuade her to play, as children say, at being Hero and Claudio."

II. iii. 83. The Folio reads:—'*Enter Prince, Leonato, Claudio and Jack Wilson*'; the latter was probably the singer who took the part of Balthasar.

III. ii. 24. '*Where is but a humour or a worm*': toothache was popularly supposed to be caused by a worm at the root of the tooth.

III. iii. It is an interesting fact that 'Dogberry,' the vulgar name of the *dogwood*, was used as a surname as far back as the time of Richard II., and that 'Verges,' a provincial corruption of *verjuice*, occurs in an ancient MS. (MS. Ashmol. 38) as the name of a usurer whose epitaph is given:—

> "*Here lies father Varges*
> *Who died to save charges.*"

III. iii. 79-80. '*Keep your fellows' counsels and your own.*' It has been pointed out by students of Shakespeare's legal acquirements that these words still form part of the oath administered by judges' marshal to the grand jurymen at the present day.

III. v. 15. '*Comparisons are odorous.*' An elaborate extension of this joke occurs in the old play of *Sir Gyles Goosecappe* (c. 1603).

III. v. 33. '*When the age is in, the wit is out*'; a blunder for the old proverbial expression, "when the ale is in, wit is out"—

> "*When ale is in, wit is out,*
> *When ale is out, wit is in,*
> *The first thou showest out of doubt,*
> *The last in thee hath not been.*"
>
> HEYWOOD's *Epigrams and Proverbs.*

IV. ii. Nearly all the speeches of Dogberry throughout the scene are given to the famous comedian 'Kemp,' those of Verges to 'Cowley.' Willam Kempe and Richard Cowley are among the 'principall actors' enumerated in the first Folio. The retention of the names of the actors "supplies a measure of the editorial care to which the several Folios were submitted." Dogberry's speech is assigned to 'Andrew,' probably a familiar appellation of Kempe, who, according to the Cambridge Edition, often played the part of 'Merry Andrew.'

IV. ii. 5, 6. '*We have the exhibition to examine.*' Verges' blunder is not quite clear: possibly '*exhibition*' is used in the sense of 'allowance' or permission; otherwise he perhaps means 'examination to exhibit.'

V. i. 16. '*Bid sorrow wag, cry "hem!"*' The Quarto and the first and second Folios read, '*And sorrow wagge, crie hem*': Folio 3,

'*And hallow, wag, cry hem*': Folio 4, '*And hollow wag, cry hem.*'
Many emendations have been suggested. Capell's '*bid sorrow
wag,*' is now generally adopted. Johnson proposed '*Cry, sorrow
wag! and hem.*' ('Sorrow wag,' like 'care away,' was probably a
proverbial phrase.) One other suggestion is perhaps noteworthy:
—'*And, sorry wag, cry "hem."*''

V. iii. 18, 21. '*Heavily, heavily*'; so reads the Quarto; the Folios
'*Heavenly, heavenly,*' adopted by many editors. The same error,
however, of '*heavenly*' for '*heavily*' occurs in the Folio reading of
Hamlet II. ii. 296.

"The slayers of the virgin knight are performing a solemn
requiem on the body of Hero, and they invoke Midnight and the
shades of the dead to assist, until *her* death be *uttered*, that is,
proclaimed, published, sorrowfully, sorrowfully" (Halliwell).

V. iv. 120-121. '*There is no staff more reverend than one
tipped with horn*'; *i.e.* having a ferrule of horn; there is, of course,
a quibbling allusion in the words of the favourite Elizabethan
joke.

LOVE'S LABOUR'S LOST

There is no list of 'Dramatis Personæ' in the Quartos and
Folios: it should be remembered that 'Biron' is spelt 'Berowne,'
rhyming with 'moon' in Act IV. iii. 227; 'Moth' was probably
pronounced 'Mote' (*cp.* the quibble on 'nothing' in *Much Ado*,
II. iii. 57, and on 'Goths' in *As You Like It*, III. iii. 6); 'Mercade'
is generally 'Marcade'; 'Armado' is sometimes given as 'Armatho';
'Boyet' rhymes with 'debt' in V. ii. 334; 'Longaville' with 'ill' in
IV. iii. 120, and with 'mile' in V. ii. 53.

I. i. 62. '*feast*'; Quartos and Folios '*fast*,' corrected by Theobald.

I. i. 82. '*Who dazzling so*'; "that when he *dazzles*, that is, has
his eye made weak, by fixing his eye upon a *fairer* eye, that
fairer eye shall be his *heed*, his direction or *lodestar*, and give him
light that was blinded by it" (Johnson).

I. i. 104. '*Any abortive*,' the reading of the Quartos and Folios;
probably an error for '*an*' as corrected by Pope.

I. i. 106. '*shows*'; Theobald substituted '*earth*' for the sake of
the rhyme; Walker proposed '*mirth.*' Malone supposes a line to be
lost after line 104.

I. i. 108-109. '*So you to study . . . little gate*'; this is one of
the instances where the reading of the first Quarto is better than
that of the Folio:—

'*So you to studie now it is too late,
That were to clymbe ore the house to unlocke the gate.*'

Various emendations have been proposed; the only real difficulty is in the loose use of the word '*so*.' Biron says that he likes of each thing that in season grows; '*so*' presupposes, however, some statement to this effect; 'to wish for, or to do, a thing out of season is huge folly'; (*so* you, now that it is too late to study, climb o'er the house, &c.).

I. i. 181. '*Tharborough*'; the reading of the Quarto '*farborough*' probably gives us Dull's actual pronunciation of his office.

I. i. 190. '*heaven*,' so Quartos and Folios. Theobald proposed '*having*'; whatever may be the exact force of the phrase, it seems most probable that '*heaven*' is the right word, and no emendation is necessary.

I. ii. 87. '*A green wit*'; a probable allusion, according to the Cambridge editors, to the 'green withes' with which Samson was bound (*cp.* note *supra* on pronunciation of 'Moth').

I. ii. 101-102. The ballad of *King Cophetua and the Beggar-Maid* may be found in Percy's *Reliques*.

II. i. 45. '*Well fitted in arts*'; the second Folio inserts '*the*,' omitted in the earlier editions.

II. i. 113-127. The speakers in Quarto 1 are 'Berowne' and 'Katharine.'

II. i. 128. Shakespeare may have got a hint for this passage from Monstrelet's *Chronicles*, according to which Charles, King of Navarre, surrendered to the King of France the castle of Cherbourg, the country of Evreux, and other lordships for the Duchy of Nemours and a promise of 200,000 gold crowns (*vide Shakespeare's Library*, ed. Hazlitt, Part I. Vol. i.).

II. i. 235. '*Impatient to speak and not see*,' *i.e.*, 'not able to endure merely the faculty of speech without that of sight.'

III. i. 15-16. "It was a common trick among some of the most indolent of the ancient masters, to place the hands in the bosom or the pockets, or conceal them in some part of the drapery, to avoid the labour of representing them, or to disguise their own want of skill to employ them with grace and propriety" (Steevens).

IV. i. 1-4. These lines, as Spedding pointed out, were most probably introduced in the corrected copy. "It was thus that Shakespeare learnt to shade off his scenes, to carry the action beyond the stage."

IV. i. 142. '*Armado o' th' one side*'; the reading is due to Rowe; the first Quarto has '*Armatho ath toothen side*,' and the Folio '*Armathor ath to the side*.' Possibly the whole passage from '*O my troth . . . nit*' should have been printed in the previous scene, after line 136, and some editors make the transposition.

IV. ii. 40. '*The allusion holds in the exchange*,' *i.e.*, 'the riddle is as good when I use the name of Adam as when I use the name of Cain.'

IV. ii. 58. '*one sorel*'; the first Quarto has '*o sorell*,' and the

Folios 'O sorell'; Capell proposed 'O sore L,' which is generally adopted.

IV. ii. 93, 94. The first Quarto and Folio give the following reading:—

'Vermiche, vencha, que non te vnde, que non te perreche';

the reading adopted by the Cambridge editors is from Florio's *Second Frutes* (1591), whence Shakespeare probably took it.

IV. ii. 117. 'apostrophas'; this is taken by some editors to refer to the apostrophes in *vow'd* and *bow'd* (ll. 104, 106), and the words are accordingly printed 'vowed' and 'bowed'; this interpretation seems unsatisfactory, but so far nothing better has been advanced. Does not Holofernes' criticism bear directly on the last line of the canzonet? Nathaniel should have read:—

'That singës heaven's praise with such an earthly tongue.'

It was usual to mark *es* with two dots when sounded: Holofernes may mean by 'apostrophas,' 'diæreses.' The poem is printed with a few variant readings (*e.g.* 'to sing') in the *Passionate Pilgrim,* where also are found ll. 57-70 and ll. 98-117 of the next scene, also with some interesting points of difference.

IV. iii. 103. 'Wish,' so the Quartos and first Folio; in the *Passionate Pilgrim* 'wish'd'; similarly in the line 109 'thorn' is due to the version printed in *England's Helicon;* the other editions read 'throne.' Rowe first proposed the change.

IV. iii. 137. The second Folio omits 'one.' Walker's suggestion 'One's' makes the line rhythmic.

IV. iii. 141. 'Faith infringed,' the reading of the Quartos and the Folio; 'faith so infringed' seems the most satisfactory emendation proposed.

IV. iii. 161. 'a gnat,' perhaps alluding to the fact that it sings, as it flies. Biron refers probably to the King's sonnets.

IV. iii. 243. 'wood'; Quartos and Folios read 'word.'

IV. iii. 251. 'School of night'; so the early editions; 'scowl,' 'stole,' 'soul,' 'scroll,' 'seal,' 'shade,' have been proposed by various scholars; possibly, as the Cambridge editors suggest, 'school' is an error for 'shoote,' *i.e.* 'suit.'

V. i. 27-28. In Quarto and Folio the line reads:—

'Bome boon for boon priscian, a little scratcht 'twill serve.'

V. i. 123. Capell proposed 'or' for 'and'; the passage is evidently corrupt.

V. ii. 67. 'perttaunt-like'; this word is the *crux* of the play, the early editions read 'perttaunt-like' and 'pertaunt-like.' Theobald reads 'pedant-like,' and other editors suggest 'portent-like,' 'pageant-like,' 'potently,' 'persuant-like.' It is perhaps worth while suggesting that the phrase (*tant*) *pour tant* (*quasi* 'tit for tat') perhaps underlies the word: it may well have been used in some game: Mr. Marshall quotes *pur Tant* from a poetical description of an old game, but no explanation has as yet been advanced.

V. ii. 332. *'To show his teeth as white as whale's bone'*; this should certainly be printed *whalës bone,* the regular name for walrus tusk in old English.

V. ii. 338. *'Madman,'* obviously an error for *'man'*; *'mad'* probably due to *'madam'* in the next line.

V. ii. 560, 561. According to Plutarch, Alexander's head had a twist towards the left; he states also that Alexander's skin had "a marvellous good savour."

V. ii. 582. *'Canis'*; *'canus'* in the old editions, required for the sake of the rhyme.

V. ii. 730-731. The meaning of these somewhat obscure lines seems to be that 'the latest minute of the hour often fashions or moulds all causes or questions to the purposes of his speed, that is, to his own intents'; "the extreme parts are the end parts, *'extremities'*—as, of our body, fingers; of chains, the final links; of given portions of time, the last of those units into which we choose to divide them." Observe *'forms'* for *'form'* by attraction of *'time.'* In the next lines the metaphor is derived from archery.

V. ii. 742. *'Double'*; so Quartos and Folios; many modern editors adopt *'dull'* from the Collier MS.

V. ii. 753. *'Strange'*; the Quartos and Folios read *'straying,'* probably merely a variant spelling of *'strange.'*

V. ii. 865. *'Jack hath not Jill,'* cp. *Midsummer-Night's Dream,* III. ii. 462:—

> "Jack shall have Jill:
> Nought shall go ill:
> The man shall have his mare again, and all shall be well."

A MIDSUMMER-NIGHT'S DREAM

I. i. 10. *'new-bent'*; Rowe's correction of *'now bent,'* the reading of the Quartos and Folios.

I. i. 11. *'Philostrate'* is the name assumed by Arcite in Chaucer's *Knight's Tale*; it occurs too in Plutarch's *Lives,* where are to be found also the names, Lysander, and Demetrius.

I. i. 27. The second Folio reads *'this hath bewitched'*; the earlier edition *'this man'*; perhaps we should read *'this man hath 'witched.'*

I. i. 44. *'our law'*; Solon's laws gave a father the power of life and death over his child.

I. i. 159, 160. These lines should perhaps be transposed.

I. i. 167. *'to do observance to a morn of May,'* cp. *Knight's Tale,* 1500; *'And for to doon his observance to May.'*

I. i. 219. *'stranger companies'*; Theobald's emendation of *'strange companions,'* which is the reading of the Quartos and Folios.

I. ii. 11. *'The most lamentable comedy,'* &c. Cp. the title of Preston's *Cambyses*, *'a lamentable tragedy mixed full of pleasant mirth'*; &c.

I. ii. 46. *'Thisne, Thisne,'* so the Quartos and Folios: perhaps this spelling was intentional to represent Bottom's attempt to speak the name 'in a monstrous little voice.' The words may, however, be an error for *'thisne, thisne,'* *i.e.* 'in this manner, in this manner,' *'thissen'* being used in this sense in various dialects.

II. i. 54, 55. The Quartos and Folios read *'coffe . . . loffe,'* for the sake of the rhyme.

II. i. 58. *'room'*; probably pronounced as a dissyllable.

II. i. 78. *'Perigenia,'* called 'Perigouna' in North's *Plutarch;* she was the daughter of the famous robber Sinnis, by whom Theseus had a son, Menaloppus.

II. i. 79. *'Ægle'*; Rowe's correction for *'Eagles'* of the Quartos and Folios; probably *'Eagles'* was for *'Ægles,'* a form due to North's *Plutarch*, where it is stated that some think Theseus left Ariadne "because he was in love with another, as by these verses should appear,

'*Ægles the nymph was lov'd of Theseus,*
  Who was the daughter of Panopeus.' "

II. i. 80. *'Antiopa,'* said to be the name of the Amazon queen, and the mother of Hippolytus.

II. i. 231. *'Daphne holds the chase'*; the story tells how Apollo pursued Daphne, who was changed into a laurel-tree as he reached her.

III. i. 33-41. This was probably suggested by an actual incident which occurred during the Kenilworth festivities, when one Harry Goldingham, who was to represent Arion upon the Dolphin's back, tore off his disguise and swore he was none of Arion (*cp.* Scott's use of this story in *Kenilworth*).

III. i. 171. *'Squash,'* *i.e.* an unripe peascod.

III. ii. 36. *'latch'd'*; the word *'latch'* in this passage, as Prof. Skeat has pointed out, is not connected with the ordinary *'latch,'* 'to catch,' but is etymologically the casual form of *'leak,'* and means 'to cause to drop, to drip.'

III. ii. 119. *'sport alone,'* *i.e.* 'by itself, without anything else'; others render *'alone'* by 'above all things, without a parallel.'

III. ii. 188. *'oes'*; o was used for anything round, among other things for circular discs of metal used for ornaments, *cp.* Bacon, Essay xxxvii.: "And Oes, and Spangs, as they are of no great cost, so they are of most glory."

III. ii. 204. *'needles,'* a monosyllable; *'needle'* was often spelt *'neeld'* in Old English.

III. ii. 212-214. "Helena says, 'we had two seeming bodies but one heart.' She then exemplifies her position by a simile—'we had two of the first, *i.e.* bodies, like the double coats in heraldry that belong to man and wife as one person, but which, like our single heart, have but one crest.' "

III. ii. 257. *'No no; he'll . . . seem'*; the first Quarto *'heele seem'*; the second *'hee'l seem'*; the first Folio *'No, no, Sir, seem.'* The passage is clearly corrupt in the old editions. I am inclined to accept Mr. Orson's ingenious suggestion:—

> *"No no, sir; still*
> *Seeme to breake loose,"*

'heele' being an easy misreading of *'stille.'*

IV. i. 27. *'a reasonable good ear in music'*; weavers were supposed to be fond of music, more especially of psalm-singing; *cp.* 1 *Henry IV.*, II. iv. 130, 131. *'I would I were a weaver, I could sing psalms.'*

IV. i. 40. *'So doth the woodbine the sweet honeysuckle'*; commonly *'woodbine'* is identical with *'honeysuckle,'* but it is also used by Elizabethans for *'convolvulus'* and *'ivy.'* Shakespeare, however, uses the word in two other passages (II. i. 251 and *Much Ado,* III. i. 30) in the sense of *'honeysuckle'*; hence Warburton suggested:—

> *"So doth the woodbine, the sweet honeysuckle,*
> *Gently entwist the maple, ivy so,"* &c.

Johnson thought that *'woodbine'* was the plant, and *'honeysuckle'* the flower. These suggestions are not satisfactory: the simplest way out of the difficulty is to take *'woodbine'* as equivalent to *'convolvulus'* or *'bindweed'*; *cp.* Ben Jonson's *Vision of Delight:*—

> *"behold!*
> *How the blue bindweed doth itself unfold*
> *With honeysuckle."*

IV. i. 71. *'Dian's bud'*; it has been thought that perhaps *'Dian's bud'* = *'Diana's rose,'* *'the rose of England's Virgin Queen'*; *'Diana's Rose'* is actually used in this complimentary sense in Greene's *Friar Bacon.*

IV. i. 80. *'Than common sleep,'* &c.; the Quartos and first two Folio read *'sleepe: of all these, fine the sense'*; the correction is Theobald's.

IV. i. 88. *'prosperity'*; so the first Quarto; the second and Folios *'posterity.'*

IV. i. 114. *'fountains'*; perhaps an error for *'mountains.'*

V. i. 47. *'my kinsman Hercules'*; *cp.* North's *Plutarch, Life of Theseus:* "they (Theseus and Hercules) were near kinsmen, being cousins removed by the mother's side."

V. i. 54. *'critical,'* *i.e.* 'censorious' as in the well-known utterance of Iago, *'I am nothing, if not critical'* (*Othello,* II. i. 119).

V. i. 59. *'wondrous strange snow'*; *'strange'* is hardly the epithet one would expect, and various emendations have been suggested: —*'strange black,'* *'strong snow,'* *'swarthy snow,'* *'sable-snow,'* *'and, wondrous strange! yet snow.'* Perhaps the most plausible conjecture is Mr. S. W. Orson's *'wondrous flaming snow,'* cp. "What strange fits be these, Philautus, that burne thee with such a heat, that thou shakest for cold, and all thy body in a shivering sweat, in *a flaming ice*, melteth like wax and hardeneth like the adamant" (Lyly's *Euphues*, ed. Arber, p. 311).

V. i. 91. *'And what poor duty,'* &c.; Coleridge proposed:—
> "And what poor duty cannot do, yet would,
> Noble respect takes it," &c.

The metre is defective as the lines stand. Theobald read *'poor willing duty . . . Noble respect.'* The meaning is sufficiently clear, and recalls *Love's Labour's Lost*, V. ii. 517, *'That sport best pleases that doth least know how,'* &c. *'Takes it in might'* = regards the ability or effort of the performance.

V. i. 118. *'stand upon points'*; Quince's punctuation reminds one of the reading of Roister Doister's letter to Mistress Constance in the old comedy (*cp. Roister Doister*, iii. 3).

V. i. 138. *'name'*; as there is no rhyme to *name*, the loss of a line is to be inferred, or perhaps we should read *'which by name Lion hight.'*

V. i. 205. *'mural down'*; the Quartos read *'Moon used'*; the Folios *'morall downe'*; the emendation *'mural'* was due to Pope.

V. i. 221. *'a lion-fell'*; the Quartos and Folios read *'a lion fell,'* *i.e.* a fierce lion, but Snug wishes to say 'he is not a lion,' wherefore the words have been hyphened by most modern editors, *'lion-fell,'* *i.e.* 'a lion's skin.' Johnson understood *'neither'* before *'a lion fell'*; Rowe read *'No lion fell.'* There is, I think, a more obvious emendation, and I propose:—
> "Then know that I, one Snug the joiner, n'am
> A lion fell, nor else no lions dam,"

'n'am' being an archaic form, like *nill* (*i.e.* ne will). In Gascoigne's *Steele Glas* the following couplet occurs, remarkably suggestive of our text:—
> "I n'am a man, as some do think I am;
> (Laugh not good lord), I am indede a dame."

V. i. 261, 262. Spedding proposed to invert these lines.

V. 1. 265. *'gleams'*; the Quartos and Folio 1 read *'beams'*; Folio 2 *'streams.'*

V. i. 311-312. *'he for a man—God bless us,'* omitted in the Folios, probably in consequence of the statute of James I. forbidding profane speaking, or use of 'the holy name of God.'

V. i. 315. *'means,'* changed by Theobald to *'moans.'* *'Mean'* in the sense of 'to lament,' an archaic form, is really more correct than *'moan,'* and probably intentionally used by Shakespeare to harmonise with the archaisms of the interlude.

V. ii. 2. *'behowls'*; Theobald's emendation of *'beholds,'* the reading of the Quartos and Folios.

V. ii. 25. *'this ditty'*; Johnson supposes that two songs are lost, one led by Titania, and one by Oberon.

THE MERCHANT OF VENICE

The name 'Shylock' may have been derived by Shakespeare from a pamphlet called 'Caleb Shillocke his prophecies, or the Jewes Prediction'; the Pepysian ballad on this subject belongs to the year 1607; to the same year belongs a prose piece printed at the end of a rare tract called 'A Jewes prophecie, or Newes from Rome of two mighty armies,' &c. Its ultimate origin is unknown; it may have been an Italian name Sciolocca. According to Hunter, Scialac was the name of a Maronite of Mount Libanus, who was living in 1614.

I. i. 27. 'dock'd'; Rowe's emendation for 'docks,' the reading of the Quartos and Folios.

I. i. 113. 'Is that any thing new?' The old editions read 'Is that any thing now,' changed to 'new' by Johnson. Rowe first suggested the interrogation.

I. ii. 70. 'the Scottish lord'; in the first Folio 'Scottish' is changed to 'other.'

I. ii. 72-74. "Alluding to the constant assistance, or rather, constant promises of assistance, that the French gave the Scots in their quarrels with the English" (Warburton).

I. ii. 111. 'The four strangers'; allusion has been made to six strangers. An interesting oversight on the poet's part.

I. iii. 60, 61. 'Is he yet possess'd How much ye would,' so read the second and third Quartos; the Folios read 'he would'; the first Quarto 'are you resolv'd how much he would have': this is one of the important points in which the second Quarto is superior to the first.

I. iii. 67. Cp. Genesis xxx.

I. iii. 70. 'the third,' i.e. 'reckoning Abraham himself as the first.'

I. iii. 130. 'A breed for barren metal'; the reading of the Folio 'a breed of'; 'for' must be equivalent to 'in exchange for'; 'breed' = 'interest money bred from the principal' (cp. Gr. τόκος).

II. i. The old stage direction ran as follows:—'Enter Morochus a tawnie Moore all in white, and three or four followers accordingly, with Portia, Nerissa and their traine.'

II. i. 25. 'the Sophy,' cp. "Sofi, and Sofito, an ancient word signifying a wise man, learned and skillful in Magike Naturale. It has grown to be the common name of the Emperour of Persia" (Abraham Hartwell's translation of Minadoi's History of the Wars between the Turks and the Persians).

The 'Sefii of Persia' is mentioned in the German play Der Jude von Venedig.

II. i. 35. '*page*'; Theobald's emendation for '*rage*,' the reading of all the old editions.

II. ii. 84. Gobbo's '*you*,' as a mark of respect, changes to '*thou*,' after the recognition.

II. ii. 148. "Long and deep lines from the Mount of Venus (the ball of the thumb) towards the line of life, signifieth so many wives.
. . . These lines visible and deep, so many wives the party shall have" (Saunder's *Chiromancie*, quoted by Halliwell).

II. iii. 11. '*did*'; the Quartos and first Folio read '*doe*'; the reading '*did*' was first given in the second Folio; if this is adopted, '*get*' = 'beget.'

II. v. 24. '*Black-Monday*,' *i.e.* Easter Monday, so called, because of a storm which occurred on April 14, 1360, being Easter Monday, when Edward III was lying with his army before Paris, and when many of his men-at-arms died of cold (Stowe).

II. v. 35. '*Jacob's staff*'; *cp.* Gen. xxxii. and Heb. xi. 21. 'A Jacob's staff' was generally used in the sense of 'a pilgrim's staff,' because St. James (or Jacob) was the patron saint of pilgrims.

II. v. 42. 'A *Jewess' eye*'; the Quartos and Folios read '*a Jewes eye*,' probably pronounced '*Jewës*'; 'worth a Jew's eye' was a proverbial phrase: 'that worth was the price which the Jews paid for immunity from mutilation and death.' The reading '*Jewess*' seems very doubtful.

II. vi. 51. '*by my hood*'; this phrase is found nowhere else in Shakespeare; according to Malone, Gratiano is in a masqued habit, to which it is probable that formerly, as at present, a large cape or hood was affixed.

II. vii. 41. '*the Hyrcanian deserts*'; Shakespeare three times mentions the tigers of Hyrcania, 'the name given to a district of indefinite extent south of the Caspian,' where, according to Pliny, tigers were bred.

II. vii. 53. '*undervalued*'; "in the beginning of Elizabeth's reign, gold was to silver in the proportion of 11 to 1; in the forty-third year of her reign it was in the proportion of 10 to 1" (Clarendon).

II. vii. 69. '*tombs do*'; Johnson's emendation for the old reading '*timber do*.'

II. vii. 75. Halliwell notes that this line is a paraphrastical inversion of the common old proverb: 'Farewell, frost,' which was used in the absence or departure of anything that was unwelcome or displeasing.

III. i. 9. '*Knapped ginger*'; perhaps '*to knap ginger*' is to 'nibble ginger'; old women were fond of this condiment: Cotgrave invariably gives '*knap*' as a synonym of '*gnaw*' or '*nibble*.'

III. i. 60. '*humility*,' rightly explained by Schmidt as 'kindness, benevolence, humanity.'

III. i. 105. The special value of the 'turquoise' was its supposed virtue in indicating the health of the wearer: it was said to brighten or fade as its wearer was well or ill, and to give warning of approaching danger.

III. ii. 54. '*more love*'; because Hercules rescued Hesione not for love of the lady, but for the sake of the horses promised him by Laomedon.

III. ii. 99. '*veiling an Indian beauty*'; it has been pointed out that Montaigne in his Essay on 'Beauty' says: "The Indians describe it black and swarthy, with blabbered thick lips, with a broad and flat nose." If Shakespeare gives us a reminiscence of this, he must have read Montaigne in French, as Florio's translation was not published until 1603.

III. ii. 102. '*Hard food for Midas*,' who prayed that everything he touched might turn to gold, and soon regretted his prayer.

III. ii. 106. '*paleness*'; as Bassanio uses 'pale' of silver a few lines before, Theobald, on Warburton's suggestion, proposed to read '*plainness*'; but '*pale*' is a regular epithet of lead, and there seems no reason for changing the reading here.

III. ii. 112. '*rain*'; the reading of the second Quarto, '*rein*,' is generally preferred.

III. v. 69-70. '*And if on earth he do not mean it, then In reason*'; the second Quarto '*it, it*'; the Folios '*it, it is*.' Various emendations have been suggested for '*mean*,' but no change is necessary: '*mean*' = 'aim at.' A kind correspondent, Mr. S. W. Orson, calls attention to Herbert's use of the word in '*The Church Porch*' (E. Stock's reprint of the first edition) "Shoots higher much than he that *means* a tree" (p. 12), and "Scorns his first bed of dirt, and *means* the sky" (p. 163).

IV. i. 36. '*Our holy Sabbath*'; so the first Quarto; the second reads '*Sabaoth*'; it is just possible that Shakespeare might have been misled by the expression, 'Lord God of Sabaoth,' which occurs in the New Testament. 'Sabbath' and 'Sabaoth' (*i.e.* 'hosts,' in the phrase 'Lord of hosts') were confused even by Sir Walter Scott, when in *Ivanhoe*, ch. x. he refers to "the gains of a week, aye the space between two Sabaoths." Similarly Spenser (F. Q. viii. 2):—

> '*But henceforth all shall rest eternally*
> *With him that is the God of Sabaoth hight.*'

Dr. Johnson treated the two words as identical in the first edition of his Dictionary.

IV. i. 50, 51. '*affection, Mistress of passion*'; the Quartos and Folios read '*affection. Master of passion*.' The reading now generally adopted was first suggested by Thirlby; '*Maistres*' or '*mastres*,' the old spelling of '*mistress*' evidently produced the error. '*Affection*,' when contrasted with '*passion*,' seems to denote 'emotions produced through the senses by external objects.'

IV. i. 56. *'a wollen bag-pipe'*; the reading of all the old editions; *'wawling,' 'swollen,' 'bollen,'* have been variously suggested; *'woollen'* probably refers to the covering of the wind-bag.

IV. i. 181, 182. *Cp.* "Mercy is seasonable in the time of affliction, as clouds of rain in the time of drought," Ecclesiasticus, xxxv. 20.

IV. i. 252. *'Are there balance'*; *'balance'* was frequently treated as a plural by Elizabethan writers, though this is the only instance in Shakespeare.

V. i. 4. *'Troilus'*; the image is from Chaucer's *Troilus and Cresseide:* "Upon the wallis fast eke would he walke" (Bk. v. 666).

V. i. 7-14. *'Thisbe,'* &c. Hunter (*New Illustrations,* i. 309) ingeniously suggests that the old Folio of Chaucer was lying open before Shakespeare when he wrote this dialogue, and that there he found Thisbe, Dido, and Medea, as well as Troilus. It is certainly striking that Thisbe, Dido, and Medea follow each other in the *'Legend of Good Women.'* Shakespeare has seemingly transferred to Dido what he found in Chaucer's *Legend* concerning Ariadne (*'And to the stronde bare-fote faste she went'* —*'And turne agayne, and on the stronde hire fyinde.'*). Chaucer's *Medea* directed Shakespeare's mind to Ovid, *Metam.* VII.

V. i. 15. *'Jessica'*; Medea, who stole away from her father Æetes, with the golden fleece, suggests Jessica's own story to Lorenzo.

V. i. 60, &c. "The corresponding passage in Plato is in his tenth book *De Republica* where he speaks of the harmony of the Spheres, and represents a syren sitting on each of the eight orbs, and singing to each in its proper tone, while they are thus guided through the heavens, and consent in a diapason of perfect harmony, the Fates themselves chanting to this celestial music" (Du Bois, *The Wreath,* p. 60, quoted by Furness). The Platonic doctrine is, however, blended with reminiscences of Job xxxviii. 7, "The morning stars sang together."

V. i. 65. *'close it in'*; Quarto 1 and Folios read *'in it,'* which some editors have taken as equivalent to *'close-in-it.'*

V. i. 193. A similar repetition of the word *'love'* at the end of ten consecutive lines is found in *'The Fayre Mayde of the Exchange'* (1607); *cp. Edward III.* Act II. sc. i., where *'the sun'* ends eight consecutive lines.

AS YOU LIKE IT

DRAMATIS PERSONÆ. The pronunciation of *'Jaques'* is still somewhat doubtful, though the metrical test makes it certain that it is always a dissyllable in Shakespeare: there is evidence that the name was well known in England, and ordinarily pronounced as a monosyllable; hence Harrington's *Metamorphosis of A-jax* (1596). The name of the character was probably rendered '*Jakës*'; the modern stage practice is in favour of '*Jaqowes.*'

I. i. 1. '*it was upon this fashion: bequeathed,*' &c. The Folio does not place a stop at '*fashion,*' but makes '*bequeathed*' a past participle; the words '*charged*' . . . '*on his blessing*' presuppose '*he*' or '*my father*'; the nominative may, however, be easily supplied from the context, or possibly, but doubtfully, '*a*' (= '*he*') has been omitted before '*charged.*' There is very much to be said in favour of the Folio reading; a slight confusion of two constructions seems to have produced the difficulty. Warburton, Hanmer, and Capell proposed to insert '*my father*' before '*bequeathed.*' Others punctuate in the same way as in the present text, but read '*he bequeathed*' or '*my father bequeathed*'; the Cambridge editors hold that the subject of the sentence is intentionally omitted.

I. ii. 75. The Folio prefixes '*Rosalind*' to the speech: Theobald first proposed the change to '*Celia,*' and he has been followed by most editors. Capell suggested '*Fernandine*' for '*Frederick*' in the previous speech. Shakespeare does not give us the name of Rosalind's father: he is generally referred to as '*Duke Senior*'; Celia's father is mentioned as '*Frederick*' in two other places (l. 219 of this scene, and V. iv. 151). One has, however, a shrewd suspicion that Touchstone is referring to the exiled king as '*old* Frederick,' and that Rosalind speaks the words '*my father's love is enough to honour him*'; the expression is so much in harmony with her subsequent utterance, ll. 220:

'*My father loved Sir Rowland as his soul.*'

And again, in the next scene, l. 28:—

'*The Duke my father loved his father dearly.*'

I. ii. 189. '*You mean*'; Theobald proposed '*An' you mean,*' and the Cambridge editors suggest that '*and*' for '*an*' (= if) may be the right reading, omitted by the printer, who mistook it for part of the stage-direction '*Orl. and*' for '*Orland.*'

I. ii. 254. '*the taller*'; but Rosalind is later on described as '*more than common tall,*' and Celia as '*the woman low, and browner than her brother*'; probably '*taller*' is a slip of Shakespeare's pen: '*shorter,*' '*smaller,*' '*lesser,*' '*lower,*' have been variously proposed; of these '*lesser*' strikes one perhaps as most Shakespearian.

I. iii. 97. '*change,*' &c., Folio 1; the other Folios read '*charge,*' *i.e.* 'burden,' probably the true reading.

I. iii. 123. There has been much discussion of the scansion

of this line; several critics, in their anxiety to save Shakespeare from the serious charge of using a false quantity, propose to accent *'Aliena'* on the penultimate, but for all that it seems most likely that the line is to be read:—

'No lóng|er Cél|ya bút|Ali|ena.'

II. i. 5. *'here feel we but'*; Theobald first conjectured *'but'* for *'not'* of the Folios, and his emendation has been accepted by many scholars, though violently opposed by others. Most of the discussions turn on *'the penalty of Adam,'* which ordinarily suggests toil—'in the sweat of thy brow shalt thou eat bread'—but in this passage Shakespeare makes the penalty to be "the season's difference," *cp. Paradise Lost,* x. 678, 9:—
'Else had the spring Perpetual smiled on earth with vernant flowers.'

II. i. 13-14. *'like the toad, ugly and venomous,'* &c. A favourite Euphuistic conceit, *e.g.* *'The foul toade hath a faire stone in his head,'* Euphues, p. 53 (ed. Arber), based on an actual belief in toadstones. The origin of the belief is traced back to Pliny's description of a stone as 'of the colour of a frog.'

II. iii. 12. *'no more do yours,'* a somewhat loose construction, but one easily understood, the force of the previous sentence being 'to some kind of men their graces serve them not as friends.'

II. iii. 71. *'seventeen'*; Rowe's emendation for *'seaventie'* of the Folios.

II. iv. 1. *'weary'*; Theobald's emendation for *'merry'* of the Folios, and generally adopted; some scholars are in favour of the Folio reading, and put it down to Rosalind's assumed merriment; her subsequent confession as to her weariness must then be taken as an aside.

II. iv. 46. *'from whom,'* *i.e.* from the peascod; similarly *'her'* in the next line: he was wooing the peascod instead of his mistress.

II. v. 3. *'turn,'* so the Folios: Pope substituted *'tune'*; but the change is unnecessary; according to Steevens *'to turn a tune or note'* is still a current phrase among vulgar musicians.

II. v. 56-57. *'I'll rail against all the first-born of Egypt.'* According to Johnson *'the first-born of Egypt'* was a proverbial expression for high-born persons, but it has not been found elsewhere. Nares suggests that perhaps Jaques is only intended to say that, if he cannot sleep, he will, like other discontented persons, rail against his betters. There is no doubt some subtler meaning in the words, and the following is possibly worthy of consideration:—Jaques says if he cannot sleep he'll rail against all first-borns, for it is the question of birthright which has caused him *'leave his wealth and ease,'* merely as he had previously put it *'to please a stubborn will'*; this idea has perhaps suggested

Pharaoh's stubbornness, and by some such association 'all first-borns' became 'all the first-born of Egypt'; or, by mere association, the meaningless tag 'of Egypt' is added by Jaques to round off the phrase, and to give it some sort of colour.

II. vii. 19. Touchstone of course alludes to the common saying 'Fortune favours fools,' cp. 'Every man out of his humour,' I. i.

> Sogliardo. Why, who am I, sir?
>
> Macilente. One of those that fortune favours.
>
> Carlo. [Aside] The periphrasis of a fool.

II. vii. 34, 36. 'A worthy fool' . . . 'O, worthy fool': the 'A' and 'O' should probably change places, according to an anonymous conjecture noted in the Cambridge Edition.

II. vii. 55. 'Not to seem'; the words 'not to' were first added by Theobald: the Folios read 'seem'; Collier, following his MS. corrections, proposed 'but to seem'; the meaning is the same in both cases. Mr. Furness follows Ingleby in maintaining the correctness of the text, and paraphrases thus:—"He who is hit the hardest by me must laugh the hardest, and that he must do so is plain; because if he is a wise man he must seem foolishly senseless of the bob by laughing it off. Unless he does this, viz., shows his insensibility by laughing it off, any chance hit of the fool will expose every nerve and fibre of his folly."

II. vii. 73. 'the weary very means,' the reading of the Folios (Folios 1 and 2 'wearie'; Folios 3, 4, 'weary'). Pope proposed 'very very'; Collier (MS.) 'the very means of wear'; Staunton 'weary-very,' or 'very-weary.' Others maintain the correctness of the original reading, and explained 'until that its very means, being weary or exhausted, do ebb.' A very plausible emendation was suggested by Singer, viz., 'wearer's' for 'weary,' and it has rightly been adopted by several editors: cp. Henry VIII. I. i. 83-85:—

> 'O, many
> Have broke their backs with laying manors on 'em
> For this great journey.'

II. vii. 178. 'because thou art not seen,' i.e. "as thou art an enemy that dost not brave us with thy presence" (Johnson): several unnecessary emendations have been proposed, e.g. 'Thou causest not that teen' (Hanmer); 'Because thou art foreseen' (Staunton), &c.

II. vii. 189. 'As friend remember'd not,' i.e. 'as forgotten friendship,' or 'as want an unremembered friend feels': cp. 'benefits forgot,' supra.

III. ii. 104. 'the very false gallop,' cp. Nashe's Four Letters Confuted, "I would trot a false gallop through the rest of his ragged verses but that if I should retort his rime dogrell aright, I must make my verses (as he doth his) run hobling like a

Brewer's Cart upon the stones, and observe no length in their feet."

III. ii. 146. *'pulpiter'*: Spedding's suggestion for *'Jupiter'* of the Folios.

III. ii. 384. *'living,'* *i.e.* lasting, permanent; the antithesis seems to require *'loving,'* which has been substituted by some editors: it is noteworthy that in some half-dozen instances in Shakespeare *'live'* has been printed for *'love,'* but it is questionable whether any change is justifiable here.

III. iii. 4. *'your features!* . . . *what features?'* Farmer's conjecture *'feature!* . . . *what's feature'* seems singularly plausible; *cp.* l. 17, *'I do not know what "poetical" is.'*

III. iii. 69. *'her,'* so Folios 1, 2: *'his,'* Folios 3, 4: the female bird was the falcon; the male was called 'tercel' or 'tassel.'

III. iv. 39. *'noble goose'*; Hanmer substituted *'nose-quilled'* for *'noble,'* which is, of course, used ironically.

III. v. 7. *'dies and lives,'* *i.e.* 'lives and dies,' *i.e.* 'subsists from the cradle to the grave'; the inversion of the words seems to have been an old idiom; *cp.* 'Romaunt of the Rose,' v. 5790:—

"With sorwe they both die and live,
    That unto Richesse her hertis yive."

Other passages in later literature might be adduced where the exigencies of metre do not exist.

IV. i. 136. *'like Diana in the fountain.'* Stowe mentions in his *Survey of London* (1603) that there was set up in 1596 on the east side of the cross in Cheapside "a curiously wrought tabernacle of grey marble, and in the same an alabaster image of Diana, and water conveyed from the Thames prilling from her naked breast." It is very doubtful whether Shakespeare is referring to this particular 'Diana,' as some have supposed.

IV. ii. 12. The words *'Then sing him home, the rest shall bear this burden,'* are printed as one line in the Folios. Theobald was the first to re-arrange, as in the text. Knight, Collier, Dyce, and others take the whole to be a stage-direction. Knight first called attention to the fact that possibly the original music for this song is to be found in John Hilton's *'Catch that Catch Can; or, a Choice Collection of Catches, Rounds,'* &c., 1652 (printed Furness, p. 230, 231).

IV. iii. 74. *'fair ones'*; Mr. Wright suggests that perhaps we should read 'fair one,' and Mr. Furness assents to the view that 'Shakespeare seems to have forgotten that Celia was apparently the only woman present.' But surely it is noteworthy that Oliver a few lines lower down gives the description:—'The boy is fair,' &c.

IV. iii. 86. *'like a ripe sister: the woman low'*; the pause at the woman low cæsura takes the place of a syllable.

IV. iii. 100. *'chewing the food,'* usually quoted as 'chewing the cud,' a correction of the line first suggested by Scott (*cp.* Introduction to *Quentin Durward*).

V. ii. 17. '*fair sister*'; Oliver addresses 'Ganymede' thus for he is Orlando's counterfeit Rosalind (*cp.* IV. iii. 92). Some interpreters of Shakespeare are of opinion that Oliver knows the whole secret of the situation.

V. ii. 65. '*which I tender dearly*'; probably an allusion to the Act "against Conjuracons, Inchantments, and Witchcraftes," passed under Elizabeth, which enacted that all persons using witchcraft, &c., whereby death ensued, should be put to death without benefit of clergy, &c.

V. iii. 15. Chappell printed the music of the song from a MS., now in the Advocates' Library, Edinburgh, belonging to the early part of the seventeenth century (*cp.* Furness, pp. 262, 263). In the Folios the last stanza is made the second. Mr. Roffe is of opinion that Shakespeare contemplated a trio between the Pages and Touchstone.

V. iv. 4. '*As those that fear they hope, and know they fear.*' A large number of unnecessary emendations have been proposed for this plausible reading of the Folios; *e.g.* '*fear, they hope, and know they fear*'; '*fear their hope and hope their fear*'; '*fear their hope and know their fear,*' &c. The last of these gives the meaning of the line as it stands in the text.

V. iv. 84. '*we quarrel in print, by the book*'; Shakespeare probably refers to "*Vincentio Saviolo his Practise. In two Bookes. The first intreating the use of the Rapier and Dagger. The second of Honor and honorable Quarrels*"; printed in 1594.

V. iv. 85. '*books for good manners,*' *e.g.* "*A lytle Booke of Good Manners for Chyldren with interpritation into the vulgare Englysshe tongue by R. Whittinton, Poet Laureat*"; printed at London in 1554; (*cp.* Dr. Furnivall's *Book of Norture of John Russell*, &c., published by the *Early English Text Society*, 1868). *Cp. Hamlet*, V. ii. 149, '*he (i.e. Laertes) is the card of calendar of gentry,*' a probable allusion to the title of some such 'book of manners.'

V. iv. 107. '*her hand with his*'; the first and second Folios '*his hand*'; corrected to '*her*' in the second and third Folios.

V. iv. 141. '*even daughter, welcome*'; Theobald proposed '*daughter-welcome,*' *i.e.* 'welcome as a daughter.' Folios 1, 2, 3, read '*daughter welcome*'; Folio 4, '*daughter, welcome.*' The sense is clear whichever reading is adopted, though the rhythm seems in favour of the reading in the text: 'O my dear niece,' says the Duke, 'nay, daughter, welcome to me in no less degree than daughter.'

Epilogue. 15. '*If I were a woman*'; the part of Rosalind was of course originally taken by a boy-actor: women's parts were not taken by women till after the Restoration.

THE TAMING OF THE SHREW

INDUCT. i. 7. *'go by, Jeronimy'*; a popular phrase from Kyd's *Spanish Tragedy*—"the common butt of raillery to all the poets in Shakespeare's time."

Induct. i. 13. *'Brach Merriman'*; *'brach'* usually means a female hound, as in the next line; the sequence of thought requires *'brach'* to be a verb: perhaps it is used in the sense of 'couple,' 'mate.' Hanmer proposed *'leech'*; Keightley, *'bathe'*; Singer (ed. 2), *'trash,'* &c.

Induct. i. 60. *'And when he says he is,'* &c., so the old eds. The reading is probably correct; the line means 'when he says he is mad, say that he dreams.' Rowe proposed *'And when he says he's poor'*; Keightley.*'And when he says what he is,'* &c.

Induct. i. 84. The Folios and Quarto prefix *'Sincklo,'* the name of an actor in Shakespeare's company, who is mentioned also in stage-directions of Quarto edition (1600) of 2 *Henry IV.*, V. iv., and in the Folio, 3 *Henry VI.*, III. i.

Induct. i. 84. *'Soto'* is a character in Beaumont and Fletcher's *Women Pleased.*

I. i. 32. *Cp. The Taming of a Shrew:*—
> *'Welcome to Athens, my beloved friend,*
> *To Plato's school and Aristotle's walks.'*

I. i. 42. *'If Biondello, thou wert'*; the Collier MS. reads *'now were'*; Dyce adopts this emendation.

I. i. 64. *'To comb your noddle with a three-legg'd stool'*; an old expression occurring in Skelton's *Merrie Tales.* "Hys wife would divers times in the weeke kimbe his head with a iii. footed stoole."

I. i. 231. *'I, sir! ne'er a whit.'* Rowe proposed *'Ay, sir, ne'er,'* &c.; Dyce, *'Ay, sir.—Ne'er.'* It is difficult to determine whether *'I'* is the personal pronoun, or stands, as is often the case, for *'Ay.'*

I. i. 243. *'The presenters,'* *i.e.* Sly and his attendants in the balcony above.

I. ii. 28. *'what he 'leges in Latin'*; the Folios and Quarto, *'leges,'* an authorised form for *'alleges'*; Grumio, strange to say, though an Italian, mistakes Italian for Latin.

I. ii. 146-147. *'paper'* . . . *'them'*; changed by Pope to *'papers'*: Mr. Daniel considers *'paper'* to be the note of the *'books,'* and *'them'* the books.

II. i. 75-82, arranged as verse in the Folios and Quarto, first printed as prose by Pope.

II. i. 200. *'no such jade as you'*; probably an error for *'no jade for such as you,'* as conjectured by Hudson: many other less obvious emendations have been proposed, *e.g.* "*no such load as you, sir*" (Singer), &c.

II. i. 205-207. '*buzzard*' in this passage is a crux: its three senses are, I think, punned on by the speakers:—(i.) a simpleton (l. 206); (ii.) a mean hawk (ll. 207, 208); in the latter case Petruchio interprets it as (iii.) 'a buzzing insect,' hence 'you wasp' (l. 209). Katharine's reply seems to mean:—'that, in calling her a turtle, he has mistaken a hawk for a dove'; underlying this retort there may be a suggestion of the proverbial 'blind buzzard.'

II. i. 287. '*morn*'; *cp. Troilus*, I. iii. 229:—
> '*Modest as morning when she coldly eyes*
> *The youthful Phœbus.*'

The Collier MS. has '*moone.*'

II. i. 316. '*We will have rings and things,*' probably a fragment of an old ballad. Collier quotes some lines bearing a very strong resemblance to these "from the recitation of an old lady"—a vague authority.

II. i. 368. '*Marseilles' road,*' Folio 1 and Quarto, '*Marcellus*'; the other Folios '*Marsellis*'; the word is obviously trisyllabic; the apostrophe is not needed, *cp.* '*Venice gold,*' '*Pisa walls*' in the previous speech.

III. i. 4. Theobald proposed '*she is a shrew, but, wrangling pedant, this is*'; evidently some words are lost, but it is useless to attempt the restoration of the line, as there is no evidence.

III. ii. 16. '*make friends, invite, and proclaim the banns*'; so Folio 1 and Quarto; Folios 2 and 3 insert '*yes*' before '*and.*' The more noteworthy suggestions are:—"*Make friends invite, Yes*" (Singer); "*make friends invite guests*" (Dyce); "*make feasts, invite friends*" (Dyce, ed. 2).

IV. i. 125. '*Where is the life that late I led*'; a line of an old song, quoted also by Pistol; *cp.* 2 *Henry IV.*, V. iii. 137. Similarly '*It was the friar of orders grey,*' &c., is a bit of an old ballad, now lost.

IV. i. 192. '*to kill a wife with kindness,*' a proverbial expression. Heywood's play, *A Woman Killed with Kindness,* was first produced in 1602.

IV. ii. 45. '*longeth*'; the Folios and Quartos correct '*longeth,*' without apostrophe; '*to long*' in the sense of 'to belong' is common in older English writings. Similarly '*pointed*' in old eds., III. ii. 1.

IV. ii. 61. '*An ancient angel*'; so the Folios and Quartos; Theobald suggested '*engle*' (a gull); other proposals have been *ayeul, gentle, morsel, antick,* &c., but no change is necessary. Cotgrave renders *Angelot à la grosse escaille* by "an old angell; and by metaphor, a fellow of the old, sound, honest and worthie stamp."

IV. iii. 60. *'ruffling treasure'*; Pope changed *'ruffling'* to *'rustling'*; perhaps we should read *'russling'* (for *'rustling'*). Cp. *Lear,* II. iv. 299, where the Quarto reading is *'russel,'* while the Folios have *'ruffle.'* Mrs. Quickly's *'rushling in silk and gold'* (*Merry Wives,* II. ii. 63) seems to be an important piece of evidence in favour of *'rustling.'*

IV. iv. 62. *'Cambio,'* probably an error for *'Biondello,'* as suggested by the Cambridge editors, and more satisfactory from a metrical point of view. Again, "the supposed Cambio was not acting as Baptista's servant, and moreover, had he been sent on such an errand, he would have 'flown on the wings of love' to perform it. We must suppose that Biondello apparently makes his exit, but really waits till the stage is clear for an interview with his disguised master."

V. i. 25. *'his father has come from Padua,'* so the Folios and Quartos; various changes have been proposed, *e.g.* *'to Padua,'* *'from Pisa,'* &c., but the Pedant means that he has been staying at Padua.

ALL'S WELL THAT ENDS WELL

I. i. 75-76.
> *'These great tears grace his remembrance more*
> *Than those I shed for him;'*

i.e. "the big and copious tears she then shed herself, which were caused in reality by Bertram's departure, though attributed by Lafeu and the Countess to the loss of her father; and from this misapprehension of theirs graced his remembrance more than those she actually shed for him."

I. i. 105-154. These lines are struck out by some editors; the Cambridge editors rightly call them 'a blot on the play'; they were probably "an interpolation, 'to tickle the ears of the groundlings.'" The opening words of the speech which follows are obscure, and the enumeration of 'the loves' looks like 'the nonsense of some foolish conceited player.' Hanmer proposed:—

> *'Not my virginity yet.—You're for the Court:*
> *There shall your master,'* &c.

I. ii. 54. *'He scatter'd not in ears, but grafted them,'*; *cp.* the Collect in the Liturgy: "Grant we beseech thee, Almighty God, that the words which we have heard this day with our outward ears may through thy grace be so grafted inwardly in our hearts, that they may bring forth the fruit of good living," &c.

I. ii. 56. *'this,'* so the Folio; Pope read *'Thus,'* possibly the right word here.

I. iii. 22. 'service is no heritage'; the idea seems to be that, 'if service is no blessing, children are'; Psalm cxxvii. 3 has been appropriately cited in connection with this expression:—"Lo, children are an heritage of the Lord."

I. iii. 48-49. 'Young Charbon the puritan and old Poysam the papist'; 'Charbon' possibly for 'Chair-bonne,' and 'Poysam' for 'Poisson,' alluding to the respective lenten fares of the Puritan and Papist (cp. the old French proverb, 'Jeune chair et viel poisson' = young flesh and old fish are the best).

I. iii. 104. '. . . queen of virgins'; Theobald inserted 'Dian no' before 'queen.'

II. i. 1, 2. 'lords' . . . 'lords'; probably the young noblemen are divided into two sections according as they intend to take service with the 'Florentines' or the 'Senoys' (cp. Note vi. Cambridge edition).

II. i. 12, 13. 'let higher Italy,—Those bated,' &c.; the passage is probably corrupt. 'Higher Italy' has been variously interpreted to mean (1) Upper Italy; (2) the side of Italy next to the Adriatic (but both Florence and Siena are on the other side); (3) Italy higher in rank and dignity than France; (4) the noblest of Italy, the worthiest among Italians. Johnson paraphrased as follows:—'Let upper Italy, where you are to exercise your valour, see that you come to gain honour, to the abatement, that is, to the disgrace and depression of those that have now lost their ancient military fame, and inherit but the fall of the last monarchy.' Schmidt proposed 'high' for 'higher': Coleridge 'hired': Hanmer 'bastards' for 'bated.' Knight took 'bated' to mean 'excepted,' Schmidt 'beaten down.'

II. i. 32-3. 'No sword worn but one to dance with'; alluding to the light swords worn for dancing.

II. i. 61. 'I'll fee'; Theobald's emendation. Folios, 'Ile see.'

II. i. 77. 'To give great Charlemain a pen in 's hand'; Charlemagne late in life attempted to learn to write.

II. i. 173-174.

'ne worse of worst extended,
With vilest torture let my life be ended';

So Folio 1; the other Folios read 'no' for 'ne.' Malone's 'nay' for 'ne' commends itself, though his explanation of 'extended' as 'my body being extended on the rack' seems weak: it is probably used here simply in the sense of 'meted out to me,' or merely used for the purpose of emphasising 'worse of worst.' A mass of conjectural emendations are recorded in the Cambridge edition of the play.

II. ii. 21-22. 'Tib's rush for Tom's forefinger'; 'Tib and Tom' were used like 'Jack and Jill'; Tib was a cant term for any low or vulgar woman. 'Rush rings' were sometimes used at mar-

riage ceremonies, especially where the marriages were somewhat doubtful (*cp.* Douce's *Illustrations,* p. 196).

II. iii. 1-39. Johnson changed the distribution of the speakers, so as to bring out 'the whole merriment of the scene,'
which, according to him, "consists in the pretensions of Parolles to knowledge and sentiments which he has not." Johnson
has been generally followed by modern editors. The Folio
arrangement has been kept in the Cambridge text.

II. iii. 24. '*a showing of a heavenly effect in an earthly actor*';
the title of some pamphlet is evidently ridiculed in these
words.

II. iii. 73. '*Imperial Love*'; Folio 1, '*imperiall loue*'; Folio 2,
'*imperiall Iove*'; Folio 3, '*impartiall Jove.*'

II. iii. 76. '*ames-ace,*' *i.e.* two aces; the lowest throw at dice;
one would expect it, from the context, to mean just the contrary, but Lafeu is probably making 'a comparison by contraries,'—'an ironical comparison,' used with humorous effect.
"One lauding a sweet-songed prima donna," aptly observed
Brinsley Nicholson, "says, I'd rather hear her than walk a
hundred miles with peas in my boots."

II. v. 26. '*end*'; the Folios have '*And*'; the correction, from
the Ellesmere copy of the first Folio, has been generally adopted.

II. v. 44-45. '*Have or will to deserve*'; Malone proposed '*have
qualities or will,*' &c.; Singer, '*wit or will*'; the later Folios omit
'*to,*' and read '*have, or will deserve*'; the reading in the text is
that of Folio 1.

III. i. 12-13.
'*That the great figure of a council frames
By self-unable motion*';
probably Clarke's explanation of these difficult lines is the
best:—"The reasons of our state I cannot give you, excepting
as an ordinary and uninitiated man, whom the august body
of a government-council creates with power unable of itself
to act, or with power incapable of acting of its own accord or
independently." Others make '*that*' the subject of '*frames,*' ex-
plaining '*motion*' as 'mental sight,' or 'intuition.'

III. ii. 8-9. '*sold*'; so Folios 3, 4; Folios 1, 2, '*hold*'; Harness
proposed '*holds a goodly manner for.*'

III. ii. 62. '*If thou engrossest all the griefs are thine*'; the omission of the relative is common in Shakespeare. Rowe unnecessarily altered the line to '*all the griefs as thine.*'

III. ii. 88. '*holds him much to have*'; so the Folios; Theobald
conjectured '*soils him much to have*'; others suggested '*hoves him
not much to have*'; '*fouls him much to have,*' &c. Rolfe's view of
the passage seems by far the most satisfactory:—"He has a deal
of that too-much, *i.e.* excess of vanity, which makes him fancy he
has many good qualities."

III. ii. 108. *'still-peering air'*; so Folio 1; Folio 2, *'still-piercing'*; probably an error for *'still-piecing,'* i.e. 'still-closing.' A passage in *The Wisdom of Solomon* has been appropriately compared, and may be the source of the thought:—*"As when an arrow is shot at a mark, it pareth the air, which immediately cometh together again, so that a man cannot know where it went through."*

III. v. 63. *'I write, good creature,'* so Folio 1; Folios 2, 3, 4, *'I right'*; Rowe, *'Ah! right good creature!'* The Globe edition, *'I warrant, good creature'*; Kinnear, *'I war'nt* (= warrant), *good creature'* (cp. *Hamlet*, I. ii. 242, Quarto 2, *'I war'nt'*).

III. vi. 34. *'John Drum's Entertainment'*; 'to give a person John Drum's Entertainment' probably meant to give him such an entertainment as the drum gets; hence 'to give a person a drumming,' to turn him forcibly out of your company. Theobald quotes the following from Holinshed's *Description of Ireland*:—"His porter, or none other officer, durst not, for both his ears, give the simplest man that resorted to his house, *Tom Drum his entertainment,* which is to hale a man in by the head, and thrust him out by both the shoulders." In Marston's interlude, *Jack Drum's Entertainment* (1601), Jack Drum is a servant who is constantly baffled in his knavish tricks.

IV. i. 38. *'Bajazet's mule'*; the allusion has not yet been explained; perhaps *'Bajazet's'* is a blunder on the part of Parolles for *'Balaam's.'*

IV. ii. 25. *'Jove's,'* probably substituted for the original *'God's,'* in obedience to the statute against profanity. Johnson conjectured *'Love's.'*

IV. ii. 36. *'Who then recover'*; the Folios read, *'who then recovers,'* changed unnecessarily by Pope to *'which then recover,'* but *'who'* is often used for 'an irrational antecedent personified,' though in this passage the antecedent may be *'of me'* implied in *'my'*; *'my sick desires'* = 'the sick desires of me'; in this latter case 'recovers' is the more common third person singular, instead of the first person after *'who.'*

IV. ii. 38. *'I see that men make rope's in such a scarre,'* the reading of Folios 1, 2; Folio 3, *'make ropes'*; Folio 4, *'make ropes . . . scar.'* This is one of the standing cruxes in the text of Shakespeare; some thirty emendations have been proposed for *'ropes'* and *'scarre,'* e.g. *'hopes . . . affairs'*; *'hopes . . . scenes'*; *'hopes . . . scare'*; *'slopes scarre'*: other suggestions are, *'may cope's . . . sorte'*; *'may rope's . . . snarle'*; *'may rope's . . . snare,'* &c. The apostrophe in the first and second Folios makes it almost certain that ' *'s'* stands for 'us.' Possibly *'make'* is used as an auxiliary; *'make rope's,'* would then mean 'do constrain, or ensnare us.' Or is *'make rope'* a compound verb? *'Scarre'* may be *'scare'* (i.e. 'fright'). The general sense seems to be, 'I see that men may reduce us to such a fright, that we'll forsake ourselves.'

IV. iii. 233. 'He will steal, sir, an egg out of a cloister,' i.e. 'anything, however trifling, from any place, however holy.'

IV. iii. 261. 'and a perpetual succession for it'; some such verb as 'grant' is to be supplied. Hanmer altered 'for it' to 'in it'; Kinnear conjectured 'free in perpetuity.'

IV. iv. 34. 'revives'; so the Folios; 'reviles,' 'invites,' 'requires' have been variously proposed; it is doubtful whether any change is necessary: 'Time,' says Helena, 'gives us fresh courage.'

IV. v. 35. 'an English name'; Folios 1, 2, 'maine'; Folio 3, 'main'; Folio 4, 'mean'; Rowe first suggested 'name'; the allusion is obviously to the Black Prince.

IV. v. 35-36. 'his fisnomy is more hotter'; Hanmer's proposal 'honour'd' for 'hotter' seems to be a most plausible emendation.

V. i. 6. 'Enter a Gentleman'; Folio 1 reads 'A gentle Astringer'; Folio 2, 'A gentle Astranger'; Folios 3, 4, 'A Gentleman a stranger.' 'Astringer' = a keeper of goshawks; the word occurs nowhere else in Shakespeare. There seems, however, no very particular reason for its omission in modern editions, though it is true that in the Folio the speeches given to 'the Astringer' all have the prefix 'Gent.'

V. ii. 1. 'Good Monsieur Lavache'; Folio 1, 'Lauatch'; Folio 2, 'Lavatch'; Folios 3, 4, 'Levatch'; Tollet's conjecture 'Lavache' has been generally adopted. Clark suggests that it may have been intended for Lavage, which, in familiar French, is used to express 'slop,' 'puddle,' 'washiness.' Something is to be said in favour of Jervis' proposed reading, 'Lapatch,' i.e. 'patch' = clown, with the prefix 'la' in imitation of 'Lafeu.'

V. ii. 22. 'Similes of comfort'; Theobald's certain emendation for the reading of the Folios, 'smiles of comfort.'

V. iii. 65, 66.
> 'Our own love waking cries to see what's done,
> While shameful hate sleeps out the afternoon.

Johnson conjectured 'slept' for 'sleeps,' i.e. 'love cries to see what was done while hatred slept, and suffered mischief to be done.' Mason proposed 'old' for 'own.' W. G. Clarke ingeniously emended 'shameful hate' into 'shame full late,' but the emendation destroys the antithesis between 'love' and 'hate.' It is best to leave the lines as they stand, though the words 'our own love' are somewhat doubtful: the general meaning is simple enough.

V. iii. 121. 'my fore-past proofs,' &c.; i.e. "the proofs which I have already had are sufficient to show that my fears were not vain and irrational. I have rather been hitherto more easy than sought, and have unreasonably had too little fear" (Johnson).

V. iii. 193. 'He blushes, and 'tis it'; Folios ' 'tis hit,' which has been variously explained as an Archaic form of 'it': as an error for ' 'tis his,' or 'is hit.' It seems unnecessary to alter the Folio;

''*tis hit*' can very well mean 'the blow has been well aimed, it has struck home,' 'it' being used impersonally.

V. iii. 214. '*Her infinite cunning, with her modern grace*'; Walker's certain emendation of the Folio reading '*her insuite comming*'; other suggestions have been made:—'*Her instant comity*' (Bubier); '*Her Jesuit cunning*' (Bulloch); '*Her own suit, coming*' (Perring).

Epil. 1. '*The King's a beggar*'; an allusion to the old story of 'The King and the Beggar' (*cp.* Percy's *Reliques*), often referred to by Shakespeare; *cp.* '*Is there not a ballad, boy, of the King and the Beggar?*' (*Love's Labour's Lost*, I. ii. 102-103); similarly *Richard II.*, V. iii. 79, 80:—

> '*Our scene is alter'd from a serious thing,*
> *And now chang'd to "The Beggar and the King."*'

TWELFTH NIGHT; OR, WHAT YOU WILL

I. i. 5. '*sound*'; so the Folios; Pope changed it to '*south*,' and editors have generally accepted this emendation, but it seems unnecessary: Grant White appropriately asks, "Did Pope, or the editors who have followed him, ever lie musing on the sward at the edge of a wood, and hear the low sweet hum of the summer air, as it kissed the coyly-shrinking wild flowers upon the banks, and passed on loaded with fragrance from the sweet salute?"

I. i. 22. '*like fell and cruel hounds*'; referring to the story of Actæon.

I. i. 38. '*all supplied, and filled*'; the comma after '*supplied*' is not in the Folio: its insertion simplifies the lines. Others leave the Folio reading, but bracket '*her sweet perfections*' in the next line; making them appositional to '*thrones.*'

I. ii. 14. '*Arion on the dolphin's back*'; the Folios misprint '*Orion*' for '*Arion.*'

I. iii. 64, 65. '*bring your hand to the buttery-bar and let it drink*'; "a proverbial phrase among Abigails, to ask at once for a kiss and a present" (Kenrick).

I. iii. 88. '*Then hadst thou had an excellent head of hair*'; Sir Toby evidently plays upon '*tongues*' and '*tongs*' (*i.e.* curling-tongs).

I. iii. 107. '*an old man*'; Theobald proposed to read '*a noble man,*' taking the allusion to be to Orsino. Clarke explains '*an old man*' as 'a man of experience'; "the word *old*," he adds, "gives precisely that absurd effect of refraining from competing in dancing, fencing, &c., with exactly the antagonist incapacitated by age over whom Sir Andrew might hope to prove his superiority."

I. iii. 125. *'That's sides and heart'*; Sir Andrew and Sir Toby are wrong in the parts assigned to Taurus in the old astrological figures of the human body. Taurus was supposed to govern the neck and throat.

I. iv. 3. *'three days'*; Mr. Daniel points out in his 'Time-Analysis' that this statement is inconsistent with the Duke's words in V. i. 102, *'Three months this youth hath tended upon me.'*

II. i. 15. *'Messaline'*; possibly an error for Mitylene, as Capell conjectured.

II. iii. 16. *'the picture of "we three"'*; "a common sign, in which two wooden heads are exhibited with this inscription under it, *'We three loggerheads be,'* the spectator being supposed to make the third" (Malone).

II. iii. 22-23. *'Pigrogromitus . . . of Queubus,'* &c. Mr. Swinburne sees in these 'freaks of nomenclature' the direct influence of Rabelais (*cp. A Study of Shakespeare,* pp. 155, 156).

II. iii. 37. *'O mistress mine,'* &c. "this tune is contained in both the editions of Morley's *Consort Lessons,* 1599 and 1611. It is also found in Queen Elizabeth's Virginal Book, arranged by Boyd. As it is to be found in print in 1599, it proves either that Shakespeare's *Twelfth Night* was written in or before that year, or that, in accordance with the then prevailing custom, *'O mistress mine,'* was an old song, introduced into the play" (Chappell's *Popular Music of the Olden Time*).

II. iii. 105. *'Out o' tune, sir: ye lie'*; Theobald proposed *'time, sir?'* which has been very generally adopted. The reading of the Folios may well stand without change. Sir Toby says to the Clown that he is out of tune and lies in declaring *'no, no, no, you dare not'* (*i.e.* dare not bid Malvolio go). Hence next words *'Art any more than a steward,'* addressed to Malvolio.

II. v. 35. *'the lady of the Strachy'*; this is one of the unsettled problems in Shakespeare. Hunter ingeniously suggested that Shakespeare ridicules, in the scene between the Clown, as Sir Topas, and Malvolio (IV. ii.), the exorcisms by Puritan ministers, in the case of a family named *Starchy* (1596-99), and that the difficult *Strachy* was a hint to the audience to expect subsequent allusion to the Starchy affair. Others suggest *'Strozzi,'* *'Stracci,'* *'Stratarch.'* Halliwell refers to a Russian word meaning lawyer or judge. The incident of a lady of high rank marrying her steward is the subject of Webster's *Duchess of Malfy.*

II. v. 59. *'with cars'*; so Folio 1; the later Folios, *'with cares'*; Johnson, *'with carts'*; many emendations have been proposed. Clarke defends the original reading, and compares *'A team of horse shall not pluck that from me'* (*Two Gentlemen,* III. i. 264, 265). Hanmer's suggestion *'by th' ears'* has been generally adopted.

II. v. 141-142. *'yellow stockings'*; these were much worn in

Shakespeare's time, and have still survived to our own day in the yellow stockings worn by the 'Blue Coat boys.'

III. i. 47. 'these,' *i.e.* these coins which Viola has given him.

III. i. 54. 'Cressida was a beggar'; 'according to the story Cressida finally became a leper and begged by the roadside.'

III. i. 62. 'And, like the haggard, check at every feather'; so the Folios; Johnson proposed 'not' for 'and,' and this reading has reasonably been adopted by most editors; 'to check' is "a term in falconry, applied to a hawk when she forsakes her proper game, and follows some other of inferior kind that crosses her in her flight"; the meaning therefore of the Folio reading would be 'that he must catch at every opportunity,' but this does not suit the context: the wise Clown must be discriminative; hence Johnson's 'not.'

III. i. 66. 'wise men, folly-fall'n, quite taint their wit'; Folio 1, 'wisemens folly falne'; Hanmer and Warburton, 'wise men's folly shown'; the text is Theobald's, and is generally adopted.

III. i. 120. 'a cypress, not a bosom, Hides my heart'; the force of these words has, it would seem, been missed; the point of the 'cypress' is not its blackness but its transparency. *Cp.* 'The Ballad of Robin Hood, Scarlet and John':

> "Cypress over her face,
> Through which her rose-like cheeks did blush
> All in a comely grace."

'Bosom' must, I think, be used in this passage in the sense of 'the bosom of the dress' which conceals the body. Olivia says, 'you can see my heart; a thin gauze as it were hides it, not a stomacher.'

III. ii. 23. 'sailed into the north,' &c.; perhaps this is a reference to the discovery of Northern Nova Zembla by the Dutchman Barenz in 1596. (*Cp.* C. H. Coote's paper on 'the new map,' l. 85. *New Shakespeare Society Publications,* 1878.)

III. ii. 59. 'youngest wren of nine'; Folio, 'mine,' emended by Theobald. The wren is said to lay nine or ten eggs at a time, and the last hatched nestling is usually the smallest of the whole brood.

III. ii. 71. 'the new map with the augmentation of the Indies'; no doubt a reference to the map which Hallam, in his *Literature of Europe,* calls 'the best map of the 16th century': it is found in the first edition of Hakluyt's *Voyages* (1589), but as it records discoveries made at least seven years later, it was in all probability a separate map, well known at the time, and made so as to be inserted in Hakluyt: the author was probably Mr. Emmerie Mollineux, who was also the first Englishman to make a terrestrial globe. It is noteworthy that the map shows a marked development of the geography of India proper, &c. (*Cp. Transactions of New Shakespeare Society,* 1877-79.)

III. iii. 15. 'And thanks; and ever . . . oft good turns.' The
Cambridge editors hold that some word has dropped out between
'ever' and 'oft.' Many emendations have been proposed; perhaps
the simplest reading is that of the Old spelling Shakespeare:—

'And thanks, and, ever oft, good turns . . .'

'ever oft' in the sense of 'with perpetual frequency.' Theobald
proposed:—

'And thanks, and ever thanks; and oft good turns.'

IV. i. 12-14. 'I am afraid this great lubber, the world, will prove
a cockney'; so the Folios; the lines evidently mean "I am afraid
affectation and foppery will overspread the world" (Johnson);
it has been proposed to change 'world' into 'word' (i.e. with reference to 'vent'): others read 'this great lubberly world'; Knight
explains that the words are spoken aside, and mean, 'I am afraid
the world will prove this great lubber (Sebastian) a cockney.'
This seems very strained, and probably the simplest reading of
the passage is the best.

IV. ii. 12-13. 'the old hermit of Prague'; Douce points out that
the allusion is "not to the celebrated heresiarch, Jerome of
Prague, but another of that name, born likewise at Prague, and
called the hermit of Camaldoli in Tuscany."

IV. ii. 37. 'clearstories'; Folio 1, 'cleere stores'; Folio 2, 'cleare
stones'; the reading adopted is Blakeway's conjecture in Boswell:
'clerestory' is the name given to the windows above the arches of
the nave of a Gothic church.

IV. ii. 127. 'goodman devil'; Folio 1, 'good man diuell'; Rowe's
'goodman Drivel,' seems the most plausible emendation, if any
is necessary; Folio 2 reads 'good man Direll.'

V. i. 108. 'My soul the faithfull'st offerings hath breathed out';
the Folios 'have,' corrected by Capell, but probably Shakespeare's own reading; the plural for the singular, owing to the
plural object ('faithfull'st offerings') preceding the verb.

V. i. 192. 'a passy measures pavin'; Folio 1, 'panyn'; Folio 2,
'Pavin'; various emendations have been suggested, but there is
little doubt that the reading in the text is the correct one. 'Passy
measures' is a corruption of the Italian 'passamezzo,' which word
Florio explains as 'a passa-measure in dancing, a cinque pace'; it
was a slow dance, differing little from the action of walking.
'Pavin' was a grave Spanish dance. According to Halliwell, the
passy measures pavin is described as follows in an early MS. list
of dances:—"The passinge measure Pavyon—2 singles and a
double forward, and 2 singles syde.—Reprince back." Sir Toby
means, therefore, that 'the surgeon is a rogue and a grave solemn
coxcomb.'

V. i. 351. 'against.' Tyrwhitt's conjecture 'in' has a good deal
in its favour; 'against' may have been caught from line 368.

THE WINTER'S TALE

I. ii. 44. '*What lady she her lord*'; '*she*' has been variously interpreted; Collier and Dyce proposed '*should*,' destroying the beauty of the line; Schmidt makes the phrase '*lady she*' = 'a woman that is a lady,' taking '*she*' ≅ 'woman'; others print '*lady-she*'; perhaps the word may be best explained as the pleonastic pronoun so common in popular poetry; the rhythm seems to favour this latter view.

I. ii. 70. '*The doctrine of ill-doing, nor dream'd*'; so Folio 1; the later Folios, '*no nor dream'd*'; Spedding, '*neither dream'd*'; perhaps '*doctrine*' should be read as a trisyllable; a harsh line would, however, result; and the reading of the later Folios has much to commend it.

I. ii. 133-134. '*false As o'er-dyed blacks*'; Folios 1, 2, 3, '*o're dy'd*'; the words have been variously interpreted to mean 'fabrics dyed over with some other colour,' or, 'dyed too much'; Steevens saw in the phrase an allusion to the fact that black will receive no other hue without discovering itself through it; the passage may simply contain the idea, 'the blacker the garb, the less sincere the mourning.'

I. ii. 156. '*methoughts*'; so the Folios in this and other places; this erroneous form was probably due to '*methinks*'; it is noteworthy that the correct '*methought*' occurs a few lines below.

I. ii. 285. '*that*,' *i.e.* 'that of which you accuse her.'

II. i. 11. '*Who taught you this?*' Rowe's emendation of the reading of Folio 1, '*taught 'this*' (with an apostrophe before '*this*,' indicating an elision); the later Folios, '*taught this*.'

II. i. 24. '*A sad tale's best for winter*,' hence the title of the play.

II. i. 38-39. '*There may be in the cup A spider*,' &c.; it was formerly believed that spiders were venomous.

II. i. 133-134. '*I'll keep my stables where I lodge my wife*'; *i.e.* 'I'll degrade my wife's chamber into a stable or dog kennel.'

II. i. 142. '*I would land-damn him*'; so the Folios; '*land-damm*,' '*laudanum*,' '*lamback*,' (*i.e.* 'ebat'), '*half-damn*,' '*live-damn*,' '*landan* (*lantan, rantan*),' '*land-dam*,' are among the various emendations proposed; Schmidt suggests '*I would—Lord, damn him!*' In all probability the reading of the Folios should not be departed from, and it seems likely that Antigonus, having in the previous phrase used the word '*damn'd*,' here uses 'land-damn,' as a sort of grim quibble for 'landan,'—a Gloucestershire word still in use "to express the punishment meted out to slanderers and adulterers by rustics traversing from house to house along the country side, blowing trumpets and beating drums or pans and kettles; when an audience was assembled the delinquents' names were proclaimed, and they were said to be landanned" (*cp.* Halliwell's *Dictionary of Archaic Words,* and *Notes and Queries* iii. 464): *landan, lantan, rantan,* were variants of the same word, which was probably imitative in its origin.

II. i. 152. '*As you feel doing thus,*' probably = my doing thus to you (*i.e.* touching him, or perhaps pulling his beard); '*the instruments that feel*' = my fingers.

II. iii. 177. '*to it own protection,*' so Folios 1, 2; Folios 3, 4, '*its*'; the old possessive form '*it,*' still in use in Lancashire, occurs again in this play (III. ii. 101); there are some dozen instances elsewhere: '*it own,*' may be regarded as a sort of idiomatic compound, the combination helping to maintain the archaism; '*its*' (Folio, *it 's*) *own,*' to be found in Act I. ii. 266 is said to be the only instance of its use in Shakespeare.

III. iii. 112. '*You 're a made old man*'; Theobald's emendation of the Folio reading '*mad,*' confirmed by a passage in Shakespeare's original:—"The goodman desired her to be quiet . . . if she could hold her peace they were made for ever."

IV. i. 15. '*to it,*' *i.e.* 'the present.'

IV. i. 4. '*It is fifteen years since,*' &c.; changed by Hanmer to '*sixteen,*' the number intended by Shakespeare.

IV. ii. 23, 24. '*when the kite builds, look to lesser linen*'; alluding to this bird's habit of carrying off small linen garments hung out to dry; Autolycus preferred more substantial prey.

IV. ii. 49. '*I' the name of me——*'; probably, as has been suggested, the Clown's exclamation of '*Mercy*' is interrupted by Autolycus.

IV. iii. 243. '*clamour your tongues*'; Hanmer's emendation '*charm*' has been generally adopted, but '*clamour*' is almost certainly correct (Taylor, the Water-Poet, wrote '*Clamour the promulgation of your tongues*'); '*clamour*' or rather '*clammer,*' is probably radically identical with '*clamber,*' the Scandinavian original of which '*klambra*' = 'to pinch closely together, to clamp.'

IV. iii. 269. '*another ballad of a fish*'; *cp. e.g.* "A strange report of a monstrous fish that appeared in the form of a woman from her waist upward, seen in the sea"; entered in the Stationers' Registers in 1604.

IV. iii. 428. '*Far than Deucalion off*'; '*far*' = 'farther'; the Folios all correctly read '*farre,*' *i.e.* the old form of the comparative of '*far.*'

IV. iii. 578. '*i' the rear o' her birth*'; Folios 1, 2, 3, '*'our birth*'; Rowe first emended the line as in the text, though in his second edition he read '*o' our*' for '*o' her.*'

IV. iii. 586. '*appear,*' *i.e.* appear so (like Bohemia's son).

IV. iii. 706. *'at palace'*; Folio 1, *'at 'Pallace'*; probably the apostrophe indicates "the omission of the article or its absorption in rapid pronunciation."

V. ii. 51. *'weather-bitten conduit'*; changed to *'weather-beaten'* in Folio 3; but *'weather-bitten'* is undoubtedly the correct form (*cp.* Skeat's *Etymological Dictionary*): *conduits* were frequently in the form of human figures.

V. ii. 90-91. *'that rare Italian master'*; Giulio Pippi, known as 'Giulio Romano,' was born in 1492, and died in 1546; his fame as a painter was widespread; Shakespeare, taking him as 'a type of artistic excellence,' makes him a sculptor; it must, however, be remembered that the statue was a 'painted picture.' Much has been made of this reference by the advocates of Shakespeare's alleged Italian journeys (*cp.* Elze's *Essays on Shakespeare*).

GLOSSARY

a', he. L.L.L. v. 2

abate, omit. L.L.L. v. 2; diminish. M.N.D. iii. 2

abode, delay. M. of V. ii. 6

abridgment, pastime, entertainment. M.N.D. v. 1

abstract, inventory. M.W. iv. 2

abuse, deceive. Tp. v. 1; etc.; ill-usage. M.W. v. 3; imposture. M. for M. v. 1

aby, suffer for. M.N.D. iii. 2

accountant, liable to give account. M. for M. ii. 4

adamant, diamond, loadstone. M.N.D. ii. 1

addition, title. M. W. ii. 2 A.W. ii. 3

address, prepare. M. W. iii. 5, &c.

admittance, admissibility. M. W. ii. 2; acceptance, sanction. M.W. iii. 3

adoptious christendoms, &c., christenings of adopted children for whom Cupid stands godfather. A.W. i. 2

advance, raise. Tp. i. 2; iv. 1

affied, betrothed. T. of S. iv. 4

affront, confront. W.T. v. 1

aglet-baby, doll decked with tagged laces. T. of S. i. 2

a-hold,close to the wind. Tp.i. 1

aim, guess, conjecture. Two G. iii. 1; T. of S. ii. 1

aim, cry, encourage, a term from archery. M.W. iii. 2

a-life, on my life. W.T. iv. 3

all-building, being the ground and foundation of all; or ? all-binding. M. for M. ii. 4

all hid, game of hide and seek. L.L.L. iv. 3

allicholy, allycholly, melancholy. Two G. iv. 2; M. W. i. 4

alligant, elegant. M.W. ii. 2

allottery, portion. As. i. 1

allow the wind, stand aside. A. W. v. 2

amain, at full speed. Tp. iv. 1; C. of E. i. 1

ames-ace, both aces, the lowest possible throw in dice. A. W. ii. 3

amport, dejected. T. of S. iv. 3

ample, well. A.W. iii. 5

an, if. Tp. ii. 1; &c.

anatomize, expose. As. i. 1; A. W. iv. 3

anatomy, walking skeleton. C. of E. v. 1

ancientry, elders. W.T. iii. 3; old-fashioned style. M.A. ii. 1

angel, a gold coin. M.W. i. 3; C. of E. iv. 3; M.A. ii. 3

answer, thrust after a parry. Tw. N. iii. 4

anthropophaginian, cannibal. M.W. iv. 5

ape-bearer, one who leads an ape. W.T. iv. 2

apes in hell, to lead, fancied consequence of dying a spinster. M.A. ii. 1; T. of S. ii. 1

appeached, give accusatory evidence. A.W. i. 3

apple of her eye, upon the, in obedience to her glance. L.L. L. v. 2

appliances, subservience. M. for M. iii. 1

apprehensive, fantastic. A.W. i. 2

approof, approval. M. for M. ii. 4; proof. A.W. i. 2; ii. 5

apricocks, apricots. M.N.D. iii. 1

araise, raise from the dead. A. W. ii. 1

arbitrement, decision. Tw.N. iii. 4

argosy, merchant vessel. M. of V. i. 1; T. of S. ii. 1

argument, subject for satire. M. A. i. 1; M.N.D. iii. 2; proof, token. M.A. ii. 3; L.L.L. i. 2; Tw.N. iii. 2

armigero, esquire. M.W. i. 1

armipotent, mighty in arms. L. L.L. v. 2; A.W. iv. 3

arras, tapestry placed round the walls of apartments, often at such a distance from them as to allow of people being concealed between. M.W. iii. 3; M.A. i. 3; T. of S. ii. 1

artificial, skilful. M.N.D. iii. 2

artist, medical practitioner. A. W. ii. 3

arts-man, scholar. L.L.L. v. 1

aspersion, shower, or spray. Tp. iv. 1

aspicious, blunder for suspicious. M.A. iii. 5

assay, accost, assail. M.W. ii. 1; M. for M. i. 2; test. M. for M. iii. 1; attempt. As. i. 3; make trial of. A.W. iii. 7

assured, betrothed. C. of E. iii. 2

Ates, mischiefs. L.L.L. v. 2

atomy, atom, mote. As. iii. 2; iii. 5

atone, are at one. As. v. 4

attaint, dishonour. C. of E. iii.2

attorney, duly appointed substitute. As. iv. 1

attorneyed, engaged as an attorney. M. for M. v. 1; performed by proxy. W.T. i. 1

aunt, old woman, gossip. M.N. D. ii. 1; loose woman. W.T. iv. 2

avised, advised. M.W. i. 1

avoid, begone. Tp. iv. 1; W.T. i.2

awful, law-abiding. Two G. iv. 1; awe-inspiring. T. of S. v. 2

backare, stand back, give place. T. of S. ii. 1

back-trick, caper backwards. Tw.N. i. 3

baffle, disgrace a knight with infamy. Tw.N. ii. 5; hoodwink. Tw.N. v. 1

bald, destitute of meaning. C. of E. ii. 2

balk, let slip, not forthcoming. Tw.N. iii. 2

balk logic, bandy words. T. of S. i. 1

Banbury cheese, nothing but paring. M.W. i. 1

band, bond. C. of E. iv. 2; A. W. iv. 2

bane, death. M. for M. i. 2

bare, shave. M. for M. iv. 2; A. W. iv. 1

barful, full of hindrances. Tw. N. i. 4

barm, froth, yeast. M.N.D. ii. 1

barn, barne, bairn, child. M.A. iii. 4; A.W. i. 3; W.T. iii. 3

barnacle, species of wild goose. Tp. iv. 1

base, bid the, challenge to a chase in the game of prisoners' base. Two G. i. 2

basilisk, fabulous serpent supposed to kill by its glance. W. T. i. 2

basta, enough. T. of S. i. 1

bastard, a kind of sweet wine. M. for M. iii. 2

bate, blunt with use. L.L.L. i. 1; except. M.N.D. i. 1; reduce. M. of V. iii. 3; flap the wing. T. of S. iv. 1

bat-fowling, catching birds by night, when at roost. Tp. ii. 1

batler, probably a heavy wooden implement for beating clothes in the wash. As. ii. 4

bawbling, paltry. Tw.N. v. 1

bawcock, fine fellow. Tw.N. iii. 4; W.T. i. 2

beadsman, one who prays for another. Two G. i. 1

beard, prickles on the ears of corn. M.N.D. ii. i

bearing-cloth, cloth in which a child was carried to be christened. W.T. iii. 3

bear in hand, keep in expectation. M. for M. i. 4; M.A. iv. 1; T. of S. iv. 2

bear up, take your course. Tp. iii. 2

beating in, puzzling. Tp. i. 2

beating on, thinking persistently. Tp. v. 1

become, make becoming. C. of E. iii. 2

bed-swerver, adulteress. W.T. ii. 1

beg, apply for the custody of a minor or an idiot; hence, to set down as a fool. L.L.L. v.2

being, since. M.A. iv. 1

be-mete, measure. T. of S. iv. 3

bemoiled, bemired. T. of S. iv.1

benched, raised to authority. W.T. i. 2

bent, hold the, keep the passion fresh. Tw.N. ii. 4

ben venuto, welcome. L.L.L. iv. 2; T. of S. i. 2

Bergomask, rustic dance from Bergamo. M.N.D. v. 1

Bermoothes, Bermudas. Tp. i.2

beshrew, curse, with weakened force, as 'plague on.' Two G. i. 1; &c.

bestow, acquit. Two G. iii. 1; As. iv. 3; settle or give in marriage. As. v. 4; T. of S. i. 1; iv. 4

bestraught, distracted. T. of S. Ind. 2

beteem, accord, grant. M.N.D. i. 1

betid, befallen. Tp. i. 2

bias, preponderant tendency. L.L.L. iv. 2; Tw.N. v. 1; weight on one side of a bowl which affects its direction. T. of S. iv. 5

Biddy, a fowl. Tw.N. iii. 4

bilbo, a sword noted for the temper and elasticity of its blade. M.W. i. 1; iii. 5

bill, placard. M.A. i. 1; halberd. M.A. iii. 3; bonds. M.A. iii. 3

billets, small logs. M. for M. iv. 3

birdbolt, blunt-headed arrow. M.A. i. 1; L.L.L. iv. 3; Tw.N. i. 5

birding, bird-catching, fowling. M.W. iii. 3; iv. 2

bis coctus, twice cooked. L.L.L. iv. 2

black, dark-complexioned. M.A. iii. 1; black fabric. W.T. i. 2

Black-Monday, a name for Easter Monday. M. of V. ii. 5

blank, white spot in the centre of the target. W.T. ii. 3

blazon, description (heraldry). M.A. ii. 1; Tw.N. i. 5

blench, swerve, start aside. M. for M. v. 5; W.T. i. 2

bless the mark, phrase used as apology after mentioning something horrible or indecent. Two. G. iv. 4

blow, fill with eggs. Tp. iii. 1; blossom, bloom. Two G. i. 1; &c.; inflate with vanity. Tw. N. ii. 5

blown, fly-blown, filled with eggs. L.L.L. v. 2

blue eye, a dark circle round the eye. Tp. i. 2; As. iii. 2

board, accost, make advances to, woo. M.W. ii. 1; &c.

bob, a jest, scoff. As. ii. 7

bodykins, God's body, an oath. M.W. ii. 3

boggle, take alarm. A.W. v. 3

bold-beating, brow-beating. M.W. ii. 2

bolt or shaft of it, make, risk making something or other out of it; make the venture. M.W. iii. 4

bombard, leather bottle or jug for liquor. Tp. ii. 2

bombast, padding used to stuff out garments. L.L.L. v. 2

boot, profit, avail. Two G. i. 1; &c.

boot, grace to, God help us. W. T. i. 2

boot-hose, overstocking which covered the leg like a jackboot. T. of S. iii. 2

boots, torture of the boots. Two G. i. 1

bosky, bushy. Tp. iv. 1

bossed, studded. T. of S. ii. 1

bottle, bundle. M.N.D. iv. 1

bottom, wind as a skein. Two G. iii. 2; extent. M. for M. i. 1; vessel. M. of V. i. 1; Tw.N. v. 1; dell. As. iv. 3; ball. T. of S. iv. 3

bouncing, imperious. M.N.D. ii. 1

bourn, boundary. Tp. ii. 1; W. T. i. 2

bowget, budget, wallet. W.T. iv. 2

bow-hand, left hand. L.L.L. iv. 1

brabble, brawl. Tw.N. v. 1

brach, bitch hound. T. of S. Ind. 1

braid, deceitful. A.W. iv. 2

brake, thicket. M.N.D. ii. 1

bravery, finery. M. for M. i. 3;
As. ii. 7; T. of S. iv. 3

brawl, French dance. L.L.L.
iii. 1

breach of the sea, surf. Tw.N.
ii. 1

break up, carve. L.L.L. iv. 1;
open. M. of V. ii. 4

breathe, exercise. A.W. ii. 3

breathed, in good wind. L.L.L.
v. 2; T. of S. Ind. 2; in full display of strength. As. i. 2

breeching, subject to the birch;
T. of S. iii. 1

breed-bate, mischief-maker.
M.W. i. 4

bribed buck, stolen deer. M.
W. v. 5

brief, list. M.N.D. v. 1; in brief.
As. iv. 3; contract. A.W. ii. 3;
summary. A.W. v. 3

bring out, put out, disconcert.
L.L.L. v. 2; As. iii. 2

bring to try, lay a ship with her
side close to the wind. Tp. i. 1

broach, stab. M.N.D. v. 1

brock, badger, a term of contempt. Tw.N. ii. 5

broke, negotiate. A.W. iii. 5

broken, fallen out. Two G. ii. 5;
with teeth missing. A.W. ii. 3

broken music, arranged for different instruments; part or
concerted music. As. i. 2

broker, go-between. Two G. i.2

Brownist, Independent (sect
founded by Robert Brown, *c.*
1581). Tw.N. iii. 2

buck, with reference to the
horns. M.W. iii. 3

buck-basket, washing-basket.
M.W. iii. 3; &c.

bucking, washing linen with
lye. M.W. iii. 3

buckler, shield, defend. T. of
S. iii. 2

bucklers, give the, own oneself beaten. M.A. v. 2

buck of the first head, buck of
the fifth year. L.L.L. iv. 2

bug, bug-bear. T. of S. i. 2;
W.T. iii. 2

bugle, black glass bead. As. iii.
5; W.T. iv. 3

bully, term of familiarity and
endearment. M.W. i. 3; ii. 3;
M.N.D. iii. 1

bully-rook, boon companion.
M.W. i. 3; ii. 1

bum-baily, bailiff. Tw.N. iii.
4

bush, a bush of ivy, used as a
vintner's sign. As. Epil. 3

buttery, place for storing liquor
or provisions. T. of S. Ind. i

buttonhole lower, a, without
ceremony. L.L.L. v. 2

buttons, 'tis in his, he is sure to
succeed. M.W. iii. 2

butt-shaft, blunt arrow used for
shooting at the butt. L.L.L. i.
2

by'r lakin, by our Lady. Tp. iii.
3; M.N.D. iii. 1

caddis, worsted tape used for
garters. W.T. iv. 3

caitiff, despicable wretch. M.
for M. v. 1; A.W. iii. 2

cake is dough, project has
failed of success. T. of S. i. 1;
v. 1

callat, scold. W.T. ii. 3

can, can make. Tp. iv. 1

canary, light sweet wine from
the Canary Islands. M.W. iii.
2; Tw.N. i. 3; lively Spanish
dance. A.W. ii. 1; dance the
canary. L.L.L. iii. 1; blunder
for quandary. M.W. ii. 2

candied, covered with hoar-
frost. Tp. ii. 1

canker, dog-rose. M.A. i. 3; worm. M.N.D. ii. 2

can't no other, is there no way. A.W. i. 3

canton, song. Tw.N. i. 5

canzonet, short song. L.L.L. iv. 2

capable, susceptible. As. iii. 5; A.W. i. 1

caparison, clothing. W.T. iv. 2

capon, type of dullness. C. of E. iii. 1; love-letter. L.L.L. iv. 1

capriccio, whim. A.W. ii. 3

captious, capacious. A.W. i. 3

carack, large ship of burden. C. of E. iii. 2

carbonado, score across for broiling. A.W. iv. 5; W.T. iv. 3

cardecu, quart d'écu, old French coin, worth about 2s. 1½d. A.W. iv. 3; v. 2

cardinally, blunder for 'carnally.' M. for M. ii. 1

card-maker, one who makes cards for combing wool. T. of S. Ind. 2

card of ten, face it with a, put on a bold front. T. of S. ii. 1

Carduus Benedictus, holy thistle. M.A. iii. 4

career, careire, short gallop at full speed. M.W. i. 1; M.A. v. 1; L.L.L. v. 2

carkanet, a jewelled necklace. C. of E. iii. 1

carlot, churl, peasant. As. iii. 5

carpet, table-cloth. T. of S. iv. 1

carpet consideration, for services in the Court. Tw.N. iii. 4

carpet-monger, one who frequents ladies' boudoirs or carpeted chambers. M.A. v. 2

carriage, burden. Tp. v. 1; bearing. C. of E. iii. 2; M.A. i. 3; management. W.T. iii. 1

cart, punishment akin to the ducking-stool. T. of S. i. 1

carve, ? to use great courtesy and affability. M.W. i. 3; L.L.L. v. 2

case, condition. Tp. iii. 2; to strip off the case or skin. A.W. iii. 6; skin, hide. Tw.N. v.1

cassock, a military cloak. A.W. iv. 3

cast, thrown up; with a play upon the sense of assigning parts to actors. Tp. ii. 1; emptied. M. for M. iii. 1; cast-off. As. iii. 4

Castiliano vulgo, nonsense phrase. Tw.N. i. 3

Cataian, thief, scoundrel, blackguard. M.W. ii. 1; Tw. N. ii. 3

catch, part song. Tp. iii. 2; Tw. N. ii. 3

cater-cousins, good friends. M. of V. ii. 2

cates, dainties. C. of E. iii. 1

caudle, gruel. L.L.L. iv. 3

centre, the earth, as supposed centre of universe. W.T. ii. 1

cerecloth, winding-sheet. M. of V. ii. 7

cesse, cease. A.W. v. 3

chairs of order, seats of the knights of an order. M.W. v.5

Cham, Great, Emperor of China, or Khan of Tartary. M. A. ii. 1

champian, open country. Tw. N. ii. 5

change, interchange. A.W. iii. 2; W.T. i. 2

chape, mounting of a scabbard. T. of S. iii. 2; A.W. iv. 3

charact, mark, stamp. M. for M. v. 1

character, write. Two G. ii. 7; As. iii. 2; writing. M. for M. i. 1; W.T. v. 2

charactery, expression of thought by symbols. M.W. v. 5

charge, put to expense. M.W. ii. 2; entrust. C. of E. iii. 1; cost, expense. M. of V. iv. 1; W.T. iv. 3

chargeful, expensive. C. of E. iv. 1

charge-house, school. L.L.L. v. 1

chariness, scrupulous integrity. M.W. ii. 1

cheapen, bargain for. M.A. ii. 3

'cheator, escheator, an officer who collected fines due to the Exchequer. M.W. i. 3

check, restraint. M.W. iii. 4; austere rule. T. of S. i. 1; to forsake the 'quarry' and fly at any chance bird. Tw.N. ii. 5; iii. 1

cherry-pit, game with cherry-stones. Tw.N. iii. 4

cheveril, kid-leather, very flexible. Tw.N. iii. 1

childing, fruitful. M.N.D. ii. 1

chirurgeonly, surgeon-like. Tp. ii. 1

chough, chatterer. Tp. ii. 1; bird of the crow family. M.N.D. iii. 2

chuck, term of endearment. L.L.L. v. 1; Tw.N. iii. 4

cicatrice, scar-like mark. As.iii. 5; A.W. ii. 1

cinque-pace, lively dance. M.A. ii. 1

circum circa, round and round. L.L.L. v. 1

circummured, walled round. M. for M. iv. 1

cittern-head, term of contempt, with ref. to the grotesquely carved head of a cittern or guitar. L.L.L. v. 2

civil, orderly. Two G. v. 4; grave. As. iii. 2; Tw.N. iii. 4; courteous. Tw.N. i. 4

civil doctor, doctor of civil law. M. of V. v. 1

clack-dish, wooden alms-dish with a lid, clacked by beggars to attract attention. M. for M. iii. 2

clamour, silence. W.T. iv. 3

clap, strike hands on concluding a bargain. W.T. i. 2

clapped up, concluded hastily. T. of S. ii. 1

clapper-claw, thrash. M.W. ii.3

claw, flatter. M.A. i. 3; L.L.L. iv. 2

clepe, call. L.L.L. v. 1

clew, ball of thread. A.W. i. 3

climate, sojourn. W.T. v. 1

clipping, embracing. W.T. v. 2

clodpole, blockhead. Tw.N. iii. 4

cloistress, nun. Tw.N. i. 1

clout, mark for archers. L.L.L. iv. 1

cock, perversion of 'God.' T. of S. iv. 1; woodcock (i.e. fool). W.T. iv. 2

'cock and pie, by', an asseveration, meaning possibly 'cock,' God, and 'pie,' the ordinal of the R.C. Church. M.W. i. 1

cockatrice, serpent, said to kill by its mere glance. Tw.N. iii. 4

cockled, furnished with a shell. L.L.L. iv. 3

cockney, petted child. Tw.N. iv. 1

cod, peascod. As. ii. 4

codling, half-grown apple. Tw.N. i. 5

cog, deceive, wheedle. M.W. iii. 1; &c.

coil, disturbance, confusion, ado. Tp. i. 2; &c.

collied, murky. M.N.D. i. 1

collop, piece of flesh. W.T. i. 2

colour, ensign. M.W. iii. 4; pretext. L.L.L. iv. 2; W.T. iv. 3; kind. As. i. 2

colourable, specious, plausible. L.L.L. iv. 2

colt, young or inexperienced person. M. of V. i. 2

combinate, betrothed. M. for M. iii. 1

come off, pay, disburse. M.W. iv. 3

comfect, sugar-plum. M.A. iv. 1

comfortable, of good comfort. As. ii. 6; comforting. A.W. i. 1

coming-in, income. M. of V. ii. 2

coming-on, complaisant. As. iv. 1

commerce, conversation. Tw. N. iii. 4

commixture, complexion. L.L. L. v. 2

commodity, advantage, interest. M. of V. iii. 3; W.T. iii. 2; parcel, quantity of wares. Tw. N. iii. 1

commodity of brown paper, a parcel of goods sold on credit by a usurer to a needy person, who immediately raised some cash by reselling them at a lower price, generally to the usurer himself. M. for M. iv. 3

commoner, prostitute. A.W. v. 3

commonty, blunder for 'comedy.' T. of S. Ind. 2

compact, leagued. M. for M. v. 1

companion, used as term of contempt. M.W. iii. 1; &c.

compass, accomplish. Two G. iv. 2; gain possession of. W.T. iv. 2

compassed, rounded, curved. T. of S. iv. 3

competitor, associate. Two G. ii. 6; companion. L.L.L. ii. 1; confederate. Tw.N. iv. 2

complements, accomplishments. L.L.L. i. 1

compt, account. A.W. v. 3

compter, counter. W.T. iv. 2

comptible, sensitive. Tw.N. i. 5

conceit, estimation, opinion. Two G. iii. 2; &c.; understanding. C. of E. iii. 2; a fancy article. M.N.D. i. 1; idea. W.T. iii. 2

conceited, imagined. Tw.N. iii. 4; witty, clever. W.T. iv. 3

conceitless, thoughtless. Two G. iv. 2

concern, befit. M.N.D. i. 1; is of importance. W.T. iii. 2

conclusions passed the careires, ? the end came very swiftly. M.W. i. 1

concolinel, a nonsense word. L.L.L. iii. 1

concupiscible, vehemently desirous. M. for M. v. 1

condition, social position, rank. Tp. iii. 1; character, behaviour. M.A. iii. 2; M. of V. i. 2; A.W. iv. 3

confidence, confidential communication. M.W. i. 4; M.A. iii. 5

confixed, fixed firmly, fastened. M. for M. v. 1

confound, destroy, ruin. C. of E. i. 2; M. of V. iii. 2

congee, pay one's respects at leaving. A.W. iv. 3

consort, company of musicians. Two G. iii. 2; fellowship. Two G. iv. 1; keep company with. C. of E. i. 2; L.L.L. ii. 1; M.N.D. iii. 2

constant, steady. Tp. ii. 2; self-possessed, M. of V. iii. 2; uniform. As. iii. 5; consistent. Tw.N. iv. 2

constantly, confidently. M. for M. iv. 1

conster, construe, explain. Tw. N. iii. 1

contempts, blunder for 'contents.' L.L.L. i. 1

continent, that which contains. M.N.D. ii. 1; that which comprises. M. of V. iii. 2

continue, let live. M. for M. iv. 3

contrive, conspire. M. of V. iv. 1; pass the time. T. of S. i. 2

control, to call to account. Tp. i. 2

convenience, propriety. A.W. iii. 2

convents, is convenient. Tw.N. v. 1

convented, summoned. M. for M. v. 1

conversation, behaviour. M.W. ii. 1; intercourse. A.W. i. 3

convertite, convert. As. v. 4

conveyance, *impossible*, incredible dexterity. M.A. ii. 1

cony, rabbit. As. iii. 2

cony-catch, cheat, trick. M.W. i. 1; &c.

copatain hat, high-crowned hat. T. of S. v. 1

cope, requite. M. of V. iv. 1; come into contact with. As. ii. 1; W.T. iv. 3

copulatives, persons about to be coupled in marriage. As. v. 4

coragio, courage. Tp. v. 1; A. W. ii. 5

coram, blunder for 'quorum.' M.W. i. 1

coranto, kind of dance. A.W. ii. 3; Tw.N. i. 3

cormorant, ravenous. L.L.L. i. 1

cornuto, cuckold. M.W. iii. 5

corollary, surplus, supernumerary. Tp. iv. 1

correspondent, responsive. Tp. i. 2

costard, apple of large size, head. M.W. iii. 1

Cotsall, Cotswold. M.W. i. 1

countenance, feigned appearance. M. for M. v. 1; patronage. As. i. 1; honour. T. of S. iv. 1

counter, following the scent in the reverse direction. C. of E. iv. 2; worthless wager. As. ii.7

Counter-gate, gate of prison attached to city court. M.W. iii. 3

counterpoint, quilt, counterpane. T. of S. ii. 1

county, count. M.A. iv. 1; &c.

couplement, couple, pair. L.L.L. v. 2

courses, points of the compass. Tp. i. 1

cousin, nephew. M.A. i. 2; niece. As. i. 3; Tw.N. i. 3; uncle. Tw.N. i. 5

covent, convent. M. for M. iv. 3

cowl-staff, staff thrust through the handles of a tub to carry it. M.W. iii. 3

Cox my passion, an oath, 'God's my passion.' A.W. v. 2

coy, caress. M.N.D. iv. 1

coystril, knave, base fellow. Tw.N. i. 3

cozen, cozener, cheat. M.W. iv. 5

cozier, cobbler. Tw.N. ii. 3

crack, boast. L.L.L. iv. 3; flaw. W.T. i. 2

crack-hemp, gallows'-bird. T. of S. v. 1

crazed, impaired, unsound. M. N.D. i. 1

cream, form a scum on the surface. M. of V. i. 1

credent, creditable, reputable. M. for M. iv. 4; credible. W. T. i. 2

crews, bands. Two G. iv. 1

crisp, rippled, wrinkled. Tp. iv. 1

cross, coin. L.L.L. i. 2; As. ii. 4

crowner, coroner. Tw.N. i. 5

cry, pack of hounds. M.N.D. iv. 1

cubiculo, bedchamber. Tw.N. iii. 2

cuckoo-buds, buttercup, marsh marigold, cowslip. L.L. L. v. 2

cullion, base fellow. T. of S. iv. 2

curious, particular, cautious. T. of S. iv. 4; A.W. i. 2; W.T. iv. 3

curious-knotted, laid out in elaborate plots. L.L.L. i. 1

curst, perverse, cantankerous. Two G. iii. 1; &c.

curtal, having tail docked. M. W. ii. 1; C. of E. iii. 2. *See* A. W. ii. 3

curtle-axe, cutlass. As. i. 3

cust-alorum, blunder for 'custos rotulorum.' M.W. i. 1

custard-coffin, crust of 'custard,' or open pie. T. of S. iv. 3

customer, associate. C. of E.

iv. 4; prostitute. A.W. v. 3

cut, 'cut-tail horse,' or gelding; term of abuse. Tw.N. ii. 3

cypress, ? coffin of cypress-wood. Tw.N. ii. 4; Cyprus crape. Tw.N. ? ii. 4; iii. 1; W. T. iv. 3

daff, to thrust aside. M.A. ii. 3; v. 1

danger, mischief. M. of V. iv. 1; power to injure. M. of V. iv. 1

darkling, in darkness. M.N.D. ii. 2

dash, infusion, tinge. W.T. v. 2; abash. L.L.L. v. 2

daubery, work of a dauber, coarse work. M.W. iv. 2

day-woman, dairy-woman. L. L.L. i. 2

debatement, deliberation. M. for M. v. 1

debile, weak. A.W. ii. 3

deboshed, debauched, seduced. Tp. iii. 2; A.W. ii. 3

decern, concern. M.A. iii. 5

deck, sprinkled. Tp. i. 2

deface, cancel. M. of V. iii. 2

default, in the, at a pinch. A. W. ii. 3

defeat, cheat. M.N.D. iv. 1

defeature, marring of features. C. of E. ii. 1; v. 1

defect, blunder for 'effect.' M. N.D. iii. 1

defend, forbid. M.A. ii. 1; iv. 2

defiance, rejection. M. for M. iii. 1

definitive, resolved. M. for M. v. 1

degree, step towards. Tw.N. iii. 1

deliver, relate. Tp. v. 1; &c.; liberate. Tw.N. v. 1

denay, refusal. Tw.N. ii. 4

denier, a French copper coin of very small value. T. of S. Ind. 1

denunciation, formal announcement. M. for M. i. 2

deprave, decry, disparage. M. A. v. 1

deputation, deputyship. M. for M. i. 1

derivative, transmission by descent. W.T. iii. 2

descant, accompaniment to a musical theme. Two G. i. 2

detected, accused. M. for M. iii. 2

determinate, intended. Tw.N. ii. 1

determine, assign. M. for M. i. 1; limit. M. for M. iii. 1

detest, blunder for 'protest.' M.W. i. 4; M. for M. ii. 1

device, conceptions, aims. As. i. 1

diaper, napkin. T. of S. Ind. 1

dibble, pointed instrument to make holes for planting seeds. W.T. iv. 3

diet, fix. A.W. iv. 3; limit. A.W. v. 3

difference, i. e. in our social status. W.T. iv. 3

diffused, confused. M.W. iv. 4

digression, moral deviation. L. L.L. i. 2

dig-you-den, give you good evening. L.L.L. iv. 1

dilate, relate. C. of E. i. 1

dilated, prolonged. A.W. ii. 1

dildo, a word used in the refrains of ballads. W.T. iv. 3

dimension, bodily shape. Tw. N. i. 5; v. i

disable, disparage, undervalue. M. of V. ii. 7; As. iv. 1; v. 4; cripple. M. of V. i. 1

discase, unrobe, undress. Tp. v. 1; W.T. iv. 3

discharge, performance. Tp. ii. 1; perform. M.N.D. i. 2; iv. 2; v. i

discipled, educated. A.W. i. 2

discontenting, discontented. W.T. iv. 3

disfurnish, deprive, divest. Two G. iv. 1

dishonest, dishonesty, immodest, unchastity. M.W. iv. 2; As. v. 3

disliken, disguise. W.T. iv. 3

dismount, unsheathe. Tw.N. iii. 4

dispose, control. Two G. ii. 7; C. of E. i. 1

disputable, disputatious. As. ii. 5

dissemble, disguise. Tw.N. iv. 2

dissembly, blunder for 'assembly.' M.A. iv. 2

dissolutely, dissolved, blunders for 'resolutely,' 'resolved.' M. W. i. 1

distemper, disorder. Tw.N. ii. 1

distemperature, disorder. C. of E. v. 1; M.N.D. ii. 1

disvouch, disown. M. for M. iv. 4

divulge, proclaim. M.W. iii. 2; A.W. ii. 1; Tw.N. i. 5

do, describe. W.T. v. 2

dog-ape, baboon. As. ii. 5

doit, a small Dutch coin, worth about half a farthing. Tp. ii. 2; M. of V. i. 3

dole, sorrow. M.N.D. v. 1; As. i. 2; share. A.W. ii. 3; W.T. i. 2

dominical, red letter in calendar indicating Sunday. L.L. L. v. 2

dowle, one of the fibres of a

feather. Tp. iii. 3

doxy, rogue's mistress. W.T. iv. 2

draff, refuse, swill given to pigs. M.W. iv. 2

draw, take draught of liquor. Tp. ii. 2; draw liquor for customers. M.W. i. 3; draw instrument from case, or draw bow across fiddle. M.A. v. 1; draw back. M. of V. ii. 9; Tw. N. i. 5; receive. M. of V. iv. 1

draw dryfoot, track game by the mere scent of the foot. C. of E. iv. 2

drawer, a tapster. M.W. ii. 2

drawn, with drawn swords. Tp. ii. 1; M.N.D. iii. 2; drunk. Tp. ii. 2

dribbling, falling short or wide of mark. M. for M. i. 3

drive, commute. M. of V. iv. 1

drovier, dealer in cattle. M.A. ii. 1

drumble, dawdle. M.W. iii. 3

Drum's entertainment, John, rough reception, turning an unwelcome guest out of doors. A.W. iii. 6

dry-beat, beat soundly. L.L.L. v. 2

duello, laws of the duel. L.L.L. i. 2; Tw.N. iii. 4

dump, plaintive melody or song. Two G. iii. 2; M.A. ii. 3

durance, imprisonment. M. for M. iii. 1; Tw.N. v. 1

durance, suit of, suit made of stout durable cloth (play on same word meaning 'imprisonment'). C. of E. iv. 3

eaning time, time of bearing lambs. M. of V. i. 3

eanling, young lamb. M. of V. i. 3

*ear, plough. A.W. i. 3

ecstasy, state of being 'beside oneself'; frenzy or stupor caused by fear or passion. Tp. iii. 3; &c.

effect, accomplishment. Two G. i. 1; expression. M. for M. iii. 1; sign, symptom. M.A. ii. 3; purport, significance. As. iv. 3

eggs for money, take, put up with an affront. W.T. i. 2

eke, also, moreover. M.W. i. 3; ii. 3; M.N.D. iii. 1

eld, people of the old time. M. W. iv. 4; age. M. for M. iii. 1

elder, heart of, weak, faint-hearted. M.W. ii. 3

element, air. Tw.N. i. 1; sphere. Tw.N. iii. 1

emboss, drive to extremity. A. W. iii. 6

embossed, foaming at mouth with exhaustion. T. of S. Ind. 1; swollen. As. ii. 7

embowelled, exhausted. A.W. i. 3

enchantingly, as though enchanted. As. i. 1

encounter, adversary. L.L.L. v. 2; greeting. T. of S. iv. 5; go toward. Tw.N. iii. 1; befall. W.T. ii. 1; behaviour. W. T. iii. 2

end, still an, continually. Two G. iv. 4

enfolding, garment. W.T. iv. 3

enforced, violated. M.N.D. iii. 1

enfreedoming, bringing into a state of freedom. L.L.L. iii. 1

engage, pledge. M.A. iv. 1; As. v. 4

engine, instrument of war. Tp. ii. 1; instrument. Two G. iii. 1

enlarge, release. Tw.N. v. 1

enlargement, release. L.L.L. iii. 1

enmew, mew up, keep under. M. for M. iii. 1

enow, enough. M. of V. iii. 5

ensconce, shelter. M.W. ii. 2; iii. 3

enshield, shielded, concealed. M. for M. ii. 4

entertain, hire, take into service. Two G. ii. 4; &c.; maintain. M. of V. i. 1; desire to keep. M. for M. iii. 1

entertainment, employment, service. A.W. iii. 6; iv. 1; treatment. Tw.N. i. 5

entrenched, cut. A.W. ii. 1

envy, malice, spite. Tp. i. 2; M. of V. iv. 1

Ephesian, boon companion. M.W. iv. 5

epitheton, epithet, appellation. L.L.L. i. 2

Ercles, Hercules. M.N.D. i. 2

erection, direction. M.W. iii. 5

eringoes, candied root of sea holly, used as sweetmeat. M.W. v. 5

erst, little while since. As. iii. 5

escapes, sallies. M. for M. iv. i

estate, bestow, settle. Tp. iv. 1; M.N.D. i. 1; As. v. 2; state. M. of V. iii. 2; rank. A.W. iii. 7; wealth. W.T. iv. 2; affairs. W.T. iv. 3

estimable wonder, admiring judgment. Tw.N. ii. 1

even, make, grant. A.W. ii. 1; full. A.W. v. 3

everlasting garment, ? the buff jerkin of a sergeant. C. of E. iv. 2

evitate, avoid. M.W. v. 5

examine, question. A.W. iii. 5

exceed, be pre-eminent. M.A. iii. 4

except before excepted, a legal phrase, 'make objection.' Tw. N. i. 3

excess, interest. M. of V. i. 3

excrement, hair, moustache, beard. C. of E. ii. 2; &c.

exempt, separated. C. of E. ii. 2; remote. As. ii. 1; exclude. A.W. ii. 1

exhibition, allowance, maintenance. Two G. i. 3

exorcist, raiser of spirits. A.W. v. 3

experimental seal, stamp of experience. M.A. iv. 1

exploit, action, combat. A.W. i. 2; iv. 1

exposition, blunder for 'disposition.' M.N.D. iv. 1

expostulate, discuss. Two G. iii. 1

expressive, open or emphatic in expression. A.W. ii. i

expressure, expression. Tw.N. ii. 3; image, picture. M.W. v. 5

extent, seizure. As. iii. 1; assault. Tw.N. iv. 1

extermined, exterminated. As. iii. 5

extirp, root out. M. for M. iii. 2

extracting, ? distracting. Tw. N. v. i

extravagancy, vagrancy. Tw. N. ii. 1

eyas-musket, young hawk; sprightly child. M.W. iii. 3

eye, slight shade, tinge. Tp. ii. 1; limits. M. of V. i. 1

eyne, eyes. L.L.L. v. 2; M.N.D. i. 1

face, brave. C. of E. iii. 1; T. of S. iv. 3; v. 1

face out of, bully out of,

shamelessly exclude from. Tw.N. iv. 2; v. 1

face with card of ten, bluff, carry through by effrontery. T. of S. ii. 1

facinorous, infamous. A.W. ii. 3

fact, crime, deed. M. for M. iv. 2; W.T. iii. 2

fadge, fit, be suitable. L.L.L. v. 1; succeed. Tw.N. ii. 2

fading, refrain of popular song of indecent character. W.T. iv. 3

fail, failure. W.T. ii. 3; v. i

fain, wish to. Tp. i. 1; As. i. 2

fair, fairness, beauty. C. of E. ii. 1; &c.; in state, finery. T. of S. ii. 1

fairest grant is the necessity, best gift is that which meets the needs of case. M.A. iii. i

fairing, present. L.L.L. v. 2

faithless, unbelieving. M. of V. ii. 4

fall, let fall. Tp. ii. 1; &c.; be allotted. M. of V. i. 3; give birth to. M. of V. i. 3; happen. M. of V. iii. 2; A.W. v. 1; sinking of the note, cadence. Tw.N. i. 1

fallow, of a reddish-yellow colour. M.W. i. 1

false, falsehood. M. for M. ii. 4

falsing, deceptive. C. of E. ii. 2

familiar, spirit supposed to attend at call. L.L.L. i. 2

fancy, love. M.A. iii. 2; &c.

fancy-monger, dealer in love. As. iii. 2

fantastic, fop. M. for M. *Dram. Per.*; foppish. Two G. ii. 7

fap, drunk. M.W. i. 1

fardel, little pack. W.T. iv. 3; &c.

farthingale, framework of hoops of whalebone, for extending skirts of dresses; hooped petticoat. Two G. ii. 7; &c.

fartuous, blunder for 'virtuous.' M.W. ii. 2

fashion-monging, foppish. M.A. v. 1

fashions, farcy, disease of horses. T. of S. iii. 2

fat, make fat. M.N.D. ii. 1; cloying. Tw.N. v. i

favour, appearance, aspect, face. M. for M. iv. 2; &c.; present, token of love. L.L.L. v. 2; M.N.D. ii. 1; iv. 1

fay, faith. T. of S. Ind. ii

fear, frighten. M. for M. ii. 1; M. of V. ii. 1; T. of S. i. 2; peril, cause for fear. M.N.D. v. 1; fear for. M. of V. iii. 5; T. of S. v. 2

feater, more becoming. Tp. ii. 1

featly, neatly, gracefully. Tp. i. 2; W.T. iv. 3

federary, accomplice. W.T. ii. 1

feeder, servant. As. ii. 4

feeding, pasturage. W.T. iv. 3

fee-simple, unconditional possession. A.W. iv. 3

fell, enraged, savage. M.N.D. ii. 1; Tw.N. i. 1; fleece. As. iii. 2

fellow, equal, consort. Tp. ii. 1; &c.; accompany, be a partner. W.T. i. 2

fellowly, sympathetic. Tp. v. 1

fence, swordsmanship. M.W. i. 1; M.A. v. 1; Tw.N. iii. 4

feodary, accomplice. M. for M. ii. 4

festinately, hastily, speedily. L.L.L. iii. 1

fetch in, draw confession from. M.A. i. 1

few, in, in short. Tp. i. 2; T. of S. i. 2

fico, fig, expression of contempt. M.W. i. 3

fife, wry-necked, fife with upper part resembling the beak of a bird, or musician as looking away from his instrument. M. of V. ii. 5

fights, screen used during naval engagement to protect crew of a vessel. M.W. ii. 2

figure, figure of speech. Two G. ii. 1; L.L.L. i. 2; T. of S. i. 2; horoscope. M.W. iv. 2; phantasm. M.W. iv. 2; typify. M.N.D. i. 1

file, multitude. M. for M. iii. 2

fine, punish, punishment. M. for M. ii. 2; iii. 1; aim, end. M.A. i. 1; A.W. iv. 4; smart, T. of S. iv. 1; artful. A.W. v. 3

fine and recovery, absolute possession. M.W. iv. 2; C. of E. ii. 2

fine's the crown, end crowns all. A.W. iv. 4

firago, virago. Tw.N. iii. 4

fire, will-o'-the-wisp. M.N.D. iii. i

fire-new, brand-new. L.L.L. i. 1; Tw.N. iii. 2

fives, a disease in horses. T. of S. iii. 2

fixure, direction. W.T. v. 3

flap-dragon, snap-dragon, raisin caught out of burning brandy and eaten. L.L.L. v. 1

flap-dragoned, swallowed. W. T. iii. 3

flat-long, with the flat side. Tp. ii. 1

flatness, completeness. W.T. iii. 2

flatter with, deal falsely. Tw. N. i. 5

flaunts, finery. W.T. iv. 3

flaw, passionate outburst. M. for M. ii. 3

fleer, laugh, mock. M.A. v. 1; L.L.L. v. 2

fleet, company. M.A. ii. 1; fade, die away. M. of V. iii. 2; pass. iv. 1; As. i. 1

flesh, satiate. A.W. iv. 3

flewed, having large chaps. M. N.D. iv. 1

flight, shooting with arrows the greatest possible distance. M. A. i. 1

flote, wave. Tp. i. 2

flourish, embellish, gloss over. M. for M. iv. 1; fanfare of trumpets. M. of V. iii. 2

foil, put to, defeat, repulse. Tp. iii. 1

foin, thrust. M.W. ii. 3; M.A. v. 1

foison, plenty. Tp. ii. 1; iv. 1; M. for M. i. 4

folly-fallen, fallen into folly. Tw.N. iii. 1

fond, fondly, fondness, foolish, foolishly, foolishness. Two G. i. 1; &c.; valued by fools, trivial. M. for M. ii. 2; doting. M. for M. ii. 2; &c.; dote. Tw.N. ii. 2

fool, used as a term of endearment and pity. As. ii. 1; W.T. ii. 1; jester. T. of S. i. 1

fool-begged, foolishly demanded. C. of E. ii. 1

foot, kick, spurn. M. of V. i. 3; path. M. of V. ii. 4

foppery, folly. M.W. v. 5; M. for M. i. 2; M. of V. ii. 5

force, enforce. M. for M. iii. 1; scruple. L.L.L. v. 2; necessity. M.N.D. iii. 2; M. of V. iv. 1; W.T. iv. 3

fordone, wearied out. M.N.D. v. 2

'*forehand*, done at some earlier time. M.A. iv. 1

forehorse to a smock, squire of dames. A.W. ii. 1

forfend, forbid. W.T. iv. 3

forgery, invention. M.N.D. ii. 1

forked, horned. W.T. i. 2

formal, normal, sane. C. of E. v. 1; Tw.N. ii. 5

forted, fortified. M. for M. v. 1

forth-right, straight course or path. Tp. iii. 3

fortune, happen, chance. Two G. v. 4

foundered, lame, disabled. Tp. iv. 1

frame, form. M. for M. v. 1; scheme, order. M.A. iv. 1; L. L.L. iii. 1; contrivance. M.A. iv. 1; devise, plan. M.A. v. 1; W.T. v. 1

frampold, sour-tempered, disagreeable. M.W. ii. 2

franklin, yeoman. W.T. v. 2

fraught, cargo. Tw.N. v. 1; laden. Two G. iii. 2; M. of V. ii. 8; W.T. iv. 3

fraughtage, cargo. C. of E. iv. 1

fraughting, that form a cargo. Tp. i. 2

free, liberal. M. for M. v. i; innocent. As. ii. 7; Tw.N. ii. 4; W.T. ii. 3; noble. Tw.N. i. 5; W.T. ii. 2; accessible. W.T. ii. 1; ready. W.T. iv. 3

French crown, the baldness produced by the 'French disease.' M. for M. i. 2; M.N.D. i. 2; A.W. ii. 2

fresh, spring of fresh water. Tp. iii. 2; youthful. W.T. iv. 3

fret, chafe. M. of V. iv. 1; ring of gut placed on finger-board of musical instrument to regulate fingering. T. of S. ii. 1; spoil. T. of S. ii. 1

frippery, place where cast-off clothes are sold. Tp. iv. 1

frize, coarse woollen cloth. M. W. v. 5

from, different to, apart from. M.A. iii. 1; Tw.N. i. 5; v. 1

froth and lime, make a tankard froth, and put lime into sack to make it sparkle. M.W. i. 3

froward, refractory. T. of S. i. 1

fruitful, fruitfully, abundant, fully. M. for M. iv. 3; A.W. ii. 2

frutify, a confusion of 'notify' with 'fructify.' M. of V. ii. 2

fullam, die loaded at corner. M.W. i. 3

full-fraught, fully laden. Two G. iii. 2

fulsome, lustful. M. of V. i. 3; cloying, wearisome from excess. Tw.N. v. 1

gaberdine, loose upper garment. Tp. ii. 2; M. of V. i. 3

gaged, bound. M. of V. i. 1

galimaufry, gallimaufry, hotchpotch, medley. M.W. ii. 1; W.T. iv. 3

gall, harass, oppress. W.T. i. 2

galliard, lively dance in triple time. Tw.N. i. 3

galliass, heavy low-built vessel, larger than a galley. T. of S. ii. 1

gallows, gallows-bird. L.L.L. v. 2

gambold, gambol. T. of S. Ind. 2

gamester, gambler. M.W. iii.

1; L.L.L. i. 2; athlete. As. i. 1; term of contempt. T. of S. ii. 1; lewd person. A.W. v. 3

garden-house, summer-house. M. for M. v. 1

garner, granary. Tp. iv. 1

garnish, outfit, dress. M. of V. ii. 6

gaskins, breeches or hose. Tw. N. i. 5

gaud, gawd, trifle, finery. M.N. D. i. 1; iv. 1; T. of S. ii. 1

gear, matter, purpose. M. of V. i. 1; ii. 2

geck, fool, dupe. Tw.N. v. 1

geminy, couple. M.W. ii. 2

general, populace. M. for M. ii. 4

generation, offspring. W.T. ii. 1

generative, having the power of generating. M. for M. iii. 2

generous, noble, high-born. M. for M. iv. 6; L.L.L. v. 1

genius, one of two opposed spirits by whom each person was supposed to be attended; spirit. Tp. iv. 1; C. of E. v. 1; Tw.N. iii. 4

gentility, gentle bearing, gentle birth. L.L.L. i. 1; As. i. 1

gentle, noble, well-born. Tp. i. 2; W.T. i. 2; gentleman, one of good birth. M.W. iii. 2; &c.; term of endearment. W. T. iv. 3

gentry, rank by birth. M.W. ii. 1; W.T. i. 2

germane, kin, related. W.T. iv. 3

gest, time allotted for a halt or stay. W.T. i. 2

gesture, bearing. As. v. 2

giddily, lightly. Tw.N. ii. 4

gig, whipping-top. L.L.L. iv. 3; v. 1

giglot, lewd woman. M. for M. v. 1

gild, impart flush to. Tp. v. 1

Gillian, Juliana. C. of E. iii. 1

gillyvors, gillyflowers (a variety of wall-flower). W.T. iv. 3

gin, snare. Tw.N. ii. 5

ging, gang. M.W. iv. 2

Ginn, Jenny. C. of E. iii. 1

gird, gibe, hit. T. of S. v. 2

girdle, turn one's, ? find harmless outlet for anger. M.A. v. i

give, display as armorial bearing, bear. M.W. i. 1; grant to be. W.T. iii. 2

give out, proclaim. W.T. iv. 3

glance, allude, hint. C. of E. v. 1; M.N.D. ii. 1

glances, satirical allusions, side hits. As. ii. 7

glass, hour-glass. W.T. i. 2

glasses, runnings of hour-glass. Tp. i. 2; v. i

glassy essence, essential nature of man. M. for M. ii. 2

gleek, jest or gibe. M.N.D. iii. 1

glib, castrate. W.T. ii. 1

glozes, pretences, disguises. L. L.L. iv. 3

God bless the mark, phrase used as apology after mentioning something horrible or indecent. Two G. iv. 4; M. of V. ii. 2

God dig you den, God ye good even, God give you a good evening. L.L.L. iv. 1; As. v. 1

God 'ild, God shield. As. iii. 3; v. 4

Gogs-wouns, God's wounds, an oath. T. of S. iii. 2

good, financially sound. M. of V. i. 3

good deed, in very deed. W.T. i. 2

good den, good even. M.A. iii. 2

good even and twenty, twenty good evenings. M.W. ii. 1

good-jer, good year, a meaningless expletive. M.W. i. 4; M.A. i. 3

good life, lifelike truth. Tp. iii. 3; good name. M.W. iii. 3

good life, song of, moral song. Tw.N. ii. 3

gorge, throat, stomach. W.T. ii. 1

goss, gorse. Tp. iv. 1

gossip, woman's female friend, invited to be present at a birth. Two G. iii. 1; C. of E. v. i; to act as sponsor. A.W. i. 1; make merry. C. of E. v. 1; sponsor. W.T. ii. 3

gossips' bowl, used at christening feasts. M.N.D. ii. 1

go through, deal in succession. M. for M. ii. 1

gourd, a kind of false dice. M.W. i. 3

government, in, under control. M.N.D. v. 1

grace, favour granted. M.N.D. ii. 2; T. of S. i. 2; gain honour. As. i. 1; favour. A.W. v. 2; W.T. iii. 2; virtue. Tw.N. v. 1

graceful, full of nobility. W.T. v. 1

graff, graft. As. iii. 2

grained, furrowed. C. of E. v.1

grain, in, fast, genuine, in the very nature. C. of E. iii. 2; Tw.N. i. 5

gramercy, thanks. M. of V. ii. 2; T. of S. i. 1

grange, country house. M. for M. iii. 1; granary. W.T. iv. 3

grated upon, harassed with importunities. M.W. ii. 2

gratify, fee, reward. M. of V. iv. 1; T. of S. i. 2

gratillity, blunder for 'gratuity.' Tw.N. ii. 3

gratulate, pleasing. M. for M. v. 1

grave, engrave, cut. M. of V. ii. 7

gravelled, at a standstill. As. iv. 1

greasily, indecently. L.L.L. iv. 1

Greek, roysterer. Tw.N. iv. 1

green, ? fresh, or freshly greased. T. of S. iii. 2

grize, step, stair. Tw.N. iii. 1

grizzle, sprinkling of grey hairs. Tw.N. v. 1

groat, English coin worth about 4d. M.W. i. 1

gross, palpable. M. for M. i. 2; A.W. i. 3; total. As. iv. 1

grossly, awkwardly. M.W. ii. 2; obviously, palpably. C. of E. ii. 2; A.W. i. 3; materially. M. of V. v. 1

grossness, density. M.N.D. iii. 1; enormity, flagrancy. M. of V. iii. 2; Tw.N. iii. 2

growing, accruing. C. of E. iv. 1

grow to, have a tendency. M. of V. ii. 2

guard, ornamental trimming. M. for M. iii. 1; M.A. i. 1; L.L.L. iv. 3; ornament, trim. M.A. i. 1; M. of V. ii. 2

guerdon, reward, requital. M.A. v. 3; L.L.L. iii. 1

guilder, gold coin once current in Netherlands. C. of E. i. 1; iv. 1

guiled, treacherous. M. of V. iii. 2

gull, trick, deception. M.A. ii. 3; dupe, simpleton. Tw.N. iii. 2; v. 1

gull-catcher, trickster. Tw.N. ii. 5

gust, pleasure. Tw.N. i. 3; taste, relish. W.T. i. 2

H, i. e. ache (pron. aitch). M. A. iii. 4

hack, become vile and vulgar. M.W. ii. 1

haggard, haggerd, wild female hawk. M.A. iii. 1; &c.

hag-seed, offspring of witch. Tp. i. 2

hale, haul, draw, drag. M.A. ii. 3; &c.

half-cheek, side-face. L.L.L. v. 2

halidom, holy relic, anything regarded as sacred. Two G. iv. 2

Hallowmas, feast of All Saints. Two G. ii. 1; M. for M. ii. 1

hammered of, pondered on. W.T. ii. 2

hand, lay hands on. W.T. ii. 3

hand, at or *in any,* on any account, in any case. T. of S. i. 2; A.W. iii. 6

handfast, custody. W.T. iv. 3

hands, of all, in any case. L.L. L. iv. 3

hangman boys, young rascals. Two G. iv. 4

haply, perhaps. Tw. N. i. 2

happily, haply, perhaps. M. for M. iv. 2; T. of S. iv. 4; Tw.N. iv. 2

happiness, aptitude. M.A. ii. 3

harlot, lewd fellow. C. of E. v. 1; adulterous. W.T. ii. 3

hatch, half-door. C. of E. iii. 1

haud credo, hardly I believe. L.L.L. iv. 2

have at, I'll try. W.T. iv. 3

have to, we'll go to. T. of S. i. 1

have with, I'll go with. L.L.L. iv. 2; As. i. 2

hawking, hawk-like, keen. A. W. i. 1

hawthorn-buds, dandies. M. W. iii. 3

hay, country dance. L.L.L. v. 1

head, behead. M. for M. ii. 1; face. M.A. v. 1; M.N.D. i. 1; fountain-head. A.W. i. 3

head, of the first, said of a deer at the age when the antlers are first developed. L.L.L. iv. 2

head-stall, part of bridle that fits round head. T. of S. iii. 2

heart, affection. As. i. 1

heat, run swiftly over. W.T. i. 2; course. Tw.N. i. 1

heaviness, sadness. Tp. v. 1; M. of V. ii. 8

heavings, sighs. W.T. ii. 3

heavy, drowsy. Tp. ii. 1; sad, sorrowful. M. for M. iv. 1; M. of V. v. 1; W.T. iii. 3

hedge, shift, dodge. M.W. ii. 2; restrict. M. of V. ii. 1

hedge-priest, illiterate priest of inferior status. L.L.L. v. 2

heft, heaving. W.T. ii. 1

height, highest degree. M.A. iv. 1

Helen, blunder for 'Hero.' M. N.D. v. 1

helm, steer, guide. M. for M. iii. 2; helmet. A.W. iii. 3

helpless, unavailing. C. of E. ii. 1

hent, reached, occupied. M. for M. iv. 6; lay hold of. W.T. iv. 2

herb of grace, rue. A.W. iv. 5

hereby, as it may happen. L.L. L. i. 2

hest, behest, command. Tp. i. 2; iii. 1

hic jacet (here lies), die in the attempt. A.W. iii. 6

Hiems, winter. M.N.D. ii. 1

high and low, two kinds of false dice. M.W. i. 3

high bent, turned full. A.W. v. 3

high-cross, market-cross. T. of S. i. 1

high-proof, in the highest degree. M.A. v. 1

hight, is called. L.L.L. i. 1; M.N.D. v. 1

hilding, good-for-nothing. T. of S. ii. 1; A.W. iii. 6

hind, servant, agricultural labourer. M.W. iii. 5; L.L.L. i. 2; As. i. 1; female of the deer. As. iii. 2

hint, occasion, opportunity. Tp. i. 2; ii. 1

hip, on or *upon the*, at a disadvantage. M. of V. i. 3; iv. 1

hipped, having the hip injured or dislocated. T. of S. iii. 2

hobby-horse, frivolous or foolish fellow. M.A. iii. 2; prostitute. W.T. i. 2

hob, nob, have or have not, give or take. Tw.N. iii. 4

hodge-pudding, pudding made of a medley of ingredients. M.W. v. 5

hold, remain. M.A. i. 1; keep promise. M.N.D. i. 2; maintain. A.W. i. 1

holding, consistency. A.W. iv. 2

holidame, halidom, q.v. T. of S. v. 2

holp, helped. Tp. i. 2; C. of E. iv. 1

home, thoroughly. Tp. v. 1; &c.; a home-thrust. L.L.L. v. 1

home, and home, effectively, out and out. M. for M. iv. 3

hoodman, blindfolded player in blindman's buff. A.W. iv. 3

hoodwink, to cover up from sight. Tp. iv. 1

hornbook, primer. L.L.L. v. 1

horn-mad, mad with rage at having been made a cuckold. M.W. i. 4; C. of E. ii. 1; M.A. i. 1

host, lodge, put up. C. of E. i. 2; A.W. iii. 5

host, lay at, were left at. C. of E. v. i

hot-house, bathing-house, brothel. M. for M. ii. 1

hovel-post, support of the roof of an outhouse. M. of V. ii. 2

hox, hamstring, hough. W.T. i. 2

hoy, small vessel; a sloop. C. of E. iv. 3

hull, float, anchor. Tw.N. i. 5

Hungarian, thievish, beggarly. M.W. i. 3

hungerly, hungry-looking. T. of S. iii. 2

hurly, hurly-burly. T. of S. iv. 1

hurtling, conflict. As. iv. 3

husband, housekeeper, steward. M. for M. iii. 2; T. of S. v. 1

hyen, hyena. As. iv. 1

i'fecks, in faith. W.T. i. 2

ignomy, ignominy. M. for M. ii. 4

ignorant fumes, fumes producing unconsciousness. Tp. v. i

ill-ta'en, misconceived. W.T. i. 2

illustrate, illustrious. L.L.L. iv. i; v. 1

image, idea. M.W. iv. 6

imagined speed, all speed imaginable. M. of V. iii. 4

imbrue, stain with blood. M.N. D. v. i

immediately, purposely. M.N. D. i. 1

imp, child. L.L.L. i. 2; v. 2

impawned, in pledge. W.T. i. 2

impeticos, burlesque word for 'to pocket,' perhaps intended to suggest 'petticoat.' Tw.N. ii. 3

importance, importunity. Tw. N. v. 1; import, meaning. W. T. v. 2

important, importunate. C. of E. v. 1; M.A. ii. 1

importing, of much import. A. W. v. 3

impose, injunction. Two G. iv. 3; command. M.A. v. 1

imposition, imputation, accusation, charge. M. for M. i. 2; W.T. i. 2; injunction. M. of V. i. 2; imposed task. M. of V. iii. 4; A.W. iv. 4

incardinate, incarnal, blunders for 'incarnate.' M. of V. ii. 2; Tw.N. v. 1

incense, instigate. M.A. v. 1; W.T. v. 1

inch-meal, by, by inches, inch by inch. Tp. ii. 2

incidency, incident. W.T. i. 2

include, bring to a close. Two G. v. 4

incontinent, immediately. As. v. 2

incony, pretty, 'nice.' L.L.L. iii. 1; iv. 1

incorporate, made one body. M.N.D. iii. 2

increase, vegetable produce, crops. Tp. iv. 1

incredulous, incredible. Tw.N. iii. 4

Ind, Inde, India, or the Indies

(E. or W.). Tp. ii. 2; L.L.L. iv. 3; As. iii. 2

indifferent, equally. T. of S. i. 2; of medium quality or character. T. of S. iv. 1; fairly. Tw.N. i. 3; i. 5

indubitate, undoubted. L.L.L. iv. 1

inequality, variableness. M. for M. v. 1

infection, blunder for 'affection.' M.W. ii. 2

infest, vex. Tp. v. 1

informal, ? disordered in mind. M. for M. v. 1

inherit, win. Two G. iii. 2

inkle, a kind of tape. L.L.L. iii. 1; W.T. iv. 3

inland, in or towards interior of country. As. ii. 7; having refinements characteristic of inlying parts of country. As. iii. 2

inly, inwardly. Tp. v. 1; heartfelt. Two G. ii. 7

innocent, idiot. A.W. iv. 3

insanie, madness. L.L.L. v. 1

insculped, engraved. M. of V. ii. 7

insinuate, convey notion by indirect suggestion. L.L.L. v. 1; ingratiate. As. Epil. 8; intermeddle. W.T. iv. 3

instalment, place wherein some one is installed. M.W. v. 5

intellect, purport. L.L.L. iv. 2

intelligencing, conveying information. W.T. ii. 3

intelligent, communicative. W.T. i. 2

intend, pretend. M.A. ii. 2; M. N.D. iii. 2; T. of S. iv. 1

intendment, intention. As. i. 1

intenible, incapable of holding or containing. A.W. i. 3

intermission, action to while

away time. M. of V. iii. 2

intestine, internal. C. of E. i. 1

invectively, with inveighing or denunciation. As. ii. 1

inward, secret, confidential. M. A. iv. 1; L.L.L. v. 1; familiar acquaintance. M. for M. iii. 2; inwardly. M. of V. iii. 2

inwardness, intimacy. M.A. iv. 1

issued, born, descended. Tp. i. 2

issues, purposes. M. for M. i. 1

it, them. L.L.L. i. 1

I wis, certainly, truly. M. of V. ii. 9; T. of S. i. 1

Jack, knave. Tp. iv. 1; &c.; a leather vessel for liquor. T. of S. iv. 1

Jack-a-Lent, figure set up to be pelted during Lent. M.W. iii. 3; v. 5

jade, worthless nag. T. of S. i. 2; befool. Tw.N. ii. 5

jar, discordant sound. As. ii. 7; tick. W.T. i. 2

jay, showy person. M.W. iii. 3

jerk, short sharp witty speech. L.L.L. iv. 2

jerkin, close-fitting jacket. Tp. iv. 1; Two G. ii. 4

jet, strut, swagger. Tw.N. ii. 5

jills, drinking vessels made of metal. T. of S. iv. 1

joinder, conjunction, union. Tw.N. v. 1

joint-stool, a kind of folding chair. T. of S. ii. 1

joul, knock, push. A.W. i. 3

journal, daily. M. for M. iv. 3

jump, agree. M. of V. ii. 9; T. of S. i. 1; Tw.N. v. 1

junket, sweetmeat. T. of S. iii. 2

just, justly, exactly, precisely. M. for M. iii. 1; &c.

justify, prove. Tp. v. 1; A.W. iv. 3; confirm. W.T. v. 2; v. 3

juvenal, juvenile. L.L.L. i. 2; iii. 1; M.N.D. iii. 1

keel, cool boiling liquid by stirring, skimming, or pouring in something cold. L.L.L. v. 2

keep, restrain. Two G. iv. 4; reside. M. for M. i. 3; M. of V. iii. 3; charge; an article which serves for containing something. T. of S. i. 2

keeping, maintenance. As. i. 1

Keisar, kaiser, emperor. M.W. i. 3

kennel, gutter. T. of S. iv. 3

kersey, coarse narrow cloth. M. for M. i. 2; T. of S. iii. 2; plain, homely. L.L.L. v. 2

kibe, chilblain, esp. on the heel. Tp. ii. 1; M.W. i. 3

kickchaws, toy, trifle, gewgaw. Tw.N. i. 3

kicky-wicky, ludicrous term for wife. A.W. ii. 3

kid-fox, fox-cub. M.A. ii. 3

kiln-hole, fire-hole of kiln. M. W. iv. 2; W.T. iv. 3

kind, kindred. Two G. ii. 3; natural. M.A. i. 1; respect. M. N.D. i. 1; nature. As. iv. 3; A.W. i. 3

kind, deed of, sexual function. M. of V. i. 3

kissing-comfits, perfumed comfits for sweetening the breath. M.W. v. 5

kitchen, entertain in the kitchen. C. of E. v. 1

knack, knick-knack. M.N.D. i. 1; T. of S. iv. 3; W.T. iv. 3

knap, nibble. M. of V. iii. 1

knit, texture. T. of S. iv. 1

knot (folded arms). Tp. i. 2

labras, blunder for 'labra,' plural of 'labrum,' a lip. M. W. i. 1

laced mutton, strumpet. Two G. i. 1

lakin, form of Lady; *by'r lakin* = by our Lady. Tp. iii. 3; M. N.D. iii. 1

lampass, disease of horses. T. of S. iii. 2

land-damn, make a hell on earth for. W.T. ii. 1

languishing, attack of faintness, such as proceeds from disease. A.W. i. 3

lapsed, surprised, apprehended. Tw.N. iii. 3

large, licentious, gross. M.A. ii. 3; iv. 1

latch, secure. M.N.D. iii. 2

latten, mixed metal of yellow colour. M.W. i. 1

laying on, wagering on. T. of S. v. 2

leaguer, camp, investing force. A.W. iii. 6

leasing, lying, falsehood. Tw. N. i. 5

leavened, tempered, modified. M. for M. i. 1

led, carried. A.W. iv. 3

leer, countenance. As. iv. 1

leet, court which lords of certain manors were empowered to hold. T. of S. Ind. 2

'lege, allege, say. T. of S. i. 2

leg, make a, bow, make obeisance. A.W. ii. 2

leiger, resident ambassador. M. for M. iii. 1

leisure, by my good, gradually. M. for M. iii. 2

leman, lover. M.W. iv. 2; Tw. N. ii. 3

lenten, poor, scanty. Tw. N. i. 5

l'envoy, epilogue. L.L.L. iii. 1

let, hinder, delay. Two G. iii. 1; &c.

Lethe, a river in Hades, the water of which produced forgetfulness. Tw.N. iv. 1

level, guess. M. of V. i. 2; equipoised, steady. Tw.N. ii. 4; range of missile. W.T. ii. 3; direction, aim. W.T. iii. 2

lewdster, lewd person. M.W. v. 3

libbard, leopard. L.L.L. v. 2

lie, lodge, dwell. Two G. iv. 2; &c.

light, wanton. C. of E. iv. 3

lighter, inferior. Tw.N. v. 1

liking, appearance, condition. M.W. ii. 1

Limander, Leander. M.N.D. v. 1

limbo, prison, confinement. C. of E. iv. 2; region on the border of hell. A.W. v. 3

lime, birdlime. Tp. iv. 1; Two G. iii. 2; put lime into wine. M.W. i. 3; catch as with birdlime. M.A. iii. 1; Tw.N. iii. 4

limit, appointed time. M. for M. iii. 1; appoint, fix. M. for M. iv. 2; prescribed time of repose after child-bearing. W.T. iii. 2

line, draw, trace. As. iii. 2

line-grove, grove of lime-trees. Tp. v. 1

ling, fish, meagre food. A.W. iii. 2

link, blacking, lamp-black. T. of S. iv. 1

linsey-woolsey, medley, nonsense. A.W. iv. 1

lion-fell, lion's skin. M.N.D. v. 1

liquor, dress boots with oil or grease. M.W. iv. 5

list, like, care to. Tp. iii. 2; W. T. iv. chor.; limit, boundary.

M. for M. i. 1; A.W. ii. 1; Tw.
N. iii. 1

livelihood, activity, vigour. A.
W. i. 1

lively, lifelike. As. v. 4; W.T. v.
3

liver, supposed to be the seat
of love and of passion generally. Tp. iv. 1; &c.

liver-vein, style of men in love.
L.L.L. iv. 3

lob, clown. M.N.D. ii. 1

lock, love-lock. M.A. iii. 3; v. 1

lode-star, pole-star. M.N.D. i.
1

long, belong. M. for M. ii. 2

'long of, on account of,
through. L.L.L. ii. 1; M.N.D.
iii. 2

longly, for a long time. T. of S.
i. 1

look out, blush. W.T. iv. 3

loose, last moment. L.L.L. v.
2; shoot, let fly. M.N.D. ii. 1

lordings, lordlings. W.T. i. 2

'Lord's sake, for the,' supplica-
tion of imprisoned debtors to
passers-by. M. for M. iv. 3

Lord's tokens, plague-spots. L.
L.L. v. 2

lose, forget. M.N.D. i. 1; cause
the loss of. Tw.N. ii. 2

loss of question, in the, for the
sake of argument. M. for M.
ii. 4

love-broker, go-between. Tw.
N. iii. 2

loves, affects. L.L.L. iv. 3

loves, of all, phrase of strong
entreaty. M.W. ii. 2; M.N.D.
ii. 2

love-springs, tender shoots of
love. C. of E. iii. 2

lower chair, easy chair. M. for
M. iii. 1

lower messes, people dining at
the lower end of the table;

hence, inferiors. W.T. i. 2

lozel, worthless person. W.T.
ii. 3

luce, pike, fish. M.W. i. 1

lumpish, low-spirited, dejected. Two G. iii. 2

lunes, fits of frenzy. M.W. iv.
2; W.T. ii. 2

lurch, remain about a place
furtively. M.W. ii. 2

lure, apparatus used to recall
hawks. T. of S. iv. 1

lustihood, vigour of body, ro-
bustness. M.A. v. 1

luxurious, unchaste. M.A. iv. 1

luxury, lust. M.W. v. 5; M. for
M. v. 1

maculate, spotted, defiled. L.
L.L. i. 2

Magnifico, magnate of Venice.
M. of V. iii. 2

mail, bag. L.L.L. iii. 1

main-course, main-sail. Tp. i. 1

making, outward form. C. of
E. iv. 2

malapert, presumptuous, impudent. Tw.N. iv. 1

Mall, Mary. Tp. ii. 2; Tw.N. i.
3

malmsey, strong sweet wine.
L.L.L. v. 2

malt-horse, heavy horse used
by maltsters, term of abuse.
C. of E. iii. 1; T. of S. iv. 1

manage, manager, wield,
wielder. Two G. iii. 1; L.L.L.
i. 2

mankind, masculine, furious.
T.W. ii. 3

manner, taken with the,
caught in the act. L.L.L. i. 1;
W.T. iv. 3

mantle, cloud, become covered
over. M. of V. i. 1

margent, margin with mar-
ginal notes. L.L.L. ii. 1; bor-

der, edge. M.N.D. ii. 1

mark, thirteen shillings and fourpence. M. for M. iv. 3; pattern. W.T. iv. 3

marl, clay. M.A. ii. 1

marmozet, small monkey. Tp. ii. 2

marry, asseverative exclamation. Tw.N. iv. 2

mart, bargain. T. of S. ii. 1; W. T. iv. 3

match, bargain. M. of V. iii. 1

mated, confounded, stupefied. C. of E. iii. 2; v. 1

material, full of matter or sense. As. iii. 3

matter, important matter. Tp. ii. 1

maugre, in spite of. Tw.N. iii. 1

maze, figure marked on village greens for rustic sports. M.N. D. ii. 1; perplex. M.N.D. ii. 1

meacock, effeminate. T. of S. ii. 1

mealed, spotted, stained. M. for M. iv. 2

mean, tenor or alto. Two G. i. 2; L.L.L. v. 2; W.T. iv. 2; means, method. Two G. ii. 7; &c.; opportunity. C. of E. i. 2

meander, crooked and winding path. Tp. iii. 3

measure, grave and stately dance. M.A. ii. 1; &c.; judge. W.T. ii. 1

mechanical, vulgar, vile. M.W. ii. 2; artisan. M.N.D. iii. 2

medicinable, healing. M.A. ii. 2

medicine, physician. A.W. ii. 1; W.T. iv. 3

meet, even, quits. M.A. i. 1

mell, meddle. A.W. iv. 3

men of hair, dressed in goatskins. W.T. iv. 3

mercatante, a merchant. T. of S. iv. 2

mere, absolute, downright. L. L.L. i. 1; &c.; merely. A.W. iii. 5

merely, altogether. Tp. i. 1; M. A. ii. 3

mess, group of four. L.L.L. iv. 3; v. 2; course. T. of S. iv. 4; W.T. iv. 3

mete, aim. L.L.L. iv. 1

mete-yard, measuring rod. T. of S. iv. 3

metheglin, spiced variety of mead. M.W. v. 5; L.L.L. v. 2

mew, mew up, confine. M.N. D. i. 1; T. of S. i. 1

mewl, whimper, cry feebly. As. ii. 7

mickle, much. C. of E. iii. 1

middle-earth, earth as placed between heaven and hell. M. W. v. 5

milch-kine, cows giving milk. M.W. iv. 4; T. of S. ii. 1

mill-sixpences, sixpences struck by coining-mill instead of hammer. M.W. i. 1

mind, spirit, temper. M. for M. ii. 4; M. of V. ii. 8; mean, intend. M.N.D. v. 1; remind. W.T. iii. 2

mine, undermine. As. i. 1; my kinsmen. A.W. i. 3

minimus, small insignificant creature. M.N.D. iii. 2

minion, favourite. Tp. iv. 1; &c.; spoilt favourite. Two G. i. 2; saucy wench. T. of S. ii. 1

minstrelsy, for my, instead of music. L.L.L. i. 1

misgraffed, badly matched. M. N.D. i. 1

misprise, despise, scorn. M.A. iii. 1; As. i. 1; i. 2; mistake. M. N.D. iii. 2; A.W. iii. 2

misprision, mistake, misunderstanding. M.A. iv. 1; &c.; contempt. A.W. ii. 3

miss, do without. Tp. i. 2

missingly, with sense of loss. W.T. iv. 1

misuse, deceive. M.A. ii. 2

mo, moe, more. M. for M. iii. 1; &c.

modern, ordinary, common-place. As. ii. 7; iv. 1; A.W. ii. 3; modest, or modish. A.W. v. 3

moiety, part, share. A.W. iii. 2; W.T. ii. 3; half. W.T. iii. 2

monarcho, the title assumed by Italian who fancied himself emperor of the world; one who is an object of ridicule. L.L.L. iv. 1

montant, upright blow or thrust. M.W. ii. 3

month's mind, good mind, inclination. Two G. i. 2

monument, memory. M.A. v. 2

monumental, serving as memento also as a proof of identity. A.W. iv. 3

mood, anger. Two G. iv. 1; C. of E. ii. 2

moonish, variable, fickle. As. iii. 2

mop, grimace. Tp. iv. 1

moralize, moral on, point the moral of. As. ii. 1; ii. 7

morning's love, i.e. Cephalus. M.N.D. iii. 2

morris-pike, a pike supposed of Moorish origin. C. of E. iv. 3

mort, note sounded on a horn at the death of the deer. W.T. i. 2

mortifying, killing. M.A. i. 3

mose in the chine, suffer from glanders. T. of S. iii. 2

motion, puppet-show. Two G. ii. 1; M. for M. iii. 2; W.T. iv.

2; proposal. M.W. i. 1; C. of E. i. 1; incitement. M. for M. i. 4; emotion, impulse. Tw.N. ii. 4

motive, instrument. A.W. iv. 4

motley, parti-coloured, as fool's dress. As. ii. 7; Tw.N. i. 5; fool. As. iii. 3

motley-minded, variegated, changeable. As. v. 4

mountanto, an upright blow or thrust. M.A. i. 1

move, appeal to. C. of E. ii. 2

mow, grimace. Tp. ii. 2; iv. 1

murmur, rumour. Tw.N. i. 2

murrain, plague, used as an imprecation. Tp. iii. 2

murrion, having died of disease. M.N.D. ii. 1

mystery, art of a trade guild. M. for M. iv. 2; A.W. iii. 6

napkin, handkerchief. As. iv. 3; T. of S. Ind. 1

native, by nature. L.L.L. i. 2; closely related. A.W. i. 1

natural, half-witted person. Tp. iii. 2; As. i. 2

nature, natural affection. Tp. v. 1; C. of E. i. 1; special duty. As. iii. 1; life. M. for M. ii. 4; temperament. A.W. iii. 1; way. A.W. iv. 3

naught, efface oneself, withdraw. As. i. 1

naughty, morally bad, wayward. M. for M. ii. 1; M. of V. iii. 2; good for nothing. A.W. v. 3

nayward, denial, disbelief. W.T. ii. 1

nay-word, watch word, catchword. M.W. ii. 2; v. 2; byword. Tw.N. ii. 3

neaf, fist. M.N.D. iv. 1

near-legged, knock-kneed in forelegs. T. of S. iii. 2

neat, ox, oxen. Tp. ii. 2; &c.

neat-herds, cow-herds. W.T. iv. 3

neb, mouth. W.T. i. 2

necessitied, in need of. A.W. v. 3

neeze, sneeze. M.N.D. ii. 1

nerve, sinews. Tp. i. 2

nick, reckoning, account. Two G. iv. 2; indent. C. of E. v. 1

night-rule, night revelry or riot. M.N.D. iii. 2

nine men's morris, a game between two players, each with nine disks of wood, or pegs, often played in the open. M. N.D. ii. 1

nit, gnat, or small fly; term of contempt or fun. L.L.L. iv. 1; T. of S. iv. 3

noddy, noodle. Two G. i. 1

noise, low or melodious sound. Tp. iii. 2

non-come, blunder for 'non compos' (out of one's right mind). M.A. iii. 5

note, mark of distinction. A. W. i. 3; be known. Tw.N. iv. 3; notice. W.T. i. 1; sign. W. T. i. 2; list. W.T. iv. 2

notedly, particularly. M. for M. v. 1

novum, game at dice, principal throws being nine and five. L. L.L. v. 2

nowl, head. M.N.D. iii. 2

number, metre. Tw.N. ii. 5

nuncio, messenger. Tw.N. i. 4

nuthook, beadle, constable. M. W. i. 1

O, anything round; circle, round spot, orb. L.L.L. v. 2; M.N.D. iii. 2

obscenely, blunder for 'seemly.' M.N.D. i. 2

occasion, husband's, opportunity for getting the better of one's husband. As. iv. 1

Od, minced form of 'God.' M. W. i. 1; &c.

oeilliades, amorous glances. M. W. i. 3

o'erflourished, elaborately carved. Tw.N. iii. 4

o'erlooked, perused. Two. G. i. 2; bewitched. M.W. v. 5; M. of V. iii. 2

o'erparted, with too difficult a part, or too many parts to play. L.L.L. v. 2

o'er-raught, outwitted, cheated. C. of E. i. 2

o'erslip, slips by without notice. Two G. ii. 2

offer, essay, try, endeavour. As. iii. 2; contribute. As. v. 4; make an attempt. W.T. iv. 3

office, service. M. for M. v. 1; perform by way of service. A. W. iii. 2

officed, functioned. W.T. i. 2

old, great, plentiful, excessive. M.W. i. 4; &c.

omit, neglect. Tp. i. 2; ii. 1; Two G. ii. 4

open, (of hounds) to begin to cry when in pursuit of a scent. M.W. iv. 2; clear, easy to understand. M. for M. ii. 1; Tw. N. ii. 5; openly. Tw.N. iii. 3

opinion, self-conceit. L.L.L. v. 1; reputation, estimation. M. of V. i. 1

opinioned, blunder for 'pinioned.' M.A. iv. 2

or, before. Tp. i. 2; v. 1; &c.

orb, orbit. M.A. iv. 1; circles, rings. M.N.D. ii. 1; star. M. of V. v. 1; the earth, the world. Tw.N. iii. 1

ordinary, public meal at eating-house or tavern. A.W. ii. 3

ostent, ostentation, display, appearance, exhibition. M.A. iv. 1; &c.

othergates, otherwise, in another way. Tw.N. v. 1

otherwhere, elsewhere. C. of E. ii. 1

ounce, lynx. M.N.D. ii. 2

ouph, goblin child. M.W. iv. 4; v. 5

ousel, blackbird, merle. M.N.D. iii. 1

out, completely, quite. Tp. i. 2; iv. 1; M.A. iii. 2; exhausted. Tp. iii. 2; out of practice. L.L.L. iv. 1; at a loss from failure of memory or self-possession. L.L.L. v. 2; As. iv. 1; into confusion or perplexity. L.L.L. v. 2; As. iii. 2; at variance. M. of V. iii. 5; over. A.W. i. 2; in error, mistaken. Tw.N. ii. 3; W.T. ii. 1; dislocated. W.T. iv. 2

outvied, out-done. T. of S. ii. 1

outward, uninitiated. A.W. iii. 1

overture, opening of negotiations or proceedings. A.W. iv. 3; Tw.N. i. 5; disclosure. W.T. ii. 1

owe, own, possess. Tp. i. 2; &c.

oyes, call or exclamation of 'Oyez,' 'Hear ye!' M.W. v. 5

pace, train, exercise. M. for M. iv. 3; prescribed walk. A.W. iv. 5

pack, compact, plot. M.W. iv. 2; C. of E. iv. 4; T. of S. v. 1

packed, leagued. C. of E. v. 1; M.A. v. 1

pain, penalty. M. for M. ii. 4; trouble. M. for M. v. 1; toil. T. of S. iii. 1

painted cloth, hanging for room painted or worked with figures, mottoes, or texts; tapestry. L.L.L. v. 2; As. iii. 2

palabras, i.e. pocas palabras (Sp.), few words. M.A. iii. 5

pale, bounds, region. W.T. iv. 2

panderly, base. M.W. iv. 2

pantaloon, dotard, old fool. As. ii. 7; T. of S. iii. 1

pantler, officer in charge of pantry. W.T. i . 3

parcel, part. M.W. i. 1; C. of E. v. 1; in part, partly. M. for M. ii. 1; company, collection, assemblage. L.L.L. v. 2; M. of V. i. 2; A.W. ii. 3; detail. As. iii. 5

pard, leopard, or panther. Tp. iv. 1; M.N.D. ii. 2; As. ii. 7

parfect, blunder for 'present.' L.L.L. v. 2

parish-top, top kept for the use of villagers. Tw.N. i. 3

'paritor (apparitor), summoning officer of ecclesiastical court. L.L.L. iii. 1

parle, conversation. Two G. i. 2; speak. L.L.L. v. 2; parly. T. of S. i. 1

parlous, perilous. M.N.D. iii. 1; As. iii. 2

particular, part. A.W. ii. 5

partlet, hen. W.T. ii. 3

pash, head. W.T. i. 2

pass, indulge in as a jest. M.W. i. 1; pass description. M.W. i. 1; iv. 2; thrust in fencing. M.W. ii. 1; ii. 3; Tw.N. iii. 1; pronounce verdict. M. for M. ii. 1; course of action. M. for M. v. 1; pass for. L.L.L. v. 1; transfer to. T. of S. iv. 4; transact. T. of S. iv. 4; impose. Tw.N. v. 1; surpass. W.T. ii. 2

passado, thrust in fencing. L. L.L. i. 2

passage, passing of people. C.

of E. iii. 1; occurrence. A.W. i. 1; act, transaction, proceeding. Tw.N. iii. 2; course, process. W.T. iii. 2

passant (of a beast, in heraldry), walki g. M.W. i. 1

passion, passionate speech or outburst. M.N.D. v. 1; feel deeply. Tp. v. 1; L.L.L. i. 1; grieving. Two G. iv. 4

pass of pate, sally of wit. Tp. iv. 1

passy-measures pavin, slow dance. Tw.N. v. 1

patch, fool, clown. Tp. iii. 2; &c.

patched, motley. M.N.D. iv. 1

pathetical, moving, affecting. L.L.L. i. 2; iv. 1; As. iv. 1

patine, thin circular plate of metal. M. of V. v. 1

pattern, match. W.T. iii. 2

pauca, pauca verba, paucas pallabris, few words. M.W. i. 1; L.L.L. iv. 2; T. of S. Ind. 1

paunch, stab or wound in the stomach. Tp. iii. 2

pavin, stately dance. Tw.N. v. 1

peach, impeach, betray. M. for M. iv. 3

peaking, sneaking. M.W. iii. 5

peascod, pea-pod. M.N.D. iii. 1; As. ii. 4; Tw.N. i. 5

peat, pet, spoilt girl. T. of S. i. 1

peculiar, private. M. for M. i. 2

pedant, pedascule, schoolmaster. L.L.L. iii. 1; T. of S. iii. 1; &c.

peer, appear. W.T. iv. 2; iv. 3

peevish, foolish. M.W. i. 4; C. of E. iv. 1; Tw.N. i. 5; wayward, saucy. As. iii. 5

Peg-a-Ramsey, name of old ballad. Tw.N. ii. 3

peise, weigh down. M. of V. iii. 2

pelting, paltry. M. for M. ii. 2; M.N.D. ii. 1

pensioner, gentleman-at-arms, body-guard. M.W. ii. 2; M.N.D. ii. 1

Penthesilea, queen of the Amazons. Tw.N. ii. 3

pent-house, shelter, porch, shed, outhouse. M.A. iii. 3; L.L.L. iii. 1; M. of V. ii. 6

perdurably, everlastingly. M. for M. iii. 1

perdy, Par Dieu, an oath. C. of E. iv. 4; Tw.N. iv. 2

peregrinate, having air of a traveller. L.L.L. v. 1

perfect, instruct or inform completely. Tp. i. 2; M. for M. iv. 3; sure. W.T. iii. 3

perge, go on, proceed. L.L.L. iv. 2

perpend, ponder, consider. M.W. ii. 1; As. iii. 2; Tw.N. v. 1

persever, persevere. As. v. 2

personage, personal appearance. M.N.D. iii. 2; Tw.N. i. 5

perspective, magnifying glass, telescope. A.W. v. 3; picture or figure constructed so as to produce a fantastic effect. Tw.N. v. 1

persuaded, best, having the best opinion. Tw.N. ii. 3

pertly, promptly, quickly. Tp. iv. 1

perttaunt-like, a word not yet explained. L.L.L. v. 2

pettitoes, pigs' trotters; W.T. iv. 3

phantasime, fantastic being. L.L.L. iv. 1; v. 1

pheezar, see 'pheeze' below. M.W. i. 3

pheeze, beat, pay you out. T. of S. Ind. 1

Phibbus, Phoebus. M.N.D. i. 2

Philip and Jacob, St. Philip's and St. James's Day. M. for M. iii. 2

physics, heals, cures. W.T. i. 1

pia mater, brain. L.L.L. iv. 2; Tw.N. i. 5

picked, finical, particular. L.L.L. v. 1

piece, exemplification. Tp. i. 2; work of art. W.T. v. 2; v. 3; complete. W.T. v. 2

piety, blunder for 'impiety.' M. A. iv. 2

piled, having a pile or long nap, as velvet. M. for M. i. 2

pilot's glass, hour-glass. A.W. ii. 1

pin, mere nothing. M.W. i. 1; stud fixed in centre of target. L.L.L. iv. 1

pin and web, disease of the eye; ?cataract. W.T. i. 2

pinched, made ridiculous. W. T. ii. 1

pinfold, place for confining stray cattle. Two G. i. 1

pioned, ? dug, excavated, trenched; ? covered with marsh-marigolds. Tp. iv. 1

pip, each of the spots on playing-cards. T. of S. i. 2 (allusion to card-game called 'one-and-thirty')

pipe-wine, wine drawn directly from cask or 'wood' (with play upon musical 'pipe' and 'canary' the dance). M.W. iii. 2

pitch, degree, elevation, status. Tw.N. i. 1

place, house, dwelling. As. ii. 3; precedence. A.W. i. 1; position, station. W.T. i. 2

placket, pocket, especially in woman's skirt. L.L.L. iii. 1; W.T. iv. 3

plain, mere, absolute. Tp. v. 1

plain-song, singing simple melody. M.N.D. iii. 1

planched, planked, boarded. M. for M. iv. 1

plantain, plantain leaf used to stop bleeding. L.L.L. iii. 1

plash, pool, puddle. T. of S. i. 1

plausive, plausible, pleasing, specious. A.W. i. 2; iv. 1

pleached, formed by inter-twisting of boughs and twigs. M.A. i. 2; iii. 1

please, pay. C. of E. iv. 4

please-man, man-pleaser, sycophant. L.L.L. v. 2

pluck up, rouse thyself. M.A. v. 1

plummet, 'Ignorance itself is a plummet o'er me' = 'I am a plummet's depth below ignorance itself.' M.W. v. 5

point, smallest detail. Tp. i. 2; suggest. L.L.L. ii. 1; tagged lace for attaching hose to doublet. T. of S. iii. 2; Tw.N. i. 5; W.T. iv. 3

point-device, -devise, extremely neat, precise, scrupulous. L.L.L. v. 1; As. iii. 2; exactly. Tw.N. ii. 5

poising us, adding our weight (of patronage). A.W. ii. 3

poke, pocket. As. ii. 7

poking-sticks, rods used for stiffening plaits of ruffs. W.T. iv. 3

pole, quarter-staff. L.L.L. v. 2

pole-clipt, hedged in by poles. Tp. iv. 1

pollusion, blunder for 'allusion.' L.L.L. iv. 2

pomander, ball of perfume. W. T. iv. 3

pomewater, large juicy apple. L.L.L. iv. 2

Poor-John, hake (or ? other fish) salted and dried for food. Tp. ii. 2

porpentine, porcupine. C. of E. iii. 1

porringer, small basin. T. of S. iv. 3

port, gate. A.W. iii. 5; deportment, style of living, importance. M. of V. i. 1; iii. 2; T. of S. i. 1

possess, inform. M. for M. iv. 1; &c.

possession, mental endowment. Two G. v. 2; i.e. by the devil. C. of E. v. 1

possitable, blunder for 'positively.' M.W. i. 1

post, letter-carrier. Tp. ii. 1; &c.; post-haste. C. of E. i. 2; iii. 2; W.T. ii. 1; tavern doorpost on which reckonings were scored. C. of E. i. 2

posy (i.e. poesy), short motto, line of poetry, inscribed on a knife or in a ring. M. of V. v. 1

pottle, two quarts. M.W. ii. 1; iii. 5

powdered, salted and pickled. M. for M. iii. 2

practice, scheming, machination, trickery. M. for M. v. 1; &c.

practise, intrigue. Two G. iv. 1; As. i. 1; play a trick. T. of S. Ind. i

praise, appraise, value. Tw.N. i. 5

prank, dress. Tw.N. ii. 4; W.T. iv. 3

preceptial, instructive. M.A. v. 1

preeches, breeched for flogging. M.W. iv. 1

prefer, promote. Two G. ii. 4;

recommend. M. of V. ii. 2; T. of S. i. 1; press forward. M. for M. i. 1; submitted for approval. M.N.D. iv. 2

pregnant, clear, obvious. M. for M. ii. 1; W.T. v. 2; inventive, resourceful. M. for M. i. 1; Tw.N. ii. 2; receptive, disposed, ready. Tw.N. iii. 1

prejudicates, prejudices. A.W. i. 2

premises, previous circumstances. Tp. i. 2

prenzie, doubtful word, prob. an error. M. for M. iii. 1

preposterous, blunder for 'prosperous.' W.T. v. 2

prest, constrained. M. of V. i. 1

Prester John, a legendary Christian king and priest ruling in the extreme East, or in Abyssinia. M.A. ii. 1

prevailment, influence, ascendancy. M.N.D. i. 1

pribbles and prabbles, petty wranglings. M.W. i. 1

prick, the spine. Tp. ii. 2; spot in centre of target. L.L.L. iv. 1; sting. As. iii. 2; stick. T. of S. iii. 2; incite. T. of S. iii. 2

pricket, buck in its second year. L.L.L. iv. 2

prig, thief. W.T. iv. 2

primero, gambling card-game. M.W. iv. 5

principality, one of the nine orders of angels. Two G. ii. 4

print, in, with exactness or preciseness. Two G. ii. 1; L.L.L. iii. 1; As. v. 4

priser, prize-fighter. As. ii. 3

probation, proof. M. for M. v. 1; trial. Tw.N. ii. 5

process, course, story. M. of V. iv. 1

prolixious, long in duration. M. for M. ii. 4

prolonged, postponed. M.A. iv. 1

prompture, instigation. M. for M. ii. 4

proper-false, handsome and deceitful. Tw.N. ii. 2

property, mere means to an end. M.W. iii. 4; fulfilment. A.W. ii. 1; make a tool of, exploit. Tw.N. iv. 2

proportions, fortune. M. for M. v. 1

propose, converse, conversation. M.A. iii. 1

propriety, individuality. Tw. N. v. 1

provincial, belonging to an ecclesiastical province. M. for M. v. 1

provoke, invoke. M. for M. iii. 1

pruning, adorning. L.L.L. iv. 3

puddings, bowels, entrails. M. W. ii. 1

pugging, ? 'pigging,' thievish, or 'pug-tooth,' eye-tooth. W. T. iv. 2

puisny, puny, insignificant. As. iii. 4

pumpion, pumpkin. M.W. iii. 3

punk, prostitute. M.W. ii. 2; M. for M. v. 1

punto, stroke or thrust with sword-point. M.W. ii. 3

purgation, vindication, proof. As. i. 3; v. 4; W.T. iii. 2

push, pish! make a push at = treat with disdain. M.A. v. 1; impulse, impetus. W.T. v. 3

push-pin, child's game. L.L.L. iv. 3

put, compelled; called upon. M. for M. i. 1

put in, plead, intercede. M. for M. i. 2

put on, urge onward. M. for M.

iv. 2; ? to lay on as a blow. L. L.L. iv. 1; communicate, impart. As. i. 2; Tw.N. v. 1

putter-on, instigator. W.T. ii. 1

putter-out, one who lends money at interest. Tp. iii. 3

quail, overpower. M.N.D. v. 1; fail. As. ii. 2

quarter, to add another's coat to one's hereditary coat-of-arms. M.W. i. 1; conduct, relations. C. of E. ii. 1

quatch-buttock, squat buttock. A.W. ii. 2

quean, ill-behaved woman. M. W. iv. 2

queasy, nice, delicate. M.A. ii. 1

quell, kill. M.N.D. v. 1

quern, handmill. M.N.D. ii. 1

quest, inquiry, pursuit, search. M. for M. iv. 1; M. of V. i. 1

questant, seeker. A.W. ii. 1

question, consideration. M. for M. i. 1; that's the question. M.A. v. 2; talk, discourse. M.N.D. ii. 1; &c.

question, loss of, for the sake of argument. M. for M. ii. 4

quick, running. Tp. iii. 2; living. M.W. iii. 4; &c.; pregnant. L.L.L. v. 2

quillets, casuistries. L.L.L. iv. 3

quintain, stout post, used as mark in tilting. As. i. 2

quire, company. M.N.D. ii. 1; sing in concert. M. of V. v. 1

quirk, witty turn, conceit. M.A. ii. 3; fit, sudden stroke. A.W. iii. 2; trick of behaviour. Tw. N. iii. 4

quit, leave. Tp. i. 2; M. for M. ii. 4; remit. C. of E. i. 1; M. of V. iv. 1; acquit. As. iii. 1; A.

W. v. 3; renounce, dismiss. Tw.N. v. 1

quittance, receipt. M.W. i. 1

quoif, cap. W.T. iv. 3

quote, regard, mention. L.L.L. iv. 3; v. 2; A.W. v. 3

quotidian, intermittent fever. As. iii. 2

rabato, kind of stiff collar. M. A. iii. 4

race, natural or inherited disposition. Tp. i. 2; M. for M. ii. 4; a herd of horses. M. of V. v. 1; root. W.T. iv. 2

rack, driving mist. Tp. iv. 1; stretch or raise beyond the normal degree. M.A. iv. 1; M. of V. i. 1

ragged, harsh, discordant. As. ii. 5

rank, abundantly. M.W. iv. 6; lustful. M. of V. i. 3; position. As. i. 2; movement in line or file. As. iii. 2; row. As. iv. 3

rankness, pride, rebellion. As. i. 1

rascal, inferior deer of a herd. As. iii. 3

rate, estimation, consideration. Tp. i. 2; ii. 1; value. M. for M. ii. 2; M. of V. ii. 7; mode of living. M. of V. i. 1; scold. T. of S. i. 1; price. A.W. v. 3

rato-lorum, blunder for 'rotu-lorum.' M.W. i. 1

raught, reached. L.L.L. iv. 2

ravel, become entangled. Two G. iii. 2

ravin, ravenously devour. M. for M. i. 2; ravenous. A.W. iii. 2

rayed, befouled, soiled. T. of S. iii. 2; iv. 1

razure, effacement. M. for M. v. 1

reason, anything reasonable.

Tp. iii. 2; possibility of action. Two G. ii. 4; T. of S. ii. 1; discourse. L.L.L. v. 1; As. i. 2; argue. M. of V. ii. 8; 'it is just.' W.T. iv. 3

reave, deprive. A.W. v. 3

rebate, make blunt. M. for M. i. 4

rebused, blunder for 'abused.' T. of S. i. 2

recheat, notes sounded on a horn to call together the hounds in a hunt. M.A. i. 1

reclusive, secluded. M.A. iv. 1

record, render in song. Two G. v. 4; memory. Tw.N. v. 1

recorder, wind instrument. M. N.D. v. 1

recountment, relation, recital. As. iv. 3

red-lattice, lattice painted red as the mark of an inn, hence an alehouse or inn. M.W. ii. 2

reechy, smoky, dirty. M.A. iii. 3

reed, reedy or squeaking. M. of V. iii. 4

reeling-ripe, drunk to the point of reeling. Tp. v. i

refell, refuse, reject. M. for M. v. 1

refer, have recourse. M. for M. iii. 1

reformed, blunder for 'in-formed.' M.A. v. 1

regreet, greeting. M. of V. ii. 9

rehearse, sing over. M.N.D. v. 2

rein, submit to the rein. Tw.N. iii. 4

religious, faithful. A.W. ii. 3

relish, realize. W.T. ii. 1

remember thy curtsy, put on thy hat. L.L.L. v. 1

remorse, compassion. Tp. v. 1, &c.

remorseful, compassionate. Two G. iv. 3

remove, absence. M. for M. i. 1; post-stage. A.W. v. 3

removed, removedness, secluded, seclusion. M. for M. i. 3; &c.; distant in relationship. As. v. 4; separated by time. Tw.N. v. 1

render, describe as. As. iv. 3; pay, exhibit. M.A. v. 3; to make. M. of V. iii. 2

renegado, apostate. Tw.N. iii. 2

rent, rend. M.N.D. iii. 2

repair, come back. L.L.L. v. 2; restores, revives. A.W. i. 2; restoration. W.T. v. 1

repasture, repast. L.L.L. iv. 1

repetition, remembrance. A. W. v. 3

report, reputation. M. for M. ii. 3; M.A. iii. 1; testimony. L.L.L. ii. 1

reportingly, by report or hearsay. M.A. iii. 1

reprehend, misused for 'represent.' L.L.L. i. 1

reproach, blunder for 'approach.' M. of V. ii. 5

reprove, disprove. M.A. ii. 3

require, deserve. W.T. ii. 3; iii. 2

requit, repay, requite. Tp. iii. 3

rere-mice, bats. M.N.D. ii. 2

resolve, bring to a clear understanding. Tp. v. 1; M. for M. iv. 2; inform. M. for M. iii. 1; answer. L.L.L. ii. 1; T. of S. iv. 2; solve. As. iii. 2

resolvedly, definitely. A.W. v. 3

resolve you, prepare yourselves. W.T. v. 3

respect, value. Two G. i. 2; regard, care for. Two G. iii. 1; &c.; consideration, estimation. L.L.L. v. 2; M.N.D. ii. 1; regard to circumstances. M. of

V. v. 1; reason. A.W. ii. 5

respected, blunder for 'suspected.' M. for M. ii. 1

respecting, in comparison with. W.T. v. 1

respective, worthy of regard. Two G. iv. 4; careful. M. of V. v. 1

'rest, arrest. C. of E. iv. 2; &c.

restrained, forbidden. M. for M. ii. 4; drawn tightly. T. of S. iii. 2

rest, set up one's, resolve, determine. C. of E. iv. 3; M. of V. ii. 2; A.W. ii. 1

retention, power to retain. Tw. N. ii. 4

retort, refer back. M. for M. v. 1

reverse, back-handed stroke. M.W. ii. 3

rheum, cold or catarrh. M. for M. iii. 1; C. of E. iii. 2; W.T. iv. 3; saliva. M. of V. i. 3; tears. M.A. v. 2

rheumatic, inducing catarrhal affections. M.W. iii. 1; characterized by rheum. M.N.D. ii. 1

Rialto, quarter of Venice in which the Exchange was situated. M. of V. i. 3

rib, enclose as with ribs. M. of V. ii. 7

rid, destroy. Tp. i. 2

right, exactly. M.N.D. iv. 2

ring-carrier, go-between. A.W. iii. 5

Ringwood, name of a dog. M. W. ii. 1

riping, point of becoming ripe. M. of V. ii. 8

ronyon, abusive term applied to a woman. M.W. iv. 2

rope-tricks, ? blunder or pun for 'rhetoric.' T. of S. i. 2

round, bring to completeness.

Tp. iv. 1; plain spoken. C. of E. ii. 1; Tw.N. ii. 3; circle. M.N.D. ii. 1; encircle. M.N.D. iv. 1; whisper. W.T. i. 2; develop to a full round form. W.T. ii. 1

roundel, round dance. M.N.D. ii. 2

roundly, promptly. As. v. 3; T. of S. v. 2; bluntly. T. of S. iii. 2; without needless ceremony. T. of S. iv. 4

rout, rabble. C. of E. iii. 1

roynish, coarse, base. As. ii. 2

rub, encounter (in playing bowls) some impediment which diverts the bowl from its proper course. L.L.L. iv. 1

rubious, ruby-coloured. Tw.N. i. 4

rudesby, insolent fellow. T. of S. iii. 2; Tw.N. iv. 1; ruffling, rising in ruffles. T. of S. iv. 3

rule, procedure. M. of V. iv. 1; Tw.N. ii. 3

rushling, blunder for 'rustling.' M.W. ii. 2

russet, homespun. L.L.L. v. 2

russet-pated, grey-headed. M.N.D. iii. 2

ruttish, lustful. A.W. iv. 3

sack, white wine. Tp. ii. 2; T. of S. Ind. 2; Tw.N. ii. 3

Sackerson, name of a famous bear. M.W. i. 1

sad, sadness, serious, seriousness. Two G. i. 3; &c.

sain, said. L.L.L. iii. 1

sale-work, ready-made goods. As. iii. 5

salt, salt-cellar. Two G. iii. 1; lustful. M. for M. v. 1

saltiers, blunder for 'satyrs.' W.T. iv. 3

sanctimonious, holy, consecrated. Tp. iv. 1

sanctimony, sanctity. A.W. iv. 3

sand-blind, half-blind, dim-sighted, purblind. M. of V. ii. 2

sanded, of a sandy colour. M.N.D. iv. 1

sans, without. Tp. i. 2; L.L.L. v. 2; As. ii. 7

saucy, wanton, lascivious. M. for M. ii. 4; A.W. iv. 4

scale, weigh as in scales, estimate. M. for M. iii. 1

scall, scabby. M.W. iii. 1

scambling, scrambling. M.A. v. 1

scamel, meaning uncertain. Tp. ii. 2

scandaled, scandalous. Tp. iv. 1

scape, transgression. W.T. iii. 3

scarfed, beflagged. M. of V. ii. 6

scarfs and bannerets, silken ornaments worn on various parts of the attire. A.W. ii. 3

scathful, hurtful, harmful. Tw.N. v. 1

sconce, head. C. of E. i. 2; ii. 2; defence. C. of E. ii. 2

scour, to depart in haste, run away, decamp. W.T. ii. 1

scrip, written list. M.N.D. i. 2; small bag. As. iii. 2

scrippage, contents of a scrip. As. iii. 2

scrubbed, stunted. M. of V. v. 1

scruple, quantity. M. for M. i. 1

scut, tail. M.W. v. 5

search, probe. As. ii. 4

season, influence. M. for M. ii. 2; opportunity. C. of E. iv. 2; that which preserves. M.A. iv. 1; preserve. A.W. i. 1; Tw.N. i. 1

second, helpful. W.T. ii. 3

secure, careless. M.W. ii. 1

seedness sowing of the seed. M. for M. i. 1

seeming, appearance, hypocrisy. M. for M. ii. 4; M.A. iv. 1; seemingly, becomingly. As. v. 4; freshness. W.T. iv. 3

seen, well, well-skilled. T. of S. i. 2

seldom when, rarely. M. for M. iv. 2

semblative, resembling, like. Tw.N. i. 4

se'nnight, a week. As. iii. 2

Senoys, Sienese. A.W. i. 2

sense, feelings. Tp. ii. 1; sensual passions. M. for M. ii. 2; reason. M. of V. v. 1; A.W. i. 1

sensible, sensitive. Tp. ii. 1; C. of E. iv. 4; M. of V. ii. 8; capable of feeling. M.N.D. v. 1; substantial. M of V. ii. 9

sentences, sententious sayings. M.A. ii. 3

sequent, following. M. for M. v. 1; follower. L.L.L. iv. 2

serpigo, skin eruption. M. for M. iii. 1

sessa, exclamation urging to speed. T. of S. Ind. 1

set, set to music, value. Two G. i. 2; seated. Two G ii. 1; a set at tennis. L.L.L. v. 2

several, belonging to private owner. L.L.L. ii. 1; individual. W.T. i. 2

Shafalus, i.e. Cephalus. M.N.D. v. 1

sheep-biter, sheep-biting, thief, thieving. Tw.N. ii. 5; M. for M. v. 1

sheep-whistling, sheep-tending. W.T. iv. 3

sheer, mere, nothing but. T. of S. Ind. 2

shent, rated, reviled. M.W. i. 4; Tw.N. iv. 2

sheriff's post, post to which proclamations were affixed. Tw.N. i. 5

shield, defend, grant. M. for M. iii. 1

ship-tire, headdress. M.W. iii. 3

shot, reckoning. Two G. iii. 5

shoulder-shotten, with dislocated shoulder. T. of S. iii. 2

shovel-board, shilling used in game of that name. M.W. i. 1

'shrew, beshrew, plague. W.T. i. 2

shrewd, mischievous, bad. M.W. ii. 2; &c.; shrewish. M.A. ii. 1

shrieve, sheriff. A.W. iv. 3

shrift, absolution. M. for M. iv. 2

shrow, shrew. L.L.L. v. 2

sicles, shekels. M. for M. ii. 2

side sleeves, long hanging sleeves. M.A. iii. 4

siege, stool, excrement. Tp. ii. 2; seat. M. for M. iv. 2

significant, something to express meaning. L.L.L. iii. 1

signory, lordship, domain, territory. Tp. i. 2

silly, defenceless. Two G. iv. 1; homely. Tw.N. ii. 4

simple, herb used in medicine. M.W. i. 4; iii. 3; As. iv. 1; foolish. T. of S. v. 2

since once, that once upon a time. M.N.D. ii. 1; T. of S. Ind. 1; when. W.T. v. 1

singled, separated. L.L.L. v. 1

sinister, left. M.N.D. v. 1; A.W. ii. 1

sink, make fall. Tp. ii. 1

sinking-ripe, ready to sink. C. of E. i. 1

sirrah, familiar style of address. Tp. v. 1

sir-reverence, corruption of

'save-reverence,' an apologetic expression. C. of E. iii. 2

Sisters Three, the Fates. M.N.D. v. 1

sith, since. M. for M. i. 3; &c.

sithence, since. A.W. i. 3

skill, matter. T. of S. iii. 2; Tw.N. v. 1; cunning. W.T. ii. 1; reason. W.T. iv. 3

skill-less, skilless, ignorant. Tp. iii. 1; Tw.N. iii. 3

skipper, thoughtless fellow. T. of S. ii. 1

slack, neglect. M.W. iii. 4

sleeve-hand, a wristband. W.T. iv. 3

'slid, God's lid, an oath. M.W. iii. 4; Tw.N. iii. 4

'slight, God's light, an oath. Tw.N. ii. 5; iii. 2

slighted, chucked, threw contemptuously. M.W. iii. 5

slop, slops, loose breeches. M.A. iii. 2; L.L.L. iv. 3

slubber, slur over. M. of V. ii. 8

sluggardized, made indolent. Two G. i. 1

smack, savour. M. for M. ii. 2; M. of V. ii. 2; the small of the leg. L.L.L. v. 2; smattering. A.W. iv. 1

small, boy's or woman's treble voice; shrill-voiced. M.N.D. i. 2; Tw.N. i. 4

smother, suffocating smoke. As. i. 2

smug, trim, spruce. M. of V. iii. 1

snatches, repartees. M. for M. iv. 2

sneap, check, nip. L.L.L. i. 1; W.T. i. 2

sneck up, expression of contempt. Tw.N. ii. 3

snipt-taffeta, dressed in silks and ribbons. A.W. iv. 5

snuff, object of loathing. A.W. i. 2

sod, sodden. L.L.L. iv. 2

solely, absolutely. A.W. i. 1; alone. W.T. ii. 3

solemn, ceremonious. A.W. iv. 3

something, somewhat. M. of V. i. 1

sonties, ? corruption of 'sante,' 'sanctity,' or 'saints.' M. of V. ii. 2

sooth, truth. M.N.D. ii. 2; &c.

Sophy, Shah of Persia. Tw.N. ii. 5; iii. 4

sore, buck of the fourth year. L.L.L. iv. 2

sorel, buck of the third year. L.L.L. iv. 2

sot, fool. Tp. iii. 2; C. of E. ii. 2; Tw.N. i. 5

soud, a sigh of fatigue. T. of S. iv. 1

sovereignty, efficacy. A.W. i. 3

spare, forbear to offend. M. for M. ii. 3

specialties, articles of a contract. L.L.L. ii. 1; T. of S. ii. 1

speciously, blunder for 'specially.' M.W. iii. 4; iv. 5

sped, done for, prospered. M. of V. ii. 9; W.T. i. 2

speed, succeed. Two G. iv. 4; T. of S. i. 2; help. As. i. 2; fortune, progress. T. of S. ii. 1; W.T. iii. 2

sphery, starry. M.N.D. ii. 2

spinner, spider. M.N.D. ii. 2

splay, castrate. M. for M. ii. 1

spleen, supposed seat of emotion of laughter. M. for M. ii. 2; quick movement. M.N.D. i. 1; passion. As. iv. 1; ill-temper. T. of S. iii. 2; laughter. Tw.N. iii. 2; &c.

sprag, quick, sharp. M.W. iv. 1

sprat, worthless fellow. A.W. iii. 6

spring, beginning. M.N.D. ii. 1

springe, trap. W.T. iv. 2

spurs, roots. Tp. v. 1

squandered, scattered. M. of V. i. 3

squandering, random. As. ii. 7

square, quarrel. M.N.D. ii. 1; embroidery about the bosom of garment. W.T. iv. 3; shape. W.T. v. 1

squarer, brawler, braggart. M. A. i. 1

squash, unripe peascod. M.N. D. iii. 1; Tw.N. i. 5; W.T. i. 2

squire, squier, square, rule, measure. L.L.L. v. 2; W.T. iv. 3

stage, exhibit. M. for M. i. 1

stagger, staggering, hesitate, hesitation. M.W. iii. 3; M. for M. i. 2; As. iii. 3

staggers, apoplexy in horses. T. of S. iii. 2; bewilderment. A. W. ii. 3

stain, tinge, characteristic. A. W. i. 1

stale, decoy. Tp. iv. 1; T. of S. iii. 1; dupe, laughing-stock. M.W. ii. 3; T. of S. i. 1; prostitute. C. of E. ii. 1; M.A. ii. 2; iv. 1

stall, keep close, as in a stall. A. W. i. 3

stamps, impressed coins. M.W. iii. 4

stand, withstand. T. of S. i. 2; fight. W.T. iii. 2

standing, duration. W.T. i. 2

standing-bed, bed standing on posts. M.W. iv. 5

standing water, between ebb and flood of tide. Tw.N. i. 5

stand upon, be of importance to. C. of E. iv. 1

staniel, kestrel-hawk. Tw.N. ii. 5

stanze, stanzo, stanza. L.L.L. iv. 2; As. ii. 5

staple, thread. L.L.L. v. 1

star, pole star. M.A. iii. 4; fortune. Tw.N. ii. 5

start-up, upstart. M.A. i. 3

starve, nip with cold. Two G. iv. 4

state, attitude. L.L.L. iv. 3; estate, fortune. M. of V. iii. 2; &c.; chair of state. Tw.N. ii. 5; authority. Tw.N. ii. 5; condition. Tw.N. v. 1

statute-caps, woollen caps, worn by citizens in accordance with an Act of Parliament of 1571. L.L.L. v. 2

stead, be of service. Tp. i. 2; &c.

stead up, supply, take the place of. M. for M. iii. 1

steely, unyielding. A.W. i. 1

stew, cauldron. M. for M. v. 1

stigmatical, marked with deformity. C. of E. iv. 2

still an end, perpetually. Two G. iv. 4

still-piecing, doubtful word. A.W. iii. 2

still-vexed, always disturbed. Tp. i. 2

stoccado, thrust in fencing. M. W. ii. 1

stock, thrust in fencing. M.W. ii. 3; stocking. T. of S. iii. 2; Tw.N. i. 3

stock-fish, dried cod. Tp. iii. 2; M. for M. iii. 2

stockish, insensible. M. of V. v. 1

stomach, courage. Tp. i. 2; temper. Two G. i. 2; appetite. C. of E. i. 2; M.A. i. 3; T. of S. iv. 1; pride. T. of S. v. 2; inclination. A.W. iii. 6

stone-bow, cross-bow for shooting stones. Tw.N. ii. 5

story, subject of mirth. M. for M. i. 4

stoup, drinking-cup. Tw.N. ii. 3

stout, haughty, proud. Tw.N. ii. 5

stover, fodder for cattle. Tp. iv. 1

strain, pervert oneself. W.T. iii. 2

strained, constrained. M. of V. iv. 1; turned from right course. W.T. iii. 2

strait, strict. M. for M. ii. 1

straited, at a loss. W.T. iv. 3

straitness, strictness. M. for M. iii. 2

strange, original. L.L.L. v. 1; reserved, distant. Tw.N. ii. 5; estranged. Tw.N. v. 1

strangely, extraordinarily well. Tp. iv. 1

strangeness, reserve, distant manner. Tw.N. iv. 1

strayed, led astray. C. of E. v. 1

stricture, strictness. M. for M. i. 3

strond, strand. M. of V. i. 1

struck, advanced. T. of S. ii. 1

stuck-in, thrust in fencing. Tw. N. iii. 4

studied, practised, instructed. M. of V. ii. 2

stuffed, complete. M.A. i. 1; W.T. ii. 1

subscribe, be surety. A.W. iii. 6; iv. 5; admit, acknowledge. M. for M. ii. 4; declare. M.A. v. 2

subscribe to, admit, acknowledge. Two G. v. 4; A.W. v. 3

substractors, detractors. Tw.N. i. 3

subtilties, illusions, false appearances. Tp. v. 1

succeed, inherit. M. for M. ii. 4; descend by order of succession; A.W. iii. 7

succeeding, consequence. A. W. ii. 3

success, the issue. M.A. iv. 1; succession. W.T. i. 2

succession, others from doing the same. A.W. iii. 5

sufferance, suffering. M.W. iv. 2; &c.

sufficiency, ability. W.T. ii. 1

suffigance, blunder for 'sufficient.' M.A. iii. 5

suggest, tempt. Two G. iii. i; L.L.L. v. 2; A.W. iv. 5

suggestion, prompting, temptation. Tp. ii. 1; iv. 1; L.L.L. i. 1

suit, service due to a feudal superior. M. for M. iv. 4; fit. M.A. v. 1; Tw.N. i. 2; furnish. As. i. 3; petition, dress. As. ii. 7

suits, respects. T. of S. Ind. 1

suits with fortune, out of, dismissed from Fortune's service. As. i. 2

superfluous, luxurious. A.W. i. 1

superscript, address. L.L.L. iv. 2

supportance, keeping. Tw.N. iii. 4

supposed, blunder for 'deposed,' M. for M. ii. 1; spurious. M. of V. iii. 2

supposition, beguile the, deceive the opinion. A.W. iv. 3

suspect, suspicion. C. of E. iii. 1; blunder for 'respect.' M.A. ii. 2

swabber, one who scrubs the deck of a ship. Tp. ii. 2; Tw. N. i. 5

swarth, grass cut by one sweep of scythe. Tw.N. ii. 3

swashing, swaggering. As. i. 3

swayed, strained. T. of S. iii. 2

sweat, plague. M. for M. i. 2; sweated. M. of V. iii. 2; As. ii. 3

sweetness, self-indulgence. M. for M. ii. 4

sweet-suggesting, sweetly tempting. Two G. ii. 6

swinge, beat. Two G. ii. 1; &c.

sworn out, forsworn. L.L.L. ii. 1

sympathized, mutually suffered. C. of E. v. 1; suitably matched. L.L.L. iii. 1

table, writing tablet. Two G. ii. 7; palm of the hand. M. of V. ii. 2; tablet. A.W. i. 1

table-book, memorandum-book. W.T. iv. 3

tables, backgammon. L.L.L. v. 2

tabor, small drum. Tp. iii. 2; &c.

ta'en, given. T. of S. i. 2

ta'en up, arranged amicably. As. v. 4

taffeta, plain wove glossy silk. L.L.L. v. 2; Tw.N. ii. 4; florid, bombastic. L.L.L. v. 2

take, strike. M. for M. ii. 1; T. of S. iii. 2; Tw.N. ii. 5; strike with disease. M.W. iv. 4; captivate. Tp. v. 1; W.T. iii. 2; iv. 3; take to. C. of E. i. 2

take air, get abroad. Tw.N. iii. 4

take in, conquer. W.T. iv. 3

take order, take measures. M. for M. ii. 1

taken up, arrested; and obtained on credit. M.A. iii. 3

take up, take to task. Two G. i. 2; make up, arrange amicably. As. v. 4; Tw.N. iii. 4; assume. Tw.N. v. 1

tall, fine, doughty. M.W. i. 4; &c.

tang, ? pungent or stinging effect; or an unpleasant tone, twang. Tp. ii. 2; utter with a ringing tone. Tw.N. ii. 5; iii. 4

tardy, retard. W.T. iii. 2

targe, light shield or buckler. L.L.L. v. 2

tarriance, tarrying, delay, procrastination. Two G. ii. 7

Tartar, Tartarus, hell. C. of E. iv. 2; Tw.N. ii. 5

taste, experience. Tp. v. 1; to try, to test. Tw.N. iii. 1; iii. 4

tawdry-lace, woman's silk necktie. W.T. iv. 3

tax, taxing, charge, accusation, censure. M.A. i. 1; As. ii. 7; A.W. ii. 1

taxation, censure, satire. As. i. 2

tear a cat, rant. M.N.D. i. 2

teen, grief. Tp. i. 2; L.L.L. iv. 2

tell, count. Tp. ii. 1; W.T. iv. 3

temper, mix. M.A. ii. 2

temperance, temperature. Tp. ii. 1

temperate, chaste. Tp. iv. 1

tempered, disposed. As. i. 2

temporary meddler, cleric who meddles with temporal affairs. M. for M. v. 1

tender, regard, especially with care or tenderness. Tp. ii. 1; &c.; dear. Two G. v. 4; tend. T. of S. Ind. 1; introduce. W. T. iv. 3

tents, bed hangings. T. of S. ii. 1

terminations, terms. M.A. ii. 1

tester, sixpence, money in general. M.W. i. 3

testern, present with a tester. Two G. i. 1

testimonied, attested. M. for M. iii. 2

testril, sixpence. Tw.N. ii. 3

tharborough, constable. L.L.L. i. 1

theorick, theory. A.W. iv. 3

thereabouts, of that import. W. T. i. 2

thereto, in addition, besides. W.T. i. 2

thick-pleached, thickly intertwined. M.A. i. 2

thick-skin, blockhead. M.W. iv. 5; M.N.D. iii. 2

thill-horse, shaft-horse. M. of V. ii. 2

third-borough, constable. T. of S. Ind. 1

thought, care, anxiety, melancholy. As. iv. 1; Tw.N. ii. 4; the swiftness of thought. Tp. iv. 1

Thracian singer, Orpheus. M. N.D. v. i

thrasonical, boastful. L.L.L. v. 1; As. v. 2

thread and thrum, everything in general. M.N.D. v. 1

three-pile, richest kind of velvet. W.T. iv. 2

three-piled, having a thick pile, richest. M. for M. i. 2; superfine. L.L.L. v. 2

thrift, success. M. of V. i. 1; profits. M. of V. i. 3

throughly, thoroughly. Tp. iii. 3; Two G. i. 2; T. of S. iv. 4

throw, venture (as in dice). Tw.N. v. 1

thrum, tufted end of a thread in weaving. M.N.D. v. 1

thrummed hat, hat made of very coarse woollen stuff. M. W. iv. 2

tickle, tottering. M. for M. i. 2

tick-tack, sort of backgammon. M. for M. i. 2

'tide, betide. M.N.D. v. 1

tightly, briskly, smartly. M.W. i. 3; ii. 3

tillyvally, an expression of contempt. Tw.N. ii. 3

tilth, tillage. Tp. ii. 1; M. for M. i. 4

time, youth. M. of V. i. 1

timeless, untimely. Two G. iii. 1

tinct, grand elixir sought by alchemists. A.W. v. 3

tire, headdress. Two G. iv. 4; M.W. iii. 3; M.A. iii. 4

tire-valiant, fanciful headdress. M.W. iii. 3

tiring-house, dressing-room of a theatre. M.N.D. iii. 1

tithe, ? tilth. M. for M. iv. 1

tittles, trifles. L.L.L. iv. 1

to, compared to. Tp. i. 2; ii. 1; L.L.L. ii. 1; A.W. ii. 3; for, as. Tp. ii. 1; Two G. ii. 4; at. Two G. i. 1; with. M.A. ii. 1

toaze, drag out. W.T. iv. 3

tod, 28 lbs. of wool, yield a tod. W.T. iv. 2

tofore, before. L.L.L. iii. 1

tongue, to denounce. M. for M. iv. 4

tongues, foreign languages. Two G. iv. 1; M.A. v. 1

took, gave. T. of S. iii. 2

top, forelock. M.A. i. 2; head. A.W. i. 2

torcher, torch-bearer. A.W. ii. 1

touch, action. M.N.D. iii. 2; trait. As. iii. 2; v. 4

touse, pull, tear. M. for M. v. 1

toward, in preparation. M.N. D. iii. 1; As. v. 4; T. of S. i. 1; tractable. T. of S. v. 2

trace, traverse. M.A. iii. 1; M. N.D. ii. 1

train, entice, allure. C. of E. iii. 2

traject, ferry. M. of V. iii. 4

translate, change, transform. M.N.D. i. 1; iii. 1

transport, remove to another world. M. for M. iv. 3; M.N.D. iv. 2; carried away by feeling. W.T. iii. 2; v. 3

trash, lop, cut off high branches. Tp. i. 2

travel of regard, grave survey. Tw.N. ii. 5

traverse, make a thrust. M.W. ii. 3; crosswise. As. iii. 4

tray-trip, a game of dice in which success depended on throwing the three. Tw.N. ii. 5

tremor cordis, trembling of the heart. W.T. i. 2

trench, cut. Two G. iii. 2

trencher-knight, servant who waits at table. L.L.L. v. 2

trencher-man, good feeder. M. A. i. 1

trick, custom, habit. M. for M. v. 1; toy. T. of S. iv. 3; W.T. ii. 1; special peculiarity of look, voice, &c. A.W. i. 1; W. T. ii. 3

tricking, ornaments, costumes. M.W. iv. 4

tricksy, sportive. Tp. v. 1; M. of V. iii. 5

trifle, appearance. Tp. v. 1; toy. M.N.D. i. 1

triple, third. A.W. ii. 1

triplex, triple-time in music. Tw.N. v. 1

triumph, festival. Two G. v. 4; M.N.D. i. 1

troll, sing in rotation. Tp. iii. 2

trol-my-dames, French game of 'trou madame.' W.T. iv. 2

trot, troth. M.W. iv. 5; term of

contempt. M. for M. iii. 2; hag. T. of S. i. 2

troth, truth. M.W. i. 4; M.N.D. ii. 2

trow, wonder. M.W. i. 4; ii. 1; think ye. M.A. iii. 4; know. As. iii. 2

Troyan, used as term of contempt. L.L.L. v. 2

truant, play truant. C. of E. iii. 2

truckle-bed, low bed, which can be pushed under another. M.W. iv. 5

trumpet, herald. W.T. ii. 2

trunk sleeve, full sleeve. T. of S. iv. 3

try, bring a ship as close to wind as possible. Tp. i. 1

tub, process of curing venereal disease by sweating. M. for M. iii. 2

tuck, rapier. Tw.N. iii. 4

tucket, flourish on a trumpet. M. of V. v. 1; A.W. iii. 5, stage direction

tug, contend. W.T. iv. 3

tuition, guardianship. M.A. i. 1

tundish, funnel. M. for M. iii. 2

Turk, turn, become wicked. M. A. iii. 4

turn, change. Two G. ii. 2; modulate, tune. As. ii. 5

turtle, turtle-dove. T. of S. ii. 1

twelve score, twelve score yards. M.W. iii. 2

twilled, covered with reeds. Tp. iv. 1

twink, twinkling, instant. Tp. iv. 1; T. of S. ii. 1

tyrant, pitiless critic. M.A. i. 1

umber, red ochre. As. i. 3

unadvised, unintentionally. Two G. iv. 4

unbreathed, unexercised. M.N. D. v. 1

uncape, uncouple, throw off the hounds. M.W. iii. 3

uncase, undress. L.L.L. v. 2; T. of S. i. 1

unchary, carelessly. Tw.N. iii. 4

unchecked, not contradicted. M. of V. iii. 1

unconfirmed, inexperienced. M.A. iii. 3; L.L.L. iv. 2

uncurrent, extraordinary. W.T. iii. 2

underbear, face, trim. M.A. iii. 4

undertaker, surety, or agent for others. Tw.N. iii. 4

undervalued, inferior in value. M. of V. i. 1; ii. 7

unfolding star, the star that bids shepherd let sheep out of fold. M. for M. iv. 2

unfool, take away reproach of folly. M.W. iv. 2

unfurnish, deprive. W.T. v. 1

unfurnished, without companion. M. of V. iii. 2

ungalled, unblemished. C. of E. iii. 1

ungenitured, without power of procreation. M. for M. iii. 2

ungot, unbegotten. M. for M. v. 1

unhandsome, unsuitable. As. Epil.

unhappiness, mischief. M.A. ii. 1

unhappy, mischievous. C. of E. iv. 4; L.L.L. v. 2; A.W. iv. 5

unhatched, undrawn, undisclosed. Tw.N. iii. 4

unintelligent, unconscious. W. T. i. 1

unjust, dishonest. W.T. iv. 3

unkind, unnatural. As. ii. 7

unlike, unlikely. M. for M. v. 1

unmuzzled, as of dogs worrying bear. Tw.N. iii. 1

unpeeled, stripped, desolate. L.L.L. ii. 1

unpinked, not pierced with eyelet holes. T. of S. iv. 1

unpitied, unmerciful. M. for M. iv. 2

unpregnant, dull, without sense. M. for M. iv. 4

unprizable, invaluable. Tw.N. v. 1

unprofited, with nothing gained. Tw.N. i. 4

unquestionable, unwilling to be conversed with. As. iii. 2

unraked, not made up for night. M.W. v. 5

unreverend, unreverent, irreverent. Two G. ii. 6; T. of S. iii. 2

unrolled, struck off the roll. W. T. iv. 2

unroosted, henpecked. W.T. ii. 3

unseasoned, inexperienced. A. W. i. 1

unshape, throw into disorder. M. for M. iv. 4

unshunned, unavoidable. M. for M. iii. 2

unsisting, ? unresting. M. for M. iv. 2

unstanched, incontinent. Tp. i. 1

unthrift, unthrifty, good-fornothing. M. of V. i. 3; v. 1

unthrifty to, not to increase. W.T. v. 2

untoward, unmannerly. T. of S. iv. 5

untowardly, unluckily. M.A. iii. 2

untread, retrace. M. of V. ii. 6

untried, unexamined. W.T. iv. Chorus

untrussing, unloosing 'points' of hose. M. for M. iii. 2

up and down, exactly. Two G. ii. 3; M.A. ii. 1

upshoot, deciding shot. L.L.L. iv. 1

up-staring, standing on end. Tp. i. 2

urchin, hedgehog, goblin. Tp. i. 2; M.W. iv. 4

urchin-shows, apparitions of goblins. Tp. ii. 2

usance, interest of money. M. of V. i. 3

use, interest. M. for M. i. 1; M. A. ii. 1; Tw.N. iii. 1; custom. M. for M. i. 4; A.W. v. 1; trust. M. of V. iv. 1

usurping, counterfeit, false. L. L.L. iv. 3

utter, pass from one to another. L.L.L. ii. 1; cause so to pass. W.T. iv. 3

vagrom, mistake for 'vagrant.' M.A. iii. 3

vail, lower, let fall. M. for M. v. 1; L.L.L. v. 2; M. of V. i. 1; T. of S. v. 2

vain, 'for vain' = uselessly. M. for M. ii. 4; light of tongue. C. of E. iii. 2

vanity, illusion. Tp. iv. 1

vantage, opportunity. M.W. iv. 6; M. for M. v. 1; M. of V. iii. 2; superiority. M.N.D. i. 1

vara, very. L.L.L. v. 2

varlet, knave. Tp. iv. 1; M.A. iv. 2

vast, dreary stretch of sea. W. T. i. 1

vastidity, extent, immensity. M. for M. iii. 1

vaward, vanguard. M.N.D. iv. 1

velure, velvet. T. of S. iii. 2

venew, veney, a bout at fencing. M.W. i. 1; L.L.L. v. 1

vengeance, mischief. As. iv. 3

ventricle, cavity. L.L.L. iv. 2

verse love, make love in verse. M.N.D. ii. 1

via, go forward; away with you. M.W. ii. 2; M. of V. ii. 2; come on. L.L.L. v. 1

vice, the buffoon. Tw.N. iv. 2; screw. W.T. i. 2

vie, stake, as at cards. T. of S. ii. 1

viewless, invisible. M. for M. iii. 1

vigitant, blunder for 'vigilant.' M.A. iii. 3

villagery, village people. M.N. D. ii. 1

villain, used good-humouredly. C. of E. i. 2; Tw.N. ii. 5; W.T. i. 2; serf. As. i. 1

viol-de-gamboys (blunder for 'da gamba'), violoncello. Tw. N. i. 3

virginalling, playing with fingers, as upon virginal. W.T. i. 2

virtue, essence, very being. Tp. i. 2; M.N.D. iv. 1; efficacy. M. of V. v. 1

visited, infected. L.L.L. v. 2

visor, mask. M.A. ii. 1; L.L.L. v. 2

vizaments, advisements, counsel. M.W. i. 1

vizarded, masked. M.W. iv. 6

vlouting-stog, laughing-stock. M.W. iii. 1

voice, name, behalf. M. for M. i. 2; vote. M.N.D. i. 1; As. ii. 4

void, emit. M. of V. i. 3

volable, quick-witted. L.L.L. iii. 1

vow-fellow, companions in oath. L.L.L. ii. 1

vulgar, vulgar tongue. As. v. 1; common. Tw.N. iii. 1; common person. W.T. ii. 1

vulgarly, publicly. M. for M. v. 1

waft, beckon. C. of E. ii. 2; M. of V. v. 1; turn. W.T. i. 2

waftage, passage by water. C. of E. iv. 1

wag, to go one's way. M.W. i. 3; ii. 1; M.A. v. 1; shake. M. of V. iv. 1

wailful, doleful. Two G. iii. 2

wainropes, waggon-ropes. Tw. N. iii. 2

waist, part of ship between quarterdeck and forecastle. Tp. i. 2

wake, late revels. L.L.L. v. 2; W.T. iv. 2

wanton, luxuriant. M.N.D. ii. 1; play, dally. W.T. ii. 1

wantonness, lasciviousness. M. W. iv. 2

ward, guard in fencing. Tp. i. 2; M.W. ii. 2; W.T. i. 2; defence. L.L.L. iii. 1

warden, large baking pear. W. T. iv. 2

warp, deviate. M. for M. i. 1; twist, pervert. As. ii. 7; A.W. v. 3

warrant, secure, protect. M. for M. iv. 2; C. of E. iv. 4; As. iii. 3; attest. M.A. iv. 1

warranted need, upon a, if the question required a guarantee. M. for M. iii. 2

warrener, gamekeeper. M.W. i. 4

watch, tame by keeping awake. M.W. v. 5; T. of S. iv. 1

waters, for all, fit for anything. Tw.N. iv. 2

watery star, the moon. W.T. i. 2

waxen, grow, increase. M.N.D. ii. 1

wear, fashion. M. for M. iii. 2; &c.; wear out, tire. As. ii. 4; A.W. v. 1; are in fashion. A. W. i. 1; grow fitted by use. Tw.N. ii. 4

weather-fend, shelter. Tp. v. 1

web, disease of the eye, ? cataract. W.T. i. 2

weed, garment. Two G. ii. 7; &c.

weeding, weeds. L.L.L. i. 1

welkin, sky. Tp. i. 2; Tw.N. ii. 3; iii. 1; blue. W.T. i. 2

well, at rest. W.T. v. 1

well-advised, deliberate, in right mind. L.L.L. v. 2

well entered, being initiated. A.W. ii. 1

well found, found to be well skilled. A.W. ii. 1

well-liking, in good condition. L.L.L. v. 2

wezand, windpipe. Tp. iii. 2

whelm, overwhelm. M.W. ii. 2

when, exclamation of impatience. Tp. i. 2; T. of S. iv. 1

whe'r, whether. Tp. v. 1; C. of E. iv. 1

where, whereas. Two G. iii. 1; L.L.L. ii. 1; M. of V. iv. 1; to where. M.N.D. iv. 1

wherein, in what dress. As. iii. 2

where you are, what you mean. As. v. 2

whey-face, covered with youthful down. M.W. i. 4

while-ere, not long ago. Tp. iii. 2

whist, hushed, silent. Tp. i. 2

white, bull's-eye in target. T. of S. v. 2

whiting-time, bleaching-time. M.W. iii. 3

whitster, bleacher. M.W. iii. 3

whoo-bub, hubbub. W.T. iv. 3

whooping, out of all, beyond expression. As. iii. 2

whoreson, bastard. Tp. i. 1; &c.

wide, far from, indifferent to. M.W. iii. 1; distractedly. M. A. iv. 1

wide-chapped, open-mouthed. Tp. i. 1

widow, dower. M. for M. v, 1

widowhood, rights of a widow. T. of S. ii. 1

wightly, nimble. L.L.L. iii. 1

wild, rash, heedless. W.T. ii. 1; iv. 3

wilderness, wildness. M. for M. iii. 1

wimpled, blindfolded. L.L.L. iii. 1

wind, blow. M.A. i. 1; to fold. M.N.D. iv. 1

windgalls, swelling in horse's legs. T. of S. iii. 2

windring, winding. Tp. iv. 1

windy, windward, safe. M.A. ii. 1; Tw.N. iii. 4

wish, commend. T. of S. i. 1; i. 2; desire. M. for M. v. 1

wit, wisdom. Two G. i. 1; &c.; sense. M.A. i. 1

witcracker, jester. M.A. v. 4

withal, not do, not help it. M. of V. iii. 4

withering out, delaying enjoyment of. M.N.D. i. 1

without-door, external. W.T. ii. 1

witness, evidence. M.W. iv. 2

wit-snapper, man ready at repartee. M. of V. iii. 5

'wit, whither wilt?' expression used to check anyone talking too much. As. iv. 1

wittol, contented cuckold. M. W. ii. 2

woe, sorry. Tp. v. 1

woman'me to it, make me show my woman's weakness. A.W. iii. 2

woman-tired, henpecked. W.T. ii. 3

womb, enclose. W.T. iv. 3

wonder, wondering, admiration. W.T. iv. chor.; v. 1

wondered, wonder-working. Tp. iv. 1

wood, mad. Two G. ii. 3; M.N. D. ii. 1

woodbine, bindweed, honeysuckle, or convolvulus. M.N. D. ii. 1; iv. 1

woodcock, fool. M.A. v. 1; &c.

woollen, blankets. M.A. ii. 1

woolward, go, wear wool instead of linen next skin. L. L.L. v. 2

word, promise. A.W. ii. 1

word, at a, in short. M.W. i. 1; as good as my word. M.W. i. 3

working, scope. As. i. 2

working-day, common, ordinary. As. i. 3

world, wonder. M.A. iii. 5; T. of S. ii. 1

world, go to the, be married. M.A. ii. 1; A.W. i. 3

worm, creature. Tp. iii. 1; M. W. v. 5; serpent. M. for M. iii. 1; M.N.D. iii. 2

worn times, old age. W.T. v. 1

worship, honour, dignity. W.T. i. 2

wort, root. M.W. i. 1; sweet unfermented beer. L.L.L. v. 2

wot, wotting, know, knowing. L.L.L. i. 1; W.T. iii. 2

wrack of sea, shipwreck. C. of E. v. 1

wrath, wrathful. M.N.D. ii. 1; ardour. As. v. 2

wring, writhe. M.A. v. 1

writ, scripture. A.W. ii. 1; written, claimed. A. W. ii. 3

write, claim to be. A.W. ii. 3
wroth (so spelt for rhyme),
  wrath. M. of V. ii. 9
wry-necked, see *fife.*

yare, yarely, ready, readily;
  nimble, active, briskly. Tp. i.
  1; &c.
Yead, diminutive for 'Edward.'
  M.W. i. 1,
yearn, grieve, vex. M.W. iii. 5
years, in, into wrinkles. L.L.L.
  v. 2

yellow, emblem of jealousy. W.
  T. ii. 3
yellowness, jealousy. M.W. i. 3
yellows, jaundice in horses. T.
  of S. iii. 2
yest, foam, froth. W.T. iii. 3
yield you forth, expose you. M.
  for M. v. 1
younker, youth. M. of V. ii. 6

zany, buffoon. L.L.L. v. 2;
  Tw.N. i. 5
zodiacs, years. M. for M. i. 2

